D0793211

Best Books for Young Adult Readers

Best Books for Young Adult Readers™

Stephen J. Calvert
EDITOR

R. R. BOWKER
New Providence, New Jersey

Published by R. R. Bowker, a division of Reed Elsevier Inc.

Printed and bound in the United States of America

Library of Congress Cataloging-in-Publication Data

Calvert, Stephen.
Best books for young adult readers / Stephen J. Calvert, editor.
p. cm.
Includes bibliographical references and index.
ISBN 0-8352-3832-6 (alk. paper)
1. Teenagers—United States—Books and reading. 2. Young adult literature, English—Bibliography. I. Title.
Z1037.C176 1997
011.62'5—dc21 97-478
CIP

Contents

History and Geography

Major Subjects Arranged Alphabetically

Preface

The Best Books series was established to help librarians, teachers, and other media-related professionals meet both the curriculum-related and recreational reading needs of their students. *Best Books for Young Adult Readers,* the newest title in the series, covers recommended material for readers in grades 7–12, or roughly ages 12–18. The book supplements the previously published titles *Best Books for Children* (5th edition, 1994), *Best Books for Junior High Readers* (1991), and *Best Books for Senior High Readers* (1991).

In view of society's intellectual concerns, we hope the selection and arrangement of materials in this volume will help users to:

Respond to changes within the juvenile population. Today's student is different from yesterday's, just as tommorrow's student will be different from today's. The proportion of school-age children who are members of minority groups, fall below the poverty line, and/or live in single-parent homes has expanded dramatically in recent years. Moreover, preteen and teenage readers boast experience and awareness levels unthinkable as recently as 20 years ago. As a result, publishers have produced more books on problematic themes as well as titles geared to readers from a variety of cultural and socioeconomic backgrounds.

Support new trends in education. In view of our global society, more attention is being devoted to geography and foreign languages. Science instruction is less textbook-oriented and more inclined to embrace experimentation, field trips, and trade books. Finally, as libraries and schools have assumed a greater responsibility for the development of the nation's youth, information on family life, sex education, abuse, and other realities of twentieth-century life must be made available.

Serve the interests of individuals. As important as cooperative planning and societal concerns may be, it is personal attention that inspires the love and habit of reading.

General Scope and Criteria for Inclusion

There are 6,586 titles—2,165 fiction and 4,421 nonfiction titles—listed in *Best Books for Young Adult Readers,* titles that were published between the last quarter of 1990 and the first quarter of 1996. In previous volumes in the Best Books series, approximately 10 percent of the titles listed were cited within the annotations of other titles by the same authors. Because these titles—primarily nonfiction series titles—were not always cited in the correct place in the book's subject arrangement, we have provided separate, full bibliographic entries for such titles in this volume.

Excluded from this bibliography, for the most part, are general reference works (dictionaries, encyclopedias, etc.), professional books for librarians and teachers, and mass market series books.

For most titles, at least two recommendations were required from the sources consulted for a title to be included. Among the titles included that were reviewed by only one source, many received starred reviews in *Booklist* and/or *School Library Journal* or were recipients of a prominent book award. The vast majority of the titles were in print at the time they were added to the database from which this volume was created, although certainly some of them are now out of stock or out of print. On the other hand, some out-of-print hardcover editions will be available in paperback editions that may not be cited in this volume.

Sources Used

In compiling this annotated bibliography, several retrospective sources were used: *Senior High School Library Catalog,* 14th edition (H. W. Wilson); *Middle and Junior High School Library Catalog,* 7th edition (H. W. Wilson); *Books for You: A Booklist for Senior High Students,* 11th edition (National Council of Teachers of English); *Your Reading: A Booklist for Junior High and Middle School* (National Council of Teachers of English); and *Books for the Teen Age,* 1995 edition (New York Public Library).

In addition, the following book-reviewing periodicals were consulted: *Booklist, School Library Journal,* and *VOYA* (Voice of Youth Advocates). Reviews were drawn from journal issues from January 1991 through March 1996.

Uses of This Book

Best Books for Young Adult Readers was designed to help librarians and media specialists with four vital tasks: (1) to evaluate the adequacy of existing collections; (2) to build new collections or strengthen existing holdings; (3) to provide reading guidance to young adults; and (4) to prepare bibliographies and reading lists. To increase the book's usefulness—particularly when it comes to bibliographies and suggested reading—titles are arranged under broad areas of interest or, in the case of nonfiction works, by curriculum-oriented subjects rather than the Dewey decimal classifications. Suggested Dewey classification numbers are nevertheless provided within most nonfiction entries.

Subject Arrangement

To help users integrate material from all the volumes in the Best Books series, we have categorized books under the same subject headings whenever possible. The subject headings and subheadings used in this book can be found on pages v–xii (Contents) and xiii–xiv (Major Subjects Arranged Alphabetically).

As in all bibliographies of this type, some arbitrary decisions had to be made concerning placement of books under specific subjects. For example, books of mathematical puzzles will be found in the Mathematics section rather than in the Jokes, Puzzles, Riddles, and Word Games section.

Indexes

Following the main body of text are the book's three indexes. The Author Index cites authors, book titles, and entry numbers. Joint authors are listed separately. The Title Index cites titles and entry numbers. Works of fiction (including poetry and drama) in both of these indexes are indicated by (F) following the title. Finally, an extensive Subject/Grade Level Index lists entries under thousands of subject headings and specific grade level suitability for each entry. With very few exceptions, the subject headings and subheadings are those found in *Sears List of Subject Headings,* 15th edition (H. W. Wilson, 1994). One exception is that "United States" is not used as a subheading in this book, unlike Sears, for it is assumed that subjects refer to the United States unless otherwise noted.

The following codes are used to identify general grade levels:

IJ (Intermediate–Junior High) grades 5–8
IS (Intermediate–Senior High) grades 5–12

JS	(Junior–Senior High) grades 7–12
S	(Senior High) grades 9–12
SA	(Senior High–Adult) grades 9–adult

Because all reviewing sources cite different reading levels for each book—sometimes, reading levels that do not overlap!—we have arbitrarily used those cited by reviewers for *Booklist* in most cases.

Entries

A typical entry contains the following information, where applicable: (1) author(s) or editor(s); (2) title and subtitle; (3) grade levels in parentheses; (4) series title in parentheses (new to this edition); (5) translator or adapter; (6) indication of illustrations; (7) publication date; (8) publisher; (9) price of hardbound edition (LB = library binding); (10) International Standard Book Number (ISBN) of hardbound edition; (11) paperback publisher ("paper"); if no paperback publisher is listed, it is the same as that for the hardbound edition; (12) paperback price; (13) ISBN of the paperback edition; (14) a descriptive annotation; (15) noteworthy awards given to the title (new to this edition); (16) review citations, with an asterisk indicating a starred review; and (17) Dewey decimal classification number for nonfiction titles.

Some entries may appear without annotations when they are part of a series that has been recommended, or when the title reveals the content of the book. Some recommended series are:

Peter Bedrick—Masters of Art
Chelsea House—Black Americans of Achievement; Earth at Risk; Encyclopedia of Health; Hispanics of Achievement; Immigrant Experience; Indians of North America; Milestone in Black American History, et al.
Children's Press—Enchantment of the World
Dillon—Ecology Watch
Dorling Kindersley—Eyewitness Art; Eyewitness Science
Enslow—Contemporary Women; Diseases and People; Drug Library; Multicultural Issues; Sports Greats, et al.
Gloucester—Green Issues; Save Our Earth
Greenhaven—Current Controversies; Opposing Viewpoints
Knopf—Eyewitness Books
Lerner—Then and Now; Visual Geography
Lucent—Encyclopedia of Discovery and Invention; The Importance Of; Overview; World History
Macmillan—First Families; History Mystery; Past and Present
Marshall Cavendish—Cultures of the World
Messner—Issues for the 1990s
Millbrook—American Albums; Investigate!

Oxford University Press—Extraordinary Explorers
Raintree/Steck-Vaughn—Causes and Consequences
Rosen—Drug Abuse Prevention Library; In Their Own Voices; Need to Know Library
Rourke—American Voices
Silver Burdett—Pioneers in Change
Thomas Learning—People and Places
Twenty-First Century—Issues of Our Time; Understanding Illness
VGM Career Horizons
Viking—What Makes a. . .
Watts—Fun with Science

Review Citations

Review citations are given for books published and reviewed from late 1990 through the first quarter of 1996. These review citations will give librarians sources from which to find more-detailed information about each of the books listed. The abbreviations used in this book for these sources are:

BL	*Booklist*
BTA	*Books for the Teen Age*
BY	*Books for You*
MJHS	*Middle and Junior High School Library Catalog*
SHS	*Senior High School Library Catalog*
SLJ	*School Library Journal*
SLJS	*School Library Journal Star Track*
VOYA	*Voice of Youth Advocates*
YR	*Your Reading*

New Features

In addition to the aforementioned listing of full bibliographic citations for all titles in this volume, we have added series titles to entries. Also new to this volume is the inclusion of many prominent national (and a few international) book awards won by the titles listed. Among the awards cited are the following: Association for Library Service to Children (ALSC) Notable Children's Book Award; Booklist (BL) Editors' Choice; Boston Globe/Horn Book Award; Carter G. Woodson Book Award; Child Study Children's Book Award; Christopher Award; Coretta Scott King Award; Edgar; Friends of American Writers Juvenile Book Merit Award; Golden Kite Award; International Reading Association (IRA) Children's Books Award; Jane Addams Children's Book Award; John Newbery Medal and Honor Books; Kate Greenaway

Medal; Mildred L. Batchelder Award; National Jewish Book Award; School Library Journal (SLJ) Best Books of the Year; Scott O'Dell Award for Historical Fiction; Western Heritage Award; and Young Adult Library Services Association (YALSA) Best Book for Young Adults.

The listings in *Best Books for Young Adult Readers* contains approximately 910 awards won by more than 600 titles. In addition, the listings include about 900 entries that received starred reviews in *Booklist* and/or *School Library Journal.*

Acknowledgments

Many people contributed to the preparation of this bibliography. For their excellent editorial assistance, I would like to thank Michelle Brown, Keith Farrey, Vicki Farrey, Linda Loeffelholz, Paul Morrissey, Sue Reindollar, Peg Roberts, Gwen Stauffacher, Tony Wells, and Marcia Weuve. I am also deeply indebted to Catherine Barr for her unflagging support and to Nancy Bucenec, Bowker's Production Managing Editor, for her patience and diligent efforts to bring this title to print.

Literary Forms

Fiction

Adventure and Survival

1 Avi. *"Who Was That Masked Man, Anyway?"* (5–7). 1992, Orchard/Richard Jackson LB $14.99 (0-531-08607-0); 1994, Avon/Camelot paper $3.99 (0-380-72113-9). Toward the end of World War II, 6th-grader Frankie tries to transform his life into a script from "Superman," "The Lone Ranger," etc., where the future of the free world depends on the outcome of his adventures. Awards: ALSC Notable Children's Book; BL Editors' Choice; SLJ Best Book. (Rev: BL 8/92*; MJHS; SLJ 10/92*; YR)

2 Baillie, Allan. *Adrift* (5–7). 1992, Viking $14 (0-670-84474-8). Children are accidentally swept out to sea in a makeshift boat in this survival adventure set in Australia. (Rev: BL 3/15/92; SLJ 5/92)

3 Bainbridge, Beryl. *The Birthday Boys* (9–adult). 1994, Carroll & Graf $18.95 (0-7867-0071-8). A fictional account of an early twentieth-century expedition to Antarctica, narrated by Captain Robert Scott and 4 fellow explorers who were doomed to die. (Rev: BL 4/1/94; SLJ 10/94)

4 Bauer, Marion Dane. *Face to Face* (5–9). 1991, Clarion $13.95 (0-395-55440-3). This novel of a troubled father-son relationship describes their reunion on a failed whitewater rafting trip and the painful aftermath when they separate again. (Rev: BL 9/15/91; MJHS; SLJ 10/91)

5 Bawden, Nina. *The House of Secrets* (5–7). 1992, Clarion $13.95 (0-395-58670-4). When 3 siblings come to live with a strict older aunt, they find a houseful of secrets, an orphan, a "witch," and ultimately a happy ending. (Rev: BL 3/15/92; MJHS)

6 Benchley, Peter. *The Beast* (9–adult). 1991, Random $21 (0-679-40355-8). *Jaws* revisited, this time with a giant squid as villain. (Rev: BL 5/15/91; SLJ 11/91)

7 Benchley, Peter. *White Shark* (9–adult). 1994, Random $22 (0-679-40356-6). An evil Nazi scientist creates a water-breathing superkiller that is sunk in a U-boat at the end of World War II and gets loose 50 years later. (Rev: BL 1/15/94; SHS; SLJ 11/94)

8 Bunting, Eve. *The Hideout* (5–7). 1991, Harcourt $15.95 (0-15-233990-6). When Andy, 12, runs away from home because he resents his stepfather, he finds a hotel key and moves into a plush suite, until the staff threaten his security. (Rev: BL 4/1/91; MJHS; SLJ 5/91)

9 Byars, Betsy. *Coast to Coast* (5–8). 1992, Delacorte $14 (0-385-30787-X). The adventures of Birch, 13, and her grandfather, who fly a Piper Cub from South Carolina to California. (Rev: BL 12/1/92; MJHS; SLJ 1/93; YR)

10 Campbell, Eric. *The Place of Lions* (6–9). 1991, Harcourt $15.95 (0-15-262408-2). When their plane crashes over the Serengeti, Chris and his injured father must learn a lesson in survival, surrounded by a pride of lions and poachers. Awards: YALSA Best Book for Young Adults. (Rev: BL 11/15/91; SLJ 11/91)

11 Campbell, Eric. *The Shark Callers* (7–10). 1994, Harcourt $10.95 (0-15-200007-0); paper $4.95 (0-15-200010-0). Parallel stories of 2 boys' survival in Papua New Guinea during a volcanic eruption and tidal wave. (Rev: BL 11/15/94; BTA; SLJ 9/94; VOYA 10/94)

12 Castelli, Alfredo. *The Snowman* (9–12). Illus. 1990, Catalan Communications (43 E. 19th St., New York, NY 10003) paper $9.95 (0-87416-124-X). A reporter on an Everest expedition encounters huge figures in the snow and later awakens in a lamasery, where, after terrifying dreams, he discovers the monks' secret. (Rev: BL 9/1/91)

13 Cooney, Caroline B. *Flash Fire* (7–10). 1995, Scholastic $14.95 (0-590-25253-4). A girl's wish for a more exciting life comes true when a fire sweeps the wealthy neighborhood where she lives in Los Angeles. (Rev: BL 11/1/95; SLJ 12/95; VOYA 12/95)

14 Cooney, Caroline B. *Flight No. 116 Is Down* (7–10). 1992, Scholastic $13.95. With a lightning pace, the author depicts the drama and human interest inherent in disaster. Awards: YALSA Best Book for Young Adults. (Rev: BL 1/15/92; MJHS; YR)

15 Corcoran, Barbara. *Stay Tuned* (6–9). 1991, Atheneum $13.95 (0-689-31673-9). The adventures of Stevie, 14; Alex, 18; and 2 young neighbors at an abandoned summer camp, where they begin to reshape their lives. (Rev: BL 3/15/91; SLJ 4/91)

16 Cottonwood, Joe. *Danny Ain't* (6–10). 1992, Scholastic $13.95 (0-590-45067-0). His mother is dead and his father is in a VA hospital, but Danny manages to endure poverty alone and forge a value system. (Rev: BL 9/1/92; SLJ 10/92)

17 Cottonwood, Joe. *Quake!* (5–8). 1995, Scholastic $13.95 (0-590-22232-5). Based on California's 1989 earthquake and seen through the eyes of a 14-year-old girl. (Rev: BL 5/1/95; SLJ 5/95)

18 Crichton, Michael. *The Lost World* (9–adult). 1995, Knopf $25.95 (0-679-41946-2). Five years after *Jurassic Park*, carcasses of the supposedly extinct saurians wash up on shore and precipitate another action-filled hunt. (Rev: BL 9/1/95)

19 Di Mercurio, Michael. *Attack of the Seawolf* (9–adult). 1993, Donald I. Fine $21.95 (1-55611-360-9). Michael "Patch" Pacino returns to action commanding the *U.S.S. Seawolf* on a mission to rescue an American submarine from Chinese rebels. (Rev: BL 6/1–15/93; SLJ 12/93)

20 Disher, Garry. *Ratface* (5–9). 1994, Ticknor & Fields $10.95 (0-395-69451-5). Kidnapped by the racist Australian cult known as the White League, Max, Christina, and Stefan escape captivity and are pursued by Ratface, a cult deputy. (Rev: BL 11/1/94; SLJ 12/94; VOYA 2/95)

21 Ferris, Jean. *All That Glitters* (7–10). 1996, Farrar $16 (0-374-30204-9). In this adventure, Brian, 16, goes on a scuba-diving expedition with his father and an archeologist investigating a shipwrecked Spanish galleon. (Rev: BL 2/15/96; SLJ 3/96)

22 Gilman, Dorothy. *Caravan* (9–adult). 1992, Doubleday $19 (0-385-42361-6). A teenage carnival huckster marries, travels to the Sahara, witnesses her husband's murder, and eventually falls in love again. Awards: BL Editors' Choice. (Rev: BL 4/15/92; SHS)

23 Goldman, E. M. *Money to Burn* (6–8). 1994, Viking $14.99 (0-670-85339-9). Two 14-year-old boys anticipate a boring summer until they find a suitcase containing $400,000—the loot of a dead drug dealer—and decide to keep it. (Rev: BL 3/1/94; BTA; SLJ 4/94)

24 Hafen, Lyman. *Over the Joshua Slope* (6–8). 1994, Bradbury $14.95 (0-02-741100-1). A gritty, fast-paced adventure where a father and son come to an understanding after an accident caused by the boy cripples his father. (Rev: BL 5/1/94; MJHS; SLJ 6/94; VOYA 6/94)

25 Hahn, Mary Downing. *The Spanish Kidnapping Disaster* (5–7). 1991, Clarion $13.95 (0-395-55696-1). Felicia doesn't get along with her stepsiblings until they're kidnapped and must survive and escape. (Rev: BL 3/15/91; MJHS; SLJ 5/91)

26 Heneghan, James. *Torn Away* (7–10). 1994, Viking $14.99 (0-670-85180-9). A teenager, forced to leave his home in Northern Ireland where he wants to stay and fight with the IRA, must join his uncle's family in Canada. (Rev: BL 2/15/94; MJHS; SLJ 9/94; VOYA 4/94)

27 Hillerman, Tony. *Finding Moon* (9–adult). 1995, HarperCollins $24 (0-06-017772-1). In Vietnam in 1975, Moon Mathias, a newspaper editor, searches for the daughter of his younger brother, who died in the war. (Rev: BL 9/15/95*)

28 Hobbs, Will. *The Big Wander* (7–10). 1992, Atheneum $13.95 (0-689-31767-0); 1994, Avon/Camelot paper $3.99 (0-380-72140-6). Clay Lancaster, 14, and his brother Mike are on a "big waner," their last trip together before Mike goes away to college. Awards: YALSA Best Book for Young Adults. (Rev: BL 10/15/92*; MJHS; SLJ 11/92)

29 Hobbs, Will. *Downriver* (9–12). 1991, Atheneum $13.95 (0-689-31690-9); 1992, Bantam/Starfire paper $3.50 (0-553-29717-1). Jessie, 15, is one of 8 problem teens in an outdoor survival program that almost ends in disaster. Awards: YALSA Best Book for Young Adults. (Rev: BL 3/1/91; MJHS; SLJ 3/91)

30 Kehret, Peg. *Danger at the Fair* (5–8). 1995, Dutton/Cobblehill $14.99 (0-525-65182-9). Ellen and Corey are back, this time sharing a thrill-a-minute adventure set at a county fair, where a fortune-teller tells Ellen that her brother Corey is in danger. (Rev: BL 12/1/94; MJHS; SLJ 2/95)

31 McCarthy, Cormac. *The Crossing* (9–adult). 1994, Knopf $23 (0-679-43158-6). A parallel novel to *All the Pretty Horses*. Billy, 16, and his kid brother, Boyd, grow up on a desert New Mexico ranch. A she-wolf wreaks havoc with the cattle until Billy captures her. (Rev: BL 5/15/94*)

32 McCutchan, Philip. *Apprentice, to the Sea* (9–adult). 1995, St. Martin's $17.95 (0-312-11743-4). A sea adventure with Tom Chatto, 16, beginning his officer-in-training duty aboard an aging windjammer. (Rev: BL 3/1/95; SLJ 8/95)

33 Macken, Walter. *The Flight of the Doves* (6–9). 1992, Simon & Schuster $14 (0-671-73801-1). Attempting to escape abuse from their stepfather, Finn, 12, and his sister Derval, 7, flee England for their grandmother's home in Ireland. (Rev: BL 1/1/93; BTA)

34 Macken, Walter. *Island of the Great Yellow Ox* (5–8). 1991, Simon & Schuster $14 (0-671-73800-3). An Irish boy and 2 American friends are shipwrecked on an uninhabited island, where they are held captive by ruthless archeologists and must solve a mystery to survive. (Rev: BL 10/15/91; SLJ 10/91)

35 Marsden, John. *Tomorrow, When the War Began* (9–12). 1995, Houghton $13.95 (0-395-70673-4). A girl and her friends return from a camping trip in the bush to find that their country has been invaded and their families taken prisoner. (Rev: BL 4/15/95; SLJ 6/95)

36 Martin, Susan D. *I Sailed with Columbus* (5–7). Illus. 1991, Overlook $17.95 (0-87951-431-0). An adventure tale, based on actual events, told from the viewpoint of a fictional boy who was a passenger on the *Santa Maria* in 1492. (Rev: BL 9/1/91; SLJ 9/91)

37 Masterton, David. *Get Out of My Face* (7–9). 1991, Atheneum $13.95 (0-689-31675-5). A canoe accident on a camping trip manages to bond a 15-year-old with her new stepbrother and stepsister when they work together for survival. (Rev: BL 10/15/91)

38 Mikaelsen, Ben. *Sparrow Hawk Red* (6–8). 1993, Hyperion LB $14.89 (1-56282-388-4); paper $4.50 (0-7868-1002-5). Ricky, 13, wanting to avenge his mother's murder by drug smugglers, steals the smugglers' plane. (Rev: BL 8/93*; SLJ 5/93)

39 Morey, Walt. *Death Walk* (6–10). 1991, Blue Heron Publishing (24450 N.W. Hansen Rd., Hillsboro, OR 97124) $13.95 (0-936085-18-5). After being stranded in the Alaskan wilderness, a teenage boy must learn to survive in the harsh climate while on the run from killers. (Rev: BL 6/1/91; MJHS; SLJ 6/91)

40 Murphy, Claire Rudolf. *To the Summit* (7–12). 1992, Dutton/Lodestar $15 (0-525-67383-0). A 17-year-old girl climbs Mt. McKinley to gain her father's respect. (Rev: BL 5/15/92; BTA; YR)

41 Naylor, Phyllis Reynolds. *The Fear Place* (5–7). 1994, Atheneum $14.95 (0-689-31866-9). This is a literal cliffhanger about Doug Brillo, 12, who overcomes his terror of heights to rescue the older brother he hates. (Rev: BL 12/15/94; BTA; MJHS; SLJ 12/94; VOYA 4/95)

42 Paulsen, Gary. *Brian's Winter* (5–9). 1996, Delacorte $15.95 (0-385-32198-8). An elemental story of wilderness survival, a sequel to *Hatchet* (1987). (Rev: BL 12/15/95)

43 Paulsen, Gary. *The Cookcamp* (5–7). 1991, Orchard/Richard Jackson LB $13.99 (0-531-08527-9). A lyrical novel in which a boy, age 5, is sent to the Minnesota woods to live with his grandmother, a cook for a road-building crew, because his father is fighting in World War II. Awards: SLJ Best Book. (Rev: BL 3/1/91; SLJ 2/91*)

44 Paulsen, Gary. *The Haymeadow* (6–9). Illus. 1992, Delacorte $15 (0-385-30621-0); 1994, Dell/Yearling paper $3.99 (0-440-40923-3). A 14-year-old boy takes 9,000 sheep out to pasture for the summer and tries to gain the acceptance of his father. Awards: YALSA Best Book for Young Adults. (Rev: BL 5/15/92*; SLJ 6/92; YR)

45 Paulsen, Gary. *The River* (5–12). 1991, Delacorte $14.95 (0-385-30388-2). In this sequel to *Hatchet* (1987), Paulsen takes the wilderness adventure beyond self-preservation and makes teen Brian responsible for saving someone else. (Rev: BL 5/15/91; BY; MJHS)

46 Pausewang, Gudrun. *Fall-out* (7–12). Tr. by Patricia Crampton. 1995, Viking $13.99 (0-670-86104-9). An accident at a nuclear power plant forces a 14-year-old to assume the responsibility of finding a way to safety. (Rev: BL 9/15/95; SLJ 8/95)

47 Peck, Robert Newton. *Arly's Run* (6–9). 1991, Walker $16.95 (0-8027-8120-9). Orphaned Arly escapes from an early nineteenth-century Florida work farm and journeys to Moore Haven, where shelter has been arranged for him. (Rev: BL 12/15/91; SLJ 2/92)

48 Pike, Christopher. *Bury Me Deep* (7–10). 1991, Pocket/Archway paper $3.50 (0-671-69057-4). A scuba-diving vacation in Hawaii turns into an adventure involving murder, ghosts, and underwater thrills. (Rev: BL 9/1/91)

49 Pullman, Philip. *The Tin Princess* (9–12). 1994, Knopf $16 (0-679-84757-X). In the tiny Germanic kingdom of Razkavia, Adelaide, the unlikely Cockney queen, and her companion/ translator, Becky Winter, are involved in political intrigue and romance. (Rev: BL 2/15/94; BTA; MJHS; SLJ 4/94; VOYA 8/94)

50 Rauprich, Nina. *Una extraña travesía* (9–12). Tr. from German by Dolores Abalos. 1994, Ediciones SM (Madrid, Spain) paper $7.95 (84-348-4422-2). In this adventure novel, set in the 1800s, Carl—a young man rejected by everyone in his hometown in Germany—flees by sea to New Zealand, where many search for gold. English title: *Strange Voyage*. (Rev: BL 10/15/95)

51 Shusterman, Neal. *Speeding Bullet* (6–10). 1991, Little, Brown $14.95 (0-316-78905-4). Action-packed story of a Manhattan teen with low self-esteem who suddenly becomes a superhero. Awards: SLJ Best Book. (Rev: BL 1/1/91; MJHS; SLJ 2/91*)

52 Smith, Roland. *Thunder Cave* (5–8). 1995, Hyperion $16.95 (0-7868-0068-2). A boy searches for his biological father in Kenya and encounters a dangerous ring of wildlife poachers. (Rev: BL 5/1/95; SLJ 5/95)

53 Snyder, Zilpha Keatley. *Fool's Gold* (5–7). 1993, Delacorte $14 (0-385-30908-2). Barney is trapped in a mine, and Rudy, 14, must overcome his claustrophobia to rescue him. (Rev: BL 3/1/ 93; SLJ 5/93)

54 *Tales of the Sea: An Illustrated Collection of Adventure Stories* (7–12). 1992, Rizzoli $24.95 (0-8478-1578-1). Sea adventures from Heyerdahl, Melville, London, and Christina Rossetti, among others. Color and B&W illustrations. (Rev: BL 12/15/92; BTA; MJHS)

55 Taylor, Theodore. *Timothy of the Cay: A Prequel-Sequel* (5–7). 1993, Harcourt $13.95 (0-15-288358-4); 1994, Avon/Flare paper $3.99 (0-380-72119-8). An intertwining of 2 personal narratives: One takes place before Timothy and Phillip are shipwrecked on the cay; the other, after Phillip is saved. (Rev: BL 9/15/93; SLJ 10/ 93; VOYA 12/93)

56 Taylor, Theodore. *The Weirdo* (9–12). 1991, Harcourt $15.95 (0-15-294952-6). After his friend mysteriously disappears, Chip assumes leadership of the fight to protect bears living in the local swamp. Awards: YALSA Best Book for Young Adults. (Rev: BL 12/15/91; MJHS; SLJ 1/ 92)

57 Temple, Frances. *Tonight, by Sea* (6–10). 1995, Orchard/Richard Jackson LB $15.99 (0-531-08749-2). A docunovel about Haitian boat people who struggle for social justice after harrowing escapes to freedom. (Rev: BL 3/15/95; SLJ 4/95)

58 Ure, Jean. *Plague* (7–12). 1991, Harcourt/ Jane Yolen $16.95 (0-15-262429-5); 1993, Puffin paper $4.99 (0-14-036283-5). Three teenagers must band together to survive in a hostile, nearly deserted London after a catastrophe has killed almost everyone. Awards: YALSA Best Book for Young Adults. (Rev: BL 11/15/91*; MJHS; SLJ 10/91)

59 Vigor, John. *Danger, Dolphins, and Ginger Beer* (5–7). 1993, Atheneum $14.95 (0-689-31817-0). While Sally, 12, and her 2 younger brothers are camping on Crab Island in the Caribbean, they discover a wounded dolphin, watch a boat crash on a reef, and uncover a drug-smuggling operation. (Rev: BL 8/93; SLJ 7/93; VOYA 8/93)

60 Walker, Mary Willis. *Under the Beetle's Cellar* (9–adult). 1995, Doubleday $22.50 (0-385-46859-8). A female crime reporter tries to negotiate the release of 11 children and a school bus driver who are buried in a bus by a cult leader who believes the world's end is imminent. Awards: SLJ Best Book. (Rev: BL 8/95*; SLJ 12/95)

61 Watkins, Paul. *The Promise of Light* (9–adult). 1993, Random $20 (0-679-41974-8). After discovering in 1921 that his late parents had adopted him, recent college grad Ben returns to his Irish homeland to uncover their past. (Rev: BL 12/15/92*; BTA; SLJ 6/93)

62 Watson, Harvey. *Bob War and Poke* (6–9). 1991, Houghton $13.95 (0-395-57038-7). City slicker bank robbers and cardsharps Lucinda and Randolph take on the services of country boys Warren and Ralph, and they tour local towns and hills. (Rev: BL 11/15/91; SLJ 12/91)

63 Westall, Robert. *The Kingdom by the Sea* (6–9). 1991, Farrar $14.95 (0-374-34205-9). This World War II survival adventure concerns a 12-year-old boy who is on his own on the northern English coast after his family home is bombed. Awards: Guardian Award for Children's Fiction; YALSA Best Book for Young Adults. (Rev: BL 11/1/91; MJHS; SLJ 11/91)

64 Williams, Barbara. *Titanic Crossing* (5–8). 1995, Dial LB $14.89 (0-8037-1791-1). A 13-year-old boy is aboard the *Titanic* with his mother and sister when it begins to sink. (Rev: BL 5/15/95; SLJ 6/95)

Animal Stories

65 Adler, C. S. *That Horse Whiskey!* (6–8). 1994, Clarion $13.95 (0-395-68185-5); 1996, Avon/Camelot paper $3.99 (0-380-72601-7). Lainey, 13, disappointed that she didn't get a horse for her birthday, works at a stable training a stubborn horse and falls for a city boy. Awards: Newbery Medal. (Rev: BL 11/1/94; MJHS; SLJ 11/94; VOYA 12/94)

66 Arnosky, Jim. *Long Spikes* (5–7). 1992, Clarion $12.95 (0-395-58830-8). A young deer grows into an adventuresome adulthood. (Rev: BL 5/1/92; SLJ 5/92)

67 Bakker, Robert T. *Raptor Red* (9–adult). 1995, Bantam $21.95 (0-553-10124-2). An animal lover's novel by a paleontologist who imagines an action-filled year in the life of a young adult female dinosaur, Raptor Red. (Rev: BL 8/95*; VOYA 2/96)

68 Bauer, Marion Dane. *A Question of Trust* (5–7). 1994, Scholastic $13.95 (0-590-47915-6). After Brad's parents separate and his mother leaves, he and his brother, Brad, find a half-wild cat that kills one of her kittens and they protect the surviving kittens. Awards: SLJ Best Book (Rev: BL 1/15/94*; MJHS; SLJ 3/94*; VOYA 4/94)

69 Bruchac, Joseph. *Native American Animal Stories* (5–8). Illus. 1992, Fulcrum paper $12.95 (1-55591-127-7). Animal stories from various Native American tribes, for reading aloud and storytelling. (Rev: BL 9/1/92; SLJ 11/92) [398.2]

70 Burgess, Melvin. *The Cry of the Wolf* (5–8). 1992, Morrow/Tambourine $13 (0-688-11744-9). The Hunter sets out with cold, deadly precision to wipe out the last pack of wolves in England. (Rev: BL 10/15/92; SLJ 9/92; YR)

71 Buyukmihci, Hope Sawyer. *Hoofmarks* (9–adult). 1994, J. N. Townsend $22.95 (1-880158-05-1). A memoir of the author's childhood on a farm. While working with horses, she developed a lifelong love for them. (Rev: BL 8/94) [813.54]

72 Cleary, Beverly. *Strider* (5–9). Illus. 1991, Morrow LB $13.88 (0-688-09901-7). In this sequel to *Dear Mr. Henshaw*, the hero is now 4 years older, beginning high school and still writing in his diary, with his beloved dog, Strider, by his side. (Rev: BL 7/91*; SLJ 9/91)

73 Corcoran, Barbara. *Wolf at the Door* (6–8). 1993, Atheneum $14.95 (0-689-31870-7). Lee, age 13, feels inferior to her beautiful sister until Lee rescues a young wolf and opposition from neighbors unite them. (Rev: BL 10/1/93; VOYA 12/93)

74 Crompton, Anne Eliot. *The Snow Pony* (5–9). 1991, Holt $14.95 (0-8050-1573-6). New in town, a lonely 8th-grade girl is offered a job by her shy, misunderstood neighbor taming and grooming a pony for his grandson. (Rev: BL 9/15/91)

75 Cross, Gillian. *Wolf* (6–12). 1991, Holiday $13.95 (0-8234-0870-1). Cassy, 13, learns all about wolves, both in animal and human form, while growing up in London. (Rev: BL 1/15/91; SLJ 4/91)

76 Ellis, Ella Thorp. *Swimming with the Whales* (6–9). 1995, Holt $14.95 (0-8050-3306-8). Paolo—a boy living on the Patagonian peninsula, where there are more whales, sea lions, and guanacos than people—must face moving to San Francisco and falling in love. (Rev: BL 7/95)

77 Evans, Nicholas. *The Horse Whisperer* (9–adult). 1995, Delacorte $23.95 (0-385-31523-6). After a teenager loses her leg in a riding accident, her mother moves them to Montana, where the "horse whisperer," a man of mystical powers, tries to rebuild their lives. (Rev: BL 8/95*)

78 Fromenthal, Jean-Luc. *Broadway Chicken* (5–8). Tr. by Suzi Baker. Illus. 1995, Hyperion LB $14.89 (0-7868-2048-9). A tale of success and failure with, yes, a dancing chicken as the protagonist. (Rev: BL 12/15/95)

79 George, Jean Craighead. *The Missing 'Gator of Gumbo Limbo: An Ecological Mystery* (5–7). 1992, HarperCollins LB $13.89 (0-06-020397-8). Liza and her mother live in the Everglades, where they scheme to protect an alligator threatened by an armed official, oblivious to its importance to the delicate ecology. (Rev: BL 6/1/92; MJHS; SLJ 6/92)

80 Greenberg, Martin H., and Charles G. Waugh, eds. *A Newbery Zoo: A Dozen Animal Stories by Newbery Award–Winning Authors* (5–7). 1995, Delacorte $16.95 (0-385-32263-1). This anthology ranges from fireflies to moose, from fable to ecological observations, and from Cleary to Byars. (Rev: BL 1/15/95; SLJ 4/95)

81 Hall, Lynn. *The Soul of the Silver Dog* (5–8). 1992, Harcourt $16.95 (0-15-277196-4). A handicapped dog bonds with his new teenage owner living in a troubled family. (Rev: BL 4/15/92; MJHS; SLJ 6/92; YR)

82 Henkes, Kevin. *Protecting Marie* (5–7). 1995, Greenwillow $15 (0-688-13958-2). Fanny, 12, worries about the reactions of her moody artist father when she receives a dog that she loves very much. Awards: SLJ Best Book. (Rev: BL 3/15/95; SLJ 5/95; VOYA 5/95)

83 Henry, Marguerite. *Misty's Twilight* (5–7). 1992, Macmillan $12.95 (0-02-743623-3). Dr. Sandy Price and her 2 children move to Virginia and buy a horse that foals Misty's Twilight, which is first a cutting horse and jumper before becoming a dressage horse. (Rev: BL 9/1/92; SLJ 9/92)

84 Hobbs, Will. *Beardance* (7–12). 1993, Atheneum $14.95 (0-689-31867-7). Prospector Cloyd Atcity stays the winter in the Colorado mountains to ensure the survival of the last 2 grizzly cubs in the state after their mother and sibling die. Awards: YALSA Best Book for Young Adults. (Rev: BL 11/15/93; BTA; MJHS; SLJ 12/93; VOYA 12/93)

85 Katz, Welwyn Wilton. *Whalesinger* (7–10). 1991, Macmillan/Margaret K. McElderry $14.95 (0-689-50511-6). Two Vancouver teens spending their summer on the California coast encounter a corrupt research scientist, endangered whales, and natural disasters. (Rev: BL 2/1/91; SLJ 5/91)

86 Kendall, Sarita. *Ransom for a River Dolphin* (5–8). 1993, Lerner $18.95 (0-8225-0735-8). The story of a Colombian girl who discovers her stepfather's harpoon head in a wounded Amazon River dolphin and nurses it back to health. (Rev: BL 2/1/94; SLJ 3/94)

87 Kincaid, Beth. *Back in the Saddle* (5–9). (Silver Creek Riders) 1994, Berkley/Jove paper $3.50 (0-515-11480-4). This first book in the series focuses on 4 girls attending a summer riding camp, and their relationships with each other and their horses. (Rev: BL 1/1/95; SLJ 12/94)

88 Klass, David. *California Blue* (7–10). 1994, Scholastic $13.95 (0-590-46688-7). A 17-year-old California boy who cares about track and butterflies finds a chrysalis that turns out to be an unknown species. Awards: SLJ Best Book. (Rev: BL 3/1/94; BTA; MJHS; SHS; SLJ 4/94*; VOYA 6/94)

89 Levin, Betty. *Away to Me, Moss* (5–7). 1994, Greenwillow $14 (0-688-13439-4). Zanna, 10, lives on Ragged Mountain and deals with her father's job-related absence and her mother's exhaustion from overwork. She finds joy by befriending Moss, a collie. (Rev: BL 10/1/94; SLJ 10/94)

90 McCaig, Donald. *Nop's Hope* (9–adult). 1994, Crown $20 (0-517-58488-3). A heartwarming but unsentimental story of a border collie named Hope and a woman whose husband and daughter are killed. (Rev: BL 5/15/94; BTA; SLJ 9/94; VOYA 10/94)

91 Michener, James A. *Creatures of the Kingdom: Stories of Animals and Nature* (9–adult). 1993, Random $22 (0-679-41367-7). Sections from Michener's novels that deal with animals and other aspects of nature, e.g., the volcanoes of Hawaii, the habits of the *diplodocus* dinosaur, and the life of the salmon. (Rev: BL 7/93; SLJ 5/94)

92 Mikaelsen, Ben. *Rescue Josh McGuire* (6–9). 1991, Hyperion LB $14.89 (1-56282-100-8). Josh, age 13, rescues an orphaned bear cub; when he is told it must be turned over to game authorities, he runs away into the mountains. Awards: IRA Children's Book. (Rev: BL 12/15/91)

93 Mikaelsen, Ben. *Stranded* (6–8). 1995, Hyperion LB $15.89 (0-7868-2059-4). Koby—a 12-year-old girl who feels as isolated and stranded as the wounded pilot whales she helps rescue—learns a great deal about emotional barriers and reconciliation. (Rev: BL 8/95*; SLJ 6/95; VOYA 12/95)

94 Monson, A. M. *The Deer Stand* (6–8). 1992, Lothrop $13 (0-688-11057-6); 1994, Morrow/Beech Tree paper $4.95 (0-688-13623-0). Bits, 12, is desperately unhappy about moving from Chicago to rural Wisconsin, but when she succeeds in taming a young deer, her loneliness is eased. Awards: Friends of American Writers Juvenile Book. (Rev: BL 1/15/93; SLJ 1/93)

95 Naylor, Phyllis Reynolds. *The Grand Escape* (5–7). 1993, Atheneum $13.95 (0-689-31722-0); 1994, Dell/Yearling paper $3.99 (0-440-40968-3). The adventures of 2 cats, Marco and his brother Polo, who must solve 3 "Great Mysteries" before they can join the Club of Mysteries. (Rev: BL 7/93; MJHS)

96 Naylor, Phyllis Reynolds. *Shiloh* (5–8). 1991, Atheneum $12.95 (0-689-31614-3). Set in the West Virginia hills, this novel of an 11-year-old and a neighbor's abused beagle that he loves explores the complex nature of right and wrong. Awards: ALSC Notable Children's Book; Fisher Children's Book; Newbery Medal. (Rev: BL 12/1/91*; MJHS; SLJ 9/91)

97 Nelson, Drew. *Wild Voices* (5–8). Illus. 1991, Putnam/Philomel $15.95 (0-399-21798-3). Told from wild animals' viewpoints, these stories relate their daily tasks of hunting, fighting, and escaping, in the constant struggle to survive. (Rev: BL 10/1/91)

98 Parnall, Peter. *Marsh Cat* (5–7). 1991, Macmillan $12.95 (0-02-770120-4). A huge, wild black cat is drawn into the world of a barn cat, is caught in a forgotten trap, and is nursed back to health by a girl who wants to tame him. (Rev: BL 10/15/91; SLJ 1/92)

99 Peck, Sylvia. *Kelsey's Raven* (5–7). 1992, Morrow $14 (0-688-09583-6). An old, injured raven is adopted by a family and changes their lives. (Rev: BL 5/1/92; SLJ 6/92; YR)

100 Polikoff, Barbara Garland. *Riding the Wind* (5–7). 1995, Holt $14.95 (0-8050-3492-7). This sequel to *Life's a Funny Proposition, Horatio* (1992) tells Angie's reaction to her favorite horse being hurt by a tough new girl and her nursing him back to health. (Rev: BL 6/1–15/95; SLJ 9/95)

101 Ramachander, Akumal. *Little Pig* (5–7). Illus. 1992, Viking $15 (0-670-84350-4). Combines photography, collage, and painting, showing a woman wearing a series of elaborately sculptured masks that capture her imaginings. (Rev: BL 11/15/92; SLJ 1/93) [398.245]

102 Reaver, Chap. *Bill* (6–8). 1994, Delacorte $14.95 (0-385-31175-3). Jessica, 13, is torn between loyalty to her father, a Kentucky moonshiner, and her growing realization that his drinking and lifestyle benefit no one. Awards: SLJ Best Book. (Rev: BL 4/1/94*; MJHS; SLJ 6/94*; VOYA 6/94)

103 Savage, Deborah. *To Race a Dream* (6–9). 1994, Houghton $14.95 (0-395-69252-0). In early twentieth-century Minnesota, young Theodora dreams of being a harness-racing driver. She disguises herself as a boy and works as a stable hand. (Rev: BL 11/1/94*; BTA; SLJ 12/94; VOYA 10/94)

104 Sherlock, Patti. *Four of a Kind* (5–9). 1991, Holiday $13.95 (0-8234-0913-9). Andy's grandfather agrees to lend him money to buy a pair of horses, and he sets his sights on winning the horse-pulling contest at a state fair. (Rev: BL 12/1/91; SLJ 10/91)

105 Sherlock, Patti. *Some Fine Dog* (5–8). 1992, Holiday $13.95 (0-8234-0947-3). A star soloist in the boys' choir would rather spend time with his gifted dog than practice his singing. (Rev: BL 3/15/92; SLJ 4/92; YR)

106 Slade, Michael. *The Horses of Central Park* (5–7). 1992, Scholastic $12.95 (0-590-44659-2). A boy and his best friend decide to free the carriage horses of New York's Central Park. (Rev: BL 2/1/92; YR)

107 Springer, Nancy. *The Boy on a Black Horse* (6–9). 1994, Atheneum $14.95 (0-689-31840-5). A story about a gypsy youth (a rom, as they prefer to be called) who has run off from his abusive father. (Rev: BL 4/15/94; SLJ 6/94; VOYA 6/94)

108 Tamar, Erika. *Junkyard Dog* (5–7). 1995, Knopf $15 (0-679-87057-1). A girl's heart goes out to a mistreated junkyard dog, and she gains self-confidence as her stepfather helps her to build a doghouse. (Rev: BL 5/1/95; SLJ 6/95)

109 Taylor, Theodore. *Tuck Triumphant* (5–7). 1991, Doubleday $14.95 (0-385-41480-3); 1992, Avon/Camelot paper $3.50 (0-380-71323-3). A sequel to *The Trouble with Tuck*, the story of a blind dog and his owners continues when the family decides to adopt a small Korean boy. (Rev: BL 2/1/91; MJHS; SLJ 3/91)

110 Tryon, Thomas. *The Adventures of Opal and Cupid* (6–8). 1992, Viking LB $14 (0-670-82239-6). A girl and her amazing performing elephant leave home to find fame and fortune in New York. (Rev: BL 9/15/92; SLJ 1/93)

111 Turnbull, Ann. *Speedwell* (5–7). 1992, Candlewick $14.95 (1-56402-112-2). To escape the privations of the 1930s depression in England, Mary races pigeons and wants to enter her pigeon in a race in France for the prize money. (Rev: BL 12/15/92; SLJ 10/92)

112 Welch, Sheila Kelly. *A Horse for All Seasons: Collected Stories* (5–8). 1995, Boyds Mills $15.95 (1-56397-415-0). Twelve stories of young people and the horses in their lives. (Rev: BL 4/1/95; SLJ 1/95) [813.54]

Classics

Europe

GENERAL AND MISCELLANEOUS

113 Cervantes Saavedra, Miguel de. *Don Quijote de la Mancha, Vols. 1 and 2* (9–adult). Illus. 1993, Anaya (Madrid, Spain) $199 (84-207-5629-6). This expensive edition of the Spanish-language masterpiece (weighing 16 pounds!) contains more than 1,000 double-page watercolors and B&W drawings and a luxurious binding and design. The original spelling and punctuation have been updated for contemporary Spanish speakers. Full Spanish titles: *El ingenioso hidalgo Don Quijote de la Mancha* (Vol. 1) and *El ingenioso caballero Don Quijote de la Mancha* (Vol. 2). English title: *Don Quijote de la Mancha*. (Rev: BL 10/15/95; BTA; MJHS; SHS)

114 Delamare, David. *Cinderella* (7–12). 1993, Simon & Schuster $15 (0-671-76944-8). The familiar story is set in a locale much like Venice and enhanced by Delamare's paintings, both realistic and surreal. (Rev: BL 9/15/93; SLJ 12/93) [398.2]

115 Perrault, Charles, and Naomi Lewis. *Puss in Boots* (5–7). Illus. 1994, North-South $14.95 (1-

55858-099-9). A different artistic interpretation of the famed tale that is menacing and darkly enigmatic. Awards: SLJ Best Book. (Rev: BL 4/15/94; MJHS; SLJ 7/94) [398.24]

GREAT BRITAIN AND IRELAND

116 Dickens, Charles. *A Christmas Carol* (5–8). Illus. 1995, Macmillan/Margaret K. McElderry $19.95 (0-689-80213-7). The familiar Dickens tale with Blake's scraggly cartoon-type illustrations. (Rev: BL 10/15/95; MJHS)

117 Dickens, Charles. *David Copperfield* (8–12). Illus. 1995, North-South LB $18.88. Includes some little-known episodes that Dickens excerpted from his book for public readings, information about dramatic performance, and illustrations. (Rev: BL 12/15/95; MJHS; SHS)

118 Lester, Julius, reteller. *Othello* (8–12). 1995, Scholastic $12.95 (0-590-41967-6). Although significant changes have been made in the characterizations, the original story line is followed in Lester's "re-imagining" of Shakespeare's play. (Rev: BL 2/15/95; SLJ 4/95*; VOYA 5/95)

119 Schmidt, Gary D. *Pilgrim's Progress* (5–7). Illus. 1994, Eerdmans $24.99 (0-8028-5080-4). Retells the allegory of Christian, who leaves the city of Destruction in search of the Celestial City and encounters such characters as Goodwill, Despair, and Deceiver. (Rev: BL 11/1/94; SLJ 12/94)

120 Stevenson, Robert Louis. *Treasure Island* (5–12). Illus. 1992, Viking $20 (0-670-84685-6). The classic tale in a large-size format, with full-page watercolors and B&W drawings. (Rev: BL 11/15/92; SHS)

121 Swift, Jonathan. *Gulliver in Lilliput* (5–7). Retold by Margaret Hodges. Illus. 1995, Holiday LB $15.95 (0-8234-1147-8). Detailed watercolors add intricacy to Gulliver's strange adventures. Awards: SLJ Best Book. (Rev: BL 4/15/95; SLJ 6/95)

122 Swift, Jonathan. *Gulliver's Travels* (5–7). Adapt. by James Riordan. Illus. 1992, Oxford Univ. $18 (0-19-279897-9). An adaptation of Swift's satiric fantasies about Lilliput and Brobdingnag. (Rev: BL 11/15/92; MJHS; SHS) [823]

United States

123 Gallico, Paul. *The Snow Goose* (7–12). Illus. 1992, Knopf LB $16.99 (0-679-90683-5). A hunchbacked artist and a young child nurse a wounded snow goose back to health, and it later returns to protect them in this large, fiftieth-anniversary illustrated edition of this classic. (Rev: BL 9/15/92; SHS)

124 Irving, Washington. *The Legend of Sleepy Hollow: Found Among the Papers of the Late Diedrich Knickerbocker* (5–8). (Books of Wonder) Illus. 1992, Boyds Mills/Caroline House $15.95 (1-56397-027-9). The classic about Ichabod Crane and his encounter with a headless horseman. (Rev: BL 11/1/92)

Other Countries

125 Alderson, Brian. *The Arabian Nights; or, Tales Told by Sheherezade During a Thousand Nights and One Night* (5–8). Illus. 1995, Morrow $20 (0-688-14219-2). The tales this time are written in a colloquial style, retaining more of the earthiness and vigor of the original. Border pictures like Persian miniatures and double-page spreads grace the pages. (Rev: BL 10/15/95; SLJ 9/95) [398.22]

126 Kipling, Rudyard. *The Jungle Books: The Mowgli Stories* (5–7). Illus. 1995, Morrow $20 (0-688-09979-3). Eight Mowgli stories, richly illustrated with 18 watercolors. (Rev: BL 10/15/95; MJHS; SLJ 11/95)

Contemporary Life and Problems

General and Miscellaneous

127 Carpenter, William. *A Keeper of Sheep* (9–adult). 1994, Milkweed Editions (430 First Ave. N., Suite 400, Minneapolis, MN 55401) $21.95 (1-57131-000-2). On summer break, Penelope cares for her neighbor's lover, a composer dying of AIDS, while battling with her affluent community determined to drive him out. (Rev: BL 8/94; BTA)

128 Cooper, Ilene. *Lights, Camera, Attitude!* (6–9). (Hollywood Wars) 1993, Penguin paper $3.99 (0-14-036155-3). In the series' second book, the show's about to go on, and Alison is finding that her TV series has totally changed her life. Sequel to *My Co-Star, My Enemy*. (Rev: BL 5/1/93)

129 Cooper, Ilene. *My Co-Star, My Enemy* (6–9). (Hollywood Wars) 1993, Penguin/Puffin paper $3.25 (0-14-036156-1). Shy Alison, 15, accompanies a friend to an audition and ends up starring in a TV show, but her onscreen stepsister resents almost everything about her. (Rev: BL 5/1/93; SLJ 6/93)

130 Geras, Adèle. *Happy Endings* (7–12). 1991, Harcourt $14.95 (0-15-233375-4). The backstage drama of an English production of *Three Sisters*, in which Mel has won a role. (Rev: BL 5/1/91; SLJ 5/91)

131 Gilmore, Kate. *Jason and the Bard* (8–12). 1993, Houghton $14.95 (0-395-62472-X). A leisurely novel about Jason and 6 other apprentices at a summer Shakespeare festival. (Rev: BL 3/15/93; SLJ 6/93)

132 Hausman, Gerald. *Doctor Moledinky's Castle: A Hometown Tale* (7–12). 1995, Simon & Schuster $15 (0-689-80019-3). First-person stories about the narrator's town full of eccentrics. (Rev: BL 12/1/95; SLJ 10/95; VOYA 2/96)

133 Johnston, Janet. *Ellie Brader Hates Mr. G* (5–7). 1991, Clarion $13.95 (0-395-58195-8). Describes Ellie's life in her 5th-grade class when her beloved teacher is replaced by strict Mr. Garrett at the end of the school year. (Rev: BL 11/15/91; SLJ 12/91)

134 Ladew, Donald P. *Stradivarius* (9–adult). 1995, Carroll & Graf $21.95 (0-7867-0136-6). A mixture of fact and fancy in a well-told tale of one of Stradivarius's violins, "Hercules." (Rev: BL 1/1/95; SLJ 4/95)

135 Malcolm, Jahnna N. *Makin' the Grade* (5–7). (Rock 'n' Rebels) 1991, Bantam/Skylark paper $2.99 (0-553-15955-0). A record producer chooses a cross-cultural mix for a new superstar band, but its members discover success isn't worth the phoniness of a manufactured image. (Rev: BL 12/15/91)

136 Malcolm, Jahnna N. *Sticking Together* (5–7). (Rock 'n' Rebels) 1991, Bantam/Skylark paper $2.99 (0-553-15956-9). The members of a rock band begin to argue, and their jealousies and irritations affect the band's ability to deliver a professional performance. (Rev: BL 12/15/91)

137 Nunes, Lygia Bojunga. *My Friend the Painter* (5–7). Tr. by Giovanni Pontiero. 1991, Harcourt $13.95 (0-15-256340-7). In this Brazilian story, Claudio, 11, describes to his adult friend the grief and bewilderment he's felt since his friend's suicide. (Rev: BL 4/1/91; SLJ 10/91)

138 Paulsen, Gary. *The Monument* (6–9). 1991, Delacorte $15 (0-385-30518-4). A 13-year-old girl's friendship with an artist who is hired to create a monument in her small town transforms her into dedicating herself to art. Awards: SLJ Best Book; YALSA Best Book for Young Adults. (Rev: BL 9/15/91; MJHS; SLJ 10/91*)

139 Rodowsky, Colby. *Sydney, Invincible* (7–10). 1995, Farrar $14 (0-374-37365-5). In this sequel to *Sydney, Herself*, a girl yearns to write and struggles with the idea of responsible journalism. (Rev: BL 4/15/95)

140 Sullivan, Charles, ed. *Hispanic-American Literature and Art for Young People* (7–12). 1994, Abrams $24.95 (0-8109-3422-1). Collects Latino prose, poetry, painting, and photography, with profiles of leading figures from Cervantes to singer Gloria Estefan. Awards: BL Editors' Choice. (Rev: BL 7/94*)

141 Tamar, Erika. *Out of Control* (9–12). 1991, Atheneum $14.95 (0-689-31689-5). The story of a high school rock band and the relationships of the members, who each rely on the band for identity and friendship but resent being controlled by the others. (Rev: BL 9/15/91)

142 Theroux, Paul. *Millroy the Magician* (9–adult). 1994, Random $23 (0-679-40247-0). Jilly, a teenage runaway, joins Millroy, a mysterious magician, to proclaim his gospel of good nutrition, with humorous results. (Rev: BL 10/15/93*; SLJ 10/94; VOYA 8/94)

143 Willis, Patricia. *A Place to Claim As Home* (6–8). 1991, Clarion $13.95 (0-395-55395-4). Orphan Henry, 13, is hired to work for Miss Sarah on an Ohio farm in 1943, and he soon comes to wonder whether he might be the illegitimate child she gave away 13 years before. Awards: Friends of American Writers Juvenile Book. (Rev: BL 5/15/91; SLJ 8/91)

Ethnic Groups and Problems

144 Banks, Jacqueline Turner. *The New One* (5–7). 1994, Houghton $13.95 (0-395-66610-4). A fresh, honest story of friendship, family, and prejudice among a group of 6th-grade kids in Kentucky. (Rev: BL 4/15/94; SLJ 6/94; VOYA 10/94)

145 Beake, Lesley. *Song of Be* (6–12). 1993, Holt $14.95 (0-8050-2905-2); 1995, Penguin/Puffin paper $3.99 (0-14-037498-1). The tragedy of Namibian natives who are caught in a changing world is told by the character Be, a 15-year-old girl working on a white man's ranch. Awards: SLJ Best Book. (Rev: BL 12/1/93*; BTA; SLJ 3/94; VOYA 4/94)

146 Beatty, Patricia. *Who Comes with Cannons?* (5–7). 1992, Morrow $14 (0-688-11028-2). Quakers Truth Hopkins, 12, and her aunt and uncle live on a North Carolina farm at the start of the Civil War, and the farm becomes a station on the

Underground Railroad. (Rev: BL 1/1/93; BTA; SLJ 10/92; YR)

147 Bedford, Simi. *Yoruba Girl Dancing* (9–adult). 1992, Viking $19 (0-670-84045-9). A semi-autobiographical novel about a Nigerian girl's adjustment to life at an English boarding school in the 1950s. Awards: SLJ Best Book. (Rev: BL 10/1/92; SLJ 3/93*)

148 Bennett, James. *Dakota Dream* (8–10). 1994, Scholastic $13.95 (0-590-46680-1). A teen orphan in a group home dreams he is a Dakota warrior and flees to the reservation, where a chief guides him in his quest. Awards: SLJ Best Book; YALSA Best Book for Young Adults. (Rev: BL 1/15/94; BTA; MJHS; SLJ 3/94)

149 Bertrand, Diane Gonzales. *Sweet Fifteen* (8–12). 1995, Arte Público $12.95 (1-55885-122-4); paper $7.95 (1-55885-133-X). While making a party dress for Stefanie Bonilla, age 14, Rita Navarro falls in love with her uncle and befriends her widowed mother, maturing in the process. (Rev: BL 6/1–15/95; SLJ 9/95)

150 Bolden, Tonya, ed. *Rites of Passage: Stories about Growing Up by Black Writers from Around the World* (7–12). 1994, Hyperion $16.95 (1-56282-688-3). A collection of 17 stories that focus on growing up black in the United States, Africa, Australia, Great Britain, the Caribbean, and Central America. (Rev: BL 3/1/94; BTA; MJHS; SLJ 6/94)

151 Boyd, Candy D. *Fall Secrets* (5–7). 1994, Penguin/Puffin paper $3.99 (0-14-036583-4). Jessie wants to become an actress but must also keep up her grades. (Rev: BL 9/15/94; SLJ 12/94)

152 Brown, Linda Beatrice. *Crossing over Jordon* (9–adult). 1995, Ballantine $22 (0-345-37857-1). From the time of slavery to the early twenty-first century, the women of an African American family experience love, suffering, and a struggle to be free. (Rev: BL 2/15/95; SLJ 9/95)

153 Burgess, Barbara Hood. *Oren Bell* (6–12). 1991, Delacorte $13.95 (0-385-30325-4). This novel about a 7th-grader who lives in a declining Detroit neighborhood features a "strong family and is rich in character, humor, and moral fiber." (Rev: BL 5/15/91; MJHS)

154 Buss, Fran Leeper, and Daisy Cubias. *Journey of the Sparrows* (7–12). 1991, Dutton/Lodestar $14.95 (0-525-67362-8). Describes the cruel journey from El Salvador to a difficult life in Chicago of a strong, loving 15-year-old and her siblings. Awards: YALSA Best Book for Young Adults. (Rev: BL 10/1/91; SLJ 10/91)

155 Campbell, Bebe Moore. *Your Blues Ain't Like Mine* (9–adult). 1992, Putnam $22.95 (0-399-13746-7); 1993, Ballantine paper $12 (0-345-38395-8). A fictionalization of the 1955 Emmett Till murder, in which a teenage boy from Chicago was lynched in Mississippi after speaking French in the presence of a young white girl. Awards: BL Editors' Choice. (Rev: BL 8/92; BTA; SLJ 1/93)

156 Cansino, Eliacer. *Yo, Robinsón Sánchez, habiendo naufragado* (7–10). 1992, Ediciones Toray (Barcelona, Spain) paper $8.95 (84-310-3406-8). A teenager relates his experiences at home and at a new school when his father is reassigned from Salamanca to a new job in Seville, Spain. English title: *I, Robinson Sanchez, Having Shipwrecked*. (Rev: BL 10/1/94)

157 Cheong, Fiona. *The Scent of the Gods* (9–adult). 1991, Norton $19.95 (0-393-03024-5). This novel of an extended family and the coming-of-age of its youngest member is set in Singapore during the violent 1960s. (Rev: BL 9/15/91*)

158 Chocolate, Debbi. *NEATE to the Rescue!* (5–7). 1992, Just Us Books (301 Main St., Suite 22–24, Orange, NJ 07050) paper $3.95 (0-940975-42-4). An African American girl, Naimah, 13, campaigns for her mother's reelection to the city council, in opposition to a racist challenger. (Rev: BL 3/15/93; SLJ 7/93)

159 Cofer, Judith Ortiz. *An Island Like You* (7–12). 1995, Orchard/Melanie Kroupa LB $15.99 (0-531-08747-6). Stories of Puerto Rican immigrant kids experiencing the tensions between 2 cultures. Awards: SLJ Best Book. (Rev: BL 2/15/95*; SLJ 7/95)

160 Curry, Constance. *Silver Rights* (9–adult). 1995, Algonquin $21.95 (1-56512-095-7). The title comes from what older black country people call their civil rights: *silver rights*. This is the backdrop for the story of the Carters, a family of Mississippi sharecroppers who wanted a top-notch education for 7 of their 13 children. (Rev: BL 9/1/95) [976.2]

161 Curtis, Christopher Paul. *The Watsons Go to Birmingham–1963* (5–8). 1995, Delacorte $14.95 (0-385-32175-9). Fourth-grader Kenny Watson tells of conflicts in his African American family, especially with his tough older brother, that cause them to return to the South during the 1960s civil rights movement. Awards: Child Study Children's Book; Golden Kite. (Rev: BL 8/95; SLJ 10/95; VOYA 12/95)

162 Davis, Ossie. *Just Like Martin* (5–8). 1992, Simon & Schuster $14 (0-671-73202-1). A docunovel of 13-year-old Isaac's struggles with family problems and a vow of nonviolence during the 1960s civil rights movement. (Rev: BL 9/1/92; MJHS; SLJ 10/92; YR)

163 Davis, Thulani. *1959* (9–adult). 1992, Grove/Weidenfeld $18.95 (0-8021-1230-7). Life in a small Virginia town on the verge of violent social change, as seen through the eyes of a 12-year-old girl. (Rev: BL 1/1/92*)

164 Egli, Werner J. *Tarantino* (8–12). Tr. from German by José A. Santiago. 1992, Ediciones SM (Madrid, Spain) paper $10.95. Three youth leave Guatemala for San Diego in search of a life free from misery and political persecution, but it is not easy for poor, undocumented immigrants to deal with gangs, drug traffic, and crime. (Rev: BL 2/1/94)

165 Gallo, Donald R., ed. *Join In: Multiethnic Short Stories by Outstanding Writers for Young Adults* (7–12). 1993, Delacorte $15.95 (0-385-31080-3). Seventeen stories concerning the problems teenagers of other ethnic backgrounds have living in the United States. (Rev: BL 1/15/94; BTA; MJHS; SLJ 11/93; VOYA 10/93)

166 Gardner, Mary. *Boat People* (9–adult). 1995, Norton $21 (0-393-03738-X). A sympathetic fictional portrait of Vietnamese refugees in Galveston, Texas. Awards: Associated Writing Programs. (Rev: BL 2/15/95*)

167 Greene, Patricia Baird. *The Sabbath Garden* (7–12). 1993, Dutton/Lodestar $15.99 (0-525-67430-6). One night, Opal Tyler takes refuge from her abusive brother with Jewish neighbor Soloman Lesho. The resulting bond lets them help their community. (Rev: BL 12/1/93; SLJ 2/94)

168 Guy, Rosa. *The Music of Summer* (9–12). 1992, Delacorte $15 (0-385-30599-0). Sarah, age 17, weighs the pain of peer pressure against the excitement of first love during one summer on Cape Cod. Awards: YALSA Best Book for Young Adults. (Rev: BL 4/15/92; SHS; SLJ 2/92; YR)

169 Hamilton, Virginia. *Plain City* (5–7). 1993, Scholastic $13.95 (0-590-47364-6). Buhlaire Sims, age 12, must come to terms with her new identity when her almost-white presumed-dead father walks back into her Midwestern town. Awards: ALSC Notable Children's Book; SLJ Best Book. (Rev: BL 9/15/93*; BTA; MJHS; SLJ 11/93*; VOYA 2/94)

170 Haynes, David. *Right by My Side* (9–adult). 1993, New Rivers paper $9.95 (0-89823-147-7). African American teen Marshall Field Finney describes a year of his life—the year his mother left him and his father ran away to Las Vegas to find himself. (Rev: BL 2/15/93*; BTA; SLJ 12/93)

171 Hiçyilmaz, Gaye. *The Frozen Waterfall* (7–10). 1994, Farrar $16 (0-374-32482-4). Selda, 12, is a Turkish immigrant living in Switzerland. Using her grandmother as role model, she searches for her identity as a woman. Awards: Korczak Literary Competition. (Rev: BL 10/1/94; SLJ 10/94; VOYA 12/94)

172 Higginsen, Vy, and Tonya Bolden. *Mama, I Want to Sing* (6–12). 1992, Scholastic $13.95 (0-590-44201-5). African American Doris, 10, devastated by her father's death, turns to music for consolation; but when, as a teenager, she plays secular music, her mother disapproves. (Rev: BL 12/1/92; SLJ 10/92)

173 Hill, Anthony. *The Burnt Stick* (5–7). 1995, Houghton $12.95 (0-395-73974-8). John Jagamarra, a boy of mixed Australian Aborigine and white heritage, is taken from his mother at age 5 to be raised in a white missionary community. (Rev: BL 7/95; SLJ 10/95)

174 Houston, James. *Drifting Snow: An Arctic Search* (5–10). 1992, Macmillan/Margaret K. McElderry $13.95 (0-689-50563-9). Elizabeth Queen, 13, searches for her Inuk family roots on Nesak Island in the Canadian Arctic. (Rev: BL 10/15/92; SLJ 10/92; YR)

175 Johnson, Angela. *Toning the Sweep* (7–12). 1993, Orchard/Richard Jackson LB $13.99 (0-531-08626-7); 1994, Scholastic/Point Signature paper $3.95 (0-590-48142-8). Captures the innocence, vulnerability, and love of human interaction, as well as the melancholy, self-discovery, and introspection of an African American adolescent. Awards: Coretta Scott King; SLJ Best Book. (Rev: BL 4/1/93*; MJHS; SLJ 4/93*)

176 Johnson, Stacie. *Sort of Sisters* (5–8). (18 Pine Street). 1992, Bantam paper $3.50 (0-553-29719-8). The series' first book focuses on what happens when orphaned cousin Tasha comes to live with Sarah's family and the adjustments the 2 girls must make before they can be friends. (Rev: BL 8/92; YR)

177 Killingsworth, Monte. *Circle Within a Circle* (7–9). 1994, Macmillan/Margaret K. McElderry $14.95 (0-689-50598-1). A runaway teenage boy and a Chinook Indian join a crusade to save a stretch of sacred land from commercial development. (Rev: BL 3/1/94; BTA; MJHS; SLJ 6/94; VOYA 6/94)

178 Kincaid, Jamaica. *The Autobiography of My Mother* (9–adult). 1996, Farrar $20 (0-374-10732-7). Kincaid's essay *A Small Place* is expanded into this novel about a woman's search for identity as she searches for her mother. (Rev: BL 12/1/95*)

179 Kingsolver, Barbara. *Pigs in Heaven* (9–12). 1993, HarperCollins $23 (0-06-016801-3). Taylor and her 6-year-old adopted Cherokee daughter flee authorities to escape separation. Awards: SLJ Best Book. (Rev: SLJ 11/93*)

180 Laird, Elizabeth. *Kiss the Dust* (6–10). 1992, Dutton $15 (0-525-44893-4); 1994, Penguin/ Puffin paper $3.99 (0-14-036855-8). A docunovel about a refugee Kurdish teen caught up in the 1984 Iran-Iraq War. Awards: YALSA Best Book for Young Adults. (Rev: BL 6/15/92; BTA; MJHS; YR)

181 Lee, Gus. *China Boy* (9–adult). 1991, Dutton $19.94 (0-525-24994-X); NAL/Signet paper $5.99 (0-451-17434-8). Kai—or "China Boy," as he is called by the neighborhood bullies—turns his life around when he learns to stand his ground and fight back. (Rev: BL 3/1/91; SHS)

182 Lee, Gus. *Honor and Duty* (9–adult). 1994, Knopf $24 (0-679-41258-1). A Chinese American cadet at West Point demonstrates honor and devotion to duty by implicating classmates and friends in a cheating incident. (Rev: BL 1/1/94*)

183 Lee, Marie G. *Finding My Voice* (7–12). 1992, Houghton $13.95 (0-395-62134-8); 1994, Dell/Laurel Leaf paper $3.99 (0-440-21896-9). Pressured by her strict Korean parents to get into Harvard, senior Ellen Sung tries to find time for friendship, romance, and fun in her small Minnesota town. Awards: Friends of American Writers Juvenile Book. (Rev: BL 9/1/92; MJHS; SLJ 10/92)

184 Lehrman, Robert. *The Store That Mama Built* (5–7). 1992, Macmillan $12.95 (0-02-754632-2). A Russian immigrant family moves to Pittsburgh, Pennsylvania, to start a grocery store. (Rev: BL 4/15/92; SLJ 7/92)

185 Lipsyte, Robert. *The Brave* (8–12). 1991, HarperCollins/Charlotte Zolotow $14.95 (0-06-023915-8); 1993, HarperTrophy paper $4.50 (0-06-447079-2). A Native American heavyweight boxer is rescued—by a tough-but-tender ex-boxer/New York City cop—from drugs, pimps, and hookers. Awards: SLJ Best Book; YALSA Best Book for Young Adults. (Rev: BL 10/15/91; MJHS; SHS; SLJ 10/91*)

186 Lipsyte, Robert. *The Chief* (7–10). 1993, HarperCollins LB $14.89 (0-06-021068-0). Sonny Bear can't decide whether to go back to the reservation, continue boxing, or become Hollywood's new Native American darling. Sequel to *The Brave*. (Rev: BL 6/1–15/93; BTA; MJHS; VOYA 12/93)

187 López, Tiffany Ana, ed. *Growing Up Chicana/o* (9–adult). 1993, Morrow $18 (0-688-11467-9). This anthology presents the writings of 20 current Chicano authors, including Rudolfo Anaya and Sandra Cisneros, on multicultural issues. (Rev: BL 12/1/93; BTA)

188 Maartens, Maretha. *Paper Bird: A Novel of South Africa* (5–9). Tr. by Madeleine van Biljon. 1991, Clarion $13.95 (0-395-56490-5). This novel (translated from Afrikaans) describes growing up amid poverty in a South African black township and the terrifying effects of political violence. (Rev: BL 9/15/91*; SLJ 10/91)

189 Marino, Jan. *The Day That Elvis Came to Town* (7–10). 1991, Little, Brown $14.45 (0-316-54618-6). Wanda is thrilled when a room in her parents' boarding house is rented to Mercedes, who makes her feel pretty and smart—and who once went to school with Elvis Presley. Awards: BL Editors' Choice; SLJ Best Book. (Rev: BL 12/15/90*; SLJ 1/91*)

190 Markle, Sandra. *The Fledglings* (6–9). 1992, Bantam/Starfire $15 (0-553-07729-5). With her parents dead, Kate, 14, runs away to live with her Cherokee grandfather and immerses herself happily in his world. (Rev: BL 6/15/92; YR)

191 Mazer, Anne. *Moose Street* (5–7). 1992, Knopf/Borzoi LB $13.99 (0-679-93233-X). An eccentric story of a Jewish girl worried about her religious identity among her gentile neighbors. (Rev: BL 11/1/92*)

192 Mazzio, Joann. *The One Who Came Back* (7–10). 1992, Houghton $13.95 (0-395-59506-1). A New Mexico teen must prove he didn't kill his best friend. (Rev: BL 4/1/92; SLJ 5/92)

193 Moore, Yvette. *Freedom Songs* (6–12). 1991, Orchard LB $14.99 (0-531-08412-4); 1992, Penguin/Puffin paper $3.99 (0-14-036017-4). In 1968, Sheryl, 14, witnesses and then experiences acts of prejudice while visiting relatives in North Carolina. (Rev: BL 4/15/91; SHS; SLJ 3/91)

194 Mowry, Jess. *Way Past Cool* (9–adult). 1992, Farrar $17 (0-374-28669-8). Kids struggle to survive in a violent California ghetto. Awards: BL Editors' Choice; YALSA Best Book for Young Adults. (Rev: BL 3/15/92; SHS)

195 Murray, Albert. *The Spyglass Tree* (9–adult). 1991, Pantheon $20 (0-394-58887-8). An African American college student from Alabama remembers his charmed youth, adored by both his natural and adopted mothers and carefully nurtured by teachers. (Rev: BL 11/1/91*)

196 Myers, Walter Dean. *The Glory Field* (7–10). 1994, Scholastic $14.95. Follows a family's 200-year history, from the capture of an African boy in the 1750s through the lives of his descendants on a small plot of South Carolina land called the Glory Field. Awards: SLJ Best Book. (Rev: BL 10/1/94; BTA; MJHS)

197 Namioka, Lensey. *April and the Dragon Lady* (7–12). 1994, Harcourt $10.95 (0-15-276644-8). A Chinese American high school junior must relinquish important activities to care for her ailing grandmother and struggle with the constraints of her traditional female role. (Rev: BL 3/1/94; BTA; SLJ 4/94; VOYA 6/94)

198 Namioka, Lensey. *Yang the Third and Her Impossible Family* (5–7). Illus. 1995, Little, Brown $15.95 (0-316-59726-0). Cross-cultural awkwardness and a young Chinese girl who is desperately trying to be American. (Rev: BL 4/15/95; SLJ 8/95; VOYA 5/95)

199 Ng, Fae Myenne. *Bone* (9–adult). 1993, Hyperion $19.95 (1-56282-944-0). A look at the barriers and the love between generations in a Chinese American family. (Rev: BL 9/15/92*; SHS)

200 Okimoto, Jean Davies. *Molly by Any Other Name* (6–12). 1990, Scholastic $13.95 (0-590-42993-0). A teenage adoptee searches for her birth mother. (Rev: BL 1/15/91)

201 Okimoto, Jean Davies. *Talent Night* (6–10). 1995, Scholastic $14.95 (0-590-47809-5). In this story, Rodney Suyama, 17, wants to be the first Japanese American rapper and to date beautiful Ivy Ramos. (Rev: BL 6/1–15/95; SLJ 5/95)

202 Oughton, Jerrie. *Music from a Place Called Half Moon* (6–10). 1995, Houghton $13.95 (0-395-70737-4). Small-town bigotry and personal transformation in the 1950s. Awards: Child Study Children's Book. (Rev: BL 5/1/95; SLJ 4/95)

203 Perkins, Mitali. *The Sunita Experiment* (7–10). 1993, Little, Brown/Joy Street $14.95 (0-316-69943-8); 1994, Hyperion paper $4.95 (1-56282-671-9). An Asian American 8th-grade teen is confused about self-identity and is trying to fit into a "normal" high school. (Rev: BL 5/1/93; BTA; MJHS; SLJ 6/93; VOYA 10/93)

204 Pettit, Jayne. *My Name Is San Ho* (5–7). 1992, Scholastic $13.95 (0-590-44172-8). A young Vietnamese boy must adjust to a new culture when his mother marries an American soldier and moves the family to Philadelphia. (Rev: BL 3/1/92; BTA; MJHS; YR)

205 Pinkney, Andrea Davis. *Hold Fast to Dreams* (5–8). 1995, Morrow $15 (0-688-12832-7). A young African American girl moves from her neighborhood into an all-white suburb, where she is challenged by her new situation as "the other." (Rev: BL 2/15/95; SLJ 4/95)

206 Pullman, Philip. *The Broken Bridge* (8–12). 1992, Knopf LB $15.99 (0-679-91972-4). A biracial girl learns the truth about her heritage. (Rev: BL 2/15/92; SLJ 3/92*)

207 Qualey, Marsha. *Revolutions of the Heart* (7–12). 1993, Houghton $13.95 (0-395-64168-3). Cory lives in a small Wisconsin town that is torn by bigotry about Chippewa Indians who are reclaiming their hunting and fishing rights. Awards: SLJ Best Book; YALSA Best Book for Young Adults. (Rev: BL 4/1/93; SLJ 5/93*)

208 Rana, Indi. *The Roller Birds of Rampur* (7–12). 1993, Holt $15.95 (0-8050-2670-3); 1994, Ballantine/Fawcett Juniper paper $3.99 (0-449-70434-3). This coming-of-age story of a young woman caught between British and Indian cultures is a lively account of the immigration experience and of Indian culture. (Rev: BL 7/93; SLJ 5/93; VOYA 2/94)

209 Robinet, Harriette Gillem. *Children of the Fire* (5–7). 1991, Atheneum $12.95 (0-689-31655-0). An indomitable 11-year-old orphan girl born into slavery spends the night of October 8, 1871, following the path of the Great Chicago Fire. Awards: Friends of American Writers Juvenile Book. (Rev: BL 10/15/91; SLJ 10/91)

210 Savage, Deborah. *A Stranger Calls Me Home* (9–12). 1992, Houghton $14.95 (0-395-59424-3). A mystical tale of 3 friends' search for cultural identity. (Rev: BL 3/15/92; BTA; SLJ 5/92)

211 Silver, Norman. *No Tigers in Africa* (7–12). 1992, Dutton $15 (0-525-44733-4); 1994, Penguin/Puffin paper $3.99 (0-14-036935-X). A white South African teenager arrives in England, haunted by guilt that he caused the death of a black teenager. When he fails to adjust to school, he breaks down and attempts suicide. (Rev: BL 6/1/92; MJHS; SHS; SLJ 11/92)

212 Silver, Norman. *Python Dance* (8–12). 1993, Dutton $14.99 (0-525-45161-7). In South Africa, Ruth grapples with an abusive stepfather, the pressures of high school, her social life, and her fear that she has an abnormally large bust. (Rev: BL 10/15/93; BTA; MJHS; SLJ 2/94; VOYA 2/94)

213 Sinykin, Sheri Cooper. *The Buddy Trap* (5–7). 1991, Atheneum $13.95 (0-689-31674-7). A musically gifted Korean American boy is drawn into escalating war games at a summer camp and courageously does the right thing. (Rev: BL 9/1/91)

214 Smothers, Ethel Footman. *Down in the Piney Woods* (5–8). 1992, Knopf LB $14.99 (0-679-90360-7); 1994, Random/Bullseye paper

$3.99 (0-679-84714-6). The daily life of a strong African American sharecropper family in 1950s rural Georgia is described in a colloquial voice. (Rev: BL 12/15/91; SLJ 1/92)

215 Smothers, Ethel Footman. *Moriah's Pond* (5–7). 1995, Knopf $14 (0-679-84504-6). This sequel to *Down in the Piney Woods* is a strongly autobiographical family story about growing up black in rural Georgia in the 1950s. (Rev: BL 1/15/95; SLJ 2/95)

216 Soto, Gary. *Jesse* (10–12). 1994, Harcourt $14.95 (0-15-240239-X). Mexican American Jesse, 17, leaves high school in 1968, moves in with his poor older brother, takes college classes, worries about the draft, and faces racism. (Rev: BL 10/1/94; BTA; SHS; SLJ 12/94; VOYA 2/95)

217 Soto, Gary. *Local News* (5–7). 1993, Harcourt $13.95 (0-15-248117-6); 1994, Scholastic/Point Signature paper $3.95 (0-590-48446-X). Thirteen short stories about young Hispanics—at home, at school, and at the mall. (Rev: BL 4/15/93; MJHS; SLJ 5/93; VOYA 8/93)

218 Soto, Gary. *Pacific Crossing* (6–9). 1992, Harcourt $14.95 (0-15-259188-5); paper $6.95 (0-15-259188-5). As part of a summer exchange program, Lincoln Mendoza adapts to life on a Japanese farm, practices a martial art, embraces Japanese customs, and shares his own. (Rev: BL 11/1/92; SLJ 11/92; YR)

219 Tan, Amy. *The Kitchen God's Wife* (9–adult). 1991, Putnam $21.95 (0-399-13578-2). The mesmerizing story a Chinese émigré mother tells her daughter. Awards: SLJ Best Book. (Rev: BL 4/15/91*; SHS; SLJ 12/91)

220 Tan, Amy. *The Moon Lady* (5–8). Illus. 1992, Macmillan $16.95 (0-02-788830-4). An adaptation of "The Moon Lady" from Tan's adult best-seller *The Joy Luck Club*, which speaks to our common nightmares and secret wishes. (Rev: BL 9/1/92; SLJ 9/92)

221 Taylor, Mildred D. *The Well: David's Story* (5–7). 1995, Dial LB $14.89 (0-8037-1803-9). This novella revisits the long-suffering Logan family, focusing on the boyhood of David in the early 1900s in Mississippi. Awards: ALSC Notable Children's Book; Jane Addams Children's Book Award. (Rev: BL 12/15/94; SLJ 2/95)

222 Taylor, Theodore. *Maria: A Christmas Story* (5–7). 1992, Harcourt $13.95 (0-15-217763-9). Although Maria's Mexican American ranch family cannot afford to enter an elaborate float in the local Christmas parade, the community bands together to create a small miracle. (Rev: BL 9/15/92; SLJ 1/93; YR)

223 Temple, Frances. *Taste of Salt: A Story of Modern Haiti* (7–12). 1992, Orchard/Richard Jackson LB $14.99 (0-531-08609-7). A first novel simply told in the voices of 2 Haitian teenagers who find political commitment and love. Awards: BL Editors' Choice; Jane Addams Children's Book Award; SLJ Best Book. (Rev: BL 8/92; BTA; SLJ 9/92*)

224 Ugwu-Oju, Dympna. *What Will My Mother Say: A Tribal African Girl Comes of Age in America* (9–adult). 1995, Bonus $24.95 (1-56625-042-0). An African American mother, born in Nigeria, struggles with culture conflict in raising her American-born daughter. (Rev: BL 11/1/95) [306]

225 Velásquez, Gloria. *Maya's Divided World* (7–12). 1995, Arte Público paper $12.95 (1-55885-126-7). A Chicana, who seemingly leads a charmed life, discovers that her parents are divorcing, and her world falls apart. (Rev: BL 3/1/95; SLJ 4/95)

226 Wartski, Maureen. *Candle in the Wind* (9–12). 1995, Fawcett/Juniper paper $4.50 (0-449-70442-4). Drawn from newspaper headlines, the shocking story of the murder of a Japanese American teen and the climate of racial hate that led to it. (Rev: BL 11/15/95; SLJ 3/96; VOYA 2/96)

227 West, Dorothy. *The Wedding* (9–adult). 1995, Doubleday $20 (0-385-47143-2). In an African American community on Martha's Vineyard, Massachusetts, Lute tries to win Shelby away from her white fiancé. Awards: SLJ Best Book. (Rev: BL 12/1/94; SLJ 7/95)

228 Wilkinson, Brenda. *Definitely Cool* (5–7). 1993, Scholastic $13.95 (0-590-46186-9). Roxanne—an African American starting junior high in an upscale New York community—learns that traveling with an in-group can lead to unexpected problems. (Rev: BL 2/15/93)

229 Williams, Michael. *Crocodile Burning* (7–12). 1992, Dutton/Lodestar $15 (0-525-67401-2); 1994, Penguin/Puffin paper $3.99 (0-14-036793-4). For Sowetan teen Seraki Nzule, getting a role in a township musical is a chance to escape violence and oppression. Awards: YALSA Best Book for Young Adults. (Rev: BL 8/92; SLJ 11/92; YR)

230 Williams, Michael. *Into the Valley* (7–10). 1993, Putnam/Philomel $14.95 (0-399-22516-1). A morality play about factional fighting among blacks in South Africa. (Rev: BL 8/93; SLJ 10/93; VOYA 12/93)

231 Williams-Garcia, Rita. *Fast Talk on a Slow Track* (9–12). 1991, Dutton/Lodestar $14.95 (0-

525-67334-2). After graduating from high school as valedictorian, Denzel attends Princeton's summer session for minority students and fails for the first time in his life. Awards: SLJ Best Book; YALSA Best Book for Young Adults. (Rev: BL 4/1/91; SLJ 4/91*)

232 Woods, Paula L., and Felix H. Liddell, eds. *I Hear a Symphony: African Americans Celebrate Love* (9–adult). 1994, Doubleday/Anchor $27.95 (0-385-47502-0). Fiction, essays, poetry, and artwork that celebrate romance and the love of self, family, community, and country. (Rev: BL 10/1/94; BTA) [810.8]

233 Woodson, Jacqueline. *The Dear One* (6–9). 1991, Delacorte $14 (0-385-30416-1). A pregnant African American teenager lives with the family of her mother's friend until the baby is born in this exploration of issues of women's sexuality. (Rev: BL 11/15/91; MJHS)

234 Woodson, Jacqueline. *From the Notebooks of Melanin Sun May* (6–10). 1995, Scholastic/Blue Sky $14.95 (0-590-45880-9). A 13-year-old black boy's mother announces that she loves a fellow student, a white woman. (Rev: BL 4/15/95; SLJ 8/95)

235 Woodson, Jacqueline. *I Hadn't Meant to Tell You This* (5–9). 1994, Delacorte $14.95 (0-385-32031-0). Two young teenage girls resist the bigotry in their school and the sorrow in their families and give each other strength to go on. Awards: ALSC Notable Children's Book; BL Editors' Choice; SLJ Best Book; YALSA Best Book for Young Adults. (Rev: BL 2/15/94*; BTA; MJHS; SLJ 5/94*; VOYA 4/94)

236 Woodson, Jacqueline. *Maizon at Blue Hill* (5–8). 1992, Delacorte $14 (0-385-30796-9); 1994, Dell/Yearling paper $3.50 (0-440-40899-7). Seventh-grader Maizon reluctantly leaves her Brooklyn home, her best friend, and her grandmother to attend a private girls' boarding school, where she must confront issues of race, class, prejudice, and identity. Awards: YALSA Best Book for Young Adults. (Rev: BL 7/92; MJHS; SLJ 11/92; YR)

237 Wright, Richard. *Rite of Passage* (7–12). 1994, HarperCollins LB $12.89 (0-06-023420-2). This newly discovered novella, written in the 1940s, concerns a gifted 15-year-old who runs away from his loving Harlem home and survives on the streets with a violent gang. (Rev: BL 1/1/94; MJHS; SLJ 2/94; VOYA 4/94)

238 Yep, Laurence. *The Star Fisher* (6–10). 1991, Morrow $12.95 (0-688-09365-5); 1992, Penguin/Puffin paper $3.99 (0-14-036003-4). Drawing on his mother's childhood, Yep depicts a Chinese family's experiences when they arrive in West Virginia in 1927 to open a laundry. Awards: Christopher. (Rev: BL 5/15/91; MJHS; SLJ 5/91)

239 Yep, Laurence. *Thief of Hearts* (5–8). 1995, HarperCollins LB $13.89 (0-06-025342-8). Stacy learns of her mixed Chinese and American heritage when she, her mother, and great-grandmother travel to San Francisco's Chinatown. (Rev: BL 7/95; SLJ 8/95)

240 Young, Ronder Thomas. *Learning by Heart* (5–7). 1993, Houghton $13.95 (0-395-65369-X); 1995, Penguin/Puffin paper $3.99 (0-14-037252-0). In a small 1960s Southern town, the slow awakening of a 10-year-old's consciousness of racial divisions. Awards: ALSC Notable Children's Book; SLJ Best Book. (Rev: BL 12/15/93; MJHS; SLJ 10/93*)

Family Life and Problems

241 Adler, C. S. *Daddy's Climbing Tree* (5–7). 1993, Clarion $13.95 (0-395-63032-0). When her father is killed, Jessica suffers terrible grief, raging fury, denial, rejection–the loss of a world—until she achieves a final, sad acceptance. (Rev: BL 6/1–15/93; SLJ 5/93)

242 Adler, C. S. *Tuna Fish Thanksgiving* (5–7). 1992, Clarion $13.95 (0-395-58829-4). A 13-year-old wishes for a real family Thanksgiving after her parents are divorced and her siblings separated. (Rev: BL 4/15/92; SLJ 5/92; YR)

243 Adler, C. S. *Willie, the Frog Prince* (5–7). 1994, Clarion $13.95 (0-395-65615-X). An 11-year-old boy has trouble in school and at home with his dad until he meets some friends who help him find self-worth. (Rev: BL 4/15/94; MJHS; SLJ 6/94)

244 Alcock, Vivien. *A Kind of Thief* (5–8). 1994, Dell paper $3.50 (0-440-40916-0). The tale of a girl who imagines herself an accomplice to her father's crime. (Rev: BL 1/15/92; YR)

245 Apple, Max. *Roommates: My Grandfather's Story* (9–12). 1994, Warner $19.95 (0-446-51826-3). Irascible Rocky Goodstein, 103, takes charge of his grandson's family. Awards: SLJ Best Book. (Rev: SLJ 12/94)

246 Auch, Mary Jane. *Out of Step* (5–7). 1992, Holiday $13.95 (0-8234-0985-6). Auch combines sensitivity with a light touch as she covers the turmoil of family change after bereavement and sibling rivalry. (Rev: BL 1/15/93; SLJ 9/92; YR)

247 Avi. *The Barn* (5–8). 1994, Orchard/Richard Jackson LB $13.99 (0-531-08711-5). After their widowed father is paralyzed, Ben and his siblings must run their 1850s Oregon farm alone. He decides they must build a barn for their incapacitated father. Awards: ALSC Notable Children's Book; BL Editors' Choice. (Rev: BL 9/1/94*; SLJ 10/94)

248 Banks, Lynne Reid. *Broken Bridge* (7–12). 1995, Morrow $15 (0-688-13595-1). A sequel to *One More River*. A woman's daughter sees her cousin killed by an Arab terrorist while living in a kibbutz, posing some tough moral questions. (Rev: BL 3/15/95; SLJ 4/95; VOYA 5/95)

249 Bechard, Margaret. *Really No Big Deal* (5–7). 1994, Viking $13.99 (0-670-85444-1); 1996, Penguin paper $3.99 (0-14-036912-0). The mother of 7th-grader Jonah is dating the principal of his school, and he finds himself attracted to the principal's step-granddaughter. (Rev: BL 3/15/94; SLJ 5/94*)

250 Blacker, Terence. *Homebird* (6–12). 1993, Bradbury $13.95 (0-02-710685-3). A complex story about Nicky, who runs away from an English boarding school, then from his family, to become a squatter with several other teenagers who support themselves through crime. (Rev: BL 7/93; VOYA 8/93)

251 Blair, David Nelson. *Fear the Condor* (7–12). 1992, Dutton/Lodestar $15 (0-525-67381-4). An Aymaran Indian girl in Bolivia doesn't fight oppression when the rest of her village wages war. (Rev: BL 5/15/92; BTA; YR)

252 Block, Francesca Lia. *The Hanged Man* (9–adult). 1994, HarperCollins LB $13.89 (0-06-024537-9). Against a backdrop of Hollywood excess, alienated Laura struggles to cope with her dead father's acts of incest, while her mother lives in denial. (Rev: BL 9/15/94; BTA; SLJ 9/94; VOYA 12/94)

253 Blume, Judy. *Here's to You, Rachel Robinson* (6–8). 1993, Orchard LB $14.99 (0-531-08651-8); 1994, Dell/Yearling paper $4.50 (0-440-40946-2). This sequel to *Just As Long As We're Together* is full of multidimensional characters. (Rev: BL 9/1/93; MJHS; SLJ 11/93; VOYA 12/93)

254 Bond, Nancy. *Truth to Tell* (6–8). 1994, Macmillan $17.95 (0-689-50601-5). A 14-year-old girl finds herself on her way to New Zealand with her mother without understanding a clear reason for the relocation. (Rev: BL 4/15/94; BTA; MJHS; SLJ 6/94; VOYA 8/94)

255 Boswell, Robert. *Mystery Ride* (9–adult). 1993, Knopf $22 (0-679-41292-1). Angela, unable to control her defiant daughter Dulcie, 15, drives her to Iowa, where she's expected to spend the summer with Angela's compassionate ex-husband. (Rev: BL 12/15/92*)

256 Boyd, Candy Dawson. *Chevrolet Saturdays* (5–10). 1993, Macmillan $14.95 (0-02-711765-0). After his parents divorce, Joey's mother remarries Mr. Johnson, but Joey rejects and alienates his kindly stepfather. When Joey makes amends, new family ties are formed. (Rev: BL 5/15/93; SLJ 5/93)

257 Bradley, Virginia. *Wait and See* (5–7). 1994, Dutton/Cobblehill $14.99 (0-525-65158-6). Amy's life is disrupted when her longtime nanny returns home to England. The lonely girl befriends Violetta, a new girl in her class with a dependent mother. (Rev: BL 8/94; SLJ 8/94; VOYA 12/94)

258 Brown, James. *Lucky Town* (9–adult). 1994, Harcourt $22.95 (0-15-100067-0). In this coming-of-age novel, Bobby Barlow recalls his teen years, when he lived a lawless life with his ex-convict father. Awards: BL Editors' Choice. (Rev: BL 4/1/94)

259 Brown, John Gregory. *Decorations in a Ruined Cemetery* (9–adult). 1994, Houghton $19.95 (0-395-67025-X). Using 3 narrators—a young girl, her stepmother, and an elderly African American man—Brown reveals the secrets of a family's multiracial past. (Rev: BL 12/1/93*)

260 Brown, Larry. *Joe* (9–adult). 1991, Algonquin Books of Chapel Hill (P.O. Box 2225, Chapel Hill, NC 27515-2225) $19.95 (0-945575-61-0). Hard-drinking Joe helps turn the life of a neglected teenager around. (Rev: BL 8/91*)

261 Brown, Susan M. *You're Dead, David Borelli* (5–7). 1995, Atheneum $15 (0-689-31959-2). David's whole life changes when his mother dies and his father disappears. Now this previously rich kid must deal with a foster home and public middle school. (Rev: BL 6/1–15/95)

262 Bunting, Eve. *Sharing Susan* (5–7). 1991, HarperCollins LB $13.89 (0-06-021694-8); 1994, HarperTrophy paper $3.95 (0-06-440430-7). A 12-year-old is caught between 2 couples when her natural parents suddenly demand her back upon discovering that she is their daughter. (Rev: BL 9/15/91; MJHS; SLJ 10/91)

263 Cadnum, Michael. *Taking It* (9–12). 1995, Viking $14.99 (0-670-86130-8). Anna shoplifts as a way to test her limits amid her parents' divorce and her feelings of alienation from family and friends. But it eventally catches up to her. (Rev: BL 7/95*; SLJ 8/95; VOYA 2/96)

264 Campbell, Bebe Moore. *Brothers and Sisters* (9–adult). 1994, Putnam $22.95 (0-399-13929-X). Contemporary family relationships, romance, and friendship among African Americans and whites in the corporate banking world. Awards: SLJ Best Book. (Rev: BL 6/94; SLJ 2/95)

265 Cannon, A. E. *Amazing Gracie* (6–9). 1991, Delacorte $15 (0-385-30487-0). Gracie, age 16, is burdened with a depressed mother who is marrying a high school sweetheart and with an unwelcome 5-year-old stepbrother. Awards: SLJ Best Book; YALSA Best Book for Young Adults. (Rev: BL 11/1/91; MJHS; SLJ 8/91*)

266 Casey, Maude. *Over the Water* (7–12). 1994, Holt $14.95 (0-8050-3276-2). A young girl's rite of passage from dissension with her controlling mother to understand her mother as a person. Awards: SLJ Best Book. (Rev: BL 5/15/94; BTA; MJHS; SLJ 6/94*; VOYA 8/94)

267 Christiansen, C. B. *I See the Moon* (5–7). 1994, Atheneum $14.95 (0-689-31928-2). In a memoir addressed to a niece, Isabella, on the eve of her twelfth birthday, Bitte looks back at her own twelfth year and the time of Isabella's birth. Awards: ALSC Notable Children's Book. (Rev: BL 2/1/95; BTA; MJHS; SLJ 1/95; VOYA 4/95)

268 Coman, Carolyn. *What Jamie Saw* (5–8). 1995, Front Street $13.95 (1-886910-02-2). A tale about a young boy with an abusive father from whom he, his mother, and baby sister flee. Awards: ALSC Notable Children's Book. (Rev: BL 12/15/95*; SLJ 12/95*)

269 Conly, Jane Leslie. *Crazy Lady!* (5–8). 1993, HarperCollins/Laura Geringer LB $12.89 (0-06-021360-4). In a poor city neighborhood, Vernon, failing 7th grade, befriends Maxine—who hollers and screams on the street when she's drunk—and helps care for her disabled teenage son. Awards: SLJ Best Book. (Rev: BL 5/15/93*; BTA; MJHS; SLJ 4/93*)

270 Cooney, Caroline B. *Whatever Happened to Janie?* (6–11). 1993, Delacorte $15.95 (0-385-31035-8); 1994, Dell/Laurel Leaf paper $3.99 (0-440-21924-8). Janie, 15, after discovering she's a missing child on a milk carton, returns to her birth family, which has been searching for her since her kidnapping at age 3. Sequel to *The Face on the Milk Carton*. (Rev: BL 6/1–15/93; MJHS; SLJ 6/93; VOYA 8/93)

271 Cooper, Bernard. *A Year of Rhymes* (9–adult). 1993, Viking $20 (0-670-84732-1). Short stories set in early 1960s Los Angeles are united by the Zerkin family and its neighbors; the leukemia of Bob, the oldest son; and 11-year-old Burt's dawning awareness of his homosexuality. (Rev: BL 7/93*)

272 Cooper, Ilene. *Buddy Love: Now on Video* (5–8). 1995, HarperCollins LB $13.89 (0-06-024664-2). A boy gets a camcorder and begins to see his family, friends, and eventually himself through a new lens. (Rev: BL 9/15/95; SLJ 10/95; VOYA 4/96)

273 Cooper, Melrose. *Life Riddles* (5–7). 1994, Holt $14.95 (0-8050-2613-4). The life of a poor inner-city family struggling for food, shelter, education, and medical care as seen through the eyes of 12-year-old Janelle. (Rev: BL 2/15/94; SLJ 4/94)

274 Corcoran, Barbara. *Family Secrets* (5–8). 1992, Atheneum $14.95 (0-689-31744-1). A teenager contemplates the advantages and disadvantages of family after discovering she was adopted. (Rev: BL 3/1/92; SLJ 2/92)

275 Corey, Deborah Joy. *Losing Eddie* (9–adult). 1993, Algonquin Books of Chapel Hill (P.O. Box 2225, Chapel Hill, NC 27515-2225) $15.95 (0-945575-67-X). This novel's young heroine uses love and faith to overcome the realities of poverty, spousal abuse of her sister, death of her brother, mother's breakdown, and father's drinking. (Rev: BL 9/15/93; SLJ 2/94)

276 Creech, Sharon. *Walk Two Moons* (7–9). 1994, HarperCollins LB $15.89 (0-06-023337-0). Tells the story of Sal, 13, who goes to Idaho with her grandparents to be with her mother, who has actually been killed after a bus accident. Awards: Newbery Medal; SLJ Best Book. (Rev: BL 11/15/94; MJHS; SLJ 10/94*; VOYA 2/95)

277 Crosby, Caroline. *The Haldanes* (9–adult). 1993, St. Martin's $21.95 (0-312-09303-9). In 1920s England, Pauline, 15, leaves her childhood home for St. Austin's, where school friendships help her cope with loneliness and family complications in this coming-of-age story. (Rev: BL 6/1–15/93; SLJ 1/94)

278 Deaver, Julie Reece. *Chicago Blues* (6–10). 1995, HarperCollins LB $15 (0-06-024675-8). Two sisters make it on their own because of an alcoholic mother, with successes, struggles, and eventual forgiveness resulting from their forced independence. (Rev: BL 9/1/95; SLJ 8/95; VOYA 12/95)

279 Deem, James M. *3 NBs of Julian Drew* (7–12). 1994, Houghton $14.95 (0-395-69453-1). Julian, 15, is emotionally and physically abused by his father and his demented stepmother. He finds strength by writing to his deceased mother in coded notebooks. (Rev: BL 10/15/94; BTA; SLJ 10/94*; VOYA 12/94)

280 Derby, Pat. *Grams, Her Boyfriend, My Family and Me* (7–10). 1994, Farrar $16 (0-374-38131-3). A laid-back teenager finds himself becoming involved in family politics when his mother returns to work and his grandmother comes to live in their tiny house. Awards: SLJ Best Book. (Rev: BL 3/15/94; SHS; SLJ 11/94*; VOYA 4/94)

281 De Vito, Cara. *Where I Want to Be* (6–10). 1993, Houghton $13.95 (0-395-64592-1). Abandoned by her mother 9 years earlier, Kristie, 14, is cared for by her much-older half-brothers and must piece together the secrets of her unusual family. (Rev: BL 4/1/93; SLJ 6/93)

282 Donovan, Stacey. *Dive* (9–adult). 1994, Dutton $14.99 (0-525-45154-4). Virginia, 15, deals with her injured dog, her alcoholic mother, her precocious sister, her drug-addicted brother, her terminally ill father, and her attraction to her friend Jane. (Rev: BL 11/1/94; SLJ 1/95; VOYA 4/95)

283 Dubosarsky, Ursula. *The White Guinea-Pig* (5–7). 1995, Viking $14.99 (0-670-85738-6). Geraldine, 12, must cope with a troubled sister, an escaped guinea pig, and the possiblity her father's business is failing. (Rev: BL 7/95)

284 Duffey, Betsy. *Coaster* (5–8). 1994, Viking $13.99 (0-670-85480-8). Hart, age 12, barely sees his father since his parents' divorce and desperately hopes he will show up for their annual roller-coaster trip. (Rev: BL 8/94; BTA; SLJ 9/94; VOYA 4/95)

285 Duffey, Betsy. *Utterly Yours, Booker Jones* (5–7). 1995, Viking $13.99 (0-670-86007-7). An aspiring science fiction writer, age 12, has problems with the way he perceives reality. He is living under the dining room table, which is affecting him and his work strangely. (Rev: BL 9/15/95; SLJ 9/95; VOYA 4/96)

286 Duffy, James. *Cleaver and Company* (6–8). 1991, Scribner $12.95 (0-684-19371-X). Cleaver, a lovable Bernese mountain dog, provides comic relief in this story of a worried 13-year-old girl whose parents are separated. (Rev: BL 11/15/91; SLJ 12/91)

287 Dunlop, Eileen. *Finn's Search* (5–7). 1994, Holiday $14.95 (0-8234-1099-4). Chris's family farm is threatened by a planned gravel pit in a Roman field. In order to stop the pit, Chris and his pal, Finn, try to find Roman artifacts. (Rev: BL 10/1/94; SLJ 10/94; VOYA 4/95)

288 Egan, Jennifer. *The Invisible Circus* (9–adult). 1995, Doubleday $22.95 (0-385-47379-6). Phoebe comes of age believing that her older sister's era, the much ballyhooed 1960s, was more real and important than her own teenage years, following her father's death. (Rev: BL 12/15/94*)

289 Ehrlich, Amy. *The Dark Card* (9–12). 1991, Viking $13.95 (0-670-83733-4). A compelling story of a New Jersey teen whose double life takes her to the casinos of Atlantic City. (Rev: BL 2/15/91*)

290 Ellis, Sarah. *Out of the Blue* (5–7). 1995, Macmillan/Margaret K. McElderry $15 (0-689-80025-8). A story of adjustment and acceptance: A 12-year-old girl discovers that she has a 24-year-old sister who was given up for adoption at birth. (Rev: BL 5/1/95; SLJ 5/95)

291 Ellis, Sarah. *Pick-up Sticks* (5–8). 1992, Macmillan/Margaret K. McElderry $13.95 (0-689-50550-7); 1993, Penguin/Puffin paper (0-14-036340-8). A disgruntled teen learns a lesson in life after being sent to live with relatives. Awards: SLJ Best Book. (Rev: BL 1/15/92; MJHS; SLJ 3/92*)

292 Ewing, Kathryn. *Family Karate* (5–7). 1992, Boyds Mills/Caroline House $13.95 (1-56397-117-8). When her family's spats become intolerable, Jennifer decides to take an advice columnist's suggestion and put herself in other people's shoes. (Rev: BL 1/15/93; SLJ 10/92)

293 Fakih, Kimberly Olson. *High on the Hog* (5–7). 1994, Farrar $16 (0-374-33209-6). A sense of family connectedness allows Trapp, 12, to face her move from a farm to New York City and the aging of her great-grandparents. (Rev: BL 6/1–15/94; SLJ 5/94*; VOYA 8/94)

294 Ferris, Jean. *Relative Strangers* (6–10). 1993, Farrar $16 (0-374-36243-2). The child of separated parents, Berkeley must learn to accept her father as less than the idealized fantasy she imagined when he takes her to Europe with his new family. (Rev: BL 10/1/93; MJHS; VOYA 12/93)

295 Feuer, Elizabeth. *Lost Summer* (5–8). 1995, Farrar $16 (0-374-31020-3). A 12-year-old girl is shipped off to camp one summer as her parents reconstruct their lives following divorce. (Rev: BL 5/15/95; SLJ 5/95)

296 Fine, Anne. *The Book of the Banshee* (6–9). 1992, Little, Brown $13.95 (0-316-28315-0); 1994, Scholastic paper $2.95 (0-590-46926-6). English teenager Will Flowers's younger sister, Estelle, has become a banshee, and he decides his family life is like an account of World War I he is reading. Awards: SLJ Best Book. (Rev: BL 12/1/91*; SLJS 1/92*)

297 Fletcher, Ralph. *Fig Pudding* (5–7). 1995, Clarion $14.95 (0-395-71125-8). The oldest of 6 children, 12-year-old Cliff, recalls the past year in episodes focusing on his brothers and sisters. Awards: ALSC Notable Children's Book. (Rev: BL 5/15/95)

298 Fox, Paula. *The Eagle Kite* (6–10). 1995, Orchard/Richard Jackson LB $14.99 (0-531-08742-5). Liam goes through a tangle of denial, anger, shame, grief, and empathy after learning that his father is dying of AIDS. His mother says he got it from a blood tranfusion, but Liam remembers seeing his father embrance a young man 2 years before. Awards: SLJ Best Book. (Rev: BL 2/1/95*; SLJ 4/95*; VOYA 5/95)

299 Fox, Paula. *Western Wind* (6–9). 1993, Orchard/Richard Jackson LB $14.99 (0-531-08652-6). Elizabeth is sent to live for a month with her beloved Gran on an island off Maine, but she's not told of Gran's serious heart condition. Awards: SLJ Best Book. (Rev: BL 10/15/93; MJHS; SLJ 12/93*; VOYA 12/93)

300 Frank, Lucy K. *I Am an Artichoke* (6–9). 1995, Holiday $14.95 (0-8234-1150-8). Sarah, 15, spends a summer as a mother's helper for Emily, who is 12 and anorexic and whose mother alternates between denial and obsession. (Rev: BL 2/1/95; SLJ 3/95)

301 Franklin, Kristine L. *Eclipse* (6–9). 1995, Candlewick $14.95 (1-56402-544-6). A young girl feels confused and powerless when her father becomes ill and her family seems to fall apart. (Rev: BL 3/15/95; SLJ 4/95)

302 Fraustino, Lisa Rowe. *Grass and Sky* (5–7). 1994, Orchard LB $15.99 (0-531-08673-9). Timmi spends time in a cabin in the Maine woods with the grandfather she has never been allowed to know and learns of his past alcoholism. (Rev: BL 3/15/94; SLJ 4/94; VOYA 6/94)

303 Gaeddert, Louann. *Hope* (5–7). 1995, Atheneum $14 (0-689-80128-9). Shaker life is the background of this story of 2 children whose mother dies and father has gone panning for gold. After a year in a Shaker community, they must make some tough decisions when their father returns. (Rev: BL 12/15/95; SLJ 11/95; VOYA 12/95)

304 Gándara, Alejandro. *Falso movimiento* (9–12). 1992, Ediciones SM (Madrid, Spain) $12.95 (84-348-3708-0). The fears and anxieties of 15-year-old Carlota's parents, along with their doubts about their marriage, combine to produce a realistic, powerful novel. English title: *False Movement*. (Rev: BL 6/1–15/93)

305 Garden, Nancy. *Lark in the Morning* (7–10). 1991, Farrar $14.95 (0-374-34338-1). Gillie tries to keep 2 secrets from her parents: that she has discovered 2 abused runaways are living on the family's property; and that she is gay. (Rev: BL 7/91; SLJ 6/91)

306 Garland, Sherry. *Shadow of the Dragon* (6–12). 1993, Harcourt $10.95 (0-15-273530-5); paper $3.95 (0-15-273532-1). Danny Vo has grown up American since he emigrated from Vietnam as a child. Now traditional Vietnamese ways, new American culture, and skinhead prejudice clash, resulting in his cousin's death. Awards: YALSA Best Book for Young Adults. (Rev: BL 11/15/93*; BTA; MJHS; SLJ 11/93; VOYA 12/93)

307 Goodman, Joan Elizabeth. *Songs from Home* (5–7). 1994, Harcourt $10.95 (0-15-203590-7); paper $4.95 (0-15-203591-5). Anna, 12, and her father travel Europe, surviving by singing in restaurants for tips. She wants a home and information about her deceased mother. (Rev: BL 9/1/94; BTA; SLJ 10/94; VOYA 12/94)

308 Grant, Cynthia D. *Keep Laughing* (7–10). 1991, Atheneum $14.95 (0-689-31514-7). When 15-year-old Shepherd's father who abandoned him as a child returns and asks for forgiveness, Shepherd moves in with him and learns about his selfishness and irresponsibility. Awards: SLJ Best Book. (Rev: BL 11/1/91; MJHS; SLJ 9/91*)

309 Grant, Cynthia D. *Mary Wolf* (7–12). 1995, Atheneum $16 (0-689-80007-X). A tale of a homeless family in which the only person who is logical and reasonable is the 16-year-old daughter. (Rev: BL 10/1/95; SLJ 10/95; VOYA 12/95)

310 Grant, Cynthia D. *Shadow Man* (7–12). 1992, Atheneum $13.95 (0-689-31772-7). Chapters are narrated by various inhabitants of a California town where Gabriel, 18, is found dead in a car accident after leaving a party alone and drunk. Awards: YALSA Best Book for Young Adults. (Rev: BL 11/1/92; MJHS; SLJ 10/92)

311 Greene, Constance C. *Nora: Maybe a Ghost Story* (6–8). 1993, Harcourt $10.95 (0-15-277696-6); paper $3.95 (0-15-276895-5). When Nora and Patsy's father announces his intention to marry after 3 years of widowhood, they have to deal with resentment and their mother's ghostly presence. (Rev: BL 10/1/93; MJHS; VOYA 12/93)

312 Griffin, Peni R. *Vikki Vanishes* (6–9). 1995, Macmillan/Margaret K. McElderry $15 (0-689-80028-2). A long-absent dad shows up and seduces and steals away his 16-year-old daughter. (Rev: BL 5/15/95; SLJ 9/95)

313 Grove, Vicki. *Rimwalkers* (6–10). 1993, Putnam $14.95 (0-399-22430-0). On an Illinois farm for the summer, Tory develops improved self-esteem as she unravels a mystery involving the apparition of a small boy. (Rev: BL 10/15/93; SLJ 10/93; VOYA 12/93)

314 Haas, Jessie. *Uncle Daney's Way* (5–7). 1994, Greenwillow $14 (0-688-12794-0). A family moves to a rural area, where they hope to create a better future for themselves. An uncle moves in with his horse and teaches them about making positive changes. (Rev: BL 4/15/94; SLJ 4/94)

315 Hall, Lynn. *Flying Changes* (7–12). 1991, Harcourt $13.95 (0-15-228790-6). An awkward Kansas teenager must give up her romantic dreams after her father is paralyzed and her mother, who abandoned her years before, returns home. Awards: YALSA Best Book for Young Adults. (Rev: BL 6/15/91*; SHS)

316 Hamilton, Virginia. *Primos* (6–10). Tr. by Amalia Bermejo. 1993, Santillana (Madrid, Spain) paper $12.50 (84-204-4747-1). Although she lives with her mother and brother, Camy misses her grandmother, who is in a nursing home. Her main problem, however, is her beautiful, smart cousin Patty Ann. English title: *Cousins*. (Rev: BL 4/1/94)

317 Hathorn, Libby. *Thunderwith* (7–10). 1991, Little, Brown $15.95 (0-316-35034-6). This story of an unhappy 15-year-old girl and a beautiful dingolike dog she finds is set in the Australian rain forest. Awards: SLJ Best Book; YALSA Best Book for Young Adults. (Rev: BL 9/1/91; SLJ 5/91*)

318 Hermes, Patricia. *Mama, Let's Dance* (5–7). 1991, Little, Brown $14.95 (0-316-35861-4). When 3 children, ages 7–16, are abandoned, they must fend for themselves to avoid being split up and put in foster homes. Awards: SLJ Best Book. (Rev: BL 12/1/91; SLJ 9/91)

319 Hermes, Patricia. *Someone to Count On* (5–7). 1993, Little, Brown $14.95 (0-316-35925-4). Samantha, 11, is dragged by her mother to her grandfather's Colorado ranch. She loves the ranch, shares a love of books with her grandfather, and is taught to ride horses by a boy her age. (Rev: BL 10/15/93; MJHS; SLJ 12/93; VOYA 12/93)

320 Hernández, Irene Beltran. *The Secret of Two Brothers* (7–10). 1995, Arte Público $14.95 (1-55885-141-0); paper $7.95 (1-55885-142-9). An action-packed story about 2 Mexican American boys who meet many challenges. Especially appealing to those whose first language is Spanish or for reluctant readers. (Rev: BL 10/1/95; SLJ 11/95)

321 Hickman, Janet. *Jericho* (5–8). 1994, Greenwillow $14 (0-688-13398-3). Angela, 12, resents having to care for her elderly, increasingly forgetful grandmother, Arminda. As Angela learns of Arminda's life, she begins to connect it to her own. (Rev: BL 9/1/94; MJHS; SLJ 9/94)

322 High, Linda Oatman. *Maizie* (5–8). 1995, Holiday $14.95 (0-8234-1161-3). The mother of tough, resilient Maizie has left, and Maizie must care for her sister and her father, who drinks too much. (Rev: BL 4/15/95; SLJ 4/95)

323 Hill, Elizabeth Starr. *Broadway Chances* (5–7). 1992, Viking $14 (0-670-84197-8). In this sequel to *The Street Dancers*, Fitzi comes out of show business retirement for the allure of a dance solo in a Broadway musical. (Rev: BL 10/1/92; SLJ 5/92; YR)

324 Hill, Elizabeth Starr. *Curtain Going Up!* (5–7). 1995, Viking $14.99 (0-670-85919-2). Fitzi Wolper, performing in a Broadway show, tries to get the attention of the show's young lead, who's focused solely on his career. (Rev: BL 1/15/95; SLJ 3/95)

325 Hill, Elizabeth Starr. *The Street Dancers* (5–7). 1991, Viking $13.95 (0-670-83435-1). The daughter in a family of street performers seeks a "normal" life. (Rev: BL 6/15/91)

326 Hite, Sid. *An Even Break* (5–7). 1995, Holt $14.95 (0-8050-3837-X). A wholesome look at small-town America as a background for a story about a 12-year-old boy who lands a job at the billiard parlor to help out his hard-working mom. (Rev: BL 11/1/95; SLJ 12/95; VOYA 2/96)

327 Hite, Sid. *It's Nothing to a Mountain* (6–9). 1994, Holt $15.95 (0-8050-2769-6). Tells the story of 2 teens' parents' deaths and the teens' response to their loss. Awards: SLJ Best Book; YALSA Best Book for Young Adults. (Rev: BL 5/15/94; BTA; SLJ 6/94; VOYA 8/94)

328 Hodge, Merle. *For the Life of Laetitia* (5–9). 1993, Farrar $15 (0-374-32447-6). Rooted in Caribbean culture and language, this novel celebrates place and community as it confronts divisions of race, class, and gender. Awards: YALSA Best Book for Young Adults. (Rev: BL 12/1/92; BTA; SLJ 1/93)

329 Honeycutt, Natalie. *Ask Me Something Easy* (6–9). 1991, Orchard/Richard Jackson LB $13.99 (0-531-08494-9). A teenager analyzes her fractured family and tries to cope with her parents' bitter divorce. (Rev: BL 6/1/91; MJHS; SLJ 3/91)

330 Howard, Ellen. *The Tower Room* (5–7). 1993, Atheneum $13.95 (0-689-31856-1). After her unmarried mother dies of an abortion in the 1950s, Mary Brooke Edwards goes to live with her maiden aunt in her castlelike home. (Rev: BL 12/15/93)

331 Howker, Janni. *The Topiary Garden* (7–12). Illus. 1995, Orchard $13.95 (0-531-06891-9). Fleeing her all-male family in a rage, Liz meets ancient Sally, who invites her into a topiary garden to tell her how she once became a boy. (Rev: BL 4/1/95; SLJ 4/95)

332 Huong, Duong Thu. *Paradise of the Blind* (9–adult). Tr. by Phan Huy Duong and Nina McPherson. 1993, Morrow $20 (0-688-11445-8). Huong's book, banned in her homeland, introduces us to daily life in Vietnam under communism in the 1970s in this coming-of-age tale of a young girl. Awards: SLJ Best Book. (Rev: BL 1/15/93*; SLJ 7/93*)

333 Insel, Deborah. *Clouded Dreams* (9–adult). 1995, Delphinium $19.95 (1-883285-04-6). Tells the story of an inner-city African American family—headed by teenager Cirri—torn apart by drugs, gangs, and hustlers. (Rev: BL 1/15/95; SLJ 12/95)

334 James, Mary. *Frankenlouse* (5–8). 1994, Scholastic $13.95 (0-590-46528-7). Nick, 14, is enrolled at Blister Military Academy, which is run by his father. He escapes into his own comic book creations featuring an insect named Frankenlouse. (Rev: BL 10/15/94; BTA; MJHS; SLJ 11/94; VOYA 12/94)

335 Johnson, Emily Rhoads. *A House Full of Strangers* (5–8). 1992, Dutton/Cobblehill $14 (0-525-65091-1). When unknown relatives move in to care for Flora, 12, she resists being drawn into her new family. (Rev: BL 7/92; SLJ 6/92; YR)

336 Khashoggi, Soheir. *Mirage* (9–adult). 1996, Tor/Forge $22.95 (0-312-85835-3). A novel with the plight of a Middle Eastern Islamic woman at its heart, from an author who is a product of a similar culture. (Rev: BL 12/1/95*)

337 Kimmel, Eric A. *One Good Tern Deserves Another* (6–9). 1994, Holiday $14.95 (0-8234-1138-9). After his stepfather is killed, Peebee, 14, moves with his mother to Oregon. He falls for Lani, an avid bird watcher, and his mother falls for Lani's widowed father. (Rev: BL 11/1/94; BTA; SLJ 10/94; VOYA 4/95)

338 Klass, Sheila Solomon. *Next Stop: Nowhere* (6–10). 1995, Scholastic $14.95 (0-590-46686-0). Exiled to Vermont to live with her eccentric father, Beth must deal with separation from her close friend and from her new romantic interest, Josef, who's moved to Israel. (Rev: BL 1/15/95; SLJ 4/95; VOYA 2/95)

339 Klein, Robin. *All in the Blue Unclouded Weather* (6–8). 1992, Viking LB $11.95 (0-670-83909-4). Follows the adventures of 4 sisters and their cousin growing up in a small, gossipy Australian town in the 1940s. (Rev: BL 3/15/92)

340 Koertge, Ron. *The Harmony Arms* (7–9). 1992, Little, Brown/Joy Street $15.95 (0-316-50104-2); 1994, Avon/Flare paper $3.99 (0-380-72188-0). Gabriel and his father have gone to Los Angeles to break into the movies. By summer's end, Gabriel has embarked on his first romance and confronted death for the first time. Awards: ALSC Notable Children's Book; SLJ Best Book; YALSA Best Book for Young Adults. (Rev: BL 10/15/92; SLJ 8/92*; YR)

341 Koertge, Ron. *Tiger, Tiger, Burning Bright* (6–10). 1994, Orchard/Melanie Kroupa LB $15.99 (0-531-08690-9). This story of a boy and his ailing grandfather is set in a small, economically depressed town in the desert hills of California. Awards: SLJ Best Book. (Rev: BL 2/15/94; BTA; MJHS; SLJ 3/94; VOYA 6/94)

342 Koller, Jackie French. *The Last Voyage of the Misty Day* (6–9). 1992, Atheneum $13.95 (0-689-31731-X). The story of a young girl and her friendship with an ailing neighbor. (Rev: BL 5/1/92; SLJ 6/92)

343 Koller, Jackie French. *A Place to Call Home* (7–10). 1995, Atheneum $16 (0-689-80024-X). Biracial Anna, age 15, is a strong character in search of love and roots following sexual abuse and rejection from her own family. (Rev: BL 10/15/95; SLJ 10/95; VOYA 2/96)

344 Lasky, Kathryn. *Memoirs of a Bookbat* (5–9). 1994, Harcourt $10.95 (0-15-215727-1). A free-thinking teen evaluates her conservative, religious parents as weird and affirms that her free-ranging reading makes her free. (Rev: BL 4/15/94; MJHS; SLJ 7/94; VOYA 6/94)

345 Letts, Billie. *Where the Heart Is* (9–adult). 1995, Warner $17.95 (0-446-51972-3). The troubles of a pregnant teen abandoned by her boyfriend. The plot follows the next 5 years of her life in a soap-opera plot. (Rev: BL 9/1/95; SLJ 4/96)

346 Levinson, Marilyn. *No Boys Allowed* (5–8). 1993, Troll/Bridgewater LB $13.95 (0-8167-3135-7). After her father leaves her family to marry his young law partner, Cassie must learn to trust men again. (Rev: BL 10/1/93; SLJ 11/93)

347 Levit, Rose. *With Secrets to Keep* (7–9). 1991, Betterway/Shoe Tree $12.95 (1-55870-197-4). Incest and child abuse are confronted in this optimistic story of the child of an immigrant Greek family and her sister. (Rev: BL 9/1/91; SLJ 6/91)

348 London, Jonathan. *Where's Home?* (5–7). 1995, Viking $13.99 (0-670-86028-X). Homeless 14-year-old Adrian and his Vietnam vet dad have a hard life but find love for each other as they travel from West Virginia to Detroit to San Francisco. (Rev: BL 6/1–15/95; SLJ 8/95)

349 Lynch, Chris. *Shadow Boxer* (6–10). 1993, HarperCollins LB $13.89 (0-06-023028-2). Their father's death leaves 14-year-old George and his hyperactive younger brother in conflict that can only be resolved by dispelling their father's shadow. Awards: SLJ Best Book. (Rev: BL 12/15/93; MJHS; SLJ 9/93*; VOYA 12/93)

350 McDermott, Alice. *At Weddings and Wakes* (9–adult). 1992, Farrar $20 (0-374-10674-6). The joys and sorrows of an Irish American family told by its younger members. (Rev: BL 3/1/92; SHS; SLJ 9/92)

351 McEwan, Ian. *The Daydreamer* (5–7). Illus. 1994, HarperCollins $14 (0-06-024426-7). Peter, 10, is a quiet loner, and he lets his imagination run wild by having elaborate, surreal daydreams. Awards: SLJ Best Book. (Rev: BL 9/1/94*; SLJ 10/94*)

352 McKay, Hilary. *The Exiles at Home* (5–7). 1994, Macmillan/Margaret K. McElderry $15.95 (0-689-50610-4). The adventures of the Conroy sisters from just before Christmas throughout the following year in Cumbria, England. A sequel to *The Exiles*. (Rev: BL 1/15/95*; MJHS; SLJ 2/95; VOYA 4/95)

353 MacKinnon, Bernie. *Song for a Shadow* (8–12). 1991, Houghton $14.95 (0-395-55419-5). Concerns 18-year-old Aaron's attempts to sort out his relationships with his parents—his father has always seemed too wrapped up in his career, and his mother is emotionally troubled. (Rev: BL 3/15/91; SLJ 4/91)

354 MacLachlan, Patricia. *Baby* (5–10). 1993, Delacorte $13.95 (0-385-31133-8). In this beautifully written, moving story, "Baby" refers to Larkin's brother (who died before the story begins) and Sophie, who's left in a basket on the driveway of the Larkin home. Awards: ALSC Notable Children's Book; YALSA Best Book for Young Adults. (Rev: BL 9/1/93; SLJ 11/93; VOYA 10/93)

355 MacLachlan, Patricia. *Journey* (5–7). Illus. 1991, Delacorte $13.50 (0-385-30427-7). Journey, abandoned by his mother and making a new life with his sister on his grandparents' farm, develops a loving relationship with his grandfather. Awards: ALSC Notable Children's Book; SLJ Best Book; YALSA Best Book for Young Adults. (Rev: BL 9/15/91; MJHS; SLJ 9/91*)

356 McNamer, Deirdre. *Rima in the Weeds* (9–adult). 1991, HarperCollins $19.95 (0-06-016523-5). A young, single mother tries to pull her life together after returning to her disapproving Montana hometown. (Rev: BL 1/15/91*; SHS)

357 Mahy, Margaret. *Fortunate Name* (5–7). (Cousins Quartet) Illus. 1993, Delacorte $13.95 (0-385-31135-4). Lolly Bancroft becomes Lorelei Fortune and assumes a new persona as a strong and beautiful girl who takes her place in a gang formed by her cousins. (Rev: BL 2/15/94; SLJ 11/93)

358 Mahy, Margaret. *The Other Side of Silence* (7–10). 1995, Viking $14.99 (0-670-86455-2). A gothic story with a menacing tone about a young woman's quest for individuality and personal power. (Rev: BL 10/1/95*; SLJ 10/95; VOYA 4/96)

359 Marino, Jan. *The Mona Lisa of Salem Street* (5–7). 1995, Little, Brown $15.95 (0-316-54614-3). A 12-year-old and her younger brother are shunted around to various relatives after their parents die. (Rev: BL 3/1/95; SLJ 4/95)

360 Marsden, John. *Letters from the Inside* (8–12). 1994, Houghton $13.95 (0-395-68985-6). Two teenage girls begin a correspondence, their initial letters describing ideal fictitious lives. With time, they reveal that one has a violent brother and the other is in prison. Awards: SLJ Best Book; YALSA Best Book for Young Adults. (Rev: BL 10/15/94; BTA; MJHS; SHS; SLJ 9/94*; VOYA 12/94)

361 Masters, Susan Rowan. *Summer Song* (5–7). 1995, Clarion $14.95 (0-395-71127-4). A young girl, abandoned at birth, grows up with her grandparents, one of whom dies and the other, who is ill. (Rev: BL 9/15/95; SLJ 12/95; VOYA 12/95)

362 Mayfield, Sue. *I Carried You on Eagle's Wings* (7–9). 1991, Lothrop $12.95 (0-688-10597-1). Fourteen-year-old Tony's mother is terminally ill, and a friendship with a classmate, Clare, blossoms when she helps him care for an injured gull. (Rev: BL 11/1/91; SLJ 9/91)

363 Mazer, Harry. *Who Is Eddie Leonard?* (7–10). 1993, Delacorte $14.95 (0-385-31136-2). When his grandmother dies, Eddie sees a missing-child poster that convinces him he's really the kidnapped Jason Diaz. But the Diazes aren't the perfect family he imagined. Awards: YALSA Best Book for Young Adults. (Rev: BL 11/15/93; SLJ 11/93; VOYA 4/94)

364 Mazer, Norma Fox. *D, My Name Is Danita* (6–8). 1991, Scholastic $13.95 (0-590-43655-4). The latest in this light series presents an interesting premise: Girl meets boy who turns out to be her older half-brother. (Rev: BL 4/1/91; BY; SLJ 3/91)

365 Mazer, Norma Fox. *Missing Pieces* (7–10). 1995, Morrow $15 (0-688-13349-5). A 14-year-old seeks a missing part of her life by looking for a father who abandoned her. (Rev: BL 4/1/95; SLJ 4/95*; VOYA 5/95)

366 Mead, Alice. *Junebug* (5–7). 1995, Farrar $14 (0-374-33964-3). A boy lives in the projects and takes care of his sister while dreaming of escaping his glum existence. (Rev: BL 9/15/95; SLJ 11/95; VOYA 2/96)

367 Mickle, Shelley Fraser. *Replacing Dad* (9–adult). 1993, Algonquin $17.95 (1-56512-017-5). A teenage son and his mother relate their experiences and the emotional upheaval that followed the mother's divorce, told in alternating chapters. (Rev: BL 5/15/93; BTA)

368 Miller, Mary Jane. *Upside Down* (5–7). 1992, Viking $13 (0-670-83648-6). A junior high student tries to keep her widowed mother from dating the divorced father of the class geek. (Rev: BL 2/1/92; YR)

369 Mori, Kyoko. *One Bird* (8–12). 1995, Holt $15.95 (0-8050-2983-4). A coming-of-age story set in Japan about a 15-year-old girl, Megumi, who loses her mother yet finds people who understand and love her. (Rev: BL 10/15/95; SLJ 11/95; VOYA 2/96)

370 Mosher, Howard Frank. *Northern Borders* (9–adult). 1994, Doubleday $22.95 (0-385-47337-0). Austen Kittredge recounts his eccentric relatives and hilarious adolescence in Vermont. Awards: SLJ Best Book. (Rev: SLJ 2/95)

371 Moulton, Deborah. *Summer Girl* (5–9). 1992, Dial $15 (0-8037-1153-0). As her mother is dying of cancer, 13-year-old Tamara must rebuild a relationship with a father she hasn't seen in 10 years. (Rev: BL 2/1/92; MJHS; SLJ 6/92; YR)

372 Murphy, Barbara Beasley. *Fly Like an Eagle* (7–12). 1994, Delacorte $14.95 (0-385-32035-3); 1995, Dell/Laurel Leaf paper (0-440-21948-5). This sequel to *Ace Hits the Big Time* (1981) finds Ace on a quest with his dad, Barney, to find Barney's natural parents, which takes them all over the country. (Rev: BL 12/15/93; MJHS; SLJ 3/94; VOYA 4/94)

373 Murphy, Claire Rudolf. *Gold Star Sister* (6–8). 1994, Dutton/Lodestar $14.99 (0-525-67492-6). Gram, who has moved into Carrie's home, is dying of cancer, and Carrie wants to do something generous as a final gift to her. (Rev: BL 11/15/94*; MJHS; SLJ 11/94; VOYA 2/95)

374 Myers, Anna. *Rosie's Tiger* (5–8). 1994, Walker $14.95 (0-8027-8305-8). When Rosie's brother returns from the Korean War, he brings a wife and son with him. She becomes consumed by the tiger of jealousy. (Rev: BL 9/15/94; SLJ 11/94)

375 Myers, Walter Dean. *Somewhere in the Darkness* (7–12). 1992, Scholastic $14.95 (0-590-42411-4). A father and son get to know each other after Dad is released from prison. Awards: ALSC Notable Children's Book; BL Editors' Choice; Coretta Scott King Honor Book; Newbery Honor Book; SLJ Best Book; YALSA Best Book for Young Adults. (Rev: BL 2/1/92*; MJHS; SHS; SLJ 4/92*; YR)

376 Nasaw, Jonathan. *Shakedown Street* (7–12). 1993, Delacorte $14.95 (0-385-31071-4). Caro and her mother are forced to live on the street after being ripped off by a religious group. Caro almost becomes a prostitute to survive before things get better. (Rev: BL 12/15/93; VOYA 10/93)

377 Naylor, Phyllis Reynolds. *Being Danny's Dog* (5–7). 1995, Atheneum $15 (0-689-31756-5). Danny and his loyal, protective brother T.R. move to a townhouse and make some new friends, who present some challenging situations. (Rev: BL 10/1/95; SLJ 10/95; VOYA 12/95)

378 Naylor, Phyllis Reynolds. *Ice* (6–8). 1995, Atheneum $16 (0-689-80005-3). A 13-year-old girl learns about herself and about relationships in her search for her father and her isolation from her mother. (Rev: BL 8/95; SLJ 10/95; VOYA 12/95)

379 Nelson, Theresa. *Earthshine* (5–9). 1994, Orchard/Richard Jackson LB $15.99 (0-531-08717-4). "Slim" decides to live with her father and his lover, who is dying of AIDS. At a support group, she meets Isaiah, whose pregnant mother also has AIDS. Awards: ALSC Notable Children's Book; Child Study Children's Book; SLJ Best Book; YALSA Best Book for Young Adults. (Rev: BL 9/1/94; BTA; SLJ 9/94*; VOYA 10/94)

380 Nunez, Sigrid. *A Feather on the Breath of God* (9–adult). 1995, HarperCollins $18 (0-06-017151-0). The daughter of a Chinese/Panamanian father and German mother ponders the connection between love and pain, the results of cultural displacement, and the arbitrariness of life. (Rev: BL 12/15/94*)

381 Okimoto, Jean Davies. *Take a Chance, Gramps!* (5–7). 1990, Little, Brown/Joy Street $13.95 (0-316-63812-9). An unpopular junior high student and her lonely grandfather both find romance and acceptance at a dance. (Rev: BL 1/15/91; SLJ 12/90)

382 O'Nan, Stewart. *Snow Angels* (9–adult). 1994, Doubleday $20 (0-385-47574-8). In a small Pennsylvania town in winter, Arthur, 15, copes with his parents' divorce and finds the drowned body of his former babysitter's 3-year-old daughter. (Rev: BL 10/15/94*)

383 Park, Barbara. *Mick Harte Was Here* (5–7). 1995, Knopf/Apple Soup LB $15.99 (0-679-97088-6). A look at the effects of a brother's death on an entire family through the eyes of his 13-year-old sister. Awards: SLJ Best Book. (Rev: BL 3/1/95; SLJ 5/95)

384 Paterson, Katherine. *Flip-Flop Girl* (5–7). 1994, Dutton/Lodestar $13.99 (0-525-67480-2). Vinnie and her traumatized family move to a small Virginia town when her father dies. Her only friend is Lupe, a half-Latina outsider, and she falls in love with a teacher. Awards: ALSC Notable Children's Book; SLJ Best Book. (Rev: BL 12/15/93; MJHS; SLJ 5/94*)

385 Pearson, Gayle. *The Fog Doggies and Me* (5–7). 1993, Atheneum $13.95 (0-689-31845-6). A San Francisco teenager feels betrayed when her 13-year-old best friend leaps into the world of boyfriends and diets. (Rev: BL 1/15/94; SLJ 1/94; VOYA 2/94)

386 Pearson, Gayle. *One Potato, Tu: Seven Stories* (5–8). 1992, Atheneum $12.95 (0-689-31706-9). Loosely connected stories surrounding a 12-year-old girl, her family, and friends in their Oakland, California, neighborhood. (Rev: BL 4/1/92; SLJ 5/92)

387 Peck, Robert Newton. *A Part of the Sky* (5–7). 1994, Knopf $18 (0-679-43277-9). In this autobiographical novel, Rob, 13, must take care of his mother and run his family's small farm after the death of his father. Sequel to *A Day No Pigs Would Die*. (Rev: BL 9/15/94; BTA; SHS)

388 Pevsner, Stella. *I'm Emma: I'm a Quint* (5–7). 1993, Clarion $13.95 (0-395-64166-7). The sequel to *Sister of the Quints* (1987) finds Emma struggling to decide whether to accept TV coverage of herself and her siblings or be known for who she is. (Rev: BL 10/1/93; SLJ 12/93)

389 Pevsner, Stella. *Jon, Flora, and the Odd-Eyed Cat* (6–8). 1994, Clarion $13.95 (0-395-67021-7). Jon, 14, moves with his family to South Carolina, where he receives late-night visits from a cat. Soon he meets Flora, 12, the cat's crazy owner. (Rev: BL 11/1/94; SLJ 10/94; VOYA 12/94)

390 Pevsner, Stella. *The Night the Whole Class Slept Over* (5–7). 1991, Clarion $13.95 (0-89919-983-6). Dan attends school in his grandparents' small Wisconsin town while his mother looks for a cabin in the woods and makes new friendships, including a new romance. (Rev: BL 10/1/91; SLJ 11/91)

391 Pfeffer, Susan Beth. *April Upstairs* (9–adult). 1990, Holt $13.95 (0-8050-1306-7). A young girl develops a close relationship with a cousin after her parents divorce. (Rev: BL 1/1/91; SLJ 3/91)

392 Pfeffer, Susan Beth. *Darcy Downstairs* (6–8). 1990, Holt $13.95 (0-8050-1307-5). Young cousins become good friends when their families move into the same apartment building. (Rev: BL 1/1/91)

393 Pfeffer, Susan Beth. *Family of Strangers* (9–12). 1992, Bantam/Starfire $15 (0-553-08364-3); 1994, Dell/Laurel Leaf paper $3.99 (0-440-21895-0). Characters in a dysfunctional family are examined through the letters and essays of an introverted young daughter. Awards: YALSA Best Book for Young Adults. (Rev: BL 2/1/92; SHS; YR)

394 Pfeffer, Susan Beth. *Make Believe* (5–7). 1993, Holt $14.95 (0-8050-1754-2). A complicated story about the effect of divorce on 2 families with 6th-grade daughters. (Rev: BL 10/15/93; SLJ 12/93; VOYA 2/94)

395 Pfeffer, Susan Beth. *Most Precious Blood* (7–12). 1991, Bantam/Starfire $13.95 (0-553-07109-2). Concerns the daughter of a tycoon who confronts her family when she discovers that her father is not her biological parent. (Rev: BL 9/1/91)

396 Polikoff, Barbara Garland. *Life's a Funny Proposition, Horatio* (5–7). 1992, Holt $13.95 (0-8050-1972-3). A quietly wrenching story about grief across generations, starring Horatio, age 12. Awards: ALSC Notable Children's Book; SLJ Best Book. (Rev: BL 6/15/92; SLJ 8/92*)

397 Porte, Barbara Ann. *Something Terrible Happened* (6–10). 1994, Orchard/Richard Jackson LB $16.99 (0-531-08719-0); 1996, Troll paper $4.50 (0-8167-3868-8). Part white, part West Indian, Gillian, 12, must adjust to living with her deceased father's "plain white" relatives when her mother contracts AIDS. Awards: SLJ Best Book; YALSA Best Book for Young Adults. (Rev: BL 9/15/94; MJHS; SLJ 10/94; VOYA 10/94)

398 Pringer, Nancy. *Toughing It* (7–10). 1994, Harcourt $10.95 (0-15-200008-9); paper $4.95 (0-15-200011-9). Tuff lives in a trailer with his alcoholic mother and her abusive boyfriend. When Tuff is murdered, Dillon, his younger brother, runs to the man who could be his father. Awards: Edgar; SLJ Best Book; YALSA Best Book for Young Adults. (Rev: BL 9/1/94; SLJ 9/94; VOYA 8/94)

399 Provoost, Anne. *My Aunt Is a Pilot Whale* (6–9). Tr. by Ria Bleumer. 1995, Women's Press paper $9.95 (0-88961-202-1). A story of family relationships and friendship but also of incest. (Rev: BL 3/1/95)

400 Quindlen, Anna. *Object Lessons* (9–adult). 1991, Random $19 (0-394-56965-2). Maggie, 12, learns important lessons in life while spending the summer of 1960 in a suburb of the Bronx. (Rev: BL 1/15/91; SLJ 9/91)

401 Quinn, Eric Shaw. *Say Uncle* (9–adult). 1994, Dutton $20.95 (0-525-93780-3). Describes the antics of a gay man who gains custody of his recently deceased sister's newborn son despite concerns about his sexual orientation. (Rev: BL 7/94; BTA)

402 Radley, Gail. *The Golden Days* (5–7). 1991, Macmillan $12.95 (0-02-775652-1). Foster child Cory, 11—not believing he's really wanted—runs away with new friend Carlotta, who, at 75, hates the nursing home life. Awards: SLJ Best Book. (Rev: BL 4/1/91; SLJ 3/91*)

403 Reed, Don C. *The Kraken* (6–10). 1995, Boyds Mills/Caroline House $15.95 (1-56397-216-6). In Newfoundland in the late 1800s, a boy struggles to survive against the impersonal rich and the harsh environment. (Rev: BL 3/15/95; SLJ 2/95)

404 Reiss, Kathryn. *The Glass House People* (10–12). 1992, Harcourt $16.95 (0-15-231040-1); paper $6.95 (0-15-231041-X). A woman returns to the dysfunctional family she left 20 years earlier, and her children uncover the accident-murder that tore their relationships apart. (Rev: BL 3/15/92; SLJ 5/92; YR)

405 Rhodes, Judy Carole. *The King Boy* (5–9). 1991, Bradbury $13.95 (0-02-776115-0). Benjy loves his Grandpa King, but everyone else in the small Arkansas town hates him. After the old man's death, Benjy finally learns the truth about him. (Rev: BL 12/15/91; SLJ 12/91)

406 Roberts, Willo Davis. *What Are We Going to Do about David?* (5–8). 1993, Atheneum/Jean Karl $14.95 (0-689-31793-X). Because his parents are considering divorce, David, 11, is sent to live with his grandmother, an understanding woman who helps him gain self-reliance and confidence. (Rev: BL 3/15/93; MJHS; SLJ 4/93)

407 Rodowsky, Colby. *Hannah in Between* (5–8). 1994, Farrar $15 (0-374-32837-4). Hannah struggles with what to do when she discovers that her mother is a secret alcoholic. Awards: SLJ Best Book; YALSA Best Book for Young Adults. (Rev: BL 4/1/94; BTA; MJHS; SLJ 5/94; VOYA 10/94)

408 Ross, Ramon Royal. *The Dancing Tree* (5–7). 1995, Atheneum $14 (0-689-80072-X). A mother leaves home to recenter her life while her daughter struggles to understand the tensions between her parents. A wise grandmother helps her understand. (Rev: BL 9/1/95; SLJ 2/96)

409 Ross, Rhea Beth. *Hillbilly Choir* (6–9). 1991, Houghton $13.95 (0-395-53356-2). Laurie, 15, and her mother, a failed actress, return to Laurie's grandmother's Arkansas home. None of Laurie's family or friends has the talent or means to escape the small town—except for Laurie. (Rev: BY; SLJ 7/91)

410 Roy, Jacqueline. *Soul Daddy* (7–10). 1992, Harcourt/Gulliver $16.95 (0-15-277193-X). Twin sisters cope with being abandoned, black, and poor. (Rev: BL 5/1/92; SLJ 4/92; YR)

411 Ryan, Mary E. *My Sister Is Driving Me Crazy* (6–8). 1991, Simon & Schuster $15 (0-671-73203-X). The frustrations and consolations of being a twin are described in this story of sisters who are attracted to the same teenage boy. (Rev: BL 9/1/91; BTA; SLJ 9/91)

412 Rylant, Cynthia. *Missing May* (5–7). 1992, Orchard/Richard Jackson LB $12.99 (0-531-08596-1); 1993, Dell/Yearling paper $3.99 (0-440-40865-2). An orphaned girl and her uncle learn how to grieve and how to heal after losing someone they love. Awards: ALSC Notable Children's Book; BL Best of Editors' Choice; Boston Globe/Horn Book; Newbery Medal; YALSA Best Book for Young Adults. (Rev: BL 2/15/92*; BTA; MJHS; SLJ 3/92*)

413 Sachs, Marilyn. *What My Sister Remembered* (5–7). 1992, Dutton LB $15 (0-525-44953-1); 1994, Penguin/Puffin paper $3.99 (0-14-036944-9). After 8 years apart, 2 sisters are reunited, and Molly discovers why her sister left the family, in this tale of a dysfunctional family. (Rev: BL 6/15/92*; MJHS; SLJ 8/92; YR)

414 Salat, Cristina. *Living in Secret* (5–7). 1993, Bantam/Skylark $15 (0-553-08670-7); 1994, Dell/Yearling paper $3.99 (0-440-40950-0). After her parents' divorce, Amelia, age 11, wants to live with her mother. But her mother is a lesbian and believes she must "kidnap" her daughter and move to California. (Rev: BL 2/15/93; SLJ 2/93)

415 Sargent, Sarah. *Between Two Worlds* (5–7). 1995, Ticknor & Fields $14.95 (0-395-66425-X). A young girl experiences many of the familiar problems of families, but this time with a fresh twist and no easy solutions. (Rev: BL 8/95; SLJ 8/95)

416 Sebestyen, Ouida. *Out of Nowhere* (6–9). 1994, Orchard/Melanie Kroupa LB $15.99 (0-531-08689-5). The story of the bonding into a sort of family of a quirky group of characters: Harley, 13, who's left home; his dog Ishmael; Bill, a junk collector; May, the "queen of clean";

et al. Awards: SLJ Best Book. (Rev: BL 4/1/94; MJHS; SHS; SLJ 3/94; VOYA 4/94)

417 Shea, Lisa. *Hula* (9–adult). 1993, Norton $17.95 (0-393-03589-1). Two sisters are abused by their violent father—a war casualty—in a Virginia town while their mother remains unhelpful. This surreal story never names any of the family members. Awards: BL Editors' Choice. (Rev: BL 11/15/93)

418 Shusterman, Neal. *What Daddy Did* (7–10). 1991, Little, Brown $15.95 (0-316-78906-2). A young boy recounts the story of how is father murdered his mother and how he ultimately comes to understand and forgive him. Awards: YALSA Best Book for Young Adults. (Rev: BL 7/91; SLJ 6/91)

419 Sinykin, Sheri Cooper. *Next Thing to Strangers* (6–9). 1991, Lothrop $12.95 (0-688-10694-3). A teenage boy and girl form a half-romantic relationship while visiting their grandparents in neighboring trailers in a retirement park. Awards: SLJ Best Book. (Rev: BL 11/15/91; SLJ 8/91*)

420 Sleator, William. *Oddballs* (9–12). 1993, Dutton $14.99 (0-525-45057-2). These stories, which constitute a memoir of Sleator's adolescence, introduce his oddball parents and siblings. Awards: YALSA Best Book for Young Adults. (Rev: BL 8/93; BTA; MJHS; VOYA 12/93)

421 Smith, Barbara A. *Somewhere Just Beyond* (5–8). 1993, Atheneum $12.95 (0-689-31877-4). When 12-year-old Callie's Gramma becomes critically ill, Callie must deal with her loved one's new debility and find the maturity to accept death as inevitable. (Rev: BL 12/15/93; SLJ 1/94)

422 Smith, Doris Buchanan. *Best Girl* (5–8). 1993, Viking $13.99 (0-670-83752-0). Nealy, 11, has divorced parents, a runaway sister, and a stressed-out mother. Her only refuge is under Mrs. Dees's porch—until the house burns down. Awards: SLJ Best Book. (Rev: BL 1/15/93; SLJ 1/93*)

423 Smith, Jane Denitz. *Mary by Myself* (5–7). 1994, HarperCollins LB $13.89 (0-06-024518-2). This deeply felt novel about Mary, 11, speaks with spare drama about grief, anger, and kindness. (Rev: BL 11/1/94; MJHS; SLJ 11/94; VOYA 4/95)

424 Smith, Lee. *Saving Grace* (9–12). 1995, Putnam $22.95 (0-399-14050-6). The story of Florida Grace Shepherd, a spirited Southern women of humble background who endures difficult, often tragic times. (Rev: BL 4/1/95; SLJ 1/96)

425 Stevens, Diane. *Liza's Blue Moon* (6–8). 1995, Greenwillow $15 (0-688-13542-0). A coming-of-age story where a young girl feels she has been left behind by all that matters in life. (Rev: BL 4/1/95; SLJ 4/95)

426 Stevenson, James. *The Bones in the Cliff* (5–7). 1995, Greenwillow $15 (0-688-13745-8). A boy is alone and afraid, constantly alert for the arrival of a hit man who is after his father. (Rev: BL 5/1/95*; SLJ 4/95)

427 Sweeney, Joyce. *Shadow* (7–10). 1994, Delacorte $15.95 (0-385-32051-5). Sarah's cat, Shadow, has mysteriously returned from the dead. Sarah and Cissy, the psychic housemaid, try to figure out why. Awards: SLJ Best Book; YALSA Best Book for Young Adults. (Rev: BL 7/94; MJHS; SLJ 9/94; VOYA 10/94)

428 Sweeney, Joyce. *The Tiger Orchard* (9–12). 1993, Delacorte $15 (0-385-30841-8). Zack leaves home to find his father, which is the key to understanding himself and shapes his maturation. Awards: YALSA Best Book for Young Adults. (Rev: BL 4/1/93; SLJ 5/93)

429 Talbert, Marc. *A Sunburned Prayer* (5–8). 1995, Simon & Schuster LB $14 (0-689-80125-4); 1997, paper $4.50 (0-689-81326-0). Eloy walks 17 miles under the New Mexico sun to ask God for a miracle to save his grandmother's life. Awards: SLJ Best Book. (Rev: BL 8/95; SLJ 7/95)

430 Tate, Eleanora E. *A Blessing in Disguise* (5–8). 1995, Delacorte $14.95 (0-385-32103-1). Zambia, 12, wants to live with her father, Snake, who's involved in criminal activities, but he disappoints and humiliates her and she learns valuable lessons about caring, loyalty, and honesty. (Rev: BL 1/1/95; SLJ 2/95; VOYA 4/95)

431 Thesman, Jean. *The Rain Catchers* (7–12). 1991, Houghton $13.95 (0-395-55333-4). Grayling learns the importance of storytelling in keeping the past alive, understanding others and herself, and surviving difficult times. Awards: Golden Kite; SLJ Best Book. (Rev: BL 4/15/91*; BY; SLJ 3/91)

432 Tyler, Anne. *Saint Maybe* (9–adult). 1991, Knopf $22 (0-679-40361-2). The story of an eccentric Baltimore family's guilt and redemption spanning 4 generations. (Rev: BL 6/1/91; SHS; SLJ 12/91)

433 Wallace, Bill. *True Friends* (5–7). 1994, Holiday $14.95 (0-8234-1141-9). When 6th-grader Courtney's brother is arrested, she is abandoned by friends and her stepmother leaves. She makes friends with a new kid who walks with a cane. (Rev: BL 10/15/94; SLJ 10/94; VOYA 4/95)

434 Wallace-Brodeur, Ruth. *The Godmother Tree* (5–7). Rev. ed. 1992, HarperCollins LB $12.89 (0-06-022458-4). Laura's summer on her family's new farm is full of surprises, but she keeps everything in perspective, perhaps because of the godmother tree. (Rev: BL 7/92; SLJ 5/92*)

435 Wartski, Maureen. *Dark Silence* (7–10). 1994, Ballantine/Fawcett Juniper paper $3.99 (0-449-70418-1). Teenager Randy must deal with her mother's recent death and the abuse of her neighbor, Delia. (Rev: BL 4/1/94; SLJ 7/94; VOYA 6/94)

436 Watson, Larry. *Justice* (9–adult). 1995, Milkweed Editions (430 First Ave. N., Suite 400, Minneapolis, MN 55401) $17.95 (1-57131-002-9). This prequel to *Montana 1948* treats men's relationships with their fathers. (Rev: BL 1/1/95; SLJ 9/95)

437 Wieler, Diana. *Last Chance Summer* (5–9). 1991, Delacorte $14.95 (0-385-30317-3). Chronicles a few weeks in the lives of 8 boys who are on the verge of being sent to a juvenile-hall-like facility for petty crimes and running away. (Rev: BL 4/15/91; SLJ 5/91)

438 Wilde, Nicholas. *Down Came a Blackbird* (6–8). 1992, Holt $14.95 (0-8050-2001-2). James, 13, must resort to a dream world to deal with his anger and grief over his mother's neglect, at his killing of a blackbird, and with a life beyond his control. Awards: SLJ Best Book. (Rev: BL 12/1/92; SLJS 6/93*; YR)

439 Willey, Margaret. *The Melinda Zone* (6–9). 1993, Bantam $16 (0-553-09215-4); 1994, Dell/Laurel Leaf paper $3.50 (0-440-21902-7). Melinda, 14, who has shuttled between divorced parents, spends the summer in Michigan with her aunt, uncle, and cousin and learns how to establish her identity and care for others. (Rev: BL 1/15/93; YR)

440 Williams, Carol Lynch. *Adeline Street* (5–7). 1995, Delacorte $14.95 (0-385-31075-7). A sequel to *Kelly and Me*. The Orton family during the year after the death of the youngest daughter. (Rev: BL 4/1/95)

441 Williams-Garcia, Rita. *Like Sisters on the Homefront* (8–12). 1995, Dutton/Lodestar $14.99 (0-525-67465-9). A candid story of a 14-year-old pregnant teen who has an abortion and is sent to Southern relatives, where there is a collision of culture and class. A funny, yet heartbreaking story told in snappy dialogue. Awards: SLJ Best Book. (Rev: BL 9/1/95*; SLJ 10/95; VOYA 4/96)

442 Willis, Patricia. *Out of the Storm* (5–7). 1995, Clarion $14.95 (0-395-68708-X). After World War II, a 12-year-old girl, who has lost her father in the war, is forced to move in with relatives she does not like. (Rev: BL 4/15/95; SLJ 4/95)

443 Wolff, Virginia Euwer. *Make Lemonade* (7–12). 1993, Holt $15.95 (0-8050-2228-7); 1994, Scholastic/Point Signature paper $3.95 (0-590-48141-X). Rooted in the community of poverty, the story offers a penetrating view of the conditions that foster ignorance, destroy self-esteem, and challenge strength. Awards: ALSC Notable Children's Book; Child Study Children's Book; Golden Kite; SLJ Best Book; YALSA Best Book for Young Adults. (Rev: BL 6/1–15/93*; BTA; MJHS; SLJ 7/93*; VOYA 10/93)

444 Wood, June Rae. *A Share of Freedom* (6–8). 1994, Putnam $15.95 (0-399-22767-9). Freedom, an intelligent, independent 7th-grader, has never met her father. Her mother's severe alcoholism lands Freedom and her brother in a foster home. Awards: Friends of American Writers Juvenile Book; SLJ Best Book. (Rev: BL 9/1/94; SLJ 10/94*; VOYA 4/95)

445 Wood, June Rae. *When Pigs Fly* (5–8). 1995, Putnam $15.95 (0-399-22911-6). A 13-year-old girl learns to cope with many problems, one of which is a younger sister with Down's syndrome. (Rev: BL 12/1/95; SLJ 10/95; VOYA 12/95)

Physical and Emotional Problems

446 Anderson, Rachel. *Black Water* (6–9). 1995, Holt $14.95 (0-8050-3847-7). A portrait of a disabled child in Victorian England's back streets. Awards: SLJ Best Book. (Rev: BL 5/15/95; SLJ 7/95)

447 Anderson, Rachel. *The Bus People* (8–12). 1992, Holt $13.95 (0-8050-2297-X). Six stories that focus on the physically, emotionally, and mentally disabled passengers who ride Bertram's Bus to a special school daily. Awards: SLJ Best Book; YALSA Best Book for Young Adults. (Rev: BL 11/15/92; MJHS; SLJ 1/93*)

448 Arrick, Fran. *What You Don't Know Can Kill You* (7–12). 1992, Bantam/Starfire $15 (0-553-07471-7); 1994, Dell/Laurel Leaf paper $3.99 (0-440-21894-2). Birth control, sexual activity, and safe-sex practices are addressed in this novel about a girl who tests HIV positive and the suicide of her boyfriend. (Rev: BL 12/15/91; MJHS)

449 Arter, Jim. *Gruel and Unusual Punishment* (6–9). 1991, Delacorte $13.95 (0-385-30298-3). Arnold, an obnoxious kid who's disliked by teachers and students alike, has no friends until he meets Edward—who makes Arnold's antics seem tame. Awards: YALSA Best Book for Young Adults. (Rev: BL 2/15/91; MJHS)

450 Bantle, Lee F. *Diving for the Moon* (5–7). 1995, Simon & Schuster $14 (0-689-80004-5). A young girl's friendship deepens for her hemophiliac friend who acquires AIDS from a transfusion. (Rev: BL 9/1/95; SLJ 10/95)

451 Bennett, James. *I Can Hear the Mourning Dove* (8–12). 1990, Houghton $14.95 (0-395-53623-5). A 16-year-old girl battles mental illness. (Rev: BL 1/15/91; MJHS; SLJ 9/90)

452 Buchanan, Dawna Lisa. *The Falcon's Wing* (6–9). 1992, Orchard LB $13.99 (0-531-08586-4). A teenage girl learns to understand and defend her retarded cousin. (Rev: BL 2/1/92; MJHS; SLJ 4/92)

453 Calvert, Patricia. *Picking Up the Pieces* (5–9). 1993, Scribner $14.95 (0-684-19558-5). A story of adjustments: Megan, 14, is wheelchair-bound for life after an accident, and Julia, an aging actress, is trying to adjust to her declining career. (Rev: BL 5/1/93; MJHS; SLJ 6/93; VOYA 8/93)

454 Caseley, Judith. *My Father, the Nutcase* (9–12). 1992, Knopf/Borzoi LB $15.99 (0-679-93394-8). Life for Zoe, age 15, takes a nose dive when her father becomes clinically depressed. (Rev: BL 3/15/93; SLJ 11/92)

455 Cooper, Ilene. *The New, Improved Gretchen Hubbard* (5–7). 1992, Morrow $14 (0-688-08432-X). Since Gretchen has lost weight, life still isn't quite right; and when a boy asks her out on a date, those camouflaging pounds don't seem so bad. (Rev: BL 8/92; SLJ 10/92; YR)

456 Cooper, Ilene. *Stupid Cupid* (5–7). (Holiday Five) 1995, Viking $13.99 (0-670-85059-4). Seventh-grader Maddy faces 2 problems: She's the biggest girl in her class, and her widowed mother has no social life. (Rev: BL 1/1/95; SLJ 2/95)

457 Covington, Dennis. *Lizard* (9–12). 1991, Delacorte $15 (0-385-30307-6); Dell/Laurel Leaf paper $3.50 (0-440-21490-4). Explores the themes of gaining worldly wisdom and resolving adolescent fears of being different—in this case, having a facial deformity and other birth defects. Awards: BL Editors' Choice. (Rev: BL 5/1/91*; BY; SHS; SLJ 6/91)

458 Crutcher, Chris. *Staying Fat for Sarah Byrnes* (7–12). 1993, Greenwillow $14 (0-688-11552-7). The only friend of overweight Eric is Sarah, whose face was severely burned as a child. Their attempt to escape her unbalanced father leads to an almost deadly climax. Awards: SLJ Best Book; YALSA Best Book for Young Adults. (Rev: BL 3/15/93; BTA; MJHS; SLJ 3/93*; VOYA 8/93)

459 Dale, Mitzi. *Round the Bend* (6–8). 1991, Delacorte $15 (0-385-30308-4). This first-person story is a 15-year-old's account of her nervous breakdown, hospitalization, treatment by a sympathetic therapist, and eventual understanding of her problems. (Rev: BL 10/15/91)

460 Davis, Deborah. *My Brother Has AIDS* (6–9). 1994, Atheneum $14.95 (0-689-31922-3). In this realistic, accurate portrait of the caretaking families that love people with AIDS, Lacy, 13, is unprepared for the announcement that her beloved older brother is homosexual and dying of AIDS. (Rev: BL 11/15/94; BTA; MJHS; SLJ 1/95; VOYA 5/95)

461 Draper, Sharon M. *Tears of a Tiger* (7–10). 1994, Atheneum $15.95 (0-689-31878-2). A star basketball player is killed in an accident after he and his friends drink and drive. The driver, who survives, is depressed and ultimately commits suicide. (Rev: BL 11/1/94; BTA; MJHS; SLJ 2/95)

462 Durant, Penny Raife. *When Heroes Die* (6–9). 1992, Atheneum $13.95 (0-689-31764-6). Gary, 12, has to face the fact that his uncle-hero is homosexual and has contracted AIDS. (Rev: BL 10/15/92; SLJ 11/92; YR)

463 Farrell, Mame. *Marrying Malcolm Murgatroyd* (5–7). 1995, Farrar $14 (0-374-34838-3). With the 6th-grader Hannah, we confront our own conflicts about friendship, shame, and loyalty as she sticks up for an unpopular boy who has befriended her disabled brother. (Rev: BL 11/1/95; SLJ 11/95; VOYA 2/96)

464 Fenner, Carol. *Randall's Wall* (5–7). 1991, Macmillan/Margaret K. McElderry $11.95 (0-689-50518-3). Fifth-grader Randall Lord is shunned by all his classmates, except spunky Jean, as the poorest, dirtiest kid in town, until she persuades him to take a bath. (Rev: BL 4/1/91*; MJHS; SLJ 4/91)

465 Ferris, Jean. *Signs of Life* (6–10). 1995, Farrar $14 (0-374-36909-7). Hannah and her parents must come to grips with their grief over her twin's death while on vacation at the painted caves in Lascaux, France. (Rev: BL 7/95; SLJ 4/95)

466 Fraustino, Lisa Rowe. *Ash* (9–12). 1995, Orchard LB $16.99 (0-531-08739-5). A 15-year-old recalls, in diary form, his older brother's slide into schizophrenia. (Rev: BL 4/1/95; SLJ 4/95; VOYA 5/95)

467 Fromm, Pete. *Monkey Tag* (5–7). 1994, Scholastic $14.95 (0-590-46525-2). While playing a dangerous game, Thad, 12, falls and becomes paralyzed. His twin, Eli, feels guilty and questions his Catholic faith. (Rev: BL 10/15/94; BTA; SLJ 10/94; VOYA 12/94)

468 Garland, Sherry. *The Silent Storm* (5–7). 1993, Harcourt $14.95 (0-15-274170-4). Alyssa has been mute since her mother was killed and her father disappeared in a hurricane, and now another hurricane approaches and Alyssa must save her grandfather. Awards: SLJ Best Book. (Rev: BL 6/1–15/93; BTA; MJHS; SLJ 7/93*; VOYA 8/93)

469 Gelb, Alan. *Real Life: My Best Friend Died* (7–12). 1995, Pocket/Archway paper $3.50 (0-671-87273-7). A high school senior, living a happy, normal life, finds his world exploding when he feels responsible for his friend's death. (Rev: BL 4/1/95; SLJ 6/95; VOYA 5/95)

470 Geras, Adèle. *Watching the Roses* (7–12). 1992, Harcourt $16.95 (0-15-294816-3). A retelling of *The Sleeping Beauty* in a realistic contemporary setting. (Rev: BL 10/1/92; SLJ 11/92; YR)

471 Gibbons, Kaye. *Sights Unseen* (9–adult). 1995, Putnam $19.95 (0-399-13986-9). Hattie recounts her childhood growing up with a manic-depressive mother and the struggle it was for the entire family. (Rev: BL 6/1–15/95; SLJ 11/95)

472 Gleitzman, Morris. *Blabber Mouth* (6–8). 1995, Harcourt $11 (0-15-200369-X); paper $5 (0-15-200370-3). A mute girl is anything but silent as she talks with her hands and inside her head. (Rev: BL 5/1/95; SLJ 6/95)

473 Grima, Tony, ed. *Not the Only One: Lesbian and Gay Fiction for Teens* (10–12). 1995, Alyson paper $7.95 (1-55583-275-X). This collection of lesbian/gay fiction deals with young-adult characters, including works by Leslea Newman, Laurel Winter, Emily Ormand, and Raymond Luczak. (Rev: BL 7/95; VOYA 4/96)

474 Grunwald, Lisa. *The Theory of Everything* (9–adult). 1991, Knopf $20 (0-394-58149-0). Science and magic conflict in this often perplexing but very readable tale of a physicist who escapes into his work rather than face emotional uncertainty. (Rev: BL 3/1/91*)

475 Harnett, Sonya. *Wilful Blue* (10–12). 1994, Viking $13.99 (0-670-85718-1). The story of Guy, a young Australian artist who kills himself. Guy's newly found friend, Jesse, obsesses over his death. (Rev: BL 10/15/94; SLJ 12/94)

476 Helfman, Elizabeth. *On Being Sarah* (7–9). Illus. 1992, Albert Whitman $11.95 (0-8075-6068-5). Based on the life of a real person, this is the story of Sarah, 12, who has cerebral palsy, cannot vocalize and is confined to a wheelchair, and communicates through Blissymbols. (Rev: BL 12/15/92; SLJ 1/93)

477 Holland, Isabelle. *The House in the Woods* (6–9). 1991, Little, Brown $15.95 (0-316-37178-5). Bridget, 14, struggles to find self-worth and inner peace one summer at a cottage with her mute brother, twin sisters, father, and new nanny. (Rev: BL 5/1/91; SLJ 6/91)

478 Hosie-Bounar, Jane. *Life Belts* (7–12). 1993, Delacorte $14.95 (0-385-31074-9). This collection tells the exploits of 2 girls—including a joyride by boat down the Long Island coast—each from a different character's viewpoint. (Rev: BL 12/1/93; SLJ 11/93; VOYA 12/93)

479 Hurwin, Davida Wills. *A Time for Dancing* (7–12). 1995, Little, Brown $15.95 (0-316-38351-1). A powerful story of 2 friends, one of whom is diagnosed with lymphoma. Their friendship becomes a story of saying good-bye and death. (Rev: BL 11/1/95*; SLJ 10/95; VOYA 12/95)

480 Janover, Caroline. *The Worst Speller in Jr. High* (5–7). 1994, Free Spirit (400 First Ave. N., Suite 616, Minneapolis, MN 55401) paper $4.95 (0-915793-76-8). Katie, 13, finds junior high difficult because she's dyslexic, she can't find her academic or social niche, and she faces increased home responsibilities. (Rev: BL 2/1/95; BTA; SLJ 2/95; VOYA 5/95)

481 Johnson, Angela. *Humming Whispers* (8–12). 1995, Orchard/Richard Jackson LB $14.99 (0-531-08748-4). Sophy, 14, reveals the impact of her 24-year-old sister Nicole's schizophrenia on the lives of those who love her. (Rev: BL 2/15/95; SLJ 4/95; VOYA 5/95)

482 Johnston, Julie. *Hero of Lesser Causes* (5–8). 1993, Little, Brown/Joy Street $14.95 (0-316-46988-2). When 12-year-old Keely's adored older brother Patrick is paralyzed by polio, she tries to connect him to some sort of normal life. Awards: ALSC Notable Children's Book; SLJ Best Book. (Rev: BL 7/93; SLJ 6/93*; VOYA 8/93)

483 Kirby, Susan E. *Shadow Boy* (9–12). 1991, Orchard/Richard Jackson LB $15.99 (0-531-08469-8). Artie suffers a traumatic head injury and must relearn how to function normally. (Rev: BL 6/1/91; BY)

484 Klass, Sheila Solomon. *Kool Ada* (5–7). 1991, Scholastic $13.95 (0-590-43902-2). Ada, age 12, retreats into a world of silence and fighting after the death of her parents and brother, but a remarkable teacher helps her control her anger. Awards: SLJ Best Book. (Rev: BL 10/15/91; SLJ 8/91*)

485 Klass, Sheila Solomon. *Rhino* (7–10). 1993, Scholastic $13.95 (0-590-44250-3). Fourteen-year-old Annie suffers from a nose that is a family characteristic and looks too big for her face. (Rev: BL 1/15/94; BTA; SLJ 11/93; VOYA 12/93)

486 Le Mieux, A. C. *The TV Guidance Counselor* (8–12). 1993, Morrow/Tambourine $13 (0-688-12402-X). Michael Madden, 17, tells of the events, specifically his parents' divorce, that led to his attempted suicide despite a good job, supportive girlfirend, and photography talent. (Rev: BL 12/15/93; SLJ 10/93)

487 Mahon, K. L. *Just One Tear* (5–10). 1994, Lothrop $10 (0-688-13519-6). The diary of a 14-year-old girl tells the story of a 13-year-old boy whose father is shot in front of him and tells how the boy deals with his grief. (Rev: BL 5/15/94; SLJ 5/94; VOYA 10/94)

488 Metzger, Lois. *Barry's Sister* (6–9). 1992, Atheneum $15.95 (0-689-31521-X); 1993, Penguin/Puffin paper $4.50 (0-14-036484-6). A child with cerebral palsy has a huge impact on his family. (Rev: BL 4/15/92; SLJ 6/92)

489 Metzger, Lois. *Ellen's Case* (7–12). 1995, Atheneum $16 (0-689-31934-7). In this sequel to *Barry's Sister*, Ellen—now 16 and more understanding of her brother's cerebral palsy—is involved in an intense malpractice trial. (Rev: BL 8/95; SLJ 10/95; VOYA 12/95)

490 Miklowitz, Gloria D. *Desperate Pursuit* (9–12). 1992, Bantam/Starfire paper $3.99 (0-553-29746-5). A teenage love triangle takes a deadly turn. (Rev: BL 2/1/92; SLJ 7/92)

491 Miklowitz, Gloria D. *Past Forgiving* (8–10). 1995, Simon & Schuster $14 (0-671-88442-5). A teenage girl caught in an abusive relationship with her boyfriend. (Rev: BL 5/1/95; SLJ 6/95)

492 Nelson, Theresa. *The Beggar's Ride* (6–8). 1992, Orchard/Richard Jackson LB $14.99 (0-531-08496-5); 1994, Dell/Laurel Leaf paper $3.99 (0-440-21887-X). A compelling chronicle of a runaway's time on the tawdry boardwalks of Atlantic City. Awards: SLJ Best Book. (Rev: BL 11/1/92; SLJ 11/92*)

493 Newman, Lesléa. *Fat Chance* (6–9). 1994, Putnam $14.95 (0-399-22760-1). Judi, who thinks she's fat, becomes obsessed with her weight. When feelings of guilt and disgust lead her to bulimic behavior, an overweight teacher tries to help. (Rev: BL 9/1/94; SLJ 1/95)

494 Perl, Lila. *Fat Glenda Turns Fourteen* (6–9). 1991, Clarion $13.95 (0-395-53341-4). Fat Glenda returns home after a summer of romance—and slenderness—only to find that depression has caused her to gain 10 pounds. (Rev: BL 4/15/91; MJHS; SLJ 6/91)

495 Philbrick, Rodman. *Freak the Mighty* (7–10). 1993, Scholastic/Blue Sky $13.95 (0-590-47412-X). When Maxwell Kane, the son of Killer Kane, makes a friend in Kevin, a new boy with a birth defect, he gains a new identity. Yet Kevin's death and Max's kidnapping threaten it. (Rev: BL 12/15/93; BTA; MJHS; SLJ 12/93*; VOYA 4/94)

496 Randle, Kristen D. *The Only Alien on the Planet* (8–12). 1995, Scholastic $14.95 (0-590-46309-8). Ginny and Caulder try to break through to Smitty (the Alien), who is mute and isolated due to abuse he's suffered. (Rev: BL 1/15/95; SLJ 3/95; VOYA 4/95)

497 Reid, P. Carey. *Swimming in the Starry River* (9–adult). 1994, Hyperion $19.95 (0-7868-6005-7). A chronicle of courage, frustration, and compassion: A father forges a powerful bond with his young child who has a debilitating disease. (Rev: BL 5/15/94; BTA)

498 Rodowsky, Colby. *Remembering Mog* (7–10). 1996, Farrar $14.95 (0-374-34663-1). Annie remembers too clearly the killing of her older sister on the eve of high school graduation; so as her own graduation approaches, she seeks guidance from a counselor. (Rev: SLJ 3/96*)

499 Rosofsky, Iris. *My Aunt Ruth* (7–10). 1991, HarperCollins/Charlotte Zolotow LB $13.89 (0-06-025088-7). The tale of Patty's first forays on stage and her relationships with cast members, as well as of her Aunt Ruth, a diabetic who must have her legs amputated. (Rev: BL 4/1/91; SLJ 5/91)

500 Rubin, Susan Goldman. *Emily Good As Gold* (6–8). 1993, Harcourt $10.95 (0-15-276632-4). Emily's parents see their developmentally disabled child as never being able to grow up, but Emily begins to do so on her own, especially sexually. (Rev: BL 11/1/93; SLJ 10/93)

501 Ruby, Lois. *Miriam's Well* (7–12). 1993, Scholastic $13.95 (0-590-44937-0). Explores the boundaries of religious freedom while telling a story of teenage love. Awards: YALSA Best Book for Young Adults. (Rev: BL 3/1/93; MJHS; SLJ 5/93)

502 Sachs, Marilyn. *Thirteen Going on Seven* (5–7). 1993, Dutton $12.99 (0-525-45096-3). A candid, funny story about a girl with a learning disability growing up in a loving family. (Rev: BL 5/1/93; SLJ 6/93)

503 Shepard, Elizabeth. *H* (9–adult). 1995, Viking $16.95 (0-670-85927-3). A 12-year-old finds friends and comfort in the make-believe world of his mental illness. (Rev: BL 4/1/95; SLJ 9/95)

504 Shreve, Susan. *The Gift of the Girl Who Couldn't Hear* (5–7). 1991, Morrow/Tambourine $12.95 (0-688-10318-9). Concerns the relationship between two 7th-grade girls, one of whom is deaf and has been raised in the oral method, without sign language. Awards: BL Editors' Choice; SLJ Best Book. (Rev: BL 10/15/91*; MJHS; SLJ 8/91*)

505 Sirof, Harriet. *Because She's My Friend* (7–10). 1993, Atheneum $14.95 (0-689-31844-8). Two girls of opposite temperament become friends when strong-willed Valerie's right leg is paralyzed after an accident and she meets well-behaved Terri. (Rev: BL 9/15/93; MJHS; SLJ 10/93; VOYA 12/93)

506 Smith, Doris Buchanan. *Remember the Red-Shouldered Hawk* (6–8). 1994, Putnam $14.95 (0-399-22443-2). Sensitively explores the problems of a close-knit family coping with Alzheimer's and racism. (Rev: BL 4/1/94; SLJ 6/94)

507 Springer, Nancy. *Colt* (5–9). 1991, Dial $14.95 (0-8037-1022-4). Colt, in a wheelchair with spina bifida, enjoys a physical therapy program of horseback riding. (Rev: BL 11/1/91)

508 Tamar, Erika. *Fair Game* (9–12). 1993, Harcourt $10.95 (0-15-278537-X); paper $3.95 (0-15-227065-5). Based on a real-life tragedy, this explicit story tells of the sexual assault of a mentally disabled girl by a group of high school jocks. (Rev: BL 11/15/93; SLJ 10/93; VOYA 12/93)

509 Tamar, Erika. *The Truth about Kim O'Hara* (7–10). 1992, Atheneum $14.95 (0-689-31789-1). A coming-of-age story where Andy, 15, struggles with the conflict between sexual feelings for and friendship with the beautiful Vietnamese-born Kim. Sequel to *It Happened at Cecilia's*. (Rev: BL 12/1/92; SLJ 1/93; YR)

510 Thesman, Jean. *Summerspell* (7–10). 1995, Simon & Schuster $15 (0-671-50130-5). A web of lies and secrets are behind a girl's escape from sexual harassment to a cabin where life had been safe and happy in the past. (Rev: BL 5/1/95; SLJ 6/95)

511 Voigt, Cynthia. *When She Hollers* (7–12). 1994, Scholastic $13.95 (0-590-46714-X). Tish, 17, endures her stepfather's sexual abuse. She deals with shame, anger, and denial before revealing her secret to a classmate's father, who is a lawyer. Awards: SLJ Best Book. (Rev: BL 10/15/94; BTA; MJHS; SHS; SLJ 11/94*; VOYA 12/94)

512 Werlin, Nancy. *Are You Alone on Purpose?* (5–8). 1994, Houghton $13.95 (0-395-67350-X). Opposites attract when Alison, 13, hesitantly falls in love with the unruly Harry, who has an accident that confines him to a wheelchair. (Rev: BL 8/94; BTA; SLJ 9/94; VOYA 10/94)

513 White, Ruth. *Weeping Willow* (7–10). 1992, Farrar $16 (0-374-38255-7); paper $3.95 (0-374-48280-2). This uplifting novel conveying hill country life is about a girl who overcomes abuse to make her own way. Awards: YALSA Best Book for Young Adults. (Rev: BL 6/15/92; SLJ 7/92; YR)

514 Willey, Margaret. *Facing the Music* (7–10). 1996, Delacorte $14.95 (0-385-32104-X). After their mother's sudden death, Lisa and her brother Mark join a band to escape their grief. (Rev: BL 3/15/96; SLJ 2/96; VOYA 4/96)

515 Williams, Karen Lynn. *A Real Christmas This Year* (5–8). 1995, Clarion $13.95 (0-395-70115-5). Megan worries that she won't have a happy Christmas because her brother Kevin suffers from physical and emotional problems that exhaust their mother and strain their finances. Eventually, she gets the Christmas she wants—and some unexpected lessons about life. (Rev: BL 9/15/95; VOYA 12/95)

516 Wilson, Nancy Hope. *Bringing Nettie Back* (5–7). 1992, Macmillan $13.95 (0-02-793075-0). Dramatizes the joy of friendship and the loss when things go wrong for Clara, 11, and her classmate Nettie, who become best friends one summer in the country. (Rev: BL 1/1/93; MJHS; SLJ 10/92)

517 Wilson, Nancy Hope. *The Reason for Janey* (5–7). 1994, Macmillan $14.95 (0-02-793127-7). A girl's parents divorce and a new person, a mentally disabled adult, moves into the household. The girl learns how to confront the past and move on. (Rev: BL 4/15/94; SLJ 5/94*)

518 Wood, June Rae. *The Man Who Loved Clowns* (5–8). 1992, Putnam $14.95 (0-399-21888-2). Delrita's views of living and dying, appreciating and surrendering, are transformed after the death of her parents in an auto accident and the death of her uncle from Down's syndrome. Awards: SLJ Best Book. (Rev: BL 11/15/92; MJHS; SLJ 9/92*; YR)

Personal Problems and Growing into Maturity

519 Abraham, Pearl. *The Romance Reader* (9–adult). 1995, Putnam/Riverhead $21.95 (1-57322-015-9). An introduction to Orthodox Jewish culture through the experiences of a 12-year-old girl who grows into a 19-year-old married woman. (Rev: BL 8/95; SLJ 12/95)

520 Aitkens, Maggi. *Kerry, a Teenage Mother* (6–9). Photos. Illus. 1994, Lerner LB $14.21 (0-8225-2556-9). A day in the life of an 18-year-old mother on welfare who is trying to make a better life for her and her daughter. (Rev: BL 12/15/94; SLJ 12/94) [362.83]

521 Amis, Kingsley. *We Are All Guilty* (7–10). 1992, Viking LB $14 (0-670-84268-0). An alienated teenager gets into trouble and must reexamine his values. (Rev: BL 3/15/92; YR)

522 Arvin, Reed. *The Wind in the Wheat* (9–adult). 1994, Thomas Nelson $12.99 (0-7852-8146-0). Andrew enters the world of professional Christian music and eventually realizes he must follow his conscience—and possibly lose everything—or yield to his producer's wishes. (Rev: BL 12/15/94*; VOYA 4/95)

523 Avi. *Blue Heron* (5–8). 1992, Bradbury $14.95 (0-02-707751-9). A young girl with a troubled family life finds comfort in nature and a beautiful bird. Awards: YALSA Best Book for Young Adults. (Rev: BL 1/15/92*; BTA; MJHS; SLJ 4/92)

524 Banks, Russell. *Rule of the Bone* (9–adult). 1995, HarperCollins $22 (0-06-017275-4). A first-person narration of a teenage boy who becomes a drifter, convinced that he is destined for a criminal career. Awards: SLJ Best Book. (Rev: BL 3/1/95; SLJ 4/95)

525 Barrett, Elizabeth. *Free Fall* (10–12). 1994, HarperCollins $14.89 (0-06-024465-8). Ginnie, 17, must cope with exile to her grandmother's for the summer, with her parents' failing marriage, and with her rocky romantic relationships. (Rev: BL 11/15/94; BTA)

526 Bell, Mary S. *Sonata for Mind and Heart* (7–10). 1992, Atheneum $15.95 (0-689-31734-4). A 16-year-old violinist is torn between his father's encourgement and his mother's desire for him to pursue another career. (Rev: BL 5/15/92; SLJ 5/92)

527 Berg, Elizabeth. *Durable Goods* (9–adult). 1993, Random $17 (0-679-42208-0). Katie, 12, narrates this tender, poignant, funny, totally believable coming-of-age story. Awards: SLJ Best Book; YALSA Best Book for Young Adults. (Rev: BL 4/15/93; SLJ 11/93*; VOYA 12/93)

528 Betancourt, Jeanne. *Kate's Turn* (5–8). 1992, Scholastic $13.95 (0-590-43103-X). This story of the young ballerina Kate, who decides the price of fame is too high, shows the grueling, often painful life of a dancer. (Rev: BL 1/1/92; SLJ 2/92; YR)

529 Block, Francesca Lia. *Baby Be-Bop* (8–12). 1995, HarperCollins/Joanna Cotler LB $13.89 (0-06-024880-7). Dirk is gay and struggles with self-loathing, among any number of debilitating emotions and experiences, until his grandmother shares her wisdom about loving and living. (Rev: BL 10/1/95*; SLJ 9/95)

530 Bridgers, Sue Ellen. *Keeping Christina* (7–10). 1993, HarperCollins LB $14.89 (0-06-021505-4). Annie takes sad newcomer Christina under her wing, but she turns out to be a liar and troublemaker and this creates conflicts with Annie's family, friends, and boyfriend. (Rev: BL 7/93; MJHS; SLJ 7/93)

531 Brooks, Bruce. *What Hearts* (8–12). 1992, HarperCollins/Laura Geringer LB $13.89 (0-06-021132-6). Four long stories about the boy Asa, especially the child's relationship with his emotionally fragile mother and his hostile competition with his stepfather. (Rev: BL 9/1/92*; SHS; SLJ 11/92; YR)

532 Bunin, Sherry. *Dear Great American Writers School* (9–12). 1995, Houghton $14.95 (0-395-71645-4). A sensitive, bittersweet story of a young aspiring writer who is drawn into a magazine's scheme to train young writers. (Rev: BL 11/15/95; SLJ 10/95; VOYA 12/95)

533 Bunting, Eve. *Jumping the Nail* (7–12). 1991, Harcourt $15.95 (0-15-241357-X). A dependent, unstable girl becomes unhinged when she is persuaded by her danger-seeking boyfriend to jump off a cliff with him. (Rev: BL 11/1/91; MJHS; SHS; SLJ 12/91)

534 Cadnum, Michael. *Breaking the Fall* (8–12). 1992, Viking $15 (0-670-84687-2). To help him forget that his parents are separating and he isn't playing baseball anymore, Stanley and Jared start housebreaking, taking token items to mark their daring. (Rev: BL 11/15/92; SLJ 9/92; YR)

535 Camus, Albert. *First Man* (9–12). Tr. by David Hapgood. 1995, Knopf $23 (0-679-43937-4). A remarkable autobiographical novel of childhood, just published 34 years after the manuscript was discovered in the car wreckage where Camus was killed. (Rev: BL 8/95; SLJ 2/96)

536 Cannon, Bettie. *Begin the World Again* (8–12). 1991, Scribner $13.95 (0-684-19292-6). After growing up in a commune, a teen moves to Michigan to live with her grandmother. She is torn between the communal and "establishment" lifestyles but ultimately defines her own life. (Rev: BL 6/15/91; SLJ 7/91)

537 Cardella, Lara. *Good Girls Don't Wear Trousers* (9–adult). Tr. by Diana Di Carcaci. 1994, Arcade $16.95 (1-55970-263-X). After being caught kissing a boy in her gossipy Sicilian village, teenager Annetta is wrapped in scandal and exiled to live with a drunken, abusive uncle. (Rev: BL 9/1/94; BTA; SLJ 11/94)

538 Carney, Mary Lou. *How Do You Hug an Angel? A Devotional Novel for Junior Highers* (5–7). 1993, Zondervan paper $6.99 (0-310-59411-1). After having surgery to restore her hearing, Elise must depend on her new friends and her guardian angel to adjust to the hearing world. (Rev: BL 10/1/93; SLJ 2/94; VOYA 2/94) [242]

539 Carter, Alden R. *Dogwolf* (7–10). 1994, Scholastic $13.95 (0-590-46741-7). In this coming-of-age novel, Pete realizes that a dogwolf that he's set free must be found and killed before it kills a human. (Rev: BL 1/1/95; BTA; SLJ 4/95)

540 Castañeda, Omar S. *Imagining Isabel* (9–12). 1994, Dutton/Lodestar $15.99 (0-525-67431-4). Isabel, a poor Guatemalan villager, dreams of being a teacher. The city offers her a teaching job that leads to involvement in a dangerous guerrilla movement. Sequel to *Under the Volcano*. (Rev: BL 10/1/94; BTA; MJHS; SLJ 9/94)

541 Charyn, Jerome. *Back to Bataan* (5–7). 1993, Farrar $15 (0-374-30476-9). Part Hollywood romance, part realistic coming-of-age story, this novel about Jack Dalton, 11, in New York City during World War II is both absurd and painful. (Rev: BL 6/1–15/93; SLJ 6/93; VOYA 8/93)

542 Choi, Sook Nyul. *Gathering of Pearls* (7–10). 1994, Houghton $13.95 (0-395-67437-9). Sookan Bak leaves Korea in 1954 to attend a New York women's college, where she struggles to fit in. Second sequel to *The Year of Impossible Goodbyes*. (Rev: BL 9/1/94; BTA; MJHS; VOYA 10/94)

543 Christian, Mary Blount. *Linc* (7–10). 1991, Macmillan $12.95 (0-02-718580-X). An artistic, nonathletic son rejected by his superjock father discovers the real meaning of manhood when he saves his father's life on a hunting trip. (Rev: BL 11/15/91)

544 Cole, Sheila. *What Kind of Love?* (8–10). 1995, Lothrop $14 (0-688-12848-3). A 15-year-old becomes pregnant and deals with hard decisions. (Rev: BL 3/15/95; SLJ 5/95)

545 Coles, William E., and Stephen Schwandt. *Funnybone* (8–12). 1992, Atheneum $14.95 (0-689-31666-6). A dysfunctional family grapples with codependency. (Rev: BL 2/15/92; SLJ 5/92)

546 Coman, Carolyn. *Tell Me Everything* (6–9). 1993, Farrar $15 (0-374-37390-6). When Roz Jacoby's mother dies rescuing Nate from a mountain, Roz seeks him out and tries to find freedom from her pain through forgiveness and God. Awards: ALSC Notable Children's Book; SLJ Best Book. (Rev: BL 9/15/93*; MJHS; SLJ 11/93*; VOYA 12/93)

547 Cooney, Caroline B. *Twenty Pageants Later* (7–9). 1991, Bantam/Starfire $14.95 (0-553-07254-4). As the younger, plainer sister of a frequent beauty contest winner, 14-year-old Scottie-Ann has mixed feelings when she finds herself a reluctant contestant in a middle-school pageant. (Rev: BL 4/1/91; MJHS)

548 Covington, Vicki. *Night Ride Home* (9–adult). 1992, Simon & Schuster $20 (0-671-74345-7). A newly married 19-year-old tries to sort out his complicated personal life in a small Southern mining town. (Rev: BL 9/15/92*)

549 Creech, Sharon. *Absolutely Normal Chaos* (5–8). 1995, HarperCollins LB $14.89 (0-06-02699-28). Mary Lou, 13, keeps a journal during summer vacation, chronicling the roller coaster process of adolescence—evolving friendships, the first kiss, and the gradual appreciation of people different from her. (Rev: BL 10/1/95; SLJ 11/95)

550 Crew, Gary. *Angel's Gate* (8–12). 1995, Simon & Schuster $16 (0-689-80166-1). A murder mystery/coming-of-age story about a dead man's children who have escaped to live in the wild and a 13-year-old girl who draws them back to civilization. Awards: Australian Children's Book. (Rev: BL 10/1/95; SLJ 10/95; VOYA 4/96)

551 Crew, Gary. *No Such Country* (6–9). 1994, Simon & Schuster $15 (0-671-79760-3). A mystery with elements of fantasy about an Australian fishing village with a secret. The text is strong on adolescent self-questioning and aboriginal history. (Rev: BL 5/1/94; SLJ 7/94)

552 Cruse, Howard. *Stuck Rubber Baby* (9–adult). 1995, DC Comics/Paradox $24.95 (1-56389-241-3); 1996, HarperCollins paper $14 (0-06-097713-2). A graphic novel about a gay young Southerner who learns about the agonizing struggles of racist bombings, civil rights activities, and encounters with aggressive gays, both black and white. (Rev: BL 9/1/95*) [741.5]

553 Davis, Donald. *Thirteen Miles from Suncrest* (9–adult). 1994, August House $19.95 (0-87483-379-5). The youngest child of a farm family comes of age in quaint Close Creek, North Carolina. This journal chronicles his life from 1910 to 1913. (Rev: BL 9/15/94; SLJ 1/95)

554 Davis, Terry. *If Rock and Roll Were a Machine* (8–12). 1992, Delacorte $15 (0-385-30762-

4); 1994, Dell/Laurel Leaf paper $3.99 (0-440-21908-6). In this coming-of-age novel, Bert, 16, must cope with his hatred of a vindictive teacher, sexual fantasies, his love of motorcycles, and his education as a writer. Awards: YALSA Best Book for Young Adults. (Rev: BL 11/1/92*; MJHS; SHS; SLJ 11/92)

555 De Clements, Barthe. *Breaking Out* (5–7). 1991, Delacorte $14 (0-385-30503-6). Jerry's father has been arrested for shoplifting, and preacher's kid Grace's overly restrictive mother forces her to wear outdated clothes. (Rev: BL 11/15/91; SLJ 8/91)

556 Demsky, Andy. *Dark Refuge: A Story of Cults and Their Seductive Appeal* (9–adult). 1995, Pacific paper $11.95 (0-8163-1241-9). A coming-of-age story in which young Anita is inadvertently abused by her mother and then falls into the hands of a so-called prophet of a cult. (Rev: BL 11/1/95*)

557 Doherty, Berlie. *Dear Nobody* (7–12). 1992, Orchard LB $14.99 (0-531-08611-9); 1994, Morrow/Beech Tree paper $4.95 (0-688-12764-9). This complex novel explores the consequences of a teenager's pregnancy and the resultant tensions with her boyfriend. Awards: BL Editors' Choice; Carnegie Medal; SLJ Best Book; YALSA Best Book for Young Adults. (Rev: BL 10/1/92*; BTA; MJHS; SLJ 10/92*)

558 Dracup, Angela. *The Placing* (7–10). 1991, Victor Gollancz $19.95 (0-575-04890-5). Jonathan has a dysfunctional mother; and after enduring an unsuccessful foster placement and 3 years in a children's home, he eventually finds a loving relationship with a foster mother. (Rev: BL 11/15/91)

559 Emmons, Jasen. *Cowboy Angst* (9–adult). 1995, Soho (853 Broadway, New York, NY 10003) $20 (1-56947-021-9). In a world of deeply disturbed and disturbing characters, Dennis returns to his Montana home to tell his parents that he's dropped out of law school and wants to play drums in a country band. (Rev: BL 12/1/94*)

560 Filene, Peter. *Home and Away* (9–adult). 1992, Zoland Books (384 Huron Ave., Cambridge, MA 02138) $19.95 (0-944072-22-4). A coming-of-age story set against the backdrop of the anticommunist hysteria of 1951. (Rev: BL 9/15/92; SLJ 1/93)

561 Fischer, John. *The Saints' and Angels' Song* (9–adult). 1995, Bethany paper $8.99 (1-55661-474-8). In this sequel to *Saint Ben*, Jonathan, now a teenager, remains troubled by Ben's death and seems to be receiving messages from him on how to deal with a particular girl. (Rev: BL 3/15/95*)

562 Fitch, Janet. *Kicks* (8–12). 1995, Clarion $14.95 (0-395-69624-0). When Laurie's domineering parents make her think her friend's life is ideal, she becomes involved in seamy adventures that can only end in disaster. (Rev: BL 8/95; SLJ 6/95)

563 Fox, Paula. *Monkey Island* (5–10). 1991, Orchard/Richard Jackson LB $14.99 (0-531-08562-7). A homeless, abandoned 11-year-old boy in New York City contracts pneumonia and is cared for by an African American teenager and a retired teacher, who share their place in the park with him. Awards: ALSC Notable Children's Book; BL Editors' Choice; YALSA Best Book for Young Adults. (Rev: BL 9/1/91*; MJHS; SLJ 8/91)

564 Frankel, Ellen, and Sarah Levine. *Tell It Like It Is: Tough Choices for Today's Teens* (7–9). 1995, KTAV $16.95 (0-88125-522-X). A 14-year-old Jewish girl meets the challenges of school cliques, gang intimidation, and antisemitism with strong moral conviction. (Rev: BL 9/1/95; SLJ 9/95)

565 Gabhart, Ann. *Bridge to Courage* (6–8). 1993, Avon/Flare paper $3.50 (0-380-76051-7). Luke is afraid of bridges and walks away from the initiation rites of the elite Truelanders, who then shun him. Luke finally learns self-confidence in this deftly plotted tale. (Rev: BL 5/15/93; VOYA 10/93)

566 Gifaldi, David. *Toby Scudder, Ultimate Warrior* (5–7). 1993, Clarion $13.95 (0-395-66400-4). A humorous, moving portrait of a 6th-grade bully from a troubled family who begins to come to terms with his life through a teacher's aide. Awards: SLJ Best Book. (Rev: BL 10/15/93; SLJ 10/93*)

567 Gilchrist, Ellen. *Net of Jewels* (9–adult). 1992, Little, Brown $21.95 (0-316-31423-4). A disillusioned Southern belle wants to escape the stifling customs of the 1950s. (Rev: BL 1/15/92; SLJ 5/92)

568 Godden, Rumer. *Pippa Passes* (9–adult). 1994, Morrow $22 (0-688-13397-5). Pippa goes with a ballet company to Venice, where she becomes fascinated with the city, confused by romantic overtures by both sexes, and challenged by the demands of the troupe. (Rev: BL 11/15/94; BTA)

569 Grove, Vicki. *The Crystal Garden* (5–8). 1995, Putnam $15.95 (0-399-21813-0). A girl learns to evaluate her choices in friends and fun in order to survive. (Rev: BL 9/1/95; SLJ 5/95)

570 Gunesekera, Romesh. *Reef* (9–adult). 1995, New Press $20 (1-56584-219-7). This coming-of-age story tells of defiance and growth during the Marxist rebellion in Sri Lanka in 1962. Awards: SLJ Best Book. (Rev: SLJ 4/95)

571 Haas, Jessie. *Skipping School* (7–10). 1992, Greenwillow $14 (0-688-10179-8). A realistic, ultimately upbeat portrait of a boy's reluctant coming-of-age and of a family's eventual acceptance of death. (Rev: BL 11/15/92; SLJ 11/92; YR)

572 Hall, Barbara. *Fool's Hill* (7–10). 1992, Bantam $16 (0-553-08993-5); 1995, Dell/Laurel Leaf paper $3.99 (0-440-21939-6). Captures the essence of small-town life, where people know your family and secrets, and beautifully depicts those moments of reckoning that all teens face to become adults. Awards: YALSA Best Book for Young Adults. (Rev: BL 11/15/92; YR)

573 Hamilton, Morse. *Yellow Blue Bus Means I Love You* (8–10). 1994, Greenwillow $15 (0-688-12800-9). A teenage Russian immigrant attends a prep school, where he falls passionately in love with an American girl. (Rev: BL 9/1/94; BTA; SLJ 6/94; VOYA 10/94)

574 Haseley, Dennis. *Getting Him* (6–9). 1994, Farrar $16 (0-374-32536-7). Donald wants revenge, and the bullies in his neighborhood are only too happy to teach him how to get it, but he must decide if the lesson is worth learning. (Rev: BL 12/15/94; SLJ 11/94; VOYA 12/94)

575 Haugen, Tormod. *Keeping Secrets* (5–7). Tr. from Norwegian by David R. Jacobs. 1994, HarperCollins $15 (0-06-020881-3). A Norwegian version of the Sleeping Beauty story with a surprising reversal. (Rev: BL 4/15/94; SLJ 9/94)

576 Hayes, Sheila. *The Tinker's Daughter* (5–8). 1995, Dutton/Lodestar $14.99 (0-525-67497-7). Mother-daughter conflicts and peer issues propel the plot of this story about a young girl with a single mom and friends who present challenges. (Rev: BL 9/15/95; SLJ 11/95; VOYA 2/96)

577 Hazelgrove, William Elliot. *Ripples* (9–adult). 1992, Pantonne Press (329 W. 18th St., Chicago, IL 60616) paper $5.95 (0-9630052-9-4). Branton, age 18, feels betrayed when his best friend steals his summer love. Awards: BL Editors' Choice. (Rev: BL 3/15/92)

578 Hazelgrove, William Elliot. *Tobacco Sticks* (9–adult). 1995, Pantonne Press (329 W. 18th St., Chicago, IL 60616) $18.95 (0-9630052-8-6). Racial tensions come to a peak in 1945 Richmond, Virginia, when 13-year-old Lee Hartwell's lawyer father defends an African American maid in court. (Rev: BL 7/95; SLJ 9/95)

579 Henkes, Kevin. *Words of Stone* (5–7). 1992, Greenwillow $14 (0-688-11356-7). Two loners find comfort and friendship with each other during one summer in rural Wisconsin. Awards: ALSC Notable Children's Book; SLJ Best Book. (Rev: BL 9/15/92; SLJ 9/92*; YR)

580 Herman, Charlotte. *A Summer on Thirteenth Street* (5–7). 1991, Dutton $13.95 (0-525-44642-7). In the summer of 1944, 11-year-old Shirley Cohen and next-door-neighbor Morton share the simple pleasures of being kids in a simpler time. (Rev: BL 11/15/91)

581 Hood, Ann. *Places to Stay the Night* (9–adult). 1993, Doubleday $19.95 (0-385-42556-2). A tale of teenagers grappling with self-identity, uncertainty, and fear of the future, looking for answers on alcohol, drugs, and sex. (Rev: BL 12/1/92*)

582 Hopper, Nancy J. *The Interrupted Education of Huey B.* (7–12). 1991, Dutton/Lodestar $14.95 (0-525-67336-9). A glimpse at ecological problems, peer relationships, and responsibility as seen through the eyes of a high school senior. (Rev: BL 6/15/91; SLJ 6/91)

583 Hopper, Nancy J. *What Happened in Mr. Fisher's Room* (5–7). 1995, Dial $14.99 (0-8037-1841-1). An 8th-grader gradually becomes aware of human complexity through problems with boy-girl relations and teachers. (Rev: BL 9/1/95; SLJ 8/95; VOYA 2/96)

584 Horowitz, Eve. *Plain Jane* (9–adult). 1992, Random $20 (0-679-41261-1). Jane, 18, grapples with her parents' divorce and her older sister's marriage to an orthodox Jew. For mature readers. (Rev: BL 8/92; SLJ 5/93)

585 Howe, Norma. *Shoot for the Moon* (7–9). 1992, Crown LB $15.99 (0-517-58151-5). A self-centered smart aleck has her attitude adjusted by family, friends, and a trip to Italy. (Rev: BL 2/15/92; SLJ 4/92)

586 *Into the Widening World: International Coming-of-Age Stories* (9–adult). 1995, Persea paper $11.95 (0-89255-204-2). The innocence and daring of youth are elegantly captured in this anthology of brilliant voices from 22 countries. (Rev: BL 1/1/95; SLJ 8/95; VOYA 5/95)

587 Johnson, Lissa Halls. *Just Like Ice Cream* (6–10). 1995, Tyndale paper $4.99 (0-8423-1989-1). An update of the 1985 book, with current information about birth control, AIDS, etc. This story deals with a pregnant 16-year-old who chooses not to have an abortion. She gains support from a woman friend. The message: abstention from premarital sex. Also, abortion is a frightening option. (Rev: BL 9/1/95; SLJ 10/95)

588 Johnson, Scott. *One of the Boys* (8–12). 1992, Atheneum $15.95 (0-689-31520-1). A teen must part ways with his manipulative best friend when a prank takes a criminal turn. Awards: YALSA Best Book for Young Adults. (Rev: BL 4/1/92; SLJ 5/92)

589 Johnson, Scott. *Overnight Sensation* (7–12). 1994, Atheneum $16.95 (0-689-31831-6). An engrossing story of a young woman's moral deterioration and subsequent redemption, involving issues of antisemitism, teen alcoholism, and the use of condoms to prevent AIDS. (Rev: BL 4/1/94; SHS; SLJ 5/94; VOYA 6/94)

590 Johnston, Julie. *Adam and Eve and Pinch-Me* (9–12). 1994, Little, Brown $14.95 (0-316-46990-4); 1995, Penguin/Puffin paper $4.99 (0-14-037588-0). A neglected child learns the meaning of love in this coming-of-age story. Awards: ALSC Notable Children's Book; Schwartz Children's Book; SLJ Best Book. (Rev: BL 5/15/94*; BTA; SLJ 7/94; VOYA 8/94)

591 Kaye, Marilyn. *The Atonement of Mindy Wise* (6–9). 1991, Harcourt $15.95 (0-15-200402-5). A Jewish girl reviews a year's worth of sins on Yom Kippur and realizes she isn't as bad as she had thought. (Rev: BL 6/15/91)

592 Kaye, Marilyn. *Real Heroes* (5–7). 1993, Harcourt/Gulliver $16.95 (0-15-200563-3); 1994, Avon/Camelot paper $3.50 (0-380-72283-6). Presents the personal dilemmas facing Kevin, 11—his problems with his separated parents and the plight of his gym teacher, who is gay and HIV positive. (Rev: BL 4/1/93; MJHS; SLJ 6/93)

593 Kehret, Peg. *Cages* (6–9). 1991, Dutton/Cobblehill $13.95 (0-525-65062-8). A 9th-grader resorts to shoplifting after encountering huge disappointments at home and at school, but he rebuilds a strong self-concept with the help of a concerned teacher and an elderly friend. (Rev: BL 6/15/91; MJHS; SLJ 6/91)

594 Kennedy, Barbara. *The Boy Who Loved Alligators* (7–9). 1994, Atheneum $14.95 (0-689-31876-6). When young Jim's "friend," an alligator, eats the neighbor's dog, he's forced to face some hard truths. (Rev: BL 4/1/94; SLJ 6/94)

595 Kerr, M. E. *Deliver Us from Evie* (7–12). 1994, HarperCollins LB $14.89 (0-06-024476-3). Evie, 18, falls in love with a banker's preppy daughter, Patty. When Patty's father tries to stop the relationship, the youth flee to New York. Awards: BL Editors' Choice; SLJ Best Book; YALSA Best Book for Young Adults. (Rev: BL 9/15/94*; BTA; MJHS; SHS; SLJ 11/94*; VOYA 10/94)

596 Koertge, Ron. *Mariposa Blues* (6–9). 1991, Little, Brown $15.95 (0-316-50103-4). Adolescence makes Graham ill-tempered with nearly everyone, especially his racehorse trainer father, so he goes to work for a rival trainer. (Rev: BL 4/15/91; SLJ 5/91)

597 Le Mieux, A. C. *Do Angels Sing the Blues?* (7–10). 1995, Morrow/Tambourine $14 (0-688-13725-3). A problem novel with romantic themes of a rich boy falling for a girl from the wrong side of the tracks. (Rev: BL 9/1/95; SLJ 9/95)

598 Lester, Jim. *Fallout* (7–10). 1996, Delacorte $15.95 (0-385-32168-6). A fast-paced, clever coming-of-age story about Kenny, who's sent to prep school for his junior year, told in a stream-of-consciousness form. (Rev: BL 1/1/96; SLJ 2/96; VOYA 2/96)

599 Levoy, Myron. *Kelly 'n' Me* (7–10). 1992, HarperCollins/Charlotte Zolotow LB $14.89 (0-06-020839-2). Anthony, 15, an accomplished street musician, merges his guitar playing with Kelly's incredible voice, but she is elusive about her family and home life. (Rev: BL 1/1/93; SLJ 10/92; YR)

600 Levy, Elizabeth. *Cheater, Cheater* (5–8). 1993, Scholastic $13.95 (0-590-45865-5). Lucy Lovello has been labeled a cheater and even her teachers don't trust her; but when she finds her best friend cheating, she faces a moral dilemma. (Rev: BL 10/1/93; MJHS; SLJ 10/93; VOYA 12/93)

601 Levy, Marilyn. *Is That Really Me in the Mirror?* (7–10). 1991, Ballantine/Fawcett Juniper paper $3.95 (0-449-70343-6). Joanne is envious of her beautiful, popular older sister until an automobile accident and plastic surgery transform Joanne into a very pretty stranger. (Rev: BL 11/1/91)

602 Lewis, Beverly. *Whispers down the Lane* (5–8). (Summerhill Secrets) 1995, Bethany paper $4.99 (1-55661-476-4). While helping a friend escape an abusive father, Merry comes to deal with her own grief for her dead twin sisters. (Rev: BL 9/1/95; SLJ 2/96)

603 Lynch, Chris. *Gypsy Davey* (9–12). 1994, HarperCollins LB $13.89 (0-06-023587-X). Davey—who ages from 2 to 12 in this story—learns to rise above the problems of his dysfunctional family. Awards: SLJ Best Book; YALSA Best Book for Young Adults. (Rev: BL 10/1/94; BTA; SHS; SLJ 10/94*; VOYA 12/94)

604 Lynch, Chris. *Slot Machine* (8–10). 1995, HarperCollins LB $13.89 (0-06-023585-3). Elvin is a 13-year-old boy, overweight, and expected to perform with exuberance everything forced upon him. (Rev: BL 9/1/95*; SLJ 10/95; VOYA 12/95)

605 McColley, Kevin. *Pecking Order* (6–9). 1994, HarperCollins LB $15.89 (0-06-023555-1).

This tragic, yet comic coming-of-age novel follows 2 years in the life of its adolescent narrator on the family farm in Minnesota. (Rev: BL 3/1/94; SLJ 4/94; VOYA 6/94)

606 Macdonald, Caroline. *Speaking to Miranda* (7–10). 1992, HarperCollins/Willa Perlman LB $13.89 (0-06-021103-2). In Australia and New Zealand, Ruby, 18, leaves her boyfriend, travels with her father, and gradually decides to explore the mysteries of her life: Who was her mother? Who is her family? Who is she? (Rev: BL 12/15/92*; SLJ 10/92; YR)

607 McKenna, Colleen O'Shaughnessy. *The Brightest Light* (6–10). 1992, Scholastic $13.95 (0-590-45347-5). A young girl discovers the secret behind her hometown's strange behavior during one long, hot summer. (Rev: BL 9/15/92; SLJ 12/92)

608 Maguire, Gregory. *Missing Sisters* (6–9). 1994, Macmillan/Margaret K. McElderry $14.95 (0-689-50590-6). An orphan with speech and hearing impediments living with a group of nuns discovers she has an identical twin sister. (Rev: BL 3/15/94; MJHS; SLJ 5/94; VOYA 12/94)

609 Marino, Jan. *For the Love of Pete* (6–8). 1993, Little, Brown $14.95 (0-316-54627-5). Phoebe is on her way from Georgia to Maine to find the father she's never met. Awards: SLJ Best Book. (Rev: BL 6/1–15/93; MJHS; SLJ 5/93*)

610 Marino, Jan. *Like Some Kind of Hero* (7–10). 1992, Little, Brown $14.95 (0-316-54626-7). Ted, a talented 15-year-old classical guitarist, wants to join a lifeguard trainee program to impress the girls, but he has promised to continue his music and summer job. (Rev: BL 12/1/91)

611 Marsh, Fabienne. *The Moralist of the Alphabet Streets* (9–adult). 1991, Algonquin Books of Chapel Hill (P.O. Box 2225, Chapel Hill, NC 27515-2225) $15.95 (0-945575-47-5). A long, hot, unruly summer tests 18-year-old Meredith's theories of morality and encourages her tendency for frankness and cynicism. (Rev: BL 2/15/91; SHS)

612 Mazer, Norma Fox. *E, My Name Is Emily* (6–8). 1991, Scholastic $13.95 (0-590-43653-8). Emily, age 14, realizes her divorced mother is attracted to their landlord and then discovers the boy who has a crush on her is the landlord's nephew. (Rev: BL 12/1/91; MJHS; SLJ 11/91)

613 Merrick, Monte. *Shelter* (9–adult). 1993, Hyperion $19.95 (1-56282-862-2). Nelson, 13, and 2 friends investigate what they wrongly believe to be the murder of a developmentally disabled neighbor boy. Awards: YALSA Best Book for Young Adults. (Rev: BL 6/1–15/93; BTA)

614 Meyer, Carolyn. *Drummers of Jericho* (6–9). 1995, Harcourt $11 (0-15-200441-6); paper $5 (0-15-200190-5). Jewish Pazit Trujillo goes to live with her father in the small town of Jericho, but trouble breaks out when she objects to Christian symbols at school. (Rev: BL 6/1–15/95; SLJ 9/95; VOYA 5/95)

615 Miller, Frances A. *Cutting Loose* (9–12). 1991, Fawcett/Juniper paper $3.95 (0-449-70384-3). In this sequel to *The Truth Trap*, Matt—now adopted by a policeman—takes his best friend, Meg, to a summer job on a ranch, where they must come to grips with their relationships with each other and their families. (Rev: BL 10/1/91; BY)

616 Mills, Claudia. *Dinah Forever* (5–7). 1995, Farrar $14 (0-374-31788-7). Another in Mills's series about Dinah, who is now entering 7th grade, enjoying friends, and quarreling with her enemies—plus a little romance. (Rev: BL 10/1/95; SLJ 11/95; VOYA 12/95)

617 Mills, Claudia. *The Secret Life of Bethany Barrett* (5–7). 1994, Macmillan $14.95 (0-02-767013-9). Middle-child Bethany feels caught between a perfect older sister and a little brother who may be developmentally delayed. (Rev: BL 1/1/95; SLJ 2/95)

618 Moore, Martha. *Under the Mermaid Angel* (5–8). 1995, Delacorte $14.95 (0-385-32160-0). A 13-year-old girl meets a glamorous 30-year-old woman, Roxanne, the archetypal stranger who brings excitement and lessons about life and then leaves town. Awards: ALSC Notable Children's Book; Delacorte Prize for First Young Adult Novel. (Rev: BL 8/95; SLJ 10/95; VOYA 12/95)

619 Mori, Kyoko. *Shizuko's Daughter* (9–12). 1993, Holt $15.95 (0-8050-2557-X). After an adolescence in protective, self-imposed isolation, Yuki leaves home in Kobe, Japan, to study art in Nagasaki. (Rev: BL 2/1/93; BTA; SLJ 6/93; VOYA 10/93)

620 Morrow, Bradford. *Trinity Fields* (9–adult). 1995, Viking $22.95 (0-670-85728-9). A dark, yet hopeful novel about 2 young men haunted by their fathers' involvement with the atomic bomb, their own conflicting feelings about the Vietnam War, and their love for the same woman. (Rev: BL 2/1/95*)

621 Murphy, Catherine Frey. *Alice Dodd and the Spirit of Truth* (5–7). 1993, Macmillan $14.95 (0-02-767702-8). Alice's search for identity leads her to pretend that she's a medium for a dead princess from Atlantis. (Rev: BL 6/1–15/93; SLJ 5/93)

622 Murray, Katherine. *Jake* (9–adult). 1995, Thomas Nelson paper $8.99 (0-7852-8095-2). In this allegory of the Christ figure who walks the earth as a mortal, an adolescent girl is drawn to a gentle, mysterious man who lives by the sea. (Rev: BL 5/15/95*)

623 Naylor, Phyllis Reynolds. *Alice in April* (5–8). 1993, Atheneum/Jean Karl $14.95 (0-689-31805-7). Alice is back, this time caught between her desire to be a perfect housekeeper and her fascination with her developing body. (Rev: BL 3/1/93; MJHS; SLJ 6/93)

624 Paulsen, Gary. *The Car* (6–9). 1994, Harcourt $13.95 (0-15-292878-2). The cross-country adventures of Terry, 14, and Waylon, a 45-year-old Vietnam vet, who sometimes suffers flashback memories and becomes violent. (Rev: BL 4/1/94; BTA; MJHS; SLJ 5/94; VOYA 6/94)

625 Paulsen, Gary. *A Christmas Sonata* (5–7). 1992, Delacorte $14 (0-385-30441-2); 1994, Dell/Yearling paper $4.99 (0-440-40958-6). As Christmas 1943 approaches, a preschool boy inadvertently makes 2 weighty discoveries that provide a poignant emotional reading experience. (Rev: BL 9/1/92*)

626 Paulsen, Gary. *Sisters/Hermanas* (8–10). Tr. by Gloria de Aragón Andújar. 1993, Harcourt $10.95 (0-15-275323-0); paper $3.95 (0-15-275324-9). The bilingual story of 2 girls, age 14, in a Texas town, one an illegal Mexican immigrant prostitute, the other a superficial blond cheerleader. (Rev: BL 1/1/94; SLJ 1/94; VOYA 12/93)

627 Paulsen, Gary. *The Tent: A Parable in One Sitting* (6–10). 1995, Harcourt $14 (0-15-292879-0). A 14-year-old struggles to keep his values when his father fraudulently poses as an itinerant preacher. (Rev: BL 3/15/95; SLJ 5/95)

628 Peck, Richard. *Unfinished Portrait of Jessica* (7–10). 1991, Delacorte $15 (0-385-30500-1). A 13-year-old who blames her mother for the departure of her beloved father makes a Christmas visit to his Mexican beach house and must face the pain of his betrayal. (Rev: BL 9/15/91*; MJHS)

629 Plummer, Louise. *My Name Is Sus5an Smith: The 5 Is Silent* (9–12). 1991, Delacorte $14.95 (0-385-30043-3). A coming-of-age story about a young artist with an unconventional style and a romantic vision of her disreputable relatives. Awards: SLJ Best Book; YALSA Best Book for Young Adults. (Rev: BL 7/91*; MJHS; SLJ 6/91*)

630 Porter, David. *Vienna Passage* (9–adult). 1995, Crossway paper $9.99 (0-89107-824-X). A deeply religious young Englishman matures to an understanding of the evils of antisemitism and the fulfillment of a life lived with the love of a woman, art, and music. (Rev: BL 9/1/95*)

631 Qualey, Marsha. *Everybody's Daughter* (7–10). 1991, Houghton $13.95 (0-395-55870-0). A teenager struggles for independence after her family's hippie commune group disbands. Awards: SLJ Best Book. (Rev: BL 7/91; BY; SLJ 4/91*)

632 Reynolds, Marilyn. *Beyond Dreams* (9–12). 1995, Morning Glory Press (6595 San Haroldo Way, Buena Park, CA 90620) $15.95 (1-885356-01-3); paper $9.95 (1-885356-00-5). Using alternate male and female voices, Reynolds presents short stories of teens in crisis. (Rev: BL 11/15/95; SLJ 9/95; VOYA 2/96)

633 Reynolds, Marilyn. *Detour for Emmy* (8–12). 1993, Morning Glory Press (6595 San Haroldo Way, Buena Park, CA 90620) $15.95 (0-930934-75-X); paper $8.95 (0-930934-76-8). Although Emmy is a good student and a hunk's girlfriend, her home life includes a deserter father and an alcoholic mother. Emmy's pregnancy causes more hardship when she keeps the baby. (Rev: BL 10/1/93; SLJ 7/93)

634 Reynolds, Marilyn. *Too Soon for Jeff* (8–12). 1994, Morning Glory Press (6595 San Haroldo Way, Buena Park, CA 90620) $15.95 (0-930934-90-3); paper $8.95 (0-930934-91-1). Jeff's hopes of going to college on a debate scholarship are put into jeopardy when his girlfriend happily announces she's pregnant. Jeff reluctantly prepares for fatherhood. Awards: SLJ Best Book; YALSA Best Book for Young Adults. (Rev: BL 9/15/94; BTA; SHS; SLJ 9/94; VOYA 12/94)

635 Rhodes, Judy Carole. *The Hunter's Heart* (7–10). 1993, Bradbury $13.95 (0-02-775935-0). This sequel to *The King Boy* (1991) finds 18-year-old Benjy King working his newly inherited farm. But change threatens his Arkansas town, and he may lose his best friend because of it. (Rev: BL 11/15/93; SLJ 11/93; VOYA 12/93)

636 Rosen, Roger, and Patra McSharry Sevastiades, eds. *Coming of Age: The Art of Growing Up* (9–12). 1994, Rosen LB $16.95 (0-8239-1805-X); paper $8.95 (0-8239-1806-8). This multicultural anthology of short fiction and essays confronts traditional—and more complex—coming-of-age issues. (Rev: BL 1/1/95; BTA; SHS; SLJ 1/95) [808.8]

637 Rosenthal, C. P. *Elena of the Stars* (9–adult). 1995, St. Martin's $18.95 (0-312-13482-7). Elena, on the threshold of adulthood, is sent to Wyoming, where she loses her innocence and meets evil in the land of big sky, mountains, and horses. (Rev: BL 9/1/95*)

638 Roth, Henry. *A Star Shines over Mt. Morris Park* (9–adult). 1994, St. Martin's $23 (0-312-10499-5). This first book in a forthcoming series charts a Jewish boy's life in Harlem from age 8 to 15, including his family life, school, jobs, the war, racism, and sexuality. (Rev: BL 11/15/93*)

639 Roth-Hano, Renée. *Safe Harbors* (8–12). 1993, Four Winds $15.95 (0-02-777795-2). This autobiographical novel is an account of the post-war coming-of-age of a Jewish governess in New York City. (Rev: BL 1/1/94; SLJ 12/93)

640 Roybal, Laura. *Billy* (7–9). 1994, Houghton $14.95 (0-395-67649-5). A teenage New Mexico cowhand is forced to leave his biological father, who kidnapped him 6 years earlier, and return to his Iowa family. Awards: SLJ Best Book; YALSA Best Book for Young Adults. (Rev: BL 3/15/94; BTA; MJHS; SLJ 5/94; VOYA 6/94)

641 Rumbaut, Hendle. *Dove Dream* (6–9). 1994, Houghton $13.95 (0-395-68393-9). Dove's parents are on the verge of a breakup, so she's sent to live with her aunt Anna, who helps her come of age and find love and independence through a Chickasaw vision quest. (Rev: BL 4/1/94; BTA; SLJ 5/94)

642 Ryan, Mary E. *The Trouble with Perfect* (5–8). 1995, Simon & Schuster $15 (0-689-80276-5). Problems with honesty, cheating, failure, and the value of competition plus a father who drinks too much lead Kyle to understanding himself and others. (Rev: BL 10/1/95; SLJ 11/95; VOYA 2/96)

643 Schaeffer, Frank. *Portofino* (9–adult). 1992, Macmillan $18 (0-02-607051-0). An insecure adolescent remembers vacations during the 1960s with his eccentric "born-again" family. Awards: BL Editors' Choice. (Rev: BL 9/15/92)

644 Semel, Nava. *Flying Lessons* (7–12). Tr. by Hillel Halkin. 1995, Simon & Schuster $14 (0-689-80161-0). In an Israeli village in the 1950s, a 12-year-old girl dreams of flying and takes lessons from a shoemaker with a history, not only in the circus but in concentration camps. (Rev: BL 8/95; SLJ 11/95; VOYA 12/95)

645 Shalant, Phyllis. *Shalom, Geneva Peace* (6–9). 1992, Dutton $14 (0-525-44868-3). This novel juggles many subjects: peer group pressure, budding sexuality, divorce, sibling relationships, religious values, and social problems. (Rev: BL 7/92; MJHS; YR)

646 Sharpe, Susan. *Real Friends* (7–9). 1994, Bradbury $14.95 (0-02-782352-0). Trying to fit in at her new high school, Cassie first loses her identity, then decides to reclaim her own life. (Rev: BL 11/15/94; SLJ 12/94)

647 Sheldon, Dyan. *Tall, Thin, and Blonde* (7–9). 1993, Candlewick $14.95 (1-56402-139-4). When Jenny and Amy enter high school, Amy discovers hairstyles, clothes, and diets, while Jenny finds herself drawn toward a different set of friends. (Rev: BL 11/1/93; SLJ 11/93; VOYA 2/94)

648 Shriver, Jean Adair. *Mayflower Man* (7–10). 1991, Delacorte $14.95 (0-385-30295-9). An adolescent boy descended from Pilgrims learns an important lesson about truth, acceptance, and responsibility after his grandmother dies. (Rev: BL 6/1/91)

649 Sierra i Fabra, Jordi. *Banda sonora* (8–12). 1993, Ediciones Siruela $11.95 (84-7844-159-X). In this frank coming-of-age novel, 17-year-old Vic reencounters his divorced father, one of Spain's great rock music figures. English title: *Sonorous Band*. (Rev: BL 4/1/94)

650 Sinclair, April. *Coffee Will Make You Black* (9–adult). 1994, Hyperion $19.95 (1-56282-796-0). Set in late 1960s Chicago, 11-year-old "Stevie" Stevenson's growth from child to woman parallels the growth of African American pride and equality. Awards: SLJ Best Book. (Rev: BL 12/15/93; BTA; SHS)

651 Sinykin, Sheri Cooper. *Slate Blues* (6–9). 1993, Lothrop $12 (0-688-11212-9). When Reina, 13, learns that she has an aunt who's a rock singer, Slate, she decides to use Slate to help her become a member of the 8th-grade in-crowd. (Rev: BL 6/1–15/93; VOYA 10/93)

652 Skinner, David. *The Wrecker* (6–9). 1995, Simon & Schuster $14 (0-671-79771-9). A bully, a genius, and a newcomer (the narrator) are part of a story with elements as compelling as Robert Cormier or Stephen King. (Rev: BL 8/95*; VOYA 5/95)

653 Smith, Doris Buchanan. *The Pennywhistle Tree* (5–7). 1991, Putnam $14.95 (0-399-21840-8). A belligerent 6th-grader invades another boy's private space, secretly envies him, and finally discloses his illiteracy. Awards: ALSC Notable Children's Book; SLJ Best Book. (Rev: BL 11/1/91; SLJ 10/91*)

654 Somtow, S. P. *Jasmine Nights* (9–adult). 1995, St. Martin's $22.95 (0-312-11834-1). Justin, who is Thai, must overcome the keen angst of growing up by sorting out his feelings and emotions, the strangeness of his body and of the world, and the meaning of friendship and love. (Rev: BL 1/15/95*)

655 Staples, Donna. *Arena Beach* (9–12). 1993, Houghton $14.95 (0-395-65366-5). When Terra barely survives a California earthquake, she realizes she must provide the stability that her family, boyfriend, and friends don't offer her. (Rev: BL 9/1/93; VOYA 12/93)

656 Stinson, Susan. *Fat Girl Dances with Rocks* (9–adult). 1994, Spinsters Ink (32 E. First St., Suite 330, Duluth, MN 55803) paper $10.95 (1-883523-02-8). Char, 17 and overweight, struggles with her identity, the meaning of beauty, and her confusion when her best friend, Felice, kisses her on the lips. (Rev: BL 9/1/94; VOYA 5/95)

657 Straight, Susan. *I Been in Sorrow's Kitchen and Licked Out All the Pots* (9–adult). 1992, Hyperion/Disney $19.95 (1-56282-963-7). Lyrical story of an African American women who rises from rural poverty in North Carolina and raises twin sons to see them make good as football stars. (Rev: BL 6/1/92*; SLJ 1/93)

658 Strasser, Todd. *How I Changed My Life* (7–12). 1995, Simon & Schuster $16 (0-671-88415-8). Introverted Bo, the theater department stage manager, works on her self-image and weight problem when handsome football captain Kyle joins a production. (Rev: BL 5/1/95; SLJ 5/95)

659 Tamar, Erika. *The Things I Did Last Summer* (7–9). 1994, Harcourt $10.95 (0-15-282490-1); paper $3.95 (0-15-200020-8). A teenager spending the summer on Long Island with his pregnant stepmother loses his virginity when he meets a deceptive older woman. (Rev: BL 3/15/94; BTA; SLJ 4/94; VOYA 6/94)

660 Thesman, Jean. *Cattail Moon* (6–9). 1994, Houghton $14.95 (0-395-67409-3); 1995, Avon/Flare paper $3.99 (0-380-72504-5). Julia, 14, is at odds with her mother, who wants to transform her from a classical musician into a cheerleader. (Rev: BL 4/1/94; BTA; SLJ 5/94; VOYA 8/94)

661 Thomas, Joyce Carol. *When the Nightingale Sings* (6–8). 1992, HarperCollins LB $13.89 (0-06-020295-5); 1994, HarperTrophy paper $3.95 (0-06-440524-9). Marigold's only joy in her stepfamily is singing, which leads her to audition for a Baptist Church choir, where she discovers her worth, her family, and her happiness. (Rev: BL 1/1/93; MJHS; SLJ 2/93)

662 Thompson, Julian F. *The Fling* (7–10). 1994, Holt $15.95 (0-8050-2881-1). A story on paper becomes the story in reality in this book about a mysterious woman living in a mansion with other enigmatic characters. (Rev: BL 5/1/94; BTA; SLJ 6/94; VOYA 8/94)

663 Thompson, Julian F. *Philo Fortune's Awesome Journey to His Comfort Zone* (8–12). 1995, Hyperion $16.95 (0-7868-0067-4). A story of a young man, caught with his pants down, who discovers the possibilities of the man he might become. (Rev: BL 5/1/95; SLJ 5/95; VOYA 2/96)

664 Thon, Melanie Rae. *Iona Moon* (9–adult). 1993, Poseidon $21 (0-671-79687-9). The tragedies of incest, illness, and suicide that befall Iona and her friends lead her to seek solace in casual sex. (Rev: BL 5/15/93; BTA; SHS)

665 Tomey, Ingrid. *Savage Carrot* (7–9). 1993, Scribner $14.95 (0-684-19633-6). When the death of Carrot's father robs her of her hero, she withdraws from everyone except his developmentally disabled brother. (Rev: BL 3/1/94; SLJ 2/94; VOYA 4/94)

666 Trevor, William. *Juliet's Story* (5–7). 1994, Simon & Schuster $15 (0-671-87442-X). Juliet loves to hear stories; and as she realizes that stories connect her to the people around her, she looks for hidden tales in dreams, events, and the things people say. (Rev: BL 7/94; SLJ 6/94)

667 Vail, Rachel. *Do-Over* (5–9). 1992, Orchard/Richard Jackson LB $14.99 (0-531-08610-0); 1994, Avon/Flare paper $3.99 (0-380-72180-5). The story of 13-year-old Whitman Levy's first crush, first kiss, first heartbreak, and first real boy-girl relationship, as well as assorted family problems. Awards: BL Editors' Choice. (Rev: BL 8/92*; MJHS; SLJ 9/92; YR)

668 Vail, Rachel. *Ever After* (5–9). 1994, Orchard/Richard Jackson LB $15.95 (0-531-08688-7); 1995, Avon/Flare paper $3.99 (0-380-72465-0). Describes a 14-year-old starting high school and her concerns about dieting, friendship, family, and the future. (Rev: BL 3/1/94; BTA; MJHS; SLJ 5/94*; VOYA 6/94)

669 Velásquez, Gloria. *Tommy Stands Alone* (7–10). 1995, Arte Público/Piñata $14.95 (1-55885-146-1); paper $7.95 (1-55885-147-X). An engaging story about a Latino gay teen who is humiliated and rejected but finds understanding from a Chicano therapist. Helpful for teens to understand the consequences of homophobia. (Rev: BL 10/15/95; SLJ 11/95; VOYA 12/95)

670 Verdelle, A. J. *The Good Negress* (9–adult). 1995, Algonquin $19.95 (1-56512-085-X). Neesey, 13, returns to Detroit from grandma's in the South and rages internally over family obligations and a desire for white people's education. (Rev: BL 2/15/95; SLJ 10/95)

671 Walker, Kate. *Peter* (7–12). 1992, Houghton $13.95 (0-395-64722-3). A coming-of-age novel in which a 15-year-old Australian boy struggles with his sexual identity. Awards: ALSC Notable

Children's Book; YALSA Best Book for Young Adults. (Rev: BL 4/15/93; BTA; SLJ 6/93)

672 Watkins, Graham. *Virus* (9–12). 1995, Carroll & Graf $25 (0-7867-0194-3). A doctor, a psychiatrist, and a computer expert join to look deeper into the dangers of computer addiction. (Rev: BL 8/95; SLJ 1/96)

673 Watson, Larry. *Montana* (9–adult). 1993, Milkweed Editions (430 First Ave. N., Suite 400, Minneapolis, MN 55401) $17.95 (0-915943-13-1).Awards: YALSA Best Book for Young Adults. (Rev: BL 9/1/93*)

674 Weaver, Will. *Striking Out* (8–12). 1993, HarperCollins LB $14.89 (0-06-023347-8); 1995, Harper/Trophy paper $3.95 (0-06-447113-6). When Minnesota farmboy Billy picks up a stray baseball and fires it back to the pitcher, his baseball career begins, but his family isn't enthusiastic. (Rev: BL 11/1/93; BTA; SLJ 10/93; VOYA 12/93)

675 Wesley, Valerie Wilson. *Where Do I Go from Here?* (7–12). 1993, Scholastic $13.95 (0-590-45606-7). When African American Nia is suspended from the exclusive Endicott Academy for defending a friend against racism, she goes home only to realize her old friends are too far behind her. (Rev: BL 12/15/93; SLJ 11/93; VOYA 2/94)

676 Wieler, Diana. *Bad Boy* (9–12). 1992, Delacorte $15 (0-385-30415-3). Two teenage boys' friendship is tested when one admits he's gay. Awards: YALSA Best Book for Young Adults. (Rev: BL 1/15/92)

677 Wilson, Johnniece Marshall. *Poor Girl, Rich Girl* (5–7). 1992, Scholastic $13.95 (0-590-44732-7). Miranda copes with a camp-couseling job, a stint in a grocery, and her own rent-a-kid service, maturing as she begins to overcome her fears. (Rev: BL 8/92; SLJ 4/92; YR)

678 Wimsley, Jim. *Dream Boy* (9–12). 1995, Algonquin $18.95 (1-56512-106-6). Nathan—bookish and slight and sexually abused by his father—moves to a farm, where he meets and falls in love with Roy, the outgoing and popular boy next door. (Rev: BL 9/15/95; SLJ 3/96; VOYA 2/96)

679 Winton, Tim. *Lockie Leonard, Human Torpedo* (6–8). 1992, Little, Brown/Joy Street $13.95 (0-316-94753-9). Set in Australia, the story of a 14-year-old surfer and his confusion as he begins a more intimate relationship with his girlfriend. (Rev: BL 12/15/91; SLJ 12/91)

680 Wojciechowski, Susan. *Promises to Keep* (6–8). 1991, Crown LB $14.99 (0-517-58187-6). Patty Dillman's determination to be popular nearly causes her to be manipulated by a rich, pretty 8th-grader she wants to accept her as a friend. (Rev: BL 10/1/91)

681 Wolff, Virginia Euwer. *The Mozart Season* (9–adult). 1991, Holt $15.95 (0-8050-1571-X). Violinist and softball player Allegra Shapiro learns about life through sports analogies when she becomes a finalist in a large youth music contest. (Rev: BL 6/1/91; MJHS; SLJ 7/91)

682 Woodson, Jacqueline. *Between Madison and Palmetto* (5–7). 1993, Delacorte $13.95 (0-385-30906-6); 1995, Dell paper $3.50 (0-440-41062-2). Maizon is back home in Brooklyn from prep school and faces issues about growing up female, about family, and about racism. (Rev: BL 9/15/93; MJHS; SLJ 11/93; VOYA 6/94)

683 Zindel, Paul. *David and Della* (7–12). 1993, HarperCollins LB $13.89 (0-06-023354-0). High school playwright David hires Della—who pretends to be blind and to have studied under Lee Strasberg—to be his coach until he overcomes writer's block. (Rev: BL 12/1/93; BTA; SLJ 12/93; VOYA 2/94)

World Affairs and Contemporary Problems

684 Alphin, Elaine Marie. *The Proving Ground* (6–8). 1992, Holt $14.95 (0-8050-2140-X). The people of Hadley resent the army's takeover of farms to make way for a test site, and some people hate "army brats" like 9th-grader Kevin. (Rev: BL 11/15/92; SLJ 1/93)

685 Anderson, Mary. *The Unsinkable Molly Malone* (7–10). 1991, Harcourt $16.95 (0-15-213801-3). Molly, age 16, sells her collages outside New York's Metropolitan Museum, starts an art class for kids on welfare, and learns that her boyfriend is rich. (Rev: BL 11/15/91)

686 Avi. *Nothing but the Truth: A Documentary Novel* (7–12). 1991, Orchard/Richard Jackson LB $14.99 (0-531-08559-7). A boy's expulsion from school is reported in a biased, inflammatory newspaper story and takes on patriotic and political overtones. Awards: ALSC Notable Children's Book; Newbery Honor Book; SLJ Best Book; YALSA Best Book for Young Adults. (Rev: BL 9/15/91*; MJHS; SLJ 9/91*)

687 Barre, Shelly A. *Chive* (5–7). 1993, Simon & Schuster $14 (0-671-75641-9). Terry is at first suspicious when his mother invites homeless Chive for dinner, but the friendship they develop is challenged when he learns Chive gets handouts from several homes. (Rev: BL 10/1/93; SLJ 11/93; VOYA 2/94)

688 Bennett, Jay. *Skinhead* (8–12). 1991, Watts LB $13.90 (0-531-11001-X). A tale of Jonathan, 19; his girlfriend, Jenny; the father who abandoned him; a bigoted grandfather; and neo-Nazi skinheads. (Rev: BL 5/1/91; MJHS; SLJ 5/91)

689 Castañeda, Omar S. *Among the Volcanoes* (7–10). 1991, Dutton/Lodestar $14.95 (0-525-67332-6). Set in a remote Guatemalan village, this story is about a Mayan woodcutter's daughter, Isabel, who is caught between her respect for the old ways and her yearning for something more. (Rev: BL 5/15/91; MJHS; SLJ 3/91)

690 Coupland, Douglas. *Microserfs* (9–adult). 1995, HarperCollins $23 (0-06-039148-0). Another Coupland look at Gen-X computer nerds trying to make sense of love and life in Silicon Valley. (Rev: BL 5/15/95*)

691 Covington, Dennis. *Lasso the Moon* (7–10). 1995, Delacorte $15.95 (0-385-32101-5). After April and her divorced doctor father move to Saint Simons Island, April takes a liking to Fernando, an illegal alien from El Salvador being treated by her father. (Rev: BL 1/15/95; BTA; SLJ 3/95; VOYA 4/95)

692 Crew, Linda. *Fire on the Wind* (6–9). 1995, Delacorte $14.95 (0-385-32185-6). A 13-year-old girl's maturation through her experiences as a "log camp kid" in Depression-era Oregon. (Rev: BL 8/95; SLJ 11/95)

693 Davis, Jenny. *Checking on the Moon* (6–9). 1991, Orchard/Richard Jackson LB $14.99 (0-531-08560-0). A 13-year-old forced to spend the summer in a run-down Pittsburgh neighborhood with the grandmother she has never met discovers community activism and her own abilities. Awards: SLJ Best Book. (Rev: BL 9/15/91; MJHS; SLJ 10/91*)

694 De Felice, Cynthia. *Lostman's River* (5–7). 1994, Macmillan $14.95 (0-02-726466-1). A 13-year-old boy is tempted to accept money to show an eccentric scientist where exotic waterfowl are in the Everglades. (Rev: BL 5/15/94; BTA; SLJ 7/94; VOYA 8/94)

695 Evans, Sanford. *Naomi's Geese* (5–7). 1993, Simon & Schuster $15 (0-671-75623-0). Having befriended a mated pair of Canada geese the summer before, Naomi must keep them from coming back, or they may be hurt by chemicals dumped in their pond. (Rev: BL 12/1/93; SLJ 11/93; VOYA 4/94)

696 Golio, Janet, and Mike Golio. *A Present from the Past* (6–8). 1995, Portunus Publishing (3435 Ocean Pk. Blvd., Suite 203, Santa Monica, CA 90405) paper $8.95 (0-9641330-5-9). In this blend of fact and fiction, Sarah and her friend become concerned about their environment after they discover some petroglyphs. (Rev: BL 12/1/95; SLJ 11/95)

697 Hesse, Karen. *Phoenix Rising* (6–8). 1994, Holt $15.95 (0-8050-3108-1). A 13-year-old and her grandmother on a Vermont farm hope to avoid radiation contamination from a nuclear plant. They are visited by Boston evacuees, one of them a boy with whom the girl falls in love. Awards: ALSC Notable Children's Book; SLJ Best Book; YALSA Best Book for Young Adults. (Rev: BL 5/15/94; BTA; MJHS; SLJ 6/94*; VOYA 8/94)

698 Inglehart, Donna Walsh. *Breaking the Ring* (7–10). 1991, Little, Brown $13.95 (0-316-41867-6). Two friends' quiet summer vacation is disrupted when they accidentally stumble onto a drug ring. (Rev: BL 6/15/91)

699 Killingsworth, Monte. *Eli's Songs* (5–8). 1991, Macmillan/Margaret K. McElderry $12.95 (0-689-50527-2). The 12-year-old son of a Los Angeles rock musician is sent to live with relatives in a small Oregon town, where he defies the establishment to save an old-growth forest. (Rev: BL 10/1/91; SLJ 11/91)

700 Konigsburg, E. L. *T-Backs, T-Shirts, Coat, and Suit* (5–8). 1993, Atheneum/Jean Karl $13.95 (0-689-31855-3). Conformity and freedom of expression are looked at in this story of a girl and her ex-hippy stepaunt. Awards: SLJ Best Book. (Rev: BL 11/1/93; BTA; SLJ 10/93*; VOYA 12/93)

701 Krisher, Trudy. *Spite Fences* (8–12). 1994, Delacorte $14.95 (0-385-32088-4). Through the anonymity of photography, Maggie, 13, is able to face the evil of segregation and racism around her in 1960 Georgia. Awards: IRA Children's Book; SLJ Best Book; YALSA Best Book for Young Adults. (Rev: BL 12/1/94*; BTA; SHS; SLJ 11/94; VOYA 10/94)

702 Lightman, Alan. *Einstein's Dreams* (9–adult). 1993, Pantheon $17 (0-679-41646-3). In this simple, thought-provoking book about the place of time in our lives, Einstein mulls over his theories and his dreams depict time moving in alternative dimensions and directions. (Rev: BL 11/15/92*)

703 Lutzeier, Elizabeth. *The Wall* (7–12). 1992, Holiday $14.95 (0-8234-0987-2). In East Berlin in the 1980s, 2 adolescent girls become friends, get involved in peace marches, and risk their lives to bring change to Germany. (Rev: BL 10/15/92; SLJ 1/93)

704 McDaniel, Lurlene. *Baby Alicia Is Dying* (8–10). 1993, Bantam paper $3.50 (0-553-29605-

1). In an attempt to feel needed, Desi volunteers to care for HIV-positive babies and discovers a deep commitment in herself. (Rev: BL 10/1/93; SLJ 7/93; VOYA 8/93)

705 Mazer, Norma Fox, and Harry Mazer. *Bright Days, Stupid Nights* (7–10). 1992, Bantam/Starfire $15 (0-553-08126-8). Charts the course of 4 youth who are brought together for a special summer newspaper internship. (Rev: BL 6/15/92; SLJ 7/92; YR)

706 Myers, Bill. *The Society* (7–9). (Forbidden Doors) 1994, Tyndale paper $4.99 (0-8423-5922-2). Scott and Becka have left Brazil and begun the year at their new U.S. school when they discover that a local bookshop is the hub of a Ouija board cult. (Rev: BL 1/15/95)

707 Neville, Emily Cheney. *The China Year* (5–8). 1991, HarperCollins LB $15.89 (0-06-024384-8). Henri, 14, has left his New York City home, school, and friends to go to Peking University for a year with his father. (Rev: BL 5/1/91; SLJ 5/91)

708 Oates, Joyce Carol. *Foxfire: Confessions of a Girl Gang* (9–adult). 1993, Dutton $21 (0-525-93632-7). A former member of a 1950s outlaw girl gang recounts the group's increasingly lawless adventures in this novel for older readers. (Rev: BL 3/15/93*)

709 Paulsen, Gary. *The Rifle* (7–9). 1995, Harcourt $16 (0-15-292880-4). An exploration of the history of a flintlock rifle, from its use in the Revolutionary War into the twentieth century, where it ends up killing a teen in a freak accident. (Rev: BL 9/15/95; SLJ 10/95; VOYA 2/96)

710 Peck, Richard. *The Last Safe Place on Earth* (7–10). 1995, Delacorte $15.95 (0-385-32052-3). Todd has a crush on Laura, who baby-sits his sister, but he discovers that she's a fundamentalist Christian who brainwashes and terrifies the child by telling her about witches and devils. (Rev: BL 1/15/95; SHS; SLJ 4/95; VOYA 2/95)

711 Qualey, Marsha. *Hometown* (7–10). 1995, Houghton $14.95 (0-395-72666-2). A new resident in a small Minnesota town takes flak when the Persian Gulf War breaks out and he learns that his father escaped to Canada during the Vietnam War. (Rev: BL 10/1/95; SLJ 12/95; VOYA 12/95)

712 Reeder, Carolyn. *Grandpa's Mountain* (5–7). 1991, Macmillan $13.95 (0-02-775811-7). Carrie, age 11, spends the summer at her grandparents' home in the Blue Ridge Mountains, and they learn the house is condemned for the creation of Shenandoah National Park. (Rev: BL 11/15/91)

713 Ruby, Lois. *Skin Deep* (8–12). 1994, Scholastic $14.95 (0-590-47699-8). Dan, the frustrated new kid in town, falls in love with popular senior Laurel, but he destroys their relationship when he joins a neo-Nazi skinhead group. (Rev: BL 11/15/94*; BTA; MJHS; SLJ 3/95; VOYA 12/94)

714 Taylor, Theodore. *The Bomb* (7–10). 1995, Harcourt $16 (0-15-200867-5). In this tale—built on Taylor's memory of a visit to Bikini Atoll as it was being prepared for testing of the atomic bomb—a 14-year-old boy suspects that the Americans are less than honest about their plans. (Rev: BL 10/1/95*; SLJ 12/95; VOYA 4/96)

715 Temple, Frances. *Grab Hands and Run* (6–12). 1993, Orchard/Richard Jackson LB $14.99 (0-531-08630-5). Jacinto opposes the oppressive government of El Salvador. When he disappears, his wife, Paloma, and their son, 12-year-old Felipe, try to escape to freedom in Canada. Awards: SLJ Best Book. (Rev: BL 5/1/93*; BTA; MJHS; SLJ 4/93*)

716 Testa, Maria. *Dancing Pink Flamingos and Other Stories* (8–12). 1995, Lerner LB $13.13 (0-8225-0738-2). Unsentimental short stories about young women who must face the difficult realities of life and rediscover the positive directions they must go. (Rev: BL 10/1/95; SLJ 9/95)

717 Tolan, Stephanie S. *Save Halloween!* (5–7). 1993, Morrow $14 (0-688-12168-3). When Johnna is asked to write the 6th-grade Halloween pageant, she's caught between her fundamentalist family's beliefs and the truth her research reveals. (Rev: BL 9/1/93*; SLJ 10/93)

Fantasy

718 Aiken, Joan. *Is Underground* (6–8). 1993, Delacorte $15 (0-385-30898-1); 1995, Dell/Yearling paper $3.99 (0-440-41068-1). Is Twite seeks the whereabouts of Arun, her cousin, and Davy Suart, the king's son, who vanished in London under suspicious circumstances. (Rev: BL 4/1/93; BTA; MJHS)

719 Alexander, Lloyd. *The Arkadians* (6–9). 1995, Dutton $15.99 (0-525-45415-2). A focus on the goddess culture and its role in history and myth. Lucian and Fronto are forced to flee a castle and hunt for the goddess who can help them. (Rev: BL 5/1/95; SLJ 5/95; VOYA 12/95)

720 Alexander, Lloyd. *The Remarkable Journey of Prince Jen* (6–9). 1991, Dutton $14.95 (0-525-44826-8); 1993, Dell/Yearling paper $3.99 (0-440-

40890-3). Prince Jen searches for the legendary court of T'ien-kuo; finds a flute girl; faces death by a bandit; and learns how to be a man and a ruler. Awards: BL Best of Editors' Choice; SLJ Best Book. (Rev: BL 12/1/91*; SLJ 12/91*)

721 Anthony, Piers. *Demons Don't Dream* (9–adult). (Xanth Saga) 1993, Tor $19.95 (0-312-85389-0). An interactive video game transports a 16-year-old boy to the infamous land of Xanth. (Rev: BL 12/15/92; SHS; VOYA 8/93)

722 Anthony, Piers. *Geis of the Gargoyle* (9–adult). (Xanth Saga) 1995, Tor $22.95 (0-312-85391-2). An environmentally conscious gargoyle searches for a spell to purify a polluted river. (Rev: BL 1/1/95; SHS)

723 Anthony, Piers. *Harpy Thyme* (9–adult). 1994, Tor $21.95 (0-312-85390-4). In search of a mate, half-harpy/half-goblin Gloha adventures through the underworld and Xanth with her friends Magician Trent and a flying centaur. (Rev: BL 12/1/93; VOYA 8/94)

724 Anthony, Piers. *Killobyte* (9–adult). 1993, Putnam $19.99 (0-399-13781-5). A wheelchair-bound policeman and a teen diabetic playing the roles of princess and wizard in a virtual-reality game join forces to foil a 15-year-old hacker determined to control their lives. Awards: BL Editors' Choice. (Rev: BL 11/15/92; SHS; VOYA 8/93)

725 Anthony, Piers. *Roc and a Hard Place* (9–adult). (Xanth Saga) 1995, Tor $23.95 (0-312-85392-0). Demoness Metria must find a jury to acquit Roxanne Roc of bizarre crimes. (Rev: BL 9/1/95; VOYA 4/96)

726 Anthony, Piers, and Philip Jose Farmer. *The Caterpillar's Question* (9–adult). 1992, Berkley/Ace $18.95 (0-441-09488-0). When aspiring art student Jack takes Tappy, an almost catatonic girl, to a Vermont clinic, strange events send them into a bewildering netherworld. (Rev: BL 9/1/92; SHS)

727 Anthony, Piers, and Richard Gilliam, eds. *Tales from the Great Turtle* (9–adult). 1994, Tor $21.95 (0-312-85628-8). Fantasy stories based on Native American myths, themes, and images. (Rev: BL 11/1/94; VOYA 5/95)

728 Anthony, Piers, and Mercedes Lackey. *If I Pay Thee Not in Gold* (9–adult). 1993, Simon & Schuster $20 (0-671-72175-5). Xylina must retrieve a powerful shard of crystal from a distant, dangerous land. (Rev: BL 4/15/93; VOYA 12/93)

729 Asimov, Isaac. *Magic: The Final Fantasy Collection* (9–adult). 1996, HarperPrism $22 (0-06-105205-1). Includes short fiction, essays on the raw materials of fantasy, and essays on the techniques of fantasy writing. (Rev: BL 12/15/95) [813]

730 Askounis, Christina. *The Dream of the Stone* (7–12). 1993, Farrar $17 (0-374-31877-8). Orphan Sarah, 15, flees evil agents from CIPHER into an alternative universe. (Rev: BL 6/1–15/93; SLJ 6/93; VOYA 8/93)

731 Avi. *City of Light, City of Dark: A Comic-Book Novel* (6–9). Illus. 1993, Orchard LB $15.99 (0-531-08650-X). In a B&W comic book format, Sarah and her friend Carlos must save her father from the evil Underton and pay tribute to the Kurbs before Manhattan freezes. (Rev: BL 9/15/93; BTA; VOYA 2/94) [741.5]

732 Babson, Marian. *Nine Lives to Murder* (9–adult). 1994, St. Martin's $18.95 (0-312-10511-8). A mystery involving the exchange of bodies between England's leading Shakespearean actor and a theater cat. (Rev: BL 2/15/94; SLJ 8/94)

733 Bakken, Harald. *The Fields and the Hills: The Journey, Once Begun* (5–9). 1992, Clarion $15.95 (0-395-59397-2). Feared in his Tam village for his ability to extend his senses over great distances, Weyr, age 13, overhears a cruel man plotting to take him in after Weyr's grandmother's death. (Rev: BL 11/15/92; SLJ 12/92)

734 Ball, Margaret. *No Earthly Sunne* (9–adult). 1994, Baen paper $5.99 (0-671-87633-3). A new version of the classic fantasy concerning the rescue of a mortal from the land of faerie. (Rev: BL 12/15/94; VOYA 5/95)

735 Ball, Margaret. *The Shadow Gate* (9–adult). 1991, Baen paper $4.95 (0-671-72032-5). A young secretary is drawn into a magical world where she is hailed as a long-exiled queen. (Rev: BL 1/1/91; SLJ 9/91)

736 Banks, Lynne Reid. *The Mystery of the Cupboard* (5–8). Illus. 1993, Morrow LB $13.88 (0-688-12635-9). The fourth book in the "cupboard" series deals with a diary describing a magic cupboard and a box containing plastic Indian figures that come to life and explain the cupboard's secrets. (Rev: BL 4/1/93; SLJ 6/93; VOYA 10/93)

737 Barker, Clive. *The Thief of Always* (9–adult). 1992, HarperCollins $20 (0-06-017724-1). An eerie tale about young Harvey and the seductive Mr. Hood's Holiday House, which may or may not be every child's dream. Awards: BL Editors' Choice. (Rev: BL 10/15/92; SHS; SLJ 2/93)

738 Barron, T. A. *The Ancient One* (6–9). 1992, Putnam/Philomel $17.95 (0-399-21899-8); 1994, Tor paper $4.99 (0-812-53654-1). A fight to save a stand of Oregon redwoods occupies Kate, 13, in this time-travel fantasy. (Rev: BL 9/1/92; SLJ 11/92; YR)

739 Barron, T. A. *The Merlin Effect* (6–9). 1994, Putnam/Philomel $17.95 (0-399-22689-3). Kate, 13, accompanies her father, a King Arthur expert, to a remote lagoon where they search a sunken ship for the magical horn of Merlin. Sequel to *Heartlight* and *The Ancient One*. (Rev: BL 11/1/94; SLJ 11/94; VOYA 12/94)

740 Beagle, Peter S. *The Innkeeper's Song* (9–adult). 1993, Penguin/ROC $20 (0-451-45288-7). Three powerful women with secret pasts, a stable boy, a weaver's son, and an innkeeper are brought face to face with the forces of magic and fate. (Rev: BL 10/15/93*; BTA)

741 Beagle, Peter S., and Janet Berliner, eds. *Peter S. Beagle's Immortal Unicorn* (9–adult). 1995, HarperPrism paper $25 (0-06-105224-8). Twenty-seven fantasy stories with the unicorn motif collected by Beagle, the author of the classic fantasy *The Last Unicorn*. (Rev: BL 10/15/95; VOYA 4/96)

742 Bedard, Michael. *Painted Devil* (7–10). 1994, Atheneum $16.95 (0-689-31827-8). A girl helping to renovate an old puppet theater discovers that the vicious-looking devil puppet has evil powers. (Rev: BL 3/1/94; MJHS; SLJ 4/94; VOYA 6/94)

743 Bell, Clare E. *Ratha's Challenge* (6–12). 1994, Macmillan/Margaret K. McElderry $16.95 (0-689-50586-8). When a tribe of prehistoric cats faces challenges to survival, their leader, Ratha, hopes to domesticate the tusked face-tails to ensure a steady food supply. (Rev: BL 1/1/95; SLJ 1/95; VOYA 5/95)

744 Block, Francesca Lia. *Witch Baby* (7–12). 1991, HarperCollins/Charlotte Zolotow LB $13.89 (0-06-020548-2). This sequel to *Weetzie Bat* focuses on the foundling Witch Baby as she searches for her parents. (Rev: BL 8/91; SHS; SLJ 9/91*)

745 Bradley, Marion Zimmer. *The Forest House* (9–adult). 1994, Viking $21.95 (0-670-84454-3). In ancient Britain, the last remaining Druid priestesses practice sacred rituals and attempt to keep peace with Roman invaders. (Rev: BL 1/15/94; SLJ 10/94)

746 Bradshaw, Gillian. *Beyond the North Wind* (5–9). 1993, Greenwillow $14 (0-688-11357-5). In a land of one-eyed giants and griffins, Aristeas tries to prevent a bloody war, but he doesn't know whose side he's on. (Rev: BL 3/15/93; SLJ 4/93; VOYA 10/93)

747 Bradshaw, Gillian. *The Dragon and the Thief* (7–10). 1991, Greenwillow $13.95 (0-688-10575-0). An ancient Egyptian fantasy, where teenage Prahotep accidentally meets an immortal dragon and tries to protect her and her fortune from an evil magician. (Rev: BL 7/91; MJHS; SLJ 10/91)

748 Bradshaw, Gillian. *The Land of Gold* (5–8). 1992, Greenwillow $14 (0-688-10576-9). In this sequel to *The Dragon and the Thief*, a clever Egyptian thief and his sidekicks save a princess from being sacrificed and help her reclaim her throne. (Rev: BL 9/15/92; SLJ 10/92; YR)

749 Brittain, Bill. *Wings* (5–7). 1991, HarperCollins LB $13.89 (0-06-020649-7). Ian, age 12, sprouts batlike wings, his father knows they will cause difficulty in his mayoral campaign, and aggressive reporters force the boy to flee into the woods. (Rev: BL 11/1/91; SLJ 10/91)

750 Brooke, William J. *A Brush with Magic* (5–7). Illus. 1993, HarperCollins LB $14.89 (0-06-022974-8). In ancient China, a peasant boy whose painted pictures become reality discovers that the magic resides within himself, not in his paintbrush. (Rev: BL 1/1/94; SLJ 1/94; VOYA 4/94)

751 Brooks, Terry. *The Elf Queen of Shannara* (9–adult). (Heritage of Shannara) 1992, Ballantine/Del Rey $22 (0-345-36299-3). Wren and her friend Garth must survive the perils of the jungle to find the Elves and then persuade them to return to the environmentally endangered Westlands. (Rev: BL 12/15/91; SHS)

752 Brooks, Terry. *The Talismans of Shannara* (9–adult). (Heritage of Shannara) 1993, Ballantine/Del Rey $22 (0-345-36300-0); paper $5.99 (0-345-38674-4). With their quests fulfilled, Par, Walker Bob, and Wren are drawn back together to face the Shadowen in the final book of the Shannara saga. (Rev: BL 1/1/93; SHS)

753 Brooks, Terry. *The Tangle Box* (9–adult). 1994, Ballantine/Del Rey $22 (0-345-38699-X). This humorous fantasy concerns Ben Holiday, sovereign of the magic kingdom of Landover, and some exiled sorcerers seeking revenge upon the fairy folk. (Rev: BL 3/15/94; SHS; VOYA 8/94)

754 Brouwer, Sigmund. *Magnus* (9–adult). 1994, Scripture Press/Victor (1825 College Ave., Wheaton, IL 60187) paper $10.99 (1-56476-296-3). Thomas lives in Magnus, a mythical British kingdom ruled by Druid thugs, and encounters Merlin the Magician and Robin Hood in his adventures. (Rev: BL 10/15/94*)

755 Brown, Mary. *Pigs Don't Fly* (9–adult). 1994, Baen paper $5.99 (0-671-87601-5). With her unknown father's magic ring, the daughter of a village whore sets out to seek her fortune, accompanied by an assortment of animal characters and a blind, amnesiac knight. Awards: SLJ Best Book. (Rev: BL 3/1/94; BTA; VOYA 10/94)

756 Brust, Steven. *Five Hundred Years After* (9–adult). 1994, Tor $23.95 (0-312-85179-0). In this fantasy swashbuckler, reunited companions from the *Phoenix Guards* stop a rash of assassinations and unrest sparked by scheming sorcerers. (Rev: BL 3/1/94; VOYA 8/94)

757 Bull, Emma. *Finder* (9–adult). 1994, Tor $21.95 (0-312-85418-8). Set in Bordertown, just outside the Elflands, this is the story of a cop who exploits a finder's talents to track down a killer sorcerer. Awards: SLJ Best Book; YALSA Best Book for Young Adults. (Rev: BL 2/15/94; BTA; SLJ 6/95; VOYA 6/94)

758 Bunch, Chris, and Allan Cole. *The Warrior's Tale* (9–adult). 1994, Ballantine/Del Rey $21 (0-345-38733-3). Warrior Rali Emilie Antero journeys on the high seas battling magic with his sister, Amalric, who leads the all-woman Maranon Guard. Sequel to *The Far Kingdoms*. (Rev: BL 10/15/94; VOYA 5/95)

759 Burgess, Melvin. *An Angel for May* (5–8). 1995, Simon & Schuster $14 (0-671-89004-2). A 12-year-old boy travels in time back 50 years with a homeless girl and her dog. (Rev: BL 5/1/95; SLJ 6/95)

760 Cady, Jack. *The Off Season* (9–adult). 1995, St. Martin's $23.95 (0-312-13574-2). In a story with elements of fantasy/science fiction and filled with eccentric characters who have returned as ghosts to a small village, a defrocked preacher comes to town and brings back the most evil man who ever lived there. (Rev: BL 10/15/95; VOYA 2/96)

761 Callander, Don. *Geomancer* (9–adult). 1994, Berkley/Ace paper $4.99 (0-441-28036-6). Captured apprentice Douglas Brightgale races to crack the spell of an ancient geomancer and to pass his firemaster examination in time for his wedding. (Rev: BL 1/1/94; VOYA 6/94)

762 Card, Orson Scott. *Alvin Journeyman* (9–adult). (Tales of Alvin Maker) 1995, Tor $23.95 (0-312-85053-0). In this continuation of a sci-fi saga, 20-year-old Alvin Maker becomes embroiled in a trial and is accused of stealing the golden plough and helping fugitive slaves. (Rev: BL 8/95*; VOYA 4/96)

763 Carter, Robert. *The Collectors* (7–12). 1994, Lothrop $14 (0-688-13763-6). Edward K, an iconoclastic insect who challenges the socioreligious ways of his colony, searches with his friends for the "mooocal," which will guarantee their ascent to heaven. (Rev: BL 11/1/94; SLJ 9/94)

764 Charnas, Suzy McKee. *The Kingdom of Kevin Malone* (7–10). 1993, Harcourt $16.95 (0-15-200756-3). Melds the world of the teenage problem novel with that of fantasy in a story that pokes gentle fun at the conventions of fantasy fiction. (Rev: BL 6/1–15/93; SLJ 1/94; VOYA 8/93)

765 Chetwin, Grace. *Child of the Air* (5–8). 1991, Bradbury $14.95 (0-02-718317-3). Two abused orphans discover they have the magical ability to fly. (Rev: BL 6/1/91; SLJ 6/91)

766 Chetwin, Grace. *The Chimes of Alyafaleyn* (5–8). 1993, Bradbury $14.95 (0-02-718222-3). Born with extraordinary powers, Caidrun wears a helmet that shuts her in sensory deprivation, which doesn't stop her from almost destroying the world. (Rev: BL 10/1/93; MJHS; SLJ 11/93; VOYA 2/94)

767 Chetwin, Grace. *Friends in Time* (5–7). 1992, Bradbury $13.95 (0-02-718318-1). Emma, 12, wishes for just one real friend and finds herself face to face with Abigail, a 10-year-old who has somehow traveled through time from 1846. (Rev: BL 7/92; SLJ 7/92)

768 Cochran, Molly, and Warren Murphy. *The Forever King* (9–adult). 1992, Tor $21.95 (0-312-85227-4). Reincarnated as Arthur Blessing, age 10, King Arthur battles a psychotic killer with the help of Merlin and Galahad, now a drunken former FBI agent. Awards: SLJ Best Book. (Rev: BL 7/92; SLJ 12/92)

769 Coelho, Paulo. *The Alchemist* (9–adult). 1993, HarperSan Francisco $16 (0-06-250217-4). Parable about a boy who must learn to listen to his heart before he can find his treasure. (Rev: BL 5/1/93; BTA; SLJ 7/93)

770 Cooney, Caroline B. *Both Sides of Time* (6–10). 1995, Delacorte $10.95 (0-385-32174-0). A girl, ripe for romance, finds it at an old mansion when she travels back to the 1890s. (Rev: BL 9/15/95)

771 Cooney, Caroline B. *Out of Time* (8–10). 1996, Delacorte $10.95 (0-385-32226-7). In this sequel to *Both Sides of Time*, Annie returns from her own time to the 1890s, where she discovers that her beloved Strat is being held shackled in an insane asylum. (Rev: BL 2/15/96; SLJ 1/96; VOYA 1/96)

772 Cooper, Louise. *Sleep of Stone* (7–12). Illus. 1991, Atheneum $14.95 (0-689-31572-4). A romantically tragic fantasy involving a prince, princess, sorcerer, and a creature that changes shape at will. Awards: YALSA Best Book for Young Adults. (Rev: BL 1/1/92; SLJ 3/92)

773 Cooper, Susan. *The Boggart* (5–7). 1993, Macmillan/Margaret K. McElderry LB $14.95 (0-689-50576-0); Aladdin paper $3.95 (0-689-80173-4). A Scottish boggart arrives in modern Canada and wreaks havoc, combining ancient magic and modern technology. Awards: Fisher Children's Book; SLJ Best Book. (Rev: BL 1/15/93; SLJ 1/93)

774 Copperfield, David, and Janet Berliner, eds. *David Copperfield's Tales of the Impossible* (9–adult). 1995, HarperCollins $23.95 (0-06-105228-0). A collection of short stories revolving around magic and illusion. (Rev: BL 11/15/95)

775 Costikyan, Greg. *By the Sword* (9–adult). 1993, Tor $18.95 (0-312-85489-7). Nijon grows from outcast boy to powerful lord in this picaresque tale of quests and dragon slaying. (Rev: BL 5/15/93; SLJ 12/93)

776 Crew, Gary. *Strange Objects* (8–12). 1993, Simon & Schuster $14 (0-671-79759-X). When Stephen, 16, finds an iron pot holding a mummified hand and a 300-year-old journal, it sets off events that end in the death of an aborigine and his own disappearance. (Rev: BL 6/1–15/93*; BTA; SLJ 5/93; VOYA 8/93)

777 Crompton, Anne Eliot. *Merlin's Harp* (9–adult). 1995, Donald I. Fine $20.95 (1-55611-463-X). The Arthurian cycle retold, with the main characters being female fairies living in unsentimental harmony with nature and raising human changelings. (Rev: BL 10/15/95; SLJ 12/95)

778 Cross, Gillian. *New World* (6–9). 1995, Holiday $15.95 (0-8234-1166-4). Miriam and Stuart, both 14, have been chosen to test a new virtual-reality game and sworn to secrecy about it, but scenes in it enact their most secret fears. (Rev: BL 2/1/95; SLJ 3/95; VOYA 12/95)

779 Datlow, Ellen, and Terri Windling, eds. *The Year's Best Fantasy and Horror: Fourth Annual Collection* (9–adult). 1991, St. Martin's $27.95 (0-312-06005-X); paper $15.95 (0-312-06007-6). Horror and fantasy tales, poems, and essays ranging from contemporary to gothic, humorous to frightening, and experimental to traditional. (Rev: BL 7/91; VOYA 12/94)

780 de Lint, Charles. *Dreams Underfoot: The Newford Collection* (9–adult). 1993, Tor $22.95 (0-312-85205-3). Nineteen interrelated stories of magic involving eccentric characters and plots. Awards: SLJ Best Book. (Rev: BL 3/15/93; SLJ 12/93*)

781 de Lint, Charles. *Memory and Dream* (9–adult). 1994, Tor $22.95 (0-312-85572-9). A Canadian painter unleashes ancient spirits with his art in a story weaving in and out of the spirit world over 20 years of Ontario history. Awards: BL Editors' Choice. (Rev: BL 10/1/94*)

782 Dickson, Gordon R. *The Dragon, the Earl, and the Troll* (9–adult). 1994, Berkley/Ace $21.95 (0-441-00098-3). The latest in the series about Dragon Knight, a twentieth-century American transported into an analogue of medieval England. (Rev: BL 12/1/94; VOYA 4/95)

783 Downer, Ann. *The Books of the Keepers* (7–10). 1993, Atheneum $15.95 (0-689-31519-8). Traces the adventures of intriguing characters in a medieval world complete with fairies, goblins, and an old magic awaiting rediscovery. Sequel to *The Spellkey* and *The Glass Salamander*. (Rev: BL 6/1–15/93; SLJ 6/93; VOYA 8/93)

784 Doyle, Debra, and James D. Macdonald. *The Knight's Wyrd* (6–9). 1992, Harcourt/Jane Yolen $16.95 (0-15-200764-4). On the eve of his knighting, young Will learns his *wyrd* (fate) from his father's wizard, which sets off a series of adventures. (Rev: BL 11/15/92; SLJ 11/92; YR)

785 Duane, Diane. *The Door into Sunset* (9–adult). 1993, Tor $21.95 (0-312-85184-7). As Eftgan and her armies prepare for war, Freelorn sets off to seek initiation and regain his kingdom. (Rev: BL 2/15/93; VOYA 10/93)

786 Duel, John. *Wide Awake in Dreamland* (5–8). Illus. 1992, Stargaze Publishing (2300 Foothill Blvd., Suite 403, La Verne, CA 91750) $15.95 (0-9630923-0-8). An evil warlock threatens to steal a 9-year-old's imagination, unless the young boy can find a friendly wizard first. (Rev: BL 3/1/92; SLJ 5/92)

787 Duncan, David. *The Living God* (9–adult). 1994, Ballantine $20 (0-345-37899-7). Using sorcery and sacrifice, Rap draws the resistance together to face a powerful coven of wizards controlled by the dwarf Zinixo. (Rev: BL 4/1/94; VOYA 10/94)

788 Duncan, David. *The Stricken Field* (9–adult). (Handful of Men) 1993, Ballantine/Del Rey $19 (0-345-37898-9). In the third book of the series, the magic-wielding King Rap and his comrades must fight the evil dwarf Zinixo and his legions of sorcerers. (Rev: BL 8/93; VOYA 2/94)

789 Duncan, David. *Upland Outlaws* (9–adult). (Handful of Men) 1993, Ballantine/Del Rey $18 (0-345-37897-0). The imperor Shandie and his supporters are in flight from a powerful sorcerer. (Rev: BL 4/1/93; VOYA 10/93)

790 Eddings, David. *The Shining Ones: Book Two of the Tamuli* (9–adult). 1993, Ballantine/Del Rey $22 (0-345-37322-7). Sparhawk and his companions leave Queen Ehlana to rescue the Bhelliom Stone from the ocean bottom and face formidable enemies, the Shining Ones. (Rev: BL 8/93; VOYA 2/94)

791 Ende, Michael. *The Night of Wishes; or, The Satanarchaeolidealcohellish Notion Potion* (7–10). 1992, Farrar $17 (0-374-19594-3). It's New Year's Eve, and Shadow Sorcery Minister Beelzebub Preposteror has fallen hopelessly behind in meeting contract deadlines. (Rev: BL 8/92; BTA; SLJ 8/92)

792 Farmer, Nancy. *The Warm Place* (5–7). 1995, Orchard/Richard Jackson LB $15.99 (0-531-08738-7). Told from the animal's point of view, a giraffe that is brought from Africa to the San Francisco Zoo finds her way back to Africa. (Rev: BL 4/1/95; SLJ 3/95)

793 Fienberg, Anna. *Ariel, Zed and the Secret of Life* (5–7). 1994, Independent Publishers Group paper $5.99 (1-86373-276-4). Sent to a magical island by her mother, Ariel, 12, journeys with her friend Zed to encounter such characters as an insomniac Sleeping Beauty and a treasure-giving Ali Baba. (Rev: BL 7/94; SLJ 6/94)

794 Fletcher, Susan. *Flight of the Dragon Kyn* (5–7). 1993, Atheneum $15.95 (0-689-31880-4). When Kara is taken to the king and commanded to use her special powers to call down dragons so he can slay them, she escapes and vows to save the creatures. Awards: SLJ Best Book; YALSA Best Book for Young Adults. (Rev: BL 1/15/94; MJHS; SHS; SLJ 11/93; VOYA 2/94)

795 Friedman, C. S. *Crown of Shadows* (9–adult). 1995, NAL/DAW $21.95 (0-88677-664-3). Racing against time to prevent the enslavement of their world, warrier priest Damien Vryce and immortal sorcerer Gerald Tarrant find themselves trapped between justice and retribution. (Rev: BL 9/15/95; VOYA 2/96)

796 Friesner, Esther. *Majyk by Accident* (9–adult). 1993, Berkley/Ace paper $4.99 (0-441-51376-X). When a clumsy young apprentice wizard accidentally acquires magical powers, he also gets a clever cat companion from the streets of twentieth-century L.A. (Rev: BL 7/93; BTA; VOYA 12/93)

797 Friesner, Esther. *Wishing Season* (7–10). (Dragonflight) 1993, Atheneum $14.95 (0-689-31574-0). Two student genies, Khalid and Gamal, vie for the affections of another genie, the expert magic-worker Tamar—and the hilarious, magical adventures begin. (Rev: BL 8/93; VOYA 10/93)

798 Furlong, Monica. *Juniper* (7–12). 1991, Knopf/Borzoi LB $13.99 (0-394-93220-X). A rich coming-of-age novel about Ninnoc, the only child of King Mark of Cornwall as Christianity is beginning to overcome the ancient Celtic religion of the Mother Goddess. (Rev: BL 2/15/91; SLJ 5/91)

799 Goldstein, Lisa. *Strange Devices of the Sun and Moon* (9–adult). 1993, Tor $19.95 (0-312-85460-9). A widowed bookseller searches 1590s London, looking for her missing son, who claims to be the king of the fair folk. (Rev: BL 2/15/93; VOYA 8/93)

800 Goldstein, Lisa. *Summer King Winter Fool* (9–adult). 1994, Tor $21.95 (0-312-85632-6). A young aristocrat, Valemar, must unravel the mystery of his exile through a whirlpool of events. (Rev: BL 5/15/94; VOYA 10/94)

801 Goodkind, Terry. *Wizard's First Rule* (9–adult). 1994, Tor $23.95 (0-312-85705-5). With the sword of Truth, young Richard Cypher goes on a quest, encountering wizards, dragons, and other evils with a modern touch of ambiguity. (Rev: BL 9/1/94; VOYA 2/95)

802 Griffin, Peni R. *A Dig in Time* (5–7). 1991, Macmillan/Margaret K. McElderry $13.95 (0-689-50525-6). When Nan and Tim are staying in Texas with their grandmother, they excavate their backyard and discover that the objects they dig up transport them back in time. (Rev: BL 6/15/91; SLJ 6/91)

803 Griffin, Peni R. *Hobkin* (5–7). 1992, Macmillan/Margaret K. McElderry $14.95 (0-689-50539-6); 1993, Penguin/Puffin paper $3.99 (0-14-036356-4). Runaway sisters try to build a new life in an bewitched farm house. (Rev: BL 3/15/92; SLJ 6/92)

804 Griffin, Peni R. *Switching Well* (5–9). 1993, Macmillan $15.95 (0-689-50581-7); 1994, Penguin/Puffin paper $3.99 (0-14-036910-4). Ada lives in 1891 San Antonio; Amber lives there in 1991. Each wishes she lived in the other's time, and their wishes are granted. Predictably, they soon wish they were back in familiar surroundings. Awards: SLJ Best Book. (Rev: BL 6/1–15/93*; MJHS; SLJ 6/93*; VOYA 8/93)

805 Gurney, James. *Dinotopia: A Land Apart from Time* (6–9). 1992, Turner $29.95 (1-878685-23-6). When their schooner is destroyed in a typhoon, a biologist and his son find themselves on an island inhabited by dinosaurs and humans living in a peaceful, cooperative society. Awards: YALSA Best Book for Young Adults. (Rev: BL 10/1/92*; SLJ 12/92)

806 Hague, Michael, ed. & illus. *The Book of Dragons* (5–7). 1995, Morrow $18 (0-688-10879-2). For dragon lovers everywhere: 17 classic dragon tales, including Kenneth Grahame's *Reluctant Dragon,* J. R. R. Tolkien's *Bilbo Baggins and the Smaug,* and others. (Rev: BL 10/1/95; SLJ 10/95)

807 Highwater, Jamake. *Rama: A Legend* (5–9). 1994, Holt $14.95 (0-8050-3052-2). When he's wrongfully banished from his father's kingdom and his wife, Sita, is kidnapped, valiant Prince Rama charges back to avenge the evil that's befallen his world. (Rev: BL 11/15/94; BTA; SLJ 12/94; VOYA 2/95)

808 Hilgartner, Beth. *The Feast of the Trickster* (7–12). 1991, Houghton LB $14.95 (0-395-55008-4). The quest-adventure tale of the search for Zan, who is the only one who can stop the Trickster. (Rev: BL 9/1/91*; SLJ 11/91)

809 Hite, Sid. *Answer My Prayer* (7–10). 1995, Holt $15.95 (0-8050-3406-4). A girl meets a fortune teller who forecasts a strange future that includes a sleeping stranger. (Rev: BL 5/1/95*)

810 Hite, Sid. *Dither Farm* (6–10). 1992, Holt $15.95 (0-8050-1871-9). An 11-year-old orphan is taken in by a farm family and discovers joys and miracles. (Rev: BL 5/15/92*; SLJ 5/92)

811 Hobbs, Will. *Kokopelli's Flute* (6–9). 1995, Atheneum $15 (0-689-31974-6). A teen finds a bone flute at an ancient Anaszi cliff dwelling that grave robbers have plundered. Strange events occur each night when the boy plays this ancient flute. (Rev: BL 10/1/95; SLJ 10/95; VOYA 2/96)

812 Hoffman, Alice. *Practical Magic* (9–adult). 1995, Putnam $22.95 (0-399-14055-7). Magic, fantasy, and love at first sight figure in this tale about 4 generations of Massachusetts sisters. (Rev: BL 3/15/95*; SLJ 11/95)

813 Hoppe, Joanne. *Dream Spinner* (6–10). 1992, Morrow $14 (0-688-08559-8). Unable to adjust to a new stepmother and -brother, a new home, and a new school, Mary begins to time-travel through her dreams and finds herself a young lady a century ago. (Rev: BL 10/1/92; MJHS; SLJ 9/92; YR)

814 Hughes, Monica. *The Promise* (6–8). 1992, Simon & Schuster $13 (0-671-75033-X). This fantasy, a sequel to *Sandwriter*, is part romance and part coming-of-age story. (Rev: BL 10/15/92; MJHS; YR)

815 Hughes, Ted. *The Iron Woman* (5–8). Illus. 1995, Dial $14.99 (0-8037-1796-2). A sinister allegorical story of contagious environmental pollution brought on by an enraged monster, an iron woman. (Rev: BL 8/95; SLJ 9/95)

816 Iles, Greg. *Black Cross* (9–adult). 1995, Dutton $19.95 (0-525-93829-X). An American physician and a German Jew attempt to thwart Hitler's plan to use nerve gas by destroying a laboratory in a concentration camp. (Rev: BL 11/1/94*)

817 Jacques, Brian. *The Bellmaker* (5–7). (Redwall Saga) 1995, Putnam/Philomel $17.95 (0-399-22805-5). The seventh adventure in the Redwall saga, in which groups of good and bad animals battle and a mouse-maid is abducted. (Rev: BL 4/1/95; MJHS; SLJ 8/95)

818 Jacques, Brian. *Mariel of Redwall* (5–7). Illus. 1992, Putnam/Philomel $17.95 (0-399-22144-1). Good eventually conquers evil in the continuing fantasy saga about the animals of Redwall Abbey. (Rev: BL 2/1/92*; MJHS; SLJ 3/92; YR)

819 Jacques, Brian. *Martin the Warrior* (5–7). (Redwall Saga) Illus. 1994, Putnam/Philomel $16.95 (0-399-22670-2). A young mouse is enslaved by the chieftain of a horde of weasels, ferrets, foxes, and rats using slave labor to build a fortress, which leads to a bloody battle. (Rev: BL 3/1/94; MJHS; SLJ 1/94)

820 Jacques, Brian. *Salamandastron* (5–7). (Redwall Saga) Illus. 1993, Putnam/Philomel $17.95 (0-399-21992-7). Centers mainly on the badgers and hares of the castle in the mountains by the sea, under attack by Ferahgo the Assassin. (Rev: BL 3/15/93; MJHS)

821 James, Betsy. *Dark Heart* (7–12). 1992, Dutton $14 (0-525-44951-5). In this sequel to *Long Night Dance*, Kat, now 17, has trained for the ritual that will enable her to join the Women's Circle, but her attempt fails. (Rev: BL 6/15/92; SLJ 7/92; YR)

822 Jones, Diana Wynne. *Aunt Maria* (6–10). 1991, Greenwillow $13.95 (0-688-10611-0). In this fantasy about family obligations, a sweet but demanding old lady turns her rebellious nephew into a wolf and sets the villagers to hunt him down. (Rev: BL 10/1/91; SLJ 10/91)

823 Jones, Diana Wynne. *The Crown of Dalemark* (7–10). 1995, Greenwillow $15 (0-688-13363-0). Treachery, magic, humor, and mystery are part of this story about 15-year-old Mitt, who is urged to assassinate Noreth, who is determined to claim the crown of Dalemark. (Rev: BL 12/15/95)

824 Jones, Robin D. *The Beginning of Unbelief* (6–9). 1993, Atheneum $13.95 (0-689-31781-6). A mental dialogue with his imaginary alter ego, Zach, helps Hal, age 15, to sort out his feelings about the dramatic changes in his life. (Rev: BL 2/15/93; SLJ 5/93)

825 Jordan, Robert. *Lord of Chaos* (9–adult). (Wheel of Time Saga) 1994, Tor $25.95 (0-312-85428-5). Rand al'Thor teaches magic to men while being pursued by the hostile Aes Sedai. Mat Cauthon is advised by dead generals and Nynaeve learns to restore magic. (Rev: BL 10/15/94; VOYA 5/95)

826 Jordan, Robert. *The Shadow Rising* (9–adult). (Wheel of Time Saga) 1992, Tor $24.95 (0-312-85431-5). The fourth volume in the saga is ambitious, rich, and detailed. (Rev: BL 10/1/92*)

827 Jordan, Sherryl. *The Juniper Game* (7–9). 1991, Scholastic $13.95 (0-590-44728-9). Dylan, age 14, and his lab partner Juniper try telepathic experiments that take them back to the fifteenth century, where a woman is accused of witchcraft. (Rev: BL 11/15/91; SLJ 10/91)

828 Kelleher, Victor. *Brother Night* (7–9). 1991, Walker LB $14.95 (0-8027-8100-4). Rabon, 15, was raised by a foster father in a small town and ends up on a quest to the city with his dark, ugly twin, both learning about their heritage along the way. (Rev: BL 6/15/91; SLJ 5/91)

829 Kempton, Kate. *The World Beyond the Waves: An Environmental Adventure* (5–7). 1995, Portunus Publishing (3435 Ocean Pk. Blvd., Suite 203, Santa Monica, CA 90405) $14.95 (0-9641330-6-7); paper $8.95 (0-9641330-1-6). A 12-year-old is thrown overboard and awakens in a world beyond the waves in a refuge for ocean animals who are injured. (Rev: BL 4/15/95; SLJ 3/95)

830 Kindl, Patrice. *Owl in Love* (5–9). 1993, Houghton $13.95 (0-395-66162-5). Owl, a shapeshifter, is an ordinary high school girl by day, and she falls in love with her science teacher. Awards: ALSC Notable Children's Book; SLJ Best Book; YALSA Best Book for Young Adults. (Rev: BL 9/1/93; BTA; MJHS; SLJS 1/94*; VOYA 12/93)

831 King, Stephen. *Insomnia* (9–adult). 1994, Viking $27.95 (0-670-85503-0). After his wife dies from a brain tumor, Ralph finds it difficult to sleep and begins to witness strange things, including the violent behavior of his neighbor. (Rev: BL 8/94; SLJ 5/95)

832 King, Stephen. *The Waste Lands* (9–adult). (Dark Tower) 1992, NAL/Plume paper $14.95 (0-452-26740-4). This third installment tells of Roland of Mid-World and 3 New Yorkers who proceed ever nearer the Dark Tower, where the source of the planet's cultural degradation lies. (Rev: BL 10/15/91*; SHS; SLJ 8/92)

833 Kipling, Rudyard. *Kipling's Fantasy* (9–adult). Edited by John Brunner. 1992, Tor $17.95 (0-312-85354-8). Atmospheric tales of myth and horror, with rich language and image. (Rev: BL 10/15/92; SLJ 6/93)

834 Kirwan-Vogel, Anna. *The Jewel of Life* (6–8). Illus. 1991, Harcourt/Jane Yolen $15.95 (0-15-200750-4). Young orphan Duffy travels to other worlds, brings back a precious cockatrice feather, and creates the Philosopher's Stone. (Rev: BL 6/15/91; SLJ 6/91)

835 Kisling, Lee. *The Fools' War* (7–12). 1992, HarperCollins LB $13.89 (0-06-020837-6). A strange, but wonderful fantasy, a mix of theology and slapstick that requires a well-developed sense of humor and a slight knowledge of Latin. (Rev: BL 10/15/92; SLJ 10/92)

836 Koller, Jackie French. *If I Had One Wish . . .* (6–8). 1991, Little, Brown $14.95 (0-316-50150-6). When 8th-grader Alec is granted his wish that his little brother had never been born, he learns a lesson about charity, kindness, and old-fashioned family values. (Rev: BL 11/1/91; SLJ 11/91)

837 Kurtz, Katherine, and Deborah Turner Harris. *The Adept* (9–adult). 1991, Berkley/Ace paper $4.95 (0-441-00343-5). Strange events in museums, ruined abbeys, and Loch Ness lead Adam Sinclair, a Scottish psychiatrist, to the discovery that evil magic is being revived. (Rev: BL 3/1/91; SLJ 9/91)

838 Kurtz, Katherine, and Deborah Turner Harris. *The Adept, No. 3: The Templar Treasure* (9–adult). 1993, Berkley paper $4.99 (0-441-00345-1). Psychiatrist Adam Sinclair and companions call upon the powers of King Solomon and the Knights Templar to prevent a crazed academic from freeing the powers of evil. (Rev: BL 6/1–15/93; VOYA 10/93)

839 Kurtz, Katherine, and Deborah Turner Harris. *The Lodge of the Lynx* (9–adult). (Adept, No. 2) 1992, Berkley/Ace paper $4.99 (0-441-00344-3). Black magic and the occult are investigated by a would-be detective and his assistant. (Rev: BL 5/15/92; SLJ 9/92)

840 Lackey, Mercedes. *The Eagle and the Nightingales* (9–adult). (Bardic Voices) 1995, Baen $22 (0-671-87636-8). One of the nightingales is a gypsy bard, who is up to her eyebrows in intrigues both mundane and magical at the Kingsford Faire. (Rev: BL 12/15/94; VOYA 5/95)

841 Lackey, Mercedes. *Sacred Ground* (9–adult). 1994, Tor $23.95 (0-312-85281-9). Jennifer Talldeer, a Native American private investigator and shaman, uses magic to trail a real estate developer involved in an insurance scam. (Rev: BL 2/15/94; BTA; SLJ 10/94; VOYA 8/94)

842 Lackey, Mercedes. *Winds of Fate* (9–adult). (Mage Winds) 1991, NAL/DAW $18.95 (0-88677-489-6). Princess Elspeth, heir to Valdemar's throne, rides in search of a mage to save the realm from the magical machinations of Ancar of Hardom. (Rev: BL 8/91; SLJ 5/92)

843 Lackey, Mercedes, and Larry Dixon. *The Black Gryphon* (9–adult). 1994, NAL/DAW $22 (0-88677-577-9). Set a thousand years before Lackey's Valdemar series, Skandranon Rashke (the Black Gryphon) and his human friend/healer Amberdrake are involved in a war of magic. (Rev: BL 12/15/93; VOYA 4/94)

844 Lee, Tanith. *Black Unicorn* (7–10). Illus. 1991, Atheneum $14.95 (0-689-31575-9). The 16-year-old daughter of a sorceress reconstructs a unicorn from a cache of golden bones, that impels her to run away from her desert home to a seaside city. Awards: YALSA Best Book for Young Adults. (Rev: BL 10/15/91; MJHS; SLJ 11/91)

845 Lee, Tanith. *Gold Unicorn* (7–10). 1994, Atheneum $15.95 (0-689-31814-6). This sequel to *Black Unicorn* continues the adventures of Tanaquil, 16, runaway daughter of an odd sorceress, who turns out to be her half-sister. (Rev: BL 1/15/95; BTA; VOYA 4/95)

846 Levin, Betty. *Mercy's Mill* (6–8). 1992, Greenwillow $14 (0-688-11122-X). In this part time-warp fantasy, part historical novel, Sarah finds companionship with a former slave who is hunting for a child whose mother was persecuted as a witch in the 1600s. (Rev: BL 12/1/92; MJHS; SLJ 9/92; YR)

847 Levitin, Sonia. *The Golem and the Dragon Girl* (5–9). 1993, Dial LB $13.89 (0-8037-1281-2); 1994, Ballantine/Fawcett Juniper paper $3.99 (0-449-70441-6). Jonathan, age 12, and his parents move into a new house, which may be inhabited by the spirit of a former tenant. (Rev: BL 2/15/93; BTA)

848 Levy, Robert. *Clan of the Shape-Changers* (6–9). 1994, Houghton $13.95 (0-395-66612-0). The hair-raising adventures of Susan, 16, and Jeffrey, who are shape-changers being pursued by the evil shaman Ometerer. (Rev: BL 4/1/94; SLJ 5/94)

849 Levy, Robert. *Escape from Exile* (6–8). 1993, Houghton $13.95 (0-395-64379-1). Daniel, 13, is struck by lightning and transported to Lithia, where his new telepathic powers help him cope with a bitter civil war. (Rev: BL 3/15/93; SLJ 5/93; VOYA 8/93)

850 Levy, Robert. *The Misfit Apprentice* (6–9). 1995, Houghton $14.95 (0-395-68077-8). In this revisit to the world created in *Clan of the Shape-Changers*, a 15-year-old apprentice magician's mastery of her power has gone awry. (Rev: BL 8/95; SLJ 4/95)

851 Lindbergh, Anne. *Three Lives to Live* (6–8). 1992, Little, Brown $14.95 (0-316-52628-2). A teenager discovers that her laundry chute is a conduit through time and that she, her grandmother, and her little sister are all the same person. (Rev: BL 4/15/92; SLJ 6/92; YR)

852 Lindbergh, Anne. *Travel Far, Pay No Fare* (5–8). 1992, HarperCollins LB $13.89 (0-06-021776-6). A fantasy/adventure dealing with parental remarriage, time travel, and reading appreciation. (Rev: BL 11/1/92; MJHS; SLJ 12/92; YR)

853 Lipsyte, Robert. *The Chemo Kid* (9–12). 1992, HarperCollins LB $13.89 (0-06-020285-8); 1993, Keypoint paper $3.95 (0-06-447101-2). A high school junior gains superhuman strength after undergoing cancer treatments. (Rev: BL 3/1/92; SLJ 3/92; YR)

854 Lisle, Janet Taylor. *Forest* (5–7). 1993, Orchard LB $15.99 (0-531-08653-4). In this satire, Amber Padgett, 12, and the squirrel Woodbine combine forces to battle adults who are thoughtless about the environment. Awards: SLJ Best Book. (Rev: BL 10/15/93; SLJ 11/93*)

855 Lisle, Janet Taylor. *The Lampfish of Twill* (5–8). Illus. 1991, Orchard LB $15.99 (0-531-08563-5). Lisle tackles issues of freedom and control, as young Eric confronts the dark forces of nature and death. Awards: SLJ Best Book. (Rev: SLJ 9/91*)

856 Lowry, Lois. *The Giver* (6–9). 1993, Houghton $13.95 (0-395-64566-2); 1994, Dell/Laurel Leaf paper $4.50 (0-440-21907-8). A dystopian fantasy in which Jonas receives his life assignment as Receiver of Memory and learns that a land with no war, poverty, fear, or hardship is also one where "misfits" are killed. Awards: ALSC Notable Children's Book; Newbery Medal; SLJ Best Book; YALSA Best Book for Young Adults. (Rev: BL 4/15/93*; BTA; MJHS; SLJ 5/93*; VOYA 8/93)

857 Luenn, Nancy. *Goldclimbers* (6–10). 1991, Atheneum $13.95 (0-689-31585-6). Aracco, 15, longs for adventure and dreams of climbing the cliffs, perhaps joining the goldclimbers and finding the legendary city of Terenger, with its streets of gold. (Rev: BL 6/1/91; SLJ 6/91)

858 Lyon, George Ella. *Here and Then* (6–8). 1994, Orchard/Richard Jackson LB $14.99 (0-531-08716-6). Abby, 13, becomes connected across time to Eliza, a nurse she portrays in a

Civil War reenactment, and goes back in time to help her. (Rev: BL 10/1/94; SLJ 10/94; VOYA 10/94)

859 MacAvoy, R. A. *The Belly of the Wolf* (9–adult). (Lens of the World) 1994, Morrow $20 (0-688-09601-8). The aging, exiled Nazhuret must make a long journey home to end the civil war now that his friend King Rudolf is dead. (Rev: BL 1/1/94; SLJ 9/95)

860 MacAvoy, R. A. *King of the Dead* (9–adult). 1991, Morrow $19 (0-688-09600-X). Nazhuret, an orphaned nobleman, and his knife-wielding mistress, Arlin, travel to the empire of an ancient foe to avert a new war. (Rev: BL 11/1/91*)

861 McCaffrey, Anne. *All the Weyrs of Pern* (9–adult). (Pern) 1991, Ballantine/Del Rey $20 (0-345-36892-4). In this sequel to *Dragonsdawn*, human settlers of Pern rediscover their original landing site and revitalize a long-lost artificial intelligence system. (Rev: BL 10/1/91*; BTA; MJHS; SHS)

862 McCaffrey, Anne. *Damia's Children* (9–adult). 1993, Putnam $21.95 (0-399-13817-X); 1994, Berkley/Ace paper $5.99 (0-441-00007-X). The saga of a telepathic/telekinetic family and alien contact, with teenage main characters. (Rev: BL 12/1/92; SHS; SLJ 11/93)

863 McCaffrey, Anne. *Dragonflight* (6–12). (Dragonriders of Pern) Adapt. by Brynne Stephens. Illus. 1991, Eclipse Books (P.O. Box 1099, Forestville, CA 95436) paper $4.95 (1-56060-074-8). Book one of a 3-part graphic novel based on *Dragonflight* from the Dragonriders of Pern series. (Rev: BL 9/1/91; MJHS)

864 McCaffrey, Anne. *The Girl Who Heard Dragons* (9–adult). 1994, Tor $22.95 (0-312-93173-5). Fifteen short fiction pieces that demonstrate the range and scope of the author's work. (Rev: BL 3/15/94; SHS; VOYA 10/94)

865 McGowen, Tom. *A Question of Magic* (6–8). (Age of Magic) 1993, Dutton/Lodestar $14.99 (0-525-67380-6). Magi, forewarned by visions of Earthdoom, plot to stop an invasion by aliens but are unsure what to do until Lithim, 12, and his father travel to the oracle Gurda for advice. (Rev: BL 10/15/93; VOYA 10/93)

866 McGowen, Tom. *A Trial of Magic* (5–9). (Age of Magic) 1992, Dutton/Lodestar $15 (0-525-67376-8). In the sequel to *The Magical Fellowship*, the mages gather at Soonchan, where the chieftain seems to be wasting away and Lithim comes under a spell forcing him to kill his own father. (Rev: BL 5/15/92; SLJ 6/92; YR)

867 McHargue, Georgess. *Beastie* (5–7). 1992, Delacorte $14 (0-385-30589-3). Four children try to save the Loch Ness Monster. (Rev: BL 2/1/92; YR)

868 McKenzie, Ellen Kindt. *A Bowl of Mischief* (5–8). 1992, Holt $14.95 (0-8050-2090-X). The clever mischief of young Ranjii, combined with visions, dreams, portents, and luck, leads to the freeing of the ruler Superus and his people. (Rev: BL 11/15/92; SLJ 11/92)

869 McKiernan, Dennis L. *Caverns of Socrates* (9–adult). 1995, Penguin/ROC $24.95 (0-451-45455-3); paper $9.95 (0-451-45476-6). Role-playing meets virtual reality, and both meet a mad computer. (Rev: BL 12/15/95; VOYA 4/96)

870 McKillip, Patricia A. *The Cygnet and the Firebird* (9–adult). 1993, Berkley/Ace $17.95 (0-441-12628-6). *The Sorceress and the Cygnet*'s sequel shows cousins Nyx Ro and Meguet Vervaine encountering a sorcerer in search of an ancient key, a firebird with amnesia, and a city of dragons. (Rev: BL 9/15/93; SLJ 5/94; VOYA 12/93)

871 McKillip, Patricia A. *Something Rich and Strange* (9–adult). (Brian Froud's Faerielands) 1994, Bantam $19.95 (0-553-09674-5). An artist hires a fantasy author to write Faerie prose for his paintings. He and an art-store owner receive Faerie visitors. (Rev: BL 10/1/94; VOYA 4/95)

872 McKillip, Patricia A. *The Sorceress and the Cygnet* (9–adult). 1991, Berkley/Ace $17.95 (0-441-77564-0). The banished Gold King tries to fight a ruling family in this fantasy of the conflict between the desire for power and the need for love. (Rev: BL 3/15/91; SHS)

873 McKinley, Robin. *Deerskin* (9–adult). 1993, Berkley/Ace $17.95 (0-441-14226-5). A compelling story of a princess who, after being brutally raped by her father, flees into the mountains with her loyal dog. Awards: SLJ Best Book; YALSA Best Book for Young Adults. (Rev: BL 4/1/93; SLJ 9/93*)

874 McKinley, Robin. *A Knot in the Grain and Other Stories* (9–12). 1994, Greenwillow $14 (0-688-09201-2). Four love stories set in Damar, a world mixing the real and the magical, featuring magicians, witches, and healers. (Rev: BL 8/94; SHS; SLJ 5/94; VOYA 10/94)

875 Mason, Patrick. *Wolfgang Amadeus Mozart's The Magic Flute* (7–12). Illus. 1990, Eclipse Books (P.O. Box 1099, Forestville, CA 95436) paper $4.95 (1-56060-049-7). This 3-volume graphic novel retells the story of the Mozart opera, conveying the farce as well as the drama and fantasy. (Rev: BL 9/1/91) [741.59]

876 Matas, Carol, and Perry Nodelman. *Of Two Minds* (5–8). 1995, Simon & Schuster $16 (0-689-80138-6). Two youths, trapped in a strange land

and stripped of their power of ESP, must work together to triumph over evil. Awards: SLJ Best Book. (Rev: SLJ 10/95; VOYA 4/96)

877 Melling, Orla. *The Druid's Tune* (6–10). 1993, O'Brien Press paper $9.95 (0-86278-285-6). Peter, a Druid lost in the twentieth century, involves 2 teenagers in a time-travel spell that sends them back to Ireland's Iron Age. (Rev: BL 2/15/93)

878 Modesitt, L. E. *The Death of Chaos* (9–adult). 1995, Tor $24.95 (0-312-85721-7). A sequel to *The Magic of Recluce*. The mad emperor of Hamor tries to conquer the world with armies and magic. (Rev: BL 9/1/95; VOYA 2/96)

879 Morpurgo, Michael. *The War of Jenkins' Ear* (6–9). 1995, Putnam/Philomel $15.95 (0-399-22735-0). Set in England at a prep school, where Toby meets a boy who is different from the rest, taking the role of peacemaker. Could this unusual boy be Jesus disguised as a British schoolboy? Awards: SLJ Best Book. (Rev: BL 9/1/95; SLJ 9/95; VOYA 12/95)

880 Murphy, Shirley Rousseau. *The Catswold Portal* (9–adult). 1992, Penguin/ROC $20 (0-451-45146-5). Feline fantasy set on 1957 Earth, as well as in the Netherworld, ties an evil queen and a human artist together. Awards: BL Editors' Choice; SLJ Best Book. (Rev: BL 4/15/92*; SLJ 8/92)

881 Nimmo, Jenny. *Rainbow and Mr. Zed* (6–9). 1994, Dutton $14.99 (0-525-45150-1). Nell is a guest of Mr. Zed, her uncle and a sorcerer, who is determined to control the world and seek revenge on Nell's father. Sequel to *Ultramarine*. (Rev: BL 2/15/95; SLJ 2/95)

882 Nimmo, Jenny. *Ultramarine* (6–9). 1992, Dutton $15 (0-525-44869-1). A brother and sister try to discover why they are so drawn to the sea. (Rev: BL 5/1/92; SLJ 5/92; YR)

883 Nodelman, Perry. *The Same Place but Different* (5–9). 1995, Simon & Schuster $15 (0-671-88415-8). A teen visits the land of Strangers, evil fairies, to rescue his sister. In this reversal of expectations, good fairies and benevolent creatures become sinister and terrifying. (Rev: BL 10/1/95)

884 Norton, Andre, and others. *Flight of Vengeance* (9–adult). 1992, Tor $21.95 (0-312-85014-X). Two novellas chronicle a young girl's developing powers and the changes among the Falconers after the Turning. (Rev: BL 12/15/92; MJHS)

885 Norton, Andre. *Golden Trillium* (9–adult). 1993, Bantam $21.95 (0-553-09507-2). Warrior Princess Kadiya reluctantly takes up her sword against a deadly plague that springs from an ancient evil. Sequel to *Black Trillium*. (Rev: BL 5/15/93; VOYA 4/94)

886 Norton, Andre, and others. *On Wings of Magic* (9–adult). (Witch World) 1994, Tor $23.95 (0-312-85026-3). Two stories set in Estcarp after the destruction of the Turning concerning Falconer women who must build new lives and potential witches treated as experimental animals. (Rev: BL 1/1/94; MJHS; VOYA 8/94)

887 Norton, Andre, and Lyn McConchie. *The Key of the Keplian* (9–adult). 1995, Warner paper $5.50 (0-446-60220-5). A part-Native American, part-Celtic girl passes into Witch World, where she must develop her own magic to survive in the realm. (Rev: BL 7/95; VOYA 2/96)

888 Oberndorf, Charles. *Testing* (9–adult). 1993, Bantam/Spectra paper $3.99 (0-553-56181-2). Centers mainly on a fateful week in the life of Karl, 17, whose personal dilemmas mirror his simulated school problems. (Rev: BL 6/1–15/93; VOYA 2/94)

889 O'Donohoe, Nick. *Under the Healing Sign* (9–adult). 1995, Berkley/Ace paper $4.99 (0-441-00180-7). A sequel to *The Magic and the Healing*. The community fights an amoral villain, which brings back veterinarian B. J. Vaugh. (Rev: BL 3/15/95; VOYA 5/95)

890 Ogiwara, Noriko. *Dragon Sword and Wind Child* (7–10). Tr. by Cathy Hirano. 1993, Farrar $16 (0-374-30466-1). Drawing on Japanese mythology, this story centers on Saya, who learns that she is the reincarnation of the Water Maiden, dedicated to the Goddess of Darkness. Awards: SLJ Best Book. (Rev: BL 8/93; BTA; SLJS 1/94*; VOYA 8/93)

891 Osborne, Mary Pope. *Haunted Waters* (7–10). 1994, Candlewick $14.95 (1-56402-119-X). Lord Huldbrand travels through a demon-haunted peninsula and falls in love with the sea-loving Undine, but the demon follows them. (Rev: BL 11/1/94; BTA; SLJ 12/94; VOYA 2/95)

892 Park, Ruth. *My Sister Sif* (6–10). 1991, Viking/Kestrel $12.95 (0-670-83924-8). In this ecological fantasy, Riko, age 14, and her older sister, Sif, are unable to cope with city life in Australia and return to their islet home, threatened by pollution. Awards: SLJ Best Book. (Rev: BL 4/1/91; SLJ 8/91*)

893 Park, Ruth. *Things in Corners* (5–7). 1991, Viking $12.95 (0-670-82225-6). Five stories of psychological horror by the Australian author. (Rev: BL 2/15/91; SLJ 5/91)

894 Pattou, Edith. *Hero's Song* (7–10). 1991, Harcourt $16.95 (0-15-233807-1). This fantasy-quest novel, infused with Irish myth and folklore, concerns a youth's search for his beloved sister, a wicked queen, and a clash between good and evil. (Rev: BL 10/15/91; SLJ 1/92)

895 Paxson, Diana L., and Adrienne Martine-Barnes. *Master of Earth and Water* (9–adult). 1993, Avon/AvoNova $22 (0-688-12505-0). A young boy, raised in the forest by a sorceress and a warrior, discovers that he has exceptional physical and mystical powers. (Rev: BL 4/1/93*)

896 Peck, Richard. *Lost in Cyberspace* (5–7). 1995, Dial $14.99 (0-8037-1931-0). In this mix of humor and science, a 6th-grader whose parents have just separated finds himself involved with a time machine that brings intriguing visitors from the past. (Rev: BL 10/15/95*; SLJ 9/95; VOYA 4/96)

897 Peña Gutiérrez, Joaquín, ed. *Cuentos fantásticos* (9–adult). 1992, Cooperativa Editorial Magisterio (Bogota, Colombia) paper $6.95 (958-20-0019-8). A collection of short fantasies by some of the best contemporary Latin American writers. English title: *Fantastic Short Stories*. (Rev: BL 2/1/94)

898 Pierce, Meredith Ann. *Dark Moon* (7–12). 1992, Little, Brown/Joy Street $16.95 (0-316-70744-9). Sequel to *Birth of the Firebringer*. A unicorn and princess battle the forces of evil. (Rev: BL 5/15/92; YR)

899 Pierce, Tamora. *Emperor Marge* (6–10). (Immortals) 1995, Atheneum/Jean Karl $17 (0-689-31989-4). The third book in the series finds Daine, 15, as part of a delegation of peace to a barbarian emperor, as her own healing magic grows. (Rev: BL 6/1–15/95)

900 Pierce, Tamora. *Wild Magic: The Immortals* (6–10). 1992, Atheneum/Jean Karl $14.95 (0-689-31761-1). An exciting tale in which teenager Daine gradually accepts the fact that she possesses wild magic. (Rev: BL 10/15/92; SLJ 11/92)

901 Pierce, Tamora. *Wolf-Speaker* (7–9). 1994, Atheneum $15.95 (0-689-31833-2). A girl who speaks the language of animals works to help humans and animals move beyond species prejudice to prevent an ecological disaster. (Rev: BL 3/15/94; MJHS; SLJ 5/94; VOYA 8/94)

902 Pini, Wendy, and Richard Pini. *The Complete Elfquest Graphic Novel: Book Seven: The Cry from Beyond* (9–12). (Elfquest) 1991, Warp Graphics/Father Tree Press (43 Haight Ave., Poughkeepsie, NY 12603) paper $16.95 (0-936861-23-1). The quest-adventure tale continues in this seventh volume of the Elfquest saga. (Rev: BL 9/1/91)

903 Pratchett, Terry. *Diggers: The Second Book of the Bromeliad* (5–8). (Bromeliad) 1991, Delacorte $14.95 (0-385-30152-9). Further adventures of a race of tiny people called the "nomes," who move to a rural quarry where their ingrained cultural attitudes make them ill equipped for life. (Rev: BL 9/1/91)

904 Price, Susan. *Ghost Dance: The Czar's Black Angel* (7–9). 1994, Farrar $16 (0-374-32537-5). A young shaman's apprentice, Shingebiss, is moved by the plight of the Northmen, who are worried about their land being destroyed by the czar's orders. (Rev: BL 11/15/94; SLJ 12/94)

905 Price, Susan. *Ghost Song* (6–9). 1992, Farrar $15 (0-374-32544-8). Fantasy set in the far North, where the heroes must battle cold, darkness, and powerful beings from other worlds. (Rev: BL 9/15/92*; SLJ 1/93; YR)

906 Reiss, Kathryn. *Time Windows* (6–9). 1991, Harcourt $15.95 (0-15-288205-7). Miranda, age 13, finds a dollhouse in the attic that replicates the details of her new home. When she looks inside, she witnesses disturbing past events. Awards: YALSA Best Book for Young Adults. (Rev: BL 11/1/91; SLJ 10/91)

907 Rodda, Emily. *Finders Keepers* (5–7). Illus. 1991, Greenwillow $12.95 (0-688-10516-5). Patrick receives an invitation via computer to participate in a quiz show named "Finders Keepers" in a parallel world beyond the "great barrier." (Rev: BL 11/15/91; SLJ 8/91)

908 Rogers, Mark E. *Samurai Cat Goes to the Movies* (9–adult). 1994, Tor paper $10.95 (0-312-85744-6). Japanese feline Miowara and his nephew, Shiro, take on Hollywood and satirize assorted film classics. (Rev: BL 9/15/94; VOYA 4/95)

909 Root, Phyllis. *The Listening Silence* (5–7). Illus. 1992, HarperCollins LB $13.89 (0-06-025093-3). A medicine man's orphaned apprentice ponders her future. (Rev: BL 3/15/92; SLJ 6/92)

910 Rosenberg, Joel. *Hour of the Octopus* (9–adult). 1994, Berkley/Ace paper $4.99 (0-441-16975-9). Former acrobat Kami Khuzud, now a detective, experiences the intricacies of D'Shai, a world ruled by an elite that loves to kill, dine well, and enjoy its courtesans. (Rev: BL 3/1/94; VOYA 8/94)

911 Ryan, Mary C. *Me Two* (5–7). Illus. 1991, Little, Brown $15.95 (0-316-76376-4). A comedy of errors begins when a boy clones himself as part of a science project. (Rev: BL 7/91; SLJ 6/91)

912 Salsitz, Rhondi Vilott. *The Twilight Gate* (6–10). Illus. 1993, Walker $16.95 (0-8027-8213-2).

Distressed by the upheaval disrupting their lives, teen George and his younger sisters seek protection through magic and instead upset the balance between light and darkness. (Rev: BL 4/15/93; SLJ 5/93; VOYA 8/93)

913 Salvatore, R. A. *The Dragon's Dagger* (9–adult). 1994, Berkley/Ace paper $4.99 (0-441-00078-9). Gary Leger, the reluctant hero of Faerie, must return to battle Robert the Dragon and the wicked witch with his magic, talking lance. (Rev: BL 8/94; VOYA 12/94)

914 Salvatore, R. A. *The Sword of Bedwyr* (9–adult). 1995, Warner $18.95 (0-446-51726-7). Luthien's blind loyalty to his father turns to contempt when he realizes that his father is powerless against the agents of the evil Wizard-King. (Rev: BL 1/15/95; VOYA 4/95)

915 Salvatore, R. A. *The Woods Out Back* (9–adult). 1993, Berkley/Ace paper $4.99 (0-441-90872-1). A young factory worker's imaginative daydreams become reality when a leprechaun transports him to the fairy realm to take part in a quest. (Rev: BL 10/15/93; VOYA 2/94)

916 Schnur, Steven. *The Shadow Children* (5–7). Illus. 1994, Morrow $13.93 (0-688-13831-4). Etienne, 11, is spending the summer at his grandfather's farm in France. When he sees ragged refugee children no one else notices, he comes to realize that he's reliving events of World War II. (Rev: BL 11/15/94; SLJ 10/94)

917 Schultz, Mark. *Dinosaur Shaman: Nine Tales from the Xenozoic Age* (9–12). 1990, Kitchen Sink $29.95 (0-87816-117-1); paper $14.95 (0-87816-118-X). These stories are set in the Xenozoic Age—a future time when humans and prehistoric beasts coexist—and describe the further adventures of Jack Tennrec and Hannah Dundee. (Rev: BL 9/1/91)

918 Service, Pamela F. *Being of Two Minds* (5–7). 1991, Atheneum/Jean Karl $13.95 (0-689-31524-4). Connie secretly knows that her mind merges with another child born at the same moment she was born: Rudolph, crown prince of a Central European kingdom. (Rev: BL 11/1/91; SLJ 10/91)

919 Service, Pamela F. *Weirdos of the Universe Unite!* (5–7). 1992, Atheneum/Jean Karl $13.95 (0-689-31746-8). A school project goes too far as mythological characters show up in an Iowa town. (Rev: BL 5/1/92; MJHS; SLJ 6/92)

920 Seymour, Tres. *Life in the Desert* (7–12). 1992, Orchard/Richard Jackson LB $12.99 (0-531-08608-9). O. Z. Bell has created a world of his own, a desert, to withstand his parents' pressure. When his world is revealed, he seeks a way out through suicide, but he is saved by his friend Rebecca. (Rev: BL 9/1/92; SLJ 11/92)

921 Shachtman, Tom. *Driftwhistler: A Story of Daniel au Fond* (5–7). 1991, Holt $14.95 (0-8050-1285-0). Sea lion Daniel au Fond becomes a Driftwhistler and leads the 13 tribes of creatures to the utopia where humans and animals live harmoniously. (Rev: BL 12/1/91)

922 Sherman, Josepha. *Child of Faerie, Child of Earth* (6–10). 1992, Walker $14.95 (0-8027-8112-8). A Faerie Prince falls in love with a human girl and gives her magical powers to fight an evil stepmother. Awards: YALSA Best Book for Young Adults. (Rev: BL 2/15/92*; SLJ 5/92*; YR)

923 Sherman, Josepha. *Gleaming Bright* (5–8). 1994, Walker $16.95 (0-8027-8296-5). Princess Finola flees an arranged marriage and searches for a magical box that she can use to save her kingdom. (Rev: BL 3/1/94; MJHS; SLJ 5/94; VOYA 6/94)

924 Sherman, Josepha. *Windleaf* (7–12). 1993, Walker $14.95 (0-8027-8259-0). Count Thierry falls in love with half-faerie Glinfinial, only to have her father, the Faerie Lord, steal her away. (Rev: BL 11/1/93*; SLJ 12/93; VOYA 2/94)

925 Shetterly, Will. *Elsewhere* (8–12). 1991, Harcourt/Jane Yolen $16.95 (0-15-200731-8). Set in Bordertown, between the real world and Faerie world, home to runaway elves and humans, this is a fantasy of integration, survival, and coming of age. (Rev: BL 10/15/91; SLJ 11/91)

926 Shetterly, Will. *Nevernever* (8–12). 1993, Harcourt/Jane Yolen $16.95 (0-15-257022-5); Tor paper $4.99 (0-8125-5151-6). This sequel to *Elsewhere* shows Wolfboy trying to protect Florida, the heir of Faerie, from gangs of Elves out to get her, while one of his friends is framed for murder. (Rev: BL 9/15/93; SLJ 10/93; VOYA 12/93)

927 Shippey, Tom, ed. *The Oxford Book of Fantasy Stories* (9–adult). 1994, Oxford Univ. $25 (0-19-214216-X). Stories written from 1888 through 1992 that illustrate the growth of the fantasy tradition in literature. (Rev: BL 3/15/94*)

928 Singer, Marilyn. *Charmed* (6–9). 1990, Atheneum $14.95 (0-689-31619-4). A 12-year-old girl travels through time and space with a friend from another world, trying to find ways to thwart the evil Charmer, who is threatening the universe. (Rev: BL 1/1/91; MJHS; SLJ 12/90)

929 Slepian, Jan. *Back to Before* (5–7). 1993, Putnam/Philomel $14.95 (0-399-22011-9). Hilary and her cousin Linny, both 11, are flung back in time a year, before Linny's mother died and

Hilary's parents divorced. (Rev: BL 9/1/93*; MJHS; SLJ 10/93)

930 Smith, Sherwood. *Wren's Quest* (5–9). 1993, Harcourt/Jane Yolen $16.95 (0-15-200976-0). Wren takes time out from magician's school to search for clues to her parentage. Sequel to *Wren to the Rescue*. (Rev: BL 4/1/93*; BTA; SLJ 6/93)

931 Smith, Sherwood. *Wren's War* (5–8). 1995, Harcourt $17 (0-15-200977-9). A sequel to *Wren to the Rescue* and *Wren's Quest*. Princess Teressa struggles to control herself and her destiny when she finds her parents murdered. (Rev: BL 3/1/95*; SLJ 5/95)

932 Smith, Stephanie A. *Other Nature* (9–adult). 1995, Tor $21.95 (0-312-85638-5). Genetic experiments in the not-so-distant future propel the plot and stir heroic characters. (Rev: BL 9/15/95; VOYA 2/96)

933 Snyder, Zilpha Keatley. *Song of the Gargoyle* (5–7). 1991, Delacorte $14.95 (0-385-30301-7); 1994, Dell/Yearling paper $3.99 (0-440-40898-9). A young man in a medieval world searches for his kidnapped father with the help of an enchanted gargoyle. (Rev: BL 2/1/91; MJHS; SLJ 2/91)

934 Sobol, Donald J. *"My Name Is Amelia"* (5–8). 1994, Atheneum/Jean Karl $14.95 (0-689-31970-3). Lisa, 16, is thrown overboard while sailing in the Bahamas and ends up on an island where an evil scientist has assembled history's most gifted statesmen and inventors. (Rev: BL 1/1/95; BTA; SLJ 1/95; VOYA 2/95)

935 Spencer, William Browning. *Zod Wallop* (9–adult). 1995, St. Martin's $21.95 (0-312-13629-3). An adult fairy tale with a zany, wonderfully sinister plot where the characters interact in an institutionalized setting. (Rev: BL 10/15/95; VOYA 2/96)

936 Springer, Nancy. *The Friendship Song* (5–7). 1992, Atheneum $12.95 (0-689-31727-1). When her favorite rock star collapses and dies, a teenage fan tries to contact him in the spirit world. (Rev: BL 1/15/92; SLJ 4/92)

937 Stasheff, Christopher. *The Oathbound Wizard* (9–adult). 1993, Ballantine/Del Rey $20 (0-345-34713-7). In a sequel to *The Majesty's Wizard*, a college student-turned-wizard in an alternate world vows to conquer a neighboring kingdom and win the queen's hand. (Rev: BL 2/15/93; VOYA 10/93)

938 Staub, Wendy Corsi. *Witch Hunt* (7–12). 1995, Kensington/Z-Fave paper $3.99 (0-8217-4878-5). Abbey leaves her own reality in 1963 and travels back to the days of the Salem witch trials. (Rev: BL 5/1/95)

939 Stearns, Michael, ed. *A Wizard's Dozen: Stories of the Fantastic* (7–12). 1993, Harcourt/Jane Yolen $16.95 (0-15-200965-5). This collection of 13 strange and magical tales includes works by Vivian Vande Velde, Patricia Wrede, and Bruce Coville. (Rev: BL 12/15/93; SLJ 12/93; VOYA 4/94)

940 Stevenson, Laura C. *The Island and the Ring* (7–10). 1991, Houghton $15.95 (0-395-56401-8). Princess Tania's kingdom and family are destroyed by Ascanet, who plans to conquer the world, and she realizes her destiny is to drive him away. (Rev: BL 12/1/91; SLJ 9/91)

941 Stevermer, Caroline. *A College of Magics* (9–adult). 1994, Tor $22.95 (0-312-85689-X). In this alternative-world fantasy, a young noblewoman in quasi-Edwardian society goes to college to learn magic and upon graduation encounters perilous intrigues. (Rev: BL 3/1/94; BTA; VOYA 8/94)

942 Stevermer, Caroline. *River Rats* (7–10). 1992, Harcourt/Jane Yolen $16.95 (0-15-200895-0). This action-packed story begins in the years following a nuclear disaster when 6 orphans, living on an old paddle wheeler, are threatened by a fugitive with a menacing past. Awards: YALSA Best Book for Young Adults. (Rev: BL 4/1/92; MJHS; SLJ 8/92; YR)

943 Strauss, Victoria. *Guardian of the Hills* (7–10). 1995, Morrow $15 (0-688-06998-3). Pamela, who is part Quapaw Indian, experiences cultural conflict when her grandfather organizes an excavation of the sacred burial grounds to learn more of their spiritual heritage. (Rev: BL 10/15/95*)

944 Strickland, Brad. *Dragon's Plunder* (6–8). Illus. 1992, Atheneum $14.95 (0-689-31573-2). A pirate story, with sea battles, a kidnapping, a daring rescue, and a search for treasure. (Rev: BL 1/15/93; YR)

945 Strieber, Whitley. *The Wild* (9–adult). 1991, Tor paper $5.95 (0-812-51277-4). Bob Duke stares at a wolf one day at a zoo, and its gaze seems to invade his soul. Soon Bob is transformed into a wolf and must flee the police. (Rev: BL 5/1/91*)

946 Sutcliff, Rosemary. *Chess-Dream in a Garden* (6–9). Illus. 1993, Candlewick $16.95 (1-56402-192-0). A picture book for older readers that is an unusual combination of chess, fantasy, and fable. (Rev: BL 9/1/93; SLJ 11/93)

947 Tarr, Judith. *His Majesty's Elephant* (6–9). 1993, Harcourt $16.95 (0-15-200737-7). Set in the court of Charlemagne, this fantasy tells of a teenage princess who joins forces with a witch and an enchanted elephant to save her father. (Rev: BL 1/1/94; VOYA 2/94)

948 Taylor, L. A. *Cat's Paw* (9–adult). 1995, Berkley/Ace paper $4.99 (0-441-00181-5). A woman searches for her husband in a kingdom where magic is outlawed and people find it safer to look the other way. (Rev: BL 3/15/95; SLJ 6/95; VOYA 5/95)

949 Tepper, Sheri S. *Beauty* (9–adult). 1991, Doubleday $20 (0-385-41939-2); 1991, paper $12 (0-385-41940-6). Retelling of the *Sleeping Beauty* fairy tale combines fantasy and science fiction. Awards: YALSA Best Book for Young Adults. (Rev: BL 7/91)

950 Tolkien, J. R. R. *The Hobbit; or, There and Back Again* (5–12). Adapted by Charles Dixon and Sean Deming. Illus. 1990, Eclipse Books (P.O. Box 1099, Forestville, CA 95436) paper $12.95 (0-345-36858-4). The classic story of Bilbo Baggins and his companions is introduced to reluctant readers in this full-color graphic novel. (Rev: BL 9/1/91; MJHS; SHS)

951 Turner, Ann. *Rosemary's Witch* (5–8). 1991, HarperCollins/Charlotte Zolotow LB $13.89 (0-06-026128-5); paper $3.95 (0-06-440494-3). Rosemary discovers that her new home is haunted by the spirit of a girl named Mathilda, who's become a witch because of her pain and anger. Awards: SLJ Best Book. (Rev: BL 4/1/91; SLJ 5/91*)

952 Vande Velde, Vivian. *Dragon's Bait* (7–10). 1992, Harcourt/Jane Yolen $15.95 (0-15-200726-1). A young girl accused of being a witch and sentenced to be killed by a dragon becomes friends with a shape-changer who promises to help her take revenge. (Rev: BL 9/15/92; MJHS; SLJ 9/92; YR)

953 Vande Velde, Vivian. *User Unfriendly* (7–10). 1991, Harcourt/Jane Yolen $16.95 (0-15-200960-4). Arvin and his mother are hooked up to a computer game in which cerebral stimulation creates the illusion of reality, and they go on a violent fantasy quest. (Rev: BL 12/1/91; MJHS; SLJ 11/91)

954 Varley, John, and Ricia Mainhardt, eds. *Superheroes* (9–adult). 1995, Berkley/Ace paper $12 (0-441-00137-8). Spotlights comic book champions' often tongue-in-cheek literary cousins, from Captain Cosmos to Captain Housework. (Rev: BL 1/15/95; SLJ 9/95; VOYA 5/95)

955 Vick, Helen Hughes. *Walker's Journey Home* (7–10). 1995, Harbinger House (P.O. Box 42948, Tucson, AZ 85733-2948) $14.95 (1-57140-000-1); paper $9.95 (1-57140-001-X). Walker leads the Sinagua Indians through treacherous challenges from both old enemies and new. He learns that greed and jealousy have been destructive forces throughout history. Sequel to *Walker of Time*. (Rev: BL 8/95)

956 Voigt, Cynthia. *The Wings of a Falcon* (7–12). 1993, Scholastic $14.95 (0-590-46712-3). An epic tale of heroism and cowardice, love and loss, loyalty and betrayal. Also use *On Fortune's Wheel* (1990) and *Jackaroo* (1985). (Rev: SLJ 10/93*; VOYA 12/93)

957 Volsky, Paula. *The Wolf of Winter* (9–adult). 1993, Bantam paper $12.95 (0-553-37210-6). Prince Varis overthrows his ruthless brother Ulor's reign by using black magic to kill all the other heirs. (Rev: BL 11/1/93; VOYA 6/94)

958 Wangerin, Walter. *The Crying for a Vision* (6–10). 1994, Simon & Schuster $15 (0-671-79911-8). An epic account of a boy's sacrifice to save a Native American nation from the aftermath of a near-apocalyptic war. (Rev: BL 12/15/94; SHS; SLJ 1/95; VOYA 4/95)

959 Watt-Evans, Lawrence, and Esther Friesner. *Split Heirs* (9–adult). 1993, Tor $18.95 (0-312-85320-3). When a plot to hide royal triplets backfires, the 3 are raised separately. Their eventual reunion leads to mistaken identitites and many gags in this sword-and-sorcery spoof. (Rev: BL 7/93; VOYA 12/93)

960 Weis, Margaret, and Tracy Hickman. *The Seventh Gate* (9–adult). (Death Gate Cycle) 1994, Bantam $22.95 (0-553-09647-8). Facing capture by dragons and death, several adventurers escape through the "seventh gate," which transports them to an apocalyptic confrontation. The seventh and final volume in the series. (Rev: BL 8/94; VOYA 2/95)

961 Willey, Elizabeth. *The Well-Favored Man: The Tale of the Sorcerer's Nephew* (9–adult). 1993, Tor $22.95 (0-312-85590-7). When his mother slips into the Spring of Power and his father and uncle disappear, a sorcerer prince must face dragons, illusions, and court intrigue. (Rev: BL 10/15/93; VOYA 4/94)

962 Williams, A. Susan, and Richard Glyn-Jones. *The Penguin Book of Modern Fantasy by Women* (9–adult). 1995, Viking $27.95 (0-670-85907-9). Includes selections from Elizabeth Bowen, Daphne du Maurier, and others. A good companion to the *Women of Wonder*. (Rev: BL 9/15/95)

963 Williams, Ruth L. *The Silver Tree* (5–7). 1992, HarperCollins/Charlotte Zolotow LB $13.89 (0-06-020297-1). When Micki discovers a dollhouse with real people in it, she is transported back 100 years into the body of her cousin, who is near death. (Rev: BL 9/1/92; SLJ 6/92)

964 Williams, Tad. *To Green Angel Tower* (9–adult). 1993, NAL/DAW $25 (0-88677-521-3). The concluding volume of the epic Memory, Sorrow and Thorn trilogy about the exploits of Simon, the scullery boy turned knight. (Rev: BL 2/1/93; SLJ 11/93)

965 Williams, Tad, and Nina Kiriki Hoffman. *Child of an Ancient City* (7–10). Illus. 1992, Atheneum $14.95 (0-689-31577-5). A fantasy in which soldiers in the Middle East long ago had to tell sad stories to keep a "vampyr" at bay. (Rev: BL 12/1/92; SLJ 1/93)

966 Winthrop, Elizabeth. *The Battle for the Castle* (5–7). 1993, Holiday $14.95 (0-8234-1010-2). William receives a magic token for his birthday, along with a note about love, courage, and loyalty and a reminder that at 12 he's ready to become a squire. (Rev: BL 9/1/93; SLJ 5/93)

967 Wrede, Patricia C. *Calling on Dragons* (6–10). (Enchanted Forest Chronicles) 1993, Harcourt/Jane Yolen $16.95 (0-15-200950-7). The Society of Wizards steals King Mendanbar's magic sword, which helps maintain the spell that protects the forest from wizards. (Rev: BL 5/1/93; MJHS; SLJ 6/93; VOYA 8/93)

968 Wrede, Patricia C. *Mairelon the Magician* (9–adult). 1991, Tor $17.95 (0-312-85041-7); paper $3.99 (0-812-50896-3). A female street waif is taken up by a magician who uses her skills for thievery, and they are launched on an adventurous, perilous quest across England. (Rev: BL 5/15/91; SLJ 2/92)

969 Wrede, Patricia C. *The Raven Ring* (9–adult). 1994, Tor $21.95 (0-312-85040-9). Set in the world of Lyra, a woman from Cilhar travels to the city of Ciaron and finds danger and magic. (Rev: BL 10/15/94; BTA)

970 Wrede, Patricia C. *Searching for Dragons* (6–12). (Enchanted Forest Chronicles) 1991, Harcourt/Jane Yolen $16.95 (0-15-200898-5). Cimorene goes on a quest with Mendanbar, king of the forest, to find the dragon king Kazul by borrowing a faulty magic carpet from a giant. Awards: ALSC Notable Children's Book; YALSA Best Book for Young Adults. (Rev: BL 10/1/91; MJHS; SLJ 12/91)

971 Wrede, Patricia C. *Talking to Dragons* (6–10). (Enchanted Forest Chronicles) 1993, Harcourt $16.95 (0-15-284247-0). The fourth book in the series opens 16 years after *Calling on Dragons* with King Menenbar still imprisoned in his castle by a wizard's spells. (Rev: BL 8/93; MJHS; VOYA 12/93)

972 Wynne-Jones, Diana. *Fantasy Stories* (5–8). 1994, Kingfisher Books (95 Madison Ave., New York, NY 10016) paper $6.95 (1-85697-982-2). Fantasies and folktales, primarily excerpts from classics, from 18 authors. (Rev: BL 3/1/95; SLJ 11/94)

973 Yep, Laurence. *Dragon Cauldron* (6–10). 1991, HarperCollins LB $16.89 (0-06-026754-2); 1994, HarperTrophy paper $4.95 (0-06-440398-X). Monkey narrates this sequel to *Dragon Steel* (1985), continuing the quest of the band of humans and wizards and Shimmer, a dragon princess, in her task of repairing the damaged cauldron. (Rev: BL 5/15/91; MJHS; SLJ 6/91)

974 Yep, Laurence. *Dragon War* (6–10). 1992, HarperCollins LB $14.89 (0-06-020303-X); paper $4.95 (0-06-440525-7). In this sequel to *Dragon Cauldron*, the heroes use shape-changing magic and the help of a Dragon King to save the day. (Rev: BL 4/15/92; MJHS; SLJ 6/92)

975 Yolen, Jane. *Briar Rose* (9–adult). 1992, Tor $17.95 (0-312-85135-9). A young girl makes a promise to her dying grandmother and discovers her roots in Poland and the Holocaust. Awards: SLJ Best Book; YALSA Best Book for Young Adults. (Rev: BL 9/15/92; MJHS; SHS; SLJ 4/93*)

976 Yolen, Jane. *Here There Be Unicorns* (6–10). Illus. 1994, Harcourt $16.95 (0-15-209902-6). Stories and poems incorporating traditional themes associated with unicorn myth, such as healing, goodness, and unconditional love. (Rev: BL 11/1/94; SLJ 1/95; VOYA 4/95)

977 Yolen, Jane. *The Wild Hunt* (6–12). 1995, Harcourt $17 (0-15-200211-1). The myth of the Wild Hunt is combined with other European legends when Jerold and Gerund become pawns in a game between the Horned King Winter and his wife. (Rev: BL 6/1–15/95; SLJ 6/95; VOYA 12/95)

978 Yolen, Jane, ed. *Xanadu* (9–adult). 1993, Tor $21.95 (0-312-85367-X). An anthology of sci-fi tales and poems, many with youthful protagonists and situations. (Rev: BL 1/15/93; VOYA 8/93)

979 Yolen, Jane, ed. *Xanadu 3* (9–adult). 1995, Tor $21.95 (0-312-85898-1). An anthology of previously unpublished fairy tales, ghost stories, and fables. (Rev: BL 1/1/95; SHS; VOYA 5/95)

980 Yolen, Jane, ed. *Xanadu 2* (9–adult). 1994, St. Martin's $18.95 (0-312-85368-8). Focuses on twisted versions of reality. Authors include Megan Lindholm, Richard Kearn, and Carol Jane Bang. (Rev: BL 12/15/93; SLJ 3/95)

981 Zambreno, Mary Frances. *Journeyman Wizard* (5–7). 1994, Harcourt $16.95 (0-15-200022-4). A blend of mystery and magic in this sequel to *A Plague of Sorcerers*. A student wizard is studying with a moody master spellmaker when a freak accident occurs. (Rev: BL 5/1/94; BTA; SLJ 6/94; VOYA 6/94)

982 Zambreno, Mary Frances. *A Plague of Sorcerers* (5–7). 1991, Harcourt/Jane Yolen $16.95 (0-15-262430-9). Young Jermyn, apprenticed to the Master Theoretician, and his familiar, a skunk named Delia, must come to the rescue when a plague afflicts the city's wizards. Awards: YALSA Best Book for Young Adults. (Rev: BL 11/15/91; SLJ 10/91)

983 Zuroy, Michael. *Second Death* (9–adult). 1992, Walker $19.95 (0-8027-1181-2). A Special Intelligence Squad must track down the creator of a violent zombielike killer. (Rev: BL 2/15/92; SLJ 11/92)

Historical Fiction

Prehistory

984 Brennan, J. H. *Shiva Accused: An Adventure of the Ice Age* (6–9). 1991, HarperCollins LB $13.89 (0-06-020742-6). A prehistoric orphan girl is accused of murder by a rival tribe. A sequel to *Shiva*. (Rev: BL 8/91; SLJ 11/91)

985 Brennan, J. H. *Shiva's Challenge: An Adventure of the Ice Age* (6–9). 1992, HarperCollins LB $16.89 (0-06-020826-0). In the third entry in the series, the Cro-Magnon Shiva is spirited away by the shamanistic Crones to test her powers and see if she can survive the ordeals that will maker her a Crone, too. (Rev: BL 12/15/92; YR)

986 Cowley, Marjorie. *Dar and the Spear-Thrower* (5–7). 1994, Clarion $13.95 (0-395-68132-4). A Cro-Magnon adolescent approaching manhood worries about his adult hunting responsibilities and searches to trade his sun stones for a bow and arrow. (Rev: BL 8/94; MJHS; SLJ 9/94)

987 Denzel, Justin. *Hunt for the Last Cat* (5–7). 1991, Putnam/Philomel $14.95 (0-399-22101-8). A prehistoric Indian youth is ordered to kill the girl he loves in order to save his clan. (Rev: BL 2/1/92; YR)

988 Denzel, Justin. *Land of the Thundering Herds* (6–9). Illus. 1993, Putnam/Philomel $14.95 (0-399-21894-7). Prehistoric animals are the main characters in this novel, showing their fierceness and tenderness as they deal with migrations and natural disasters. (Rev: BL 11/1/93; SLJ 10/93; VOYA 12/93)

989 Dickinson, Peter. *A Bone from a Dry Sea* (7–10). 1993, Delacorte $16 (0-385-30821-3); 1995, Dell/Laurel Leaf paper $3.99 (0-440-21928-0). The protagonists are Li, a girl in a tribe of "sea apes" living 4 million years ago, and Vinny, the teenage daughter of a modern-day paleontologist. Awards: ALSC Notable Children's Book; BL Editors' Choice; SLJ Best Book; YALSA Best Book for Young Adults. (Rev: BL 2/1/93; BTA; MJHS; SLJ 4/93*; YR)

990 James, Carollyn. *Digging Up the Past* (5–7). Illus. 1990, Watts LB $11.90 (0-531-10878-3). A fictional examination of measuring and mapping an archeological site and digging and labeling what is unearthed. (Rev: BL 2/15/91; SLJ 2/91)

991 Jordan, Sherryl. *Wolf-Woman* (6–9). 1994, Houghton $13.95 (0-395-70932-6). Tanith, 16, must choose among the familiar but unhapy world of her clan, a growing fondness for a warrior of a nearby tribe, and the lure of the wolf pack. Awards: SLJ Best Book; YALSA Best Book for Young Adults. (Rev: BL 11/15/94; MJHS; SLJ 10/94; VOYA 12/94)

992 Wolf, Joan. *The Reindeer Hunters* (9–adult). 1994, Dutton $20.95 (0-525-93848-6). Tells the story of Cro-Magnons living at the end of the Ice Age. Warring clans make peace in order to fight invading proto-Britons. (Rev: BL 10/1/94; SLJ 4/95)

Ancient and Medieval History

GENERAL AND MISCELLANEOUS

993 Cushman, Karen. *Catherine, Called Birdy* (6–9). 1994, Clarion $14.95 (0-395-68186-3). Life in the last decade of the twelfth century as seen through the eyes of a teenage girl. Awards: ALSC Notable Children's Book; BL Editors' Choice; Golden Kite; IBBY; Newbery Honor Book; Sandburg Award for Literary Excellence; SLJ Best Book; YALSA Best Book for Young Adults. (Rev: BL 4/15/94; BTA; MJHS; SLJ 6/94*; VOYA 6/94)

994 Levitin, Sonia. *Escape from Egypt* (8–10). 1994, Little, Brown $15.95 (0-316-52273-2). Historical fiction concerning the biblical tale of the Exodus told from the point of view of 2 teens. Awards: BL Editors' Choice; SLJ Best Book; YALSA Best Book for Young Adults. (Rev: BL 5/1/94*; BTA; MJHS; SHS; SLJ 4/94; VOYA 4/94)

995 Rivers, Francine. *Echo in the Darkness* (9–adult). (Mark of the Lion) 1994, Tyndale paper $11.99 (0-8423-1307-9). Christian fiction by the popular author. (Rev: BL 10/15/94*)

996 Rivers, Francine. *A Voice in the Wind* (9–adult). (Mark of the Lion) 1993, Tyndale paper $11.99 (0-8423-7750-6). After the crucifixion of Christ, Hadassah, a persecuted Christian woman, endures the sacking of Jerusalem and a Roman slave ship. (Rev: BL 10/15/94*)

997 Tarr, Judith. *Lord of the Two Lands* (9–adult). 1993, Tor $19.95 (0-312-85362-9). Unveils the destiny of Alexander the Great as supported and guided by the Egyptian priestess Meriamon, daughter of a pharaoh. (Rev: BL 2/15/93; VOYA 8/93)

GREECE AND ROME

998 Tarr, Judith. *Throne of Isis* (9–adult). 1994, Tor/Forge $22.95 (0-312-85363-7). A carefully researched story about Antony and Cleopatra. (Rev: BL 4/15/94; VOYA 8/94)

MIDDLE AGES

999 Cushman, Karen. *The Midwife's Apprentice* (7–12). 1995, Clarion paper $10.95 (0-395-69229-6). A homeless young woman in medieval England becomes strong as she picks herself up and learns from a midwife to be brave. Awards: Newbery Medal; SLJ Best Book. (Rev: BL 3/15/95*; SLJ 5/95)

1000 Dana, Barbara. *Young Joan* (6–10). 1991, HarperCollins/Charlotte Zolotow LB $17.89 (0-06-021423-6). A fictional account of Joan of Arc that questions how a simple French farm girl hears, assimilates, and acts upon a message from God. (Rev: BL 5/15/91*; MJHS; SLJ 5/91)

1001 McGraw, Eloise. *The Striped Ships* (6–8). 1991, Macmillan/Margaret K. McElderry $15.95 (0-689-50532-9). An 11-year-old Saxon girl survives the 1066 invasion of her village by the Normans and is forced to rely on her wits in a world of clashing cultures. (Rev: BL 11/15/91; SLJ 9/91)

1002 Matas, Carol. *The Burning Time* (6–9). 1994, Delacorte $15.95 (0-385-32097-3). Rose tells the story of her mother, a healer in a medieval village who so frightens those in power that they accuse her of witchcraft and torture her. (Rev: BL 9/1/94; BTA; MJHS; SHS; SLJ 10/94; VOYA 10/94)

1003 Penman, Sharon Kay. *The Reckoning* (9–adult). 1991, Holt $22.95 (0-8050-1014-9). A battle over the Welsh throne leads to vows of revenge and acts of heroism in the thirteenth century. Awards: SLJ Best Book. (Rev: BL 8/91; SLJ 7/92)

1004 Rosen, Sidney, and Dorothy Rosen. *The Magician's Apprentice* (5–8). 1994, Carolrhoda $14.96 (0-87614-809-7). An orphan in a French abbey in the Middle Ages is accused of having a heretical document in his possession and is sent to spy on Roger Bacon, the English scientist. (Rev: BL 5/1/94; SLJ 6/94)

1005 Temple, Frances. *The Ramsay Scallop* (7–10). 1994, Orchard/Richard Jackson LB $17.99 (0-531-08686-0). In 1299, 14-year-old Elenor and her betrothed nobleman are sent on a chaste pilgrimage to Spain and hear the stories of their fellow travelers. Awards: BL Editors' Choice (Top of the List—Fiction); SLJ Best Book; YALSA Best Book for Young Adults. (Rev: BL 3/15/94*; MJHS; SLJ 5/94; VOYA 4/94)

1006 Tomlinson, Theresa. *The Forestwife* (8–12). 1995, Orchard LB $15.99 (0-531-08750-6). A Robin Hood legend with Marian as the benevolent Green Lady of the forest. (Rev: BL 3/1/95*; SLJ 3/95; VOYA 5/95)

1007 Walsh, Jill Paton. *Knowledge of Angels* (9–adult). 1994, Houghton $21.95 (0-395-68666-0). In the Middle Ages, a cardinal on a Mediterranean island tries to determine whether a criminal and a girl raised by wolves are acts of angels. Awards: SLJ Best Book. (Rev: SLJ 12/94)

Africa

1008 Campbell, Eric. *The Year of the Leopard Song* (7–10). 1992, Harcourt $16.95 (0-15-299806-3). An engrossing story in which African tribal ritual becomes as powerful and believable as the friendship that binds two 18-year-old boys, Alan and Kimathi. (Rev: BL 10/15/92; SLJ 11/92)

1009 Case, Dianne. *Love, David* (5–7). Illus. 1991, Dutton/Lodestar $14.95 (0-525-67350-4). In a one-room shanty in a mixed-race community on the desolate South African Cape Flats, universal family conflicts are acted out. (Rev: BL 10/15/91)

1010 Case, Dianne. *92 Queens Road* (6–10). 1995, Farrar $16 (0-374-35518-5). Tells a story of vitality and sorrow about a coloured (mixed-race) child in South Africa in the 1960s. (Rev: BL 2/1/95; SLJ 8/95; VOYA 5/95)

1011 Dickinson, Peter. *AK* (7–10). 1992, Delacorte $15 (0-385-30608-3); 1994, Dell/Laurel Leaf paper $3.99 (0-440-21897-7). A young soldier survives a bloody civil war but must use his gun again after his father is kidnapped during a military coup. Awards: YALSA Best Book for Young Adults. (Rev: BL 4/15/92; BTA; MJHS; SHS; SLJ 7/92; YR)

1012 Fabian, Stella. *Is Your Heart Happy? Is Your Body Strong?* (6–12). 1992, Brighton & Lloyd (P.O. Box 2903, Costa Mesa, CA 92628) paper $3.75 (0-922434-37-9). Gives a glimpse of a North African people whose lives depend on mutual cooperation and harmony with nature. (Rev: BL 6/15/92; SLJ 1/93)

1013 Rupert, Janet E. *The African Mask* (6–9). 1994, Clarion $13.95 (0-395-67295-3). The story of a Yoruba girl living 900 years ago in Africa. Layo and her grandmother compete with another clan to make a death mask. (Rev: BL 7/94; SLJ 9/94)

1014 Weaver-Gelzer, Charlotte. *In the Time of Trouble* (6–9). 1993, Dutton LB $15.99 (0-525-44973-6). In western Africa in the 1950s, Jessie, 14, struggles with defining her relationship with her parents, siblings, friends, and God. (Rev: BL 2/1/93; SLJ 7/93; YR)

Asia and the Pacific

1015 Bell, William. *Forbidden City* (9–12). 1990, Bantam $14.95 (0-553-07131-9); paper $3.50 (0-553-28864-4). A 17-year-old accompanies his cameraman father on assignment to Beijing, learns about life in Communist China, and changes his mind about the glamour of war. Awards: Schwartz Children's Book. (Rev: BL 1/15/91*)

1016 Binstock, R. C. *Tree of Heaven* (9–adult). 1995, Soho (853 Broadway, New York, NY 10003) $22 (1-56947-038-3). Two lovers try to escape doom during the Japanese invasion of China in the 1930s. Awards: SLJ Best Book. (Rev: BL 8/95; SLJ 10/95)

1017 Bosse, Malcolm. *Deep Dream of the Rain Forest* (6–10). 1993, Farrar $15 (0-374-31757-7). Orphaned Harry Windsor goes to Borneo to join his uncle, where he's forced to join a native warrior's dreamquest. Awards: SLJ Best Book. (Rev: BL 10/1/93; BTA; SLJ 10/93*; VOYA 12/93)

1018 Bosse, Malcolm. *The Examination* (8–12). 1994, Farrar $17 (0-374-32234-1). During the Ming Dynasty, 2 very different Chinese brothers try to understand one another as they travel to Beijing, where one brother hopes to pass a government examination. Awards: BL Editors' Choice; SLJ Best Book; YALSA Best Book for Young Adults. (Rev: BL 11/1/94*; BTA; SHS; SLJ 12/94)

1019 Bosse, Malcolm. *Tusk and Stone* (8–12). 1995, Front Street $15.95 (1-886910-01-4). A blend of history and fiction about a young Brahman of seventh-century India who struggles to make sense of random disasters in his life. (Rev: BL 12/1/95; VOYA 2/96)

1020 Choi, Sook Nyul. *Echoes of the White Giraffe* (7–10). 1993, Houghton $13.95 (0-395-64721-5). Sookan, 15, struggles for independence within the restrictions of life in a refugee camp during the Korean War. (Rev: BL 4/1/93; MJHS; SLJ 5/93)

1021 Choi, Sook Nyul. *Year of Impossible Goodbyes* (6–10). 1991, Houghton $13.95 (0-395-57419-6). An autobiographical novel of 2 children in North Korea following World War II who become separated from their mother while attempting to cross the border into South Korea. Awards: ALSC Notable Children's Book; SLJ Best Book; YALSA Best Book for Young Adults. (Rev: BL 9/15/91; MJHS; SLJ 10/91*)

1022 Disher, Garry. *The Bamboo Flute* (5–8). 1993, Ticknor & Fields $10.95 (0-395-66595-7). In this brief, quiet novel of self-discovery, an Australian boy, age 12, brings music back into the life of his impoverished family. Awards: SLJ Best Book. (Rev: BL 9/1/93; SLJS 1/94*)

1023 Garland, Sherry. *Song of the Buffalo Boy* (7–10). 1992, Harcourt $16.95 (0-15-277107-7); paper $3.95 (0-15-200098-4). An Amerasian teenager wants to escape the prejudice of a Vietnam village and tries to find her father. Awards: YALSA Best Book for Young Adults. (Rev: BL 4/1/92; MJHS; SLJ 6/92; YR)

1024 Gee, Maurice. *The Champion* (6–10). 1993, Simon & Schuster $14 (0-671-86561-7). Rex, age 12, must overcome his own racism and recognize a true hero when an African American war veteran is sent to recuperate in his New Zealand home. Awards: YALSA Best Book for Young Adults. (Rev: BL 10/1/93*; BTA; SLJ 10/93; VOYA 2/94)

1025 Haugaard, Erik Christian. *The Boy and the Samurai* (6–9). 1991, Houghton $14.95 (0-395-56398-4). Despite his prejudice against samurai, Saru concocts a plot to rescue the imprisoned wife of a samurai. (Rev: BL 5/1/91*; SLJ 4/91)

1026 Haugaard, Erik Christian. *The Revenge of the Forty-Seven Samurai* (7–12). 1995, Houghton $14.95 (0-395-70809-5). In a true story set in feudal Japan, a young servant is a witness to destiny when his master meets an unjust death. (Rev: BL 5/15/95; SLJ 4/95)

1027 Ho, Minfong. *The Clay Marble* (5–9). 1991, Farrar $13.95 (0-374-31340-7). After fleeing from her Cambodian home in the early 1980s, 12-year-old Dara is separated from her family during an attack on a refugee camp on the Thailand border. (Rev: BL 11/15/91; SLJ 10/91)

1028 Klein, Robin. *Dresses of Red and Gold* (6–8). 1993, Viking $12.50 (0-670-84733-X). The Melling girls, the lively heroines of *All in the Blue Unclouded Weather*, are back in another novel about small-town life in post–World War II Australia. (Rev: BL 6/1–15/93; MJHS)

1029 Lord, Bette Bao. *The Middle Heart* (9–adult). 1996, Knopf $25 (0-394-53432-8). A tale of the horrible realities of modern China—with the cultural revolution and the Tiananmen Square uprising as the background—the story of 3 youth who forge an unlikely alliance that survives 5 decades. (Rev: BL 12/15/95*)

1030 Namioka, Lensey. *The Coming of the Bear* (6–9). 1992, HarperCollins LB $13.89 (0-06-020289-0). Two unemployed samurai, running from powerful enemies, are taken in by a strange island tribe. (Rev: BL 3/1/92; BTA; SLJ 3/92*; YR)

1031 Robson, Lucia St. Clair. *The Tokaido Road: A Novel of Feudal Japan* (9–adult). 1991, Ballantine $19.95 (0-345-37026-0). This picaresque romance is based on an actual feud and steeped in the customs and culture of eighteenth-century Japan. (Rev: BL 4/1/91*; MJHS)

1032 Staples, Suzanne Fisher. *Haveli: A Young Woman's Courageous Struggle for Freedom in Present-Day Pakistan* (9–12). 1993, Knopf $18 (0-679-84157-1); 1995, Random/Sprinter paper $4.99 (0-679-86569-1). Presents the issue of a woman's role in a traditional society (Pakistan), intrigue, tough women characters, and fluid writing. Sequel to *Shabanu*. (Rev: BL 6/1–15/93*; BTA; SLJS 1/94*; VOYA 12/93)

1033 Tsukiyama, Gail. *The Samurai's Garden* (9–adult). 1995, St. Martin's $18.95 (0-312-11813-9). A cultural and individual metamorphosis seen through the journal of a 20-year-old Chinese student as China stirs to the threat of Japanese invasion in 1937. (Rev: BL 3/1/95*)

1034 Watkins, Yoko Kawashima. *My Brother, My Sister, and I* (6–10). 1994, Bradbury $16.95 (0-02-792526-9). Tells of a once-secure middle-class child who is now homeless, hungry, and in danger. A sequel to the fictionalized autobiography *So Far from the Bamboo Grove*. (Rev: BL 5/1/94; BTA; MJHS; SLJ 9/94; VOYA 8/94)

Europe and the Middle East

1035 Alder, Elizabeth. *The King's Shadow* (7–12). 1995, Farrar $16 (0-374-34182-6). Set in medieval Britain, mute Evyn is sold into slavery, but as Earl Harold of Wessex's squire and eventually foster son, he chronicles the king's life and becomes a storyteller. Awards: Friends of American Writers Juvenile Book; IRA Children's Books; SLJ Best Book. (Rev: BL 7/95; SLJ 7/95)

1036 Avery, Gillian. *Maria's Italian Spring* (5–8). Illus. 1993, Simon & Schuster $15 (0-671-79582-1). Avery's engaging period tale skillfully depicts the Victorian era and the restrictions women faced. Sequel to *Maria Escapes*. (Rev: BL 5/15/93; SLJ 6/93; VOYA 10/93)

1037 Climent, Paco. *Sissi no quiere fotos* (8–12). 1993, Ediciones Toray (Barcelona, Spain) paper $6.95 (84-310-3515-3). Climent re-creates the 1898 murder by an Italian anarchist of Sissi, the wife of Emperor Francis Joseph of Austria, through the eyes of Leticia, an 18-year-old journalist. Award: Infanta Elena International Award for adolescent literature (Spain). English title: *Sissi Doesn't Want Any Photos*. (Rev: BL 4/1/94)

1038 Cole, Sheila. *The Dragon in the Cliff: A Novel Based on the Life of Mary Anning* (5–8). Illus. 1991, Lothrop $12.95 (0-688-10196-8). The life of Mary Anning, who, while gathering fossils from the Dorset, England, cliffs in the early 1800s, discovered the first ichthyosaur skeleton when she was 13. (Rev: BL 3/1/91; SLJ 9/91)

1039 Cooperstein, Claire. *Johanna* (9–adult). 1995, Scribner $22 (0-684-80234-1). Fictionalizes the story of Vincent van Gogh's posthumous fame through the character of Johanna, his brother's widow, who saves his paintings and letters after his death. (Rev: BL 6/1–15/95; SLJ 4/96)

1040 Dickinson, Peter. *Shadow of a Hero* (7–12). 1994, Delacorte $15.95 (0-385-32110-4). Letta's grandfather fights for the freedom of Varina, her family's Eastern European homeland. Living in England, she becomes interested in Varina's struggle. (Rev: BL 9/15/94*; BTA; SLJ 11/94; VOYA 10/94)

1041 Doherty, Berlie. *Street Child* (5–7). 1994, Orchard LB $14.99 (0-531-08714-X). Jim Jarvis escapes from a workhouse in Victorian London, struggles to survive in cold, crowded slums, where he's forced to steal food, and searches for a home. (Rev: BL 9/1/94; BTA; MJHS; SLJ 10/94)

1042 Forman, James D. *Prince Charlie's Year* (7–10). 1991, Scribner $13.95 (0-684-19242-X). A MacDonald clan member leaves the Scottish Highlands in 1745 to follow Prince Charlie in his attempt to regain the British throne; he is captured and sold into indentured service. (Rev: BL 12/1/91)

1043 Garden, Nancy. *Dove and Sword: A Novel of Joan of Arc* (6–8). 1995, Farrar $18 (0-374-34476-0). A first-person narrative about a boy growing up with Joan of Arc as his neighbor. He follows her across France and watches her last moments as she is burned at the stake. (Rev: BL 12/15/95; SLJ 11/95; VOYA 2/96)

1044 Geras, Adèle. *Golden Windows and Other Stories of Jerusalem* (5–7). 1993, HarperCollins LB $13.89 (0-06-022942-X). A collection of 5 interconnected stories of the life of Zehava Genzel and her family—refugees from a Russian pogrom—in Jerusalem in the early 1900s. Awards: National Jewish Book. (Rev: BL 10/15/93; SLJ 10/93; VOYA 2/94)

1045 Grover, Wayne. *Ali and the Golden Eagle* (6–8). 1993, Greenwillow $14 (0-688-11385-0). A novel based on fact, in which Grover finds the walled village of Ezratu, Saudi Arabia; meets Ali and is accepted into the boy's family; and watches the village move into the twentieth century. (Rev: BL 3/15/93; SLJ 4/93; VOYA 10/93)

1046 Gunn, Neil. *Morning Tide* (9–adult). 1993, Walker $19.95 (0-8027-1228-2). A 12-year-old boy recalls life in a Scottish fishing village with his close-knit family. (Rev: BL 1/15/93*)

1047 Hersom, Kathleen. *The Half Child* (5–7). 1991, Simon & Schuster $13.95 (0-671-74225-6). In a Yorkshire village in 1650, Lucy tells of her life and that of her sister Sarah, who is shunned by the villagers and some of her own family as a changeling. Awards: SLJ Best Book. (Rev: BL 10/1/91; SLJ 11/91*)

1048 Hiçyilmaz, Gaye. *Against the Storm* (6–12). 1992, Little, Brown/Joy Street $14.95 (0-316-36078-3). Addresses the hardships of displaced people in modern Turkey. Awards: ALSC Notable Children's Book; SLJ Best Book. (Rev: BL 4/15/92; BTA; SLJ 5/92)

1049 Kordon, Klaus. *Brothers Like Friends* (6–10). Tr. by Elizabeth D. Crawford. 1992, Putnam/Philomel $14.95 (0-399-22137-9). Two brothers in post–World War II East Berlin cope with a soccer injury that will kill one of them. (Rev: BL 5/1/92; SLJ 6/92; YR)

1050 Llorente, Pilar Molina. *The Apprentice* (5–7). Tr. by Robin Longshaw. Illus. 1993, Farrar $14 (0-374-30389-4). Set in Renaissance Florence, this tale from Spain is about Arduino, 13, who convinces his father to apprentice him to a master painter, only to find that the Maestro has imprisoned a gifted apprentice in the attic. Awards: ALSC Notable Children's Book; Batchelder. (Rev: BL 8/93; BTA; VOYA 2/94)

1051 Marsh, Jean. *The House of Eliott* (9–adult). 1994, St. Martin's $20.95 (0-312-10996-2). Based on the BBC television series, this is the story of 2 determined sisters in 1920s London who open a dressmaking salon, as well as the men in their lives. (Rev: BL 2/1/94; SLJ 8/94)

1052 Matas, Carol. *Sworn Enemies* (7–10). 1993, Bantam $16 (0-553-08326-0). In czarist Russia, the enemies are Aaron, a young Jewish scholar, and Zev, hired to kidnap fellow Jews to fulfill military quotas. (Rev: BL 2/1/93; BTA; MJHS; SLJ 2/93; YR)

1053 Orlev, Uri. *The Lady with the Hat* (7–10). Tr. by Hillel Halkin. 1995, Houghton $14.95 (0-395-69957-6). Yulek, a concentration camp survivor, encounters antisemitism on return to Poland, while a Jewish girl, hidden from the Nazis, wants to be a nun. Awards: Batchelder. (Rev: BL 3/15/95; SLJ 5/95)

1054 Pargeter, Edith. *The Heaven Tree Trilogy* (9–adult). 1993, Warner $24.95 (0-446-51708-9). *The Heaven Tree* (1960), *The Green Branch* (1962), and *The Scarlet Seed* (1963) make up this trilogy set in medieval Britain about a family of artisans and their power-hungry benefactors. (Rev: BL 10/1/93*)

1055 Phillips, Ann. *A Haunted Year* (5–8). 1994, Macmillan $14.95 (0-02-774605-4). A 12-year-old in Edwardian England finds a picture of her mysterious dead cousin and uses a magic circle of stones to summon his spirit, with dire consequences. (Rev: BL 3/15/94; SLJ 4/94)

1056 Pullein-Thompson, Christine. *The Long Search* (5–7). 1993, Bradbury $13.95 (0-02-775445-6). A 12-year-old boy is caught up in the Romanian Revolution of 1989 when he leaves his village in search of his parents, who are political prisoners. (Rev: BL 1/15/94; SLJ 12/93; VOYA 12/93)

1057 Schur, Maxine Rose. *The Circlemaker* (6–10). 1994, Dial $14.99 (0-8037-1354-1). A 12-year-old Jewish boy in a Ukrainian shtetl escapes 25 years of forced conscription in the czar's army in 1852. (Rev: BL 1/15/94; MJHS; SLJ 2/94)

1058 Segal, Jerry. *The Place Where Nobody Stopped* (5–10). Illus. 1991, Orchard/Richard Jackson LB $14.99 (0-531-08497-3). A gentle combination of Jewish folktale, historical fiction, and farce, set in early-1900s Russia. (Rev: BL 2/15/91; MJHS; SLJ 3/91)

1059 Turnbull, Ann. *No Friend of Mine* (5–7). 1995, Candlewick $15.95 (1-56402-565-9). This story portrays the friendship of 2 young boys despite the class differences of their parents: impoverished laborers in the English coal mines and the wealthy mine owners. (Rev: BL 8/95; SLJ 10/95)

1060 Wakefield, Tom. *War Paint* (9–adult). 1994, St. Martin's $19.95 (0-312-11094-4). Miss Kay Roper, a flamboyant and enigmatic school teacher, brightens a war-weary English mining village in 1942, teaching the inhabitants lessons in love and passion. Awards: BL Editors' Choice. (Rev: BL 7/94)

1061 Walsh, Jill Paton. *Grace* (9–12). 1992, Farrar $16 (0-374-32758-0); paper $5.95 (0-374-42792-5). Based on the life of Grace Darling, the young English woman who became a hero when she rowed out from a lighthouse in 1838 to save shipwreck survivors. Awards: SLJ Best Book. (Rev: BL 6/15/92; MJHS; SLJ 7/92*)

1062 Williams, Jeanne. *Daughter of the Storm* (9–adult). 1994, St. Martin's $20.95 (0-312-10441-3). The story of a waif in a nineteenth-century Scots island village who grows up to become a teacher. (Rev: BL 3/1/94; SLJ 11/94)

Latin America and Canada

1063 Alvarez, Julia. *In the Time of the Butterflies* (9–adult). 1994, Algonquin $21.95 (1-56512-038-8). Follows the real-life struggles of the Mirabel sisters from girlhood to womanhood as they struggle under, and ultimately resist, the political dictatorship of the Dominican Republic. Awards: YALSA Best Book for Young Adults. (Rev: BL 7/94; BTA)

1064 Berry, James. *Ajeemah and His Son* (6–12). 1992, HarperCollins/Willa Perlman LB $12.89 (0-06-021044-3). Ajeemah and his son Atu each struggle to escape slavery in Jamaica. Awards: ALSC Notable Children's Book; BL Editors' Choice; Boston Globe/Horn Book; SLJ Best Book; YALSA Best Book for Young Adults. (Rev: BL 10/1/92; BTA; MJHS; SLJ 9/92*; YR)

1065 Dorris, Michael. *Morning Girl* (5–9). 1992, Hyperion $12.95 (1-56282-284-5). The lovely and surprising coming-of-age story of Morning Girl and Star Boy, Arawak Indians on the eve of Columbus's exploration of the West Indies. Awards: BL Editors' Choice; O'Dell Award for Historical Fiction; SLJ Best Book. (Rev: BL 8/92*; MJHS; SLJ 10/92)

1066 Foster, Cecil. *No Man in the House* (9–adult). 1992, Ballantine $17 (0-345-38067-3). Barbados on the eve of independence is the setting for this moving story of a poor family's struggle for dignity and survival. (Rev: BL 11/15/92; BTA)

1067 Gantos, Jack. *Jack's New Power: Stories from a Caribbean Year* (5–8). 1995, Farrar $16 (0-374-33657-1). A follow-up to *Heads or Tails*. Eight stories, some laugh-out-loud funny, tell more from Jack's journal when his family moves to the Caribbean. (Rev: BL 12/1/95; SLJ 11/95)

1068 Haugaard, Erik Christian. *Under the Black Flag* (5–7). 1994, Roberts Rinehart (P.O. Box 666, Niwot, CO 80544) paper $8.95 (1-879373-63-7). William, 14, is the son of an eighteenth-century Jamaican plantation owner. After he's kidnapped en route to England by the pirate Blackbeard, he plots his escape with Sam, a 15-year-old slave. (Rev: BL 4/1/94; SLJ 5/94)

1069 Lingard, Joan. *Between Two Worlds* (7–9). 1991, Dutton/Lodestar $14.95 (0-525-67360-1). The disorienting immigrant experience is described in this story of Latvian refugees who arrive in Canada following World War II. (Rev: BL 11/15/91)

1070 Merino, José María. *Beyond the Ancient Cities* (7–10). Tr. by Helen Lane. 1994, Farrar $16 (0-374-34307-1). The perils and adventures of Miguel and his godfather, who are traveling from Mexico to Panama, among Mayan, Incan, and Spanish cultures. (Rev: BL 4/1/94; SLJ 5/94; VOYA 10/94)

1071 Merino, José María. *The Gold of Dreams* (6–9). Tr. by Helen Lane. 1992, Farrar $14.95 (0-374-32692-4); paper $4.95 (0-374-42584-1). A young explorer hunts for a golden treasure and discovers his real family instead. (Rev: BL 1/15/92; BTA; YR)

1072 Slaughter, Charles H. *The Dirty War* (6–9). 1994, Walker $15.95 (0-8027-8312-0). Arte, 14, lives in Buenos Aires, Argentina. When his father is taken prisoner by the government, his grandmother stages public protests. (Rev: BL 11/1/94; BTA; SLJ 12/94; VOYA 2/95)

1073 Talbert, Marc. *Heart of a Jaguar* (7–10). 1995, Simon & Schuster $16 (0-689-80282-X). In the heart of a Mayan village, a death-inducing drought is taking its toll. (Rev: BL 9/15/95; SLJ 11/95; VOYA 12/95)

1074 Turner, Bonnie. *The Haunted Igloo* (5–7). 1991, Houghton $13.95 (0-395-57037-9). The story of a French Canadian family living north of the Arctic Circle in the 1930s and their relationship with an Eskimo family. (Rev: BL 11/15/91; SLJ 2/92)

United States

INDIANS OF NORTH AMERICA

1075 Banks, Sara H. *Remember My Name* (5–7). Illus. 1993, Roberts Rinehart (P.O. Box 666, Niwot, CO 80544) paper $8.95 (1-879373-38-6). The story of a young Cherokee/Scot girl, Annie Rising Fawn, who avoids the forced removal of the Cherokee from Georgia in 1838 by escaping to her grandmother's home in the hills. (Rev: BL 9/1/93; SLJ 6/93)

1076 Blevins, Win. *Stone Song* (9–adult). 1995, Tor/Forge $22.95 (0-312-85567-2). Blevins has fictionalized this story of His Crazy Horse and the Lakota Sioux culture he tried to protect. (Rev: BL 7/95*)

1077 Bruchac, Joseph. *Turtle Meat and Other Stories* (9–adult). 1992, Holy Cow! Press (P.O. Box 3170, Mt. Royal Sta., Duluth, MN 55803) $18.95 (0-930100-48-4); paper $10.95 (0-930100-49-2). Abenaki writer Bruchac provides mythic, historical, and contemporary stories with wit and a fine sense of character. (Rev: BL 11/15/92; SLJ 12/92)

1078 Burks, Brian. *Runs with Horses* (6–10). 1995, Harcourt $11 (0-15-200264-2); paper $5 (0-15-200994-9). A story of a Native American boy, Runs with Horses, who must past the test to become one of Geronimo's warriors. The story breaks with the tradition of portraying Indians as passive and peaceable. (Rev: BL 11/1/95; SLJ 11/95; VOYA 2/96)

1079 Conley, Robert J. *Mountain Windsong* (9–adult). 1992, Univ. of Oklahoma $19.95 (0-8061-2452-0). Beautiful teenager Oconeechee and handsome Waguli plan to marry until the government forces them to separate by decreeing that Cherokee tribes relocate. (Rev: BL 11/15/92; BTA)

1080 Donnell, Susan. *Pocahontas* (9–adult). 1991, Berkley paper $8.95 (0-425-12617-X). A direct descendant of Pocahontas uses family records as the basis for this famous Native American's life story. (Rev: BL 2/1/91; SLJ 8/91)

1081 Dorris, Michael. *Guests* (5–7). 1994, Hyperion LB $13.89 (0-7868-2036-5). A Native American boy leaves home after his father invites white strangers to the harvest festival. He befriends a runaway girl while hiding in the forest. Awards: ALSC Notable Children's Book. (Rev: BL 10/1/94; SLJ 10/94)

1082 Hogan, Linda. *Solar Storms* (9–adult). 1995, Scribner $22 (0-684-81227-4). A 17-year-old girl searches for her Native American roots and becomes involved in intertribal conflicts developing from a planned hydroelectric dam. (Rev: BL 9/15/95*)

1083 O'Dell, Scott, and Elizabeth Hall. *Thunder Rolling in the Mountains* (5–9). 1992, Houghton $14.95 (0-395-59966-0); 1993, Dell/Yearling paper $3.99 (0-440-40879-2). From the viewpoint of Chief Joseph's daughter, this historical novel concerns the forced removal of the Nez Perce from their homeland in 1877. (Rev: BL 6/15/92*; MJHS; SLJ 8/92)

1084 Rodolph, Stormy. *Quest for Courage* (5–7). (Council for Indian Education) Illus. 1993, Roberts Rinehart (P.O. Box 666, Niwot, CO 80544) paper $8.95 (1-879373-57-2). A disabled Blackfoot teenager is unable to join the tribe's hunting parties with his friends, and he must learn the courage to pursue his own vision quest. (Rev: BL 3/15/94)

1085 Stewart, Elisabeth J. *On the Long Trail Home* (5–7). 1994, Clarion $13.95 (0-395-68361-0). A Cherokee girl flees from her soldier captives on the Trail of Tears in the 1830s. She struggles to survive in the wilderness while heading homeward. (Rev: BL 10/15/94; SLJ 12/94)

DISCOVERY AND EXPLORATION

1086 Garland, Sherry. *Indio* (7–10). 1995, Harcourt/Gulliver $11 (0-15-238631-9); paper $5 (0-15-200021-6). Ipa-ta-chi's life is destroyed when Spaniard conquistadors enslave her. When her brother is injured and sister raped in the silver mines, Ipa attempts to escape but is charged with murder. (Rev: BL 6/1–15/95; SLJ 6/95)

COLONIAL PERIOD AND FRENCH AND INDIAN WARS

1087 Armstrong, Jennifer. *Bridie of the Wild Rose Inn* (6–9). 1994, Bantam paper $3.99 (0-553-29866-6). A teenage girl in the Massachusetts Colony discovers she must suppress the religion and healing arts she learned as a child in Scotland in order to conform to Puritan society. (Rev: BL 3/15/94)

1088 Keehn, Sally M. *I Am Regina* (8–10). 1991, Putnam/Philomel $15.95 (0-399-21797-5). A white girl was kidnapped by Indians when she was 10 and became so absorbed into the tribe's culture that she couldn't remember anything about her early years when she was rescued 9 years later. Based on a true story. (Rev: BL 7/91; SLJ 6/91)

1089 Keehn, Sally M. *Moon of Two Dark Horses* (6–9). 1995, Putnam/Philomel $16.95 (0-399-22783-0). A friendship sensitively drawn between a Native American boy and a white settler. (Rev: BL 11/15/95*; SLJ 11/95; VOYA 12/95)

1090 Koller, Jackie French. *The Primrose Way* (7–10). 1992, Harcourt $17.95 (0-15-256745-3). A historical romance in which Rebekah, 16, falls in love with Mishannock, a Pawtucket holy man. Awards: YALSA Best Book for Young Adults. (Rev: BL 10/15/92; SLJ 9/92; YR)

1091 Lasky, Kathryn. *Beyond the Burning Time* (7–12). 1994, Scholastic $13.95 (0-590-47331-X). A documentary novel capturing the ignorance, violence, and hysteria of the Salem witch trials. Mary, 12, tries to save her mother, accused of witchcraft. Awards: ALSC Notable Children's Book; SLJ Best Book. (Rev: BL 10/15/94; BTA; MJHS; SLJ 1/95; VOYA 12/94)

1092 Rinaldi, Ann. *A Break with Charity: A Story about the Salem Witch Trials* (7–10). 1992, Harcourt/Gulliver $16.95 (0-15-200353-3). This blend of history and fiction brings to life the dark period in American history of the Salem witch trials. Awards: YALSA Best Book for Young Adults. (Rev: BL 10/1/92; MJHS; SLJ 9/92)

1093 Rinaldi, Ann. *The Fifth of March: A Story of the Boston Massacre* (7–12). 1993, Harcourt $10.95 (0-15-200343-6); paper $3.95 (0-15-227517-7). In 1770, 14-year-old Rachel, an indentured servant in the household of John Adams, becomes caught up in political turmoil when she befriends a young British soldier. (Rev: BL 1/15/94*; BTA; MJHS; SLJ 1/94)

REVOLUTIONARY PERIOD (1775–1809)

1094 Gaeddert, Louann. *Breaking Free* (5–8). 1994, Atheneum $14.95 (0-689-31883-9). In upstate New York, about 1800, orphan Richard, 12, works on his uncle's farm and secretly teaches a young slave to read and then to escape with her father to Canada. (Rev: BL 4/1/94; MJHS; SLJ 5/94; VOYA 8/94)

1095 Reit, Seymour. *Guns for General Washington: A Story of the American Revolution* (6–8). 1990, Harcourt $15.95 (0-15-200466-1). The true account of Colonel Henry Knox's attempt to bring cannons and artillery to the Continental Army during the blockade of 1775–76. (Rev: BL 1/1/91; SLJ 1/91)

1096 Rinaldi, Ann. *Finishing Becca: The Story of Peggy Shippen and Benedict Arnold* (7–10). 1994, Harcourt $10.95 (0-15-200880-2). Historical fiction based on the author's contention that it was Peggy Shippen Arnold, wife of Benedict, who was responsible for her husband's betrayal of the American Revolution. (Rev: BL 11/15/94; SLJ 12/94; VOYA 2/95)

1097 Rinaldi, Ann. *A Ride into Morning: The Story of Temple Wick* (7–10). 1991, Harcourt/Gulliver $15.95 (0-15-200573-0). Historical adventure set during the Revolutionary War, when a woman hid her horse in her house to keep it from rebellious soldiers. (Rev: BL 8/91; SLJ 5/91)

1098 Rinaldi, Ann. *The Secret of Sarah Revere* (7–10). 1995, Harcourt/Gulliver $11 (0-15-200393-2); paper $5 (0-15-200392-4). The daughter of Paul Revere recalls the events of her past 2 years against a background of historically significant events. (Rev: BL 11/15/95; SLJ 11/95; VOYA 12/95)

1099 Rinaldi, Ann. *A Stitch in Time* (7–10). (Quilt Trilogy) 1994, Scholastic $13.95 (0-590-46055-2). This historical novel set in eighteenth-century Salem, Massachusetts, concerns the tribulations of a 16-year-old girl and her family. (Rev: BL 3/1/94; BTA; MJHS; SLJ 5/94; VOYA 4/94)

1100 Rinaldi, Ann. *Wolf by the Ears* (8–12). 1991, Scholastic $13.95 (0-590-43413-6). Harriet Hemmings—the alleged illegitimate daughter of Thomas Jefferson and his slave mistress—faces moral dilemmas in regard to freedom, equal rights, and her future. Awards: YALSA Best Book for Young Adults. (Rev: BL 2/1/91; BY; MJHS; SHS; SLJ 4/91)

1101 Thornton, Lawrence. *Ghost Woman* (9–adult). 1992, Ticknor & Fields $19.95 (0-395-61592-5). Tragic historical tale of an Indian woman who is rescued from an island following 10 years of solitary survival. Awards: BL Editors' Choice. (Rev: BL 4/15/92)

1102 Walter, Mildred Pitts. *Second Daughter: The Story of a Slave Girl* (6–9). 1996, Scholastic $15.95 (0-590-48282-3). The events leading up to the 1781 trial of a slave woman, Mum Bett, who took her owner to court and won her freedom under the Massachusetts constitution. (Rev: BL 2/15/96; SLJ 2/96)

NINETEENTH CENTURY TO THE CIVIL WAR (1809–1861)

1103 Armstrong, Jennifer. *Steal Away* (7–10). 1992, Orchard/Richard Jackson LB $14.99 (0-531-08583-X). Two unhappy 13-year-old girls—one a slave, and the other a white orphan—

disguise themselves as boys and escape. (Rev: BL 2/1/92; MJHS)

1104 Cary, Lorene. *The Price of a Child* (9–adult). 1995, Knopf $23 (0-679-42106-8). A woman is forced to leave her baby son when she escapes to freedom. (Rev: BL 4/15/95; SLJ 12/95)

1105 Charbonneau, Eileen. *In the Time of the Wolves* (6–9). 1994, Tor paper $3.99 (0-812-53361-5). In this story set in New York State 170 years ago, twin Josh struggles for his identity within his family and copes with prejudice against his Dutch/English/French/Native American heritage. (Rev: BL 12/1/94; VOYA 4/95)

1106 Chase-Riboud, Barbara. *The President's Daughter* (9–adult). 1994, Crown $23 (0-517-59861-2). Harriet—daughter of Thomas Jefferson and his mistress and slave, Sally Hemings—passes as white and starts a new life as a free woman. Sequel to *Sally Hemings*. (Rev: BL 9/1/94; BTA)

1107 Collier, James Lincoln, and Christopher Collier. *The Clock* (5–7). Illus. 1992, Delacorte $15 (0-385-30037-9). Three young millworkers try to expose an evil overseer in 1810 Connecticut. (Rev: BL 2/1/92)

1108 Conlon-McKenna, Marita. *Wildflower Girl* (5–7). 1992, Holiday $14.95 (0-8234-0988-0); 1994, Penguin/Puffin paper $3.99 (0-14-036292-4). In this sequel to *Under the Hawthorn Tree*, Peggy, 13, after her parents' deaths in the Irish famine, travels to Boston, where she must cope with hardships, fear, and loneliness. (Rev: BL 9/1/92; SLJ 11/92)

1109 Cooper, J. California. *Family* (9–adult). 1991, Doubleday $18.95 (0-385-41171-5). An African American slave commits suicide but returns as a spirit to watch her children mature and experience freedom after the Civil War. Awards: YALSA Best Book for Young Adults. (Rev: BL 1/15/91; SLJ 8/91)

1110 Crook, Elizabeth. *Promised Lands* (9–adult). 1994, Doubleday $22.50 (0-385-41858-2). Centers on 2 Texas families and the battle for independence in the Texas rebellion of 1836. Awards: SLJ Best Book. (Rev: BL 3/15/94; SLJ 12/94)

1111 D'Aguiar, Fred. *The Longest Memory* (9–adult). 1995, Pantheon $20 (0-679-43962-5). Guyanese poet D'Aguiar lyrically portrays the wide range of psychological and emotional conflicts shared by masters and slaves during the era of American slavery. (Rev: BL 12/15/94*)

1112 Finley, Mary Peace. *Soaring Eagle* (5–9). 1993, Simon & Schuster $14 (0-671-75598-6). In this coming-of-age story, Julio searches for his heritage among mid-nineteenth-century Cheyenne Indians. (Rev: BL 8/93; VOYA 2/94)

1113 Fuller, Jamie. *The Diary of Emily Dickinson* (9–adult). 1993, Mercury $18 (1-56279-048-X). This imagined diary combines made-up entries with Dickinson's own poetry, clarified by biographical information. It delves into her life, unrequited loves, relationship with her father, faith, and love of writing. (Rev: BL 9/15/93*)

1114 Graham, Heather. *Runaway* (9–adult). 1994, Delacorte $18.95 (0-385-31264-4). Framed for murder, Tara seeks refuge with a gambler in 1830s New Orleans. They flee to the Florida wilderness, where whites and Seminoles engage in battle. (Rev: BL 8/94; SLJ 1/95)

1115 Gutman, Bill. *Across the Wild River* (5–7). 1993, HarperCollins paper $3.50 (0-06-106159-X). The adventures of a wagon train that takes the pioneer families to the Snake River in the Oregon Territory. (Rev: BL 3/1/94)

1116 Gutman, Bill. *Along the Dangerous Trail* (5–7). 1993, HarperCollins paper $3.50 (0-06-106152-2). Pioneer families begin their wagon train journey in Independence, Missouri, in 1848 and travel as far as Chimney Rock in the Unorganized Territory. (Rev: BL 3/1/94)

1117 Hermes, Patricia. *On Winter's Wind* (5–7). 1995, Little, Brown $14.95 (0-316-35978-5). An 11-year-old girl is faced with heavy family responsibilities and difficult decisions about a runaway slave when her mother becomes too ill and her father is missing. (Rev: BL 10/1/95; SLJ 9/95; VOYA 12/95)

1118 Jones, Douglas C. *This Savage Race* (9–adult). 1993, Holt $23 (0-8050-2243-0). A resilient frontier family survives devastating earthquakes, land swindles, and near starvation. (Rev: BL 5/1/93*)

1119 Karr, Kathleen. *Gideon and the Mummy Professor* (5–8). 1993, Farrar $16 (0-374-32563-4). After Gideon, 12, finds a golden scarab in the mummy of the vaudeville act he shares with his father, they are pursued by various scoundrels in this 1855 New Orleans adventure. (Rev: BL 7/93; MJHS; SLJ 6/93)

1120 Lyons, Mary E. *Letters from a Slave Girl: The Story of Harriet Jacobs* (7–12). 1992, Scribner $14.95 (0-684-19446-5). Based on Jacobs's autobiography, these "letters," written to lost relatives and friends, provide a look at what slavery meant for a young female in the mid-1800s. Awards: ALSC Notable Children's Book; Golden Kite; SLJ Best Book; YALSA Best

Book for Young Adults. (Rev: BL 10/1/92; BTA; MJHS; SLJ 12/92*; YR)

1121 Olds, Bruce. *Raising Holy Hell* (9–adult). 1995, Holt $22.50 (0-8050-3856-6). A fascinating study of U.S. slavery and one of its most ardent opponents, John Brown, told through real and fabricated quotations by witnesses and participants. (Rev: BL 8/95*)

1122 Paterson, Katherine. *Lyddie* (9–12). 1991, Dutton/Lodestar $14.95 (0-525-67338-5). The life and hard times of a young girl growing up in the mid-nineteenth century. Awards: ALSC Notable Children's Book; BL Editors' Choice; IBBY; SLJ Best Book; YALSA Best Book for Young Adults. (Rev: BL 1/1/91*; MJHS; SLJ 2/91*)

1123 Paulsen, Gary. *Nightjohn* (6–12). 1993, Delacorte $14 (0-385-30838-8). Told in the voice of Sarny, 12, Paulsen exposes the popular myths that African American slaves were really content, well cared for, ignorant, and childlike and that brave, resourceful slaves frequently and easily escaped. Awards: ALSC Notable Children's Book; SLJ Best Book; YALSA Best Book for Young Adults. (Rev: BL 12/15/92; BTA; MJHS; SLJS 6/93*)

1124 Ruby, Lois. *Steal Away Home* (7–10). 1994, Macmillan $14.95 (0-02-777883-5). Dana, 12, finds a skeleton in a secret room of her Kansas home that turns out to be the remains of Lizbet, a conductor on the Underground Railroad. (Rev: BL 1/1/95; SLJ 2/95; VOYA 4/95)

1125 Stolz, Mary. *Cezanne Pinto: A Memoir* (6–10). 1994, Knopf $15 (0-679-84917-3). This fictionalized memoir of a runaway slave who became a soldier, cowboy, and teacher includes quotations and stories of the great figures of the time. Awards: SLJ Best Book; YALSA Best Book for Young Adults. (Rev: BL 1/15/94; MJHS; SLJ 12/93; VOYA 6/94)

1126 Whelan, Gloria. *Once on This Island* (5–7). 1995, HarperCollins LB $14.89 (0-06-026249-4). A fictionalized account of a young girl and her older siblings who must take responsibility for the family farm in Michigan when their father leaves to fight the British in the War of 1812. (Rev: BL 10/1/95; SLJ 11/95; VOYA 2/96)

1127 Zelazny, Roger, and Gerald Hausman. *Wilderness* (9–adult). 1994, Tor/Forge $21.95 (0-312-85654-7). Alternating between 2 remarkable survival stories, this is a tribute to those who triumphed over the American wilderness in the early nineteenth century. (Rev: BL 2/15/94; BTA; SLJ 7/94)

THE CIVIL WAR (1861–1865)

1128 Bass, Cynthia. *Sherman's March* (9–adult). 1994, Villard $21 (0-679-43033-4). A fast-paced fictionalized account of Sherman's infamous march to the sea. Awards: SLJ Best Book. (Rev: SLJ 12/94)

1129 Beatty, Patricia. *Jayhawker* (6–9). 1991, Morrow $13.95 (0-688-09850-9). The story of 12-year-old Elijah, son of a Kansas abolitionist, who becomes a spy and infiltrates Charles Quantrill's infamous Bushwhacker network. Awards: SLJ Best Book. (Rev: BL 9/1/91*; MJHS; SLJ 9/91*)

1130 Collier, James Lincoln, and Christopher Collier. *With Every Drop of Blood: A Novel of the Civil War* (6–10). 1994, Delacorte $15.95 (0-385-32028-0). A docunovel about Johnny, a young rebel soldier during the Civil War who is captured by Cush, a black Union soldier. Together, the men must endure the horrors of war and bigotry. (Rev: BL 7/94; MJHS; SLJ 8/94; VOYA 12/94)

1131 Curtis, Jack. *Pepper Tree Rider* (9–adult). 1994, Walker $19.95 (0-8027-4137-1). A subtle Western where a fast gun isn't always the answer; from the pen of the screenplay writer of *Gunsmoke*. (Rev: BL 5/1/94; SLJ 10/94)

1132 Donahue, John. *An Island Far from Home* (5–7). 1994, Carolrhoda LB $14.96 (0-87614-859-3). A 12-year-old wants to avenge the death of his father, who was in the Union Army, by fighting against the hated rebels. (Rev: BL 2/15/95; SLJ 2/95)

1133 Fleischman, Paul. *Bull Run* (6–12). 1993, HarperCollins/Laura Geringer LB $13.89 (0-06-021447-3). Spotlights the diary entries of 16 fictional characters, 8 each from the South and the North, throughout the battle. Awards: O'Dell Award for Historical Fiction; SLJ Best Book. (Rev: BL 1/15/93*; BTA; MJHS; SLJ 3/93*)

1134 Forman, James D. *Becca's Story* (5–8). 1992, Scribner $14.95 (0-684-19332-9). Forman uses his ancestors' Civil War–era letters and diaries to weave the story of Becca, who is courted by 2 young men who go off to fight in the Union Army. Awards: SLJ Best Book; YALSA Best Book for Young Adults. (Rev: BL 12/1/92; MJHS; SHS; SLJ 11/92*; YR)

1135 Forrester, Sandra. *Sound the Jubilee* (7–10). 1995, Dutton/Lodestar $14.99 (0-525-67486-1). A docu-novel—as well as a coming-of-age story—about a community of runaway slaves who land on Roanoke Island during the Civil War. (Rev: BL 3/1/95)

1136 Houston, Gloria. *Mountain Valor* (5–7). Illus. 1994, Putnam/Philomel $14.95 (0-399-

22519-6). Based on the life of a relative of the author, the story shows a frontier settler whose major goal was survival rather than blind allegiance to either the North or the South in the Civil War. (Rev: BL 4/1/94; SLJ 6/94; VOYA 6/94)

1137 Jones, Ted. *Fifth Conspiracy* (9–12). 1995, Presidio $21.95 (0-89141-515-7). In this sequel to *Hard Road to Gettysburg*, Jones immerses readers in Civil War battlefields and behind-the-front planning and espionage. (Rev: BL 8/95; SLJ 3/96)

1138 Jones, Ted. *Hard Road to Gettysburg* (9–adult). 1993, Lyford $21.95 (0-89141-445-2). A richly detailed Civil War novel finds twin brothers pitted against each other when one brother impersonates the other to spy on the Confederate Army. (Rev: BL 5/1/93; SLJ 1/94)

1139 Meriwether, Louise. *Fragments of the Ark* (9–adult). 1994, Pocket $21 (0-671-79947-9). Based on a true account, this historical novel concerns slaves who escaped to join Union forces and the bigotry they faced from their "rescuers." (Rev: BL 2/15/94; BTA; SLJ 11/94)

1140 Nixon, Joan Lowery. *A Dangerous Promise* (6–8). 1994, Delacorte $15.95 (0-385-32073-6). Mike Kelly, 12, and Todd Blakely run away to help the Union forces in the Civil War and experience the terrors of war. (Rev: BL 9/1/94; MJHS; SLJ 11/94; VOYA 10/94)

1141 Nixon, Joan Lowery. *Keeping Secrets* (5–8). (Orphan Train) 1995, Delacorte $15.95 (0-385-32139-2). Set in Missouri during the Civil War, Peg, age 11, is unwittingly involved with a Union spy. (Rev: BL 3/1/95; SLJ 3/95; VOYA 4/95)

1142 Rinaldi, Ann. *In My Father's House* (7–10). 1993, Scholastic $13.95 (0-590-44730-0). A coming-of-age novel set during the Civil War about 7-year-old Oscie. Awards: YALSA Best Book for Young Adults. (Rev: BL 2/15/93; MJHS)

1143 Travis, L. *Captured by a Spy* (6–10). 1995, Baker paper $5.99 (0-8010-8915-8). A story of mercy and heart during the Civil War, when 2 Northern boys, one white and one African American, are taken to Canada and placed in the hands of an infamous, exiled Confederate sympathizer. (Rev: BL 9/15/95)

1144 Wisler, G. Clifton. *Mr. Lincoln's Drummer* (5–7). 1994, Dutton/Lodestar $14.99 (0-525-67463-2). Willie, 11, enters the Civil War as a drummer boy, and his war consists mainly of camp life, discomfort, and retreat, but he meets Lincoln and receives the Medal of Honor. (Rev: BL 1/15/95; VOYA 5/95)

1145 Wisler, G. Clifton. *Red Cap* (6–8). 1991, Dutton/Lodestar $14.95 (0-525-67337-7); 1994, Penguin/Puffin paper $3.99 (0-14-036936-8). An adolescent boy lies about his age in order to join the Union Army, but he ends up as a prisoner of war in the infamous Andersonville camp. Awards: YALSA Best Book for Young Adults. (Rev: BL 8/91; MJHS; SLJ 8/91)

WESTERN EXPANSION AND PIONEER LIFE

1146 Blair, Clifford. *The Guns of Sacred Heart* (9–adult). 1991, Walker $18.95 (0-8027-4123-1). Outlaws trying to free their leader who is a prisoner at a remote mission school are fought off by a marshal, a cowboy, and the school's staff and students. (Rev: BL 11/1/91; SLJ 5/92)

1147 Bonner, Cindy. *Lily* (9–adult). 1992, Algonquin Books of Chapel Hill (P.O. Box 2225, Chapel Hill, NC 27515-2225) $17.95 (0-945575-95-5). An old-fashioned Western romance, where innocent girl falls in love with a worldly guy from an outlaw family. Awards: SLJ Best Book; YALSA Best Book for Young Adults. (Rev: BL 9/1/92*; BTA; SLJ 12/92)

1148 Brown, Lois, ed. *Tales of the Wild West: An Illustrated Collection of Adventure Stories* (9–adult). 1993, Rizzoli $24.95 (0-8478-1748-2). Old West stories that stay true to the classic tradition, including works by Bret Harte, Zane Grey, O. Henry, and Theodore Roosevelt. (Rev: BL 9/15/93; SLJ 10/93) [813]

1149 Calvert, Patricia. *Bigger* (5–8). 1994, Scribner $14.95 (0-684-19685-9). Accompanied by an abused stray dog named Bigger, Tyler, 12, sets out on an 800-mile trip from Missouri to the Rio Grande to find his father after the Civil War. (Rev: BL 4/1/94; BTA; SLJ 4/94; VOYA 4/94)

1150 Coville, Bruce. *Fortune's Journey* (5–8). 1995, Troll/Bridgewater $13.95 (0-8167-3650-2). A teen romance in which a 16-year-old girl leads a troupe of actors west along the Oregon Trail in a Conestoga wagon. (Rev: BL 10/15/95; SLJ 11/95; VOYA 2/96)

1151 Eidson, Tom. *The Last Ride* (9–adult). (St. Agnes' Stand) 1995, Putnam $21.95 (0-399-14057-3). Samuel Jones, an aging Indian warrior, wants to make amends with his daughter, whom he deserted 30 years before. (Rev: BL 3/15/95*)

1152 Eidson, Tom. *St. Agnes' Stand* (9–adult). 1994, Putnam $19.95 (0-399-13915-X). En route to California in 1858, a hunted murderer inadvertently rescues 3 nuns and 7 nearly starving orphans, and Sister St. Agnes helps him out of a jam. (Rev: BL 4/1/94; SLJ 7/94)

1153 Estleman, Loren D. *Sudden Country* (9–adult). 1991, Doubleday $15 (0-385-24727-3). In this coming-of-age novel set in 1890s Texas, David discovers a map showing the location of gold stolen by Quantrill's Raiders. (Rev: BL 6/15/91; SLJ 5/92)

1154 Fleischman, Paul. *The Borning Room* (5–10). 1991, HarperCollins LB $13.89 (0-06023785-6). Georgina remembers her life's "turnings," most of which occurred in the room set aside for giving birth and dying in her grandfather's house in nineteenth-century rural Ohio. Awards: SLJ Best Book. (Rev: BL 10/1/91*; MJHS; SLJ 9/91*)

1155 Gregory, Kristiana. *Jimmy Spoon and the Pony Express* (6–8). 1994, Scholastic $13.95 (0-590-46577-5). Jimmy answers an ad for Pony Express riders, but he's haunted by his previous life with the Shoshone (see *The Legend of Jimmy Spoon*, 1990), especially the beautiful Nahanee. (Rev: BL 11/15/94; SLJ 11/94; VOYA 4/95)

1156 Hurmence, Belinda. *Dixie in the Big Pasture* (5–8). 1994, Clarion $13.95 (0-395-52002-9). A 13-year-old and her family move near the land of the Kiowas, who teach her about their way of life. (Rev: BL 4/15/94; MJHS; SLJ 5/94)

1157 Irwin, Hadley. *Jim-Dandy* (5–7). 1994, Macmillan/Margaret K. McElderry $14.95 (0-689-50594-9). A lonely boy and a colt develop a close relationship until the animal is sold to Custer's Seventh Cavalry for much needed cash. The boy follows the horse to look after it. (Rev: BL 4/15/94; BTA; MJHS; SLJ 5/94; VOYA 6/94)

1158 Karr, Kathleen. *Oh, Those Harper Girls!* (6–9). 1992, Farrar $16 (0-374-35609-2). Faced with the foreclosure of their Texas ranch, 6 sisters are determined to help their unlucky father save their homestead. (Rev: BL 4/15/92; MJHS; YR)

1159 Matheson, Richard. *Gunfight* (9–adult). 1993, Evans $16.95 (0-87131-726-5). A young girl's plot to make her boyfriend jealous backfires when he's forced into a gunfight to defend her honor. (Rev: BL 3/15/93*)

1160 Mazzio, Joann. *Leaving Eldorado* (6–9). 1993, Houghton $13.95 (0-395-64381-3). The adventures of Maude, 14, in 1896 New Mexico Territory. (Rev: BL 3/15/93; BTA; SLJ 5/93)

1161 Meyer, Carolyn. *Where the Broken Heart Still Beats: The Story of Cynthia Ann Parker* (7–12). 1992, Harcourt/Gulliver $16.95 (0-15-200639-7); paper $5.95 (0-15-295602-6). A fictional retelling of the abduction of Parker, who was stolen by Comanches as a child and lived with them for 24 years, first as a slave, then as a chief's wife. Awards: YALSA Best Book for Young Adults. (Rev: BL 12/1/92; SHS; SLJ 9/92; YR)

1162 Morpurgo, Michael. *Twist of Gold* (5–8). 1993, Viking $14.95 (0-670-84851-4). Two kids leave their dying mother in Ireland in the 1840s and travel across the sea and the United States to find their father in California. (Rev: BL 4/1/93; MJHS; SLJ 2/93; VOYA 8/93)

1163 Paine, Lauran. *Riders of the Trojan Horse* (9–adult). 1991, Walker $18.95 (0-8027-4116-9). A brave stagecoach driver pursues thieves who have stolen his vehicle and kidnapped the sheriff. (Rev: BL 7/91; SLJ 10/91)

1164 Paine, Lauran. *The Squaw Men* (7–10). 1992, Walker $19.95 (0-8027-4126-6). Two white men married to Native American women and living with the tribe are caught in the middle when tribe leaders want to force white settlers out. (Rev: BL 4/15/92)

1165 Paulsen, Gary. *Call Me Francis Tucket* (5–8). 1995, Delacorte $14 (0-385-32116-3). In this sequel to *Mr. Tucket* (1994), 15-year-old Francis becomes separated from a wagon train headed for Oregon and must survive the wilderness. (Rev: BL 7/95; SLJ 6/95; VOYA 5/95)

1166 Paulsen, Gary. *Mr. Tucket* (6–9). 1994, Delacorte $14.95 (0-385-31169-9). A 14-year-old boy strays from his family's wagon on the Oregon Trail and ends up with the Pawnees. A trapper helps him escape and teaches him much about life and survival. (Rev: BL 5/1/94; BTA; MJHS; VOYA 4/94)

1167 Roberts, Willo Davis. *Jo and the Bandit* (6–8). 1992, Atheneum/Jean Karl $14.95 (0-689-31745-X). Orphans Jo and her brother are sent to live with their uncle in 1860s Texas. When the stagecoach is robbed, Jo hides the son of the gang leader and helps him escape. (Rev: BL 6/1/92; SLJ 7/92)

1168 Sauerwein, Leigh. *The Way Home* (7–12). Illus. 1994, Farrar $15 (0-374-38247-6). Short stories set in the American West that evoke the struggles of frontier life, past and present. Several describing relationships between whites and Native Americans. (Rev: BL 3/15/94; MJHS; SLJ 4/94; VOYA 6/94)

1169 Svee, Gary. *Single Tree* (9–adult). 1994, Walker $19.95 (0-8027-4142-8). Runs Towards is adopted by a roaming Montana cowboy in the 1880s. Years later, as Towards journeys to their reunion, he rides with a ruthless vigilante. Awards: BL Editors' Choice. (Rev: BL 9/15/94*)

1170 Thoene, Brock. *The Legend of Storey County* (9–adult). 1995, Thomas Nelson $16.99

(0-7852-8070-7). The author and his wife wrote the best-selling *Twilight of Courage* with the same sly, good humor as this tall tale told from the point of view of Jim, who turns out to be the Jim of *Huck Finn* fame. (Rev: BL 11/1/95*)

1171 Wallace, Bill. *Buffalo Gal* (6–8). 1992, Holiday $13.95 (0-8234-0943-0). Amanda's plans for an elegant sixteenth birthday party evaporate when her mother drags her to the wilds of Texas to search for buffalo with cowboys. (Rev: BL 6/15/92; SLJ 5/92; YR)

1172 Windle, Janice Woods. *True Women* (9–adult). 1994, Putnam $22.95 (0-399-13813-7). Based on the author's own family, the adventures of Texans Euphemia, Georgia, and Bettie, as well as other female relatives of differing racial backgrounds. (Rev: BL 11/1/93; SLJ 9/94)

1173 Yep, Laurence. *Dragon's Gate* (6–9). 1993, HarperCollins LB $14.89 (0-06-022972-1). The adventures of a privileged Chinese teenager who travels to California in 1865 to join his father and uncle working on the transcontinental railroad. (Rev: BL 1/1/94; BTA; MJHS; SLJ 1/94; VOYA 12/93)

RECONSTRUCTION TO WORLD WAR I (1865–1914)

1174 Collier, James Lincoln. *My Crooked Family* (6–8). 1991, Simon & Schuster $15 (0-671-74224-8). Roger, age 14 and living in the slums in the early 1900s, steals in order to feed himself and becomes involved with the gang that killed his father. (Rev: BL 12/1/91; MJHS; SLJ 10/91)

1175 Cross, Gillian. *The Great American Elephant Chase* (5–8). 1993, Holiday $14.95 (0-8234-1016-1). In 1881, Tad, age 15, and Cissie attempt to get to Nebraska with her showman father's elephant, pursued by 2 unsavory characters who claim they had bought the elephant. Awards: SLJ Best Book. (Rev: BL 3/15/93*; SLJ 5/93*; VOYA 10/93)

1176 Dillard, Annie. *The Living* (9–adult). 1992, HarperCollins $22.50 (0-06-016870-6). Pioneers labor to build a new life in the Pacific Northwest. (Rev: BL 2/15/92*; SHS)

1177 Duffy, James. *Radical Red* (5–8). 1993, Scribner $13.95 (0-684-19533-X). This shows the plight of women in 1894 through the character of Connor O'Shea, 12, who is drawn into a suffrage demonstration while she and her mother are abused at home. (Rev: BL 12/1/93; SLJ 1/94; VOYA 2/94)

1178 Gibbons, Kaye. *Charms for the Easy Life* (9–adult). 1993, Putnam $21.50 (0-399-13791-2). Appealing characters and carefully selected period details make this intergenerational novel a delight. Awards: SLJ Best Book; YALSA Best Book for Young Adults. (Rev: BL 1/15/93; SLJ 9/93*)

1179 Gregory, Kristiana. *Earthquake at Dawn* (5–9). (Great Episodes) 1992, Harcourt/Gulliver $15.95 (0-15-200446-7). Based on actual letters and photos, this historical fiction depicts the devastating 1906 San Francisco earthquake. Awards: YALSA Best Book for Young Adults. (Rev: BL 4/15/92; BTA; SLJ 8/92; YR)

1180 Hesse, Karen. *A Time of Angels* (5–8). 1995, Hyperion LB $15.89 (0-7868-2072-1). Influenza sweeps a city and kills thousands. The sickened protagonist, Hannah, tries to escape its ravages by moving to Vermont, where an old farmer helps her. (Rev: BL 12/1/95; SLJ 12/95)

1181 Jackson, Dave, and Neta Jackson. *Danger on the Flying Trapeze* (6–8). 1995, Bethany paper $4.99 (1-55661-469-1). A 14-year-old joins the circus with his family to escape a dreary life. The boy hears the great evangelist D. L. Moody and learns something about the meaning of courage and faith. (Rev: BL 9/1/95; SLJ 12/95)

1182 Kirkpatrick, Katherine. *Keeping the Good Light* (7–12). 1995, Delacorte $14.95 (0-385-32161-9). In this coming-of-age story set in the early 1900s at a lighthouse on Long Island Sound, a young girl yearns to escape isolation. (Rev: BL 9/15/95; SLJ 8/95)

1183 Lawlor, Laurie. *Addie's Long Summer* (5–7). Illus. 1992, Albert Whitman $11.95 (0-8075-0167-0). In this third story about the farm life of the Mills family in the late nineteenth century, Addie can't wait to share the summer with her cousins, but they don't fit in easily at first. (Rev: BL 8/92; SLJ 11/92)

1184 Leonard, Laura. *Finding Papa* (5–7). 1991, Atheneum/Jean Karl $14.95 (0-689-31526-0). Three motherless children journey by train from Kansas to San Francisco in 1905 to join their irresponsible father, a would-be miner and full-time adventurer they hardly know. (Rev: BL 10/15/91; SLJ 9/91)

1185 Nixon, Joan Lowery. *Land of Dreams* (6–9). (Ellis Island) 1994, Delacorte $14.95 (0-385-31170-2). A Swedish immigrant in rural Minnesota who longs to move to Minneapolis learns the importance of community support when fire strikes her home. (Rev: BL 2/15/94; MJHS; SLJ 2/94)

1186 Nixon, Joan Lowery. *Land of Hope* (6–9). (Ellis Island) 1992, Bantam/Starfire $16 (0-553-08110-1). Rebekah, 15, and her family escape persecution in Russia in the early 1900s and flee to New York City to join Uncle Avir, where life is harsh but hopeful. (Rev: BL 12/15/92; MJHS; SLJ 10/92; YR)

1187 Nixon, Joan Lowery. *Land of Promise* (6–9). (Ellis Island) 1993, Bantam $16 (0-553-08111-X); 1994, Dell/Laurel Leaf paper $3.99 (0-440-21904-3). Focuses on Irish Rosie, one of 3 immigrant girls arriving in the United States in the early 1900s, and her adjustment to life in Chicago. (Rev: BL 12/1/93; MJHS; VOYA 10/93)

1188 Pfeffer, Susan Beth. *Nobody's Daughter* (5–7). 1995, Delacorte $14.95 (0-385-32106-6). Emily, 11, has been placed in an orphanage, but she's convinced her stay will last only until her "true" family is located. (Rev: BL 1/1/95; SLJ 3/95; VOYA 4/95)

1189 Sherman, Eileen Bluestone. *Independence Avenue* (5–9). 1990, Jewish Publication Society $13.95 (0-8276-0367-3). This Jewish immigration story (from Russia to Texas) set in 1907 has a resourceful, engaging hero, an unusual setting, and plenty of action. (Rev: BL 2/15/91; SLJ 1/91)

1190 Shivers, Louise. *A Whistling Woman* (9–adult). 1993, Longstreet $15 (1-56352-085-0). Set in North Carolina after the Civil War, this novel critically examines the relationship between a mother and daughter. (Rev: BL 8/93*)

1191 Shreve, Susan Richards. *Daughters of the New World* (9–adult). 1992, Doubleday $20 (0-385-26796-7). Chronicles a family of strong, resilient, loving women, from an 1890 transatlantic crossing through World War I. (Rev: BL 11/1/91*; SHS)

1192 Weitzman, David. *Thrashin' Time: Harvest Days in the Dakotas* (5–8). 1991, Godine $24.95 (0-87923-910-7). A young boy describes his first experience with a new-fangled steam engine threshing machine in 1912. (Rev: BL 3/1/92*)

1193 Wyman, Andrea. *Red Sky at Morning* (5–7). 1991, Holiday $13.95 (0-8234-0903-1). On an Indiana farm in 1909, 2 sisters and their grandfather must pull together when the girls' mother dies in childbirth. (Rev: BL 12/1/91; SLJ 9/91)

1194 Yektai, Niki. *The Secret Room* (5–7). 1992, Orchard LB $14.99 (0-531-08606-2). In 1903 New York City, Katharine and her brother Freddie discover a secret room they can hide in to escape their governess. (Rev: BL 10/1/92; YR)

BETWEEN WARS AND THE GREAT DEPRESSION (1919–1941)

1195 Corbin, William. *Me and the End of the World* (5–8). 1991, Simon & Schuster $15 (0-671-74223-X). When fringe religious leaders announce the world will end on May 1, 1928, Tim believes he has only a few months to live and assigns himself important challenges. (Rev: BL 11/1/91; SLJ 9/91)

1196 Crofford, Emily. *A Place to Belong* (5–7). 1994, Carolrhoda $19.95 (0-87614-808-9). A historical novel of family love and anger in hard times, told from the perspective of a 6th-grader. (Rev: BL 5/15/94; SLJ 6/94)

1197 French, Albert. *Billy* (9–adult). 1993, Viking $20 (0-670-85013-6). The tragedy of racism is underlined when 10-year-old Billy is tried as an adult in rural Mississippi for stabbing a 15-year-old girl in self-defense. Awards: SLJ Best Book; YALSA Best Book for Young Adults. (Rev: BL 10/1/93)

1198 Green, Connie Jordan. *Emmy* (5–8). 1992, Macmillan/Margaret K. McElderry $13.95 (0-689-50556-6). The story of perseverence and survival in a 1924 Kentucky mining town by Emmy, 11; her brother Gene, 14; their depressed father; and their mother, who is forced to take in boarders. (Rev: BL 12/1/92; SLJ 12/92; YR)

1199 Hesse, Karen. *Letters from Rifka* (5–8). 1992, Holt $14.95 (0-8050-1964-2); 1993, Penguin/Puffin paper $3.99 (0-14-036391-2). In letters to Russia, Rifka, 12, tells of her journey to the United States in 1919, from the dangerous escape over the border, across Europe and the sea, to America. Awards: ALSC Notable Children's Book; Barbara Cohen Memorial; Batchelder; Christopher; IRA Children's Book; National Jewish Book; SLJ Best Book; YALSA Best Book for Young Adults. (Rev: BL 7/92; MJHS; SLJ 8/92*)

1200 Horvath, Polly. *The Happy Yellow Car* (5–7). 1994, Farrar $15 (0-374-32845-5). Pork-Fry Queen Betty Grunt, 12, lives in a small Missouri town with her wacky family, including a father who has just spent her college fund on a new car. (Rev: BL 8/94; SLJ 9/94; VOYA 12/94)

1201 Karr, Kathleen. *The Cave* (5–7). 1994, Farrar $15 (0-374-31230-3). Christine's Depression-era farm family routinely fights dust storms, and her brother's asthma may force the family from their home. (Rev: BL 9/15/94; BTA; SLJ 9/94; VOYA 12/94)

1202 Koller, Jackie French. *Nothing to Fear* (5–7). 1991, Harcourt $15.95 (0-15-200544-7). Focuses on Danny's growing up as a first-generation Irish American in a New York City tenement in 1933. (Rev: BL 3/1/91; SLJ 5/91)

1203 Little, Jean. *His Banner over Me* (6–9). 1995, Viking $13.99 (0-670-85664-9). A child of missionaries moves from Taiwan to Canada, where her parents leave her to grow up many years on her own and a terminally ill woman changes her life dramatically. (Rev: BL 11/15/95; SLJ 12/95)

1204 Lord, Athena V. *Z.A.P., Zoe and the Musketeers* (5–7). 1992, Macmillan $13.95 (0-02-759561-7). A group of children call themselves "ZAP" and find adventure in the summer of 1941. (Rev: BL 4/1/92)

1205 Meyer, Carolyn. *White Lilacs* (6–9). 1993, Harcourt $10.95 (0-15-200641-9); paper $3.95 (0-15-200626-5). Shows how the "colored" section of Dillion, Texas, was turned into a park through intimidation, as told by teenager Rose Lee Jefferson. Based on a true story. Awards: YALSA Best Book for Young Adults. (Rev: BL 11/1/93; MJHS; SLJ 10/93; VOYA 12/93)

1206 Myers, Anna. *Red-Dirt Jessie* (5–7). 1992, Walker $13.95 (0-8027-8172-1); paper $4.95 (0-8027-7435-0). A poignant tale of a Depression-era Oklahoma family struggling valiantly against hard times, told by 12-year-old Jessie. (Rev: BL 1/15/93; SLJ 11/92*)

1207 Reeder, Carolyn. *Moonshiner's Son* (7–10). 1993, Macmillan $14.95 (0-02-775805-2). It's Prohibition, and Tom, 12, is learning the art of moonshining from his father—until he becomes friendly with the new preacher's daughter. (Rev: BL 6/1–15/93; SLJ 5/93; VOYA 8/93)

1208 Robinet, Harriette Gillem. *Mississippi Chariot* (6–10). 1994, Atheneum $14.95 (0-689-31960-6). Life in the 1930s Mississippi Delta is vividly evoked in this story of Shortning Bread, 12, whose father has been wrongfully convicted of a crime and sent to a chain gang. (Rev: BL 11/15/94; BTA; SLJ 12/94; VOYA 5/95)

1209 Singer, Isaac Bashevis. *The Certificate* (9–adult). Tr. by Leonard Wolf. 1992, Farrar $22 (0-374-12029-3). A shy, 19-year-old aspiring writer enters into a "fictive marriage" with an aristocratic woman who loves another man. (Rev: BL 10/15/92; SHS)

1210 Snyder, Zilpha Keatley. *Cat Running* (5–7). 1994, Delacorte $14.95 (0-385-31056-0). During the Great Depression, a young girl and boy race against time, the weather, and prejudice for medical help for his little sister. Awards: SLJ Best Book. (Rev: SLJ 11/94)

1211 Tsukiyama, Gail. *Women of the Silk* (9–adult). 1991, St. Martin's $18.95 (0-312-06465-9). Spanning the years between the world wars, this tale of a young Chinese girl forced to work in a silk factory describes the sisterhood of workers she discovers there. Awards: SLJ Best Book. (Rev: BL 9/15/91; SLJ 3/92)

1212 Van Raven, Pieter. *A Time of Troubles* (6–10). 1990, Scribner $13.95 (0-684-19212-8). A young boy and his ex-convict father seek work in California during the Depression. Awards: O'Dell Award for Historical Fiction. (Rev: BL 1/15/91)

1213 Whittaker, Dorothy Raymond. *Angels of the Swamp* (6–8). 1991, Walker $15.95 (0-8027-8129-2). Two teenage orphans survive on an island off the Florida coast, then discover they're not alone. (Rev: BL 1/15/92; SLJ 4/92; YR)

Twentieth-Century Wars

WORLD WAR I

1214 Kinsey-Warnock, Natalie. *The Night the Bells Rang* (5–7). Illus. 1991, Dutton/Cobblehill $12.95 (0-525-65074-1). Growing up on a Vermont farm during World War I, Mason has an ambivalent relationship with the school bully, Aden, who enlists in the army and is killed. (Rev: BL 11/15/91; SLJ 2/92)

1215 Skurzynski, Gloria. *Good-bye, Billy Radish* (5–7). 1992, Bradbury $14.95 (0-02-782921-9). Against a backdrop of Pennsylvania steel mills during World War I, the story of 2 boys' bond despite different backgrounds. Awards: Jefferson Cup Honor Book; SLJ Best Book. (Rev: BL 10/15/92; SLJ 12/92*; YR)

WORLD WAR II AND THE HOLOCAUST

1216 Almagor, Gila. *Under the Domim Tree* (6–9). 1995, Simon & Schuster $15 (0-671-89020-4). An autobiographical novel about young Holocaust survivors in an agricultural youth village in Israel in 1953. Awards: National Jewish Book. (Rev: BL 5/1/95; SLJ 6/95)

1217 Anderson, Rachel. *Paper Faces* (6–12). 1993, Holt $14.95 (0-8050-2527-8). Dot has lived her life in poverty in World War II London with her mother. The end of the war brings change—including her father's return—that she dreads. Awards: Guardian Award for Children's Fiction. (Rev: BL 11/1/93*; SLJ 12/93; VOYA 12/93)

1218 Atlan, Lilane. *The Passersby* (9–12). Tr. by Rochelle Owens. Illus. 1993, Holt $13.95 (0-8050-3054-9). This prose poem pictures No, an anorexic teenager, as searching for an ideal, purpose, and friends while confronted with the reality of her adopted brother's experiences in Auschwitz. (Rev: BL 12/1/93; SLJ 12/93; VOYA 2/94)

1219 Bawden, Nina. *The Real Plato Jones* (5–8). 1993, Clarion $13.95 (0-395-66972-3). British teen Plato Jones and his mother return to Greece for his grandfather's funeral, where Plato discovers that his grandfather may have been a coward and traitor in the Greek resistance. Awards: SLJ Best Book. (Rev: BL 10/15/93; BTA; SLJ 11/93*)

1220 Baylis-White, Mary. *Sheltering Rebecca* (5–7). 1991, Dutton/Lodestar $14.95 (0-525-67349-0). As two 6th-grade girls in England during World War II become friends, one of them, a Jewish refugee, tells of her escape from Nazi Germany. (Rev: BL 10/15/91)

1221 Bergman, Tamar. *Along the Tracks* (6–9). Tr. by Michael Swirsky. 1991, Houghton $14.95 (0-395-55328-8). The story of an 8-year-old Jewish boy who is separated from his parents during World War II and wanders through Russia for 4 years in search of them. Awards: ALSC Notable Children's Book; SLJ Best Book. (Rev: BL 9/15/91; MJHS; SLJ 12/91) [940.53]

1222 Bunting, Eve. *Spying on Miss Miller* (6–8). 1995, Clarion $13.95 (0-395-69172-9). During World War II in Belfast, Jessie, 13, believes her half-German teacher is a spy. (Rev: BL 3/15/95*; SLJ 5/95)

1223 Carter, Peter. *The Hunted* (8–12). 1994, Farrar $17 (0-374-33520-6). In 1943, Vito Salvani is traveling from Italy to his home in France with a small Jewish boy, pursued by the Milici (Italy's Gestapo). (Rev: BL 4/1/94; BTA; MJHS; SHS; SLJ 6/94; VOYA 10/94)

1224 Coerr, Eleanor. *Mieko and the Fifth Treasure* (5–7). 1993, Putnam $14.95 (0-399-22434-3); 1994, Dell/Yearling paper $3.50 (0-440-40947-0). When the atom bomb drops on Nagasaki, Mieko's life is changed forever: She cuts her hand on glass, leaving a terrible scar, and she's convinced that she'll never paint again. (Rev: BL 4/1/93*; SLJ 7/93)

1225 Cormier, Robert. *Tunes for Bears to Dance To* (6–12). 1992, Delacorte $15 (0-385-30818-3); 1994, Dell/Laurel Leaf paper $3.99 (0-440-21903-5). In a stark morality tale set in a Massachusetts town after World War II, Henry, age 11, is tempted, corrupted, and redeemed. Awards: YALSA Best Book for Young Adults. (Rev: BL 6/15/92; MJHS; SLJ 9/92; YR)

1226 Cutler, Jane. *My Wartime Summers* (5–7). 1994, Farrar $15 (0-374-35111-2). Tomboy Ellen, 11, comes of age during World War II. Her uncle fights in France, and her friends, including a Holocaust refugee, begin to like boys. (Rev: BL 10/1/94*; SLJ 11/94; VOYA 4/93)

1227 Dillon, Ellis. *Children of Bach* (7–10). 1992, Scribner $13.95 (0-684-19440-6). When a group of Hungarian Jewish children return from school to find that their parents have been taken away by Nazis, they must escape over the mountains to safety in Italy. (Rev: BL 12/1/92; BTA; MJHS; SLJ 12/92; YR)

1228 Drucker, Malka, and Michael Halperin. *Jacob's Rescue: A Holocaust Story* (6–10). 1993, Bantam/Skylark $15 (0-553-08976-5); 1994, Dell/Yearling paper $3.99 (0-440-40965-9). The fictionalized true story of 2 Jewish children saved from the Holocaust in Poland by "Righteous Gentiles." (Rev: BL 2/15/93; MJHS; SLJ 5/93)

1229 Hahn, Mary Downing. *Stepping on the Cracks* (5–8). 1991, Clarion $13.95 (0-395-58507-4). Describes the moral conflict of a 6th-grade girl in a small town who must decide whether to help a pacifist deserter from World War II. Awards: O'Dell Award for Historical Fiction; SLJ Best Book. (Rev: BL 10/15/91*; MJHS; SLJ 12/91*)

1230 Hotze, Sollace. *Summer Endings* (5–7). 1991, Clarion $13.95 (0-395-56197-3). The large events and minutiae of the summer of 1945 as they affect 12-year-old Christine in Chicago. (Rev: BL 5/1/91; MJHS; SLJ 6/91)

1231 Kennedy, Raymond. *The Bitterest Age* (9–adult). 1994, Ticknor & Fields $19.95 (0-395-68629-6). A young girl's extraordinary effort to survive with her faith and dignity intact during the bleak final year of World War II. Awards: BL Editors' Choice. (Rev: BL 4/15/94; BTA)

1232 Kertesz, Imre. *Fateless* (9–adult). Tr. by Christopher C. Wilson. 1992, Northwestern Univ. $58.95 (0-8101-1024-5); paper $12.95 (0-8101-1049-0). A Holocaust survival tale told from the viewpoint of a Hungarian Jewish teenager. Awards: BL Editors' Choice. (Rev: BL 9/15/92)

1233 Laird, Christa. *But Can the Phoenix Sing?* (7–10). 1995, Greenwillow $15 (0-688-13612-5). A Holocaust survivor story where a young boy learns that cruelty and tenderness can reside at the same time in one person. (Rev: BL 11/15/95; SLJ 10/95)

1234 Levitin, Sonia. *Annie's Promise* (6–10). 1993, Atheneum $14.95 (0-689-31752-2). Set near the end of World War II, this sequel to *Silver Days* focuses on 13-year-old Annie's break from her overprotective Jewish immigrant parents. (Rev: BL 2/1/93; MJHS; SLJ 4/93)

1235 Levitin, Sonia. *Journey to America* (5–7). Illus. 1993, Atheneum $13.95 (0-689-31829-4). The story of a courageous Jewish family that flees Hitler's Germany for Switzerland in 1938. (Rev: BL 9/1/93; MJHS)

1236 Manley, Joan B. *She Flew No Flags* (7–10). 1995, Houghton $14.95 (0-395-71130-4). A strongly autobiographical World War II novel about a 10-year-old's voyage from India to her new home in the United States and the people she meets on the ship. (Rev: BL 3/15/95; SLJ 4/95; VOYA 5/95)

1237 Matas, Carol. *Daniel's Story* (6–9). 1993, Scholastic $13.95 (0-590-46920-7). In this companion to an exhibit at the U.S. Holocaust Memorial Museum, Daniel symbolizes the millions of young people who suffered or died under Hitler's regime. (Rev: BL 5/15/93; BTA; MJHS)

1238 Michener, James A. *South Pacific* (5–9). Illus. 1992, Harcourt/Gulliver LB $16.95 (0-15-200618-4). A retelling of *South Pacific* for youth. (Rev: BL 9/1/92; SLJ 11/92)

1239 Morpurgo, Michael. *Waiting for Anya* (5–8). 1991, Viking $12.95 (0-670-83735-0). Set in occupied France, Jo, age 12, helps a group of Jewish children hide from the Germans and then escape over the mountains to Spain. Awards: SLJ Best Book; YALSA Best Book for Young Adults. (Rev: BL 5/15/91; SLJ 4/91*)

1240 Nolan, Han. *If I Should Die Before I Wake* (7–10). 1994, Harcourt $10.95 (0-15-238040-X). Teenager Hilary—who hangs out with neo-Nazis—is in a hospital after an accident. Next to her is a Holocaust survivor, Chana; and before Hilary regains consciousness, she slips into Chana's memory and travels back in time to Auschwitz. (Rev: BL 4/1/94; BTA; SLJ 4/94; VOYA 6/94)

1241 Orlev, Uri. *The Man from the Other Side* (6–10). Tr. by Hillel Halkin. 1991, Houghton $13.95 (0-395-53808-4). The story of a teenager in Nazi-occupied Warsaw who helps desperate Jews despite his dislike of them. Awards: ALSC Notable Children's Book; BL Editors' Choice; Batchelder; IBBY; National Jewish Book; SLJ Best Book; YALSA Best Book for Young Adults. (Rev: BL 6/15/91*; MJHS; SLJ 9/91*)

1242 Ray, Karen. *To Cross a Line* (7–10). 1994, Orchard/Richard Jackson LB $15.99 (0-531-08681-X). The story of a 17-year-old Jewish boy who is pursued by the Gestapo and encounters barriers in his desperate attempts to escape Nazi Germany. (Rev: BL 2/15/94; BTA; SLJ 6/94; VOYA 6/94)

1243 Reuter, Bjarne. *The Boys from St. Petri* (7–10). Tr. by Anthea Bell. 1994, Dutton $14.99 (0-525-45121-8). Danish teenager Lars and his friends fight the Nazi occupation of their home town during World War II and plan to blow up a train. Awards: ALSC Notable Children's Book; Batchelder; SLJ Best Book; YALSA Best Book for Young Adults. (Rev: BL 2/1/94; BTA; MJHS; SLJ 2/94; VOYA 4/94)

1244 Rochman, Hazel, and Darlene Z. McCampbell, eds. *Bearing Witness: Stories of the Holocaust* (7–12). 1995, Orchard/Melanie Kroupa LB $15.99 (0-531-08788-3). This anthology of 24 works revolving around the Holocaust includes memoirs, poetry, short stories, a film script, a letter, and a comic strip. (Rev: BL 6/1–15/95; SLJ 9/95; VOYA 12/95) [808]

1245 Rylant, Cynthia. *I Had Seen Castles* (6–12). 1993, Harcourt $10.95 (0-15-238003-5). A strong message about the physical and emotional costs of war—in this story, the toll of World War II on John, a Canadian adolescent. (Rev: BL 9/1/93; VOYA 2/94)

1246 Salisbury, Graham. *Under the Blood-Red Sun* (5–9). 1994, Delacorte $15.95 (0-385-32099-X). Tomi, born in Hawaii of Japanese parents, struggles during World War II, facing suspicion and hatred from classmates. His father is sent to a U.S. prison camp. Awards: O'Dell Award for Historical Fiction; SLJ Best Book. (Rev: BL 10/15/94*; BTA; MJHS; SLJ 10/94; VOYA 10/94)

1247 Savin, Marcia. *The Moon Bridge* (5–7). 1992, Scholastic $13.95 (0-590-45873-6). Fifth-grader Ruthie defends Japanese American Mitzi from schoolyard persecution and becomes her best friend in 1941 San Francisco. (Rev: BL 11/15/92; SLJ 1/93)

1248 Thesman, Jean. *Molly Donnelly* (6–9). 1993, Houghton $13.95 (0-395-64348-1); 1994, Avon/Flare paper $3.99 (0-380-72252-6). The saga of a young girl's growing up in Seattle during World War II and coping with not only the changes wrought by war but typical adolescent concerns. (Rev: BL 4/1/93; MJHS; SLJ 5/93; VOYA 8/93)

1249 van Dijk, Lutz. *Damned Strong Love: The True Story of Willi G. and Stefan K.* (8–12). Tr. by Elizabeth D. Crawford. 1995, Holt $15.95 (0-8050-3770-5). Nazi persecution of homosexuals, based on the life of Stefan K., a Polish teenager. Awards: ALSC Notable Children's Book. (Rev: BL 5/15/95; SLJ 8/95)

1250 Voigt, Cynthia. *David and Jonathan* (8–12). 1992, Scholastic $14 (0-590-45165-0). A holocaust survivor darkens the life of his American cousin with gruesome stories of the prison camps. (Rev: BL 3/1/92; SHS; SLJ 3/92; YR)

1251 Vos, Ida. *Anna Is Still Here* (5–7). Tr. by Terese Edelstein and Inez Smidt. 1993, Houghton $13.95 (0-395-65368-1). Re-creates the Holocaust survivor experience from the viewpoint of Anna, 13, who's trying to adjust to home and school in the Netherlands after the war. (Rev: BL 4/15/93*; SLJ 5/93)

1252 Vos, Ida. *Dancing on the Bridge at Avignon* (5–8). Tr. by Terese Edelstein and Inez Smidt. 1995, Houghton $14.95 (0-395-72039-7). A translation from the Dutch of wartime experiences for the Jews in the Netherlands and one particular young Jewish girl, Rosa. (Rev: BL 10/15/95; SLJ 10/95; VOYA 2/96)

1253 Westall, Robert. *Echoes of War* (7–12). 1991, Farrar $13.95 (0-374-31964-2). Five short stories about ordinary people caught up in war and its aftermath. (Rev: BL 8/91; SLJ 8/91)

1254 Westall, Robert. *The Promise* (6–10). 1991, Scholastic $13.95 (0-590-43760-7). Bob's friendship with beautiful, sickly Valerie becomes romantic; when she dies, only Bob know that her spirit still lingers among the living. (Rev: BL 3/1/91; MJHS; SLJ 3/91)

1255 Yep, Laurence. *Hiroshima* (5–7). 1995, Scholastic $9.95 (0-590-20832-2); paper $2.99 (0-590-20833-0). A sparely fictionalized account of the dropping of the bomb on Hiroshima in 1945 told through many points of view. (Rev: BL 3/15/95*; SLJ 5/95)

KOREAN, VIETNAM, AND OTHER WARS

1256 Baillie, Allan. *Little Brother* (5–7). 1992, Viking $14 (0-670-84381-4); 1994, Penguin/Puffin paper $3.99 (0-14-036862-0). A boy must try to survive on his own after losing his family in the Cambodian war. (Rev: BL 1/15/92; SLJ 3/92)

1257 Emerson, Zack. *Welcome to Vietnam* (8–12). 1991, Scholastic paper $2.95 (0-590-44591-X). A 19-year-old infantryman in Vietnam faces the boredom, fear, and danger of the war and performs a courageous act. (Rev: BL 11/191; SLJ 2/92)

1258 Forsyth, Frederick. *The Fist of God* (9–adult). 1994, Bantam $23.95 (0-553-09126-3). Two British brothers who are espionage experts organize an elaborate mission to find a secret weapon that's in Saddam Hussein's possession. (Rev: BL 3/1/94)

1259 Kerr, M. E. *Linger* (7–12). 1993, HarperCollins LB $14.89 (0-06-022882-2). In a story filled with wit and sadness, Kerr tells of kids entangled in love, war, and work. (Rev: BL 6/1–15/93; BTA; MJHS; SLJ 7/93; VOYA 8/93)

1260 Potok, Chaim. *I Am the Clay* (9–adult). 1992, Knopf $20 (0-679-41195-X). An injured orphan boy touches the hearts of a crusty Korean refugee and his more compassionate wife. (Rev: BL 4/1/92; SHS; SLJ 12/92)

1261 Qualey, Marsha. *Come in from the Cold* (9–12). 1994, Houghton $14.95 (0-395-68986-4). In 1969, Maud's sister is killed while protesting the Vietnam War. Jeff's brother dies fighting in it. Maud and Jeff are drawn together by mutual grief and hope. Awards: SLJ Best Book; YALSA Best Book for Young Adults. (Rev: BL 9/15/94; BTA; SLJ 12/94; VOYA 10/94)

1262 Talbert, Marc. *The Purple Heart* (5–8). 1991, HarperCollins/Willa Perlman LB $13.89 (0-06-020429-X). Luke's father has returned from Vietnam an anguished, brooding war hero, and Luke loses his father's Purple Heart, leading to confrontation and reconciliation. (Rev: BL 12/15/91*; MJHS; SLJ 2/92)

1263 Whelan, Gloria. *Goodbye, Vietnam* (5–7). 1992, Knopf/Borzoi LB $13.99 (0-679-92263-6); 1993, Random/Bullseye paper $3.99 (0-679-82376-X). A voyage of tragic dimensions of Mai and her family, from Vietnam's Mekong Delta swamps to the sea and to Hong Kong and freedom. (Rev: BL 1/1/93; BTA; SLJ 9/92)

1264 White, Ellen Emerson. *The Road Home* (8–12). 1995, Scholastic $15.95 (0-590-46737-9). Re-creates a Vietnam War medical base in claustrophobic and horrific detail, starring Rebecca Phillips, from the Echo Company series. (Rev: BL 1/15/95; SLJ 4/95; VOYA 4/95)

Horror Stories and the Supernatural

1265 Aiken, Joan. *A Fit of Shivers: Tales for Late at Night* (7–10). 1992, Delacorte $15 (0-385-30691-1). Vengeful ghosts, eerie dreams, and haunted houses abound in these 10 tales. (Rev: BL 9/1/92; MJHS)

1266 Aiken, Joan. *A Foot in the Grave* (6–10). Illus. 1992, Viking LB $15.95 (0-670-84169-2). A series of ghost stories illustrated by surrealistic paintings. (Rev: BL 3/15/92; SLJ 5/92)

1267 Alphin, Elaine Marie. *The Ghost Cadet* (5–7). 1991, Holt $13.95 (0-8050-1614-7). While visiting his grandmother in Virginia, Benjy learns lessons about the Civil War and has adventures with the ghost of a cadet who was killed nearby. (Rev: BL 5/1/91; SLJ 5/91)

1268 Bauer, Marion Dane. *A Taste of Smoke* (5–7). 1993, Clarion $13.95 (0-395-64341-4); 1995, Dell/Yearling paper $3.99 (0-440-41034-7). Caitlin, age 13, goes camping in Minnesota with her sister Pam. When Pam's boyfriend joins them, Caitlin feels angry and abandoned. It's then that she begins to see the ghost of an orphan boy. (Rev: BL 10/15/93; MJHS; SLJ 12/93; VOYA 2/94)

1269 Bellairs, John, and Brad Strickland. *The Drum, the Doll, and the Zombie* (5–7). 1994, Dial LB $14.89 (0-8037-1463-7). Johnny Dixon, Fergie Ferguson, Father Higgins, and Professor Childermass join together again, this time battling zombies and demons invoked by the evil Madame Sinestra. Sequel to *The Secret of the Underground Room*. (Rev: BL 7/94; MJHS; SLJ 10/94; VOYA 5/95)

1270 Bellairs, John, and Brad Strickland. *The Ghost in the Mirror* (5–7). 1993, Dial LB $14.89 (0-8037-1371-1). Good-witch Mrs. Zimmerman travels with Rose Rita, 14, to Pennsylvania to regain her lost magical powers, when they are transported to 1828. (Rev: BL 2/15/93; VOYA 10/93)

1271 Block, Francesca Lia. *Missing Angel Juan* (8–12). (Weetzie Bat Saga) 1993, HarperCollins LB $13.89 (0-06-023007-X). Witch Baby, aided by her grandfather's ghost, roams New York City, looking for Angel Juan, who's left her behind to play music on the city streets. Awards: SLJ Best Book. (Rev: BL 10/15/93; BTA; SLJ 10/93*; VOYA 12/93)

1272 Bradbury, Ray. *The Ray Bradbury Chronicles, Vol. 5* (9–adult). Illus. 1994, NBM Publishing (185 Madison Ave., Suite 1502, New York, NY 10016) $19.95 (1-56163-080-2). One of 7 volumes containing new stories in comic book format with subtle, complex artwork. (Rev: BL 2/1/94) [741.5]

1273 Brown, Roberta Simpson. *The Queen of the Cold-Blooded Tales* (6–9). 1993, August House $19 (0-87483-332-9). A collection of 23 contemporary horror stories. (Rev: BL 9/1/93; VOYA 4/94) [813]

1274 Buffie, Margaret. *Someone Else's Ghost* (8–12). 1995, Scholastic $14.95 (0-590-46922-3). A girl's brother dies and haunts the family both literally and figuratively, for the family's new home seems to have a presence. (Rev: BL 3/1/95; SLJ 3/95; VOYA 4/95)

1275 Buffie, Margaret. *The Warnings* (7–12). 1991, Scholastic $13.95 (0-590-43665-1). Rachel leads a lonely life with the old people (the Fossils) until she receives the Warnings, strange psychic messages that let her know of a grave threat. (Rev: BL 3/15/91; BY; MJHS)

1276 Burgess, Melvin. *Burning Issy* (7–10). 1994, Simon & Schuster $15 (0-671-89003-4). Burgess's story, set in medieval times, asks What if there really were witches, and What if they were ordinary women and men who were secret followers of a religion of nature worship? (Rev: BL 1/1/95; SLJ 12/94; VOYA 4/95)

1277 Butler, Beverly. *Witch's Fire* (5–7). 1993, Dutton $14.99 (0-525-65132-2). Kirsty, paralyzed after an accident that killed her mother and sister, lives with her father and stepmother and she must come to grips with a witch trying to get her home back. (Rev: BL 8/93; MJHS; VOYA 12/93)

1278 Campbell, Ramsey. *Alone with the Horrors: The Great Short Fiction of Ramsey Campbell, 1961–1991* (9–adult). 1993, Arkham $26.95 (0-87054-165-X). This horror collection contains uneasy spirits, brutal revenge, black magic, atmospheric settings, taut language, and many plot twists. (Rev: BL 2/1/93; VOYA 8/93)

1279 Cavanagh, Helen. *Panther Glade* (5–8). 1993, Simon & Schuster $15 (0-671-75617-6). Bill spends a summer in Florida with his great-aunt Cait. He's afraid of the Everglades and alligators, but he comes to appreciate Indian history and crafts. (Rev: BL 6/1–15/93; SLJ 6/93; VOYA 10/93)

1280 Cohen, Daniel. *Phantom Animals* (6–9). 1991, Putnam $13.95 (0-399-22230-8). Short selections featuring ghostly dogs, scary kangaroos, menacing birds, and phantom cats. (Rev: BL 8/91; MJHS; SLJ 7/91)

1281 Cooney, Caroline B. *Night School* (7–10). 1995, Scholastic paper $3.50 (0-590-47878-8). Four California teens enroll in a mysterious night school course and encounter an evil instructor and their own worst character defects. (Rev: BL 5/1/95)

1282 Coville, Bruce. *Oddly Enough* (6–9). 1994, Harcourt/Jane Yolen $15.95 (0-15-200093-3). Nine short horror stories involving blood drinking, elves, unicorns, ghosts, werewolves, and executioners. Awards: SLJ Best Book; YALSA Best Book for Young Adults. (Rev: BL 10/1/94; MJHS; SLJ 12/94; VOYA 2/95)

1283 Cramer, Alexander. *A Night in Moonbeam County* (6–8). 1994, Scribner $15.95 (0-684-19704-9). City kids are hosted by some hobo spirits who tell these 10 mystical stories. (Rev: BL 5/15/94; SLJ 6/94; VOYA 10/94)

1284 Cullen, Lynn. *The Backyard Ghost* (5–7). 1993, Clarion $13.95 (0-395-64527-1). A skillful blending of ghost story and the politics of junior high popularity. (Rev: BL 6/1–15/93; SLJ 5/93)

1285 Dark, Larry, ed. *The Literary Ghost: Great Contemporary Ghost Stories* (9–adult). 1991, Atlantic Monthly $22.95 (0-87113-474-8). Twenty-eight ghost stories from such celebrated authors as Oates, Gordimer, Greene, Sexton, Singer, and Bowles. (Rev: BL 10/15/91; SHS)

1286 Dean, Jan. *Finders* (6–9). 1995, Macmillan/Margaret K. McElderry $15 (0-689-50612-0). Helen Draper, 16, inherits her grandfather's gift of "finding" people and things, but when kelpie Nicholas Morgan asks her to find a special stone, her life is in jeopardy. (Rev: BL 5/1/95)

1287 Farmer, Penelope. *Thicker Than Water* (5–7). 1993, Candlewick $14.95 (1-56402-178-5). Will is haunted by a ghost of a boy trapped in an English mine. (Rev: BL 3/1/93; SLJ 4/93)

1288 Fremont, Eleanor. *Tales from the Crypt, Vol. 1* (5–7). 1991, Random paper $2.99 (0-679-81799-9). Adaptations of gruesome horror tales, several of which have made the transition to television. (Rev: BL 9/1/91)

1289 Gale, David, ed. *Don't Give Up the Ghost: The Delacorte Book of Original Ghost Stories* (5–7). 1993, Delacorte paper $14.95 (0-385-31109-5). A satisfying roundup of original ghost stories by 12 of the best children's authors. (Rev: BL 8/93; MJHS; VOYA 12/93)

1290 Gallo, Donald R., ed. *Short Circuits: Thirteen Shocking Stories by Outstanding Writers for Young Adults* (7–10). 1992, Delacorte $16 (0-385-30785-3). More scary stories, with much humor, a little voodoo, ghosts, werewolves, etc. (Rev: BL 12/1/92; MJHS; SHS; SLJ 11/92; YR)

1291 Galloway, Priscilla. *Truly Grim Tales* (7–12). 1995, Delacorte $10.95 (0-385-32200-3). A newer, grim version of familiar tales. (Rev: BL 9/15/95; SLJ 9/95)

1292 Garden, Nancy. *My Sister, the Vampire* (6–8). 1992, Knopf/Bullseye LB $8.99 (0-679-92659-3); paper $3.99 (0-679-82659-9). The traditional vampire story has been modernized and moved to a small town in Maine, where strange events affect Sarah, age 13, Tim, 12, and Jenny, 5. (Rev: BL 7/92; SLJ 9/92)

1293 Gordon, John. *The Burning Baby* (9–12). 1993, Candlewick $14.95 (1-56402-067-3). Five macabre tales of murder or suicide victims returning to exact gruesome revenge. (Rev: BL 10/15/93; BTA; SLJ 11/93)

1294 Gorog, Judith. *On Meeting Witches at Wells* (5–8). 1991, Putnam/Philomel $14.95 (0-399-21803-3). A procession of odd storytellers appears to a class of 8th-graders assembling story pillows and spin the tales that will stuff the pillows. (Rev: BL 12/15/91; SLJ 1/92)

1295 Gorog, Judith. *Please Do Not Touch* (6–12). 1993, Scholastic $13.95 (0-590-46682-8). The reader enters a different fantasy for each of the 11 horror stories. (Rev: BL 9/1/93; VOYA 12/93)

1296 Griffiths, Barbara. *Frankenstein's Hamster: Ten Spine-Tingling Tales* (6–9). 1992, Dial $15 (0-8037-0952-8). Ten creepy stories, often with offbeat humor, in various settings—e.g., an Egyptian tomb, a housing development, and a child's birthday party. (Rev: BL 6/15/92; SLJ 8/92; YR)

1297 Hahn, Mary Downing. *Look for Me by Moonlight* (7–10). 1995, Clarion $13.95 (0-395-69843-X). A 16-year-old girl, grateful for friendship, meets a boy whose attention has dangerous strings attached. (Rev: BL 3/15/95; SLJ 5/95)

1298 Hambly, Barbara. *Traveling with the Dead* (9–adult). 1995, Ballantine/Del Rey $22 (0-345-38102-5). A retired British Intelligence officer discovers an Austrian spymaster who can command the services of the undead as well as the living. A sequel to *Those Who Hunt the Night.* (Rev: BL 9/15/95; VOYA 4/96)

1299 Haskins, James. *The Headless Haunt and Other African American Ghost Stories* (5–8). 1994, HarperCollins LB $13.89 (0-06-022997-7). Anecdotes and background information about each tale. (Rev: BL 10/1/94; MJHS; SLJ 10/94; VOYA 2/95) [398.25]

1300 Henry, Maeve. *A Gift for a Gift: A Ghost Story* (6–9). 1992, Delacorte $14 (0-385-30562-1). Sick of the squalid English household where her family depends on her to cook, clean, and cope, Fran, age 15, walks out on them one night. (Rev: BL 6/15/92; YR)

1301 Hill, Mary, ed. *Creepy Classics: Hair-Raising Horror from the Masters of the Macabre* (6–10). 1994, Random paper $4.99 (0-679-86692-2). Gothic horror stories, poems, and novel excerpts by masters of the genre. Includes selections from Poe and an excerpt from Shelley's *Frankenstein*. (Rev: BL 10/15/94; SLJ 11/94)

1302 Hodges, Margaret. *Hauntings: Ghosts and Ghouls from Around the World* (5–8). Illus. 1991, Little, Brown $16.95 (0-316-36796-6). A diverse collection of 16 familiar and lesser-known tales about the supernatural. (Rev: BL 11/15/91; SLJ 11/91) [398.2]

1303 Hotze, Sollace. *Acquainted with the Night* (8–12). 1992, Clarion $13.95 (0-395-61576-3). Combines a tantalizing mystery/ghost story (based on a true story) with an exploration of the relationship between Molly, 17, and her cousin Caleb, recovering from the Vietnam War and his father's suicide. Awards: YALSA Best Book for Young Adults. (Rev: BL 12/1/92*; SLJ 11/92)

1304 Hughes, Dean. *Nutty's Ghost* (6–8). 1993, Atheneum $13.95 (0-689-31743-3). Nutty lands the lead in a terrible movie, and the ghost of a Shakespearean actor uses Nutty to gain revenge on the movie's director. (Rev: BL 2/15/93; SLJ 5/93)

1305 Jacques, Brian. *Seven Strange and Ghostly Tales* (5–7). 1991, Putnam/Philomel $14.95 (0-399-22103-4). Although they take place in contemporary English settings of home and school, each story in this humorous collection contains horrifying supernatural elements. (Rev: BL 11/1/91*; SLJ 12/91)

1306 James, J. Alison. *Runa* (7–9). 1993, Atheneum $13.95 (0-689-31708-5). Runa, 13, spends the summer on a Swedish island, where she becomes caught up in a family curse imposed by Norse gods. (Rev: BL 7/93; SLJ 7/93; VOYA 10/93)

1307 Jennings, Paul. *Undone! More Mad Endings* (5–8). 1995, Viking $14.99 (0-670-86005-0). In this collection of 8 stories, the Australian author steps into fantastical realms without ever losing touch with firm ground. (Rev: BL 1/1/95; SLJ 1/95)

1308 Jennings, Paul. *Unmentionable! More Amazing Stories* (8–12). 1993, Viking $13.99 (0-670-84734-8). The fourth in a series of short stories of the supernatural, set in Australia. (Rev: BL 3/15/93; MJHS)

1309 Jennings, Paul. *Unreal! Eight Surprising Stories* (5–8). 1991, Viking $12.95 (0-670-84175-7). An assortment of short stories ranging from funny to scary to gross, all told by young boys. Awards: SLJ Best Book. (Rev: BL 8/91; SLJ 12/91*) [823.54]

1310 Katz, Welwyn Wilton. *Come Like Shadows* (10–12). 1993, Viking $13.99 (0-670-84861-1). The superstition that Shakespeare's *Macbeth* is cursed comes alive when 2 young people involved in its production see visions in a prop mirror. (Rev: BL 12/1/93; SLJ 12/93; VOYA 10/93)

1311 Kehret, Peg. *Horror at the Haunted House* (5–7). 1992, Dutton/Cobblehill $14 (0-525-65106-3). When Ellen and her brother Corey join a Halloween haunted house project, she discovers that she's haunted by the ghost of Lydia, who died 3 years before. (Rev: BL 9/1/92; MJHS; SLJ 9/92)

1312 Kelleher, Victor. *Del-Del* (7–12). Illus. 1992, Walker $16.95 (0-8027-8154-3). A family believes its son is possessed by an evil alien. (Rev: BL 3/1/92; SLJ 6/92; YR)

1313 Klein, Robin. *Tearaways* (6–10). 1991, Viking $12.95 (0-670-83212-X). This short-story collection combines shivery horror with laughter. (Rev: BL 6/15/91; SLJ 6/91)

1314 Lehr, Norma. *The Shimmering Ghost of Riversend* (5–7). 1991, Lerner LB $12.95 (0-8225-0732-3). Kathy spends the summer at an old family mansion and is contacted by a ghostly black-clothed woman who may be the murderer or the victim in a long-ago scandal. (Rev: BL 10/1/91)

1315 Levy, Elizabeth. *The Drowned* (7–12). 1995, Hyperion $16.95 (0-7868-0135-2). A supernatural potboiler with a demented mother who ritually drowns a teenager and a drowned victim who returns to life. (Rev: BL 12/1/95; SLJ 12/95)

1316 Locke, Joseph. *Game Over* (7–10). 1993, Bantam paper $3.50 (0-553-29652-3). Joe, a video game champ, finds himself in Hades, locked in combat with the arcade's owner, Mr. Blacke. (Rev: BL 8/93; SLJ 7/93; VOYA 4/94)

1317 Lyons, Mary E., ed. *Raw Head, Bloody Bones: African-American Tales of the Supernatural* (5–7). 1991, Scribner $11.95 (0-684-19333-7). These bone-chilling tales include information on their sources. Awards: SLJ Best Book. (Rev: BL 1/1/92; SLJ 12/91*) [398.2]

1318 Macdonald, Caroline. *Hostilities: Nine Bizarre Stories* (7–10). 1994, Scholastic $13.95 (0-590-46063-3). A collection of 9 tales with strange, unsettling themes and Australian locales. (Rev: BL 1/15/94; SLJ 3/94; VOYA 10/94)

1319 Macdonald, Caroline. *Secret Lives* (8–12). 1995, Simon & Schuster $14 (0-671-51081-9). When imaginary rebel Gideon begins taking over Ian's life, committing crimes Ian doesn't remember, Ian must bring him under control. (Rev: BL 6/1–15/95; SLJ 6/95)

1320 McDonald, Collin. *The Chilling Hour: Tales of the Real and Unreal* (6–8). 1992, Dutton/Cobblehill $14 (0-525-65101-2). Eight scary stories with unexpected twists. (Rev: BL 12/1/92; MJHS; SLJ 8/92)

1321 McDonald, Collin. *Shadows and Whispers: Tales from the Other Side* (5–7). 1994, Dutton $13.99 (0-525-65184-5). Eight short stories with supernatural elements, often involving dreams, including a vengeful whale and a tuxedo that retains the personalities of its owners. (Rev: BL 9/1/94; SLJ 10/94)

1322 McKissack, Patricia. *The Dark-Thirty: Southern Tales of the Supernatural* (5–8). Illus. 1992, Knopf/Borzoi LB $15.99 (0-679-91863-9). Ten original stories rooted in African American history and the oral-storytelling tradition—e.g., slavery, belief in "the sight," the Montgomery bus boycott, etc. Awards: Coretta Scott King; SLJ Best Book. (Rev: BL 12/15/92; MJHS; SLJ 12/92*)

1323 Mahy, Margaret. *Dangerous Spaces* (5–7). 1991, Viking $12.95 (0-670-83734-2). Anthea and her cousin Flora are drawn into a dream world where past occupants of the house are exercising a mysterious hold on them. Awards: SLJ Best Book. (Rev: BL 5/15/91; SLJ 4/91*)

1324 Moore, Robin. *When the Moon Is Full* (5–8). 1994, Knopf $15 (0-679-85642-0). Six stories with supernatural overtones, most of which center upon animals. (Rev: BL 1/15/95; BTA; SLJ 12/94; VOYA 5/95)

1325 Murphy, Jim. *Night Terrors* (6–9). 1993, Scholastic $13.95 (0-590-45341-6). Five gruesome horror stories dealing with vampires, mummies, cannibals, etc. (Rev: BL 10/1/93; MJHS; VOYA 12/93)

1326 Patneaude, David. *Dark Starry Morning: Stories of This World and Beyond* (5–8). 1995, Albert Whitman $13.95 (0-8075-1474-8). Six tales about beneficial encounters with the unknown, the world beyond. (Rev: BL 9/1/95; SLJ 9/95)

1327 Pepper, Dennis, ed. *The Oxford Book of Scary Tales* (5–8). 1992, Oxford Univ. $19 (0-19-278131-6). Scary stories and poems, meant for reading aloud and sharing. (Rev: BL 1/15/93; MJHS; SLJ 1/93) [808.8]

1328 Pike, Christopher. *The Lost Mind* (9–12). 1995, Pocket/Archway paper $3.99 (0-671-87269-9). A supernatural tale of terror and mysticism. The protagonist awakens with no memory and a dead body beside her. (Rev: BL 11/15/95)

1329 Pines, T., ed. *Thirteen: 13 Tales of Horror by 13 Masters of Horror* (8–12). 1991, Scholastic paper $3.50 (0-590-45256-8). Popular horror writers' stories of revenge, lust, and betrayal. (Rev: BL 3/1/92)

1330 Poe, Edgar Allan. *Tales of Edgar Allan Poe* (7–12). 1991, Morrow $19.95 (0-688-07509-6). Eerie watercolor paintings illustrate 14 of Poe's most unsettling stories. (Rev: BL 8/91; MJHS; SHS)

1331 Preiss, Byron, and John Betancourt, eds. *The Ultimate Zombie* (9–adult). 1993, Dell paper $11.95 (0-440-50534-8). A creepy roundup of horror tales involving zombies in various guises, some of them unexpected. (Rev: BL 10/15/93*)

1332 Preston, Douglas, and Lincoln Child. *Relic* (9–adult). 1995, Tor/Forge $22.95 (0-312-85630-X). Preston teams up with the editor of numerous horror anthologies in an occult thriller about a mysterious relic from the Amazon. (Rev: BL 12/1/94; SLJ 10/95)

1333 Price, Susan, ed. *Horror Stories* (6–12). 1995, Kingfisher Books (95 Madison Ave., New York, NY 10016) paper $6.95 (1-85697-592-4). Two dozen Halloween read-alouds from such writers as Joan Aiken, Stephen King, Edgar Allan Poe, and John Steinbeck. (Rev: BL 10/15/95)

1334 Ragz, M. M. *French Fries up Your Nose* (5–8). 1994, Pocket paper $2.99 (0-671-88410-7). When the class clown runs for student council president, he struggles to maintain his irresponsible image while developing serious, election-winning habits. (Rev: BL 3/15/94)

1335 Reiss, Kathryn. *Dreadful Sorry* (7–10). 1993, Harcourt $16.95 (0-15-224213-9). A horror tale involving nightmares, terror of drowning, visions, and a handsome boy who is somehow connected to Molly's fears. Awards: SLJ Best Book. (Rev: BL 7/93; SLJ 6/93*; VOYA 8/93)

1336 Rice, Bebe Faas. *The Year the Wolves Came* (5–8). 1994, Dutton $14.99 (0-525-45209-5). In Canada in 1906, wolves have returned to a village to menace the homesteaders and kill livestock, looking for their leader. (Rev: BL 1/15/95; MJHS; SLJ 12/94)

1337 Sargent, Sarah. *Jerry's Ghosts: The Mystery of the Blind Tower* (5–8). 1992, Bradbury $13.95 (0-02-778035-X). Two ghost children befriend a live boy and then help him escape from their uncle's bizarre immortality experiments. (Rev: BL 3/15/92; SLJ 3/92)

1338 Saul, John. *Shadows* (9–adult). 1992, Bantam $19.50 (0-553-07474-1). After a 10-year old genius transfers from a public school to a private academy, strange deaths start to occur. (Rev: BL 5/1/92; BTA; SHS)

1339 Schwartz, Alvin. *Scary Stories 3: More Tales to Chill Your Bones* (5–7). Illus. 1991, HarperCollins LB $13.89 (0-06-021795-2); HarperTrophy paper $3.95 (0-06-440418-8). These modernized versions of spooky tales handed down through history seem to rest within the realm of possibility. (Rev: BL 8/91; SLJ 11/91) [398.2]

1340 Seabrooke, Brenda. *The Haunting of Holroyd Hill* (6–8). 1995, Dutton/Cobblehill $14.99 (0-525-65167-5). Ghosts and a murder mystery, combined with some Civil War history, are the background for the adventures of an 11-year-old girl and her brother. (Rev: BL 9/1/95; SLJ 4/95)

1341 Silverberg, Robert, and Martin H. Greenberg, eds. *The Horror Hall of Fame* (9–adult).

1991, Carroll & Graf $19.95 (0-88184-692-9). Eighteen classic horror stories by 18 famous authors, including "The Fall of the House of Usher" and "The Monkey's Paw." (Rev: BL 8/91; SHS)

1342 Sinykin, Sheri Cooper. *Sirens* (7–10). 1993, Lothrop $13 (0-688-12309-0). Chantal, 14, acquires a magical statue that attracts boys, but each meets with a serious accident and she races to prevent more victims from being claimed. (Rev: BL 1/1/94; VOYA 4/94)

1343 Sleator, William. *Dangerous Wishes* (5–9). 1995, Dutton $14.99 (0-525-45283-4). In this sequel to *The Spirit House*, Dominic Kamen travels to Thailand, where he seeks to return a jade carving to escape a vengeful spirit. (Rev: BL 8/95; SLJ 11/95; VOYA 4/96)

1344 Sleator, William. *The Spirit House* (6–9). 1991, Dutton $13.95 (0-525-44814-4). A Thai exchange student living with an American family reveals sinister mystical powers when one of his hosts builds a traditional spirit house as a gift for him. (Rev: BL 10/1/91; MJHS; SLJ 12/91)

1345 Snyder, Zilpha Keatley. *The Trespassers* (5–7). 1995, Delacorte $14.95 (0-385-31055-2). Neely Bradford, 10, and her younger brother, Grub, adopt the abandoned Halcyon House as their own, until new owners move in. (Rev: BL 6/1–15/95; SLJ 8/95)

1346 Stine, R. L. *Superstitious* (9–adult). 1995, Warner $21.95 (0-446-51953-7). A graduate student marries a folklore scholar whose adherence to rituals and obsession with superstitions leads her to suspect that he may be connected to gruesome campus murders. (Rev: BL 8/95; SLJ 11/95)

1347 Strieber, Whitley. *The Forbidden Zone* (9–adult). 1993, Dutton $21 (0-525-93683-1). Among the weird things that threaten a small town are screaming that comes from under the earth and strange insects that attack humans. (Rev: BL 5/15/93*)

1348 Tolan, Stephanie S. *Who's There?* (5–8). 1994, Morrow $14 (0-688-04611-8). Drew, 14, and her younger brother, who has been mute since their parents died, are living with their father's family. She becomes convinced their house is haunted. (Rev: BL 9/1/94; BTA; SLJ 10/94)

1349 Tolan, Stephanie S. *The Witch of Maple Park* (5–8). 1992, Morrow $14 (0-688-10581-5). In this suspense story: Is Mackenzie really psychic? Is the old woman who always watches her a witch? Is she a kidnapper? (Rev: BL 9/1/92; SLJ 10/92)

1350 Vande Velde, Vivian. *Companions of the Night* (7–10). 1995, Harcourt/Jane Yolen $17 (0-15-200221-9). A 16-year-old finds herself caught in a life-and-death chase after she helps an injured young man who is perhaps a vampire. (Rev: BL 4/1/95; SLJ 5/95)

1351 Welch, R. C. *Scary Stories for Stormy Nights* (5–7). 1995, Lowell House paper $4.95 (1-56565-262-2). Ten contemporary horror tales with predictable plots. (Rev: BL 5/1/95)

1352 Westall, Robert. *The Call and Other Stories* (7–12). 1993, Viking $13 (0-670-82484-4). A collection of 6 spine-tinglers set in England. (Rev: BL 1/1/93; MJHS)

1353 Westall, Robert. *Demons and Shadows* (7–11). 1993, Farrar $16 (0-374-31768-2). One previously unpublished and 10 out-of-print ghost stories are combined in this collection of dark tales. (Rev: BL 10/1/93; BTA; MJHS; SLJ 10/93; VOYA 12/93)

1354 Westall, Robert. *Gulf* (6–9). 1996, Scholastic $14.95 (0-590-22218-X). A savage tale of a psychic child witnessing the terrors of the Gulf War through the eyes of Latif, a 13-year-old Iraqi soldier. (Rev: SLJ 1/96; VOYA 4/96)

1355 Westall, Robert. *Shades of Darkness: More of the Ghostly Best Stories of Robert Westall* (7–12). 1994, Farrar $17 (0-374-36758-2). Eleven eerie tales, not the guts-and-gore variety of supernatural fiction but haunting and insightful tales. (Rev: BL 4/15/94; MJHS; SHS; SLJ 5/94; VOYA 8/94)

1356 Westall, Robert. *The Stones of Muncaster Cathedral* (8–12). 1993, Farrar $11 (0-374-37263-2). Joe is repairing a cathedral tower, and when his partner and 2 boys die in mysterious falls, Joe, a policeman, and a chaplain uncover and destroy the evil that has possessed the tower for centuries. (Rev: BL 5/1/93; BTA; MJHS; SLJ 6/93)

1357 Westwood, Chris. *Calling All Monsters* (7–12). 1993, HarperCollins LB $14.89 (0-06-022462-2). Joanne is a huge fan of a horror writer, so when she starts seeing nightmare creatures from his books, she recognizes them. (Rev: BL 6/1–15/93; SLJ 7/93; VOYA 12/93)

1358 Westwood, Chris. *He Came from the Shadows* (5–8). 1991, HarperCollins LB $14.89 (0-06-021659-X). In a cautionary tale about the dangers of wishing for too much, odd things start to happen after a stranger comes to town. (Rev: BL 4/1/91; SLJ 6/91)

1359 Wright, Betty Ren. *A Ghost in the House* (5–7). 1991, Scholastic $13.95 (0-590-43606-6). Sarah, age 12, and her invalid great-aunt experience bizarre happenings and confront a dangerous ghost who wants revenge on the old woman. (Rev: BL 11/1/91; SLJ 11/91)

1360 Wright, Betty Ren. *The Ghosts of Mercy Manor* (5–7). 1993, Scholastic $13.95 (0-590-43601-5). When Gwen Maxwell is fostered with the Mercys, she discovers the ghost of a young girl and the secrets hidden by Mrs. Mercy. Awards: SLJ Best Book. (Rev: BL 9/15/93; MJHS; SLJS 1/94*; VOYA 12/93)

1361 Wyss, Thelma Hatch. *A Stranger Here* (7–12). 1993, HarperCollins LB $13.89 (0-06-021439-2). Jada, 16, falls in love with the ghost of Starr Freeman, a World War II flyer killed on the day Jada was born. (Rev: BL 5/1/93; SLJ 5/93; VOYA 10/93)

1362 Yolen, Jane. *Here There Be Witches* (6–10). 1995, Harcourt $17 (0-15-200311-8). Short stories and poetry about witches in all shapes and forms. (Rev: BL 10/15/95; SLJ 12/95; VOYA 12/95)

1363 Yolen, Jane, and Martin H. Greenberg, eds. *Vampires: A Collection of Original Stories* (7–12). 1991, HarperCollins LB $14.89 (0-06-026801-8). This collection of vampire tales spans the centuries from tribal clan to suburban shopping mall, and the undead include piano teachers and the girl next door. (Rev: BL 9/1/91*; MJHS; SHS; SLJ 11/91)

1364 Young, Richard, and Judy Dockery Young. *Ozark Ghost Stories* (5–12). 1995, August House paper $10.95 (0-87483-410-4). Spooky Ozark stories are the focus of the Youngs' latest horror anthology, including old favorites and less well-known jokes and tales. (Rev: BL 6/1–15/95) [398.2]

1365 Young, Richard, and Judy Dockery Young. *The Scary Story Reader* (6–9). 1993, August House $19 (0-87483-271-3). Forty-one scary urban legends are presented, including traditional tales of horror as well as less well-known stories from Alaska and Hawaii. (Rev: BL 11/15/93; SLJ 5/94) [398.25]

1366 Zelazny, Roger. *A Night in the Lonesome October* (9–adult). 1993, Avon/AvoNova $20 (0-688-12508-5). A rollicking, suspenseful fantasy set near nineteenth-century London. (Rev: BL 7/93; BTA; VOYA 12/93)

1367 Zindel, Paul. *The Doom Stone* (6–10). 1995, HarperCollins LB $14.89 (0-06-024727-4). A slimy, truly evil creature stalks the moors and inhabits the mind of the protagonist's aunt. (Rev: BL 12/15/95; SLJ 12/95; VOYA 4/96)

1368 Zindel, Paul. *Loch* (7–10). 1994, HarperCollins $14.89 (0-06-024543-3). Lovable, though human-eating, creatures trapped in a Vermont lake become prey for a ruthless man. (Rev: BL 11/15/94; BTA; SLJ 1/95; VOYA 4/95)

Humor

1369 Adams, Cecil. *Return of the Straight Dope* (9–adult). 1994, Ballantine paper $10 (0-345-38111-4). Irreverent columns that provide funny, reasoned responses to goofy, obscure, and interesting questions. (Rev: BL 3/15/94; SLJ 8/94) [031]

1370 Avi. *Punch with Judy* (6–8). Illus. 1993, Bradbury $14.95 (0-02-707755-1); 1994, Avon/Flare paper $3.99 (0-380-72253-4). The orphan boy Punch encounters tragedy and comedy in his attempt to keep a medicine show alive with the help of the owner's daughter. (Rev: BL 3/15/93; SLJ 6/93; VOYA 8/93)

1371 Baker, Russell, ed. *Russell Baker's Book of American Humor* (9–adult). 1993, Norton $30 (0-393-03592-1). Divides 100+ humorous pieces into 12 categories, such as "Shameless Frivolity" and "This Sex Problem." (Rev: BL 11/1/93) [818.02]

1372 Barry, Lynda. *My Perfect Life* (9–adult). 1992, HarperPerennial paper $9 (0-06-096505-3). The continuing saga of Maybonne Mullen's coming of age. Awards: BL Editors' Choice. (Rev: BL 5/15/92*) [741.5]

1373 Bauer, Joan. *Squashed* (7–10). 1992, Delacorte $15 (0-385-30793-4). A humorous tale of Ellie Morgan, 16, who struggles to best the odious Cyril Pool by growing the biggest pumpkin in Iowa. Awards: Delacorte Press Prize; SLJ Best Book. (Rev: BL 9/1/92; BTA; MJHS; SLJ 9/92*; YR)

1374 Bellarosa, James M. *Virgil Hunter* (9–adult). 1993, John Daniel & Co. (P.O. Box 21922, Santa Barbara, CA 93121) paper $9.95 (1-880284-00-6). Virgil, a disrespectful bumpkin, finds himself mixed up with a nervous psychiatrist, a lusty farm girl, and a fake faith healer in this broad, scatological comedy. (Rev: BL 4/15/93; BTA)

1375 Byars, Betsy. *Wanted . . . Mud Blossom* (5–7). Illus. 1991, Delacorte $14 (0-385-30428-5). The Blossoms return in this hilarious story of truth, justice, sibling rivalry, and unrequited love, centering upon the trial of the dog Mud for "murdering" the class's hamster. Awards: ALSC

Notable Children's Book; Edgar; SLJ Best Book. (Rev: BL 9/15/91; SLJ 7/91*)

1376 Carkeet, David. *Quiver River* (7–10). 1991, HarperCollins/Laura Geringer LB $14.89 (0-06-022454-1). Two 16-year-old boys spending the summer working at a California campground find their relationship changing when one has his first sexual experience with a college girl. (Rev: BL 10/15/91)

1377 Clarke, J. *Al Capsella and the Watchdogs* (7–10). 1991, Holt $14.95 (0-8050-1598-1). Al Capsella, 15, and his Australian high school friends spend much of their time bemoaning the tactics their parents use to be involved in all phases of their lives. (Rev: BL 8/91; SLJ 8/91)

1378 Conford, Ellen. *Dear Mom, Get Me Out of Here!* (6–9). 1992, Little, Brown $14.95 (0-316-15370-2). A slapstick comedy in which Paul, 13, discovers that his new boys' school is a dismal place where teachers are as weird as the kids. (Rev: BL 10/15/92; SLJ 11/92)

1379 Conford, Ellen. *I Love You, I Hate You, Get Lost* (7–10). 1994, Scholastic $13.95 (0-590-45558-3). A collection of humorous short stories about the emotions that young people experience, each story about a different common problem. (Rev: BL 3/1/94; SLJ 4/94; VOYA 6/94)

1380 Cooper, Ilene. *Seeing Red* (6–9). (Hollywood Wars) 1993, Penguin/Puffin paper $3.25 (0-14-036157-X). Jamie and Alison head to New York for a publicity tour, but Alison develops paralyzing stage fright on live TV. (Rev: BL 8/93)

1381 Davis, Donald. *Barking at a Fox-Fur Coat* (9–adult). 1991, August House $19.95 (0-87483-141-5); paper $9.95 (0-87483-140-7). Seventeen original tales based on the author's childhood and family experiences in rural North Carolina, each highlighting a set of human foibles and ending with an ironic twist. (Rev: BL 10/15/91; SLJ 4/92)

1382 Deaver, Julie Reece. *You Bet Your Life* (8–10). 1993, HarperCollins/Charlotte Zolotow LB $14.89 (0-06-021517-8). Bess, 17, begins to shape a new life after her mother's suicide by becoming an intern on a TV comedy show and by writing letters to her mother. (Rev: BL 8/93; MJHS; SLJ 7/93; VOYA 8/93)

1383 Feiffer, Jules. *The Man in the Ceiling* (5–7). 1993, HarperCollins/Michael di Capua LB $14.89 (0-06-205036-2); paper $3.95 (0-06-205907-6). To earn the respect of his dysfunctional family, Jimmy creates a superhero cartoon, but he finds his abilities blocked when he must choose whether to compormise his art. (Rev: BL 11/15/93*; SLJ 2/94)

1384 Fine, Anne. *Flour Babies* (5–9). 1994, Little, Brown $14.95 (0-316-28319-3). English schoolboy Simon must take part in a parenting project by carrying around a flour baby, resulting in hilarity and newfound wisdom. Awards: ALSC Notable Children's Book; Greenaway Medal; SLJ Best Book. (Rev: BL 4/1/94*; BTA; MJHS; SLJ 6/94*; VOYA 6/94)

1385 Fleischman, Paul. *A Fate Totally Worse Than Death* (7–12). Illus. 1995, Candlewick $15.95 (1-56402-627-2). An offbeat mix of horror story and satire about self-centered rich girls who want to teach a beautiful exchange student a lesson. (Rev: BL 10/15/95; SLJ 10/95; VOYA 4/96)

1386 Fleischman, Sid. *Jim Ugly* (5–7). Illus. 1992, Greenwillow LB $14 (0-688-10886-5). A parody of a Western melodrama involving a 12-year-old boy and his half-breed dog, Jim Ugly. Awards: ALSC Notable Children's Book. (Rev: BL 5/15/92; SLJ 4/92*)

1387 Foley, June. *Susanna Siegelbaum Gives Up Guys* (6–9). 1991, Scholastic $13.95 (0-590-43699-6). A no-boys-for-a-month bet with a friend is the premise for this story in which Susanna invents a fake boyfriend for her parents' benefit. (Rev: BL 9/1/91; BTA)

1388 Frazetta, Frank. *Small Wonders: The Funny Animal Art of Frank Frazetta* (9–adult). 1991, Kitchen Sink paper $9.95 (0-87816-146-5). Collection of works created when the artist was a teenager. (Rev: BL 2/1/92) [741.5]

1389 Gale, David, ed. *Funny You Should Ask: The Delacorte Book of Original Humorous Short Stories* (5–7). 1992, Delacorte $15 (0-385-30535-4); 1994, Dell/Yearling paper $3.99 (0-440-40922-5). An entertaining collection of humorous short stories. (Rev: BL 2/1/92; MJHS; YR) [817.54]

1390 Gleitzman, Morris. *Misery Guts* (6–8). 1993, Harcourt $12.95 (0-15-254768-1). Keith Shipley hates that his parents are always worried and arguing, so he tries everything to lighten them up, including moving from London to Australia. (Rev: BL 7/93; SLJ 7/93)

1391 Gleitzman, Morris. *Worry Warts* (6–8). 1993, Harcourt $12.95 (0-15-299666-4). In this sequel to *Misery Guts*, Keith tries—and fails—to save his parents' marriage by going off to Australian opal fields to make money. (Rev: BL 7/93; SLJ 5/93)

1392 Greenburg, Dan. *Young Santa* (5–9). Illus. 1991, Viking $13.95 (0-670-83905-1). A tongue-in-cheek account of the boyhood and adolescence of Santa Claus, his first job in a department store, his first driver's license, and so on. (Rev: BL 10/1/91*)

1393 Hall, Lynn. *Dagmar Schultz and the Green-Eyed Monster* (5–7). 1991, Scribner $11.95 (0-684-19254-3). When a blonde with naturally curly hair moves to her Iowa hometown, Dagmar, 13, is overwhelmed by jealousy, until good sense and her down-to-earth family come to the rescue. (Rev: BL 6/15/91; SLJ 6/91)

1394 Handford, Martin. *¿Dónde está Waldo? en Hollywood* (5–8). Tr. by Jaume Ribera. 1993, Ediciones B (Barcelona, Spain) $13.95 (84-406-3798-5). This large-format Waldo book contains detailed, colorful illustrations depicting various Hollywood scenes: silent movies, musicals, Westerns, dinosaur films. English title: *Where's Waldo? in Hollywood.* (Rev: BL 10/1/94)

1395 Hayes, Daniel. *Eye of the Beholder* (5–8). 1992, Godine $14 (0-87923-881-X). Tyler and Lymie are in trouble again when they sculpt some rocks and throw them in the river, to be found as "lost treasures" of a sculptor who once lived in the town. (Rev: BL 2/1/93; MJHS; SLJ 12/92)

1396 Howe, James. *The New Nick Kramer; or, My Life as a Baby-Sitter* (5–8). 1995, Hyperion LB $13.89 (0-7868-2053-5). A rivalry between boys for the pretty newcomer gets this light-hearted plot moving. (Rev: BL 12/15/95)

1397 Hughes, Langston. *Black Misery* (6–12). Illus. 1994, Oxford Univ. $12.95 (0-19-509114-0). A collection of jokes often told by and for African Americans during the civil rights movement, many mocking stereotypes and presenting painful truisms. (Rev: BL 10/1/94) [818]

1398 Kalman, Maira. *Max in Hollywood, Baby* (6–9). 1992, Viking LB $15 (0-670-84479-9). Max the dog has gone Hollywood. Everybody's favorite poet pooch just couldn't resist the call of the Big Screen. The ongoing saga of Max the dog—in words, in pictures, in typography. Awards: BL Editors' Choice. (Rev: BL 12/1/92*; SLJ 11/92)

1399 Kalman, Maira. *Swami on Rye: Max in India* (5–9). 1995, Viking $14.99 (0-670-85646-0). Max the dog is whisked away by a swami to exotic India, where Kalman ridicules adult affectations and silliness in their search for meaning in life. (Rev: BL 10/15/95)

1400 Karl, Herb. *The Toom County Mud Race* (8–10). 1992, Delacorte $15 (0-385-30540-0). An offbeat, often hilarious adventure that involves the annual mud race through a swamp; a 4WD, dead-of-night treasure hunt; and near-fatal run-ins with X Slocum. (Rev: BL 6/15/92; YR)

1401 Kidd, Ronald. *Sammy Carducci's Guide to Women* (5–7). 1991, Dutton/Lodestar $14.95 (0-525-67363-6); 1994, Penguin/Puffin paper $3.99 (0-14-036481-1). The battle of the sexes set in the 6th grade: When Sammy tries to impress Becky, both learn lessons about life and relationships. (Rev: BL 1/1/92)

1402 Korman, Gordon. *Macdonald Hall Goes Hollywood* (5–7). 1991, Scholastic $12.95 (0-590-43940-5). The boys from Macdonald Hall are back and in trouble again when a movie crew comes to their school. (Rev: BL 6/15/91; MJHS)

1403 Korman, Gordon. *The Twinkie Squad* (5–7). 1992, Scholastic $13.95 (0-590-45249-5). A brainy 6th-grader with postnasal drip and the class jock are sentenced to join their school's Special Discussion Group, a gathering of oddball kids led by eccentric husband-and-wife counselors. (Rev: BL 9/15/92; MJHS; SLJ 9/92)

1404 Lowry, Lois. *Anastasia at This Address* (5–9). 1991, Houghton $13.95 (0-395-56263-5); 1992, Dell/Yearling paper $3.50 (0-440-40652-8). The Newbery Medalist's irrepressible heroine is in top form as, deciding she's ready for romance, she answers a personal ad, with typically hilarious results. (Rev: BL 4/1/91; MJHS)

1405 McCann, Helen. *What's French for Help, George?* (5–7). Illus. 1993, Simon & Schuster $13 (0-671-74689-8). George, age 13, desperately wants to win a free trip to France, but he needs to invade a computer program to guarantee that he's chosen. He wins, and with his friends sets off to terrorize the French. (Rev: BL 10/15/93; SLJ 6/93)

1406 McKay, Hilary. *The Exiles* (5–7). 1992, Macmillan/Margaret K. McElderry $14.95 (0-689-50555-8). The thoughtless adventures of the 4 Conroe sisters, ages 6–13, at Big Grandma's for the summer. Awards: Guardian Award for Children's Fiction. (Rev: BL 1/1/93*; MJHS; SLJ 10/92)

1407 McKenna, Colleen O'Shaughnessy. *Camp Murphy* (5–7). 1993, Scholastic $13.95 (0-590-45807-8). Collette, 12, and her girlfriends decide to run a week-long day camp for children, but countless unexpected problems beset them. (Rev: BL 3/15/93; SLJ 4/93)

1408 McKenna, Colleen O'Shaughnessy. *Mother Murphy* (5–7). 1992, Scholastic $13.95 (0-590-44820-X). A girl tries to make her ornery brothers and sisters behave when she becomes Mother for a day. (Rev: BL 2/1/92; YR)

1409 McKenna, Colleen O'Shaughnessy. *Murphy's Island* (5–7). 1990, Scholastic $12.95 (0-590-43552-3). The fourth book about Collette and her family, this time on an island, away for the first 4 months of 6th grade at her school. (Rev: BL 1/1/91; SLJ 12/90)

1410 Manes, Stephen. *Comedy High* (7–10). 1992, Scholastic $13.95 (0-590-44436-0). A comic story of a new high school, designed to graduate jocks, performers, gambling experts, and hotel workers. (Rev: BL 12/1/92; SLJ 11/92)

1411 Mills, Claudia. *Dinah in Love* (5–7). 1993, Macmillan $13.95 (0-02-766998-X). Dinah doesn't believe her friend Suzanne when she says Nick Tribble torments her because he really likes her. And she definitely won't invite him to the sock hop. (Rev: BL 11/15/93; MJHS; SLJ 12/93; VOYA 4/94)

1412 Mulford, Philippa Greene. *Making Room for Katherine* (5–9). 1994, Macmillan $14.95 (0-02-767652-8). A 16-year-old is recovering from her father's death when a 13-year-old cousin arrives from Paris to visit for the summer. Good for reluctant readers. (Rev: BL 4/15/94; SLJ 5/94; VOYA 8/94)

1413 Myers, Mike, and Robin Ruzan. *Wayne's World: Extreme Close-up* (9–adult). 1992, Hyperion paper $7.95 (1-56282-979-3). A collection of Wayne and Garth's most famous *Saturday Night Live* sketches. (Rev: BL 2/1/92) [791.45]

1414 Myers, Walter Dean. *The Righteous Revenge of Artemis Bonner* (5–9). 1992, HarperCollins LB $13.89 (0-06-020846-5). Set in the late 1800s, this spoof chronicles Artemis Bonner's quest to avenge his uncle's death and recover a treasure. (Rev: BL 10/1/92; BTA; SLJ 10/92; YR)

1415 Naylor, Phyllis Reynolds. *Alice In-Between* (5–7). 1994, Atheneum $14.95 (0-689-31890-1). A gentle comedy about that in-between age where Alice, 13, is part young girl and part budding young woman. (Rev: BL 5/1/94; BTA; MJHS; SLJ 6/94; VOYA 8/94)

1416 Naylor, Phyllis Reynolds. *Alice the Brave* (5–7). 1995, Atheneum $15 (0-689-80095-9). Alice learns to take chances and expresses fears about what every young person tries to experience as normal. (Rev: BL 5/1/95; MJHS; SLJ 5/95)

1417 Naylor, Phyllis Reynolds. *All but Alice* (5–8). 1992, Atheneum/Jean Karl $12.95 (0-689-31773-5); 1994, Dell/Yearling paper $3.50 (0-440-40918-7). A nerd suddenly becomes popular in 7th grade, but she may have to risk her new status for a friendship. Awards: ALSC Notable Children's Book; SLJ Best Book. (Rev: BL 3/1/92; BTA; MJHS; SLJ 5/92*)

1418 Naylor, Phyllis Reynolds. *Reluctantly Alice* (5–8). 1991, Atheneum/Jean Karl $13.95 (0-689-31681-X); 1992, Dell/Yearling paper $3.25 (0-440-40685-4). Klutzy 7th-grader copes with class bullies and raging hormones. Awards: SLJ Best Book. (Rev: BL 2/1/91; MJHS; SLJ 3/91*; YR)

1419 Paulsen, Gary. *Harris and Me: A Summer Remembered* (6–12). 1993, Harcourt $13.95 (0-15-292877-4). The 11-year-old narrator is dumped on his aunt and uncle's farm for the summer by his alcoholic parents, but through his exploits with his cousin Harris, it becomes his home. Awards: YALSA Best Book for Young Adults. (Rev: BL 12/1/93*; MJHS; SLJ 1/94; VOYA 2/94)

1420 Peck, Richard. *Bel-Air Bambi and the Mall Rats* (5–7). 1993, Delacorte $14.95 (0-385-30823-X). The bankrupt Babcock family is forced to move to Hickory Fork, where a gang has taken over the mall. Bambi and Buffie decide that it's up to them to set things straight, with hilarious results. Awards: SLJ Best Book. (Rev: BL 9/1/93; SLJ 9/93*; VOYA 12/93)

1421 Peck, Robert Newton. *Soup* (5–7). 1995, Knopf $15 (0-679-87320-1). This fourteenth story about Soup and his sidekick is filled with broad comedy and exaggerated characters that make the predictable mayhem hilarious. (Rev: BL 9/1/95)

1422 Peck, Robert Newton. *Soup in Love* (5–7). Illus. 1992, Delacorte $14 (0-385-30563-X). A boy falls for twins and plans to win the Most Creative Valentine contest, with unexpected results. (Rev: BL 1/15/92; SLJ 4/92)

1423 Peña Gutiérrez, Joaquín, ed. *Cuentos picarescos* (9–adult). 1992, Cooperativa Editorial Magisterio (Bogota, Colombia) paper $6.95 (958-20-0015-5). A collection of short, humorous stories by some of the best contemporary Latin American writers. Includes a 2- or 3-page introduction to the life and achievements of each author. English title: *Humorous Short Stories*. (Rev: BL 2/1/94)

1424 Robbins, Trina. *A Century of Women Cartoonists* (9–adult). 1993, Kitchen Sink $24.95 (0-87816-201-1); paper $16.95 (0-87816-200-3). Robbins uses reproductions of their comics in this documentation of women cartoonists from about 1900 to the present, giving sexism as the deterrant to women's success. (Rev: BL 11/15/93) [741.5]

1425 Ryan, Mary E. *Me, My Sister, and I* (5–7). 1992, Simon & Schuster $15 (0-671-73851-8). Follows Mattie and her twin sister Pru through the ups and downs of being 13: finding a date, playing in a rock band, and uncovering a political scandal. (Rev: BL 12/15/92; SLJ 10/92)

1426 Sachar, Louis. *Dogs Don't Tell Jokes* (5–7). 1991, Knopf LB $14.99 (0-679-92017-X). A 7th-grader aspires to become a stand-up comic and enters a talent contest, despite his nerdy reputation. (Rev: BL 7/91; MJHS; SLJ 9/91)

1427 Sachs, Marilyn. *Circles* (7–10). 1991, Dutton $14.95 (0-525-44683-4). A good-natured acount of romantic blindman's buff, in which Mark and Beebe, although both juniors in the same high school, don't meet until the last page. Awards: SLJ Best Book. (Rev: BL 3/15/91; MJHS; SLJ 3/91*)

1428 Soto, Gary. *Summer on Wheels* (5–8). 1995, Scholastic $13.95 (0-590-48365-X). In a sequel to *Crazy Weekend*, Hector and Mando take an 8-day bike ride from their East L.A. barrio to Santa Monica, moving from relative to relative. (Rev: BL 1/15/95; SLJ 4/95; VOYA 4/95)

1429 Talbott, Hudson. *Your Pet Dinosaur: An Owner's Manual* (5–8). Illus. 1992, Morrow LB $14.93 (0-688-11338-9). A tongue-in-cheek guide to living with your pet dinosaur. (Rev: BL 9/15/92; SLJ 5/93) [818]

1430 Taylor, William. *Agnes the Sheep* (5–7). 1991, Scholastic $13.95 (0-590-43365-2). What starts as a simple class project for Belinda and Joe turns into a "wild and woolly" sheep chase. Awards: BL Editors' Choice. (Rev: BL 5/15/91*; SLJ 3/91)

1431 Townsend, Sue. *Adrian Mole: The Lost Years* (9–adult). 1994, Soho (853 Broadway, New York, NY 10003) $22 (1-56947-014-6). Adrian's diary chronicles his struggle with the raging hormones of adolescence and his search for a suitable career. Sequel to *The Adrian Mole Diaries*. (Rev: BL 8/94; SLJ 1/95)

1432 Vail, Rachel. *Wonder* (5–7). 1991, Orchard/Richard Jackson LB $13.99 (0-531-08564-3). In this funny novel, Jess and her 7th-grade classmates begin to discover the boundaries of friendship, self-confidence, and boy-girl relationships. Awards: BL Editors' Choice; SLJ Best Book. (Rev: BL 9/1/91; SLJ 8/91*; SLJ 8/91)

1433 Wersba, Barbara. *You'll Never Guess the End* (7–12). 1992, HarperCollins/Charlotte Zolotow LB $13.89 (0-06-020449-4). A send-up of the New York City literary scene, rich dilettantes, and Scientology. (Rev: BL 11/15/92; SLJ 9/92; YR)

1434 White, Bailey. *Mama Makes Up Her Mind and Other Dangers of Southern Living* (9–adult). 1993, Addison-Wesley $17.95 (0-201-63295-0). A charming, humorous reflection on life in Georgia with her eccentric mother, by a National Public Radio commentator. (Rev: BL 3/15/93*) [814]

1435 Wynne-Jones, Tim. *The Book of Changes* (5–7). 1995, Orchard/Melanie Kroupa LB $14.99 (0-531-08789-1). Short stories that celebrate the spontaneous, wild, and crazy adolescent world. (Rev: BL 10/1/95; SLJ 10/95)

Mysteries, Thrillers, and Spy Stories

1436 Aellen, Richard. *The Cain Conversion* (9–adult). 1993, Donald I. Fine $21.95 (1-55611-348-X). Secret Service agent Sullivan irrationally pulls a gun on the president, prompting a discovery that he's actually a Soviet sleeper agent. (Rev: BL 4/1/93; SLJ 10/93)

1437 Alcott, Louisa May. *From Jo March's Attic* (9–adult). 1993, Northeastern Univ. $21.95 (1-55553-177-6). As in 4 earlier collections, newly discovered works that were originally released under a pseudonym make up this volume. (Rev: BL 11/1/93) [813.4]

1438 Alexander, Gary. *Blood Sacrifice* (9–adult). 1993, Doubleday $17 (0-385-46895-4). This tale of a Mexican serial killer is both a gripping mystery and a funny look at common stereotypes found in tourist meccas. (Rev: BL 7/93*)

1439 Anastasio, Dina. *The Case of the Glacier Park Swallow* (5–7). 1994, Roberts Rinehart (P.O. Box 666, Niwot, CO 80544) paper $6.95 (1-879373-85-8). Juliet, a student veterinarian, uncovers a drug-smuggling ring and drives to Canada to check out a lead. (Rev: BL 12/1/94; SLJ 10/94)

1440 Arkin, Anthony Dana. *Captain Hawaii* (7–10). 1994, HarperCollins $14.89 (0-06-021509-7). Aaron, 16, is on vacation in Hawaii, where he stumbles onto a mystery involving a tourist boat company, a dead scientist, and an evil hotel owner who plots to over-develop Hawaii. (Rev: BL 11/15/94*; BTA; SLJ 11/94; VOYA 12/94)

1441 Armstrong, Campbell. *A Concert of Ghosts* (9–adult). 1993, HarperCollins $20 (0-06-017946-5). A 1960s burnout has his life threatened when a journalist convinces him to return to San Francisco and reconstruct his past. (Rev: BL 12/1/92*)

1442 Avi. *Windcatcher* (5–7). 1991, Bradbury $12.95 (0-02-707761-6). Tony, 11, has bought a sailboat and takes it to his grandmother's home on the Connecticut shore, where he tries to learn the whereabouts of a buried treasure. (Rev: BL 3/1/91; SLJ 4/91)

1443 Barnard, Robert. *A Fatal Attachment* (9–adult). 1992, Scribner $20 (0-684-19412-0). By taking control of her nephews' lives, Lydia alienated her sister and brother-in-law from their adolescent sons. Twenty years later, history seems to be repeating itself. (Rev: BL 8/92; SLJ 2/93)

1444 Barnes, Linda. *Snapshot: A Carlotta Carlyle Novel.* (9–adult). 1993, Delacorte $19.95 (0-385-30612-1). In the fifth book in the series, 6-foot, red-headed, Boston PI Carlotta Carlyle is tangled up in a convoluted case involving drug counterfeiting. (Rev: BL 6/1–15/93; SLJ 10/93)

1445 Barr, Nevada. *A Superior Death* (9–adult). 1994, Putnam $19.95 (0-399-13916-8). Park ranger Anna Pigeon must solve a puzzle involving a mysterious sunken ship and a deep-sea diver who is murdered on his wedding night. (Rev: BL 3/1/94; SLJ 8/94)

1446 Barrow, Adam. *Flawless* (9–adult). 1995, Dutton $22.95 (0-525-94047-2). A father who has spent time in prison for killing his wife is released to live with his son, who was 9 when he witnessed the killing. (Rev: BL 9/1/95*)

1447 Bell, Mary Ann. *The Secret of the Mezuzah* (5–10). 1995, NavPress paper $5 (0-89109-872-0). A 13-year-old makes life more interesting for himself in Vienna when he tracks down a spy and finds that the spy is his mother. (Rev: BL 3/15/95)

1448 Bellairs, John. *The Mansion in the Mist* (5–7). 1992, Dial LB $14.89 (0-8037-0846-7). A fantasy/mystery in which Anthony Monday, librarian Ms. Eels, and her brother find a chest that can transport them to a parallel world run by maniacs intent on controlling the universe. (Rev: BL 8/92; MJHS; SLJ 6/92)

1449 Bennett, Jay. *Coverup* (8–10). 1991, Watts LB $13.90 (0-531-11091-5). Realizing his friend has killed a pedestrian on a deserted road after a party, Brad returns to the accident scene and meets a girl searching for her homeless father. (Rev: BL 11/1/91; MJHS; SHS)

1450 Black, Veronica. *Vow of Obedience* (9–adult). 1994, St. Martin's $18.95 (0-312-10573-8). A whodunit involving Sister Joan, who ventures out of her cloister to solve 2 loathsome murders. Awards: BL Editors' Choice. (Rev: BL 4/15/94; SLJ 9/94)

1451 Block, Barbara. *Chutes and Adders* (9–adult). 1994, Kensington $18.95 (0-8217-4533-6). Robin is managing her late husband's pet store when her assistant is mysteriously killed by a snake. Police discover a hidden $50,000 and suspect Robin of murdering her husband. (Rev: BL 8/94*)

1452 Brandon, Jay. *Rules of Evidence* (9–adult). 1992, Pocket $20 (0-671-73174-2). A loner cop accused of murder hires an African American lawyer to defend him. (Rev: BL 1/1/92*)

1453 Burke, Jan. *Goodnight, Irene* (9–adult). 1993, Simon & Schuster $17 (0-671-78200-2). When a fellow reporter and friend becomes the victim of a bomb, Irene Kelly must investigate, in a plot with countless twists. (Rev: BL 2/15/93*)

1454 Carris, Joan. *Beware the Ravens, Aunt Morbelia* (5–7). 1995, Little, Brown $14.95 (0-316-12961-5). Todd, 12, his eccentric Aunt Morbelia, and his best friend, Jeff, are off to an eerie English manor house to settle her inheritance and they're stalked by menacing strangers. (Rev: BL 12/15/94; SLJ 4/95)

1455 Carroll, Jonathan. *After Silence* (9–adult). 1993, Doubleday $22.50 (0-385-41974-0). Lincoln, a rebellious teen, discovers the terrible truth about his identity: that his mother had kidnapped him as an infant. (Rev: BL 4/1/93; SLJ 4/94)

1456 Chaplin, Elizabeth. *Hostage to Fortune* (9–adult). 1993, Mysterious $17.95 (0-89296-504-5). A sudden windfall changes the lives of Susan and her husband in this dark, intense psychological murder mystery. (Rev: BL 2/15/93*)

1457 Chapman, Sally. *Love Bytes* (9–adult). 1994, St. Martin's $20.95 (0-312-11023-5). An intriguing mystery about the computer business and the protagonist Julie Blake, first introduced in *Raw Data*. (Rev: BL 4/15/94*; BTA)

1458 Clancy, Tom. *Without Remorse* (9–adult). 1993, Putnam $24.95 (0-399-13825-0). Vietnam vet John Kelly's revenge against the murderers of his 20-year-old girlfriend is an integral part of this complex thriller. (Rev: BL 6/1–15/93; SLJ 11/93)

1459 Clark, Carol Higgins. *Iced* (9–12). 1995, Warner Books $19.95 (0-446-51764-X). Los Angeles PI Regan Reilly, vacationing in Colorado, stumbles across a series of art thefts. (Rev: BL 5/15/95; SLJ 1/96)

1460 Clark, Mary Higgins. *All Around the Town* (9–adult). 1992, Simon & Schuster $21.50 (0-671-67365-3). A traumatized college student is defended against murder charges by her level-headed attorney sister. (Rev: BL 4/15/92; SHS)

1461 Clark, Mary Higgins. *I'll Be Seeing You* (9–adult). 1993, Simon & Schuster $23 (0-671-67366-1). The puzzling death of the heroine's father, unethical procedures at a fertility clinic, dual identities, and hidden motives. (Rev: BL 4/15/93; SLJ 11/93)

1462 Clark, Mary Higgins, ed. *The International Association of Crime Writers Presents Bad Behavior* (8–12). 1995, Harcourt/Gulliver $20 (0-15-200179-4); paper $10 (0-15-200178-6). Features many stories with young characters and less overt violence than adult fare. Includes works by Sara Paretsky, P. D. James, Lawrence Block, and Liza Cody. (Rev: BL 7/95)

1463 Clark, Mary Higgins. *Let Me Call You Sweetheart* (9–adult). 1995, Simon & Schuster $24 (0-684-80396-8). Prosecutor Kerry McGrath scours the world of gem thieves, child stalkers, the Irish Mafia, and more to solve the murder of the beautiful Suzanne Reardon. (Rev: BL 4/1/95; SLJ 9/95)

1464 Cleary, Jon. *Bleak Spring* (9–adult). 1994, Morrow $21 (0-688-12332-5). An Australian police inspector faces a difficult case when he comes to believe his wife and her lesbian lover are involved in the murder of a neighbor. (Rev: BL 3/1/94; SLJ 8/94)

1465 Cook, Robin. *Terminal* (9–adult). 1993, Putnam $21.95 (0-399-13771-8). A thriller involving medical students, cancer research, and a murderous housekeeper. (Rev: BL 12/1/92; SHS; SLJ 5/93)

1466 Cormier, Robert. *In the Middle of the Night* (10–12). 1995, Delacorte $15.95 (0-385-32158-9). An exploration of the dark underside of human emotions: A 16-year-old is drawn into a telephone game that drags him close to disaster. (Rev: BL 4/1/95; SLJ 5/95; VOYA 5/95)

1467 Cornwell, Patricia. *All That Remains* (9–adult). 1992, Scribner $20 (0-684-19395-7). A whodunit about the baffling serial murders of 5 college-age couples. (Rev: BL 6/1/92; SLJ 12/92)

1468 Cornwell, Patricia. *Cruel and Unusual* (9–adult). 1993, Scribner $21 (0-684-19530-5). An edge-of-your-seat thriller with plenty of action, a gripping plot, and a mind-boggling climax. (Rev: BL 4/15/93; SLJ 11/93)

1469 Cornwell, Patricia. *From Potter's Field* (9–adult). 1995, Scribner $24 (0-684-19598-4); 1996, Berkley paper $6.99 (0-425-15409-2). The Central Park (New York) murder of a young, homeless woman on Christmas sends medical examiner Scarpetta, her friend Captain Marino, and her niece on a chase that ends in the subway. (Rev: BL 5/1/95*)

1470 Davis, Lindsey. *The Iron Hand of Mars* (9–adult). 1993, Ballantine paper $4.99 (0-345-38024-X). Roman history and the detective story meet: Marcus Didius Falco, an A.D. 70 private eye, becomes involved with a rebel chief, a priestess, a legion, and a missing legate. (Rev: BL 9/15/93; SLJ 3/94)

1471 Davis, Lindsey. *Venus in Copper* (9–adult). 1992, Crown $20 (0-517-58477-8). Witty PI Marcus Falco romps through ancient Rome on the trail of a suspected gold digger. (Rev: BL 3/15/92*; SLJ 2/93)

1472 Dawson, Janet. *Nobody's Child* (9–adult). 1995, Ballantine/Fawcett Columbine $21 (0-449-90976-X). A spunky heroine searches for an HIV-positive baby whose mother has been murdered. (Rev: BL 10/1/95; SLJ 4/96)

1473 De Felice, Cynthia. *The Light on Hogback Hill* (5–8). 1993, Macmillan $13.95 (0-02-726453-X). When 11-year-olds Hadley and Josh discover that the Witch Woman of Hogback Hill is really a shy, deformed woman, they help her find the courage to return to town. (Rev: BL 11/1/93; SLJ 11/93)

1474 Deighton, Len. *Faith* (9–adult). 1995, HarperCollins $24 (0-06-017622-9). Bernard Sampson heads to the Orient to find VERDI, a source that can reveal information about espionage in the post–cold-war era. Sequel to *Spy Sinker*. (Rev: BL 11/1/94*)

1475 Dexter, Colin. *Morse's Greatest Mystery and Other Stories* (9–adult). 1995, Crown $23 (0-517-79992-8). Arrogant, brilliant Inspector Morse and gentle, modest Sergeant Lewis combine detective skills in 11 complex stories of suspense, intrigue, and humor. (Rev: BL 10/1/95*)

1476 Doctorow, E. L. *The Waterworks* (9–adult). 1994, Random $23 (0-394-58754-5). A young freelance writer in post–Civil War New York City disappears after being disowned by his conniving father. Some overtones of Sherlock Holmes. (Rev: BL 4/15/94*; SLJ 1/95)

1477 Dorf, Fran. *Flight* (9–adult). 1992, Dutton $20 (0-525-93482-0). After awakening from a 20-year coma, a woman is hunted by the man who injured her. (Rev: BL 5/15/92*)

1478 Doyle, Arthur Conan. *The Adventures of Sherlock Holmes* (6–12). Illus. 1992, Morrow/Books of Wonder $20 (0-688-10782-6). Twelve adventures of the ingenious detective are illustrated by vivid watercolors. (Rev: BL 9/15/92; MJHS)

1479 Duffy, James. *The Graveyard Gang* (6–8). 1993, Scribner $14.95 (0-684-19449-X). It's up to the teenage Graveyard Gang to clear Amy of the charge of murdering "Bigmouth" Jenkins. (Rev: BL 7/93; SLJ 5/93; VOYA 8/93)

1480 Dunant, Sarah. *Fatlands* (9–adult). 1994, Penzler Books (129 W. 56th St., New York, NY 10019) $21 (1-883402-82-4). Investigator Hannah Wolfe babysits a famous scientist's daughter. When a bomb kills the child, Hannah feels it was meant for the scientist so she hunts for the killers. (Rev: BL 11/1/94*)

1481 Dunlap, Susan. *Time Expired* (9–adult). 1993, Delacorte $18.95 (0-385-30444-7). Homicide detective Jill Smith tracks a murderer and tries to learn who's playing dangerous tricks on parking-meter minders. (Rev: BL 5/15/93; VOYA 10/93)

1482 Dunlop, Eileen. *Green Willow* (6–8). 1993, Holiday $14.95 (0-8234-1021-8). When her sister dies, Kit Crawford and her mother move to an apartment, where Kit discovers an old Japanese man, a ghost, and a new friend. (Rev: BL 12/1/93; SLJ 1/94; VOYA 4/94)

1483 Dunning, John. *The Bookman's Wake* (9–adult). 1995, Scribner $21 (0-684-80003-9). Ex-cop-turned book dealer Cliff Janeway tracks down a priceless edition of a book and encounters intrigue and murder. (Rev: BL 4/1/95*)

1484 Egleton, Clive. *Hostile Intent* (9–adult). 1993, St. Martin's $18.95 (0-312-08812-4). Hostile Russian agents are pitted against the best of the British SIS in the post–Cold War era of intelligence gathering. (Rev: BL 6/1–15/93*)

1485 Eisenberg, Lisa. *Mystery at Camp Windingo* (5–8). 1991, Dial $13.95 (0-8037-0950-1). Kate Clancy is back on vacation, surrounded by mysterious doings—valuable birds are missing and almost everyone is sick from food poisoning. (Rev: BL 3/15/91; SLJ 4/91)

1486 Emerson, Kathy Lynn. *The Mystery of the Missing Bagpipes* (5–7). 1991, Avon/Camelot paper $2.95 (0-380-76138-6). Ancient bagpipes and jeweled daggers are stolen from a Maine estate where a millionaire runs a school for bagpipe instruction, and 2 kids solve the mystery. (Rev: BL 9/15/91)

1487 Evanovich, Janet. *One for the Money* (9–adult). 1994, Scribner $20 (0-684-19639-5). An out-of-work discount-lingerie buyer becomes a bounty hunter for the reward money. She is hired to find a wanted cop from her past. (Rev: BL 9/1/94*)

1488 Feder, Harriet K. *Mystery of the Kaifeng Scroll* (6–9). 1995, Lerner LB $13.13 (0-8225-0739-0). In this sequel to *Mystery in Miami Beach* (1992), Vivi Hartman, age 15, must use her wits and knowledge of the Torah to save her mother from Palestinian terrorists. (Rev: BL 6/1–15/95)

1489 Ferguson, Alane. *Overkill* (7–10). 1992, Bradbury $13.95 (0-02-734523-8); 1994, Avon/Flare paper $3.99 (0-380-72167-8). Lacey is seeing a therapist about nightmares in which she stabs her friend Celeste; when Celeste is found dead, Lacey is falsely arrested for the crime. (Rev: BL 1/1/93; SLJ 1/93; YR)

1490 Francis, Dick. *Come to Grief* (9–adult). 1995, Putnam $23.95 (0-399-14082-4). Ex-jockey-turned-sleuth Sid Halley searches for the culprit who has committed senseless acts of mutilation on prized race horses and discovers it is his old pal and rival. Awards: Edgar. (Rev: BL 8/95*)

1491 Francis, Dick. *Decider* (9–adult). 1993, Putnam $22.95 (0-399-13871-4). Lee Morris is drawn into a family dispute when an inherited racecourse grandstand is blown up. (Rev: BL 8/93; VOYA 10/94)

1492 Francis, Dick. *Driving Force* (9–adult). 1992, Putnam $21.95 (0-399-13776-9). An ex-jockey who transports thoroughbreds from race to race must unravel a mystery when a hitchiker he picks up dies suddenly. (Rev: BL 9/15/92; SHS; SLJ 2/93)

1493 Francis, Dick. *Wild Horses* (9–adult). 1994, Putnam $22.95 (0-399-13974-5). A filmmaker's latest movie is based upon a real-life horse-racing tragedy involving a hanging death ruled a suicide. As the film producer uncovers new secrets, he suspects murder. (Rev: BL 8/94; SLJ 1/95)

1494 Freemantle, Brian. *The Button Man* (9–adult). 1993, St. Martin's $21.95 (0-312-08716-0). FBI agent Crowley and Russian detective Danilov join forces to solve the brutal murder of a beautiful attaché in the American Embassy in Moscow. (Rev: BL 7/93*)

1495 Freemantle, Brian. *No Time for Heroes* (9–adult). 1995, St. Martin's $22.95 (0-312-11866-X). A Russian and an American investigator carry out a global search for the killer of a Russian diplomat. (Rev: BL 2/15/95*)

1496 Gaines, Ernest J. *A Lesson Before Dying* (9–12). (Borzoi Reader) 1993, Knopf $23 (0-679-41477-0); Random/Vintage paper $12 (0-679-74166-6). In the 1940s in rural Louisiana, an uneducated African American man is sentenced to die for a crime he was incapable of committing. Awards: SLJ Best Book. (Rev: SLJ 7/93*; VOYA 10/93)

1497 Garber, Joseph R. *Vertical Run* (9–adult). 1995, Bantam $21.95 (0-553-10033-5). David Elliott performs commando-style tricks to outwit his enemies. (Rev: BL 8/95*)

1498 Gardner, John. *Maestro* (9–adult). 1993, Penzler Books (129 W. 56th St., New York, NY 10019) $23 (1-883402-24-7). Not a James Bond novel, but a multigenerational epic spanning 10 decades that focuses on a world-famous orchestra conductor who becomes a spy. (Rev: BL 9/1/93*)

1499 Gavin, Thomas. *Breathing Water* (9–adult). 1994, Arcade $21.95 (1-55970-232-X). The mystery of a young boy's identity confuses the citizens of Rising Sun and causes tragedy to the boy. Awards: SLJ Best Book. (Rev: SLJ 7/94)

1500 Gee, Maurice. *The Fire-Raiser* (6–12). 1992, Houghton $13.95 (0-395-62428-2). A thriller set in New Zealand during World War I dramatizes the secret fury of a pyromaniac and relates it to the mob violence let loose in the community by jingoism and war. Awards: BL Editors' Choice. (Rev: BL 10/15/92*; SLJ 9/92; YR)

1501 George, Elizabeth. *Missing Joseph* (9–adult). 1993, Bantam $21.95 (0-553-09253-7). An English woman is accused of poisoning the village vicar in this exploration of relationships, love, and morality. (Rev: BL 6/1–15/93*)

1502 George, Elizabeth. *Playing for the Ashes* (9–adult). 1994, Bantam $21.95 (0-553-09262-6). Complex relationships and provocative moral, emotional, and ethical questions are the background for the capers of 2 homicide detectives in search of the murderer of a cricket player. (Rev: BL 5/15/94*)

1503 George, Jean Craighead. *The Fire Bug Connection* (5–7). 1993, HarperCollins LB $13.89 (0-06-021491-0). A teen mystery, in which Maggie tries to figure out what environmental factor is killing some Czech fire bugs. (Rev: BL 5/15/93; SLJ 6/93)

1504 Gibbs, Tony. *Shadow Queen* (9–adult). 1992, Mysterious paper $4.99 (0-446-40108-0). The security of the House of Windsor is threatened by a girl possessed by the spirit of her ancestor, Mary, Queen of Scots, and having letters supposedly written by her. (Rev: BL 12/15/91*)

1505 Gilpin, T. G. *Death of a Fantasy Life* (9–adult). 1993, St. Martin's $16.95 (0-312-09270-9). Includes an imaginative plot, humorous eccentricities of "hero" Ponton, and his pairing with a stripper to solve a series of murders in London's seedy Soho. (Rev: BL 5/1/93*)

1506 Goddard, Ken. *Prey* (9–adult). 1992, Tor $21.95 (0-312-85112-X). A special government investigation team seeks justice for environmental crimes. (Rev: BL 9/15/92; BTA)

1507 Goldman, E. M. *Getting Lincoln's Goat: An Elliot Armbruster Mystery* (7–10). 1995, Delacorte $14.95 (0-385-32098-1). What happens when 10th-grader Elliot Armbruster announces that he wants to become a private investigator? (Rev: BL 4/15/95; SLJ 3/95; VOYA 5/95)

1508 Gosling, Paula. *Death Penalties* (9–adult). 1991, Mysterious $17.95 (0-89296-458-8). Tess must care for her son, traumatized by the death in a car accident of his father, and deal with financial ruin. When anonymous phone callers demand money, detective Abbott investigates. (Rev: BL 8/91; SLJ 1/92)

1509 Grace, C. L. *The Merchant of Death* (9–adult). 1995, St. Martin's $19.95 (0-312-13124-0). Set in medieval Britain, healer Kathryn Swinbrooke and soldier Colum Murtagh must find a tax collector's murderer to recover the royal taxes stolen from him. (Rev: BL 6/1–15/95; SLJ 11/95)

1510 Grace, C. L. *Shrine of Murders: Being the First of the Canterbury Tales of Kathryn Swinbrooke, Leech and Physician* (9–adult). 1993, St. Martin's $17.95 (0-312-09388-8). After the War of the Roses, Colum Murtagh is sent to Canterbury, where warlocks and wizards encourage black magic and evil prevails. (Rev: BL 4/15/93; SLJ 12/93)

1511 Grant, Charles L. *Fire Mask* (6–8). 1991, Bantam/Starfire $14.95 (0-553-07167-X); paper $3.99 (0-553-29673-6). The lives of Cliff and his friends are threatened when they become entangled in a dangerous investigation of the last words of a dying man. (Rev: BL 4/15/91; SLJ 3/91)

1512 Green, Kate. *Black Dreams* (9–adult). 1992, HarperCollins $20 (0-06-017984-8). As in the previous *Shattered Moon* (1986), psychic Theresa Fortunato teams up with L.A.P.D. Lieutenant Jardine, this time to save a kidnapped girl. (Rev: BL 9/15/93; SLJ 5/94)

1513 Grimes, Martha. *The Horse You Came in On* (9–adult). 1993, Knopf $21 (0-679-42523-3). Scotland Yard detective Jury is in the United States, trying to solve 3 seemingly unrelated murders in this complicated mystery. (Rev: BL 5/15/93*)

1514 Grisham, John. *The Client* (9–adult). 1993, Doubleday $23.50 (0-385-42471-X). Mark Sway, 11, witnesses a Mafia lawyer's suicide, which puts him in danger from Barry the Blade and a politically ambitious U.S. attorney. (Rev: BL 2/1/93*; SLJ 7/93; VOYA 8/93)

1515 Grisham, John. *The Pelican Brief* (9–adult). 1992, Doubleday $22 (0-385-42198-2). A law student runs for her life after discovering who murdered 2 supreme court justices. Awards: YALSA Best Book for Young Adults. (Rev: BL 1/15/92)

1516 Hall, Barbara. *The House Across the Cove* (7–12). 1995, Dell/Laurel Leaf paper $3.99 (0-440-21938-8). A love story and a mystery in which Tyler Crane stumbles into an empty house where there is suspicious activity. (Rev: BL 9/15/95; SLJ 2/96)

1517 Hallinan, Timothy. *A Man with No Time* (9–adult). 1993, Morrow $21 (0-688-10344-8). A gritty, sometimes graphically violent thriller starring Simeon Grist, who's quick-witted, adept, agile, and appealing. (Rev: BL 7/93*)

1518 Haugaard, Erik Christian. *The Death of Mr. Angel* (7–12). 1992, Roberts Rinehart (P.O. Box 666, Niwot, CO 80544) $13.95 (1-879373-26-2). A compelling, dark tale about an outsider that's also an intensely disturbing portrait of a dysfunctional family and a malignant society. (Rev: BL 1/15/93; SLJ 11/92)

1519 Hayden, Jan, and Mary Kistler. *Has Anyone Seen Allie?* (6–9). 1991, Dutton/Cobblehill $13.95 (0-525-65057-1). Judy, 16, is being pursued by the murderer of her best friend, Allie. (Rev: BL 3/1/91; SLJ 3/91)

1520 Hayes, Daniel. *The Trouble with Lemons* (5–8). 1991, Godine $14.95 (0-87923-825-9). Tyler, 14, has all kinds of problems—allergies, asthma, and nightmares—and then he finds a dead body. Awards: YALSA Best Book for Young Adults. (Rev: BL 5/1/91; MJHS; SLJ 6/91)

1521 Haynes, Betsy. *Deadly Deception* (7–10). 1994, Delacorte $14.95 (0-385-32067-1); 1995, Dell/Laurel Leaf paper $3.99 (0-440-21947-7). A 17-year-old gets involved in the murder of a favorite school counselor. (Rev: BL 5/15/94; BTA; SLJ 6/94)

1522 Heisel, Sharon E. *A Little Magic* (5–7). 1991, Houghton $13.95 (0-395-55722-4). Jessica and her cousin Corky one day notice strange lights and mysterious noises and glimpse ghostly figures in the woods, followed by the disappearance of their friend Georgette. (Rev: BL 5/15/91; SLJ 4/91)

1523 Higgins, Jack. *The Eagle Has Flown* (9–adult). 1991, Simon & Schuster $21.95 (0-671-72458-4). The sequel to *The Eagle Has Landed*, in which Devlin is asked by the Germans to parachute into England and free the formerly believed-dead Steiner. (Rev: BL 3/1/91; SHS)

1524 Higgins, Jack. *The Eagle Has Landed* (9–adult). 1991, Simon & Schuster $21.95 (0-671-73310-9). A revision of the 1975 edition, published in its complete form as the author originally wished it, with 10 percent new material. (Rev: BL 3/1/91; SHS)

1525 Hill, Reginald. *Pictures of Perfection* (9–adult). 1994, Delacorte $19.95 (0-385-31270-9). A classic, witty English mystery with wonderfully eccentric characters and an ingenious plot about a missing constable and 3 detectives. (Rev: BL 10/1/94*)

1526 Hillerman, Tony, ed. *The Mysterious West* (9–adult). 1994, HarperCollins $23 (0-06-017785-3). Collects 20 mystery and suspense stories with Western themes that feature humor, action, and murder. (Rev: BL 10/1/94; SLJ 3/95)

1527 Hillerman, Tony. *Sacred Clowns* (9–adult). 1993, HarperCollins $23 (0-06-016767-X). Police officers must sort through a host of pieces to solve 2 murders—one a school shop teacher and the other a sacred clown. (Rev: BL 9/1/93*; BTA)

1528 Holton, Hugh. *Presumed Dead* (9–adult). 1994, Tor/Forge $21.95 (0-312-85710-1). Commander Larry Cole unravels the secrets of the National Science and Space Museum, where 200 people have vanished since 1900. (Rev: BL 7/94; VOYA 8/94)

1529 Hornsby, Wendy. *77th Street Requiem* (9–adult). 1995, Dutton $20.95 (0-525-93998-9). A documentary filmmaker investigates a 20-year-old murder, with background on the 1974 kidnapping of Patty Hearst. (Rev: BL 9/15/95*)

1530 Ignatius, David. *Siro* (9–adult). 1991, Farrar $19.95 (0-374-26506-2). CIA operative Edward Stone neglects to inform his superiors of his plan to spread disinformation among Soviet southern republics. (Rev: BL 3/15/91; SLJ 10/91)

1531 Irving, Clifford. *Final Argument* (9–adult). 1993, Simon & Schuster $22 (0-671-74868-8). In this fast-paced courtroom drama, Irving focuses on a young African American man falsely accused of murder. (Rev: BL 4/1/93*)

1532 Irwin, Hadley. *The Original Freddie Ackerman* (5–7). 1992, Macmillan/Margaret K. McElderry $14.95 (0-689-50562-0). When Trevor, 12—who belongs to a complicated blended family—is exiled to a Maine island to live with great-aunts, he gets involved in solving mysteries for an author, about himself, and about the nature of families. Awards: SLJ Best Book. (Rev: BL 1/1/93; MJHS; SLJ 8/92*)

1533 Isaacs, Susan. *After All These Years* (9–adult). 1993, HarperCollins $23 (0-06-016768-8).

A story of midlife crises, divorce, suburban sex, and murder among the rich, with a funny, gutsy heroine and an imaginative plot. (Rev: BL 5/15/93; SLJ 12/93)

1534 Iverson, Marc. *Persian Horse* (9–adult). 1991, Crown/Orion $20 (0-517-58310-0). This military thriller delivers a satisfactory amount of tension, technology, gunplay, and dead bodies. (Rev: BL 5/15/91; SLJ 10/91)

1535 James, Bill. *Take* (9–adult). 1994, Countryman/Foul Play $20 (0-88150-294-4). A small-time crook gets involved in a plan to steal a payroll, that turns out to be much more than expected. (Rev: BL 5/15/94*)

1536 James, P. D. *Original Sin* (9–adult). 1995, Knopf $24 (0-679-43889-0). Set in the modern publishing world, where traditions may crumble but such timeless emotions as grief, rage, love—and murder—prevail. (Rev: BL 1/1/95*)

1537 Johnston, Norma. *The Dragon's Eye* (7–10). 1990, Four Winds $13.95 (0-02-747701-0). The life of junior Jenny begins to unravel when nasty, cryptic messages start appearing at school. (Rev: BL 1/15/91; SLJ 12/90)

1538 Jones, Jill. *Emily's Secret* (9–adult). 1995, St. Martin's paper $4.99 (0-312-95576-6). A mysterious diary telling of Emily Brontë's passion for a Gypsy horse trader, a secret she carried to her grave, is the basis for this contemporary story, where the protagonists are attracted to each other through their search for the truth behind Brontë's death. (Rev: BL 8/95; SLJ 4/96)

1539 Kaminsky, Stuart. *Lieberman's Day* (9–adult). 1994, Holt $19.95 (0-8050-2575-8). Two Chicago policemen deal with murder, brutality, drugs, and difficult moral issues in this action-filled novel. (Rev: BL 2/15/94*)

1540 Karas, Phyllis. *The Hate Crime* (7–10). 1995, Avon paper $3.99 (0-380-78214-6). A docunovel/whodunit about a teen who scrawls the names of 7 concentration camps on a Jewish temple. (Rev: BL 12/1/95; VOYA 2/96)

1541 Kehret, Peg. *Night of Fear* (6–10). 1994, Dutton/Cobblehill $14.99 (0-525-65136-5). This suspense novel for reluctant readers concerns the escape attempts of a boy who is abducted and taken on the road by a man who fits the description of a bank robber. (Rev: BL 2/15/94; MJHS; SLJ 4/94; VOYA 2/94)

1542 Kehret, Peg. *Terror at the Zoo* (5–7). 1992, Dutton $14 (0-525-65083-0). An overnight camping trip at the zoo turns into a night of terror as a sister and brother foil an escaped convict's attempt to steal a valuable animal. (Rev: BL 12/1/91; MJHS; SLJ 1/92)

1543 Kellerman, Jonathan. *Devil's Waltz* (9–adult). 1993, Bantam $22.95 (0-553-09205-7). A complicated, intriguing mystery with Alex Delaware as its hero. (Rev: BL 10/15/92; SLJ 5/93)

1544 Kellerman, Jonathan. *The Web* (9–adult). 1996, Bantam $23.95 (0-553-08921-8). A must for mystery collections. Full of psychologically fascinating characters and suspense-filled action on a remote island. (Rev: BL 10/15/95*)

1545 Kelly, Mary Anne. *Foxglove* (9–adult). 1992, St. Martin's $17.95 (0-312-08195-2). After moving to a new home with her son and police officer husband, a woman becomes involved in the mystery of the death of an old friend. (Rev: BL 12/1/92*)

1546 Kemelman, Harry. *The Day the Rabbi Resigned* (9–adult). 1992, Ballantine/Fawcett Columbine $20 (0-449-90681-7). A rabbi joins forces with police to discover the real reason a prominent professor died. (Rev: BL 3/1/92; SLJ 9/92)

1547 Kerr, M. E. *Fell Down* (7–12). 1991, HarperCollins/Charlotte Zolotow LB $14.89 (0-06-021764-2). Fell has dropped out of prep school but is haunted by the death of his best friend there, so he returns to find a mystery of kidnapping, murder, and obsession. Awards: BL Editors' Choice. (Rev: BL 9/15/91*; BTA; SLJ 10/91)

1548 Kijewski, Karen. *Alley Kat Blues* (9–12). 1995, Doubleday $22.95 (0-385-46852-0). Kat Colorado is often on the road between Sacramento, where she investigates a hit-and-run, and Las Vegas, where she tries to find out why Hank, her beau, isn't returning her calls. (Rev: BL 6/1/95; SLJ 1/96)

1549 Kijewski, Karen. *Copy Kat* (9–adult). 1992, Doubleday $18.50 (0-385-42096-X). Hard-boiled female PI Kat Colorado is back in the series' fourth novel, with a new identity as bartender Kate, who tries to discover who murdered Diedre Durkin. (Rev: BL 10/1/92; SLJ 5/93)

1550 King, Laurie R. *The Beekeeper's Apprentice; or, On the Segregation of the Queen* (9–adult). 1994, St. Martin's $21.95 (0-312-10423-5). Sherlock Holmes and a brilliant 15-year-old girl become a detective duo and match wits with great criminal minds in England during World War I. Awards: SLJ Best Book; YALSA Best Book for Young Adults. (Rev: BL 2/1/94*; BTA; SLJ 7/94)

1551 King, Laurie R. *A Grave Talent* (9–adult). 1993, St. Martin's $19.95 (0-312-08804-3). Kate Martinelli, a lesbian homicide detective, investigates the murders of 3 little girls, with a world-renowned painter as the prime suspect. (Rev: BL 2/1/93*)

1552 King, Laurie R. *A Monstrous Regiment of Women* (9–12). 1995, St. Martin's $22.95 (0-312-13565-3). Using disguise, guile, and ruse, Mary, 21—and a partner with Sherlock Holmes—investigates murders in the inner circle of feminist preacher Margery Childe in 1920s London. (Rev: BL 9/1/95; SLJ 2/96)

1553 Kritlow, William. *A Race Against Time* (7–10). 1995, Thomas Nelson paper $4.99 (0-7852-7923-7). A scientist experiments with a deadly virus and before his death reveals that the cure is hidden in a virtual reality computer. With his knowledge of the virus's cure, an evil brother deals in blackmail. (Rev: BL 10/15/95)

1554 Landers, Gunnard. *The Violators* (9–adult). 1991, Walker $18.95 (0-8027-1179-0). An undercover agent for the U.S. Fish and Wildlife Services must bring poachers to justice. (Rev: BL 1/15/92; SLJ 6/92)

1555 Lasky, Kathryn. *Double Trouble Squared* (5–7). 1991, Harcourt $14.95 (0-15-224126-4); paper $5.95 (0-15-224127-2). Two sets of twins with telepathic powers attempt to solve bizarre mysteries in London. (Rev: BL 1/15/92; SLJ 2/92; YR)

1556 Lehane, Dennis. *A Drink Before the War* (9–adult). 1994, Harcourt $22.95 (0-15-100093-X). Patrick and Angelo are hired by 2 state senators to locate a black cleaning woman who filched several sensitive documents. (Rev: BL 11/15/94*)

1557 Lehrer, Jim. *Fine Lines* (9–adult). 1994, Random $20 (0-679-42823-2). In the sixth tale of the lieutenant governor of Oklahoma, someone is killing members of the state legislature. (Rev: BL 5/1/94; SLJ 11/94)

1558 L'Engle, Madeleine. *Troubling a Star* (7–10). 1994, Farrar $16 (0-374-37783-9). Vicki Austin, 16, travels to Antarctica and meets a Baltic prince looking for romance. They try to solve a mystery involving nuclear waste. (Rev: BL 8/94; BTA; SLJ 10/94; VOYA 12/94)

1559 Lewin, Michael Z. *Underdog* (9–adult). 1993, Mysterious $18.95 (0-89296-440-5). When homeless Jan Moro uncovers a police sting to catch thug Billy Cigar, his own entrepreneurial plan, which depends on Cigar's partnership, is endangered. (Rev: BL 10/1/93*)

1560 Lieberman, Herbert. *Sandman, Sleep* (9–adult). 1993, St. Martin's $22.95 (0-312-08886-8). A combined sci-fi/mystery wherein a billionaire has discovered a way to produce a master race of children with perfect genes. (Rev: BL 3/1/93; VOYA 12/93)

1561 Linscott, Gillian. *Stage Fright* (9–adult). 1993, St. Martin's $17.95 (0-312-09812-X). Suffragist Nell Bray was supposed to protect playwright George Bernard Shaw's leading lady from her estranged husband, but she ends up having to prove her innocent of murder. (Rev: BL 12/1/93; SLJ 7/94)

1562 Locke, Joseph. *Kill the Teacher's Pet* (8–12). 1991, Bantam/Starfire paper $2.99 (0-553-29058-4). A favorite high school teacher disappears and the replacement arrives—a man believed to be involved in the murders of several students across the country. (Rev: BL 12/15/91; SLJ 3/92)

1563 Lovesey, Peter. *The Last Detective* (9–adult). (Perfect Crime Books) 1991, Doubleday $18.50 (0-385-42114-1). In this intricately plotted crime novel, detective Peter Diamond struggles against bureaucratic intervention in the murder investigation of a former soap opera star. (Rev: BL 9/1/91*)

1564 Lupoff, Richard A. *The Bessie Blue Killer* (9–adult). 1994, St. Martin's $20.95 (0-312-10425-1). Hobart and Marvia are drawn into a mystery involving kidnapping, drugs, and airplanes when a murder occurs on the set of a World War II film. (Rev: BL 3/15/94*; BTA; VOYA 6/94)

1565 McCammon, Robert R. *Gone South* (9–adult). 1992, Pocket $22 (0-671-74306-6). This tale about a killer on the run is more thriller than horror story, though with a hefty dose of violence. (Rev: BL 8/92; SLJ 5/93)

1566 McCrumb, Sharyn. *The Hangman's Beautiful Daughter* (9–adult). (Ballad) 1992, Scribner $18.95 (0-684-19407-4). A minister's wife unravels the mystery of one family's murder-suicide in Appalachia. (Rev: BL 3/15/92*)

1567 McCrumb, Sharyn. *Missing Susan* (9–adult). 1991, Ballantine $17 (0-345-36575-5). A royalty-adoring forensic anthropologist takes a group tour of England's most famous murder sites, led by a guide who has been paid to kill one of his charges. (Rev: BL 9/1/91*)

1568 McCrumb, Sharyn. *She Walks These Hills* (9–adult). (Ballad) 1994, Scribner $21 (0-684-19556-9). A radio talk show host, a graduate student, and a police dispatcher travel the haunted foothills of the Appalachian Trail, each searching for clues to troubled pasts. Awards: SLJ Best Book. (Rev: BL 8/94; BTA; SLJ 3/95)

1569 McGraw, Eloise. *Tangled Webb* (5–7). 1993, Macmillan/Margaret K. McElderry $13.95

(0-689-50573-6). After her widowed father remarries, Juniper, 12, believes that his bride is hiding something, so she plays detective and gradually unravels her stepmother's story. (Rev: BL 6/1–15/93; MJHS; SLJ 6/93; VOYA 8/93)

1570 McInerny, Ralph. *The Case of the Constant Caller* (7–10). 1995, St. Martin's $16.95 (0-312-13037-6). Youths investigate the theft of a laptop computer, with the primary suspect a paroled criminal. (Rev: BL 8/95; SLJ 9/95; VOYA 4/96)

1571 McInerny, Ralph. *The Case of the Dead Winner* (7–10). 1995, St. Martin's $15.95 (0-312-13038-4). From the author of the Father Dowling series, this tale of 3 teenagers who practice their sleuthing on a suspicious mother-and-daughter reunion leads to several deaths. (Rev: BL 8/95; SLJ 9/95; VOYA 4/96)

1572 McMullan, Kate. *Under the Mummy's Spell* (5–8). 1992, Farrar $16 (0-374-38033-3). Interweaves the tales of Peter, a present-day 12-year-old New Yorker, and Nephia, an Egyptian princess who lived 3,000 years ago. (Rev: BL 7/92; SLJ 7/92; YR)

1573 McQuillan, Karin. *The Cheetah Chase* (9–adult). 1994, Ballantine $20 (0-345-38183-1). Safari specialist Jazz Jasper witnesses her friend Nick being stung to death by a scorpion, teams with Inspector Ormondi to investigate the suspicious death, and uncovers murder. (Rev: BL 8/94; SLJ 12/94)

1574 Mahoney, Dan. *Detective First Grade* (9–adult). 1993, St. Martin's $21.95 (0-312-09288-1). A realistic look at big-city cops trying to solve a violent terrorist kidnapping in time to save the victim. (Rev: BL 4/15/93; SLJ 10/93)

1575 Mahy, Margaret. *Underrunners* (5–7). 1992, Viking $14 (0-670-84179-X); 1994, Penguin/Puffin paper $3.99 (0-14-036869-8). Dreams of adventure become frighteningly real when an 11-year-old and his friend are kidnapped. Awards: SLJ Best Book. (Rev: BL 2/1/92*; MJHS; SLJ 2/92*; YR)

1576 Malashenko, Alexei. *The Last Red August* (9–adult). Tr. by Anthony Olcott. 1993, Scribner $21 (0-684-19571-2). An absorbing, action-packed tale of political intrigue, kidnapping, and murder set in modern-day Russia. (Rev: BL 5/1/93*)

1577 Margolin, Phillip. *After Dark* (9–adult). 1995, Doubleday $23.95 (0-385-47548-9). Part courtroom drama, psychological thriller, murder mystery, and love story, starring young lawyer Tracy Cavanaugh. (Rev: BL 5/1/95*)

1578 Maron, Margaret. *Bootlegger's Daughter* (9–adult). 1992, Mysterious $18.95 (0-89296-445-6). A North Carolina lawyer agrees to do some amateur sleuthing for an 18-year-old troubled by her mother's unsolved murder. Awards: Edgar. (Rev: BL 4/15/92)

1579 Maron, Margaret. *Southern Discomfort* (9–adult). 1993, Mysterious $18.95 (0-89296-446-4). A disturbed teen turns murderer and creates havoc in a small Southern town. The portrait of small-town life is poignant and funny. (Rev: BL 6/1–15/93*)

1580 Marston, Edward. *The Ravens of Blackwater* (9–adult). 1994, St. Martin's $20.95 (0-312-11330-7). A soldier and a lawyer are hired by William the Conquerer to inventory the estate of a rapacious family. They uncover a murder and the prime suspect is an abbey prioress. (Rev: BL 9/15/94; SLJ 4/95)

1581 Masters, Anthony. *A Watching Silence* (5–8). 1992, Simon & Schuster $15 (0-671-79173-7). When young Martin, an American living on Shetland Island, stumbles on a mysterious knife, intrigue follows, involving smuggling, Norse traditions, a Nigerian cabin boy, and the violence of nature. (Rev: BL 11/15/92; SLJ 10/92)

1582 Michaels, Barbara. *Stitches in Time* (9–adult). 1995, HarperCollins $22 (0-06-017763-2). Weaves an incredible mystery based on a haunted quilt. (Rev: BL 5/1/95; SLJ 11/95)

1583 Morrell, David. *The Covenant of the Flame* (9–adult). 1991, Warner $19.95 (0-446-51563-9). Fatal attacks on polluters around the world are investigated by a writer and a New York Police Department lieutenant. (Rev: BL 4/1/91*)

1584 Muller, Marcia. *Till the Butchers Cut Him Down* (9–adult). 1994, Mysterious $18.95 (0-89296-455-3). Sharon McCone, private investigator, must uncover the truth about what happened to her troubleshooting computer guru friend. (Rev: BL 4/15/94*)

1585 Mystery Scene Staff, eds. *The Year's 25 Finest Crime and Mystery Stories* (9–12). 1995, Carroll & Graf $24 (0-7867-0251-6). A collection of 25 crime and mystery short stories, 12 of the authors being women. (Rev: SLJ 3/96)

1586 Nickolae, Barbara. *Ties That Bind* (9–adult). 1993, Berkley paper $4.99 (0-425-13573-X). A young photographer searching for her uncle finds her life in danger when she witnesses the discovery of a corpse. (Rev: BL 1/1/93; SLJ 5/93)

1587 Nixon, Joan Lowery. *A Candidate for Murder* (6–12). 1991, Delacorte $14.95 (0-385-30257-6); 1992, Dell/Laurel Leaf paper $3.50 (0-440-21212-X). While Cary's father enters the political limelight, his daughter gets embroiled in a series of strange events. (Rev: BL 3/1/91; BY; MJHS)

1588 Nixon, Joan Lowery. *A Deadly Promise* (5–7). 1992, Bantam/Starfire $16 (0-553-08054-7). Western heroine Sarah Lindley, her sister, and a stagecoach driver attempt to solve the mystery behind her father's death and recover his honor. Sequel to *High Trail to Danger*. (Rev: BL 3/1/92; MJHS; SLJ 3/92; YR)

1589 Nixon, Joan Lowery. *The Name of the Game Was Murder* (6–8). 1993, Delacorte $15 (0-385-30864-7). Teenager Samantha must work with her uncle's houseguests to find a damning manuscript and uncover the murderer of its author. Awards: Edgar. (Rev: BL 3/1/93; BTA)

1590 Nixon, Joan Lowery. *Shadowmaker* (7–9). 1994, Delacorte $14.95 (0-385-32030-2). When Katie's mother, an investigative journalist, is brought evidence of toxic-waste dumping and must probe into the case, Katie discovers that events at her school are related. Awards: Edgar. (Rev: BL 3/1/94; MJHS; SLJ 5/94; VOYA 8/94)

1591 Nixon, Joan Lowery. *Spirit Seeker* (6–9). 1995, Delacorte $15.95 (0-385-32062-0). Holly Campbell is pitted against her police detective father in a race to exonerate her boyfriend of a charge of double murder. (Rev: BL 9/15/95; SLJ 9/95; VOYA 2/96)

1592 Nixon, Joan Lowery. *The Weekend Was Murder!* (6–10). 1992, Delacorte $15 (0-385-30531-1); 1994, Dell/Laurel Leaf paper $3.99 (0-440-21901-9). A teen sleuth and her boyfriend attend a murder-mystery-enactment weekend and discover a real murder. (Rev: BL 2/15/92; MJHS; SHS; SLJ 3/92)

1593 O'Connell, Carol. *Mallory's Oracle* (9–adult). 1994, Putnam $21.95 (0-399-13975-3). Kathleen Mallory, once a street urchin, has grown up to be a computer-whiz cop. She hits the streets again to track down the killer of her adoptive father. (Rev: BL 7/94*)

1594 O'Connell, Carol. *The Man Who Cast Two Shadows* (9–adult). 1995, Putnam $22.95 (0-399-14064-6). Kathy Mallory pits her uncanny intelligence and computer skills against a compulsive and evasive adversary. (Rev: BL 3/1/95*)

1595 Olson, Toby. *At Sea* (9–adult). 1993, Simon & Schuster $19 (0-671-73641-8). Detective Blue becomes embroiled in a complicated rape/murder/drug-smuggling case in a Cape Cod tourist town full of shady secrets. (Rev: BL 4/15/93*)

1596 Paretsky, Sara. *Guardian Angel* (9–adult). 1992, Delacorte $20 (0-385-29931-1). Intrepid female private eye V. I. Warshawski is involved with greedy Yuppies offloading dodgy bonds on Chicago seniors. (Rev: BL 12/1/91; SLJ 9/92)

1597 Paretsky, Sara. *Tunnel Vision* (9–adult). 1994, Delacorte $21.95 (0-385-29932-X). The latest adventure of the spunky, tough, one-woman-crime-crusader V. I. Warshawski is gripping, intriguing, and long. (Rev: BL 4/1/94*; SLJ 1/95)

1598 Patneaude, David. *Someone Was Watching* (6–9). 1993, Albert Whitman $13.95 (0-8075-7531-3). David, 13, who must solve the mystery of whether his baby sister drowned at a picnic or was kidnapped, embarks on a cross-country chase of possible kidnappers. (Rev: BL 7/93; SLJ 7/93)

1599 Pearce, Michael. *The Mamur Zapt and the Men Behind* (9–adult). 1993, Mysterious $17.95 (0-89296-487-1). Authentic portrait of early twentieth-century, British-occupied Egypt, with a sophisticated hero and plenty of action and mystery. (Rev: BL 7/93; BTA)

1600 Perry, Anne. *Cain His Brother* (9–adult). 1995, Ballantine/Fawcett Columbine $22.95 (0-449-90847-X). Victorian detective William Monk investigates the case of the missing husband whose thug of a twin brother is suspected of doing the deed. (Rev: BL 8/95*)

1601 Perry, Thomas. *Vanishing Act* (9–adult). 1995, Random $23 (0-679-43536-0). Native American Jane Whitefield helps people disappear. In this case, she helps John Felker, accused of embezzlement, attain a new identity. (Rev: BL 12/15/94; SLJ 8/95)

1602 Perutz, Leo. *Master of the Day of Judgment* (9–adult). 1994, Arcade $19.95 (1-55970-171-4). In 1909 Vienna, Baron von Yosch is accused of killing an actor whose wife was once his lover. He finds a terrifying secret when he investigates. (Rev: BL 10/15/94*)

1603 Peters, Elizabeth. *The Snake, the Crocodile and the Dog* (9–adult). 1992, Warner $19.95 (0-446-51585-X). The eccentric Emersons begin their annual archeological trek to Egypt, and feisty Amelia's husband is mysteriously abducted. (Rev: BL 8/92; SLJ 2/93)

1604 Peters, Ellis. *The Holy Thief* (9–adult). 1993, Mysterious $17.95 (0-89296-524-X). Thievery and murder intrude upon crafty Brother Cadfael's well-ordered life. (Rev: BL 3/1/93; SLJ 7/93)

1605 Petersen, P. J. *Liars* (6–9). 1992, Simon & Schuster $14 (0-671-75035-6). Sam, 14, discovers that he knows when someone is lying. His ESP makes him suspicious of almost everyone, even his father. (Rev: BL 6/1/92; SLJ 4/92*; YR)

1606 Pickard, Nancy. *Confession* (9–adult). 1994, Pocket $20 (0-671-78261-4). The discovery that Geof fathered a now-teenage boy sets the plot in motion. The boy's mother and stepfather were murdered, and Geof insists that the case be reopened. (Rev: BL 5/15/94*)

1607 Pickard, Nancy. *I.O.U.* (9–adult). 1992, Pocket paper $4.99 (0-671-68043-9). A multilayered novel in which amateur sleuth Jenny Cain examines her deceased mother's insanity, delves into the family business bankruptcy, and deals with an attempt on her own life. (Rev: BL 2/15/91*)

1608 Piesman, Marissa. *Heading Uptown* (9–adult). 1993, Delacorte $18.95 (0-385-30537-0). A clever, often hilarious mystery with eccentric characters. (Rev: BL 1/15/93*)

1609 Prather, Ray. *Fish and Bones* (6–9). 1992, HarperCollins LB $13.89 (0-06-025122-0). Bones, 13, tries to unravel the mystery of a pig-masked bandit who robs the bank in Sun City, Florida. Awards: SLJ Best Book. (Rev: SLJ 2/93*)

1610 Prowell, Sandra West. *The Killing of Monday Brown* (9–adult). 1994, Walker $19.95 (0-8027-3184-8). Private eye Phoebe Siegel investigates a missing dealer in Native American artifacts. (Rev: BL 5/15/94*)

1611 Reaver, Chap. *A Little Bit Dead* (9–12). 1992, Delacorte $15 (0-385-30801-9); 1994, Dell/Laurel Leaf paper $3.99 (0-440-21910-8). When Reece saves an Indian boy from lynching by U.S. marshals, lawmen claim that he murdered one of the marshals and he must clear himself. Awards: Edgar; YALSA Best Book for Young Adults. (Rev: BL 9/1/92; SLJ 9/92; YR)

1612 Rendell, Ruth. *The Crocodile Bird* (9–adult). 1993, Crown $20 (0-517-59576-1). Liza, 16, learns to live in the world and recounts to her lover the tale of her isolated childhood and her mother's obsession and acts of murder. Awards: YALSA Best Book for Young Adults. (Rev: BL 7/93*; BTA; SLJ 3/94)

1613 Rendell, Ruth. *Kissing the Gunner's Daughter* (9–adult). 1992, Mysterious $19.95 (0-89296-390-5). The inspector tries to solve a complex puzzle when a famous novelist and her family are slaughtered, leaving only a 17-year-old survivor. (Rev: BL 4/15/92*)

1614 Rigbey, Liz. *Total Eclipse* (9–adult). 1995, Pocket $22 (0-671-79579-1). Recently divorced astronomer Lomax must prove his coworker and love interest Julia innocent of the murder of her husband and stepdaughter. (Rev: BL 7/95*)

1615 Roberts, Les. *The Cleveland Connection* (9–adult). 1993, St. Martin's $19.95 (0-312-08746-2). Cleveland PI Jacovich, trying to locate a missing Serbian grandfather, must sort through age-old Balkan animosities and modern wise-guy rules of conduct. (Rev: BL 1/15/93*)

1616 Roberts, Les. *The Lake Effect* (9–adult). 1994, St. Martin's $21.95 (0-312-11537-7). Private-eye Milan Jacovich returns a favor for a mobster and helps run Barbara Corn's mayoral campaign. When the competing candidate's wife is murdered, Jacovich investigates. (Rev: BL 11/1/94*)

1617 Roberts, Willo Davis. *The Absolutely True Story: My Trip to Yellowstone Park with the Terrible Rupes (No Names Have Been Changed to Protect the Guilty)* (5–7). 1994, Atheneum $14.95 (0-689-31939-8). Lewis, 12, thinks he's lucky to be invited to go to Yellowstone with the Rupes—who eat junk food, don't assign chores, and do what they want—until all the children are kidnapped by 2 menacing men. Awards: Edgar. (Rev: BL 1/15/95; SLJ 3/95; VOYA 4/95)

1618 Roberts, Willo Davis. *Caught!* (5–7). 1994, Atheneum $14.95 (0-689-31903-7). Vickie, 13, and her younger sister hop a bus to California to stay with their dad, but he has disappeared and they become immersed in a web of intrigue. Awards: Edgar. (Rev: BL 4/1/94; SLJ 5/94)

1619 Roberts, Willo Davis. *Scared Stiff* (5–7). 1991, Atheneum/Jean Karl $13.95 (0-689-31692-5). Rick, 11, and his younger brother Kenny explore an amusement park in search of their missing mother. (Rev: BL 2/15/91; MJHS; SLJ 3/91)

1620 Robinson, Peter. *A Dedicated Man* (9–adult). 1991, Scribner $17.95 (0-684-19265-9). A 16-year-old girl may know who murdered an archeologist, but then she disappears, leaving the chief inspector with an even bigger puzzle to solve. (Rev: BL 8/91*)

1621 Ross, Kate. *Whom the Gods Loved* (9–adult). 1995, Viking $19.95 (0-670-86207-X). Set in early nineteenth-century London, society gentleman Julian Kestrel investigates the murder of his old acquaintance Alexander Falkland. (Rev: BL 6/1–15/95; SLJ 10/95)

1622 Ross, Ramon Royal. *Harper and Moon* (6–8). 1993, Atheneum/Jean Karl $13.95 (0-689-31803-0). Set in 1942, the story of Harper and Moon deals with child abuse, animal abuse, suspected murder, and a suicide attempt. Awards: ALSC Notable Children's Book; SLJ Best Book. (Rev: BL 5/15/93; SLJ 9/93*)

1623 Rubinstein, Gillian. *Galax-Arena* (7–10). 1995, Simon & Schuster $15 (0-689-80136-X). A 13-year-old girl and 20 other children from Earth are removed to another planet and trained to perform dangerous acrobatic tricks. (Rev: BL 10/15/95*; SLJ 10/95)

1624 Rushford, Patricia H. *Dying to Win: Lost in a World Where Drugs Reign . . .* (7–12). (Jennie McGrady Mystery) 1995, Bethany paper $3.99 (1-55661-559-0). In the series' sixth episode, Jennie, 16, unravels a puzzle surrounding a rebellious schoolmate. (Rev: BL 1/1/96; SLJ 2/96)

1625 Rushford, Patricia H. *Without a Trace: Nick Is Missing and Now They Are After Her . . .* (6–9). (Jennie McGrady Mystery) 1995, Bethany paper $3.99 (1-55661-558-2). In the fifth book in the series, Jennie practices her sleuthing skills when her young brother and one of his friends disappear. (Rev: BL 9/1/95; SLJ 9/95; VOYA 2/96)

1626 Safire, William. *Sleeper Spy* (9–12). 1995, Random $24 (0-679-43447-X). Reporter Irving Fein is investigating a sleeper spy—a man sent by the KGB to the United States as a normal citizen who is waiting to be "activated"—with double and triple crosses, the Russian Mafia, murder, and a suicide. (Rev: BL 9/1/95; SLJ 3/96)

1627 Saul, John. *Black Lightning* (9–adult). 1995, Ballantine/Fawcett Columbine $23 (0-449-90864-X). Two years after the execution of serial killer Richard Kraven, reporter Anne Jeffer finds her husband has changed and the murders have begun again. (Rev: BL 6/1–15/95; SLJ 12/95)

1628 Sedley, Kate. *The Plymouth Cloak: The Second Tale of Roger the Chapman* (9–adult). 1993, St. Martin's $16.95 (0-312-08875-2). A medieval peddler-sleuth is enlisted by the Duke of Gloucester to unmask the murderer of a suspected double agent. (Rev: BL 2/1/93; BTA)

1629 Sedley, Kate. *The Weaver's Tale* (9–adult). 1994, St. Martin's $20.95 (0-312-10474-X). A medieval adventure with Roger the Chapman, an itinerant peddler, as sleuth, investigating the disappearance and death of a widow's father. (Rev: BL 5/15/94; SLJ 1/95)

1630 Shreve, Susan Richards. *The Train Home* (9–adult). 1993, Doubleday $19 (0-385-42357-8). An Irish actor, posing as a priest, seeks revenge against the murderer of his brother, and a beautiful opera singer is trapped in a loveless marriage. (Rev: BL 7/93*)

1631 Siciliano, Sam. *The Angel of the Opera: Sherlock Holmes Meets the Phantom of the Opera* (9–adult). 1994, Penzler Books (129 W. 56th St., New York, NY 10019) $21 (1-883402-46-8). Sherlock Holmes's cousin is the narrator in this mystery where one case is ending just as the Paris Opera case is beginning. (Rev: BL 5/15/94; SLJ 12/94)

1632 Smith, April. *North of Montana* (9–adult). 1994, Knopf $23 (0-679-43197-7). FBI agent Ana, hungry for a career-making case, investigates movie star Jayne Mason's claim that her doctor has hooked her on painkillers. (Rev: BL 9/15/94*; SLJ 5/95)

1633 Smith, Charlie. *Chimney Rock* (9–adult). 1993, Holt $22.50 (0-8050-2244-9). Actor Will Blake and his father, a screen director, are locked in a battle to claim actress Kate Dunn, Will's wife. (Rev: BL 4/1/93*)

1634 Stabenow, Dana. *A Cold-Blooded Business* (9–adult). 1994, Berkley $17.95 (0-425-14173-X). Aleut private eye Kate Shugak travels north of the Arctic Circle to investigate a rise in cocaine use among Alaskan oil field workers. (Rev: BL 3/1/94*; SLJ 9/94)

1635 Stabenow, Dana. *Play with Fire* (9–adult). 1995, Berkley $19.95 (0-425-14717-7). A female Alaskan investigator checks into the mysterious disappearance of the son of a local preacher. (Rev: BL 3/15/95*)

1636 Steiner, Barbara. *Dreamstalker* (8–12). 1992, Avon/Flare paper $3.50 (0-380-76611-6). A girl wonders if she's psychic when her terrifying nightmares start coming true. (Rev: BL 3/15/92)

1637 Vine, Barbara. *Anna's Book* (9–adult). 1993, Crown/Harmony $22 (0-517-58796-3). Mature readers will enjoy the darkness and complexity, mesmerizing plot, and unconventional characters in this story of 3 generations of London women and the diaries that unite them. (Rev: BL 4/15/93*)

1638 Vine, Barbara. *No Night Is Too Long* (9–adult). 1995, Crown/Harmony $23 (0-517-79964-2). A man who thinks he has gotten away with murder begins receiving mysterious letters in this tale of psychological suspense. (Rev: BL 12/1/94*)

1639 Voigt, Cynthia. *The Vandemark Mummy* (6–9). 1991, Atheneum $14.95 (0-689-31476-0). Involves a break-in at a museum of Egyptian antiquities and 2 teenage siblings who attempt to solve the mystery. (Rev: BL 9/1/91; SLJ 9/91)

1640 Walker, Mary Willis. *The Red Scream* (9–adult). 1994, Doubleday $19.95 (0-385-46858-X). Journalist Molly Cates obsessively researched serial-killer Louie Bronk for years, ultimately writing a book on his life. Before his execution,

Bronk screams innocence and Molly investigates. (Rev: BL 8/94*)

1641 Waterhouse, Jane. *Graven Images* (9–adult). 1995, Putnam $22.95 (0-399-14080-8). Garner Quinn writes popular true-crime books, but because of a victim's unexpected about-face, her subject—a serial murderer—walks free. (Rev: BL 9/15/95*)

1642 Westall, Robert. *Stormsearch* (5–7). 1992, Farrar $14 (0-374-37272-1). When Tim finds a model ship on a beach, he helps his uncle retrieve the ship, sail it, research its history, and dig for treasure. Awards: YALSA Best Book for Young Adults. (Rev: BL 10/15/92; BTA; SLJ 11/92; YR)

1643 Westall, Robert. *Yaxley's Cat* (7–10). 1992, Scholastic $13.95 (0-590-45175-8). A family rents a cottage once owned by a mysterious old man and fight to stay after townspeople try to run them out. Awards: YALSA Best Book for Young Adults. (Rev: BL 3/15/92; BTA; MJHS; SLJ 3/92; YR)

1644 Westlake, Donald E. *Don't Ask* (9–adult). 1993, Mysterious $18.95 (0-89296-469-3). The bumbling Dortmunder gang tries to steal the leg bone of a thirteenth-century saint. (Rev: BL 3/1/93; BTA)

1645 Wilde, Nicholas. *Death Knell* (7–12). 1991, Holt $14.95 (0-8050-1851-4). Two teenage boys on holiday in Norfolk, England, discover the murdered body of a recluse while investigating a tolling church bell. (Rev: BL 12/1/91)

1646 Wilson, F. Paul. *The Select* (9–adult). 1994, Morrow $22 (0-688-04618-5). A young woman resorts to subterfuge to gain admission to a highly selective medical school and discovers the institution is not what it seemed. (Rev: BL 1/1/94; SLJ 6/94)

1647 Windsor, Patricia. *The Christmas Killer* (7–10). 1991, Scholastic $13.95 (0-590-43311-3). Rosecleer solves the mystery of a serial killer of teenage girls who is haunting the town where she lives with her parents and twin brother. (Rev: BL 10/15/91; MJHS)

1648 Woods, Paula L., ed. *Spooks, Spies, and Private Eyes: Black Mystery, Crime, and Suspense Fiction* (9–adult). 1995, Doubleday $22.95 (0-385-48082-2). Short mysteries by such African American writers as Richard Wright (*The Man Who Killed a Shadow*) and George Schuyler (*The Shoemaker Murder*). (Rev: BL 11/15/95)

1649 Wright, L. R. *A Touch of Panic* (9–adult). 1994, Scribner $20 (0-684-19672-7). Canadian policeman Karl Alberg takes a case involving a master burglar, a mate-hunting psychopath, and various idiosyncratic characters. (Rev: BL 9/15/94*)

1650 Yastrow, Shelby. *Under Oath* (9–adult). 1994, Eakin/Diamond paper $5.50 (0-7865-0005-0). A legal thriller about an obstetrician facing a malpractice suit. (Rev: BL 5/15/94; SLJ 10/94)

1651 *The Year's 25 Finest Crime and Mystery Stories* (9–adult). 1992, Carroll & Graf $21 (0-88184-903-0). Well-known and unfamiliar writers provide a wonderful variety of entertaining crime/mystery stories, from macabre to humorous. (Rev: BL 12/15/92*)

1652 Yorke, Margaret. *A Small Deceit* (9–adult). 1991, Viking $18.95 (0-670-83977-9). A convicted rapist plots revenge against the judge who sentenced him to prison. (Rev: BL 8/91*)

1653 Zubro, Mark Richard. *Political Poison* (9–adult). 1993, St. Martin's $17.95 (0-312-09364-0). The intrigue of Chicago politics, a single father who happens to be gay, and the murder of a popular alderman. (Rev: BL 6/1–15/93)

Romances

1654 Aikath-Gyaltsen, Indrani. *Daughters of the House* (9–adult). 1993, Ballantine $16 (0-345-38073-8). Set in modern India, Chchanda, 18, tells of her household of 3 generations of self-sufficient women and how love, lust, betrayal, and loyalty change them. (Rev: BL 1/1/93; BTA)

1655 Alcott, Louisa May. *A Long Fatal Love Chase* (9–12). 1995, Random $21 (0-679-44510-2). Written in 1866, this racy tale about Rosamond is melodramatic but intriguing, dramatizing the tragic plight of women in oppressive times. (Rev: BL 9/15/95; SLJ 2/96)

1656 Applegate, Katherine. *Sharing Sam* (7–10). 1995, Bantam paper $3.50 (0-553-56660-1). A sacrificial love story where a best friend is dying of a brain tumor and the boyfriend Sam is shared. (Rev: BL 3/15/95; SLJ 2/95)

1657 Applegate, Katherine, and others. *See You in September* (7–10). 1995, Avon paper $3.99 (0-380-78088-7). Four chaste but charming short stories by 4 popular YA "romance" authors. (Rev: BL 1/1/96; SLJ 3/96)

1658 Bauer, Joan. *Thwonk* (7–10). 1995, Delacorte $14.95 (0-385-32092-2). "Thwonk" is the sound of Cupid's bow when A. J.'s wish comes true that hunky Peter become hers alone. Unfortunately, Peter's adoration is more than she bargained for. (Rev: BL 1/1/95; BTA; SLJ 1/95)

1659 Binchy, Maeve. *The Glass Lake* (9–adult). 1995, Delacorte $23.95 (0-385-31354-3). Helen is presumed to have drowned in an Irish lake, but she's fled to London with her lover. Years later, she tries to reestablish contact with her teenaged daughter, Kit. (Rev: BL 1/1/95; SLJ 8/95)

1660 Blake, Michael. *Airman Mortensen* (9–adult). 1991, Seven Wolves Publishing (8928 National Blvd., Los Angeles, CA 90034) $20 (0-9627387-7-8). The poignant summer romance between an 18-year-old airman awaiting court martial and the base commander's daughter is described in this story of the loss of innocence. (Rev: BL 10/1/91; SLJ 11/91)

1661 Bonner, Cindy. *Looking after Lily* (9–adult). 1994, Algonquin $18.95 (1-56512-045-0). Lily's outlaw husband has been sentenced to jail and asks his brother to care for his pregnant wife, whereupon he falls in love with her. Awards: SLJ Best Book; YALSA Best Book for Young Adults. (Rev: BL 2/15/94*; BTA; SLJ 5/94; VOYA 10/94)

1662 Brooks, Martha. *Two Moons in August* (7–12). 1992, Little, Brown $14.95 (0-316-10979-7). A midsummer romance in the 1950s between a newcomer to a small Canadian community and a 16-year-old girl who is mourning her mother's death. Awards: YALSA Best Book for Young Adults. (Rev: BL 11/15/91*; SLJ 3/92*)

1663 Byars, Betsy. *Bingo Brown's Guide to Romance* (5–8). 1992, Viking $14 (0-670-84491-8). Romance, confusion, and comedy occur when Bingo Brown meets his true love in the produce section of the grocery store. (Rev: BL 4/1/92; MJHS; SLJ 4/92)

1664 Cormier, Robert. *We All Fall Down* (8–12). 1991, Delacorte $16 (0-385-30501-X); Dell paper $3.99 (0-440-21556-0). Random violence committed by 4 high school seniors is observed by the Avenger, who also witnesses the budding love affair of one of the victims of the attack. Awards: SLJ Best Book. (Rev: BL 9/15/91*; MJHS; SHS; SLJ 9/91*)

1665 Coulter, Catherine. *Lord of Falcon Ridge* (9–adult). 1995, Berkley/Jove paper $6.50 (0-515-11584-3). In this conclusion to the trilogy, set in Britain in A.D. 922, Cleve and Chessa meet and fall in love as he's transporting her to her intended husband and she's pursued by a kidnapper. (Rev: BL 1/15/95; SLJ 9/95)

1666 Danzinger, Paula. *Thames Doesn't Rhyme with James* (7–10). 1994, Putnam $14.95 (0-399-22526-9). Kendra and her family take a joint vacation to London with the Lees and their son Frank, her long-distance boyfriend. (Rev: BL 12/1/94; BTA; SLJ 1/95; VOYA 4/95)

1667 Driscoll, Jack. *Skylight* (9–12). 1991, Orchard/Richard Jackson LB $14.99 (0-531-08561-9). A middle-class teenage boy falls in love with a rich girl who betrays him. (Rev: BL 2/1/92)

1668 Erdrich, Louise. *The Bingo Palace* (9–adult). 1994, HarperCollins $23 (0-06-017080-8). Comedy and romance meld in this story of ne'er-do-well Lipsha Morrisey, who proves his worth to his Chippewa beloved, Shawnee Ray Toose, and resolves his relationship with his dead mother. (Rev: BL 12/15/93*)

1669 Fiedler, Lisa. *Curtis Piperfield's Biggest Fan* (5–9). 1995, Clarion $13.95 (0-395-70728-5). A young girl in an all-girl Catholic school experiences teen erotic fascinations. (Rev: BL 9/15/95; VOYA 12/95)

1670 Gelman, Jan. *Marci's Secret Book of Dating* (5–8). 1991, Knopf/Bullseye LB $7.99 (0-679-91106-5); paper $2.95 (0-679-81106-0). Marci is asked out by good-looking but inconsiderate Patrick but she comes to her senses after he takes her to a beach kegger. (Rev: BL 12/15/91)

1671 Geras, Adèle. *Pictures of the Night* (7–12). 1993, Harcourt $16.95 (0-15-261588-1). A modern reworking of *Snow White,* with the heroine an 18-year-old singer in London and Paris. (Rev: BL 3/1/93; SLJ 6/93)

1672 Geras, Adèle. *The Tower Room* (7–12). 1992, Harcourt $15.95 (0-15-289627-9). The fairy tale *Rapunzel* is updated and set in an English girls' boarding school in the 1960s. (Rev: BL 2/15/92; YR)

1673 Gilchrist, Ellen. *Starcarbon: A Meditation on Love* (9–adult). 1994, Little, Brown $21.95 (0-316-31327-0). Love is the theme of this novel about half-Cherokee Olivia Hand and her high school sweetheart as well as a group of related couples. (Rev: BL 1/15/94*)

1674 Hahn, Mary Downing. *The Wind Blows Backward* (8–12). 1993, Clarion $13.95 (0-395-62975-6); 1994, Avon/Flare paper $3.99 (0-380-77530-1). Spencer's downward emotional spiral and Lauren's deep commitment evoke a fantasy love gone awry. Awards: YALSA Best Book for Young Adults. (Rev: BL 5/1/93; MJHS; SLJ 5/93)

1675 Harper, Karen. *Circle of Gold* (9–adult). 1992, Dutton $20 (0-525-93453-7). A spirited mountain girl finds passion but not contentment when she marries an English lord. Awards: SLJ Best Book. (Rev: BL 4/15/92; SLJ 12/92)

1676 Hendry, Diana. *Double Vision* (7–9). 1993, Candlewick $14.95 (1-56402-125-4). In 1950s England, Eliza, 15, must deal with first love, insecurity, betrayal, and her friend's pregnancy. (Rev: BL 3/1/93*; BTA)

1677 Hobbs, Valerie. *How Fat Would You Have Gotten If I Hadn't Called You Back?* (8–12). 1995, Orchard/Richard Jackson LB $19.99 (0-531-08780-8). A coming-of-age story that deals with all the important emotions: love, friendship, responsibilities, rebellion, and identity in 1950s small-town America. (Rev: BL 10/1/95; SLJ 10/95; VOYA 12/95)

1678 Holt, Victoria. *Daughter of Deceit* (9–adult). 1991, Doubleday $20 (0-385-41949-X). The daughter of a recently deceased London actress must call off her wedding when it is revealed that her fiancé is probably her half-brother. (Rev: BL 9/1/91; SLJ 4/92)

1679 Kaplow, Robert. *Alessandra in Between* (8–12). 1992, HarperCollins LB $13.89 (0-06-023298-6). A young heroine has a lot on her mind, including her grandfather's deteriorating health, her friendships, and an unrequited love. (Rev: BL 9/15/92; SLJ 9/92)

1680 Kay, Susan. *Phantom* (9–adult). 1991, Delacorte $19.95 (0-385-30296-7). Fans of *Phantom of the Opera* will recognize Erik, whose character is well drawn in his dual roles of adored hero and hated villain. Awards: SLJ Best Book. (Rev: BL 2/15/91; SLJ 9/91)

1681 King, Tabitha. *One on One* (9–adult). 1993, Dutton $23 (0-525-93590-8). A coming-of-age story featuring the fierce, unexpected attraction between 2 mismatched high school basketball stars: Deannie, female, who's a pierced, tatooed skinhead, and Sam, a virgin who's an Adonis with a ponytail. (Rev: BL 2/1/93; SLJ 7/93)

1682 Kline, Suzy. *Who's Orp's Girlfriend?* (5–7). 1993, Putnam/Grosset $14.95 (0-399-22431-9). Orp's involved in the school musical. As it progresses, so does his understanding of the opposite sex, mainly by learning what not to do concerning girls. (Rev: BL 8/93; MJHS; SLJ 7/93)

1683 Lachtman, Ofelia Dumas. *The Girl from Playa Bianca* (7–12). 1995, Arte Público $14.95 (1-55885-148-8); paper $7.95 (1-55885-149-6). A gothic romance where the major players are Hispanic. (Rev: BL 11/15/95; SLJ 10/95; VOYA 12/95)

1684 McCants, William D. *Anything Can Happen in High School (and It Usually Does)* (6–8). 1993, Harcourt $10.95 (0-15-276604-9); paper $3.95 (0-15-276605-7). In his attempts to win back his summer love, Janet, by starting a school club, T. J. Burant realizes her shallowness isn't for him. (Rev: BL 10/1/93; SLJ 10/93; VOYA 12/93)

1685 McCants, William D. *Much Ado about Prom Night* (9–12). 1995, Harcourt/Browndeer $11 (0-15-200083-6); paper $5 (0-15-200081-X). Becca's ordeals form the basis for a witty novel joining the angst of high school with sly points about love and sex, politics, and peer pressure. (Rev: BL 7/95; SLJ 6/95)

1686 McDaniel, Lurlene. *Don't Die, My Love* (7–12). 1995, Bantam paper $3.99 (0-553-56715-2). A couple, "engaged" since 6th grade, discover that Luke has Hodgkin's lymphoma. (Rev: BL 9/15/95; SLJ 10/95; VOYA 12/95)

1687 Magorian, Michelle. *Not a Swan* (9–12). 1992, HarperCollins/Laura Geringer LB $17.89 (0-06-024215-9). During World War II, Rose, 17, and her 2 older sisters are evacuated to the English countryside, where Rose falls in love with a veteran who supports her efforts to become a writer. (Rev: BL 8/92; BTA)

1688 Morrison, Toni. *Jazz* (9–adult). 1992, Knopf $21 (0-679-41167-4). The lives, loves, and losses of African Americans in Harlem during the late 1920s. (Rev: BL 3/1/92*; SHS)

1689 Mullins, Hilary. *The Cat Came Back* (7–12). 1993, Naiad $9.95 (1-56280-040-X). When Stevie, a prep school girl, falls in love with classmate Andrea, attraction, doubt, and denial eventually lead to acceptance. (Rev: BL 10/1/93; BTA; VOYA 12/93)

1690 Narayan, Kirin. *Love, Stars, and All That* (9–adult). 1994, Pocket $20 (0-671-79395-0). A studious, naive, convent-educated Indian graduate student at Berkeley searches for her ideal mate in academia. (Rev: BL 1/1/94; SLJ 8/94)

1691 Newton, Suzanne. *Where Are You When I Need You?* (7–10). 1991, Viking $13.95 (0-670-81702-3); Penguin/Puffin paper $3.99 (0-14-034454-3). A young woman must choose between going to college or staying home and marrying her childhood sweetheart. Awards: SLJ Best Book. (Rev: BL 1/1/91; SLJS 8/91*)

1692 Nixon, Joan Lowery. *High Trail to Danger* (6–10). 1991, Bantam/Starfire $15 (0-553-07314-1). A determined 17-year-old girl runs away from her cruel guardian to find her long-lost father in a wild Colorado mining town of the 1870s. (Rev: BL 7/91; SLJ 7/91)

1693 Pearson, Kit. *Looking at the Moon* (6–9). 1992, Viking $12.95 (0-670-84097-1). Norah, 13, and her brother Gavin, 8, have been sent from England to Canada for the duration of World War II, and Norah experiences the pangs of first love. A sequel to *The Sky Is Falling,* (Rev: BL 8/92*; YR)

1694 Plummer, Louise. *The Unlikely Romance of Kate Bjorkman* (7–10). 1995, Delacorte $15.95 (0-385-32049-3). A brainy teen foils a beautiful, evil temptress and gets the man of her dreams. Awards: SLJ Best Book. (Rev: SLJ 10/95; VOYA 12/95)

1695 Powell, Randy. *Is Kissing a Girl Who Smokes Like Licking an Ashtray?* (7–12). 1992, Farrar $15 (0-374-33632-6); paper $3.95 (0-374-43627-4). High school senior Biff has never had a girlfriend until he meets the wild, beautiful loner Heidi, who is as troubled and mouthy as he is shy and fumbling. Awards: YALSA Best Book for Young Adults. (Rev: BL 6/1/92*; SLJ 6/92; YR)

1696 Riefe, Barbara. *For Love of Two Eagles* (9–adult). 1995, Tor/Forge $22.95 (0-312-85703-9). A seventeenth-century love story about an English woman's marriage to an Oneida chief. (Rev: BL 2/15/95; SLJ 9/95)

1697 Roberts, Nora. *Born in Fire* (9–adult). 1994, Berkley/Jove paper $5.99 (0-515-11469-3). The story of talented glass artist Maggie's contentious relationship with Dublin gallery owner Rogan. First in a projected trilogy about the lives of 3 Irish sisters. (Rev: BL 10/1/94; SLJ 6/95)

1698 Rodowsky, Colby. *Lucy Peale* (8–12). 1992, Farrar $15 (0-374-36381-1); 1994, Farrar/Aerial paper $3.95 (0-374-44659-8). Lucy is pregnant, alone, and terrified when she meets Jake, and their friendship slowly evolves into love. (Rev: BL 7/92; SLJ 7/92; YR)

1699 Rostkowski, Margaret I. *Moon Dancer* (7–10). 1995, Harcourt/Browndeer $11 (0-15-276638-3); paper $5 (0-15-200194-8). A 15-year-old accompanies others to view ancient canyon rock art of Native American women and feels connections to the archetypal images. (Rev: BL 5/1/95; SLJ 9/95)

1700 Sonnenmark, Laura. *The Lie* (6–10). 1992, Scholastic $13.95 (0-590-44740-8). A teenage girl goes to great lengths to get the attention of a handsome classmate. (Rev: BL 4/15/92; SLJ 4/92; YR)

1701 Stanek, Lou Willett. *Katy Did* (8–12). 1992, Avon/Flare paper $2.99 (0-380-76170-X). A shy country girl and popular city boy fall in love, with tragic consequences. (Rev: BL 3/15/92)

1702 Stewart, Mary. *The Stormy Petrel* (9–adult). 1991, Morrow $18 (0-688-11035-5). A genteel romance set in Scotland's Hebrides Islands. (Rev: BL 8/91; SLJ 3/92)

1703 Sweeney, Joyce. *Piano Man* (7–9). 1992, Delacorte $15 (0-385-30534-6); 1994, Dell/Laurel Leaf paper $3.99 (0-440-21915-9). A 14-year-old girl develops a crush on the 20-something musician living in the apartment above her. (Rev: BL 4/1/92; YR)

1704 Thompson, Julian F. *Shepherd* (9–12). 1993, Holt $15.95 (0-8050-2106-X). When popular Mary Sutherland makes advances toward Shep Catlett, he declares himself in love and tries to save her from her drinking. (Rev: BL 12/15/93; BTA; SLJ 11/93; VOYA 2/94)

1705 Vine, Barbara. *The Brimstone Wedding* (9–adult). 1996, Crown/Harmony $24 (0-517-70339-4). The story of a 70-year-old woman and a 30-year-old whose paths cross in a nursing home. The elder serves as a wise confidante based on years of pain. (Rev: BL 10/1/95*)

1706 Voigt, Cynthia. *Glass Mountain* (9–adult). 1991, Harcourt $19.95 (0-15-135825-7). A wealthy New Yorker posing as a butler falls in love with his employer's fiancée but doesn't know she is engaged, and she doesn't know he loves her. (Rev: BL 11/1/91; SHS; SLJ 4/92)

1707 Waddell, Martin. *Tango's Baby* (9–12). 1995, Candlewick $16.95 (1-56402-615-9). With a British setting, this funky story concerns a very young couple (Crystal is 15) who try to hold onto their baby in a world of offbeat characters. (Rev. BL 12/15/95; SLJ 11/95)

1708 Westall, Robert. *Falling into Glory* (9–12). 1995, Farrar $18 (0-374-32256-2). Set in 1950s Britain, 17-year-old Robbie has it all, but compromises it when he falls in love with his teacher Emma Harris, who returns that love. (Rev: BL 6/1–15/95)

1709 Whitney, Phyllis A. *Daughter of the Stars* (9–adult). 1994, Crown $20 (0-517-59929-5). Lacy discovers the family that has been her mother's secret for years. She ventures to Harper's Ferry in order to help them and learns of her father's unsolved murder. (Rev: BL 9/15/94; SLJ 3/95)

1710 Wittlinger, Ellen. *Lombardo's Law* (7–10). 1993, Houghton $13.95 (0-395-65969-8); 1995, Morrow paper $4.95 (0-688-05294-0). The conventions of romance are thrown aside when sophomore Justine and 8th-grader Mike find themselves attracted to each other, despite hardships they must overcome. Awards: YALSA Best Book for Young Adults. (Rev: BL 9/15/93; BTA; VOYA 12/93)

1711 Wittlinger, Ellen. *Noticing Paradise* (6–10). 1995, Houghton $14.95 (0-395-71646-2). Told in alternate first-person narration, a story about 16-

year-olds who fall in love while on an excursion to the Galápagos Islands. Includes much about endangered species. (Rev: BL 11/1/95; SLJ 10/95; VOYA 2/96)

1712 Wolitzer, Hilma. *Tunnel of Love* (9–adult). 1994, HarperCollins $20 (0-06-118007-6). The misadventures of a gullible, naive young widow and her rebellious teenage stepdaughter. (Rev: BL 4/1/94; BTA)

Science Fiction

1713 Adams, Douglas. *Mostly Harmless* (9–adult). (Hitchhiker's Trilogy) 1992, Crown/Harmony $20 (0-517-57740-2). The intergalactic adventures of Arthur Dent and Ford Prefect continue as the heroes are whipped between parallel universes that eventually collide. (Rev: BL 9/15/92; SHS)

1714 Allen, Roger MacBride. *Isaac Asimov's Inferno* (9–adult). 1994, Berkley/Ace paper $12 (0-441-00023-1). In this sequel to *Caliban*, the Three Laws of Robotics are further explored when a murder takes place on a planet of Earth Settlers and Spacers. (Rev: BL 9/15/94; VOYA 4/95)

1715 Anderson, Kevin J., and Doug Beason. *Assemblers of Infinity* (9–adult). 1993, Bantam paper $4.99 (0-553-29921-2). Scientists work frantically to keep the Earth from being taken over by miscroscopic machines capable of infiltrating humans. (Rev: BL 2/15/93; VOYA 8/93)

1716 Anderson, Poul. *Harvest of Stars* (9–adult). 1993, Tor $22.95 (0-312-85277-0). Sweeping, fast-paced, and intricate sci-fi for more-sophisticated readers. (Rev: BL 6/1–15/93; VOYA 2/94)

1717 Anthony, Piers. *Chaos Mode* (9–adult). (Mode) 1994, Berkley/Ace $19.95 (0-399-13893-5). Colene, Darius, and the telepathic horse Sequiro are joined by an alien in a journey back to Earth, where Colene hopes to make peace with her family. (Rev: BL 1/1/94; SHS; VOYA 6/94)

1718 Anthony, Piers. *Fractal Mode* (9–adult). (Mode) 1992, Berkley/Ace $18.95 (0-399-13649-5). Colene, her lover, a telepathic horse, and a woman who "remembers" the future stumble into a reality under tyranny, are captured, and escape with the help of various phenomena. (Rev: BL 10/15/91; SHS)

1719 Anthony, Piers. *Virtual Mode* (9–adult). 1991, Berkley/Ace $15.95 (0-399-13661-4). Fantasy coming-of-age story about a 14-year-old who enters an alternate reality. (Rev: BL 1/1/91; SHS)

1720 Asaro, Catherine. *Primary Inversion* (9–adult). 1995, Tor $21.95 (0-312-85764-0). A female fighter pilot is the protagonist in this story of interstellar warfare, psychic power, and romance. (Rev: BL 2/15/95*)

1721 Asimov, Isaac. *The Complete Stories, Vol. 2* (9–adult). 1992, Doubleday/Foundation paper $12 (0-385-42079-X). Forty stories by the prolific science fiction author. (Rev: BL 3/15/92; SHS)

1722 Asimov, Isaac. *Forward the Foundation* (9–adult). 1993, Doubleday $23.50 (0-385-24793-1); 1994, Bantam/Spectra paper $5.99 (0-553-56507-9). The conclusion to Asimov's efforts to bind his various universes together into one vast future history. (Rev: BL 2/15/93; BTA; SLJ 3/94)

1723 Asimov, Isaac. *Gold* (9–adult). 1995, HarperPrism $20 (0-06-105206-X). Previously uncollected work: cerebral tales, introductions to anthologies, and essays on writing science fiction. (Rev: BL 2/15/95) [813]

1724 Asimov, Isaac, and Roger MacBride Allen. *Caliban* (9–adult). 1993, Berkley/Ace paper $9.95 (0-441-09079-6). A sheriff trails a rogue robot that has escaped from a lab. (Rev: BL 3/1/93; VOYA 8/93)

1725 Asimov, Isaac, and Robert Silverberg. *The Positronic Man* (9–adult). 1993, Doubleday $22.50 (0-385-26342-2). An expansion on Asimov's classic *The Bicentennial Man*, this explores the philosophical line between human and robot through the character of NDR-113/Andrew Martin. (Rev: BL 9/15/93)

1726 Bear, Greg. *Moving Mars* (9–adult). 1993, Tor $23.95 (0-312-85515-X). A physicist on Mars links up with an artificial intelligence and a revolutionary woman determined to give her world a future. (Rev: BL 9/15/93; VOYA 4/94)

1727 Bechard, Margaret. *Star Hatchling* (5–7). 1995, Viking $13.99 (0-670-86149-9). A speculative sci-fi novel about a girl who accidentally lands on a planet without her family and examines the alien culture. (Rev: BL 9/15/95; SLJ 8/95)

1728 Benford, Gregory. *Furious Gulf* (9–adult). 1994, Bantam $22.95 (0-553-09661-3). The adventure-packed chronicle of the voyage of the starship *Argo*, pursued by hostile cybernetic entities. Told from the viewpoint of an 18-year-old captain's son. (Rev: BL 5/15/94; SLJ 11/94; VOYA 4/95)

1729 Bishop, Michael. *Brittle Innings* (9–adult). 1994, Bantam $21.95 (0-553-08136-5). An elaborate mix of fantasy and an inspirational baseball story. (Rev: BL 4/15/94; VOYA 10/94)

1730 Bisson, Terry. *Bears Discover Fire and Other Stories* (9–adult). 1993, Tor $19.95 (0-312-85411-0). The collection is named for a story in which bears give up hibernation upon discovering fire and goes on to more traditional science fiction. (Rev: BL 10/1/93; SHS)

1731 Bojold, Lois McMaster. *Mirror Dance* (9–adult). 1994, Baen $21 (0-671-72210-7). Miles Vorkosigan's cloned brother Mark goes on a mission that goes awry. Miles comes to the rescue, but his body is put in cryogenic suspension and lost. Awards: BL Editors' Choice. (Rev: BL 1/1/94*; VOYA 6/94)

1732 Bova, Ben. *Death Dream* (9–adult). 1994, Bantam $22.95 (0-553-08234-5). The designer of CyberWorld, a virtual-reality theme park, finds all is not fun and games when he becomes caught up in sinister plots. (Rev: BL 7/94*; SHS; SLJ 3/95; VOYA 2/95)

1733 Bova, Ben. *Mars* (9–adult). 1992, Bantam $20 (0-553-07892-5). A panoramic story of the first expedition to Mars, told from the viewpoint of a Native American geologist who joins the mission at the last minute. (Rev: BL 4/15/92; BTA)

1734 Bowkett, Stephen. *Frontiersville High* (6–9). 1991, Victor Gollancz $17.95 (0-575-04755-0). The adventures of students who attend an orbiting high school space laboratory in the year 2090. (Rev: BL 2/15/92)

1735 Brin, David. *Glory Season* (9–adult). 1993, Bantam $22.95 (0-553-07645-0). Portrays the values and traditions of Stratos, a world dominated by families of cloned females, where men and other "variants" are oppressed. (Rev: BL 3/15/93; BTA; VOYA 12/93)

1736 Brin, David. *Otherness* (9–adult). 1994, Bantam/Spectra paper $5.99 (0-553-29528-4). Short fiction, essays, and commentaries that strive to define the term *otherness*, including stories about extraterrestrial contact and the limits of our perception of reality. (Rev: BL 8/94; VOYA 2/95) [813.54]

1737 Brittain, Bill. *Shape-Changer* (5–8). 1994, HarperCollins LB $13.89 (0-06-024239-6). Three 7th-graders meet an extraterrestrial, a policeman from the planet Rodinam, who is escorting a dangerous criminal to an asteroid. (Rev: BL 4/15/94; MJHS; SLJ 6/94)

1738 Brunner, John. *A Maze of Stars* (9–adult). 1992, Ballantine/Del Rey paper $4.99 (0-345-37554-8). Past, present, and future are mixed together in this tale about Ship, a biotechnological wonder created to seed more than 600 planets. (Rev: BL 5/15/91*)

1739 Butler, Octavia E. *Parable of the Sower* (9–adult). 1993, Four Walls Eight Windows (39 W. 14th St., Suite 503, New York, NY 10011) $19.95 (0-941423-99-9). After her neighborhood is overrun by a pyromaniac cult, adolescent Lauren Olamina gains followers on her way toward refuge in California. Awards: SLJ Best Book; YALSA Best Book for Young Adults. (Rev: BL 11/15/93; BTA; SLJ 7/94)

1740 Caraker, Mary. *The Faces of Ceti* (7–10). 1991, Houghton $14.95 (0-395-54698-2). Colonists on the planet Ceti see their new home as a chance to avoid the ecological disasters that spoiled Earth. (Rev: BL 5/1/91; BY; SLJ 5/91)

1741 Card, Orson Scott. *The Call of Earth* (9–adult). (Homecoming Saga) 1993, Tor $21.95 (0-312-93037-2). Teenagers are at the heart of the story featuring a sentient computer whose plans involve a return to Earth. (Rev: BL 11/15/92; SHS; VOYA 8/93)

1742 Card, Orson Scott. *The Memory of Earth: Homecoming, Vol. 1* (9–adult). (Homecoming Saga) 1992, Tor $20.95 (0-312-93036-4). Science fiction saga set on the planet Harmony, where a computer rules the population. (Rev: BL 1/1/92; SHS)

1743 Card, Orson Scott. *Pastwatch: The Redemption of Christopher Columbus* (9–adult). 1996, Tor $23.95 (0-312-85058-1). Time travelers from a ruined future Earth journey to the time of Columbus, hoping to reshape those events. (Rev: BL 12/1/95; VOYA 4/96)

1744 Card, Orson Scott. *The Ships of Earth* (9–adult). (Homecoming Saga) 1994, Tor $22.95 (0-312-85659-8). Guided by the Oversoul, the prophet Nafai and his band of pilgrims flee across the desert from ruined Basilica and its conquerors. (Rev: BL 1/15/94; VOYA 6/94)

1745 Card, Orson Scott. *Xenocide* (9–adult). 1991, Tor $21.95 (0-312-85056-5). Ender and his family search for a miracle that will preserve the existence of 3 intelligent but vastly different species. Awards: SLJ Best Book. (Rev: BL 5/15/91; SHS; SLJ 12/91)

1746 Carter, Carmen. *The Devil's Heart* (9–adult). 1993, Pocket $20 (0-671-79325-X). A complicated *Star Trek* story featuring Captain Picard, who becomes the guardian of a mysterious artifact. (Rev: BL 3/1/93; SLJ 11/93)

1747 Carver, Jeffrey A. *Dragon Rigger* (9–adult). 1993, Tor $22.95 (0-312-85061-1). The dragons need the aid of their human friend, starrigger Jael Le Brae, to defeat the deadly evil that threatens the Realm. (Rev: BL 6/1–15/93; VOYA 12/93)

1748 Carver, Jeffrey A. *A Neptune Crossing* (9–adult). 1994, Tor $23.95 (0-312-85640-7). While doing survey work on Neptune's moon Triton, loner John Bandicut becomes the reluctant accomplice to aliens' efforts to save Earth. (Rev: BL 3/15/94; VOYA 12/94)

1749 Chalker, Jack L. *Echoes of the Well of Souls* (9–adult). (Well World) 1993, Ballantine/Del Rey paper $10 (0-345-36201-2). A meteor that strikes Earth is the agent summoning Nathan and Mavra back to the Well World to reset the computer that runs the universe. (Rev: BL 5/15/93; VOYA 12/93)

1750 Cherryh, C. J. *Foreigner* (9–adult). 1994, NAL/DAW $20 (0-88677-590-6). A human is attacked by an assassin on a distant planet, where they trade technical knowledge for the right to peaceful coexistence with the natives. (Rev: BL 1/15/94; BTA; VOYA 4/94)

1751 Clarke, Arthur C. *The Hammer of God* (9–adult). 1993, Bantam $19.95 (0-553-09557-9). The struggle to avert an asteroid on course to collide with Earth. (Rev: BL 4/15/93; BTA; VOYA 12/93)

1752 Clarke, Arthur C., and Gentry Lee. *Rama Revealed* (9–adult). (Rama) 1994, Bantam $22.95 (0-553-09536-6). The fourth book of the series focuses on the New Eden colony, which is ruled by Nakamura, a dictator who overthrew the governess and wages war on the octospiders. (Rev: BL 12/1/93; VOYA 6/94)

1753 Clarke, J. *Al Capsella Takes a Vacation* (7–12). 1993, Holt $14.95 (0-8050-2685-1). Al and his friend Lou set off for a fantasy beach vacation, but nothing turns out as they dreamed and they're too embarrassed to admit it. (Rev: BL 7/93; BTA)

1754 Coppel, Alfred. *Glory* (9–adult). 1993, St. Martin's $21.95 (0-312-85469-2). A spaceship crew lands in the midst of a violent racial struggle when they deliver cargo to a planet ruled by descendants of the Boers of South Africa. (Rev: BL 4/15/93; SLJ 4/94; VOYA 2/94)

1755 Datlow, Ellen, and Terri Windling, eds. *Black Thorn, White Rose* (9–adult). 1994, Avon/AvoNova $22 (0-688-13713-X). Variations of famous European folktales involving dwarves, witches, elves, trolls, etc., including a retelling of "Rumpelstiltskin." (Rev: BL 8/94; BTA; VOYA 4/95)

1756 Dexter, Catherine. *Alien Game* (5–8). 1995, Morrow $15 (0-688-11332-X). The new girl in the 8th grade is a true alien from another planet. (Rev: BL 5/1/95; SLJ 4/95)

1757 Dozois, Gardner, ed. *Modern Classic Short Novels of Science Fiction* (9–adult). 1994, St. Martin's $27.95 (0-312-10504-5). Thirteen short science fiction novels by such noted writers as Poul Anderson, Brian Aldiss, Gene Wolfe, Joanna Russ, Nancy Kress, and Kate Wilhelm. (Rev: BL 2/1/94; VOYA 8/94)

1758 Dozois, Gardner, ed. *The Year's Best Science Fiction: Eleventh Annual Collection* (9–adult). 1994, St. Martin's $26.95 (0-312-11105-3); paper $16.95 (0-312-11104-5). Excellent sci-fi short stories. (Rev: BL 7/94; VOYA 2/95)

1759 Drake, David. *The Sharp End* (9–adult). 1993, Baen $20 (0-671-72192-5). Set in the universe of his Hammer's Slammers series, 6 misfits from their government of mercenaries decide to "clean out" 2 drug empires on the planet Cantilucca. (Rev: BL 9/15/93; VOYA 6/94)

1760 Drake, David. *The Voyage* (9–adult). 1994, Tor $23.95 (0-312-85158-8). The epic voyage of a group of handpicked mercenaries who set out to reclaim a fortune stolen 70 years before. (Rev: BL 1/1/94; VOYA 10/94)

1761 Duncan, Dave. *The Cursed* (9–adult). 1995, Ballantine/Del Rey $22 (0-345-38951-4). Clans battle in a world of power and passion. (Rev: BL 5/1/95; VOYA 12/95)

1762 Dunlop, Eileen. *Webster's Leap* (5–7). 1995, Holiday $15.95 (0-8234-1193-1). A brother and sister are visiting their father's old castle and experience a strange shift back 400 years to previous lives spent there. (Rev: BL 10/1/95; SLJ 10/95)

1763 Engh, M. J. *Rainbow Man* (9–adult). 1993, Tor $17.95 (0-312-85468-4). A starshipper stops at what appears to be a utopian planet but discovers that the inhabitants' perfect behavior is enforced through the threat of torture. (Rev: BL 4/15/93; VOYA 12/93)

1764 Farmer, Nancy. *The Ear, the Eye and the Arm* (7–10). 1994, Orchard/Richard Jackson LB $17.99 (0-531-08679-8). In Zimbabwe, in 2194, the military ruler's son, 13, and his younger siblings leave their technologically overcontrolled home and embark on a series of perilous adventures. Awards: ALSC Notable Children's Book; Newbery Honor Book; SLJ Best Book; YALSA Best Book for Young Adults. (Rev: BL 4/1/94; BTA; MJHS; SLJ 6/94; VOYA 6/94)

1765 Findley, Timothy. *Headhunter* (9–adult). 1994, Crown $22 (0-517-59827-2). A darkly satiric, horrifying tale of decadence and evil. A self-proclaimed psychic plays with the minds of some of the most powerful men and women of Toronto. (Rev: BL 4/15/94*)

1766 Foreman, Leila Rose. *Shatter World* (5–7). 1995, Eerdmans $13.99 (0-8028-5097-9). A 12-year-old girl and her brother struggle to find their identities in a world determined by their parents' religious choices. (Rev: BL 5/15/95; SLJ 4/95; VOYA 12/95)

1767 Forward, Robert L. *Camelot 30K* (9–adult). 1993, Tor $20.95 (0-312-85215-0). Beyond Neptune orbits the planet Ice, which a human expedition finds is actually designed to spread its insectlike population throughout space. (Rev: BL 9/15/93; VOYA 4/94)

1768 French, Jackie. *Somewhere Around the Corner* (5–7). 1995, Holt $14.95 (0-8050-3889-2). A shift back and forth in time in Sydney, Australia, from 1994 to 1932 when a girl learns about the precariousness of life. (Rev: BL 5/15/95)

1769 Gilden, Mel. *The Pumpkins of Time* (5–7). 1994, Harcourt/Browndeer $10.95 (0-15-276603-0); paper $4.95 (0-15-200889-6). Young comic book collector Myron, his friend Princess, and a cat named H. G. Wells become involved with time-traveling pumpkins and dubious time-travelers. (Rev: BL 10/15/94; SLJ 10/94; VOYA 12/94)

1770 Goldman, E. M. *The Night Room* (6–10). 1995, Viking $14.99 (0-670-85838-2). Seven high school juniors take part in an experiment with virtual reality: a simulation of their 10-year reunion. (Rev: BL 1/1/95; SLJ 5/94)

1771 Goonan, Kathleen Ann. *Queen City Jazz* (9–adult). 1994, Tor $23.95 (0-312-85678-4). Futuristic Ohio is ravaged by nanotechnology that promises utopian ideals but kills with a nanoplague. Verity, 16, goes to Cincinnati, hoping to revive her murdered brother and dog. (Rev: BL 10/1/94; VOYA 5/95)

1772 Haddix, Margaret Peterson. *Running Out of Time* (5–7). 1995, Simon & Schuster $15 (0-689-80084-3). A new twist on time-travel fiction: A woman who has always believed she was living in the 1840s escapes the boundaries of her home to discover life in 1996. (Rev: BL 10/1/95; SLJ 10/95; VOYA 12/95)

1773 Haldeman, Jack C., and Jack Dann. *High Steel* (9–adult). 1993, Tor $18.95 (0-312-93163-8). A space-age steelworker—who has close ties to Native American medicine—is exploited by corporations when his psychic talents are discovered. (Rev: BL 7/93; VOYA 12/93)

1774 Harrison, Harry. *Galactic Dreams* (9–adult). 1994, Tor $19.95 (0-312-85246-0). Twelve satirical action stories about supertrooper Bill the Galactic Hero present a tough, sometimes violent, vision of the future. (Rev: BL 3/1/94; VOYA 12/94)

1775 Harrison, Harry. *The Stainless Steel Rat Sings the Blues* (9–adult). 1994, Bantam $19.95 (0-553-09612-5). Slippery Jim Di Griz, caught in a bank robbery, must infiltrate a prison planet and recover an alien artifact in order to escape the penalty. (Rev: BL 1/15/94; VOYA 8/94)

1776 Harrison, Harry. *Stainless Steel Visions* (9–adult). 1993, Tor $18.95 (0-312-85245-2). Sci-fi tales with quirky plot twists, incorrigible heroes, ecological themes, and moderate violence. (Rev: BL 1/15/93; VOYA 10/93)

1777 Haycock, Kate. *Science Fiction Films* (5–8). 1992, Macmillan/Crestwood LB $12.95 (0-89686-716-1). This overview of cinematic science fiction covers early silent films, comic strip serials, 1950s UFO movies, and modern special-effects blockbusters. (Rev: BL 10/15/92; SLJ 1/93) [791.43]

1778 Heintze, Ty. *Valley of the Eels* (5–8). 1993, Eakin $14.95 (0-89015-904-1). A dolphin leads 2 boys to an underwater station where friendly aliens are cultivating trees for replanting on their own planet. (Rev: BL 3/1/94)

1779 Hightower, Lynn S. *Alien Blues* (9–adult). 1992, Berkley/Ace paper $4.50 (0-441-64460-0). Futuristic homicide detective tries to deal with a bad marriage, an alien partner, and a dangerous serial killer. (Rev: BL 1/15/92; SLJ 6/92)

1780 Hoover, H. M. *Only Child* (5–7). 1992, Dutton $14 (0-525-44865-9). Cody, 12, vacations on an Earthlike planet, is captured by aliens, and risks his life to preserve the world for its original inhabitants. (Rev: BL 5/15/92; SLJ 7/92)

1781 Hoover, H. M. *The Winds of Mars* (6–9). 1995, Dutton $14.99 (0-525-45359-8). Annalyn, age 17, believes that the president of Mars is her father but she discovers after a revolution that he's actually an android. (Rev: BL 8/95; SLJ 8/95; VOYA 12/95)

1782 Houghton, John. *A Distant Shore* (9–adult). 1994, Thomas Nelson paper $10.99 (0-7852-8228-9). In a world where most people live on boats, a painter is compelled to track the source of a green light emanating from a rock. In his search he encounters ways of living—rationalist, New Age, libertine—that he must first experience to reject. (Rev: BL 11/15/94*)

1783 Howarth, Lesley. *Maphead* (6–8). 1994, Candlewick $14.95 (1-56402-416-4). Maphead, living in a parallel universe, wants to meet his mortal mother, so he assumes human form, attends school, and befriends his mother's other son. Awards: Guardian Award for Children's Fiction. (Rev: BL 10/1/94; SLJ 10/94; VOYA 2/95)

1784 Howarth, Lesley. *Weather Eye* (6–8). 1995, Candlewick $14.95 (1-56402-616-7). A 13-year-old has special powers as she monitors the weather in her small English town. (Rev: BL 9/15/95*; SLJ 11/95)

1785 Hughes, Monica. *The Crystal Drop* (6–8). 1993, Simon & Schuster $14 (0-671-79195-8). Megan's mother is dead and her father has deserted the family, so she must take her brother on a long trek across Canada's barren plains to their uncle's home. (Rev: BL 3/15/93; MJHS; SLJ 6/93; VOYA 12/93)

1786 Hughes, Monica. *Invitation to the Game* (7–10). 1991, Simon & Schuster $14 (0-671-74236-1); paper $3.95 (0-671-86692-3). In 2154, a high school graduate and her friends face life on welfare in a highly robotic society and are invited to participate in a sinister government "Game." Awards: SLJ Best Book. (Rev: BL 9/15/91; MJHS; SLJS 1/92*)

1787 Jablokov, Alexander. *The Breath of Suspension* (9–adult). 1994, Arkham $20.95 (0-87054-167-6). Short stories with such themes as time-traveling detectives, a cyborg whale that explores Jupiter's atmosphere, and manmade alternate universes. (Rev: BL 8/94; VOYA 12/94)

1788 Klause, Annette Curtis. *Alien Secrets* (5–8). 1993, Delacorte $14.95 (0-385-30928-7). Modern variations on the best of 1950s–1960s science fiction by Heinlein, Norton, Bova, et al. Awards: ALSC Notable Children's Book; BL Editors' Choice; SLJ Best Book. (Rev: BL 6/1–15/93*; MJHS; SLJ 9/93*; VOYA 8/93)

1789 Knight, Damon. *Why Do Birds* (9–adult). 1992, Tor $17.95 (0-312-85174-X). An apocalyptic fable of ingenious originality and dark comedic overtones, set in the early twenty-first century. (Rev: BL 11/1/92*)

1790 Kress, Nancy. *Beggars and Choosers* (9–adult). 1994, Tor $22.95 (0-312-85749-7). The future world is divided between 3 feuding groups: the superhuman Sleepless, the genetically altered ruling elite called "homo superior," and the poor masses. Sequel to *Beggars in Spain*. (Rev: BL 10/1/94; SLJ 5/95; VOYA 4/95)

1791 Kritlow, William. *Backfire* (7–10). (Virtual Reality) 1995, Thomas Nelson paper $4.99 (0-7852-7925-3). Teens obtain access to a virtual-reality machine and live out their fantasies until an evil programmer comes along. (Rev: BL 12/1/95)

1792 Kritlow, William. *The Deadly Maze* (7–10). (Virtual Reality) 1995, Thomas Nelson paper $4.99 (0-7852-7924-5). Teens don virtual-reality suits and enter a strange computer-generated world where evil is pervasive. (Rev: BL 12/1/95)

1793 Lawrence, Louise. *Andra* (6–10). 1991, HarperCollins LB $14.89 (0-06-023705-8). This novel is set 2,000 years in the future, when humanity, having destroyed Earth's environment, lives in rigidly governed, sealed, underground cities. (Rev: BL 5/1/91; SLJ 5/91)

1794 Lawrence, Louise. *Keeper of the Universe* (7–10). 1993, Clarion $13.95 (0-395-64340-6). The issues of freedom of choice and moral responsibility are adeptly handled in this provocative sci-fi adventure. (Rev: BL 4/1/93; MJHS; SLJ 6/93)

1795 Lawrence, Louise. *The Patchwork People* (7–10). 1994, Clarion $14.95 (0-395-67892-7). This brooding story takes place in a bleak Wales of the future, where natural resources are nearly depleted and jobs are scarce. (Rev: BL 12/15/94*; SLJ 11/94)

1796 Le Guin, Ursula K., and Brian Attebery. *The Norton Book of Science Fiction, 1960–1990* (9–adult). 1993, Norton $27.50 (0-393-03546-8). The last 3 decades of North American science fiction are represented in 60 stories that focus on themes rather than author reputation. (Rev: BL 10/1/93)

1797 Lewitt, S. N. *Song of Chaos* (9–adult). 1993, Berkley/Ace paper $4.99 (0-441-77529-2). A teenage boy who is considered a misfit because of his severe asthma and heightened sensory perceptions finds acceptance in a renegade society. (Rev: BL 10/15/93; VOYA 4/94)

1798 Lucas, George, and Chris Claremont. *Shadow Moon: First in the Chronicles of the Shadow War* (9–adult). 1995, Bantam $22.50 (0-553-09596-X). Lucas of *Star Wars* fame and Claremont of Marvel Comics offer the first in a planned trilogy of sci-fi novels. (Rev: BL 10/1/95; VOYA 2/96)

1799 McCaffrey, Anne. *The Chronicles of Pern: First Fall* (9–adult). 1993, Ballantine $23 (0-345-36898-3). Five original stories by the author of the popular Pern series offer a glimpse into the early history of the Dragonriders. (Rev: BL 9/1/93; MJHS; VOYA 4/94)

1800 McCaffrey, Anne. *Damia* (9–adult). (Rowan) 1992, Putnam $21.95 (0-399-13648-7). Focuses on the strong-willed daughter of the Rowan, who inherits a stormy nature and powerful telepathic powers. Second in a trilogy. Awards: SLJ Best Book. (Rev: BL 4/1/92; SHS; SLJ 12/92)

1801 McCaffrey, Anne. *The Dolphins of Pern* (9–adult). (Pern) 1994, Ballantine/Del Rey $22 (0-345-36894-0). Young dragonrider T'lion rebuilds the world of Pern's ancient relationship with the "shipfish," dolphins that came to Pern with its early human settlers. (Rev: BL 9/15/94; MJHS; SHS; VOYA 2/95)

1802 McCaffrey, Anne. *Freedom's Landing* (9–adult). 1995, Berkley/Ace $22.95 (0-399-14062-X). An alien race of slavers is settling a habitable but dangerous planet with slaves from other races. (Rev: BL 4/15/95; SLJ 8/95)

1803 McCaffrey, Anne. *Lyon's Pride* (9–adult). 1994, Putnam $22.95 (0-399-13907-9). An alliance between humans and aliens searches for creatures that destroy indigenous life forms on any planet they inhabit. (Rev: BL 1/1/94; SLJ 9/94; VOYA 10/94)

1804 McCaffrey, Anne, and Elizabeth Ann Scarborough. *Power Lines* (9–adult). 1994, Ballantine/Del Rey $20 (0-345-38174-2). In this riveting sequel to *The Powers That Be*, the planet Petaybee becomes an active force in its inhabitants' battle to prevent the ruling Intergal Company's rape of the planet. (Rev: BL 4/1/94; SHS; VOYA 12/94)

1805 McCaffrey, Anne, and Elizabeth Ann Scarborough. *The Powers That Be* (9–adult). 1993, Ballantine/Del Rey $20 (0-345-38173-4). Major Yanaba Maddock has been retired to the icy planet Petaybee, where she's assigned to spy on civilians. (Rev: BL 4/15/93; SLJ 1/94; VOYA 12/93)

1806 McDevitt, Jack. *The Engines of God* (9–adult). 1994, Berkley $21.95 (0-441-00077-0). An interstellar archeologist races to uncover the secrets of planet Quragua's alien artifacts before it is settled by humans fleeing an environmentally destroyed Earth. (Rev: BL 9/15/94; VOYA 12/94)

1807 McHugh, Maureen F. *Half the Day Is Night* (9–adult). 1994, Tor $21.95 (0-312-85479-X). French-speaking war-vet David Dai moves to Caribe, a futuristic underwater metropolis and becomes Mayla Ling's bodyguard, protecting her from terrorists. (Rev: BL 10/15/94; VOYA 4/95)

1808 McIntyre, Vonda N. *The Crystal Star* (9–adult). 1994, Bantam $21.95 (0-553-08929-3). In this *Star Wars* novel, Leia and Han Solo's children are kidnapped by Lord Hethrir. Leia rescues them while Luke and Han look for lost Jedi knights. (Rev: BL 10/1/94; VOYA 5/95)

1809 Manson, Cynthia, and Charles Ardai, eds. *FutureCrime: An Anthology of the Shape of Crime to Come* (9–adult). 1992, Donald I. Fine $21.95 (1-55611-312-9). Robocops and cyberpunks match wits in a dark future. (Rev: BL 1/15/92; SLJ 9/92)

1810 Modesitt, L. E. *Of Tangible Ghosts* (9–adult). 1994, Tor $22.95 (0-312-85720-9). In a world where ghosts are very real, a former spy investigates the "awful secret," a method of killing them. (Rev: BL 10/1/94; VOYA 4/95)

1811 Mohan, Kim, ed. *Amazing Stories: The Anthology* (9–adult). 1995, Tor $23.95 (0-312-85882-5); paper $13.95 (0-312-89048-6). Classic science fiction short stories. (Rev: BL 4/15/95)

1812 Morrow, James, ed. *Nebula Awards 28: SFWA's Choices for the Best Science Fiction and Fantasy of the Year* (9–adult). 1994, Harcourt $24.95 (0-15-100082-4). A compilation of the 1992 science fiction offerings. (Rev: BL 4/15/94)

1813 Morrow, James, ed. *Nebula Awards 27: SFWA's Choices for the Best Science Fiction and Fantasy of the Year* (9–12). 1993, Harcourt $24.95 (0-15-164935-9); Harcourt/Harvest paper $12.95 (0-15-164935-9). The best science fiction stories of 1991, including a series of tributes to Isaac Asimov. (Rev: BL 3/15/93; VOYA 10/93)

1814 Morrow, James, ed. *Nebula Awards 26: SFWA's Choices for the Best Science Fiction and Fantasy of the Year* (9–12). 1992, Harcourt/Harvest paper $12.95 (0-15-665472-5). The best science fiction stories of 1990. (Rev: BL 3/15/92)

1815 Nemecek, Larry. *The Star Trek: The Next Generation Companion* (9–adult). 1992, Pocket paper $13 (0-671-79460-4). Chronicles the genesis of the *Star Trek* series, with production notes for each of the episodes during the first 5 seasons. (Rev: BL 10/15/92) [791.45]

1816 Niven, Larry. *Playgrounds of the Mind* (9–adult). 1991, Tor $22.95 (0-312-85219-3). A mix of short fiction, fantasy, essays, letters, introductions, and novel excerpts—a continuation of the author's previous book, *N-Space*. (Rev: BL 9/1/91) [813]

1817 Niven, Larry, and Jerry Pournelle. *The Gripping Hand* (9–adult). 1993, Pocket $22 (0-671-79573-2). The formation of a new star allows the Moties to bridge the blockade and again confront the Empire in this complex sequel to *The Mote in God's Eye*. (Rev: BL 12/15/92; VOYA 8/93)

1818 Norton, Andre, and P. M. Griffin. *Redline the Stars* (9–adult). 1993, Tor $19.95 (0-312-85314-9). The Free Trader starship *Solar Queen* and its crew face their archrival Rael Cofort's half-sister. (Rev: BL 2/15/93; VOYA 10/93)

1819 Oppel, Kenneth. *Dead Water Zone* (7–10). 1993, Little, Brown/Joy Street $14.95 (0-316-65102-8). Set in the near future, Paul and his physically handicapped brother, Sam, have always had an unhealthy symbiotic relationship. Sam finds a way to break the tie. Awards: SLJ Best Book. (Rev: SLJS 6/93*)

1820 Ore, Rebecca. *Gaia's Toys* (9–adult). 1995, Tor $22.95 (0-312-85781-0). Eco-terrorist Allison is caught and brainwashed by the government to catch a scientist developing insects whose bite drugs people into pacifism. (Rev: BL 7/95*)

1821 Perry, Steve. *Spindoc* (9–adult). 1994, Berkley/Ace paper $4.99 (0-441-00008-8). Venture Silk uses highly sophisticated technology to control or twist the media in a spaceport and refuses to believe the "spin" on his lover's murder. (Rev: BL 1/15/94; VOYA 6/94)

1822 Piercy, Marge. *He, She and It* (9–adult). 1991, Knopf $22 (0-679-40408-2). Two tales of humans vs. machines, one in the year 2059 of psycho-engineers and cyborgs, the other in 1599 of Jewish mysticism and a golem (artificial being). (Rev: BL 9/1/91*)

1823 Pohl, Frederik. *The Voices of Heaven* (9–adult). 1994, St. Martin's $21.95 (0-312-85643-1). Nebula Grand Master Pohl weaves an absorbing tale of Barry di Hoa, who supervises antimatter fuel transfer to a spacecraft while trying to keep his past mental disorder under control. (Rev: BL 5/1/94; SHS; VOYA 10/94)

1824 Pratchett, Terry. *Wings: The Last Book of the Bromeliad* (5–8). (Bromeliad) 1991, Delacorte $15 (0-385-30436-6). Gnomes hitchhike to Florida on the Concorde in order to get close enough to a communication satellite to summon their ship to take them away from Earth. (Rev: BL 12/1/91)

1825 Reiss, Kathryn. *Pale Phoenix* (7–10). 1994, Harcourt $10.95 (0-15-200030-5); paper $3.95 (0-15-200031-3). Miranda Browne's parents take in an orphan girl who can disappear at will and who was the victim of a tragedy in a past life in Puritan Massachusetts. Awards: Edgar. (Rev: BL 3/15/94; BTA; SLJ 5/94; VOYA 6/94)

1826 Resnick, Mike. *Inferno: A Chronicle of a Distant World* (9–adult). 1993, Tor $20.95 (0-312-85437-4). Within decades, the peaceful world of Faligor changes to a society led by genocidal tyrants. Revolution brings the hope of a return to native traditions. (Rev: BL 12/1/93; VOYA 4/94)

1827 Resnick, Mike. *A Miracle of Rare Design: A Tragedy of Transcendence* (9–adult). 1994, Tor $21.95 (0-312-85484-6). A space-traveling adventurer is maimed and left for dead by a group of aliens. Rescued by another alien species, he is transformed into one of them. (Rev: BL 11/1/94; VOYA 5/95)

1828 Robinson, Kim Stanley, ed. *Future Primitive: The New Ecotopias* (9–adult). 1994, Tor $23.95 (0-312-85474-9). Science fiction–themed writings, from poems to novel excerpts, promoting ecological awareness and exploring man's past, present, and future relationship with nature. (Rev: BL 7/94; VOYA 2/95) [813]

1829 Robinson, Kim Stanley. *Green Mars* (9–adult). 1994, Bantam $22.95 (0-553-09640-0); paper $12.95 (0-553-37335-8). The terraforming of Mars into a habitable world is under way, and the divided colonists advocate everything from gutting the planet's resources to leaving it virginal. (Rev: BL 2/1/94; SLJ 2/95)

1830 Robinson, Kim Stanley. *Red Mars* (9–adult). 1993, Bantam $22.50 (0-553-09204-9); paper $11 (0-553-37134-7). The original settlers of Mars are pulled apart by personal jealousies and professional differences, leading to revolution. (Rev: BL 1/1/93*; SLJ 5/94)

1831 Rubinstein, Gillian. *Skymaze* (5–7). 1991, Orchard $14.95 (0-531-08529-5). In this sequel to *Space Demons*, 4 young heroes are plunged into the realm of a new video game, where they must play for their lives. (Rev: BL 7/91; SLJ 4/91)

1832 Rusch, Kristine Kathryn, and Edward L. Ferman, eds. *The Best from Fantasy and Science Fiction: A 45th Anniversary Anthology* (9–adult). 1994, St. Martin's $23.95 (0-312-11246-7). Stories by such authors as Gene Wolf, Harlan Ellison, and Joe Haldeman from *The Magazine of Fantasy and Science Fiction*. (Rev: BL 9/15/94; VOYA 12/94)

1833 Saberhagen, Fred. *Berserker Kill* (9–adult). 1993, Tor $24.95 (0-312-85266-5). In the latest in his military science fiction saga, a berserker captures a ship full of human germ plasm, which the humans must rescue. (Rev: BL 9/15/93; VOYA 4/94)

1834 Sargent, Pamela, ed. *Nebula Awards 29: SFWA's Choices for the Best Science Fiction and Fantasy of the Year* (9–adult). 1995, Harcourt $25 (0-15-100107-3); Harcourt/Harvest paper $13 (0-15-600119-5). A collection of science fiction and fantasy. (Rev: BL 4/15/95; SHS; SLJ 10/95)

1835 Sargent, Pamela, ed. *Women of Wonder: The Classic Years: Science Fiction by Women from the 1940s to the 1970s* (9–adult). 1995, Harcourt/Harvest paper $15 (0-15-600031-8). The first of 2 new volumes updating the previous

3 out-of-print *Women of Wonder* titles. Includes 21 stories and a perceptive introductory overview of women in science fiction. (Rev: BL 8/95)

1836 Sargent, Pamela, ed. *Women of Wonder: The Contemporary Years: Science Fiction by Women from the 1970s to the 1990s* (9–adult). 1995, Harcourt/Harvest paper $15 (0-15-600033-4). The second of 2 volumes updating the out-of-print *Women of Wonder* titles includes 21 stories published between 1978 and 1993, with suggestions for further reading. (Rev: BL 8/95)

1837 Shatner, William. *Tek Vengeance* (9–adult). 1993, Berkley/Ace $19.95 (0-399-13788-2). Detective Jake Cardigan leaves a trail of stunned informers and zapped androids across Europe in a futuristic thriller. (Rev: BL 10/15/92; VOYA 10/93)

1838 Sheffield, Charles. *Cold As Ice* (9–adult). 1992, Tor $19.95 (0-312-85139-1). Nine sleeping infants, once nestled in pods and ejected from a doomed ship, have grown up to become the key to an extraordinary race. (Rev: BL 6/15/92*)

1839 Sheffield, Charles. *Georgia on My Mind and Other Places* (9–adult). 1995, Tor $21.95 (0-312-85663-6). A collection of the author's short stories. (Rev: BL 2/15/95; SHS)

1840 Sheffield, Charles. *Godspeed* (9–adult). 1993, Tor $21.95 (0-312-85317-3). Teenager Jay Hara falls into a space voyage to find the Godspeed Drive, which would make interstellar travel possible and bring Jay's home planet out of isolation. (Rev: BL 11/15/93; VOYA 4/94)

1841 Shippey, Tom, ed. *The Oxford Book of Science Fiction Stories* (9–adult). 1992, Oxford Univ. $22.50 (0-19-214204-6). A wide-reaching collection of 30 sci-fi stories covers a variety of themes, writing, and authors. (Rev: BL 9/15/92; SHS)

1842 Sleator, William. *Others See Us* (8–12). 1993, Dutton $14.99 (0-525-45104-8). When Jared, 16, falls into a toxic swamp, he acquires the ability to "visit" other people's minds and things quickly get complicated. (Rev: BL 10/15/93; BTA; MJHS; SLJ 10/93; VOYA 2/94)

1843 Stabenow, Dana. *Red Planet Run* (9–adult). 1995, Berkley/Ace paper $5.50 (0-441-00135-1). The feisty heroine, Star Svensdottir, and her twins go through a series of fast-paced adventures, beginning with trouble over the design of an asteroid being turned into a space habitat. (Rev: BL 1/1/95; VOYA 5/95)

1844 Stearns, Michael, ed. *A Starfarer's Dozen: Stories of Things to Come* (8–12). 1995, Harcourt $17 (0-15-299871-3). Teens are pushed to their limits of self-discovery in these 13 often funny and unsettling stories, a companion to *A Wizard's Dozen*. (Rev: BL 10/1/95; SLJ 11/95; VOYA 2/96)

1845 Steele, Allen. *The Jericho Iteration* (9–adult). 1994, Berkley/Ace paper $11 (0-441-00097-5). In 2012, a reporter uncovers the militaristic Emergency Relief Agency's scheme to use an antimissle satellite to stop civilian unrest by implementing martial law. (Rev: BL 10/1/94; VOYA 12/94)

1846 Stith, John E. *Reunion on Neverend* (9–adult). 1994, Tor $21.95 (0-312-85687-3). Lan Dillian returns to his home world for a vacation, which is interrupted when he becomes entangled in a murder case involving his former flame. (Rev: BL 7/94; VOYA 2/95)

1847 Sullivan, Tricia. *Lethe* (9–adult). 1995, Bantam/Spectra paper $5.50 (0-553-56858-2). After the Gene War leaves Earth ravaged, psychic Jenae is used by the governing powers to stabilize 4 newly discovered stargates. (Rev: BL 7/95; VOYA 12/95)

1848 Tepper, Sheri S. *A Plague of Angels* (9–adult). 1993, Bantam $21.95 (0-553-09513-7). The story of how Orphan and Abasio come together to save a crime-ridden, overpopulated, plague-filled world. (Rev: BL 8/93; SLJ 5/94; VOYA 2/94)

1849 Tepper, Sheri S. *Shadow's End* (9–adult). 1994, Bantam $22.95 (0-553-09514-5). The Alliance has asked Lutha to return to Dinadh to track down her missing former lover, who may hold the key to the invading Ularians' identity. (Rev: BL 11/15/94; BTA; VOYA 4/95)

1850 Tyers, Kathy. *Star Wars: The Truce at Bakura* (9–adult). 1993, Bantam $21.95 (0-553-09541-2). Chronicles the further adventures of the characters from the *Star Wars* movies. (Rev: BL 10/15/93; VOYA 6/94)

1851 Watt-Evans, Lawrence. *Out of This World* (9–adult). 1994, Ballantine/Del Rey $20 (0-345-37245-X). In this science fiction spoof, earthlings join with humans from alternate universes to battle the evil shadow threatening their realms. (Rev: BL 2/1/94; VOYA 8/94)

1852 Wesley, Mary. *Haphazard House* (5–7). 1993, Overlook $14.95 (0-87951-470-1). An eccentric artist buys a magic Panama hat and is drawn to acquire a run-down English country estate where time runs haphazardly. (Rev: BL 1/1/94)

1853 Williams, Sheila, ed. *The Loch Moose Monster: More Stories from Isaac Asimov's Science Fiction Magazine* (9–12). 1993, Delacorte $16 (0-385-30600-8). These 14 sci-fi stories feature mostly young protagonists and not-very-technical situations. (Rev: BL 3/1/93; MJHS)

1854 Willis, Connie. *Doomsday Book* (9–adult). 1992, Bantam $22 (0-553-08131-4); paper $10 (0-553-35167-2). When an Oxford student is mistakenly sent back to 1348 and the site of the Black Plague, her mentor battles technical failures and a devastating virus to get her back. (Rev: BL 6/15/92*)

1855 Willis, Connie. *Impossible Things* (9–adult). 1994, Bantam paper $5.99 (0-553-56436-6). In this second collection of her science fiction short stories, Willis presents 11 works, including award-winning "The Last of the Winnebagos," "Even the Queen," and "At the Rialto." (Rev: BL 12/15/93*; SLJ 3/95; VOYA 6/94)

1856 Willis, Connie. *Uncharted Territory* (9–adult). 1994, Bantam/Spectra paper $3.99 (0-553-56294-0). Planetary surveyors Fin and Carson battle hostile terrain, bureaucratic red tape, and renegade "planet crashers." (Rev: BL 5/1/94; VOYA 12/94)

1857 Wilson, Robert Charles. *Mysterium* (9–adult). 1994, Bantam paper $11.95 (0-553-37365-X). A Midwestern town is transported to another time by humanoids who want to ransack its culture and ravage the population. Awards: SLJ Best Book. (Rev: BL 4/1/94; VOYA 10/94)

1858 Wolverton, David, ed. *L. Ron Hubbard Presents Writers of the Future, Vol. 8* (9–adult). 1992, Bridge Publications paper $5.99 (0-88404-772-5). Outstanding submissions to the Writers of the Future contest, matched with work by Illustrators of the Future contest entrants. (Rev: BL 10/1/92) [813]

1859 Womack, Jack. *Random Acts of Senseless Violence* (9–adult). 1994, Atlantic Monthly $21 (0-87113-577-9). Lola Hart, living in future Manhattan, uses her diary to chronicle a violent, crumbling society. When her parents move her family to Harlem, she joins a gang. (Rev: BL 7/94; BTA)

1860 Yolen, Jane, ed. *2041: Twelve Short Stories about the Future by Top Science-Fiction Writers* (5–9). 1991, Delacorte $16 (0-385-30445-5); 1994, Dell/Laurel Leaf paper $3.99 (0-440-21898-5). Contains varied stories that address the question of what the world will be like in 50 years. Awards: SLJ Best Book. (Rev: BL 9/1/91; MJHS; SLJ 7/91*)

Sports

1861 Anderson, Peggy King. *Safe at Home!* (5–8). 1992, Atheneum $12.95 (0-689-31686-0). Because of his family's problems, including alcoholism, Tony feels safe and in control only on the baseball field. (Rev: BL 10/1/92; SLJ 9/92)

1862 Bannon, Troy. *Aggro Moves: Street Wizards, Book 1* (5–8). 1991, Dell/Yearling paper $2.99 (0-440-40506-8). Bobby Clarke organizes a team of the best of the skateboard gangs to challenge vandalizing thrashers from the Chain Gang. (Rev: BL 12/15/91)

1863 Bennett, James. *The Squared Circle* (9–12). 1995, Scholastic $14.95 (0-590-48671-3). A high school all-American basketball player finds pressures building among academics, sports, and his social life. (Rev: BL 12/15/95; SLJ 12/95)

1864 Bouton, Jim, and Eliot Asinof. *Strike Zone* (9–adult). 1994, Viking $20.95 (0-670-85214-7). A rookie Chicago Cubs pitcher and an aging umpire who's been paid to fix a pivotal game go head-to-head in this baseball novel. (Rev: BL 4/1/94; BTA; SLJ 12/94)

1865 Christopher, Matt. *Fighting Tackle* (5–7). Illus. 1995, Little, Brown $14.95 (0-316-14010-4). Terry is shocked when his football coach moves him from safety to nose tackle, and he's unsettled to learn that his younger brother, who has Down's syndrome, now runs faster than he. (Rev: BL 2/1/95; SLJ 2/95)

1866 Christopher, Matt. *Return of the Home Run Kid* (5–7). Illus. 1992, Little, Brown $14.95 (0-316-14080-5). This sequel to *The Kid Who Only Hit Homers* opens at the start of a new season, when the young hero receives more coaching from a baseball great. (Rev: BL 4/15/92; SLJ 5/92)

1867 Christopher, Matt. *The Winning Stroke* (5–8). 1994, Little, Brown $14.95 (0-316-14266-2). A 12-year-old faces months of therapy after breaking his leg in a baseball game. Lessons learned during recovery transform Jerry into a stronger competitor. (Rev: BL 5/1/94; SLJ 6/94; VOYA 6/94)

1868 Crutcher, Chris. *Ironman* (8–12). 1995, Greenwillow $15 (0-688-13503-X). A psychological/sports novel in which a 17-year-old carries around an attitude that fuels the plot. Awards: SLJ Best Book. (Rev: BL 3/1/95*; SHS; SLJ 3/95; VOYA 5/95)

1869 Deuker, Carl. *Heart of a Champion* (8–10). 1993, Little, Brown $14.95 (0-316-18166-8);

1994, Avon/Flare paper $3.50 (0-380-72269-0). Explores the ups and downs of the 5-year friendship of Seth and Jimmy, from their first meeting on a baseball field at age 12. Awards: YALSA Best Book for Young Adults. (Rev: BL 6/1–15/93; BTA; MJHS; SLJ 6/93)

1870 Drumtra, Stacy. *Face-off* (5–10). 1992, Avon/Flare paper $3.50 (0-380-76863-1). Twin brothers' competition for friends, recognition, and hockey greatness turns bitter when T.J. transfers to his brother's school. (Rev: BL 4/1/93; VOYA 8/93)

1871 Duder, Tessa. *Alex in Rome* (8–12). 1992, Houghton $13.95 (0-395-62879-2). Focuses on the gradually evolving affection of Tom, 23, a New Zealander in Italy to study music, and Alex, in Rome to represent New Zealand in women's swimming in the 1960 Olympics. (Rev: BL 10/15/92; SLJ 10/92)

1872 Dygard, Thomas J. *Backfield Package* (6–12). 1992, Morrow $14 (0-688-11471-7). High school football stars want to play together in college, but only one of them is offered a scholarship. (Rev: BL 9/15/92; MJHS; SLJ 9/92; YR)

1873 Dygard, Thomas J. *Game Plan* (6–9). 1993, Morrow $14 (0-688-12007-5); 1995, Penguin/Puffin paper $3.99 (0-14-036970-8). Beano, a high school football student manager, must coach the team when the team's coach is injured in a car accident. (Rev: BL 9/1/93; MJHS; SLJ 10/93; VOYA 2/94)

1874 Dygard, Thomas J. *Infield Hit* (6–9). 1995, Morrow $15 (0-688-14037-8). A boy's struggle to make new friends through playing baseball. (Rev: BL 4/15/95; SLJ 3/95)

1875 Dygard, Thomas J. *The Rebounder* (7–10). 1994, Morrow $14 (0-688-12821-1). Chris quits playing basketball after accidentally injuring an opponent. Transferring to a new school, he is guided back to the sport by a sensitive coach. (Rev: BL 9/1/94, BTA; SLJ 10/94)

1876 Emerson, Mark. *The Mean Lean Weightlifting Queen* (7–12). 1992, Tudor (P.O. Box 38366, Greensboro, NC 27438) $17.95 (0-936389-26-5). Determined to change her appearance and improve her self-esteem, Susan takes up weightlifting. Her success raises questions about her ability and femininity. (Rev: BL 1/15/93; BTA; SLJ 8/92)

1877 Gallo, Donald R. *Ultimate Sports* (7–12). 1995, Delacorte $15.95 (0-385-32152-X). The 16 sports stories here, by popular young-adult authors, have varied ethnic backgrounds, a number of cognitive and physical levels, and male and female protagonists. (Rev: BL 11/15/95; SLJ 10/95; VOYA 4/96)

1878 Hayes, Daniel. *No Effect* (6–8). 1993, Godine $15.95 (0-87923-989-1). An 8th-grade boy deals with unattainable love and a very attainable outlet for his frustrations and energies: wrestling. Awards: SLJ Best Book; YALSA Best Book for Young Adults. (Rev: BL 5/1/94; BTA; MJHS; SLJ 1/94; VOYA 2/94)

1879 Hoffius, Stephen. *Winners and Losers* (7–10). 1993, Simon & Schuster $15 (0-671-79194-X). When star runner Daryl collapses during a meet, the coach, his father, starts to ignore him and push Daryl's friend Curt to train harder. (Rev: BL 7/93; BTA; MJHS; VOYA 2/94)

1880 Hughes, Dean. *End of the Race* (5–7). 1993, Atheneum $13.95 (0-689-31779-4). White Jared and African American Davin are on the junior track team and feel pressure from their fathers, but prejudice keeps them from being friends. (Rev: BL 11/1/93; BTA; SLJ 12/93; VOYA 2/94)

1881 Jackson, Alison. *Crane's Rebound* (5–7). Illus. 1991, Dutton $12.95 (0-525-44722-9). An 11-year-old attending a basketball camp is assigned an obnoxious roommate and participates in a prank with him that gets him in trouble with his dorm adviser. (Rev: BL 9/15/91; SLJ 9/91)

1882 Klass, David. *Danger Zone* (7–10). 1996, Scholastic $16.95 (0-590-48590-3). Jimmy, a star high school basketball player in Minnesota, is chosen for a national Teen Dream Team that travels to a Rome tournament. (Rev: SLJ 3/96; VOYA 4/96)

1883 Kline, Suzy. *Orp Goes to the Hoop* (5–7). 1991, Putnam $13.95 (0-399-21834-3). The comic adventures of a 7th-grader who plays a crucial part in his basektball team's big game. (Rev: BL 7/91; MJHS)

1884 Korman, Gordon. *The Toilet Paper Tigers* (5–7). 1993, Scholastic $13.95 (0-590-46230-X). A Texas baseball team sponsored by Feather-Soft Bathroom Tissue is whipped into shape by Coach Pendergast's 12-year-old granddaughter. (Rev: BL 10/1/93)

1885 Lynch, Chris. *Iceman* (8–12). 1994, HarperCollins $15 (0-06-023341-9). An emotionally fragile teenager expresses his anger in violent hockey games and spends time at the local mortuary with a disturbed recluse who works there. Awards: BL Editors' Choice; SLJ Best Book; YALSA Best Book for Young Adults. (Rev: BL 2/1/94; BTA; MJHS; SLJ 3/94; VOYA 4/94)

1886 Maclean, John. *When the Mountain Sings* (6–9). 1992, Houghton $14.95 (0-395-59917-2). Sam, 13, pushes himself past his limits and achieves more than he believes he can as a competitive skier. (Rev: BL 11/15/92; SLJ 12/92)

1887 Manes, Stephen. *An Almost Perfect Game* (5–7). 1995, Scholastic $14.95 (0-590-44432-8). Jake and Randy spend every summer with their baseball-fan grandparents, until Jake finds he can control the game through his scorecard. (Rev: BL 6/1–15/95; SLJ 6/95)

1888 Murrow, Liza Ketchum. *Twelve Days in August* (8–11). 1993, Holiday $14.95 (0-8234-1012-9). In the course of a school year, Todd, age 16, must deal with a soccer team bully, homophobia, peer pressure, and girlfriend problems. Awards: SLJ Best Book. (Rev: BL 3/1/93; SLJS 6/93*; VOYA 10/93)

1889 Neumann, Peter J. *Playing a Virginia Moon* (8–12). 1994, Houghton $14.95 (0-395-66562-0). A fiercely competitive high school senior is determined to win a cross-country championship and plans his race strategy as if for battle, like his hero, General Lee. (Rev: BL 3/15/94; BTA; SLJ 5/94; VOYA 6/94)

1890 Powell, Randy. *Dean Duffy* (8–12). 1995, Farrar $15 (0-374-31754-2). A Little League baseball great has problems with his pitching arm and sees his career collapse. (Rev: BL 4/15/95; SLJ 5/95)

1891 Pressfield, Steven. *The Legend of Bagger Vance: Golf and the Game of Life* (9–adult). 1995, Morrow $20 (0-688-14048-3). The narrator is instructed in the interconnectedness of golf and spirituality. (Rev: BL 4/15/95; SLJ 12/95)

1892 Quies, Werner. *Soccer Shots* (6–9). 1995, Frontier (1427A S.E. 122nd Ave., Portland, OR 97233-1204) paper $10.95 (0-939116-37-5). A 16-year-old East German boy pursues his dream of becoming a professional soccer player in the West. (Rev: BL 12/1/95)

1893 Raven, James. *Entering the Way* (6–8). Illus. 1993, Bantam paper $3.25 (0-553-29929-8). The Dojo Rats, 4 teenage karate students, must confront a gang that has stolen their master's heirloom sword. The first in a new series. (Rev: BL 3/1/93; SLJ 2/93)

1894 Riddell, Ruth. *Ice Warrior* (5–7). 1992, Atheneum $13.95 (0-689-31710-7). A boy moves from California to Minnesota, where he builds and races an ice boat. (Rev: BL 5/1/92; SLJ 7/92)

1895 Salkeld, Audrey, and Rosie Smith, eds. *One Step in the Clouds: An Omnibus of Mountaineering Novels and Short Stories* (9–adult). 1991, Sierra Club $25 (0-87156-638-9). Short stories, a play, 2 novellas, and 4 novels—31 works altogether—on mountain climbing. (Rev: BL 2/15/91*) [808.83]

1896 Soto, Gary. *Taking Sides* (6–9). 1991, Harcourt $14.95 (0-15-284076-1). Lincoln Mendoza moves from his inner-city San Francisco neighborhood to a middle-class suburb and must adjust to life in a new high school. (Rev: BL 12/1/91; MJHS; SLJ 11/91)

1897 Spinelli, Jerry. *There's a Girl in My Hammerlock* (5–8). 1991, Simon & Schuster $13 (0-671-74684-7). This story of a girl who goes out for junior high wrestling, to the consternation of almost everyone but her mother, raises questions about gender roles and personal identity. Awards: SLJ Best Book. (Rev: BL 10/15/91; MJHS; SLJ 9/91*)

1898 Staudohar, Paul D., ed. *Baseball's Best Short Stories* (9–adult). 1995, Chicago Review $20 (1-55652-247-9). Baseball stories from such renowned authors as Zane Grey, Robert Penn Warren, and James Thurber. (Rev: BL 11/15/95)

1899 Wallace, Bill. *Never Say Quit* (5–7). 1993, Holiday $14.95 (0-8234-1013-7). Unfairly denied places on the soccer team, a motley group of youngsters forms its own team and learns what's important in life. (Rev: BL 4/15/93; VOYA 10/93)

1900 Weaver, Will. *Farm Team* (7–12). 1995, HarperCollins LB $14.89 (0-06-023589-6). Shy Billy Baggs, with many responsibilities for his age, finds success playing baseball. A sequel to *Striking Out*. (Rev: BL 9/1/95)

1901 Wilbur, Richard. *A Game of Catch* (5–7). Illus. 1994, Harcourt $15.95 (0-15-230563-7). This short story—originally published in the 1950s and now illustrated with full-page watercolors—concerns a boy's pain at being an outsider. (Rev: BL 3/1/94)

1902 Willner-Pardo, Gina. *Jason and the Losers* (5–7). 1995, Clarion $14.95 (0-395-70160-0). A 5th-grader finds himself living with relatives, the result of a divorce, and he loses himself and his sorrow in a good game of ball. (Rev: BL 4/15/95; SLJ 4/95)

Short Stories and General Anthologies

1903 Allen, Paula Gunn, ed. *Voice of the Turtle: American Indian Literature, 1900–1970* (9–adult). 1994, Ballantine $25 (0-345-37526-2). An anthology of twentieth-century Native American literature (the first of 2 volumes), including fiction, essays, and autobiographies on such subjects as spiritual loss and displacement. (Rev: BL 7/94; SLJ 5/95) [813]

1904 Aparicio, Frances R., ed. *Latino Voices* (8–12). (Writers of America) 1994, Millbrook LB $15.90 (1-56294-388-X). Poetry, fiction, and true stories by 24 Latino writers describing experiences with immigration, family, work, discrimination, and love. (Rev: BL 10/1/94; BTA; SLJ 12/94; VOYA 2/95) [860.8]

1905 Asher, Sandy. *Out of Here: A Senior Class Yearbook* (7–10). 1993, Dutton/Lodestar $14.99 (0-525-67418-7); 1995, Penguin/Puffin paper $3.99 (0-14-037441-8). The senior year as seen through the eyes of 9 grads in Eli, Missouri. (Rev: BL 6/1–15/93; MJHS; SLJ 7/93; VOYA 12/93)

1906 Augenbraum, Harold, and Ilan Stavans, eds. *Growing Up Latino: Memoirs and Stories* (9–adult). 1993, Houghton $22.95 (0-395-62231-X); paper $12.95 (0-395-66124-2). The "Hispanic journey from darkness to light, from rejection to assimilation, from silence to voice," in 25 diverse, eloquent voices. (Rev: BL 2/1/93; BTA; MJHS; SHS) [813]

1907 Barnes, Kim, and Mary Clearman Blew, eds. *Circle of Women: An Anthology of Contemporary Western Women Writers* (9–adult). 1994, Penguin paper $10.95 (0-14-023524-8). Essays, poems, and fiction by women authors about the American West, dealing with such themes as love, loss, and land. (Rev: BL 7/94; SHS) [810.8]

1908 Bauer, Marion Dane, ed. *Am I Blue?* (8–12). 1994, HarperCollins $15 (0-06-024253-1). Sixteen short stories from well-known young-adult writers who have something meaningful to share about gay awareness and want to present positive, credible gay role models. Awards: ALSC Notable Children's Book; SLJ Best Book. (Rev: BL 5/1/94*; BTA, MJHS; SHS; SLJ 6/94; VOYA 8/94)

1909 Bernard, Robert, ed. *A Short Wait Between Trains: A Collection of War Short Stories by American Writers* (9–adult). 1991, Delacorte $18 (0-385-30486-2). Most of the 22 adult stories in this collection have antiwar themes and are by some of America's greatest writers, including Hemingway, Faulkner, and Malamud. (Rev: BL 11/1/91; SLJ 2/92) [813]

1910 Berry, James. *The Future-Telling Lady and Other Stories* (5–7). 1993, HarperCollins/Willa Perlman LB $12.89 (0-06-021435-X). Stories of contemporary Jamaica, rooted in the country's oral tradition. (Rev: BL 2/15/93; MJHS; SLJ 2/93)

1911 *Best-Loved Stories Told at the National Storytelling Festival* (9–adult). 1991, National Storytelling Press $19.95 (1-879991-01-2); paper $11.95 (1-879991-00-4). The 37 traditional stories collected here cover a wide range of ethnic backgrounds, genres, and colloquial voices. (Rev: BL 10/15/91) [398.2]

1912 Boyd, Herb, and Robert L. Allen, eds. *Brotherman: The Odyssey of Black Men in America* (9–adult). 1995, Ballantine $27.50 (0-345-37670-6). An anthology of fiction, memoir, essays, and poetry from African American men. (Rev: BL 2/15/95) [810.8]

1913 Briscoe, Stuart, and Jill Briscoe. *The Family Book of Christian Values: Timeless Stories for Today's Family* (9–adult). 1995, Chariot Family/Christian Parenting $24.99 (0-7814-0245-X). Inspirational and popular writers have been chosen to emphasize Christian values. (Rev: BL 11/15/95) [808.8]

1914 Brooks, Martha. *Traveling On into the Light* (7–12). 1994, Orchard/Melanie Kroupa LB $14.99 (0-531-08713-1). Stories about runaways, suicide, and desertion, featuring romantic, sensitive, and smart teenage outsiders. Awards: SLJ Best Book; YALSA Best Book for Young Adults. (Rev: BL 6/94; BTA; MJHS; SHS; SLJ 8/94*; VOYA 10/94)

1915 Brown, Wesley, and Amy Ling, eds. *Imagining America: Stories from the Promised Land* (9–adult). 1992, Persea $24.95 (0-89255-161-5); paper $12.95 (0-89255-167-4). A multicultural anthology of 37 stories by distinguished writers about emigration to and migration within the United States during the twentieth century. (Rev: BL 12/15/91*; SLJ 6/92)

1916 Carlson, Lori M., ed. *American Eyes: New Asian-American Short Stories for Young Adults* (8–12). 1994, Holt $14.95 (0-8050-3544-3). These stories present widely varied answers to the question What does it mean to Asian American adolescents to grow up in a country that views them as aliens? (Rev: BL 1/1/95; BTA; SHS; SLJ 1/95; VOYA 5/95)

1917 Cofer, Judith Ortiz. *The Latin Deli* (9–adult). 1993, Univ. of Georgia $19.95 (0-8203-1556-7). At the heart of this collection of Ortiz Coffer's stories, essays, and poems is the conflict of her childhood as a first-generation immigrant. (Rev: BL 11/15/93*; BTA) [810.8]

1918 Crawford, E. A., and Teresa Kennedy, eds. *A Christmas Sampler: Classic Stories of the Season, from Twain to Cheever* (9–adult). 1992,

Hyperion $19.95 (1-56282-933-5). This chronologically arranged anthology of short stories features pieces by such familiar authors as Mark Twain and Washington Irving. (Rev: BL 10/15/92) [813.010833]

1919 Crutcher, Chris. *Athletic Shorts: 6 Short Stories* (8–12). 1991, Greenwillow $13.95 (0-688-10816-4). Focuses on themes important to teens, such as father-son friction, insecurity, and friendship and mixes poignancy with humor. Awards: SLJ Best Book; YALSA Best Book for Young Adults. (Rev: BL 10/15/91; SHS; SLJ 9/91*)

1920 Dillard, Annie. *The Annie Dillard Reader* (9–adult). 1994, HarperCollins $25 (0-06-017158-8). A gathering of poems, short stories, essays, and chapters of novels from the author's diverse body of work. (Rev: BL 11/15/94; SHS) [818]

1921 Divakaruni, Chitra. *Arranged Marriage* (9–adult). 1995, Doubleday/Anchor $21 (0-385-47558-6). This collection of short stories revolves around arranged marriages, both in India and the United States, and the differences in women's lives in both countries. (Rev: BL 7/95*; SLJ 12/95)

1922 Gallo, Donald R., ed. *Within Reach: Ten Stories* (7–12). 1993, HarperCollins LB $14.89 (0-06-021441-4). A collection of short stories, including science fiction and horror. (Rev: BL 6/1–15/93; MJHS; VOYA 2/94)

1923 Golden, Lilly, ed. *A Literary Christmas: Great Contemporary Christmas Stories* (9–adult). 1992, Atlantic Monthly $20 (0-87113-490-X). Twenty-seven stories and novel excerpts from such authors as Annie Dillard, Raymond Carver, Leo Rosten, Tobias Wolf, and Ntozake Shange. (Rev: BL 10/15/92) [808.83]

1924 Gordimer, Nadine. *Crimes of Conscience* (9–adult). (African Writers) 1991, Heinemann paper $8.95 (0-435-90668-2). The themes of these dark, beautiful stories by the great South African writer are betrayal and its opposite: the unexpected good people find in themselves. (Rev: BL 5/1/91; SHS)

1925 Greer, Colin, and Herbert Kohl. *A Call to Character: A Family Treasury of Stories, Poems, Plays, Proverbs, and Fables to Guide the Development of Values . . .* (9–adult). 1995, HarperCollins $25 (0-06-017339-4). A book to be read to children stressing values that are important through their psychological development. (Rev: BL 11/15/95) [808.8]

1926 Harvey, Karen, ed. *American Indian Voices* (7–12). (Writers of America) 1995, Millbrook $16.90 (1-56294-382-0). Thirty selections giving insights into the cultures and experiences of American Indians. (Rev: BL 5/15/95; SLJ 5/95) [810.8]

1927 Heynen, Jim. *The One-Room Schoolhouse: Stories about the Boys* (9–adult). 1993, Knopf $20 (0-679-41786-9). Lovingly captures the simple experienes of a group of Midwest farm boys: drinking from puddles, hurling rotten eggs, helping with heifer calving, etc. (Rev: BL 5/15/93*)

1928 Hill, Susan. *The Christmas Collection* (5–7). Illus. 1994, Candlewick $19.95 (1-56402-341-9). Four stories and a poem that capture the essence of traditional Christmas celebrations. Includes woodcut illustrations. (Rev: BL 10/15/94)

1929 Hong, Maria, ed. *Growing Up Asian American* (9–adult). 1993, Morrow $20 (0-688-11266-8). This collection of stories and essays looks at the Asian American experience through such issues as education stratification, kinship, beauty standards, and intraethnic conflicts. (Rev: BL 12/15/93; BTA) [810.8]

1930 Hurston, Zora Neal. *Novels and Stories* (9–adult). 1995, Library of America (14 E. 60th St., New York, NY 10022) $35 (0-940450-83-6). Includes all 4 of Hurston's novels plus many of her short stories. (Rev: BL 1/1/95; SHS)

1931 Jones, Edward P. *Lost in the City* (9–12). Photos. 1992, Morrow $19 (0-688-11526-8). Compelling short stories featuring African Americans, ages 8–80, in Washington, D.C. Awards: SLJ Best Book. (Rev: SLJ 1/93*)

1932 Killens, John Oliver, and Jerry W. Ward, eds. *Black Southern Voices: An Anthology of Fiction, Poetry, Drama, Nonfiction, and Critical Essays* (9–adult). 1992, NAL/Meridian paper $15 (0-452-01096-9). Essays, poetry, drama, and fiction by such familiar names as Arna Bontemps, Alice Walker, and Nikki Giovanni, as well as less-well-known writers. (Rev: BL 10/15/92) [810.8]

1933 King, Stephen. *Nightmares and Dreamscapes* (9–adult). 1993, Viking $27.50 (0-670-85108-6). A collection of short stories, including pastiches of Doyle and Chandler, a vampire story, and a sports story. (Rev: BL 7/93*)

1934 Kuper, Peter. *Give It Up! And Other Short Stories by Franz Kafka* (9–adult). (ComicLit) 1995, NBM Publishing (185 Madison Ave., Suite 1502, New York, NY 10016) $14.95 (1-56163-125-6). Kuper uses a scratchboard style, resembling woodcuts of German expressionists, to accentuate the dark humor found in 9 of Kafka's stories. (Rev: BL 8/95) [741.5]

1935 Lesley, Craig, and Katheryn Stavrakis, eds. *Talking Leaves: Contemporary Native American*

Short Stories (9–adult). 1991, Dell/Laurel Leaf paper $10 (0-440-50344-2). Firmly rooted in the oral tradition, this anthology of 38 stories by contemporary Native American writers includes many with modern settings. (Rev: BL 11/15/91; MJHS)

1936 Lewis, David L., ed. *The Portable Harlem Renaissance Reader* (9–adult). 1994, Viking $27.95 (0-670-84510-8). The best literature that emerged from a flowering of African American culture centered in Harlem between the world wars. (Rev: BL 3/15/94; SHS) [810.8]

1937 Loughery, John, ed. *First Sightings: Stories of American Youth* (9–adult). 1993, Persea $29.95 (0-89255-186-0); paper $11.95 (0-89255-187-9). An anthology of 20 dramatic stories about children and teens, by John Updike, Philip Roth, Alice Walker, Joyce Carol Oates, et al. (Rev: BL 4/15/93; BTA)

1938 Madison, D. Soyini, ed. *The Woman That I Am: The Literature and Culture of Contemporary Women of Color* (9–adult). 1994, St. Martin's $35 (0-312-10012-4). Latina, Asian, African American, and Native American women writers such as Angelou, Erdich, Morrison, and Tan make up this anthology delving into the culture of contemporary women of color. (Rev: BL 12/15/93) [810.9]

1939 Mahy, Margaret. *The Door in the Air and Other Stories* (6–10). Illus. 1991, Delacorte $13.95 (0-385-30252-5). A series of fantasy sketches about how the power of art makes simple things seem new. (Rev: BL 2/1/91; MJHS; SLJ 4/91)

1940 Major, Clarence, ed. *Calling the Wind: Twentieth-Century African-American Short Stories* (9–adult). 1993, HarperCollins $25 (0-06-018337-3); paper $12 (0-06-098201-2). Includes stories by Langston Hughes, Zora Neale Hurston, James Baldwin, Toni Morrison, and dozens more. (Rev: BL 12/1/92*; BTA)

1941 Mandelbaum, Paul, ed. *First Words: Earliest Writings from 42 Favorite Authors* (9–adult). 1993, Algonquin Books of Chapel Hill (P.O. Box 2225, Chapel Hill, NC 27515-2225) $24.95 (0-945575-71-8). First attempts at writing by 42 authors—such as Jill McCorkle, Michael Crichton, Stephen King, and Gore Vidal—accompanied by profiles and childhood photos. (Rev: BL 11/15/93) [813.54]

1942 Mazer, Anne, ed. *America Street: A Multicultural Anthology of Stories* (5–8). 1993, Persea $14.95 (0-89255-190-9); paper $4.95 (0-89255-191-7). Fourteen short stories about growing up in America's diverse society by Robert Cormier, Langston Hughes, Grace Paley, Gary Soto, et al. (Rev: BL 9/1/93; SLJ 11/93; VOYA 12/93)

1943 Mee, Susie, ed. *Downhome: An Anthology of Southern Women Writers* (9–12). 1995, Harcourt $16 (0-15-600121-7). A selection of 21 stories that illustrate women's memories of being down home in the South. (Rev: BL 10/15/95; SLJ 2/96)

1944 *More Best-Loved Stories Told at the National Storytelling Festival* (9–adult). 1992, National Storytelling Press $19.95 (1-879991-09-8); paper $11.95 (1-879991-08-X). Stories featuring familiar folklore, family anecdotes, and tales from many cultures, with a brief note on each storyteller. (Rev: BL 11/15/92) [808.83]

1945 Mullane, Deirdre. *Crossing the Danger Water: Three Hundred Years of African-American Writing* (9–adult). 1993, Doubleday/Anchor $16 (0-385-42243-1). The history of African Americans is explored in their writings, narratives, letters, editorials, speeches, lyrics, and folktales, from U.S. colonization to today. (Rev: BL 11/1/93) [810.8]

1946 Muse, Daphne, ed. *Prejudice: Stories about Hate, Ignorance, Revelation, and Transformation* (7–12). 1995, Hyperion $16.95 (0-7868-0024-0). Fifteen stories about prejudice. (Rev: BL 5/15/95; VOYA 2/96)

1947 Naylor, Gloria, ed. *Children of the Night: The Best Short Stories by Black Writers, 1967 to the Present* (9–adult). 1996, Little, Brown $24.95 (0-316-59926-3). A short-story collection, balanced thematically, from the editorial hands of one of the finest black female writers. (Rev: BL 12/1/95)

1948 Newcombe, Jack, ed. *A New Christmas Treasury* (9–adult). Rev. ed. 1991, Viking $25 (0-670-83960-4). These classic Yuletide short stories, poems, letters, and essays include favorite selections by Dickens, O. Henry, and others, as well as 14 new contributions. (Rev: BL 10/15/91) [808.8]

1949 Nye, Naomi Shihab, ed. *The Tree Is Older Than You Are: A Bilingual Gathering of Poems and Stories from Mexico with Paintings by Mexican Artists* (6–12). 1995, Simon & Schuster $19.95 (0-689-80297-8). Mexican poems and traditional stories are presented side-by-side in this bilingual volume. (Rev: BL 9/15/95; SLJ 10/95; VOYA 12/95) [860.9]

1950 Oates, Joyce Carol, ed. *The Oxford Book of American Short Stories* (9–adult). 1992, Oxford Univ. $24.95 (0-19-507065-8). For college-bound students, short stories from Washington Irving to the present. (Rev: BL 8/92; SHS)

1951 Paterson, Katherine. *A Midnight Clear: Stories for the Christmas Season* (5–12). 1995, Dutton/Lodestar $16 (0-525-67529-9). Stories that reveal the spirit of Christmas in contemporary life—hope and light in a dark, uncertain world. (Rev: BL 9/15/95)

1952 Power, Susan. *The Grass Dancer* (9–adult). 1994, Putnam $22.95 (0-399-13911-7). Anna Thunder, a Sioux living in North Dakota, is the central character in this novel that tells the generational stories of Anna's family. Awards: BL Editors' Choice; SLJ Best Book; YALSA Best Book for Young Adults. (Rev: BL 8/94; BTA; SHS; SLJ 5/95; VOYA 12/94)

1953 Rebolledo, Tey Diana, and Eliana S. Rivero, eds. *Infinite Divisions: An Anthology of Chicana Literature* (9–adult). 1993, Univ. of Arizona $40 (0-8165-1252-3); paper $19.95 (0-8165-1384-8). Spans the history of prose and poetry by Mexican American women and that of the settlement of the so-called New World. (Rev: BL 6/1–15/93; SHS) [810.8]

1954 Rochman, Hazel, and Darlene Z. McCampbell, eds. *Who Do You Think You Are? Stories of Friends and Enemies* (7–12). 1993, Little, Brown/Joy Street $15.95 (0-316-75355-6). Fifteen stories about friendship and its loss, by Erdrich, Updike, Bradbury, Oates, Cisneros, et al. Awards: SLJ Best Book; YALSA Best Book for Young Adults. (Rev: BL 4/1/93; MJHS; SLJ 5/93*; VOYA 8/93) [813]

1955 Rollins, Charlemae Hill, ed. *Christmas Gif': An Anthology of Christmas Poems, Songs, and Stories* (5–12). Illus. 1993, Morrow $14 (0-688-11667-1). A reissue of this Christmas anthology, newly illustrated by Ashley Bryan, of African American songs, stories, poems, spirituals, and recipes. (Rev: BL 7/93; MJHS) [810.8]

1956 Rosen, Roger, and Patra McSharry, eds. *East-West: The Landscape Within* (7–12). (World Issues) 1992, Rosen LB $16.95 (0-8239-1375-9); paper $8.95 (0-8239-1376-7). Short stories and nonfiction selections by diverse authors of varied nationalities on their culture's beliefs and values, among them Dalai Lama, Joseph Campbell, Lydia Minatoya, and Aung Aung Taik. (Rev: BL 12/15/92; SLJ 2/93) [909]

1957 Ruoff, A. La Vonne Brown. *Literatures of the American Indian* (7–12). Illus. 1991, Chelsea House $17.95 (1-55546-688-5). Ritual dramas, pictographs, songs, speeches, myths, legends, autobiographies, poems, and stories describe the Native American cultural heritage. (Rev: BL 3/1/91; MJHS) [973]

1958 Salisbury, Graham. *Blue Skin of the Sea* (8–12). 1992, Delacorte $15 (0-385-30596-6). In these 11 stories, one finds a strong sense of time and place, fully realized characters, stylish prose, and universal themes. Awards: Child Study Children's Book; SLJ Best Book; YALSA Best Book for Young Adults. (Rev: BL 6/15/92*; BTA; SLJ 6/92*)

1959 Schwartz, Steven. *Lives of the Fathers* (9–adult). 1991, Univ. of Illinois $16.95 (0-252-01815-X). Ten short stories portray the powerful, often complicated relationships between fathers and sons. (Rev: BL 7/91*)

1960 Silver, Norman. *An Eye for Color* (8–12). 1993, Dutton $14.99 (0-525-44859-4). Autobiographical stories about what it's like to grow up white, male, and Jewish in South Africa. (Rev: BL 1/15/93; SLJ 7/93; YR)

1961 Soto, Gary. *Beisbol en abril y otras historias* (5–9). Tr. by Tedi López Mills. Illus. 1993, Fondo de Cultura Económica (Mexico) paper $7.49 (968-16-3854-9). This translation of Soto's popular collection of 11 short stories tells about the trials of growing up in California. English title: *Baseball in April and Other Stories*. (Rev: BL 10/1/94)

1962 Stepto, Michele, ed. *African-American Voices* (7–12). (Writers of America) 1995, Millbrook $16.90 (1-56294-474-6). Selections by W. E. B. Du Bois, Toni Morrison, Ralph Ellison, and others plus traditional chants, speeches, and poetry. (Rev: BL 5/15/95; SLJ 3/95) [810.8]

1963 Sumrall, Amber Coverdale, ed. *Love's Shadow: Writings by Women* (9–adult). 1993, Crossing LB $26.95 (0-89594-584-3); paper $14.95 (0-89594-583-5). Stories and poems by women dealing with the end of love (both heterosexual and lesbian) and its emotional effects. (Rev: BL 9/15/93) [808.83]

1964 Thomas, Roy Edwin. *Come Go with Me* (9–adult). 1994, Farrar $15 (0-374-37089-3). Ninety-four stories collected from interviews in the Appalachians, Ozarks, and Ouachita Mountain regions. (Rev: BL 5/1/94; SLJ 7/94) [976.7]

1965 Vázquez, Montalbán Manuel, and others. *Breve antología de cuentos 4: Latinoamérica y España* (9–12). 1993, Editorial Sudamericana (Buenos Aires, Argentina) paper $8.90 (950-07-0897-3). Seven short stories by Vázquez Montalbán (Spain), Arreola (Mexico), Borges (Argentina), Piñera (Cuba), Allende (Chile), Rosa (Brazil), and Céspedes (Bolivia), with brief biographical sketches, glossary, and notes. (Rev: BL 10/1/94)

1966 Velie, Alan R., ed. *The Lightning Within: An Anthology of Contemporary American Indian Fiction* (9–adult). 1991, Univ. of Nebraska

$19.95 (0-8032-4659-5). Offers a thoughfully selected sampling of fiction by 7 noted modern Native American writers, e.g., Momaday, Erdrich, Dorris, Silko, Vizenor, and Ortiz. (Rev: BL 5/15/91; SHS; SLJ 9/91)

1967 Villaseñor, Victor. *Walking Stars: Stories of Magic and Power* (7–12). 1994, Arte Público/Piñata $14.95 (1-55885-118-6). True short stories describing the everyday magic and family love found in the author's Mexican and Native American heritage. (Rev: BL 10/15/94; SLJ 11/94; VOYA 4/95) [813]

1968 Washington, James Melvin, ed. *Conversations with God: Two Centuries of Prayer by African-Americans* (9–adult). 1994, HarperCollins $20 (0-06-017161-8). A collection of 200 prayers, poems, hymns, and stories by authors ranging from the famous to the unknown. (Rev: BL 11/15/94*) [242.8]

1969 Washington, Mary Helen, ed. *Memory of Kin: Stories about Family by Black Writers* (9–adult). 1991, Doubleday $22.95 (0-385-24782-6); paper $12.95 (0-385-24783-4). Wide-ranging collection of short stories and poetry dealing with the African American family experience. (Rev: BL 1/1/91; SHS; SLJ 7/91) [810.8]

1970 West, Dorothy. *The Richer, the Poorer: Stories, Sketches, and Reminiscences* (9–adult). 1995, Doubleday $22 (0-385-47145-9). Short stories and autobiographical essays by West, the only living participant in the Harlem Renaissance; includes her early writing as well as that on issues of today. (Rev: BL 7/95) [813]

1971 Wilson, Budge. *The Dandelion Garden* (6–10). 1995, Putnam/Philomel $15.95 (0-399-22768-7). A collection of 10 stories, mostly reflecting emotional growth but also some science fiction. (Rev: BL 9/1/95; SLJ 6/95)

1972 Wilson, Budge. *The Leaving and Other Stories* (6–10). 1992, Putnam/Philomel $14.95 (0-399-21878-5). Accounts of their mothers are told by different Nova Scotia women. Awards: ALSC Notable Children's Book; SLJ Best Book; YALSA Best Book for Young Adults. (Rev: BL 5/1/92; SLJ 6/92*; YR)

1973 Wynne-Jones, Tim. *Some of the Kinder Planets* (5–8). 1995, Orchard/Melanie Kroupa LB $14.99 (0-531-08751-4). Nine stories with ordinary boys and girls in offbeat situations. Awards: Boston Globe/Horn Book; SLJ Best Book. (Rev: BL 3/1/95*; SLJ 4/95)

1974 Young, Richard Alan, and Judy Dockery Young. *Stories from the Days of Christopher Columbus: A Multicultural Collection for Young Readers* (5–9). 1992, August House $17.95 (0-87483-199-7); paper $8.95 (0-87483-198-9). Anthology of stories that were being told in 1492, translated from Spanish, Aztec, and other languages. (Rev: BL 9/15/92; SLJ 7/92) [398]

Plays

General and Miscellaneous Collections

1975 Beard, Jocelyn A., ed. *The Best Men's Stage Monologues of 1993* (9–adult). 1994, Smith & Kraus paper $8.95 (1-880399-43-1). Includes 52 monologues from 1993 plays. (Rev: BL 4/1/94; SHS; VOYA 8/94) [808.82]

1976 Beard, Jocelyn A., ed. *The Best Men's Stage Monologues of 1992* (9–adult). 1993, Smith & Kraus paper $8.95 (1-880399-11-3). Monologues for men from outstanding 1992 theatrical works. (Rev: BL 6/1–15/93; SHS) [792]

1977 Beard, Jocelyn A., ed. *The Best Women's Stage Monologues of 1993* (9–adult). 1994, Smith & Kraus paper $8.95 (1-880399-42-3). Includes 58 monologues from 1993 plays. (Rev: BL 4/1/94; SHS; VOYA 8/94) [808.82]

1978 Beard, Jocelyn A., ed. *The Best Women's Stage Monologues of 1992* (9–adult). 1993, Smith & Kraus paper $8.95 (1-880399-10-5). Monologues for women from outstanding 1992 theatrical works. (Rev: BL 6/1–15/93; SHS) [792]

1979 Beard, Jocelyn A., ed. *Monologues from Classic Plays 468 B.C. to 1960 A.D.* (9–adult). 1993, Smith & Kraus paper $11.95 (1-880399-09-1). Monologues from early Greek, Roman, medieval, and Restoration plays and the modern works of Williams, Pinter, and Beckett. (Rev: BL 6/1–15/93) [808.82]

1980 Horvath, John, and others, eds. *Duo! The Best Scenes for the 90's* (9–adult). 1995, Applause paper $12.95 (1-55783-030-4). From established playwrights of the 1980s and 1990s are these 130 scenes for 2 actors. (Rev: BL 4/15/95) [792]

1981 Kamerman, Sylvia, ed. *The Big Book of Large-Cast Plays: 27 One-Act Plays for Young Actors* (5–10). 1994, Plays $18.95 (0-8238-0302-3). Thirty short plays arranged according to audience appeal, with varied topics. (Rev: BL 3/15/95; SHS) [812]

1982 Kraus, Eric, ed. *Monologues from Contemporary Literature, Vol. 1* (9–adult). 1993, Smith & Kraus paper $8.95 (1-880399-04-0). Monologues extracted from such literary sources as Paul Theroux's *Chicago Loop*. (Rev: BL 6/1–15/93) [792]

1983 Lazarus, John. *Not So Dumb: Four Plays for Young People* (7–12). 1993, Coach House paper $14.95 (0-88910-453-0). Four loosely connected plays that examine the nature of friendship and the problems of growing up. (Rev: BL 1/1/94) [812]

1984 Slaight, Craig, and Jack Sharrar, eds. *Great Monologues for Young Actors* (9–12). 1992, Smith & Kraus paper $11.95 (1-880399-03-2). Offers 84 selections from classic and contemporary stage plays and other literature. (Rev: BL 9/1/92; BTA; MJHS; SHS; SLJ 9/92) [808.8245]

1985 Slaight, Craig, and Jack Sharrar, eds. *Great Scenes and Monologues for Children* (5–8). (Young Actors) 1993, Smith & Kraus paper $11.95 (1-880399-15-6). Includes selections from children's novels and fairy tales, as well as adult drama and short stories. (Rev: BL 10/1/93; MJHS; SLJ 11/93) [808.82]

1986 Slaight, Craig, and Jack Sharrar, eds. *Great Scenes for Young Actors from the Stage* (9–12). 1991, Smith & Kraus paper $11.95 (0-9622722-6-4). A collection of 45 scenes from the contemporary and classic theater, graded according to ability level and including a brief synopsis of each play. (Rev: BL 11/1/91; MJHS; SHS) [808.82]

1987 Slaight, Craig, and Jack Sharrar, eds. *Multicultural Monologues for Young Actors* (9–12). 1995, Smith & Kraus paper $11.95 (1-880399-47-4). Includes 20 poems, plays, and other fiction, arranged by gender. Monologues represent various cultures and dramatic literatures, both contemporary and classic. Some strong language and mature themes. (Rev: BL 8/95; SLJ 9/95) [808.82]

1988 Slaight, Craig, and Jack Sharrar, eds. *Multicultural Scenes for Young Actors* (9–12). 1995, Smith & Kraus paper $11.95 (1-880399-48-2). Contemporary and classic materials for groups and pairs from a variety of cultural and dramatic literatures. Some strong language and mature themes. (Rev: BL 8/95) [808.82]

Geographical Regions

Europe

GREAT BRITAIN AND IRELAND

1989 Garfield, Leon. *Shakespeare Stories II* (6–10). Illus. 1995, Houghton $24.95 (0-395-70893-1). Nine plot synopses of *Julius Caesar* and less familiar plays. (Rev: BL 4/1/95; MJHS; SHS; SLJ 6/95) [823]

1990 Shakespeare, William, and John Fletcher. *Cardenio; or, The Second Maiden's Tragedy* (9–adult). Commentary by Charles Hamilton. 1994, Glenbridge Publishing (4 Woodland Lane, Macomb, IL 61455) $24.95 (0-944435-24-6). A handwriting expert has discovered a lost manuscript of one of Shakespeare's plays. (Rev: BL 4/15/94) [822.33]

OTHER COUNTRIES

1991 Goldoni, Carlo. *Villeggiatura: A Trilogy Condensed* (9–12). (Young Actors) Tr. by Robert Cornthwaite. 1995, Smith & Kraus paper $14.95 (1-880399-72-5). A 3-act comedy of manners in eighteenth-century Italian court life that is perfect for drama classes or theater groups. (Rev: BL 2/1/95; SLJ 4/95) [852]

United States

1992 Dove, Rita. *The Darker Face of the Earth* (9–adult). 1994, Story Line (27006 Gap Rd., Brownsville, OR 97327-9718) paper $10.95 (0-934257-74-4). This verse play, based on the story of Oedipus and placed within the context of slavery, is set on a plantation in antebellum South Carolina. (Rev: BL 2/15/94*; BTA) [812.54]

1993 Gardner, Herb. *Conversations with My Father* (9–adult). 1994, Pantheon $20 (0-679-42405-9); paper $11 (0-679-74766-4). This play—set in a New York City bar in the 1930s and 1940s—concerns the relationship of a Jewish immigrant father with his 2 sons. (Rev: BL 1/1/94; BTA) [812]

1994 Graham, Kristen, ed. *The Great Monologues from the Women's Project* (9–adult). 1995, Smith & Kraus paper $7.95 (1-880399-35-0). Fifty-three monologues provide dramatic, funny, angry, and sexy performance opportunities. (Rev: BL 2/15/95) [812]

1995 Haskins, James. *The March on Washington* (5–9). 1993, HarperCollins LB $14.89 (0-06-021290-X). These plays, written for the National Children's Repertory Theatre, are filled with slapstick humor. One play has an environmental message. (Rev: BL 5/15/93*; BTA; MJHS; VOYA 8/93) [323.1]

1996 Kamerman, Sylvia, ed. *The Big Book of Holiday Plays* (6–9). 1990, Plays $16.95 (0-8238-0291-4). An assortment of one-act plays and adaptations, both dramas and comedies, geared to 14 holidays. (Rev: BL 2/1/91; MJHS; SLJ 1/91)

1997 Kamerman, Sylvia, ed. *Plays of Black Americans: The Black Experience in America, Dramatized for Young People* (7–12). 1994, Plays paper $13.95 (0-8238-0301-5). Eleven dramas focus on the history of African Americans. (Rev: BL 5/15/95; MJHS; SLJ 2/95) [812]

1998 Lamb, Wendy, ed. *Hey Little Walter* (9–12). 1991, Dell paper $3.99 (0-440-21025-9). Six plays—with the common theme of identity and belonging—written by teenagers for the annual Young Playwrights Festival. (Rev: BL 1/15/92) [812.54]

1999 Lamb, Wendy, ed. *Ten out of Ten: Ten Winning Plays Selected from the Young Playwrights Festival, 1982–1991* (7–12). 1992, Delacorte $18 (0-385-30811-6). Nine plays highlighted in previous anthologies and one from the 1991 festival appearing in print for the first time.

(Rev: BL 11/15/92; BTA; MJHS; SHS; SLJ 11/92) [812]

2000 Love, Douglas. *Be Kind to Your Mother (Earth) and Blame It on the Wolf: Two Original Plays* (5–8). 1993, HarperFestival LB $13.89 (0-06-021290-X). These plays, written for the National Children's Repertory Theatre, are filled with slapstick humor. One play has an environmental message. (Rev: BL 3/1/93; VOYA 8/93) [812]

2001 Simon, Neil. *Lost in Yonkers* (9–adult). 1992, Random $17 (0-679-40890-8). Prize-winning play about 2 brothers forced to live with their strict grandmother and ditzy aunt after their mother dies. Awards: YALSA Best Book for Young Adults. (Rev: BL 3/15/92; SHS; SLJ 6/92) [812]

2002 Slaight, Craig, ed. *New Plays from A.C.T.'s Young Conservatory* (9–12). 1993, Smith & Kraus $14.95 (1-880399-25-3). Five contemporary plays written from the viewpoints of young actors ages 13–22, who perform them. (Rev: BL 8/93; VOYA 8/93) [812.54008]

2003 Wilson, August. *The Piano Lesson* (9–adult). 1990, Dutton $16.95 (0-525-24926-5); 1990, NAL/Plume paper $6.95 (0-452-26534-7). Pulitzer Prize–winning play about an African American family in Pittsburgh in the 1930s. (Rev: BL 1/1/91; SHS) [812.54]

Poetry

General and Miscellaneous Collections

2004 Carter, Anne, sel. *Birds, Beasts, and Fishes: A Selection of Animal Poems* (9–adult). Illus. 1991, Macmillan $16.95 (0-02-717776-9). An illustrated collection of poetry from ancient and modern sources on many different animal species. Awards: SLJ Best Book. (Rev: BL 10/1/91; SLJ 10/91*) [808.81]

2005 Duffy, Carol Ann, ed. *I Wouldn't Thank You for a Valentine: Poems for Young Feminists* (6–12). Illus. 1994, Holt $14.95 (0-8050-2756-4). This anthology draws on poets from many cultures and includes works by Nikki Giovanni, Sharon Olds, and Mary Oliver. (Rev: BL 3/1/94*; MJHS; SLJ 1/94; VOYA 4/94) [808.81]

2006 Gilbert, Sandra M., and others, eds. *Mother Songs: Poems for, by, and about Mothers* (9–adult). 1995, Norton $22.50 (0-393-03771-1). Poems by men and women covering the maternal cycle. (Rev: BL 5/1/95) [811.008]

2007 Gillan, Maria Mazziotti, and Jennifer Gillan, eds. *Unsettling America: An Anthology of Contemporary Multicultural Poetry* (9–adult). 1994, Penguin paper $13.95 (0-14-023778-X). Features poets from various cultures and backgrounds, including Native American Joy Harjo, Hawaiian Garrett Hongo, and African American Rita Dove. (Rev: BL 10/1/94; SLJ 5/95) [811]

2008 Gordon, Ruth, ed. *Peeling the Onion* (8–12). 1993, HarperCollins LB $14.89 (0-06-021728-6). Poets from all over the world capture the echoing quiet "when the game has ended." (Rev: BL 6/1–15/93*; BTA; MJHS; SLJ 7/93; VOYA 8/93) [808.81]

2009 Gordon, Ruth, ed. *Pierced by a Ray of Sun* (7–12). 1995, HarperCollins LB $15.89 (0-06-023614-0). A compilation of poems from across cultures and eras dealing with topics from the timely to the timeless and emotions from hope to despair. (Rev: BL 5/1/95*; SLJ 6/95) [808.81]

2010 Hall, Linda, ed. *An Anthology of Poetry by Women: Tracing the Tradition* (9–adult). 1995, Cassell $55 (0-304-32415-9); paper $14.95 (0-304-32434-5). Traces the tradition of women's poetry from early times, organized by themes. (Rev: BL 3/1/95) [811]

2011 Harrison, Michael, and Christopher Stuart-Clark, eds. *The Oxford Book of Story Poems* (5–7). 1990, Oxford Univ. $17.95 (0-19-276087-4). The works of dozens of poets, ranging from traditional ballads to contemporary poems. Illustrated. (Rev: BL 2/1/91; MJHS) [821]

2012 Harvey, Anne, ed. *Shades of Green* (5–8). Illus. 1992, Greenwillow $18 (0-688-10890-3). Lyrics about our human need for "weeds and wilderness"—about 200 poems on grass, trees, flowers, weeds, etc. Awards: Signal Poetry. (Rev: BL 6/15/92; SLJ 7/92; YR) [821.008]

2013 Hempel, Amy, and Jim Shepard, eds. *Unleashed: Poems by Writers' Dogs* (9–adult). 1995, Crown $15 (0-517-70140-5). The dogs of such writers as Natalie Kusz, Gordon Lish, Kathryn Walker, and John Irving present poetry on subjects like "Chow," "Theology," "The Good Life," and "Substance Abuse." (Rev: BL 6/1–15/95) [811.008]

2014 Hirshfield, Jane, ed. *Women in Praise of the Sacred: 43 Centuries of Spiritual Poetry by Women* (9–adult). 1994, HarperCollins $22.50 (0-06-016987-7). Personal interpretations of visions and other mystical realizations of life's sacredness spanning 4,000 years and embracing numerous cultures. (Rev: BL 3/15/94*) [808.81]

2015 Hollis, Jill, ed. *Love's Witness: Five Centuries of Love Poetry by Women* (9–adult). 1993, Carroll & Graf paper $10.95 (0-7867-0030-0). Hollis draws from the love poetry of 5 centuries of women in this anthology showing the similarities and differences of love through the ages. (Rev: BL 11/15/93) [821]

2016 Janeczko, Paul B., ed. *Looking for Your Name: A Collection of Contemporary Poems* (9–12). 1993, Orchard/Richard Jackson LB $15.99 (0-531-08625-9). A wide variety of poems, by men and women, about soldiers' war memories, family violence, gay/lesbian lives, sports, love, AIDS, suicide, etc. Awards: SLJ Best Book. (Rev: BL 1/15/93*; BTA; MJHS; SLJS 6/93*) [811]

2017 Janeczko, Paul B., ed. *Wherever Home Begins: 100 Contemporary Poems* (8–12). 1995, Orchard/Richard Jackson LB $15.99 (0-531-08781-6). One hundred contemporary poems that express various aspects of a sense of place. (Rev: BL 10/1/95; SLJ 11/95; VOYA 12/95) [811]

2018 Livingston, Myra Cohn, ed. *Call Down the Moon: Poems of Music* (6–12). 1995, Macmillan/Margaret K. McElderry $16 (0-689-80416-4). A collection of poems by Tennyson, Whitman, and others, who use words to express how we listen and make music. (Rev: BL 10/1/95; SLJ 11/95; VOYA 2/96) [821.008]

2019 Livingston, Myra Cohn. *Riddle-Me Rhymes* (5–7). 1994, Macmillan/Margaret K. McElderry $13.95 (0-689-50602-3). A collection of 86 riddles and puzzles of varying difficulty from such authors as Jonathan Swift, Robert Frost, Carl Sandburg, and Emily Dickinson. (Rev: BL 8/94; SLJ 5/94) [398.6]

2020 Livingston, Myra Cohn, ed. *A Time to Talk: Poems of Friendship* (7–12). 1992, Macmillan/Margaret K. McElderry $12.95 (0-689-50558-2). Poems from many times and places express how friends bring us joy and support; how they betray and leave us; how we miss them when they're gone; etc. (Rev: BL 10/15/92; MJHS; SLJ 11/92; YR) [808.81]

2021 Marcus, Leonard S. *Lifelines: A Poetry Anthology Patterned on the Stages of Life* (10–12). 1994, Dutton $16.99 (0-525-45164-1). Poems, both classical and new, arranged according to the stages of life from birth through old age and death. (Rev: BL 9/1/94; BTA; MJHS; SLJ 10/94; VOYA 2/95) [821.008]

2022 Merrill, Christopher, ed. *The Forgotten Language: Contemporary Poets and Nature* (9–adult). 1991, Gibbs Smith/Peregrine Smith paper $14.95 (0-87905-376-3). This collection focuses on nature and our endangered world. (Rev: BL 5/1/91; SHS; SLJ 4/92) [811]

2023 Moyers, Bill. *The Language of Life: A Festival of Poets* (9–adult). 1995, Doubleday $29.95 (0-385-47917-4). An accompaniment to Moyers's TV series, presenting longer versions of 15 interviews, along with interviews with 19 more poets. (Rev: BL 6/1–15/95) [811]

2024 Neuberger, Julia, ed. *The Things That Matter: An Anthology of Women's Spiritual Poetry* (9–adult). 1995, St. Martin's/Thomas Dunne $21 (0-312-11899-6). The spriritual expressions of women in poetry with a Christian orientation. (Rev: BL 3/1/95) [821.008]

2025 Nye, Naomi Shihab, ed. *This Same Sky: A Collection of Poems from Around the World* (7–12). 1992, Four Winds $15.95 (0-02-768440-7). An extraordinary collection of 129 contemporary poets from 68 countries, with an index by country. Awards: ALSC Notable Children's Book; BL Editors' Choice. (Rev: BL 10/15/92*; BTA; SHS; SLJ 12/92; YR) [808.81]

2026 Oliver, Mary. *A Poetry Handbook* (9–adult). 1994, Harcourt/Harvest paper $8.95 (0-15-672400-6). A handbook on the formal aspects and structure of poetry from a Pulitzer Prize–winning poet. (Rev: BL 7/94; SHS) [808.1]

2027 Soto, Gary. *A Fire in My Hands: A Book of Poems* (6–10). Illus. 1991, Scholastic $11.95 (0-590-45021-2). Illustrated collection of 23 poems, along with advice to young poets. (Rev: BL 4/1/92; BTA; SLJ 3/92) [811]

2028 Strand, Mark, ed. *The Golden Ecco Anthology: 100 Great Poems of the English Language* (9–adult). 1994, Ecco $22 (0-88001-366-4). A collection of 100 "great" poems, including many by women and African Americans. (Rev: BL 8/94) [821.008]

2029 Swenson, May. *The Complete Poems to Solve* (5–8). Illus. 1993, Macmillan $13.95 (0-02-788725-1). Collects intelligent, accessible free verse with a puzzle aspect, from riddles to verse requiring less-pointed, more-subtle solutions. (Rev: BL 6/1–15/93; BTA; SLJ 5/93) [811]

2030 Sword, Elizabeth Hauge, and Victoria McCarthy. *A Child's Anthology of Poetry* (5–7). 1995, Ecco $20 (0-88001-378-8). A wide range of narrative and lyrical poetry from the traditional literary canon, with a few contemporary voices thrown in. (Rev: BL 11/15/95) [808.81]

Geographical Regions

Europe

GREAT BRITAIN AND IRELAND

2031 Berry, James, ed. *Classic Poems to Read Aloud* (5–8). 1995, Kingfisher $16.95 (1-85697-987-3). Jamaican writer Berry has collected favorites, mostly British, along with new voices usually excluded from the literary canon. (Rev: BL 5/1/95; SLJ 5/95) [808.81]

2032 Coleridge, Samuel Taylor. *The Rime of the Ancient Mariner* (7–12). Illus. 1992, Atheneum $16.95 (0-689-31613-5). Haunting interpretation of a 200-year-old poem that tells the story of a sailor locked in a living nightmare after he shoots an innocent albatross and watches all his shipmates die. (Rev: BL 3/15/92; MJHS; SLJ 4/92) [821]

2033 Opie, Iona, and Peter Opie. *I Saw Esau: The Schoolchild's Pocket Book* (7–12). Illus. 1992, Candlewick Press $19.95 (1-56402-046-0). Traces schoolyard folk rhymes to their roots. Awards: ALSC Notable Children's Book; BL Editors' Choice. (Rev: BL 4/15/92*; MJHS; SLJ 6/92)

2034 Pollinger, Gina, ed. *Something Rich and Strange: A Treasury of Shakespeare's Verse* (7–12). Illus. 1995, Kingfisher $16.95 (1-85697-597-5). A thematic arrangement of Shakespeare's sonnets and poetry from his plays with many bright pictures. (Rev: BL 11/1/95; SLJ 12/95) [822.3]

OTHER COUNTRIES

2035 Glatstein, Jacob. *I Keep Recalling: The Holocaust Poems of Jacob Glatstein* (9–adult). Tr. by Barnett Zumoff. 1993, KTAV $29.50 (0-88125-429-0). This Yiddish and English volume is a collection of works from Glatstein's previous 6, focusing on Jewish fortitude during the Holocaust while honoring those who died. (Rev: BL 12/15/93) [839.09]

2036 Schiff, Hilda, ed. *Holocaust Poetry* (9–adult). 1995, St. Martin's $18.95 (0-312-13086-4). An anthology of 85 poems provide a stark memoir of the Holocaust. (Rev: BL 5/15/95*) [808.81]

2037 Striar, Marguerite, ed. *Rage Before Pardon: Poets of the World Bearing Witness to the Holocaust* (9–adult). 1995, Paragon House $26.95 (1-55778-724-7). Striar has collected 280 poems arranged historically, with contributors from all walks of life bearing witness to this horrific event. (Rev: BL 11/1/95) [808.81]

United States

2038 Ackerman, Diane. *Jaguar of Sweet Laughter: New and Selected Poems* (9–adult). 1991, Random $18 (0-679-40214-4). This selection of new work and poems from earlier volumes accentuates Ackerman's range of voices and moods. (Rev: BL 4/1/91*) [811]

2039 Adoff, Arnold. *Slow Dance Heartbreak Blues* (7–10). 1995, Lothrop LB $14 (0-688-10569-6). Gritty, hip-hop poetry for modern, urban teens. (Rev: BL 12/15/95; SLJ 9/95) [811]

2040 Baker, Paul. *Joker, Joker, Deuce* (9–adult). 1994, Penguin paper $12.95 (0-14-058723-3). This hip-hop poetry expresses the emotions of the youth of the inner city. (Rev: BL 2/15/94) [811]

2041 Bates, Katharine Lee. *O Beautiful for Spacious Skies* (5–8). Illus. 1994, Chronicle $14.95 (0-8118-0832-7). A pairing of contemporary art with America's unofficial anthem. (Rev: BL 11/15/94; SLJ 1/95) [811.4]

2042 Begay, Shonto. *Navajo: Visions and Voices Across the Mesa* (7–12). 1995, Scholastic $15.95 (0-590-46153-2). Poetry that speaks to the ongoing struggle of living in a "dual society" and paintings firmly rooted in Navajo culture. Awards: ALSC Notable Children's Book. (Rev: BL 4/1/95; SLJ 3/95) [811]

2043 Berry, Wendell. *Entries* (9–adult). 1994, Pantheon $20 (0-679-42609-4). In the words and rhythms of ordinary speech, Berry's poems are about family, farm, and community with the natural world. (Rev: BL 4/1/94*) [811]

2044 Bruchac, Joseph, ed. *Returning the Gift: Poetry and Prose from the First North American Nature Writers Festival* (9–adult). 1994, Univ. of Arizona $45 (0-8165-1376-7). An anthology of native North American fiction and poetry, including selections from Mexico, Central America, and Canada. (Rev: BL 8/94; SHS) [810.9]

2045 Cannon, Hal, and Thomas West, eds. *Buckaroo: Visions and Voices of the American Cowboy* (9–adult). 1993, Simon & Schuster $45 (0-671-88054-3). This collection of cowhand poems is accompanied by a CD that provides the voices of 16 prominent reciters and photos and watercolors depicting the cowboy personality. (Rev: BL 11/15/93) [978]

2046 Carlson, Lori M., ed. *Cool Salsa: Bilingual Poems on Growing Up Latino in the United States* (7–12). 1994, Holt $14.95 (0-8050-3135-9). An anthology of poetry that describes the experience of growing up with a dual heritage. Awards: SLJ Best Book. (Rev: BL 11/1/94; BTA; MJHS; SHS; SLJ 8/94*; VOYA 2/95) [811]

2047 Christopher, Nicholas, ed. *Walk on the Wild Side: Urban American Poetry since 1975* (9–adult). 1994, Macmillan/Collier paper $12 (0-02-042725-5). An anthology of 120 modern poems with urban perspectives and urban settings. (Rev: BL 4/1/94; SHS) [811]

2048 Conarroe, Joel, ed. *Eight American Poets* (9–adult). 1994, Random $25 (0-679-42779-1). Collects selected works from such modern poets as Theodore Roethke, Sylvia Plath, and Allen Ginsberg, with the personal and literary history of each. Sequel to *Six American Poets*. (Rev: BL 10/1/94; SHS) [811.008]

2049 Cruz, Victor Hernández, and others, eds. *Paper Dance: 55 Latin Poets* (9–adult). 1995, Persea paper $13.95 (0-89255-201-8). A collection of poetry from 55 Latinos/as. (Rev: BL 3/1/95) [811]

2050 Daniels, Jim, ed. *Letters to America: Contemporary American Poetry on Race* (9–adult). 1995, Wayne State Univ. paper $19.95 (0-8143-2542-4). Accessible, readable poems that speak to our nation's nightmare and call into question the purpose of poetry. (Rev: BL 11/15/95) [811]

2051 Dove, Rita. *Mother Love* (9–adult). 1995, Norton $17.95 (0-393-03808-4). Sonnets drawn on the timeless tragedy of Demeter and Persephone. (Rev: BL 5/1/95*) [811]

2052 Dove, Rita. *Selected Poems* (9–adult). 1993, Random/Vintage paper $12 (0-679-75080-0). Three collections of poetry by the U.S. poet laureate are gathered here into one volume: *The Yellow House on the Corner; Museum;* and the Pulitzer Prize–winning *Thomas and Beulah*. Dove's images draw on African American history and family experiences to illuminate our contemporary world. (Rev: BL 10/15/93; BTA) [811]

2053 Elledge, Jim, ed. *Sweet Nothings: An Anthology of Rock and Roll in American Poetry* (9–adult). 1994, Indiana Univ. $29.95 (0-253-31936-6). An anthology of rock and roll in American poetry. (Rev: BL 4/1/94; SHS) [811]

2054 Ferlinghetti, Lawrence, ed. *City Lights Pocket Poets Anthology* (9–adult). 1995, City Lights $18.95 (0-87286-311-5). A who's who of post–World War II American modernism, the poetry of the 1950s and 1960s avant-garde. (Rev: BL 11/15/95) [808.81]

2055 Fletcher, Ralph. *I Am Wings: Poems about Love* (5–7). Illus. 1994, Macmillan $13.95 (0-02-735395-8). These poems tell the story of a boy falling in and out of love, using contemporary images and everyday language. Awards: SLJ Best Book. (Rev: BL 3/15/94; BTA; MJHS; SLJ 6/94*; VOYA 6/94) [811]

2056 Forman, Ruth. *We Are the Young Magicians* (9–adult). 1993, Beacon $22 (0-8070-6820-9); paper $12 (0-8070-6821-7). This poetry collection covers such themes as being an African American, family, growing up, and lesbianism. (Rev: BL 3/15/93*) [811]

2057 Giovanni, Nikki. *Ego-Tripping and Other Poems for Young People* (9–12). Illus. 1994, Chicago Review/Lawrence Hill $14.95 (1-55652-188-X). Ten poems have been added to her 1973 collection to make 23 poems celebrating ordinary folks and their struggles and liberation. (Rev: BL 4/15/94; MJHS) [811]

2058 Giovanni, Nikki, ed. *Grand Mothers: Poems, Reminiscences, and Short Stories about the Keepers of Our Traditions* (7–12). 1994, Holt $15.95 (0-8050-2766-1). An anthology of 27 poems, memories, and stories about grandmothers, containing a diverse range of styles, sentiments, and experiences. (Rev: BL 9/15/94; BTA; MJHS; SHS; SLJ 10/94; VOYA 12/94) [820]

2059 Giovanni, Nikki. *The Selected Poems of Nikki Giovanni (1968–1995)* (9–adult). 1996, Morrow $20 (0-688-14047-5). A rich synthesis of her work that reveals the evolution of her poetic voice. (Rev: BL 12/15/95) [811]

2060 Glenn, Mel. *My Friend's Got This Problem, Mr. Candler: High School Poems* (8–12). Photos. 1991, Clarion $14.95 (0-89919-833-3). A book of poetry, with photos, about high school students, presented through the eyes of a guidance counselor during a typical school week. Awards: YALSA Best Book for Young Adults. (Rev: BL 9/15/91; MJHS; SHS) [811]

2061 Harper, Michael S., and Anthony Walton, eds. *Every Shut Eye Ain't Asleep: An Anthology of Poetry by African Americans since 1945* (9–adult). 1994, Little, Brown $24.95 (0-316-34712-4); paper $12.95 (0-316-34710-8). Presents the work of 35 African American poets who wrote, or are still writing, in the postwar era. (Rev: BL 2/15/94*; BTA) [811]

2062 Hearne, Betsy. *Polaroid and Other Poems of View* (7–12). Illus. 1991, Macmillan/Margaret K. McElderry $12.95 (0-689-50530-2). Collection of short poems using the camera as a metaphor, drawing connections between word pictures created by the poet and those taken by a photographer. (Rev: BL 8/91; SHS) [811]

2063 Hopkins, Lee Bennett. *Been to Yesterdays: Poems of a Life* (5–7). Illus. 1995, Boyds Mills LB $14.95 (1-56397-467-3). These poems explore the psyche of the author at age 13, including the devastation of his parents' divorce. Awards: Christopher; SLJ Best Book. (Rev: BL 1/1/96; SLJ 9/95)

2064 Hopkins, Lee Bennett, ed. *Hand in Hand* (5–8). 1994, Simon & Schuster $19.95 (0-671-73315-X). A browsable collection that includes selections from Frost, Longfellow, Whitman, Hughes, and Sandberg, among others. (Rev: BL 1/1/95; MJHS; SLJ 12/94; VOYA 4/95) [811]

2065 Hudgins, Andrew. *The Glass Hammer: A Southern Childhood* (9–adult). 1994, Houghton $18.95 (0-395-70011-6). Poetic childhood memoirs about growing up in a family with a father who could be brutal, yet express familial love. (Rev: BL 5/15/94) [811]

2066 Hughes, Langston. *The Block* (6–12). Illus. 1995, Viking $15.99 (0-670-86501-X). Poetry by Langston Hughes coupled with sections of a 6-panel collage, a picture of a city block, which is housed in New York City's Metropolitan Museum of Art. (Rev: BL 11/1/95; SLJ 12/95) [811]

2067 Hughes, Langston. *The Dream Keeper and Other Poems* (5–12). Illus. 1994, Knopf LB $12.99 (0-679-94421-4). A classic poetry collection by the renowned African American, originally published in 1932, is presented in a new, illustrated edition. (Rev: BL 3/15/94; BTA; MJHS; VOYA 6/94) [811]

2068 Hughes, Langston, and others, eds. *The Collected Poems of Langston Hughes* (9–adult). 1994, Knopf $30 (0-679-42631-0). A large collection of the African American poet's work. Hughes speaks in jazzlike rhythms of the pain of everyday life, Harlem street life, prejudice, Southern violence, and love. (Rev: BL 10/1/94*; SHS) [811]

2069 Janeczko, Paul B., comp. *Preposterous: Poems of Youth* (7–12). 1991, Orchard/Richard Jackson Books LB $14.99 (0-531-08501-5). Poems by 82 American poets who have recorded their memories of being teenagers. (Rev: BL 3/1/91; BY; SLJ 3/91)

2070 Janeczko, Paul B. *Stardust Otel* (7–9). 1993, Orchard/Richard Jackson LB $14.99 (0-531-08648-8). A series of free-verse poems create impressions of a 15-year-old boy's family, friends, and neighbors. (Rev: BL 1/1/94; SLJ 11/93; VOYA 12/93) [811]

2071 Kherdian, David, ed. *Beat Voices: An Anthology of Beat Poetry* (9–12). 1995, Holt $14.95 (0-8050-3315-7). An introduction to the best Beat writers in all their outrageousness and music. (Rev: BL 5/15/95; SLJ 11/95) [811]

2072 Kingsolver, Barbara. *Another America/Otra América* (9–adult). Tr. into Spanish by Rebeca Cartes. 1992, Seal Press $14.95 (1-878067-14-1); paper $10.95 (1-878067-15-X). Poems with Spanish translations about severe political oppression, but also about kindness, hope, and survival. (Rev: BL 2/15/92; SLJ 8/92) [811]

2073 Lawrence, Jacob. *Harriet and the Promised Land* (6–12). 1993, Simon & Schuster $15 (0-671-86673-7). The efforts of Tubman to bring slaves to the freedom of the North is retold in rhythmic text and narrative paintings. (Rev: BL 10/1/93*) [811]

2074 Livingston, Myra Cohn, ed. *Lots of Limericks* (5–12). Illus. 1991, Macmillan/Margaret K. McElderry $13.95 (0-689-50531-0). Arranged by subject, 210 absurd and amusing verses, many of them anonymous. (Rev: BL 10/1/91; SLJ 1/92) [821]

2075 Loewen, Nancy, ed. *Walt Whitman* (5–12). 1994, Creative Education LB $18.95 (0-88682-608-X). A dozen selections from *Leaves of Grass* are juxtaposed with brief biographical vignettes and sepia photos. (Rev: SLJ 7/94*)

2076 McClatchy, J. D., ed. *The Vintage Book of Contemporary American Poetry* (9–adult). 1990, Random/Vintage paper $14.95 (0-679-72858-9). A representative collection of diverse American poetry at the turn of the mellennium, including poems by Clampitt, Bidart, Rich, Sexton, and Cunningham. (Rev: BL 2/15/91; SHS) [811]

2077 McNeill, Louise. *Hill Daughter: New and Selected Poems* (9–adult). 1991, Univ. of Pittsburgh $24.95 (0-8229-3685-2); paper $12.95 (0-8229-5456-7). This collection by a major American poet includes many poems in which Appalachian hillfolk tell their life stories and recent work lamenting nuclear endangerment. (Rev: BL 11/15/91*; SLJ 6/92) [811]

2078 Marius, Richard, and Keith Frome, eds. *The Columbia Book of Civil War Poetry* (9–adult). 1994, Columbia Univ. $24.95 (0-231-10002-7). An anthology of Civil War poetry, including famous songs and semi-anonymous newspaper verses. (Rev: BL 9/15/94; SHS; SLJ 11/94) [811.008]

2079 Medearis, Angela Shelf. *Skin Deep and Other Teenage Reflections* (6–9). 1995, Macmillan $15 (0-02-765980-1). Poetry in free verse candidly reflects contemporary teenage concerns: bulimia, growing up black, making it as a cheerleader, and being a teenage mother. (Rev: BL 8/95; SLJ 6/95) [811.54]

2080 Millay, Edna St. Vincent. *The Ballad of the Harp Weaver* (5–7). Illus. 1991, Putnam/Philomel $14.95 (0-399-21611-1). An illustrated edition of the famous Millay poem about a mother and child. (Rev: BL 12/1/91) [811]

2081 Morrison, Lillian, comp. *At the Crack of the Bat: Baseball Poems* (5–7). Illus. 1992, Hyperion LB $14.89 (1-56282-177-6). Morrison's poetry celebrates spring training, the thrill of hitting for a win, the disappointment of missing a catch. (Rev: BL 8/92; SLJ 6/92*)

2082 Oliver, Mary. *White Pine: Poems and Prose Poems* (9–adult). 1994, Harcourt $19.95 (0-15-100131-6); paper $11.95 (0-15-600120-9). Forty poems on nature from the Pulitzer Prize–winning author. (Rev: BL 11/15/94*; SHS) [811]

2083 Panzer, Nora, ed. *Celebrate America: In Poetry and Art* (5–7). 1994, Hyperion $18.89 (1-56282-665-4). Awards: ALSC Notable Children's Book; SLJ Best Book; YALSA Best Book for Young Adults. (Rev: BL 11/15/94; BTA; SLJ 11/94*) [811.008]

2084 Philip, Neal, ed. *Singing America* (7–12). Illus. 1995, Viking $19.99 (0-670-86150-2). These poems express the diversity that has been a part of the United States throughout its history. Includes works by Whitman, Dickinson, Sandburg, and Howe. (Rev: BL 6/1–15/95; SLJ 9/95; VOYA 12/95) [811]

2085 Rylant, Cynthia. *Something Permanent* (7–12). Illus. 1994, Harcourt $16.95 (0-15-277090-9). Combines Rylant's poetry with Evans's photos to evoke stong emotions of Southern life during the Depression. Awards: BL Editors' Choice; SLJ Best Book; YALSA Best Book for Young Adults. (Rev: BL 7/94*; BTA; MJHS; SHS; SLJ 8/94; VOYA 12/94) [811]

2086 Schmidt, Gary D., ed. *Robert Frost* (5–7). Illus. 1994, Sterling $14.95 (0-8069-0633-2). This book in the Poetry for Young People series includes 25 poems to introduce Frost to the younger set. (Rev: BL 12/1/94; SLJ 2/95) [811]

2087 Simic, Charles, ed. *The Best American Poetry, 1992* (9–adult). 1992, Scribner $25 (0-684-19501-1); Macmillan/Collier paper $13 (0-02-069845-3). A selection of works by newer poets, all of whom relish language for its own sake. (Rev: BL 9/15/92) [811]

2088 Stafford, William. *Learning to Live in the World: Earth Poems* (8–12). 1994, Harcourt $15.95 (0-15-200208-1). Fifty nature poems that will appeal to teens. (Rev: BL 1/1/95; SLJ 12/94) [811]

2089 Steig, Jeanne. *Alpha Beta Chowder* (5–8). Illus. 1992, HarperCollins/Michael di Capua LB $14.89 (0-06-205007-9). A collection of nonsense verses celebrating the joy of words—their sound and meaning—each verse playing with a letter of the alphabet. (Rev: BL 11/15/92; SLJ 12/92) [811]

2090 Sumrall, Amber Coverdale, and Patrice Vecchione, eds. *Bless Me, Father: Stories of Catholic Childhood* (9–adult). 1994, NAL/Plume paper $11.95 (0-452-27154-1). Poetry and fiction by authors raised in a Catholic environment. Includes stories about religious confusion and blossoming sexuality. (Rev: BL 11/1/94) [810.8]

2091 Turner, Ann. *Grass Songs* (7–12). Illus. 1993, Harcourt $16.95 (0-15-136788-4). Dramatic monologues that express courage and despair, passion and loneliness, and the struggle to find a home in the wilderness. (Rev: BL 6/1–15/93; BTA; VOYA 8/93) [811]

2092 Viorst, Judith. *Sad Underwear and Other Complications* (5–7). 1995, Atheneum $15 (0-689-31929-0). Poems enjoyable for their snap and vigor and fun with language. (Rev: BL 4/1/95; SLJ 5/95) [811]

2093 Walker, Alice. *Her Blue Body Everything We Know: Earthling Poems, 1965–1990, Complete* (9–adult). 1991, Harcourt $22.95 (0-15-140040-7). Walker brings a woman's wisdom to bear on love, life's unavoidable tragedies, blacks' struggle for equality and justice, and a world committing eco-suicide. (Rev: BL 4/15/91*; SHS) [811]

2094 Whipple, Laura, ed. *Celebrating America: A Collection of Poems and Images of the American Spirit* (5–10). 1994, Putnam/Philomel $19.95 (0-399-22036-4). An anthology of poetry and art that reflects the diverse range of American cultures, styles, and periods. (Rev: BL 9/1/94*; SLJ 9/94) [811.008]

Other Regions

2095 Alarcón, Francisco X. *Snake Poems: An Aztec Invocation* (9–adult). 1992, Chronicle paper $10.95 (0-8118-0161-6). Verses written about Mexican Americans, based on poems and prayers of the ancient Aztecs. (Rev: BL 3/1/92) [811]

2096 Chipasula, Stella, and Frank Chipasula, eds. *Heinemann Book of African Women's Poetry* (9–adult). 1995, Heinemann paper $10.95 (0-435-90680-1). A wide range of poetic voices celebrating Africa's racial and cultural diversity. (Rev: BL 2/15/95*) [821]

2097 Lee, Jeanne M. *The Song of Mu Lan* (5–9). 1995, Front Street $15.95 (1-886910-00-6). A Chinese folk poem from between A.D. 420 and 589 that explores sex roles and women in the military. Includes Chinese text in original calligraphy. (Rev: BL 11/15/95; SLJ 12/95) [895.1]

2098 Mado, Michio. *The Animals: Selected Poems* (5–12). Tr. by the Empress Michiko of Japan. Illus. 1992, Macmillan/Margaret K. McElderry $16.95 (0-689-50574-4). Twenty Japanese poems—with English versions on facing pages—about animals. (Rev: BL 12/1/92; SLJ 2/93) [895.6]

2099 Neruda, Pablo. *Selected Odes of Pablo Neruda* (9–adult). Tr. by Margaret Sayers Peden. 1990, Univ. of California $40 (0-520-05944-1); paper $12.95 (0-520-07172-7). A bilingual selection of the Chilean laureate's renowned "elemental odes." (Rev: BL 2/15/91*; SHS) [861]

Folklore, Fairy Tales, and Fables

General and Miscellaneous

2100 Brooke, William J. *Teller of Tales* (9–12). 1994, HarperCollins LB $14.89 (0-06-023400-8). Teller, a strange old scribe who writes fanciful stories, is cared for by an independent girl who becomes the inspiration for his latest fiction. (Rev: BL 11/1/94; SLJ 12/94; VOYA 4/95)

2101 Creeden, Sharon. *Fair Is Fair: World Folktales of Justice* (9–adult). 1995, August House $19.95 (0-87483-400-7). Thirty folktales adapted from different times and places. (Rev: BL 5/15/95; SLJ 10/95) [398]

2102 De Caro, Frank, ed. *The Folktale Cat* (9–adult). 1993, August House paper $12.95 (0-87483-303-5). An international collection of 51 classic and lesser-known feline folktales, including a discussion of the domestic cat's role in folklore. (Rev: BL 4/15/93; SLJ 11/93) [398.2]

2103 Jaffe, Nina. *Patakin* (6–12). 1994, Holt $14.95 (0-8050-3005-0). Folktales from around the world about drums and drummers, including stories about sacred drums and magical drummers. (Rev: BL 8/94*; BTA; MJHS; SLJ 9/94) [398.27]

2104 Jaffe, Nina, and Steve Zeitlin. *While Standing on One Foot: Puzzle Stories and Wisdom Tales from the Jewish Tradition* (5–7). Illus. 1993, Holt $14.95 (0-8050-2594-4). Seventeen diverse Jewish folktales presented as intellectual puzzles designed to challenge creative thinking skills. (Rev: BL 1/1/94*; SLJ 1/94; VOYA 2/94) [296.1]

2105 Lang, Andrew. *A World of Fairy Tales* (5–7). Edited by Neil Philip. 1994, Dial $20 (0-8037-1250-2). Collects 24 illustrated fairy tales from various countries, including Zimbabwe, Japan, and Iceland. Points out common motifs and includes notes on sources. (Rev: BL 9/1/94; SLJ 8/94) [398.21]

2106 Lurie, Alison, ed. *The Oxford Book of Modern Fairy Tales* (9–adult). 1993, Oxford Univ. $25 (0-19-214218-6). The writers here show all kinds of transformations in their magical stories, including Oscar Wilde, Tanith Lee, and Ursula Le Guin. (Rev: BL 5/1/93; SLJ 5/94)

2107 MacDonald, Margaret Read. *Peace Tales: World Folktales to Talk About* (5–7). 1992, Shoe String/Linnet $22.50 (0-208-02328-3); paper $13.95 (0-208-02329-1). Tales and proverbs illustrate how suspicion, stubbornness, and fear cause conflict and how cooperation, patience, and understanding help build loving relationships. (Rev: BL 6/15/92; SLJ 10/92) [398.2]

2108 Mazer, Anne. *The Oxboy* (5–7). 1993, Knopf $13 (0-679-84191-1). This allegory reveals a world in which the time when humans married animals has given way to reviling the children of these unions. Awards: ALSC Notable Children's Book. (Rev: BL 11/1/93; SLJ 11/93)

2109 Sherman, Josepha, ed. *Orphans of the Night* (6–10). 1995, Walker $16.95 (0-8027-8368-6). Brings together 11 short stories and 2 poems about creatures from local folklore, most with teen protagonists. (Rev: BL 6/1–15/95; SLJ 6/95; VOYA 12/95)

2110 Shuker, Karl. *Dragons: A Natural History* (9–adult). 1995, Simon & Schuster $22.50 (0-684-81443-9). Helps the reader identify the various species of dragons. Charmingly written and beautifully illustrated. (Rev: BL 11/1/95) [398.24]

Geographical Regions

2111 McLaurin, Melton. *Celia: A Slave* (9–adult). 1991, Univ. of Georgia $19.95 (0-8203-1352-1). This novelistic account uses the 1855 case of a slave who murders her master as a forum for exploring the politics, attitudes, and events preceding the Civil War. Awards: SLJ Best Book. (Rev: BL 11/15/91; SLJ 6/92) [345.73]

Africa

2112 Berry, Jack. *West African Folktales* (9–adult). Edited by Richard Spears. 1991, Northwestern Univ. $24.95 (0-8101-0979-4); paper $10.95 (0-8101-0993-X). Vivid folktales imparting basic life lessons collected over 35 years by a linguist who specialized in the spoken art of Sierra Leone, Ghana, and Nigeria. (Rev: BL 10/15/91; SHS) [398.2]

2113 Fairman, Tony. *Bury My Bones but Keep My Words* (5–7). Illus. 1993, Holt $15.95 (0-8050-2333-X). Retellings of stories from various African countries. Awards: SLJ Best Book. (Rev: BL 2/15/93; SLJS 6/93*) [398.2]

2114 Gatti, Anne. *Tales from the African Plains* (5–7). Illus. 1995, Dutton $18.99 (0-525-45282-6). Tales from various peoples in Africa, with the best showing universal themes. (Rev: BL 5/1/95; SLJ 6/95) [398.2]

2115 Greaves, Nick. *When Lion Could Fly and Other Tales from Africa* (5–8). Illus. 1993, Barron's $13.95 (0-8120-6344-9); paper $8.95 (0-8120-1625-4). A collection of African folktales combined with factual information about various animal species. (Rev: BL 1/1/94; SLJ 4/94) [398.24]

Asia and the Middle East

2116 Livo, Norma J., and Dia Cha, eds. *Folk Stories of the Hmong: Peoples of Laos, Thailand, and Vietnam* (9–adult). 1991, Libraries Unlimited $18.50 (0-87287-854-6). The unique culture and heritage of the ancient Hmong people is celebrated in this collection of folktales. Includes an introduction to Hmong history. (Rev: BL 10/1/91; MJHS) [398.2]

2117 Mayer, Marianna. *Turandot* (6–8). Illus. 1995, Morrow LB $15.93 (0-688-09074-5). The tale of the princess who will consent to marry only the one man who can answer her 3 riddles. Set in China and beautifully illustrated. (Rev: BL 10/15/95; SLJ 10/95)

2118 Meeker, Clare Hodgson. *A Tale of Two Rice Birds: A Folktale from Thailand* (5–8). Illus. 1994, Sasquatch (1008 Western Ave., Suite 300, Seattle, WA 98104) $14.95 (1-57061-008-8). (Rev: BL 1/15/95; SLJ 11/94) [398.24]

2119 Watkins, Yoko Kawashima. *Tales from the Bamboo Grove* (5–7). Illus. 1992, Bradbury $14.95 (0-02-792525-0). A retelling of 6 classic Japanese folktales. (Rev: BL 9/15/92; SLJ 11/92) [398.2]

2120 Yep, Laurence. *Tongues of Jade* (6–9). Illus. 1991, HarperCollins LB $14.89 (0-06-022471-1). This retelling of 17 fanciful tales from a variety of Chinese American communities includes stories of talking animals, helpful spirits, and a fisherman wizard. (Rev: BL 12/15/91; MJHS; SLJ 12/91) [398.2]

Australia and the Pacific Islands

2121 Oodgeroo. *Dreamtime: Aboriginal Stories* (6–10). Illus. 1994, Lothrop $16 (0-688-13296-0). Traditional and autobiographical stories of Aboriginal culture and its roots. Also examines current Aboriginal life alongside white civilization. (Rev: BL 10/1/94; BTA; SLJ 10/94)

Europe

2122 Day, David. *The Search for King Arthur* (9–adult). 1995, Facts on File $24.95 (0-8160-3370-6). Filled with illustrations from noted artists, this volume traces the legend of Arthur from its historical roots and analyzes the social and political forces that shaped his story. (Rev: BL 11/15/95; SLJ 2/96) [942.01]

2123 Kuniczak, W. S. *The Glass Mountain: Twenty-Six Ancient Polish Folktales and Fables* (5–7). Illus. 1992, Hippocrene $14.95 (0-7818-0087-0). Varied traditional and exotic tales of high adventure, daring deeds, and lessons learned, with beautiful princesses, clever peasants, and wicked relatives. (Rev: BL 5/1/93) [398.2]

2124 Llywelyn, Morgan. *Finn MacCool* (9–adult). 1994, Tor/Forge $23.95 (0-312-85476-5). This historical novel concerns a self-mythologizing outsider in royal Celtic society and how his legends were created. (Rev: BL 2/1/94; SLJ 12/94)

2125 Markale, Jean. *King of the Celts: Arthurian Legends and Celtic Tradition* (9–adult). Tr. by Christine Hauch. 1994, Inner Traditions paper $14.95 (0-89281-452-7). A survey of Arthurian lore in Celtic history that points out how the legends were misappropriated by propagandists of the courtly nobility. (Rev: BL 3/1/94) [942.01]

2126 Morpurgo, Michael. *Arthur: High King of Britain* (5–7). Illus. 1995, Harcourt $19.95 (0-15-200080-1). A fresh retelling of nine familiar Arthurian stories, with Arthur narrating them to a 12-year-old boy who awakes in Arthur's cave. (Rev: BL 8/95)

2127 Napoli, Donna Jo. *The Magic Circle* (6–12). 1993, Dutton LB $14.99 (0-525-45127-7). A possible "history" of the witch in *Hansel and Gretel.* (Rev: BL 7/93; SLJS 1/94*; VOYA 8/93)

2128 Perham, Molly. *King Arthur and the Legends of Camelot* (5–7). Illus. 1993, Viking $22 (0-670-84990-1). A detailed version of the Arthurian legends in a large-size volume, with romantic paintings and drawings of knights, dragons, and lovely maidens. (Rev: BL 7/93; SLJ 4/94) [942.01]

2129 Phillips, Graham, and Martin Keatman. *King Arthur: The True Story* (9–adult). 1994, Arrow paper $9.95 (0-09-929681-0). A scholarly examination of the Arthurian legend that attempts to document its roots and determine whether the king ever existed. (Rev: BL 1/15/94) [942.01]

2130 Spariosu, Mihai I., and Dezso Benedek. *Ghosts, Vampires, and Werewolves: Eerie Tales from Transylvania* (6–10). 1994, Orchard LB $16.99 (0-531-08710-7). An anthology of horror tales by authors who heard the stories as children living in the Transylvanian Alps. (Rev: BL 10/15/94; MJHS; SLJ 10/94) [398.2]

2131 Tolkien, J. R. R. *Bilbo's Last Song* (5–12). Illus. 1990, Houghton $14.95 (0-395-53810-6). An elaborately illustrated book centered around a poem. (Rev: BL 1/15/91; SLJ 1/91) [821]

2132 Wein, Elizabeth. *The Winter Prince* (7–12). 1993, Atheneum $15.95 (0-689-31747-6). Renaming the main characters in Arthurian legend, Wein looks at the psyche of Medraut, son of King Artos, and his half-sister, Modgause, and his relationship with Artos's legitimate son, Lleu. (Rev: BL 11/15/93; BTA; MJHS; SLJ 10/93; VOYA 12/93)

2133 Wilde, Oscar. *Fairy Tales of Oscar Wilde, Vol. 1: The Selfish Giant; The Star Child* (5–8). Illus. 1992, NBM Publishing (185 Madison Ave., Suite 1502, New York, NY 10016) $15.95 (1-56163-056-X). A comic strip retelling of two of Wilde's short stories, the first of a planned series. (Rev: BL 1/15/93; SLJ 4/93) [823]

2134 Wilde, Oscar. *Fairy Tales of Oscar Wilde, Vol. 2: The Young King; The Remarkable Rocket* (5–8). Illus. 1994, NBM Publishing (185 Madison Ave., Suite 1502, New York, NY 10016) $15.95 (1-56163-085-3). A comic strip retelling of two of Wilde's short stories, the second of a planned series of five titles. (Rev: BL 9/1/94)

North America

INDIANS OF NORTH AMERICA

2135 Bierhorst, John. *The White Deer and Other Stories Told by the Lenape* (8–12). 1995, Morrow $15 (0-688-12900-5). This collection of Lenape/Delaware tribal stories is organized by type and includes a history of the tribe. (Rev: BL 6/1–15/95; SLJ 9/95) [398.2]

2136 Bruchac, Joseph. *Flying with the Eagle, Racing the Great Bear: Stories from Native North America* (5–8). 1993, Troll/Bridgewater $13.95 (0-8167-3026-1). This collection includes 16 Native American rites-of-passage stories for young males, organized geographically with B&W illustrations. (Rev: BL 12/15/93; BTA; MJHS) [398.2]

2137 Bruchac, Joseph, and Gayle Ross. *The Girl Who Married the Moon: Tales from Native North America* (9–adult). 1994, Troll/Bridgewater $13.95 (0-8167-3481-X). Sixteen stories from various North American native peoples that explore the roles of women in the culture. (Rev: BL 10/1/94; SLJ 11/94) [398.2]

2138 Greene, Jacqueline Dember. *Manabozho's Gifts: Three Chippewa Tales* (5–7). Illus. 1994, Houghton $13.95 (0-395-69251-2). Elements from Algonquin, Menominee, and Ojibwa legends emphasize the philosophy of living in harmony with nature. (Rev: BL 3/15/95; SLJ 1/95) [398.2]

2139 Mullett, G. M., ed. *Cuentos de la Mujer Araña: Leyendas de los indios hopis* (8–12). Tr. by Angela Pérez. 1994, José J. de Olañeta (Palma de Mallorca) paper $13.95 (84-7651-213-9). These translations of Hopi legends are accompanied by colorful illustrations of kachinas. English title: *Stories of Spiderwoman: Legends of the Hopi Indians.* (Rev: BL 10/15/95)

2140 Pijoan, Teresa. *White Wolf Woman: Native American Transformation Myths* (7–12). 1992, August House $17.95 (0-87483-201-2); paper $8.95 (0-87483-200-4). Drawn from a wide range of Indian tribes, a collection of 37 stories about animal and human transformation and connection. (Rev: BL 10/1/92; MJHS) [398.2]

2141 Rockwell, David. *Giving Voice to Bear: North American Indian Rituals, Myths, and Images of the Bear* (9–adult). Illus. 1991, Roberts Rinehart (P.O. Box 666, Niwot, CO 80544) $25 (0-911797-97-1). Explains what the bear symbolized to Native Americans and examines its place in ceremonies, traditions, and myths. (Rev: BL 2/1/92) [299.7]

2142 Ude, Wayne. *Maybe I Will Do Something: Seven Coyote Tales* (7–12). Illus. 1993, Houghton $14.95 (0-395-65233-2). Ude retells 7 Native American coyote stories in this volume, including the creation of the world and the creation of man. (Rev: BL 12/15/93; SLJ 2/94) [398.24]

UNITED STATES

2143 Avila, Alfred. *Mexican Ghost Tales of the Southwest* (7–9). Edited by Kat Avila. 1994, Arte Público/Piñata paper $9.95 (1-55885-107-0). (Rev: BL 10/1/94; SLJ 9/94) [398.25]

2144 Block, Francesca Lia. *Cherokee Bat and the Goat Guys* (9–12). 1992, HarperCollins/Charlotte Zolotow LB $13.89 (0-06-020270-X). In Block's third punk fairy tale, the youth form a rock band, which finds success until corruption sets in, when wise Coyote puts them right and heals them. (Rev: BL 8/92; SLJ 9/92; YR)

2145 Cohn, Amy L., comp. *From Sea to Shining Sea: A Treasury of American Folklore and Folk Songs* (6–12). Illus. 1993, Scholastic LB $29.95 (0-590-42868-3). Contains 140+ folk songs and stories, from traditional American Indian to more modern tellings. Illustrated by 15 Caldecott winners and honor artists. Awards: ALSC Notable Children's Book; SLJ Best Book. (Rev: BL 9/15/93*; MJHS; SLJ 11/93*)

2146 Del Rey, Lester, and Risa Kessler, eds. *Once upon a Time: A Treasury of Modern Fairy Tales* (9–adult). 1991, Ballantine/Del Rey $25 (0-345-36263-2). Ten original fairy tales for adults by Asimov, Cherryh, Hambly, McCaffrey, and others. (Rev: BL 11/15/91; SLJ 8/92)

2147 Garry, Jim. *This Ol' Drought Ain't Broke Us Yet (But We're All Bent Pretty Bad)* (9–adult). 1992, Crown/Orion $18 (0-517-58814-5). Colorful anecdotes, stories, myths, and legends humorously celebrate Western life. (Rev: BL 9/15/92; SLJ 2/93) [978]

2148 Hamilton, Virginia. *Her Stories: African American Folktales, Fairy Tales, and True Tales* (5–8). Illus. 1995, Scholastic/Blue Sky $19.95 (0-590-47370-0). Nineteen tales about African American females retold in the wonderful style of Virginia Hamilton. Awards: ALSC Notable Children's Book; Coretta Scott King; SLJ Best Book. (Rev: BL 11/1/95*; SLJ 11/95) [398.2]

2149 Hausman, Gerald. *Duppy Talk: West Indian Tales of Mystery and Magic* (5–8). 1994, Simon & Schuster $14 (0-671-89000-X). Six tales built on legends brought from Africa to the Caribbean, which have supernatural or mystical elements. (Rev: BL 1/15/95; SLJ 1/95) [398.2]

2150 Kimmel, Eric A. *The Witch's Face: A Mexican Tale* (7–12). Illus. 1993, Holiday $15.95 (0-8234-1038-2). Kimmel uses a picture book format for this Mexican tale of a man who rescues his love from becoming a witch, only to lose her to his own doubt. (Rev: BL 11/15/93; SLJ 2/94) [398.22]

2151 Lester, Julius. *The Last Tales of Uncle Remus* (5–9). Illus. 1994, Dial LB $17.89 (0-8037-1304-5). This fourth volume in the Uncle Remus series draws together 39 African American tall tales, ghost stories, and trickster tales with 8 color and 26 B&W illustrations. Awards: BL Editors' Choice. (Rev: BL 12/15/93*; MJHS; SLJ 1/94) [398.2]

2152 Osborne, Mary Pope. *American Tall Tales* (5–7). Illus. 1991, Knopf/Borzoi LB $18.99 (0-679-90089-6). Wild versions of 9 tall tales mix history with fantasy. Awards: SLJ Best Book. (Rev: BL 3/15/92; SLJ 12/91*) [398.22]

2153 Reneaux, J. J. *Cajun Folktales* (6–8). 1992, August House $19.95 (0-87483-283-7); paper $9.95 (0-87483-282-9). An assortment of Cajun folktales are divided into broad groups: animal tales, fairy tales, funny folk tales, and ghost stories. (Rev: BL 9/15/92) [398.2]

2154 Turenne Des Prés, François. *Children of Yayoute: Folktales of Haiti* (6–9). 1994, Universe $19.95 (0-87663-791-8). Traditional folktales that depict Haitian history and customs. Includes paintings that illustrate island life. (Rev: BL 10/1/94; SLJ 1/95) [398.2]

2155 Wigginton, Eliot, and others, ed. *Foxfire: 25 Years* (9–adult). 1991, Doubleday $24.95 (0-385-41345-9); paper $14.95 (0-385-41346-7). Fascinating stories and characters constituting the Foxfire legend told by the author and his students. (Rev: BL 4/15/91; SHS) [370]

2156 Willard, Nancy. *Beauty and the Beast* (6–12). Illus. 1992, Harcourt LB $19.95 (0-15-206052-9). A reworking of the foundations of the tale that surprises, with a setting in New York at the turn of the century and the plot remarkably true to the original. Awards: SLJ Best Book. (Rev: BL 11/1/92; MJHS; SLJ 10/92*) [398.2]

Mythology

General and Miscellaneous

2157 Belting, Natalia M. *Moon Was Tired of Walking on Air* (5–7). Illus. 1992, Houghton $15.95 (0-395-53806-8). A retelling of creation myths of various South American Indian tribes. (Rev: BL 9/15/92; SLJ 2/93) [398.2]

2158 Larungu, Rute. *Myths and Legends from Ghana for African-American Cultures* (5–7). Illus. 1992, Tell Publications/Telcraft (3800 Mogadore Ind. Pkwy., Mogadore, OH 44260) LB $14.95 (1-878893-21-1); paper $8.95 (1-878893-20-3). Eight fast-paced Hausa and Ashanti folk tales. (Rev: BL 12/1/92; SLJ 10/92) [996.3385]

2159 Philip, Neil. *The Illustrated Book of Myths: Tales and Legends of the World* (5–8). Illus. 1995, Dorling Kindersley $19.95 (0-7894-0202-5). An ambitious collection of the world's oral traditions and folklore, with charts of the Norse and Greek pantheons. (Rev: BL 12/1/95; SLJ 12/95; VOYA 4/96) [291.1]

Greece and Rome

2160 Alcock, Vivien. *Singer to the Sea God* (6–12). 1993, Delacorte $15 (0-385-30866-3). Weaves together some epic tales—from Scylla and Charybdis to Perseus and the Gorgon—with the story of a group of runaway slaves who act out scary travelers' tales they've only half-believed. Awards: YALSA Best Book for Young Adults. (Rev: BL 5/1/93; BTA)

2161 Edmondson, Elizabeth. *The Trojan War* (5–8). (Great Battles and Sieges) Illus. 1992, Macmillan/New Discovery LB $13.95 (0-02-733273-X). (Rev: BL 11/1/92) [939]

2162 McCaughrean, Geraldine. *The Odyssey* (6–12). 1995, Oxford Univ. $19.95 (0-19-274130-6). Retells Odysseus' encounters with Circe, Poseidon, the Lotus-eaters, and Calypso, on his way home to Penelope, who is overridden with suitors. (Rev: BL 7/95) [883]

2163 Mikolaycak, Charles. *Orpheus* (9–12). 1992, Harcourt LB $19.95 (0-15-258804-3). This picture book version of the Orpheus myth combines classical and romantic images that celebrate the human body. (Rev: BL 10/15/92; SLJ 9/92) [398.21]

2164 Orgel, Doris. *Ariadne, Awake!* (5–12). Illus. 1994, Viking $15.99 (0-670-85158-2). The Greek story of Theseus and the Minotaur, told from the perspective of the young princess Ariadne, who helps Theseus. (Rev: BL 5/1/94*; SLJ 6/94)

2165 Sutcliff, Rosemary. *Black Ships Before Troy: The Story of the Iliad* (5–12). Illus. 1993, Delacorte $19.95 (0-385-31069-2). A re-creation of the classic epic, with a compelling vision and sensitivity to language, history, and heroics. Awards: Greenaway Medal; YALSA Best Book for Young Adults. (Rev: BL 10/15/93; MJHS) [883]

Speeches, Essays, and General Literary Works

2166 Abdallah, Anouar, and others, eds. *For Rushdie: A Collection of Essays by 100 Arabic and Muslim Writers* (9–adult). Tr. by Kirk Anderson and Kenneth Whitehead. 1994, Braziller $27.50 (0-8076-1354-1). A brave work, the result of invitations to about 100 well-known Arab or Muslim writers to contribute on behalf of Salman Rushdie. (Rev: BL 4/15/94) [823]

2167 Bell-Scott, Patricia, ed. *Life Notes: Personal Writings by Contemporary Black Women* (9–adult). 1994, Norton $25 (0-393-03593-X). Excerpts from journals and notebooks of contemporary African American women on such topics as childhood, identity, love, abuse, and work. (Rev: BL 2/15/94; BTA; SLJ 9/94) [305.48]

2168 Bradbury, Ray. *Yestermorrow: Obvious Answers to Impossible Futures* (9–adult). 1992, Capra Press (P.O. Box 2068, Santa Barbara, CA 93120) $19.95 (1-877741-04-3). The famous sci-fi author sketches his vision of the future, including plans for electronic malls and imaginative high-tech museums. (Rev: BL 3/1/92) [814]

2169 Carroll, Rebecca. *I Know What the Red Clay Looks Like: The Voice and Vision of Black Women Writers* (9–adult). 1994, Crown/Carol Southern $22.50 (0-517-88261-2); paper $12 (0-517-88261-2). Insightful interviews with black women writers, followed by excerpts from their works. (Rev: BL 11/15/94; BTA; SLJ 3/95) [810.9]

2170 Crouch, Stanley. *The All-American Skin Game; or, The Decoy of Race: The Long and the Short of It, 1990–1994* (9–adult). 1995, Pantheon $24 (0-679-44202-2). A collection of pieces by a Negro (as he calls himself) thinker who has a flair for provoking the reader to refuse facile thought and reflect on the less obvious aspects of race and racism. (Rev: BL 10/15/95*) [305.896]

2171 Giovanni, Nikki. *Racism 101* (9–adult). 1994, Morrow $20 (0-688-04332-1). This best-selling poet's sixteenth book looks at the African American community, education, and historical perspective in a collection of essays. (Rev: BL 12/1/93*) [811]

2172 Gonzalez, Ray. *Memory Fever: A Journey Beyond El Paso del Norte* (9–adult). 1993, Broken Moon Press (P.O. Box 24585, Seattle, WA 98124-0585) paper $13.95 (0-913089-49-4). Essays by a poet of Mexican ancestry that evoke memories of growing up in the 1960s in the U.S. Southwest. (Rev: BL 4/15/93) [814]

2173 Halliburton, Warren J., ed. *Historic Speeches of African Americans* (7–12). (African American Experience) 1993, Watts LB $13.40 (0-531-11034-6). Chronologically organized speeches by such leaders as Sojourner Truth, Frederick Douglass, Marcus Garvey, James Baldwin, Angela Davis, and Jesse Jackson. (Rev: BL 4/15/93; MJHS; SLJ 7/93) [815]

2174 Hirschfelder, Arlene, and Beverly R. Singer. *Rising Voices: Writings of Young Native Americans* (5–8). 1992, Scribner $12.95 (0-684-19207-1). A variety of young Native American voices, many of them youth, covering identity, family, homelands, rituals, education, etc. Awards: SLJ Best Book. (Rev: BL 7/92; BTA; MJHS; SLJ 12/92*) [810.8]

2175 Jones, Lisa. *Bulletproof Diva: Tales of Race, Sex, and Hair* (9–adult). 1994, Doubleday $25.95 (0-385-47122-X). A writer—the daughter of a white mother (Hettie Jones) and an African American father (Amiri Baraka)—explores race, gender, and style in 40 dynamic essays. (Rev: BL 4/15/94*) [305.896]

2176 MacArthur, Brian, ed. *The Penguin Book of Twentieth-Century Speeches* (9–adult). 1993, Viking $35 (0-670-83126-3). Chosen from political and social-justice realms, this collection of over 150 speeches is largely from British sources. (Rev: BL 6/1–15/93) [808.8504]

2177 Meltzer, Milton, ed. *Lincoln in His Own Words* (6–9). Illus. 1993, Harcourt $22.95 (0-15-245437-3). A collection of excerpts of Lincoln's statements framed with facts about his life. (Rev: BL 9/1/93; VOYA 12/93) [973.7]

2178 Miller, Lee, ed. *From the Heart: Voices of the American Indian* (9–adult). 1995, Knopf $24 (0-679-43549-2). An anthology of 4 centuries of Northern Hemisphere Native American speeches, excerpts, and quotes. (Rev: BL 5/15/95) [973]

2179 Raspberry, William. *Looking Backward at Us* (9–adult). 1991, Univ. Press of Mississippi $17.95 (0-87805-535-5). These *Washington Post* columns offer commentary on a wide range of social and political issues in education, criminal justice, and family and racial matters. (Rev: BL 11/15/91) [361.1]

2180 Reed, Ishmael. *Airing Dirty Laundry* (9–adult). 1993, Addison-Wesley $20 (0-201-62462-1). Reed's provocative essays on reading, writing, and racism challenge both liberal and conservative views, especially regarding prejudice against African American males. (Rev: BL 10/15/93) [305.896]

2181 Safire, William, ed. *Lend Me Your Ears: Great Speeches in History* (9–adult). 1992, Norton $35 (0-393-03368-6). Over 250 orations are individually analyzed within their historical context, with comments on their forensic elements. (Rev: BL 9/15/92; MJHS; SHS) [808.85]

2182 Yep, Laurence, ed. *American Dragons: Twenty-Five Asian American Voices* (7–12). 1993, HarperCollins LB $14.89 (0-06-021495-3). Autobiographical stories, poems, and essays about children whose parents come from China, Japan, Korea, and Tibet, struggling to find "an identity that isn't generic." (Rev: BL 5/15/93; BTA; SLJ 7/93; VOYA 10/93) [810.9]

Literary History and Criticism

General and Miscellaneous

2183 Knox, Bernard, ed. *The Norton Book of Classical Literature* (9–adult). 1993, Norton $29.95 (0-393-03426-7). More than 300 pieces of classical literature, primarily Greek but also some Roman. (Rev: BL 2/15/93; SHS) [880]

2184 Sullivan, Charles, ed. *Children of Promise: African-American Literature and Art for Young People* (7–12). 1991, Abrams $24.95 (0-8109-3170-2). An anthology of African American literature and art from the time of slavery to the present day. Awards: YALSA Best Book for Young Adults. (Rev: BL 11/16/91; MJHS; SLJ 1/92) [700]

Fiction

General and Miscellaneous

2185 Clute, John. *Science Fiction: The Illustrated Encyclopedia* (9–12). 1995, DK $39.95 (0-7894-0185-1). This collection of sci-fi information includes chapters on visions of the future, themes in history, influential magazines, classic titles, graphic works, and genre films. (Rev: BL 1/1/96; SLJ 1/96)

2186 Rainey, Richard. *The Monster Factory* (6–12). 1993, Macmillan $13.95 (0-02-775663-7). A discussion of 7 famous monster-story writers and their most-loved works. (Rev: BL 8/93; BTA; MJHS; VOYA 10/93) [809.3]

2187 Zipes, Jack. *Spells of Enchantment: The Wondrous Fairy Tales of Western Culture* (9–adult). 1991, Viking $30 (0-670-83053-4). A collection of 67 literary fairy tales for adults from some of the greatest European and American authors, including Rousseau, Goethe, Yeats, Thackeray, Twain, and Thurber. (Rev: BL 10/15/91; SHS) [398]

United States

2188 Johnson-Feelings, Dianne. *Presenting Laurence Yep* (8–12). 1995, Twayne $20.95 (0-8057-8201-X). A biocritical study drawn from the Chinese American artist Laurence Yep's autobiography *The Lost Garden*. (Rev: BL 12/15/95) [813]

2189 Russell, Sandi. *Render Me My Song: African-American Women Writers from Slavery to the Present* (9–adult). 1991, St. Martin's $18.95 (0-312-05288-X). Informal literary history intoduces the lives and works of African American women writers from slavery to the present. (Rev: BL 2/1/91*; MJHS) [810.9]

Plays

Europe

Great Britain and Ireland

SHAKESPEARE

2190 Ross, Stewart. *Shakespeare and Macbeth: The Story Behind the Play* (5–8). Illus. 1994, Viking $16.99 (0-670-85629-0). An approach grounded in ordinary daily life and what Shakespeare's main commercial considerations were at the time. Awards: SLJ Best Book; YALSA Best Book for Young Adults. (Rev: BL 3/15/95; MJHS; SLJ 1/95) [822.3]

2191 Whalen, Richard F. *Shakespeare: Who Was He? The Oxford Challenge to the Bard of Avon* (9–adult). 1994, Praeger $19.95 (0-275-94850-1). Probes the questionable authorship of the works of Shakespeare. Presents evidence suggesting the plays were written by others. (Rev: BL 11/1/94) [822.3]

Language and Communication

Signs and Symbols

2192 Aaseng, Nathan. *Navajo Code Talkers* (6–9). 1992, Walker LB $15.85 (0-8027-8183-7). Describes how Navajos were recruited during World War II to create an unbreakable code that allowed the marines to transmit information quickly, accurately, and safely. (Rev: BL 12/1/92; BTA; MJHS; SLJ 12/92) [940.54]

2193 Hausman, Gerald. *Turtle Island Alphabet: A Lexicon of Native American Symbols and Culture* (9–adult). 1992, St. Martin's $19.95 (0-312-07103-5). From *arrow* to *zigzag*, an alphabet of important Native American symbols. (Rev: BL 3/15/92; MJHS; SHS) [398.2]

2194 Jean, Georges. *Writing: The Story of Alphabets and Scripts* (7–12). (Discoveries) 1992, Abrams paper $12.95 (0-8109-2893-0). Traces the beginnings of writing through the development of alphabets to printing and bookmaking, emphasizing the physical rather than intellectual aspects of the process. (Rev: BL 7/92; BTA) [652.1]

2195 Morris, Desmond. *Bodytalk: The Meaning of Human Gestures* (9–adult). 1995, Crown paper $17 (0-517-88355-4). An illustrated guide to the origin and meaning of more than 600 informal body gestures. (Rev: BL 3/15/95; SHS) [302.2]

Symbols, Words, and Languages

2196 Beard, Henry, and Chris Cerf. *The Official Politically Correct Dictionary and Handbook* (9–adult). 1992, Villard paper $10 (0-679-74113-5). An irreverent dictionary of current terms and euphemisms. (Rev: BL 4/15/92) [818]

2197 Cox, Brenda S. *Who Talks Funny? A Book about Languages for Kids* (7–12). 1995, Shoe String/Linnet $25 (0-208-02378-X). Explores the importance of learning another language, their development and common elements, and interesting facts, such as how to say the days of the week in 27 languages. (Rev: BL 7/95; SLJ 4/95) [400]

2198 Fakih, Kimberly Olson. *Off the Clock: A Lexicon of Time Words and Expressions* (6–10). 1995, Ticknor & Fields $13.95 (0-395-66374-1). A look at how we talk about time in folklore, anthropology, myth, history, semantics, and physics. (Rev: BL 1/1/95; SLJ 3/95) [428.1]

2199 Feinberg, Barbara Silberdick. *Words in the News: A Student's Dictionary of American Government and Politics* (5–8). 1993, Watts $13.40 (0-531-11164-4). This guide to 500 words and phrases that make up the language of American government and politics includes trivia and cartoons. (Rev: BL 3/1/94; MJHS; SLJ 5/94) [320.973]

2200 Gay, Kathlyn. *Getting Your Message Across* (6–12). 1993, Macmillan/New Discovery $13.95 (0-02-735815-1). Obstacles to communication are examined using examples of body language, expression, listening, and clothing. Also covers advertising. (Rev: BL 10/1/93; BTA; SLJ 11/93; VOYA 2/94) [302.2]

2201 Graham-Barber, Lynda. *Doodle Dandy! The Complete Book of Independence Day Words* (5–7). Illus. 1992, Bradbury $13.95 (0-02-736675-8). Provides the etymologies of 34 words or phrases that we use but seldom think about, e.g., *boycott, colony, stars and stripes, Uncle Sam, fireworks, barbecue, watermelon, etc.* (Rev: BL 7/92; SLJ 3/92) [394.2]

2202 Harlan, Judith. *Bilingualism in the United States: Conflict and Controversy* (7–12). 1991, Watts LB $12.90 (0-531-13001-0). A discussion of assimilation versus pluralism, of the historical importance of Spanish in America, and of experiences with bilingualism in other countries. (Rev: BL 11/15/91; SHS; SLJ 12/91) [306.4]

2203 Klausner, Janet. *Talk about English: How Words Travel and Change* (6–10). Illus. 1990, HarperCollins/Crowell LB $14.89 (0-690-04833-5). A history of the development of the English language and an explanation of various linguistic inventions. (Rev: BL 1/1/91; MJHS) [422.2]

2204 Kramer, Patricia. *Discovering Self-Expression and Communication* (7–12). (Self-Esteem Library) 1991, Rosen $14.95 (0-8239-1276-0). Perspectives on how words and gestures are used to communicate, as well as suggestions for positive self-expression. (Rev: BL 2/15/92; SLJ 9/92) [302.2]

2205 Lederer, Richard. *Adventures of a Verbivore* (9–adult). 1994, Pocket $21 (0-671-70941-0). Excerpts from the author's *Writer's Digest* columns that revel in puns, word games, and the fun of language. (Rev: BL 2/15/94) [428.2]

2206 Lederer, Richard. *The Miracle of Language* (9–adult). 1991, Pocket $20 (0-671-70939-9). A collection of humorous essays examining the English language, literature, and libraries by a noted columnist. (Rev: BL 12/1/91) [428]

2207 Lederer, Richard. *More Anguished English* (9–adult). 1993, Delacorte $17.95 (0-385-31017-X). Lederer draws from court transcripts, term papers, etc. to illustrate errors of English usage and help readers learn to improve their sentence structure. (Rev: BL 10/15/93) [428]

2208 Macrone, Michael. *It's Greek to Me!* (9–adult). 1991, HarperCollins $16.95 (0-06-270022-7). Explains the Greek and Latin origins of many common English words and phrases. (Rev: BL 8/91) [422]

2209 Martin, Russell. *Out of Silence: A Journey into Language* (9–adult). 1994, Holt $22.50 (0-8050-1998-7). Documents the continuing odyssey of the author's nephew, who was diagnosed as autistic after receiving a routine childhood inoculation. (Rev: BL 3/15/94) [616.8]

2210 Muschell, David. *What in the Word? Origins of Words Dealing with People and Places* (9–adult). 1996, McGuinn & McGuire Publishing (P.O. Box 20603, Bradenton, FL 34203) paper $14.95 (1-881117-14-6). Explains the origins of real and imaginary person- and place-names. (Rev: BL 1/1/91; SHS) [422]

2211 Proctor, William. *The Terrible Speller: A Quick and Easy Guide to Enhancing Your Spelling Ability* (9–adult). 1993, Morrow $12 (0-688-09981-5). Following a few basic spelling rules, Proctor cites 200 of the most common spelling errors and provides suggestions for imprinting their correct spelling. (Rev: BL 10/15/93) [428.1]

2212 Rawson, Hugh. *Devious Derivations: Popular Misconceptions—and More Than 1,000 True Origins of Common Words and Phrases* (9–adult). 1994, Crown $22.50 (0-517-58066-7). Rawson blends folklore, history, and literary quotations in his explanations of how more than 1,000 words came into popular usage. (Rev: BL 10/15/93) [422]

2213 Safire, William. *Coming to Terms* (9–adult). 1992, Henry Holt paper $14.95 (0-8050-2005-5). Contains 160 essays (with letters commenting on them) compiled from Safire's column "On Language," from the *New York Times Magazine*. For teens who care about writing well. (Rev: BL 4/1/91; SHS) [428]

2214 Safire, William. *Quoth the Maven* (9–adult). 1993, Random $25 (0-679-42324-9). Selections from the author's "On Language" column in *New York Magazine* plus numerous quarrelsome and enlightening reader responses. (Rev: BL 4/15/93) [428]

2215 Shipman, Robert Oliver. *A Pun My Word: A Humorously Enlightened Path to English Usage* (9–adult). 1991, Littlefield Adams paper $14.95 (0-8226-3011-7). Humorous examples help explain common problems in grammar and word usage. (Rev: BL 7/91) [428]

2216 Soukhanov, Anne H. *Watch Word: The Stories Behind the Words of Our Lives* (9–adult). 1995, Holt $25 (0-8050-3564-8). The editor of the *American Heritage Dictionary* looks at new words in our vernacular and gives definitions, usage, and some history. (Rev: BL 6/1–15/95) [422]

2217 Terban, Marvin. *Hey, Hay! A Wagonful of Funny Homonym Riddles* (5–7). 1991, Clarion $13.95 (0-395-54431-9); paper $5.95 (0-395-56183-3). Zany combination of puns, riddles, and other word play. (Rev: BL 6/1/91) [818]

2218 Warburton, Lois. *The Beginning of Writing* (5–8). 1990, Lucent LB $11.95 (1-56006-113-8). Discusses communication strategies invented by pre-alphabetic societies. (Rev: BL 5/1/91; MJHS; SLJ 5/91) [652]

Writing and the Media

General and Miscellaneous

2219 Kemper, Dave, and others. *Writers Express: A Handbook for Young Writers, Thinkers and Learners* (5–7). 1994, Write Source (P.O. Box 460, Burlington, WI 53105) $13.95 (0-939045-94-X); paper $10.45 (0-939045-93-1). Advice on writing everything from a school report to a tall tale, with guidelines for increasing vocabulary, preparing a speech, taking tests, and reading maps. (Rev: BL 7/94; SLJ 7/94) [808]

2220 *Scrawl! Writing in Ancient Times* (5–8). (Buried Worlds) 1994, Lerner LB $17.21 (0-8225-3209-3). A history of writing worldwide, from prehistoric symbols to the invention of printing. Revised, updated edition of *Ancient Scrolls*. (Rev: BL 1/15/95; MJHS) [411]

Books and Publishing

2221 Brookfield, Karen. *Book* (5–9). (Eyewitness Books) 1993, Knopf LB $15.99 (0-679-94012-X). The evolution of writing and the forms in which it has been recorded. (Rev: BL 10/1/93; MJHS) [002]

2222 Madama, John. *Desktop Publishing: The Art of Communication* (7–12). 1993, Lerner $14.95 (0-8225-2303-5). Introduces desktop-publishing elements and terminology to beginning computer users, with advice on writing, editing, layout, type, illustration, and printing. (Rev: BL 5/15/93; MJHS; SLJ 6/93) [686.2]

2223 Olmert, Michael. *The Smithsonian Book of Books* (9–adult). 1992, Smithsonian $45 (0-89599-030-X). Celebrates the powerful link between readers and the printed page as it follows books from the days of scribes to moveable type to children's book illustration. Awards: SLJ Best Book. (Rev: BL 9/1/92; SHS; SLJ 1/93*) [002]

2224 Wilson, Elizabeth B. *Bibles and Bestiaries: A Guide to Illuminated Manuscripts* (6–9). 1994, Farrar $25 (0-374-30685-0). Describes how a book was made in the Middle Ages. Awards: SLJ Best Book. (Rev: BL 1/1/95; BTA; SLJ 12/94*) [745.6]

Newspapers, Magazines, Comics, and Journalism

2225 Benton, Mike. *Horror Comics: The Illustrated History* (9–adult). 1991, Taylor $21.95 (0-87833-734-2). An illustrated history of and collector's guide to horror comic books. (Rev: BL 5/15/91; BTA) [745.1]

2226 Benton, Mike. *Superhero Comics of the Silver Age: The Illustrated History* (9–adult). 1992, Taylor $24.95 (0-87833-746-6). Illustrated descriptions of comic book superheroes, artists, publishers, and popular titles from the late 1950s to 1970, with a historical perspective. (Rev: BL 12/15/91) [741.5]

2227 Bova, Ben. *Challenges* (9–adult). 1993, Tor $21.95 (0-312-85550-8). Bova, in a blend of essay and fiction, shares a sampling of tightly plotted, low-violence tales and the incidents that sparked them. (Rev: BL 4/1/93; SLJ 10/93; VOYA 12/93) [813.54]

2228 Braden, Maria. *She Said What? Interviews with Women Newspaper Columnists* (9–adult). 1993, Univ. Press of Kentucky $24 (0-8131-1819-0). Discusses the history and influence of female columnists, followed by interviews with 13 well-known women journalists and excerpts from their columns. (Rev: BL 4/15/93) [070.92]

2229 Daniels, Les. *Marvel: Five Fabulous Decades of the World's Greatest Comics* (9–adult). 1991, Abrams $45 (0-8109-3821-9). The story of the development of Marvel Comics is told with artwork, biographies, and profiles of the publishers' foremost heroes and villains. (Rev: BL 11/1/91; SHS) [741.5]

2230 De Bartolo, Dick. *Good Days and Mad* (9–adult). 1994, Thunder's Mouth $29.95 (1-56025-077-1); paper $16.95 (1-56025-091-7). Reminiscences about the founder and staff of *Mad* magazine, from its creation to the present. Awards: SLJ Best Book. (Rev: SLJ 5/95)

2231 Feelings, Tom. *Tommy Traveler in the World of Black History* (5–8). 1991, Black Butterfly Children's Books (625 Broadway, New York, NY 10012) $13.95 (0-86316-202-9). Illustrates African American history through the eyes of a protagonist who imagines himself participating in the important events. (Rev: BL 9/15/91; SLJ 2/92) [741.5]

2232 Hinds, Patricia Mignon, ed. *Essence: 25 Years Celebrating Black Women* (9–adult). 1995, Abrams $35 (0-8109-3256-3). A celebration of one of the most important publications for the African American woman, with excellent photography and articles by poets, writers, and scholars. (Rev: BL 11/1/95) [305.48]

2233 Janello, Amy, and Brennon Jones. *The American Magazine* (9–adult). 1991, Abrams $60 (0-8109-1909-5). This illustrated retrospective celebrates over 2 centuries of the magazine publishing business, covering changing gender roles, race relations, politics, etc. (Rev: BL 12/1/91) [051]

2234 Jeffords, Susan, and Lauren Rabinovitz, eds. *Seeing Through the Media: The Persian Gulf War* (9–adult). 1994, Rutgers Univ. $45 (0-8135-2041-X); paper $16 (0-8135-2042-8). Sixteen essays on the Gulf War that analyze the ways in which the internal imperatives of government, the military, and the media interacted to shape and distort events. (Rev: BL 3/15/94) [070.4]

2235 Kessler, Judy. *Inside People: The Stories Behind the Stories* (9–adult). 1994, Villard $20 (0-679-42186-6). Tracks the evolution of *People* magazine and gives an account of the stories behind the interviews. (Rev: BL 3/15/94) [051]

2236 Knobler, Peter, and Greg Mitchell, eds. *Very Seventies: A Cultural History of the 1970s, from the Pages of Crawdaddy* (9–adult). 1995, Simon & Schuster/Fireside paper $14 (0-02-022005-7). A collection of articles published in *Crawdaddy* magazine in the 1970s. (Rev: BL 4/15/95) [973.924]

2237 Love, Robert, ed. *The Best of Rolling Stone: 25 Years of Journalism on the Edge* (9–adult). 1993, Doubleday paper $15 (0-385-47051-7). A collection of 37 articles spanning 25 years of popular history. Includes portraits of the magazine's inner workings. (Rev: BL 9/15/93) [051]

2238 McCloud, Scott. *Understanding Comics* (9–adult). 1993, Kitchen Sink/Tundra (320 Riverside Dr., Northampton, MA 01060) paper $19.95 (1-56862-019-5). The history of comics in a comic book format. (Rev: BL 9/1/93*; BTA) [741.5]

2239 Reidelbach, Maria. *Completely Mad: A History of the Comic Book and Magazine* (9–adult). 1991, Little, Brown $39.95 (0-316-73890-5). Hundreds of reprinted examples of irreverence from 4 decades of *Mad* are found in this chronicle of the influential cult comic book and popular magazine. Awards: YALSA Best Book for Young Adults. (Rev: BL 10/15/91; BTA; SHS; SLJ 6/92) [741.5]

2240 Sabato, Larry J. *Feeding Frenzy: How Attack Journalism Has Transformed American Politics* (9–adult). 1991, Free Press $22.95 (0-02-927635-7). Claims that democracy is being undermined because meaningful news and commentary are being overshadowed by political pseudoscandals. (Rev: BL 9/1/91) [302.23]

2241 Senna, Carl. *The Black Press and the Struggle for Civil Rights* (7–12). (African American Experience) 1993, Watts $13.90 (0-531-11036-2). The history of many African American publications is traced, from *Freedom's Journal* of 1827 to influential present-day newspapers. (Rev: BL 1/1/94; BTA; MJHS; SHS; SLJ 1/94; VOYA 2/94) [071]

2242 Tebbel, John, and Mary Ellen Waller-Zuckermann. *The Magazine in America, 1741–1990* (9–adult). 1991, Oxford Univ. $35 (0-19-505127-0). A comprehensive history of the American magazine, with special focus on the growth of mass-market publications from 1919 to 1945. (Rev: BL 6/15/91) [051]

Philosophy and Religion

Philosophy

2243 Fulghum, Robert. *Maybe (Maybe Not): Second Thoughts from a Secret Life* (9–adult). 1993, Villard $19 (0-679-41960-8). Fulghum shares insights into observed and imagined events. (Rev: BL 8/93; SLJ 4/94) [814.54]

2244 Karnos, David D., and Robert G. Shoemaker, eds. *Falling in Love with Wisdom: American Philosophers Talk about Their Calling* (9–adult). 1993, Oxford Univ. $23 (0-19-507201-4). Down-to-earth, personal, and often humorous accounts of the factors and events that led 64 modern philosophers to love philosophy. (Rev: BL 1/15/93; SLJ 10/93) [191]

World Religions

General and Miscellaneous

2245 Aaseng, Rolf E. *A Beginner's Guide to Studying the Bible* (9–adult). 1991, Augsburg paper $6.95 (0-8066-2571-6). Outlines basic techniques and resources for enriching Bible study. (Rev: BL 4/1/92) [220.07]

2246 Bach, Alice, and J. Cheryl Exum. *Miriam's Well: Stories about Women in the Bible* (9–adult). 1991, Delacorte $16 (0-385-30435-8). The stories of a diverse group of women mentioned in the Bible are told by a children's author and a biblical scholar. (Rev: BL 10/1/91; MJHS; SLJ 1/92) [221.9]

2247 Bachrach, Deborah. *The Inquisition* (8–12). (World History) 1995, Lucent LB $14.95 (1-56006-247-9). (Rev: BL 2/15/95) [272]

2248 Batchelor, Mary, ed. *Children's Prayers from Around the World* (5–7). 1995, Augsburg $13.99 (0-8066-2830-8). More than 200 prayers, grouped thematically, express children's concerns. A revision of *The Lion Book of Children's Prayers* with new illustrations. (Rev: BL 9/1/95) [242]

2249 Bonvillain, Nancy. *Native American Religion* (6–12). (Indians of North America) 1995, Chelsea LB $18.95 (0-7910-2652-3); paper $8.95 (0-7910-3479-8). Explanations of native spiritual life that emphasize the natural world and the Earth. Also discusses holistic approaches taken toward illness and well-being. (Rev: BL 3/1/96; SLJ 2/96)

2250 Gellman, Marc, and Thomas Hartman. *How Do You Spell God? Answers to the Big Questions from Around the World* (5–8). Illus. 1995, Morrow $15 (0-688-13041-0). This survey of a variety of religions poses major questions about life, then presents answers according to the beliefs of Judaism, Islam, Christianity, Buddhism, and Hinduism. (Rev: BL 6/1–15/95; SLJ 5/95) [200]

2251 Hewitt, Catherine. *Buddhism* (5–8). 1995, Thomson Learning $15.95 (1-56847-375-3). An easily understood text with a map of the world showing where Buddhism flourishes. (Rev: BL 9/1/95) [294.3]

2252 Hoobler, Thomas, and Dorothy Hoobler. *Confucianism* (6–9). (World Religions) 1993, Facts on File LB $17.95 (0-8160-2445-6). Describes how the teachings of Confucius evolved from a social order to a religion, permeating all phases of Chinese life for 2,000 years. (Rev: BL 3/1/93; MJHS; SHS) [299]

2253 Lyden, John, ed. *Enduring Issues in Religion* (10–12). (Enduring Issues) 1995, Greenhaven LB $17.95 (1-56510-260-6); paper $9.95 (1-56510-259-2). In this series, the editors pose a general question and present several contradicting source materials to develop a debate. (Rev: BL 7/95) [200]

2254 Occhiogrosso, Peter. *The Joy of Sects: A Spirited Guide to the World's Religious Traditions* (9–adult). 1994, Doubleday $23.95 (0-385-42564-3). Covers the history, terms, and practices of Hinduism, Buddhism, Christianity, Islam, Judaism, Taoism, and "New Age" religions. Awards: BL Editors' Choice. (Rev: BL 9/15/94) [291]

2255 Phipps, William E. *Muhammad and Jesus: A Comparison of the Prophets and Their Teachings* (9–adult). 1995, Paragon House $18.95 (1-55778-718-2). An introduction to 2 important spiritual leaders and the religions they represent. (Rev: BL 9/1/95) [297]

2256 Segal, Lore. *The Story of King Saul and King David* (5–8). 1991, Shocken $20 (0-8052-4088-8). The biblical stories of Saul and David are translated into direct, modern, colloquial English prose. (Rev: BL 11/15/91) [222]

2257 Singh, Nikky-Guninder Kaur. *Sikhism* (6–9). (World Religions) 1993, Facts on File $17.95 (0-8160-2446-4). (Rev: BL 7/93) [294.6]

2258 Stoltzfus, Louise. *Amish Women: Lives and Stories* (9–adult). 1994, Good Books $14.95 (1-56148-129-7). Amish women reveal their uniqueness, hopes, and aspirations. (Rev: BL 12/1/94; SLJ 6/95) [305.48]

2259 Tutu, Desmond, ed. *The African Prayer Book* (9–adult). 1995, Doubleday $15 (0-385-47730-9). African Christian and non-Christian prayers, poems, and litanies. (Rev: BL 5/1/95) [242]

2260 Vardey, Lucinda, ed. *God in All Worlds: An Anthology of Contemporary Spiritual Writing* (9–adult). 1995, Pantheon $35 (0-679-44214-6). Prayers and devotional readings, with a backdrop of a world filled with evil, that yield their comforts when read selectively. (Rev: BL 9/1/95*) [291.4]

2261 Viswanathan, Ed. *Am I a Hindu?* (9–adult). 1992, Halo Books (P.O. Box 2529, San Francisco, CA 94126) paper $14.95 (1-879904-06-3). A comprehensive introduction to Hinduism written in a "catechism" form, with questions and answers grouped according to topic. (Rev: BL 10/15/92) [294.5]

2262 Wangu, Madhu Bazaz. *Buddhism* (6–9). (World Religions) 1993, Facts on File LB $17.95 (0-8160-2442-1). Describes Buddha's life, the spread of Buddhism, and its existence today. (Rev: BL 3/1/93; MJHS; SHS) [294.3]

2263 Wangu, Madhu Bazaz. *Hinduism* (6–9). (World Religions) 1991, Facts on File LB $17.95 (0-8160-2447-2). A detailed, complex look at this major religion. (Rev: BL 4/15/92; MJHS; SHS) [294.5]

2264 Ward, Kaari, ed. *ABC's of the Bible: Intriguing Questions and Answers about the Greatest Book Ever Written* (9–adult). 1991, Reader's Digest $32 (0-89577-375-9). Presented in a question-and-answer format, this book covers the history of the biblical period and gives definitions of terms. (Rev: BL 10/1/91; SLJ 2/92) [220]

Christianity

2265 Allen, Thomas B. *Possessed: The True Story of an Exorcism* (9–adult). 1993, Doubleday $20 (0-385-42034-X). Investigates the evidence on which the filmed novel *The Exorcist* was based, explaining the relevant theological and scientific viewpoints. (Rev: BL 6/1–15/93) [264]

2266 Armstrong, Carole. *Lives and Legends of the Saints: With Paintings from the Great Art Museums of the World* (5–7). 1995, Simon & Schuster $17 (0-689-80277-3). The lives of 20 saints in paintings from the world's great museums grace the text of this book, with a brief introduction for each. (Rev: BL 9/1/95*; SLJ 12/95) [270]

2267 Bernos de Gasztold, Carmen. *Prayers from the Ark* (5–7). Tr. by Rumer Godden. Illus. 1992, Viking $16 (0-670-84496-9). These poems/prayers, written by a woman during World War II, are offered by the animals aboard Noah's ark. Awards: SLJ Best Book. (Rev: BL 9/1/92; SLJ 8/92*) [841]

2268 Biffi, Inos. *An Introduction to the Liturgical Year* (5–9). 1995, Eerdmans $16.99 (0-8028-5103-7). Helps clarify the annual cycle of dates that celebrate the life of Christ. (Rev: BL 9/1/95) [263]

2269 Bolick, Nancy O'Keefe, and Sallie G. Randolph. *Shaker Villages* (6–8). Illus. 1993, Walker LB $13.85 (0-8027-8210-8). Offers insights into one of the world's longest-lived communal societies, its founder, its faith, its daily life, and its village organization. (Rev: BL 3/15/93; BTA; SLJ 6/93) [289]

2270 Brown, Stephen F. *Christianity* (6–9). (World Religions) 1991, Facts on File $17.95 (0-8160-2441-3). Describes the historical and contemporary impact of Christianity. (Rev: BL 4/15/92) [200]

2271 Chaikin, Miriam. *Children's Bible Stories: From Genesis to Daniel* (5–7). Illus. 1993, Dial LB $17.89 (0-8037-0990-0). Features 26 Old Testament stories, with opulent colored-pencil art. (Rev: BL 2/15/93*; SLJ 1/93) [221.9]

2272 Cornwell, John. *The Hiding Places of God: A Personal Journey into the World of Religious Visions, Holy Objects, and Miracles* (9–adult). 1991, Warner $19.95 (0-446-51468-3). An examination of supernatural aspects and several miraculous incidents in the lives of contemporary religious persons. (Rev: BL 10/1/91) [248.2]

2273 Dudley, William, and Teresa O'Neill, eds. *Puritanism* (9–12). (Opposing Viewpoints) 1994, Greenhaven LB $17.95 (1-56510-082-4); paper $9.95 (1-56510-081-6). The opinions of Puritans in terms of what they believed constituted an ideal community and the role of the individual in it. (Rev: BL 3/1/94; MJHS) [285]

2274 Durham, Michael S. *Miracles of Mary: Apparitions, Legends, and the Miraculous Works of the Blessed Virgin Mary* (9–adult). 1995, HarperSan Francisco $25 (0-06-062131-1). A variety of images and stories about Mary, grouped thematically with carefully documented sources for the illustrations. (Rev: BL 12/1/95) [232.91]

2275 Gordon, Anne. *A Book of Saints: True Stories of How They Touch Our Lives* (9–adult). 1994, Bantam paper $12.95 (0-553-37272-6). How the saints, from missionaries to mystics, can have a positive impact in our modern lives with the use of devotional prayer. (Rev: BL 7/94) [282.092]

2276 Kenna, Kathleen. *A People Apart* (5–8). Illus. 1995, Houghton $17.95 (0-395-67344-5). A carefully thought-out photo essay on the lives of the Mennonite from a woman who attended the church as a child. Interviews and the history of the group flesh out the text. (Rev: BL 11/1/95*; SLJ 12/95*; SLJ 12/95) [289.7]

2277 McCary, P. K. *Rappin' with Jesus: The Good News According to the Four Brothers* (9–adult). (Black Bible Chronicles) 1994, African American Family (575 Madison Ave., Suite 1006, New York, NY 10022) paper $14.95 (1-56977-005-0). The Gospels of Matthew, Mark, Luke, and John are presented in a translation to black vernacular. (Rev: BL 2/15/94) [226.05209]

2278 Paterson, Katherine. *Who Am I?* (5–7). 1992, Eerdmans paper $9.95 (0-8028-5072-3). Drawing on history, the Bible, personal stories, and fiction, reflects on the questions Where in the world is God? Where do I belong? Who is my neighbor? and What is my purpose? (Rev: BL 12/15/92; SLJ 11/92) [248.8]

2279 Schouweiler, Thomas. *The Devil* (6–9). (Opposing Viewpoints/Great Mysteries) 1992, Greenhaven $17.50 (0-89908-091-X). Examines the question of the devil's existence and the beginnings of devil mythology, worship, and possession, looking at both sides and giving no definitive answers. (Rev: BL 5/1/93; MJHS) [133.4]

2280 Stein, Stephen J. *The Shaker Experience in America: A History of the United Society of Believers* (9–adult). 1992, Yale Univ. $40 (0-300-05139-5). A history of these seemingly radical religious people from the classic eighteenth-century Shaker period to their modern resurgence. (Rev: BL 5/1/92)

2281 Stivender, Ed. *Raised Catholic (Can You Tell?)* (9–adult). 1992, August House $19.95 (0-87483-277-2). A nostalgic look at growing up Catholic in the 1950s. (Rev: BL 9/15/92) [282]

2282 *The Story of Christmas* (5–12). Illus. 1991, Dutton $15.95 (0-525-44768-7). Selections from the Gospels of Matthew and Luke are matched with distinctive folk art in this seasonal volume. Awards: ALSC Notable Children's Book; SLJ Best Book. (Rev: BL 11/15/91*) [232.92]

2283 Wilke, Angela. *Mi primer libro de Navidad* (5–8). Tr. by Conchita Peraire del Molino. 1994, Editorial Molino (Barcelona, Spain) $17.50 (84-272-1712-9). This large-format book includes numerous ideas for Christmas decorations, gifts, cards, and recipes, with color photos. English title: *My First Christmas Book*. (Rev: BL 10/15/95)

Islam

2284 Barboza, Steven. *American Jihad: Islam after Malcolm X* (9–adult). 1994, Doubleday $25 (0-385-47011-8). Interviews with dozens of American Muslims, including such prominent figures as Muhammad Ali, Kareem Abdul-Jabbar, and Louis Farrakhan. (Rev: BL 1/1/94; BTA) [297]

2285 Child, John. *The Rise of Islam* (6–8). 1995, Peter Bedrick LB $16.95 (0-87226-116-6). A historical approach to Islam's effect on world history. Discusses its beginnings and middle development but only briefly discusses Islam today. (Rev: BL 9/1/95; SLJ 8/95) [297]

2286 De Caro, Louis A. *On the Side of My People: A Religious Life of Malcolm X* (9–adult). 1995, New York Univ. $29.95 (0-8147-1864-7). Scholarly and thorough, yet very accessible—a correction to the often provincial interpretation of Malcolm X's religious dimension. (Rev: BL 11/1/95) [297]

2287 Gordon, Matthew S. *Islam* (6–9). (World Religions) 1991, Facts on File $17.95 (0-8160-2443-X). An overview of the history of Islam, its branches, the Koran, and Islam's place in the modern world. (Rev: BL 4/15/92; MJHS; SHS; SLJ 1/92) [297]

2288 Gumley, Frances, and Brian Redhead. *The Pillars of Islam: An Introduction to the Islamic Faith* (9–adult). 1992, Parkwest paper $7.95 (0-

563-20879-1). This short history of Islam includes traditions, rituals, and doctrine of the faith. (Rev: BL 3/15/92) [297.2]

2289 Spencer, William. *Islam Fundamentalism in the Modern World* (7–10). 1995, Millbrook $15.90 (1-56294-435-5). Explains the tenets of Islam and the general nature of religious fundamentalism. (Rev: BL 4/15/95; SLJ 5/95) [320.5]

2290 Winters, Paul A., ed. *Islam* (8–12). (Opposing Viewpoints) 1995, Greenhaven LB $17.95 (1-56510-248-7); paper $9.95 (1-56510-247-9). Looks at the Islamic religion, politics, and culture in relation to the West, including essays and articles on clashes, goals, fundamentalism, terrorism, and women. (Rev: BL 6/1–15/95; SHS) [320.5]

2291 Wormser, Richard. *American Islam: Growing Up Muslim in America* (6–12). 1994, Walker LB $15.85 (0-8027-8344-9). A portrait of Muslim American youth and their faith. (Rev: BL 12/15/94; BTA; SLJ 3/95) [297]

Judaism

2292 Chaikin, Miriam. *Menorahs, Mezuzas, and Other Jewish Symbols* (5–9). 1990, Clarion $14.95 (0-89919-856-2). A Jewish historian explores and explains some of the symbols of the faith. (Rev: BL 1/15/91; SLJ 1/91) [296.4]

2293 Frommer, Myrna Katz, and Harvey Frommer, eds. *Growing Up Jewish in America: An Oral History* (9–adult). 1995, Harcourt $25 (0-15-100132-4). A fascinating oral collection of anecdotes, memories, and wisdom of Jewish life in the U.S. (Rev: BL 11/1/95) [973]

2294 Goldin, Barbara Diamond. *Bat Mitzvah: A Jewish Girl's Coming of Age* (5–7). 1995, Viking $14.99 (0-670-86034-4). The companion to Kimmel's *Bar Mitzvah: A Jewish Boy's Coming of Age* discusses the roles of Jewish women through the ages, how to celebrate the bat mitzvah, and etiquette for those attending the service. (Rev: BL 9/1/95; SLJ 11/95) [296.4]

2295 Goldin, Barbara Diamond. *The Passover Journey: A Seder Companion* (5–8). Illus. 1994, Viking $15.99 (0-670-82421-6). This illustrated celebration of the Jewish holiday mixes biblical excerpts with rabbinic Passover stories and explains the origins and symbolism of the Seder. Awards: ALSC Notable Children's Book. (Rev: BL 3/1/94*; SLJ 2/94) [269.4]

2296 Kimmel, Eric A. *Bar Mitzvah: A Jewish Boy's Coming of Age* (5–7). 1995, Viking $14.99 (0-670-85540-5). A comprehensive look at the coming-of-age Jewish ceremony. (Rev: BL 2/15/95; SLJ 3/95) [296.4]

2297 Morrison, Martha, and Stephen F. Brown. *Judaism* (6–9). (World Religions) Illus. 1991, Facts on File LB $17.95 (0-8160-2444-8). An illustrated study of the effect Judaism has had on civilization and a look at its evolution, branches, holidays, and traditions. (Rev: BL 4/15/92; SLJ 3/92) [296]

2298 Wood, Angela. *Judaism* (5–8). 1995, Thomson Learning $15.95 (1-56847-376-1). An informative text on Judaism, with a glossary, bibliography, and map of where the religion flourishes. (Rev: BL 9/1/95; SLJ 11/95) [296]

Religious Cults

2299 Cohen, Daniel. *Cults* (7–10). 1994, Millbrook LB $15.90 (1-56294-324-3). Describes cults throughout American history, including Pilgrims, Quakers, Moonies, and Satanists. Examines the recruiting methods they use. (Rev: BL 11/1/94; BTA; SLJ 2/95; VOYA 2/95) [291.9]

2300 Singer, Margaret, and Janja Lalich. *Cults in Our Midst* (9–adult). 1995, Jossey-Bass $25 (0-7879-0051-6). An analysis of the cult phenomenon. (Rev: BL 4/15/95) [291.9]

2301 Streissguth, Thomas. *Charismatic Cult Leaders* (7–12). 1995, Oliver Press (5707 W. 36th St., Minneapolis, MN 55416) $14.95 (1-881508-21-8). A balanced presentation of a potentially sensational topic. Includes biblical references, where appropriate, in the discussion of various cults and their leaders. (Rev: BL 8/95) [291]

Society and the Individual

General Sociology

2302 Stern, Michael, and Jane Stern. *Jane and Michael Stern's Encyclopedia of Pop Culture: An A to Z Guide of Who's Who and What's What from Aerobics and Bubble Gum to Valley of the Dolls and Moon Unit Zappa* (9–adult). 1992, HarperCollins $25 (0-06-271523-2); paper $17 (0-06-273064-9). Covers all areas of pop culture and offers clues as to why the items belong in the pop pantheon. (Rev: BL 10/1/92) [973.9]

2303 Trimble, Stephen. *The People: Indians of the American Southwest* (9–adult). 1993, SAR $50 (0-933452-36-5); paper $29.95 (0-933452-37-3). Essays and photos illustrating the current economic, political, and social climate of Southwestern Native Americans, based on hundreds of interviews. (Rev: BL 10/1/93; VOYA 4/94) [979]

Government and Political Science

United Nations and Other International Organizations

2304 Jacobs, William Jay. *Search for Peace: The Story of the United Nations* (7–10). 1994, Scribner $14.95 (0-684-19652-2). Describes the formation of the United Nations and discusses the organization's difficulty in maintaining peace. (Rev: BL 7/94; BTA; MJHS; SHS; SLJ 8/94) [341.23]

2305 Janello, Amy, and Brennon Jones, eds. *A Global Affair: An Inside Look at the United Nations* (9–adult). 1995, Jones & Janello (267 Fifth Ave., Rm. 800, New York, NY 10016) $35 (0-9646322-0-9). A celebration in essay form of the political and humanitarian work of the United Nations. (Rev: BL 9/15/95) [341.23]

2306 Woog, Adam. *The United Nations* (6–8). (Overview) 1994, Lucent LB $14.95 (1-56006-145-6). A well-organized overview of the birth, evolution, and historical successes and failures of the United Nations. (Rev: BL 3/15/94; MJHS) [341.23]

International Relations, Peace, and War

2307 Altman, Linda Jacobs. *Genocide: The Systematic Killing of a People* (7–12). (Issues in Focus) 1995, Enslow LB $17.95 (0-89490-664-X). Directs its attention to the history of genocide, the ongoing apartheid between Them and Us that gruesomely reminds us that racism everywhere uses the same stereotypes. (Rev: BL 10/15/95; SLJ 11/95; VOYA 12/95) [364.15]

2308 Barry, Tom, and others. *The Great Divide: The Challenge of U.S.–Mexico Relations for the 1990s* (9–adult). 1994, Grove/Atlantic $24 (0-8021-1559-4). The complex relationships linking Mexico and the United States, placing the North American Free Trade Agreement within the context of this relationship. (Rev: BL 5/15/94) [303.48]

2309 Carter, Jimmy. *Talking Peace: A Vision for the Next Generation* (8–12). 1993, Dutton $16.99 (0-525-44959-0). Carter encourages youth to work for world peace by improving human rights, civil liberties, environmental protection, and aid for the poor. The 1995 revised edition updates events in some of the war-torn areas Carter discussed previously and includes a chapter about his peace missions to Korea, Haiti, Bosnia, and Sudan. Awards: SLJ Best Book. (Rev: BL 8/93; BTA; SLJ 10/93*; SLJ 1/96) [327.1]

2310 Chalberg, John C., ed. *Isolationism* (9–12). (Opposing Viewpoints/American History) 1995, Greenhaven LB $17.95 (1-56510-223-1); paper $9.95 (1-56510-222-3). Excerpts from historical speeches, editorials, and essays espousing and opposing isolationist views. (Rev: BL 3/15/95) [327.73]

2311 Kort, Michael. *The Cold War* (7–12). 1994, Millbrook $16.90 (1-56294-353-7). A suspenseful account of the battle-by-battle events of the cold war, interweaving what we knew then with what we know now. (Rev: BL 4/15/94; SLJ 3/94; VOYA 6/94) [909.82]

2312 Kronenwetter, Michael. *Covert Action* (9–12). 1991, Watts LB $12.90 (0-531-13018-5). An overview of the history and impact of covert activity in the U.S. government from Washington to Reagan. (Rev: BL 3/1/91; SHS; SLJ 5/91) [327.12]

2313 Ousseimi, Maria. *Caught in the Crossfire: Growing Up in a War Zone* (6–10). 1995, Walker LB $20.85 (0-8027-8364-3). Examines the effects of violence on children and how children's perception of the world changes because of it. (Rev: BL 9/1/95; SLJ 9/95; VOYA 12/95) [305.23]

2314 Polesetsky, Matthew, ed. *The New World Order* (7–12). (Opposing Viewpoints) 1991, Greenhaven LB $15.95 (0-89908-183-5); paper $8.95 (0-89908-158-4). (Rev: BL 10/1/91; MJHS; SHS) [327.09]

2315 Rosen, Roger, and Patra McSharry, eds. *Teenage Soldiers, Adult Wars* (9–12). (Icarus World Issues) 1991, Rosen LB $16.95 (0-8239-1304-X); paper $8.95 (0-8239-1305-8). Short stories and essays by teenage soldiers in troubled areas around the world—from Northern Ireland to the Middle East—who express their front-line views of military conflict. Awards: SLJ Best Book. (Rev: BL 6/15/91; SLJ 4/91) [808.8]

2316 Ross, Stewart. *Spies and Traitors* (5–7). (Fact or Fiction) 1995, Millbrook/Copper Beech LB $15.90 (1-56294-648-X); paper $5.95 (1-56294-188-7). An overview of the world of espionage in the past and present. (Rev: BL 11/15/95) [355.3]

2317 Schecter, Jerrold L., and Peter S. Deriabin. *The Spy Who Saved the World: How a Soviet Colonel Changed the Course of the Cold War* (9–adult). 1992, Scribner $14.95 (0-684-19068-0). The story of a Soviet military officer who gave Russian secrets to the United States and Great Britain after World War II. (Rev: BL 3/1/92) [327.12]

2318 Thompson, Leroy. *Dirty Wars: Elite Forces vs. the Guerrillas* (9–adult). 1991, David & Charles $27.95 (0-7153-9441-X). An illustrated history of counterinsurgency warfare and its guerrilla opposition, emphasizing the post–World War II era. (Rev: BL 9/1/91) [355.0218]

2319 Volkman, Ernest. *Spies: The Secret Agents Who Changed the Course of History* (9–adult). 1994, Wiley $24.95 (0-471-55714-5). Forty-five true spy stories featuring famous and less-familiar moles, defectors, and spy masters. (Rev: BL 1/15/94) [355.3]

2320 Wekesser, Carol, ed. *American Foreign Policy* (9–12). (Opposing Viewpoints) 1993, Greenhaven LB $17.95 (0-89908-199-1); paper $9.95 (0-89908-174-6). A completely revamped edition with new opposing viewpoints on the subject of American foreign relations. (Rev: BL 6/1–15/93; MJHS; SLJ 7/93) [217.73]

2321 Woodward, Bob. *The Commanders* (9–adult). 1991, Simon & Schuster $24.95 (0-671-41367-8). How George Bush's national security team decided to wage war against Manuel Noriega and Saddam Hussein. (Rev: BL 6/1/91) [973.928]

United States Government and Institutions

General and Miscellaneous

2322 Hoig, Stan. *It's the Fourth of July!* (5–8). 1995, Dutton/Cobblehill $14.99 (0-525-65175-6). After telling the history behind the Declaration of Independence, Hoig describes different ways the Fourth of July has been celebrated throughout the country since then. (Rev: BL 7/95; SLJ 6/95) [394.2]

2323 Kronenwetter, Michael. *How Democratic Is the United States?* (7–12). (Democracy in Action) 1994, Watts LB $13.93 (0-531-11155-5). Presents the problems affecting politics and government in the United States and discusses proposals for change. (Rev: BL 11/15/94; SHS) [324.6]

2324 Sedeen, Margaret. *Star-Spangled Banner: Our Nation and Its Flag* (9–adult). 1993, National Geographic $37.50 (0-87044-944-3). Legends—such as the tale of Betsy Ross—are sorted from facts in this history of the U.S. flag, from Francis Scott Key to the modern controversy about flag desecration. Color photos. (Rev: BL 10/15/93) [929.9]

The Constitution

2325 Bernstein, Richard B., and Jerome Angel. *Amending America: If We Love the Constitution So Much, Why Do We Keep Trying to Change It?* (9–adult). 1993, Times Books $25 (0-8129-2038-4). A well-documented account of the U.S. Constitution's amendment process, which examines the 27 amendments adopted and many that were rejected. (Rev: BL 3/15/93) [342.73]

2326 Burger, Warren. *It Is So Ordered: A Constitution Unfolds* (9–adult). 1995, Morrow $22 (0-688-09595-X). Brief reviews of 15 Supreme Court cases. (Rev: BL 3/1/95) [342.73]

2327 Dudley, William, ed. *The Bill of Rights* (9–12). (Opposing Viewpoints) 1994, Greenhaven LB $17.95 (1-56510-088-3). Presents differing views on various civil rights issues arising from contemporary interpretations of constitutional intent. (Rev: BL 3/1/94; MJHS; SHS) [342.73]

2328 Dudley, William, ed. *The Creation of the Constitution* (9–12). (Opposing Viewpoints/American History) 1995, Greenhaven paper $9.95 (1-56510-220-7). An in-depth look at the controversies surrounding the creation and ratification of the U.S. Constitution. (Rev: BL 7/95) [342.73]

2329 Gay, Kathlyn. *Church and State: Government and Religion in the United States* (9–12). 1992, Millbrook LB $14.90 (1-56294-063-5). Explores the legal, political, and social questions surrounding the doctrine of separation of church and state, using actual court cases. (Rev: BL 9/1/92; MJHS; SLJ 10/92) [322]

2330 Hentoff, Nat. *Free Speech for Me—But Not for Thee: How the American Left and Right Relentlessly Censor Each Other* (9–adult). 1992, HarperCollins $25 (0-06-019006-X). A report on the assaults on free speech in the United States from all sides. (Rev: BL 8/92; MJHS; SHS) [342.73]

2331 Lang, Susan S., and Paul Lang. *Censorship* (8–12). 1993, Watts $12.90 (0-531-10999-2). Discusses a wide range of issues relating to First Amendment rights, arguing for free exchange of ideas and speech, however distasteful. (Rev: BL 6/1–15/93; BTA; MJHS; SLJ 7/93; VOYA 10/93) [363.3]

2332 Leinwand, Gerald. *Do We Need a New Constitution?* (7–12). (Democracy in Action) 1994, Watts $13.40 (0-531-11127-X). Discusses whether or not the U.S. Constitution is adequate to cope with problems unforeseen by its founders. (Rev: BL 9/15/94; SHS) [342.73]

2333 Leone, Bruno, ed. *Free Speech* (9–12). (Current Controversies) 1994, Greenhaven LB $16.95 (1-56510-078-6); paper $9.95 (1-56510-077-8). Places current censorship battles in a historical context. (Rev: BL 4/15/94; MJHS; SHS) [323.44]

2334 Marsh, Dave, and others. *50 Ways to Fight Censorship and Important Facts to Know about the Censors* (9–adult). 1991, Thunder's Mouth paper $5.95 (1-56025-011-9). A how-to manual on defending freedom of speech. (Rev: BL 6/1/91; SHS; SLJ 3/92) [363.3]

2335 Meltzer, Milton. *The Bill of Rights: How We Got It and What It Means* (6–10). 1990, HarperCollins/Crowell LB $14.89 (0-690-04807-6). Includes the text and a brief explanation of each amendment, how each has worked in practice, and legal cases related to the Bill of Rights. Awards: SLJ Best Book. (Rev: BL 10/1/90; SLJ 5/91*)

2336 Pascoe, Elaine. *Freedom of Expression: The Right to Speak Out in America* (7–10). 1992, Millbrook LB $14.90 (1-56294-255-7). A concise presentation of the debate about such issues as flag burning, Nazi marches, and "hate speech." (Rev: BL 11/15/92; BTA; MJHS; SLJ 12/92) [342.73]

2337 Sherrow, Victoria. *Separation of Church and State* (6–10). (Impact) 1992, Watts LB $12.90 (0-531-13000-2). A summary of church-and-state issues in the United States. (Rev: BL 2/1/92; BTA; SLJ 11/92) [322.1]

2338 Steffens, Bradley. *Censorship* (7–12). (Overview) 1996, Lucent LB $16.95 (1-56006-166-9). Presents a historical overview of the issue and deals with the right of free speech. (Rev: BL 2/15/96; SLJ 3/96)

2339 Steins, Richard. *Censorship: How Does It Conflict with Freedom?* (6–9). (Issues of Our Time) 1995, Twenty-First Century LB $15.98 (0-8050-3879-5). (Rev: BL 7/95) [363.3]

2340 Zeinert, Karen. *Free Speech: From Newspapers to Music Lyrics* (7–10). 1995, Enslow $17.95 (0-89490-634-8). The censorship battle, in the context of various mediums, from a historical perspective. (Rev: BL 4/1/95; SLJ 6/95) [323.44]

The Presidency

2341 Aaseng, Nathan. *You Are the President* (7–10). 1994, Oliver Press (5707 W. 36th St., Minneapolis, MN 55416) LB $14.95 (1-881508-10-2). Devotes one chapter each to a crisis faced by 8 presidents in this century, e.g., Theodore Roosevelt, Eisenhower, and Nixon. (Rev: BL 4/1/94; SLJ 7/94; VOYA 8/94) [973.9]

2342 Andrew, Christopher. *For the President's Eyes Only: Secret Intelligence and the American Presidency from Washington to Bush* (9–adult). 1995, HarperCollins $30 (0-06-017037-9). Analyzes the use of intelligence operations spending of chief executives from George Washington to George Bush. (Rev: BL 1/15/95*) [327.1273]

2343 Black, Christine M. *The Pursuit of the Presidency: '92 and Beyond* (7–12). 1993, Oryx paper $22.50 (0-89774-845-X). Using the presidential campaign of 1992, the author explains the inner workings of a political campaign and how campaigns relate to actual governing. (Rev: BL 4/15/94) [324.973]

2344 Freidel, Frank, and William Pencak, eds. *The White House: The First Two Hundred Years* (9–adult). 1993, Northeastern Univ. $24.95 (1-55553-170-9). Essays that illustrate the evolving function of the White House as both a national emblem and a presidential residence. (Rev: BL 1/1/94) [975.3]

2345 Heller, David. *Mr. President, Why Don't You Paint Your White House Another Color!* (9–adult). 1991, Ballantine $18 (0-345-36551-8). A Harvard psychologist provides the disarming results of his innovative interviewing techniques with children on their attitudes about U.S. and world politics and government. (Rev: BL 9/15/91) [320.973]

2346 Lindop, Edmund. *Presidents by Accident* (7–12). 1991, Watts LB $14.90 (0-531-11059-1). This collective biography focuses on the 9 men who "accidentally" assumed the U.S. presidency, and presents an overview of the status of the vice presidency. (Rev: BL 9/1/91; SLJ 11/91) [973]

2347 Nardo, Don. *The U.S. Presidency* (6–8). (Overview) 1995, Lucent LB $14.95 (1-56006-157-X). (Rev: BL 7/95) [353.03]

2348 Nelson, W. Dale. *The President Is at Camp David* (9–adult). 1995, Syracuse Univ. $24.95 (0-8156-0318-5). The changes that each president has brought to Camp David. (Rev: BL 5/15/95) [973.9]

2349 Paludan, Phillip Shaw. *The Presidency of Abraham Lincoln* (9–adult). 1994, Univ. Press of Kansas $29.95 (0-7006-0671-8). Told from the perspective that saving the Union and freeing the slaves were 2 of the most critical issues in Lincoln's mind. (Rev: BL 5/15/94) [973.7]

2350 Pious, Richard M. *The Young Oxford Companion to the Presidency of the United States* (7–12). 1993, Oxford Univ. $35 (0-19-507799-7). Profiles of all presidents and vice presidents and some first ladies are provided, as well as discussions of elections, policies, and theories about the use of presidential power. (Rev: BL 3/15/94; MJHS; SHS) [351]

2351 Shogan, Robert. *The Riddle of Power: Presidential Leadership from Truman to Bush* (9–adult). 1991, Dutton $19.95 (0-525-24956-7). A political reporter reviews 9 U.S. presidencies, beginning with Truman, and assesses what each achieved. (Rev: BL 1/15/91; SHS) [353.63]

2352 Stuckey, Mary E. *The President As Interpreter-in-Chief* (9–adult). 1991, Chatham House paper $14.95 (0-934540-92-6). Examines the relationship between mass media and modern U.S. presidents. (Rev: BL 3/1/92) [353.03]

Federal Government, Its Agencies, and Public Administration

2353 Ashabranner, Brent. *A New Frontier: The Peace Corps in Eastern Europe* (7–10). Photos. 1994, Dutton/Cobblehill $15.99 (0-525-65155-1). A photo-essay depicting the lives and working environments of Peace Corps volunteers stationed in formerly communist Eastern European countries. (Rev: BL 10/1/94; SLJ 11/94; VOYA 4/95) [361.6]

2354 Bernotas, Bob. *The Department of Housing and Urban Development* (7–10). (Know Your Government) 1991, Chelsea House $14.95 (0-87754-841-2). Describes the cabinet department's history, functions, and structure. (Rev: BL 9/15/91; MJHS) [353.85]

2355 Dio Guardi, Joseph J. *Unaccountable Congress: It Doesn't Add Up* (9–adult). 1992, Regnery Gateway $19.95 (0-89526-521-4). A former congressman highlights government's inaction and mishandling of the budget. (Rev: BL 3/1/92) [336.73]

2356 Fireside, Bryna J. *Is There a Woman in the House . . . or Senate?* (6–10). 1994, Albert Whitman $14.95 (0-8075-3662-8). An examination of the careers of 10 women who have served in Congress. (Rev: BL 5/15/94; BTA; MJHS; SLJ 3/94) [328.73]

2357 Fisher, David. *Hard Evidence: How Detectives Inside the FBI's Sci-Crime Lab Have Helped Solve America's Toughest Cases* (9–adult). 1995, Simon & Schuster $23 (0-671-79369-1). An introduction to the FBI crime laboratory in Washington, D.C. (Rev: BL 3/1/95) [363.2]

2358 Kessler, Ronald. *The FBI: Inside the World's Most Powerful Law Enforcement Agency* (9–adult). 1993, Pocket $22 (0-671-78657-1). The author of *Inside the CIA* now tackles the FBI since 1972, focusing on technology use, espionage, terrorism, and internal politics, such as director Sessions' dismissal. (Rev: BL 9/15/93) [353.0074]

2359 Kohut, John. *Stupid Government Tricks: Outrageous (but True) Stories of Bureaucratic Bungling and Washington Waste* (9–adult). 1995, NAL/Plume paper $8.95 (0-452-27314-5). Anecdotal material about government waste. (Rev: BL 3/1/95) [336.73]

2360 Landau, Elaine. *Big Brother Is Watching: Secret Police and Intelligence Services* (7–12). 1992, Walker LB $15.85 (0-8027-8161-6). Describes the activities and methods of intelligence and police services in several Western and Eastern-bloc nations, including the KGB, the

Mossad, the CIA, and Honduran death squads. (Rev: BL 6/1/92; SLJ 8/92) [363.2]

2361 Rehnquist, William H. *Grand Inquests: The Historic Impeachments of Justice Samuel Chase and President Andrew Johnson* (9–adult). 1992, Morrow $23 (0-688-05142-1). Examines impeachment and the separation of powers as outlined by the U.S. Constitution. (Rev: BL 4/1/92) [353.03]

2362 Ritchie, Donald A. *The Young Oxford Companion to the Congress of the United States* (7–12). 1993, Oxford Univ. $35 (0-19-507777-6). Selected biographies of members of Congress and concise articles on events, documents, policies, and procedures. (Rev: BL 3/15/94; MJHS; SHS) [328.73]

2363 Sandak, Cass R. *Congressional Committees* (7–9). (Inside Government) 1995, 21st Century Books LB $15.98 (0-8050-3425-0). An overview of how congressional committees came into existence, how they control legislation, and their role within Congress.. (Rev: BL 12/15/95; SLJ 1/96)

2364 Sandak, Cass R. *Lobbying* (7–9). (Inside Government) 1995, 21st Century Books LB $15.98 (0-8050-3424-2). A look at how legislation is influenced, including a brief history of lobbies and descriptions of domestic and foreign public-interest groups. (Rev: BL 12/15/95; SLJ 1/96)

2365 Schwarz, Karen. *What You Can Do for Your Country: An Oral History of the Peace Corps* (9–adult). 1991, Morrow $21 (0-688-07559-2). Personal accounts provide a comprehensive look at the Peace Corps from 1960 to 1990. (Rev: BL 5/15/91; SHS) [361.6]

2366 Tally, Steve W. *Bland Ambition: From Adams to Quayle—The Cranks, Criminals, Tax Cheats and Golfers Who Made It to Vice President* (9–adult). 1992, Harcourt/Harvest paper $10.95 (0-15-613140-4). A tongue-in-cheek examination of the nation's 44 Vice Presidents, from John Adams to Dan Quayle. (Rev: BL 9/15/92) [353.003]

State and Municipal Governments and Agencies

2367 Conway, W. Fred. *Firefighting Lore: Strange but True Stories from Firefighting History* (9–adult). 1993, Fire Buff House (P.O. Box 711, New Albany, IN 47151) paper $9.95 (0-925165-14-X). Written by a former fire chief, this history of American firefighting provides short accounts of famous and lesser-known great fires. (Rev: BL 1/1/94) [363.378]

Libraries and Other Educational Institutions

2368 Conaway, James. *The Smithsonian: 150 Years of Adventure, Discovery, and Wonder* (9–adult). 1995, Knopf/Smithsonian $60 (0-679-44175-1). Provides historical background and a multitude of photos, with sidebars about many of the museum's scientific expeditions. (Rev: BL 11/1/95) [069]

2369 Goodrum, Charles A. *Treasures of the Library of Congress* (9–adult). Rev. ed. 1991, Abrams $75 (0-8109-3852-9). An impressive and exciting tour of a major national resource. (Rev: BL 4/1/91; SHS) [027.573]

2370 Weinberg, Jeshajahu, and Rina Elieli Weinberg. *The Holocaust Museum in Washington* (9–12). 1995, Rizzoli $45 (0-8478-1906-X). Insights given into the design, plan, and construction of the museum and its exhibits. (Rev: BL 1/1/96; SLJ 3/96)

The Law and the Courts

2371 Abramson, Jeffrey. *We the Jury: The Jury System and the Ideal of Democracy* (9–adult). 1994, Basic Books $25 (0-465-03698-8). The author proposes jury reform based on examinations of historical and contemporary court cases. (Rev: BL 12/1/94; SHS) [347.73]

2372 Alderman, Ellen, and Caroline Kennedy. *In Our Defense: The Bill of Rights in Action* (9–adult). 1991, Morrow $22.95 (0-688-07801-X). A series of hard-hitting cases challenge the historic meaning of a fundamental American document. (Rev: BL 1/15/91; SHS; SLJ 5/91) [342.73]

2373 Bender, David L., and Bruno Leone, eds. *The Death Penalty* (9–12). Rev. ed. 1991, Greenhaven $15.95 (0-89908-180-0); paper $8.95 (0-89908-155-X). This edition provides a historical perspective on the death penalty and the controversy surrounding it. (Rev: BL 1/15/92; SLJ 7/92) [364.6]

2374 Biskup, Michael D., ed. *Criminal Justice* (9–12). (Opposing Viewpoints) 1993, Greenhaven LB $17.95 (0-89908-624-1); paper $9.95 (0-89908-623-3). A completely revamped edition with new opposing viewpoints on the criminal justice system. (Rev: BL 6/1–15/93; MJHS) [364.098]

2375 Blake, Arthur. *The Scopes Trial: Defending the Right to Teach* (5–7). (Spotlight on American History) 1994, Millbrook LB $15.40 (1-56294-

407-X). Describes the 1925 "Monkey Trial" after teacher John Scopes was arrested for discussing evolution. Examines Darwin's theory, divine creation, and freedom of speech. (Rev: BL 10/15/94; MJHS; SLJ 10/94) [344.73]

2376 Carrel, Annette. *It's the Law! A Young Person's Guide to Our Legal System* (8–12). 1994, Volcano Press (P.O. Box 270, Volcano, CA 95689) paper $12.95 (1-884244-01-7). The book's goal is voter responsibility through understanding of the kinds of laws there are, their developmental history, and how they can be changed. (Rev: BL 2/15/95; VOYA 12/95) [349.73]

2377 Courter, Gay. *I Speak for This Child: True Stories of a Child Advocate* (9–adult). 1995, Crown $24 (0-517-59541-9). Stories of children and adolescents at the mercy of the child welfare system and adults who help them. (Rev: BL 2/1/95) [362.7]

2378 Dershowitz, Alan M. *Contrary to Popular Opinion* (9–adult). 1992, Pharos $22.95 (0-88687-701-6). An outspoken attorney gives his opinons on a variety of timely legal and ethical topics. (Rev: BL 9/15/92*) [814]

2379 Dudley, Mark E. *Gideon v. Wainwright (1963): Right to Counsel* (6–10). (Supreme Court Decisions) 1995, Twenty First Century LB $15.98 (0-8050-3914-7). Looks at how the case was built, argued, and decided and discusses its present-day impact. (Rev: BL 6/1–15/95) [347.3]

2380 Ehrenfeld, Norbert, and Lawrence Treat. *You're the Jury: Solve Twelve Real-Life Court Cases along with the Juries Who Decided Them* (9–adult). 1992, Holt/Owl paper $9.95 (0-8050-1951-0). Presents the testimony and evidence of 12 actual court cases, with analysis, pertinent questions, and the courtroom verdict. (Rev: BL 7/92; SLJ 9/92) [347.73]

2381 Fireside, Harvey, and Sarah Betsy Fuller. *Brown v. Board of Education: Equal Schooling for All* (6–10). (Landmark Supreme Court Cases) 1994, Enslow LB $17.95 (0-89490-469-8). Presents background information, the case itself, and the long-ranging impact it has had on our society. (Rev: BL 11/15/94; MJHS) [344.73]

2382 Gold, Susan Dudley. *Miranda v. Arizona (1966)* (6–10). (Supreme Court Decisions) 1995, Twenty-First Century LB $15.98 (0-8050-3915-5). Provides historical background about the case and discusses its impact today. (Rev: BL 6/1–15/95) [345.73]

2383 Gold, Susan Dudley. *Roberts v. U.S. Jaycees (1984): Women's Rights* (6–10). (Supreme Court Decisions) 1995, Twenty-First Century LB $15.98 (0-8050-4238-5). The American struggle for women's rights is re-examined in light of this case. (Rev: BL 11/15/95) [342.73]

2384 Goodman, James. *Stories of Scottsboro* (9–adult). 1994, Pantheon $27.50 (0-679-40779-0). A narrative history of the infamous Scottsboro case, in which 9 African American youths were falsely accused of raping 2 white women in Alabama in 1931. (Rev: BL 3/15/94) [345.761]

2385 Harrington, Mon. *Women Lawyers: Rewriting the Rules* (9–adult). 1994, Knopf $24 (0-394-58025-7). Through interviews with female graduates of Harvard Law School, the author paints a disturbing picture of sexism in the legal profession and offers practical solutions. (Rev: BL 1/15/94*) [349.73]

2386 Harrison, Maureen, and Steve Gilbert, eds. *Landmark Decisions of the United States Supreme Court II* (9–adult). 1992, Excellent Books (P.O. Box 7121, Beverly Hills, CA 90212-7121) paper $15.95 (0-9628014-2-9). Synopses of important Supreme Court rulings, including decisions on slavery, women's suffrage, Bible reading in public schools, book banning, and the death penalty. (Rev: BL 1/1/92) [347]

2387 Herda, D. J. *Furman v. Georgia: The Death Penalty Case* (6–10). (Landmark Supreme Court Cases) 1994, Enslow LB $17.95 (0-89490-489-2). Summarizes the historical background of this case, the case itself, and the impact it has had on our society. (Rev: BL 11/15/94; MJHS) [345.73]

2388 Milch, David, and Bill Clark. *True Blue: The Real Stories Behind NYPD Blue* (9–adult). 1995, Morrow $23 (0-688-14081-5). The inside dope from the chief scriptwriter of *NYPD Blue*, David Milch, and the "creative consultant" and real detective, Bill Clark. (Rev: BL 11/1/95) [363.2]

2389 O'Neill, Laurie A. *Little Rock: The Desegregation of Central High* (5–7). (Spotlight on American History) 1994, Millbrook LB $15.40 (1-56294-354-5). Describes the integration of public schools in Little Rock, Ark., after the 1954 Supreme Court case *Brown* v. *Board of Education*. (Rev: BL 10/15/94; SLJ 10/94) [373.767]

2390 Osborn, Kevin. *Justice* (5–10). (Values Library) 1992, Rosen LB $13.95 (0-8239-1231-0). Gives a brief history of our system of justice and discusses why in some societies community welfare is all-important while in others individual rights are more important. (Rev: BL 8/92; SLJ 8/92) [320]

2391 Patrick, John J. *The Young Oxford Companion to the Supreme Court of the United States* (7–12). (Young Oxford Companion) 1994, Oxford Univ. $35 (0-19-507877-2). A comprehensive guide to the Supreme Court including biographies, court decisions, concepts, ideas, issues, terms, phrases, procedures, and practices. (Rev: BL 8/94; MJHS; SHS) [347.73]

2392 Rudolph, Robert. *The Boys from New Jersey: How the Mob Beat the Feds* (9–adult). 1992, Morrow $22 (0-688-09259-4). The U.S. government's crackdown on the mob backfires as a result of the longest trial in federal court history. (Rev: BL 3/15/92) [354.73]

2393 Sabbag, Robert. *Too Tough to Die: Down and Dangerous with the United States Marshals* (9–adult). 1992, Simon & Schuster $22 (0-671-66094-2). A history of the oldest federal law enforcement agency and a look at some of its famous cases of the past century. (Rev: BL 3/15/92) [363.2]

Politics

GENERAL AND MISCELLANEOUS

2394 Birnbaum, Jeffrey H. *The Lobbyists: How Business Gets Its Way in Washington* (9–adult). 1992, Times Books $25 (0-8129-2086-4). A look at the activities of several of the thousands of lobbyists representing corporate, trade, and special interests. (Rev: BL 10/15/92; SHS)

2395 Buchwald, Art. *Lighten Up, George* (9–adult). 1991, Putnam $19.95 (0-399-13667-3). These newspaper columns deal with the absurdities of government life during the Bush administration. (Rev: BL 10/1/91) [814]

2396 Buckley, William F. *Happy Days Were Here Again: Reflections of a Libertarian Journalist* (9–adult). 1993, Random $25 (0-679-40398-1). Essays by the conservative TV pundit on subjects ranging from the Thomas/Hill hearings to Elizabeth Taylor's eighth wedding. (Rev: BL 7/93) [814]

2397 Cunningham, Liz. *Talking Politics: Choosing the President in the Television Age* (9–adult). 1995, Praeger $19.95 (0-275-94187-6). Ten well-known media and political personalities discuss the relationship between presidential candidates and television broadcasters. (Rev: BL 4/15/95) [791.45]

2398 Feinberg, Barbara Silberdick. *American Political Scandals: Past and Present* (8–12). 1992, Watts $13.40 (0-531-11126-1). This fact book deals thematically with a variety of political scandals, from Andrew Jackson's "bigamy" in 1791 to Neil Bush's 1991 savings and loan difficulties. (Rev: BL 11/1/92; BTA; MJHS; SLJ 1/93) [320.973]

2399 Garment, Suzanne. *Scandal: The Culture of Mistrust in American Politics* (9–adult). 1991, Times Books $23 (0-8129-1942-4). Catalogs many of the political scandals that occurred during the 1970s and '80s, among them such notabless as Bert Lance, Geraldine Ferraro, and Oliver North. (Rev: BL 12/1/91) [320.973]

2400 Gay, Kathlyn. *The New Power of Women in Politics* (6–9). 1994, Enslow LB $17.95 (0-89490-584-8). Women in federal, state, and local government, with biographical profiles and their particular focus. (Rev: BL 2/15/95; SLJ 3/95) [320]

2401 Hart, Roderick P. *Seducing America: How Television Charms the Modern Voter* (9–adult). 1994, Oxford Univ. $22 (0-19-508656-2). Explores the psychological realm and argues that television changes the way viewers *feel* about politics. (Rev: BL 4/15/94) [324.7]

2402 Melder, Keith. *Hail to the Candidate: Presidential Campaigns from Banners to Broadcasts* (9–adult). 1992, Smithsonian $39.95 (1-56098-177-6); paper $19.95 (1-56098-178-4). A look at the many components of a presidential campaign and how they help determine the course of history. (Rev: BL 5/1/92; SLJ 6/92) [324.973]

2403 Tipp, Stacey L., and Carol Wekesser, eds. *Politics in America* (5–8). (Opposing Viewpoints) 1992, Greenhaven LB $15.95 (0-89908-189-4); paper $8.95 (0-89908-164-9). Strongly differing viewpoints are presented in order to foster critical thinking skills regarding politics. (Rev: BL 5/1/92; MJHS; SHS) [320.973]

2404 Wills, Garry. *Certain Trumpets: The Call of Leaders* (9–adult). 1994, Simon & Schuster $23 (0-671-65702-X). Well-reasoned profiles of outstanding leaders and the nature of their leadership. (Rev: BL 4/15/94; SLJ 11/94) [303.3]

ELECTIONS

2405 Ceaser, James, and Andrew Busch. *Upside Down and Inside Out: The 1992 Elections and American Politics* (9–adult). 1993, Rowman & Littlefield $42.50 (0-8476-7846-6); paper $12.95 (0-8226-3023-0). This presidential-campaign analysis expounds the idea of "outsiderism" to explain the candidates' fluctuating fortunes, discussing Buchanan's and Perot's roles. (Rev: BL 4/15/93) [324.973]

2406 *Choosing the President, 1992: A Citizen's Guide to the Electoral Process* (9–adult). 1992, Lyons & Burford $15.95 (1-55821-171-3); paper $9.95 (1-55821-169-1). The League of Women Voters' guide explains the party system and how the electoral college works, as well as how delegates are selected to attend party conventions. (Rev: BL 4/1/92) [324.973]

2407 Coil, Suzanne M. *Campaign Financing: Politics and the Power of Money* (7–12). 1994, Millbrook $15.90 (1-56294-220-4). Some shocking but well-supported facts about what it takes to run a campaign. (Rev: BL 4/15/94; BTA; MJHS; SLJ 3/94; VOYA 8/94) [324.7]

2408 Gould, Lewis L. *1968: The Election That Changed America* (9–adult). 1993, Ivan R. Dee (1332 N. Halsted St., Chicago, IL 60622-2632) $18.95 (1-56663-009-6). A concise, well-documented overview of the major figures and their campaigns in the 1968 presidential election—at a time of urban riots and the Vietnam War. (Rev: BL 3/1/93) [324.973]

2409 Kerbel, Matthew Robert. *Edited for Television: CNN, ABC, and the 1992 Presidential Election* (9–adult). 1994, Westview $55 (0-8133-1699-5); paper $16.95 (0-8133-1700-2). An analysis of the 1992 presidential election as covered on ABC and CNN television. (Rev: BL 4/15/94) [324.973]

2410 Reische, Diana. *Electing a U.S. President* (7–12). 1992, Watts LB $13.90 (0-531-11043-5). A straightforward look at the presidential campaign process and the people involved in it. (Rev: BL 4/15/92; SLJ 8/92) [324.0973]

2411 Sherrow, Victoria. *Image and Substance: The Media in U.S. Elections* (7–10). 1992, Millbrook $14.90 (1-56294-075-9). Recounts the history of the media's role in political campaigns and describes the increasing influence of image over substance. (Rev: BL 10/1/92; BTA; MJHS; SLJ 11/92) [324.7]

The Armed Forces

2412 Arnold, James R. *Presidents under Fire: Commanders in Chief in Victory and Defeat* (9–adult). 1994, Crown/Orion $27.50 (0-517-58863-3). Four case studies illustrate the point that we often block the decisive behaviors that we admire in our elected officials. (Rev: BL 5/15/94) [353.03]

2413 Ashabranner, Brent. *A Grateful Nation: The Story of Arlington National Cemetery* (5–8). Photos. 1990, Putnam $15.95 (0-399-22188-3). Factual information on the cemetery's history and operations, including stories about the people buried there and anecdotes from visitors and staff. (Rev: BL 2/1/91; MJHS) [975.5]

2414 Howarth, Stephen. *To Shining Sea: A History of the United States Navy, 1775–1990* (9–adult). 1991, Random $25 (0-394-57662-4). A general history of the U.S. Navy with anecdotes and personality sketches. (Rev: BL 4/1/91; SHS) [359]

2415 Kelly, Orr. *Never Fight Fair! Navy SEALs' Stories of Combat and Adventure* (9–adult). 1995, Presidio $22.95 (0-89141-519-X). A history of the Navy SEALs told through reminiscences and anecdotes. (Rev: BL 1/15/95; SLJ 12/95) [359.9]

2416 Kohlhagen, Gale Gibson, and Ellen Heinbach. *The United States Naval Academy: A Pictorial Celebration of 150 Years* (9–adult). 1995, Abrams $49.50 (0-8109-3932-0). A pictorial retrospective of the United States Naval Academy. (Rev: BL 3/15/95) [359]

2417 Melchior, Ib. *Case by Case: A U.S. Army Counterintelligence Agent in World War II* (9–adult). 1993, Presidio $21.95 (0-89141-444-4). A chronicle of Melchior's hair-raising escapades as an agent for the OSS and the U.S. Army in World War II. (Rev: BL 3/1/93) [940.54]

2418 Moran, Tom. *The U.S. Army* (5–8). (Armed Services) 1990, Lerner LB $14.95 (0-8225-1434-6). Overview of the U.S. Army's development from colonial militia to the 1989 action in Panama. (Rev: BL 1/1/91; SLJ 1/91) [335]

2419 Muir, Kate. *Arms and the Woman* (9–adult). 1994, Sinclair-Stevenson $24.95 (1-85619-115-X). The pros and cons of women in the military, especially in the front lines, with both British and American soldiers' reactions to women's service. (Rev: BL 5/1/94) [355.0082]

2420 Reef, Catherine. *Black Fighting Men: A Proud History* (5–8). (African American Soldiers) 1994, Twenty-First Century LB $14.95 (0-8050-3106-5). The heroic action of each soldier is examined, as well as his life before and after the conflict. (Rev: BL 9/15/94; MJHS) [355]

2421 Stewart, Robert. *The Brigade in Review: A Year at the U.S. Naval Academy* (9–adult). 1993, Naval Institute $39.95 (1-55750-776-7). This illustrated volume covers the Annapolis year, from the introduction of the academy plebes to the senior midshipmen's graduation. (Rev: BL 2/1/94) [359]

2422 Stillwell, Paul, ed. *The Golden Thirteen: Recollections of the First Black Naval Officers* (9–adult). 1993, Naval Institute $22.95 (1-55750-779-1). Oral histories of African Americans who faced prejudice and overcame limitations to become the first commissioned officers of their race in the Navy. (Rev: BL 1/15/93; SHS) [359]

2423 Stremlow, Mary V. *Coping with Sexism in the Military* (7–12). 1990, Rosen $14.95 (0-8239-1025-3). An analysis of the military from the perspective of the female recruit. (Rev: BL 2/15/91; SHS) [355]

2424 Sullivan, George. *Modern Combat Helicopters* (7–12). (Military Aircraft) 1993, Facts on File $17.95 (0-8160-2353-0). (Rev: BL 8/93) [358.4]

2425 Waller, Douglas C. *The Commandos: The Inside Story of America's Secret Soldiers* (9–adult). 1994, Simon & Schuster $23 (0-671-78717-9). This history of U.S. military special operations gives an account of the training of special forces and the SEALs and describes their activities in Panama and the Persian Gulf. (Rev: BL 1/1/94) [356]

2426 Wekesser, Carol, and Matthew Polesetsky, eds. *Women in the Military* (9–12). (Current Controversies) 1991, Greenhaven LB $16.95 (0-89908-579-2); paper $9.95 (0-89908-585-7). An up-to-date look at the pros and cons of women serving in the armed forces. (Rev: BL 6/15/92; SHS) [355.4]

Taxes and Public Expenditure

2427 Gross, Martin. *The Government Racket: Washington Waste from A to Z* (9–adult). 1992, Bantam paper $7.99 (0-553-37175-4). This exposé of the bureaucracy and extravagant perks that continue to inflate the federal budget also proposes solutions. (Rev: BL 10/1/92) [336.73]

Citizenship and Civil Rights

Civil and Human Rights

2428 Alderman, Ellen, and Caroline Kennedy. *The Right to Privacy* (9–adult). 1995, Knopf $26.95 (0-679-41986-1). A review of model cases of encroachment on the right to privacy in the workplace, in the press, and by computer. (Rev: BL 10/1/95) [323.44]

2429 Anderson, Kelly C. *Police Brutality* (6–10). (Overview) 1995, Lucent $14.95 (1-56006-164-2). A discussion of the reasons for police behaviors and the stress and danger of the job. (Rev: BL 4/15/95; SLJ 3/95) [363.2]

2430 Bornstein, Jerry. *Police Brutality: A National Debate* (7–12). 1993, Enslow LB $17.95 (0-89490-430-2). The Rodney King affair is used as a prime example of racism and police brutality, as its definition, causes, and solutions are discussed. (Rev: BL 9/15/93; BTA; SLJ 11/93) [363.2]

2431 Bowe, Frank. *Equal Rights for Americans with Disabilities* (9–12). 1993, Watts LB $12.90 (0-531-13030-4). Explores the extent to which access to and attitudes toward education, transportation, housing, and jobs for the physically/mentally disabled have changed in recent years and suggests what's to come. (Rev: BL 4/1/93; MJHS; SHS) [346.7301]

2432 Burns, James MacGregor, and Stewart Burns. *A People's Charter: The Pursuit of Rights in America* (9–adult). 1991, Knopf $30 (0-394-57763-9). An impartial overview of the concept of individual human rights as it has evolved over time, from slavery to abortion. (Rev: BL 11/15/91) [323]

2433 Chafe, William H. *The Road to Equality: American Women since 1962* (8–12). (Young Oxford History of Women in the United States) 1994, Oxford Univ. $20 (0-19-508325-3). (Rev: BL 12/15/94; SHS) [305.42]

2434 Dolan, Edward F. *Your Privacy: Protecting It in a Nosy World* (7–12). 1995, Dutton/Cobblehill $14.99 (0-525-65187-X). A historical and practical look at one of our most important rights. (Rev: BL 1/1/95; SLJ 2/95) [323.44]

2435 Dudley, William, ed. *Police Brutality* (9–12). (Current Controversies) 1991, Greenhaven LB $16.95 (0-89908-580-6); paper $9.95 (0-89908-586-5). Examines the social, economic, and psychological causes of brutality. (Rev: BL 6/15/92; SLJ 3/92) [363.2]

2436 Evans, J. Edward. *Freedom of Religion* (5–8). 1990, Lerner LB $9.95 (0-8225-1754-X). Discusses the history of religious freedom in America. (Rev: BL 1/15/91; SLJ 4/91) [323.44]

2437 French, Marilyn. *The War Against Women* (9–adult). 1992, Summit $20 (0-671-77829-3). A report on the repression of women worldwide, told with a combination of facts and passion. (Rev: BL 3/15/92*) [305.42]

2438 Gottfried, Ted. *Privacy: Individual Rights v. Social Needs* (8–12). 1994, Millbrook LB $15.90 (1-56294-403-7). Discusses debates involving law enforcement, surveillance, abortion, AIDS, and media coverage. (Rev: BL 9/15/94; SHS; SLJ 10/94; VOYA 2/95) [342.73]

2439 Greenberg, Keith E. *Adolescent Rights: Are Young People Equal under the Law?* (6–9). (Issues of Our Time) 1995, Twenty-First Century LB $15.98 (0-8050-3877-9). Integrates historical information with the various positions regarding adolescent rights and offers possible solutions. (Rev: BL 7/95) [346.7301]

2440 Hammer, Trudy J. *Affirmative Action: Opportunity for All?* (8–12). (Issues in Focus) 1993, Enslow LB $17.95 (0-89490-451-5). A look at affirmative action in education and employment, including its history, examples of its successes and failures, statistics, and photos. (Rev: BL 10/1/93; SLJ 12/93; VOYA 2/94) [331.13]

2441 Hempelman, Kathleen A. *Teen Legal Rights: A Guide for the '90s* (7–12). 1994, Greenwood $39.95 (0-313-28760-0). Covers teenage legal issues and concerns, including students' rights, sexual privacy, personal appearance, and juvenile court. (Rev: BL 9/15/94; SHS; VOYA 10/94) [346.7301]

2442 Kronenwetter, Michael. *Under 18: Knowing Your Rights* (7–12). 1993, Enslow LB $17.95 (0-89490-434-5). A discussion of the legal rights of children in such areas as privacy, grooming and dress codes, freedom of the press for school publications, and the classroom. (Rev: BL 2/1/94; BTA; MJHS; SLJ 11/93; VOYA 2/94) [323.3]

2443 Landau, Elaine. *Your Legal Rights: From Custody Battles to School Searches, the Headline-Making Cases That Affect Your Life* (6–10). 1995, Walker LB $15.85 (0-8027-8360-0). A review of advances in protections for children. (Rev: BL 5/15/95; SLJ 8/95) [346.7301]

2444 Meyers, Madeleine, ed. *Forward into Light: The Struggle for Woman's Suffrage* (5–8). (Perspectives on History) 1994, Discovery Enterprises paper $4.95 (1-878668-25-0). (Rev: BL 8/94) [324.6]

2445 Mills, Nicolaus, ed. *Debating Affirmative Action: Race, Gender, Ethnicity, and the Politics of Inclusion* (9–adult). 1994, Dell/Delta paper $10.95 (0-385-31221-0). Essays by various writers look at affirmative action from political, legal, and personal perspectives. (Rev: BL 2/15/94) [331.13]

2446 Payne, Charles M. *I've Got the Light of Freedom: The Organizing Tradition and the Mississippi Freedom Struggle* (9–adult). 1995, Univ. of California $30 (0-520-08515-9). Community organizing for civil rights, the groundwork laid by the local NAACP, and its impact in the Mississippi Delta. (Rev: BL 4/15/95*) [323.0972]

2447 Peck, Rodney. *Working Together Against Human Rights Violations* (7–12). (Library of Social Activism) 1995, Rosen LB $14.95 (0-8239-1778-9). Presents a wide range of human rights issues. (Rev: BL 4/15/95) [323]

2448 Rappaport, Doreen. *Tinker vs. Des Moines: Student Rights on Trial* (7–12). 1993, HarperCollins LB $14.89 (0-06-025118-2). An intriguing account of a recent period of history that conscientiously presents both sides of the issue. (Rev: BL 8/93; MJHS; SLJ 1/94) [342.73]

2449 Shapiro, Joseph P. *No Pity: How the Disability Rights Movement Is Changing America* (9–adult). 1993, Times Books $25 (0-8129-1964-5). A history of the struggle to overcome negative public perception of the disabled. Discusses the movement's diversity and its aggressive attack on myths and stereotypes. (Rev: BL 4/15/93) [323.3]

2450 Walker, Samuel. *Hate Speech: The History of an American Controversy* (9–adult). 1994, Univ. of Nebraska $25 (0-8032-4763-X); paper $11.95 (0-8032-9751-3). The first comprehensive history of hate speech. (Rev: BL 4/15/94) [342.73]

Immigration

2451 Anderson, Kelly C. *Immigration* (6–8). (Overview) 1993, Lucent $14.95 (1-56006-140-5). (Rev: BL 6/1–15/93; MJHS) [325.73]

2452 Andryszewski, Tricia. *Immigration: Newcomers and Their Impact on the U.S.* (7–9). 1995, Millbrook $15.90 (1-56294-499-1). A detailed study of immigration as it pertains to the United States. (Rev: BL 1/15/95; SHS; SLJ 5/95) [304.8]

2453 Ashabranner, Brent. *Still a Nation of Immigrants* (7–12). 1993, Dutton $15.99 (0-525-65130-6). Looks at the present influx of immigrants, talks about why they come, and what they bring with them. (Rev: BL 9/1/93; MJHS; VOYA 2/94) [325.73]

2454 Barbour, William, ed. *Illegal Immigration* (9–12). (Current Controversies) 1994, Greenhaven LB $16.95 (1-56510-072-7); paper $9.95 (1-56510-071-9). An anthology of articles representing a variety of viewpoints regarding the seriousness of the problem of illegal immigration. (Rev: BL 4/15/94; MJHS; SHS) [353.0081]

2455 Brimelow, Peter. *Alien Nation: Common Sense about Immigration and the American Future* (9–adult). 1995, Random $23 (0-679-43058-X). A British immigrant probes the adverse impact of immigration in the United States and the consequences of current immigration policy. (Rev: BL 3/15/95) [304.8]

2456 Cox, Vic. *The Challenge of Immigration* (7–12). (Multicultural Issues) 1995, Enslow LB $17.95 (0-89490-628-3). An introduction to the controversial issues concerning immigration. (Rev: BL 5/1/95; SLJ 5/95) [325.73]

2457 Emsden, Katharine, ed. *Coming to America: A New Life in a New Land* (5–8). (Perspectives on History) 1993, Discovery Enterprises paper $4.95 (1-878668-23-4). Presents diaries, journals, and letters of immigrants from many countries to give insight into their lives. (Rev: BL 11/15/93) [325.73]

2458 Eoyang, Eugene. *Coat of Many Colors: Reflections on Diversity by a Minority of One* (9–adult). 1995, Beacon $24 (0-8070-0420-0). Celebrates diversity, attacks the separation between "us" and "them," and shows that the greatness of the United States has always depended on its immigrants. (Rev: BL 2/1/95) [305.8]

2459 Halliburton, Warren J. *The West Indian–American Experience* (7–10). 1994, Millbrook LB $15.40 (1-56294-340-5). Tells the story of one Jamaican family's emigration to the United States in the 1980s, as well as the history of the Caribbean and emigration to the United States. (Rev: BL 4/1/94; SLJ 7/94) [973]

2460 Hoobler, Dorothy, and Thomas Hoobler. *The Chinese American Family Album* (6–10). 1994, Oxford Univ. $19.95 (0-19-508130-7). The text is excerpted from letters, journals, oral histories, and newspaper accounts of Chinese Americans who describe life in China, their travels to North America, the difficulties encountered, and the jobs they undertook. (Rev: BL 4/1/94; MJHS; SHS; VOYA 2/95) [973]

2461 Katz, William Loren. *The Great Migrations: History of Multicultural America* (7–12). (History of Multicultural America) 1993, Raintree/Steck-Vaughn $15.96 (0-8114-6278-1). Shows the impact that women and minorities have had in the formation and development of this country. (Rev: BL 6/1–15/93; MJHS) [973]

2462 Knight, Margy Burns. *Who Belongs Here? An American Story* (5–7). Illus. 1993, Tilbury $16.95 (0-88448-110-7). The adjustment of a 10-year-old Cambodian refugee to his new home challenges readers to confront difficult questions about immigration and racism. (Rev: BL 3/1/94; SLJ 10/93) [305.895]

2463 Koral, April. *An Album of the Great Wave of Immigration* (5–7). 1992, Watts LB $14.40 (0-531-11123-7). Covering 1890–1924, explains some of the reasons why southern and eastern Europeans left their homelands, the often deplorable shipboard conditions, and the inspections that immigrants were subjected to on Ellis Island. (Rev: BL 1/15/93; MJHS) [304.8]

2464 Krull, Kathleen. *City Within a City: How Kids Live in New York's Chinatown* (5–7). (World of My Own) 1994, Dutton/Lodestar $15.99 (0-525-67437-3). Photo-essays showing what it's like to be an immigrant child in a strongly ethnic neighborhood. (Rev: BL 4/15/94; SLJ 7/94) [305.23]

2465 Krull, Kathleen. *The Other Side: How Kids Live in a California Latino Neighborhood* (5–7). (World of My Own) 1994, Dutton/Lodestar $15.99 (0-525-67438-1). Photo-essays about a Latino neighborhood in California where the young people continue their contact across the border. (Rev: BL 4/15/94; SLJ 6/94) [979.4]

2466 Lee, Kathleen. *Illegal Immigration* (7–12). (Overview) 1996, Lucent LB $16.95 (1-56006-171-5). Distinguishes differences between legal and illegal immigrants and explains why illegal immigrants come to the United States, their impact on the economy, and America's response to them. (Rev: BL 1/1/96; SLJ 3/96)

2467 Leinwand, Gerald. *American Immigration: Should the Open Door Be Closed?* (7–12). 1995, Watts $13.93 (0-531-13038-X). A historical perspective on the current immigration debate reveals the racism that still underlies the melting-pot argument. (Rev: BL 8/95; VOYA 12/95) [325.73]

2468 Miller, Kerby, and Paul Wagner. *Out of Ireland: The Story of Irish Emigration to America* (9–adult). 1994, Elliott & Clark $24.95 (1-880216-25-6). Describes such events as the potato famine, using actual letters written by immigrants and exiles to family members back home. (Rev: BL 9/15/94) [973]

2469 Mills, Nicolaus, ed. *Arguing Immigration: The Debate over the Changing Face of America* (9–adult). 1994, Simon & Schuster/Touchstone paper $12 (0-671-89558-3). Authors such as Toni Morrison discuss immigration, its costs, benefits, and cultural consequences. (Rev: BL 9/1/94) [325.73]

2470 Poynter, Margaret. *The Uncertain Journey: Stories of Illegal Aliens in El Norte* (6–10). 1992, Atheneum $14.95 (0-689-31623-2). The stories of 12 illegal aliens who overcame huge odds in order to succeed in the United States. (Rev: BL 3/1/92) [325.73]

2471 Reimers, David M. *A Land of Immigrants* (5–8). (Immigrant Experience) 1995, Chelsea House $18.95 (0-7910-3361-9); paper $8.95 (0-7910-3373-2). An overview of immigration to the United States and Canada. (Rev: BL 10/15/95) [304.8]

2472 Rosen, Roger, and Patra McSharry, eds. *Border Crossings: Emigration and Exile* (8–12). (Icarus World Issues) 1992, Rosen LB $16.95 (0-8239-1364-3); paper $8.95 (0-8239-1365-1). Twelve fiction and nonfiction selections that illustrate the lives of those affected by geopolitical change. (Rev: BL 11/1/92) [808.8]

2473 Sagan, Miriam. *Tracing Our Jewish Roots* (5–7). (American Origins) 1993, John Muir $12.95 (1-56261-151-8). A description of life in the shtetls of Eastern Europe, the first wave of Jewish immigration, the process of assimilation, and what life is like for Jews in the United States today. (Rev: BL 2/15/94) [973]

2474 St. Pierre, Stephanie. *Teenage Refugees from Cambodia Speak Out* (7–12). 1995, Rosen $14.95 (0-8239-1848-3). The grim stories of the escape from the "killing fields" and powerful testimony to the reality of refugee life. (Rev: BL 5/15/95; SLJ 5/95) [973]

2475 Sawyer, Kem K. *Refugees: Seeking a Safe Haven* (7–12). (Multicultural Issues) 1995, Enslow LB $17.95 (0-89490-663-1). (Rev: BL 6/1–15/95) [362.87]

2476 Strazzabosco-Hayn, Gina. *Teenage Refugees from Iran Speak Out* (7–12). 1995, Rosen $14.95 (0-8239-1845-9). Iranian teens tell their grim stories as powerful testimony to the reality of refugee life. (Rev: BL 5/15/95; SLJ 5/95) [973]

2477 Takaki, Ronald. *A Different Mirror: A History of Multicultural America* (9–adult). 1993, Little, Brown $27.95 (0-316-83112-3). Describes the immigrant experiences of Japanese, African, Irish, and Jewish Americans, exposing the abuses suffered by Native Americans, slaves, and workers who built the country. Awards: Christopher. (Rev: BL 6/1–15/93*; SLJ 1/94) [973]

2478 Takaki, Ronald. *From Exiles to Immigrants: The Refugees from Southeast Asia* (6–10). (Asian American Experience) 1995, Chelsea House $18.95 (0-7910-2185-8). A personal history of the refugee Southeast Asians in America. (Rev: BL 8/95) [978]

2479 Tekavec, Valerie. *Teenage Refugees from Bosnia-Herzegovina Speak Out* (7–12). 1995, Rosen $14.95 (0-8239-1843-2). Short, first-person accounts of those escaping the holocaust engulfing their homeland. (Rev: BL 5/15/95) [305.23]

2480 Ungar, Sanford J. *Fresh Blood: The New American Immigrants* (9–adult). 1995, Simon & Schuster $25 (0-684-80860-9). From the former host of National Public Radio's *All Things Considered* comes this look at the new immigrants—"the illegal aliens"—their relationship to their current communities, and their reception by earlier immigrants. (Rev: BL 10/15/95) [305.8]

Ethnic Groups and Prejudice

General and Miscellaneous

2481 Able, Deborah. *Hate Groups* (8–12). 1995, Enslow LB $17.95 (0-89490-627-5). Traces the hate crime phenomenon through American history and looks at the psychology behind it. (Rev: BL 4/15/95; SLJ 5/95) [305.8]

2482 Banfield, Susan. *Ethnic Conflicts in Schools* (7–12). (Multicultural Issues) 1995, Enslow LB $17.95 (0-89490-640-2). (Rev: BL 6/1–15/95) [371.5]

2483 *CityKids Speak on Prejudice* (7–12). 1995, Random paper $5.99 (0-679-86552-7). Identifies areas in which intolerance is common and cites unexpected examples of discrimination. (Rev: BL 5/1/95) [303.3]

2484 Cook, Bernard A., and Rosemary Petralle Cook. *German Americans* (7–10). (American Voices) 1991, Rourke LB $12.95 (0-86593-140-2). (Rev: BL 2/15/92) [973]

2485 Cozic, Charles P., ed. *Ethnic Conflict* (8–12). (At Issue) 1995, Greenhaven LB $12.95 (1-56510-265-7); paper $7.95 (1-56510-298-3). (Rev: BL 3/15/95) [305.8]

2486 Duvall, Lynn. *Respecting Our Differences: A Guide to Getting Along in a Changing World* (7–12). 1994, Free Spirit Publishing (400 First Ave. N., Suite 616, Minneapolis, MN 55401) $12.95 (0-915793-72-5). Promotes cultural diversity and decries racial prejudice, discussing stereotypes, immigration, and bigotry. (Rev: BL 11/1/94; SHS; VOYA 4/95) [177]

2487 Ezekiel, Raphael S. *The Racist Mind: Portraits of American Neo-Nazis and Klansmen* (9–adult). 1995, Viking $23.95 (0-670-83958-2). Klansmen and neo-Nazis speak of their lives, many times revealing cases of poverty, poor education, medical problems, ignorance, and dysfunctional families as the root of their hatred. (Rev: BL 7/95) [320.5]

2488 Franklin, Paula A. *Melting Pot or Not? Debating Cultural Identity* (7–12). (Multicultural Issues) 1995, Enslow LB $17.95 (0-89490-644-5). Explores cultural identity as a kaleidoscope rather than a melting pot, looking at the histories of different ethnic groups and current opinions about identity. (Rev: BL 6/1–15/95) [305.8]

2489 Gay, Kathlyn. *I Am Who I Am: Speaking Out about Multiracial Identity* (7–12). 1995, Watts LB $13.93 (0-531-11214-4). Gay looks at what it's like to grow up in a mixed-race environment, including cultural, historical, and political perspectives and opinions from experts. (Rev: BL 6/1–15/95; SLJ 8/95) [305.8]

2490 Gillam, Scott. *Discrimination: Prejudice in Action* (7–12). (Multicultural Issues) 1995, Enslow LB $17.95 (0-89490-643-7). (Rev: BL 6/1–15/95) [303.3]

2491 Herda, D. J. *Ethnic America: The North Central States* (5–7). (American Scene) 1991, Millbrook LB $13.90 (1-56294-016-3). (Rev: BL 2/1/92) [572.973]

2492 Herda, D. J. *Ethnic America: The Northeastern States* (5–7). (American Scene) 1991, Millbrook LB $13.90 (1-56294-014-7). A broad overview of the major ethnic groups that have settled in the Northeastern states. (Rev: BL 2/1/92) [572.973]

2493 Herda, D. J. *Ethnic America: The Northwestern States* (5–7). 1991, Millbrook $13.90 (1-56294-018-X). Regions of the country highlighted through unique territorial characteristics. Includes a history of Indians native to the area, followed by a study of white immigration. (Rev: BL 1/15/92; SLJ 3/92) [572.973]

2494 Herda, D. J. *Ethnic America: The South Central States* (5–7). (American Scene) 1991, Millbrook LB $13.90 (1-56294-017-1). Economic and political history of the major ethnic groups in the South Central states. (Rev: BL 2/1/92) [572.973]

2495 Herda, D. J. *Ethnic America: The Southeastern States* (5–7). 1991, Millbrook LB $13.90 (1-56294-015-5). A focus on unique regional characteristics. Includes histories of Indians native to the area and the progressions of white immigrations. (Rev: BL 1/15/92; SLJ 2/92) [572.973]

2496 Herda, D. J. *Ethnic America: The Southwestern States* (5–7). (American Scene) 1991, Millbrook LB $13.90 (1-56294-019-8). Economic and political history of the major ethnic groups in the Southwestern states. (Rev: BL 2/1/92) [572.973]

2497 Katz, William Loren. *Minorities Today* (7–9). (Multicultural America) 1993, Raintree/Steck-Vaughn $15.96 (0-8114-6281-1). Explores minorities and their trials in today's America. (Rev: BL 10/1/93; MJHS) [305.8]

2498 Kranz, Rachel. *Straight Talk about Prejudice* (7–10). (Straight Talk About) 1992, Facts on File $16.95 (0-8160-2488-X). A look at prejudice and how it has affected several racial, ethnic, and religious groups in the U.S. (Rev: BL 5/15/92; SLJ 7/92) [303.3]

2499 Kronenwetter, Michael. *Prejudice in America: Causes and Cures* (7–12). 1993, Watts LB $13.40 (0-531-11163-6). Focuses on race, religion, and ethnicity in an exploration of how prejudice is engendered by fear and fostered by stereotypes. (Rev: BL 2/15/94; VOYA 4/94) [303.3]

2500 Kuklin, Susan. *Speaking Out: Teenagers Take on Sex, Race and Identity* (7–12). 1993, Putnam $15.95 (0-399-22343-6); paper $8.95 (0-399-22532-3). Students are interviewed in order to gauge the prejudices of young adults. (Rev: BL 8/93; BTA; SLJ 7/93) [305.2]

2501 Langone, John. *Spreading Poison: A Book about Racism and Prejudice* (7–12). 1993, Little, Brown $15.95 (0-316-51410-1). Examines the events and social conditions that have led to racial, religious, and sexual discrimination and consequences of prejudice. (Rev: BL 3/15/93; MJHS; SLJ 1/93) [305.8]

2502 McSharry, Patra, and Roger Rosen, eds. *Apartheid: Calibrations of Color* (6–10). (Icarus World Issues) 1991, Rosen LB $16.95 (0-8239-1330-9); paper $8.95 (0-8239-1331-7). Stories, articles, and photos provide insight into South Africa today. Preface by Archbisop Desmond Tutu. (Rev: BL 7/91, SLJ 10/91) [305.8]

2503 Milios, Rita. *Working Together Against Racism* (7–12). (Library of Social Activism) 1995, Rosen $14.95 (0-8239-1840-8). A history of civil rights in America and ways to protect citizens from racism. (Rev: BL 4/15/95) [305.8]

2504 Mizell, Linda. *Think about Racism* (6–10). 1991, Walker LB $15.85 (0-8027-8113-6); paper $8.95 (0-8027-7365-6). Focuses on the experiences of African Americans, Indians, Latinos, and Asian Americans from their early history to the 1960s civil rights movements. (Rev: BL 6/1/92; SLJ 2/92) [305.8]

2505 Schlesinger, Arthur M. *The Disuniting of America* (9–adult). 1992, Norton $14.95 (0-393-03380-5). A famous historian argues against the idea of multiculturalism in the United States. (Rev: BL 1/1/92; SHS) [973]

2506 Streissguth, Thomas. *Hatemongers and Demagogues* (6–10). 1995, Oliver Press (5707 W. 36th St., Minneapolis, MN 55416) $14.95 (1-881508-23-4). A study of the mongers of hate and bigotry, starting with the Salem witch trials and including Louis Farrakhan. (Rev: BL 12/15/95; SLJ 2/96) [920.073]

2507 Winters, Paul A., ed. *Race Relations* (8–12). 1996, Greenhaven LB $19.95 (1-56510-357-

2); paper $11.55 (1-56510-356-4). Confronts the present climate of anger and discusses the pros and cons of affirmative action, among other topics. (Rev: BL 12/15/95; SLJ 1/96) [305.8]

2508 Wright, David K. *A Multicultural Portrait of Life in the Cities* (7–12). (Perspectives) 1993, Marshall Cavendish LB $18.95 (1-85435-659-3). An upbeat discussion of 8 representative cities: New York, Los Angeles, Chicago, Detroit, San Francisco, New Orleans, Miami, and San Antonio. (Rev: BL 3/15/94; MJHS; SLJ 3/94) [305.8]

African Americans

2509 Archer, Jules. *They Had a Dream: The Civil Rights Struggle from Frederick Douglass to Marcus Garvey to Luther King and Malcolm X* (7–12). 1993, Viking $15.99 (0-670-84494-2). A collective political biography of 4 great African American leaders, integrating their stories with a history of civil rights from slavery to the 1960s. (Rev: BL 6/1–15/93; MJHS; SLJ 12/93) [323]

2510 Bing, Léon. *Do or Die: For the First Time, Members of L.A.'s Most Notorious Teenage Gangs . . . Speak for Themselves* (9–adult). 1991, HarperCollins $19.95 (0-06-016326-7). Los Angeles gang members describe their incredibly violent world. Awards: YALSA Best Book for Young Adults. (Rev: BL 7/91*) [364.3]

2511 Carson, Clayborne, and others, eds. *The Eyes on the Prize Civil Rights Reader: Documents, Speeches, and Firsthand Accounts from the Black Freedom Struggle, 1954–1990* (9–adult). 1991, Viking $25 (0-670-84217-6); Penguin paper $14.95 (0-14-015403-5). Contains much of the material that is basic to the American civil rights movement, including speeches by Martin Luther King, Jr. and writings by Malcolm X. (Rev: BL 9/15/91; SHS) [973]

2512 Cohen, Ellis A. *Dangerous Evidence* (9–adult). 1995, Berkley paper $5.99 (0-425-14725-8). Racism within the Marine Corps is shown in the wrongful arrest and conviction of African American Marine Corporal Lindsey Scott. (Rev: BL 5/1/95) [343]

2513 Collins, Charles M., and David Cohen, eds. *The African Americans* (9–adult). 1993, Viking $45 (0-670-84982-0). In choosing African Americans past and present to honor here, the editors selected both famous and everyday heroes to represent with photographs and commentary. (Rev: BL 12/15/93; BTA; SHS) [973]

2514 Dalton, Harlon L. *Racial Healing: Confronting the Fear Between Blacks and Whites* (9–adult). 1995, Doubleday $22.50 (0-385-47516-0). The author's goal is to engage constructive dialogue between European and African Americans. (Rev: BL 9/15/95*) [305.8]

2515 Dolan, Sean. *Pursuing the Dream: From the Selma–Montgomery March to the Formation of PUSH (1965–1971)* (7–10). (Milestones in Black American History) 1995, Chelsea House LB $18.95 (0-7910-2254-4); paper $7.95 (0-7910-2680-9). (Rev: BL 7/95) [323.1]

2516 Dornfeld, Margaret. *The Turning Tide: From the Desegregation of the Armed Forces to the Montgomery Bus Boycott* (7–10). (Milestones in Black American History) 1995, Chelsea House $18.95 (0-7910-2256-0); paper $7.95 (0-7910-2681-7). Surveys this period in African American history. (Rev: BL 8/95) [973]

2517 Feagin, Joe R., and Melvin P. Sikes. *Living with Racism: The Black Middle-Class Experience* (9–adult). 1994, Beacon $25 (0-8070-0924-5). A thorough study of the African American middle class today through interviews with 209 members. (Rev: BL 5/15/94) [305.96]

2518 Hacker, Andrew. *Two Nations: Black and White, Separate, Hostile, Unequal* (9–adult). 1992, Scribner $24.95 (0-684-19148-2). Interprets research results on race relations in the United States. (Rev: BL 2/15/92; SHS) [305.8]

2519 Hamilton, Virginia. *Many Thousand Gone: African Americans from Slavery to Freedom* (5–9). Illus. 1993, Random LB $16.99 (0-394-92873-3). Combining history with personal slave narratives and biography, Hamilton tells of the famous—Douglass, Truth, Tubman—and the obscure—slaves, rebels, and conductors. Awards: SLJ Best Book. (Rev: BL 12/1/92*; BTA; MJHS; SLJ 5/93*) [973.7]

2520 Harrington, Walt. *Crossings: A White Man's Journey into Black America* (9–adult). 1993, HarperCollins $25 (0-06-016558-8). Harrington—a white man married to an African American–describes his year-long journey into black America, from Colonial Williamsburg to Hollywood studios to an Ice-T concert. (Rev: BL 1/1/93; SLJ 7/93) [305.896]

2521 Harris, Eddy. *South of Haunted Dreams: A Ride Through Slavery's Old Back Yard* (9–adult). 1993, Simon & Schuster $19 (0-671-74896-3). The African American author rides a motorcycle through the South to discover his past and the prejudices that shaped him. (Rev: BL 5/1/93) [818.5403]

2522 Harris, Jacqueline L. *History and Achievement of the NAACP* (9–12). 1992, Watts LB $13.40 (0-531-11035-4). A history of the NAACP from its 1908 founding following race riots in Illinois to the retirement of President Benjamin Hooks. Includes photos, bibliography, chronology, and texts of primary documents. (Rev: BL 2/15/93) [973]

2523 Haskins, James. *The Day Martin Luther King, Jr., Was Shot: A Photo History of the Civil Rights Movement* (5–9). 1992, Scholastic paper $5.95 (0-590-43661-9). A photo history of the African American struggle from the time of slavery to the present. (Rev: BL 2/1/92; SLJ 5/92) [323.4]

2524 Haskins, James. *Freedom Rides: Journey for Justice* (5–7). 1995, Little, Brown LB $14.89 (0-7868-2037-3). An overview of the nonviolent civil rights protest movement. (Rev: BL 1/1/95; SLJ 4/95) [323.1]

2525 Haskins, James. *Get on Board: The Story of the Underground Railroad* (5–9). 1993, Scholastic $14.95 (0-590-45418-8). Covers the routes and stations, signs and signals, "conductors," and passengers on the Underground Railroad. Includes slave narratives, timeline, and a bibliography. (Rev: BL 2/15/93; BTA; MJHS; SLJ 2/93; VOYA 10/93) [973.7]

2526 Hauser, Pierre. *Great Ambitions: From the "Separate but Equal" Doctrine to the Birth of the NAACP (1896–1909)* (7–10). (Milestones in Black American History) 1995, Chelsea House $18.95 (0-7910-2264-1); paper $7.95 (0-7910-2690-6). (Rev: BL 2/15/95) [323.1]

2527 Henry, Christopher. *Forever Free: From the Emancipation Proclamation to the Civil Rights Bill of 1875 (1863–1875)* (7–10). (Milestones in Black American History) 1995, Chelsea House LB $18.95 (0-7910-2253-6); paper $7.95 (0-7910-2679-5). (Rev: BL 7/95) [323.1]

2528 Hine, Darlene Clark. *The Path to Equality: From the Scottsboro Case to the Breaking of Baseball's Color Barrier* (7–10). (Milestones in Black American History) 1995, Chelsea House $18.95 (0-7910-2251-X); paper $7.95 (0-7910-2677-9). (Rev: BL 8/95) [973]

2529 Hoobler, Dorothy, and Thomas Hoobler. *The African American Family Album* (6–10). (American Family Albums) 1995, Oxford Univ. LB $22.95 (0-19-508128-5). A social and cultural pictorial history of the African American experience. (Rev: BL 4/15/95; SHS) [973]

2530 Hooks, Bell. *Killing Rage: Ending Racism* (9–adult). 1995, Holt $20 (0-8050-3782-9). Passionate essays about race and racism from a African American and feminist point of view. (Rev: BL 9/15/95) [305.8]

2531 Jordan, June. *Technical Difficulties: African American Notes on the State of the Union* (9–adult). 1992, Pantheon $24 (0-679-40625-5). Essays and speeches by an African American poet present her thoughts on racism, individuality, violence, and patriotism. (Rev: BL 10/1/92) [973.92]

2532 King, Wilma. *Toward the Promised Land: From Uncle Tom's Cabin to the Onset of the Civil War (1851–1861)* (7–10). (Milestones in Black American History) 1995, Chelsea House LB $18.95 (0-7910-2265-X); paper $7.95 (0-7910-2691-4). Examines the major trends and personalities in the struggle to end slavery. (Rev: BL 7/95) [973]

2533 Landau, Elaine. *The White Power Movement: America's Racist Hate Groups* (7–10). 1993, Millbrook $14.90 (1-56294-327-8). Landau presents the historical background of the white supremacist movement and takes a closer look at such organizations as the KKK, skinheads, and WAR. (Rev: BL 12/1/93; BTA; SLJ 1/94; VOYA 2/94) [305.8]

2534 Levine, Ellen. *Freedom's Children: Young Civil Rights Activists Tell Their Own Stories* (6–12). 1993, Putnam $15.95 (0-399-21893-9); 1994, Avon/Flare paper $3.99 (0-380-72114-7). In this collection of oral histories, 30 African Americans who were children or teenagers in the 1950s and 1960s talk about what it was like for them in the South. Awards: Jane Addams Children's Book Award; SLJ Best Book; YALSA Best Book for Young Adults. (Rev: BL 12/15/92*; BTA; MJHS; SLJ 3/93*; YR) [973]

2535 Mabry, Marcus. *White Bucks and Black-Eyed Peas: Coming of Age Black in White America* (9–adult). 1995, Scribner $23 (0-684-19669-7). The *Newsweek* Paris correspondent recalls the women who raised him, their practicality and stubbornness, and their sacrifices and commitment to the dream they had for his future. (Rev: BL 8/95) [305.896]

2536 McKissack, Patricia, and Fredrick McKissack. *The Civil Rights Movement in America from 1865 to the Present* (5–10). 1991, Children's Press $39.93 (0-516-00579-0). This newly updated resource surveys minorities' struggles for equality in the United States. (Rev: BL 3/1/92; BTA; MJHS) [973]

2537 Madhubuti, Haki R., ed. *Why L.A. Happened: Implications of the '92 Los Angeles Rebellion* (9–adult). 1993, Third World Press (7524 S. Cottage Grove, P.O. Box 30, Chicago, IL 60619) paper $14.95 (0-88378-094-1). Probing essays, articles, and poetry generated by the 1992 Los Angeles riots. Contributors include Terry Mc-

Millan and Gwendolyn Brooks. (Rev: BL 3/15/93) [305.8]

2538 Myers, Walter Dean. *Now Is Your Time! The African-American Struggle for Freedom* (6–9). 1991, HarperCollins LB $17.89 (0-06-024371-6). The author traces the path of African Americans through history, interweaving events with biographical sketches of slaves, soldiers, inventors, political leaders, and artists. Awards: Coretta Scott King. (Rev: BL 11/1/91; MJHS; SLJ 3/92) [973]

2539 Newman, Gerald, and Eleanor Newman Layfield. *Racism: Divided by Color* (7–12). (Multicultural Issues) 1995, Enslow LB $17.95 (0-89490-641-0). (Rev: BL 9/15/95) [305.8]

2540 Parks, Rosa, and Gregory J. Reed. *Quiet Strength: The Faith, the Hope, and the Heart of a Woman Who Changed a Nation* (9–adult). 1995, HarperCollins/Zondervan $12.99 (0-310-50150-4). A celebration of Rosa Parks's lifelong commitment to justice for Black Americans. (Rev: BL 1/1/95; SHS) [323]

2541 Powledge, Fred. *We Shall Overcome: Heroes of the Civil Rights Movement* (7–10). 1993, Scribner $14.95 (0-684-19362-0). This history of the civil rights movement: why the movement began, the system of segregation that existed with the government's tacit approval, and the movement's milestones. (Rev: BL 6/1–15/93; BTA; MJHS; VOYA 8/93) [323.1]

2542 Ridgeway, James. *Blood in the Face: The Ku Klux Klan, Aryan Nations, Nazi Skinheads, and the Rise of a New White Culture* (9–adult). 1991, Thunder's Mouth $29.95 (1-560250-02-X); paper $18.95 (1-560250-03-8). Analysis of the racist far right and its organized hatred. (Rev: BL 1/15/91; SHS) [305.8]

2543 Robeson, Paul, Jr. *Paul Robeson, Jr. Speaks to America* (9–adult). 1993, Rutgers Univ. $17.95 (0-8135-1985-3). Essays precisely defining the issues at stake in "the struggle between the mosaic and the melting pot" and the nation's angry cultural wars. (Rev: BL 6/1–15/93) [305.8]

2544 Rogers, James T. *The Antislavery Movement* (7–12). 1994, Facts on File $17.95 (0-8160-2907-5). Traces slavery and its repercussions from 1619 to post–World War II. (Rev: BL 1/1/95; SLJ 12/94; VOYA 5/95) [973]

2545 Segal, Ronald. *The Black Diaspora* (9–adult). 1995, Farrar $27.50 (0-374-11396-3). The first white South African to join the African National Congress and a political exile in Britain, Segal brings a rich personal background to his history of the black experience outside Africa over 5 centuries. (Rev: BL 8/95*) [970.004]

2546 Shipman, Pat. *The Evolution of Racism: Human Differences and the Use and Abuse of Science* (9–adult). 1994, Simon & Schuster $23 (0-671-75460-2). Demonstrates how evolutionary theory has been manipulated to condemn or support racism, the latter most notoriously by the Nazi eugenics movement. (Rev: BL 7/94) [305.5]

2547 Stepto, Michele, ed. *Our Song, Our Toil: The Story of American Slavery As Told by Slaves* (5–7). 1994, Millbrook LB $17.90 (1-56294-401-0). A compact book recounting the story of American slavery as told through excerpts from autobiographies and other historical documents. (Rev: BL 5/15/94; MJHS; SLJ 10/94)

2548 Terkel, Studs. *Race: How Blacks and Whites Think and Feel about the American Obsession* (9–adult). 1992, New Press $24.95 (1-56584-000-3). A provocative look at contemporary race relations. (Rev: BL 1/15/92; BTA; SHS) [305.8]

2549 Walter, Mildred Pitts. *Mississippi Challenge* (7–12). 1992, Bradbury $18.95 (0-02-792301-0). This in-depth history of the civil rights struggle in Mississippi tells how ordinary people worked to change the political system. Awards: Christopher; Coretta Scott King Honor Book. (Rev: BL 11/1/92; MJHS; SLJ 1/93; YR) [305.896]

2550 Weisbrot, Robert. *Marching Toward Freedom.* (7–12). (Milestones in Black American History) 1994, Chelsea House $18.95 (0-7910-2256-0); paper $7.95 (0-7910-2682-5). A description of the milestones of the civil rights movement. (Rev: BL 11/15/94; BTA; SLJ 9/94; VOYA 10/94) [973]

2551 Wells, Diana, ed. *We Have a Dream: African-American Visions of Freedom* (9–adult). 1993, Carroll & Graf $21.95 (0-88184-941-3); paper $11.95 (0-88184-925-1). Collection of 32 selections from renowned figures focusing on the dimensions of the African American dream of a remade world. (Rev: BL 5/15/93) [323.1]

2552 West, Cornel. *Race Matters* (9–adult). 1993, Beacon $15 (0-8070-0918-0). West ruminates on such racial issues as black antisemitism, sexuality, and the lack of quality African American leaders. (Rev: BL 2/15/93; SLJ 12/93) [305.8]

2553 Whittemore, Katharine, and Gerald Marzorati. *Voices in Black and White: Writings on Race in America from Harper's Magazine* (9–adult). 1992, Franklin Square Press (666 Broadway, New York, NY 10012) $21.95 (1-879957-07-8); paper $14.95 (1-879957-06-X). This collection of articles on the American obsession with race includes writings by Twain, Faulkner, James Baldwin, Shelby Steele, and Jesse Jackson. (Rev: BL 11/15/92) [305.8]

2554 Wiley, Ralph. *What Black People Should Do Now: Dispatches from Near the Vanguard* (9–adult). 1993, Ballantine $22 (0-345-38045-2). This essay collection deals with U.S. racism, citing recent events—such as the Thomas-Hill hearings and the Mike Tyson rape case—to support his arguments. (Rev: BL 9/15/93) [305.896]

Asian Americans

2555 Auerbach, Susan. *Vietnamese Americans* (7–10). (American Voices) 1991, Rourke LB $12.95 (0-86593-136-4). Traces the history of Vietnamese Americans, from their first struggles after arriving in the United States to their status in society today. (Rev: BL 2/15/92; SLJ 2/92) [973]

2556 Bandon, Alexandra. *Chinese Americans* (6–12). (Footsteps to America) 1994, Silver Burdett/New Discovery LB $13.95 (0-02-768149-1). A look at the Chinese people in America from their initial immigration in the mid nineteenth century to their current status. (Rev: BL 10/15/94) [973]

2557 Bandon, Alexandra. *Filipino Americans* (6–10). (Footsteps to America) 1993, Macmillan/New Discovery $14.95 (0-02-768143-2). Looks at the Philippines and why immigrants left it, as well as their culture, politics, education, religion, and holidays in the U.S. (Rev: BL 12/15/93; SLJ 12/93) [973]

2558 Kitano, Harry. *The Japanese Americans* (5–8). (Land of Immigrants) 1995, Chelsea House $18.95 (0-7910-3358-9); paper $8.95 (0-7910-3380-5). Provides extensive information on the history of Japanese Americans. (Rev: BL 10/15/95; VOYA 2/96) [305.895]

2559 Rolater, Fred S., and Jeannette Baker Rolater. *Japanese Americans* (7–10). (American Voices) 1991, Rourke LB $12.95 (0-86593-138-0). (Rev: BL 2/15/92) [973]

2560 She, Colleen. *Teenage Refugees from China Speak Out* (7–12). (In Their Own Voices) 1995, Rosen $14.95 (0-8239-1847-5). Interviews with native Chinese teenagers who are now living in the United States. (Rev: BL 6/1–15/95) [305.23]

2561 Stanley, Jerry. *I Am an American: A True Story of Japanese Internment* (5–10). 1994, Crown LB $15.99 (0-517-59787-X). A photo-essay detailing the experiences of Japanese Americans during World War II. Focuses on war hysteria and the unjust use of internment camps. Awards: SLJ Best Book. (Rev: BL 10/15/94*; BTA; MJHS; SLJ 11/94*) [940.53]

2562 Takaki, Ronald. *Ethnic Islands: The Emergence of Urban Chinese America* (6–10). (Asian American Experience) 1994, Chelsea House $18.95 (0-7910-2180-7). First-person accounts of the Chinese American experience in the twentieth century. (Rev: BL 9/15/94; MJHS) [973]

2563 Takaki, Ronald. *From the Land of Morning Calm: The Koreans in America* (6–10). (Asian American Experience) 1994, Chelsea House $18.95 (0-7910-2181-5). Uses oral histories and local documents to challenge stereotypes that plague Korean Americans. Photos and a chronology. (Rev: BL 9/1/94; MJHS; SLJ 9/94; VOYA 12/94) [973]

2564 Takaki, Ronald. *In the Heart of Filipino America: Immigrants from the Pacific Isles* (6–10). (Asian American Experience) 1994, Chelsea House $18.95 (0-7910-2187-4). A historical overview of the Filipino experience in America. (Rev: BL 12/15/94) [973]

2565 Takaki, Ronald. *India in the West: South Asians in America* (6–10). (Asian American Experience) 1994, Chelsea House $18.95 (0-7910-2186-6). A historical overview of the Asian Indian experience in America. (Rev: BL 12/15/94) [970.004914]

2566 Wapner, Kenneth. *Teenage Refugees from Vietnam Speak Out* (7–12). (In Their Own Voices) 1995, Rosen $14.95 (0-8239-1842-4). Interviews with native Vietnamese teenagers who are now living in the United States. (Rev: BL 6/1–15/95) [305.23]

2567 Wilson, John. *Chinese Americans* (7–10). (American Voices) 1991, Rourke LB $12.95 (0-86593-135-6). (Rev: BL 2/15/92) [973]

2568 Wu, Dana Ying-Hui, and Jeffrey Dao-Sheng Tung. *The Chinese-American Experience* (5–7). (Coming to America) 1993, Millbrook LB $14.90 (1-56294-271-9). Discusses why the Chinese came to America, what they left behind, the transpacific journey, what they found here, and how they are doing today. (Rev: BL 6/1–15/93; MJHS; SLJ 7/93*) [973]

Hispanic Americans

2569 Aliotta, Jerome J. *The Puerto Ricans* (5–8). (Land of Immigrants) 1995, Chelsea House $18.95 (0-7910-3360-0); paper $8.95 (0-7910-3382-1). Provides an extensive history of Puerto Ricans as Americans. (Rev: BL 10/15/95) [305.868]

2570 Bandon, Alexandra. *Mexican Americans* (6–10). (Footsteps to America) 1993, Macmillan/New Discovery $14.95 (0-02-768142-4). Looks at

Mexico and the culture of immigrants to the United States. Includes first-person narratives of immigrant experiences. (Rev: BL 12/15/93; SLJ 12/93; VOYA 2/94) [305.868]

2571 Catalano, Julie. *The Mexican Americans* (5–8). (Immigrant Experience) 1995, Chelsea House $18.95 (0-7910-3359-7); paper $7.95 (0-7910-3381-3). Following a brief survey of Mexico's history, traces the growth of immigration of Mexicans to the U.S. from the late 1800s to the present. (Rev: BL 11/15/95; SLJ 1/96) [973]

2572 Cerar, K. Melissa. *Teenage Refugees from Nicaragua Speak Out* (7–12). (In Their Own Voices) 1995, Rosen $14.95 (0-8239-1849-1). (Rev: BL 6/1–15/95) [973]

2573 Cockcroft, James D. *The Hispanic Struggle for Social Justice: The Hispanic Experience in the Americas* (8–12). (Hispanic Experience in the Americas) 1994, Watts LB $14.84 (0-531-11185-7). Discusses the diverse experiences of Mexican Americans, Puerto Ricans, and other Latinos and relates their ethnic history to national issues of labor, immigration, civil rights, and feminism. (Rev: BL 2/1/95; SHS) [305.868]

2574 Cockcroft, James D. *Latinos in the Making of the United States* (8–12). (Hispanic Experience in the Americas) 1995, Watts LB $14.84 (0-531-11209-8). Shows the important roles Latino immigrants have played in such areas as farm work, health care, and the arts. (Rev: BL 7/95; SLJ 11/95) [973]

2575 Garza, Hedda. *Latinas: Hispanic Women in the United States* (8–12). (Hispanic Experience in the Americas) 1994, Watts LB $14.84 (0-531-11186-5). Blasts the old stereotypes of weak, submissive, housebound women dominated by macho men. (Rev: BL 2/1/95; SHS) [305.48]

2576 Hoobler, Dorothy, and Thomas Hoobler. *The Mexican American Family Album* (6–10). (American Family Albums) 1994, Oxford Univ. LB $22.95 (0-19-508129-3). A clear, informative history of Mexican Americans. (Rev: BL 4/15/95; MJHS; SHS) [973]

2577 Lannert, Paula. *Mexican Americans* (7–10). (American Voices) 1991, Rourke LB $12.95 (0-86593-139-9). Traces the history of Mexican Americans, from the earliest visitors to America to the group's present status. (Rev: BL 2/15/92) [973]

2578 Martinez, Elizabeth Coonrod. *The Mexican-American Experience* (5–7). (Coming to America) 1995, Millbrook LB $15.90 (1-56294-515-7). (Rev: BL 6/1–15/95) [973]

2579 Mendez, Adriana. *Cubans in America* (5–7). (In America) 1994, Lerner LB $11.96 (0-8225-1953-4). A brief but accurate overview of Cuban history, Cuban immigration to the United States, and Cuban American culture. (Rev: BL 8/94) [973]

2580 Novas, Himilce. *Everything You Need to Know about Latino History* (9–adult). 1994, NAL/Plume paper $11.95 (0-452-27100-2). Surveys Latino culture and contributions to history, including both the Spanish-American War and the Mexican War. (Rev: BL 9/15/94; BTA) [973]

2581 Stavans, Ilan. *The Hispanic Condition: Reflections on Culture and Identity in America* (9–adult). 1994, HarperCollins $25 (0-06-017005-0). Autobiographical essays concerning the author's culture and identity as a Jewish Mexican American. (Rev: BL 3/15/95) [305.868]

Indians and Other Native Americans

2582 Curtis, Edward. *Native Nations: First Americans as Seen by Edward S. Curtis* (9–adult). 1993, Little, Brown/Bulfinch $60 (0-8212-2052-7). One hundred plates and excerpts of Curtis's work in documenting the tribes of North America illustrate this downsizing of the original. (Rev: BL 11/15/93) [306]

2583 Fixico, Donald L. *Urban Indians* (7–12). (Indians of North America) 1991, Chelsea House $17.95 (1-55546-732-6). A challenge to current stereotypes about Native Americans and their role in modern society. (Rev: BL 7/91; MJHS; SLJ 12/91) [307.76]

2584 Green, Rayna. *Women in American Indian Society* (7–12). 1992, Chelsea House LB $17.95 (1-55546-734-2). Discusses the strong role of women before Europeans came to the United States and their changing role as Indians were stripped of their land and forced to assimilate in white culture. Awards: SLJ Best Book. (Rev: BL 9/1/92; MJHS; SLJ 8/92*) [305.48]

2585 Hall, Edward T. *West of the Thirties: A Story of Discoveries Among the Navajo and Hopi* (9–adult). 1994, Doubleday $21.95 (0-385-42421-3). An anthropologist recounts his experiences as a young man working on Arizona's Navajo and Hopi reservations, 1933–1937. (Rev: BL 3/1/94) [973]

2586 Hoig, Stan. *People of the Sacred Arrows: The Southern Cheyenne Today* (6–8). 1992, Dutton/Cobblehill $15 (0-525-65088-1). Portrayal of modern life of the Southern Cheyenne, including some of the problems they face: poverty, illness, etc. (Rev: BL 9/1/92; BTA; SLJ 11/92; YR) [976.6]

2587 Kane, Joe. *Savages* (9–adult). 1995, Knopf $25 (0-679-41191-7). An environmentalist recounts recent journeys to Amazonia, where he investigated the issues and parties involved in the destruction of the rain forest. (Rev: BL 9/15/95*) [333.3]

Jews

2588 Hoobler, Dorothy, and Thomas Hoobler. *The Jewish American Family Album* (6–10). (American Family Albums) 1995, Oxford Univ. LB $22.95 (0-19-508135-8). The history, sociology, and pivotal people of the Jewish American experience. (Rev: BL 11/15/95) [973]

2589 Muggamin, Howard. *The Jewish Americans* (5–8). (Immigrant Experience) 1995, Chelsea House $19.95 (0-7910-3365-1); paper $8.95 (0-7910-3387-2). (Rev: BL 11/15/95; MJHS) [973]

Other Ethnic Groups

2590 Ashabranner, Brent. *An Ancient Heritage: The Arab-American Minority* (5–9). Photos. 1991, HarperCollins LB $14.89 (0-06-020049-9). Interviews with a wide variety of Arab Americans. (Rev: BL 3/15/91; MJHS) [973]

2591 Bandon, Alexandra. *West Indian Americans* (6–12). (Footsteps to America) 1994, Silver Burdett/New Discovery LB $13.95 (0-02-768148-3). Describes immigration from the West Indies. (Rev: BL 10/15/94) [973]

2592 Brooks, Geraldine. *Nine Parts of Desire: The Hidden World of Islamic Women* (9–adult). 1995, Doubleday/Anchor $22.95 (0-385-47576-4). Journalist Brooks wore a "hijab," the black veil worn by Islamic women, to discover how they are treated in various Islamic countries. (Rev: BL 9/15/94) [305.48]

2593 Cavan, Seamus. *The Irish-American Experience* (5–7). (Coming to America) 1993, Millbrook LB $14.90 (1-56294-218-2). Discusses why the Irish came to the United States, what they left behind, the transatlantic journey, what they found here, and how they are doing today. (Rev: BL 6/1–15/93; MJHS) [973]

2594 Hoobler, Dorothy, and Thomas Hoobler. *The Irish American Family Album* (6–10). (American Family Albums) 1995, Oxford Univ. $19.95 (0-19-509461-1). An arresting picture of what it has meant to be of Irish heritage in America. (Rev: BL 3/15/95; SHS) [973]

2595 Hoobler, Dorothy, and Thomas Hoobler. *The Italian American Family Album* (6–10). (American Family Albums) 1994, Oxford Univ. LB $22.95 (0-19-508126-9). Traces the Italian American experience through diaries, letters, and oral histories. (Rev: BL 5/15/94; MJHS; SHS) [973]

2596 Kuropas, Myron B. *Ukrainians in America* (6–12). (In America) Rev. ed. 1996, Lerner LB $13.13 (0-8225-1043-X). An account of Ukrainian immigrants in the United States, as well as a historical overview of Ukrainians who struggled under centuries of foreign domination. (Rev: BL 3/15/96; SLJ 3/96)

2597 Lee, Kathleen. *Tracing Our Italian Roots* (5–7). (American Origins) 1993, John Muir $12.95 (1-56261-149-6). Describes life in Italy, the causes for immigration to the United States, and the challenges of assimilation. (Rev: BL 2/15/94) [973]

2598 Magocsi, Paul R. *The Russian Americans* (5–8). (Immigrant Experience) Rev. ed. 1995, Chelsea House $19.95 (0-7910-3367-8). A coherent survey of Russian/Soviet history provides the background for understanding the reasons for the waves of immigrants to the United States. (Rev: BL 11/15/95; MJHS; SLJ 1/96) [973]

2599 Moscinski, Sharon. *Tracing Our Irish Roots* (5–7). (American Origins) 1993, John Muir $12.95 (1-56261-148-8). Describes what life is like in Ireland, why the Irish have immigrated to the United States, and the challenges of assimilation. (Rev: BL 2/15/94) [973]

2600 Tekavec, Valerie. *Teenage Refugees from Haiti Speak Out* (7–12). (In Their Own Voices) 1995, Rosen $14.95 (0-8239-1844-0). Interviews with native Haitian teenagers who are now living in the United States. (Rev: BL 6/1–15/95) [305.23]

2601 Watts, J. F. *The Irish Americans* (5–8). (Immigrant Experience) 1995, Chelsea House $18.95 (0-7910-3366-X); paper $8.95 (0-7910-3388-0). (Rev: BL 10/15/95) [973]

2602 Witkoski, Michael. *Italian Americans* (7–10). (American Voices) 1991, Rourke LB $12.95 (0-86593-137-2). Traces the history of Italian Americans, from early explorers to the group's present status. (Rev: BL 2/15/92; SLJ 2/92) [973]

2603 Zamenova, Tatyana. *Teenage Refugees from Russia Speak Out* (7–12). (In Their Own Voices) 1995, Rosen $14.95 (0-8239-1846-7). (Rev: BL 6/1–15/95) [973]

Social Concerns and Conflicts

General and Miscellaneous

2604 Cozic, Charles P., and Paul A. Winters, eds. *Gambling* (7–12). (Current Controversies) 1995, Greenhaven LB $17.95 (1-56510-234-7); paper $9.95 (1-56510-235-5). A collection of differing viewpoints regarding gambling. (Rev: BL 8/95) [363.4]

2605 Davis, Bertha. *Gambling in America: A Growth Industry* (9–adult). 1992, Watts LB $12.90 (0-531-13021-5). Provides a brief history of gaming, then explains odds, various games (casino gambling games, lotteries, etc.), how people bet and why they gamble, and implications of states' legalization. (Rev: BL 11/15/92; MJHS; SHS; SLJ 12/92) [795]

2606 Hackman, Peggy, and Don Oldenburg, eds. *Dear Mr. President* (5–7). 1993, Avon $4 (0-380-77473-9). A collection of children's letters to President Clinton expressing their concerns on major national issues. (Rev: BL 1/15/94) [816]

2607 Hutchinson, Earl Ofari. *Beyond O.J.: Race, Sex, and Class Lessons for America* (9–adult). 1996, Middle Passage $19.95 (1-881032-12-4); paper $14.95 (0-881032-07-8). A discussion about the implications of the Simpson case regarding race, class, and sex in America. (Rev: BL 12/15/95) [305.8]

2608 Hyde, Margaret O. *Gambling: Winners and Losers* (6–9). 1995, Millbrook LB $16.40 (1-56294-532-7). A general overview of gambling as a sociopolitical issue. (Rev: BL 12/15/95; SLJ 3/96) [363.4]

2609 Maquire, Stephen, and Bonnie Wren, eds. *Torn by the Issues: An Unbiased Review of the Watershed Issues in American Life* (9–adult). 1994, Fithian (P.O. Box 1525, Santa Barbara, CA 93102) paper $15.95 (1-56474-093-5). Presents the opposing viewpoints surrounding our most contentious social issues: abortion, AIDS, animal rights, global warming, homelessness, gun control, welfare, etc. (Rev: BL 7/94) [306]

2610 Rosen, Roger, and Patra McSharry Sevastiades, eds. *On Heroes and the Heroic: In Search of Good Deeds* (7–12). (Icarus World Issues) 1993, Rosen LB $16.95 (0-8239-1384-8); paper $8.95 (0-8239-1385-6). This installment of the series asserts, through 9 fiction and nonfiction pieces, that heroes are more media hype than reality. (Rev: BL 9/15/93; SLJ 1/94; VOYA 12/93) [808.8]

2611 Weiss, Ann E. *Lotteries: Who Wins, Who Loses?* (8–12). (Issues in Focus) 1991, Enslow LB $17.95 (0-89490-242-3). This analysis of games of chance covers historical aspects of betting from colonial times to modern-day "lottomania," as well as the social and political issues surrounding gambling. (Rev: BL 11/15/91; MJHS; SLJ 11/91) [336.1]

2612 Wekesser, Carol, ed. *Violence in the Media* (7–12). (Current Controversies) 1995, Greenhaven LB $17.95 (1-56510-237-1); paper $9.95 (1-56510-236-3). A collection of differing viewpoints regarding violence in the media. (Rev: BL 8/95; SHS) [303.6]

Environmental Issues

General and Miscellaneous

2613 Anderson, Joan. *Earth Keepers* (5–7). (Gulliver Green Books) Illus. 1993, Harcourt $17.95

(0-15-242199-8). A photo-essay focusing on persons whose daily lives are devoted to restoring the earth and protecting wildlife. (Rev: BL 10/15/93; MJHS) [363.7]

2614 Andryszewski, Tricia. *The Environment and the Economy: Planting the Seeds for Tomorrow's Growth* (7–12). 1995, Millbrook $16.40 (1-56294-524-6). Traces the emergence of environment-versus-economy questions, with a historical perspective. (Rev: BL 12/1/95; SLJ 11/95) [363.7]

2615 Billings, Charlene W. *Pesticides: Necessary Risk* (7–12). (Issues in Focus) 1993, Enslow LB $17.95 (0-89490-299-7). Examines the history and uses of pesticides, their advantages and disadvantages, and their regulation in the United States. (Rev: BL 3/15/93) [363.17]

2616 Caldicott, Helen. *If You Love This Planet: A Plan to Heal the Earth* (9–adult). 1992, Norton paper $19.95 (0-393-30835-9). Presents, in medical terms, the diagnosis and tough cure for an ailing planet Earth. (Rev: BL 3/1/92*; BTA) [363.7]

2617 Fumento, Michael. *Science under Siege* (9–adult). 1993, Morrow $25 (0-688-10795-8). Investigates the conflicting claims of politicians, scientists, and others who argue about pressing environmental issues. (Rev: BL 1/1/93*) [363.1]

2618 Gay, Kathlyn. *Cleaning Nature Naturally* (6–12). 1991, Walker LB $16.85 (0-8027-8119-5). This discussion of the uses of chemicals in pest control techniques advocates environmentally sensitive management practices. (Rev: BL 11/15/91; MJHS; SLJ 12/91) [632]

2619 Goldsmith, Edward, and others. *Imperiled Planet: Restoring Our Endangered Ecosystems* (9–adult). 1990, MIT $29.95 (0-262-07132-0). An in-depth overview of current ecological problems. (Rev: BL 1/1/91; SHS) [363.7]

2620 Harms, Valerie. *The National Audubon Society Almanac of the Environment: The Ecology of Everyday Life* (9–adult). 1994, Putnam paper $16.95 (0-399-13942-7). The ecology of the body, the home, the community, the ocean, and the land and the complex politics of environmentalism. (Rev: BL 3/15/94; SHS; SLJ 10/94) [363.7]

2621 Hirschi, Ron. *Save Our Prairies and Grasslands* (5–8). Illus. 1994, Doubleday $17.95 (0-385-31149-4); paper $9.95 (0-385-31199-0). Divides a particular environment in the Midwest and West into subgroups, describes the habitat, and suggests preservation projects. (Rev: BL 4/15/94; MJHS; SLJ 5/94) [574.5]

2622 Hirschi, Ron. *Save Our Wetlands* (5–8). Illus. 1994, Doubleday $17.95 (0-385-31152-4); paper $9.95 (0-385-31197-4). Covers many regions of the United States, describing habitats and suggesting preservation projects. (Rev: BL 4/15/94; MJHS; SLJ 5/94) [574.5]

2623 Lee, Sally. *Pesticides* (9–12). 1991, Watts LB $12.90 (0-531-13017-7). Traces the development, uses, and risks of pesticides and also presents alternatives to chemical pest control, including biological, physical, mechanical, and cultural controls. (Rev: BL 4/15/91; SHS; SLJ 8/91) [363.17]

2624 Murphy, Pamela, and others. *The Garbage Primer: A Handbook for Citizens* (9–adult). 1993, Lyons & Burford paper $10.95 (1-55821-250-7). This describes how we deal with garbage and what we need to know to dispose of it responsibly. Includes a disposal milestone timeline. (Rev: BL 11/15/93) [363.72]

2625 Robbins, Ocean, and Sol Solomon. *Choices for Our Future* (7–12). 1994, Book Publishing (P.O. Box 99, Summertown, TN 38483) paper $9.95 (1-57067-002-1). The founders of Youth for Environmental Sanity believe that young people have an influence in adopting more ecologically responsible lifestyles. (Rev: BL 3/15/95) [363.7]

2626 Rosen, Roger, and Patra McSharry, eds. *Planet Earth: Egotists and Ecosystems* (9–12). 1991, Rosen LB $16.95 (0-8239-1334-1); paper $8.95 (0-8239-1335-X). Short stories, articles, and photo-essays addressing environmental abuse. (Rev: BL 2/15/92; SLJ 4/92) [809]

2627 Rubin, Charles T. *The Green Crusade: Rethinking the Roots of Environmentalism* (9–adult). 1994, Free Press $22.95 (0-02-927525-3). A critical examination of the utopianism of the environmental movement and the anticapitalist ethics of the leading authors in the field. (Rev: BL 2/1/94) [363.7]

2628 Student Environmental Action Coalition. *The Student Environmental Action Guide: By the Student Environmental Action Coalition (SEAC)* (9–adult). 1991, EarthWorks Press (1400 Shattuck Ave., P.O. Box 25, Berkeley, CA 94709) paper $4.95 (1-879682-04-4). This brief manual describing opportunities for recycling in the campus environment includes campus success stories that encourage collective student action. (Rev: BL 10/15/91) [363.7]

2629 Tesar, Jenny. *Global Warming* (6–9). (Our Fragile Planet) 1991, Facts on File $18.95 (0-8160-2490-1). The causes and probable future of global warming, with background information on the atmosphere and ways individuals and governments can affect change. (Rev: BL 11/1/91; MJHS; SLJ 11/91) [363.73]

2630 Wade, Nicholas, and others, eds. *The New York Times Book of Science Literacy, Vol. 2: The Environment from Your Backyard to the Ocean Floor* (9–adult). 1994, Times Books $25 (0-8129-2215-8). Pieces by 28 *New York Times* writers on the facts and controversies surrounding environmental issues, including pollution, endangered species, and habitat restoration. (Rev: BL 7/94; SHS) [363.7]

2631 Yount, Lisa. *Pesticides* (5–8). (Overview) 1995, Lucent LB $14.95 (1-56006-156-1). The history and controversy over pesticides are looked into from an ecologically friendly approach, yet explaining economic motivations as well. (Rev: BL 6/1–15/95; SLJ 5/95) [363.73]

Pollution

2632 Asimov, Isaac, and Frederik Pohl. *Our Angry Earth* (9–adult). 1991, Tor $19.95 (0-312-85252-5). Two famous science fiction authors have created a handbook for environmental damage control and repair. (Rev: BL 9/15/91) [363.7]

2633 Blashfield, Jean F., and Wallace B. Black. *Oil Spills* (5–8). (Saving Planet Earth) 1991, Children's Press LB $18.95 (0-516-05508-9). A close look at this huge threat to the environment, along with suggestions on getting involved in solving the problem. (Rev: BL 3/1/92; SLJ 5/92) [363.73]

2634 Bullard, Robert D., ed. *Unequal Protection: Environmental Justice and Communities of Color* (9–adult). 1994, Sierra Club $25 (0-87156-450-5). Academics, journalists, activists, and others provide details on environmental racism throughout the United States. (Rev: BL 5/1/94) [363.703]

2635 Carlson-Finnerty, La Vonne. *Environmental Health* (7–12). (Encyclopedia of Health) 1994, Chelsea House $19.95 (0-7910-0082-6). (Rev: BL 8/94; SHS) [616.9]

2636 Carr, Terry. *Spill! The Story of the Exxon Valdez* (5–7). 1991, Watts LB $18.90 (0-531-10998-4). A straightforward, nonpolitical account of one of the worst ecological disasters of our time, covering the collision, the oil spread, and the effects on wildlife and the coast. Awards: SLJ Best Book. (Rev: BL 6/1/91; SLJ 7/91*)

2637 Collinson, Alan. *Pollution* (5–8). (Repairing the Damage) 1992, Macmillan/New Discovery LB $13.95 (0-02-722995-5). A historical overview covering such topics as nuclear wastes, river pollution, overpopulation, and the like. (Rev: BL 9/15/92) [363.73]

2638 Cozic, Charles P., ed. *Pollution* (9–12). (Current Controversies) 1994, Greenhaven LB $16.95 (1-56510-076-X); paper $9.95 (1-56510-075-1). (Rev: BL 4/15/94; SHS) [363.73]

2639 Dolan, Edward F. *Our Poisoned Sky* (7–12). 1991, Dutton/Cobblehill $14.95 (0-525-65056-3). A discussion of 4 different aspects of polluted air: the pollutants, the ozone layer, acid rain, and the greenhouse effect. (Rev: BL 3/1/91; SLJ 7/91) [363.73]

2640 Dolan, Edward F., and Margaret M. Scariano. *Nuclear Waste: The 10,000-Year Challenge* (8–12). 1990, Watts LB $13.90 (0-531-10943-7). A discussion of the challenges of radioactive waste disposal. (Rev: BL 3/15/91; SHS; SLJ 2/91) [363.72]

2641 Ganeri, Anita. *Rivers, Ponds and Lakes* (5–8). (Ecology Watch) 1992, Dillon LB $13.95 (0-87518-497-9). (Rev: BL 11/1/92) [574.5]

2642 Gay, Kathlyn. *Air Pollution* (7–12). (Impact) 1991, Watts LB $12.90 (0-531-13002-9). An examination of the alarming ecological effects and health risks of atmospheric pollution and an outline of combative strategies. (Rev: BL 12/1/91; MJHS; SHS) [363.73]

2643 Gay, Kathlyn. *Global Garbage: Exporting Trash and Toxic Waste* (9–12). 1992, Watts $13.40 (0-531-13009-6). Documents the many ways humans—through greed, ignorance, or overconsumption—have polluted land, sea, air, and outer space. (Rev: BL 3/15/93; BTA; MJHS; SHS) [363.72]

2644 Gay, Kathlyn. *Water Pollution* (7–12). 1990, Watts LB $12.90 (0-531-10949-6). Veteran environmental-affairs writer discusses threats to water supplies and methods of protection. (Rev: BL 1/1/91; SHS; SLJ 4/91) [363.73]

2645 Hare, Tony. *Habitat Destruction* (5–8). (Save Our Earth) 1991, Gloucester LB $11.90 (0-531-17307-0). Basic facts on who and what is destroying the habitat. (Rev: BL 3/1/92) [333.95]

2646 Hare, Tony. *Polluting the Air* (5–8). (Save Our Earth) 1992, Gloucester LB $11.90 (0-531-17346-1). (Rev: BL 10/1/92) [363.73]

2647 Hare, Tony. *Toxic Waste* (5–8). (Save Our Earth) Illus. 1991, Gloucester LB $11.90 (0-531-17308-9). Basic information about toxic waste. (Rev: BL 3/1/92) [363.72]

2648 Lucas, Eileen. *Acid Rain* (5–8). (Saving Planet Earth) 1991, Children's Press LB $18.95 (0-516-05503-8). Thought-provoking study of the environmental problem. (Rev: BL 3/1/92) [363.73]

2649 Mowrey, Marc, and Tim Redmond. *Not in Our Backyard: The People and Events That Shaped America's Modern Environmental Movement* (9–adult). 1993, Morrow $23 (0-688-10644-7). The growth of the evnironmental movement is looked at from a personal approach, as each chapter profiles someone who fought for a clean environment. (Rev: BL 12/1/93) [363.7]

2650 Nadis, Steve, and others. *Car Trouble* (9–adult). (Guides to the Environment) 1993, Beacon $27.50 (0-8070-8522-7); paper $12 (0-8070-8523-5). Addresses the impact of automobile pollution on the Earth's resources and examines strategies to alleviate the problem. (Rev: BL 1/15/93) [363.73]

2651 O'Neill, Mary. *Air Scare* (5–7). Illus. 1991, Troll LB $9.89 (0-8167-2082-7); paper $2.95 (0-8167-2083-5). Key background information demonstrates how this resource is currently being abused. (Rev: BL 6/15/91) [363.73]

2652 O'Neill, Mary. *Water Squeeze* (5–7). Illus. 1991, Troll LB $9.89 (0-8167-2080-0); paper $2.95 (0-8167-2081-9). Historical background information explains why and how water is being abused. Also discusses the mass die-off of seals in 1988. (Rev: BL 6/15/91) [363.73]

2653 Pringle, Laurence. *Oil Spills: Damage, Recovery, and Prevention* (5–8). 1993, Morrow LB $14.93 (0-688-09861-4). Petroleum's formation, removal from the ground, and benefits are described, as well as the damage caused by spills and cleanup and prevention efforts. (Rev: BL 9/15/93) [363.73]

2654 Rock, Maxine. *The Automobile and the Environment* (9–12). (Earth at Risk) 1992, Chelsea House $19.95 (0-7910-1592-0). (Rev: BL 12/1/92) [363.73]

2655 Stenstrup, Allen. *Hazardous Waste* (5–8). (Saving Planet Earth) 1991, Children's Press LB $18.95 (0-516-05506-2). Analysis of a dangerous environmental problem. (Rev: BL 3/1/92) [363.72]

2656 Tesar, Jenny. *The Waste Crisis* (5–9). (Our Fragile Planet) 1991, Facts on File $18.95 (0-8160-2491-X). Emphasizes the urgency of the problem and offers possibilities for solutions. (Rev: BL 11/15/91; MJHS; SLJ 11/91) [363.72]

2657 Wekesser, Carol, ed. *Water* (7–12). (Opposing Viewpoints) 1994, Greenhaven paper $11.95 (1-56510-063-8). (Rev: BL 1/1/94; MJHS; SHS) [333.91]

Recycling

2658 Becklake, Sue. *Waste Disposal and Recycling* (6–8). (Green Issues) 1991, Gloucester LB $12.90 (0-531-17305-4). (Rev: BL 11/1/91) [363.72]

2659 *50 Simple Things Kids Can Do to Recycle* (5–7). 1994, EarthWorks Press (1400 Shattuck Ave., P.O. Box 25, Berkeley, CA 94709) paper $6.95 (1-879682-00-1). Lists projects and activities for recycling at home, at school, and in the community. Provides instructions for handling certain materials. (Rev: BL 7/94; MJHS; SLJ 8/94) [363.7]

2660 Gay, Kathlyn. *Garbage and Recycling* (6–12). 1991, Enslow LB $17.95 (0-89490-321-7). This analysis of current solid, toxic, and nuclear waste disposal methods focuses on the leading recycling solutions for the garbage crisis. (Rev: BL 11/15/91; SLJ 11/91) [363.72]

2661 Gutnik, Martin J. *Recycling: Learning the Four R's: Reduce, Reuse, Recycle, Recover* (7–10). 1993, Enslow LB $17.95 (0-89490-399-3). A consciousness-raising overview that explores how each person can make a difference. (Rev: BL 8/93; MJHS; VOYA 8/93) [363.72]

2662 McVicker, Dee. *Easy Recycling Handbook* (9–adult). 1994, Grassroots (P.O. Box 86, Gilbert, AZ 85299-0086) paper $8.95 (0-9638428-5-4). A guide to getting acquainted with recycling methods and waste management, with advice on overcoming time and space constraints. (Rev: BL 3/15/94) [363.7]

2663 Stefoff, Rebecca. *Recycling* (9–12). (Earth at Risk) 1991, Chelsea House LB $16.95 (0-7910-1573-4). Wide-ranging overview of the common types of materials recycled, specific recycling procedures, and challenges. (Rev: BL 6/15/91) [363.72]

Population Issues

General and Miscellaneous

2664 Adams, Patricia, and Jean Marzollo. *The Helping Hands Handbook: A Guidebook for Kids Who Want to Help People, Animals and the World We Live In* (5–10). 1992, Random LB $11.99 (0-679-92816-2); paper $4.99 (0-679-82816-8). Suggests 100+ projects that kids can do to help people, animals, and the world in general. (Rev: BL 1/15/93; MJHS) [302]

2665 Barbour, Scott, ed. *Hunger* (7–12). (Current Controversies) 1995, Greenhaven LB $17.95 (1-56510-239-8); paper $9.95 (1-56510-238-X). This compilation of articles, essays, and book excerpts written by journalists, scholars, and activists, will challenge YAs to evaluate the information and develop their own conclusions. (Rev: BL 8/95) [363.8]

2666 Bernards, Neal. *Population: Detecting Bias* (5–7). (Opposing Viewpoints Juniors) 1992, Greenhaven LB $10.95 (0-89908-622-5). (Rev: BL 1/15/93; MJHS) [304.6]

2667 Burby, Liza N. *World Hunger* (6–8). (Overview) 1995, Lucent LB $14.95 (1-56006-120-0). A historical and contemporary look at world hunger that examines the complexities of the issue. (Rev: BL 7/95) [363.8]

2668 Cohen, Joel E. *How Many People Can the Earth Support?* (9–adult). 1995, Norton $27.50 (0-393-03862-9). For the nondemographer trying to develop informed opinions, Cohen gives an overview of the history of the human population and a number of other key issues. (Rev: BL 12/1/95) [304.6]

2669 Hohm, Charles, and Lori Jones, eds. *Population* (7–12). (Opposing Viewpoints) 1995, Greenhaven LB $17.95 (1-56510-215-0); paper $9.95 (1-56510-214-2). Different sides of major questions on population are discussed by experts. (Rev: BL 7/95; SHS) [304.6]

2670 Newton, David E. *Population: Too Many People?* (7–12). (Issues in Focus) 1992, Enslow $18.95 (0-89490-295-4). A well-balanced account of the question: Is each new person an asset or a liability to life on earth? (Rev: BL 10/15/92) [304.6]

2671 Roberts, Sam. *Who Are We: A Portrait of America Based on the 1990 Census* (9–adult). 1994, Times Books $18 (0-8129-2192-5). This analysis of the 1990 census results points out troubling changes in American society, such as increased polarization and economic discrimination. (Rev: BL 2/1/94) [304.6]

2672 Spencer, William. *The Challenge of World Hunger* (7–12). (Environmental Issues) 1991, Enslow LB $15.95 (0-89490-283-0). An overview of the science, technology, and politics of hunger. (Rev: BL 9/1/91) [363.8]

2673 Winckler, Suzanne, and Mary M. Rodgers. *Population Growth* (5–7). (Our Endangered Planet) 1991, Lerner LB $14.95 (0-8225-2502-X). Covers the effects of rapid population growth on the environment and the great impact of developed nations that use the earth's resources. (Rev: BL 6/15/91; MJHS; SLJ 5/91) [304.6]

Aging

2674 Terkel, Studs. *Coming of Age: Passion, Power, and the Old* (9–adult). 1995, New Press $25 (1-56584-284-7). Sixty-nine well-known and everyday people over 70 years of age remember the past century and describe their experiences. (Rev: BL 7/95*) [305.26]

Crime and Prisons

2675 Almonte, Paul, and Theresa Desmond. *Capital Punishment* (5–10). 1991, Macmillan/Crestwood $11.95 (0-89686-660-2). Case histories that dramatize such problems as discrimination in the use of capital punishment, while attempting to remain neutral on controversial aspects. (Rev: BL 12/15/91) [364.6]

2676 Anderson, David C. *Crime and the Politics of Hysteria: How the Willie Horton Story Changed American Justice* (9–adult). 1995, Times Books $25 (0-8129-2061-9). Anderson argues against "expressive justice," such as in the William Horton case, that sentences death and other excessive punishments so victims will feel better. (Rev: BL 7/95) [364.973]

2677 Archer, Jules. *Rage in the Streets: Mob Violence in America* (7–12). Illus. 1994, Harcourt $16.95 (0-15-277691-5). A compendium of examples of mob violence across American history, with an introductory chapter on the psychology of riots. (Rev: BL 4/15/94; BTA; MJHS; SHS; SLJ 9/94; VOYA 8/94) [303.6]

2678 Ballinger, Erich. *Detective Dictionary: A Handbook for Aspiring Sleuths* (5–8). 1994, Lerner LB $14.21 (0-8225-0721-8). Focuses on the elements of detective work, including deductive puzzles and instructions on creating a crime lab. (Rev: BL 9/15/94; MJHS) [363.2]

2679 Barbour, Scott, and Karin L. Swisher, eds. *Violence* (7–12). (Opposing Viewpoints) 1996, Greenhaven LB $19.95 (1-56510-355-6); paper $11.55 (1-56510-354-8). Presents possible causes of violence with emphasis on the problems of domestic and youth violence. (Rev: SLJ 3/96)

2680 Baumann, Ed, and John O'Brien. *Murder Next Door* (9–adult). 1991, Bonus $19.95 (1-55773-916-1). Describes 18 bizarre murders, many of them in the Midwest. (Rev: BL 8/91)

2681 Bender, David L., and Bruno Leone, eds. *America's Prisons* (9–12). 5th ed. 1991, Greenhaven $15.95 (0-89908-178-9); paper $8.95 (0-89908-153-3). Includes discussion of the purpose of prisons, their effect on criminals the rising prison population, and alternatives to prisons. (Rev: BL 1/15/92; SLJ 7/92) [365]

2682 Bender, David, and Bruno Leone, eds. *Crime and Criminals* (9–12). (Opposing Viewpoints) 1995, Greenhaven LB $17.95 (1-56510-176-6); paper $9.95 (1-56510-177-4). A look at the causes and prevention of crime, gun control, and dealing with young offenders. (Rev: BL 4/1/95) [364.973]

2683 Bing, Léon. *Smoked: A True Story about the Kids Next Door* (9–adult). 1993, HarperCollins $22 (0-06-016920-6). Chronicles the shotgun murders of 3 teenage girls by 2 male friends, revealing the shocking underside to growing up in a moneyed "all-American" community. (Rev: BL 6/1–15/93; BTA) [364.1]

2684 Boostrom, Ron, ed. *Enduring Issues in Criminology* (10–12). (Opposing Viewpoints/Enduring Issues) 1995, Greenhaven LB $17.95 (1-56510-256-8); paper $9.95 (1-56510-255-X). Attempts to stir debate on issues of criminology by presenting a general question and essays supporting differing viewpoints. (Rev: BL 7/95) [364]

2685 Brown, Arnold R. *Lizzie Borden: The Legend, the Truth, the Final Chapter* (9–adult). 1991, Rutledge Hill $18.95 (1-55853-099-1). A reexamination of the 1892 hatchet murders of Andrew and Abby Borden. Brown offers convincing evidence that they were killed by Lizzie Borden's half-brother. (Rev: BL 8/91)

2686 Brown, Gene. *Violence on America's Streets* (5–8). (Headliners) 1992, Millbrook LB $14.90 (1-56294-155-0). Focuses on the proliferation of drugs and guns, police brutality, and black-on-black crime. (Rev: BL 12/1/92; MJHS) [364]

2687 Cauffiel, Lowell. *Eye of the Beholder* (9–adult). 1994, Kensington $20 (0-8217-4614-6). Probes the murder of television newscaster Diane King. Evidence soon points to her husband, a criminal-justice teacher. (Rev: BL 7/94) [364.1]

2688 Cope, Carol Soret. *In the Fast Lane: A True Story of Murder in Miami* (9–adult). 1993, Simon & Schuster $23 (0-671-73026-6). An account of a murder case in which the greedy wife of a Miami builder hired thugs to kill him. (Rev: BL 7/93) [364.1]

2689 Cozic, Charles P., ed. *Gangs* (8–12). (Opposing Viewpoints) 1995, Greenhaven LB $19.95 (1-56510-363-7); paper $11.55 (1-56510-362-9). A thought-provoking, alarming, and moving discussion of gangs and violence in the United States. (Rev: BL 12/15/95) [364.1]

2690 Dershowitz, Alan M. *The Abuse Excuse: Sob Stories and Other Evasions of Responsibility* (9–adult). 1994, Little, Brown $22.95 (0-316-18135-8). Argues that the legal system is hampered by a defense tactic increasingly used to blame the defendant's crimes on past traumas, such as "black rage." (Rev: BL 9/15/94) [345.04]

2691 De Santis, John. *For the Color of His Skin: The Murder of Yusuf Hawkins and the Trial of Bensonhurst* (9–adult). 1991, Pharos $18.95 (0-88687-621-4). Uncovers events leading up to the murder of Hawkins and chronicles the murder itself, the activism, the investigation, the trial, and its aftermath. (Rev: BL 11/15/91*) [364.1]

2692 De Santis, John. *The New Untouchables: How America Sanctions Police Violence* (9–adult). 1994, Noble Press (111 E. Chestnut, Suite 48A, Chicago, IL 60611) $55 (1-879360-31-4). Explores the modern role of law enforcement, the dangers of police brutality, excessive use of force, and the loss of constitutional freedoms. (Rev: BL 11/1/94) [363.2]

2693 Duncan, Lois. *Who Killed My Daughter? The True Story of a Mother's Search for Her Daughter's Murderer* (9–adult). 1992, Delacorte $20 (0-385-30781-0). The true story of how the author tracked her daughter's killer with the help of a psychic. Awards: SLJ Best Book; YALSA Best Book for Young Adults. (Rev: BL 4/15/92; BTA; MJHS; SHS; SLJ 8/92) [364.1]

2694 Fine, John Christopher. *Racket Squad* (6–10). 1993, Atheneum $14.95 (0-689-31569-4). A former assistant district attorney and federal government counsel describes the poisonous effect of organized crime on the environment and health care. (Rev: BL 5/15/93; BTA) [364.1]

2695 Franklin, Eileen, and William Wright. *Sins of the Father: The Landmark Franklin Case: A Daughter, a Memory, and a Murder* (9–adult). 1991, Crown $22 (0-517-58207-4). The murder case of a girl that remained unsolved for 20 years until the victim's best friend recalled witnessing her own father as the rapist/murderer. (Rev: BL 11/1/91) [364.1]

2696 Gardner, Robert. *Crime Lab 101: Experimenting with Crime Detection* (6–9). 1992, Walker LB $14.85 (0-8027-8159-4). Details how law enforcement agencies use science and technology to solve crimes, with 25 crime lab activities and 8 exercises. (Rev: BL 8/92; MJHS; SLJ 10/92) [363.2]

2697 Garrison, J. Gregory, and Randy Roberts. *Heavy Justice: The State of Indiana v. Michael G. Tyson* (9–adult). 1994, Addison-Wesley $22.95 (0-201-62275-0). The prosecutor in the trial of heavyweight-champion Tyson discusses the case. (Rev: BL 4/15/94) [345.73]

2698 Gelman, Mitch. *Crime Scene: On the Streets with a Rookie Police Reporter* (9–adult). 1992, Times Books $20 (0-8129-2084-8). A recollection of the author's stint as a rookie crime reporter for *New York Newsday*. (Rev: BL 8/92; BTA) [070.4]

2699 Good, Jeffrey, and Susan Goreck. *Poison Mind* (9–adult). 1995, Morrow $22 (0-688-11947-6). An undercover officer recounts her efforts to befriend and thus reveal the perpetrator of an atrocious crime. (Rev: BL 9/1/95) [364.1]

2700 Gordon, Nicholas. *Murders in the Mist: Who Killed Dian Fossey* (9–adult). 1994, Hodder & Stoughton $29.95 (0-340-59880-8). About illegal trading and the violent death in Rwanda of Dian Fossey and at least seven others associated with Fossey. (Rev: BL 5/15/94) [364.152]

2701 Greenberg, Keith E. *Out of the Gang* (5–8). 1992, Lerner LB $12.95 (0-8225-2553-4). Reveals what gang life is like and offers portraits of a man who escaped gang life and a boy who has managed to stay out of it. B&W photos. (Rev: BL 6/15/92; SLJ 9/92; YR) [364.1]

2702 Guernsey, JoAnn Bren. *Should We Have Capital Punishment?* (7–10). (Pro/Con) 1993, Lerner $17.50 (0-8225-2602-6). Informs readers of both sides of the capital punishment debate, with graphic photos. (Rev: BL 7/93; MJHS) [364.6]

2703 Hammer, Richard. *Beyond Obsession* (9–adult). 1992, Morrow $22 (0-688-09479-1). Bizarre true-crime story of a Connecticut teenager who murdered his girlfriend's mother. (Rev: BL 3/1/92) [364.1]

2704 Harris, Ellen. *Guarding the Secrets: Palestinian Fanaticism and a Father's Murder of His Too-American Daughter* (9–adult). 1995, Scribner $23 (0-02-548335-8). An account of the 1989 "honor killing" by the parents of an Americanized Palestinian teenage girl whose crime was dating an African American boy. (Rev: BL 3/1/95) [364.1]

2705 Hinojosa, Maria. *Crews: Gang Members Talk to Maria Hinojosa* (9–12). 1995, Harcourt $17 (0-15-292873-1); paper $9 (0-15-200283-9). An NPR correspondent interviews New York City gang members after a subway stabbing. (Rev: BL 3/15/95; SLJ 4/95*; VOYA 5/95) [302.3]

2706 Humes, Edward. *Buried Secrets: A True Story of Serial Murder, Black Magic, and Drug-Running on the U.S. Border* (9–adult). 1991, Dutton $19.95 (0-525-24946-X). Chilling account of a Mexican satanic cult and its bizarre activities. (Rev: BL 1/15/91) [364.1]

2707 Humes, Edward. *Mississippi Mud: Southern Justice and the Dixie Mafia* (9–adult). 1994, Simon & Schuster $23 (0-671-88998-2). The story of Margaret and Judge Vincent Shery, a prominent Biloxi African American couple whose daughter uncovered political and mob links to their murders. (Rev: BL 9/1/94) [364.1]

2708 Hutchinson, Earl Ofari. *The Mugging of Black America* (9–adult). 1990, African American Images (1909 W. 95th St., Chicago, IL 60643) paper $8.95 (0-913543-21-7). An angry firsthand account of what defines African Americans as the perpetrators and victims of crime and as the casualties of the criminal justice system. Also offers guidelines for action. (Rev: BL 9/1/91) [305.896073]

2709 Hyde, Margaret O. *Kids in and out of Trouble* (6–9). 1995, Dutton/Cobblehill $13.99 (0-525-65149-7). A dark picture of the juvenile justice system and juvenile violence. (Rev: BL 5/15/95; SLJ 5/95; VOYA 12/95) [364.3]

2710 Jah, Yusuf, and Sister Shah'Keyah. *Uprising: Crips and Bloods Tell the Story of America's Youth in the Crossfire* (9–adult). 1995, Scribner $23 (0-684-80460-3). Probing interviews with gang members, who talk about the worthwhile aspects of gang membership and how it must be channeled into peaceful, productive activities. (Rev: BL 11/1/95) [364.1]

2711 Kaminer, Wendy. *It's All the Rage: Crime and Culture* (9–adult). 1995, Addison-Wesley $22 (0-201-62274-2). Uses high-profile cases to stimulate discussion of the criminal justice system, cultural mores, and violence. (Rev: BL 4/1/95) [364.1]

2712 Landsman, Susan. *Who Shot JFK?* (6–8). (History Mystery) 1992, Avon/Camelot paper $3.50 (0-380-77063-6). Takes on the tricky subject of JFK's assassination and examines the maze of theories, charges, and countercharges. (Rev: BL 4/1/93) [364.1]

2713 Larson, Erik. *Lethal Passage: How the Travels of a Single Handgun Expose the Roots of America's Gun Crisis* (9–adult). 1994, Crown $20 (0-517-59677-6). This important indictment of the American gun industry exposes historic myths, National Rifle Association propaganda, and an industry badly in need of comprehensive regulation. (Rev: BL 1/15/94*) [364.1]

2714 La Valle, John J. *Coping When a Parent Is in Jail* (8–12). (Coping) 1995, Rosen $15.95 (0-8239-1967-6). Discusses the effects of a parent in jail on his/her children and gives them a view of their parent's new circumstances. (Rev: BL 7/95) [362.7]

2715 Lindop, Edmund. *Assassinations That Shook America* (7–12). 1992, Watts LB $13.40 (0-531-11049-4). A recounting of the events leading to and the repercussions of the assassinations of American presidents and Huey Long, Martin Luther King, Jr., and Robert Kennedy. (Rev: BL 11/15/92; SHS) [364.1]

2716 McGinniss, Joe. *Cruel Doubt* (9–adult). 1991, Simon & Schuster $25 (0-671-67947-3). An account of the circumstances surrounding a brutal murder and a description of a family torn apart by a son's involvement with drugs and fantasy games. (Rev: BL 9/1/91) [364.1]

2717 McKee, La Vonne, and Ted Schwarz. *"Get Ready to Say Goodbye". A Mother's Story of Senseless Violence, Tragedy, and Triumph* (9–adult). 1994, New Horizon $22.95 (0-88282-079-6). A mother describes the bizarre shooting of her 13-year-old son by his best friend and the quadriplegic boy's continuing legal and medical battles. (Rev: BL 3/15/94; SLJ 11/94) [362.88]

2718 Maier, Anne McDonald. *Mother Love, Deadly Love: The Texas Cheerleader Murder Plot* (9–adult). 1992, Birch Lane $18.95 (1-55972-137-5). The case of the mother who plotted to have 2 people killed to further her daughter's chance to make the high school cheerleading squad. (Rev: BL 11/1/92) [364.1]

2719 Martingale, Moira. *Cannibal Killers: The History of Impossible Murders* (9–adult). 1994, Carroll & Graf paper $10.95 (0-7867-0096-3). Takes a philosophical look at cannibal killings from ancient China to the present. (Rev: BL 8/94) [364.1]

2720 Meltzer, Milton. *Crime in America* (6–10). 1990, Morrow $12.95 (0-688-08513-X). Survey of crime, law enforcement, and the justice system, including both the strengths and weaknesses of the current judicial structure. (Rev: BL 1/1/91; MJHS; SHS; SLJ 12/90) [364.973]

2721 Micheels, Peter A. *The Detectives* (9–adult). 1994, St. Martin's $21.95 (0-312-09785-9). Eight oral testimonies by New York City police detectives describing the gritty realities of their profession. (Rev: BL 3/1/94) [363.2]

2722 Morris, Norval, and David J. Rothman, eds. *The Oxford History of the Prison: The Practice of Punishment in Western Society* (9–adult). 1995, Oxford Univ. $39.95 (0-19-506153-5). A collection of 8 historical essays and 6 articles about prisons. (Rev: BL 12/15/95) [365]

2723 Oliver, Marilyn Tower. *Gangs: Trouble in the Streets* (5–8). 1995, Enslow LB $17.95 (0-89490-492-2). Discusses the nineteenth-century beginnings of gangs, aspects of modern gang life, and how a member (sometimes) quits a gang. (Rev: BL 8/95)

2724 Otfinoski, Steven. *Whodunit? Science Solves the Crime* (7–10). 1995, W. H. Freeman $19.95 (0-7167-6538-1); paper $13.95 (0-7167-6539-X). A look at the techniques used by forensic science on real cases. (Rev: BL 12/1/95) [363.2]

2725 Owens, Lois Smith, and Vivian Verdell Gordon. *Think about Prisons and the Criminal Justice System* (6–10). (Think) 1991, Walker LB $15.85 (0-8027-8121-7); paper $9.95 (0-8027-7370-2). Basic information on incarceration, crime and its consequences, the criminal justice system, and the whys of laws. (Rev: BL 6/1/92; MJHS, SLJ 2/92) [364.973]

2726 Owens, Tom, and Rod Browning. *Lying Eyes: The Truth Behind the Corruption and Brutality of the LAPD and the Brutal Beating of Rodney King* (9–adult). 1994, Thunder's Mouth $22.95 (1-56025-074-7). A former LAPD officer who was hired as a private investigator on Rodney King's behalf gives his perspective on the famous case and its aftermath. (Rev: BL 2/15/94) [363.2]

2727 Platt, Richard. *Pirate* (5–9). (Eyewitness Books) 1995, Knopf $17 (0-679-87255-8). Full-color photographs illustrate this book on piracy from the time of ancient Greece to the nineteenth century. (Rev: BL 8/95; SLJ 8/95) [364.1]

2728 Prejean, Helen. *Dead Man Walking: An Eyewitness Account of the Death Penalty in the United States* (9–adult). 1993, Random $20 (0-679-40358-2). A Catholic nun describes her relationship with a death row inmate whose sentence she worked to get commuted but whose execution she had to witness. Awards: Christopher. (Rev: BL 5/15/93) [364.6]

2729 Protess, David, and Rob Warden. *Gone in the Night: The Dowaliby Family's Encounter with Murder and the Law* (9–adult). 1993, Delacorte $21.95 (0-385-30619-9). A detailed examination of the unsolved 1988 murder case of a 7-year-old girl in suburban Chicago. Contends that the criminal justice system failed the accused. (Rev: BL 4/15/93) [345.773]

2730 Prothrow-Stith, Deborah, and Michaele Weissman. *Deadly Consequences* (9–adult). 1991, HarperCollins $22.50 (0-06-016344-5). Violence among young men treated as a public health issue. (Rev: BL 6/1/91) [364.3]

2731 Radish, Kris. *Run, Bambi, Run* (9–adult). 1992, Birch Lane $18.95 (1-55972-103-0). A former Milwaukee policewoman escapes from prison after being convicted of killing her husband's ex-wife. (Rev: BL 3/1/92) [364.1]

2732 Rappaport, Doreen. *The Alger Hiss Trial* (7–12). (Be the Judge, Be the Jury) 1993, HarperCollins LB $14.89 (0-06-025120-4); paper $4.95 (0-06-446115-7). A presentation of the evidence in the 1948 Alger Hiss case, from opening statements to final verdict. (Rev: BL 1/1/94; MJHS; SLJ 2/94; VOYA 6/94) [345.747]

2733 Rivlin, Gary. *Drive-by* (9–adult). 1995, Holt $25 (0-8050-2921-4). In this compassionate study of a drive-by shooting, Rivlin examines the history of the victims, their families, and their impoverished living conditions. (Rev: BL 8/95) [364.1]

2734 Ross, Eileen, and others. *Savage Shadows: Eileen Ross's True Story of Blindness, Rape and Courage* (9–adult). 1992, New Horizon $21.95 (0-88282-105-9). The true story of how a blind woman helped convict her rapist. (Rev: BL 1/15/92) [382.883]

2735 Ross, Stewart. *Bandits and Outlaws* (5–7). (Fact or Fiction) 1995, Millbrook/Copper Beech LB $15.90 (1-56294-649-8); paper $5.95 (1-56294-189-5). A whirlwind tour of banditry from ancient China to today's drug gangs. Covers 20 individuals or groups, chiefly from the Northern Hemisphere. (Rev: BL 11/15/95; SLJ 1/96) [364.1]

2736 Ross, Stewart. *Pirates* (5–7). (Fact or Fiction) 1995, Millbrook/Copper Beech LB $15.90 (1-56294-619-6). Historical piracy in each of 4 geographical areas is explored, as well as modern piracy. (Rev: BL 7/95; SLJ 5/95) [904]

2737 Ryan, Patrick J. *Organized Crime* (10–12). (Contemporary World Issues) 1995, ABC-Clio $39.50 (0-87436-746-8). An objective description of various crime organizations, from the 1850s to the present. (Rev: BL 11/1/95; SLJ 3/96)

2738 Salak, John. *Violent Crime: Is It Out of Control?* (6–9). (Issues of Our Time) 1995, 21st Century Books LB $15.98 (0-8050-4239-3). Outlines aggressive behavior, with an emphasis on finding underlying causes and encouraging rehabilitation. (Rev: SLJ 2/96)

2739 Simon, David. *Homicide: A Year on the Killing Streets* (9–adult). 1991, Houghton $24.95 (0-395-48829-X). Gritty account of the year a *Baltimore Sun* reporter spent with the homicide unit. (Rev: BL 6/15/91) [363.2]

2740 Slatalla, Michele, and Joshua Quittner. *Masters of Deception: The Gang That Ruled Cyberspace* (9–adult). 1995, HarperCollins $23 (0-06-017030-1). The adventures of on-line hackers, whose escapades landed them in jail. (Rev: BL 1/15/95*) [364.1]

2741 Steele, Philip. *Smuggling* (5–9). (Past and Present) 1993, Macmillan/New Discovery $12.95 (0-02-786884-2). (Rev: BL 8/93) [364.1]

2742 Steins, Richard. *The Death Penalty: Is It Justice?* (6–9). (Issues of Our Time) 1993, Twenty-First Century $14.95 (0-8050-2571-5). First presenting Gary Gilmore's execution, this book looks at the death penalty through history and presents the current debate. (Rev: BL 11/1/93) [364.6]

2743 Stewart, Gail B. *Drug Trafficking* (6–8). 1990, Lucent LB $11.95 (1-56006-116-2). The author follows the drugs (marijuana, cocaine, and heroin) from the fields through the refinement process. (Rev: BL 4/15/91; SLJ 3/91) [363.4]

2744 Stewart, Gail B. *What Happened to Judge Crater?* (6–9). (History Mystery) Illus. 1992, Macmillan/Crestwood LB $11.95 (0-89686-617-3). (Rev: BL 9/15/92) [347.747]

2745 Streissguth, Thomas. *Hoaxers and Hustlers* (7–10). 1994, Oliver Press (5707 W. 36th St., Minneapolis, MN 55416) $14.95 (1-881508-13-7). Chronicles cons from the 1800s to the present, including the pyramid schemes, the "Martian invasion" radio hoax, and Jim and Tammy Faye Bakker's real-estate scam. (Rev: BL 9/1/94; BTA; SLJ 7/94) [364.1]

2746 Taylor, Lawrence. *To Honor and Obey* (9–adult). 1992, Morrow $22 (0-688-09854-1). The true story of a Manhattan socialite accused of stabbing and killing her estranged husband. (Rev: BL 1/15/92) [364.1]

2747 Vernon, Robert. *L.A. Justice* (9–adult). 1993, Focus on the Family Publishing $17.99 (1-56179-124-5). An insider's account of the Los Angeles Police Department at the time of the L.A. riots, including the author's views on the causes and what must be done now. (Rev: BL 1/1/93; VOYA 12/93) [303.6]

2748 Vollers, Maryanne. *Ghosts of Mississippi: The Murder of Medger Evers, the Trials of Byron De La Beckwith, and the Haunting of the New South* (9–adult). 1995, Little, Brown $24.95 (0-316-91485-1). An exposé of a racist found guilty in 1991 for the 1963 murder of an African American civil rights activist. (Rev: BL 4/1/95) [364.1]

2749 Warburton, Lois. *Prisons* (6–9). (Overview) 1993, Lucent $14.95 (1-56006-138-3). The author outlines the historical background of prisons and discusses the trends in treatment; views of current practices; issues; and takes a look at everyday life behind bars. (Rev: BL 5/1/93; MJHS) [365]

2750 Watkins, Ronald J. *Evil Intentions* (9–adult). 1992, Morrow $22 (0-688-10270-0). The true account of the rape and murder of a 26-year-old woman by 2 drifters in Arizona. (Rev: BL 2/15/92) [364.1]

2751 Wormser, Richard. *Juveniles in Trouble* (8–12). 1994, Messner $16 (0-671-86775-X). Extensive use of first-person narratives of troubled youth with hard-hitting, factual information on important choices kids in trouble need to make. (Rev: BL 5/15/94; SHS; SLJ 6/94) [364.3]

Poverty, Homelessness, and Hunger

2752 Berck, Judith. *No Place to Be: Voices of Homeless Children* (7–12). 1992, Houghton $14.95 (0-395-53350-3). Honest testimony of homeless young people and their poetry. Awards: ALSC Notable Children's Book; BL Editors' Choice. (Rev: BL 4/1/92*; BTA; MJHS; SLJ 6/92; YR) [362.7]

2753 Blau, Joel. *The Visible Poor: Homelessness in the United States* (9–adult). 1992, Oxford Univ. $22.95 (0-19-505743-0). Focuses on the political, social, and economic aspects of homelessness. (Rev: BL 2/15/92; SHS) [362.5]

2754 Davis, Bertha. *Poverty in America: What We Do about It* (7–10). 1991, Watts LB $12.90 (0-531-13016-9). A timely discussion about a critical issue in easy-to-understand language. (Rev: BL 5/15/91; MJHS; SLJ 6/91) [362.5]

2755 DeKoster, Katie, ed. *Poverty* (7–12). (Opposing Viewpoints) 1994, Greenhaven paper $11.95 (1-56510-065-4). Differing viewpoints are taken on such questions as what causes poverty and why women and minorities suffer from higher rates of poverty than white males. (Rev: BL 1/1/94; MJHS) [362.5]

2756 Flood, Nancy Bohac. *Working Together Against World Hunger* (7–12). (Library of Social Activism) 1995, Rosen $14.95 (0-8239-1773-8). (Rev: BL 4/15/95) [363.8]

2757 Homeless Joe. *My Life on the Street: Memoirs of a Faceless Man* (9–adult). 1992, New Horizon $19.95 (0-88282-102-4). After being evicted from his apartment, an unemployed contractor finds himself homeless on the New York City streets. (Rev: BL 3/15/92) [305.569]

2758 Johnson, Joan J. *Kids Without Homes* (7–12). 1991, Watts LB $13.90 (0-531-11064-8). Actual case histories are used to illustrate what makes families homeless, what homelessness is like, and what can be done about it. (Rev: BL 9/15/91; MJHS; SHS; SLJ 10/91) [362.7]

2759 Le Vert, Marianne. *The Welfare System* (7–12). 1995, Millbrook LB $15.90 (1-56294-455-X). A look at the questions surrounding the great welfare debate. (Rev: BL 4/15/95; SHS; SLJ 4/95) [361.6]

2760 McCauslin, Mark. *Homelessness* (6–9). 1994, Macmillan/Crestwood LB $13.95 (0-89686-805-2); paper $4.95 (0-382-24757-4). Surveys and analyzes the decline of affordable housing in the past few decades, along with other economic and employment factors that have led to homelessness. (Rev: BL 2/1/95; SLJ 3/95) [362.5]

2761 Rozakis, Laurie. *Homelessness: Can We Solve the Problem?* (6–9). (Issues of Our Time) 1995, Twenty-First Century LB $15.98 (0-8050-3878-7). A well-rounded discussion that will encourage readers to form their own conclusions. (Rev: BL 7/95) [362.5]

2762 Schatz, Howard. *Homeless: Portraits of Americans in Hard Times* (9–adult). 1993, Chronicle paper $22.95 (0-8118-0512-3). Presents portraits of 75 of San Francisco's homeless, ages 3 to 94, accompanied by their own stories in some cases. (Rev: BL 10/1/93) [362.5]

2763 Seymour-Jones, Carole. *Homelessness* (5–9). (Past and Present) 1993, Macmillan/New Discovery $12.95 (0-02-786882-6). (Rev: BL 8/93; MJHS) [362.5]

2764 Shames, Stephen. *Outside the Dream: Child Poverty in America* (9–adult). 1991, Aperture paper $19.95 (0-89381-475-X). This collection of sobering photos begins with a passionate introduction revealing the magnitude of child poverty in the United States and ends with a plea from the president of the Children's Defense Fund. (Rev: BL 9/1/91) [362.53]

2765 Switzer, Ellen. *Anyplace but Here: Young, Alone, and Homeless: What to Do* (7–12). 1992, Atheneum $13.95 (0-689-31694-1). A description of the dreary future that awaits most teen runaways, with comments from interviews with members of 2 runaway "families." (Rev: BL 10/1/92; BTA; MJHS; SHS; SLJ 11/92; YR) [362.7]

2766 Urrea, Luis Alberto. *Across the Wire: Life and Hard Times on the Mexican Border* (9–adult). 1993, Doubleday/Anchor paper $9 (0-385-42530-9). A memoir by a Mexican that describes the poverty in Tijuana, Mexico, "the place from which you never get away." Awards: Christopher. (Rev: BL 3/15/93) [972]

Unemployment and Labor Problems

2767 Altman, Linda Jacobs. *Migrant Farm Workers: The Temporary People* (7–12). 1994, Watts LB $13.40 (0-531-13033-9). Examines the economic and social factors that have created and supported a U.S. migrant labor market, from the 1849 gold rush to leader César Chávez. (Rev: BL 10/15/94; SLJ 8/94) [331.5]

2768 Freedman, Russell. *Kids at Work: Lewis Hine and the Crusade Against Child Labor* (5–9). Photos. 1994, Clarion $16.95 (0-395-58703-4). Profiles the investigative photographer who exposed the horrors of forced child labor in the United States during the early twentieth century. Photos. Awards: ALSC Notable Children's Book; Golden Kite; Jane Addams Children's Book Award; SLJ Best Book; YALSA Best Book for Young Adults. (Rev: BL 8/94; BTA; MJHS; SLJ 9/94*) [331.3]

2769 Meltzer, Milton. *Cheap Raw Material: How Our Youngest Workers Are Exploited and Abused* (9–12). 1994, Viking $14.99 (0-670-83128-X). Survey of the history of child labor that reveals the ongoing exploitation of young people in the American workplace. (Rev: BL 3/1/94*; BTA; MJHS; SLJ 7/94) [331.3]

2770 St. Pierre, Stephanie. *Everything You Need to Know When a Parent Is Out of Work* (6–12). (Need to Know Library) 1991, Rosen LB $12.95 (0-8239-1217-5). Explains the ways parents can lose jobs and the effects unemployment can have on a parent's behavior, family routines, and relationships. (Rev: BL 10/1/91) [331.137]

Public Morals

2771 Bernards, Neal. *Gun Control* (6–9). 1991, Lucent LB $12.95 (1-56006-127-8). Examines many aspects of gun control in the United States, including various approaches to control, how the Second Amendment is interpreted, whether gun control reduces crime, and its status in Canada, Japan, and Great Britain. (Rev: BL 8/92; SLJ 6/92) [363.3]

2772 Cozic, Charles P., and Bruno Leone, eds. *Sexual Values* (9–12). (Opposing Viewpoints) 1995, Greenhaven LB $17.95 (1-56510-211-8); paper $9.95 (1-56510-210-X). Debates eroding moral values, how homosexuals should be regarded by society, and sexual values for children. (Rev: BL 4/1/95; SLJ 2/95; VOYA 5/95) [306.7]

2773 Davidson, Osha Gray. *Under Fire: The NRA and the Battle for Gun Control* (9–adult). 1993, Holt $25 (0-8050-1904-9). Focuses on the history, influence, and agenda of the powerful NRA, which has experienced recent setbacks. (Rev: BL 4/1/93*) [363.3]

2774 Dolan, Edward F., and Margaret M. Scariano. *Guns in the United States* (7–12). 1994, Watts LB $13.93 (0-531-11189-X). Discusses the rising gun violence in America—without taking sides in the gun-control debate—to encourage readers to investigate and take a knowledgeable stand on gun control. (Rev: BL 1/15/95; SHS; VOYA 5/95) [363.3]

2775 Johnson, Joan J. *Teen Prostitution* (8–12). 1992, Watts LB $13.90 (0-531-11099-0). Explores what makes teenage boys and girls turn to prostitution and what keeps some turning tricks even after they have a chance to escape. (Rev: BL 12/1/92; BTA; SHS; SLJ 12/92) [306.74]

2776 Landau, Elaine. *Armed America: The Status of Gun Control* (7–12). 1990, Messner LB $12.98 (0-671-72386-3); paper $5.95 (0-671-72387-1). A thorough examination of the gun control issue. (Rev: BL 3/15/91; BY; SLJ 7/91) [363.3]

2777 Miller, Maryann. *Working Together Against Gun Violence* (7–12). (Library of Social Activism) 1994, Rosen $14.95 (0-8239-1779-7). Presents various sides of the issue and attempts to get young people involved in working against hate groups and gun violence. (Rev: BL 4/15/95) [363.3]

2778 Newton, David E. *Gun Control: An Issue for the Nineties* (6–10). 1992, Enslow LB $17.95 (0-89490-296-2). A balanced look at both sides of the emotional gun control issue. (Rev: BL 2/15/92; SLJ 6/92) [363.3]

2779 Otfinoski, Steven. *Gun Control: Is It a Right or a Danger to Bear Arms?* (6–9). (Issues of Our Time) 1993, Twenty-First Century $14.95 (0-8050-2570-7). Reviews laws, the gun culture, violence and its effect on children, and the debate over gun control. (Rev: BL 11/1/93) [363.3]

2780 Sugarmann, Josh. *NRA: Money, Firepower and Fear* (9–adult). 1991, National Press Books (7200 Wisconsin Ave., Suite 212, Bethesda, MD 20814) $19.95 (0-915765-88-8). An in-depth review of the National Rifle Association and the methods it's used to transform a constitutional right into the social nightmare of the unregulated possession of weapons. (Rev: BL 12/1/91) [363.3]

2781 Whitehead, Fred. *Culture Wars* (8–12). (Opposing Viewpoints) 1994, Greenhaven LB $17.95 (1-56510-101-4); paper $9.95 (1-56510-100-6). Includes discussions from a variety of writers on such cultural topics as intellectual freedom, artistic quality, and public morality. (Rev: BL 5/1/94; MJHS; SLJ 3/94) [306]

Sex Roles

2782 Archer, Jules. *Breaking Barriers: The Feminist Revolution from Susan B. Anthony to Margaret Sanger and Betty Friedan* (7–10). 1991, Viking $14.95 (0-670-83104-2). A history of feminism, focusing on the lives and work of 3 women: Susan B. Anthony, Margaret Sanger, and Betty Friedan. (Rev: BL 7/91; MJHS; SLJ 5/91)

2783 Bell-Scott, Patricia, and others, eds. *Double Stitch: Black Women Write about Mothers and Daughters* (9–adult). 1991, Beacon $19.95 (0-8070-0910-5). Fiction, personal narratives, essays, and poetry presenting insights into African American mother-daughter relationships and the legacy of survival passed down from one generation to the next. (Rev: BL 11/1/91; SLJ 4/92) [810.8]

2784 Bender, David, and Bruno Leone, eds. *Feminism* (7–12). (Opposing Viewpoints) 1995, Greenhaven LB $17.95 (1-56510-178-2); paper $9.95 (1-56510-179-0). Essays supporting different viewpoints are presented. Topics include feminism's effects on women, society, and its future and goals. (Rev: BL 7/95; SLJ 2/95) [305.42]

2785 Bender, David, and Bruno Leone, eds. *Male/Female Roles* (9–12). (Opposing Viewpoints) 1995, Greenhaven LB $17.95 (1-56510-174-X); paper $9.95 (1-56510-175-8). A discussion of how sex roles are established, whether they have changed for the better, and predictions for the future. (Rev: BL 4/1/95; SLJ 2/95) [305.3]

2786 Brooks, Bruce. *Boys Will Be* (5–adult). 1993, Holt $14.95 (0-8050-2420-4). Geared for both young boys and their parents, this looks at growing up and issues like reading, dangerous friends, and ice hockey. (Rev: BL 12/1/93; SLJ 12/93; VOYA 2/94) [305.23]

2787 Connor, Marlene Kim. *What Is Cool? Understanding Black Manhood in America* (9–adult). 1995, Crown $20 (0-517-79965-0). Growing up as an African American male and the importance of the peer group are examined in their historical and contemporary context. (Rev: BL 5/1/95) [305.38]

2788 Davis, Flora. *Moving the Mountain: The Women's Movement in America since 1960* (9–adult). 1991, Simon & Schuster $23 (0-671-60207-1). A comprehensive history of the feminist movement that focuses on the actions women have taken and concludes that the revolution is only half won. (Rev: BL 11/1/91) [305.42]

2789 Deutsch, Sarah Jane. *From Ballots to Breadlines: American Women 1920–1940* (8–12). (Young Oxford History of Women in the United States) 1994, Oxford Univ. $20 (0-19-508063-7). Examines women's history between the wars, discussing social position, race, and sexuality, including lesbianism. (Rev: BL 8/94; BTA; SHS) [305.4]

2790 Faludi, Susan. *Backlash: The Undeclared War Against American Women* (9–adult). 1991, Crown $24 (0-517-57698-8). A scathing presentation of the evidence of increasing antifeminism and misogyny in popular culture, in politics, and in women's everyday lives. (Rev: BL 9/1/91*) [305.42]

2791 Findlen, Barbara, ed. *Listen Up: Voices from the Next Feminist Generation* (9–adult). 1995, Seal Press paper $12.95 (1-878067-61-3). Young feminist voices in urgent essays about racism, sex, gender, AIDS, and abortion. (Rev: BL 5/1/95) [305.42]

2792 Gilbert, Roland, and Chico Tyehimba-Taylor. *The Ghetto Solution* (9–adult). 1994, WRS (P.O. Box 21207, Waco, TX 76702-1207) $19.95 (1-56796-021-9). The story of the founding of Simba, the influential organization of successful African American men who attempt to provide role models and help for young boys. (Rev: BL 1/15/94) [305.896]

2793 Liptak, Karen. *Coming of Age: Traditions and Rituals Around the World* (7–10). 1994, Millbrook $15.90 (1-56294-243-3). A description of ritual isolation, tests of endurance, and food sharing among various tribes, in world religions, and in contemporary industrialized countries. (Rev: BL 3/1/94; MJHS; SLJ 4/94) [392]

2794 May, Elaine Tyler. *Pushing the Limits: American Women 1940–1961* (8–12). (Young Oxford History of Women in the United States) 1994, Oxford Univ. $20 (0-19-508084-X). Discusses women's roles during and after World War II, including women in the work force, the struggle to be more than homemakers, and reproductive rights. (Rev: BL 8/94; BTA; SHS; SLJ 5/94*) [305.4]

2795 Mills, Kay. *From Pocahontas to Power Suits: Everything You Need to Know about Women's History in America* (9–adult). 1995, NAL/Plume paper $10.95 (0-452-27152-5). A celebration of women in America's history, from civil rights and women in the workplace to education, arts, and sports. (Rev: BL 3/15/95) [305.4]

2796 Nelson, Mariah Burton. *The Stronger Women Get, the More Men Love Football: Sexism and the American Culture of Sports* (9–adult). 1994, Harcourt $22.95 (0-15-181393-0). A hard-hitting account asserting that women are better athletes than men and capable of competing with men. Written by a reporter who was sexually abused by a coach when a teen. (Rev: BL 5/15/94) [796]

2797 Roessel, Monty. *Kinaaldá: A Navajo Girl Grows Up* (5–7). (We Are Still Here) 1993, Lerner $19.95 (0-8225-2655-7); paper $6.95 (0-8225-9641-5). A typical American teenager returns to the Navajo reservation to celebrate her coming-of-age in a 2-day ceremony of prayer, ritual, feasting, and rejoicing. (Rev: BL 1/15/94; SLJ 2/94) [392]

2798 Shaaban, Bouthaina. *Both Right and Left Handed: Arab Women Talk about Their Lives* (9–adult). 1991, Indiana Univ. $35 (0-253-35189-8); paper $12.95 (0-253-20688-X). A disowned Arab woman weaves her story with that of other Syrian, Lebanese, Palestinean, and Algerian women and corrects many stereotypes. (Rev: BL 11/1/91) [305.48]

2799 Sigerman, Harriet. *Laborers for Liberty: American Women, 1865–1890* (7–12). 1994, Oxford Univ. $20 (0-19-508046-7). The problems women faced in the post–Civil War period, especially the issues faced by Native Americans, Hispanics, and freed slaves. (Rev: BL 5/1/94; SHS) [305.42]

2800 Smith, Karen Manners. *New Paths to Power: American Women 1890–1920* (8–12). (Young Oxford History of Women in the United States) 1994, Oxford Univ. $20 (0-19-508111-0). (Rev: BL 12/15/94; SHS) [305.4]

Social Action, Social Change, and Futurism

2801 Adelman, Deborah. *The "Children of Perestroika": Moscow Teenagers Talk about Their Lives and the Future* (7–12). 1991, M. E. Sharpe $24.95 (1-56324-000-9). This collection of 11 interviews with Soviet teens overturns stereotypes and reveals their strong political and class consciousness and conservative attitudes toward sex. (Rev: BL 12/15/91*; SLJ 8/94) [305.2]

2802 Adelman, Deborah. *The "Children of Perestroika" Come of Age: Young People of Moscow Talk about Life in the New Russia* (10–12). 1994, M. E. Sharpe $30 (1-56324-286-9). Muscovites first interviewed as teenagers, now young adults, discuss their careers, love, and the Soviet Union's collapse. Sequel to *Children of Perestroika: Moscow Teenagers Talk*. (Rev: BL 9/1/94; BTA; SHS) [305.23]

2803 Anderson, Terry H. *The Movement and the Sixties* (9–adult). 1995, Oxford Univ. $25 (0-19-507409-2). A history of social activism as it unfolded in the 1960s. (Rev: BL 4/15/95*) [303.48]

2804 Carlson, Richard, and Bruce Goldman. *2020 Visions: Long View of a Changing World* (9–adult). 1991, Stanford Alumni Association (Bowman Alumni House, Stanford, CA 94305-4005) paper $11.95 (0-916318-44-3). Optimistic futurist speculation that concentrates on the long-term impact of such trends as an aging population, a restructured economy, and a divided society. (Rev: BL 11/1/91) [303.4973]

2805 Cohen, David. *America: Then and Now* (9–adult). 1992, HarperCollins $40 (0-06-250176-3). Photos of various aspects of American life from the mid-nineteenth to the mid-twentieth century are joined with a contemporary photo of the same or a comparable scene. Awards: SLJ Best Book. (Rev: BL 10/15/92; SLJ 6/93*) [973]

2806 Hoose, Phillip. *It's Our World, Too! Stories of Young People Who Are Making a Difference* (5–10). 1993, Little, Brown $19.95 (0-316-37241-2). Stories of young, contemporary movers and shakers and the influence these young people have had on their world. Awards: ALSC Notable Children's Book; Christopher. (Rev: BL 9/1/93; MJHS; SLJ 7/93) [302]

2807 Kennedy, Geraldine, ed. *From the Center of the Earth: Stories out of the Peace Corps* (9–adult). 1991, Clover Park Press (P.O. Box 5067, Santa Monica, CA 90409-5067) paper $12.95 (0-9628632-0-3). Maps of exotic, often unfamiliar locales are included in this collection of 9 fictional and 4 autobiographical tales by former Peace Corps members. (Rev: BL 10/15/91) [361.26]

2808 Markley, Oliver W., and Walter R. McCuan, eds. *21st Century Earth* (7–12). (Opposing Viewpoints) 1996, Greenhaven LB $19.95 (1-56510-415-3); paper $11.55 (1-56510-414-5). An assortment of forecasts for the near future, including the effects of overpopulation and the impacts of new technologies. (Rev: SLJ 3/96)

2809 Salzman, Marian, and others. *150 Ways Teens Can Make a Difference: A Handbook for Action* (8–12). 1991, Peterson's Guides paper

$7.95 (1-56079-093-8). Resource for teens who want to use their time and talents to help others. Includes a state-by-state list of association addresses. (Rev: BL 2/1/92; MJHS; SHS; SLJ 4/92) [302]

2810 Sims, Grant. *Leaving Alaska* (9–adult). 1994, Atlantic Monthly $22 (0-87113-476-4). A memoir of the social environment of the writer's stay in Alaska, with all the intimate violences he experienced, along with the nightmare of the *Exxon Valdez*. (Rev: BL 5/15/94) [363.7]

2811 Zimmerman, Richard. *What Can I Do to Make a Difference? A Positive Action Sourcebook* (9–adult). 1992, NAL/Plume paper $12.95 (0-452-26632-7). A guide to humanitarian activism covering the environment, human welfare, animal rights, health issues, and world peace. (Rev: BL 12/15/91) [361.6]

Social Customs

2812 Goss, Linda, and Clay Goss. *It's Kwanzaa Time!* (5–7). 1995, Putnam $19.95 (0-399-22505-6). Stories illustrate the 7 principles of the Kwanzaa celebration. (Rev: BL 12/15/95) [394.2]

2813 Harris, Jessica. *A Kwanzaa Keepsake: Celebrating the Holiday with New Traditions and Feasts* (9–adult). 1995, Simon & Schuster $22 (0-684-80045-4). A collection of ethnic recipes for celebrating Kwanzaa plus definitions of the 7 principles that are part of the meaning of the celebration. (Rev: BL 11/15/95) [394.2]

2814 Kennedy, Pagan. *Platforms: A Microwaved Cultural Chronicle of the 1970s* (9–adult). 1994, St. Martin's paper $13.95 (0-312-10525-8). This examination of the 1970s covers ecology, television, sex, disco, and the cult of nostalgia. (Rev: BL 4/1/94) [973.92]

2815 Landau, Elaine. *Interracial Dating and Marriage* (7–12). 1993, Messner LB $13.98 (0-671-75258-8); paper $7.95 (0-671-75261-8). Narratives from 10 young adults and 5 adults tell of their experiences with and reactions to interracial relationships. (Rev: BL 11/1/93) [306.73]

2816 Santino, Jack. *All Around the Year: Holidays and Celebrations in American Life* (9–adult). 1994, Univ. of Illinois $24.95 (0-252-02049-9). An evaluation of the effect of holidays on American life. (Rev: BL 4/15/94; SHS) [394.26973]

2817 Seymour, Tryntje Van Ness. *The Gift of Changing Woman* (5–8). 1993, Holt $16.95 (0-8050-2577-4). Seymour describes the Apache initiation rite for young women in a picture book format using illustrations by Apache artists. (Rev: BL 11/15/93; MJHS; SLJ 3/94) [299]

Terrorism

2818 Landau, Elaine. *Terrorism: America's Growing Threat* (7–10). 1992, Dutton/Lodestar $15 (0-525-67382-2). Provides a definition of terrorism, some rationales for its use, and information on major terrorist organizations (primarily Middle Eastern, but also the KKK and skinheads) and their leaders. (Rev: BL 6/15/92; MJHS; SLJ 7/92; YR) [363.4]

2819 MacDonald, Eileen. *Shoot the Women First: Inside the Secret World of Female Terrorists* (9–adult). 1992, Random $20 (0-679-41596-3). Interviews with female terrorists from a half-dozen countries reveal what ideologies have convinced them to engage in political violence. (Rev: BL 9/15/92) [303.6]

Urban and Rural Life

2820 Aldis, Rodney. *Towns and Cities* (5–8). (Ecology Watch) 1992, Dillon LB $13.95 (0-87518-496-0). (Rev: BL 12/15/92) [574.5]

2821 Barr, Roger. *Cities* (6–8). (Overview) 1995, Lucent LB $14.95 (1-56006-158-8). An introductory overview that presents a historical as well as a contemporary look at cities. (Rev: BL 7/95) [307.76]

2822 Cozic, Charles P., ed. *America's Cities* (7–12). (Opposing Viewpoints) 1993, Greenhaven LB $17.95 (0-89908-195-9). (Rev: BL 5/1/93; SHS) [307.76]

2823 Leuzzi, Linda. *Urban Life* (6–9). 1995, Chelsea House $14.95 (0-7910-2841-0). Leuzzi looks at urban life in American cities a century ago, both from our perspective looking back and from the viewpoint of someone living then. (Rev: BL 7/95; SLJ 9/95) [973]

2824 Pichaske, David R., ed. *Late Harvest* (9–adult). 1991, Paragon House $25.95 (1-55778-049-8). Contemporary essays, fiction, and poetry, with a rural American theme, by many acclaimed writers. (Rev: BL 9/15/91) [810.8]

2825 Toth, Jennifer. *The Mole People: Life in the Tunnels Beneath New York City* (9–adult). 1993, Chicago Review $19.95 (1-55652-190-1). A study of the "houseless" living in the subways of New York City, including the effects of AIDS, crack, death, and violence on them. (Rev: BL 9/15/93; BTA) [305.5]

2826 Vergara, Camilo José. *The New American Ghetto* (9–adult). 1995, Rutgers Univ. $49.95 (0-8135-2209-9). Chilean-born Vergara has photographed American ghettos since 1977 and gathered his work as a documentation of their geography and ecology. (Rev: BL 12/1/95*) [307.3]

Economics and Business

General and Miscellaneous

2827 Heilbroner, Robert L., and Lester C. Thurow. *Economics Explained: Everything You Need to Know about How the Economy Works and Where It's Going* (9–adult). 1994, Simon & Schuster/Touchstone $12 (0-671-88422-0). Two well-known economists present a primer on economics and provide an overview of the history of economic thought. (Rev: BL 1/15/94; SHS) [330]

2828 Katz, Donald. *Just Do It! The Nike Spirit in the Corporate World* (9–adult). 1994, Random $23 (0-679-43275-2). Katz examines all aspects of Nike—its Oregon "campus," its Far East factories, its retailers, the symbiotic relationship between athletes and Nike, its company culture, its successes, and its failures. (Rev: BL 5/1/94; SLJ 11/94) [338.7]

2829 Menzel, Peter. *Material World* (9–adult). 1994, Sierra Club $30 (0-87156-437-8). Photo spreads, with brief commentaries, of possessions of families in more than 50 countries. Awards: SLJ Best Book. (Rev: SLJ 5/95; VOYA 4/96)

2830 Strasser, J. B., and Laurie Becklund. *Swoosh: The Story of Nike and the Men Who Played There* (9–adult). 1992, Harcourt $24.95 (0-15-187430-1). This biographical history of the Nike corporation and its key figures describes the company's rise to the top in the athletic-shoe business. (Rev: BL 12/1/91) [338.7]

2831 Waterman, Robert H. *What America Does Right: Learning from Companies That Put People First* (9–adult). 1994, Norton $22 (0-393-03597-2). Examines the successful operations of companies that are organized in order to recognize, understand, and fulfill their employees' needs. (Rev: BL 2/15/94) [658.5]

Economic Systems and Institutions

General and Miscellaneous

2832 Buchholz, Todd G. *From Here to Economy: A Shortcut to Economic Literacy* (9–adult). 1995, Dutton $21.95 (0-525-93902-4). A clear explanation of American economic philosophies and the political platforms and government branches that enact or influence national and international policies. (Rev: BL 2/1/95) [330]

2833 Calleo, David P. *The Bankrupting of America: How the Federal Budget Is Impoverishing the Nation* (9–adult). 1992, Morrow $22 (0-688-05162-6). An economist explains the federal deficit, its size, and how it is financed. (Rev: BL 3/1/92) [339.5]

2834 Madrick, Jeffrey. *The End of Affluence: The Causes and Consequences of America's Economic Decline* (9–adult). 1995, Random $20 (0-679-43623-5). An investigation of America's current economic status. (Rev: BL 9/15/95) [330.973]

2835 O'Neill, Terry, and Karin L. Swisher, eds. *Economics in America* (7–10). (Opposing Viewpoints) 1992, Greenhaven LB $15.95 (0-89908-187-8); paper $8.95 (0-89908-162-2). Thoroughly updated edition that looks at the state of the U.S. economy, the budget deficit, taxation, the banking system, and the future of labor. (Rev: BL 6/15/92; SHS) [338.973]

2836 Reich, Charles A. *Opposing the System* (9–adult). 1995, Crown $23 (0-517-59777-2). The author of *Greening of America* now speaks frankly about the tyranny of economics, that creates a pervasive sense of social insecurity. (Rev: BL 10/1/95*) [306]

Stock Exchanges

2837 Davies, Nancy M. *The Stock Market Crash of 1929* (7–12). (American Events) 1994, Macmillan/New Discovery $14.95 (0-02-726221-9). (Rev: BL 7/94; MJHS) [338.5]

2838 Feinberg, Barbara Silberdick. *Black Tuesday: The Stock Market Crash of 1929* (5–7). (Spotlight on American History) 1995, Millbrook LB $15.90 (1-56294-574-2). (Rev: BL 10/15/95) [338.5]

Consumerism

2839 Klein, David, and Marymae E. Klein. *Getting Unscrewed and Staying That Way: The Sourcebook of Consumer Protection* (9–adult). 1993, Holt $25 (0-8050-2590-1). Provides addresses and phone numbers for obtaining redress for consumer problems. (Rev: BL 7/93) [381.3]

2840 Milios, Rita. *Shopping Savvy* (9–12). (Lifeskills Library) 1992, Rosen $12.95 (0-8239-1455-0). Basic guidelines for shopping, budgeting, and prioritizing needs are presented. (Rev: BL 2/15/93; MJHS) [640]

Employment and Jobs

2841 Atkin, S. Beth, ed. *Voices from the Fields: Children of Migrant Farmworkers Tell Their Stories* (7–12). 1993, Little, Brown/Joy Street $16.95 (0-316-05633-2). Oral histories from 9 children, each interview exhibiting a strong sense of family devotion, providing a reminder that education is the key to escaping the fields. Awards: SLJ Best Book; YALSA Best Book for Young Adults. (Rev: BL 5/1/93*; BTA; MJHS; SLJS 1/94*; VOYA 2/94) [305.23]

2842 Baxandall, Rosalyn, and Linda Gordon, eds. *America's Working Women: A Documentary History 1600 to the Present* (9–adult). 1995, Norton $27.50 (0-393-03653-7); paper $12.95 (0-393-31262-3). Chronologically arranged overview of the changing roles and contributions of women. (Rev: BL 3/15/95*; SHS) [331.4]

2843 Colman, Penny. *Rosie the Riveter* (6–12). 1995, Crown LB $16.99 (0-517-59791-8). An overview of the role women played in the wartime workplace. Awards: ALSC Notable Children's Book; SLJ Best Book. (Rev: BL 4/15/95; SLJ 5/95) [331.4]

2844 Greene, Laura Offenhartz. *Child Labor: Then and Now* (9–12). 1993, Watts $12.90 (0-531-13008-8). A history of child labor and an exploration of the factors that justify child labor, while decrying its abusive aspects. (Rev: BL 4/1/93; SHS) [331.3]

2845 Packard, Gwen K. *Coping When a Parent Goes Back to Work* (8–12). (Coping) 1995, Rosen $15.95 (0-8239-1698-7). Gives children whose parents are back in the workforce tips on adapting to the new situation, as well as case studies. (Rev: BL 7/95) [306.874]

Labor Unions

2846 Colman, Penny. *Strike! The Bitter Struggle of American Workers from Colonial Times to the Present* (6–9). 1995, Millbrook LB $16.90 (1-56294-459-2). An overview of 200 years of labor stuggles, including a comprehensive list of major strikes and full-page B&W photos. (Rev: BL 11/95; SLJ 1/96)

2847 Dash, Joan. *We Shall Not Be Moved: The Women's Factory Strike of 1909* (7–12). 1996, Scholastic $15.95 (0-590-48409-5). Chronicles the effective action taken to improve working conditions, especially for immigrant workers, in the garment industry. (Rev: BL 1/1/96; SLJ 2/96; VOYA 4/96)

2848 de Ruiz, Dana Catharine, and Richard Larios. *La causa: The Migrant Farmworkers' Story* (5–7). Illus. 1993, Raintree LB $14.94 (0-8114-7231-0); paper $4.95 (0-8114-8071-2). A history of the United Farm Workers union and the role of their leaders and organizers, César Chávez and Dolores Huerta. (Rev: BL 6/1–15/93; SLJ 7/93) [331.88]

Money and Trade

2849 Lewis, Brenda Ralph. *Monedas y billetes* (7–12). (Mis aficiones/My Hobby) 1993, Editorial Debate (Madrid, Spain) $12.99 (84-7444-645-7). Includes simple explanations, numerous practical suggestions, and photos, charts, and drawings in color. Large format. English title: *Coins and Bills*. Previous series titles: *Observación de pájaros (Bird Watching)* and *Sellos (Stamps)*. (Rev: BL 4/1/94)

2850 Resnick, Abraham. *Money* (6–8). (Overview) 1995, Lucent LB $14.95 (1-56006-165-0). (Rev: BL 7/95) [332.4]

2851 *Sold! The Origins of Money and Trade* (5–8). (Buried Worlds) 1994, Runestone $17.21 (0-8225-3206-9). A beautifully illustrated account of early forms of money, how coins were made, and what they reveal to archaeologists about the people who used them. (Rev: BL 9/15/94; MJHS) [737.4]

Marketing and Advertising

2852 Bernards, Neal. *Advertising: Distinguishing Between Fact and Opinion* (5–7). (Opposing Viewpoints Juniors) 1991, Greenhaven LB $9.95 (0-89908-614-4). A how-to book for looking at how we choose what to buy. (Rev: BL 5/15/92; SLJ 7/92) [659.1]

2853 Fraser, James. *The American Billboard: 100 Years* (9–adult). 1991, Abrams $49.50 (0-8109-3116-8). Examples of highway advertising signs that connect the history of billboards to trends in society, graphic arts, and the advertising industry. (Rev: BL 11/15/91) [659.13]

2854 Gay, Kathlyn. *Caution! This May Be an Advertisement: A Teen Guide to Advertising* (7–12). 1992, Watts LB $13.90 (0-531-11039-7). Carefully documented guide to the world of advertising, featuring a brief history of ads, what motivates consumers to buy, market research, target groups, and industry trends. (Rev: BL 4/15/92; BTA; MJHS; SHS; SLJ 5/92) [659.1]

2855 McSharry, Patra, and Roger Rosen, eds. *Coca-Cola Culture: Icons of Pop* (10–12). (Icarus World Issues) 1994, Rosen LB $16.95 (0-8239-1593-X); paper $8.95 (0-8239-1594-8). Essays and fiction on how America's commercial products have influenced the way other countries perceive us as well as how we see ourselves. (Rev: BL 3/1/94) [306.4]

2856 Stabiner, Karen. *Inventing Desire: The Hottest Shop, the Coolest Players, the Big Business of Advertising* (9–adult). 1993, Simon & Schuster $25 (0-671-72346-4). An inside look at the Chiat/Day advertising agency, detailing in dramatic episodes a pivotal year in the "hot" company's corporate operations. (Rev: BL 5/15/93) [338.7]

2857 Stauber, John C., and Sheldon Rampton. *Toxic Sludge Is Good for You: Damn Lies, and the Public Relations Industry* (9–adult). 1995, Common Courage (P.O. Box 702, Monroe, ME 04951) $29.95 (1-56751-061-2); paper $16.95 (1-56751-060-4). The authors assess the role of public relations in the marketing of various crucial items, such as nuclear power and infant formula. (Rev: BL 12/1/95) [659.2]

Guidance and Personal Development

Education and the Schools

General and Miscellaneous

2858 Atlas, James. *Battle of the Books: The Curriculum Debate in America* (9–adult). 1992, Norton $17.95 (0-393-03413-5). Translating politically correct jargon into plain language, this book airs the controversial issues surrounding the multiculturalism debate. (Rev: BL 10/1/92) [370.19]

2859 Cohen, Leah Hagar. *Train Go Sorry: Inside a School for the Deaf* (9–adult). 1994, Houghton $21.95 (0-395-63625-6). The author personalizes the issues facing the deaf culture by writing about her own family at a New York City school for the deaf. (Rev: BL 2/1/94; BTA; SLJ 12/94) [371.91]

2860 Cozic, Charles P., ed. *Education in America* (5–8). (Opposing Viewpoints) 1992, Greenhaven LB $15.95 (0-89908-188-6); paper $8.95 (0-89908-163-0). A valuable collection of well-chosen, readable articles that bring most of today's major educational issues into focus. (Rev: BL 5/1/92; MJHS; SHS) [370]

2861 Feiler, Bruce S. *Learning to Bow: An American Teacher in a Japanese School* (9–adult). 1991, Ticknor & Fields $19.95 (0-395-58521-X). Chronicles the author's year as an English teacher in Japan, describes the unusual customs he witnessed, and explodes many of the American-made myths about the Japanese. Awards: SLJ Best Book. (Rev: BL 9/1/91; SLJ 3/92) [373.52]

2862 Harvard Lampoon, ed. *A Harvard Education in a Book* (9–adult). 1991, Putnam/Perigee paper $7.95 (0-399-51665-4). This spoof covers campus photo tours, history, study skills, courses offered, dorm life, etc. The *Lampoon* editors try to give nongrads the ability to drop the right names with ease. (Rev: BL 9/1/91) [378.744]

2863 Kahlenberg, Richard D. *Broken Contract: A Memoir of Harvard Law School* (9–adult). 1992, Hill & Wang $22.95 (0-8090-3165-5). This account of the author's student days at Harvard Law School illustrates the hidebound conservatism of legal education in today's graduate schools. (Rev: BL 12/15/91) [362.58]

2864 Kane, Pearl Rock, ed. *The First Year of Teaching: Real-World Stories from America's Teachers* (9–adult). 1991, Walker $21.95 (0-8027-1170-7); paper $11.95 (0-8027-7359-1). A collection of the best essays by educators asked to describe the trials and rewards of their initial year as teachers. (Rev: BL 10/1/91) [371.1]

2865 Kozol, Jonathan. *Savage Inequalities* (9–adult). 1991, Crown $20 (0-517-58221-X). An examination of the shocking conditions found in selected racially segregated urban schools. Reports that de facto segregation still exists in today's inner-city schools. (Rev: BL 8/91*; SHS) [371.96]

2866 Llewellyn, Grace. *The Teenage Liberation Handbook: How to Quit School and Get a Real Life and Education* (9–12). 1991, Lowry House (P.O. Box 1014, Eugene, OR 97440-1014) paper $14.95 (0-9629591-0-3). A former teacher enthusiastically endorses home schooling as a viable alternative to public and private schools, giving advice on overcoming parental and legal roadblocks. (Rev: BL 10/15/91) [371.3]

2867 Meier, Deborah. *The Power of Their Ideas: Lessons for America from a Small School in Harlem* (9–adult). 1995, Beacon $20 (0-8070-3110-0). A passionate defense of public schools by a New York City principal. (Rev: BL 5/1/95) [372.1]

2868 Mernit, Susan. *Everything You Need to Know about Changing Schools* (7–10). (Need to Know Library) 1992, Rosen LB $12.95 (0-8239-1326-0). Tips on making new friends and getting along with teachers. (Rev: BL 4/15/92) [371.2]

2869 Oleksy, Walter. *Education and Learning* (6–12). (Information Revolution) 1995, Facts on File $17.95 (0-8160-3074-X). A book of breadth rather than depth concerning computer/online/multimedia use in the K–12 environment. (Rev: BL 11/15/95; VOYA 12/95) [371.3]

2870 Postman, Neil. *The End of Education: Redefining the Value of Schools* (9–adult). 1995, Knopf $22 (0-679-43006-7). A redefinition of current educational models to encourage a sense of purpose and respect for learning. (Rev: BL 9/15/95*) [370]

2871 Randolph, Sallie G. *Putting On Perfect Proms, Programs, and Pageants* (9–12). 1991, Watts $12.90 (0-531-11061-3). This guide for organizers and participants illustrates current trends and gives thematic ideas for school social events. (Rev: BL 12/1/91; MJHS; SHS) [793.3]

2872 Schneider, Meg. *Help! My Teacher Hates Me* (5–8). 1994, Workman paper $7.95 (1-56305-492-2). Helpful hints on achieving a productive attitude in school. (Rev: BL 3/15/95) [371.8]

2873 Sherrow, Victoria. *Challenges in Education* (7–12). (Issues for the 90s) 1991, Messner LB $13.98 (0-671-70556-3). An overview of the major questions and concerns facing today's educators. (Rev: BL 11/1/91) [370]

Development of Academic Skills

Study Skills

2874 Krieger, Melanie Jacobs. *How to Excel in Science Competitions* (9–12). 1991, Watts $12.90 (0-531-11004-4). Practical guidance on participating in major science competitions for students interested in pursuing independent research projects. (Rev: BL 12/15/91; MJHS; SHS; SLJ 2/92) [507.973]

2875 Schumm, Jeanne Shay. *School Power: Strategies for Succeeding in School* (5–8). Illus. 1992, Free Spirit (400 First Ave. N., Suite 616, Minneapolis, MN 55401) paper $11.95 (0-915793-42-3). Sensible suggestions for improving study skills: organization, note taking, improving reading, and writing reports. (Rev: BL 3/1/93; BTA) [371.3]

Writing and Speaking Skills

2876 Amberg, Jay, and Mark Larson. *The Creative Writing Handbook* (9–adult). 1992, Scott Foresman/GoodYear paper $7.95 (0-673-36013-X). A guide to putting effective words on a page. Does not cover marketing techniques. (Rev: BL 3/1/92) [808.02]

2877 Bauer, Marion Dane. *What's Your Story? A Young Person's Guide to Writing Fiction* (5–10). 1992, Clarion $13.95 (0-395-57781-0); paper $6.95 (0-395-57780-2). Award-winning writer gives advice to young authors, including suggestions for planning, writing, and revising. Awards: ALSC Notable Children's Book. (Rev: BL 4/15/92; MJHS; SLJ 6/92*) [808.3]

2878 Bauer, Marion Dane. *A Writer's Story from Life to Fiction* (5–8). 1995, Clarion $14.95 (0-395-72094-X); paper $6.95 (0-395-75053-9). A writer for 20 years helps young writers find their writer's voice and discusses her own life. (Rev: BL 9/15/95; SLJ 10/95; VOYA 2/96) [813]

2879 Bugeja, Michael J. *The Art and Craft of Poetry* (9–adult). 1994, Writer's Digest $19.95 (0-89879-633-4). Describes various genres of poetry, the elements of poems, styles, and forms, including exercises and examples from master poets. (Rev: BL 3/15/94) [808.1]

2880 Ehrlich, Henry. *Writing Effective Speeches* (9–adult). 1992, Paragon House paper $8.95 (1-55778-484-1). How to write high-quality speeches for others. Also includes advice on recognizing a client's needs, style, and subject. (Rev: BL 3/1/92) [808.5]

2881 Everhart, Nancy. *How to Write a Term Paper* (7–12). 1995, Watts LB $13.93 (0-531-11200-4). This revised edition of *So You Have to Write a Term Paper* (1987) includes new information on electronic sources and data management by computer. (Rev: BL 6/1–15/95; MJHS; SLJ 5/95) [808]

2882 Gilbert, Sara. *You Can Speak Up in Class* (5–9). Illus. 1991, Morrow LB $12.88 (0-688-09867-3); paper $6.95 (0-688-10304-9). A look at what's behind speaker's fright and suggestions for overcoming it. (Rev: BL 8/91; SLJ 6/91) [372.6]

2883 James, Elizabeth, and Carol Barkin. *Sincerely Yours: How to Write Great Letters* (5–7). 1993, Clarion $14.95 (0-395-58831-6); paper $6.95 (0-395-58832-4). Explains the parts of a letter, types of business and personal correspondence, and what and how to write, with examples by Joe Cool and Mary Sunshine. (Rev: BL 5/1/93; MJHS; SLJ 5/93; VOYA 8/93) [808.6]

2884 Janeczko, Paul B. *Poetry from A to Z: A Guide for Young Writers* (5–7). 1994, Bradbury $15.95 (0-02-747672-3). Presents poetry and offers commentary and suggestions toward the writing of poetry. (Rev: BL 12/15/94; VOYA 5/95) [808.1]

2885 Kowit, Steve. *In the Palm of Your Hand: The Poet's Portable Workshop* (9–adult). 1995, Tilbury paper $12.95 (0-88448-149-2). Informally discusses the technical demands of poetry, along with the creative sources of poetry. (Rev: BL 9/1/95) [808.1]

2886 Ledoux, Denis. *Turning Memories into Memoirs: A Handbook for Writing Lifestories* (9–adult). 1993, Soleil Press (RFD 1, Box 452, Lisbon Falls, ME 04252) paper $17.95 (0-9619373-2-7). A step-by-step handbook that encourages individuals to record their oral histories as a legacy for their families. (Rev: BL 3/15/93) [808.06692]

2887 Lester, James D., Sr., and James D. Lester, Jr. *The Research Paper Handbook* (9–adult). 1992, Scott Foresman/GoodYear paper $7.95 (0-673-36016-4). A manual with chapters covering topic selection, note taking, outlining, and bibliographies. (Rev: BL 2/15/92; BTA) [808.023]

2888 Livingston, Myra Cohn. *Poem-Making: Ways to Begin Writing Poetry* (5–9). 1991, HarperCollins/Charlotte Zolotow LB $15.89 (0-06-024020-2). Focuses on technical voice, metrics, form and figures of speech, as well as the excitement and strange power of poetry. (Rev: BL 4/1/91; MJHS; SLJ 6/91) [372.6]

2889 Mungo, Ray. *Your Autobiography: More Than 300 Questions to Help You Write Your Personal History* (9–adult). 1994, Macmillan/Collier paper $8 (0-02-029545-6). This guide to creating a memoir provides suggestions, quotations, and questions designed to stimulate recollection. (Rev: BL 2/1/94; SHS) [808]

2890 Nolan, William F. *How to Write Horror Fiction* (9–adult). 1991, Writer's Digest $15.95 (0-89879-442-0). Advice for aspiring authors includes samples from modern horror novels and profiles of successful authors in this genre, such as Koontz, Rice, and King. (Rev: BL 2/1/91; SHS) [808.3]

2891 Ochoa, George, and Jeff Osier. *The Writer's Guide to Creating a Science Fiction Universe* (9–adult). 1993, Writer's Digest $18.95 (0-89879-536-2). An overview of all the sciences to help the sci-fi writer avoid scientific errors. (Rev: BL 3/1/93) [808.3]

2892 Otfinoski, Steven. *Putting It in Writing* (5–8). (Scholastic Guides) 1993, Scholastic $10.95 (0-590-49458-9). Uses student samples to teach the basics of writing letters, invitations, reports, essays, and reviews. (Rev: BL 10/1/93; SLJ 4/94) [808]

2893 Policoff, Stephen Phillip, and Jeffrey Skinner. *Real Toads in Imaginary Gardens: Suggestions and Starting Points for Young Creative Writers* (8–12). 1992, Chicago Review paper $11.95 (1-55652-137-5). Includes discussion of poems and plays as well as fiction. For older readers. (Rev: BL 6/1/92; BTA; SLJ 4/92) [372.6]

2894 Ryan, Elizabeth A. *How to Be a Better Writer* (5–9). 1991, Troll LB $9.89 (0-8167-2462-8); paper $3.95 (0-8167-2463-6). Emphasis on basic but overlooked essentials of writing, such as understanding the assignment, length of the piece, and getting the topic approved. (Rev: BL 4/1/92) [372.6]

2895 Ryan, Elizabeth A. *How to Build a Better Vocabulary* (5–9). 1991, Troll LB $9.89 (0-8167-2460-1); paper $3.95 (0-8167-2461-X). A traditional study of prefixes, suffixes, and roots. Includes chapters on foreign words. (Rev: BL 4/1/92; SLJ 4/92) [372.6]

2896 Ryan, Elizabeth A. *How to Make Grammar Fun (and Easy!)* (5–9). 1991, Troll LB $9.89 (0-8167-2456-3); paper $3.95 (0-8167-2457-1). Devotes a chapter to each of the parts of speech, defines them, and gives correct-usage examples. (Rev: BL 4/1/92) [428]

2897 Ryan, Elizabeth A. *How to Write Better Book Reports* (5–9). 1991, Troll LB $9.89 (0-8167-2458-X); paper $3.95 (0-8167-2459-8). Recommendations for brainstorming, outlining, rough drafts, and rewriting the perfect book report. (Rev: BL 4/1/92; SLJ 4/92) [372.6]

2898 Ryan, Margaret. *How to Give a Speech* (7–12). 1995, Watts LB $13.93 (0-531-11199-7). This revision of *So You Have to Give a Speech* (1987) includes new information on electronic sources and data management by computer. (Rev: BL 6/1–15/95; MJHS; SLJ 6/95) [808.5]

2899 Ryan, Margaret. *How to Read and Write Poems* (5–8). 1991, Watts LB $11.90 (0-531-20043-4). Young people are encouraged to express themselves through poetry. Advice is given on language and style. (Rev: BL 1/1/92; SLJ 1/92) [808.1]

2900 Safire, William, and Leonard Safir, eds. *Good Advice on Writing: Writers Past and Present on How to Write Well* (9–adult). 1992, Simon

& Schuster $22 (0-671-77005-5). Authors counsel would-be writers on technical skills and how to avoid bad opening lines. (Rev: BL 9/15/92) [808]

2901 Stanek, Lou Willett. *Thinking Like a Writer: A Handy Guide Guaranteed to Inspire You!* (5–7). 1994, Random paper $5.99 (0-679-86217-X). Ideas and advice for writing stories, with helpful exercises. (Rev: BL 2/15/95; SLJ 3/95; VOYA 5/95) [372.6]

2902 Stevens, Carla. *A Book of Your Own: Keeping a Diary or Journal* (5–8). 1993, Clarion $14.95 (0-89919-256-4); paper $7.95 (0-395-67887-0). Instructions on keeping a journal and examples of diary entries from such familiar writers as Anne Frank and Louisa May Alcott, (Rev: BL 1/15/94; MJHS; SLJ 11/93; VOYA 2/94) [808]

2903 Terban, Marvin. *Checking Your Grammar* (5–8). (Scholastic Guides) 1993, Scholastic $10.95 (0-590-49454-6). A guide to grammar that also covers sexist language, spelling, homonyms, and confused words. (Rev: BL 10/1/93; SLJ 2/94) [428.2]

2904 Writer's Digest. *The Writer's Digest Guide to Good Writing* (9–adult). 1994, Writer's Digest $18.95 (0-89879-640-7). This retrospective anthology organized by decade contains essays providing advice and information for writers, by writers. (Rev: BL 3/15/94) [808.02]

Academic Guidance

General and Miscellaneous

2905 Unger, Harlow G. *But What If I Don't Want to Go to College? A Guide to Success Through Alternative Education* (10–12). 1991, Facts on File $19.95 (0-8160-2534-7). Discusses alternate forms of training, job descriptions, résumé and cover-letter writing, application completion, and interviewing techniques. (Rev: BL 1/1/92; MJHS; SHS; SLJ 5/92) [370.11]

Colleges and Universities

2906 Carroll, Joan. *The Black College Career Guide* (9–12). 1992, Zulema Enterprises (108 William Howard Taft Rd., Cincinnati, OH 45219) paper $6.95 (1-881223-00-0). Presents information on 104 African American colleges: location, history, enrollment, curriculum, costs, financial aid, and scholarships. (Rev: BL 2/15/93) [378.7]

2907 Edelstein, Scott. *The Truth about College: How to Survive and Succeed as a Student in the 90's* (10–12). 1991, Lyle Stuart paper $9.95 (0-8184-0546-5). A straightforward presentation of what may be encountered in college and the options available for handling problems. (Rev: BL 9/1/91) [378.1]

2908 Halberstam, Joshua. *Acing College: A Professor Tells Students How to Beat the System* (9–adult). 1991, Penguin paper $6.95 (0-14-013998-2). Commonsense advice for college students on topics ranging from how to select professors and class participation to test-taking skills and term paper requirements. (Rev: BL 7/91) [378.1]

2909 Mayer, Barbara. *How to Succeed in College* (9–12). 1992, VGM Career Books paper $9.95 (0-8442-4166-0). Topics include self-esteem, attitude, coping with change, and ego building. (Rev: BL 2/15/93) [378.1]

2910 Needle, Stacy. *The Other Route into College: Alternative Admission* (9–adult). 1991, Random paper $11 (0-679-73140-7). For those who don't meet regular college admission standards, but who don't want to settle for less or give up on college altogether. (Rev: BL 6/1/91; SHS; SLJ 8/91) [378.1]

2911 Paul, Bill. *Getting In: An Inside Look at the Admissions Process* (9–adult). 1995, Addison-Wesley $20 (0-201-62256-4). Paul, a journalist and a Princeton interviewer, reveals the story behind college admissions as he tracks 5 applicants. (Rev: BL 10/1/95) [378.1]

Financial Aid

2912 Blum, Laurie. *Free Money for Private Schools* (9–adult). 1992, Simon & Schuster/Fireside paper $12 (0-671-74591-3). Geographically arranged resource for locating grants, loans, scholarships, and matching funds. (Rev: BL 2/15/92) [378.3]

2913 Carpenter, Donna Sammons. *Bright Ideas: The Ins and Outs of Financing a College Education* (9–adult). 1992, Simon & Schuster/Fireside paper $11 (0-671-66633-9). No-frills guide to college financing with tips on savings programs, loan sources, scholarships, and grants. (Rev: BL 3/15/92) [378.3]

2914 Deutschman, Alan. *Winning Money for College: The High School Student's Guide to Scholarship Contests* (9–12). 3rd ed. 1992, Peterson's Guides paper $10.95 (1-56079-059-8). Provides information on 50 programs sponsored by private agencies that present awards based on special skills and achievements. (Rev: BL 2/15/93) [378.3]

2915 Ragins, Marianne. *Winning Scholarships for College: An Insider's Guide* (9–adult). 1994, Holt/Owl paper $10.95 (0-8050-3072-7). A guide for hunting down scholarship funds. Provides tips on finding scholarship money, taking tests, writing essays, and interviewing. (Rev: BL 9/15/94; SHS) [378.3]

Careers and Occupational Guidance

General and Miscellaneous

2916 Dunbar, Robert E. *Guide to Military Careers* (9–12). 1992, Watts LB $12.90 (0-531-11118-0). Includes much material on fringe benefits of a military career, as well as specialties for enlisted men and women officers. (Rev: BL 2/15/93) [355]

2917 Kaplan, Andrew. *Careers for Number Lovers* (9–12). Photos. 1991, Millbrook $11.90 (1-878841-21-1). Fourteen professionals profile their work, offering relevant personal insights about the joy of working with numbers. (Rev: BL 3/1/91; SLJ 11/91) [510.23]

2918 Kaplan, Andrew. *Careers for Wordsmiths* (9–adult). 1991, Millbrook LB $12.90 (1-56294-024-4). Prospective writers, editors, and journalists will find job descriptions from professional wordsmiths in this book. (Rev: BL 9/1/91; SLJ 1/92) [381]

2919 McFarland, Rhoda. *The World of Work: The Lifeskills Library* (9–12). (Lifeskills Library) 1993, Rosen $12.95 (0-8239-1467-4). Takes readers through the process of job hunting, with information on résumés, interviews, applications, general skills, and time management. (Rev: BL 6/1–15/93) [650.14]

2920 *Resumes for High School Graduates* (9–12). 1992, VGM Career Books paper $9.95 (0-8442-4151-2). Includes numerous sample résumés that depict the type of skills and background a high school graduate could present, with sample cover letters. (Rev: BL 2/15/93) [808]

2921 Rivers, Wilga M. *Opportunities in Foreign Language Careers* (9–12). 1992, VGM Career Books $13.95 (0-8442-4042-7); paper $10.95 (0-8442-4043-5). (Rev: BL 1/1/93) [402.3]

2922 Seelye, H. Ned, and J. Laurence Day. *Careers for Foreign Language Aficionados and Other Multilingual Types* (9–12). 1992, VGM Career Books $12.95 (0-8442-8130-1); paper $8.95 (0-8442-8129-8). Employment from volunteer work to corporate and international experiences is thoroughly addressed, with sources of information listed. (Rev: BL 6/1/92) [402]

2923 Stanley, Sandra Carson. *Women in the Military—Vocational Guidance* (9–adult). 1993, Simon & Schuster LB $14.98 (0-671-75549-8); paper $8.95 (0-671-75550-1). The history, politics, and psychological and sociological aspects of women in military life, with comments and stories from service women. (Rev: BL 3/15/94; MJHS; SLJ 1/94) [355]

Careers

General and Miscellaneous

2924 Camenson, Blythe. *Careers for History Buffs and Others Who Learn from the Past* (9–12). 1994, VGM Career Books $12.95 (0-8442-4108-3); paper $9.95 (0-8442-4109-1). (Rev: BL 8/94; VOYA 4/95) [907.2]

2925 Curless, Maura. *Kids* (6–9). (Careers Without College) 1993, Peterson's Guides paper $7.95 (1-56079-251-5). Describes professions that deal with children, such as teachers, caregivers, and museum staff. (Rev: BL 10/1/93) [649]

2926 De Galan, Julie, and Stephen Lambert. *Great Jobs for Foreign Language Majors* (9–12).

1994, VGM Career Books paper $11.95 (0-8442-4351-5). A guide for those interested in careers relating to foreign languages, discussing how to secure employment in various occupations. (Rev: BL 8/94) [650.14]

2927 Dunlop, Reginald. *Come Fly with Me! Your Nineties Guide to Becoming a Flight Attendant* (9–adult). 1993, Maxamillian (P.O. Box 10034, Chicago, IL 60610) paper $15.95 (0-9632749-9-6). Gives specifics on increasing the chances of employment in a competitive field. Provides a tutorial for presenting oneself in the best light. (Rev: BL 6/1–15/93) [387.7]

2928 Fasulo, Michael, and Jane Kinney. *Careers for Environmental Types* (9–12). 1993, VGM Career Books $12.95 (0-8442-4102-4); paper $9.95 (0-8442-4103-2). Outlines the educational preparation necessary to enter the world of environmental careers. (Rev: BL 5/15/93) [363.7]

2929 Field, Shelly. *Careers As an Animal Rights Activist* (9–12). 1993, Rosen LB $13.95 (0-8239-1465-8); paper $9.95 (0-8239-1722-3). Concentrates on jobs within animal rights organizations, with lists of organizations and trade associations and a cruelty-free shopping guide. (Rev: BL 5/15/93; SLJ 6/93; VOYA 8/93) [179.4]

2930 Fry, Ron. *Your First Job: For College Students—and Anyone Preparing to Enter Today's Tough Job Market* (9–adult). 1993, Career Press paper $9.95 (1-56414-053-9). Discusses the job-hunting process, résumé writing, company researching, interviewing, accepting the job offer, negotiating salary and benefits, etc. (Rev: BL 5/1/93) [650.14]

2931 Frydenborg, Kay. *They Dreamed of Horses: Careers for Horse Lovers* (6–9). 1994, Walker LB $16.85 (0-8027-8284-1). Suggests career possibilities that involve working with horses, telling the stories of 13 women who love and work with them. (Rev: BL 7/94; SLJ 7/94; VOYA 8/94) [636.1]

2932 Gartner, Robert. *Exploring Careers in the National Parks* (9–12). 1993, Rosen LB $13.95 (0-8239-1414-3); paper $9.95 (0-8239-1726-6). Describes the employment opportunities available within the close-knit family atmosphere of the National Parks Service. (Rev: BL 5/15/93; BTA; SLJ 11/93; VOYA 10/93) [363.6]

2933 Gould, Jay R., and Wayne A. Losano. *Opportunities in Technical Writing and Communication Careers* (9–12). 1994, VGM Career Books $13.98 (0-8442-4128-8); paper $10.95 (0-8442-4129-6). (Rev: BL 8/94) [808]

2934 Hole, Dorothy. *The Air Force and You* (9–12). (Armed Forces) 1993, Macmillan/Crestwood $12.95 (0-89686-764-1). (Rev: BL 3/15/94) [358.4]

2935 Hole, Dorothy. *The Army and You* (9–adult). (Armed Forces) 1993, Macmillan/Crestwood $12.95 (0-89686-765-X). Not written as a recruitment text, this volume is an examination of how to go about choosing the army as a career. (Rev: BL 3/15/94; SLJ 1/94) [355]

2936 Hole, Dorothy. *The Coast Guard and You* (9–adult). (Armed Forces) 1993, Macmillan/Crestwood $12.95 (0-89686-766-8). A straightforward, factual description of life in the Coast Guard. (Rev: BL 3/15/94; SLJ 1/94) [359.9]

2937 Hole, Dorothy. *The Marines and You* (9–12). (Armed Forces) 1993, Macmillan/Crestwood $12.95 (0-89686-768-4). (Rev: BL 3/15/94) [359.9]

2938 Hole, Dorothy. *The Navy and You* (9–12). (Armed Forces) 1993, Macmillan/Crestwood $12.95 (0-89686-767-6). (Rev: BL 3/15/94) [359]

2939 Kaplan, Andrew. *Careers for Outdoor Types* (9–adult). 1991, Millbrook LB $12.90 (1-56294-022-8). Job descriptions from those employed in outdoor settings. (Rev: BL 9/1/91; SLJ 1/92) [790]

2940 Kaplan, Andrew. *Careers for Sports Fans* (9–adult). 1991, Millbrook LB $12.90 (1-56294-023-6). Job descriptions from those already working in the sports industry. (Rev: BL 9/1/91; SLJ 1/92) [796]

2941 Kennedy, Don. *Exploring Careers on Cruise Ships* (9–12). (Careers) 1993, Rosen LB $13.95 (0-8239-1665-0); paper $9.95 (0-8239-1714-2). Analyzes the modern cruise ship business and stresses the need for applicants to be persistent and seriously committed. (Rev: BL 10/1/93) [385]

2942 Kirkwood, Tim. *The Flight Attendant Career Guide* (9–12). 1993, TKE paper $14.95 (0-9637301-4-2). Explores the lifestyle of a flight attendant, including information helpful for interviewing. (Rev: BL 10/1/93) [387.7]

2943 Krebs, Michelle. *Cars* (9–12). (Careers Without College) 1992, Peterson's Guides paper $7.95 (1-56079-221-3). Presents 5 types of employment that may require further education but not a 4-year degree. (Rev: BL 2/15/93) [629.2]

2944 Lee, Mary Price. *Opportunities in Animal and Pet Care Careers* (9–12). 1993, VGM Career Books $13.95 (0-8442-4079-6); paper $10.95 (0-8442-4081-8). All aspects of these careers are considered, including the perceptions of society, and stresses on the job. (Rev: BL 3/15/94) [636]

2945 Leshay, Jeff. *How to Launch Your Career in TV News* (9–12). 1993, VGM Career Books $14.95 (0-8442-4138-5). Depicts careers in TV news, from the interviewing process on. Includes interviews with those in the business and information on college programs and scholarships. (Rev: BL 10/1/93) [070]

2946 Mason, Helen. *Great Careers for People Who Like Being Outdoors* (9–12). (Career Connections) 1993, Gale $16.95 (0-8103-9390-5). Profiles persons in the profession, explains what the jobs entail, preparation requirements, special activities and information, the outlook for the future, and a list of related occupations. (Rev: BL 3/15/94) [796.5023]

2947 Miller, Louise. *Careers for Animal Lovers and Other Zoological Types* (9–adult). 1991, VGM Career Books paper $9.95 (0-8442-8125-5). Information on animal care employment, from pet-sitter to veterinarian. (Rev: BL 6/1/91) [636]

2948 Munday, Marianne F. *Opportunities in Word Processing Careers* (9–adult). 1991, VGM Career Books $12.95 (0-8442-8164-6); paper $9.95 (0-8442-8165-4). Comprehensive guide to understanding word processing in today's business world and what the future holds for those interested in pursuing a career in the field. (Rev: BL 6/1/91) [652.5]

2949 Pitz, Mary Elizabeth. *Careers in Government* (9–12). 1994, VGM Career Books $14.95 (0-8442-4194-6); paper $12.95 (0-8442-4195-4). A guide for those looking for employment with the government. Explains the hiring processes for many nonelective occupations and federal jobs. (Rev: BL 8/94) [350]

2950 Shenk, Ellen. *Outdoor Careers: Exploring Occupations in Outdoor Fields* (9–12). 1992, Stackpole paper $14.95 (0-8117-2542-1). Provides job descriptions, profiles of men and women in various fields, resources, market information, government employment, etc. (Rev: BL 2/15/93; SLJ 5/93) [331.7]

2951 Shorto, Russell. *Careers for Animal Lovers* (9–12). (Choices) 1992, Millbrook $12.90 (1-56294-160-7). Based on interviews with a zookeeper, snake handler, veterinarian, and pet groomer. Includes career lists and an index of organizations. (Rev: BL 1/1/92; SLJ 2/92) [636]

2952 Shorto, Russell. *Careers for People Who Like People* (9–12). (Choices) 1992, Millbrook $12.90 (1-56294-157-7). (Rev: BL 1/1/92) [331.7]

2953 VGM Career Horizons, eds. *VGM's Careers Encyclopedia* (9–adult). 3rd ed. 1991, VGM Career Books $39.95 (0-8442-8692-3). An updated, comprehensive report on 200 careers, arranged alphabetically. (Rev: BL 6/1/91) [331.7]

Arts, Entertainment, and Sports

2954 Beckett, Kathleen. *Fashion* (9–12). (Careers Without College) 1992, Peterson's Guides paper $7.95 (1-56079-220-5). (Rev: BL 2/15/93) [687]

2955 Blumenthal, Howard J. *Careers in Television* (9–12). 1992, Little, Brown $16.95 (0-316-10076-5). Firsthand advice from successful television professionals. (Rev: BL 1/1/92; SLJ 12/91) [791.45]

2956 Blumenthal, Howard J. *You Can Do It! Careers in Baseball* (9–12). 1993, Little, Brown $16.95 (0-316-10095-1). Interviews with 17 people working in a variety of baseball jobs, each concluding with advice for those interested in their particular job. (Rev: BL 5/15/93; BTA; YR) [796.357]

2957 Curless, Maura. *Fitness* (9–12). (Careers Without College) 1992, Peterson's Guides paper $7.95 (1-56079-223-X). (Rev: BL 2/15/93) [613.7]

2958 Fry, Ron, ed. *Radio and Television Career Directory* (9–adult). 1991, Career Press (P.O. Box 687, Franklin Lakes, NJ 07417-1322) paper $19.95 (0-934829-82-9). Individuals with extensive experience in the broadcasting industry offer vocational advice and information. (Rev: BL 9/1/91) [384.54]

2959 Greenspon, Jaq. *Careers for Film Buffs and Other Hollywood Types* (9–12). 1993, VGM Career Books $12.95 (0-8442-4100-8); paper $9.95 (0-8442-4101-6). An encyclopedia of job descriptions, covering such departments as production, camera and sound, special effects, grip and electric, makeup and costumes, etc. (Rev: BL 5/15/93) [791.43]

2960 Greenwald, Ted. *Music* (9–12). (Careers Without College) 1992, Peterson's Guides paper $7.95 (1-56079-219-1). Presents 5 types of employment that may require further education but not a 4-year degree. (Rev: BL 2/15/93) [780]

2961 Henderson, Kathy. *Market Guide for Young Artists and Photographers* (9–adult). 1990, Betterway/Shoe Tree paper $10.95 (1-55870-176-1). This manual for beginners includes information on poster and art competitions as well as art submission policies and hints. (Rev: BL 1/1/91; SLJ 3/91) [706.8]

2962 Henderson, Kathy. *Market Guide for Young Writers* (6–12). 1990, Betterway/Shoe

Tree paper $10.95 (1-55870-175-3). Supplies useful tips on manuscript preparation and submission guidelines for a variety of publications. (Rev: BL 1/1/91; MJHS; SHS) [808.02]

2963 Hopkins, Del, and Margaret Hopkins. *Careers As a Rock Musician* (9–12). 1993, Rosen LB $13.95 (0-8239-1518-2); paper $9.95 (0-8239-1725-8). Emphasizes that a clear understanding of the business side of the profession is vital for success. (Rev: BL 5/15/93; VOYA 10/93) [781.66]

2964 Kaplan, Andrew. *Careers for Artistic Types* (9–12). Photos. 1991, Millbrook $11.90 (1-878841-20-3). Presents an interesting assortment of artistic careers with information gathered directly from individuals employed in these particular occupations. (Rev: BL 3/1/91; SLJ 11/91) [702.3]

2965 Lantz, Fran. *Rock, Rap, and Rad: How to Be a Rock or Rap Star* (6–12). 1992, Avon/Flare paper $3.99 (0-380-76793-7). Lantz takes rock star wannabes through the basic steps of choosing an instrument, finding other musicians and a place to play, lining up gigs, etc. (Rev: BL 7/93; BTA; YR) [781.66]

2966 Menzel-Gerrie, Sharon. *Careers in Comedy* (9–adult). 1993, Rosen LB $13.95 (0-8239-1517-4); paper $9.95 (0-8239-1713-4). A comprehensive description of what it takes to become a stand-up comedian. It strongly encourages completing a college education. (Rev: BL 3/15/94; BTA; SLJ 1/94) [792.7]

2967 Mirault, Don. *Dancing . . . for a Living: Where the Jobs Are, What They Pay, What Choreographers Look For, What to Ask* (9–adult). 1994, Rafter Publishing (10800 Peachgrove St., Apt. 5, North Hollywood, CA 91601) $15.95 (0-9637864-4-X). An experienced professional describes available employment opportunities and gives practical career suggestions for dancers. (Rev: BL 1/15/94) [792.8]

2968 Moss, Miriam. *Fashion Designer* (6–9). 1991, Macmillan/Crestwood LB $11.95 (0-89686-610-6). Points out the prestige and perks, as well as the downside, of the world of fashion design. (Rev: BL 5/15/91; SLJ 7/91) [746.9]

2969 Moss, Miriam. *Fashion Model* (6–9). 1991, Macmillan/Crestwood LB $11.95 (0-89686-609-2). The prestige and perks, as well as the downside, of fashion modelling are discussed. (Rev: BL 5/15/91; SLJ 7/91) [659.1]

2970 Moss, Miriam. *Fashion Photographer* (6–9). 1991, Macmillan/Crestwood LB $11.95 (0-89686-608-4). Points out the prestige and perks, as well as the downside, of fashion photography. (Rev: BL 5/15/91; SLJ 7/91) [778.9]

2971 Munday, Marianne F. *Opportunities in Crafts Careers* (9–12). 1993, VGM Career Books $13.95 (0-8442-4068-0); paper $10.95 (0-8442-4069-9). (Rev: BL 3/15/94) [745.023973]

2972 Piper, Robert J., and Richard D. Rush. *Opportunities in Architectural Careers* (9–12). 1992, VGM Career Books $13.95 (0-8442-4038-9); paper $10.95 (0-8442-4039-7). (Rev: BL 1/1/93) [720.23]

2973 Powell, Stephanie. *Hit Me with Music: How to Start, Manage, Record, and Perform with Your Own Rock Band* (8–12). 1995, Millbrook LB $16.40 (1-56294-653-6). A good source for young rockers wanting to start their own band, with a bibliography and recommended reading. (Rev: BL 11/15/95; SLJ 2/96; VOYA 4/96) [781.66]

2974 Ritchie, Carol L., ed. *My First Year in Television: Real-World Stories from America's TV Professionals* (9–adult). (First Year Career) 1995, Walker $19.95 (0-8027-1293-2); paper $9.95 (0-8027-7424-5). A collection of interviews with TV professionals discussing their first years in television. (Rev: BL 10/15/95; VOYA 2/96) [791.45]

2975 Rosenbaum, Jean, and Mary Prine. *Opportunities in Fitness Careers* (9–adult). 1991, VGM Career Books $12.95 (0-8442-8185-9); paper $9.95 (0-8442-8167-0). Information on educational requirements and income expectations for one of the fastest growing industries in the U.S. today. (Rev: BL 6/1/91) [613.7]

2976 Salmon, Mark. *Opportunities in Visual Arts Careers* (9–12). 1992, VGM Career Books $13.95 (0-8442-4031-1); paper $10.95 (0-8442-4033-8). Discusses working for a company, freelance work, teaching art, and art therapy. (Rev: BL 2/15/93) [702.3]

2977 Shorto, Russell. *Careers for People Who Like to Perform* (9–12). (Choices) 1992, Millbrook $12.90 (1-56294-158-5). Covers an array of professions such as juggler, rock musician, talk-show host, pastor, and teacher. (Rev: BL 1/1/92) [790.2]

2978 Steele, William Paul. *Stay Home and Star! A Step-by-Step Guide to Starting Your Regional Acting Career* (9–adult). 1992, Heinemann paper $13.95 (0-435-08603-0). Practical advice about acting opportunities on the local level, emphasizing a businesslike approach and the basic requirements for success. (Rev: BL 2/1/92) [792]

2979 Taylor, John. *How to Get a Job in Sports: The Guide to Finding the Right Sports Career* (9–adult). 1992, Macmillan/Collier paper $9.95 (0-

02-082091-7). This alphabetically arranged guide to sports-related careers contains information on salaries, training requirements, and job descriptions. (Rev: BL 4/1/92) [796]

2980 Wilson, Lee. *Making It in the Music Business: A Business and Legal Guide for Songwriters and Performers* (9–adult). 1995, NAL/Plume paper $10.95 (0-452-26848-6). A practical handbook of copyright law, trademarks, and other issues, by a music attorney. (Rev: BL 4/1/95) [780]

Business

2981 Basye, Anne. *Opportunities in Direct Marketing Careers* (9–12). 1992, VGM Career Books $13.95 (0-8442-4036-2); paper $10.95 (0-8442-4037-0). (Rev: BL 1/1/93) [658.8]

2982 Basye, Anne. *Opportunities in Telemarketing Careers* (9–12). 1994, VGM Career Books $13.98 (0-8442-4133-4); paper $10.95 (0-8442-4134-2). (Rev: BL 8/94) [658.85]

2983 Burnett, Rebecca. *Careers for Number Crunchers and Other Quantitative Types* (9–12). 1992, VGM Career Books $12.95 (0-8442-8136-0); paper $9.95 (0-8442-8137-9). Includes facts and case studies about such jobs as buying, management, and marketing. (Rev: BL 2/15/93) [510]

2984 Dolber, Roslyn. *Opportunities in Fashion Careers* (9–12). 2nd ed. 1992, VGM Career Books $13.95 (0-8442-4022-2); paper $10.95 (0-8442-4023-0). (Rev: BL 1/1/93) [687]

2985 Healy, Lisa, ed. *My First Year in Book Publishing: Real-World Stories from America's Book Publishing Professionals* (9–adult). 1994, Walker $21.95 (0-8027-1294-0); paper $9.95 (0-8027-7425-3). A guide for those interested in book publishing, including testimony from agents, editors, publicists, and indexers describing their first year of work. (Rev: BL 9/1/94; VOYA 12/94) [070.5]

2986 Mogel, Leonard. *Making It in Advertising: An Insider's Guide to Career Opportunities* (9–adult). 1993, Macmillan paper $10 (0-02-034552-6). Based on interviews with ad agency professionals, an introduction to advertising, describing available positions and the talents needed to succeed. (Rev: BL 4/15/93) [659.1]

2987 Mogel, Leonard. *Making It in Public Relations* (9–adult). 1993, Macmillan paper $10 (0-02-070180-2). This career guide describes where the PR jobs are and what is required to work in the field. (Rev: BL 4/15/93) [659.2]

2988 Noronha, Shonan F. R. *Careers in Communications* (9–adult). 1993, VGM Career Books $16.95 (0-8442-4182-2); paper $12.95 (0-8442-4183-0). Information on the fields of journalism, photography, film, radio, multimedia, television and video, advertising, and public relations. (Rev: BL 3/15/94) [384]

2989 Plawin, Paul. *Careers for Travel Buffs and Other Restless Types* (9–12). 1992, VGM Career Books $12.95 (0-8442-8109-3); paper $8.95 (0-8442-8127-1). Covers—for typical travel careers but also positions that involve traveling as a small aspect—job descriptions, getting into the businesses, and future success. (Rev: BL 6/1/92; SLJ 3/92) [331.7]

2990 Ring, Gertrude. *Careers in Finance* (9–12). 1993, VGM Career Books $16.95 (0-8442-4186-5); paper $12.95 (0-8442-4187-3). (Rev: BL 5/15/93) [332]

2991 Rosenthal, Lawrence. *Exploring Careers in Accounting* (9–12). Rev. ed. 1993, Rosen LB $13.95 (0-8239-1501-8); paper $9.95 (0-8239-1721-5). Covers positions available and criteria required, with appendices of definitions, associations, accounting schools, etc. (Rev: BL 5/15/93; SLJ 6/93) [657]

2992 Rowh, Mark. *Opportunities in Warehousing Careers* (9–12). 1992, VGM Career Books $13.95 (0-8442-4034-6); paper $10.95 (0-8442-4035-4). Includes a bibliography and lists of warehousing organizations, magazines and newsletters, and technical schools and colleges. (Rev: BL 2/15/93) [658.7]

2993 Schiff, Kenny. *Opportunities in Desktop Publishing Careers* (9–12). 1993, VGM Career Books $13.95 (0-8442-4064-8); paper $10.95 (0-8442-4065-6). Notes the specialized areas where jobs are available and includes interviews with those employed in the field. (Rev: BL 5/15/93) [686.2]

2994 Shaw, Eva. *Writing and Selling Magazine Articles* (9–adult). 1992, Paragon House paper $8.95 (1-55778-443-4). Helpful hints for getting published include focusing an article, directing it to the right editor, and writing spin-off pieces. (Rev: BL 3/15/92) [808]

2995 Steinberg, Margery. *Opportunities in Marketing Careers* (9–12). 1993, VGM Career Books $13.95 (0-8442-4076-1); paper $10.95 (0-8442-4078-8). (Rev: BL 3/15/94) [658.8]

Construction and Mechanical Trades

2996 Garvey, Lonny D. *Opportunities in the Machine Trades* (9–12). 1994, VGM Career Books $13.98 (0-8442-4123-7); paper $10.95 (0-8442-4124-5). (Rev: BL 8/94) [671]

2997 Lytle, Elizabeth Stewart. *Careers in the Construction Industry* (9–12). 1992, Rosen LB $12.95 (0-8239-1348-1). Describes the variety of positions available and the process of advancement, with extensive information concerning education and training. (Rev: BL 6/1/92) [624]

2998 Rowh, Mark. *Careers for Crafty People and Other Dexterous Types* (9–12). 1993, VGM Career Books $12.95 (0-8442-4106-7); paper $9.95 (0-8442-4107-5). (Rev: BL 3/15/94) [745]

2999 Santilli, Chris. *Opportunities in Masonry Careers* (9–12). (VGM Career Guides) 1993, VGM Career Books $13.95 (0-8442-4066-4); paper $10.95 (0-8442-4067-2). (Rev: BL 5/15/93) [693]

Education and Librarianship

3000 Edelfelt, Roy A., and Blythe Camenson. *Careers in Education* (9–12). 1992, VGM Career Books $16.95 (0-8442-4176-8); paper $12.95 (0-8442-4177-6). (Rev: BL 2/15/93) [370]

Law, Police, and Other Society-Oriented Careers

3001 Eberts, Marjorie, and Margaret Gisler. *Careers for Kids at Heart and Others Who Adore Children* (9–12). 1994, VGM Career Books $12.95 (0-8442-4110-5); paper $9.95 (0-8442-4111-3). A career guide for those interested in working with children, focusing on jobs in child care, education, recreation, and health. (Rev: BL 8/94) [362.7]

3002 Eberts, Marjorie, and Margaret Gisler. *Careers in Child Care* (9–12). 1994, VGM Career Books $14.95 (0-8442-4191-1); paper $12.95 (0-8442-4193-8). Profiles occupations relating to child care, including teaching, sports, recreation, welfare, the arts, and entertainment. (Rev: BL 8/94) [362.7]

3003 Lee, Mary Price, and Richard S. Lee. *Careers in Firefighting* (9–12). 1993, Rosen LB $13.95 (0-8239-1515-8). An in-depth study describing the different levels of employment, including a chapter on women in the field. (Rev: BL 5/15/93; SLJ 6/93)

3004 Munneke, Gary. *Opportunities in Law Careers* (9–12). 1993, VGM Career Books $13.95 (0-8442-4086-9); paper $10.95 (0-8442-4087-7). (Rev: BL 3/15/94) [340]

3005 Paradis, Adrian A. *Opportunities in Nonprofit Organization Careers* (9–adult). 1993, VGM Career Books $13.95 (0-8442-4088-5); paper $10.95 (0-8442-4089-3). Emphasizes the variety of nonprofit organizations and provides sources for further information and direction. (Rev: BL 3/15/94) [331.7]

3006 Parker, Julie F. *Careers for Women As Clergy* (9–12). 1993, Rosen LB $13.95 (0-8239-1424-0). The various positions open to clergywomen of the United Methodist Church are discussed. (Rev: BL 10/1/93; BTA; VOYA 8/93) [253]

3007 Selden, Annette, ed. *Handbook of Government and Public Service Careers* (9–adult). 1993, VGM Career Books paper $12.95 (0-8442-4142-3). A reference book presenting basic information about 47 careers that are specific to government or can be found in a government context. (Rev: BL 3/15/94) [353.001]

3008 Simenhoff, Mark, ed. *My First Year As a Lawyer: Real-World Stories from America's Lawyers* (9–adult). 1994, Walker $19.95 (0-8027-1289-4); paper $9.95 (0-8027-7417-2). A guide for those interested in the legal profession, including testimony from attorneys, litigators, and law clerks describing their first year of work. (Rev: BL 9/1/94; VOYA 2/95) [340]

3009 Simpson, Carolyn, and Dwain Simpson. *Careers in Social Work* (9–12). 1992, Rosen $12.95 (0-8239-1407-0). Contains job descriptions, advantages, disadvantages, and opportunities within each profession. (Rev: BL 6/1/92) [361.3]

Medicine and Health

3010 Cardoza, Anne. *Opportunities in Homecare Services Careers* (9–12). 1993, VGM Career Books $13.95 (0-8442-4061-3); paper $10.95 (0-8442-4062-1). Information about careers in professional child care, various types of therapy, and post–intensive-surgery assistance. (Rev: BL 5/15/93) [362.1]

3011 Clayton, Lawrence. *Careers in Psychology* (9–12). 1992, Rosen $12.95 (0-8239-1457-7). Uses clinical scenarios in a description of various careers in mental-health care. (Rev: BL 6/1/92; BTA; SLJ 5/92) [150]

3012 Edwards, Lois. *Great Careers for People Interested in the Human Body* (9–adult). (Career Connections) 1993, Gale $16.95 (0-8103-9386-7). Information from representatives of various medical fields, with challenges to further investigation through activities and suggestions. (Rev: BL 3/15/94; SLJ 12/93) [610.69]

3013 Fry, Ron, ed. *Healthcare Career Directory* (9–adult). 1991, Career Press (P.O. Box 687, Franklin Lakes, NJ 07417-1322) paper $19.95 (0-934829-83-7). Commentary from medical professionals and a discussion of getting into medical school, plus a section on finding an entry level job in the medical field. (Rev: BL 9/1/91) [610.69]

3014 Garner, Geraldine O. *Careers in Social and Rehabilitation Services* (9–12). 1993, VGM Career Books $16.95 (0-8442-4188-1); paper $12.95 (0-8442-4190-3). (Rev: BL 3/15/94) [361]

3015 Gordon, Susan, and Kristin Hohenadel. *Health Care* (9–12). (Careers Without College) 1992, Peterson's Guides paper $7.95 (1-56079-222-1). Presents 5 types of employment that may require further education but not a 4-year degree. (Rev: BL 2/15/93) [610]

3016 Ramsdell, Melissa, ed. *My First Year As a Doctor: Real-World Stories from America's M.D.'s* (9–adult). 1994, Walker $19.95 (0-8027-1290-8); paper $9.95 (0-8027-7418-0). A guide for those interested in careers in medicine, including testimony from professionals describing their first year of working in the field. (Rev: BL 9/1/94; SHS; VOYA 4/95) [610.69]

3017 Sacks, Terrence J. *Careers in Medicine* (9–12). (VGM Professional Careers) 1992, VGM Career Books $16.95 (0-8442-4178-4); paper $12.95 (0-8442-4179-2). Covers educational expenses, internships, and areas of specialty for physicians. Lists U.S. and Canadian medical schools, organizations, and specialty boards. (Rev: BL 2/15/93) [610.69]

3018 Selden, Annette, ed. *VGM's Handbook of Health Care Careers* (9–12). 1992, VGM Career Books paper $12.95 (0-8442-4148-2). Briefly covers a large number of jobs, with information on résumés, cover letters, and interviews. (Rev: BL 2/15/93) [610]

3019 Sherry, Clifford J. *Opportunities in Medical Imaging Careers* (9–12). 1993, VGM Career Books $13.95 (0-8442-4070-2); paper $10.95 (0-8442-4071-0). (Rev: BL 3/15/94) [616.07]

3020 Simpson, Carolyn, and Penelope Hall. *Careers in Medicine* (9–adult). 1993, Rosen LB $13.95 (0-8239-1711-8); paper $9.95 (0-8239-1712-6). This description of various broad types of doctors and their specialties includes schooling and licensing procedures and a section on medical ethics. (Rev: BL 3/15/94; SLJ 1/94) [610.69]

Science and Engineering

3021 Czerneda, Julie. *Great Careers for People Interested in Living Things* (9–12). (Career Connections) 1993, Gale $16.95 (0-8103-9387-5). Practitioners in their fields are profiled, with information on their educational backgrounds and descriptions of a typical workday. (Rev: BL 3/15/94) [574.023]

3022 Grand, Gail L. *Student Science Opportunities* (7–12). 1994, Wiley paper $14.95 (0-471-31088-3). A guide to science programs offered throughout the U.S. during the summer. (Rev: BL 5/1/94; MJHS; SHS) [507]

3023 Grant, Lesley. *Great Careers for People Concerned about the Environment* (9–12). (Career Connections) 1993, Gale $16.95 (0-8103-9388-3). Profiles various professionals and their educational backgrounds, and includes science-oriented activities aimed to pique interest in various areas. (Rev: BL 3/15/94) [363.7]

Technical and Industrial Careers

3024 Bone, Jan. *Opportunities in Cable Television* (9–12). 2nd ed. 1992, VGM Career Books $13.95 (0-8442-4026-5); paper $10.95 (0-8442-4027-3). (Rev: BL 1/1/93) [384.55]

3025 Bone, Jan. *Opportunities in CAD/CAM Careers* (9–12). 1993, VGM Career Books $13.95 (0-8442-4084-2); paper $10.95 (0-8442-4085-0). (Rev: BL 3/15/94)

3026 Dudzinski, George A. *Opportunities in Tool and Die Careers* (9–12). 1993, VGM Career Books $13.95 (0-8442-4047-8); paper $10.95 (0-8442-4048-6). (Rev: BL 5/15/93) [621.9]

3027 Eberts, Marjorie, and Margaret Gisler. *Careers for Computer Buffs and Other Technological Types* (9–adult). 1993, VGM Career Books $12.95 (0-8442-4104-0); paper $9.95 (0-8442-4105-9). Industries that use computers are covered in this text, developed around informative statements by individuals in the field. (Rev: BL 3/15/94) [004]

3028 Kaplan, Andrew. *Careers for Computer Buffs* (9–adult). 1991, Millbrook LB $12.90 (1-56294-021-X). Employees in the computer industry describe their jobs. (Rev: BL 9/1/91; SLJ 1/92) [004]

3029 Lytle, Elizabeth Stewart. *Exploring Careers As an Electrician* (9–12). (Careers) 1993, Rosen LB $13.95 (0-8239-1513-1); paper $9.95 (0-8239-1716-9). A wide range of opportunities are discussed. (Rev: BL 10/1/93) [621.319]

3030 Noronha, Shonan F. R. *Opportunities in Television and Video Careers* (9–12). 1993, VGM Career Books $13.95 (0-8442-4090-7); paper $10.95 (0-8442-4091-5). (Rev: BL 3/15/94) [384.55]

3031 Richardson, Peter, and Bob Richardson. *Great Careers for People Interested in How Things Work* (9–adult). (Career Connections) 1993, Gale $16.95 (0-8103-9389-1). Information about a variety of careers, traditional and nontraditional. (Rev: BL 3/15/94; SLJ 1/94) [602.3]

3032 Richardson, Peter, and Bob Richardson. *Great Careers for People Interested in Math and Computers* (9–12). (Career Connections) 1993, Gale $16.95 (0-8103-9385-9). (Rev: BL 3/15/94) [004.023]

3033 Rowh, Mark. *Opportunities in Drafting Careers* (9–12). 1993, VGM Career Books $13.95 (0-8442-4082-6); paper $10.95 (0-8442-4083-4). (Rev: BL 3/15/94) [604.2]

3034 Rowh, Mark. *Opportunities in Electronics Careers* (9–12). 1992, VGM Career Books $12.95 (0-8442-8183-2); paper $9.95 (0-8442-8184-0). An overview of the types of careers available, providing information on the background and skills needed, along with future demands and prospects. (Rev: BL 6/1/92) [621.281]

3035 Rowh, Mark. *Opportunities in Installation and Repair Careers* (9–12). VGM Career Books $13.98 (0-8442-4135-0); paper $10.95 (0-8442-4136-9). (Rev: BL 8/94) [602]

3036 Scharnberg, Ken. *Opportunities in Trucking Careers* (9–12). 1992, VGM Career Books $12.95 (0-8442-8181-6); paper $9.95 (0-8442-8182-4). Thoroughly discusses how the complexities involved in scheduling and organizing driver, vehicle, client/customer, freight, and destination are handled, as well as salary structures. (Rev: BL 6/1/92) [388.3]

3037 Southworth, Scott. *Exploring High-Tech Careers* (9–12). Rev. ed. 1993, Rosen LB $13.95 (0-8239-1502-6); paper $9.95 (0-8239-1717-7). Describes technical writing, illustrating, and engineering positions, but concentrates on computer careers, emphasizing the importance of entry-level job experience. (Rev: BL 5/15/93) [001.64]

3038 Weintraub, Joseph. *Exploring Careers in the Computer Field* (9–12). Rev. ed. 1993, Rosen LB $14.95 (0-8239-1601-4); paper $9.95 (0-8239-1723-1). Provides informational interviews, describes future trends, and lists colleges offering computer science majors and associations. (Rev: BL 5/15/93) [001.64]

3039 Williams, Linda. *Computers* (9–12). (Careers Without College) 1992, Peterson's Guides paper $7.95 (1-56079-224-8). (Rev: BL 2/15/93) [004]

Personal Finances

Money-Making Ideas

General and Miscellaneous

3040 Bernstein, Daryl. *Better Than a Lemonade Stand! Small Business Ideas for Kids* (5–8). Illus. 1992, Beyond Words (4443 N.E. Airport Rd., Hillsboro, OR 97124-6074) paper $7.95 (0-941831-75-2). The author, a 15-year old entrepreneur, provides ideas for starting 51 different small businesses and offers advice on start-up costs, billing, and customer relations. (Rev: BL 10/1/92; SLJ 1/93) [650.1]

3041 Casewit, Curtis. *Summer Adventures* (9–adult). 1994, Macmillan/Collier paper $13 (0-02-079331-6). Offers descriptions of a wide variety of summer earning and learning opportunities, with addresses for further information. (Rev: BL 4/1/94) [790]

3042 Deem, James M. *How to Hunt Buried Treasure* (5–7). Illus. 1992, Houghton $15.95 (0-395-58799-9). The lore and logistics of treasure hunting. (Rev: BL 9/15/92; MJHS; SLJ 10/92) [622]

3043 Green, Paul, and Kit Kiefer. *101 Ways to Make Money in the Trading-Card Market* (9–adult). 1994, Bonus paper $8.95 (1-56625-002-1). Advice on investing in, as opposed to collecting, trading cards, including information on identifying undervalued items and when to buy and sell. (Rev: BL 3/15/94) [790.132]

Baby-sitting

3044 Barkin, Carol, and Elizabeth James. *The New Complete Babysitter's Handbook* (5–7). 1995, Clarion $16.95 (0-395-66557-4); paper $7.95 (0-395-66558-2). Serious, practical, and full of good advice. (Rev: BL 5/1/95; MJHS; SHS; SLJ 6/95) [649]

Managing Money

3045 Rendon, Marion, and Rachel Kranz. *Straight Talk about Money* (7–12). (Straight Talk About) 1992, Facts on File $16.95 (0-8160-2612-2). Provides a brief history and description of money and the U.S. economy, followed by suggestions young adults can use when earning and managing money. (Rev: BL 6/15/92; MJHS; SHS) [332.4]

Health and the Human Body

General and Miscellaneous

3046 Barbour, William, ed. *Mental Illness* (7–12). (Opposing Viewpoints) 1995, Greenhaven LB $17.95 (1-56510-209-6); paper $9.95 (1-56510-208-8). Each thematic chapter contains opinion pieces and excerpts from scientific studies supporting various viewpoints on mental health issues. (Rev: BL 7/95; SHS) [362.2]

3047 Farrell, Warren. *The Myth of Male Power: Why Men Are the Disposable Sex* (9–adult). 1993, Simon & Schuster $23 (0-671-79349-7). Farrell contends that our male-dominated society actually kills off men early and blames them for too many problems. (Rev: BL 7/93) [305.32]

3048 *The Good Health Fact Book: A Complete Question-and-Answer Guide to Getting Healthy and Staying Healthy* (9–adult). 1992, Reader's Digest $27 (0-89577-416-X). Answers 1,000–plus nutrition, health, and fitness questions and contains a medical emergency guide. (Rev: BL 10/1/92) [613]

3049 McCoy, Kathy, and Charles Wibbelsman. *The New Teenage Body Book* (7–12). Rev. ed. Illus. 1992, Putnam/Perigee $14.95 (0-399-51725-1). This revised edition provides information and advice concerning the use of drugs, alcohol, and cigarettes; how to handle peer pressure; contraceptive methods; and abortion. (Rev: BL 6/15/92; BTA; MJHS; SHS; SLJ 5/92) [613]

3050 Villarosa, Linda, ed. *Body and Soul: The Black Women's Guide to Physical Health and Emotional Well-Being* (9–adult). 1994, Harper-Perennial $40 (0-06-055359-6); paper $20 (0-06-095085-4). Contributors to this straight-from-the-heart guide include black female scientists, academics, health care practitioners, and writers. (Rev: BL 11/15/94*) [613]

Aging and Death

3051 Bloyd, Sunni. *Euthanasia* (7–10). 1995, Lucent LB $14.95 (1-56006-141-3). A comprehensive look at a difficult subject, with actual cases, photos, and a wide variety of views. Useful for preparation for debates. (Rev: BL 8/95; SLJ 9/95) [179]

3052 Bode, Janet. *Death Is Hard to Live With: Teenagers and How They Cope with Death* (7–12). 1993, Delacorte $16.95 (0-385-31041-2). Bode uses interviews with both teenagers and professionals to talk about death and its effect on those left behind. (Rev: BL 9/15/93; BTA; MJHS; VOYA 4/94) [155.9]

3053 Bratman, Fred. *Everything You Need to Know When a Parent Dies* (7–10). (Need to Know Library) 1992, Rosen LB $12.95 (0-8239-1324-4). (Rev: BL 4/15/92; MJHS) [155.9]

3054 Digiulio, Robert, and Rachel Kranz. *Straight Talk about Death and Dying* (7–12). (Straight Talk About) 1995, Facts on File $16.95 (0-8160-3078-2). (Rev: BL 9/15/95) [155.9]

3055 Dudley, William, ed. *Death and Dying* (7–12). (Opposing Viewpoints) 1992, Greenhaven LB $17.95 (0-89908-192-4); paper $9.95 (0-89908-167-3). A discussion of the best treatment for the terminally ill, the determination of death, how dying patients can control the decision to end treatment, and how to cope with grief. (Rev: BL 11/15/92; MJHS; SHS) [179]

3056 Edelson, Edward. *Aging* (7–12). 1990, Chelsea House $18.95 (0-7910-0035-4). (Rev: BL 2/15/91; MJHS) [612.6]

3057 Gay, Kathlyn. *The Right to Die: Public Controversy, Private Matter* (7–12). (Issue and Debate) 1993, Millbrook $15.90 (1-56294-325-1). Discusses euthanasia and assisted suicide in depth—from Greek times to the present—along with actual recent cases. (Rev: BL 10/1/93; MJHS) [179]

3058 Grollman, Earl A. *Straight Talk about Death for Teenagers: How to Cope with Losing Someone You Love* (7–12). 1993, Beacon $22.50 (0-8070-2500-3); paper $7.95 (0-8070-2501-1). Grollman validates the painful feelings teens experience following the death of a loved one, conveying a sense of the grief as well as getting on with life. (Rev: BL 4/1/93; MJHS; SLJ 6/93; VOYA 8/93) [155.9]

3059 Grosshandler-Smith, Janet. *Coping When a Parent Dies* (7–12). (Coping) 1995, Rosen LB $15.95 (0-8239-1514-X). A high school guidance counselor offers a wide range of coping skills to meet the issues experienced when a parent dies. Glossary and a list for further reading. (Rev: BL 8/95; VOYA 12/95) [155.9]

3060 Jussim, Daniel. *Euthanasia: The Right to Die Issue* (7–10). 1993, Enslow LB $17.95 (0-89490-429-9). A balanced presentation that explains the complex emotional and legal entanglements surrounding this issue. (Rev: BL 10/15/93; BTA; MJHS; SLJ 11/93; VOYA 12/93) [179]

3061 Landau, Elaine. *The Right to Die* (7–12). 1993, Watts $13.95 (0-531-13015-0). A balanced, in-depth examination of the controversial issue, including a chapter on the rights of adolescents to refuse medical treatment. (Rev: BL 1/15/94; BTA; MJHS; SLJ 2/94; VOYA 2/94) [174]

3062 Langone, John. *Growing Older: What Young People Should Know about Aging* (7–12). 1991, Little, Brown $14.95 (0-316-51459-4). Misconceptions about the elderly are discussed to help teens come to terms with the aging process. (Rev: BL 1/15/91*; MJHS; SHS) [305.26]

3063 Wekesser, Carol, ed. *Euthanasia* (7–12). (Opposing Viewpoints) 1995, Greenhaven LB $17.95 (1-56510-244-4); paper $9.95 (1-56510-243-6). (Rev: BL 7/95; MJHS; SHS) [179]

Alcohol, Drugs, and Smoking

3064 Berger, Gilda. *Addiction* (7–12). Rev. ed. 1992, Watts LB $13.40 (0-531-11144-X). A revised 1982 edition that contains new information on the upsurge in the use of crack cocaine and the risk of AIDS among users. (Rev: BL 1/15/93; MJHS; SHS; SLJ 12/92) [616.86]

3065 Berger, Gilda. *Alcoholism and the Family* (8–12). (Changing Family) 1993, Watts $13.40 (0-531-12548-3). This discussion of alcoholism, presented in question-and-answer format, focuses on its effects on the family and covers causes, prevention, treatment, and recovery. (Rev: BL 1/15/94; MJHS; SLJ 12/93; VOYA 2/94) [362.29]

3066 Berger, Gilda, and Nancy Levitin. *Crack* (6–12). 1995, Watts LB $13.93 (0-531-11188-1). Emphasizes the dangers of crack to users, the cost to society, and crack's ability to claim innocent victims: crack babies. (Rev: BL 5/1/95; MJHS; SHS) [362.29]

3067 Carroll, Marilyn. *Cocaine and Crack* (9–12). (Drug Library) 1994, Enslow LB $17.95 (0-89490-472-8). Everything you need to know about crack and cocaine. (Rev: BL 4/15/95; SLJ 4/95; VOYA 5/95) [616.86]

3068 Clayton, Lawrence. *Amphetamines and Other Stimulants* (5–10). (Drug Abuse Prevention Library) 1994, Rosen LB $14.95 (0-8239-1534-4). In addition to describing these drugs and what they do to the body, it also provides suggestions for avoiding peer pressure. (Rev: BL 4/15/95; MJHS) [362.29]

3069 Clayton, Lawrence. *Barbiturates and Other Depressants* (5–10). (Drug Abuse Prevention Library) 1994, Rosen LB $14.95 (0-8239-1535-2). (Rev: BL 4/15/95; MJHS) [362.29]

3070 Clayton, Lawrence. *Designer Drugs* (5–10). (Drug Abuse Prevention Library) 1994, Rosen $13.95 (0-8239-1519-0). (Rev: BL 4/15/94) [362.29]

3071 Cozic, Charles P., and Karin L. Swisher, eds. *Chemical Dependency* (7–12). (Opposing Viewpoints) 1991, Greenhaven LB $15.95 (0-89908-179-7); paper $8.95 (0-89908-154-1). (Rev: BL 10/1/91; MJHS; SHS) [362.29]

3072 Currie, Elliott. *Dope and Trouble: Portraits of Delinquent Youth* (9–adult). 1992, Pantheon $22 (0-394-56151-1). Interviews with troubled kids in a juvenile facility; displays the effectiveness of the current juvenile justice system.

Awards: YALSA Best Book for Young Adults. (Rev: BL 1/1/92) [363.3]

3073 Currie, Elliott. *Reckoning: Drugs, the Cities, and the American Future* (9–adult). 1993, Hill & Wang $25 (0-8090-8049-4). The author sees drug abuse as a social problem and traces sources, not symptoms, of drug use. (Rev: BL 12/1/92) [362.29]

3074 De Stefano, Susan. *Drugs and the Family* (5–7). Illus. 1991, Twenty-First Century LB $14.95 (0-941477-61-4). Explains the way roles and relationships change when a family member has a drug problem and how that person can be helped. (Rev: BL 6/1/91; SLJ 6/91) [262.29]

3075 Dolan, Edward F. *Drugs in Sports* (7–12). 2nd ed. 1992, Watts LB $13.90 (0-531-11041-9). An updated edition that focuses on substances most often abused by athletes: steroids, amphetamines, cocaine, and marijuana. B&W photos. (Rev: BL 6/15/92; SHS; SLJ 3/92) [362.29]

3076 Falco, Mathea. *The Making of a Drug-Free America: Programs That Work* (9–adult). 1992, Times Books $22 (0-8129-1957-2). Detailed discussion of drug programs that work: education, moving dealers out of neighborhoods, treatment, establishing effective community coalitions, and changing public attitudes. (Rev: BL 11/15/92) [362.29]

3077 Friedman, David. *Alerta a las drogas y el cerebro* (5–7). (Libro de alerta sobre los drogas) Illus. 1991, Children's Press $15.95 (0-516-37353-6). The first title in this Spanish-language series defines psychoactive drugs without undue proselytizing. English title: *Focus on Drugs and the Brain*. (Rev: BL 1/1/92)

3078 Harris, Jacqueline L. *Drugs and Disease* (5–8). (Bodies in Crisis) 1993, Twenty-First Century $14.95 (0-8050-2602-9). Case studies are included in this book about drug abuse. (Rev: BL 1/15/94; MJHS) [616.86]

3079 Harris, Jonathan. *Drugged America* (7–12). 1991, Four Winds $14.95 (0-02-742745-5). A look at the enormous U.S. drug problem describes commonly abused illicit drugs as well as information on treatment programs. (Rev: BL 8/91; SHS; SLJ 8/91) [362.29]

3080 Harris, Jonathan. *This Drinking Nation* (7–12). 1994, Four Winds $16.95 (0-02-742744-7). Discusses America's alcohol consumption from 1607 to the present, including information on the prohibition period of 1920–1933. Also examines teenage drinking and alcoholism. (Rev: BL 7/94; MJHS; SLJ 9/94; VOYA 10/94) [394.1]

3081 Hurwitz, Ann Ricki, and Sue Hurwitz. *Hallucinogens* (5–10). (Drug Abuse Prevention Library) 1992, Rosen LB $14.95 (0-8239-1461-5). (Rev: BL 12/15/92; MJHS) [362.29]

3082 Johnson, Joan J. *America's War on Drugs* (8–12). Illus. 1990, Watts LB $13.90 (0-531-10954-2). Broad coverage of the war on drugs offers no easy solutions. (Rev: BL 1/15/91; SHS) [363.4]

3083 Kronenwetter, Michael. *Drugs in America* (9–12). (Issues for the 1990s). 1990, Messner LB $12.98 (0-671-70557-1). (Rev: BL 4/1/91; MJHS) [362.29]

3084 Landau, Elaine. *Hooked: Talking about Addictions* (6–10). 1995, Millbrook LB $15.90 (1-56294-469-X). A discussion of addictive behvior that explains causes, effects, and the recovery process. (Rev: BL 1/1/96; SLJ 1/96) [362.29]

3085 Landau, Elaine. *Teenage Drinking* (7–12). (Issues in Focus) 1994, Enslow LB $17.95 (0-89490-575-9). (Rev: BL 11/15/94) [362.29]

3086 Langone, John. *Tough Choices: A Book about Substance Abuse* (7–12). 1995, Little, Brown $14.95 (0-316-51407-1). An overview of the contradictory medical evidence involving the use of alcohol, drugs, and nicotine. (Rev: BL 4/1/95; SHS; SLJ 2/95; VOYA 2/95) [362.29]

3087 Lee, Mary Price, and Richard S. Lee. *Drugs and Codependency* (5–10). (Drug Abuse Prevention Library) 1995, Rosen $15.95 (0-8239-2065-8). (Rev: BL 9/15/95) [616.869]

3088 Lukas, Scott E. *Steroids* (7–10). (Drug Library). 1994, Enslow LB $17.95 (0-89490-471-X). Considers the physical, psychological, and legal consequences of using the drug. (Rev: BL 1/1/95; SLJ 1/95; VOYA 4/95) [362.29]

3089 McMillan, Daniel. *Winning the Battle Against Drugs: Rehabilitation Programs* (7–12). 1991, Watts LB $13.90 (0-531-11063-X). Various rehabilitation programs are described, from the Hazelden treatment center and a Narcotics Anonymous group to a methadone maintenance clinic. (Rev: BL 11/1/91; MJHS; SLJ 1/92) [362.29]

3090 Miller, Maryann. *Drugs and Date Rape* (5–10). (Drug Abuse Prevention Library) 1995, Rosen $15.95 (0-8239-2064-X). (Rev: BL 9/15/95) [362.88]

3091 Miller, Maryann. *Drugs and Gun Violence* (5–10). (Drug Abuse Prevention Library) 1995, Rosen $15.95 (0-8239-2060-7). (Rev: BL 9/15/95) [364.2]

3092 Monroe, Judy. *Nicotine* (7–10). (Drug Library) 1995, Enslow LB $17.95 (0-89490-505-8). (Rev: BL 7/95) [613.85]

3093 Myers, Arthur. *Drugs and Peer Pressure* (5–10). (Drug Abuse Prevention Library) 1995, Rosen $15.95 (0-8239-2066-6). (Rev: BL 9/15/95) [362.29]

3094 Nevitt, Amy. *Fetal Alcohol Syndrome* (7–12). (Drug Abuse Prevention Library) 1996, Rosen LB $15.95 (0-8239-2061-5). Explains the signs and symptoms of babies born to women who drink during pregnancy and what happens to these children as they grow up. (Rev: SLJ 3/96)

3095 Newer, Hank. *Steroids* (7–12). 1990, Watts LB $12.90 (0-531-10946-1). Basic facts about steroids, their uses in sports, and their effects. Alternatives to steroids are also examined. (Rev: BL 1/15/91) [362.29]

3096 O'Neill, Catherine. *Alerta al alcohol* (5–7). (Libro de alerta sobre los drogas/Drug Free Kids) 1991, Children's Press $15.95 (0-516-37351-X). Includes basic facts about alcohol and its abuse, a history of its use, relevant facts and myths, and a glossary. English title: *Focus on Alcohol*. (Rev: BL 1/1/92)

3097 Peck, Rodney. *Drugs and Sports* (7–10). (Drug Abuse Prevention Library) 1992, Rosen $14.95 (0-8239-1420-8). Part of a high/low series for reluctant readers. (Rev: BL 12/15/92; SLJ 2/93) [362.29]

3098 Perry, Robert. *Alerta a la nicotína y la cafeína* (5–7). (Libro de alerta sobre los drogas/Drug Free Kids) Illus. 1991, Children's Press $15.95 (0-516-37355-2). Includes basic facts about nicotine and caffeine and the consequences of their abuse, a history of their use, relevant facts and myths, and a glossary. English title: *Focus on Nicotine and Caffeine*. (Rev: BL 1/1/92)

3099 Robbins, Paul R. *Designer Drugs* (7–12). (Drug Library) 1995, Enslow LB $17.95 (0-89490-488-4). An exploration of the growing problem of synthetic substances made by "kitchen chemists." (Rev: BL 5/1/95; SLJ 5/95) [362.29]

3100 Rogak, Lisa Angowski. *Steroids: Dangerous Game* (6–9). 1992, Lerner LB $11.96 (0-8225-0048-5). Discusses what steroids are and why they are so dangerous physically and psychologically. Covers drug testing, use of steroids in sports, and tips for training without them. (Rev: BL 2/15/93; SLJ 12/92; YR) [362.29]

3101 Rosenberg, Maxine B. *On the Mend: Getting Away from Drugs* (9–12). 1991, Bradbury $14.95 (0-02-777914-9). Based on personal interviews, this book follows teens from their initial drug involvement, through their crises, their counseling, and the usually successful resolution of their drug problems. (Rev: BL 10/15/91; SLJ 12/91) [362.29]

3102 Salak, John. *Drugs in Society: Are They Our Suicide Pill?* (6–9). (Issues of Our Time) 1993, Twenty-First Century $14.95 (0-8050-2572-3). (Rev: BL 1/15/94) [362.29]

3103 Santamaria, Peggy. *Drugs and Politics* (5–10). (Drug Abuse Prevention Library) 1994, Rosen $15.95 (0-8239-1703-7). (Rev: BL 3/15/95) [363.4]

3104 Sherry, Clifford. *Inhalants* (5–10). 1994, Rosen $15.95 (0-8239-1704-5). Definitions of inhalants and how they affect the body. (Rev: BL 2/15/95; SLJ 3/95) [362.29]

3105 Shuker-Haines, Frances. *Everything You Need to Know about a Drug-Abusing Parent* (7–12). (Need to Know Library) 1994, Rosen $13.95 (0-8239-1529-8). (Rev: BL 4/15/94; MJHS) [362.29]

3106 Shulman, Jeffrey. *Alerta a la cocaína y el crack* (5–7). (Libro de alerta sobre los drogas/Drug Free Kids) Illus. 1991, Children's Press $15.95 (0-516-37352-8). Includes basic facts about cocaine and crack and the consequences of their abuse, a history of their use, relevant facts and myths, and a glossary. English title: *Focus on Cocaine and Crack*. (Rev: BL 1/1/92)

3107 Shulman, Jeffrey. *Drugs and Crime* (5–7). Illus. 1991, Twenty-First Century LB $14.95 (0-941477-60-6). A blend of statistics and emotional appeals dramatizes how drug use generates criminal activity. (Rev: BL 6/1/91; SLJ 6/91) [363.4]

3108 Silverstein, Alvin, and others. *Steroids: Big Muscles, Big Problems* (7–10). 1992, Enslow LB $17.95 (0-89490-318-7). After defining natural and synthetic (anabolic) steroids, offers an overview of the use and abuse of steroids, with a focus on their use in sports. (Rev: BL 7/92; MJHS) [362.29]

3109 Smith, C. Fraser. *Lenny, Lefty, and the Chancellor* (9–adult). 1992, Bancroft Press (P.O. Box 65360, Baltimore, MD 21209) paper $12.95 (0-9631246-0-9). When a college basketball star dies of a drug overdose, school officials attempt to avoid a scandal. (Rev: BL 3/15/92; SLJ 8/92) [796.323]

3110 Smith, Judie. *Drugs and Suicide* (5–10). (Drug Abuse Prevention Library) 1992, Rosen LB $14.95 (0-8239-1421-6). (Rev: BL 12/15/92) [362.2]

3111 Sonder, Ben. *Dangerous Legacy: The Babies of Drug-Taking Parents* (7–12). 1994, Watts LB $13.93 (0-531-11195-4). Discusses the effects drugs have on the developing fetus. (Rev: BL 12/1/94; SHS; SLJ 2/95; VOYA 4/95) [362.29]

3112 Steffens, Bradley. *Addiction: Distinguishing Between Fact and Opinion* (5–7). (Opposing Viewpoints Juniors) 1994, Greenhaven LB $10.95 (1-56510-094-8). (Rev: BL 1/1/94) [362.29]

3113 Steins, Richard. *Alcohol Abuse: Is This Danger on the Rise?* (6–9). (Issues of Our Time) 1995, Twenty-First Century $15.98 (0-8050-3882-5). Includes a definition of alcoholism, the disease's short- and long-term effects on a family, the physical effects on youth, peer pressure, and drinking and driving. (Rev: BL 10/15/95; SLJ 2/96) [362.29]

3114 Swisher, Karin L. *Drug Trafficking* (9–12). (Current Controversies) 1991, Greenhaven LB $16.95 (0-89908-576-8); paper $9.95 (0-89908-582-2). The pros and cons of waging the war on drugs, legalizing drugs, and U.S. campaigns for stemming the flow of drugs are addressed. (Rev: BL 6/15/92; MJHS) [363.4]

3115 Swisher, Karin L., and Katie DeKoster. *Drug Abuse* (7–12). (Opposing Viewpoints) 1994, Greenhaven LB $17.95 (1-56510-060-3); paper $9.95 (1-56510-059-X). (Rev: BL 4/15/94; MJHS) [362.29]

3116 Talmadge, Katherine S. *Drugs and Sports* (5–7). Illus. 1991, Twenty-First Century LB $14.95 (0-941477-59-2). A focus on steroids, cocaine, and alcohol, supported with quotes by sports figures who have come back from addiction. (Rev: BL 6/1/91; SLJ 6/91) [362.29]

3117 Terkel, Susan Neiburg. *Should Drugs Be Legalized?* (7–12). 1990, Watts LB $13.90 (0-531-10944-5). An impartial, easy-to-understand examination of the drug legalization debate. (Rev: BL 1/1/91*; MJHS; SHS) [363.4]

3118 Wax, Wendy. *Say No and Know Why: Kids Learn about Drugs* (5–7). Photos. 1992, Walker LB $13.85 (0-8027-8141-1). Takes a sobering look at the roles played by hospitals and courts in the drug abuse dilemma. (Rev: BL 1/15/93; SLJ 10/92) [362.29]

3119 Webb, Margot. *Drugs and Gangs* (7–12). (Drug Abuse Prevention Library) 1996, Rosen LB $15.95 (0-8239-2059-3). Discussion includes advice on how to stay clear of gangs and where to go for help. (Rev: SLJ 3/96)

3120 Weir, William. *In the Shadow of the Dope Fiend: America's War on Drugs* (9–adult). 1995, Shoe String/Archon $32.50 (0-208-02384-4). A social history of drug usage. (Rev: BL 4/1/95; VOYA 12/95) [363.4]

3121 Wekesser, Carol, ed. *Alcoholism* (9–12). (Current Controversies) 1994, Greenhaven LB $16.95 (1-56510-074-3); paper $9.95 (1-56510-073-5). (Rev: BL 4/15/94; MJHS; SHS) [362.29]

3122 Wells, Tim, and William Triplett. *The Drug Wars: Voices from the Street* (9–adult). 1992, Morrow $20 (0-688-09548-8). Heroin, crack, and cocaine viewed from multiple perspectives, allowing readers to draw their own conclusions. (Rev: BL 4/1/92) [363.4]

3123 Woods, Geraldine. *Heroin* (7–10). (Drug Library). 1994, Enslow LB $17.95 (0-89490-473-6). A well-researched, clearly written and carefully sourced book about heroin abuse and addiction. (Rev: BL 1/1/95; SLJ 1/95; VOYA 4/95) [362.29]

3124 Yoslow, Mark. *Drugs in the Body* (9–12). 1992, Watts LB $13.90 (0-531-12507-6). This scientific perspective on drug abuse examines what happens to the body from the first moment of use to what occurs after weeks, months, and years of repeated use. (Rev: BL 4/1/92; SLJ 5/92) [616.86]

3125 Zeller, Paula Klevan. *Alerta a la marihuana* (5–7). (Libro de alerta sobre los drogas/Drug Free Kids) Illus. 1991, Children's Press $15.95 (0-516-37354-4). Includes basic facts about marijuana and the consequences of its abuse, a history of its use, relevant facts and myths, and a glossary. English title: *Focus on Marijuana*. (Rev: BL 1/1/92; SLJ 2/92)

Bionics and Transplants

3126 Durrett, Deanne. *Organ Transplants* (6–8). (Overview) 1993, Lucent $14.95 (1-56006-137-5). (Rev: BL 6/1–15/93; MJHS) [617.9]

3127 Leinwand, Gerald. *Transplants: Today's Medical Miracles* (7–12). Rev. ed. 1993, Watts LB $13.90 (0-531-13026-6). Provides arguments for and against fetal transplants, the buying and selling of organs, and the role of the free market in prosthesis development, among other topics. (Rev: BL 3/15/93; MJHS; SHS) [617.9]

Diseases and Illnesses

3128 Aaseng, Nathan. *Cerebral Palsy* (7–12). 1991, Watts $12.40 (0-531-12529-7). Case studies of the causes, prevention, detection, and treatment of cerebral palsy. (Rev: BL 1/15/92; MJHS; SHS; SLJ 2/92) [616.8]

3129 Aaseng, Nathan. *The Common Cold and the Flu* (7–12). 1993, Watts LB $12.90 (0-531-12537-8). Provides clear explanations of how viruses attack and how our immune system responds, and offers theories about virus transmission. (Rev: BL 3/15/93; MJHS; SHS) [616.2]

3130 Beshore, George. *Sickle Cell Anemia* (7–12). 1994, Watts LB $13.93 (0-531-12510-6). An informative overview that includes a history of the disease, how it is transmitted from parent to child, and the importance of genetic testing. (Rev: BL 1/1/95; SHS; SLJ 1/95; VOYA 4/95) [616.1]

3131 Biddle, Wayne. *Field Guide to Germs* (9–12). 1995, Holt $22.50 (0-8050-3531-1). Historical information on the various bacteria and viruses that attack humans, presented in an informal, humorous way. (Rev: BL 8/95; SLJ 1/96)

3132 Biskup, Michael D., and Karin L. Swisher, eds. *AIDS* (7–12). (Opposing Viewpoints) 1992, Greenhaven LB $17.95 (0-89908-190-8); paper $9.95 (0-89908-165-7). The pros and cons of AIDS as a moral issue, the effectiveness of testing and treatment, and the prevention of the disease's spread. (Rev: BL 11/15/92; MJHS; SHS) [362.1]

3133 Blake, Jeanne. *Tiempos de riesgo: Entérate del SIDA para mantenerte saludable* (7–12). Tr. by Aída E. Marcuse. 1993, Workman paper $5.95 (1-56305-436-1). The author discusses the problem of AIDS and explains important related issues, such as sexual relationships, the use of condoms, drug abuse, and ways of dealing with HIV-infected people. English title: *Risky Times: How to Be AIDS-Smart and Stay Healthy*. (Rev: BL 10/1/93)

3134 Brodman, Michael, and others. *Straight Talk about Sexually Transmitted Diseases* (7–12). (Straight Talk About) 1993, Facts on File $16.95 (0-8160-2864-8). Discusses the ways sexually transmitted diseases are contracted, symptoms, possible consequences, and treatment. (Rev: BL 3/15/94; BTA; MJHS; SLJ 6/94) [616.95]

3135 Burkett, Elinor. *The Gravest Show on Earth: America in the Age of AIDS* (9–adult). 1995, Houghton $22.95 (0-395-74537-3). There are 3 essential books on AIDS—Shilts's *And the Band Played On*, Fumento's *Myth of Heterosexual AIDS*, and this one, in which Burkett exposes the profiteering and exploitation of AIDS. (Rev: BL 10/1/95*) [362]

3136 Clayton, Lawrence, and Betty Sharon Smith. *Coping with Sports Injuries* (6–12). 1992, Rosen LB $13.95 (0-8239-1453-4). Discusses the physical and emotional consequences of sports injuries and the importance of age-appropriate conditioning. (Rev: BL 2/15/93; SHS; SLJ 9/92) [617.1]

3137 Corrick, James A. *Muscular Dystrophy* (9–12). 1993, Watts LB $12.90 (0-531-12540-8). Discusses the incurable, sometimes fatal hereditary disease, its symptoms, diagnosis, and treatment. (Rev: BL 3/15/93; MJHS) [616.7]

3138 Cozic, Charles, and Karin L. Swisher. *The AIDS Crisis* (9–12). (Current Controversies) 1991, Greenhaven LB $16.95 (0-89908-578-4); paper $9.95 (0-89908-584-9). Addresses such topics as funding, treatment, testing, and controlling the spread of HIV. (Rev: BL 6/15/92; MJHS; SLJ 5/92) [362.1]

3139 Daugirdas, John T. *S.T.D. Sexually Transmitted Diseases, Including HIV/AIDS* (8–12). 3rd ed. 1992, MedText (15W560 89th St., Hinsdale, IL 60521) paper $14.95 (0-9629279-1-0). This overview simplifies the language and prunes unnecessary medical terminology. (Rev: BL 10/1/92; SLJ 11/92) [616.951]

3140 Desowitz, Robert S. *The Malaria Capers: More Tales of Parasites and People, Research and Reality* (9–adult). 1991, Norton $22.95 (0-393-03013-X). Describes the early work and the current status of research on malaria and kala-azar, and gives accounts of the personalities and scientific organizations involved. (Rev: BL 10/15/91) [616.9]

3141 Facklam, Howard, and Margery Facklam. *Viruses* (5–7). (The Invaders). 1994, Twenty-First Century LB $15.95 (0-8050-2856-0). Clear photos and text of viruses that invade our bodies. (Rev: BL 1/1/95; SLJ 3/95) [576]

3142 Flynn, Tom, and Karen Lound. *AIDS: Examining the Crisis* (7–12). 1995, Lerner LB $13.13 (0-8225-2625-5). An informative explanation in clear language about HIV and AIDS. (Rev: BL 5/1/95; SLJ 6/95) [362.1]

3143 Ford, Michael Thomas. *100 Questions and Answers about AIDS: A Guide for Young People* (8–12). 1992, Macmillan/New Discovery $14.95 (0-02-735424-5). Answers to common queries that clarify background, distinguish misinformation, and guide readers toward safer behaviors. Awards: SLJ Best Book; YALSA Best Book for Young Adults. (Rev: BL 8/92; SHS; SLJ 1/93*) [616.97]

3144 Ford, Michael Thomas. *The Voices of AIDS* (8–12). 1995, Morrow $15 (0-688-05322-X).

Dedicated to getting the word out about AIDS, told by 12 people, many of them women. (Rev: BL 8/95*; SLJ 11/95) [362.1]

3145 Gallo, Robert. *Virus Hunting: Cancer, AIDS, and the Human Retrovirus: A Story of Scientific Discovery* (9–adult). 1991, Basic Books $22.95 (0-465-09806-1). (Rev: BL 3/1/91; SHS) [616]

3146 Galperin, Anne. *Gynecological Disorders* (9–12). (Encyclopedia of Health). 1990, Chelsea House $18.95 (0-7910-0075-3). (Rev: BL 3/15/91; MJHS) [618.1]

3147 Giblin, James Cross. *When Plague Strikes: The Black Death, Smallpox, AIDS* (6–12). (Women of Our Time) 1995, HarperCollins LB $14.89 (0-06-025864-0). A discussion, combining social history, science, and technology, of the great plagues in history. Awards: ALSC Notable Children's Book; SLJ Best Book. (Rev: BL 10/15/95; SLJ 10/95; VOYA 4/96) [614.4]

3148 Greenberg, Lorna. *AIDS: How It Works in the Body* (5–8). 1992, Watts LB $11.90 (0-531-20074-4). Discusses the history of the spread of AIDS, current research, and the meaning of viruses and the body's defense system. (Rev: BL 12/1/92; SLJ 7/92) [616.97]

3149 Harris, Jacqueline L. *Communicable Diseases* (5–8). (Bodies in Crisis). 1993, Twenty-First Century $14.95 (0-8050-2599-5). Information on how contagious diseases are transmitted, how the body responds, and what methods are available for treatment and prevention. (Rev: BL 1/15/94) [616.9]

3150 Harris, Jacqueline L. *Hereditary Diseases* (5–8). (Bodies in Crisis) 1993, Twenty-First Century $14.95 (0-8050-2603-7). Discusses chromosomes, their makeup, defects, external factors, and research in genetic engineering. (Rev: BL 1/15/94; MJHS) [616]

3151 Henig, Robin Marantz. *A Dancing Matrix: Voyages along the Viral Frontier* (9–adult). 1993, Knopf $23 (0-394-58878-9). An engrossing, informative account of modern viral research, including the origins of AIDS and the disease-generating impact of human encroachment on the environment. (Rev: BL 1/15/93*) [576]

3152 Johnson, Earvin "Magic." *What You Can Do to Avoid AIDS* (9–adult). 1992, Times Books paper $3.99 (0-8129-2063-5). Facts, answers to common questions, and interviews comprise this excellent guide to AIDS for teens. Awards: BL Editors' Choice; YALSA Best Book for Young Adults. (Rev: BL 6/1/92) [616.97]

3153 Joseph, Stephen C. *Dragon Within the Gates: The Once and Future AIDS Epidemic* (9–adult). 1992, Carroll & Graf $21 (0-88184-905-7). A former New York City health commissioner gives an overview of the AIDS epidemic and suggests ways to combat it. (Rev: BL 9/15/92) [362.19]

3154 Karlen, Arno. *Man and Microbes* (9–12). 1995, Putnam $24.95 (0-87477-759-3). A history of communicable diseases, featuring plagues and epidemics, listed in chronological order. Also includes discussions on AIDS and sexually transmitted diseases. (Rev: BL 4/1/95; SLJ 1/96)

3155 Kittredge, Mary. *Teens with AIDS Speak Out* (8–12). 1992, Messner LB $14.98 (0-671-74542-5); paper $8.95 (0-671-74543-3). Combines facts and interviews on AIDS' history, transmission, treatment, and prevention, as well as safer-sex practices and discrimination against people with AIDS. Awards: YALSA Best Book for Young Adults. (Rev: BL 6/1/92; SLJ 7/92; YR) [362.1]

3156 Kolodny, Nancy J. *When Food's a Foe: How to Confront and Conquer Eating Disorders* (8–12). Rev. ed. 1992, Little, Brown paper $7.95 (0-316-50181-6). Includes self-help and self-awareness approaches to dealing with eating disorders. (Rev: BL 5/15/92; MJHS; SHS; SLJ 5/92) [616.85]

3157 Kubersky, Rachel. *Everything You Need to Know about Eating Disorders: Anorexia and Bulimia* (7–10). (Need to Know Library) 1992, Rosen LB $13.95 (0-8239-1321-X). A candid look at psychological, historical, and sociocultural aspects of these disorders. (Rev: BL 5/15/92; SLJ 9/92) [616.85]

3158 Landau, Elaine. *Allergies* (5–7). (Understanding Illness) 1994, Twenty-First Century $15.95 (0-8050-2989-3). Describes the symptoms, diagnosis, and treatment of the illness and addresses preventative measures. (Rev: BL 12/15/94) [616.97]

3159 Landau, Elaine. *Blindness* (5–7). (Understanding Illness) 1994, Twenty-First Century $15.95 (0-8050-2992-3). (Rev: BL 12/15/94) [617.7]

3160 Landau, Elaine. *Cancer* (5–7). (Understanding Illness) 1994, Twenty-First Century $15.95 (0-8050-2990-7). (Rev: BL 12/15/94) [616.99]

3161 Landau, Elaine. *Epilepsy* (5–7). (Understanding Illness) 1994, Twenty-First Century $15.95 (0-8050-2991-5). (Rev: BL 12/15/94) [616.8]

3162 Little, Marjorie. *Diabetes* (7–12). (Encyclopedia of Health). 1990, Chelsea House $18.95 (0-

7910-0061-3). (Rev: BL 3/15/91; MJHS; SHS) [616.4]

3163 McIvor, Kirsten. *Exposure: Victims of Radiation Speak Out* (9–adult). 1992, Kodansha $25 (4-77001-623-9). Reporters present data on radiation contamination in 15 countries, hoping their effort will help reduce the use of nuclear power for any purpose. (Rev: BL 9/15/92) [363.17]

3164 Mactire, Sean P. *Lyme Disease and Other Pest-Borne Illnesses* (7–12). 1992, Watts/Venture LB $12.40 (0-531-12523-8). This nontechnical but scientific examination addresses the history of the disease, transmission, symptoms, treatments, and current research. (Rev: BL 10/1/92; MJHS; SHS; SLJ 7/92) [616.9]

3165 Maloney, Michael, and Rachel Kranz. *Straight Talk about Eating Disorders* (7–12). 1991, Facts on File $16.95 (0-8160-2414-6). This subject is addressed in a matter-of-fact manner and includes recommendations for solving the problem. (Rev: BL 4/15/91; MJHS; SHS) [616.85]

3166 Manning, Karen. *AIDS: Can This Epidemic Be Stopped?* (6–9). (Issues of Our Time) 1995, 21st Century Books LB $15.98 (0-8050-4240-7). An overview of the status of HIV/AIDS research, treatment, and issues surrounding the disease. (Rev: SLJ 2/96; VOYA 4/96)

3167 Miller, Martha J. *Kidney Disorders* (7–12). (Encyclopedia of Health) 1992, Chelsea House LB $18.95 (0-7910-0066-4). (Rev: BL 12/1/92; MJHS) [616.6]

3168 Moe, Barbara. *Coping with Eating Disorders* (7–10). 1991, Rosen $12.95 (0-8239-1343-0). Actual case histories are used to explain the characteristics of bulimia, anorexia, and complusive-eating patterns. Practical coping suggestions also offered. (Rev: BL 7/91; SHS; SLJ 11/91) [616.85]

3169 Newman, Gerald, and Eleanor Newman Layfield. *Allergies* (7–10). 1992, Watts/Venture LB $12.40 (0-531-12516-5). This overview for allergy sufferers explains how the body reacts to different allergens, along with information on treatments. (Rev: BL 9/15/92; MJHS; SHS; SLJ 7/92) [616.97]

3170 Nourse, Alan E. *The Virus Invaders* (8–10). 1992, Watts LB $12.40 (0-531-12511-4). Virology is explained in lay terms, including a history of viruses and the prognosis for treatment of killers like malaria and AIDS. (Rev: BL 9/15/92; SHS; SLJ 7/92) [616]

3171 Powers, Mary C. *Arthritis* (7–12). (Encyclopedia of Health) 1992, Chelsea House LB $18.95 (0-7910-0057-5). (Rev: BL 10/1/92; MJHS) [616.7]

3172 Preston, Richard. *The Hot Zone* (9–adult). 1994, Random $23 (0-679-43094-6). Chronicles the nearly disastrous leak of the deadly Ebola virus from the Reston Primate Quarantine Unit that was prevented by the U.S. Army Veterinary Corps. Awards: SLJ Best Book. (Rev: BL 10/1/94; BTA; SLJ 1/95) [614.5]

3173 Radetsky, Peter. *The Invisible Invaders: The Story of the Emerging Age of Viruses* (9–adult). 1991, Little, Brown $22.95 (0-316-73216-8). What is known about viruses and recent genetic discoveries based on viral research. (Rev: BL 1/1/91; SHS) [616.0194]

3174 Ryan, Frank. *The Forgotten Plague: How the Battle Against Tuberculosis Was Won—and Lost* (9–adult). 1993, Little, Brown $20.45 (0 316-76380-2). Describes the work of pioneer investigators and recent research efforts to control the spread of emerging drug-resistant TB strains. (Rev: BL 5/15/93) [614.5]

3175 Siegel, Dorothy Schainman, and David E. Newton. *Leukemia* (7–12). 1994, Watts LB $13.93 (0-531-12509-2). An introductory survey emphasizing the cure rate for leukemia. (Rev: BL 2/15/95; SLJ 1/95; VOYA 4/95) [616.99]

3176 Silverstein, Alvin, and others. *Cystic Fibrosis* (7–12). 1994, Watts LB $13.40 (0-531-12552-1). Explains the often-fatal hereditary disease, how it is transmitted, and how it affects the body. Outlines current treatment and research. (Rev: BL 9/15/94; SLJ 8/94; VOYA 10/94) [616.37]

3177 Silverstein, Alvin, and others. *Mononucleosis* (7–10). (Diseases and People). 1994, Enslow LB $17.95 (0-89490-466-3). Examines this disease in terms of history, causes, treatment, prevention, and societal consequences. (Rev: BL 1/15/95; SLJ 3/95) [616.9]

3178 Silverstein, Alvin, and others. *So You Think You're Fat?* (7–12). 1991, HarperCollins LB $13.89 (0-06-021642-5). A book written to help teenagers think more intelligently about their eating habits, to decide whether they have problems, and to work toward solving them. (Rev: BL 4/15/91; MJHS; SHS) [616.85]

3179 Silverstein, Alvin, and Virginia Silverstein. *AIDS: Deadly Threat* (8–12). 1991, Enslow LB $18.95 (0-89490-175-3). This revised edition has been expanded to include chapters on the medical, social, and political aspects of HIV and AIDS. (Rev: BL 6/15/91; MJHS; SHS; SLJ 6/92) [616.97]

3180 Simpson, Carolyn. *Coping with Asthma* (5–7). 1995, Rosen LB $15.95 (0-8239-2069-0). A discussion of asthma that benefits both those who have it and those who don't. (Rev: BL 9/15/95; VOYA 12/95) [616.2]

3181 Thayne, Emma Lou, and Becky Thayne Markosian. *Hope and Recovery: A Mother-Daughter Story about Anorexia Nervosa, Bulimia, and Manic Depression* (9–12). 1992, Watts LB $13.90 (0-531-11140-7). One family's experiences with anorexia nervosa, bulimia, and manic depression, told by a mother and daughter. (Rev: BL 2/15/92; MJHS; SLJ 5/92) [362.1]

3182 Weiss, Jonathan H. *Breathe Easy: Young People's Guide to Asthma* (5–7). 1994, Magination (19 Union Square W., 8th Fl., New York, NY 10003) paper $9.95 (0-945354-62-2). An accessible self-help approach to asthma. (Rev: BL 2/15/95; VOYA 5/95) [618.92]

3183 Wilkinson, Beth. *Coping When a Grandparent Has Alzheimer's Disease* (9–12). 1992, Rosen $12.95 (0-8239-1415-1). Addresses a wide range of issues through testimony of teens whose grandparents are in various stages of Alzheimer's. (Rev: BL 4/1/92; BTA; MJHS; SHS) [362.1]

3184 Yancey, Diane. *The Hunt for Hidden Killers: Ten Cases of Medical Mystery* (7–12). 1994, Millbrook $15.90 (1-56294-389-8). A description of the determined efforts of health workers attempting to unravel such medical enigmas as AIDS and Lyme disease. (Rev: BL 3/15/94; BTA; MJHS; SLJ 7/94) [614.4]

3185 Yount, Lisa. *Cancer* (9–12). 1991, Lucent LB $12.95 (1-56006-125-1). A report on detection, treatment, and prevention of cancer. (Rev: BL 5/1/92; MJHS; SLJ 5/92) [616.99]

3186 Zonderman, Jon, and Laurel Shader. *Environmental Diseases* (5–8). (Bodies in Crisis) 1993, Twenty-First Century $14.95 (0-8050-2600-2). Focuses on several present-day diseases, with illustrations and charts explaining such ailments as Lyme disease. (Rev: BL 7/94; SLJ 4/94) [616.9]

3187 Zonderman, Jon, and Laurel Shader. *Nutritional Diseases* (5–8). (Bodies in Crisis) 1993, Twenty-First Century $14.95 (0-8050-2601-0). Discusses the causes and possible treatments for such nutritional disorders as obesity, anorexia, bulimia, and bingeing. (Rev: BL 7/94; MJHS; SLJ 4/94) [616.3]

Doctors, Hospitals, and Medicine

3188 Almonte, Paul, and Theresa Desmond. *Medical Ethics* (5–10). 1991, Macmillan/Crestwood $11.95 (0-89686-662-9). Using well-known examples, offers an unopinionated perspective on such controversial issues as euthanasia, AIDS testing, and surrogate mothering. (Rev: BL 12/15/91) [174.2]

3189 Armstrong, David, and Elizabeth Metzger Armstrong. *The Great American Medicine Show: Being an Illustrated History of Hucksters, Healers, Health Evangelists, and Heroes from Plymouth Rock to the Present* (9–adult). 1991, Prentice-Hall $18 (0-13-364027-2). An illustrated historical account of the fads and fashions of the American medical industry. (Rev: BL 11/1/91) [615.8]

3190 Carpineto, Jane F. *R.N.: The Commitment, the Heartache and the Courage of Three Dedicated Nurses* (9–adult). 1992, St. Martin's $18.95 (0-312-07095-0). Profiles the private and professional lives of 3 nurses. (Rev: BL 1/15/92) [610.73]

3191 Colen, B. D. *O.R.: The True Story of 24 Hours in a Hospital Operating Room* (9–adult). 1993, Dutton $20 (0-525-93518-5). Vividly describes treatment procedures, patients, and professional staff in 16 rooms of a New York City hospital during 24 hours. (Rev: BL 3/15/93) [617]

3192 Fleming, Robert. *Rescuing a Neighborhood: The Bedford-Stuyvesant Volunteer Ambulance Corps* (5–8). 1995, Walker LB $16.85 (0-8027-8330-9). A chronicle of a volunteer emergency corps in Bedford-Stuyvesant, Brooklyn. (Rev: BL 5/1/95; SLJ 9/95) [362.1]

3193 Koop, C. Everett. *Koop: The Memoirs of the Former Surgeon General* (9–adult). 1991, Random $22.50 (0-394-57626-8). The author's carefully reasoned opinions on AIDS, abortion, the right to die, and other controversial medical issues are expressed in this memoir. (Rev: BL 9/1/91*) [610]

3194 Levitin, Nancy. *America's Health Care Crisis: Who's Responsible?* (7–12). 1994, Watts LB $13.93 (0-531-11187-3). Analyzes the major health care debates. (Rev: BL 4/15/95; SHS; SLJ 3/95) [338.4]

3195 McCoy, J. J. *Animals in Research: Issues and Conflicts* (8–12). 1993, Watts $19.14 (0-531-13023-1). A balanced, carefully researched overview of this emotional issue. (Rev: BL 8/93; BTA; MJHS) [179]

3196 Murphy, Wendy, and Jack Murphy. *Nuclear Medicine* (7–12). (Encyclopedia of Health) 1993, Chelsea House $19.95 (0-7910-0070-2); paper $7.95 (0-7910-0497-X). (Rev: BL 12/1/93; MJHS; SHS) [616.07]

3197 Nardo, Don. *Medical Diagnosis* (7–12). (Encyclopedia of Health) 1992, Chelsea House LB $18.95 (0-7910-0067-2). (Rev: BL 10/1/92; MJHS) [616.07]

3198 Roueché, Berton. *The Man Who Grew Two Breasts: And Other Tales of Medical Detection* (9–adult). 1995, Dutton/Truman Talley $18.95 (0-525-93934-2). Eight medical cases that originally stumped doctors. (Rev: BL 4/15/95) [610]

3199 Sherrow, Victoria. *The U.S. Health Care Crisis: The Fight over Access, Quality, and Cost* (7–12). 1994, Millbrook LB $15.90 (1-56294-364-2). Examines U.S. health care options, current and past controversies, and the possibility of providing universal coverage. (Rev: BL 10/15/94; SHS; SLJ 11/94; VOYA 2/95) [362.1]

3200 Stetter, Cornelius. *The Secret Medicine of the Pharaohs: Ancient Egyptian Healing* (9–adult). 1993, Quintessence paper $19.95 (0-86715-265-6). Uses Egyptian papyri to reconstruct ancient Egyptian medicine and explain it in a modern scientific context. Many color illustrations. (Rev: BL 9/15/93) [610]

3201 Stewart, Gail B. *Alternative Healing* (7–10). (Opposing Viewpoints) 1990, Greenhaven LB $13.95 (0-89908-083-9). (Rev: BL 4/1/91; MJHS; SHS) [615.8]

3202 Terkel, Susan Neiburg. *Colonial American Medicine* (5–8). (Colonial America) 1993, Watts $12.90 (0-531-12539-4). An account of traditional medicine that addresses the colonists' problems with illness and the risks of seeking help from medical practitioners. (Rev: BL 1/1/94; MJHS; SLJ 11/93) [632.1]

3203 Van Steenwyk, Elizabeth. *Frontier Fever: The Silly, Superstitious—and Sometimes Sensible—Medicine of the Pioneers* (5–8). 1995, Walker LB $16.85 (0-8027-8403-8). The medicine of European settlers and indigenous peoples are contrasted, and medicine through the Civil War up to the twentieth century is explored. (Rev: BL 7/95; SLJ 12/95; VOYA 12/95) [610]

3204 Verghese, Abraham. *My Own Country: A Doctor's Story of a Town and Its People in the Age of AIDS* (9–adult). 1994, Simon & Schuster $23 (0-671-78514-1). Verghese interjects humor and pathos into his memoir detailing work with AIDS patients in eastern Tennessee during the mid-1980s. (Rev: BL 4/1/94; BTA) [362.1]

3205 Wolfson, Evelyn. *From the Earth to Beyond the Sky: Native American Medicine* (5–8). 1993, Houghton $14.95 (0-395-55009-2). This look at Native American medicine describes how some common plants are used, as well as the practices, training, roles, sacred objects, and ceremonies of medicine men. (Rev: BL 12/15/93; MJHS; SLJ 12/93) [615.8]

Genetics

3206 Bryan, Jenny. *Genetic Engineering* (7–9). 1995, Thomson Learning LB $15.95 (1-56847-268-4). Recounts the advances of gene research, including a discussion of the ethical questions involved. (Rev: BL 8/95) [575.1]

3207 Brynie, Faith Hickman. *Genetics and Human Health: A Journey Within* (6–9). 1995, Millbrook LB $15.90 (1-56294-545-9). An introduction to genetics and health, including the history of genetics, current uses, and such diseases as cystic fibrosis, Marfan's syndrome, and sickle-cell anemia. (Rev: BL 6/1–15/95; SHS; SLJ 5/95) [616]

3208 Byczynski, Lynn. *Genetics: Nature's Blueprints* (6–10). (Encyclopedia of Discovery and Invention) 1991, Lucent LB $15.95 (1-56006-213-4). (Rev: BL 4/15/92) [575.1]

3209 Jones, Steve. *The Language of Genes: Unraveling the Mysteries of Human Genetics* (9–adult). 1994, Doubleday/Anchor $24.95 (0-385-47372-9). Explains the importance of genetics, exploring such topics as disease-causing genetic mutations, Darwinism, and the eugenics movement. (Rev: BL 8/94; SHS) [573.2]

3210 Kingsley, Jason, and Mitchell Levitz. *Count Us In: Growing Up with Down Syndrome* (9–adult). 1994, Harcourt $19.95 (0-15-150447-4). The 2 authors write about their own experiences of living with Down's syndrome, including families, marriage, sex, employment, ambitions, and education. (Rev: BL 11/15/93; BTA; SLJ 6/94) [362.1]

3211 Lee, Thomas F. *The Human Genome Project: Cracking the Genetic Code of Life* (9–adult). 1991, Plenum $24.50 (0-306-43965-4). Provides background information on DNA and genes, examines the Human Genome Project, and discusses genetic diseases and their possible therapeutic treatment. (Rev: BL 9/15/91; SHS) [573.2]

3212 Marion, Robert. *Was George Washington Really the Father of Our Country? A Clinical*

Geneticist Looks at World History (9–adult). 1994, Addison-Wesley $21.95 (0-201-62255-6). An exploration of the impact of genetic abnormalities on world history, including Washington's sterility, Napoleon's growth hormone deficiency, and Lincoln's Marfan's syndrome. (Rev: BL 1/15/94) [909.08]

3213 Thro, Ellen. *Genetic Engineering: Shaping the Material of Life* (7–12). 1993, Facts on File $17.95 (0-8160-2629-7). Many charts and drawings are used to enhance the author's explanations of DNA and cell structure as well as the chromosomes and genes that are the determinants of heredity. (Rev: BL 9/1/93; MJHS; SHS) [660]

3214 Wekesser, Carol, ed. *Genetic Engineering* (8–12). (Opposing Viewpoints) 1995, Greenhaven LB $19.95 (1-56510-359-9); paper $11.55 (1-56510-358-0). (Rev: BL 12/15/95) [174]

Grooming, Personal Appearance, and Dress

3215 Baker, Patricia. *Fashions of a Decade: The 1950s* (7–12). (Fashions of a Decade) 1991, Facts on File $16.95 (0-8160-2468-5). An illustrated overview of fashions of the 1950s, with historical background on the major international events of the times. (Rev: BL 12/15/91; MJHS; SLJ 2/92) [391]

3216 Delio, Michelle. *Tattoo: The Exotic Art of Skin Decoration* (9–adult). 1994, St. Martin's paper $14.95 (0-312-10148-1). Describes the art and business of tattooing, shows impressive examples, and provides a brief directory of tattooists. (Rev: BL 2/1/94; BTA) [391]

3217 Herald, Jacqueline. *Fashions of a Decade: The 1920s* (7–12). (Fashions of a Decade) 1991, Facts on File $16.95 (0-8160-2465-0). An illustrated overview of fashions and trends of the 1920s and a discussion of the development of modern life after World War I. (Rev: BL 12/15/91; MJHS; SLJ 2/92) [391]

3218 Landau, Elaine. *The Beauty Trap* (8–12). 1994, Macmillan/New Discovery $13.95 (0-02-751389-0). An examination of society's obsession with an unrealistic standard of feminine beauty and the damage it causes. (Rev: BL 3/15/94; MJHS; SHS; SLJ 3/94; VOYA 2/95) [155.6]

3219 Marano, Hara Estroff. *Style Is Not a Size: Looking and Feeling Great in the Body You Have* (9–adult). 1991, Bantam $15 (0-553-35270-9). Comprehensive style manual aimed at the full-figured woman. (Rev: BL 6/1/91) [646]

3220 Mathis, Darlene. *Women of Color: The Multicultural Guide to Fashion and Beauty* (9–adult). 1994, Ballantine $23 (0-345-38929-8). Suggests color palettes, wardrobe selections, hairstyles, and other fashion tips for African, Asian, Hispanic, and Native American women. (Rev: BL 10/1/94; BTA; SHS) [646.7]

The Human Body

General and Miscellaneous

3221 Almonte, Paul, and Theresa Desmond. *The Immune System* (5–10). 1991, Macmillan/Crestwood $11.95 (0-89686-661-0). A basic description of the way the immune system works and a catalog of familiar medical problems related to its dysfunction. (Rev: BL 12/15/91) [616.07]

3222 Day, Trevor. *The Random House Book of 1001 Questions and Answers about the Human Body* (5–8). 1994, 1994, Random paper $13 (0-679-85432-0). (Rev: BL 12/1/94; MJHS) [512]

3223 *Diccionario visual Altea del cuerpo humano* (5–12). 1992, Santillana (Madrid, Spain) $24.95 (84-372-4528-1). This large-format dictionary includes more than 200 detailed, eye-catching photos and drawings in color, with brief texts explaining the human body. Index. English title: *The Visual Dictionary of the Human Body*. (Rev: BL 4/1/94)

3224 Dillner, Luisa. *El cuerpo humano* (5–8). Tr. by Graciela Jáurequi Lorda de Castro. 1993, Editorial Sigmar (Buenos Aires, Argentina) $29.95 (950-11-0926-7). This large-format book provides a unique view of the human body and its functions through plastic overlays, color illustrations, and straightforward text. Originally published in Great Britain. English title: *The Human Body*. (Rev: BL 2/1/94)

3225 Edelson, Edward. *Sleep* (7–10). (Encyclopedia of Health) 1991, Chelsea House $18.95 (0-7910-0092-3). (Rev: BL 11/15/91; MJHS; SHS) [612.8]

3226 Knutson, Roger M. *Furtive Fauna: A Field Guide to the Creatures Who Live on You* (9–adult). 1992, Penguin paper $8 (0-14-015378-0). Facts—often humorous—about flies, bedbugs, and other tiny critters that live and feed on the human body. (Rev: BL 6/1/92; BTA) [616.9]

3227 Orlock, Carol. *Inner Time: The Science of Body Clocks and What Makes Us Tick* (9–adult). 1993, Birch Lane $18.95 (1-55972-194-4). A lively overview of the discoveries and science of biological clocks. (Rev: BL 8/93; BTA) [574.1882]

3228 Parker, Steve. *Cuerpo humano* (6–12). (Ciencia visual) Tr. by Rafael Lozano Guillén. 1994, Santillana (Madrid, Spain) $23.95 (84-372-4547-8). This large-format guide illustrates the ideas, processes, and discoveries that have changed our conception of the human body. Detailed color photos of anatomic models and microscopic images. English title: *Human Body*. (Rev: BL 10/15/95)

3229 Parker, Steve. *Human Body* (5–8). (Eyewitness Science) 1993, Dorling Kindersley LB $15.95 (1-56458-325-2). (Rev: BL 11/15/93; MJHS) [612]

3230 Stein, Sara. *The Body Book* (6–9). 1992, Workman $19.95 (1-56305-298-9); paper $11.95 (0-89480-805-2). Follows human development from conception to birth and discusses what shapes us and how our bodies work. (Rev: BL 11/1/92; SLJ 12/92) [612]

3231 Whitfield, Philip, ed. *The Human Body Explained: A Guide to Understanding the Incredible Living Machine* (9–adult). 1995, Holt $40 (0-8050-3752-7). A guide to the body, discussing all the major organs in terms of day-to-day life and their function in the survival of the species. (Rev: BL 12/1/95) [612]

3232 Young, John K. *Hormones: Molecular Messengers* (8–12). 1994, Watts LB $13.40 (0-531-12545-9). Explains the workings and functions of the body's hormones. Discusses protein, steroid, sex, adrenal, pituitary, and thyroid hormones. (Rev: BL 9/15/94; MJHS; SHS; SLJ 7/94; VOYA 10/94) [612.4]

Brain and Nervous System

3233 Alkon, Daniel. *Memory's Voice: Deciphering the Mind-Brain Code* (9–adult). 1992, HarperCollins $22.50 (0-06-018300-4). Describes the author's research on the effect of trauma on memory and the processes the brain uses to make and retain associations. (Rev: BL 10/1/92) [612.8]

3234 Barrett, Susan L. *It's All in Your Head: A Guide to Understanding Your Brain and Boosting Your Brain Power* (6–10). Illus. 1992, Free Spirit (400 First Ave. N., Suite 616, Minneapolis, MN 55401) paper $9.95 (0-915793-45-8). Covers subjects as diverse as brain anatomy, intelligence, biofeedback, creativity, ESP, and brain scans. (Rev: BL 2/15/93; MJHS) [153]

3235 Cytowic, Richard E. *The Man Who Tasted Shapes: A Neurologist Reveals the Illusion of the Rational Mind* (9–adult). 1993, Putnam/Tarcher $21.95 (0-87477-738-0). Describes a study of synesthesia, a disease that haphazardly blends the 5 senses, and shows that emotion plays a large role in brain function. (Rev: BL 5/15/93) [152]

3236 Falk, Dean. *Braindance* (9–adult). 1992, Holt $24.95 (0-8050-1282-6). A paleoanthropologist describes key stages in the evolution of the human brain. (Rev: BL 1/15/92) [569]

3237 Kittredge, Mary. *Pain* (7–12). (Encyclopedia of Health) 1991, Chelsea House $18.95 (0-7910-0072-9). (Rev: BL 1/15/92; MJHS; SHS) [616]

3238 Parker, Steve. *Brain Surgery for Beginners: And Other Major Operations for Minors* (5–7). 1995, Millbrook $15.40 (1-56294-604-8); paper $6.95 (1-56294-895-4). A detailed discussion of the central nervous system, other body systems, and the brain's role in controlling each. (Rev: BL 5/1/95) [612]

3239 Powledge, Tabitha. *Your Brain: How You Got It and How It Works* (7–12). 1994, Scribner $14.95 (0-684-19659-X). An informative overview of brain composition, development, and function. (Rev: BL 12/1/94; SHS; SLJ 9/95) [612.8]

3240 Restak, Richard. *The Brain Has a Mind of Its Own: Insights from a Practicing Neurologist* (9–adult). 1991, Crown/Harmony $18 (0-517-57483-7). Explores the indivisible connection of human behavior and emotions to the biology of the brain in this series of essays. (Rev: BL 10/15/91) [612.8]

3241 Restak, Richard. *Brainscapes: An Introduction to What Neuroscience Has Learned about the Structure, Function, and Abilities of the Brain* (9–adult). 1995, Hyperion $19.95 (0-7868-6113-4). A neurologist discusses major advances in the knowledge of the brain. (Rev: BL 10/1/95) [612.8]

3242 Restak, Richard. *Receptors* (9–adult). 1994, Bantam $23.95 (0-553-08198-5). This study focuses on receptors for neurotransmitters and provides theory, examples of brain functions, and discussion of various drugs' effects on the brain. (Rev: BL 2/15/94) [612.8]

3243 Sacks, Oliver. *An Anthropologist on Mars: Seven Paradoxical Tales* (9–adult). 1995, Knopf $24 (0-679-43785-1). (Rev: BL 1/15/95*) [616.8]

Musculoskeletal System

3244 Feinberg, Brian. *The Musculoskeletal System* (7–12). (Encyclopedia of Health) 1993, Chelsea House $19.95 (0-7910-0028-1); paper $7.95 (0-7910-0463-5). (Rev: BL 12/1/93; MJHS; SHS) [612.7]

Senses

3245 Silverstein, Alvin, and others. *Smell, the Subtle Sense* (6–9). Illus. 1992, Morrow LB $13.93 (0-688-09397-3). Classifies types of smells, types of noses (insect, reptile, human), and the steps the body goes through to detect an odor. (Rev: BL 7/92; MJHS) [612.8]

Teeth

3246 Siegel, Dorothy. *Dental Health* (7–12). (Encyclopedia of Health) 1994, Chelsea House $19.95 (0-7910-0014-1); paper $7.95 (0-7910-0454-6). (Rev: BL 1/1/94; MJHS; SHS) [617.6]

Hygiene and Physical Fitness

3247 Dixon, Barbara M., and Josleen Wilson. *Good Health for African-Americans* (9–adult). 1994, Crown $25 (0-517-59170-7). Nutritionist Dixon places African Americans' health challenges and solutions in historical context and offers advice on lifestyle improvement through a 24-week diet. (Rev: BL 2/15/94) [613]

3248 Feuerstein, Georg, and Stephan Bodian, eds. *Living Yoga: A Comprehensive Guide for Daily Life* (9–adult). 1993, Putnam/Tarcher paper $15.95 (0-87477-729-1). Interviews, essays, and articles on yoga's practices and teachings. (Rev: BL 3/15/93) [181.45]

3249 Hoy, Suellen. *Chasing Dirt: The American Pursuit of Cleanliness* (9–adult). 1995, Oxford Univ. $25 (0-19-509420-4). The history of how cleanliness became unusually integral to American culture. (Rev: BL 5/15/95) [614]

3250 Schwarzenegger, Arnold, and Charles Gaines. *Arnold's Fitness for Kids Ages 11–14: A Guide to Health, Exercise, and Nutrition* (6–9). 1993, Doubleday $15 (0-385-42268-7). Focuses on nutrition games and exercises that will help parents and kids reach their fitness goals. Includes stories of Arnold's youth. (Rev: BL 7/93)

Mental Disorders and Emotional Problems

3251 Ayer, Eleanor H. *Teen Suicide: Is It Too Painful to Grow Up?* (6–9). (Issues of Our Time) 1993, Twenty-First Century $14.95 (0-8050-2573-1). Discusses who commits suicide and why, recognizing the signs, overcoming grief, and prevention. (Rev: BL 11/1/93) [362.2]

3252 Crisfield, Deborah. *Eating Disorders* (6–9). 1994, Macmillan/Crestwood LB $13.95 (0-89686-807-9); paper $4.95 (0-382-24756-6). The psychological/behavioral disorders anorexia nervosa, bulimia, and overeating. (Rev: BL 3/1/95; SLJ 3/95) [616.85]

3253 Dunbar, Robert E. *Mental Retardation* (6–9). 1991, Watts LB $12.90 (0-531-12502-5). Covers the causes of mental retardation, modern preventative research, and a brief history of treatment, as well as the rights of the developmentally disabled. (Rev: BL 11/15/91; SLJ 1/92) [362.3]

3254 Grob, Gerald N. *The Mad among Us: A History of the Care of America's Mentally Ill* (9–adult). 1994, Free Press $24.95 (0-02-912695-9). A description of the changing attitudes toward and the treatment of mental illness, showing the twentieth-century progression from an asylum-related to a private-office practice. (Rev: BL 2/1/94) [362.2]

3255 Gutkind, Lee. *Stuck in Time: The Tragedy of Childhood Mental Illness* (9–adult). 1993, Holt $25 (0-8050-1469-1). An eye-opening view of a health care system ill-equipped to deal with the problems of mentally ill youth. (Rev: BL 7/93; SLJ 1/94) [616.89]

3256 Hall, David E. *Living with Learning Disabilities: A Guide for Students* (5–8). 1993, Lerner $15.95 (0-8225-0036-1). A pediatrician gives background information on learning disabilities, as well as coping strategies. (Rev: BL 1/1/94; SLJ 4/94) [371.9]

3257 Hayden, Torey L. *Ghost Girl: The Story of a Child Who Refused to Talk* (9–adult). 1991, Little, Brown $19.95 (0-316-35167-9). The story of a traumatized 8-year-old who refused to speak and was helped by a caring, committed teacher. Awards: YALSA Best Book for Young Adults. (Rev: BL 5/15/91; SHS) [362.1]

3258 Kuklin, Susan. *After a Suicide: Young People Speak Up* (7–12). 1994, Putnam $15.95 (0-399-22605-2); paper $9.95 (0-399-22801-2). Focuses on failed suicide attempts. Also looks at friends and family members who suffer shock, guilt, and loss when suicide succeeds. Awards: ALSC Notable Children's Book; SLJ Best Book; YALSA Best Book for Young Adults. (Rev: BL 10/15/94; BTA; SLJ 12/94; VOYA 2/95) [362.2]

3259 Maloney, Michael, and Rachel Kranz. *Straight Talk about Anxiety and Depression* (7–12). 1991, Facts on File $16.95 (0-8160-2434-0). Discusses teenage emotional pressures, stress, and sexual concerns, identifies the causes of depression and anxiety, and suggests coping strategies and techniques. (Rev: BL 10/15/91; MJHS; SHS; SLJ 3/92) [155.5]

3260 Quinn, Patricia O. *Adolescents and ADD: Gaining the Advantage* (8–12). 1996, Magination paper $12.95 (0-945354-70-3). Attention deficit disorder is defined and several treatments are discussed, including medication and coping strategies. (Rev: BL 1/1/96; SLJ 3/96)

3261 Sebastian, Richard. *Compulsive Behavior* (7–12). (Encyclopedia of Health) 1993, Chelsea House LB $18.95 (0-7910-0044-3). (Rev: BL 1/1/93; MJHS) [616.85]

3262 Sherrow, Victoria. *Mental Illness* (7–12). (Overview) 1996, Lucent LB $16.95 (1-56006-168-5). An overview of mental illness; includes a historical perspective and reforms now in progress. (Rev: BL 3/1/96; SLJ 2/96)

3263 Smith, Douglas W. *Schizophrenia* (7–12). 1993, Watts $12.90 (0-531-12514-9). An informative discussion of the causes, characteristics, and treatment of this common mental illness. (Rev: BL 7/93; MJHS; SLJ 6/93) [616]

3264 Sonder, Ben. *Eating Disorders: When Food Turns Against You* (7–10). 1993, Watts $12.90 (0-531-11175-X). Discusses the psychology of eating disorders such as anorexia nervosa and bulimia, the effects of pop culture, research on weight and eating, and dieting hazards. (Rev: BL 10/1/93; MJHS; SLJ 6/93; VOYA 8/93) [616.85]

Nutrition and Diet

3265 Arneson, D. J. *Nutrition and Disease: Looking for the Link* (7–12). 1992, Watts LB $12.90 (0-531-12504-1). Explains how fats, proteins, vitamins, and minerals correlate with good health. (Rev: BL 3/1/93) [621.3]

3266 Craig, Jenny, and Brenda L. Wolfe. *Jenny Craig's What Have You Got to Lose? A Personalized Weight Management Program* (9–adult). 1992, Villard $20 (0-679-40527-5). Guide to weight-management principles through a program of nutritious foods and regular exercise. (Rev: BL 3/1/92) [613.2]

3267 Krizmanic, Judy. *A Teen's Guide to Going Vegetarian* (7–12). 1994, Viking $14.99 (0-670-85114-0); paper $6.99 (0-14-036589-3). Explains the health, ethical, and environmental benefits of switching to a vegetarian diet. Discusses nutrition and provides recipes. (Rev: BL 10/1/94; BTA; SHS; VOYA 2/95) [613.2]

3268 Le Bow, Michael D. *Overweight Teenagers: Don't Bear the Burden Alone* (6–12). 1995, Plenum/Insight $23.95 (0-306-45047-X). By a sympathetic director of an obesity clinic; does not include food plans. (Rev: BL 12/1/95) [613.2]

3269 Levenstein, Harvey. *Paradox of Plenty: A Social History of Eating in Modern America* (9–adult). 1993, Oxford Univ. $24 (0-19-505543-8). Explores the links between social and culinary history: eating habits, nutritional breakthroughs, and food fads from the 1930s to the present. (Rev: BL 1/1/93*) [394.1]

3270 MacClancy, Jeremy. *Consuming Culture: Why You Eat What You Eat* (9–adult). 1993, Holt $23 (0-8050-2578-2). A multicultural romp through the history of world cuisine, presenting little-known facts about food taboos, fads, nutritional illogic, food politics, even cannibalism. (Rev: BL 6/1–15/93) [394.1]

3271 McMillan, Daniel. *Obesity* (7–12). 1995, Watts LB $13.93 (0-531-11201-2). A thorough resource on a topic that is difficult to define. (Rev: BL 4/15/95; SLJ 4/95) [616.3]

3272 Nardo, Don. *Vitamins and Minerals* (7–12). (Encyclopedia of Health) 1994, Chelsea House $19.95 (0-7910-0032-X). (Rev: BL 8/94; SHS) [613.2]

3273 Robbins, John. *May All Be Fed: Diet for a New World* (9–adult). 1992, Morrow paper $23 (0-688-11625-6). Low-fat, vegetarian ideals are promoted as a way to foster worldwide harmony. (Rev: BL 9/15/92) [613.2]

3274 Salter, Charles A. *Food Risks and Controversies: Minimizing the Dangers in Your Diet* (6–10). (Teen Nutrition) 1993, Millbrook $15.40 (1-56294-259-X). A nutritionist/research scientist answers questions about the dangers in a teenager's diet. (Rev: BL 12/1/93; MJHS; SLJ 11/93) [615.9]

3275 Salter, Charles A. *Looking Good, Eating Right: A Sensible Guide to Proper Nutrition and*

Weight Loss for Teens (7–10). 1991, Millbrook LB $13.90 (1-56294-047-3). Basic principles of nutrition are explained, along with discussions of fad dieting, eating disorders, and proper exercise. (Rev: BL 10/1/91; MJHS; SLJ 11/91) [616.85]

3276 Salter, Charles A. *The Nutrition-Fitness Link: How Diet Can Help Your Body and Mind* (6–10). (Teen Nutrition) 1993, Millbrook $15.40 (1-56294-260-3). The professional nutritionist/researcher discusses the dos and don'ts of nutrition for athletes. (Rev: BL 12/1/93; MJHS; SLJ 11/93; VOYA 2/94) [613.2]

3277 Salter, Charles A. *The Vegetarian Teen: A Teen Nutrition Book* (7–10). 1991, Millbrook LB $13.90 (1-56294-048-1). A positive introduction to vegetarianism that addresses the special concerns of teenagers and gives advice on achieving proper nutritional balance. (Rev: BL 10/1/91; MJHS; SHS; SLJ 11/91) [613.2]

3278 Silverstein, Alvin, and others. *Carbohydrates* (5–7). (Food Power!) Illus. 1992, Millbrook LB $13.90 (1-56294-207-7). Discusses the kinds and sources of carbohydrates and what happens when the body cannot process them properly. (Rev: BL 12/15/92; SLJ 1/93) [612.3]

3279 Silverstein, Alvin, and others. *Fats* (5–7). (Food Power!) Illus. 1992, Millbrook LB $13.90 (1-56294-208-5). Crammed with logically and concisely presented information, with many easy-to-read charts and humorous color illustrations. (Rev: BL 12/15/92) [612.3]

3280 Silverstein, Alvin, and others. *Proteins* (5–7). (Food Power!) Illus. 1992, Millbrook LB $13.90 (1-56294-209-3). Crammed with logically and concisely presented information, with many easy-to-read charts and humorous color illustrations. (Rev: BL 12/15/92) [612.3]

3281 Silverstein, Alvin, and others. *Vitamins and Minerals* (5–7). (Food Power!) Illus. 1992, Millbrook LB $13.90 (1-56294-206-9). Includes a history of vitamins and looks at theories about what kinds and how much are needed to ensure a balanced system. (Rev: BL 12/15/92; SLJ 1/93) [612.3]

3282 Spies, Karen Bornemann. *Everything You Need to Know about Diet Fads* (7–12). (Need to Know Library) 1993, Rosen $13.95 (0-8239-1533-6). (Rev: BL 10/1/93) [613.2]

3283 Stare, Frederick J., and others. *Your Guide to Good Nutrition* (9–adult). 1991, Prometheus paper $13.95 (0-87975-692-6). Professional, no-nonsense answers are given to basic questions about nutrition, weight control, dietary supplements, and the claims of the health food industry. (Rev: BL 10/1/91; SLJ 12/91) [613.2]

Physical Disabilities and Problems

3284 Barrie, Barbara. *Adam Zigzag* (6–9). 1994, Delacorte $14.95 (0-385-31172-9). This story of a dyslexic boy and his sister chronicles his problems with making sense of schoolwork and the despair he and his parents feel. (Rev: BL 2/1/94; MJHS; SLJ 3/94; VOYA 2/94)

3285 Bernstein, Joanne E., and Bryna J. Fireside. *Special Parents, Special Children* (5–7). Illus. 1991, Albert Whitman $11.50 (0-8075-7559-3). Profiles 4 families in which at least one parent is physically challenged. (Rev: BL 8/91; SLJ 2/92) [306.874]

3286 Cheney, Glenn Alan. *Teens with Physical Disabilities: Real-Life Stories of Meeting the Challenges* (6–9). 1995, Enslow LB $17.95 (0-89490-625-9). Accounts of teens' daily lives as they struggle and triumph over the challenges imposed by disabilities. Includes short biographies and photos. (Rev: BL 8/95; SLJ 8/95) [362.4]

3287 Crisfield, Deborah. *Sports Injuries* (5–10). 1991, Macmillan/Crestwood $11.95 (0-89686-663-7). Fictional scenarios lead to informative discussion of common injuries, the healing process, and the necessity of heeding the body's pain signals. (Rev: BL 12/15/91) [617.1]

3288 Kettelkamp, Larry. *High Tech for the Handicapped: New Ways to Hear, See, Talk, and Walk* (6–10). 1991, Enslow LB $17.95 (0-89490-202-4). A succinct overview of the new technologies that enable the physically challenged to become more self-sufficient. (Rev: BL 4/1/91; MJHS; SLJ 7/91) [362.4]

3289 Krementz, Jill. *How It Feels to Live with a Physical Disability* (6–9). 1992, Simon & Schuster $18 (0-671-72371-5). Twelve young people, ages 6–16, who have been challenged by physical disabilities. (Rev: BL 5/15/92*; BTA; MJHS) [305.908]

3290 Mango, Karin N. *Hearing Loss* (7–12). 1991, Watts LB $12.40 (0-531-12519-X). The hearing-impaired author describes the difficulties that complicate life for the deaf in a hearing world and what can be done to ease them. (Rev: BL 6/1/91; MJHS; SHS; SLJ 8/91) [617.8]

3291 Nardo, Don. *The Physically Challenged* (6–9). 1994, Chelsea House. $19.95 (0-7910-0073-7). A focus on the psychology of living with physical challenges and the adaptations used by individuals to participate in everyday life. (Rev: BL 8/94; MJHS; SHS) [362.4]

3292 Walker, Lou Ann. *Hand, Heart, and Mind: The Story of the Education of America's Deaf People* (7–12). 1994, Dial $14.99 (0-8037-1225-1). A discussion of the prejudice, ignorance, and conflicting philosophies that have marked the history of the education of deaf people. (Rev: BL 3/1/94; BTA; SLJ 4/94) [371.91]

Reproduction, Sex Education, and Child Care

3293 Baulieu, Étienne-Émile, and Mort Rosenblum. *The "Abortion Pill": RU-486, a Woman's Choice* (9–adult). 1991, Simon & Schuster $22 (0-671-73816-X). The developer of RU-486 describes how the drug's action against pregnancy works, traces its turbulent history, and answers antiabortion rhetoric with reason and compassion. (Rev: BL 11/1/91) [613.9]

3294 Bender, David L., and Bruno Leone, eds. *Abortion* (9–12). Rev. ed. 1991, Greenhaven $15.95 (0-89908-181-9); paper $8.95 (0-89908-156-8). A debate on abortion centering on whose rights are violated, the woman's or the unborn child's. (Rev: BL 1/15/92; SLJ 1/92) [363.4]

3295 Bode, Janet. *Kids Still Having Kids: People Talk about Teen Pregnancy* (7–12). Illus. 1992, Watts LB $14.40 (0-531-11132-6). Interviews with teens, mostly girls, on sex, pregnancy, abortion, adoption, foster care, and parenting. (Rev: BL 1/1/93; BTA; MJHS; SHS) [306.85]

3296 Bourgeois, Paulette, and Martin Wolfish. *Changes in You and Me: A Book about Puberty, Mostly for Boys* (5–7). 1994, Andrews & McMeel $14.95 (0-8362-2814-6). Attends to issues of puberty, pregnancy, and related sexual matters, including decision making. (Rev: BL 2/1/95; SLJ 3/95) [612.6]

3297 Bourgeois, Paulette, and Martin Wolfish. *Changes in You and Me: A Book about Puberty, Mostly for Girls* (5–7). 1994, Andrews & McMeel $14.95 (0-8362-2815-4). Attends to issues of puberty, pregnancy, and related sexual matters, including decision making. (Rev: BL 2/1/95; SLJ 3/95) [612.6]

3298 Bryan, Jenny. *El milagro de la vida* (5–8). Tr. by Reis Camilleri Abelló. 1994, Beascoa (Madrid, Spain) $26.95 (84-488-0194-6). This large-format book views the development of a baby during pregnancy through computer-designed plastic overlays and color drawings. English title: *The Miracle of Life*. (Rev: BL 10/15/95)

3299 Caplan, Theresa. *The First Twelve Months of Life: Your Baby's Growth Month by Month* (9–adult). 1993, Putnam/Perigee paper $14.95 (0-399-51804-5). Organized month by month, this book charts the first year of infant development. (Rev: BL 7/93) [613.9]

3300 Cozic, Charles P., and Johnathan Petrikin, eds. *The Abortion Controversy* (7–12). (Current Controversies) 1995, Greenhaven LB $17.95 (1-56510-229-0); paper $9.95 (1-56510-228-2). The morality of abortion is argued from many points of view, with information on the debate on access to abortion. (Rev: BL 3/15/95; SHS; SLJ 5/95) [363.4]

3301 Day, Nancy. *Abortion: Debating the Issue* (8–12). (Issues in Focus) 1995, Enslow LB $17.95 (0-89490-645-3). A balanced presentation of the subject, including recent developments in the antiabortion-rights movement. Black-and-white photos, glossary, and extensive notes. (Rev: BL 8/95; SLJ 12/95) [363.4]

3302 Fenwick, Elizabeth, and Richard Walker. *How Sex Works: A Clear, Comprehensive Guide for Teenagers to Emotional, Physical, and Sexual Maturity* (7–10). 1994, Dorling Kindersley $14.95 (1-56458-505-0). Discusses a wide range of topics, including puberty, love, reproduction, sexual orientation, oral sex, and sexual experimentation. (Rev: BL 9/1/94; MJHS; SHS; VOYA 12/94) [613.9]

3303 Gay, Kathlyn. *Day Care: Looking for Answers* (7–12). 1992, Enslow LB $17.95 (0-89490-324-1). Documents the need for day care, not only for children but also for the elderly and the disabled. (Rev: BL 4/1/92; SLJ 4/92) [362.7]

3304 Gay, Kathlyn. *Pregnancy: Private Decisions, Public Debates* (7–12). 1994, Watts LB $13.40 (0-531-11167-9). Discusses topics involving reproductive freedom, including the pro-choice/pro-life debate, reproductive technologies, population growth, and childbirth methods. (Rev: BL 8/94; BTA; SLJ 7/94; VOYA 10/94) [363.9]

3305 Gravelle, Karen, and Leslie Peterson. *Teenage Fathers* (7–12). 1992, Messner LB $11.98 (0-671-72850-4); paper $5.95 (0-671-72851-2). Thirteen teenage boys describe their situations and feelings when they became fathers, with qualifying comments by the authors. Awards: YALSA

Best Book for Young Adults. (Rev: BL 10/15/92; SHS) [306.85]

3306 Harris, Robie H. *It's Perfectly Normal: A Book about Changing Bodies, Growing Up, Sex, and Sexual Health* (5–7). Illus. 1994, Candlewick $19.95 (1-56402-199-8). An illustrated guide for adolescents that explores sexuality, puberty, birth, abortion, and sexual intercourse. Awards: ALSC Notable Children's Book; BL Editors' Choice; SLJ Best Book. (Rev: BL 9/15/94*; MJHS; SLJ 12/94*) [613.9]

3307 Hertz, Sue. *Caught in the Crossfire* (9–adult). 1991, Prentice-Hall $20 (0-13-381914-0). A description of the courage, tragedy, and violence of those caught up in the complex set of legal, ethical, and moral dilemmas regarding abortion. (Rev: BL 10/15/91) [363.4]

3308 Judges, Donald P. *Hard Choices, Lost Voices: How the Abortion Conflict Has Divided America, Distorted Constitutional Rights and Damaged the Courts* (9–adult). 1993, Ivan R. Dee (1332 N. Halsted St., Chicago, IL 60622-2632) $25 (1-56663-016-9). A balanced overview of the controversy, concentrating on legal issues, the Supreme Court's role, and the judicial system's seeming ambivalence. (Rev: BL 5/15/93) [363.4]

3309 Kuklin, Susan. *What Do I Do Now? Talking about Teenage Pregnancy* (8–12). 1991, Putnam $15.95 (0-399-21843-2); paper $7.95 (0-399-22043-7). A close look at what it's like to be a pregnant teenager. Features interviews with teens from different economic and racial backgrounds. Awards: YALSA Best Book for Young Adults. (Rev: BL 6/15/91; BY; SLJ 7/91*) [362.83]

3310 Lang, Paul, and Susan S. Lang. *Teen Fathers* (7–12). 1995, Watts LB $13.93 (0-531-11216-0). A fact book not often seen concerning the dilemmas teen fathers face. (Rev: BL 9/1/95; SLJ 12/95) [306.85]

3311 Lauersen, Niels H., and Eileen Stukane. *You're in Charge: A Teenage Girl's Guide to Sex and Her Body* (8–12). 1993, Ballantine/Fawcett Columbine paper $8 (0-449-90464-4). An ob-gyn discusses sexual maturation, considering pubertal change, sexually transmitted diseases, orgasm, sexual intimacy, condoms, abortion, menstruation, etc. (Rev: BL 5/1/93) [613.9]

3312 Lindsay, Jeanne Warren. *The Challenge of Toddlers: Parenting Your Child from One to Three* (7–12). (Teens Parenting) 1992, Morning Glory Press (6595 San Haroldo Way, Buena Park, CA 90620) $15.95 (0-930934-59-8); paper $9.95 (0-930934-58-X). General advice on parenting toddlers, presented in a friendly fashion, including a chapter for fathers that encourages involvement. (Rev: BL 12/15/91; SHS; SLJ 1/92) [649]

3313 Lindsay, Jeanne Warren. *Teen Dads: Rights, Responsibilities and Joys* (7–12). Illus. 1993, Morning Glory Press (6595 San Haroldo Way, Buena Park, CA 90620) $15.95 (0-930934-77-6); paper $9.95 (0-930934-78-4). (Rev: BL 10/15/93; BTA; MJHS; SLJ 10/93; VOYA 2/94) [649.1]

3314 Lindsay, Jeanne Warren. *Teens Parenting—Your Baby's First Year: A How-to-Parent Book Especially for Teenage Parents* (7–12). (Teens Parenting) 1991, Morning Glory Press (6595 San Haroldo Way, Buena Park, CA 90620) $15.95 (0-930934-53-9); paper $9.95 (0-930934-52-0). This manual on the basics of infant care combines practical information and advice, with encouragement for teenage parents. (Rev: BL 10/1/91; SLJ 12/91) [649]

3315 Lindsay, Jeanne Warren, and Jean Brunelli. *Teens Parenting—Your Pregnancy and Newborn Journey: How to Take Care of Yourself and Your Newborn If You're a Pregnant Teen* (7–12). 1991, Morning Glory Press (6595 San Haroldo Way, Buena Park, CA 90620) $15.95 (0-930934-51-2); paper $9.95 (0-930934-50-4). Personal accounts help present different options to pregnant teens, followed by an explanation of infant development. (Rev: BL 8/91) [618.2]

3316 Lindsay, Jeanne Warren, and Sally McCullough. *Teens Parenting—Discipline from Birth to Three: How to Prevent and Deal with Discipline Problems with Babies and Toddlers* (7–12). 1991, Morning Glory Press (6595 San Haroldo Way, Buena Park, CA 90620) $15.95 (0-930934-55-5); 1991, paper $9.95 (0-930934-54-7). Advice on common parental issues, including child-proofing the home, establishing bedtime, tantrums, spoiling, and toilet training. (Rev: BL 8/91) [649]

3317 Lunneborg, Patricia. *Abortion: A Positive Decision* (9–adult). 1992, Bergin & Garvey $19.95 (0-89789-243-7). A look at the pro-choice side of this controversial issue, based on interviews with more than 100 women. (Rev: BL 2/15/92) [363.4]

3318 Nathanson, Laura Walther. *The Portable Pediatrician for Parents* (9–adult). (Omnibus) 1994, HarperCollins $40 (0-06-271562-3); paper $20 (0-06-273176-9). Details what to expect at every stage of infancy and toddlerhood and counsels on broader aspects of child rearing as well. (Rev: BL 2/1/94) [618.92]

3319 Parramón, Mercé. *La maravilla de la vida* (5–9). (Mundo invisible/Invisible World) Illus. 1993, Parramón (Barcelona, Spain) $9.95 (84-342-1466-0). Explains the wonder of life through full-color drawings and diagrams and easy texts. Glossary. English title: *The Wonder of Life*. Also in this series: *Como circula nuestra sangre (How Our Blood Circulates)*. (Rev: BL 4/1/94)

3320 Riverside Mothers' Playgroup. *Entertain Me!* (9–adult). 1993, Pocket paper $8 (0-671-74536-0). Contains activities, games, songs, etc. to help newborns discover their world. (Rev: BL 7/93) [649]

3321 Rue, Nancy. *Everything You Need to Know about Getting Your Period* (6–9). (Need to Know Library) 1995, Rosen $15.95 (0-8239-1870-X). A straightforward discussion of the physiological changes that come with puberty. (Rev: BL 11/1/95; SLJ 1/96) [612.6]

3322 Stalcup, Brenda, and others, eds. *Human Sexuality* (9–12). (Opposing Viewpoints) 1995, Greenhaven LB $17.95 (1-56510-246-0); paper $9.95 (1-56510-245-2). (Rev: BL 9/15/95; SHS) [306.7]

3323 Thompson, Sharon. *Going All the Way: Teenage Girls' Tales of Sex, Romance, and Pregnancy* (9–adult). 1995, Hill & Wang $23 (0-8090-5021-8). Thompson is an advocate for the rights of teen girls to sexual pleasure, information, and birth control. She emphasizes their need for intimacy and to make choices to survive adolescence. (Rev: BL 10/1/95) [306.7]

3324 Weddington, Sarah. *A Question of Choice* (9–adult). 1992, Putnam/Grosset $21.95 (0-399-13790-4). The Texas attorney who successfully tried the *Roe* vs. *Wade* case in the U.S. Supreme Court looks back on her professional career and discusses the pro-choice agenda. (Rev: BL 9/15/92) [363.4]

3325 Westheimer, Ruth. *Dr. Ruth Talks to Kids: Where You Came From, How Your Body Changes, and What Sex Is All About* (5–9). Illus. 1993, Macmillan $13.95 (0-02-792532-3). Ranges widely over common preteen and teen concerns: puberty, sex, contraception, birth, and AIDS. (Rev: BL 7/93; MJHS; SLJ 6/93; VOYA 8/93) [306.7]

3326 Whitney, Catherine. *Whose Life? A Balanced, Comprehensive View of Abortion from Its Historical Context to the Current Debate* (9–adult). 1991, Morrow $20 (0-688-09622-0). A look at the historical context, personal experiences, and all sides of the abortion issue. (Rev: BL 7/91*) [363.4]

Safety and First Aid

3327 Chaiet, Donna. *Staying Safe at School* (7–12). (Get Prepared Library) 1995, Rosen $16.95 (0-8239-1864-5). How to stay alert and protect oneself while at school. (Rev: BL 11/15/95; SLJ 2/96) [613.6]

3328 Chaiet, Donna. *Staying Safe at Work* (7–12). (Get Prepared Library) 1995, Rosen $16.95 (0-8239-1867-X). How to stay alert and protect oneself at work. (Rev: BL 11/15/95; SLJ 2/96) [613.6]

3329 Chaiet, Donna. *Staying Safe on Public Transportation* (7–12). (Get Prepared Library) 1995, Rosen $16.95 (0-8239-1866-1). How to stay alert and protect oneself while using public transportation. (Rev: BL 11/15/95; SLJ 2/96; VOYA 4/96) [613.6]

3330 Chaiet, Donna. *Staying Safe on the Streets* (6–12). (Get Prepared Library of Violence Prevention for Young Women) 1995, Rosen LB $16.95 (0-8239-1865-3). Discusses situations young women should avoid outside the home and protection techniques. (Rev: SLJ 1/96)

3331 Chaiet, Donna. *Staying Safe While Shopping* (7–12). (Get Prepared Library) 1995, Rosen $16.95 (0-8239-1869-6). How to stay alert and protect oneself while shopping. (Rev: BL 11/15/95; SLJ 1/96) [613.6]

3332 Chaiet, Donna. *Staying Safe While Traveling* (7–12). (Get Prepared Library) 1995, Rosen $16.95 (0-8239-1868-8). How to stay alert and protect oneself while traveling. (Rev: BL 11/15/95; SLJ 2/96) [613.6]

3333 Goedecke, Christopher J., and Rosmarie Hausherr. *Smart Moves: A Kid's Guide to Self-Defense* (6–8). 1995, Simon & Schuster $16 (0-689-80294-3). A martial arts instructor offers this sourcebook of safety and survival strategies. (Rev: BL 9/15/95; SLJ 12/95; VOYA 2/96) [613.6]

3334 Grosser, Vicky, and others. *Take a Firm Stand: The Young Woman's Guide to Self-Defence* (9–12). 1993, Virago paper $11.95 (1-85381-390-7). Discusses reasons for knowing self-defense, presents case histories and pictorial demonstrations of escape techniques, and addresses the emotions following attack. (Rev: BL 5/15/93; BTA) [613.66]

3335 Wax, Nina. *Occupational Health* (7–12). (Medical Issues) 1994, Chelsea House $19.95 (0-7910-0089-3). (Rev: BL 4/15/94; MJHS; SHS) [616.9]

Sex Problems (Abuse, Harassment, etc.)

3336 Bandon, Alexandra. *Date Rape* (6–9). 1994, Macmillan/Crestwood LB $13.95 (0-89686-806-0); paper $4.95 (0-382-24755-8). A definition of the controversial subject, with information and profiles on both the victim and the attacker. (Rev: BL 3/1/95; SLJ 3/95) [362.88]

3337 Chaiet, Donna. *Staying Safe at Home* (6–12). (Get Prepared Library of Violence Prevention for Young Women) 1995, Rosen LB $16.95 (0-8239-1863-7). Information specifically for young women on stalkers and peeping Toms, domestic violence, and protection through self-defense. (Rev: SLJ 1/96; VOYA 4/96)

3338 Chaiet, Donna. *Staying Safe on Dates* (6–12). (Get Prepared Library of Violence Prevention for Young Women) 1995, Rosen LB $16.95 (0-8239-1862-9). Information for young women concerning verbal/physical abuse, invasion of boundaries, and acquaintance/date rape. (Rev: SLJ 1/96; VOYA 4/96)

3339 Gay, Kathlyn. *Rights and Respect: What You Need to Know about Gender Bias and Sexual Harassment* (7–12). 1995, Millbrook LB $16.40 (1-56294-493-2). A good source for student research on gender bias and harassment in the workplace and in education. (Rev: BL 10/1/95; SLJ 11/95) [305.42]

3340 Guernsey, JoAnn Bren. *Sexual Harassment: A Question of Power* (7–12). (Frontline) 1995, Lerner LB $13.13 (0-8225-2608-5). The issue of harassment in the workplace, school, and everyday life is discussed. Includes historical background and male perspectives. (Rev: BL 7/95; SLJ 8/95) [305.42]

3341 Landau, Elaine. *Sexual Harassment* (8–12). 1993, Walker LB $13.85 (0-8027-8266-3). Attempts to establish a sense of what constitutes inappropriate behavior, still not agreed upon in the courts or in mainstream America. (Rev: BL 6/1–15/93; BTA; MJHS) [305.42]

3342 La Valle, John. *Everything You Need to Know When You Are the Male Survivor of Rape or Sexual Assault* (6–8). (Need to Know Library) 1996, Rosen LB $15.95 (0-8239-2084-4). (Rev: BL 1/1/96; SLJ 3/96)

3343 Layman, Nancy S. *Sexual Harassment in American Secondary Schools: A Legal Guide for Administrators, Teachers, and Students* (9–adult). 1994, Contemporary Research (P.O. Box 7240, Dallas, TX 75209) $55 (0-935061-57-6); paper $18.95 (0-935061-52-5). Provides definitions of sexual harassment and examines laws regarding it in secondary schools. Outlines how schools can both avoid and deal with it. (Rev: BL 8/94; SHS; VOYA 4/95) [344.73]

3344 Levy, Barrie. *In Love and in Danger* (10–12). 1993, Seal Press paper $8.95 (1-878067-26-5). Firsthand accounts from young women who were involved in abusive relationships. (Rev: BL 8/93; BTA; VOYA 8/93) [306.73]

3345 Mazer, Norma Fox. *Out of Control* (7–12). 1993, Morrow $14 (0-688-10208-5); 1994, Avon/Flare paper $3.99 (0-380-71347-0). Deals directly and realistically with the complexities of sexual harassment. Awards: YALSA Best Book for Young Adults. (Rev: BL 6/1–15/93; BTA; MJHS; SLJS 6/93*; VOYA 8/93)

3346 Morris, Celia. *Bearing Witness: Sexual Harassment and Beyond—Everywoman's Story* (9–adult). 1994, Little, Brown $21.95 (0-316-58422-3). An examination of sexual harassment that focuses on the Anita Hill–Clarence Thomas hearings. Includes personal histories of a broad spectrum of American women. (Rev: BL 3/1/94) [305.42]

3347 Mufson, Susan, and Rachel Kranz. *Straight Talk about Date Rape* (7–12). (Straight Talk About) 1993, Facts on File $16.95 (0-8160-2863-X). (Rev: BL 9/1/93; MJHS) [362.88]

3348 Petrocelli, William, and Barbara Kate Repa. *Sexual Harassment on the Job* (9–adult). 1992, Nolo Press paper $14.95 (0-87337-177-1). Practical strategies and legal information helpful to teenagers experiencing sexual harassment at work. (Rev: BL 4/15/92) [344]

3349 Ramsey, Martha. *Where I Stopped: Remembering Rape at Thirteen* (9–adult). 1996, Putnam $23.95 (0-399-14107-3). A book written as a healing process for the author 27 years after her rape. (Rev: BL 12/1/95*) [362.88]

3350 Spies, Karen Bornemann. *Everything You Need to Know about Incest* (6–9). (Need to Know Library) 1992, Rosen LB $13.95 (0-8239-1325-2). Defines the problem of incest in simple terms, discusses its effects on victims, and tells how victims can get help. (Rev: BL 7/92; SLJ 8/92) [306.877]

3351 Stan, Adele M., ed. *Debating Sexual Correctness: Pornography, Sexual Harassment, Date Rape, and the Politics of Sexual Equality* (9–adult). 1995, Dell/Delta paper $11.95 (0-385-31384-5). Opposing viewpoints, moderate and extreme, about pornography, sexual harassment, date rape, and the politics of sexual equality. (Rev: BL 2/1/95) [305.42]

3352 Sumrall, Amber Coverdale, and Dena Taylor, eds. *Sexual Harassment: Women Speak Out* (9–adult). 1992, Crossing $20.95 (0-89594-545-2); paper $10.95 (0-89594-544-4). Eye-opening testimonies of sexual harassment victims, many of whom had the experience during their teen or college years. (Rev: BL 4/15/92) [362.83]

3353 Swisher, Karin L., and Carol Wekesser, eds. *Violence Against Women* (9–12). 1994, Greenhaven LB $16.95 (1-56510-070-0); paper $9.95 (1-56510-069-7). A diverse collection of opinions on the ramifications of violence against women. (Rev: BL 5/1/94; SLJ 5/94) [362.82]

3354 Wekesser, Carol, and others, eds. *Sexual Harassment* (9–12). (Current Controversies) 1992, Greenhaven LB $19.95 (1-56510-021-2); paper $9.95 (1-56510-020-4). Includes arguments about the causes and seriousness of the problem, what constitutes actionable behavior, and the best means to reduce harassment. (Rev: BL 4/15/93; SLJ 5/93) [331.4]

3355 Zimmerman, Jean. *Tailspin: Women at War in the Wake of Tailhook* (9–adult). 1995, Doubleday $24.95 (0-385-47789-9). Details of a sex and drinking fiasco trigger this exposé of the role of women in the military. (Rev: BL 5/15/95) [355]

Sexual Identity

3356 Bawer, Bruce. *A Place at the Table: The Gay Individual in American Society* (9–adult). 1993, Poseidon $21 (0-671-79533-3). This conservative Christian homosexual takes a middle-of-the road view in supporting gay civil rights, while criticizing both antigays and the gay subculture. (Rev: BL 10/1/93*) [305.38]

3357 Bernstein, Robert. *Straight Parents, Gay Children: Keeping Families Together* (9–adult). 1995, Thunder's Mouth $24.95 (1-56025-085-2); paper $12.95 (1-56025-086-0). Drawing on his experiences with his lesbian daughter, Bernstein describes typical parental reactions of grief and disgust and presents background information and a survival guide for those parents. (Rev: BL 6/1–15/95) [306.874]

3358 Chandler, Kurt. *Passages of Pride: Lesbian and Gay Youth Come of Age* (9–adult). 1995, Times Books $23 (0-8129-2380-4). Real-life experiences illuminate the 3 phases of homosexual life. (Rev: BL 9/15/95; VOYA 4/96) [305.2]

3359 Duberman, Martin. *Stonewall* (9–adult). 1993, Dutton $21 (0-525-93602-5). The now-legendary 1969 riot against police harassment at a Greenwich Village gay bar is placed in the context of 6 homosexuals whose political activism was affected by it. (Rev: BL 5/1/93) [306.9]

3360 Due, Linnea. *Joining the Tribe: Growing Up Gay and Lesbian in the 90's* (9–adult). 1995, Doubleday/Anchor paper $12.95 (0-385-47500-4). An enlightening, frank discussion of what gay and lesbian teens face. (Rev: BL 9/15/95; VOYA 2/96) [305.23]

3361 Dunbar, Robert E. *Homosexuality* (6–10). 1995, Enslow LB $17.90 (0-89490-665-8). A clear, mostly unbiased account for a young reader to start an investigation of homosexuality. (Rev: BL 12/15/95; VOYA 2/96) [306.76]

3362 Galas, Judith C. *Gay Rights* (7–12). (Overview) 1996, Lucent LB $16.95 (1-56006-176-6). An overview of the issue features sketches of precedent-setting cases. (Rev: BL 3/1/96; SLJ 2/96)

3363 Herman, Ellen. *Psychiatry, Psychology, and Homosexuality* (8–12). 1995, Chelsea House $24.95 (0-7910-2628-0); paper $12.95 (0-7910-2977-8). (Rev: BL 9/15/95; VOYA 12/95) [305.9]

3364 Hyde, Margaret O., and Elizabeth H. Forsyth. *Know about Gays and Lesbians* (7–12). 1994, Millbrook $15.90 (1-56294-298-0). This overview of homosexuality attacks stereotypes, surveys history, examines current controversies, and reviews religious responses to show how pervasive homophobia still is. (Rev: BL 3/1/94; BTA; MJHS; SLJ 4/94; VOYA 4/94) [305.9]

3365 MacKay, Anne. *Wolf Girls at Vassar: Lesbian and Gay Experiences, 1930–1990* (9–adult). 1993, St. Martin's paper $9.95 (0-312-08923-6). Lesbian and gay Vassar alumni recall their college years, describing campus romance, loneliness and isolation, and support networks among friends and faculty. (Rev: BL 5/15/93) [305.9]

3366 Marcus, Eric. *Is It a Choice? Answers to 300 of the Most Frequently Asked Questions about Gays and Lesbians* (9–adult). 1993, HarperSan Francisco paper $10 (0-06-250664-1). A comprehensive primer on homosexuality, answering questions about sex, relationships, discrimination, religion, coming out, AIDS, aging, and many other topics. (Rev: BL 5/1/93; BTA) [305.9]

3367 Miller, Neil. *Out of the Past: Gay and Lesbian History from 1869 to the Present* (9–adult). 1995, Random/Vintage paper $16 (0-679-74988-8). Brief biographies of famous gays and lesbians, with an overview of the gay and lesbian liberation movements. (Rev: BL 3/15/95) [306.76]

3368 Nava, Michael, and Robert Dawidoff. *Created Equal: Why Gay Rights Matter to America* (9–adult). 1994, St. Martin's $16.95 (0-312-10443-X). A book that nongays should read, focused on the civic argument only and avoiding all the other issues that tend to cloud the overriding point that homosexuals are citizens entitled to the rights all other citizens enjoy under the Constitution. (Rev: BL 4/15/94*) [305.9]

3369 Pollack, Rachel, and Cheryl Schwartz. *The Journey Out: A Guide for and about Lesbian, Gay, and Bisexual Teens* (7–12). 1995, Viking $14.99 (0-670-85845-5); Penguin/Puffin paper $6.99 (0-14-037254-7). An approachable discussion with sections on special concerns of bisexuals, terms commonly used, and the varied gay community, which offers support and opportunities for activism. (Rev: BL 12/1/95; SLJ 1/96*; VOYA 4/96) [305.23]

3370 Rench, Janice E. *Understanding Sexual Identity: A Book for Gay Teens and Their Friends* (6–10). 1990, Lerner LB $9.95 (0-8225-0044-2). A question-and-answer discussion for teens who think they are gay or who simply want to know about the subject. (Rev: BL 1/1/91; SLJ 3/91) [306.76]

3371 Shilts, Randy. *Conduct Unbecoming: Gays and Lesbians in the U.S. Military* (9–adult). 1993, St. Martin's $27.95 (0-312-09261-X). A history of the military persecution of gays and lesbians, presenting portraits of homosexual heroes who have been imprisoned or hounded from the ranks. (Rev: BL 5/15/93; SHS) [355.008]

3372 Steffan, Joseph. *Honor Bound: A Gay American Fights for the Right to Serve His Country* (9–adult). 1992, Villard $22.50 (0-679-41660-9). When Steffan—perfect high school student, track star, and devout Catholic—entered the U.S. Naval Academy, he discovered he was gay, and he was forced to resign just weeks before graduation. Awards: YALSA Best Book for Young Adults. (Rev: BL 9/1/92*; SHS) [359]

3373 Sutton, Roger. *Hearing Us Out: Voices from the Gay and Lesbian Community* (8–12). 1994, Little, Brown $16.95 (0-316-82326-0). Interviews, some with teenagers, describing the experience of growing up gay or lesbian. Includes conversations with a soldier, a minister, a lawyer, and a police officer. Awards: SLJ Best Book; YALSA Best Book for Young Adults. (Rev: BL 9/15/94; BTA; MJHS; SLJ 12/94; VOYA 2/95) [305.9]

Human Development and Behavior

General and Miscellaneous

3374 *CityKids Speak on Relationships* (7–12). 1995, Random paper $5.99 (0-679-86553-5). Quick bits on everything from meeting people and falling in love to sexual behavior and harassment. (Rev: BL 5/1/95; BTA) [302]

3375 Marzollo, Jean. *Fathers and Babies: How Babies Grow and What They Need from You from Birth to 18 Months* (9–adult). 1993, HarperCollins paper $10 (0-06-096908-3). This practical, illustrated guide describes normal chronological development and offers how-to information on such subjects as making simple toys. (Rev: BL 5/1/93) [306.874]

3376 Silver, Susan. *Baby's Best: The Best Baby (and Toddler) Products to Make a Parent's Life Easier and More Fun* (9–adult). 1993, Adams-Hall Publishing (P.O. Box 491002, Los Angeles, CA 90049) paper $9.95 (0-944708-33-1). A sourcebook for safety-conscious, environmentally aware parents, emphasizing "natural" products, with prices and phone numbers. (Rev: BL 5/1/93) [649.122]

3377 Tashlik, Phyllis, ed. *Hispanic, Female and Young: An Anthology* (6–10). 1994, Arte Público/Piñata paper $14 (1-55885-072-4). Poems, stories, and essays by 8th-grade New York City girls, exploring such topics as Hispanic culture, ethnicity, and prejudice. (Rev: BL 9/1/94; BTA; SLJ 9/94; VOYA 4/95) [810.8]

Psychology and Human Behavior

General and Miscellaneous

3378 Bode, Janet. *Beating the Odds: Stories of Unexpected Achievers* (8–12). Illus. 1991, Watts LB $13.90 (0-531-10985-2). First-person accounts by teenagers who are courageously overcoming serious problems/handicaps, with commentary by specialists on coping with difficult life situations. (Rev: BL 9/15/91*; SHS; SLJ 11/91) [305.23]

3379 Bode, Janet. *Trust and Betrayal: Real Life Stories of Friends and Enemies* (7–12). 1995, Delacorte $15.95 (0-385-32105-8). Covers peer relationships with regard to pregnancy and drug use, disability, homosexuality, sexual harassment, etc. (Rev: BL 3/1/95; SHS; SLJ 2/95; VOYA 5/95) [158]

3380 Feldman, Robert S., and Joel A. Feinman. *Who You Are: Personality and Its Development* (7–10). 1992, Watts $12.90 (0-531-12544-0). Defines personality, explains its development, discusses major personality and behavior theories, and examines various personality traits and their importance. (Rev: BL 3/15/93; MJHS) [155.2]

3381 Hunt, Morgan. *The Story of Psychology: Humankind's Ultimate Adventure: The Exploration of the Universe Within* (9–adult). 1993, Doubleday $29.95 (0-385-24762-1). A narrative history of psychology from its ancient Greek roots to contemporary therapy techniques. (Rev: BL 5/1/93) [150]

3382 Le Shan, Eda. *What Makes You So Special?* (5–8). 1992, Dial $15 (0-8037-1155-7). In a warmly anecdotal style, this introduction to human development discusses heredity and environmental issues, such as infancy, family life, and school. (Rev: BL 5/15/92; SLJ 6/92; YR) [155.2]

3383 Reynolds, Rebecca A. *Bring Me the Ocean: Nature as Teacher, Messenger, and Intermediary* (9–adult). 1995, Vander Wyk & Burnham (P.O. Box 2789, Acton, MA 01720-6789) $21.95 (0-9641089-2-5). Animals As Intermediaries, a non-profit organization that visits hospitals and other institutions, connects people to nature. (Rev: BL 5/15/95) [155.9]

3384 Schneider, Meg F. *Popularity Has Its Ups and Downs* (6–8). 1992, Messner LB $12.98 (0-671-72848-2); paper $5.95 (0-671-72849-0). Commonsense information is presented about popularity and why it may not be what it seems, as well as a discussion of self-confidence and friendship. (Rev: BL 11/15/92; BTA) [158]

Emotions and Emotional Behavior

3385 Bode, Janet, and Stan Mack. *Heartbreak and Roses: Real Life Stories of Troubled Love* (7–12). 1994, Delacorte $15.95 (0-385-32068-X). Twelve true stories about the pain of love, including abusive relationships, first-time gay love, and a disabled teen. (Rev: BL 10/1/94; BTA; MJHS; SLJ 7/94; VOYA 8/94) [306.7]

3386 Fry, Virginia. *Part of Me Died, Too: Stories of Creative Survival among Bereaved Children and Teenagers* (5–8). 1995, Dutton $14.90 (0-525-45068-8). Each of the 11 true-life stories is followed by a selection of self-help activities to aid the bereaved. Awards: ALSC Notable Children's Book. (Rev: BL 1/1/95; SLJ 2/95) [155.9]

3387 Hyde, Margaret O., and Elizabeth H. Forsyth. *The Violent Mind* (9–12). 1991, Watts LB $13.90 (0-531-11060-5). A study of theories about the causes of violence and a description of treatment programs. (Rev: BL 12/1/91; SHS; SLJ 11/91) [616.85]

3388 Kramer, Patricia. *Discovering Self-Confidence* (7–12). (Self-Esteem Library) 1991, Rosen $14.95 (0-8239-1275-2). An interactive approach to help identify feelings. (Rev: BL 2/15/92) [158]

3389 Lang, Susan S. *Teen Violence* (9–12). 1991, Watts LB $13.90 (0-531-11057-5). This study of violence committed by and against teenagers examines causes and possible solutions. (Rev: BL 12/1/91; SHS) [364.3]

Ethics and Moral Behavior

3390 Belkin, Lisa. *First, Do No Harm* (9–adult). 1993, Simon & Schuster $23 (0-671-68538-4). Offers a humanizing look at moral, ethical, and financial issues and choices facing health care professionals, patients, and families. (Rev: BL 1/15/93; SLJ 7/93) [174]

3391 Bender, David L., ed. *Constructing a Life Philosophy* (9–12). (Opposing Viewpoints) 1993, Greenhaven LB $17.95 (0-89908-198-3); paper $9.95 (0-89908-173-8). Includes new material on ecofeminism, a Native American view of religion, and selections on moral/ethical behavior. (Rev: BL 6/1–15/93) [140]

3392 Bennett, William J., ed. *The Moral Compass* (9–adult). 1995, Simon & Schuster $30 (0-684-80313-5). After the success of his earlier *The Book of Virtues*, Bennett turns out a similar title that continues the idea that verities and manners are still in style. (Rev: BL 9/1/95) [808.8]

3393 Kincher, Jonni. *The First Honest Book about Lies* (7–12). 1992, Free Spirit (400 First Ave. N., Suite 616, Minneapolis, MN 55401) paper $12.95 (0-915793-43-1). Provides tools to extract "real" information from statistics, advertisements, etc., as well as techniques for arguing persuasively. (Rev: BL 3/1/93) [155.9]

3394 Mabie, Margot C. J. *Bioethics and the New Medical Technology* (9–12). 1993, Atheneum $13.95 (0-689-31637-2). Examines a host of questions brought on by recent advances in medical technology, including the definition of life and death and how quality influences them. (Rev: BL 5/15/93; BTA; MJHS; VOYA 10/93) [174]

3395 Meltzer, Milton. *Who Cares? Millions Do . . . A Book about Altruism* (7–10). 1994, Walker $16.85 (0-8027-8325-2). Documents the stories of people who help their fellow beings, individually and through various organizations. (Rev: BL 11/15/94; BTA; SHS) [171]

3396 O'Neill, Terry, ed. *Biomedical Ethics* (7–12). (Opposing Viewpoints) 1994, Greenhaven paper $11.95 (1-56510-062-X). (Rev: BL 1/1/94; MJHS; SHS; SLJ 3/94) [174]

3397 Steins, Richard. *Morality* (5–10). (Values Library) 1992, Rosen LB $13.95 (0-8239-1230-2). Concentrates on the ability to define right and wrong and act in accordance with those beliefs, including the development of a moral sense in a child. (Rev: BL 8/92; SLJ 9/92) [170]

3398 Terkel, Susan Neiburg. *Ethics* (6–12). 1992, Dutton/Lodestar $15 (0-525-67371-7). Asks readers to examine their value systems and assess how well or poorly they live up to them. (Rev: BL 3/15/92; MJHS; SLJ 5/92; YR) [170]

3399 Tivnan, Edward. *The Moral Imagination Confronting the Ethical Issue of Our Day* (9–adult). 1995, Simon & Schuster $24 (0-671-74708-8). Essays on such controversial topics as suicide, abortion, affirmative action, and capital punishment. (Rev: BL 3/15/95) [170]

3400 Wekesser, Carol, ed. *Ethics* (7–12). (Current Controversies) 1995, Greenhaven LB $17.95 (1-56510-231-2); paper $9.95 (1-56510-230-4). Focuses on business, biomedical, and professional ethics, as well as such general issues as individual responsibility. (Rev: BL 3/15/95; SLJ 5/95) [174]

Etiquette and Manners

3401 Post, Elizabeth L. *Emily Post's Etiquette* (9–adult). 15th ed. 1992, HarperCollins $28 (0-06-270047-2). Guidebook to everything from dating to table manners to saluting the flag. (Rev: BL 4/15/92; MJHS) [395]

3402 Post, Elizabeth L., and Joan M. Coles. *Emily Post's Teen Etiquette* (7–12). 1995, HarperCollins paper $11 (0-06-273337-0). Full of information on good manners and consideration for others. (Rev: BL 10/1/95; VOYA 12/95) [395]

Intelligence and Thinking

3403 Joseph, Lawrence E. *Common Sense: Why It's No Longer Common* (9–adult). 1994, Addison-Wesley $19.95 (0-201-58116-7). This discussion concludes that recent information overload has made it more difficult to determine what qualifies as common sense. (Rev: BL 1/1/94) [149]

3404 Lucas, Eileen. *The Mind at Work: How to Make It Work Better for You* (7–10). 1993, Millbrook LB $14.90 (1-56294-300-6). Provides information on critical thinking, learning styles, and multiple intelligences. (Rev: BL 10/15/93; BTA; MJHS; SLJ 12/93; VOYA 2/94) [153]

3405 Wartik, Nancy, and La Vonne Carlson-Finnerty. *Memory and Learning* (7–12). (Encyclopedia of Health) 1993, Chelsea House LB $18.95 (0-7910-0022-2). (Rev: BL 3/15/93; MJHS) [153.1]

Personal Guidance

3406 Dentemaro, Christine, and Rachel Kranz. *Straight Talk about Student Life* (6–10). (Straight Talk About) 1993, Facts on File $16.95 (0-8160-2735-8). (Rev: BL 9/1/93; MJHS) [373.18]

3407 Feeney, Rik. *So You Want to Move Out? A Guide to Living on Your Own* (10–12). 1994, Richardson $14.95 (0-9637991-0-X). Useful tips for readers ranging from high schoolers to students preparing to leave for college to college students. (Rev: BL 4/15/94) [643]

3408 Fleming, Alice. *What Me Worry? How to Hang In When Your Problems Stress You Out* (6–10). 1992, Scribner $11.95 (0-684-19277-2). How not to let worries disrupt your everyday life is the subject of this self-help guide. (Rev: BL 5/15/92; SLJ 5/92) [152.4]

3409 Ignoffo, Matthew. *Everything You Need to Know about Self-Confidence* (7–12). (Need to Know Library) 1996, Rosen LB $15.95 (0-8239-2149-2). Guide for getting away from thought patterns that contribute to low self-esteem; outlines plans for using positive self-talk to develop self-confidence. (Rev: SLJ 3/96)

3410 Johnson, Julie Tallard. *Celebrate You! Building Your Self-Esteem* (7–10). 1991, Lerner LB $9.95 (0-8225-0046-9). Upbeat guide encourages teenagers to take pride in themselves and explains how to do it. (Rev: BL 2/1/91; SLJ 5/91; YR) [158]

3411 Johnson, Kevin. *Could Someone Wake Me Up Before I Drool on the Desk?* (6–8). 1995, Bethany paper $6.99 (1-55661-416-0). Self-help book for teens, consisting of a series of problems and suggestions for solving them through Christian principles. (Rev: BL 2/15/96; SLJ 1/96)

3412 Keltner, Nancy, ed. *If You Print This, Please Don't Use My Name* (7–12). Illus. 1992, Terra Nova Press (1309 Redwood Lane, Davis, CA 95616) paper $8.95 (0-944176-03-8). Letters from a California advice column for teens on topics ranging from sexuality to school. Bibliographies. (Rev: BL 1/1/92; BTA; SLJ 7/92) [305.23]

3413 Kohl, Candice. *The String on a Roast Won't Catch Fire in the Oven: An A–Z Encyclopedia of Common Sense for the Newly Independent Young Adult* (10–12). 1993, Gylantic Publishing (P.O. Box 2792, Littleton, CO 80161-2792) paper $12.95 (1-880197-07-3). Motherly wisdom on nearly every aspect of independent living—from apartment hunting, budgeting, shopping, traveling to everyday mundane chores. (Rev: BL 8/93; VOYA 2/94) [305.23]

3414 Kreiner, Anna. *Everything You Need to Know about School Violence* (6–8). (Need to Know Library) 1996, Rosen LB $15.95 (0-8239-2054-2). Reasons for increased violence in schools are discussed, along with ways students can protect themselves and work for positive changes. (Rev: SLJ 3/96)

3415 Lang, Denise V. *But Everyone Else Looks So Sure of Themselves: A Guide to Surviving the Teen Years* (7–9). 1991, Betterway paper $7.95 (1-55870-177-X). Self-help guide for teens covering such subjects as peer pressure, family relationships, school, and the opposite sex. (Rev: BL 8/91) [305.23]

3416 Nash, Renea D. *Everything You Need to Know about Being a Biracial/Biethnic Teen* (6–8). (Need to Know Library) 1995, Rosen $15.95 (0-8239-1871-8). (Rev: BL 11/15/95; SLJ 1/96) [306.84]

3417 Salzman, Marian, and Teresa Reisgies. *Greetings from High School* (8–12). 1991, Peterson's Guides paper $7.95 (1-56079-055-5). This collection of miscellanea covers a broad range of topics that are of concern to college-bound teenagers. (Rev: BL 9/15/91; MJHS; SLJ 11/91) [373.18]

3418 Santamaria, Peggy. *Money Smarts* (9–12). (Lifeskills Library) 1992, Rosen $12.95 (0-8239-1470-4). Explains how to handle personal finances successfully. (Rev: BL 2/15/93; MJHS) [332.024]

3419 Simpson, Carolyn. *Everything You Need to Know about Living with Your Baby and Your Parents under One Roof* (7–12). (Need to Know Library) 1996, Rosen LB $15.95 (0-8239-2150-6). Advice for teenage parents dealing with interpersonal relationships and difficult living arrangements. (Rev: BL 1/1/96; SLJ 3/96)

3420 Wirths, Claudine G., and Mary Bowman-Kruhm. *Your Circle of Friends* (5–7). Illus. 1993, Twenty-First Century $14.95 (0-8050-2073-X). A self-help book for preteens written as an imaginary dialogue between writers and an "almost teen." (Rev: BL 5/1/94) [158]

Social Groups

Family and Family Problems

3421 Bates, J. Douglas. *Gift Children: A Story of Race, Family, and Adoption in a Divided America* (9–adult). 1993, Ticknor & Fields $21.95 (0-395-63314-1). Describes transracial adoption of 2 African American infants and the impact on the entire family through their turbulent teenage and young-adult years. (Rev: BL 5/1/93; BTA) [362.7]

3422 Blomquist, Geraldine Molettiere, and Paul B. Blomquist. *Coping As a Foster Child* (7–10). (Coping) 1991, Rosen LB $12.95 (0-8239-1346-5). A look at how teens are placed in foster homes. (Rev: BL 4/15/92; SLJ 5/92) [362.7]

3423 Bode, Janet. *Truce: Ending the Sibling War* (8–12). 1991, Watts LB $12.90 (0-531-10996-8); 1993, Dell/Laurel Leaf paper $3.99 (0-440-21891-8). Case studies and interviews with teens, followed by professional analyses and potential solutions. (Rev: BL 3/15/91; SHS; SLJ 6/91) [155.44]

3424 Bollick, Nancy O'Keefe. *How to Survive Your Parents' Divorce* (7–12). (The Changing Family). 1994, Watts LB $14.42 (0-531-11054-0). Interviews with teens who have lived through the divorce of their parents, with analysis of their feelings and behaviors. (Rev: BL 1/1/95; SLJ 3/95; VOYA 4/95) [306.89]

3425 Burke, Phyllis. *Family Values: Two Moms and Their Son* (9–adult). 1993, Random $21 (0-679-42188-2). Describes the author's fight to adopt and coparent the child of her life partner, offering an insider's insight into the gay and lesbian civil rights movement. (Rev: BL 5/15/93*) [306.874]

3426 Davies, Nancy Millichap. *Foster Care* (6–12). 1994, Watts LB $13.40 (0-531-11081-8). Details foster-care laws and operational procedures, exploring the varied feelings of children in foster homes and suggesting alternatives. (Rev: BL 8/94; BTA; MJHS; SLJ 7/94; VOYA 10/94) [362.7]

3427 Dolan, Edward F. *Child Abuse* (7–12). Rev. ed. 1992, Watts LB $13.40 (0-531-11042-7). Expanded text and up-to-date information on programs to help families and children harmed by child abuse, controversy arising from new child abuse laws, etc. (Rev: BL 1/15/93; BTA; SLJ 1/93) [362.7]

3428 Gottlieb, Beatrice. *The Family in the Western World from the Black Death to the Industrial Age* (9–adult). 1992, Oxford Univ. $25 (0-19-507344-4). This documented history of the family debunks myths and examines such things as household customs, courtship, marriage, child care, birth control, and infant mortality. (Rev: BL 11/15/92; SLJ 5/93) [306.85]

3429 Gravelle, Karen, and Susan Fischer. *Where Are My Birth Parents? A Guide for Teenage Adoptees* (7–12). 1993, Walker LB $14.85 (0-8027-8258-2). Includes firsthand experiences of young people who searched for their birth families with varied success. (Rev: BL 9/1/93; MJHS; SLJ 7/93; VOYA 10/93) [362.7]

3430 Greenberg, Keith E. *Runaways* (6–10). 1995, Lerner LB $18.95 (0-8225-2557-7). Greenberg uses the personal approach to focus on the lives of 2 runaways and dispel the idea that runaways are "bad" kids. (Rev: BL 10/15/95; SLJ 12/95) [362.7]

3431 Harnack, Andrew. *Adoption* (7–12). (Opposing Viewpoints) 1995, Greenhaven LB $17.95 (1-56510-213-4); paper $9.95 (1-56510-212-6). Presents various perspectives on the hot-button issues involved with adoption, with provocative articles from well-known advocates on the topic. (Rev: BL 10/15/95; SHS) [362.7]

3432 Hyde, Margaret O. *Know about Abuse* (7–12). (Know About) 1992, Walker LB $14.85 (0-8027-8177-2). Provides facts, reasons, symptoms, examples, and solutions, covering a wide range of child abuse from obvious to subtle. (Rev: BL 11/1/92; SLJ 9/92) [362.7]

3433 Ito, Tom. *Child Abuse* (6–10). (Overview) 1995, Lucent LB $14.95 (1-56006-115-4). Researched carefully, with the author searching for change in individuals and society. (Rev: BL 4/15/95; SLJ 5/95; VOYA 5/95) [362.7]

3434 Koffinke, Carol. *"Mom, You Don't Understand!": A Mother and Daughter Share Their Views* (9–adult). 1993, Deaconess (2450 Riverside Ave. S., Minneapolis, MN 55454) paper $8.95 (0-925190-66-7). A counselor and her daughter, 15, alternately share viewpoints on dating, privacy, etc., sometimes with painful honesty. (Rev: BL 6/1–15/93; VOYA 10/93) [306.874]

3435 Koh, Frances M. *Adopted from Asia: How It Feels to Grow Up in America* (5–8). 1993, East West (P.O. Box 14149, Minneapolis, MN 55414) $14.95 (0-9606090-6-7). Interviews with 11 young people who were born in Korea and adopted by Americans. (Rev: BL 2/15/94) [306.874]

3436 Kosof, Anna. *Battered Women: Living with the Enemy* (7–12). 1995, Watts LB $13.93 (0-531-11203-9). Attempts to answer the fundamental question "Why don't you just leave?" and discusses the development of abusive relationships. (Rev: BL 4/15/95; SHS; SLJ 3/95) [362.82]

3437 Levine, Beth. *Divorce: Young People Caught in the Middle* (7–12). 1995, Enslow $17.95 (0-89490-633-X). A straightforward, commonsense manual for teens dealing with divorce. (Rev: BL 3/15/95; SLJ 6/95) [306.89]

3438 Lindsay, Jeanne Warren. *Caring, Commitment and Change: How to Build a Relationship That Lasts* (7–12). (Teenage Couples) 1995, Morning Glory Press (6595 San Haroldo Way, Buena Park, CA 90620) $15.95 (0-930934-92-X); paper $5.95 (0-930934-93-8). The personal issues involved in a marriage partnership. (Rev: BL 4/15/95; SLJ 3/95) [646.7]

3439 Lindsay, Jeanne Warren. *Coping with Reality: Dealing with Money, In-Laws, Babies and Other Details of Daily Life* (7–12). (Teenage Couples) 1995, Morning Glory Press (6595 San Haroldo Way, Buena Park, CA 90620) $15.95 (0-930934-87-3); paper $9.95 (0-930934-86-5). Counsel on the day-to-day aspects of being a part of a couple. (Rev: BL 4/15/95; SLJ 3/95) [306.81]

3440 Liptak, Karen. *Adoption Controversies* (7–12). 1993, Watts LB $13.40 (0-531-13032-0). Covers everything from adoption options and cultural attitudes toward adoption to transracial adoptions, surrogacy, and searches. (Rev: BL 3/15/94; BTA; VOYA 4/94) [362.7]

3441 Mancini, Richard E. *Everything You Need to Know about Living with a Single Parent* (7–10). (Need to Know Library) 1992, Rosen LB $12.95 (0-8239-1323-6). (Rev: BL 4/15/92) [306.85]

3442 Mufson, Susan, and Rachel Kranz. *Straight Talk about Child Abuse* (7–12). (Straight Talk About) 1991, Facts on File $15.95 (0-8160-2376-X). (Rev: BL 4/1/91; MJHS; SHS; SLJ 3/91) [362.7]

3443 Packer, Alex J. *Bringing Up Parents: The Teenager's Handbook* (8–12). Illus. 1993, Free Spirit (400 First Ave. N., Suite 616, Minneapolis, MN 55401) paper $12.95 (0-915793-48-2). Discusses in detail the art of parental manipulation: building trust, diffusing family power struggles, waging effective verbal battles, developing listening skills, and expressing feelings nonaggressively. (Rev: BL 5/1/93*; BTA; VOYA 8/93) [306.874]

3444 Pohl, Constance, and Kathy Harris. *Transracial Adoption: Children and Parents Speak* (9–12). 1992, Watts LB $13.40 (0-531-11134-2). A chronicle of the history of and controversies surrounding transracial adoption. (Rev: BL 3/15/93; SHS; SLJ 12/92) [362.7]

3445 Preston, John. *A Member of the Family: Gay Men Write about Their Closest Relations* (9–adult). 1992, Dutton $22 (0-525-93549-5). Twenty-seven highly personal recollections by gay professional writers, focusing on their relationship with the family member most important to each. (Rev: BL 10/1/92) [306.874]

3446 Rench, Janice E. *Family Violence: How to Recognize and Survive It* (6–8). 1992, Lerner LB $11.95 (0-8225-0047-7). This book speaks directly to children, with explanations of what constitutes different kinds of abuse, who is at fault, what motivates abusers, and what to do if violence occurs. (Rev: BL 11/1/92; MJHS; SLJ 9/92) [362.82]

3447 Rosenberg, Maxine B. *Living with a Single Parent* (5–7). 1992, Bradbury $14.95 (0-02-777915-7). Interviews with youth who live with only one parent, revealing their positive adjustments, the ways they handle their feelings, and suggestions for coping. (Rev: BL 11/15/92; MJHS; SLJ 12/92) [306.85]

3448 Sander, Joelle. *Before Their Time: Four Generations of Teenage Mothers* (9–adult). 1991, Harcourt $19.95 (0-15-111638-5). An oral history of 4 African American teenage mothers—great-grandmother, grandmother, mother, and daughter—that illustrates a repetitive cycle of poverty, violence, and neglect. (Rev: BL 11/1/91; SHS) [306.85]

3449 Sheehan, Susan. *Life for Me Ain't Been No Crystal Stair* (9–adult). 1993, Pantheon $21 (0-679-41472-X). (Rev: BL 9/1/93; SLJ 3/94; VOYA 2/94) [362.7]

3450 Tipp, Stacey L. *Child Abuse: Detecting Bias* (5–7). (Opposing Viewpoints Juniors) 1991, Greenhaven LB $9.95 (0-89908-611-X). Should children be allowed to testify in child abuse cases? is one of the four questions posed—and debated. (Rev: BL 5/15/92; SLJ 3/92) [362.7]

3451 Wagner, Viqi, ed. *The Family in America* (7–12). (Opposing Viewpoints) 1992, Greenhaven LB $17.95 (0-89908-194-0); paper $9.95 (0-89908-169-X). (Rev: BL 11/15/92; MJHS; SHS) [306.85]

3452 Worth, Richard. *Single-Parent Families* (6–10). 1992, Watts LB $12.90 (0-531-11131-8). Examines the social changes that led to the rise of the single-parent family, the long-term effectts of divorce, the difficulties facing single parents, etc. (Rev: BL 12/1/92; MJHS; SHS) [306.85]

Youth Groups

3453 Erickson, Judith B. *Directory of American Youth Organizations: A Guide to 500 Clubs, Groups, Troops, Teams, Societies, Lodges, and More for Young People* (6–12). 1992, Free Spirit (400 First Ave. N., Suite 616, Minneapolis, MN 55401) paper $18.95 (0-915793-36-9). Guide to hobby and sports clubs, political action groups, religious organizations, and many more catering to the interests of young people. (Rev: BL 6/1/92; SHS) [369.4]

3454 Hyde, Margaret O. *Peace and Friendship: Russian and American Teens* (6–10). 1992, Dutton/Cobblehill $14 (0-525-65107-1). General discussion about cooperative ventures (music, art, camping, etc.), a long, detailed list of organizations that promote teen exchange programs, and a chapter on how to get a pen pal. (Rev: BL 7/92; BTA; SLJ 10/92) [303.48]

3455 Lipsky, David, and Alexander Abrams. *Late Bloomers: Becoming Adult at the End of the American Century* (9–adult). 1994, Times Books $18 (0-8129-2290-5). Examines the psychology, economics, and unfavorable image of "Generation X," suggesting that high divorce rates, limited support systems, and television shaped their attitudes. (Rev: BL 9/1/94; SHS) [305.24]

The Arts and Entertainment

General and Miscellaneous

3456 Craven, Wayne. *American Art: History and Culture* (9–adult). 1994, Abrams $60 (0-8109-1942-7). Places architecture, decorative arts, painting, photography, and sculpture within cultural and historical contexts. (Rev: BL 3/15/94) [709.73]

3457 Dewey, Patrick R. *Fan Club Directory: 2000 Fan Clubs and Fan Mail Addresses in the United States and Abroad* (9–adult). 1993, McFarland paper $19.95 (0-89950-767-0). Includes 2,000 fan clubs and their addresses arranged alphabetically by keyword and indexed by subject. (Rev: BL 10/1/93; VOYA 12/93) [060]

3458 Herd, Stan. *Crop Art and Other Earthworks* (9–adult). 1994, Abrams paper $19.95 (0-8109-2575-3). This oversize paperback about an artist who turns farming landscape into artwork will intrigue art students and browsers. (Rev: BL 4/1/94*) [709]

Architecture and Building

General and Miscellaneous

3459 Garrett, Wendell, ed. *Our Changing White House* (9–adult). 1995, Northeastern Univ. $40 (1-55553-222-5). Ten authoritative essays chart the White House's evolution through the last 2 centuries with photos, facts, and anecdotes. (Rev: BL 7/95*) [975.3]

History of Architecture

3460 Brown, David J. *The Random House Book of How Things Were Built* (5–8). 1992, Random LB $19.99 (0-679-92044-7); paper $15 (0-679-82044-2). Describes materials, construction methods, and unique features of 60 notable structures around the world. (Rev: BL 6/1/92; MJHS) [720]

3461 Glenn, Patricia Brown. *Under Every Roof: A Kid's Style and Field Guide to the Architecture of American Houses* (5–8). 1993, Preservation $16.95 (0-89133-214-6). An introduction to the history and styles of American domestic architecture. Provides information on over 70 houses. (Rev: BL 7/94; SLJ 6/94) [728]

3462 Kunstler, James Howard. *The Geography of Nowhere: The Rise and Decline of America's Man-Made Landscape* (9–adult). 1993, Simon & Schuster $23 (0-671-70774-4). Explores history, economics, architecture, urban planning, and popular culture to explain why a nation so rich in natural beauty created such an ugly, depressing environment. (Rev: BL 6/1–15/93) [720.47]

3463 Scully, Vincent. *Architecture: The Natural and the Man-Made* (9–adult). 1991, St. Martin's $40 (0-312-06292-3). In this lavishly illustrated volume, a renowned art historian tours key examples of Western architecture and investigates their meaning, symbolism, and intended effect. (Rev: BL 11/1/91*) [720]

3464 Tauranac, John. *The Empire State Building: The Making of a Landmark* (9–adult). 1995, Scribner $26 (0-684-19678-6). A definitive history of the building, with anecdotes about the personalities who were involved with its construction. (Rev: BL 11/15/95) [720.4]

3465 Wilkinson, Philip. *Amazing Buildings* (5–7). Illus. 1993, Dorling Kindersley $16.95 (1-56458-234-5). An introduction to 20 famous buildings around the world, including photos, floor plans, and paintings. (Rev: BL 9/1/93; VOYA 10/93) [720]

3466 Wilkinson, Philip. *Edificios asombrosos* (5–10). Tr. by Andrés Molina. Illus. 1993, Ediciones B (Barcelona, Spain) $22.78 (84-406-3757-8). Inside and outside views of 21 of the world's most amazing buildings—such as the Coliseum (Rome), Taj Mahal (India), Temple of the Inscriptions (Mexico), and Guggenheim Museum (New York)—are beautifully reproduced in color and explained in this large-format volume. English title: *Amazing Buildings.* (Rev: BL 10/1/94)

Various Types of Buildings

3467 Bennett, David. *Skyscrapers: Form and Function* (9–adult). 1995, Simon & Schuster $35

(0-684-80318-6). A look at the inner workings of skyscrapers plus an informative history of their evolution. (Rev: BL 10/15/95) [720]

3468 Dunn, Andrew. *Skyscrapers: Structures* (5–7). (Structures) 1993, Thomson Learning $13.95 (1-56847-027-4). Discusses the advantages and disadvantages of tall buildings, why and how they are built, their future, and the limits of the technology. (Rev: BL 6/1–15/93; MJHS) [720.4]

3469 Ehlert, Willis J. *America's Heritage: Capitols of the United States* (6–12). 1993, State House Publishing (P.O. Box 5636, Madison, WI 53705-0636) $9.95 (0-9634908-3-4). Provides data on state capitals and capitol buildings, descriptions of architectural details, brief state histories, state symbols, and an extensive bibliography. (Rev: BL 4/15/93) [725]

3470 Gentry, Linnea, and Karen Liptak. *The Glass Ark: The Story of Biosphere 2* (5–8). 1991, Penguin/Puffin paper $7.95 (0-14-034928-6). An enthusiastic view of Biosphere 2, the 1991 project launched near Tucson, Arizona, to study life in a self-contained, greenhouselike structure. (Rev: BL 12/15/91) [919.9]

3471 Gravett, Christopher. *Castle* (5–9). (Eyewitness Books) 1994, Knopf LB $16.99 (0-679-96000-7). (Rev: BL 10/15/94; MJHS) [623]

3472 Hilton, Suzanne. *A Capital Capital City: 1790–1814* (6–12). 1992, Atheneum $14.95 (0-689-31641-0). The history of Washington, D.C., as viewed in period newspapers, diaries, letters, and ads. (Rev: BL 2/15/93*; MJHS; SLJ 2/93) [975.3]

3473 Monroe, Jean Guard, and Ray A. Williamson. *First Houses: Native American Homes and Sacred Structures* (6–9). 1993, Houghton $14.95 (0-395-51081-3). (Rev: BL 10/15/93; MJHS; VOYA 2/94) [299]

3474 Platt, Richard. *Castle* (5–12). (Stephen Biesty's Cross-Sections) Illus. 1994, Dorling Kindersley $16.95 (1-56458-467-4). Describes a fourteenth-century European castle, its construction and defenses, and the medieval trades, jousts, and feasts within. (Rev: BL 11/1/94; BTA; SLJ 10/94; VOYA 2/95) [940.1]

3475 Steele, Philip. *Castles* (5–7). 1995, Kingfisher $14.95 (1-85697-547-9). An oversized, heavily illustrated format with captions providing most of the information. A foldout section shows the castle inside and out. (Rev: BL 8/95; SLJ 4/95) [940.1]

3476 *Washington, D.C. A Smithsonian Book of the Nation's Capital* (9–adult). 1992, Smithsonian $39.95 (0-89599-032-6). Photo-essays by historians, journalists, and scholars on the city's history, its trappings as a capital, its artworks and documents, and its buildings, parks, and streets. (Rev: BL 11/1/92) [[975.3]

3477 Williams, Brian. *Forts and Castles* (5–8). (See Through History) 1995, Viking $15.99 (0-670-85898-6). (Rev: BL 10/15/95) [728.81]

Painting, Sculpture, and Photography

General and Miscellaneous

3478 Berkey, John. *Painted Space* (9–adult). 1991, Friedlander (740 Washington Rd., Pittsburgh, PA 15228) $19.95 (0-9627154-1-7). Collection of a science fiction artist's creations, including historical works and movie posters. (Rev: BL 1/15/92) [759.13]

3479 Bolton, Linda. *Hidden Pictures* (5–8). 1993, Dial $14.99 (0-8037-1378-9). Discussion of various artists' paintings and drawings that contain hidden images. (Rev: BL 3/1/93) [701]

3480 Cohen, David, ed. *The Circle of Life: Rituals from the Human Family Album* (9–adult). 1991, HarperCollins $39.95 (0-06-250152-6). Photos that celebrate rituals and ceremonial rites of passage from diverse cultures, showing a striking similarity of emotional depth and sense of tradition. (Rev: BL 10/15/91*) [390]

3481 Coleman, A. D. *Looking at Photographs: Animals* (6–12). 1995, Chronicle $14.95 (0-8118-0418-6). The techniques of photographing animals are revealed through full-page examples explaining viewpoint, scale, color, light, framing, and relationship. (Rev: BL 7/95; SLJ 9/95) [778.9]

3482 Cumming, Robert. *Annotated Art* (9–12). 1995, Dorling Kindersley $22.95 (1-56458-848-3). Forty-five art masterpieces from the gothic, Renaissance, neoclassic, baroque, and romantic periods are reproduced in 2-page spreads with history and technique notes on each. (Rev: BL 6/1–15/95; SLJ 8/95) [750]

3483 Davidson, Rosemary. *Take a Look: An Introduction to the Experience of Art* (5–9). 1994, Viking $18.99 (0-670-84478-0). This overview, with examples from many cultures, describes how art fits into everyday experience and how we use it to express ourselves. (Rev: BL 3/1/94; BTA; MJHS; SLJ 2/94; VOYA 6/94) [801]

3484 Lasky, Kathryn. *Think Like an Eagle: At Work with a Wildlife Photographer* (5–7). Photos by Christopher G. Knight and Jack Swedberg. 1992, Little, Brown/Joy Street $15.95 (0-316-51519-1). The authors followed wildlife photographer Swedberg across the United States in every season to document his techniques. Includes photos of eagles, alligators, and humpback whales. (Rev: BL 6/1/92; MJHS; SLJ 4/92) [778.9]

3485 Monreal y Tejada, Luís, and R. G. Haggar. *Diccionario de términos de arte* (8–12). 1992, Editorial Juventud (Barcelona, Spain) $19.95 (84-261-2701-0). A dictionary of almost 5,000 art terms, including foreign words used worldwide, for painting, sculpture, architecture, and the graphic and decorative arts. English title: *Dictionary of Art Terms*. (Rev: BL 4/1/94)

3486 Siporin, Steven. *American Folk Masters: The National Heritage Fellows* (9–adult). 1992, Abrams $49.50 (0-8109-1917-6). American folk art is celebrated with brief biographies and photos of National Heritage Fellows, spotlighting both traditional arts and multiculturalism. (Rev: BL 10/1/92) [745]

3487 Yenawine, Philip. *Key Art Terms for Beginners* (9–12). 1995, Abrams $24.95 (0-8109-1225-2). This introduction to the art world explains terms encountered in that world with more than 140 reproductions as examples. (Rev: BL 6/1–15/95) [801]

History of Art

3488 Beckett, Sister Wendy, and Patricia Wright. *The Story of Painting* (9–adult). 1994, Dorling Kindersley $39.95 (1-56458-615-4). Looks at artists, historical periods, styles, movements, aesthetics, and spirituality. (Rev: BL 11/1/94*; BTA; SLJ 5/95; VOYA 4/95) [759]

3489 Buettner, Stewart, and Reinhard G. Pauly. *Great Composers—Great Artists: Portraits* (9–adult). 1992, Timber Press/Amadeus (133 S.W. Second Ave., Suite 450, Portland, OR 97204) $44.95 (0-931340-50-0); paper $29.95 (0-931340-57-8). Profiles of famous composers, each including a reproduction of a portrait, e.g., Chopin by Delacroix, Wagner by Renoir, Satie by Picasso. (Rev: BL 10/1/92) [757]

3490 Clarke, Michael. *Watercolor* (9–adult). (Eyewitness Art) 1993, Dorling Kindersley $16.95 (1-56458-174-8). Brief text copiously illustrated with reproductions of artworks, details of paintings, photos of artists' materials, equipment, maps, and artist portraits. (Rev: BL 5/1/93; MJHS; SLJ 10/93) [751.42]

3491 Cole, Alison. *Perspective* (9–adult). (Eyewitness Art) 1993, Dorling Kindersley $16.95 (1-56458-068-7). Brief text copiously illustrated with reproductions of artworks, details of paintings, photos of artists' materials, equipments, maps, and artist portraits. (Rev: BL 5/1/93; SLJ 2/93) [701.82]

3492 Corrain, Lucia. *Giotto and Medieval Art* (6–12). (Masters of Art) 1995, Peter Bedrick LB $19.95 (0-87226-315-0). (Rev: BL 11/15/95) [759.5]

3493 Gombrich, E. H. *The Story of Art* (9–adult). Rev. ed. 1995, Chronicle $49.95 (0-7148-3355-X); paper $29.95 (0-7148-3247-2). A revision of a comprehensive standard with 443 color illustrations. (Rev: BL 10/1/95; MJHS; SHS) [709]

3494 Greenberg, Jan, and Sandra Jordan. *The Painter's Eye: Learning to Look at Contemporary American Art* (6–9). 1991, Delacorte $20 (0-385-30319-X). This introduction to the language of art uses several contemporary American paintings to illustrate the basic concepts of art and design. Awards: SLJ Best Book. (Rev: BL 10/1/91*; BTA; BY; MJHS; SLJ 9/91*) [701]

3495 Greenberg, Jan, and Sandra Jordan. *The Sculptor's Eye: Looking at Contemporary American Art* (6–12). 1993, Doubleday $19.95 (0-385-30902-3). Awards: ALSC Notable Children's Book. (Rev: BL 10/15/93; BTA; MJHS; SLJ 2/94) [709]

3496 Harris, Nathaniel. *Renaissance Art* (6–10). (Art and Artists) 1994, Thomson Learning $16.95 (1-56847-217-X). (Rev: BL 11/15/94; SLJ 10/94) [709]

3497 *La invención de la pintura* (5–8). (Biblioteca interactiva/Mundo maravilloso) Tr. from French by Fernando Bort. 1993, Ediciones SM (Madrid, Spain) $12.95 (84-348-4110-X). This "interactive" title includes numerous foldouts, flaps, and transparent plastic overlays, detailed color illustrations, and a simple explanation of the invention of painting. English title: *The Invention of Painting*. (Rev: BL 10/1/94)

3498 Isaacson, Philip M. *A Short Walk Around the Pyramids and Through the World of Art* (5–8). 1993, Knopf LB $20.99 (0-679-91523-0). Art is shown in its broadest sense as being a part of the everyday world, using examples of sculpture, architecture, photography, and painting. Awards: SLJ Best Book. (Rev: BL 9/15/93; MJHS; SLJ 8/93*) [700]

3499 MacClintock, Dorcas. *Animals Observed: A Look at Animals in Art* (6–10). 1993, Scribner $18.95 (0-684-19323-X). Celebrates the world of mammals through animal art, including works of Charles Russell, Rembrandt, and Ugo Mochi. (Rev: BL 4/1/93; MJHS; SLJ 5/93; VOYA 8/93) [704.9]

3500 Opie, Mary-Jane. *Sculpture* (7–12). (Eyewitness Art) 1994, Dorling Kindersley $16.95 (1-56458-613-8). (Rev: BL 12/1/94; BTA; MJHS; SLJ 6/95; VOYA 5/95) [730]

3501 Pekarik, Andrew. *Painting* (5–7). (Behind the Scenes) 1992, Hyperion LB $18.89 (1-56282-297-7). A companion to PBS's Behind the Scenes series, with many photos and reproductions. (Rev: BL 2/1/93; BTA; SLJ 2/93) [750]

3502 Pekarik, Andrew. *Sculpture* (5–7). (Behind the Scenes) 1992, Hyperion LB $18.89 (1-56282-295-0). A companion to PBS's Behind the Scenes series, with many photos and reproductions. (Rev: BL 2/1/93; SLJ 2/93) [730]

3503 Powell, Jillian. *Ancient Art* (6–10). (Art and Artists) 1994, Thomson Learning $16.95 (1-56847-216-1). (Rev: BL 11/15/94; SLJ 10/94) [709]

3504 Richardson, Joy. *Inside the Museum: A Children's Guide to the Metropolitan Museum of Art* (5–7). 1993, Abrams/Metropolitan Museum of Art paper $12.95 (0-8109-2561-3). This photographic tour of New York City's Metropolitan Museum of Art includes a behind-the-scenes look at organization, record keeping, and preservation. (Rev: BL 1/1/94; SLJ 2/94) [708.13]

3505 Richardson, Wendy, and Jack Richardson. *Animals: Through the Eyes of Artists* (5–7). (World of Art) 1991, Children's Press LB $14.95 (0-516-09281-2). An introduction to a variety of artists and artistic styles, featuring samples of cave art and tapestry as well as the works of masters and modernists. (Rev: BL 8/91; SLJ 8/91) [760]

3506 Richardson, Wendy, and Jack Richardson. *Cities* (5–7). (World of Art) 1991, Children's Press LB $14.95 (0-516-09282-0). City images seen through the eyes of various artists. (Rev: BL 2/1/92; SLJ 3/92) [760]

3507 Richardson, Wendy, and Jack Richardson. *Entertainers* (5–7). (World of Art) 1991, Children's Press LB $14.95 (0-516-09283-9). An eclectic series of prints and paintings depicting entertainers. (Rev: BL 2/1/92; SLJ 3/92) [760]

3508 Richardson, Wendy, and Jack Richardson. *Families: Through the Eyes of Artists* (5–7). (World of Art) 1991, Children's Press LB $14.95 (0-516-09284-7). An introduction to the works of well-known painters, focusing on how they depicted family life. (Rev: BL 8/91; SLJ 8/91) [758]

3509 Richardson, Wendy, and Jack Richardson. *The Natural World: Through the Eyes of Artists* (5–7). (World of Art) 1991, Children's Press LB $14.95 (0-516-09285-5). An introduction to a variety of artists and styles, featuring a selection of landscapes and still lifes. (Rev: BL 8/91; SLJ 8/91) [759]

3510 Richardson, Wendy, and Jack Richardson. *Water* (5–7). (World of Art) 1991, Children's Press LB $14.90 (0-516-09286-3). Introduction to the works of various artists and styles through the common theme of water. (Rev: BL 2/1/92; SLJ 3/92) [760]

3511 Roalf, Peggy. *Cats* (5–12). (Looking at Paintings) 1992, Hyperion LB $14.89 (1-56282-092-3); paper $6.95 (1-56282-091-5). Pictures of cats from Egyptian wall paintings to the Cheshire cat and more. (Rev: BL 5/15/92; SLJ 7/92) [758.3]

3512 Roalf, Peggy. *Families* (5–12). (Looking at Paintings) 1992, Hyperion LB $14.89 (1-56282-088-5); paper $6.95 (1-56282-087-7). Pictures of families from various time periods. (Rev: BL 5/15/92; SLJ 7/92) [757]

3513 Romei, Francesca. *The Story of Sculpture* (6–12). (Masters of Art) 1995, Peter Bedrick LB $19.95 (0-87226-316-9). (Rev: BL 11/15/95) [730]

3514 Sills, Leslie. *Visions: Stories about Women Artists* (5–8). 1993, Albert Whitman $18.95 (0-8075-8491-6). Melds information about the personal histories of women artists—such as Mary Cassatt, Betye Saar, Mary Frank—with insight into their art. Awards: ALSC Notable Children's Book; BL Editors' Choice; SLJ Best Book. (Rev: BL 4/1/93; BTA; MJHS; SLJ 5/93*) [709]

3515 Steffens, Bradley. *Photography: Preserving the Past* (6–10). (Encyclopedia of Discovery and Invention) 1991, Lucent LB $15.95 (1-56006-212-6). (Rev: BL 4/15/92) [770]

3516 Wakin, Edward, and Daniel Wakin. *Photos That Made U.S. History, Vol. 1: From the Civil War Era to the Atomic Age* (6–9). 1993, Walker LB $13.85 (0-8027-8231-0). Photos that altered the perceptions of people and governments during times of military and social crisis. (Rev: BL 5/1/94; MJHS; SLJ 2/94) [973.9]

3517 Wakin, Edward, and Daniel Wakin. *Photos That Made U.S. History, Vol. 2: From the Cold War to the Space Age* (6–9). 1993, Walker LB $13.85 (0-8027-8272-8). Photos that changed our perception of critical events, such as Vietnamese children fleeing napalm bombs. (Rev: BL 5/1/94; MJHS; SLJ 2/94) [973.9]

3518 Welton, Jude. *Impressionism* (9–adult). (Eyewitness Art) 1993, Dorling Kindersley $16.95 (1-56458-173-X). Brief text copiously illustrated with reproductions of artworks, details of paintings, photos of artists' materials, equipment, maps, and artist portraits (Rev: BL 5/1/93; MJHS) [759.09]

Regions

Africa

3519 Thompson, Robert Farris. *Face of the Gods: Art and Altars of Africa and the African Americas* (9–adult). 1994, Prestel $70 (3-7913-1281-2). A survey of the sacred art of Africa and its influence on the art and worship of African Americans. (Rev: BL 2/15/94) [726.5]

Asia and the Middle East

3520 Noble, Dennis L. *Forgotten Warriors: Combat Art from Vietnam* (9–adult). 1992, Praeger $29.95 (0-275-93868-9). Reproductions of drawings and paintings by combat artists illustrate actual letters, oral and official military histories, and novel excerpts about the American experience in the Vietnam War. (Rev: BL 10/1/92) [959.704]

Europe

3521 Hall, Marcia. *Michelangelo: The Sistine Ceiling Restored* (7–12). (Rizzoli Art) 1993, Rizzoli paper $7.95 (0-8478-1754-7). This volume describes the design of Michelangelo's Sistine Chapel ceiling and its restoration. (Rev: BL 1/15/94) [759.5]

3522 Kent, Sarah. *Composition* (7–12). (Eyewitness Art) 1995, Dorling Kindersley $16.95 (1-56458-612-X). An analysis of composition in art using European paintings from the Renaissance to the present. (Rev: BL 4/15/95; SLJ 8/95) [750]

3523 Mühlberger, Richard. *What Makes a Cassatt a Cassatt?* (6–12). (What Makes a . . .) 1994, Viking paper $11.99 (0-670-85742-4). (Rev: BL 1/1/95; SLJ 1/95) [759.13]

3524 Mühlberger, Richard. *What Makes a Degas a Degas?* (5–10). (What Makes a . . .) 1993, Viking $9.95 (0-670-85205-8). (Rev: BL 1/15/94; MJHS) [759.4]

3525 Mühlberger, Richard. *What Makes a Monet a Monet?* (6–12). (What Makes a . . .) 1993, Viking/Metropolitan Museum of Art $9.95 (0-670-85200-7). A presentation of biographical material, an analysis of idiosyncratic elements of the style, and full-color reproductions of the paintings of Monet. (Rev: BL 1/15/94; MJHS; SLJ 4/94) [759.4]

3526 Mühlberger, Richard. *What Makes a Picasso a Picasso?* (6–12). (What Makes a . . .) 1994, Viking paper $11.99 (0-670-85741-6). (Rev: BL 1/1/95; SLJ 1/95) [759.4]

3527 Mühlberger, Richard. *What Makes a Raphael a Raphael?* (5–10). (What Makes a . . .) 1993, Viking $9.95 (0-670-85204-X). (Rev: BL 1/15/94; MJHS) [759.5]

3528 Mühlberger, Richard. *What Makes a Rembrandt a Rembrandt?* (5–10). (What Makes a . . .) 1993, Viking $9.95 (0-670-85199-X). (Rev: BL 1/15/94; MJHS) [759.9492]

3529 Mühlberger, Richard. *What Makes a Van Gogh a Van Gogh?* (5–10). (What Makes a . . .) 1993, Viking $9.95 (0-670-85198-1). (Rev: BL 1/15/94; MJHS) [759.9492]

3530 Salvi, Francesco. *The Impressionists: The Origins of Modern Painting* (6–12). (Masters of Art) 1995, Peter Bedrick $19.95 (0-87226-314-2). An overview of Paris during the impressionists' activities. Includes large illustrations. (Rev: BL 4/1/95; BTA; VOYA 5/95) [759.05]

3531 Stuckey, Charles F. *Claude Monet, 1840–1926* (9–adult). 1995, Thames & Hudson $50 (0-500-09246-X). Includes 200 color reproductions and a 70-page illustrated chronology plus an overview of Monet's achievements and a cache of little-known letters. (Rev: BL 9/1/95) [759.4]

3532 Wood, Mara-Helen, ed. *Edvard Munch: The Frieze of Life* (9–adult). 1993, Abrams $45 (0-8109-3630-5). Commentary on and reproductions of the paintings, woodcuts, and prints that were the centerpiece of Munch's work. Includes a chronology and photos of the artist. (Rev: BL 4/15/93) [759.481]

3533 Wright, Patricia. *Manet* (9–adult). (Eyewitness Art) 1993, Dorling Kindersley $16.95 (1-56458-172-1). A brief text copiously illustrated with reproductions of artworks, details of paintings, photos of artists' materials, equipment, maps, and artist portraits. (Rev: BL 5/1/93; MJHS; SLJ 7/93) [759.4]

North America

UNITED STATES

3534 Adams, Ansel. *Ansel Adams: Our National Parks* (9–adult). 1992, Little, Brown $16.95 (0-8212-1910-3). A collection of photographs, essays, and letters. (Rev: BL 5/15/92; MJHS; SHS) [770]

3535 Easter, Eric, and others, eds. *Songs of My People: African Americans: A Self-Portrait* (9–adult). 1993, Little, Brown $39.95 (0-316-10966-5); paper $24.95 (0-316-10981-9). A photo-essay of African American life by 50 photographers who went into neighborhoods, hospitals, churches, theaters, jails, and colleges. (Rev: BL 2/15/93*) [973]

3536 Gouma-Peterson, Thalia. *Breaking the Rules: Audrey Flack, a Retrospective, 1950–1990* (9–adult). 1992, Abrams $39.95 (0-8109-3117-6). Illustrated profile of artist Audrey Flack. (Rev: BL 4/15/92) [709]

3537 Hill, Tom, and Richard W. Hill, eds. *Creation's Journey: Native American Identity and Belief* (9–adult). 1994, Smithsonian $45 (1-56098-453-8). Native American artists and academics discuss the connection of art objects to their rituals, stories, and spiritual beliefs. (Rev: BL 11/1/94; SHS) [745]

3538 Littlechild, George. *This Land Is My Land* (6–9). 1993, Children's Book Press (246 First St.,

San Francisco, CA 94105) $15.95 (0-89239-119-7). Littlechild draws on his Plains Cree background in this presentation of 17 of his full-color paintings that focus on Native American history. (Rev: BL 11/1/93; SLJ 1/94) [971]

3539 Reynolds, Donald Martin. *Masters of American Sculpture: The Figurative Tradition from the American Renaissance to the Millennium* (9–adult). 1994, Abbeville $67.50 (1-55859-276-8). A survey of a century of figurative sculpture in America. (Rev: BL 4/15/94) [730]

3540 Schaffner, Cynthia V. A. *Discovering American Folk Art* (9–adult). 1991, Abrams $24.95 (0-8109-3206-7). This basic guide to traditional folk art objects is illustrated with examples from the Museum of American Folk Art. Presents elementary projects. (Rev: BL 11/15/91) [745]

3541 Yoe, Craig, and Janet Morra-Yoe, eds. *The Art of Mickey Mouse* (9–adult). 1991, Hyperion $35 (1-56282-994-7). An affectionate homage to the pop culture icon by nearly 100 artists, each contributing his/her rendition of the mouse, with an introduction by John Updike. (Rev: BL 11/1/91; SHS) [704.9]

South and Central America

3542 Rasmussen, Waldo, and others, eds. *Latin American Artists of the Twentieth Century* (9–adult). 1993, Abrams $65 (0-8109-6121-0). This profusely illustrated volume (357 plates; 194 in color) was published as part of a Museum of Modern Art (New York) exhibit. It comprises 13 essays by art historians, who illuminate various styles of twentieth-century Latin American art and the work of selected artists. (Rev: BL 10/15/93*) [709]

Decorative Arts

3543 Giblin, James Cross. *Be Seated: A Book about Chairs* (5–8). 1993, HarperCollins LB $14.89 (0-06-021538-0). Examines the history of chairs in Egypt, India, China, Greece, Rome, Europe, and the United States, including their development, use in mythology, and use in and as art. Awards: SLJ Best Book. (Rev: BL 12/15/93; MJHS; SLJ 12/93*) [749]

3544 Heide, Robert, and John Gilman. *Popular Art Deco: Depression Era Style and Design* (9–adult). 1991, Abbeville $35 (1-55859-030-7). Explores art deco's origins and illustrates its influence on the futuristic, streamlined appearance of everything from toasters to skyscrapers. (Rev: BL 9/1/91) [709]

Music

General and Miscellaneous

3545 Ardley, Neil. *A Young Person's Guide to Music* (5–8). 1995, Dorling Kindersley $24.95 (0-7894-0313-7). A CD accompanies this volume, which focuses on classical music and the instruments that create it. (Rev: BL 12/15/95) [780]

3546 Handel, George Frideric. *Messiah: The Wordbook for the Oratorio* (5–7). Illus. 1992, HarperCollins/Willa Perlman $20 (0-06-021779-0). This illustrated libretto includes a history of the musical masterpiece's text. Awards: SLJ Best Book. (Rev: BL 10/15/92) [782.23]

3547 Lees, Gene. *Jazz Lives: Portraits of 100 Jazz Artists* (9–adult). 1992, Firefly Books $39.95 (1-895565-12-X). Profiles of well-known musicians highlighted by candid photos. (Rev: BL 9/15/92) [781.65]

3548 Marsalis, Wynton. *Marsalis on Music* (9–adult). 1995, Norton $29.95 (0-393-03881-5). Uses examples from jazz greats to teach the fundamentals of jazz and the elements of improvisation. Includes a CD. (Rev: BL 10/1/95) [780]

3549 Turnbull, Walter. *Lift Every Voice: Expecting the Most and Getting the Best from All God's Children* (9–adult). 1995, Hyperion $19.95 (0-7868-6164-9). The director of the Boys Choir of Harlem chronicles his beliefs and successes in sharing the joys of music with African American children. (Rev: BL 12/1/95) [780.7]

History of Music

3550 Davis, Francis. *The History of the Blues: The Roots, the Music, the People—From Charley Patton to Robert Cray* (9–adult). 1995, Hyperion $24.95 (0-7868-6052-9). Using a first-person perspective, Davis explores the history, evolution, and marketing of contemporary blues artists and their music. (Rev: BL 1/15/95*; SHS) [781.643]

3551 Floyd, Samuel A. *The Power of Black Music* (9–adult). 1995, Oxford Univ. $30 (0-19-508235-4). Traces African American music from Africa to the United States and explores the influence and contribution of musicians. (Rev: BL 4/1/95) [780]

3552 Gaar, Gillian. *She's a Rebel: The History of Women in Rock and Roll* (9–adult). 1992, Seal Press paper $16.95 (1-878067-08-7). The contributions of female songwriters, singers, and other musicians are tracked through 4 decades of popular music. (Rev: BL 10/1/92) [781.66]

Jazz and Popular Music (Country, Rap, Rock, etc.)

3553 Allen, Bob, ed. *The Blackwell Guide to Recorded Country Music* (9–adult). 1994, Blackwell $24.95 (0-631-19106-2). Journalists and scholars recommend the best recordings of country music from various styles and periods, including bluegrass and honky-tonk. (Rev: BL 7/94*) [016.781642]

3554 Carlin, Richard. *Jazz* (9–12). (World of Music) 1991, Facts on File $16.95 (0-8160-2229-1). (Rev: BL 9/15/91; MJHS) [781.65]

3555 Clark, Roy, and Marc Eliot. *My Life—in Spite of Myself* (9–adult). 1994, Simon & Schuster $22 (0-671-86434-3). The autobiography of the guitar- and banjo-playing country music star and mainstay of *Hee-Haw*. (Rev: BL 1/15/94) [782.42]

3556 Cohn, Lawrence, ed. *Nothing but the Blues: The Music and the Musicians* (9–adult). 1993, Abbeville $45 (1-55859-271-7). (Rev: BL 9/1/93*) [781.643]

3557 Ellison, Curtis W. *Country Music Culture: From Hard Times to Heaven* (9–adult). 1995, Univ. Press of Mississippi $40 (0-87805-721-8); paper $14.95 (0-87805-722-6). An account of the country music industry and its performers. (Rev: BL 2/15/95) [781.642]

3558 Escott, Colin, and Martin Hawkins. *Good Rockin' Tonight: Sun Records and the Birth of Rock 'n' Roll* (9–adult). Rev. ed. 1991, St. Martin's $19.95 (0-312-05439-4). (Rev: BL 4/1/91*) [781.66]

3559 Giuliano, Geoffrey. *The Beatles Album: 30 Years of Music and Memorabilia* (9–adult). 1991, Viking $29.95 (0-670-84118-8). More than 800 photos of Beatle memorabilia. (Rev: BL 1/15/92) [782.42166]

3560 Guterman, Jimmy, and Owen O'Donnell. *The Worst Rock and Roll Records of All Time: A Fan's Guide to the Stuff You Love to Hate* (9–adult). 1991, Citadel paper $14.95 (0-8065-1231-8). Opinionated guide to 50 "atrocious" rock-and-roll songs. (Rev: BL 6/1/91) [781.66]

3561 Hentoff, Nat. *Listen to the Stories: Nat Hentoff on Jazz and Country Music* (9–adult). 1995, HarperCollins $23 (0-06-019047-7). A combination of recollections and personal profiles of country music and jazz greats. (Rev: BL 4/1/95) [781.65]

3562 Heylin, Clinton. *From the Velvets to the Voidoids: A Pre-Punk History for a Post-Punk World* (9–adult). 1993, Penguin paper $14 (0-14-017970-4). Covers punk rock's precursors, the first wave, and later stages of the movement when Talking Heads and Blondie achieved mainstream success. (Rev: BL 6/1–15/93) [781.66]

3563 Lomax, Alan. *The Land Where the Blues Began* (9–adult). 1993, Pantheon $25 (0-679-40424-4). Lomax's 1940's search in the South for blues musicians vividly evoke the era. (Rev: BL 3/15/93*) [781.643]

3564 McCartney, Linda. *Linda McCartney's Sixties: Portrait of an Era* (9–adult). 1992, Little, Brown/Bulfinch $40 (0-8212-1959-6). A black-and-white pictorial retrospective of 1960s musicians. (Rev: BL 9/15/92) [781.66]

3565 Marcus, Greil. *Ranters and Crowd Pleasers: Punk in Pop Music, 1977–92* (9–adult). 1993, Doubleday $22 (0-385-41720-9). More than 60 previously published magazine essays by a fan and critic about pivotal punk rock bands and performers. (Rev: BL 5/15/93) [781.66]

3566 Martin, George, and William Pearson. *With a Little Help from My Friends: The Making of Sgt. Pepper* (9–adult). 1995, Little, Brown $22.95 (0-316-54783-2). The producer of the Beatles' records recalls his personal and professional relationship with the Fab Four. (Rev: BL 5/1/95) [782.42166]

3567 Pride, Charley, and Jim Henderson. *Pride: The Charley Pride Story* (9–adult). 1994, Morrow $20 (0-688-12638-3). The autobiography of the only African American superstar in the overwhelmingly white country music field. (Rev: BL 1/15/94) [782.42]

3568 Rose, Tricia. *Black Noise: Rap Music and Black Culture in Contemporary America* (9–adult). 1994, Wesleyan Univ. $35 (0-8195-5271-2); paper $14.95 (0-8195-6275-0). A thorough analysis of several facets of rap, including a discussion of hip-hop and the neglected role of women in rap. (Rev: BL 4/15/94; SHS) [782.42164]

3569 Scherman, Tony, ed. *The Rock Musician* (9–adult). 1994, St. Martin's paper $12.95 (0-312-09502-3). In-depth interviews of celebrated rock musicians that originally appeared in *Musician* magazine. (Rev: BL 1/15/94) [781.66]

3570 Scherman, Tony, and Mark Rowland, eds. *The Jazz Musician* (9–adult). 1994, St. Martin's paper $12.95 (0-312-09500-7). A series of profiles of jazz greats in which the legendary musicians recall important points in their lives. (Rev: BL 2/1/94) [781.65]

3571 Sexton, Adam, ed. *Rap on Rap: Straight Talk on Hip-Hop Culture* (9–adult). 1995, Dell/Delta paper $14.95 (0-385-31247-4). Articles related to hip-hop and rap, including an excerpt from a novel and television transcripts. (Rev: BL 3/1/95) [782.42164]

3572 Stanley, Lawrence A., ed. *Rap: The Lyrics* (9–adult). 1992, Penguin paper $16 (0-14-014788-8). This collection of rap lyrics includes an overview of rap's evolution in terms of African American musical traditions and American politics. (Rev: BL 10/1/92) [782.42164]

3573 Stroff, Stephen M. *Discovering Great Jazz: A New Listener's Guide to the Sounds and Styles of the Top Musicians and Their Recordings on CDs, LPs, and Cassettes* (9–adult). 1991, Newmarket $18.95 (1-55704-103-2). A balanced description of the stylistic developments in the history of jazz, with recommendations for the best recorded performances from each period. (Rev: BL 10/1/91; MJHS) [781.65]

3574 Sugerman, Danny, and Wallace Fowlie, eds. *The Doors: The Complete Illustrated Lyrics* (9–adult). 1991, Hyperion $24.95 (1-56282-996-3). A reprinting of many Doors' songs, critiqued and illustrated. (Rev: BL 8/91; SLJ 3/92) [782.42166]

3575 Wall, Mick. *Guns N' Roses: The Most Dangerous Band in the World* (9–adult). 1992, Hyperion paper $9.95 (1-56282-951-3). Details of the rock group's background, lifestyle, and career. (Rev: BL 4/1/92) [782.42166]

3576 Williams, Martin. *Jazz Changes* (9–adult). 1992, Oxford Univ. $22.95 (0-19-505847-X). Anthology of writings by an eminent jazz critic, including profiles of jazz greats. (Rev: BL 1/15/92) [781.65]

Opera and Musicals

3577 Alpert, Hollis. *The Life and Times of Porgy and Bess: The Story of an American Classic* (9–adult). 1990, Knopf $35 (0-394-58339-6). The history of a time-honored American opera. (Rev: BL 1/15/91*) [782.1]

3578 Sullivan, Arthur. *I Have a Song to Sing, O! An Introduction to the Songs of Gilbert and Sullivan* (5–8). Edited by John Langstaff. Illus. 1994, Macmillan/Margaret K. McElderry $17.95 (0-689-50591-4). (Rev: BL 12/1/94; SLJ 10/94)

3579 Townshend, Pete, and Des McAnuff. *The Who's Tommy: The Musical* (9–adult). 1993, Pantheon $40 (0-679-43066-0). This behind-the-scenes look at the rock opera by The Who includes production stills, anecdotes by cast and production members, and a CD. (Rev: BL 12/15/93) [782.1]

3580 Wilk, Max. *OK! The Story of Oklahoma!* (9–adult). 1993, Grove/Weidenfeld $24.95 (0-8021-1432-6). The story of the creation of the groundbreaking musical and its composers, songs, and performers. (Rev: BL 3/15/93) [782.1]

Orchestra and Musical Instruments

3581 Chapman, Richard. *The Complete Guitarist* (9–adult). 1993, Dorling Kindersley $29.95 (1-56458-181-0). A player's introduction to the guitar: its historic origins, a course of instruction for beginners, and issues surrounding amplification. (Rev: BL 6/1–15/93) [787.87]

3582 Gruhn, George, and Walter Carter. *Acoustic Guitars and Other Fretted Instruments: A Photographic History* (9–adult). 1993, Miller Freeman/GPI Books $39.95 (0-87930-240-2). Presents American fretted-instrument history from its beginnings to the present day, including photos of celebrity guitars. (Rev: BL 6/1–15/93) [787.87]

3583 Hart, Mickey, and others. *Planet Drum: A Celebration of Percussion and Rhythm* (9–adult). 1991, HarperCollins $39.95 (0-06-250414-2); paper $24.95 (0-06-250397-9). The percussionist for the Grateful Dead relates the worldwide origins and history of drumming and the myths associated with rhythm and percussion instruments. (Rev: BL 12/15/91) [786.9]

3584 *La música y los instrumentos 3(5–8)*. (Biblioteca interactiva/Mundo maravilloso) Tr. from French by Fernando Bort. 1993, Ediciones SM (Madrid, Spain) $12.95 (84-348-4111-8). This "interactive" title includes numerous foldouts, flaps, and transparent plastic overlays; detailed color illustrations; and a simple explanation of musical instruments. English title: *Music and the Instruments*. (Rev: BL 10/1/94)

3585 Steinberg, Michael. *The Symphony: A Concert Guide* (9–adult). 1995, Oxford Univ. $30 (0-19-506177-2). Essays based on program notes Steinberg wrote for the Boston and San Francisco orchestras over 20 years. (Rev: BL 11/1/95) [784.2]

Songs and Folk Songs

3586 Axelrod, Alan. *Songs of the Wild West* (5–9). Songs arranged by Dan Fox. 1991, Simon & Schuster $19.95 (0-671-74775-4). Collection of 45 songs from the Old West, with an overview of the Western expansionist movement and brief essays linking the music with art and history. Awards: ALSC Notable Children's Book. (Rev: BL 12/15/91; MJHS; SLJ 1/92)

3587 Downes, Belinda. *Silent Night: A Christmas Carol Sampler* (7–12). 1995, Knopf $18 (0-679-86959-X). This 32-page collection of Christmas carols is illustrated with a full-page embroidered tapestry facing each carol. Words and piano music are provided. (Rev: BL 9/15/95*) [782.281]

3588 *An Illustrated Treasury of Songs* (6–12). 1991, Rizzoli $19.95 (0-8478-1376-2). Collection of 55 classic songs, such as "Clementine" and "I've Been Working on the Railroad." Includes musical notations for voice and piano. (Rev: BL 1/15/92) [[784.6]

3589 Johnson, James Weldon. *Lift Every Voice and Sing* (6–12). Illus. 1993, Walker LB $15.85 (0-8027-8251-5). This song—the African American "national anthem"—was written for school children in 1900. It's accompanied here by dramatic linocut prints. (Rev: BL 2/15/93*; MJHS; SLJ 2/95) [782.42164]

3590 Krull, Kathleen, ed. *Gonna Sing My Head Off!* (7–12). Illus. 1992, Knopf/Borzoi $20 (0-394-81991-8). Sixty-two work songs, love songs, ballads, blues, lullabies, spirituals, protest songs, and sheer nonsense. Piano and guitar arrangements, with words to all verses. Awards: ALSC Notable Children's Book; BL Editors' Choice; SLJ Best Book. (Rev: BL 10/15/92*; SLJ 10/92*)

3591 Silverman, Jerry. *The Blues* (7–12). (Traditional Black Music) 1994, Chelsea House $15.95 (0-7910-1830-X). A collection of simple arrangements of blues standards that shows how the musical genre grew out of the despair of African American oppression. (Rev: BL 2/15/94; MJHS; SLJ 4/94) [782.421643]

3592 Silverman, Jerry. *Songs and Stories from the American Revolution* (6–10). 1994, Millbrook $18.90 (1-56294-429-0). (Rev: BL 12/1/94; MJHS; SLJ 2/95) [782.421599]

3593 Zollo, Paul, ed. *Songwriters on Songwriting* (9–adult). 1991, Writer's Digest paper $17.95 (0-89879-451-X). A collection of interviews with such luminaries as Madonna, Carole King, Paul Simon, and Frank Zappa, who discuss their songwriting methods and how their classics came to be. (Rev: BL 3/15/91; SHS) [782.42]

Theater, Dance, and Other Performing Arts

General and Miscellaneous

3594 Cushman, Kathleen, and Montana Miller. *Circus Dreams* (6–12). Illus. 1990, Little, Brown/Joy Street $15.95 (0-316-16561-1). A look at the professional college for circus artists in France, by one of its students. (Rev: BL 1/15/91; MJHS; SLJ 1/91)

3595 Fradon, Dana. *The King's Fool: A Book about Medieval and Renaissance Fools* (5–7). 1993, Dutton $14.99 (0-525-45074-2). *New Yorker* cartoonist Fradon uses a cartoon Renaissance court fool to show the highlights and dark side of the trade, with stories of individuals using their wit to make a living. (Rev: BL 11/15/93; SLJ 11/93) [792.7]

Dance (Ballet, Modern, etc.)

3596 Anderson, Joan. *Twins on Toes: A Ballet Debut* (5–7). Illus. 1993, Dutton/Lodestar paper $14.99 (0-525-67415-2). This in-depth profile of the School of American Ballet's Spring Workshop focuses on 17-year-old twins Amy and Laurel. (Rev: BL 10/1/93; SLJ 10/93) [792]

3597 Crum, Robert. *Eagle Drum: On the Powwow Trail with a Young Grass Dancer* (5–7). 1994, Four Winds $16.95 (0-02-725515-8). Explores the history, preparation, and performances of the Montana Pend Oreille people's powwow dances. Awards: Western Heritage. (Rev: BL 10/1/94; SLJ 12/94) [394]

3598 Garfunkel, Trudy. *On Wings of Joy: The Story of Ballet from the 16th Century to Today* (7–12). 1994, Little, Brown $18.95 (0-316-30412-3). Chronicles ballet's 400-year history, from Catherine de Medici's palace to contemporary dance troupes. Profiles dancers, composers, and choreographers. (Rev: BL 10/15/94; BTA; SHS; SLJ 11/94; VOYA 12/94) [792.8]

3599 Heth, Charlotte, ed. *Native American Dance: Ceremonies and Social Traditions* (9–adult). 1993, Starwood Publishing (P.O. Box 40503, Washington, DC 20016) $45 (1-56373-021-9); paper $24.95 (1-56373-020-0). Celebrates Indian dance ceremonies and social traditions, past and present, in all the Americas. Color photos. (Rev: BL 4/1/93*) [394.3]

3600 Horosko, Marian, ed. *Martha Graham: The Evolution of Her Dance Theory and Training, 1926–1991* (9–adult). 1992, Chicago Review/A Cappella $29.95 (1-55652-142-1); paper $14.95 (1-55652-141-3). Reminiscences by dancers and actors that provide insight into the development of Graham's training theories and methods. (Rev: BL 12/15/91) [792.8]

3601 Jonas, Gerald. *Dancing: The Pleasure, Power and Art of Movement* (9–adult). 1992, Abrams $45 (0-8109-3212-1). An illustrated companion to a PBS-TV series on the history of dance provides in-depth descriptions and interpretations of the roles it plays in world cultures. (Rev: BL 11/15/92; BTA) [792.8]

3602 King, Sandra. *Shannon: An Ojibway Dancer* (5–7). (We Are Still Here) Illus. 1993, Lerner $19.95 (0-8225-2652-2); paper $6.95 (0-8225-9643-1). A typical American teenage girl who is also a member of the Ojibway people learns a traditional dance in preparation for the summer powwow. (Rev: BL 1/15/94; SLJ 2/94) [394]

3603 Reynolds, Nancy, and Susan Reimer-Torn. *Dance Classics: A Viewer's Guide to the Best-Loved Ballets and Modern Dances* (9–adult). 1991, Chicago Review/A Cappella $29.95 (1-55652-109-X); paper $14.95 (1-55652-106-5). Handbook for some of the most frequently performed and popular ballets, ranging from *Swan Lake* to the dances of Twyla Tharp. (Rev: BL 6/15/91) [792.8]

Motion Pictures

3604 Arginteanu, Judy. *The Movies of Alfred Hitchcock* (7–10). 1994, Lerner LB $14.21 (0-8225-1642-X). Analyzes 8 films by the master of suspense, providing interpretation of the symbols and themes of such films as *Psycho, The Birds,* and *North by Northwest.* (Rev: BL 7/94; SLJ 8/94) [791.43]

3605 Beck, Jerry. *"I Tawt I Taw a Puddy Tat": Fifty Years of Sylvester and Tweety* (9–adult). 1991, Holt $35 (0-8050-1644-9). A tribute to Sylvester and Tweety on their 50th birthdays. Includes over 300 color-frame enlargements, cels, storyboards, and animation drawings. (Rev: BL 1/1/92) [741.5]

3606 Carnes, Mark C., and others, eds. *Past Imperfect: History According to the Movies* (9–adult). 1995, Holt $30 (0-8050-3759-4). Compares the often inaccurate portrayals of history in movies with the views of those who assert that they know the truth—for example, paleontologist Stephen Gould's discussion of the veracity of *Jurassic Park.* (Rev: BL 9/1/95*) [791.43]

3607 Cowie, Peter, ed. *World Cinema: Diary of a Day* (9–adult). 1995, Overlook $29.95 (0-87951-573-2). An overview of filmmaking, with information from directors, producers, technicians, and performers. (Rev: BL 3/15/95) [791.43]

3608 Ebert, Roger, and Gene Siskel. *The Future of the Movies* (9–adult). 1991, Andrews & McMeel paper $9.95 (0-8362-6216-6). Interviews and discussions of cinema craft with 3 influential American filmmakers: Martin Scorsese, Steven Spielberg, and George Lucas. (Rev: BL 9/1/91) [791.43]

3609 Finch, Christopher. *The Art of the Lion King* (9–adult). 1994, Hyperion $50 (0-7868-6028-6). Describes the making of the Disney film, including hundreds of production stills, sketches, animation drawings, and background paintings. (Rev: BL 9/1/94) [741.5]

3610 Fine, Marshall. *Bloody Sam: The Life and Films of Sam Peckinpah* (9–adult). 1991, Donald I. Fine $24.95 (1-55611-236-X). The turbulent life and film career of the director of *The Wild Bunch* and *Straw Dogs,* whose work has been so influential on today's violent action films. (Rev: BL 12/1/91) [791.43]

3611 Flynn, John L. *The Films of Arnold Schwarzenegger* (9–adult). 1993, Citadel paper $17.95 (0-8065-1423-X). Schwarzenegger's films, from *Hercules in New York* to his most recent, are given a critical look, with behind-the-scenes glimpses of the actor. (Rev: BL 11/1/93) [791.43]

3612 Frantz, Donald. *Beauty and the Beast: A Celebration of the Broadway Musical* (9–adult). 1995, Hyperion $35 (0-7868-6179-7). Many production photos and behind-the-scenes information from the new stage production. (Rev: BL 12/15/95) [782.1]

3613 George, Nelson. *Blackface: Reflections on African Americans and the Movies* (9–adult). 1994, HarperCollins $22 (0-06-017120-0). Examines the portrayal of African Americans in motion pictures, including the work of actor Sidney Poitier and filmmaker Spike Lee. (Rev: BL 10/15/94) [791.43]

3614 Golden, Chris, ed. *Cut! Horror Writers on Horror Film* (9–adult). 1992, Berkley paper $8.95 (0-425-13282-X). Horror writers expound on horror films, writers, and directors. (Rev: BL 3/15/92) [791.436]

3615 Hitzeroth, Deborah, and Sharon Heerboth. *Movies: The World on Film* (6–8). (Encyclopedia of Discovery and Invention) 1991, Lucent LB $15.95 (1-56006-210-X). This introduction to the world of cinema covers the history of moviemaking and the influence of films on society. (Rev: BL 12/1/91) [791.43]

3616 Hofstede, David. *Hollywood and the Comics: Film Adaptations of Comic Books and Strips* (9–adult). 1991, Zanne-3 Publishing (P.O. Box 70596, Las Vegas, NV 89170) paper $12.95 (0-9629176-4-8). This rundown of more than 50 screen adaptations of the comics supplies plot synopses, cast listings, credits, critical commentary, and a 0-to-4– star rating for each. (Rev: BL 10/15/91) [791.43]

3617 Holden, Anthony. *Behind the Oscar: The Secret History of the Academy Awards* (9–adult). 1993, Simon & Schuster $25 (0-671-70129-0). Facts and statistics about the Oscar and the Academy Awards show, as well as backstage gossip. (Rev: BL 3/15/93; SLJ 2/94) [791.43]

3618 Jameson, Richard T., ed. *They Went Thataway: Redefining Film Genres* (9–adult). 1994, Mercury paper $16.95 (1-56279-055-2). Reviews by dozens of well-known film critics are included in this collection of articles on movies that attempt to redefine film genres. (Rev: BL 1/15/94) [791.43]

3619 Johnston, Ollie, and Frank Thomas. *The Disney Villain* (9–adult). 1993, Hyperion $45 (1-56282-792-8). This retrospective of Disney animated films, up to *Aladdin,* examines cartoon villains and the philosophy behind their creation. (Rev: BL 10/15/93) [791.43]

3620 Jones, G. Williams. *Black Cinema Treasures: Lost and Found* (9–adult). 1991, Univ. of North Texas $29.95 (0-929398-26-2). A discussion of 22 films made for African American audiences by independent film producers from the 1920s through the 1950s. (Rev: BL 7/91) [701.13]

3621 Lloyd, Ann. *The Films of Stephen King* (9–adult). 1994, St. Martin's $22.95 (0-312-11329-3); paper $14.95 (0-312-11274-2). Analyzes 25 films based on books by the master of horror. Gives the cast, credits, synopsis, and critiques of each. King himself discusses several films. (Rev: BL 10/15/94) [791.43]

3622 McCarty, John. *Hollywood Gangland: The Movies' Love Affair with the Mob* (9–adult). 1993, St. Martin's $24.95 (0-312-09306-3). In this scholarly retrospective of gangster films—from a 1912 D. W. Griffith silent film to the *Godfather* saga—McCarty pays particular attention to the biggest gangster stars: Robinson, Cagney, and Bogart; to the fictionalizations of real-life gangsters; and to the genre's comeback after World War II. (Rev: BL 10/15/93) [791.43]

3623 Margulies, Edward, and Stephen Rebello. *Bad Movies We Love* (9–adult). 1993, NAL/Plume paper $12 (0-452-27005-7). A compendium of recent movies so bad that they are entertaining. (Rev: BL 7/93) [791.43]

3624 Merritt, Russell, and J. B. Kaufman. *Walt in Wonderland: The Silent Films of Walt Disney* (9–adult). 1994, Johns Hopkins Univ. $39.95 (0-8018-4907-1). Profiles Disney films of the 1920s, demonstrating how they laid the foundation for later animation techniques and conventions. (Rev: BL 9/1/94) [791.43]

3625 Perlman, Marc. *Youth Rebellion Movies* (8–12). 1993, Lerner LB $14.21 (0-8225-1640-3). Perlman summarizes movies about renegades (for example, *The Wild One, Easy Rider, Heathers*), interprets them, and discusses their impact on the culture. (Rev: BL 7/93; SLJ 6/93) [791.43]

3626 Platt, Richard. *Film* (5–9). (Eyewitness Books) 1992, Knopf LB $15.99 (0-679-91679-2). (Rev: BL 6/1/92; MJHS) [791.43]

3627 Rainer, Peter, ed. *Love and Hisses: The National Society of Film Critics Sound Off on the Hottest Movie Controversies* (9–adult). 1992, Mercury paper $14.95 (1-56279-031-5). This collection of reviews by America's best-known film critics pairs contrasting views on more than 20 years of controversial movies and on film directors. (Rev: BL 10/1/92) [791.43]

3628 Sauter, Michael. *The Worst Movies of All Time; or, What Were They Thinking?* (9–adult). 1995, Citadel paper $14.95 (0-8065-1577-5). A delight in chronicling bad movies motivates this book, with a look at some behind-the-scenes craziness. (Rev: BL 11/15/95) [791.43]

3629 Schultz, Ron. *Looking Inside Cartoon Animation* (5–8). (X-Ray Vision) Illus. 1992, John Muir paper $9.95 (1-56261-066-X). Breaks down the animator's art to its scientific underpinnings and then to the roles of key people in the process. (Rev: BL 1/15/93; MJHS; SLJ 2/93) [741.5]

3630 Scott, Elaine. *Look Alive: Behind the Scenes of an Animated Film* (5–8). 1992, Morrow LB $13.93 (0-688-09937-8). Documents the evolution of the animated Ralph and shows how various types of Ralph puppets were manipulated to create cinematic effects. (Rev: BL 9/1/92; SLJ 9/92; YR) [791.4]

3631 Sennett, Robert S. *Setting the Scene: The Great Hollywood Art Directors* (9–adult). 1994, Abrams $39 (0-8109-3846-4). (Rev: BL 12/1/94*) [791.43]

3632 Sennett, Ted. *Laughing in the Dark: Movie Comedy from Groucho to Woody* (9–adult). 1992, St. Martin's $35 (0-312-06280-X). An overview of movie comedy trends from the arrival of the talkies through the 1980s. (Rev: BL 2/15/92) [791.43]

3633 Shay, Don, and Jody Duncan. *The Making of Jurassic Park* (9–adult). 1993, Ballantine paper $18 (0-345-38122-X). Illustrated chronicle of the Crichton-Spielberg collaboration in the creation of the movie. (Rev: BL 7/93) [791.43]

3634 Skal, David J. *The Monster Show: A Cultural History of Horror* (9–adult). 1993, Norton $22.95 (0-393-03419-4). Investigates the horror genre as a cultural phenomenon. (Rev: BL 2/1/93; BTA) [791.43]

3635 Solomon, Charles. *The Disney That Never Was: The Stories and Art from Five Decades of Unproduced Animation* (9–adult). 1995, Hyperion $40 (0-7868-6037-5). The Disney projects that were abandoned, accompanied by many illustrations, concept art, and animation drawings. (Rev: BL 12/1/95) [741.5]

3636 Staskowski, Andrea. *Science Fiction Movies* (5–7). 1992, Lerner LB $13.95 (0-8225-1638-1). Production notes and plot rundowns of science fiction films, arranged chronologically from 1951 to 1982. (Rev: BL 10/15/92; SLJ 10/92) [791.43]

3637 Thomas, Bob. *Disney's Art of Animation: From Mickey Mouse to Beauty and the Beast* (9–adult). 1991, Hyperion $39.95 (1-56282-997-1). An update of the 1958 book, written with the cooperation of the Disney studio, which chronicles the history of Disney animation using art from studio archives. (Rev: BL 11/1/91; SHS; SLJ 3/92) [741.5]

3638 Thompson, Frank. *Tim Burton's Nightmare Before Christmas: The Film, the Art, the Vision* (9–adult). 1993, Hyperion $24.95 (1-56282-774-X). This companion to the Walt Disney stop-action movie uses artwork from the film to illustrate its path from idea to finished product. (Rev: BL 10/1/93) [791.43]

3639 Wright, Bruce Lanier. *Yesterday's Tomorrows: The Golden Age of Science Fiction Movie Posters, 1950 1964* (9–adult). 1993, Taylor $26.95 (0-87833-818-7); paper $19.95 (0-87833-824-1). Nearly 100 color posters for vintage sci-fi movies, including accompanying mini-essays on each film and a guide for collectors. (Rev: BL 5/1/93) [791.43]

Radio and Television

3640 Cader, Michael, ed. *Saturday Night Live: The First Twenty Years* (9–adult). 1994, Houghton $25 (0-395-70895-8). Celebrates the twentieth anniversary of the TV show *Saturday Night Live*. Includes photos and descriptions of many sketches. (Rev: BL 9/1/94; SLJ 3/95) [791.4572]

3641 Cox, Stephen. *The Addams Chronicles: Everything You Ever Wanted to Know about the Addams Family* (9–adult). 1991, HarperPerennial paper $10 (0-06-096897-4). A celebration of the 1960s television series based on the cartoon characters of Charles Addams, with profiles of the actors and synopses of each episode. (Rev: BL 12/1/91) [791.45]

3642 Day, James. *The Vanishing Vision: The Inside Story of Public Television* (9–adult). 1995, Univ. of California $29.95 (0-520-08980-4). The former head of public television takes a critical look at the restrictions and problems that riddle public television's production. (Rev: BL 10/1/95) [384.55]

3643 Finkelstein, Norman H. *Sounds in the Air: The Golden Age of Radio* (5–7). 1993, Scribner $14.95 (0-684-19271-3). A history of radio, focusing on the programs and personalities of the "golden age" of the 1930s and 1940s. (Rev: BL 6/1–15/93*; MJHS; SLJ 7/93) [384.54]

3644 Keats, Robin. *TV Land: A Guide to America's Television Shrines, Sets, and Sites* (9–adult). 1995, St. Martin's paper $12.95 (0-312-13194-1). Describes and displays a variety of settings, arranged geographically, from American TV shows, including *The Fugitive; Murder, She Wrote; The Andy Griffith Show;* and more. (Rev: BL 6/1–15/95) [791.45]

3645 Okuda, Michael, and Denise Okuda. *The Star Trek Chronology: The History of the Future* (9–adult). 1993, Pocket paper $14 (0-671-79611-9). A timeline of all the characters and events in *Star Trek* TV shows and movies. (Rev: BL 3/1/93; BTA; SLJ 11/93) [791.45]

3646 Paisner, Daniel. *Horizontal Hold: The Making and Breaking of a Network Television Pilot* (9–adult). 1992, Birch Lane $18.95 (1-55972-148-0). A behind-the-scenes look at the inception, production, and demise of a network program. (Rev: BL 9/15/92) [791.45]

3647 Ritchie, Michael. *Please Stand By: A Prehistory of Television* (9–adult). 1994, Overlook $23.95 (0-87951-546-5). The story of television before 1948, chronicling the technological struggles and advances during the medium's infancy. (Rev: BL 9/15/94; SLJ 5/95) [791.45]

3648 Shatner, William, and Chris Kreski. *Star Trek Memories* (9–adult). 1993, HarperCollins $20 (0-06-017734-9). A collection of Shatner's memories from the original TV series, including anecdotes from other stars and crew members, as well as production stills, photos, and designers' drawings. (Rev: BL 9/15/93) [791.45]

3649 Stone, Joseph, and Tim Yohn. *Prime Time and Misdemeanors: The 1950s T.V. Quiz Scandal and Investigation* (9–adult). 1992, Rutgers Univ. $22.95 (0-8135-1753-2). Firsthand report of the circumstances surrounding the television quiz show scandals of the 1950s. (Rev: BL 4/1/92) [791.45]

3650 Wang, Harvey, and David Isay. *Holding On* (9–adult). 1995, Norton $29.95 (0-393-03754-1). A celebration of a fascinating collection of ordinary but quirky Americans by Isay, producer of National Public Radio's Folklife Radio Project, and Wang, creator of *Harvey Wang's New York*. (Rev: BL 12/1/95) [973.92]

3651 West, Adam, and Jeff Rovin. *Back to the Batcave* (9–adult). 1994, Berkley paper $10 (0-425-14370-8). The actor who played the superhero Batman in the campy mid-60s television series chronicles his exploits behind the scenes. (Rev: BL 8/94) [791.45]

Recordings

3652 Early, Gerald. *One Nation under a Groove: Motown and American Culture* (9–adult). 1995, Ecco $25 (0-88001-379-6). The history of the African American record company Motown and how it brought rhythm and blues into the mainstream. (Rev: BL 6/1–15/95) [306.4]

3653 Eddy, Chuck. *Stairway to Hell: The 500 Best Heavy Metal Albums in the Universe* (9–adult). 1991, Crown/Harmony paper $14 (0-517-57541-8). In this rock-and-roll discography, heavy metal is broadly defined to include Miles Davis and the Sex Pistols, as well as Led Zeppelin and Guns N' Roses. (Rev: BL 11/1/91; SLJ 12/91) [781.66]

3654 Fong-Torres, Ben. *The Motown Album: The Sound of Young America* (9–adult). 1990, St. Martin's $50 (0-312-04517-4). Photo-essay showcasing singing stars who have recorded on Motown Records. (Rev: BL 1/15/91) [781.66]

3655 Frantz, John Parris. *Video Cinema: Techniques and Projects for Beginning Filmmakers* (9–adult). 1994, Chicago Review paper $14.95 (1-55652-228-2). (Rev: BL 11/15/94; SLJ 1/95) [791.43]

3656 Guterman, Jimmy. *The Best Rock 'n' Roll Records of All Time: A Fan's Guide to the Really Great Stuff* (9–adult). 1992, Citadel paper $12.95 (0-8065-1325-X). An interesting perspective on the "best" records of all time that will not necessarily be accepted by all readers. (Rev: BL 4/1/92) [781.66]

3657 Heylin, Clinton. *Bootleg: The Secret History of the Other Recording Industry* (9–adult). 1995, St. Martin's $29.95 (0-312-13031-7). The history of bootleg recordings, with discography. (Rev: BL 4/15/95) [364.133]

3658 O'Neil, Thomas. *The Grammys: For the Record* (9–adult). 1993, Penguin paper $14 (0-14-016657-2). Yearly listings of all Grammy nominees and winners, with essays supplying the backstage story. (Rev: BL 2/1/93; SHS) [780.26]

3659 Scott, Frank. *The Down Home Guide to the Blues* (9–adult). 1991, Chicago Review/A Cappella paper $14.95 (1-55652-130-8). A comprehensive listing of currently available blues CDs and audiotapes, alphabetized by artist. (Rev: BL 11/1/91) [016.78]

3660 Weisbard, Eric, and Craig Marks, eds. *Spin Alternative Record Guide* (9–adult). 1995, Random/Vintage $20 (0-679-75574-8). A very current and mostly alternative record guide with 500 artists listed. (Rev: BL 9/1/95; VOYA 4/96) [016.78]

Theater and Other Dramatic Forms

3661 Alberts, David. *Talking about Mim: An Illustrated Guide* (9–adult). 1994, Heinemann paper $14.95 (0-435-08641-3). Instructions on learning mime fundamentals and performance. Includes illustrations, specific exercises, and a short history of the art. (Rev: BL 11/1/94) [792.3]

3662 Baldwin, Stephen C. *Pictures in the Air: The Story of the National Theatre of the Deaf* (9–adult). 1994, Gallaudet Univ. $24.95 (1-56368-025-4). In celebration of its twenty-fifth anniversary, this tells the story of the evolution of the international touring troupe whose theater represents a unique art form. (Rev: BL 1/15/94) [792]

3663 Brown, John Russell, ed. *The Oxford Illustrated History of Theatre* (9–adult). 1995, Oxford Univ. $35 (0-19-212997-X). A well-written general history of the theater, in the form of connected essays, that avoids the usual Eurocentric approach. (Rev: BL 11/1/95; SLJ 3/96) [792]

3664 Cassady, Marsh. *The Theatre and You: A Beginning* (9–12). 1992, Meriwether (P.O. Box 7710, Colorado Springs, CO 80933) paper $14.95 (0-916260-83-6). A comprehensive introduction to theater as a performing art and craft, outlining 5 broad areas of study: theaters and stages, directing, design, acting, and theater history. (Rev: BL 11/1/92) [792]

3665 Friedman, Ginger Howard. *Callback* (9–adult). 1993, Bantam paper $4.99 (0-553-28956-X). In a companion to *The Perfect Monologue*, this experienced actor/director gives practical tips to aspiring or seasoned actors auditioning for agents, producers, or directors. (Rev: BL 9/15/93) [792]

3666 Gielgud, John, and John Miller. *Acting Shakespeare* (9–adult). 1992, Scribner $20 (0-684-19511-9). Includes fascinating personal commentary by Gielgud on roles he has played. (Rev: BL 9/15/92) [792.9]

3667 Halpern, Charna, and others. *Truth in Comedy: The Manual for Improvisation* (9–adult). 1994, Meriwether (P.O. Box 7710, Colorado Springs, CO 80933) paper $12.95 (1-56608-003-7). A thorough manual of comedic improvisation by 3 improv gurus. (Rev: BL 4/15/94) [792]

3668 Latrobe, Kathy Howard, and others. *Social Studies Readers Theatre for Young Adults: Scripts and Script Development* (7–12). (Readers Theatre) 1991, Libraries Unlimited/Teacher Ideas paper $19.50 (0-87287-864-3). (Rev: BL 9/1/91) [373.1]

3669 Sitarz, Paula Gaj. *The Curtain Rises: A History of Theater from Its Origins in Greece and Rome Through the English Restoration* (5–8). 1991, Betterway/Shoe Tree $14.95 (1-55870-198-2). Western drama from the time of Aeschylus's tragedies to the comedy of Restoration England, from the perspective of what theatergoers actually experienced in each period. (Rev: BL 9/1/91; SLJ 11/91) [792]

3670 Trussler, Simon. *The Cambridge Illustrated History of British Theatre* (9–adult). 1994, Cambridge Univ. $39.95 (0-521-41913-1). A historical overview of British theater. (Rev: BL 3/1/95) [792]

Biography, Memoirs, etc.

General and Miscellaneous

3671 Fannon, Cecilia. *Leaders* (5–8). (Women Today) 1991, Rourke LB $11.95 (0-86593-118-6). Integrates thumbnail biographics with general chapters on women achievers in politics, business, medicine, sports, and the arts. (Rev: BL 11/1/91; SLJ 2/92) [305.4]

3672 Felder, Deborah G. *The 100 Most Influential Women of All Time: A Ranking Past and Present* (9–adult). 1995, Citadel $24.95 (0-8065-1726-3). The latest in the series that includes *The Black 100* and *The Jewish 100*. (Rev: BL 12/1/95) [920.72]

3673 Foss, Joe, and Matthew Brennan. *Top Guns: America's Fighter Aces Tell Their Stories* (9–adult). 1992, Pocket paper $5.99 (0-671-68318-7). Twenty-seven aviators who served in various conflicts from World War II to Vietnam give stirring accounts of combat. (Rev: BL 5/15/91; SHS) [358.4]

3674 Handler, Andrew, and Susan V. Meschel, eds. *Young People Speak: Surviving the Holocaust in Hungary* (7–12). 1993, Watts $13.40 (0-531-11044-3). Memoirs of 11 Holocaust survivors who were children in Hungary during the Nazi occupation at the end of World War II. (Rev: BL 6/1–15/93; SLJ 7/93; VOYA 10/93) [940.53]

3675 Kessler, Lauren. *Stubborn Twig: Three Generations in the Life of a Japanese American Family* (9–adult). 1993, Random $25 (0-679-41426-6). Kessler charts the history of one Japanese American family from 1908, when Masuo Yasui and his brothers settled in the Hood River Valley, through the war and evacuation, to the present day. (Rev: BL 11/15/93; SLJ 5/94) [929]

3676 Landau, Elaine. *We Survived the Holocaust* (7–10). 1991, Watts LB $13.90 (0-531-11115-6). This series of personal accounts of survivors who were children during World War II presents a picture of ethnic and religious persecution and courageous endurance. (Rev: BL 9/15/91; MJHS; SHS; SLJ 10/91) [940.53]

3677 McCullough, David. *Brave Companions: Portraits in History* (9–adult). 1991, Prentice-Hall $20 (0-13-140104-1). Biographical essays by a popular historian, published in periodicals over 2 decades, that render portraits of persons who led lives of "active discovery." (Rev: BL 10/15/91) [973]

3678 Marvis, Barbara J. *Contemporary American Success Stories: Famous People of Asian Ancestry, Vol. 4* (5–7). 1994, Mitchell Lane $15.95 (1-883845-03-3); paper $8.95 (1-883845-09-2). Describes the lives and struggles of successful Asian Americans, including actor Dustin Nguyen and Amy Tan, author of *The Joy Luck Club*. (Rev: BL 10/1/94; SLJ 11/94) [920]

3679 Marvis, Barbara J. *Famous People of Hispanic Heritage, Vol. 1* (5–7). (Multicultural Biography) 1995, Mitchell Lane $17.95 (1-883845-21-1); paper $9.95 (1-883845-20-3). Contains sketches of 2 men and 2 women, including highlights of their lives; accounts of their struggles, triumphs, and dreams; quotes affirming the American dream; and black-and-white photos. (Rev: BL 11/15/95) [305.8]

3680 Marvis, Barbara J. *Famous People of Hispanic Heritage, Vol. 3* (5–7). (Multicultural Biography) 1995, Mitchell Lane $17.95 (1-883845-25-4); paper $9.95 (1-883845-24-6). Contains sketches of 2 men and 2 women, including highlights of their lives; accounts of their struggles, triumphs, and dreams; quotes affirming the

American dream; and black-and-white photos. (Rev: BL 11/15/95) [305.8]

3681 Marvis, Barbara J. *Famous People of Hispanic Heritage, Vol. 2* (5–7). (Multicultural Biography) 1995, Mitchell Lane $17.95 (1-883845-23-8); paper $9.95 (1-883845-22-X). Contains sketches of 2 men and 2 women, including highlights of their lives; accounts of their struggles, triumphs, and dreams; quotes affirming the American dream; and black-and-white photos. (Rev: BL 11/15/95) [305.8]

3682 Masters, Anthony. *Heroic Stories* (5–8). 1994, Kingfisher Books (95 Madison Ave., New York, NY 10016) paper $6.95 (1-85697-983-0). Attempts to isolate the qualities that prepared the 23 individuals sketched in these biographies. (Rev: BL 3/1/95) [904]

3683 Morey, Janet Nomura, and Wendy Dunn. *Famous Asian Americans* (6–10). 1992, Dutton/Cobblehill $15 (0-525-65080-6). Profiles of 14 prominent Asian Americans, including Michael Chang and Connie Chung. (Rev: BL 1/15/92; MJHS; SLJ 2/92; YR) [920]

3684 Posey, Carl, and others. *The Big Book of Weirdos* (9–adult). 1995, DC Comics/Paradox paper $12.95 (1-56389-180-8). A collection of comic strips details the lives of various renowned individuals who are considered to be weirdos. (Rev: BL 5/15/95) [741.5]

3685 Rodriguez, Luis J. *Always Running: A Memoir of La Vida Loca Gang Days in L.A.* (9–adult). 1993, Curbstone $19.95 (1-880684-06-3). Frank recollections about the author's time with a barrio gang in the 1960s and 1970s personalize crime statistics. (Rev: BL 12/15/92*; SLJ 7/93) [364.1]

3686 Salisbury, Harrison E. *Heroes of My Time* (9–adult). 1993, Walker $19.95 (0-8027-1217-7). The *New York Times* journalist emeritus profiles both famous and unknown people who strove to reform the world through deeds, not words. (Rev: BL 4/15/93; BTA; VOYA 12/93) [920.009]

3687 Scott, Kesho Yvonne. *The Habit of Surviving: Black Women's Strategies for Life* (9–adult). 1991, Rutgers Univ. $19.95 (0-8135-1646-3). Four oral histories explore ways in which African American women survive and succeed, and how these stratagies may ultimately limit them. (Rev: BL 6/15/91) [305.48]

3688 Sinnott, Susan. *Extraordinary Hispanic Americans* (5–10). (Extraordinary People) 1991, Children's Press $30.60 (0-516-00582-0). Biographies of Spanish-speaking people who made a significant impact on U.S. history from 1400 to the present. (Rev: BL 2/1/92; MJHS) [973]

3689 Wormser, Richard. *Lifers: Learn the Truth at the Expense of Our Sorrow* (9–12). 1991, Messner LB $14.98 (0-671-72548-3); paper $8.95 (0-671-72549-1). Stories of the counseling of teenage criminals on the grim realities of prison life by men sentenced to life terms. (Rev: BL 9/15/91; BY; SLJ 12/91) [365]

3690 Yount, Lisa. *Women Aviators* (6–9). 1995, Facts on File $17.95 (0-8160-3062-6). Profiles of 11 prominent female aviators. (Rev: BL 4/1/95) [629.13]

Adventure and Exploration

Collective

3691 Bernhard, Brendan. *Pizarro, Orellana, and the Exploration of the Amazon* (6–9). (World Explorers) 1991, Chelsea House $18.95 (0-7910-1305-7). (Rev: BL 9/15/91; MJHS) [981]

3692 Bonington, Chris. *Quest for Adventure* (9–adult). 1992, Hodder & Stoughton paper $24.95 (0-340-56049-5). A master risk-taker examines some of the most dangerous feats undertaken during the twentieth century. (Rev: BL 3/1/92) [907]

3693 Bruder, Gerry. *Heroes of the Horizon: Flying Adventures of Alaska's Legendary Bush Pilots* (9–adult). 1991, Alaska Northwest paper $12.95 (0-88240-363-X). The escapades of the last generation of frontier pilots who flew open planes to uncharted Alaskan settlements are told through interviews. (Rev: BL 10/1/91) [629.13]

3694 Haney, David. *Captain James Cook and the Explorers of the Pacific* (6–9). (World Explorers) 1991, Chelsea House LB $18.95 (0-7910-1310-3). (Rev: BL 4/1/92) [910]

3695 Haskins, Jim. *Against All Opposition: Black Explorers in America* (5–9). 1992, Walker LB $14.85 (0-8027-8138-1). A collective biography of African and African American explorers. (Rev: BL 2/15/92; MJHS; SLJ 6/92; YR) [910]

3696 Matthews, Rupert. *Exploradores* (5–10). (Biblioteca visual Altea) 1992, Santillana (Madrid, Spain) $18.95 (84-372-3764-5). Contains a clear, concise text on explorers, with close-up color photos, charts, and drawings. English title: *Explorers*. (Rev: BL 2/1/94)

3697 Rappaport, Doreen. *Living Dangerously: American Women Who Risked Their Lives for Adventure* (5–8). 1991, HarperCollins LB $13.89 (0-06-025109-3). Reconstructed from firsthand accounts and news articles, these biographical sketches of 6 trailblazing women emphasize their determination in the face of obstacles. (Rev: BL 10/1/91; MJHS; SLJ 12/91) [973]

3698 Stallones, Jared. *Zebulon Pike and the Explorers of the American Southwest* (6–9). (World Explorers) 1991, Chelsea House $18.95 (0-7910-1317-0). (Rev: BL 9/15/91) [978]

3699 Stefoff, Rebecca. *Accidental Explorers: Surprises and Side Trips in the History of Discovery* (6–9). (Extraordinary Explorers) 1993, Oxford Univ. LB $20 (0-19-507685-0). Focuses on swashbuckling adventurers and explorers who looked for things that weren't there or found things they weren't looking for. (Rev: BL 6/1–15/93; BTA) [910]

3700 Stefoff, Rebecca. *Scientific Explorers: Travels in Search of Knowledge* (6–9). (Extraordinary Explorers) 1993, Oxford Univ. LB $20 (0-19-507689-3). (Rev: BL 6/1–15/93; MJHS) [509]

3701 Stefoff, Rebecca. *Vasco da Gama and the Portuguese Explorers* (6–9). (World Explorers) 1993, Chelsea House LB $18.95 (0-7910-1303-0). (Rev: BL 3/15/93; MJHS) [910]

3702 Stefoff, Rebecca. *Women of the World: Women Travelers and Explorers* (6–9). (Extraordinary Explorers) 1993, Oxford Univ. LB $20 (0-19-507687-7). Focuses on little-known, nineteenth- and twentieth-century women whose explorations challenged notions of propriety and possibility. (Rev: BL 6/1–15/93; BTA) [910]

3703 Stefoff, Rebecca. *Women Pioneers* (6–12). (American Profiles) 1995, Facts on File LB $17.95 (0-8160-3134-7). Nine stories of pioneer women and their courage, ingenuity, and ultimate success. (Rev: BL 1/1/96; SLJ 2/96; VOYA 4/96)

3704 Walker, Paul Robert. *Great Figures of the Wild West* (7–10). (American Profiles) 1992, Facts on File LB $16.95 (0-8160-2576-2). (Rev: BL 9/1/92; SHS) [978]

Individual

AMUNDSEN, ROALD

3705 Flaherty, Leo. *Roald Amundsen and the Quest for the South Pole* (6–9). (World Explorers) 1992, Chelsea House LB $18.95 (0-7910-1308-1). (Rev: BL 10/1/92) [919.8]

BALLARD, ROBERT

3706 Archbold, Rick. *Deep-Sea Explorer: The Story of Robert Ballard, Discoverer of the Titanic* (7–10). 1994, Scholastic $13.95 (0-590-47232-1). A portrait of the scientist-explorer who discovered the *Titanic*, the *Bismarck*, and shipwrecks from the Battle of Guadalcanal. (Rev: BL 3/1/94; MJHS; SLJ 4/94) [551.46]

BILLBERG, RUDY

3707 Billberg, Rudy, and Jim Rearden. *In the Shadow of Eagles: From Barnstormer to Alaska Bush Pilot, a Flyer's Story* (9–adult). 1992, Alaska Northwest $12.95 (0-88240-413-X). An aviation pioneer describes his colorful career in the early days of flight. (Rev: BL 3/1/92) [628.13]

CID, EL

3708 Kislow, Philip. *El Cid* (5–9). (Hispanics of Achievement) 1993, Chelsea House LB $18.95 (0-7910-1239-5). (Rev: BL 9/15/93) [946]

CLEMENS, ARABELLA

3709 Greenberg, Judith E., and Helen Carey McKeever, eds. *A Pioneer Woman's Memoir* (6–9). (In Their Own Words) 1995, Watts LB $13.93 (0-531-11211-X). From a memoir written by the author in her eighties, this book chronicles a trek by covered wagon to Oregon. Black-and-white illustrations. (Rev: BL 9/1/95; SLJ 10/95; VOYA 2/96) [978]

COLUMBUS, CHRISTOPHER

3710 Dor-Ner, Zvi. *Columbus and the Age of Discovery* (9–adult). 1991, Morrow $40 (0-688-08545-8). This comprehensive survey of the explorer's deeds and their aftereffects is the companion volume to a PBS television documentary series. (Rev: BL 10/15/91) [970.01]

3711 Dyson, John. *Columbus: For Gold, God and Glory* (9–adult). 1991, Simon & Schuster $35 (0-671-68791-3). This narrative follows the 1990 re-creation of Columbus's first voyage in a replica of the *Niña* crewed by Spanish nautical students. It asserts that Columbus faked the route set down in his logbook. (Rev: BL 10/15/91) [970.01]

3712 Fernández-Armesto, Felipe. *Columbus* (9–adult). 1991, Oxford Univ. $21.95 (0-19-215898-8). A revisionist assessment of Columbus by an Oxford scholar, in which the popular theory that the explorer was a mystic visionary is rejected. (Rev: BL 10/15/91; SLJ 5/92) [970.01]

3713 Pelta, Kathy. *Discovering Christopher Columbus: How History Is Invented* (5–7). 1991, Lerner LB $14.95 (0-8225-4899-2). An examination of the history and legends surrounding the Columbus story, revealing the hoaxes and forgeries that have been perpetrated over the centuries and the potent myths that have remained. Awards: ALSC Notable Children's Book; SLJ Best Book. (Rev: BL 10/1/91; SLJ 11/91*) [970.01]

3714 Roop, Peter, and Connie Roop, eds. *I, Columbus: My Journal—1492–3* (5–7). Illus. 1990, Walker LB $14.85 (0-8027-6978-0). Excerpts and edited portions of the actual journal Columbus kept during his 1492 voyage. (Rev: BL 1/15/91; SLJ 5/91) [970.01]

3715 Szumski, Bonnie. *Christopher Columbus* (5–7). (Opposing Viewpoints Juniors) 1992, Greenhaven LB $10.95 (0-89908-069-3). (Rev: BL 1/15/93) [970.01]

3716 Taviani, Paolo Emilio. *Columbus: The Great Adventure: His Life, His Times, His Voyages* (9–adult). 1991, Crown/Orion $20 (0-517-58474-3). This condensation of a 4-volume account of the explorer's life, character, and achievements is written by a world-renowned Columbus scholar. (Rev: BL 9/1/91) [970.01]

3717 West, Delno C., and Jean M. West. *Christopher Columbus: The Great Adventure and How We Know about It* (5–7). 1991, Atheneum $13.95 (0-689-31433-7). A well-documented biography of the explorer that separates fact from legend. Includes reproductions of engravings, maps, and transcriptions of Columbus's log and letters. (Rev: BL 10/1/91; MJHS; SLJ 11/91) [970.01]

3718 Wilford, John Noble. *The Mysterious History of Columbus: An Exploration of the Man, the Myth, the Legacy* (9–adult). 1991, Knopf $24 (0-679-40476-7). This broad, probing investigation into the mysteries and contradictions of the explorer's life points out the subjectivity and unreliability of historical accounts. (Rev: BL 9/1/91*; SLJ 7/92) [970.01]

COOK, FREDERICK

3719 Abramson, Howard S. *Hero in Disgrace: The Life of Arctic Explorer Frederick A. Cook* (9–adult). 1991, Paragon House $21.95 (1-55778-322-5). (Rev: BL 5/15/91; SHS) [919.804]

COOK, JAMES

3720 Blumberg, Rhoda. *The Remarkable Voyages of Captain Cook* (6–12). 1991, Bradbury $18.95 (0-02-711682-4). Uses material directly from the explorer's notebooks and challenges ethnocentrism, pointing out that "New Zealanders discovered Europeans" as well. Awards: ALSC Notable Children's Book; BL Editors' Choice; SLJ Best Book. (Rev: BL 10/15/91*; SLJ 12/91*) [910]

D'ABOVILLE, GERARD

3721 D'Aboville, Gerard. *Alone: The Man Who Braved the Vast Pacific—and Won* (9–adult). 1993, Arcade $19.95 (1-55970-218-4). Journal entries describe d'Aboville's solo crossing of the Pacific in a 26-foot rowboat. (Rev: BL 7/93) [910]

DE SOTO, HERNANDO

3722 Duncan, David Ewing. *Hernando de Soto: A Savage Quest in the Americas* (9–adult). 1996, Crown $35 (0-517-58222-8). A carefully researched and documented text on a controversial conquistador. (Rev: BL 12/15/95) [970.01]

DRAKE, FRANCIS

3723 Duncan, Alice Smith. *Sir Francis Drake and the Struggle for an Ocean Empire* (6–9). (World Explorers) 1993, Chelsea House LB $18.95 (0-7910-1302-2). (Rev: BL 3/15/93) [942.05]

3724 Marrin, Albert. *The Sea King: Sir Francis Drake and His Times* (6–10). 1995, Atheneum $18 (0-689-31887-1). This biography includes Drake's trip around the world, his life as a privateer, and his role in defeating the Spanish Armada. Awards: SLJ Best Book. (Rev: BL 7/95; SLJ 9/95) [942.05]

3725 Sugden, John. *Sir Francis Drake* (9–adult). 1991, Holt $29.95 (0-8050-1489-6). (Rev: BL 4/1/91; SHS) [942.05]

HAYS, DAVID

3726 Hays, David, and Daniel Hays. *My Old Man and the Sea* (9–12). 1995, Algonquin Books $19.95 (1-56512-102-3). The adventures of a father and son who set sail in their 25-foot boat for a voyage around Cape Horn. (Rev: BL 6/1/95; SLJ 2/96)

KILEY, DEBORAH SCALING

3727 Kiley, Deborah Scaling, and Meg Noonan. *Albatross: The True Story of a Woman's Survival at Sea* (9–adult). 1994, Houghton $19.95 (0-395-65573-0). What happened when the author and 4 fellow sailors on a routine yacht delivery shipwrecked off the coast of North Carolina. (Rev: BL 4/1/94) [910.4]

MAGELLAN, FERDINAND

3728 Joyner, Tim. *Magellan* (9–adult). 1992, International Marine $24.95 (0-87742-263-X). Details the ventures of a sixteenth-century explorer best known for being the first to sail around the world. (Rev: BL 3/1/92) [910]

MCCANDLESS, CHRIS

3729 Krakauer, Jon. *Into the Wild* (9–adult). 1996, Villard $23 (0-679-42850-X). A true story expanded from Krakauer's article about a young man who starved to death one summer in Denali National Park in Alaska. (Rev: BL 12/1/95*) [917.9804]

PEARY, ROBERT

3730 Anderson, Madelyn Klein. *Robert E. Peary and the Fight for the North Pole* (8–12). 1992, Watts LB $13.90 (0-531-15246-4). Detailed account of Peary's life and accomplishments. (Rev: BL 4/1/92; SLJ 3/92) [910]

3731 Dwyer, Christopher. *Robert Peary and the Quest for the North Pole* (6–9). (World Explorers) 1992, Chelsea House LB $18.95 (0-7910-1316-2). (Rev: BL 2/1/93; MJHS) [919.804]

PONCE DE LEÓN, JUAN

3732 Dolan, Sean. *Juan Ponce de León* (5–9). (Hispanics of Achievement) 1995, Chelsea House $18.95 (0-7910-2023-1). (Rev: BL 10/15/95) [972.9]

RODGERS, CALBRAITH PERRY

3733 Taylor, Richard L. *The First Flight Across the United States: The Story of Calbraith Perry Rodgers and His Airplane, the Vin Fiz* (5–7). 1993, Watts LB $12.90 (0-531-20159-7). This biography of Rodgers captures the excitement of the early days of aviation. (Rev: BL 4/15/94; MJHS; SLJ 2/94) [629.13]

SERRA, JUNÍPERO

3734 Dolan, Sean. *Junípero Serra* (5–9). (Hispanics of Achievement) 1991, Chelsea House $17.95 (0-7910-1255-7). (Rev: BL 11/1/91; MJHS) [979.4]

VESPUCCI, AMERIGO

3735 Alper, Ann Fitzpatrick. *Forgotten Voyager: The Story of Amerigo Vespucci* (5–7). 1991, Carolrhoda LB $11.95 (0-87614-442-3). Relates the life, adventures, and influence of the explorer who mapped the coasts of the continents that bear his name. (Rev: BL 9/1/91; SLJ 9/91) [970.01]

YEADON, DAVID

3736 Yeadon, David. *Lost Worlds: Exploring the Earth's Remote Places* (9–adult). 1993, HarperCollins $27.50 (0-06-016656-8). An exploration of 9 "undiscovered" areas of the Caribbean, Venezuela, Fiji, and Australia. (Rev: BL 7/93) [910.4]

The Arts and Entertainment

Collective

3737 Bearden, Romare, and Harry Henderson. *A History of African-American Artists: From 1792 to the Present* (9–adult). 1993, Pantheon $65 (0-394-57016-2). The lives and careers of 36 African American artists born before 1925 are part of this comprehensive history of African American art. Includes more than 300 black-and-white and color prints. (Rev: BL 10/15/93*) [704]

3738 Bego, Mark. *Country Hunks* (9–adult). 1994, Contemporary paper $7.95 (0-8092-3641-9). A light read about 16 younger male country music stars who could be considered "hunks"—male pinups. (Rev: BL 5/15/94) [781.642]

3739 Benton, Mike. *Masters of Imagination: The Comic Book Artists Hall of Fame* (9–adult). 1994, Taylor $29.95 (0-87833-859-4). Profiles 13 influential comic book artists who emphasize storytelling over flashy graphics, including illustrator Jack "King" Kirby and the cocreator of Superman, Joe Shuster. (Rev: BL 10/1/94; SHS) [741.5]

3740 Cahill, Susan, ed. *Writing Women's Lives: An Anthology of Autobiographical Narratives by Twentieth-Century American Women Writers* (9–adult). 1994, HarperPerennial paper $15 (0-06-096998-9). A collection of autobiographical narratives by twentieth-century women writers, including Jane Addams and Edith Wharton. (Rev: BL 4/15/94) [810.9]

3741 Faber, Doris, and Harold Faber. *Great Lives: American Literature* (5–9). 1995, Simon & Schuster $23 (0-684-19448-1). Ten-page biographies of 30 significant American writers from Poe and Twain to Hemingway. (Rev: BL 9/1/95; SLJ 6/95; VOYA 12/95) [810.9]

3742 Gallo, Donald R., ed. *Speaking for Ourselves, Too: More Autobiographical Sketches by Notable Authors of Books for Young Adults* (6–12). 1993, National Council of Teachers of English paper $14.50 (0-8141-4623-6). Collects 89 brief pieces from popular writers and literary figures, teaching the value of reading, persistence, discipline, and journal-keeping. (Rev: BL 6/1–15/93; MJHS; SHS; VOYA 10/93) [813]

3743 Gallo, Hank. *Comedy Explosion: A New Generation* (9–adult). 1991, Thunder's Mouth paper $14.95 (1-56025-017-8). Forty contemporary comedians are profiled in this volume, each sketch containing examples of the subject's unique brand of humor. (Rev: BL 11/1/91) [792.7]

3744 Glubok, Shirley. *Painting* (5–8). 1993, Scribner $24.95 (0-684-19052-4). Profiles 23 American and European painters, including Michelangelo, Picasso, Rembrandt, and Georgia O'Keeffe. Includes a 16-page full-color insert. (Rev: BL 7/94; BTA; SLJ 7/94) [759]

3745 Gowing, Lawrence. *Biographical Dictionary of Artists* (9–12). 1995, Facts on File $50 (0-8160-3252-1). Biographical sketches summarize the individual styles and important works of 1,340 artists. (Rev: BL 1/1/96; SLJ 1/96)

3746 Greenberg, Jan, and Sandra Jordon. *The American Eye: Eleven Artists of the Twentieth Century* (6–12). 1995, Delacorte $22.50 (0-385-32173-2). The art of these 11 artists is analyzed without jargon or pretension. A list of museums displaying their artwork is included. (Rev: BL 9/1/95*; SLJ 11/95) [709]

3747 Gruen, John. *The Artist Observed: 28 Interviews with Contemporary Artists* (9–adult). 1991, Chicago Review/A Cappella $19.95 (1-55652-103-0). Detailed narrative accounts of the author's encounters with many of today's most important visual artists, with descriptions of their work. (Rev: BL 9/15/91) [709]

3748 Ione, Carole. *Pride of Family: Four Generations of American Women of Color* (9–adult). 1991, Summit $19.95 (0-671-54453-5). A writer/psychotherapist describes what it was like to grow up in a household composed almost entirely of accomplished African American women. (Rev: BL 8/91) [920.72]

3749 Jones, Hettie. *Big Star Fallin' Mama* (7–12). Rev. ed. 1995, Viking $14.99 (0-670-85621-5). A brief history of the blues and biographies of key female blues singers. (Rev: BL 2/15/95; BTA; SLJ 3/95) [782.42]

3750 Jordan, Shirley M., ed. *Broken Silences: Interviews with Black and White Women Writers* (9–adult). 1993, Rutgers Univ. $22.95 (0-8135-1932-2). Focuses on how African American and white women writers depict each other in their stories, with specific inquiries into each author's handling of race in her work. (Rev: BL 5/1/93) [810.9]

3751 Krull, Kathleen. *Lives of the Musicians: Good Times, Bad Times (And What the Neighbors Thought)* (5–8). Illus. 1993, Harcourt LB $18.95 (0-15-248010-2). Biographies of 16 musical giants, from Vivaldi, Mozart, and Beethoven to Gershwin, Joplin, and Woody Guthrie. Awards: ALSC Notable Children's Book; SLJ Best Book. (Rev: BL 4/1/93*; SLJ 5/93*)

3752 Mazer, Anne, ed. *Going Where I'm Coming From: Memoirs of American Youth* (8–12). 1995, Persea $15.95 (0-89255-205-0); paper $8.95 (0-89255-206-9). Writers from different cultures talk about growing up and the incidents in their lives that helped to establish their identities. (Rev: BL 1/15/95; VOYA 5/95) [818.540308]

3753 Nichols, Janet. *Women Music Makers: An Introduction to Women Composers* (6–12). 1992, Walker LB $19.85 (0-8027-8169-1). A glimpse into the personal lives and careers of 10 diverse female composers. (Rev: BL 9/15/92; BTA; SLJ 10/92) [780]

3754 Otfinoski, Steven. *Nineteenth-Century Writers* (7–10). (American Profiles) 1991, Facts on File $16.95 (0-8160-2486-3). A collective biography of such authors as Washington Irving, James Fenimore Cooper, Edgar Allan Poe, Herman Melville, and Henry David Thoreau. (Rev: BL 11/1/91; SHS; SLJ 11/91)

3755 Pearlman, Mickey, ed. *Between Friends: Writing Women Celebrate Friendship* (9–adult). 1994, Houghton $21.95 (0-395-65785-7); paper $12.95 (0-395-65784-9). Essays on various aspects of friendship by successful women authors, such as Joyce Carol Oates, Carolyn See, and Margot Livesey. (Rev: BL 3/15/94) [818]

3756 Reagon, Bernice Johnson. *We'll Understand It Better By and By: Pioneering African American Gospel Composers* (9–adult). 1993, Smithsonian $49.95 (1-56098-166-0); paper $19.95 (1-56098-167-9). The history and development of gospel music and its leading practitioners. (Rev: BL 2/15/93*; SLJ 7/93) [782.85]

3757 Rennert, Richard, ed. *Female Writers* (6–9). (Profiles of Great Black Americans) 1994, Chelsea House $13.95 (0-7910-2063-0); paper $5.95 (0-7910-2064-9). Biographical overviews of such writers as Alice Walker, Maya Angelou, and Toni Morrison. (Rev: BL 2/15/94; MJHS; SLJ 3/94) [810.9]

3758 Rennert, Richard, ed. *Jazz Stars* (6–9). (Profiles of Great Black Americans) 1993, Chelsea House $13.95 (0-7910-2059-2); paper $5.95 (0-7910-2060-6). Profiles of 8 jazz greats: Louis Armstrong, Count Basie, Charlie Parker, Ella Fitzgerald, Billie Holiday, Duke Ellington, Dizzy Gillespie, and John Coltrane. (Rev: BL 1/1/94; SLJ 12/93) [781.65]

3759 Rennert, Richard, ed. *Male Writers* (6–9). (Profiles of Great Black Americans) 1994, Chelsea House $13.95 (0-7910-2063-0); paper $5.95 (0-7910-2064-9). Biographical overviews of such writers as James Baldwin, Alex Haley, and Richard Wright. (Rev: BL 2/15/94; MJHS) [810.9]

3760 Rose, Phyllis, ed. *The Norton Book of Women's Lives* (9–adult). 1993, Norton $30 (0-393-03532-8). This culturally and socially diverse anthology presents biographies of 61 twentieth-century women, among them Virginia Woolf, Anaïs Nin, and Kate Simon. (Rev: BL 9/15/93) [920.72]

3761 See, Lisa. *On Gold Mountain* (9–12). 1995, St. Martin's $24.95 (0-312-11997-6). One family's history is traced from a small Chinese village to Los Angeles's Asian art community. (Rev: BL 8/95; SLJ 1/96)

3762 Smith, Lucinda Irwin. *Women Who Write, Vol. 2* (8–12). 1994, Messner LB $14.95 (0-671-87253-2). Interviews and short biographies of contemporary women writers, including Margaret Atwood and Sue Grafton. Addresses the desire to write and provides tips for aspiring authors. (Rev: BL 10/15/94; SHS; SLJ 11/94; VOYA 12/94) [809.8]

3763 Wiater, Stanley, and Stephen R. Bissette, eds. *Comic Book Rebels: Conversations with the Creators of the New Comics* (9–adult). 1993, Donald I. Fine $25 (1-55611-355-2); paper $12.95 (1-55611-354-4). Interviews with 22 comic book creators actively involved in alternative comics. (Rev: BL 7/93) [741.5]

3764 Wolf, Sylvia. *Focus: Five Women Photographers* (5–8). 1994, Albert Whitman $18.95 (0-8075-2531-6). Examines the different methods, perspectives, and attitudes toward their art of 5 women photographers. Awards: ALSC Notable Children's Book; BL Editors' Choice; SLJ Best Book; YALSA Best Book for Young Adults. (Rev: BL 10/15/94*; BTA; MJHS; SLJ 11/94) [770]

3765 Yunghans, Penelope. *Prize Winners: Ten Writers for Young Readers* (5–9). (World Writers) 1995, Morgan Reynolds $18.95 (1-883846-11-0). How some of our favorite writers of youth fiction came to pen their stories. (Rev: BL 12/15/95; SLJ 12/95; VOYA 2/96) [810.9]

Artists

AUDUBON, JOHN JAMES

3766 Kastner, Joseph. *John James Audubon* (7–12). (First Impressions) 1992, Abrams $19.95 (0-8109-1918-4). Smooth, professional writing and fine art reproduction make for a fine account of Audubon's adventurous life. (Rev: BL 10/15/92) [598]

3767 Roop, Peter, and Connie Roop, eds. *Capturing Nature: The Writings and Art of John James Audubon* (5–7). Illus. 1993, Walker LB $17.85 (0-8027-8205-1). Features excerpts from Audubon's diaries to describe his childhood in France and life in the United States as a businessman, naturalist, and artist. Includes reproductions of his work. (Rev: BL 12/15/93; MJHS; SLJ 1/94) [598]

3768 Streshinsky, Shirley. *Audubon: Life and Art in the American Wilderness* (9–adult). 1993, Villard $25 (0-679-40859-2). Traces the naturalist's life and work in documenting the birds of America. (Rev: BL 9/15/93*) [598]

BEARDEN, ROMARE

3769 Brown, Kevin. *Romare Bearden* (7–10). (Black Americans of Achievement) 1995, Chelsea House $18.95 (0-7910-1119-4); paper $7.95 (0-7910-1145-3). (Rev: BL 3/15/95) [709]

BONHEUR, ROSA

3770 Turner, Robyn Montana. *Rosa Bonheur* (5–7). (Portraits of Women Artists for Children) 1991, Little, Brown $15.95 (0-316-85648-7); 1993, paper $6.95 (0-316-85653-3). This book on Rosa Bonheur's life includes photos and high-quality reproductions of her paintings. Awards: SLJ Best Book. (Rev: BL 9/1/91; SLJ 10/91*) [759.4]

BRAQUE, GEORGES

3771 Wilkin, Karen. *Georges Braque* (9–adult). (Modern Masters) 1992, Abbeville $29.95 (0-89659-944-2); paper $19.95 (0-89659-947-7). Examines the life, works, and style of the cocreator of Cubism. (Rev: BL 3/15/92) [759.4]

CASSATT, MARY

3772 Brooks, Philip. *Mary Cassatt: An American in Paris* (5–7). 1995, Watts $13.51 (0-531-20183-X). Focuses on Cassatt's struggle to study art and be taken seriously. Well-reproduced artwork and a bibliography including sources for videotapes and print sources. (Rev: BL 10/1/95; SLJ 10/95) [759.13]

3773 Mathews, Nancy Mowll. *Mary Cassatt: A Life* (9–adult). (Rizzoli Art) 1994, Villard $26 (0-394-58497-X); 1993, Rizzoli paper $7.95 (0-8478-1611-7). This biography of the renowned American Impressionist painter details her life as a single woman in the Parisian artistic community. (Rev: BL 3/1/94*; SHS) [759.13]

3774 Plain, Nancy. *Mary Cassatt: An Artist's Life* (6–9). 1994, Dillon $13.95 (0-87518-597-5). Includes clear explanations of artistic techniques and discusses Cassatt's relationships with other Impressionists. (Rev: BL 1/15/95; BTA; SLJ 2/95) [759.13]

3775 Turner, Robyn Montana. *Mary Cassatt* (5–7). (Portraits of Women Artists for Children) 1992, Little, Brown LB $15.95 (0-316-85650-9). (Rev: BL 10/15/92; MJHS) [759.13]

CATLIN, GEORGE

3776 Sufrin, Mark. *George Catlin: Painter of the Indian West* (7–12). 1991, Atheneum $14.95 (0-689-31608-9). Catlin painted portraits and scenes in the 1830s that are now among the most significant documents of the vanishing Indian tribes west of the Mississippi. (Rev: BL 10/15/91; MJHS; SLJ 12/91) [759.13]

CURTIS, EDWARD

3777 Lawlor, Laurie. *Shadow Catcher: The Life and Work of Edward S. Curtis* (6–12). 1994, Walker LB $19.85 (0-8027-8289-2). The personal and professional highlights of the life of this little known, largely unappreciated photojournalist who was determined to preserve the lore of the American Indian. Awards: SLJ Best Book; YALSA Best Book for Young Adults. (Rev: BL 12/1/94; MJHS; SLJ 2/95; VOYA 12/94) [770]

DEGAS, EDGAR

3778 Broude, Norma. *Edgar Degas* (7–12). (Rizzoli Art) 1993, Rizzoli paper $7.95 (0-8478-1751-2). An overview of the life and work of the French artist, including large color reproductions of his paintings. (Rev: BL 1/15/94) [759.5]

3779 Meyer, Susan E. *Edgar Degas* (7–12). 1994, Abrams $19.95 (0-8109-3220-2). (Rev: BL 1/1/95; SHS; SLJ 10/94) [709]

DES JARLAIT, PATRICK

3780 Williams, Neva. *Patrick Des Jarlait: Conversations with a Native American Artist* (5–7). 1994, Lerner LB $16.13 (0-8225-3151-8). (Rev: BL 1/1/95; SLJ 1/95) [977.6]

GAUGUIN, PAUL

3781 Greenfeld, Howard. *Paul Gauguin* (7–12). (First Impressions) 1993, Abrams $19.95 (0-8109-3376-4). (Rev: BL 12/1/93; MJHS; SHS) [759.4]

3782 Pierre, Michel. *Gauguin: El descubrimiento de un pintor* (5–8). (El jardín de los pintores/The Painter's Garden) Tr. by María Durante and Jesús Peribáñez García. 1992, Grupo Anaya (Madrid, Spain) $11.95 (84-207-4762-9). Presents enough information and appealing black-and-white photos and color reproductions of Gauguin's paintings to inspire young artists. English title: *Gauguin: The Discovery of a Painter*. (Rev: BL 4/1/94)

HARING, KEITH

3783 Gruen, John. *Keith Haring: The Authorized Biography* (9–adult). 1991, Prentice-Hall $35 (0-13-516113-4). Interviews with friends and family, as well as in-depth conversations with the subject before his death, make up this oral history of the critically acclaimed graffiti artist's life. (Rev: BL 9/15/91*) [709]

KAHLO, FRIDA

3784 Drucker, Malka. *Frida Kahlo: Torment and Triumph in Her Life and Art* (9–12). 1991, Bantam/Starfire $15 (0-553-07165-3); paper $7 (0-553-35408-6). The biography of Mexico's most renowned woman painter, physically challenged from childhood, who was the political activist wife of Diego Rivera, the nation's leading artist. (Rev: BL 10/1/91; SLJ 12/91) [759]

3785 Frazier, Nancy. *Frida Kahlo: Mysterious Painter* (5–7). (Library of Famous Women) 1993, Blackbirch LB $14.95 (1-56711-012-6). (Rev: BL 2/15/93) [759.972]

3786 Garza, Hedda. *Frida Kahlo* (5–9). (Hispanics of Achievement) 1994, Chelsea House $18.95 (0-7910-1698-6); paper $7.95 (0-7910-1699-4). (Rev: BL 3/1/94) [759.972]

3787 Milner, Frank. *Frida Kahlo* (9–adult). 1995, Smithmark $14.98 (0-8317-1755-6). Contains large, full-color plates of Kahlo's paintings and photos and a biography of Kahlo. (Rev: BL 10/1/95) [759.972]

LEONARDO DA VINCI

3788 Bramly, Serge. *Leonardo: Discovering the Life of Leonardo da Vinci* (9–adult). 1991, HarperCollins $35 (0-06-016065-9). Uses Leonardo's notebooks to discover clues to his universal genius and presents previously overlooked aspects of his personal life. (Rev: BL 11/15/91; SHS) [709.2]

3789 McLanathan, Richard. *Leonardo da Vinci* (7–12). 1990, Abrams $17.95 (0-8109-1256-2). A readable, inviting introduction to the master painter, inventor, and scientist. Awards: SLJ Best Book. (Rev: BL 12/15/90; SLJ 2/91*)

3790 Pinguilly, Yves. *Leonardo da Vinci: El pintor que hablaba con los pájaros* (5–8). (El jardín de los pintores/The Painter's Garden) Tr. by María Durante and Jesús Peribáñez García. 1992, Grupo Anaya (Madrid, Spain) $11.95 (84-207-4761-0). This biography presents enough information and appealing black-and-white photos and color reproductions to inspire young artists. English title: *Leonardo da Vinci: The Painter Who Talked with Birds*. (Rev: BL 4/1/94)

3791 Romei, Francesca. *Leonardo da Vinci: Artist, Inventor and Scientist of the Renaissance* (6–12). (Masters of Art) Illus. 1995, Peter Bedrick $19.95 (0-87226-313-4). Historical and artistic overview of Leonardo. (Rev: BL 4/1/95; BTA; SLJ 2/95) [709]

MALEVICH, KAZIMIR

3792 Hilton, Alison. *Kazimir Malevich* (9–adult). (Rizzoli Art) 1993, Rizzoli paper $7.95 (0-8478-1518-8). Handsome, oversize book, mainly of reproductions. (Rev: BL 4/1/93; SLJ 8/92) [759.7]

MICHELANGELO BUONARROTI

3793 McLanathan, Richard. *Michelangelo* (7–12). (First Impressions) 1993, Abrams $19.95 (0-8109-3634-8). (Rev: BL 6/1–15/93) [700]

MIRÓ, JOAN

3794 Higdon, Elizabeth. *Joan Miró* (7–12). (Rizzoli Art) 1993, Rizzoli paper $7.95 (0-8478-1667-2). (Rev: BL 1/15/94) [709]

MODIGLIANI, AMEDEO

3795 Rose, June. *Modigliani: The Pure Bohemian* (9–adult). 1991, St. Martin's $22.95 (0-312-06416-0). Explores the personality and tracks the growth of the Italian painter/sculptor in the bohemian society of Paris. (Rev: BL 11/15/91) [709.2]

MONET, CLAUDE

3796 Waldron, Ann. *Claude Monet* (7–12). (First Impressions) 1991, Abrams $18.95 (0-8109-3620-8). This illustrated biographical study of the pioneering impressionist painter explores his fascination with nature and his experimentation with the effects of light. (Rev: BL 11/15/91; SHS; SLJ 1/92) [759.4]

MORISOT, BERTHE

3797 Higonnet, Anne. *Berthe Morisot* (7–12). (Rizzoli Art) 1993, Rizzoli paper $7.95 (0-8478-1646-X). (Rev: BL 1/15/94) [759.4]

O'KEEFFE, GEORGIA

3798 Brooks, Philip. *Georgia O'Keeffe: An Adventurous Spirit* (5–7). 1995, Watts $13.51 (0-531-20182-1). (Rev: BL 10/1/95; SLJ 10/95) [759.13]

3799 Turner, Robyn Montana. *Georgia O'Keeffe* (5–7). (Portraits of Women Artists for Children) 1991, Little, Brown $15.95 (0-316-85649-5). This biography of O'Keeffe features high-quality reproductions of the artist's work. Awards: SLJ Best Book. (Rev: BL 9/1/91; SLJ 10/91*) [759.13]

PICASSO, PABLO

3800 Antoine, Véronique. *Picasso: Un día en su estudio* (5–8). (El jardín de los pintores/The Painter's Garden) Tr. by María Durante and Jesús Peribáñez García. 1992, Grupo Anaya (Madrid, Spain) $11.95 (84-207-4763-7). Presents enough information and appealing black-and-white photos and color reproductions of Picasso's paintings to inspire young artists-to-be. English title: *Picasso: One Day in His Studio*. (Rev: BL 4/1/94)

3801 Beardsley, John. *Pablo Picasso* (7–12). (First Impressions) 1991, Abrams $18.95 (0-8109-3713-1). Succinctly describes Picasso's bohemian lifestyle and analyzes his ever-changing styles, methods, and subjects. (Rev: BL 11/15/91; MJHS; SHS; SLJ 1/92) [709]

3802 Selfridge, John W. *Pablo Picasso* (5–9). (Hispanics of Achievement) 1993, Chelsea House $18.95 (0-7910-1777-X); paper $7.95 (0-7910-1996-9). (Rev: BL 3/1/94) [759.4]

3803 Withers, Josephine. *Pablo Picasso* (7–12). (Rizzoli Art) 1993, Rizzoli paper $7.95 (0-8478-1750-4). (Rev: BL 1/15/94) [759.4]

PIPPIN, HORACE

3804 Lyons, Mary E. *Starting Home: The Story of Horace Pippin, Painter* (5–7). (African American Artists and Artisans) 1993, Scribner $15.95 (0-684-19534-8). This account of painter Horace Pippin tells how visions of World War I trenches filled his art. Awards: ALSC Notable Children's Book; Woodson Book. (Rev: BL 11/15/93; MJHS; SLJ 2/94) [759.13]

REMBRANDT VAN RIJN

3805 Bonafoux, Pascal. *A Weekend with Rembrandt* (5–9). (A Weekend With) 1992, Rizzoli $16.95 (0-8478-1441-6). (Rev: BL 8/92; MJHS) [759.9492]

3806 Schwartz, Gary. *Rembrandt* (7–12). (First Impressions) 1992, Abrams LB $18.95 (0-8109-3760-3). This jargon-free, accessible biography presents Rembrandt with all his flaws and quirks. (Rev: BL 5/1/92; SHS; SLJ 6/92*) [759.9492]

3807 Silver, Larry. *Rembrandt* (9–adult). (Rizzoli Art) 1993, Rizzoli paper $7.95 (0-8478-1519-6). Handsome, oversize book, mainly of reproductions. (Rev: BL 4/1/93; SLJ 1/93) [160]

RIVERA, DIEGO

3808 Cockcroft, James D. *Diego Rivera* (5–9). (Hispanics of Achievement) 1991, Chelsea

House $17.95 (0-7910-1252-2). (Rev: BL 11/1/91; MJHS) [759.972]

TRAYLOR, BILL

3809 Lyons, Mary E. *Deep Blues: Bill Traylor, Self-Taught Artist* (5–7). 1994, Scribner $15.95 (0-684-19458-9). (Rev: BL 11/15/94; BTA; SLJ 1/95) [759.13]

VAN GOGH, VINCENT

3810 Bonafoux, Pascal. *Van Gogh: The Passionate Eye* (7–12). (Discoveries) 1992, Abrams paper $12.95 (0-8109-2828-0). (Rev: BL 7/92; SHS) [759.9492]

3811 Loumaye, Jacqueline. *Van Gogh: La manchita amarilla* (5–8). (El jardín de los pintores/The Painter's Garden) Tr. by María Durante and Jesús Peribáñez García. Illus. 1992, Grupo Anaya (Madrid, Spain) $11.95 (84-207-4764-5). Presents enough information and appealing black-and-white photos and color reproductions of van Gogh's paintings to inspire young artists. English title: *Van Gogh: The Yellow Spot.* (Rev: BL 4/1/94)

WANG YANI

3812 Zhensun, Zheng, and Alice Low. *A Young Painter: The Life and Paintings of Wang Yani—China's Extraordinary Young Artist* (5–8). 1991, Scholastic $17.95 (0-590-44906-0). The story of a self-taught prodigy whose paintings are highly regarded in China. Includes many examples of her unique work, based on the traditional Chinese style. Awards: ALSC Notable Children's Book; BL Editors' Choice. (Rev: BL 10/1/91*; SLJ 8/91) [759.951]

WARHOL, ANDY

3813 Katz, Jonathan. *Andy Warhol* (7–12). (Rizzoli Art) 1993, Rizzoli paper $7.95 (0-8478-1752-0). Large, full-color reproductions are included in this profile of the pop artist. (Rev: BL 1/15/94) [700]

WHISTLER, JAMES MCNEILL

3814 Berman, Avis. *James McNeill Whistler* (7–12). (First Impressions) 1993, Abrams $19.95 (0-8109-3968-1). (Rev: BL 12/1/93; MJHS; SHS) [760]

WYETH, ANDREW

3815 Meryman, Richard. *Andrew Wyeth* (6–12). (First Impressions) 1991, Abrams $17.95 (0-8109-3956-8). Insights into an artist's childhood show how various events influenced his life. Awards: SLJ Best Book. (Rev: BL 8/91; MJHS; SHS; SLJS 1/92*) [759.13]

3816 Wyeth, Andrew. *Andrew Wyeth: Autobiography* (9–adult). 1995, Little, Brown/Bulfinch $50 (0-8212-2159-0). An exhibition of a lifetime of Wyeth's work, from a painting done when he was 16 to a 1933 watercolor. (Rev: BL 11/15/95; MJHS) [759.13]

ZHANG, SONG NAN

3817 Zhang, Song Nan. *A Little Tiger in the Chinese Night: An Autobiography in Art* (5–8). 1993, Tundra $19.95 (0-88776-320-0). A Canadian immigrant artist tells the story of a life buffeted by changing Chinese policies, regimes, and conditions since World War II. (Rev: BL 1/1/94*; SLJ 5/94) [759.11]

Authors

ABBOTT, SHIRLEY

3818 Abbott, Shirley. *The Bookmaker's Daughter: A Memory Unbound* (9–adult). 1991, Ticknor & Fields $19.95 (0-89919-518-0). (Rev: BL 5/1/91*) [974.7]

ALCOTT, LOUISA MAY

3819 Johnston, Norma. *Louisa May: The World and Works of Louisa May Alcott* (5–7). 1991, Four Winds $15.95 (0-02-747705-3). Based on letters and journals, this biography reveals the physical, emotional, and social stresses on the celebrated author and her family. (Rev: BL 12/15/91; SLJ 2/92*) [813]

ANGELOU, MAYA

3820 Angelou, Maya. *Wouldn't Take Nothing for My Journey Now* (9–adult). 1993, Random $17 (0-679-42743-0). (Rev: BL 9/1/93; SLJ 5/94) [818.5409]

ASIMOV, ISAAC

3821 Asimov, Isaac. *I, Asimov: A Memoir* (9–adult). 1994, Doubleday $25 (0-385-41701-2). A gathering of autobiographical writing in a series of essays. (Rev: BL 4/15/94) [813]

BALDWIN, JAMES

3822 Campbell, James. *Talking at the Gates: A Life of James Baldwin* (9–adult). 1991, Viking $21.95 (0-670-82913-7). (Rev: BL 4/1/91; SHS) [818]

3823 Kenan, Randall. *James Baldwin* (9–12). (Lives of Notable Gay Men and Lesbians) 1994, Chelsea House $19.95 (0-7910-2301-X). Chronicles the pain and poverty of Baldwin's early adult years in Paris and gives a sense of his life as a black homosexual in a white world. (Rev: BL 3/1/94; SLJ 6/94; VOYA 6/94) [818]

3824 Leeming, David. *James Baldwin: A Biography* (9–adult). 1994, Knopf $25 (0-394-57708-6). This biography of the great African American novelist/essayist was written by a personal friend. (Rev: BL 3/1/94; SHS) [818.5409]

BARAKA, IMAMU AMIRI

3825 Reilly, Charlie, ed. *Conversations with Amiri Baraka* (9–adult). (Literary Conversations) 1994, Univ. Press of Mississippi $37.50 (0-87805-686-6); paper $14.95 (0-87805-687-4). Interviews with the influential African American writer. (Rev: BL 2/15/94) [818]

BARRIE, J. M.

3826 Aller, Susan Bivin. *J. M. Barrie: The Magic Behind Peter Pan* (6–8). 1994, Lerner LB $16.13 (0-8225-4918-2). This biography of the author reveals Barrie's similarities to his character Peter Pan and his failed marriages. (Rev: BL 11/1/94; SLJ 12/94) [828]

BAUM, L. FRANK

3827 Carpenter, Angelica Shirley, and Jean Shirley. *L. Frank Baum: Royal Historian of Oz* (5–7). 1992, Lerner LB $15.95 (0-8225-4910-7). A biography of the writer who invented "a new kind of fairy tale, uniquely modern and American." (Rev: BL 7/92; MJHS; YR) [813]

BAWDEN, NINA

3828 Bawden, Nina. *In My Own Time: Almost an Autobiography* (8–12). 1995, Clarion $25.95 (0-395-74429-6). Bawden, author of numerous well-loved children's stories, writes of her own life. (Rev: BL 12/1/95) [823]

BLY, NELLIE

3829 Kroeger, Brooke. *Nellie Bly: Daredevil, Reporter, Feminist* (9–adult). 1994, Times Books $25 (0-8129-1973-4). A comprehensive biography of the pioneering nineteenth-century investigative reporter that highlights her fearlessness and instinct for drama. (Rev: BL 2/1/94*) [070]

BORGES, JORGE LUÍS

3830 Lennon, Adrian. *Jorge Luís Borges* (5–9). (Hispanics of Achievement) 1991, Chelsea House $17.95 (0-7910-1236-0). (Rev: BL 3/15/92; MJHS) [868]

BRONTË FAMILY

3831 Guzzetti, Paula. *A Family Called Brontë* (6–9). 1994, Dillon $13.95 (0-87518-592-4). An account of the Brontë family written specifically for teenagers. (Rev: BL 5/15/94; BTA; MJHS; SLJ 8/94; VOYA 8/94) [823]

3832 Knapp, Bettina L. *The Brontës: Branwell, Anne, Emily, Charlotte* (9–adult). 1991, Continuum $18.95 (0-8264-0514-2). (Rev: BL 4/15/91; SHS) [823]

BROWN, HELEN GURLEY

3833 Falkof, Lucille. *Helen Gurley Brown: The Queen of Cosmopolitan* (5–8). (Wizards of Business) 1992, Garrett Educational LB $12.95 (1-56074-013-2). An interesting, accessible, and inspiring biography of the magazine magnate. B&W photos. (Rev: BL 6/15/92, SLJ 7/92) [070.4]

BROWNING, ROBERT AND ELIZABETH BARRETT

3834 Markus, Julia. *Dared and Done: The Marriage of Elizabeth Barrett and Robert Browning* (9–adult). 1995, Knopf $30 (0-679-41602-1). Examines the social, political, and emotional forces that shaped the lives and art of nineteenth-century poets Elizabeth Barrett and Robert Browning. (Rev: BL 2/1/95*; SLJ 8/95) [821]

BURNETT, FRANCES HODGSON

3835 Carpenter, Angelica Shirley. *Frances Hodgson Burnett: Beyond the Secret Garden* (5–8). 1990, Lerner LB $14.95 (0-8225-4905-0). A glimpse into the private life of the woman who wrote *The Secret Garden*. Awards: SLJ Best Book. (Rev: BL 1/15/91; MJHS; SLJ 3/91*) [813]

BYARS, BETSY

3836 Byars, Betsy. *The Moon and I* (5–7). 1992, Messner LB $14.98 (0-671-74165-9). A memoir by the popular author that speaks of her writing, her love of snakes and other pets, her love of flying, and her love for her husband. Awards: SLJ Best Book. (Rev: BL 5/15/92*; MJHS; SLJ 4/92*) [813]

CANTWELL, MARY

3837 Cantwell, Mary. *Manhattan, When I Was Young* (9–12). 1995, Houghton $21.95 (0-395-74441-5). An autobiographical account of a fashion-magazine writer in the 1950s. (Rev: BL 8/95; SLJ 1/96)

CATHER, WILLA

3838 Keene, Ann T. *Willa Cather* (7–12). 1994, Messner $15 (0-671-86760-1). A biography examining the writer's childhood, college years, jobs as editor and teacher, travels, and friends, as well as her reputed lesbianism. (Rev: BL 10/1/94; SHS; SLJ 11/94; VOYA 4/95) [813]

3839 O'Brien, Sharon. *Willa Cather* (7–12). (Lives of Notable Gay Men and Lesbians) 1994, Chelsea House $19.95 (0-7910-2302-8); paper $9.95 (0-7910-2877-1). This biography of the author focuses on her reputed lesbianism and shows how Cather created a nurturing network of women friends and lovers. (Rev: BL 11/1/94; BTA; SLJ 11/94; VOYA 2/95) [813]

3840 Wagenknecht, Edward. *Willa Cather* (9–adult). 1993, Continuum $19.95 (0-8264-0607-6). This analysis of Cather's fiction also has sections on her life, writers who influenced her, and her personality. (Rev: BL 12/1/93) [813]

CERVANTES, MIGUEL DE

3841 Goldberg, Jake. *Miguel de Cervantes* (5–9). (Hispanics of Achievement) 1993, Chelsea House LB $18.95 (0-7910-1238-7). (Rev: BL 9/15/93; MJHS) [863]

CHESNUTT, CHARLES

3842 Thompson, Cliff. *Charles Chesnutt* (7–10). (Black Americans of Achievement) 1992, Chelsea House $17.95 (1-55546-578-1). (Rev: BL 12/1/92; MJHS) [813]

CLARKE, ARTHUR

3843 McAleer, Neil. *Arthur C. Clarke: The Authorized Biography* (9–adult). 1992, Contemporary $21.95 (0-8092-4324-5). This comprehensive, admiring biography of the science fiction writer assembles a mass of facts about Clarke's adventurous life. (Rev: BL 11/1/92) [823]

CLEARY, BEVERLY

3844 Cleary, Beverly. *My Own Two Feet* (7–adult). 1995, Morrow $15 (0-688-14267-2). In the second part of Cleary's candid autobiography, she departs for college. Although most appreciated by adults who grew up with her books, it also has a place on youth shelves. (Rev: BL 8/95*; SLJ 9/95)

CRANE, STEPHEN

3845 Sufrin, Mark. *Stephen Crane* (9–12). 1992, Atheneum $13.95 (0-689-31669-0). This balanced biography gives Crane his due as a literary artist and a seminal figure in modern American letters. Awards: SLJ Best Book. (Rev: BL 7/92; MJHS; SLJ 8/92*) [813]

DANZIGER, PAULA

3846 Krull, Kathleen. *Presenting Paula Danziger* (6–12). (United States Authors) 1995, Twayne $20.95 (0-8057-4153-4). Examines writer Danziger's personal problems, humorous teaching experiences, and group discussions of her books in 6 thematic chapters. (Rev: BL 9/1/95; VOYA 2/96) [813]

DE BLASIS, CELESTE

3847 De Blasis, Celeste N. *Graveyard Peaches* (9–adult). 1991, St. Martin's $18.95 (0-312-06362-8). A best-selling author of historical novels remembers her uncommon childhood on the family ranch near Los Angeles. (Rev: BL 11/15/91) [813]

DICKENS, CHARLES

3848 Murray, Brian. *Charles Dickens* (9–adult). 1994, Continuum $19.95 (0-8264-0565-7). (Rev: BL 1/15/95; SHS) [823]

DOIG, IVAN

3849 Doig, Ivan. *Heart Earth* (9–adult). 1993, Atheneum $19 (0-689-12137-7). A prequel to *This House of Sky* (1978), this continues the autobiography of an unconventional family in the West, stricken by illness, bad weather, and economic hardship. (Rev: BL 9/15/93*) [813]

DOYLE, ARTHUR CONAN

3850 Costello, Peter. *The Real World of Sherlock Holmes: The True Crime Casebooks of Arthur Conan Doyle* (9–adult). 1991, Carroll & Graf $19.95 (0-88184-738-0). Provides new evidence that Doyle himself participated in investigations of notorious crimes and in the mystery of the disappearance of mystery writer Agatha Christie. (Rev: BL 11/1/91) [823]

DU MAURIER, DAPHNE

3851 Shallcross, Martyn. *The Private World of Daphne du Maurier* (9–adult). 1992, St. Martin's $18.95 (0-312-07072-1). The recollections of an eccentric novelist's personal life and career. (Rev: BL 2/15/92) [823]

EDMONDS, WALTER D.

3852 Edmonds, Walter D. *Tales My Father Never Told* (9–adult). 1995, Syracuse Univ. $24.95 (0-8156-0307-X). An author's memoir of his privileged New York upbringing with a demanding father and loving mother. (Rev: BL 3/15/95) [813]

FONG-TORRES, BEN

3853 Fong-Torres, Ben. *The Rice Room: From Number Two Son to Rock 'n' Roll: Growing Up Chinese-American* (9–adult). 1994, Hyperion $22.95 (0-7868-6002-2). A coming-of-age story of an Asian American who ultimately went to work for *Rolling Stone*, chronicling rock culture. (Rev: BL 4/15/94; BTA) [973]

FROST, ROBERT

3854 Bober, Natalie S. *A Restless Spirit: The Story of Robert Frost* (7–12). Rev. ed. 1991, Holt $19.95 (0-8050-1672-4). An illustrated biography of the Pulitzer Prize–winning poet, including the complete texts of some of his work. (Rev: BL 11/15/91; SHS; SLJ 12/91) [811.52]

GATES, HENRY LOUIS, JR.

3855 Gates, Henry Louis, Jr. *Colored People* (9–adult). 1994, Knopf $22 (0-679-42179-3). A beautifully written memoir about growing up black, strengthened by family and community. (Rev: BL 4/1/94; BTA) [975.4]

HALE, JANET CAMPBELL

3856 Hale, Janet Campbell. *Bloodlines: Odyssey of a Native Daughter* (9–adult). 1993, Random $18 (0-679-41527-0). A Coeur d'Alene woman describes her painful history and that of her Native American people, and the liberating impact of her drive to become a writer. (Rev: BL 5/15/93; BTA; VOYA 12/93) [818]

HALEY, ALEX

3857 Shirley, David. *Alex Haley* (7–10). (Black Americans of Achievement) 1993, Chelsea House $18.95 (0-7910-1979-9); paper $7.95 (0-7910-1980-2). (Rev: BL 2/15/94) [813]

HELLMAN, LILLIAN

3858 Turk, Ruth. *Lillian Hellman: Rebel Playwright* (7–10). 1995, Lerner LB $16.13 (0-8225-4921-2). This biography looks at the playwright's critical work and life during the turmoil of the 1960s and the years of the House Un-American Activities Committee. (Rev: BL 6/1–15/95; SLJ 8/95) [812]

HEMINGWAY, ERNEST

3859 Lyttle, Richard B. *Ernest Hemingway: The Life and the Legend* (8–10). 1992, Atheneum $15.95 (0-689-31670-4). Tracks the events in the famous author's life and identifies the real people and events that became part of his stories. (Rev: BL 2/1/92; MJHS; SHS; SLJ 6/92) [813]

HILLERMAN, TONY

3860 Greenberg, Martin H., ed. *The Tony Hillerman Companion: A Comprehensive Guide to His Life and Work* (9–adult). 1994, HarperCollins $25 (0-06-017034-4). A comprehensive sourcebook on Tony Hillerman's life with a critical essay on his works. (Rev: BL 5/15/94; SHS) [813]

HURSTON, ZORA NEALE

3861 Calvert, Roz. *Zora Neale* (5–8). 1993, Chelsea House $14.95 (0-7910-1766-4). A biography of Hurston, the rediscovered author of the Harlem Renaissance. (Rev: BL 5/1/93; SLJ 6/93) [813]

3862 Lyons, Mary E. *Sorrow's Kitchen: The Life and Folklore of Zora Neale Hurston* (7–12). 1990, Scribner $13.95 (0-684-19198-9). A brief biography of the African American novelist whose use of dialect sometimes brought criticism from other writers and who until recently was largely forgotten. Awards: SLJ Best Book; YALSA Best Book for Young Adults. (Rev: BL 12/15/90; SLJ 1/91*)

3863 Porter, A. P. *Jump at de Sun: The Story of Zora Neale Hurston* (7–12). 1992, Carolrhoda LB $12.95 (0-87614-667-1); paper $6.95 (0-87614-546-2). A brief, easy-to-read biography that places Hurston within the context of the racism of her era. Awards: SLJ Best Book. (Rev: BL 12/15/92; SLJ 1/93*) [813]

3864 Yates, Janelle. *Zora Neale Hurston: A Storyteller's Life* (5–8). (Unsung Americans) Illus. 1991, Ward Hill Press (40 Willis Ave., Staten Island, NY 10301) paper $9.95 (0-9623380-7-9). This introduction to the life of the celebrated African American writer and folklorist features dramatic illustrations and quotations from Hurston's work. (Rev: BL 10/15/91) [813]

JEWETT, SARAH ORNE

3865 Silverthorne, Elizabeth. *Sarah Orne Jewett: A Writer's Life* (9–adult). 1993, Overlook $22.95 (0-87951-484-1). A sympathetic biography of the American realist/regionalist author that draws on unpubliched letters and diaries. (Rev: BL 3/15/93) [813]

KING, STEPHEN

3866 Keyishian, Amy, and Marjorie Keyishian. *Stephen King* (7–12). (Pop Culture Legends) 1995, Chelsea House $18.95 (0-7910-2340-0); paper $7.95 (0-7910-2365-6). Gives insight into the life of one of the world's most successful writers, covering King's childhood poverty and abandonment by his father, support by his mother, and influences on his work of such giants as C. S. Lewis, H. G. Wells, and Bram Stoker. (Rev: BL 12/15/95; SLJ 1/96) [813]

KOONTZ, DEAN

3867 Greenberg, Martin H., ed. *The Dean Koontz Companion* (9–adult). 1994, Berkley paper $13 (0-425-14135-7). An interview with the prolific author of horror fiction, commentary on his works, and short tongue-in-cheek pieces by Koontz himself. (Rev: BL 1/1/94; SHS; SLJ 5/94; VOYA 8/94) [814.54]

LAMAR, JAKE

3868 Lamar, Jake. *Bourgeois Blues: An American Memoir* (9–adult). 1991, Summit $20 (0-671-69191-0). This autobiography of a Harvard-educated middle-class African American who became a staff writer for *Time* magazine reveals the subtle and overt racism he encountered. (Rev: BL 9/1/91) [070]

L'ENGLE, MADELEINE

3869 Gonzales, Doreen. *Madeleine L'Engle: Author of "A Wrinkle in Time"* (5–8). (People in Focus) 1991, Dillon LB $12.95 (0-87518-485-5). (Rev: BL 2/15/92; SLJ 3/92) [813]

LINDBERGH, ANNE MORROW

3870 Hermann, Dorothy. *Anne Morrow Lindbergh: A Gift for Life* (9–adult). 1992, Houghton $24.95 (0-395-56114-0). Analyzes the Lindbergh marriage in contemporary terms, faulting Anne for allowing her husband to dominate her life. (Rev: BL 11/1/92) [818.5209]

LINDBERGH, CHARLES AND ANNE MORROW

3871 Milton, Joyce. *Loss of Eden: A Biography of Charles and Anne Morrow Lindbergh* (9–adult). 1993, HarperCollins $25 (0-06-016503-0). Paints a sympathetic picture of the famous couple, who dominated the news in the 1930s. (Rev: BL 11/1/92) [629.13]

LIPSYTE, ROBERT

3872 Cart, Michael. *Presenting Robert Lipsyte* (7–12). (United States Authors) 1995, Twayne $20.95 (0-8057-4151-8). A biography of Lipsyte based on personal interviews, plus a look at his works. (Rev: BL 6/1–15/95) [070.449]

LITTLE, JEAN

3873 Little, Jean. *Stars Come Out Within* (6–12). 1991, Viking $14.95 (0-670-82965-X). A Canadian children's author talks abour her blindness, work, friends, and beloved Seeing Eye dog. (Rev: BL 12/1/91; SLJ 1/92)

MATHABANE, MARK AND GAIL

3874 Mathabane, Mark, and Gail Mathabane. *Love in Black and White: The Triumph of Love over Prejudice and Taboo* (9–adult). 1992, HarperCollins $20 (0-06-016495-6). A best-selling black South African author and his wife describe their interracial marriage. (Rev: BL 12/15/91; SHS) [306.84]

MCLAURIN, TIM

3875 McLaurin, Tim. *The Keeper of the Moon* (9–adult). 1991, Norton $19.95 (0-393-02996-4). A poetic memoir of growing up and coming of age on a small North Carolina farm. (Rev: BL 11/15/91) [813]

MELVILLE, HERMAN

3876 Stefoff, Rebecca. *Herman Melville* (7–12). 1994, Simon & Schuster $15 (0-671-86771-7). A well-written, carefully researched biography of Melville. Awards: BL Editors' Choice. (Rev: BL

5/1/94*; MJHS; SHS; SLJ 6/94; VOYA 4/95) [813]

MICHENER, JAMES A.

3877 Michener, James A. *The World Is My Home: A Memoir* (9–adult). 1992, Random $25 (0-679-40134-2). An autobiography of the adventurous life of the prolific best-selling novelist, including his World War II experiences and his encounters with renowned people. (Rev: BL 11/1/91) [813]

MITCHELL, MARGARET

3878 Pyron, Darden Asbury. *Southern Daughter: The Life of Margaret Mitchell* (9–adult). 1991, Oxford Univ. $29.95 (0-19-505276-5). A history professor carefully details the personal, cultural, and historical influences on one of the most famous American novels. (Rev: BL 8/91) [813]

MOHR, NICHOLASA

3879 Mohr, Nicholasa. *Nicholasa Mohr: Growing Up Inside the Sanctuary of My Imagination* (6–12). 1994, Messner $14 (0-671-74171-3). An autobiographical account of a poor Puerto Rican girl's struggles in 1940s Manhattan, recounting her experiences with her extended family. (Rev: BL 7/94) [813]

MONTGOMERY, L. M.

3880 Andronik, Catherine M. *Kindred Spirit: A Biography of L. M. Montgomery, Creator of Anne of Green Gables* (6–9). 1993, Atheneum $14.95 (0-689-31671-2). Montgomery's biography uses her journals to portray her childhood with her grandparents on Prince Edward Island, her literary career and friendships, and her mid-life marriage to a minister. (Rev: BL 11/1/93; MJHS; SLJ 11/93; VOYA 12/93) [813]

3881 Bruce, Harry. *Maud. The Life of L. M. Montgomery* (6–8). 1992, Bantam/Starfire $16 (0-553-08770-3). This biography of the Canadian author of *Anne of Green Gables* is partially based on her journals. (Rev: BL 12/1/92; MJHS; SLJ 8/92) [813]

MORRISON, TONI

3882 Century, Douglas. *Toni Morrison* (8–12). (Black Americans of Achievement) 1994, Chelsea House $18.95 (0-7910-1877-6). A biography of the Nobel Prize–winning African American author, examining her life and the major themes of her novels. (Rev: BL 9/1/94; MJHS; SLJ 7/94; VOYA 8/94) [813]

NERUDA, PABLO

3883 Roman, Joseph. *Pablo Neruda* (7–12). (Hispanics of Achievement) 1992, Chelsea House LB $17.95 (0-7910-1248-4). Traces the great Chilean poet's life from his early years through his career as a diplomat and acclaimed writer. (Rev: BL 6/1/92; MJHS; SLJ 9/92) [861]

O'CONNOR, FLANNERY

3884 Balee, Susan. *Flannery O'Connor: Literary Prophet of the South* (8–12). 1994, Chelsea House $18.95 (0-7910-2418-0). (Rev: BL 1/1/95; SLJ 1/95; VOYA 2/95) [813]

ORWELL, GEORGE

3885 Shelden, Michael. *Orwell: A Biography* (9–adult). 1991, HarperCollins $25 (0-06-016709-2) An authorized biography of the enigmatic twentieth-century British author of *1984* and *Animal Farm.* (Rev: BL 10/1/91; SHS) [823]

PAULSEN, GARY

3886 Paulsen, Gary. *Eastern Sun, Winter Moon: An Autobiographical Odyssey* (9–adult). 1993, Harcourt $22.95 (0-15-127260-3). The vivid, sometimes horrifying story of Paulsen's incredible childhood, much of it spent in the Philippines. (Rev: BL 1/15/93)

PECK, RICHARD

3887 Peck, Richard. *Anonymously Yours* (6–9). 1992, Messner LB $14.98 (0-671-74161-6). An account of how the author became a writer, filled with commentary, quips, and advice for aspiring writers. (Rev: BL 4/15/92; MJHS; YR) [818]

PINKWATER, DANIEL

3888 Pinkwater, Daniel. *Chicago Days/Hoboken Nights* (9–adult). 1991, Addison-Wesley $17.95 (0-201-52359-0). Humorous pieces originally aired on NPR's *All Things Considered* that constitute a "fragmentary autobiography" of the author's early years. (Rev: BL 10/15/91) [813]

POE, EDGAR ALLAN

3889 Anderson, Madelyn Klein. *Edgar Allan Poe: A Mystery* (7–12). 1993, Watts $13.90 (0-531-13012-6). Photos, letters, reviews, and Poe's writings contribute to this view of him as brilliant and gifted, yet opinionated, arrogant, and impractical. (Rev: BL 10/1/93; MJHS; VOYA 10/93) [818]

3890 Loewen, Nancy. *Poe* (6–10). Illus. 1993, Creative Education $16.95 (0-88682-509-1). This photo-biography of Edgar Allan Poe presents the basics of his life in impressionistic photographs with minimal text and invented scenes. (Rev: BL 12/1/93) [818]

RINEHART, MARY ROBERTS

3891 MacLeod, Charlotte. *Had She but Known: A Biography of Mary Roberts Rinehart* (9–adult). 1994, Mysterious $21.95 (0-89296-444-8). A biography of the respected suspense writer. (Rev: BL 4/15/94) [813]

SANTIAGO, ESMERALDA

3892 Santiago, Esmeralda. *When I Was Puerto Rican* (9–adult). 1993, Addison-Wesley $20 (0-201-58117-5). Chronicles Santiago's life, its hardships and joys, from her birth in Puerto Rico, through her adolescence in Brooklyn, to her eventual escape from poverty. (Rev: BL 10/1/93; BTA; SLJ 2/94) [974.7]

SEBESTYEN, OUIDA

3893 Monseau. Virginia R. *Presenting Ouida Sebestyen* (6–12). (United States Authors) 1995, Twayne $20.95 (0-8057-8224-9). Sebestyen's unorthodox writing habits enliven this text, with detailed analysis of her 6 novels. (Rev: BL 9/1/95) [813]

SEGRÈ, CLAUDIO G.

3894 Segrè, Claudio G. *Atoms, Bombs and Eskimo Kisses: A Memoir of Father and Son* (9–adult). 1995, Viking $23.95 (0-670-86307-6). As the son of the man who helped design the first atom bomb, Claudio wants to be recognized for the path his life has taken. (Rev: BL 9/15/95) [530]

SENDER, RUTH MINSKY

3895 Sender, Ruth Minsky. *The Holocaust Lady* (9–adult). 1992, Macmillan $14.95 (0-02-781832-2). A sentimental account of a Holocaust survivor's life in America from the 1950s on, her struggle to cope with memories, bear witness, and get published. (Rev: BL 10/15/92; SLJ 12/92; YR) [940.53]

SHELLEY, MARY

3896 Miller, Calvin Craig. *Spirit Like a Storm: The Story of Mary Shelley* (7–12). (World Writers) 1996, Morgan Reynolds $18.95 (1-883846-13-7). Biography of the author of *Frankenstein*. (Rev: BL 2/15/96; SLJ 3/96)

SINGER, ISAAC BASHEVIS

3897 Perl, Lila. *Isaac Bashevis Singer: The Life of a Storyteller* (5–7). 1994, Jewish Publication Society $12.95 (0-8276-0512-9). A sensitive account of the writer's life, with many of his comments on children and reading. (Rev: BL 5/1/94; SLJ 3/95) [839]

3898 Zamir, Israel. *Journey to My Father, Isaac Bashevis Singer* (9–adult). Tr. by Barbara Harshav. 1995, Arcade $19.95 (1-55970-309-1). An account of Zamir's poignant reforging of father-son ties after 20 years of separation. (Rev: BL 11/1/95) [839]

SPEWACK, BELLA

3899 Spewack, Bella. *Streets: Memoir of the Lower East Side* (9–adult). 1995, Feminist $19.95 (1-55861-115-0). Looks back on the author's adolescent years as the daughter of a poor, Jewish single mother. (Rev: BL 9/15/95) [812]

STAPLES, BRENT

3900 Staples, Brent. *Parallel Time: Growing Up in Black and White* (9–adult). 1994, Pantheon $23 (0-679-42154-8). The autobiographical story of an African American journalist, who made his way from poverty to a University of Chicago graduate degree and the editorial board of the *New York Times*. (Rev: BL 1/15/94; BTA; SLJ 10/94; VOYA 4/95) [070.4]

STEINBECK, JOHN

3901 Ito, Tom. *John Steinbeck* (5–8). (The Importance Of) 1994, Lucent LB $14.95 (1-56006-049-2). (Rev: BL 8/94) [813]

3902 Parini, Jay. *John Steinbeck* (9–adult). 1995, Holt $30 (0-8050-1673-2). Chronicles Steinbeck's youth, friendships, marriages, travels, and the creation of each book, play, and film. A finely wrought portrait. (Rev: BL 1/15/95*; SHS) [813]

STEVENSON, ROBERT LOUIS

3903 Murphy, Jim. *Across America on an Emigrant Train* (5–12). 1993, Clarion $16.95 (0-395-63390-7). Using excerpts from Robert Louis Stevenson's journal and a variety of illustrations, Murphy paints a picture of the transcontinental railroad of the 1880s. Awards: ALSC Notable Children's Book; BL Editors' Choice; SLJ Best

Book. (Rev: BL 12/1/93*; BTA; MJHS; SLJ 12/93*) [828]

STOWE, HARRIET BEECHER

3904 Coil, Suzanne M. *Harriet Beecher Stowe* (7–12). 1993, Watts $14.95 (0-531-13006-1). An admiring biography of the celebrated author that documents the writing of *Uncle Tom's Cabin* and includes excerpts from her letters and works. (Rev: BL 1/15/94; MJHS; SLJ 1/94; VOYA 4/94) [813]

3905 Fritz, Jean. *Harriet Beecher Stowe and the Beecher Preachers* (5–9). 1994, Putnam $16.95 (0-399-22666-4). A biography of the writer of *Uncle Tom's Cabin,* examining Stowe's role as an outspoken woman author in the mid nineteenth century. (Rev: BL 8/94; BTA; MJHS; SLJ 9/94; VOYA 8/94) [813]

3906 Hedrick, Joan D. *Harriet Beecher Stowe: A Life* (9–adult). 1994, Oxford Univ. $35 (0-19-506639-1). This biography of the influential author of *Uncle Tom's Cabin* relates her complex personal story while capturing the spirit of antebellum America. (Rev: BL 1/15/94*) [813]

SWENSON, MAY

3907 Knudson, R. R. *The Wonderful Pen of May Swenson* (7–10). 1993, Macmillan $13.95 (0-02-750915-X). Knudson, Swenson's companion for 23 years, presents this biography as a collection of her poems introduced by comments about her life. (Rev: BL 11/15/93; BTA) [811]

THOREAU, HENRY DAVID

3908 Miller, Douglas T. *Henry David Thoreau: A Man for All Seasons* (8–12). 1991, Facts on File $16.95 (0-8160-2478-2). This presentation of the life and times of the author of *Walden* presents a sympathetic portrait of the famous naturalist philosopher. (Rev: BL 11/15/91; SLJ 4/92) [818]

TOLKIEN, J. R. R.

3909 Collins, David R. *J. R. R. Tolkien: Master of Fantasy* (6–9). Illus. 1992, Lerner LB $15.95 (0-8225-4906-9). A biography of this professor and author of fantasy fiction. (Rev: BL 5/15/92; SLJ 7/92; YR) [828]

TWAIN, MARK

3910 Cox, Clinton. *Mark Twain: America's Humorist, Dreamer, Prophet* (5–9). 1995, Scholastic $14.95 (0-590-45642-3). A biography that also discusses Twain's views on race and how they changed. (Rev: BL 9/15/95; SLJ 9/95; VOYA 12/95) [818]

3911 Lyttle, Richard B. *Mark Twain: The Man and His Adventures* (7–12). 1994, Atheneum $15.95 (0-689-31712-3). (Rev: BL 12/1/94; BTA; MJHS; SLJ 1/95; VOYA 2/95) [818]

3912 Press, Skip. *Mark Twain* (5–8). 1994, Lucent $14.95 (1-56006-043-3). The private, public, and literary aspects of Twain's life. (Rev: BL 5/15/94; MJHS; SLJ 4/94) [818]

3913 Rasmussen, R. Kent. *Mark Twain from A to Z: The Essential Reference to His Life and Writings* (9–12). 1995, Facts on File $45 (0-8160-2845-1). A comprehensive study of Twain's life and times. (Rev: SLJ 3/96)

UCHIDA, YOSHIKO

3914 Uchida, Yoshiko. *The Invisible Thread* (6–9). 1992, Messner LB $14.98 (0-671-74163-2). An Asian American woman recalls hardships during World War II, when her family was sent to a relocation camp in Utah. (Rev: BL 3/1/92; MJHS; SLJ 4/92*; YR) [813]

VERNE, JULES

3915 Teeters, Peggy. *Jules Verne: The Man Who Invented Tomorrow* (5–7). 1993, Walker LB $14.85 (0-8027-8191-8). A biography of the French writer, whose science-based fiction often foreordained the future. (Rev: BL 3/15/93; SLJ 5/93) [843]

WADE-GAYLES, GLORIA

3916 Wade-Gayles, Gloria. *Pushed Back to Strength: A Black Woman's Journey Home* (9–adult). 1993, Beacon $20 (0-8070-0922-9). An African American professor remembers her childhood in the Memphis housing projects at a time of intense racism, her participation in the civil rights movement, and her journey home to family and community. (Rev: BL 10/15/93) [973]

WATKINS, PAUL

3917 Watkins, Paul. *Stand Before Your God: A Boarding-School Memoir* (9–adult). 1994, Random $21 (0-679-42056-8). A candid recollection of the American-born author's youth spent in English boarding schools. (Rev: BL 1/15/94; BTA; SLJ 9/94) [813]

WHARTON, EDITH

3918 Worth, Richard. *Edith Wharton* (9–12). 1994, Messner $15 (0-671-86615-X). A discussion of Wharton's life plus an examination of her works. (Rev: BL 5/15/94; SHS; SLJ 11/94; VOYA 4/95) [813]

WHITE, E. B.

3919 Gherman, Beverly. *E. B. White: Some Writer!* (5–9). 1992, Atheneum $13.95 (0-689-31672-0). A look at the life of the author of *Charlotte's Web* reveals a man who loved words and craved solitude. (Rev: BL 4/15/92; SLJ 7/92) [818]

3920 Tingum, Janice. *E. B. White: The Elements of a Writer* (7–10). 1995, Lerner LB $17.21 (0-8225-4922-0). A quiet biography of the author of the much-beloved *Charlotte's Web* and other books. Discusses the underside of White's success: his shyness and depression. (Rev: BL 11/1/95) [818]

WHITMAN, WALT

3921 Reef, Catherine. *Walt Whitman* (7–12). 1995, Clarion $16.95 (0-395-68705-5). A biography of the nineteenth-century poet who sang of America and the self. Awards: ALSC Notable Children's Book; SLJ Best Book. (Rev: BL 5/1/95; SLJ 5/95) [811]

WILDE, OSCAR

3922 Nunokawa, Jeff. *Oscar Wilde* (10–12). (Notable Biographies) 1994, Chelsea House $19.95 (0-7910-2311-7); paper $9.95 (0-7910-2884-4). (Rev: BL 11/15/94; BTA; SLJ 11/94; VOYA 2/95) [828]

WILDER, LAURA INGALLS

3923 Anderson, William. *Laura Ingalls Wilder: A Biography* (5–8). 1992, HarperCollins LB $15.89 (0-06-020114-2). Thoroughly chronicles the life of author Wilder and fills in a few of the gaps in her stories. (Rev: BL 12/15/92; SLJ 12/92; YR) [813]

WINNEMUCCA, SARAH

3924 Scordato, Ellen. *Sarah Winnemucca: Northern Paiute Writer and Diplomat* (9–12). (North American Indians of Achievement) 1992, Chelsea House LB $17.95 (0-7910-1710-9). (Rev: BL 11/1/92; MJHS) [973]

YEP, LAURENCE

3925 Yep, Laurence. *The Lost Garden* (7–12). 1991, Messner LB $14.98 (0-671-74159-4). The nostalgic autobiography of a Chinese American writer who was raised as an outsider in an African American neighborhood. (Rev: BL 10/15/91; MJHS; SLJS 1/92*) [979.4]

ZINDEL, PAUL

3926 Zindel, Paul. *The Pigman and Me* (6–10). 1992, HarperCollins/Charlotte Zolotow LB $13.89 (0-06-020858-9). A boy recalls the valuable advice he received from an eccentric Italian housemate. Awards: SLJ Best Book. (Rev: BL 9/15/92; BTA; MJHS; SLJ 9/92*; YR) [812]

Composers

BACH, JOHANN SEBASTIAN

3927 Bettmann, Otto L. *Johann Sebastian Bach As His World Knew Him* (9–adult). 1995, Birch Lane $22.50 (1-55972-279-7). A biography of the great musician and personal essays on Bach's life. (Rev: BL 3/15/95) [780]

BEETHOVEN, LUDWIG VAN

3928 Thompson, Wendy. *Ludwig van Beethoven* (6–9). (Composer's World) 1991, Viking $15.95 (0-670-83678-8). This biography emphasizes the era in which Beethoven created his music, with details on where his concerts were performed, who played, and to whom the music was dedicated. (Rev: BL 1/15/91*; MJHS; SLJ 6/91) [780.92]

BERNSTEIN, LEONARD

3929 Chapin, Schuyler. *Leonard Bernstein: Notes from a Friend* (9–adult). 1992, Walker $17.95 (0-8027-1216-9). Recalls the working relationship and close friendship between the author and the musician. (Rev: BL 11/15/92) [780]

3930 Hurwitz, Johanna. *Leonard Bernstein: A Passion for Music* (5–8). Illus. 1993, Jewish Publication Society $12.95 (0-8276-0501-3). Acquaints readers with Bernstein as conductor, composer, pianist, and teacher and shows how his Jewish heritage was a powerful motivating influence. (Rev: BL 2/15/94; SLJ 12/93) [780]

DEBUSSY, CLAUDE

3931 Thompson, Wendy. *Claude Debussy* (6–9). (Composer's World) 1993, Viking $17.99 (0-670-84482-9). (Rev: BL 7/93; MJHS) [780]

GERSHWIN, GEORGE

3932 Peyser, Joan. *The Memory of All That: The Life of George Gershwin* (9–adult). 1993, Simon & Schuster $25 (0-671-70948-8). An in-depth examination of Gershwin's personality and what motivated him, including a portrait of his mother and his older brother. (Rev: BL 4/15/93) [780.92]

GUTHRIE, WOODY

3933 Yates, Janelle. *Woody Guthrie: American Balladeer* (6–10). 1995, Ward Hill Press (40 Willis Ave., Staten Island, NY 10301) LB $14.95 (0-9623380-0-1); paper $10.95 (0-9623380-5-2). Describes Guthrie's creative life and provides important historical information, including the many tragedies suffered by his family and his friendly relationship with labor, members of the Communist Party, and other musicians. (Rev: BL 2/1/95; SLJ 3/95) [782.42162]

HAMLISCH, MARVIN

3934 Hamlisch, Marvin, and Gerald Gardner. *The Way I Was* (9–adult). 1992, Scribner $22 (0-684-19327-2). An autobiography of Hamlisch's early life, show business successes and flops, and overdue date with love and marriage. (Rev: BL 11/15/92) [780]

HAYDN, JOSEPH

3935 Thompson, Wendy. *Joseph Haydn* (6–9). (Composer's World) 1991, Viking $17.95 (0-670-84171-4). (Rev: BL 1/1/92; MJHS) [780]

JOPLIN, SCOTT

3936 Berlin, Edward W. *Scott Joplin: King of Ragtime* (9–adult). 1994, Oxford Univ. $27.50 (0-19-508739-9). A biography of the master ragtime composer using newly discovered documents reveals that Joplin believed Irving Berlin plagiarized his work. (Rev: BL 7/94) [780]

3937 Curtis, Susan. *Dancing to a Black Man's Tune: A Life of Scott Joplin* (9–adult). 1994, Univ. of Missouri $26.95 (0-8262-0949-1). Curtis traces the life of Joplin—best known for his piano rag "The Entertainer"—from his Texas origins through his success as a performer and composer to his troubled stay in Harlem and the failure of his opera, *Treemonisha*. (Rev: BL 5/1/94) [780]

KEY, FRANCIS SCOTT

3938 Whitcraft, Melissa. *Francis Scott Key* (5–7). 1995, Watts LB $13.51 (0-531-20163-5). A discussion of Key's life and how it influenced the compostion of "The Star-Spangled Banner." (Rev: BL 2/15/95; SLJ 6/95) [349.73]

MOZART, WOLFGANG AMADEUS

3939 Switzer, Ellen. *The Magic of Mozart: Mozart, The Magic Flute, and the Salzburg Marionettes* (5–9). 1995, Atheneum/Jean Karl $15 (0-689-31851-0). A volume in 3 parts: Mozart's life, a child-friendly libretto of the opera *The Magic Flute*, and photos of the Salzburg Marionette Theater, which specializes in Mozart operas. (Rev: BL 11/15/95; SLJ 9/95; VOYA 2/96) [782.1]

3940 Thompson, Wendy. *Wolfgang Amadeus Mozart* (6–9). (Composer's World) 1991, Viking $15.95 (0-670-83679-6). Details of the composer's musical career, including where the concerts were performed, who played, and to whom the music was dedicated. (Rev: BL 1/15/91*; SLJ 6/91) [780.92]

NEWTON, JOHN

3941 Haskins, Jim. *Amazing Grace: The Story Behind the Song* (5–7). 1992, Millbrook LB $13.90 (1-56294-117-8). Profiles the man who authored the famous hymn, John Newton, a British slave trader turned minister who became an ardent abolitionist. (Rev: BL 11/1/92; SLJ 4/92) [264]

SCHUBERT, FRANZ

3942 Thompson, Wendy. *Franz Schubert* (6–9). (Composer's World) 1991, Viking $17.95 (0-670-84172-2). (Rev: BL 1/1/92; MJHS) [780]

TCHAIKOVSKY, PYOTR ILYICH

3943 Thompson, Wendy. *Pyotr Ilyich Tchaikovsky* (6–9). (Composer's World) 1993, Viking $17.99 (0-670-84476-4). (Rev: BL 7/93) [780]

Performers (Actors, Musicians, etc.)

ADAMS, NOAH

3944 Adams, Noah. *Noah Adams on "All Things Considered": A Radio Journal* (9–adult). 1992, Norton $22.95 (0-393-03043-1). Chronicles the daily life of a broadcaster, detailing one year's programs, travels, and interviews. (Rev: BL 9/15/92*) [070]

AEROSMITH

3945 Huxley, Martin. *Aerosmith: The Fall and the Rise of Rock's Greatest Band* (9–adult). 1995, St. Martin's paper $12.95 (0-312-11737-X). Picks up the Aerosmith story after their youth and looks at the elements of the rock group's rise to fame and fortune. (Rev: BL 3/1/95) [782.42165]

AILEY, ALVIN

3946 Ailey, Alvin, and Peter A. Bailey. *Revelations: The Autobiography of Alvin Ailey* (9–adult). 1995, Birch Lane $19.95 (1-55972-255-X). The African American choreographer talks about his love of music and dance, shadowed by his substance abuse and emotional illness. (Rev: BL 2/15/95) [793.3]

3947 Mitchell, Jack. *Alvin Ailey American Dance Theatre* (9–adult). 1993, Andrews & McMeel/Donna Martin $29.95 (0-8362-4509-1). After working with Ailey for 30 years, Mitchell now documents his work through this collection of photos that stop the movement of the dancers at its apex. (Rev: BL 11/1/93; BTA; MJHS) [792.8]

ALLEN, WOODY

3948 Lax, Eric. *Woody Allen* (9–adult). 1991, Knopf $24 (0-394-58349-3). (Rev: BL 4/1/91*; SHS; SLJ 11/91) [791.43]

3949 Sunshine, Linda, ed. *The Illustrated Woody Allen Reader* (9–adult). 1993, Knopf $30 (0-679-42072-X). This career scrapbook takes material from Allen's stand-up work, films, essays, plays, interviews, and stories to form a picture of his achievements. (Rev: BL 10/1/93) [812]

ALONSO, ALICIA

3950 Arnold, Sandra Martin. *Alicia Alonso: First Lady of the Ballet* (6–10). 1993, Walker LB $15.85 (0-8027-8243-4). Overcoming the lack of dance schools in her native Cuba and becoming blind in her twenties, Alicia Alonso became a prima ballerina and now teaches, studies, and performs in Cuba. (Rev: BL 12/15/93; BTA; SLJ 11/93; VOYA 2/94) [792.8]

BASIE, COUNT

3951 Kliment, Bud. *Count Basie* (7–10). (Black Americans of Achievement) 1992, Chelsea House LB $17.95 (0-7910-1118-6). (Rev: BL 9/15/92; MJHS) [781.65]

THE BEATLES

3952 Hertsgaard, Mark. *A Day in the Life: The Music and Artistry of the Beatles* (9–adult). 1995, Delacorte $23.95 (0-385-31377-2). An in-depth look at the popularity of the Beatles. (Rev: BL 3/1/95) [782.42166]

BLADES, RUBÉN

3953 Marton, Betty A. *Rubén Blades* (5–9). (Hispanics of Achievement) 1992, Chelsea House LB $17.95 (0-7910-1235-2). (Rev: BL 10/1/92) [782.42164]

BOY GEORGE

3954 Boy George, and Spencer Bright. *Take It Like a Man: The Autobiography of Boy George* (9–adult). 1995, HarperCollins $25 (0-06-017368-8). This chronicle of the rock star Boy Ceorge's life is offered without pretense and with gentle humor. It follows him through a lonely childhood to his rise to fame. (Rev: BL 9/1/95) [782.42166]

BURKE, CHRIS

3955 Burke, Chris, and Jo Beth McDaniel. *A Special Kind of Hero: Chris Burke's Own Story* (9–adult). 1991, Doubleday $18 (0-385-41645-8). This biography of Chris Burke, the star of the television series *Life Goes On,* weaves the latest information on Down's syndrome into the story of Burke's childhood struggles in a society closed to the mentally challenged. Awards: SLJ Best Book. (Rev: BL 10/15/91; SLJ 5/92) [791.45]

3956 Geraghty, Helen M. *Chris Burke* (5–10). (Great Achievers: Lives of the Physically Challenged) 1994, Chelsea House $18.95 (0-7910-2081-9). A biography of the star of TV's *Life Goes On*. Looks at Burke's family life and career success despite Down's syndrome. (Rev: BL 10/15/94) [791.45]

CALAMITY JANE

3957 Faber, Doris. *Calamity Jane: Her Life and Her Legend* (5–9). 1992, Houghton $14.95 (0-395-56396-8). Faber carefully distinguishes what is certain, what is possible, and what is blatantly untrue in the legend of Calamity Jane. (Rev: BL 8/92; MJHS; SLJ 10/92; YR) [978]

CAREY, MARIAH

3958 Nickson, Chris. *Mariah Carey: Her Story* (9–adult). 1995, St. Martin's paper $8.95 (0-312-13121-6). Traces Carey's rise to stardom due to her looks and vocal range while avoiding depravity, excess, and mania. (Rev: BL 6/1–15/95) [782.42164]

CARRERAS, JOSÉ

3959 Carreras, José. *José Carreras: Singing from the Soul: An Autobiography* (9–adult). Tr. by John E. Thomas. 1991, Y.C.P. Publications (P.O. Box 931766, Los Angeles, CA 90093) $27.95 (1-878756-89-3). (Rev: BL 5/1/91; SHS) [782]

CASALS, PABLO

3960 Garza, Hedda. *Pablo Casals* (5–9). (Hispanics of Achievement) 1993, Chelsea House LB $18.95 (0-7910-1237-9). (Rev: BL 4/1/93; MJHS) [787.4]

3961 Hargrove, Jim. *Pablo Casals: Cellist of Conscience* (5–8). (People of Distinction) 1991, Children's Press LB $12.95 (0-516-03272-0). (Rev: BL 2/15/92) [787.4]

CHARLES, RAY

3962 Ritz, David. *Ray Charles: Voice of Soul* (6–10). 1994, Chelsea House $18.95 (0-7910-2080-0); paper $7.95 (0-7910-2093-2). The story of Ray Charles Robinson, who overcame the hardships of poverty, racism, drug addiction, and blindness to become one of America's most influential musicians. (Rev: BL 11/15/94; BTA) [782.42164]

CLAPTON, ERIC

3963 Schumacher, Michael. *Crossroads: The Life and Music of Eric Clapton* (9–adult). 1995, Hyperion $24 (0-7868-6074-X). A biography of British rock star Eric Clapton. (Rev: BL 4/1/95) [787.87]

COSBY, BILL

3964 Schuman, Michael A. *Bill Cosby: Actor and Comedian* (6–12). (People to Know) 1995, Enslow LB $17.95 (0-89490-548-1). Describes the life and career of one of the most successful comedians in modern times. (Rev: BL 9/15/95; SLJ 2/96)

DAVIS, MILES

3965 Frankl, Ron. *Miles Davis* (7–10). (Black Americans of Achievement) 1995, Chelsea House $18.95 (0-7910-2156-4); paper $7.95 (0-7910-2157-2). (Rev: BL 11/15/95) [788]

DEAN, JAMES

3966 Holley, Val. *James Dean* (9–adult). 1995, St. Martin's $22.95 (0-312-13249-2). A definitive biography in the fortieth anniversary year of his death in 1955. (Rev: BL 9/15/95) [791.43]

DENVER, BOB

3967 Denver, Bob. *Gilligan, Maynard, and Me* (9–adult). 1993, Citadel paper $12.95 (0-8065-1413-2). Denver's anecdotes reveal unknown facts about his TV career as Maynard G. Krebs on *The Many Loves of Dobie Gillis* and Gilligan on *Gilligan's Island.* (Rev: BL 12/15/93) [791.45]

DOMINGO, PLÁCIDO

3968 Stefoff, Rebecca. *Plácido Domingo* (5–9). (Hispanics of Achievement) 1992, Chelsea House LB $17.95 (0-7910-1563-7). (Rev: BL 12/1/92; MJHS) [782.1]

DUNHAM, KATHERINE

3969 Dominy, Jeannine. *Katherine Dunham* (7–10). (Black Americans of Achievement) 1992, Chelsea House LB $17.95 (0-7910-1123-2). (Rev: BL 8/92; MJHS) [792.8]

DYLAN, BOB

3970 Richardson, Susan. *Bob Dylan* (7–12). (Pop Culture Legends) 1995, Chelsea House $18.95 (0-7910-2335-4); paper $7.95 (0-7910-2360-5). (Rev: BL 8/95) [782.42162]

ELLINGTON, DUKE

3971 Collier, James Lincoln. *Duke Ellington* (5–7). 1991, Macmillan $12.95 (0-02-722985-8). A biography of the legendary jazz composer and orchestral conductor that presents the essence of the man and musician. (Rev: BL 9/15/91; MJHS; SHS) [781.65]

3972 Woog, Adam. *Duke Ellington* (6–9). (The Importance Of) 1996, Lucent LB $16.95 (1-

56006-073-5). The musician's life and contributions to his profession and the world. (Rev: BL 2/15/96; SLJ 2/96)

ESTEFAN, GLORIA

3973 Stefoff, Rebecca. *Gloria Estefan* (5–9). (Hispanics of Achievement) 1991, Chelsea House $17.95 (0-7910-1244-1). Traces the singer's career from her birth in Cuba through her success with the Miami Sound Machine. (Rev: BL 8/91; MJHS; SLJ 12/91) [782.42164]

FITZGERALD, ELLA

3974 Wyman, Carolyn. *Ella Fitzgerald: Jazz Singer Supreme* (7–12). 1993, Watts LB $13.90 (0-531-13031-2). This look at the life of the jazz musician on the road also serves as a framework for a cursory history of popular music in the United States. (Rev: BL 8/93; VOYA 10/93) [782.42165]

FOSTER, JODIE

3975 Chunovic, Louis. *Jodie* (9–adult). 1995, Contemporary $19.95 (0-8092-3404-1). A straightforward biography of Jodie Foster that emphasizes the business side rather than psychoanalyzing her. (Rev: BL 12/1/95) [791.43]

GILLESPIE, DIZZY

3976 Gourse, Leslie. *Dizzy Gillespie and the Birth of Bebop* (6–10). 1994, Atheneum $14.95 (0-689-31869-3). (Rev: BL 1/1/95; SLJ 3/95) [788.92]

GOLDBERG, WHOOPI

3977 Blue, Rose, and Corinne Naden. *Whoopi Goldberg* (7–10). (Black Americans of Achievement) 1995, Chelsea House $18.95 (0-7910-2152-1); paper $7.95 (0-7910-2153-X). (Rev: BL 3/15/95; MJHS) [791]

GRAHAM, MARTHA

3978 De Mille, Agnes. *Martha: The Life and Work of Martha Graham* (9–adult). 1991, Random $30 (0-394-55643-7). A look at the professional career and personal life of the "best-known concert dancer in America." (Rev: BL 8/91*) [793.3]

3979 Graham, Martha. *Blood Memory* (9–adult). 1991, Doubleday $25 (0-385-26503-4). Autobiographical account of the famous dancer's life, including photos from her private collection. (Rev: BL 8/91*; SHS) [792.8]

3980 Pratt, Paula Bryant. *Martha Graham* (5–8). (The Importance Of) 1995, Lucent $14.95 (1-56006-056-5). (Rev: BL 1/15/95) [792.8]

3981 Probosz, Kathilyn Solomon. *Martha Graham* (6–10). (People in Focus) 1995, Silver Burdett LB $13.95 (0-87518-568-1); paper $7.95 (0-382-24961-5). (Rev: BL 8/95) [792.8]

GRODIN, CHARLES

3982 Grodin, Charles. *We're Ready for You, Mr. Grodin: Behind the Scenes at Talk Shows, Movies, and Elsewhere* (9–adult). 1994, Macmillan $22 (0-02-545795-0). Charles Grodin presents a glimpse into his life as talk show host and actor, including revealing insights about Hollywood schmoozing and many stars. (Rev: BL 10/1/94) [791.43]

HENDRIX, JIMI

3983 Green, Martin I., and Bill Sienkiewicz. *Voodoo Child: The Illustrated Legend of Jimi Hendrix* (9–adult). Illus. 1995, Penguin $34.95 (0-670-86789-6). A graphic docudrama of Jimi Hendrix, including a 30-minute CD of previously unreleased recordings. Full-color illustrations. (Rev: BL 10/15/95) [787.87]

HENSON, JIM

3984 Durrett, Deanne. *Jim Henson* (5–8). (The Importance Of) 1994, Lucent LB $14.95 (1-56006-048-4). (Rev: BL 8/94) [791.5]

3985 Finch, Christopher. *Jim Henson: The Works* (9–adult). 1993, Random $40 (0-679-41203-4). Traces the career of the creator of the Muppets from local television in the 1950s through the triumph of *Sesame Street* and his experimental work. (Rev: BL 1/15/94) [791.5]

HEPBURN, KATHARINE

3986 Leaming, Barbara. *Katharine Hepburn* (9–adult). 1995, Crown $27.50 (0-517-59284-3). (Rev: BL 3/1/95*) [791.43]

HOCKENBERRY, JOHN

3987 Hockenberry, John. *Moving Violations: War Zones, Wheelchairs, and Declarations of Independence* (9–adult). 1995, Hyperion $24.95 (0-7868-6078-2). Hockenberry—a paraplegic who covered the Middle East conflict for National Public Radio—tells how he managed to accomplish it from the confines of a wheelchair. (Rev: BL 6/1–15/95) [362.4]

HOLIDAY, BILLIE

3988 Clarke, Donald. *Wishing on the Moon: The Life and Times of Billie Holiday* (9–adult). 1994, Viking $24.95 (0-670-83771-7). Chronicles the life of the legendary jazz singer from the streets of Baltimore to New York's hottest clubs, discussing her genius and her tragic death. (Rev: BL 8/94*) [781.65092]

3989 Nicholson, Stuart. *Billie Holiday* (9–adult). 1995, Northeastern Univ. $29.95 (1-55553-248-9). A careful, factual account of the singer's tumultuous life. (Rev: BL 10/15/95) [782.42165]

HOLLY, BUDDY

3990 Amburn, Ellis. *Buddy Holly* (9–adult). 1995, St. Martin's $24.95 (0-312-13446-0). A detailed biography of one of the most influential pop music stars. Discography. (Rev: BL 10/1/95) [782.42166]

HOUDINI, HARRY

3991 Brandon, Ruth. *The Life and Many Deaths of Harry Houdini* (9–adult). 1994, Random $25 (0-679-42437-7). A biography of the escape artist, revealing his perfectionism, his obsession with death, and many of the secrets to his daring feats. (Rev: BL 9/15/94*; SHS; SLJ 5/95) [793.8]

3992 Woog, Adam. *Harry Houdini* (5–8). (The Importance Of) 1995, Lucent $14.95 (1-56006-053-0). (Rev: BL 1/15/95) [793.8]

IGLESIAS, JULIO

3993 Martino, Elizabeth. *Julio Iglesias* (5–9). (Hispanics of Achievement) 1994, Chelsea House $18.95 (0-7910-2017-7). (Rev: BL 9/15/94) [782.42164]

JACKSON, MICHAEL

3994 Nicholson, Lois. *Michael Jackson* (5–8). (Black Americans of Achievement) 1994, Chelsea House $18.95 (0-7910-1929-2); paper $7.95 (0-7910-1930-6). A biography of the pop star that examines his loneliness, his family ties, and the allegations against him of sexual abuse. (Rev: BL 10/15/94; SLJ 10/94) [782.42166]

3995 Taraborelli, J. Randy. *Michael Jackson: The Magic and the Madness* (9–adult). 1991, Birch Lane $21.95 (1-55972-064-6). (Rev: BL 4/15/91; SHS) [781.66]

JAMISON, JUDITH

3996 Jamison, Judith, and Howard Kaplan. *Dancing Spirit: An Autobiography* (9–adult). 1993, Doubleday $25 (0-385-42557-0). Jamison describes her career in dance and the childhood that led to her becoming a dancer, a choreographer, a teacher, and an artistic director of the Alvin Ailey American Dance Theatre. (Rev: BL 11/1/93) [792.8]

JOHN, ELTON

3997 Crimp, Susan, and Patricia Burstein. *The Many Lives of Elton John* (9–adult). 1992, Birch Lane $19.95 (1-55972-111-1). An intimate glimpse into the singer's life, for mature readers. (Rev: BL 4/15/92) [782.42166]

3998 Norman, Philip. *Elton John* (9–adult). 1992, Crown/Harmony $22.50 (0-517-58762-9). An exhaustive biography of the legendary pop/rock musician by a celebrated rock journalist. (Rev: BL 12/15/91) [782.42166]

JUDD, NAOMI

3999 Judd, Naomi. *Love Can Build a Bridge* (9–adult). 1993, Villard $24 (0-679-41247-6). Judd tells her rags to riches story of a hard life in Kentucky before achieving success in music and being stricken with hepatitis. (Rev: BL 12/15/93) [782.42164]

JULIA, RAUL

4000 Stefoff, Rebecca. *Raul Julia* (6–9). (Hispanics of Achievement) 1994, Chelsea House $18.95 (0-7910-1556-4). A biography of the late Puerto Rican actor, describing his theater and film work, his involvement with the Hunger Project, and his battle against ethnic stereotyping. (Rev: BL 10/1/94; MJHS; SLJ 8/94) [792]

LENNON, JOHN

4001 Conord, Bruce W. *John Lennon* (7–12). (Pop Culture Legends) 1993, Chelsea House $18.95 (0-7910-1739-7); paper $7.95 (0-7910-1740-0). Looks at Lennon's childhood in Liverpool, his career with the Beatles, and his life after their breakup. (Rev: BL 12/15/93; SLJ 11/93) [782.42166]

4002 Norman, Philip. *Days in the Life: John Lennon Remembered* (9–adult). 1991, Century $29.95 (0-7126-3922-5). (Rev: BL 3/15/91; SHS) [781.66]

MADONNA

4003 Andersen, Christopher. *Madonna Unauthorized* (9–adult). 1991, Simon & Schuster $20 (0-671-73532-2). A biography of the ubiquitous pop/rock star. (Rev: BL 11/1/91) [782.42166]

4004 Claro, Nicole. *Madonna* (7–10). (Pop Culture Legends) 1994, Chelsea House $18.95 (0-7910-2330-3); paper $7.95 (0-7910-2355-9). Examines the pop diva's childhood, the early death of her mother, her rise to stardom, her love affairs, and her controversial personality. (Rev: BL 10/15/94; BTA; SLJ 11/94; VOYA 12/94) [782.42166]

4005 Rettenmund, Matthew. *Encyclopedia Madonnica* (9–adult). 1995, St. Martin's paper $15.95 (0-312-11782-5). A quirky compendium of "all things Madonna." (Rev: BL 4/1/95) [782.42166]

4006 Thompson, Douglas. *Madonna Revealed* (9–adult). 1991, Birch Lane paper $12.95 (1-55972-099-9). The famous singer's life story. (Rev: BL 11/1/91) [782.42166]

MARLEY, BOB

4007 Boot, Adrian, and Chris Slaewicz. *Bob Marley: Songs of Freedom* (9–adult). 1995, Viking $34.95 (0-670-85784-X). A review of the life and career of Jamaican Bob Marley. (Rev: BL 4/15/95) [782.42164]

4008 Taylor, Don. *Marley and Me: The Real Bob Marley* (9–adult). 1995, Barricade Books (150 Fifth Ave., New York, NY 10011) paper $14.95 (1-56980-044-8). Marley's business manager sheds light on the complexities of this charismatic reggae musician's life. (Rev: BL 9/1/95) [782.42164]

MARSALIS, WYNTON

4009 Marsalis, Wynton. *Sweet Swing Blues on the Road* (9–adult). 1994, Norton $29.95 (0-393-03514-X). Jazz musician and composer Marsalis takes the reader with him and his band on their travels around the world. (Rev: BL 12/15/94; BTA) [788.9]

MARX, GROUCHO

4010 Tyson, Peter. *Groucho Marx* (7–12). (Pop Culture Legends) 1995, Chelsea House $18.95 (0-7910-2341-9). (Rev: BL 7/95) [792.7]

MCCARTNEY, PAUL

4011 Giuliano, Geoffrey. *Blackbird: The Life and Times of Paul McCartney* (9–adult). 1991, Dutton $22.95 (0-525-93374-3). This biography, much of it based on information from McCartney's cowriter Denny Laine, paints an occasionally negative picture of the famous Beatle. (Rev: BL 10/1/91) [781.66]

MCENTIRE, REBA

4012 Cusic, Don. *Reba McEntire: Country Music's Queen* (9–adult). 1991, St. Martin's paper $10.95. This respectful biography of the country star presents much information on the Nashville music industry and the rodeo/cowboy tradition. (Rev: BL 9/15/91) [782.42]

MONROE, MARILYN

4013 Lefkowitz, Frances. *Marilyn Monroe* (7–12). (Pop Culture Legends) 1995, Chelsea House $18.95 (0-7910-2342-7); paper $7.95 (0-7910-2367-2). (Rev: BL 8/95) [791.43]

MORENO, RITA

4014 Suntree, Susan. *Rita Moreno* (5–9). (Hispanics of Achievement) 1992, Chelsea House LB $18.95 (0-7910-1247-6). (Rev: BL 2/1/93) [782.42164]

MORRIS, MARK

4015 Acocella, Joan. *Mark Morris* (9–adult). 1993, Farrar $27.50 (0-374-20295-8). This biography of dancer/choreographer Morris reveals his disturbing work and his motives for it from the perspective of a dance/art critic. (Rev: BL 11/1/93) [792.8]

MORRISON, JIM

4016 Hopkins, Jerry. *The Lizard King: The Essential Jim Morrison* (9–adult). 1992, Scribner $19 (0-684-19524-0). Descriptions of Morrison's exploits are continued in this sequel to *No One Gets Out of Here Alive*. (Rev: BL 9/15/92) [782.42166]

4017 Jones, Dylan. *Jim Morrison: Dark Star* (9–adult). 1991, Viking $29.95 (0-670-83454-8). Illustrated biography of a doomed 1960s rock star. (Rev: BL 1/15/91; SHS) [782.421]

MURPHY, EDDIE

4018 Wilburn, Deborah A. *Eddie Murphy* (7–10). (Black Americans of Achievement) 1993, Chelsea House $18.95 (0-7910-1879-2); paper $7.95 (0-7910-1908-X). (Rev: BL 1/1/94; SLJ 1/94) [792.7]

NICHOLS, NICHELLE

4019 Nichols, Nichelle. *Beyond Uhura: Star Trek and Other Memories* (9–adult). 1994, Putnam $22.95 (0-399-13993-1). The autobiography of the African American actress famous for her role as *Star Trek*'s Lieutenant Uhura. (Rev: BL 9/15/94; VOYA 4/95) [791.45]

NIMOY, LEONARD

4020 Nimoy, Leonard. *I Am Spock* (9–adult). 1995, Hyperion $24.95 (0-7868-6182-7). This entertaining memoir of Nimoy's years with *Star Trek* follows his book, *I Am Not Spock*, by 20 years. (Rev: BL 9/15/95) [791.45]

OAKLEY, ANNIE

4021 Riley, Glenda. *The Life and Legacy of Annie Oakley* (9–adult). 1994, Univ. of Oklahoma $24.95 (0-8061-2656-6). A biography of the sharpshooter of Buffalo Bill Cody's Wild West Show, describing her personal and professional accomplishments within historical, cultural, and sociological contexts. (Rev: BL 10/1/94; SHS) [796.3]

PARKER, CHARLIE

4022 Frankl, Ron. *Charlie Parker* (7–10). (Black Americans of Achievement) 1992, Chelsea House LB $18.95 (0-7910-1134-8). (Rev: BL 2/1/93; MJHS) [788.7]

PAVAROTTI, LUCIANO

4023 Pavarotti, Luciano, and William Wright. *Pavarotti: My World* (9–adult). 1995, Crown $25 (0-517-70027-1). Pavarotti again writes of his career and life, including his happiest and saddest moments. (Rev: BL 9/1/95) [782.1]

PAVLOVA, ANNA

4024 Levine, Ellen. *Anna Pavlova: Genius of the Dance* (5–7). 1995, Scholastic $14.95 (0-590-44304-6). Dance lovers will enjoy the accounts of particular ballets—choreography, technique, style, and what went on behind the scenes. (Rev: BL 1/1/95; SLJ 4/95*; VOYA 4/95) [792.8]

PHOENIX, RIVER

4025 Glatt, John. *Lost in Hollywood: The Fast Times and Short Life of River Phoenix* (9–adult). 1995, Donald I. Fine $23.95 (1-55611-426-5); paper $12.95 (1-55611-440-0). A biography of River Phoenix, beginning with his rise to stardom and ending with a drug overdose. (Rev: BL 3/1/95) [791]

PRESLEY, ELVIS

4026 Gentry, Tony. *Elvis Presley* (7–12). (Pop Culture Legends) 1994, Chelsea House $18.95 (0-7910-2329-X); paper $7.95 (0-7910-2354-0). (Rev: BL 9/15/94) [782.42166]

4027 Guralnick, Peter. *Last Train to Memphis: The Rise of Elvis Presley* (9–adult). 1994, Little, Brown $24.95 (0-316-33220-8). Details the singer's early career, describing how a shy, naive boy made his dream of being a musician come true. The first of a projected 2-volume biography. (Rev: BL 7/94; SHS) [782.42166]

4028 Kricun, Morrie E., and Virginia M. Kricun. *Elvis 1956 Reflections* (9–adult). 1992, Morgin Press (303 W. Lancaster Ave., Suite 283, Wayne, PA 19087) $49.95 (0-9630976-0-1). A chronological record of Presley's professional career as it progressed during one year. (Rev: BL 9/15/92) [782.42166]

4029 Krohn, Katherine E. *Elvis Presley: The King* (5–7). (Achievers) 1994, Lerner $13.50 (0-8225-2877-0). Chronological biography making use of many black-and-white photos. (Rev: BL 7/94; SLJ 7/94) [782.42166]

4030 Rubel, David. *Elvis Presley: The Rise of Rock and Roll* (6–12). (New Directions) 1991, Millbrook $14.90 (1-878841-18-1). Candid account of the man who led newly powerful teenagers through the postwar boom. (Rev: BL 2/1/91; SLJ 4/91) [781.66]

PRYOR, RICHARD

4031 Pryor, Richard, and Todd Gold. *Pryor Convictions and Other Life Sentences* (9–adult). 1995, Pantheon $23 (0-679-43250-7). A painfully revealing autobiography of a publicly very funny man but privately very sad one. (Rev: BL 5/15/95*) [792.7]

QUINN, ANTHONY

4032 Amdur, Melissa. *Anthony Quinn* (5–9). (Hispanics of Achievement) 1993, Chelsea House LB $18.95 (0-7910-1251-4). (Rev: BL 9/15/93) [791.43]

RICHARDS, KEITH

4033 Booth, Stanley. *Keith: Standing in the Shadows* (9–adult). 1995, St. Martin's $19.95 (0-312-11841-4). A portrait of Keith Richards written by a friend. (Rev: BL 3/1/95) [782.42166]

ROGERS, WILL

4034 Sonneborn, Liz. *Will Rogers: Cherokee Entertainer* (9–12). (North American Indians of Achievement) 1993, Chelsea House $18.95 (0-7910-1719-2); paper $7.95 (0-7910-1988-8). (Rev: BL 12/1/93; MJHS) [792.7]

RONSTADT, LINDA

4035 Amdur, Melissa. *Linda Ronstadt* (5–9). (Hispanics of Achievement) 1993, Chelsea House LB $18.95 (0-7910-1781-8). (Rev: BL 9/15/93) [782.42164]

ROTTEN, JOHNNY (JOHN LYDON)

4036 Lydon, John, and others. *Rotten: No Irish, No Blacks, No Dogs* (9–adult). 1994, St. Martin's $22.95 (0-312-09903-7). The story of John Lydon, aka Johnny Rotten of the Sex Pistols fame. (Rev: BL 4/15/94) [782.42166]

SCHWARZENEGGER, ARNOLD

4037 Doherty, Craig A., and Katherine M. Doherty. *Arnold Schwarzenegger: Larger Than Life* (6–10). 1993, Walker LB $15.85 (0-8027-8238-8). This biography portrays Schwarzenegger as an "American hero," outlining his life and applauding his physical fitness and business sense. (Rev: BL 12/1/93; SLJ 2/94; VOYA 4/94) [646.7]

4038 Lipsyte, Robert. *Arnold Schwarzenegger: Hercules in America* (6–10). 1993, HarperCollins LB $13.89 (0-06-023003-7). Arnold Schwarzenegger is shown as the personification of mythic themes in this biography that includes such topics as power, risks, crazes, and romance. (Rev: BL 12/1/93; BTA; MJHS; SLJ 12/93; VOYA 12/93) [646.75]

SHEEN, MARTIN

4039 Hargrove, Jim. *Martin Sheen: Actor and Activist* (5–8). (People of Distinction) 1991, Children's Press paper $5.95 (0-516-03274-5). (Rev: BL 3/1/92) [791.43]

SIMON AND GARFUNKEL

4040 Morella, Joseph, and Patricia Barey. *Simon and Garfunkel: Old Friends* (9–adult). 1991, Birch Lane $19.95 (1-55972-089-1). A dual biography of the famous folk-rock singer/songwriter pair, covering their Queens boyhoods, rise to fame in the 1960s, breakup at the decade's end, and subsequent separate careers. (Rev: BL 10/1/91) [782.42164]

SIMONE, NINA

4041 Simone, Nina, and Stephen Cleary. *I Put a Spell on You: The Autobiography of Nina Simone* (9–adult). 1992, Pantheon $22 (0-679-41068-6). An ccount of singer Nina Simone's rise to fame in the late 1960s. (Rev: BL 1/15/92) [782.42164]

STIERLE, EDWARD

4042 Solway, Diane. *A Dance Against Time: The Brief, Brilliant Life of a Joffrey Dancer* (9–adult). 1994, Pocket $23 (0-671-78894-9). The biography of Eddie Stierle, a leading ballet dancer who died of AIDS at 23. Chronicles his life, examining his bisexuality and his desire to perform. (Rev: BL 11/1/94*; BTA) [792.8]

THARP, TWYLA

4043 Tharp, Twyla. *Push Comes to Shove: An Autobiography* (9–adult). 1992, Bantam $24.50 (0-553-07306-0). This intimate memoir by the famed dancer/choreographer combines career anecdotes with self-portraits of each stage of her life. (Rev: BL 11/1/92*; SHS) [792.8]

THREE STOOGES

4044 Scordato, Mark, and Ellen Scordato. *The Three Stooges* (7–12). (Pop Culture Legends) 1995, Chelsea House $18.95 (0-7910-2344-3); paper $7.95 (0-7910-2369-9). Looks at the 6 men who comprised the Three Stooges at various times. Includes black-and-white photos, a filmography, and a chronology. (Rev: BL 6/1–15/95) [791.43]

U2

4045 Flanagan, Bill. *U2 at the End of the World* (9–adult). 1995, Delacorte $22.95 (0-385-31154-0). Follows rock band U2 on an international tour. (Rev: BL 5/1/95) [782.42166]

WALLENDA, DELILAH

4046 Wallenda, Delilah, and Nan De Vicentis-Hayes. *The Last of the Wallendas* (9–adult). 1993, New Horizon $22.95 (0-88282-116-4). Master highwire artist Karl Wallenda's granddaughter describes the fading charisma and finances of the circus in the United States from a personal perspective, presenting her version of family squabbles. (Rev: BL 4/15/93) [791.3]

WELLES, ORSON

4047 Callow, Simon. *Orson Welles: The Road to Xanadu, Vol. 1* (9–adult). 1996, Viking $29.95 (0-670-86722-5). Callow questions every major intersection of Welles's life, working to get behind the myths. This volume covers his youth and early career. (Rev: BL 10/15/95*) [791.43]

YOUNG, NEIL

4048 Heatley, Michael. *Neil Young: His Life and Music* (9–adult). 1995, Hamlyn $29.95 (0-600-58541-7). A pictorial tribute to the godfather of grunge. (Rev: BL 2/15/95) [782.42166]

4049 Rolling Stone, eds. *Neil Young: The Rolling Stone Files.* (9–adult). 1994, Hyperion paper $12.95 (0-7868-8043-0). Traces Young's musical career from his stint with Crosby, Stills, and Nash to the present. (Rev: BL 8/94) [782.42166]

Miscellaneous Artists

BARNUM, P. T.

4050 Andronik, Catherine M. *Prince of Humbugs: A Life of P. T. Barnum* (6–9). 1994, Atheneum $15.95 (0-689-31796-4). (Rev: BL 12/15/94; BTA) [791.3]

4051 Fleming, Alice. *P. T. Barnum: The World's Greatest Showman* (5–8). 1993, Walker LB $15.85 (0-8027-8235-3). This biography of the circus owner describes his childhood and several of his successful entrepreneurial ventures. (Rev: BL 1/15/94; MJHS; SLJ 12/93; VOYA 2/94) [338.7]

4052 Kunhardt, Philip B., and others. *P. T. Barnum: America's Greatest Showman* (9–adult). 1995, Knopf $45 (0-679-43574-3). The story of the master of showmanship and the greatest purveyor of freaks and wonders under the big top. (Rev: BL 9/1/95) [338.7]

BOURKE-WHITE, MARGARET

4053 Ayer, Eleanor H. *Margaret Bourke-White: Photographing the World* (6–10). (People in Focus) 1992, Dillon LB $12.95 (0-87518-513-4). A lively account of the photographer's craft and technique, her long association with *Life*, and the subjects she recorded, from the Depression and Buchenwald concentration camp to Gandhi. (Rev: BL 12/1/92; SLJ 11/92) [770]

CAPRA, FRANK

4054 McBride, Joseph. *Frank Capra: The Catastrophe of Success* (9–adult). 1992, Simon & Schuster $30 (0-671-73494-6). Extensively documented biography of one of Hollywood's legendary directors. (Rev: BL 4/1/92) [791.43]

COPELAND, IAN

4055 Copeland, Ian. *Wild Thing: The Backstage, on the Road, in the Studio, off the Charts Memoirs of Ian Copeland* (9–adult). 1995, Simon & Schuster $23 (0-684-81508-7). Music agent Copeland tells of his lively life, from his childhood to his career in the alternative-music industry. (Rev: BL 11/1/95) [780.92]

DAY, TOM

4056 Lyons, Mary E. *Master of Mahogany: Tom Day, Free Black Cabinetmaker* (5–8). 1994, Scribner $15.95 (0-684-19675-1). Chronicles the life of an eighteenth-century African American cabinetmaker, using quotations from Day's diary and photos of his work. Awards: BL Editors' Choice; Woodson Book. (Rev: BL 10/1/94; SLJ 10/94*) [749.213]

DISNEY, WALT

4057 Fanning, Jim. *Walt Disney* (7–12). (Pop Culture Legends) 1994, Chelsea House $18.95 (0-7910-2331-1). (Rev: BL 10/15/94) [791.43]

4058 Greene, Katherine, and Richard Greene. *The Man Behind the Magic: The Story of Walt Disney* (6–9). 1991, Viking $16.95 (0-670-82259-0). This biography concentrates on the personal characteristics of Disney and life at the Disney Studio, clearly differentiating the man from his creations. (Rev: BL 10/1/91; SLJ 10/91) [791.43]

GEBEL-WILLIAMS, GÜNTHER

4059 Gebel-Williams, Günther, and Toni Reinhold. *Untamed: The Autobiography of the Circus's Greatest Animal Trainer* (9–adult). Illus. 1991, Morrow $19.95 (0-688-08645-4). The life story of a world-class German circus performer. (Rev: BL 2/1/91; SHS) [636.088]

JOHNSON, MARTIN AND OSA

4060 Imperato, Pascal James, and Eleanor M. Imperato. *They Married Adventure: The Wandering Lives of Martin and Osa Johnson* (9–adult). 1992, Rutgers Univ. $27.95 (0-8135-1858-X). The life and times of the popular couple who brought the unknown to movie audiences as entertainment in the years before World War II. (Rev: BL 11/1/92) [910]

LEE, SPIKE

4061 Bernotas, Bob. *Spike Lee: Filmmaker* (7–10). 1993, Enslow LB $17.95 (0-89490-416-7). Focuses on Lee's films and the controversy surrounding their themes of racism. Includes photos and a look at production problems. (Rev: BL 12/1/93; BTA; MJHS; VOYA 12/93) [791.43]

4062 Hardy, James Earl. *Spike Lee* (7–10). (Black Americans of Achievement) 1995, Chelsea House $18.95 (0-7910-1875-X); paper $7.95 (0-7910-1904-7). (Rev: BL 11/15/95) [791.43]

LESTER, RICHARD

4063 Yule, Andrew. *The Man Who "Framed" the Beatles: A Biography of Richard Lester* (9–adult). 1994, Donald I. Fine $24.95 (1-55611-390-0). This portrait of the filmmaker includes a detailed account of the filming of *A Hard Day's Night* and his other 1960s cinema successes. (Rev: BL 3/15/94) [791.43]

POWERS, HARRIET

4064 Lyons, Mary E. *Stitching Stars: The Story of Harriet Powers* (5–7). (African American Artists and Artisans) 1993, Scribner $15.95 (0-684-19576-3). The social history of story-quilt-making is looked at through the biography of quilter Harriet Powers before and after the years of the Emancipation. (Rev: BL 11/15/93; MJHS; SLJ 2/94) [746.9]

RINGGOLD, FAITH

4065 Ringgold, Faith. *We Flew over the Bridge* (9–adult). 1995, Little, Brown/Bulfinch $29.95 (0-8212-2071-3). Ringgold, the creator of the story quilt that led to her Caldecott Honor Book *Tar Beach,* recounts her struggle against racism and discrimination against women in a black community. Includes family snapshots and a 30-page color insert of her art. (Rev: BL 9/1/95) [709]

STONE, OLIVER

4066 Riordan, James. *Stone: The Controversies, Excesses and Exploits of a Radical Filmmaker* (9–adult). 1995, Hyperion $24.95 (0-7868-6026-X). The first biography written about Oliver Stone shows a complex personality who sought out the kinds of risks in life that he directs and writes about on screen. (Rev: BL 10/15/95) [791.43]

WINFREY, OPRAH

4067 Patterson, Lillie, and Cornelia H. Wright. *Oprah Winfrey, Talk Show Host and Actress* (9–adult). (Contemporary Women) 1990, Enslow LB $17.95 (0-89490-289-X). Description of the talk show hostess from childhood through her career in radio, television, and movies. (Rev: BL 1/1/91; SLJ 12/90) [791.45]

4068 Saidman, Anne. *Oprah Winfrey: Media Success Story* (5–9). 1990, Lerner LB $8.95 (0-8225-0538-X). The story of the star's life set in a fast-paced, easy-to-read format. Illustrated. (Rev: BL 1/1/91; SLJ 3/91) [791.45]

WRIGHT, FRANK LLOYD

4069 Boulton, Alexander O. *Frank Lloyd Wright, Architect: An Illustrated Biography* (8–12). 1993, Rizzoli $24.95 (0-8478-1683-4). Looks at both Wright's architecture and his private life in detail. Photos and other illustrations. (Rev: BL 12/15/93; MJHS; SLJ 11/93) [720]

4070 Rubin, Susan Goldman. *Frank Lloyd Wright* (9–adult). (First Impressions) 1994, Abrams $19.95 (0-8109-3974-6). A handsomely illustrated look at the architect's life and work. (Rev: BL 1/1/95; SHS; SLJ 1/95) [720]

Government and Other American Public Figures

Collective

4071 Beeman, Marsha Lynn. *Who Am I? Clue-by-Clue Biographical Sketches of American Historical Figures* (9–adult). 1993, McFarland paper $19.95 (0-89950-899-5). (Rev: BL 8/93; VOYA 12/93) [920]

4072 Blue, Rose, and Corinne Naden. *The White House Kids* (5–7). 1995, Millbrook LB $17.90 (1-56294-447-9). Looks at the lives of the children who have lived in the limelight of the White House, from John Adams's granddaughter to Chelsea Clinton. (Rev: BL 6/1–15/95; SLJ 8/95) [973]

4073 Davidson, Sue. *A Heart in Politics: Jeanette Rankin and Patsy T. Mink* (7–10). 1994, Seal Press paper $8.95 (1-878067-53-2). (Rev: BL 12/15/94; BTA) [328.73]

4074 Haskins, Jim. *One More River to Cross: The Stories of Twelve Black Americans* (5–8). 1992, Scholastic $13.95 (0-590-42896-9). Biographies of 12 African Americans who defied the odds to rise to the top of their fields. Awards: YALSA Best Book for Young Adults. (Rev: BL 2/1/92; MJHS; SLJ 4/92) [920]

4075 Katz, Jane, ed. *Messengers of the Wind: Native American Women Tell Their Life Stories* (9–adult). 1995, Ballantine $23 (0-345-39060-1). Native American women speak about wide-ranging topics, covering everything from political activism and childhood memories to feelings about the environment and religion. (Rev: BL 3/1/95; SHS) [970.004]

4076 Morin, Isobel V. *Women Chosen for Public Office* (5–7). 1995, Oliver Press (5707 W. 36th St., Minneapolis, MN 55416) $14.95 (1-881508-20-X). Profiles of 9 women involved in the federal government since Civil War times. (Rev: BL 5/1/95; SLJ 6/95) [920.72]

4077 Morin, Isobel V. *Women of the U.S. Congress* (6–10). 1994, Oliver Press (5707 W. 36th St., Minneapolis, MN 55416) $14.95 (1-881508-12-9). Lists all the women who have served in Congress and provides political biographies of 7 of them, citing their accomplishments and their different backgrounds and views. (Rev: BL 7/94; SLJ 5/94; VOYA 6/94) [328.73]

4078 Morin, Isobel V. *Women Who Reformed Politics* (7–12). 1994, Oliver Press (5707 W. 36th St., Minneapolis, MN 55416) $14.95 (1-881508-16-1). Describes the political activism of 8 American women, including Abby Foster's abolition fight, Carrie Catt's sufferage battle, and Gloria Steinem's feminist crusade. (Rev: BL 10/15/94; SLJ 11/94; VOYA 2/95) [303.48]

4079 Oleksy, Walter. *Military Leaders of World War II* (7–10). 1994, Facts on File $16.95 (0-8160-3008-1). (Rev: BL 1/1/95; BTA; SLJ 3/95; VOYA 5/95) [940.54]

4080 Perry, Troy D., and Thomas L.P. Swicegood. *Profiles in Gay and Lesbian Courage* (9–adult). 1991, St. Martin's $19.95 (0-312-06360-1). Biographies of 8 frontline gays in the battle against bigotry among politicians, the police and military, and religious organizations. (Rev: BL 10/1/91) [324]

4081 Phillips, Louis. *Ask Me Anything about the Presidents* (5–8). Illus. 1992, Avon/Camelot paper $2.99 (0-380-76426-1). A collection of curious facts and stories about U.S. presidents, presented in question-and-answer form. (Rev: BL 4/15/92) [920]

4082 Potter, Joan, and Constance Claytor. *African-American Firsts* (9–adult). 1994, Pinto Press (R.R. 1, P.O. Box 78, Elizabethtown, NY 12932) paper $14.95 (0-9632476-1-1). Celebrates African American contributions to history and culture from business and government to theater and the visual arts. (Rev: BL 1/15/94; BTA; MJHS; SLJ 8/94) [973]

4083 Ragaza, Angelo. *Lives of Notable Asian Americans: Business, Politics, Science* (6–10). (Asian American Experience) 1995, Chelsea House $18.95 (0-7910-2189-0). (Rev: BL 8/95) [920]

4084 Sandler, Martin W. *Presidents* (5–8). (Library of Congress) 1995, HarperCollins LB $20.89 (0-06-024535-2). Unusual tidbits about the presidents and their families. (Rev: BL 3/1/95; SLJ 4/95) [973]

4085 Sherrow, Victoria. *Political Leaders and Peacemakers* (7–12). (American Indian Lives) 1994, Facts on File $17.95 (0-8160-2943-1). Profiles 13 Native Americans who used political and diplomatic skills to protect their people from relocation and annihilation. (Rev: BL 11/1/94; SLJ 1/95) [970.004]

4086 Smith, Carter, ed. *The Founding Presidents: A Sourcebook on the U.S. Presidency* (5–8). (American Albums) 1993, Millbrook LB $18.90 (1-56294-357-X). (Rev: BL 12/1/93; MJHS) [973]

4087 Smith, Carter, ed. *Presidents in a Time of Change: A Sourcebook on the U.S. Presidency* (5–8). (American Albums) 1993, Millbrook LB $18.90 (1-56294-362-6). (Rev: BL 12/1/93; MJHS) [973.92]

4088 Smith, Carter, ed. *Presidents of a Divided Nation: A Sourcebook on the U.S. Presidency* (5–8). (American Albums) 1993, Millbrook LB $18.90 (1-56294-360-X). (Rev: BL 12/1/93; MJHS) [973.8]

4089 Smith, Carter, ed. *Presidents of a Growing Country: A Sourcebook on the U.S. Presidency* (5–8). (American Albums) 1993, Millbrook LB $18.90 (1-56294-358-8). (Rev: BL 12/1/93; MJHS) [973.8]

4090 Smith, Carter, ed. *Presidents of a World Power: A Sourcebook on the U.S. Presidency* (5–8). (American Albums) 1993, Millbrook LB $18.90 (1-56294-361-8). (Rev: BL 12/1/93; MJHS) [973.91]

4091 Smith, Carter, ed. *Presidents of a Young Republic: A Sourcebook on the U.S. Presidency* (5–8). (American Albums) 1993, Millbrook LB $18.90 (1-56294-359-6). (Rev: BL 12/1/93; MJHS) [973.5]

4092 Taylor, Kimberly Hayes. *Black Civil Rights Champions* (6–8). (Profiles) 1995, Oliver LB $14.95 (1-881508-22-6). Introduction to the history of the civil rights movement, covering the life, education, and accomplishments of 7 African American leaders and the social movements they spearheaded. (Rev: BL 1/1/96; SLJ 3/96)

4093 Truman, Margaret. *First Ladies* (9–adult). 1995, Random $25 (0-679-43439-9). A chatty, anecdotal history of 29 of the first ladies by a former resident of the White House. (Rev: BL 9/1/95; SLJ 3/96; VOYA 4/96) [973]

4094 Whitelaw, Nancy. *They Wrote Their Own Headlines: American Women Journalists* (6–10). 1994, Morgan Reynolds $17.95 (1-883846-06-4). Biographies of 7 women journalists—such as advice columnist Ann Landers and war correspondent Marguerite Higgins—examining the drive that brought success in a male-dominated field. (Rev: BL 7/94; SLJ 6/94; VOYA 8/94) [070]

Civil Rights Leaders

ABERNATHY, RALPH DAVID

4095 Reef, Catherine. *Ralph David Abernathy* (6–10). (People in Focus) 1995, Silver Burdett LB $13.95 (0-87518-653-X); paper $7.95 (0-382-24965-8). A just-the-facts approach relating the events of the civil rights worker's life. (Rev: BL 8/95) [323]

BROWN, JOHN

4096 Everett, Gwen. *John Brown: One Man Against Slavery* (5–9). Illus. 1993, Rizzoli $15.95 (0-8478-1702-4). The raid on Harper's Ferry is described from the viewpoint of abolitionist John Brown's daughter at 16. Awards: SLJ Best Book. (Rev: BL 6/1–15/93*; MJHS; SLJS 1/94*) [973.7]

DOUGLASS, FREDERICK

4097 Douglass, Frederick. *Escape from Slavery: The Boyhood of Frederick Douglass in His Own Words* (5–10). Illus. 1994, Knopf $15 (0-679-84652-2); paper $5.99 (0-679-84651-4). This shortened version of the famous abolitionist's 1845 autobiography dramatizes the abomination of slavery and the struggle of a man to break free. Awards: BL Editors' Choice. (Rev: BL 2/15/94*; MJHS; SLJ 2/94) [973.8]

4098 Meltzer, Milton, ed. *Frederick Douglass: In His Own Words* (8–12). Illus. 1995, Harcourt $22.95 (0-15-229492-9). An introduction to the articles and speeches of the great nineteenth-century abolitionist leader, which are arranged chronologically. (Rev: BL 12/15/94; SLJ 2/95) [305.8]

EDELMAN, MARIAN WRIGHT

4099 Otfinoski, Steven. *Marian Wright Edelman: Defender of Children's Rights* (5–7). (Library of Famous Women) 1992, Rosen $14.95 (0-8239-1206-X). Portrait of a strong political activist for children's rights in the United States, focusing on her work after 1960. (Rev: BL 1/15/92; MJHS) [973]

4100 Siegel, Beatrice. *Marian Wright Edelman: The Making of a Crusader* (6–9). 1995, Simon & Schuster $15 (0-02-782629-5). This biography of children's advocate and civil rights activist Edelman portrays her segregated childhood, activist teenage years, and current passion for children's issues. (Rev: BL 6/1–15/95; VOYA 12/95) [362.7]

FARMER, JAMES

4101 Skylansky, Jeff. *James Farmer* (7–10). (Black Americans of Achievement) 1991, Chelsea House $17.95 (0-7910-1126-7). (Rev: BL 3/1/92) [323]

HAMER, FANNIE LOU

4102 Mills, Kay. *This Little Light of Mine: The Life of Fannie Lou Hamer* (9–adult). 1993, Dutton $23 (0-525-93501-0). Profiles the 1960s endeavors of dedicated civil rights activist Hamer. Awards: Christopher. (Rev: BL 12/1/92*; SLJ 10/93) [973.049]

JACKSON, JESSE

4103 Haskins, James. *I Am Somebody! A Biography of Jesse Jackson* (6–9). 1992, Enslow LB $17.95 (0-89490-240-7). Presents both the public and private Jackson as a man with flaws but a charismatic leader in spite of them. (Rev: BL 7/92; MJHS; SHS; SLJ 8/92) [973.927]

KELLEY, ABBY

4104 Sterling, Dorothy. *Ahead of Her Time: Abby Kelley and the Politics of Antislavery* (9–adult). 1991, Norton $22.95 (0-393-03026-1). The biography of a nineteenth-century activist who dedicated her life to abolitionism by lecturing, organizing, and fund-raising for human rights. (Rev: BL 11/1/91*) [323]

KING, CORETTA SCOTT

4105 Henry, Sondra, and Emily Taitz. *Coretta Scott King: Keeper of the Dream* (6–9). (Contemporary Women) 1992, Enslow LB $17.95 (0-89490-334-9). Begins with Coretta Scott King's formative years in Alabama and continues through her present-day activities. (Rev: BL 8/92; MJHS) [323]

4106 King, Coretta Scott. *My Life with Martin Luther King, Jr.* (9–12). Rev. ed. 1993, Holt $16.95 (0-8050-2445-X). A revised, shortened edition of King's memoir of her life with Martin Luther King, Jr., with black-and-white photos. (Rev: BL 2/15/93; BTA; MJHS; SHS; SLJ 2/93) [323]

4107 Patrick, Diane. *Coretta Scott King* (7–9). 1991, Watts LB $13.90 (0-531-13005-3). A biographical account of Martin Luther King, Jr.'s wife, demonstrating her support of the civil rights cause and her dignity in the face of tragedy. (Rev: BL 11/1/91; SHS; SLJ 2/92) [323]

KING, MARTIN LUTHER, JR.

4108 Haskins, Jim. *I Have a Dream: The Life and Words of Martin Luther King, Jr.* (6–12). 1993, Millbrook LB $19.90 (1-56294-087-2). Contains information on King's family and schooling and the impact of the civil rights movement and beliefs that he espoused. Awards: SLJ Best Book. (Rev: BL 2/15/93; SLJ 6/93*) [323]

4109 King, Martin Luther, Jr. *The Papers of Martin Luther King, Jr., Vol. 1: Called to Serve, January 1929–June 1951* (9–adult). Edited by Clayborne Carson and Ralph E. Luker. 1992, Univ. of California $35 (0-520-07950-7). The complete texts of King's letters, speeches, sermons, student essays, and other papers, arranged chronologically. The first of 14 volumes. (Rev: BL 2/1/92) [323]

4110 Schulke, Flip. *He Had a Dream: Martin Luther King, Jr., and the Civil Rights Movement* (9–adult). 1995, Norton $39.95 (0-393-03729-0); paper $19.95 (0-393-31264-X). A photo-essay documenting the life of Dr. Martin Luther King, Jr. (Rev: BL 3/1/95) [323]

LA FLESCHE, SUSETTE

4111 Brown, Marion Marsh. *Susette La Flesche: Advocate for Native American Rights* (5–7). (People of Distinction) 1992, Children's Press LB $12.95 (0-516-03277-1). Describes the accomplishments of Omaha Indian lecturer, writer, and activist La Flesche, who rose to prominence during the trial of the Ponca chief Standing Bear. (Rev: BL 7/92; SLJ 8/92) [973]

MALCOLM X

4112 Brown, Kevin. *Malcolm X: His Life and Legacy* (7–12). 1995, Millbrook LB $19.90 (1-56294-500-9). This biography of Malcolm X covers his politics, the Nation of Islam's history, the 1960s struggle for civil rights, and Malcolm's status as a 1990s hero. (Rev: BL 6/1–15/95; SHS; SLJ 6/95; VOYA 12/95) [320.5]

4113 Collins, David R. *Malcolm X: Black Rage* (5–9). 1992, Dillon LB $12.95 (0-87518-498-7). A short biography of the influential African American activist tracing the early events that led to his belief that whites were the enemy. (Rev: BL 10/15/92; SLJ 1/93) [320.5]

4114 Evanzz, Karl. *The Judas Factor: The Plot to Kill Malcolm X* (9–adult). 1992, Thunder's Mouth $21.95 (1-56025-049-6). A detailed chronology of events following Malcolm's religious conversion to the Nation of Islam and a discussion of the evidence of a U.S. intelligence conspiracy against him. (Rev: BL 11/1/92) [364.1]

4115 Gallen, David. *Malcolm X: As They Knew Him* (9–adult). 1992, Carroll & Graf $21.95 (0-88184-851-4); paper $11.95 (0-88184-850-6). Interviews with and about Malcolm X, essays that analyze his political role, and personal memories of a wide range of people—from Angelou and Haley to Baldwin. (Rev: BL 5/15/92; SHS) [320.5]

4116 Myers, Walter Dean. *Malcolm X: By Any Means Necessary* (6–12). 1993, Scholastic $13.95 (0-590-46484-1). Pays eloquent tribute to the brilliant, radical African American leader, quoting extensively from *Autobiography of Malcolm X*. Awards: YALSA Best Book for Young Adults. (Rev: BL 11/15/92; BTA; MJHS; SHS; SLJ 2/93; YR) [297.87]

4117 Perry, Bruce. *Malcolm: A Life of the Man Who Changed Black America* (9–adult). 1991, Station Hill $24.95 (0-88268-103-6). This biography shows various sides of the African American leader. (Rev: BL 6/15/91; SHS; SLJ 3/92) [297]

4118 Stine, Megan. *The Story of Malcom X, Civil Rights Leader* (5–7). 1994, Dell/Yearling paper $3.50 (0-440-40900-4). This biography of the African American activist quotes extensively from Malcolm's autobiography. (Rev: BL 2/15/94; SLJ 8/94) [320.5]

4119 Wood, Joe, ed. *Malcolm X: In Our Own Image* (9–adult). 1992, St. Martin's $18.95 (0-312-06609-0). Leading African American intellectuals provide in-depth analyses of Malcolm X and his legacy from black, gay, and feminist perspectives. (Rev: BL 11/1/92; SHS) [320.5]

MARSHALL, THURGOOD

4120 Davis, Michael D., and Hunter R. Clark. *Thurgood Marshall: Warrior at the Bar, Rebel on the Bench* (9–adult). 1992, Birch Lane $24.95 (1-55972-133-2). Reviews the career of the first African American Supreme Court justice, who spearheaded great legal victories for desegregation and civil rights. (Rev: BL 11/1/92; SHS) [347.73]

4121 Haskins, James. *Thurgood Marshall: A Life for Justice* (6–9). 1992, Holt $14.95 (0-8050-2095-0). Readable, inspiring biography of the first African American Supreme Court justice, who devoted his life to fighting segregation and racism through the legal system. (Rev: BL 7/92*; MJHS; SLJ 8/92) [347.73]

4122 Rowan, Carl T. *Dream Makers, Dream Breakers: The World of Justice Thurgood Marshall* (9–adult). 1993, Little, Brown $24.95 (0-316-75978-3). Long, readable account of the life and times of Justice Thurgood Marshall. (Rev: BL 1/1/93*; SHS) [323]

4123 Whitelaw, Nancy. *Mr. Civil Rights: The Story of Thurgood Marshall* (7–12). (Notable Americans) 1995, Morgan Reynolds $17.95 (1-883846-10-2). This volume demonstrates Marshall's deep involvement with the civil rights movement. (Rev: BL 9/1/95) [347.73]

PARKS, ROSA

4124 Parks, Rosa, and Jim Haskins. *Rosa Parks: My Story* (6–10). 1992, Dial LB $16 (0-8037-0675-8). This autobiography of the civil rights hero becomes an oral history of the movement, including her recollections of Martin Luther King, Jr., Roy Wilkins, and others. (Rev: BL 12/15/91) [976.1]

4125 Siegel, Beatrice. *The Year They Walked: Rosa Parks and the Montgomery Bus Boycott* (6–8). 1992, Four Winds $13.95 (0-02-782631-7). The story behind a famous bus boycott and the committed work of African Americans and whites who made it a success. (Rev: BL 2/15/92; SLJ 8/92) [323]

POWELL, ADAM CLAYTON, JR.

4126 Hamilton, Charles V. *Adam Clayton Powell, Jr. The Political Biography of an American Dilemma* (9–adult). 1991, Atheneum $24.95 (0-689-12062-1). Tracks the complex series of events that led to an early civil rights leader's public disgrace and expulsion from Congress. (Rev: BL 8/91) [973.92092]

STANTON, ELIZABETH CADY

4127 Cullen-Dupont, Kathryn. *Elizabeth Cady Stanton and Women's Liberty* (6–10). 1992, Facts on File LB $16.95 (0-8160-2413-8). Presents a humanistic picture of one of the original women's rights movement leaders and provides an intimate portrait of Stanton as wife, mother, and activist. (Rev: BL 10/1/92; BTA; MJHS; SHS; SLJ 7/92) [305.42]

4128 Fritz, Jean. *You Want Women to Vote, Lizzie Stanton?* (5–7). 1995, Putnam $15.95 (0-399-22786-5). A historical biography of the spirited leader and her fight for women's suffrage. Fritz re-creates the essence of Stanton's personality and her friendship with Susan B. Anthony. Awards: ALSC Notable Children's Book. (Rev: BL 8/95*; SLJ 9/95) [324.6]

STEINEM, GLORIA

4129 Heilbrun, Carolyn G. *The Education of a Woman: The Life of Gloria Steinem* (9–adult). 1995, Dial $23.95 (0-385-31371-3). A biography of Gloria Steinem, with insights into the history and development of contemporary feminism. (Rev: BL 9/15/95*) [305.42]

4130 Hoff, Mark. *Gloria Steinem: The Women's Movement* (6–12). (New Directions) 1991, Millbrook $14.90 (1-878841-19-X). Biography of the famous feminist. (Rev: BL 2/1/91; MJHS) [305.42]

TRUTH, SOJOURNER

4131 McKissack, Patricia, and Fredrick McKissack. *Sojourner Truth: Ain't I a Woman?* (5–8). 1992, Scholastic $13.95 (0-590-44690-8). Drawing on the 1850 autobiography *Narrative of Sojourner Truth: A Northern Slave*, the authors integrate her personal story with a history of slavery, resistance, and abolitionism. (Rev: BL 11/15/92; BTA; MJHS; SLJ 2/93) [305.5]

TUBMAN, HARRIET

4132 Bentley, Judith. *Harriet Tubman* (8–12). 1990, Watts LB $13.90 (0-531-10948-8). (Rev: BL 2/15/91; SHS; SLJ 11/90) [305.5]

4133 Taylor, M. W. *Harriet Tubman* (6–8). 1990, Chelsea House $17.95. (Rev: BL 2/15/91; MJHS) [305.5]

WASHINGTON, BOOKER T.

4134 Schroeder, Alan. *Booker T. Washington* (7–10). (Black Americans of Achievement) 1992, Chelsea House LB $17.95 (1-55546-616-8). (Rev: BL 9/15/92; MJHS) [378.1]

WELLS-BARNETT, IDA B.

4135 Van Steenwyk, Elizabeth. *Ida B. Wells-Barnett: Woman of Courage* (7–12). 1992, Watts LB $13.90 (0-531-13014-2). Activist Wells-Barnett's fight for equal rights for African Americans over 40 years. (Rev: BL 4/1/92; SHS) [323]

Presidents and Their Families

ADAMS, ABIGAIL

4136 Beller, Susan Provost. *Woman of Independence: The Life of Abigail Adams* (6–10). 1992, Betterway/Shoe Tree paper $5.95 (1-55870-237-7). A history of this wife, mother, teacher, famer, patriot, historian, first lady, and first mother. (Rev: BL 5/15/92; SLJ 9/92) [973.4]

4137 Bober, Natalie S. *Abigail Adams: Witness to a Revolution* (6–12). 1995, Atheneum $16 (0-689-31760-3). A portrait of a woman and the age she lived in. Awards: Boston Globe/Horn Book; Golden Kite; SLJ Best Book. (Rev: BL 4/15/95*; SLJ 6/95) [973]

ADAMS, JOHN AND ABIGAIL

4138 Sandak, Cass R. *The John Adamses* (5–7). (First Families) 1992, Macmillan/Crestwood LB $12.95 (0-89686-640-8). (Rev: BL 12/15/92) [973.4]

BUSH, GEORGE

4139 Pemberton, William E. *George Bush* (6–12). (World Leaders) 1993, Rourke (P.O. Box 3328, Vero Beach, FL 32964) $19.93 (0-86625-478-1). (Rev: BL 12/1/93) [973.928]

BUSH, GEORGE AND BARBARA

4140 Sandak, Cass R. *The Bushes* (5–7). (First Families) 1991, Macmillan/Crestwood $11.95 (0-89686-632-7). Focuses on the former president and his family at home. Includes many informal family photos. (Rev: BL 1/15/92) [973.928]

CARTER, JIMMY AND ROSALYNN

4141 Sandak, Cass R. *The Carters* (5–7). (First Families) 1993, Macmillan/Crestwood LB $12.95 (0-89686-652-1). (Rev: BL 11/15/93) [973.926]

CLINTON, BILL

4142 Cole, Michael D. *Bill Clinton: United States President* (6–9). 1994, Enslow LB $17.95 (0-89490-437-X). Surveys Clinton's life and accomplishments prior to his presidential election, emphasizing his tenure as governor of Arkansas. (Rev: BL 7/94; MJHS; SLJ 7/94) [973.929]

4143 Cwiklik, Robert. *Bill Clinton: Our 42nd President* (5–8). 1993, Millbrook $12.40 (1-56294-387-1). (Rev: BL 9/1/93; MJHS) [973.929]

4144 Gallen, David. *Bill Clinton: As They Know Him: An Oral Biography* (9–adult). 1994, Richard Gallen (260 Fifth Ave., New York, NY 10001) $19.95 (0-9636477-2-5). Interviews with people who have known the president provide anecdotes and observations about his childhood, governorship, and candidacy. (Rev: BL 3/15/94) [973.929]

4145 Maraniss, David. *First in His Class: The Biography of Bill Clinton* (9–adult). 1995, Simon & Schuster $25 (0-671-87109-9). (Rev: BL 1/15/95; SHS) [973.929]

4146 Martin, Gene L., and Aaron Boyd. *Bill Clinton: President from Arkansas* (5–8). 1993, Tudor (P.O. Box 38366, Greensboro, NC 27438) $17.95 (0-936389-31-1). (Rev: BL 9/1/93; SLJ 6/93) [973.929]

CLINTON, HILLARY RODHAM

4147 Boyd, Aaron. *First Lady: The Story of Hillary Rodham Clinton* (5–8). 1994, Morgan Reynolds $17.95 (1-883846-02-1). A companion of sorts to *Bill Clinton: President from Arkansas*. Focuses on the first lady's accomplishments and her role in her husband's administration. (Rev: BL 4/15/94; SLJ 3/94; VOYA 12/94) [973.929]

4148 Guernsey, JoAnn Bren. *Hillary Rodham Clinton: A New Kind of First Lady* (5–7). 1993, Lerner LB $17.50 (0-8225-2875-4). Centers on how Clinton has challenged the country's expectations of the first lady and the changes she's made to tone herself down or perk herself up, accordingly. (Rev: BL 11/1/93; MJHS; SLJ 12/93) [973.929]

4149 Radcliffe, Donnie. *Hillary Rodham Clinton: A First Lady for Our Time* (9–adult). 1993, Warner $17.95 (0-446-51766-6). (Rev: BL 9/1/93; SLJ 5/94) [973.929]

EISENHOWER, DWIGHT AND "MAMIE"

4150 Sandak, Cass R. *The Eisenhowers* (5–7). 1993, Macmillan/Crestwood LB $12.95 (0-89686-653-X). (Rev: BL 11/15/93) [973.921]

FORD, GERALD

4151 Cannon, James. *Time and Chance: Gerald Ford's Appointment with History* (9–adult). 1994, HarperCollins $25 (0-06-016539-1). Chronicles Ford's rise with Nixon's decline, the Watergate scandal, and the controversial decision to grant Nixon a pardon. (Rev: BL 2/1/94) [973.924]

GRANT, ULYSSES S.

4152 Marrin, Albert. *Unconditional Surrender: U. S. Grant and the Civil War* (6–12). 1994, Atheneum $19.95 (0-689-31837-5). Part history, part biography, this is a fine study of Grant and his pivotal role in the Civil War. Awards: BL Editors' Choice; SLJ Best Book; YALSA Best Book for Young Adults. (Rev: BL 4/1/94*; BTA; MJHS; SLJ 7/94*; VOYA 6/94) [973.7]

JACKSON, ANDREW

4153 Meltzer, Milton. *Andrew Jackson and His America* (8–12). 1993, Watts $16.40 (0-531-11157-1). Presents a multifaceted picture of Jackson and his role in such historic events as the Indian removal and the abolitionist movement. (Rev: BL 1/15/94*; BTA; MJHS; SLJ 1/94) [973.5]

JACKSON, ANDREW AND RACHEL

4154 Sandak, Cass R. *The Jacksons* (5–7). (First Families) 1992, Macmillan/Crestwood LB $11.95 (0-89686-636-X). (Rev: BL 9/15/92) [973.5]

JEFFERSON, THOMAS

4155 Meltzer, Milton. *Thomas Jefferson: The Revolutionary Aristocrat* (6–10). 1991, Watts LB $15.90 (0-531-11069-9). A presentation of the major events of Jefferson's life and a discussion of some troubling inconsistencies, such as his ownership of slaves. Awards: SLJ Best Book. (Rev: BL 12/15/91*; MJHS; SHS; SLJ 12/91*) [973.4]

4156 Morris, Jeffrey. *The Jefferson Way* (5–8). (Great Presidential Decisions). 1994, Lerner LB $17.21 (0-8225-2926-2). Provides basic background information, but focuses on Jefferson's term as president. (Rev: BL 12/15/94; SLJ 12/94) [973.4]

JEFFERSON, THOMAS AND MARTHA

4157 Sandak, Cass R. *The Jeffersons* (5–7). (First Families) 1992, Macmillan/Crestwood LB $11.95 (0-89686-637-8). (Rev: BL 9/15/92) [973.4]

JOHNSON, LYNDON

4158 Eskow, Dennis. *Lyndon Baines Johnson* (8–12). (Impact Biographies). 1993, Watts $13.90 (0-531-13019-3). Well chosen episodes and anecdotes illustrate the life of this Texas-born president. (Rev: BL 9/1/93; VOYA 10/93) [973.923]

JOHNSON, LYNDON AND "LADY BIRD"

4159 Sandak, Cass R. *The Lyndon Johnsons* (5–7). 1993, Macmillan/Crestwood LB $12.95 (0-89686-644-0). (Rev: BL 9/1/93) [973.923]

KENNEDY, JOHN F.

4160 Anderson, Catherine Corley. *John F. Kennedy: Young People's President* (5–7). 1991, Lerner LB $14.95 (0-8225-4904-2). Provides solid background information about the well-known president, with an emphasis on his commitment to social reform. (Rev: BL 8/91; SLJ 8/91) [973.922]

4161 Harrison, Barbara, and Daniel Terris. *A Twilight Struggle: The Life of John Fitzgerald Kennedy* (6–10). 1992, Lothrop $18 (0-688-08830-9). A well documented, perceptive, and beautifully designed biography of JFK. Awards: ALSC Notable Children's Book; BL Editors' Choice. (Rev: BL 7/92*; MJHS; YR) [973.922]

4162 Lowe, Jacques. *JFK Remembered* (9–adult). 1993, Random $37.50 (0-679-42399-0). The photos Lowe took as Kennedy's personal photographer are now presented as full-page black-and-white spreads with identifying text. (Rev: BL 12/1/93) [973.922]

KENNEDY, JOHN F., FAMILY

4163 Sandak, Cass R. *The Kennedys* (5–7). (First Families) 1991, Macmillan/Crestwood $11.95 (0-89686-633-5). A nostalgic look at the president and his family at home. Many family photos included. (Rev: BL 1/15/92) [973.922]

LINCOLN, ABRAHAM

4164 Donald, David Herbert. *Lincoln* (9–adult). 1995, Simon & Schuster $35 (0-684-80846-3). A psychological portrait of the man from humble roots who slowly but determinedly found his niche as an attorney, then as a politician, and finally as president. (Rev: BL 8/95*) [973.7]

4165 Kunhardt, Philip B., and others. *Lincoln* (9–adult). 1992, Knopf $50 (0-679-40862-2). With many rare photos, this illustrated biography of Lincoln deserves a spot in high school collections. (Rev: BL 9/1/92; BTA; SHS; SLJ 7/93; VOYA 8/93) [973.7]

LINCOLN, ABRAHAM AND MARY TODD

4166 Sandak, Cass R. *The Lincolns* (5–7). (First Families) 1992, Macmillan/Crestwood LB $12.95 (0-89686-641-6). (Rev: BL 12/15/92) [973.7]

LINCOLN, MARY TODD

4167 Collins, David R. *Shattered Dreams: The Story of Mary Todd Lincoln* (7–10). 1994, Morgan Reynolds $17.95 (1-883846-07-2). A biography of President Lincoln's troubled widow, showing her to be a bright, ambitious woman plagued by tragedy and ultimately put on trial for insanity. (Rev: BL 8/94; SLJ 9/94; VOYA 12/94) [973.7]

MADISON, JAMES AND "DOLLEY"

4168 Sandak, Cass R. *The Madisons* (5–7). (First Families). 1992, Macmillan/Crestwood LB $12.95 (0-89686-642-4). (Rev: BL 12/15/92) [973.5]

MONROE, JAMES AND ELIZABETH

4169 Sandak, Cass R. *The Monroes* (5–7). (First Families) 1993, Macmillan/Crestwood LB $12.95 (0-89686-645-9). (Rev: BL 9/1/93) [973.5]

NIXON, RICHARD

4170 Aitken, Jonathan. *Nixon* (9–adult). 1994, Regnery Gateway $28 (0-89526-489-7). The author is a British politician and a sympathetic advocate of Nixon. (Rev: BL 4/15/94; SHS) [973.924]

4171 Ambrose, Stephen E. *Nixon, Vol. 3: Ruin and Recovery, 1973–1990* (9–adult). 1991, Simon & Schuster $27.50 (0-671-69188-0). The third and concluding volume in a series focuses on the events following the Watergate break-in and offers a balanced appraisal of the "new" Nixon in the years after his resignation. (Rev: BL 9/15/91*; SHS) [973]

4172 Larsen, Rebecca. *Richard Nixon: Rise and Fall of a President* (6–9). 1991, Watts LB $14.90 (0-531-10997-6). A balanced look at the life and career of the 37th president of the United States. (Rev: BL 8/91; MJHS; SLJ 8/91) [973.924]

4173 Nadel, Laurie. *The Great Stream of History: A Biography of Richard M. Nixon* (6–9). 1991, Atheneum $12.95 (0-689-31559-7). A former ABC news producer assesses the former president's life and career. (Rev: BL 8/91; SLJ 10/91) [973.924]

NIXON, RICHARD AND "PAT"

4174 Sandak, Cass R. *The Nixons* (5–7). (First Families). 1992, Macmillan/Crestwood LB $11.95 (0-89686-638-6). (Rev: BL 9/15/92) [973.924]

REAGAN, RONALD

4175 Sullivan, George. *Ronald Reagan* (5–8). Rev. ed. 1991, Messner $13.98 (0-671-74537-9). An updated version of the former president's life, including a new chapter on his 2nd term. (Rev: BL 1/15/92; MJHS; SHS) [973.927]

REAGAN, RONALD AND NANCY

4176 Sandak, Cass R. *The Reagans* (5–7). (First Families) 1993, Macmillan/Crestwood LB $12.95 (0-89686-646-7). (Rev: BL 9/1/93) [973.927]

ROOSEVELT FAMILIES

4177 Collier, Peter, and David Horowitz. *The Roosevelts: An American Saga* (9–adult). 1994, Simon & Schuster $27.50 (0-671-65225-7). True to Collier and Horowitz's style is this biography wherein the leading characters are psychoanalyzed and their secrets are revealed. (Rev: BL 4/15/94) [929.7]

ROOSEVELT, ELEANOR

4178 Freedman, Russell. *Eleanor Roosevelt: A Life of Discovery* (5–9). 1993, Clarion $17.95 (0-89919-862-7). This admiring photobiography captures Roosevelt's splendid public role and personal sadness. Awards: ALSC Notable Children's Book; BL Editors' Choice; Boston Globe/Horn Book; Golden Kite; Newbery Honor Book; SLJ Best Book; YALSA Best Book for Young Adults. (Rev: BL 7/93*; BTA; MJHS; SLJ 8/93*; VOYA 2/94) [973.9]

4179 Lazo, Caroline. *Eleanor Roosevelt* (5–7). (Peacemakers) 1993, Dillon $13.95 (0-87518-594-0). (Rev: BL 12/15/93) [973.917]

ROOSEVELT, FRANKLIN D.

4180 Larsen, Rebecca. *Franklin D. Roosevelt: Man of Destiny* (7–12). 1991, Watts LB $14.90 (0-531-15231-6). Discusses Roosevelt's shortcomings, the opinions of his critics, his controversial decisions, the triumphs of his presidency, and the crises overcome. (Rev: BL 11/1/91) [973.917]

ROOSEVELT, FRANKLIN AND ELEANOR

4181 Goodwin, Doris Kearns. *No Ordinary Time: Franklin and Eleanor Roosevelt: The Homefront in World War II* (9–adult). 1994, Simon & Schuster $30 (0-671-64240-5). Details the inner workings of the White House during World War II, profiling FDR's and Eleanor's eclectic assortment of guests and boarders. (Rev: BL 8/94*; SHS) [973.917]

4182 Sandak, Cass R. *The Franklin Roosevelts* (5–7). (First Families) 1992, Macmillan/Crestwood LB $11.95 (0-89686-639-4). (Rev: BL 9/15/92) [973.91]

ROOSEVELT, THEODORE

4183 Fritz, Jean. *Bully for You, Teddy Roosevelt!* (5–8). Illus. 1991, Putnam $15.95 (0-399-21769-X). Awards: SLJ Best Book. (Rev: BL 4/15/91; MJHS; SLJ 7/91*) [973.91]

4184 Meltzer, Milton. *Theodore Roosevelt and His America* (7–12). 1994, Watts LB $16.94 (0-531-11192-X). Conveys a sense of the complexities and contradictions in the president who led this country during the tumultuous first years of the century. (Rev: BL 2/1/95; SHS; VOYA 5/95) [973.91]

4185 Miller, Nathan. *Theodore Roosevelt* (9–adult). 1992, Morrow $27.50 (0-688-06784-0). A thorough account of the life of a man who overcame extremely poor health to become president. (Rev: BL 9/15/92) [973.91]

4186 Whitelaw, Nancy. *Theodore Roosevelt Takes Charge* (6–9). 1992, Albert Whitman $11.95 (0-8075-7849-5). A clear, credible biography of a larger-than-life American hero, full of contradictions. Awards: SLJ Best Book. (Rev: BL 6/1/92*; SLJ 7/92*) [973.91]

ROOSEVELT, THEODORE AND EDITH

4187 Sandak, Cass R. *The Theodore Roosevelts* (5–7). (First Families) 1991, Macmillan/Crestwood $11.95 (0-89686-634-3). (Rev: BL 1/15/92) [973.91]

TAFT, WILLIAM H. AND HELEN

4188 Sandak, Cass R. *The Tafts* (5–7). (First Families) 1993, Macmillan/Crestwood LB $12.95 (0-89686-647-5). (Rev: BL 9/1/93) [973.91]

TRUMAN, HARRY S

4189 Feinberg, Barbara Silberdick. *Harry S Truman* (7–12). 1994, Watts LB $14.40 (0-531-13036-3). Examines Truman's life and presidential administration, analyzing the events of his 2 terms and discussing his struggles and triumphs. (Rev: BL 9/1/94; BTA; SLJ 9/94) [973.918]

4190 Fleming, Thomas. *Harry S Truman, President* (6–12). 1993, Walker LB $15.85 (0-8027-8269-8). The author of this uncritical biography of the former president had access to family photos and documents. (Rev: BL 1/1/94; MJHS; SLJ 12/93; VOYA 2/94) [973.918]

4191 McCullough, David. *Truman* (9–adult). 1992, Simon & Schuster $30 (0-671-45654-7). A landmark biography of a great man and his times. (Rev: BL 4/15/92*; SHS) [973.918]

TRUMAN, HARRY S AND BESS

4192 Sandak, Cass R. *The Trumans* (5–7). (First Families) 1992, Macmillan/Crestwood LB $12.95 (0-89686-643-2). (Rev: BL 12/15/92) [973.918]

WASHINGTON, GEORGE

4193 Osborne, Mary Pope. *George Washington: Leader of a New Nation* (5–7). 1991, Dial LB $13.89 (0-8037-0949-8). Covers Washington's personal and public life in an easy-to-understand manner, drawing on his diaries, letters, and public statements. Awards: SLJ Best Book. (Rev: BL 8/91; SLJ 10/91*)

4194 Smith, Richard Norton. *Patriarch: George Washington and the New American Nation* (9–adult). 1993, Houghton $24.95 (0-395-52442-3). A detailed account of Washington's presidency, leavened with quotations and anecdotes. (Rev: BL 12/1/92) [973.4]

WASHINGTON, GEORGE AND MARTHA

4195 Sandak, Cass R. *The Washingtons* (5–7). (First Families) 1991, Macmillan/Crestwood $11.95 (0-89686-635-1). (Rev: BL 1/15/92) [973.4]

WILSON, EDITH

4196 Giblin, James Cross. *Edith Wilson: The Woman Who Ran the United States* (5–7). Illus. 1992, Viking $11 (0-670-83005-4). An overview of the life of President Wilson's wife, who some believe acted as president after he suffered a stroke. (Rev: BL 6/1/92; MJHS; SLJ 5/92) [793.91]

WILSON, WOODROW

4197 Randolph, Sallie G. *Woodrow Wilson, President* (5–9). (Presidential Biography) 1992, Walker LB $15.85 (0-8027-8144-6). Offers a concise overview of Wilson's tragic personal and political struggles, his achievements, and his place in history. (Rev: BL 12/15/91; SLJ 3/92) [973.91]

WILSON, WOODROW, FAMILY

4198 Sandak, Cass R. *The Wilsons* (5–7). (First Families) 1993, Macmillan/Crestwood LB $12.95 (0-89686-651-3). (Rev: BL 11/15/93) [973.91]

Other Government and Public Figures

BLACK HAWK

4199 Bonvillain, Nancy. *Black Hawk: Sac Rebel* (9–12). (North American Indians of Achievement) 1994, Chelsea House $18.95 (0-7910-1711-7). (Rev: BL 7/94) [973.5]

BOONE, DANIEL

4200 Faragher, John Mark. *Daniel Boone: The Life and Legend of an American Pioneer* (7–12). 1992, Holt $27.50 (0-8050-1603-1); paper $14.95 (0-8050-3007-7). A biography of the complex frontier pioneer-politician-maverick. Awards: SLJ Best Book. (Rev: BL 11/1/92*; SLJ 5/93*)

BRADLEY, BILL

4201 Bradley, Bill. *Time Present, Time Past* (9–adult). 1996, Knopf $25 (0-679-44488-2). An impressive job of writing his memoirs without boring the reader with his analysis of the larger issues. (Rev: BL 12/15/95*) [328.73]

4202 Jaspersohn, William. *Senator: A Profile of Bill Bradley in the U.S. Senate* (6–10). 1992, Harcourt $19.95 (0-15-272880-5). An in-depth photo-essay about Congress in general and Senator Bradley of New Jersey in particular, showing how his sports career led to the Senate. (Rev: BL 7/92; SLJ 10/92) [328.73]

CALHOUN, JOHN C.

4203 Celsi, Teresa. *John C. Calhoun and the Roots of War* (5–7). (History of the Civil War) 1991, Silver Burdett LB $18.98 (0-382-09936-2); paper $8.95 (0-382-24045-6). This is a biography of the influential South Carolinian, who articulated the Southern viewpoint to the nation during the pre–Civil War period. (Rev: BL 9/1/91) [973.5]

CHÁVEZ, CÉSAR

4204 Dolan, Terrance. *Julio César Chávez* (5–9). (Hispanics of Achievement) 1994, Chelsea House $18.95 (0-7910-2021-5). (Rev: BL 9/15/94) [796.8]

DAVIS, BENJAMIN, JR.

4205 Davis, Benjamin O., Jr. *Benjamin O. Davis, Jr., American: An Autobiography* (9–adult). 1991, Smithsonian $19.95 (0-87474-742-2). The first African American to graduate from West Point describes his experiences in the military and as a civilian. (Rev: BL 2/1/91; SHS; SLJ 7/91) [355]

4206 Reef, Catherine. *Benjamin Davis, Jr.* (5–8). (African American Soldiers) 1992, Twenty-First Century LB $14.95 (0-8050-2137-X). (Rev: BL 12/15/92) [358]

DOLE, ELIZABETH

4207 Mulford, Carolyn. *Elizabeth Dole: Public Servant* (6–9). (Contemporary Women) 1992, Enslow LB $18.95 (0-89490-331-4). (Rev: BL 4/1/92) [973.92]

DOOLITTLE, JAMES

4208 Doolittle, James H. *I Could Never Be So Lucky Again* (9–adult). 1991, Bantam $22.50 (0-553-07807-0). The lively recollections—written in his nineties—of the legendary aviator who commanded the first bombers to raid Japan, in 1942. (Rev: BL 9/15/91) [358.4]

EARP, WYATT

4209 Green, Carl R., and William R. Sanford. *Wyatt Earp* (5–8). (Outlaws and Lawmen of the Wild West) 1992, Enslow LB $14.95 (0-89490-367-5). An account of the life of this legendary lawman in which the violence of the times is realistically conveyed. (Rev: BL 10/1/92; MJHS) [978.02]

FARRAGUT, DAVID

4210 Foster, Leila Merrell. *David Glasgow Farragut: Courageous Navy Commander* (5–8). (People of Distinction) 1991, Children's Press LB $12.95 (0-516-03273-9). (Rev: BL 3/1/92) [940.54]

FEINSTEIN, DIANNE

4211 Roberts, Jerry. *Dianne Feinstein* (9–adult). 1994, HarperCollins $20 (0-06-258508-8). A biography of the prominent politician, chronicling her life and political career. (Rev: BL 9/1/94) [979.4]

GINSBURG, RUTH BADER

4212 Ayer, Eleanor H. *Ruth Bader Ginsburg: Fire and Steel on the Supreme Court* (5–8). 1995, Dillon LB $13.95 (0-87518-651-3); paper $7.95 (0-382-24721-3). A biography of the second woman to be named to the Supreme Court. (Rev: BL 5/15/95; SLJ 4/95; VOYA 5/95) [347.73]

GOODE, W. WILSON

4213 Goode, W. Wilson, and Joann Stevens. *In Goode Faith: Philadelphia's First Black Mayor Tells His Story* (9–adult). 1992, Judson $22.95 (0-8170-1186-2). Philadelphia's first African American mayor recounts his early life and candidly describes his turbulent political career. (Rev: BL 10/1/92) [974.8]

HOAGLAND, PETER

4214 Cwiklik, Robert. *House Rules: A Freshman Congressman's Initiation to the Backslapping, Backpedaling, and Backstabbing Ways of Washington* (9–adult). 1992, Villard $20 (0-394-58231-4). Revealing look at a Nebraska congressman's first year in Washington, D.C. (Rev: BL 2/15/92; SLJ 7/92) [328.73]

HOLLIDAY, DOC

4215 Green, Carl R., and William R. Sanford. *Doc Holliday* (5–8). (Outlaws and Lawmen of the Wild West) 1995, Enslow LB $14.95 (0-89490-589-9). (Rev: BL 6/1–15/95) [978]

HOLMES, OLIVER WENDELL

4216 White, G. Edward. *Justice Oliver Wendell Holmes: Law and the Inner Self* (9–adult). 1993, Oxford Univ. $35 (0-19-508182-X). Follows Holmes's life from childhood with his poet father to his service in the Civil War, unhappy marriage, and legal career. (Rev: BL 10/1/93) [347.73]

HOOVER, J. EDGAR

4217 Denenberg, Barry. *The True Story of J. Edgar Hoover and the FBI* (6–10). 1993, Scholastic $13.95 (0-590-43168-4). Focuses on the career, not the private life, of the feared FBI director, revealing his talents as well as his failings. (Rev: BL 4/15/93; MJHS; SLJ 6/93) [353.0074]

JORDAN, BARBARA

4218 Blue, Rose, and Corinne Naden. *Barbara Jordan* (7–10). (Black Americans of Achievement) 1992, Chelsea House LB $17.95 (0-7910-1131-3). (Rev: BL 9/15/92; MJHS) [328.73]

LEE, ROBERT E.

4219 Brown, Warren. *Robert E. Lee* (6–10). (World Leaders—Past and Present) 1991, Chelsea House $17.95 (1-55546-814-4). (Rev: BL 11/15/91) [973.7]

4220 Marrin, Albert. *Virginia's General: Robert E. Lee and the Civil War* (6–12). 1994, Atheneum $19.95 (0-689-31838-3). Details Lee's childhood, education, marriage, and career, and then concentrates on the Civil War years. Quotations from Lee, his generals, and his soldiers offer insight into the times. Awards: SLJ Best Book. (Rev: BL 12/15/94; SLJ 12/94; VOYA 4/95) [973.7]

4221 Thomas, Emory M. *Robert E. Lee* (9–adult). 1995, Norton $30 (0-393-03730-4). A large, well-researched biography of Civil War hero Robert E. Lee. (Rev: BL 4/1/95*) [973.7]

LONG, HUEY

4222 La Vert, Suzanne. *Huey Long: The Kingfish of Louisiana* (8–12). (Makers of America) 1995, Facts on File $16.95 (0-8160-2880-X). Looks at the motivations and political life of Huey Long, "Kingfish of Louisiana," including his assassination and the inner workings of the government. (Rev: BL 6/1–15/95) [976.3]

LONGSTREET, JAMES

4223 Wert, Jeffry D. *General James Longstreet: The Confederacy's Most Controversial Soldier* (9–adult). 1993, Simon & Schuster $27.50 (0-671-70921-6). Offers new information and a reinterpretation of General Longstreet, who fought in nearly every Civil War campaign of Lee's army. Also covers Longstreet's years in postwar politics. (Rev: BL 10/15/93) [973.7]

MANKILLER, WILMA

4224 Lazo, Caroline. *Wilma Mankiller* (5–7). (Peacemakers) 1995, Silver Burdett LB $13.95 (0-87518-635-1); paper $7.95 (0-382-24716-7). (Rev: BL 7/95) [973]

4225 Mankiller, Wilma, and Michael Wallis. *Mankiller: A Chief and Her People* (9–adult). 1993, St. Martin's $22.95 (0-312-09868-5). The story of the Cherokee Nation is told by Wilma Mankiller, who recounts her life and the racism she faced in her fight to lead it. (Rev: BL 10/1/93*) [973.04975]

4226 Schwarz, Melissa. *Wilma Mankiller: Principal Chief of the Cherokees* (9–12). (North American Indians of Achievement) 1994, Chelsea House $18.95 (0-7910-1715-X). (Rev: BL 10/15/94; MJHS) [973]

MARSHALL, GEORGE

4227 Saunders, Alan. *George C. Marshall* (8–12). (Makers of America) 1995, Facts on File $17.95 (0-8160-2666-1). Examines the life of the man who was an army general and secretary of state and defense. (Rev: BL 11/15/95; SLJ 2/96) [973.918]

MASTERSON, BAT

4228 Green, Carl R., and William R. Sanford. *Bat Masterson* (5–8). (Outlaws and Lawmen of the Wild West) 1992, Enslow LB $14.95 (0-89490-362-4). (Rev: BL 10/1/92) [978]

NORTH, OLIVER

4229 North, Oliver, and William Novak. *Under Fire: An American Story* (9–adult). 1991, HarperCollins/Zondervan $25 (0-06-018334-9). In this autobiography, many of the key players in the Iran-Contra affair are profiled, and it is revealed that Reagan knew about the events as they occurred. (Rev: BL 11/15/91) [921]

PARKMAN, FRANCIS

4230 Shuter, Jane, ed. *Francis Parkman and the Plains Indians* (5–8). (History Eyewitness) 1995, Raintree/Steck-Vaughn $22.80 (0-8114-8280-4). (Rev: BL 4/15/95) [978]

PERKINS, FRANCES

4231 Colman, Penny. *A Woman Unafraid: The Achievements of Frances Perkins* (6–10). 1993, Atheneum $14.95 (0-689-31853-7). Charts Perkins's career in social work that led to being New York's industrial commissioner and then U.S. secretary of labor, where she contributed to the creation of Social Security and unemployment insurance. (Rev: BL 10/1/93; MJHS; SLJ 11/93; VOYA 4/94) [973.917]

PEROT, ROSS

4232 Boyd, Aaron, and Michael Causey. *Ross Perot: Businessman Politician* (5–8). 1994, Morgan Reynolds $17.95 (1-883846-04-8). An account of Perot's rise from simple beginnings to wealth and his first presidential candidacy provide insight into his personality. (Rev: BL 3/15/94; SLJ 3/94) [973.928]

PHILIP, KING

4233 Roman, Joseph. *King Philip: Wampanoag Rebel* (9–12). (North American Indians of Achievement) 1991, Chelsea House $17.95 (0-7910-1704-4). (Rev: BL 3/1/92; MJHS) [973.2]

PINKERTON, ALLAN

4234 Green, Carl R., and William R. Sanford. *Allan Pinkerton* (5–8). (Outlaws and Lawmen of the Wild West) 1995, Enslow LB $14.95 (0-89490-590-2). (Rev: BL 11/15/95) [363.2]

4235 Wormser, Richard. *Pinkerton: America's First Private Eye* (5–9). 1990, Walker LB $18.85 (0-8027-6965-9). Biography of the founder of the detective agency best known for its pursuit of Butch Cassidy and Jesse James. (Rev: BL 1/1/91) [363.2]

POCAHONTAS

4236 Holler, Anne. *Pocahontas: Powhatan Peacemaker* (9–12). (North American Indians of Achievement) 1992, Chelsea House LB $18.95 (0-7910-1705-2). (Rev: BL 2/1/93; MJHS) [975]

POWELL, COLIN

4237 Brown, Warren. *Colin Powell* (7–10). (Black Americans of Achievement) 1992, Chelsea House LB $17.95 (0-7910-1647-1). (Rev: BL 8/92; MJHS) [355]

4238 Means, Howard. *Colin Powell: Soldier/Statesman—Statesman/Soldier* (9–adult). 1992, Donald I. Fine $23 (1-55611-335-8). Charts Powell's rapid climb through the ranks to co-commander of Desert Storm. (Rev: BL 9/15/92; SLJ 5/93) [355]

4239 Reef, Catherine. *Colin Powell* (5–8). (African American Soldiers) 1992, Twenty-First Century LB $14.95 (0-8050-2136-1). (Rev: BL 12/15/92) [355]

4240 Roth, David. *Sacred Honor: The Biography of Colin Powell* (9–adult). 1993, HarperCollins/Zondervan $18.99 (0-310-60480-X). An adulatory biography of Powell by his press secretary during the Gulf War. (Rev: BL 7/93) [355.0092]

RANDOLPH, A. PHILIP

4241 Patterson, Lillie. *A. Philip Randolph* (8–12). (Makers of America) 1995, Facts on File $17.95 (0-8160-2827-3). Recounts the life, accomplishments, and selfless devotion of the African American labor organizer/civil rights leader. (Rev: BL 11/15/95; SLJ 2/96) [323]

RENO, JANET

4242 Anderson, Paul. *Janet Reno: Doing the Right Thing* (9–adult). 1994, Wiley $22.95 (0-471-01858-9). This admiring biography by a Miami reporter relates Reno's unusual family history and tracks her through college and her years as Florida's state attorney, where she was a supporter of legal aid for the poor and an effective children's advocate. (Rev: BL 5/1/94; BTA; SHS; SLJ 11/94) [353.04]

SCHWARZKOPF, NORMAN

4243 Cohen, Roger, and Claudio Gatti. *In the Eye of the Storm: The Life of General H. Norman Schwarzkopf* (9–adult). 1991, Farrar $19.95 (0-374-17708-2). In this detailed biography of Schwarzkopf, the authors have used lengthy interviews to help tell the renowned Gulf War general's story. (Rev: BL 9/15/91; SHS) [355]

4244 Hughes, Libby. *Norman Schwarzkopf: Hero with a Heart* (6–10). (People in Focus) 1992, Dillon LB $13.95 (0-87518-521-5). (Rev: BL 1/15/93) [355]

SEWARD, WILLIAM HENRY

4245 Taylor, John M. *William Henry Seward* (9–adult). 1996, Brassey's paper $21.95 (1-57488-119-1). A biography of the antebellum lawyer, New York governor, and senator who was defeated by Lincoln at the 1860 Republican convention and became his secretary of state. (Rev: BL 9/1/91) [973.7]

SHERIDAN, PHILIP HENRY

4246 Morris, Roy. *Sheridan: The Life and Wars of General Phil Sheridan* (9–adult). 1992, Crown $25 (0-517-58070-5). A lively examination of the scrappy Union army general's career. (Rev: BL 4/15/92) [973.7]

TAYLOR, KRISTIN CLARK

4247 Taylor, Kristin Clark. *The First to Speak: A Woman of Color Inside the White House* (9–adult). 1993, Doubleday $22.50 (0-385-42510-4). A memoir about being a woman of color inside the Bush White House, where Taylor was director of media. (Rev: BL 7/93) [973.928]

THOMAS, CLARENCE

4248 Macht, Norman L. *Clarence Thomas* (6–9). 1995, Chelsea House $18.95 (0-7910-1883-0); paper $7.95 (0-7910-1912-8). Details Thomas's life journey, culminating in his controversial appointment to the Supreme Court, with frank coverage of the congressional hearings. (Rev: BL 8/95; SLJ 9/95) [347.73]

THURMOND, STROM

4249 Cohodas, Nadine. *Strom Thurmond and the Politics of Southern Change* (9–adult). 1993, Simon & Schuster $17.50 (0-671-68935-5). Biography of a pivotal figure in the emergence of the new South. (Rev: BL 12/1/92) [975.7]

YOUNG, COLEMAN

4250 Young, Coleman, and Lonnie Wheeler. *Hard Stuff: The Autobiography of Coleman Young* (9–adult). 1994, Viking $22.95 (0-670-84551-5). This autobiography by the 5-term former mayor of Detroit traces his political career and discusses the city's racial problems. (Rev: BL 1/15/94) [977.4]

Miscellaneous Persons

ADDAMS, JANE

4251 McPherson, Stephanie Sammartino. *Peace and Bread: The Story of Jane Addams* (5–8). 1993, Carolrhoda $17.50 (0-87614-792-9). An introduction to Jane Addams's work among the poor of Chicago and her leadership in international organizations on behalf of world peace. (Rev: BL 1/15/94; SLJ 2/94) [361.3]

4252 Wheeler, Leslie A. *Jane Addams* (7–12). (Pioneers in Change) 1990, Silver Burdett LB $12.98 (0-382-09962-1); paper $7.95 (0-382-09968-0). Biography of an outspoken social activist in turn-of-the-century Chicago. (Rev: BL 1/15/91) [361.3]

AMES, ALDRICH

4253 Weiner, Tim, and others. *Betrayal: The Story of Aldrich Ames, an American Spy* (9–adult). 1995, Random $25 (0-679-44050-X). Looks at the case of Aldrich Ames, an American working at the CIA who was recruited by the KGB to be a spy for the Russians. (Rev: BL 6/1–15/95) [327.12]

ANDERSON, TERRY

4254 Anderson, Terry A. *Den of Lions: Memoirs of Seven Years* (9–adult). 1993, Crown $25 (0-517-59301-7). (Rev: BL 9/1/93; SLJ 4/94) [956.9204]

ARNOLD, BENEDICT

4255 Brandt, Clare. *The Man in the Mirror: A Life of Benedict Arnold* (9–adult). 1994, Random paper $25 (0-679-40106-7). This biography of the Revolutionary War traitor exposes the underlying goals of self-promotion and future security that compelled him to commit treason. (Rev: BL 2/1/94) [973.3]

BORDEN, LIZZIE

4256 Rappaport, Doreen. *The Lizzie Borden Trial* (5–9). 1992, HarperCollins LB $13.89 (0-06-025114-X). The reader is the jury in this retelling of the 1892 Borden murder trial, in which the author shows how the legal system works and the constitutional issues involved in a trial by jury. (Rev: BL 9/1/92; MJHS; SLJ 1/93) [345.73]

BRADY, MATHEW

4257 Sullivan, George. *Mathew Brady: His Life and Photographs* (6–10). 1994, Dutton/Cobblehill $15.99 (0-525-65186-1). A biography of the photographer known for capturing the Civil War on film, including many reproductions of Brady's photos. (Rev: BL 7/94; BTA; MJHS; SLJ 12/94; VOYA 12/94) [770]

BRANT, JOSEPH

4258 Baughman, Michael. *Mohawk Blood* (9–adult). 1995, Lyons & Burford $22.95 (1-55821-376-7). Past and present struggles with Indian tradition and nonnative ways, from the grandson of the great Mohawk war chief Joseph Brant. (Rev: BL 3/1/95) [973]

CAMMERMEYER, MARGARETHE

4259 Cammermeyer, Margarethe, and Chris Fisher. *Serving in Silence* (9–adult). 1994, Viking $22.95 (0-670-85167-1). Profiles the military career of Bronze Star recipient Cammermeyer, who served honorably for 26 years before she was discharged for being a lesbian. (Rev: BL 9/15/94; BTA) [305.48]

CAPONE, AL

4260 Bergreen, Laurence. *Capone: The Man and the Era* (9–adult). 1994, Simon & Schuster $30 (0-671-74456-9). Examines the career of Chicago gangster Al Capone, recounting his actions during the 1920s, as well as his boyhood poverty and final years in prison. (Rev: BL 10/15/94) [364.1]

CASSIDY, BUTCH

4261 Green, Carl R., and William R. Sanford. *Butch Cassidy* (5–8). (Outlaws and Lawmen of the Wild West) 1995, Enslow LB $14.95 (0-89490-587-2). (Rev: BL 6/1–15/95) [364.1]

4262 Stewart, Gail B. *Where Lies Butch Cassidy?* (6–9). (History Mystery) Illus. 1992, Macmillan/Crestwood LB $11.95 (0-89686-618-1). (Rev: BL 9/15/92) [364.1]

COCHISE

4263 Schwarz, Melissa. *Cochise: Apache Chief* (9–12). (North American Indians of Achievement) 1992, Chelsea House LB $17.95 (0-7910-1706-0). (Rev: BL 10/1/92; MJHS) [973]

COCHRAN, JACQUELINE

4264 Smith, Elizabeth Simpson. *Coming Out Right: The Story of Jacqueline Cochran, the First Woman Aviator to Break the Sound Barrier* (6–8). 1991, Walker LB $14.85 (0-8027-6989-6). Cochran's accomplishments, honors, and awards are presented in detail. (Rev: BL 4/15/91; SLJ 5/91) [629.13]

CRAZY HORSE

4265 St. George, Judith. *Crazy Horse* (7–10). 1994, Putnam $16.95 (0-399-22667-2). An account of the legendary Lakota leader who struggled to save his people's culture from destruction by white soldiers and settlers. (Rev: BL 10/1/94; SLJ 11/94; VOYA 2/95) [978]

DALTON GANG

4266 Green, Carl R., and William R. Sanford. *The Dalton Gang* (5–8). (Outlaws and Lawmen of the Wild West) 1995, Enslow LB $14.95 (0-89490-588-0). (Rev: BL 11/15/95) [978]

EARHART, AMELIA

4267 Ware, Susan. *Still Missing: Amelia Earhart and the Search for Modern Feminism* (9–adult). 1993, Norton $22 (0-393-03551-4). Portrays Earhart as an inspiration to the women's movement of the 1920s and 1930s in analyzing her accomplishments. (Rev: BL 11/15/93) [629.13]

FONDA, JANE

4268 Shorto, Russell. *Jane Fonda: Political Activism* (6–12). (New Directions) 1991, Millbrook LB $14.90 (1-56294-045-7). The life of actress, activist, and entrepreneur Fonda relates her strong beliefs and deep involvement in controversial political and environmental issues, set against the backdrop of tumultuous times. (Rev: BL 10/1/91)

HIAWATHA

4269 Fradin, Dennis Brindell. *Hiawatha: Messenger of Peace* (5–7). 1992, Macmillan/Margaret K. McElderry $14.95 (0-689-50519-1). The true story of the Iroquois leader and peacemaker who lived about 500 years ago. Awards: SLJ Best Book. (Rev: BL 9/15/92; SLJ 9/92) [973]

HOFFMAN, ABBIE

4270 Hoffman, Jack, and Daniel Simon. *Run Run Run: The Lives of Abbie Hoffman* (9–adult). 1994, Putnam/Tarcher $22.95 (0-87477-760-7). A biography by Hoffman's brother detailing Abbie's radical political activities, his manic depression, and his years as a fugitive. (Rev: BL 9/15/94) [303.48]

HUNTER-GAULT, CHARLAYNE

4271 Hunter-Gault, Charlayne. *In My Place* (9–adult). 1992, Farrar $19 (0-374-17563-2). The renowned journalist writes about her early encounter with history as one of the first 2 African American students at the University of Georgia. (Rev: BL 11/1/92; SLJ 5/93) [070]

JAMES, DANIEL "CHAPPIE"

4272 Super, Neil. *Daniel "Chappie" James* (5–8). 1992, Twenty-First Century LB $14.95 (0-8050-2138-8). A well-written, inspiring account of an African American boy who grew up in the 1920s and 1930s dreaming of flying. Despite segregation and racism, he achieved his dream and became a 4-star general. (Rev: BL 12/15/92; SLJ 11/92) [355]

JAMES, JESSE

4273 Green, Carl R., and William R. Sanford. *Jesse James* (5–8). (Outlaws and Lawmen of the Wild West) 1992, Enslow LB $14.95 (0-89490-365-9). Portrays the legendary gunman as both outlaw and hero. (Rev: BL 3/1/92; MJHS; SLJ 5/92) [364.1]

4274 Stiles, T. J. *Jesse James* (6–8). 1993, Chelsea House $18.95 (0-7910-1737-0). This biography relates the details of the life and lore surrounding the notorious outlaw. (Rev: BL 2/1/94; MJHS; SLJ 11/93) [346.1]

JOSEPH, CHIEF

4275 Fox, Mary Virginia. *Chief Joseph of the Nez Perce Indians: Champion of Liberty* (5–7). (People of Distinction) 1992, Children's Press LB $13.95 (0-516-03275-5). (Rev: BL 1/15/93) [979]

4276 Yates, Diana. *Chief Joseph: Thunder Rolling from the Mountains* (7–12). 1992, Ward Hill Press (40 Willis Ave., Staten Island, NY 10301) LB $14.95 (0-9623380-9-5); paper $10.95 (0-9623380-8-7). A sensitive distillation of the life and times of Chief Joseph of the Nez Perce. (Rev: BL 12/15/92; SLJ 12/92) [979]

KOVIC, RON

4277 Moss, Nathaniel. *Ron Kovic: Antiwar Activist* (7–12). (Great Achievers: Lives of the Physically Challenged) 1994, Chelsea House $18.95 (0-7910-2076-2); paper $7.95 (0-7910-2089-4). A biography of the physically challenged Vietnam veteran, antiwar activist, and author. (Rev: BL 1/15/94; BTA) [362.1]

NADER, RALPH

4278 Celsi, Teresa. *Ralph Nader: The Consumer Revolution* (6–12). (New Directions) 1991, Millbrook LB $14.90 (1-56294-044-9). (Rev: BL 10/1/91; MJHS)

PARKER, QUANAH

4279 Wilson, Claire. *Quanah Parker: Comanche Chief* (9–12). (North American Indians of Achievement) 1991, Chelsea House $17.95 (0-7910-1702-8). Biography of the Comanche leader who fought non-Indian settlement of his lands. (Rev: BL 3/1/92; MJHS; SLJ 3/92) [973]

RATHBONE, HENRY AND CLARA

4280 Mallon, Thomas. *Henry and Clara* (9–adult). 1994, Ticknor & Fields $21.95 (0-395-59071-X). Murder and madness end the story of the Rathbones, the young couple enmeshed in Lincoln's assassination. Awards: SLJ Best Book. (Rev: SLJ 12/94)

RAY, JAMES EARL

4281 Ray, James Earl. *Who Killed Martin Luther King? The True Story by the Alleged Assassin* (9–adult). 1992, National Press Books (7200 Wisconsin Ave., Suite 212, Bethesda, MD 20814) $21.95 (0-915765-93-4). The man convicted of assassinating Martin Luther King, Jr., tells his side of the story. (Rev: BL 1/1/92) [364.1]

RED CLOUD

4282 Sanford, William R. *Red Cloud: Sioux Warrior* (5–8). (Native American Leaders of the Wild West). 1994, Enslow LB $14.95 (0-89490-513-9). Describes Red Cloud's early life and his struggle against government officials who broke promises guaranteed by numerous treaties. (Rev: BL 12/15/94; SLJ 2/95) [973]

ROSENBERG, JULIUS AND ETHEL

4283 Larsen, Anita. *The Rosenbergs* (6–9). (History Mystery) Illus. 1992, Macmillan/Crestwood LB $11.95 (0-89686-612-2). Examines the Rosenbergs and their espionage trial. For reluctant and poor readers. (Rev: BL 8/92; SLJ 10/92) [345.73]

SEQUOYAH

4284 Klausner, Janet. *Sequoyah's Gift: A Portrait of the Cherokee Leader* (5–7). 1993, HarperCollins LB $14.89 (0-06-021236-5). (Rev: BL 9/1/93; MJHS; SLJ 11/93) [973]

4285 Shumate, Jane. *Sequoyah: Inventor of the Cherokee Alphabet* (9–12). (North American Indians of Achievement) 1994, Chelsea House $18.95 (0-7910-1720-6); paper $7.95 (0-7910-1990-X). (Rev: BL 1/1/94; MJHS) [970]

SHAW, ROBERT GOULD

4286 Burchard, Peter. *"We'll Stand by the Union": Robert Gould Shaw and the Black 54th Massachusetts Regiment* (8–12). 1993, Facts on File $16.95 (0-8160-2609-2). The life and times of the Union army commander charged with training and leading Massachusetts's first black regiment. (Rev: BL 2/15/94; BTA; MJHS; VOYA 6/94) [973.7]

SITTING BULL

4287 Bernotas, Bob. *Sitting Bull: Chief of the Sioux* (9–12). (North American Indians of Achievement) 1991, Chelsea House $17.95 (0-7910-1703-6). Chronicles the life of the Native American leader. (Rev: BL 3/1/92; MJHS; SLJ 6/92) [978]

4288 Utley, Robert M. *The Lance and the Shield: The Life and Times of Sitting Bull* (9–adult). 1993, Holt $25 (0-8050-1274-5). Presents an unidealized picture of the culture of Sitting Bull's clan and re-creates the acts through which he attained its undying esteem. (Rev: BL 4/15/93) [978]

TECUMSEH

4289 Cwiklik, Robert. *Tecumseh: Shawnee Rebel* (9–12). (North American Indians of Achievement) 1993, Chelsea House LB $18.95 (0-7910-1721-4). (Rev: BL 4/1/93; MJHS) [973]

4290 Eckert, Allan W. *A Sorrow in Our Heart: The Life of Tecumseh* (9–adult). 1992, Bantam $24.50 (0-553-08023-7). A charismatic Indian leader unites North American tribes. (Rev: BL 3/1/92; SHS) [977]

WHITE, RYAN

4291 White, Ryan, and Ann Marie Cunningham. *Ryan White: My Own Story* (9–adult). 1991, Dial $16.95 (0-8037-0977-3). Firsthand account of a courageous Indiana teenager who fought hatred and prejudice in his hometown after he was diagnosed with AIDS. Awards: YALSA Best Book for Young Adults. (Rev: BL 2/1/91; BTA; MJHS; SHS; SLJ 6/91) [362.1]

Science, Medicine, Industry, and Business

Collective

4292 Aaseng, Nathan. *Twentieth-Century Inventors* (7–10). (American Profiles) 1991, Facts on File $16.95 (0-8160-2485-5). Combines historical perspective with personal profiles of important inventors to explain the events that influenced the development of such items as plastic, rockets, and television. (Rev: BL 11/1/91; MJHS; SHS; SLJ 11/91) [609.2]

4293 Curtis, Robert H. *Great Lives: Medicine* (5–8). (Great Lives) 1992, Scribner $22.95 (0-684-19321-3). Biographies of the most prominent doctors and other medical professionals throughout history. (Rev: BL 12/15/92; SHS) [610]

4294 Dash, Joan. *The Triumph of Discovery: Four Nobel Women* (7–12). 1991, Messner paper $8.95 (0-671-69333-6). (Rev: BL 3/15/91; BY; MJHS; SHS) [590.2]

4295 Davidson, Sue. *Getting the Real Story: Nellie Bly and Ida B. Wells* (6–10). 1992, Seal Press paper $8.95 (1-878067-16-8). A dual biography of 2 women who broke down barriers in journalism and how their different races shaped their individual stories. (Rev: BL 3/1/92; MJHS; SLJ 7/92) [070]

4296 Haskins, Jim. *Outward Dreams: Black Inventors and Their Inventions* (7–12). 1991, Walker LB $14.85 (0-8027-6994-2); 1992, Bantam/Starfire paper $3.50 (0-553-29480-6). Examines the lives and contributions of black men and women who, prior to the Civil War, were not given recognition for their achievements. (Rev: BL 5/15/91; MJHS) [609.2]

4297 Henderson, Harry. *Modern Mathematicians* (9–12). (Global Profiles) 1995, Facts on File LB $17.95 (0-8160-3235-1). Profiles of 9 men and 4 women who contributed to the development of modern math. (Rev: BL 1/1/96; SLJ 2/96; VOYA 2/96)

4298 Lewis, Tom. *Empire of the Air: The Men Who Made Radio* (9–adult). 1991, HarperCollins $25 (0-06-018215-6). The story of 3 men responsible for the creation of the radio and the broadcasting industry: vacuum tube inventor Lee De Forest, creator of the FM system Edwin Howard Armstrong, and RCA executive David Sarnoff. (Rev: BL 10/15/91) [621.384]

4299 Lomask, Milton. *Great Lives: Invention and Technology* (5–8). (Invention and Technology) 1991, Scribner $22.95 (0-684-19106-7). (Rev: BL 11/1/91; MJHS) [609.2]

4300 Olsen, Frank H. *Inventors Who Left Their Brand on America* (7–12). 1991, Bantam/Starfire paper $3.50 (0-553-29211-0). This reference work introduces many inventors, merchants, and entrepreneurs who have created well-known products. (Rev: BL 10/15/91) [609]

4301 Phelps, J. Alfred. *They Had a Dream: The Story of African-American Astronauts* (9–adult). 1994, Presidio $24.95 (0-89141-497-5). The story of the 7 African Americans who have been accepted as astronauts and their struggle to overcome barriers of racial and gender prejudice. (Rev: BL 1/15/94; BTA; SLJ 8/94; VOYA 8/94) [629.45]

4302 Pile, Robert B. *Top Entrepreneurs and Their Business* (6–12). 1993, Oliver Press (5707 W. 36th St., Minneapolis, MN 55416) LB $14.95 (1-881508-04-8). Pile tells the stories of 9 rags-to-riches entrepreneurs, such as L. L. Bean, Walt Disney, and Sam Walton, with photos. (Rev: BL 11/15/93; SLJ 1/94) [338]

4303 Stille, Darlene R. *Extraordinary Women Scientists* (5–8). 1995, Children's Press LB $24.60 (0-516-00585-5). A profile of 49 women scientists and their achievements, including a summary of their work, a personal portrait, and a historical overview of women in science. (Rev: BL 10/1/95; SLJ 12/95) [509.2]

4304 Veglahn, Nancy. *Women Scientists* (7–10). (American Profiles) 1991, Facts on File $16.95 (0-8160-2482-0). (Rev: BL 11/15/91) [509.2]

4305 Yount, Lisa. *Black Scientists* (7–12). (American Profiles) 1991, Facts on File $16.95 (0-8160-2549-5). The professional achievements of 8 black scientists are described, as well as the event that led each to their particular field. (Rev: BL 11/15/91; SHS; SLJ 1/92) [500]

4306 Yount, Lisa. *Twentieth-Century Women Scientists* (9–12). (Global Profiles) 1995, Facts on File LB $16.95 (0-8160-3173-8). An introduction to 11 women from around the world who have made significant contributions to twentieth-century science. (Rev: SLJ 2/96; VOYA 4/96)

Individual

ADAMSON, GEORGE AND JOY

4307 House, Adrian. *The Great Safari: The Lives of George and Joy Adamson* (9–adult). 1993, Morrow $25 (0-688-10141-0). This biography of the Adamsons uses writings, foundation materials, friends, and the author's firsthand accounts to portray them and their controversial wild-animal rehabilitation. (Rev: BL 9/15/93) [639.9]

ARLEDGE, ROONE

4308 Gunther, Marc. *The House That Roone Built: The Inside Story of ABC News* (9–adult). 1994, Little, Brown $23.95 (0-316-33151-1). A narrative account of the broadcast news organization under the 1977–1991 leadership of Roone Arledge. (Rev: BL 3/1/94) [384.55]

BARTON, CLARA

4309 Dubowski, Cathy East. *Clara Barton: Healing the Wounds* (5–7). (History of the Civil War) 1991, Silver Burdett LB $18.98 (0-382-09940-0); paper $8.95 (0-382-24049-9). A biography of the teacher and Civil War nurse best known for founding the American Red Cross. (Rev: BL 9/1/91; SLJ 8/91) [361.7]

BELL, ALEXANDER GRAHAM

4310 Lewis, Cynthia Copeland. *Hello, Alexander Graham Bell Speaking* (5–7). (Taking Part) 1991, Dillon LB $10.95 (0-87518-461-8). Focuses on Bell's personal traits, early experiences, and family background, and how, as a 29-year-old teacher of the deaf, he came to invent the telephone. (Rev: BL 9/1/91) [621.385]

BERGH, HENRY

4311 Loeper, John J. *Crusade for Kindness: Henry Bergh and the ASPCA* (5–7). 1991, Atheneum $12.95 (0-689-31560-0). Profiles the work of the founder of the American Society for the Prevention of Cruelty to Animals. (Rev: BL 6/15/91; SLJ 5/91) [179]

BRAILLE, LOUIS

4312 Bryant, Jennifer Fisher. *Louis Braille: Inventor* (5–7). (Great Achievers) 1994, Chelsea House $18.95 (0-7910-2077-0). A biography of the man whose inventions, including Braille reading, continue to aid the blind. Describes his undiminished tenacity and optimism even after he lost his sight. (Rev: BL 7/94; BTA; MJHS; SLJ 8/94) [686.2]

CARSON, RACHEL

4313 Henricksson, John. *Rachel Carson: The Environmental Movement* (6–12). (New Directions) 1991, Millbrook $14.90 (1-878841-16-5). The biologist/writer's life story, including exerpts from her own writing. (Rev: BL 2/1/91; MJHS; SLJ 5/91) [363.7]

4314 Presnall, Judith Janda. *Rachel Carson* (5–8). (The Importance Of) 1995, Lucent $14.95 (1-56006-052-2). (Rev: BL 1/15/95) [574]

4315 Stwertka, Eve. *Rachel Carson* (5–8). (First Book) 1991, Watts LB $11.90 (0-531-20020-5). Pioneer ecologist Rachel Carson's life and work. (Rev: BL 6/1/91) [574]

4316 Wadsworth, Ginger. *Rachel Carson: Voice for the Earth* (5–7). 1992, Lerner LB $15.95 (0-8225-4907-7). The life and work of the biologist and writer best known as the author of *Silent Spring*. (Rev: BL 6/1/92; SLJ 7/92; YR) [574]

4317 Wheeler, Leslie A. *Rachel Carson* (7–12). (Pioneers in Change) 1991, Silver Burdett LB $13.98 (0-382-24167-3); paper $7.95 (0-382-24174-6). (Rev: BL 2/1/92) [574]

CARTER, HOWARD

4318 Ford, Barbara. *Howard Carter: Searching for King Tut* (5–7). (Science Superstars) Illus. 1995, W. H. Freeman $14.95 (0-7167-6587-X); paper $4.95 (0-7167-6588-8). The excitement of Carter's life—the unearthing of the tomb of Tutankhamen in 1922—comes through vividly. (Rev: BL 7/95) [932]

CHÁVEZ, CÉSAR

4319 Altman, Linda Jacobs. *Cesar Chavez* (6–12). (The Importance Of) 1996, Lucent LB $16.95 (1-56006-071-9). This objective biography includes first-person comments by contemporaries and black-and-white photos. (Rev: BL 3/15/96; SLJ 2/96)

CHINN, MAY

4320 Butts, Ellen R., and Joyce R. Schwartz. *May Chinn: The Best Medicine* (5–7). (Science Superstars) Illus. 1995, W. H. Freeman $14.95 (0-7167-6589-6); paper $4.95 (0-7167-6590-X). A good portrait of the African American doctor who graduated from medical school in 1926 at age 30. (Rev: BL 7/95) [610]

CHUNG, CONNIE

4321 Malone, Mary. *Connie Chung: Broadcast Journalist* (6–9). (Contemporary Women) 1992, Enslow LB $17.95 (0-89490-332-2). Follows Chung's moves up the broadcast ladder from station to station and network to network. (Rev: BL 4/1/92) [070.4]

CORTI, JIM

4322 Kwitny, Jonathan. *Acceptable Risks* (9–adult). 1992, Poseidon $24 (0-671-73244-7). The travels of San Francisco nurse Jim Corti to procure bootleg AIDS medication in Mexico and other renegade activists' endeavors. (Rev: BL 10/1/92*) [174]

CURIE, MARIE

4323 Poynter, Margaret. *Marie Curie: Discoverer of Radium* (5–7). 1994, Enslow LB $17.95 (0-89490-477-9). (Rev: BL 1/1/95; SLJ 10/94) [540]

CURIE, MARIE AND IRENE

4324 Pflaum, Rosalynd. *Marie Curie and Her Daughter Irene* (7–10). 1993, Lerner LB $16.13 (0-8225-4915-8). A detailed account of Marie Curie's discovery of radium, polonium, and natural radiation, and Irene Curie's discovery of artificial radiation. (Rev: BL 8/93; SLJ 6/93) [540]

DARWIN, CHARLES

4325 Anderson, Margaret J. *Charles Darwin: Naturalist* (5–7). 1994, Enslow LB $17.95 (0-89490-476-0). (Rev: BL 1/1/95; SLJ 10/94) [575]

4326 Bowlby, John. *Charles Darwin: A Biography* (9–adult). 1991, Norton paper $14.95 (0-393-30930-4). (Rev: BL 3/1/91; SHS) [575]

4327 Evans, J. Edward. *Charles Darwin: Revolutionary Biologist* (6–9). (Lerner Biographies) 1993, Lerner $21.50 (0-8225-4914-X). Uses anecdotes in the telling of Darwin's life; e.g., readers learn that Darwin dropped out of medical school and that his father thought he would never amount to anything. (Rev: BL 12/1/93; SLJ 11/93) [575]

4328 Parker, Steve. *Charles Darwin and Evolution* (5–9). (Science Discoveries) 1992, Harper Collins $14 (0-06-020733-7). An introduction to a controversial scientist, supported by illustrations, charts, and glossary. (Rev: BL 9/15/92; SLJ 9/92) [575]

4329 Ventura, Piero. *Darwin: Nature Reinterpreted* (5–7). 1995, Houghton $16.95 (0-395-70738-2). An informative picture book that reveals Darwin's human side. (Rev: BL 3/1/95; SLJ 5/95) [575]

4330 White, Michael, and John Gribbin. *Darwin: A Life in Science* (9–adult). 1995, Dutton $24.95 (0-525-94002-2). An excellent first-stop biography for readers new to Darwin. (Rev: BL 12/1/95) [575]

DIX, DOROTHEA

4331 Colman, Penny. *Breaking the Chains: The Crusade of Dorothea Lynde Dix* (9–12). (Lives Well Led) 1992, Betterway/Shoe Tree paper $5.95 (1-55870-219-9). A biography of this champion of social reform for the treatment of the mentally ill. Awards: SLJ Best Book. (Rev: SLJ 7/92*)

EARLE, SYLVIA

4332 Conley, Andrea. *Window on the Deep: The Adventures of Underwater Explorer Sylvia Earle* (5–7). (New England Aquarium Books) 1991, Watts LB $13.90 (0-531-11119-9). Marine biologist and underwater explorer Earle lives on the cutting edge of deep-ocean exploration and protection. (Rev: SLJ 2/92*)

EASTMAN, CHARLES

4333 Anderson, Peter. *Charles Eastman: Physician, Reformer, Native American Leader* (5–7). (People of Distinction) 1992, Children's Press LB $12.95 (0-516-03278-X). Describes the accomplishments of the doctor Santee Sioux Charles Eastman, who was committed to improving the living conditions and legal status of Indians. (Rev: BL 7/92; MJHS; SLJ 8/92) [973]

EASTMAN, GEORGE

4334 Holmes, Burnham. *George Eastman* (7–12). (Pioneers in Change) 1992, Silver Burdett LB $13.98 (0-382-24170-3); paper $7.95 (0-382-24176-2). (Rev: BL 9/15/92) [338.7]

EDISON, THOMAS

4335 Anderson, Kelly C. *Thomas Edison* (5–8). (The Importance Of) 1994, Lucent $14.95 (1-56006-041-7). (Rev: BL 8/94) [621.3]

4336 Baldwin, Neil. *Edison: Inventing the Century* (9–adult). 1995, Hyperion $27.95 (0-7868-6041-3). A biography of the Wizard of Menlo Park. (Rev: BL 2/15/95) [621.3]

EINSTEIN, ALBERT

4337 McPherson, Stephanie Sammartino. *Ordinary Genius: The Story of Albert Einstein* (5–7). 1995, Carolrhoda LB $13.13 (0-87614-788-0). Covers Einstein's school difficulties, explanations of his discoveries, the conflict in Nazi Germany, and more, with photos of the scientist. (Rev: BL 6/1–15/95; SLJ 9/95) [530]

4338 Reef, Catherine. *Albert Einstein: Scientist of the 20th Century* (5–7). (Taking Part) 1991, Dillon LB $10.95 (0-87518-487-1). (Rev: BL 9/1/91) [530]

4339 White, Michael, and John Gribbin. *Einstein: A Life in Science* (9–adult). 1994, Dutton $21.95 (0-525-93750-1). A study of Einstein's life and scientific principles that puts his theories in social and political perspective, dispels myths, and reveals new information. (Rev: BL 2/1/94) [530.092]

EISNER, MICHAEL

4340 Flower, Joe. *Prince of the Magic Kingdom: Michael Eisner and the Re-Making of Disney* (9–adult). 1991, Wiley $22.95 (0-471-52465-4). A biography of Disney's former chief executive officer and a portrait of the corporate juggernaut. (Rev: BL 11/1/91) [384]

EPSTEIN, FRED

4341 Epstein, Fred J., and Elaine Fantle Shimberg. *Gifts of Time* (9–adult). 1993, Morrow $22 (0-688-11029-0). This memoir of a New York pediatric neurosurgeon mixes first-person recollections and descriptions of his young patients. (Rev: BL 3/1/93) [617.4]

ETHERIDGE, ANNA BLAIR

4342 Shura, Mary Francis. *Gentle Annie: The True Story of a Civil War Nurse* (5–7). 1991, Scholastic $12.95 (0-590-44367-4); 1994, paper $3.50 (0-590-43500-0). A fictionalized version of the life of Anna Etheridge, a 16-year-old Civil War nurse. (Rev: BL 3/15/91; SLJ 5/91) [973.7]

FEEHAN, JOHN M.

4343 Feehan, John M. *My Village—My World* (9–adult). 1993, Dufour/Mercier paper $12.95 (1-85635-026-6). A humorous recollection of life in an Irish village 50 years ago. (Rev: BL 3/15/93) [070.5]

FEYNMAN, RICHARD

4344 Gleick, James. *Genius: The Life and Science of Richard Feynman* (9–adult). 1992, Pantheon $27.50 (0-679-40836-3). Describes the unique life of this Nobel Prize–winning physicist, his colleagues, the story of Los Alamos, and the evolution of postwar theoretical physics. (Rev: BL 10/1/92) [530]

GAGE, LORETTA

4345 Gage, Loretta, and Nancy Gage. *If Wishes Were Horses: The Education of a Woman Veterinarian* (9–adult). 1993, St. Martin's $19.95 (0-312-08817-5). Loretta Gage's memoir of 4 grueling years as a veterinary student, begun at age 34. (Rev: BL 3/1/93; BTA; SLJ 7/93) [636.089]

GALDIKAS, BIRUTÉ

4346 Gallardo, Evelyn. *Among the Orangutans: The Biruté Galdikas Story* (5–7). 1993, Chronicle/Byron Press LB $13.95 (0-8118-0031-8); paper $6.95 (0-8118-0408-9). Offers an admiring peek into Galdikas's special world and at what the dedicated scientist discovered about orangutan behavior. (Rev: BL 4/1/93; MJHS; SLJ 6/93) [599.88]

GALILEO

4347 Reston, James, Jr. *Galileo* (9–adult). 1994, HarperCollins $25 (0-06-016378-X). Well-researched, suspenseful narrative with vigorous portraits of Galileo's opponents and supporters. (Rev: BL 4/15/94*; SHS) [520.92]

GATES, BILL

4348 Boyd, Aaron. *Smart Money: The Story of Bill Gates* (6–10). 1995, Morgan Reynolds $17.95 (1-883846-09-9). A biography of Microsoft's billionaire mogul Bill Gates. (Rev: BL 4/1/95; SLJ 4/95; VOYA 2/96) [338.7]

GODDARD, ROBERT

4349 Streissguth, Thomas. *Rocket Man: The Story of Robert Goddard* (5–7). 1995, Carolrhoda LB $13.13 (0-87614-863-1). A biography of the brilliant, secretive scientist who persevered in the engineering of rockets capable of leaving the Earth's atmosphere. (Rev: BL 10/15/95; SLJ 9/95) [621.43]

HAWKING, STEPHEN

4350 Ferguson, Kitty. *Stephen Hawking: Quest for a Theory of the Universe* (9–12). 1991, Watts LB $14.90 (0-531-11067-2). This biography of the physicist, in addition to recounting his life story, employs everyday examples to help make his complex cosmological concepts more accessible. Awards: BL Editors' Choice. (Rev: BL 9/1/91*; SLJ 4/92) [530.1]

4351 Henderson, Harry. *Stephen Hawking* (5–8). (The Importance Of) 1995, Lucent $14.95 (1-56006-050-6). (Rev: BL 1/15/95) [530]

4352 White, Michael, and John Gribbin. *Stephen Hawking: A Life in Science* (9–adult). (Great Achievers: Lives of the Physically Challenged) 1992, Dutton $23 (0-525-93447-2). A biography of one of the most important people in physics today. (Rev: BL 5/1/92; BTA; SHS; SLJ 12/92) [530]

HERRIOT, JAMES

4353 Herriot, James. *Every Living Thing* (9–adult). 1992, St. Martin's $22.95 (0-312-08188-X). Veterinarian Herriot continues his delightful recollections of work among the animals and people of the Yorkshire Dales, here in the 1950s. Awards: SLJ Best Book. (Rev: BL 8/92; BTA; SHS; SLJ 12/92) [636.089]

HEYERDAHL, THOR

4354 Heyerdahl, Thor, and Christopher Ralling. *Kon-Tiki Man: An Illustrated Biography of Thor Heyerdahl* (9–adult). 1991, Chronicle $35 (0-8118-0026-1); paper $19.95 (0-8118-0069-5). The life story of the builder of the raft *Kon-Tiki,* told in his own words and those of a fellow traveler on one of his Pacific journeys that proved that pre-Columbian ocean travel was possible. (Rev: BL 10/15/91*; SHS) [910]

HILFIKER, DAVID

4355 Hilfiker, David. *Not All of Us Are Saints: A Doctor's Journey with the Poor* (9–adult). 1994, Hill & Wang $23 (0-8090-3921-4). An account of 6 years spent treating the poor and homeless while living in inner-city Christ House, a church-based clinic and shelter. (Rev: BL 7/94) [362.1]

HORNER, JOHN R.

4356 Lessem, Don. *Jack Horner: Living with Dinosaurs* (5–7). 1994, W. H. Freeman $14.95 (0-7167-6546-2). (Rev: BL 11/15/94; MJHS) [567.9]

HUBBLE, EDWIN

4357 Christianson, Gale E. *Edwin Hubble: Mariner of the Nebulae* (9–adult). 1995, Farrar $25 (0-374-14660-8). An exploration of Hubble's contributions, personal successes, and the activities and views, inside and outside the scientific community, that sometimes annoyed his detractors. (Rev: BL 8/95*) [520]

JOHNSON, JOHN H.

4358 Falkof, Lucille. *John H. Johnson: The Man from "Ebony"* (5–8). (Wizards of Business) 1992, Garrett Educational LB $12.95 (1-56074-018-3). An interesting, accessible, and inspring biography of the magazine magnate. Black-and-white photos. (Rev: BL 6/15/92; SLJ 7/92) [070.5]

KLASS, PERRI

4359 Klass, Perri. *Baby Doctor* (9–adult). 1992, Random $23 (0-679-40957-2). A pediatrician recalls her grueling experiences while facing the harsh realities of children's illnesses. (Rev: BL 4/15/92; BTA) [618.92]

KOOP, C. EVERETT

4360 Bianchi, Anne. *C. Everett Koop: The Health of the Nation* (6–12). 1992, Millbrook $14.90 (1-56294-103-8). The story of the long, difficult road from prominent surgeon to surgeon general of the United States, where he spent 8 controversial years. (Rev: BL 9/1/92; SLJ 9/92) [610]

LATIMER, LEWIS

4361 Norman, Winifred Latimer, and Lily Patterson. *Lewis Latimer* (7–10). (Black Americans of Achievement) 1993, Chelsea House LB $18.95 (0-7910-1977-2). Follows Lattimer's career from Civil War veteran to executive at the Edison Company, where he helped Edison improve the light bulb and supervised the installation of electrical systems in several cities. (Rev: BL 11/15/93; MJHS) [609.2]

LEAKEY, LOUIS, FAMILY

4362 Morell, Virginia. *Ancestral Passions: The Leakey Family and the Quest for Humankind's Beginnings* (9–adult). 1995, Simon & Schuster $30 (0-684-80192-2). The story of the Leakey family—Louis, Mary, and their son, Richard—and their paleoanthropologic work in establishing the truth of our evolution. (Rev: BL 7/95*) [573]

LEOPOLD, ALDO

4363 Lorbiecki, Marybeth. *Of Things Natural, Wild, and Free: A Story about Aldo Leopold* (5–7). 1993, Carolrhoda $14.95 (0-87614-797-X). Aldo Leopold's love of nature developed at an early age, and his career in forestry taught him of its interdependency. Pencil sketches. (Rev: BL 11/1/93; SLJ 11/93) [333.95]

LOVELACE, ADA BYRON

4364 Wade, Mary Dodson. *Ada Byron Lovelace: The Lady and the Computer* (5–8). 1995, Silver Burdett LB $13.95 (0-87518-598-3); paper $7.95 (0-382-24717-5). Lovelace explains Babbage's analytical engine, including a computer program and ideas for its use that even its inventor hadn't imagined. (Rev: BL 5/1/95) [510]

LUCE, HENRY AND CLARE BOOTH

4365 Martin, Ralph G. *Henry and Clare: An Intimate Portrait of the Luces* (9–adult). 1991, Putnam $24.95 (0-399-13652-5). A biography of the couple who wielded great influence in communications and politics: he as founder of the Time-Life magazine empire, she as editor, playwright, congresswoman, and ambassador. (Rev: BL 9/15/91) [070.5]

MARION, ROBERT

4366 Marion, Robert. *Learning to Play God: The Coming of Age of a Young Doctor* (9–adult). 1991, Addison-Wesley $18.95 (0-201-57720-8). The clinical geneticist/teacher recalls his internship and residency, citing specific complaints on medical education while offering practical suggestions for humanizing the process. (Rev: BL 10/15/91) [610]

MCCORMACK, JOHN

4367 McCormack, John. *Fields and Pastures New: My First Year As a Country Vet* (9–12). 1995, Crown $23 (0-517-59686-5). A doctor recounts his experiences as the only veterinarian in Choctaw County, Alabama, after moving his family there in 1963. (Rev: BL 9/1/95; SLJ 1/96)

MCNAIR, RONALD E.

4368 Naden, Corinne. *Ronald McNair* (5–8). 1990, Chelsea House $17.95 (0-7910-1133-X). An inspirational biography of the second African-American astronaut, a victim of the *Challenger* disaster. (Rev: BL 4/1/91; SLJ 3/91) [629.45]

MITCHELL, MARIA

4369 Gormley, Beatrice. *Maria Mitchell: The Soul of an Astronomer* (8–12). 1995, Eerdmans $13.99 (0-8028-5116-9); paper $5.99 (0-8028-5099-5). A biography of the first woman astronomer (born 1818) and discoverer of the Mitchell Comet. (Rev: BL 9/1/95; SLJ 1/96) [520]

MONCUR, SUSAN

4370 Moncur, Susan. *They Still Shoot Models My Age* (9–adult). 1993, Serpent's Tail paper $12.99 (1-85242-230-0). An honest look at high fashion, shattering illusions of glamour and describing incidents from Moncur's European modeling career. (Rev: BL 4/15/93) [659.152]

MUIR, JOHN

4371 Wadsworth, Ginger. *John Muir: Wilderness Protector* (6–12). 1992, Lerner LB $15.95 (0-8225-4912-3). Original photos combine with Muir's letters, journals, and writings to provide a balanced overview of the conservationist's personal life, achievements, and role in the environmental movement. (Rev: BL 8/92; YR) [508.794]

NEWTON, ISAAC

4372 Hitzeroth, Deborah, and Sharon Leon. *Sir Isaac Newton* (5–8). (The Importance Of) 1994, Lucent LB $14.95 (1-56006-046-8). (Rev: BL 8/94) [530]

OPPENHEIMER, ROBERT

4373 Rummel, Jack. *Robert Oppenheimer: Dark Prince* (7–12). 1992, Facts on File $16.95 (0-8160-2598-3). The physicist credited with developing the atomic bomb is profiled in this straightforward biography. (Rev: BL 9/15/92; SLJ 9/92) [623.4]

PASTEUR, LOUIS

4374 Yount, Lisa. *Louis Pasteur* (5–8). (The Importance Of) 1995, Lucent $14.95 (1-56006-051-4). (Rev: BL 1/15/95) [509]

POGREBIN, LETTY COTTIN

4375 Pogrebin, Letty Cottin. *Deborah, Golda, and Me: Being Female and Jewish in America* (9–adult). 1991, Crown $22.95 (0-517-57517-5). The founder of *Ms.* magazine reveals her struggle to reconcile her feminisim with her Judaism. (Rev: BL 6/15/91; MJHS) [973]

PULITZER, JOSEPH, II

4376 Pfaff, Daniel W. *Joseph Pulitzer II and the Post-Dispatch: A Newspaperman's Life* (9–adult). 1991, Pennsylvania State Univ. $29.95 (0-271-00748-6). This biography of the son of the newspaper empire's founder shows him to be an astute, principled journalist who helped establish the reputation of the St. Louis newspaper. (Rev: BL 9/15/91) [070.4]

RATHER, DAN

4377 Rather, Dan. *The Camera Never Blinks Twice* (9–adult). 1994, Morrow $23 (0-688-09748-0). The TV news anchor surveys his career highlights, candidly discussing Bush, Reagan, Kennedy, Nixon, the Gulf War, and the fall of the Berlin Wall. (Rev: BL 10/1/94; SHS) [070.4]

4378 Rather, Dan, and Peter Wyden. *I Remember* (9–adult). 1991, Little, Brown $19.95 (0-316-73440-3). A famous television newsman tells what he learned from his family, teachers, and friends. (Rev: BL 8/91) [070.4]

RESTON, JAMES

4379 Reston, James. *Deadline: Our Times and the New York Times* (9–adult). 1991, Random $25 (0-394-58558-5). A *New York Times* columnist recalls his 50-year career in journalism. (Rev: BL 8/91) [070]

ROWLAND, MARY CANAGA

4380 Rowland, Mary Canaga. *As Long As Life: The Memoirs of a Frontier Woman Doctor* (9–adult). 1994, Storm Peak (157 Yesler Way, Suite 413, Seattle, WA 98104) paper $11.95 (0-9641357-0-1). The memoirs of an early nineteenth-century medicine woman who braved the wilderness to treat wounds, pull teeth, and deliver babies. (Rev: BL 11/1/94) [610]

SABIN, FLORENCE

4381 Kaye, Judith. *The Life of Florence Sabin* (5–7). (Pioneers in Health and Medicine). 1993, Twenty-First Century $14.95 (0-8050-2299-6). (Rev: BL 8/93; MJHS) [616.079]

SALK, JONAS

4382 Sherrow, Victoria. *Jonas Salk* (7–12). 1993, Facts on File $16.95 (0-8160-2805-2). Begins with polio's history, moves on to Salk's schooling and research, and ends with the Salk Institute's work on cancer and AIDS. (Rev: BL 9/15/93; MJHS) [614.5]

SCHOEN, ALLEN M.

4383 Schoen, Allen M., and Pam Proctor. *Love, Miracles, and Animal Healing: A Veterinarian's Journey from Physical Medicine to Spiritual Understanding* (9–adult). 1995, Simon & Schuster $22 (0-684-80207-4). A memoir of a veterinarian who has treated injured, ill, and abused animals. (Rev: BL 4/15/95) [636.089]

SCHWEITZER, ALBERT

4384 Bentley, James. *Albert Schweitzer: The Enigma* (9–adult). 1992, HarperCollins $20 (0-06-016364-X). A new look at the life and ideals of a Nobel Peace Prize winner. (Rev: BL 3/15/92) [610]

TESLA, NIKOLA

4385 Dommermuth-Costa, Carol. *Nikola Tesla: A Spark of Genius* (5–9). 1994, Lerner LB $16.13 (0-8225-4920-4). Traces the life and career of a pioneer in the field of electricity. (Rev: BL 12/15/94; SLJ 2/95) [621.3]

THORNTON FAMILY

4386 Thornton, Yvonne S., and Jo Coudert. *The Ditchdigger's Daughter: A Black Family's Astonishing Success Story* (9–adult). 1995, Birch Lane $19.95 (1-55972-271-1). A memoir of a childhood in a close-knit family whose father pushed his daughters to escape poverty. (Rev: BL 4/1/95) [974.9]

WALKER, MADAM C. J.

4387 Bundles, A'Lelia Perry. *Madam C. J. Walker* (5–10). (Black Americans of Achievement) 1993, Chelsea House $18.95 (1-55546-615-X); paper $7.95 (0-7910-0251-9). This biography, written by Walker's great-great-granddaughter, tells of the developer of a line of hair-care products whose entrepreneurial ability made her into the "foremost colored businesswoman in America." Awards: Woodson Book. (Rev: BL 3/1/94) [338.7]

WESTHEIMER, RUTH K.

4388 Scariano, Margaret M. *Dr. Ruth Westheimer* (7–10). 1992, Enslow LB $17.95 (0-89490-333-0). The famous Dr. Ruth recalls her unique childhood. (Rev: BL 9/15/92; SLJ 9/92) [616.85]

WILLIAMS, PAUL R.

4389 Hudson, Karen E. *The Will and the Way: Paul R. Williams, Architect* (5–7). 1994, Rizzoli $14.95 (0-8478-1780-6). A photobiography of the first African American Fellow of the American Institute of Architects. (Rev: BL 2/15/94; BTA; SLJ 3/94) [720]

WILSON, EDWARD O.

4390 Wilson, Edward O. *Naturalist* (9–adult). 1994, Island Press $24.95 (1-55963-288-7). The autobiography of the founder of sociobiology, describing his childhood love of nature and his emergence as one of the world's leading scientists. (Rev: BL 10/1/94*) [508]

WOZNIAK, STEPHEN

4391 Kendall, Martha E. *Steve Wozniak: Inventor of the Apple Computer* (6–9). 1995, Walker LB $15.85 (0-8027-8342-2). A biography of the eccentric genius who revolutionized personal computing. (Rev: BL 3/1/95; SHS; SLJ 3/95) [338.7]

WRIGHT, WILBUR AND ORVILLE

4392 Freedman, Russell. *The Wright Brothers: How They Invented the Airplane* (5–10). 1991, Holiday $16.95 (0-8234-0875-2). Chronicles the achievements of 2 brothers who built the first flying machine in an Ohio bicycle shop and ultimately saw their dream come true. Awards: ALSC Notable Children's Book; BL Best of Editors' Choice; Newbery Honor Book; SLJ Best Book; YALSA Best Book for Young Adults. (Rev: BL 6/15/91*; MJHS; SLJ 6/91*) [629.13]

Sports

Collective

4393 Aaseng, Nathan. *Athletes* (7–12). 1995, Facts on File $17.95 (0-8160-3019-7). Devoted to Native American athletes—the few who have embraced the world of professional sports. (Rev: BL 4/1/95) [796]

4394 Aaseng, Nathan. *True Champions* (6–9). 1993, Walker LB $15.85 (0-8027-8246-9). Tales of legendary athletes who have demonstrated heroism and self-sacrifice off their fields of play. (Rev: BL 8/93; BTA; MJHS; SLJ 6/93) [796]

4395 Alexander, Caroline. *Battle's End: A Seminole Football Team Revisited* (9–adult). 1995, Knopf $23 (0-679-41901-2). A factual story about a young white Rhodes scholar who became a tutor for 9 African American college football players. She follows up with an examination of their paths in life after graduation, told in their own words. (Rev: BL 12/15/95*) [305.8]

4396 Blake, Mike. *Baseball Chronicles: An Oral History of Baseball Through the Decades* (9–adult). 1994, Betterway paper $16.95 (1-55870-350-0). Oral histories from 140 former and current major-league players, organized by decade. (Rev: BL 4/15/94) [796.357]

4397 Cairns, Bob. *Pen Men: Baseball's Greatest Bullpen Stories Told by the Men Who Brought the Game Relief* (9–adult). 1992, St. Martin's $24.95 (0-312-07060-8). An inside look at bullpen antics as players endure both numbing boredom and extreme stress. (Rev: BL 3/15/92*) [796.357]

4398 Gutman, Bill. *N.B.A. Superstars* (6–9). 1995, Pocket/Archway paper $3.50 (0-671-88739-4). Profiles of 9 veteran basketball players. (Rev: BL 4/15/95) [796.323092]

4399 Hilgers, Laura. *Great Skates* (5–8). 1991, Little, Brown/Sports Illustrated paper $14.95 (0-316-36240-9). Brief biographical sketches of the world's greatest figure skaters from the 1920s to the present. (Rev: BL 2/1/92; SLJ 3/92) [796.9]

4400 Isaacs, Neil D. *Innocence and Wonder: Baseball Through the Eyes of Batboys* (9–adult). 1994, Masters Press (2647 Waterfront Pkwy. E. Dr., Indianapolis, IN 46214-2041) $14.95 (1-57028-000-2). Major league batboys from 75 years of baseball history describe their warm memories of the game and its players. (Rev: BL 9/1/94) [796.357]

4401 Jacobs, William Jay. *They Shaped the Game* (6–9). 1994, Scribner $14.95 (0-684-19734-0). Profiles the lives of baseball greats Ty Cobb, Babe Ruth, and Jackie Robinson. (Rev: BL 1/15/95; SLJ 2/95) [796.357]

4402 Kaufman, Alan S., and James C. Kaufman. *The Worst Baseball Pitchers of All Time: Bad Luck, Bad Arms, Bad Teams, and Just Plain Bad* (9–adult). 1993, McFarland paper $23.95 (0-89950-824-3). Honors pitchers since 1876 who "made a habit of losing." Includes statistics, anecdotes, and player profiles. (Rev: BL 4/1/93; VOYA 8/93) [796.357]

4403 Koppett, Leonard. *The Man in the Dugout: Baseball's Top Managers and How They Got That Way* (9–adult). 1993, Crown $22.50 (0-517-58545-6). Evaluates the lasting influences of baseball managers John McGraw, Connie Mack, and Branch Rickey on today's managers. (Rev: BL 2/15/93; VOYA 10/93) [796.357]

4404 Littlefield, Bill. *Champions: Stories of Ten Remarkable Athletes* (5–10). Illus. 1993, Little, Brown $21.95 (0-316-52805-6). Biographies of an eclectic gathering of athletes, including Pelé,

Satchel Paige, Billie Jean King, Muhammad Ali, and Julie Krone. Awards: SLJ Best Book; YALSA Best Book for Young Adults. (Rev: BL 9/1/93; SLJS 1/94*; VOYA 12/93)

4405 May, Peter. *The Big Three* (9–adult). 1994, Simon & Schuster $22 (0-671-79955-X). May, a Celtic beat reporter, explores the lives and careers of the "Big Three" of the 1980s' team: Larry Bird, Kevin McHale, and Robert Parish. (Rev: BL 12/15/93) [796.323]

4406 Reston, James, Jr. *Collision at Home Plate: The Lives of Pete Rose and Bart Giamatti* (9–adult). 1991, HarperCollins $19.95 (0-06-016379-8). (Rev: BL 4/15/91; SHS) [796.357]

4407 Ryan, Nolan, and Mickey Herskowitz. *Kings of the Hill: An Irreverent Look at the Men on the Mound* (9–adult). 1992, HarperCollins $20 (0-06-018330-6). Good-natured observations on baseball's best curveballers, best lefties, luckiest pitchers, weirdest guys, and phenomenal rookies. (Rev: BL 4/15/92) [796.357]

4408 Schulman, Arlene. *The Prizefighters: An Intimate Look at Champions and Contenders* (9–adult). 1994, Lyons & Burford $27.95 (1-55821-309-0). Interviews and photos profiling various figures in the world of boxing, including cornermen, trainers, and fighters. (Rev: BL 10/1/94; BTA) [796.8]

4409 Vecchione, Joseph J., ed. *The New York Times Book of Sports Legends* (9–adult). 1991, Times Books $25 (0-8129-1798-7). Fifty sports legends—from Jim Thorpe to Jesse Owens to Secretariat—are presented as they were in the sports pages of the *New York Times*. (Rev: BL 5/1/91; SHS; SLJ 11/91) [796]

4410 Wilber, Cynthia J. *For the Love of the Game: Baseball Memories from the Men Who Were There* (9–adult). 1992, Morrow $22 (0-688-10613-7). Heartfelt recollections from former major league baseball players of the 1940s and 1950s. (Rev: BL 2/15/92) [796.357]

Baseball

AARON, HENRY

4411 Aaron, Henry, and Lonnie Wheeler. *I Had a Hammer* (9–adult). 1991, HarperCollins $21.95 (0-06-016321-6); paper $5.50 (0-06-109956-2). The saga of "Hammerin' Hank," who broke Babe Ruth's homerun record and continued to play baseball despite the racism surrounding him and the sport. Awards: YALSA Best Book for Young Adults. (Rev: BL 2/1/91; SHS) [796.357]

4412 Rennert, Richard. *Henry Aaron* (7–10). (Black Americans of Achievement) 1993, Chelsea House $18.95 (0-7910-1859-8). (Rev: BL 5/1/93) [796.357]

ABBOTT, JIM

4413 Johnson, Rick L. *Jim Abbott: Beating the Odds* (5–7). (Taking Part) 1991, Dillon LB $10.95 (0-87518-484-7). (Rev: BL 9/1/91) [796.357]

4414 Savage, Jeff. *Sports Great Jim Abbott* (5–8). (Sports Greats) 1993, Enslow LB $15.95 (0-89490-395-0). (Rev: BL 3/1/93) [796.357]

BONILLA, BOBBY

4415 Knapp, Ron. *Sports Great Bobby Bonilla* (5–8). (Sports Greats) 1993, Enslow LB $15.95 (0-89490-417-5). (Rev: BL 9/15/93) [796.357]

4416 Rappoport, Ken. *Bobby Bonilla* (5–9). 1993, Walker LB $15.85 (0-8027-8256-6). A biography of the young New York Mets baseball player who rose from poverty in the South Bronx to superstardom and multimillionaire status. (Rev: BL 5/15/93; BTA; SLJ 5/93; VOYA 8/93) [796.357]

CLARK, WILL

4417 Knapp, Ron. *Sports Great Will Clark* (5–8). (Sports Greats) 1993, Enslow LB $15.95 (0-89490-390-X). (Rev: BL 3/1/93) [796.357]

COBB, TY

4418 Stump, Al. *Cobb* (9–adult). 1994, Algonquin Books of Chapel Hill (P.O. Box 2225, Chapel Hill, NC 27515-2225) $24.95 (0-945575-64-5). A biography of baseball legend Ty Cobb, revealing him to be a great player and a hateful, racist, nearly psychotic man. (Rev: BL 10/15/94*) [796.357]

DEAN, DIZZY

4419 Staten, Vince. *Ol' Diz: A Biography of Dizzy Dean* (9–adult). 1992, HarperCollins $22.50 (0-06-016514-6). An attempt to separate fact from fiction about one of America's best-loved baseball heroes. (Rev: BL 2/15/92) [796.357]

GIBSON, BOB

4420 Gibson, Bob, and Lonnie Wheeler. *Stranger to the Game: The Autobiography of Bob Gibson* (9–adult). 1994, Viking $22.95 (0-670-84794-1). Describes retired African American pitcher Bob Gibson's competitive nature, tracing the journey from his Omaha boyhood to the St. Louis Cardinals. (Rev: BL 7/94) [796.357]

GIBSON, JOSH

4421 Holway, John B. *Josh Gibson* (7–10). (Black Americans of Achievement) 1995, Chelsea House $18.95 (0-7910-1872-5); paper $7.95 (0-7910-1901-2). (Rev: BL 8/95) [796.357]

HERSHISER, OREL

4422 Knapp, Ron. *Sports Great Orel Hershiser* (5–8). (Sports Greats) 1993, Enslow LB $15.95 (0-89490-389-6). (Rev: BL 4/1/93) [796.357]

LEVINE, KEN

4423 Levine, Ken. *It's Gone! . . No, Wait a Minute . . . : Talking My Way into the Big Leagues at 40* (9–adult). 1993, Villard $20 (0-679-42093-2). Recounts the 1991 baseball season, during which Levine was a member of the radio broadcast team for the Baltimore Orioles. (Rev: BL 2/15/93; VOYA 10/93) [070.4]

MANTLE, MICKEY

4424 Falkner, David. *The Last Hero: The Life of Mickey Mantle* (9–adult). 1996, Simon & Schuster $24 (0-684-81424-2). Not meant to be a definitive biography but a telling of Mantle's influence as a ballplayer and as a person. (Rev: BL 12/15/95) [796.357]

4425 Mantle, Mickey, and Phil Pepe. *My Favorite Summer, 1956* (9–adult). 1991, Doubleday $18.95 (0-385-41261-4). The baseball great reflects on the season he won the Triple Crown and led his team to the World Series. (Rev: BL 2/1/91; SHS) [796.357]

MARTIN, BILLY

4426 Falkner, David. *The Last Yankee: The Turbulent Life of Billy Martin* (9–adult). 1992, Simon & Schuster $21.50 (0-671-72662-5). Biography of the highs and lows of a volatile baseball figure. (Rev: BL 2/15/92) [796.357]

MATHEWS, EDDIE

4427 Mathews, Eddie, and Bob Buege. *Eddie Mathews and the National Pastime* (9–adult). 1994, Douglas American Sports (P.O. Box 21619, Milwaukee, WI 53221) $22.95 (1-882134-41-9); paper $13.95 (1-882134-44-3). Hall-of-Famer Mathews chronicles his life and baseball career, providing anecdotes about Hank Aaron and Bob Uecker. (Rev: BL 9/15/94) [796.357]

MATHEWSON, CHRISTY

4428 Robinson, Ray. *Matty: American Hero: The Life and Career of Christy Mathewson* (9–adult). 1993, Oxford Univ. $23 (0-19-507629-X). Tracks the pitching feats of the New York Giants' pitching hero of 1900–1916. (Rev: BL 7/93) [796.357]

MITCHELL, KEVIN

4429 Dickey, Glenn. *Sports Great Kevin Mitchell* (5–8). (Sports Greats) 1993, Enslow LB $15.95 (0-89490-388-8). (Rev: BL 4/1/93) [796.357]

MUSIAL, STAN

4430 Lansche, Jerry. *Stan the Man Musial: Born to Be a Ballplayer* (9–adult). 1994, Taylor $19.95 (0-87833-846-2). A biography that sticks to baseball and avoids the fluffy, swell-guy approach. (Rev: BL 5/15/94) [796.357]

PAIGE, LEROY "SATCHEL"

4431 Ribowsky, Mark. *Don't Look Back: Satchel Paige in the Shadows of Baseball* (9–adult). 1994, Simon & Schuster $23 (0-671-77674-6). This biography of the legendary baseball pitcher places his story in the historical context of African American baseball players. (Rev: BL 2/15/94*) [796.357]

4432 Shirley, David. *Satchel Paige* (7–10). (Black Americans of Achievement). 1993, Chelsea House $18.95 (0-7910-1880-6). (Rev: BL 5/1/93) [796.357]

PATKIN, MAX

4433 Patkin, Max, and Stan Hochman. *The Clown Prince of Baseball* (9–adult). 1994, WRS (P.O. Box 21207, Waco, TX 76702-1207) $19.95 (1-56796-036-7). This autobiography of the baseball clown Max Patkin documents his long career and vagabond life. (Rev: BL 3/15/94) [796.357]

RIPKEN, CAL, JR.

4434 Macnow, Glen. *Sports Great Cal Ripken, Jr.* (5–8). (Sports Greats) 1993, Enslow LB $15.95 (0-89490-387-X). (Rev: BL 4/1/93) [796.357]

4435 Nicholson, Lois. *Cal Ripken, Jr., Quiet Hero* (6–10). 1993, Tidewater $12.95 (0-87033-445-X). This admiring biography of the Baltimore Orioles superstar describes his upbringing in a baseball family and his career successes. (Rev: BL 2/1/94) [796.357]

4436 Rosenfeld, Harvey. *Iron Man: The Cal Ripken, Jr. Story* (9–adult). 1995, St. Martin's $22.95 (0-312-13524-6). A biography of Baltimore Oriole shortstop Cal Ripken, Jr. (Rev: BL 9/1/95; SLJ 3/96) [796.357]

ROBINSON, JACKIE

4437 Reiser, Howard. *Jackie Robinson: Baseball Pioneer* (5–8). (First Book) 1992, Watts LB $11.90 (0-531-20095-7). A biography of the African American baseball star who became an American hero, with black-and-white photos. (Rev: BL 10/1/92) [796.357]

4438 Weidhorn, Manfred. *Jackie Robinson* (5–12). 1993, Atheneum $15.95 (0-689-31644-5). This biography of the African American legend who integrated baseball in 1947 focuses on the personality of the boy, the man, and the athlete. (Rev: BL 3/15/94; MJHS; SLJ 2/94; VOYA 4/94) [796.357]

RYAN, NOLAN

4439 Lace, William W. *Sports Great Nolan Ryan* (5–8). (Sports Greats) 1993, Enslow LB $15.95 (0-89490-394-2). (Rev: BL 6/1–15/93) [796.357]

SANDBERG, RYNE

4440 Sandberg, Ryne, and Barry Rozner. *Second to Home* (9–adult). 1995, Bonus $22.95 (1-56625-040-4). An autobiography of the Cubs' now-retired second baseman. (Rev: BL 4/15/95) [796.357]

STENGEL, CASEY

4441 Berkow, Ira, and Jim Kaplan. *The Gospel According to Casey: Casey Stengel's Inimitable, Instructional, Historical Baseball Book* (9–adult). 1992, St. Martin's $18.95 (0-312-06922-7). A collection of quips and quotes by and about the legendary baseball manager. (Rev: BL 2/1/92) [796.357]

WILLIAMS, TED

4442 Baldassaro, Lawrence, ed. *The Ted Williams Reader* (9–adult). 1991, Simon & Schuster/Fireside paper $11 (0-671-73536-5). A selection of literature about baseball's great hitter, from such well-known writers as Grantland Rice, Red Smith, and John Updike. (Rev: BL 12/1/91) [796.357]

4443 Cramer, Richard Ben. *Ted Williams: The Seasons of the Kid* (9–adult). 1991, Prentice-Hall $40 (0-13-515693-9). A photographic anthology of the baseball legend with a literary portrait by a Pulitzer Prize–winning author. (Rev: BL 12/1/91) [796.357]

4444 Linn, Ed. *Hitter: The Life and Turmoil of Ted Williams* (9–adult). 1993, Harcourt $23.95 (0-15-193100-3). Examines the baseball career of the legendary Boston Red Sox slugger, considered by many to be the greatest of all time. (Rev: BL 4/15/93) [796.357]

Basketball

BARKLEY, CHARLES

4445 Barkley, Charles, and Roy S. Johnson. *Outrageous! The Fine Life and Flagrant Good Times of Basketball's Irresistible Force* (9–adult). 1992, Simon & Schuster $20 (0-671-73799-6). This honest biography by the controversial Philadelphia 76er gives an insider's look at and a critique of professional basketball. (Rev: BL 11/15/91) [796.323]

4446 Macnow, Glen. *Sports Great Charles Barkley* (5–8). (Sports Greats) 1992, Enslow LB $15.95 (0-89490-386-1). (Rev: BL 10/15/92) [796.323]

BOGUES, TYRONE "MUGGSY"

4447 Bogues, Tyrone "Muggsy," and, and David Levine. *In the Land of the Giants* (9–adult). 1994, Little, Brown $19.95 (0-316-10173-7). The autobiography of the Charlotte Hornets' Muggsy Bogues, the shortest basketball player in the NBA, tells of his poverty-stricken youth and convict father. (Rev: BL 11/1/94; BTA; SLJ 5/95) [796.323]

BOL, MANUTE

4448 Montville, Leigh. *Manute: The Center of Two Worlds* (9–adult). 1993, Simon & Schuster $20 (0-671-74928-5). A blend of personal anecdotes, inside scoops, and hoop lore about the very tall Sudanese farmer who became an NBA star. (Rev: BL 2/1/93*) [796.323]

BROWN, DALE

4449 Brown, Dale, and Don Yaeger. *Tiger in a Lion's Den: Adventures in LSU Basketball* (9–adult). 1994, Hyperion $22.95 (0-7868-6044-8). Autobiography of Louisiana coach Brown, who once coached Shaquille O'Neal. Describes his controversial career. (Rev: BL 10/15/94) [796.323]

CHAMBERLAIN, WILT

4450 Chamberlain, Wilt. *A View from Above* (9–adult). 1991, Villard $20 (0-679-40455-4). The pro basketball star presents us with an opinionated autobiography, containing miscellaneous musings and "Wiltisms." (Rev: BL 9/15/91) [796.323]

GATHERS, HANK

4451 Kimble, Bo. *For You, Hank: The Story of Hank Gathers and Bo Kimble* (9–adult). 1992, Delacorte $18 (0-385-30389-0). Heartfelt memoir of a basketball player who collapsed on the court and died, by his best friend and teammate. Awards: BL Editors' Choice; YALSA Best Book for Young Adults. (Rev: BL 4/15/92) [796.323]

HARRICK, JIM

4452 Harrick, Jim, and others. *Embracing the Legend: Jim Harrick Revives the UCLA Mystique* (9–adult). 1995, Bonus $24.95 (1-56625-054-4). The story of how Jim Harrick made it as a coach. (Rev: BL 12/15/95) [796.323]

HURLEY, BOB

4453 Hurley, Bob, and Phil Pepe. *Divided Loyalties: The Diary of a Basketball Father* (9–adult). 1993, Zebra $19.95 (0-8217-4391-0). Bob Hurley's diary is the basis of this look at his work as basketball coach at an inner-city Catholic school and father to 2 basketball stars. (Rev: BL 12/1/93) [796.323]

JOHNSON, EARVIN "MAGIC"

4454 Dolan, Sean. *Magic Johnson* (7–10). 1993, Chelsea House $18.95 (0-7910-1975-6); paper $7.95 (0-7910-1976-4). (Rev: BL 9/15/93) [796.323]

4455 Greenberg, Keith E. *Magic Johnson: Champion with a Cause* (5–7). 1992, Lerner LB $9.95 (0-8225-0546-0). Depicts Magic Johnson as an enormously gifted athlete whose playing career was cut short when he learned he is HIV positive. (Rev: BL 8/92; SLJ 7/92; YR) [796.323]

4456 Haskins, James. *Sports Great Magic Johnson* (5–8). Rev. ed. 1992, Enslow LB $15.95 (0-89490-348-9). This revised edition includes a discussion of the basketball star's HIV status, his 1991 retirement from the Lakers, and his role in the fight against AIDS. (Rev: BL 10/15/92; MJHS) [796.323]

4457 Johnson, Earvin "Magic," and William Novak. *My Life* (9–adult). 1992, Random $22 (0-679-41569-6). The basketball star speaks frankly about his career, his promiscuity, and how testing HIV positive has changed his life. (Rev: BL 10/1/92; BTA; SHS) [796.323]

4458 Pascarelli, Peter F. *The Courage of Magic Johnson: From Boyhood Dreams to Superstar to His Toughest Challenge* (6–12). 1991, Bantam paper $3.99 (0-553-29915-8). Follows Johnson's life and details the player's impact on basketball history, as well as his new role as an AIDS activist. (Rev: BL 4/15/92)

JORDAN, MICHAEL

4459 Aaseng, Nathan. *Sports Great Michael Jordan* (5–8). (Sports Greats) 1992, Enslow LB $15.95 (0-89490-370-5). (Rev: BL 10/15/92) [796.323]

4460 Dolan, Sean. *Michael Jordan* (7–10). (Black Americans of Achievement) 1993, Chelsea House $18.95 (0-7910-2150-5); paper $7.95 (0-7910-2151-3). (Rev: BL 3/1/94) [796.323]

4461 Jordan, Michael, and Walter Iooss. *Rare Air: Michael on Michael* (9–adult). 1993, HarperCollins $50 (0-00-255389-9); paper $25 (0-00-638256-8). Jordan's autobiography talks about his love of basketball, his family, competitiveness, and sense of self. Supplemented by color photos. (Rev: BL 11/15/93) [796.323]

4462 Naughton, Jim. *Taking to the Air: The Rise of Michael Jordan* (9–adult). 1992, Warner $18.95 (0-446-51629-5). A former sportswriter examines the real Michael Jordan as seen by family, friends, teammates, and coaches. (Rev: BL 4/15/92; SHS) [796.323]

4463 Smith, Sam. *The Jordan Rules* (9–adult). 1991, Simon & Schuster $22 (0-671-74491-7). An honest behind-the-scenes portrayal of the Chicago Bulls basketball team and their 1990 championship season, with a revealing profile of Michael Jordan. (Rev: BL 12/15/91) [796.323]

KARL, GEORGE

4464 Sampson, Curt. *Full Court Pressure: A Tumultuous Season with Coach Karl and the Seattle Sonics* (9–adult). 1995, Doubleday $22.95 (0-385-47632-9). An anecdotal account of the 1993–1994 Seattle Sonics pro basketball team. (Rev: BL 4/1/95) [796.323]

O'NEAL, SHAQUILLE

4465 Hunter, Bruce. *Shaq Impaq* (9–adult). 1993, Bonus $19.95 (1-56625-030-7). A review of Orlando Magic center Shaquille O'Neal's rise to fame on the basketball court and in the world of marketing. (Rev: BL 1/15/94) [796.323]

OLAJUWON, HAKEEM

4466 Knapp, Ron. *Sports Great Hakeem Olajuwon* (5–8). (Sports Greats) 1992, Enslow LB $15.95 (0-89490-372-1). (Rev: BL 10/15/92) [796.323]

RIVERS, GLENN "DOC"

4467 Rivers, Glenn, and Bruce Brooks. *Those Who Love the Game: Glenn "Doc" Rivers on Life in the NBA and Elsewhere* (7–12). 1994, Holt $15.95 (0-8050-2822-6). A sports autobiography that avoids the pitfalls of similar stories, which tend to be self-serving and too much play-by-play. Awards: SLJ Best Book; YALSA Best Book for Young Adults. (Rev: BL 4/15/94; BTA; MJHS; SLJ 4/94; VOYA 6/94) [796.32364]

ROBINSON, DAVID

4468 Aaseng, Nathan. *Sports Great David Robinson* (5–8). (Sports Greats) 1992, Enslow LB $15.95 (0-89490-373-X). (Rev: BL 10/15/92) [796.323]

4469 Green, Carl R., and Roxanne Ford. *David Robinson* (5–8). (Sports Headlines) 1994, Macmillan/Crestwood $13.95 (0-89686-839-7). A biography of the basketball player that uses press quotations and photos to highlight important events in his career. (Rev: BL 10/1/94) [796.323]

4470 Savage, Jim. *The Force: David Robinson, the NBA's Newest Sky-High Sensation* (9–adult). 1992, Dell paper $4.99 (0-440-21227-8). Sports biography of the San Antonio Spurs basketball center and U.S. Olympic team member. (Rev: BL 3/15/92) [796.323]

RODMAN, DENNIS

4471 Rodman, Dennis, and others. *Rebound: The Enduring Friendship of Dennis Rodman and Bryne Rich* (9–adult). 1994, Crown $22 (0-517-59294-0). A description of the enduring relationship between professional basketball player Dennis Rodman and a teenage boy who had accidentally killed his best friend in a hunting accident. (Rev: BL 1/15/94; VOYA 8/94) [796.323]

SLOAN, NORM

4472 Sloan, Norm, and Larry Guest. *Confessions of a Coach* (9–adult). 1991, Rutledge Hill $18.95 (1-55853-129-7). A high-profile basketball coach recalls his career and defends his reputation as he reveals the pressures of big-time college coaching. (Rev: BL 11/15/91) [796.323]

THOMPSON, JOHN

4473 Shapiro, Leonard. *Big Man on Campus: John Thompson and the Georgetown Hoyas* (9–adult). 1991, Holt $19.95 (0-8050-1125-0). A profile of Georgetown University's fiery head basketball coach. (Rev: BL 1/15/91) [796.323]

WALKER, CHET

4474 Walker, Chet, and Chris Messenger. *Long Time Coming: A Black Athlete's Coming-of-Age in America* (9–adult). 1995, Grove/Weidenfeld $21 (0-8021-1504-7). Walker's autobiography deals with his career as one of the first African American NBA stars, including his rise to stardom from poverty and life as a successful businessman afterward. (Rev: BL 6/1–15/95) [796.323]

WALTON, BILL

4475 Walton, Bill, and Gene Wojciechowski. *Nothing but Net: Just Give Me the Ball and Get out of the Way* (9–adult). 1994, Hyperion $22.95 (1-56282-793-6). Walton describes his pro basketball career, his passion for the game, and his pain at not being able to play following injuries. (Rev: BL 2/1/94) [796.323]

Boxing

ALI, MUHAMMAD

4476 Conklin, Thomas. *Muhammad Ali: The Fight for Respect* (6–12). (New Directions) 1992, Millbrook $14.90 (1-56294-112-7). This well-researched account of a man whose fame transcends the boxing arena takes a close look at

Ali's conversion to the Black Muslim faith and his refusal to be inducted into the armed forces because of his religious beliefs. (Rev: BL 2/15/92; MJHS) [796.83]

4477 Diamond, Arthur. *Muhammad Ali* (5–8). (The Importance Of) 1995, Lucent $14.95 (1-56006-060-3). (Rev: BL 1/15/95) [796.8]

4478 Hauser, Thomas. *Muhammad Ali: His Life and Times* (9–adult). 1992, Simon & Schuster paper $14 (0-671-77971-0). (Rev: BL 5/15/91; SHS) [796.83]

4479 Leifer, Neil, and Thomas Hauser. *Muhammad Ali Memories* (9–adult). 1992, Rizzoli $49.50 (0-8478-1605-2); paper $29.95 (0-8478-1606-0). Ali's official biographer and a successful photographer collaborate to create a portrait of the renowned athlete in all his incarnations. (Rev: BL 11/1/92) [796.8]

LOUIS, JOE

4480 Lipsyte, Robert. *Joe Louis: A Champ for All America* (5–8). 1994, HarperCollins LB $13.89 (0-06-023410-5). The excitement of boxing plus a sympathetic biography of the Brown Bomber. (Rev: BL 3/1/95; SLJ 10/94) [796.8]

Football

AIKMAN, TROY

4481 Macnow, Glen. *Sports Great Troy Aikman* (5–8). (Sports Greats) 1995, Enslow LB $15.95 (0-89490-593-7). (Rev: BL 9/15/95) [796.332]

BYRD, DENNIS

4482 Byrd, Dennis, and Michael D'Orso. *Rise and Walk: The Trial and Triumph of Dennis Byrd* (9–adult). 1993, HarperCollins $20 (0-06-017783-7). Focuses on this New York Jets defensive lineman's recovery from a football accident that left him a quadriplegic. (Rev: BL 9/15/93) [796.332]

COURSON, STEVE

4483 Courson, Steve, and Lee R. Schreiber. *False Glory: Steelers and Steroids: The Steve Courson Story* (9–adult). 1992, Longmeadow $19.95 (0-681-41187-2). A professional football player suffers irreversible health problems after using steroids. (Rev: BL 1/15/92) [796.332]

CUNNINGHAM, RANDALL

4484 Cunningham, Randall, and Steve Wartenberg. *I'm Still Scrambling* (9–adult). 1993, Doubleday $20 (0-385-47142-4). The life of all-star quarterback Cunningham from childhood to his current pro football career. Includes the difficulties he's faced and game accounts. (Rev: BL 9/15/93) [796.332]

DAVIS, AL

4485 Dickey, Glenn. *Just Win, Baby: Al Davis and His Raiders* (9–adult). 1991, Harcourt $19.95 (0-15-146580-0). A biography of the much-admired, much-maligned coach of the Los Angeles/Oakland Raiders football team. (Rev: BL 9/15/91*) [796.332]

GIFFORD, FRANK

4486 Gifford, Frank, and Harry Waters. *The Whole Ten Yards* (9–adult). 1993, Random $22 (0-679-41543-2). Gifford's autobiography spans his impoverished early life, pro football and broadcasting careers, and his life with wife Kathy Lee. (Rev: BL 9/15/93) [796.332]

HAYES, WOODY

4487 Hornung, Paul. *Woody Hayes: A Reflection* (9–adult). 1991, Sagamore Publishing (P.O. Box 673, Champaign, IL 61824-0673) $19.95 (0-915611-42-2). A longtime friend writes an affectionate biography of the Ohio State football coach whose teams dominated the Big Ten for almost 30 years. (Rev: BL 10/1/91) [796.332]

HOSTETLER, JEFF

4488 Hostetler, Jeff, and Ed Fitzgerald. *One Giant Leap* (9–adult). 1991, Putnam $19.95 (0-399-13707-6). An autobiography of the former New York Giants quarterback. (Rev: BL 11/15/91) [796.332]

MILLS, GEORGE

4489 Mills, George R. *Go Big Red! The Story of a Nebraska Football Player* (9–adult). 1991, Univ. of Illinois $19.95 (0-252-01825-7). The author's experiences as a typical member, not a star, of the University of Nebraska football team in the mid-1970s. (Rev: BL 9/15/91) [796.332]

PRIETO, JORGÉ

4490 Prieto, Jorgé. *The Quarterback Who Almost Wasn't* (7–10). 1994, Arte Público paper $9.95 (1-55885-109-7). The autobiography of a

Mexican physician who struggled with poverty, racism, and political exile before he received a scholarship to play football at Notre Dame. (Rev: BL 8/94) [796.332]

RICE, JERRY

4491 Dickey, Glenn. *Sports Great Jerry Rice* (5–8). (Sports Greats) 1993, Enslow LB $15.95 (0-89490-419-1). (Rev: BL 9/15/93) [796.332]

SANDERS, BARRY

4492 Knapp, Ron. *Sports Great Barry Sanders* (5–8). (Sports Greats) 1993, Enslow LB $15.95 (0-89490-418-3). (Rev: BL 9/15/93) [796.331]

SMITH, EMMITT

4493 Smith, Emmitt, and Steve Delsohn. *The Emmitt Zone* (9–adult). 1994, Crown $22 (0-517-59985-6). This autobiography of the Dallas Cowboys running back describes his youth in a poor, loving family, staying in school, doing charity work, and loving football. Awards: SLJ Best Book. (Rev: BL 9/15/94; SHS; SLJ 6/95) [796.332]

WALSH, BILL

4494 Cohn, Lowell. *Rough Magic: Bill Walsh's Return to Stanford Football* (9–adult). 1994, HarperCollins $22.50 (0-06-017043-3). Bill Walsh, former head coach of the San Fransisco 49ers, returns to coach Stanford's football team. Investigates Walsh's role as coach and mentor, examining his triumphs and failures. (Rev: BL 7/94; VOYA 5/95) [796.332]

YOUNG, STEVE

4495 Morgan, Terri, and Shmuel Thaler. *Steve Young: Complete Quarterback* (5–8). (Sports Achievers) 1995, Lerner LB $14.21 (0-8225-2886-X); paper $5.95 (0-8225-9716-0). (Rev: BL 11/15/95) [796.332]

Gymnastics

KAROLYI, BELA

4496 Karolyi, Bela, and Nancy Ann Richardson. *Feel No Fear: The Power, Passion, and Politics of a Life in Gymnastics* (9–adult). 1994, Hyperion $22.95 (0-7868-6012-X). The autobiography of the gymnastics coach who has coached Nadia Comaneci, Mary Lou Retton, and Kim Szmeskal. (Rev: BL 5/1/94; BTA; VOYA 10/94) [796.44]

MILLER, SHANNON

4497 Quiner, Krista. *Shannon Miller: America's Most Decorated Gymnast* (6–9). 1996, Bradford paper $11.95 (0-9643460-1-X). The life, accomplishments, and difficulties of the Olympic gymnast are presented along with over 20 action photos. (Rev: SLJ 3/96)

Ice Skating

BLAIR, BONNIE

4498 Breitenbucher, Cathy. *Bonnie Blair: Golden Streak* (5–8). (Sports Achievers). 1994, Lerner LB $13.13 (0-8225-2883-5). Profiles Blair, who won more medals than any other U.S. athlete in Winter Olympics history. (Rev: BL 1/1/95; MJHS; SLJ 1/95) [796.91]

KERRIGAN, NANCY

4499 Morrissette, Mikki. *Nancy Kerrigan: Heart of a Champion* (5–7). 1994, Bantam paper $3.99 (0-553-48254-8). A short biography of Kerrigan written before the Olympics. (Rev: BL 5/1/94) [796.91]

Tennis

ASHE, ARTHUR

4500 Ashe, Arthur, and Arnold Rampersad. *Days of Grace: A Memoir* (9–adult). 1993, Knopf $24 (0-679-42396-6). A memoir, concentrating on the 1980s, of the deceased African American tennis player who won the Davis Cup and died from AIDS. Awards: YALSA Best Book for Young Adults. (Rev: BL 5/15/93*; BTA; SLJ 11/93) [796.342]

4501 Collins, David R. *Arthur Ashe: Against the Wind* (6–9). (People in Focus) 1994, Dillon $13.95 (0-87518-647-5). A portrait of the inspring African American sports champion, humanitarian, and civil rights activist. (Rev: BL 2/1/95; BTA; SLJ 3/95; VOYA 5/95) [796.342]

NAVRATILOVA, MARTINA

4502 Blue, Adrianne. *Martina: The Lives and Times of Martina Navratilova* (9–adult). 1995, Birch Lane $19.95 (1-55972-300-9). A biography of Navratilova, focusing on her career and, to a lesser extent, her life. (Rev: BL 9/15/95) [796.342]

ZAHARIAS, BABE DIDRIKSON

4503 Cayleff, Susan E. *Babe: The Life and Legend of Babe Didrikson Zaharias* (9–adult). 1995, Univ. of Illinois $29.95 (0-252-01793-5). Looks at Babe Didrikson Zaharias, pro golfer and Olympic gold medalist, from the viewpoints of how she lived her life, her public persona, and her lesbianism. (Rev: BL 6/1–15/95) [796.352]

Track and Field

ASHFORD, EVELYN

4504 Connolly, Pat. *Coaching Evelyn: Fast, Faster, Fastest Woman in the World* (7–10). 1991, HarperCollins LB $15.89 (0-06-021283-7). This account by her coach of the training of Olympic medal winner Evelyn Ashford gives an inside look at a runner's life and the synergy between 2 women. (Rev: BL 9/15/91; MJHS; SLJ 6/91) [796.42]

GRIFFITH JOYNER, FLORENCE

4505 Koral, April. *Florence Griffith Joyner: Track and Field Star* (5–8). (First Book) 1992, Watts LB $11.90 (0-531-20061-2). This biography of the winner of 4 Oympic track medals emphasizes her hard work and determination. (Rev: BL 10/1/92; SLJ 8/92) [796.42]

JOYNER-KERSEE, JACQUELINE

4506 Green, Carl R. *Jackie Joyner-Kersee* (5–8). (Sports Headlines) 1994, Macmillan/Crestwood $13.95 (0-89686-838-9). A biography of the track star that uses press quotations and photos to highlight important events in her career. (Rev: BL 10/1/94) [796.42]

4507 Harrington, Geri. *Jackie Joyner-Kersee: Champion Athlete* (6–10). 1995, Chelsea House $18.95 (0-7910-2085-1). Joyner-Kersee is subject to asthmatic attacks, yet she is a 4-time Olympic champion. (Rev: BL 10/1/95) [796.42]

LEWIS, CARL

4508 Klots, Steve. *Carl Lewis* (7–10). (Black Americans of Achievement) 1994, Chelsea House $18.95 (0-7910-2164-5). (Rev: BL 3/15/95) [796.42]

OWENS, JESSE

4509 Rennert, Richard. *Jesse Owens* (5–7). (Junior World Biographies) 1991, Chelsea House $12.95 (0-7910-1570-X). The life story of the great African American Olympic track athlete. (Rev: BL 9/1/91; SLJ 9/91) [796,42]

THORPE, JIM

4510 Bernotas, Bob. *Jim Thorpe: Sac and Fox Athlete* (9–12). (North American Indians of Achievement) 1992, Chelsea House LB $17.95 (0-7910-1722-2). (Rev: BL 11/1/92) [796]

4511 Lipsyte, Robert. *Jim Thorpe: 20th Century Jock* (5–8). 1993, HarperCollins LB $13.89 (0-06-022989-6). A short biography of the Native American athlete that traces his childhood in reservation schools to his Olympic triumph against enormous odds. (Rev: BL 2/1/94; MJHS; SLJ 5/94; VOYA 2/94) [796]

4512 Nardo, Don. *Jim Thorpe* (5–8). (The Importance Of) 1994, Lucent LB $14.95 (1-56006-045-X). (Rev: BL 8/94) [796]

Miscellaneous Sports

ALBERT, MARV

4513 Albert, Marv, and Rick Reilly. *I'd Love to but I Have a Game* (9–adult). 1993, Doubleday $20 (0-385-42024-2). Filled with humorous accounts of Albert's career as the voice of the Knicks, Rangers, and other sports events. (Rev: BL 11/1/93) [070.4]

FUSSELL, SAMUEL WILSON

4514 Fussell, Samuel Wilson. *Muscle: Confessions of an Unlikely Bodybuilder* (9–adult). 1991, Poseidon $18.95 (0-671-70195-9). How one man went from beanpole to bodybuilder after moving to New York City. Includes material on use and abuse of steroids in bodybuilding. Awards: SLJ Best Book; YALSA Best Book for Young Adults. (Rev: BL 1/15/91; SHS; SLJ 9/91) [646.7]

HARTJE, TOD

4515 Hartje, Tod, and Lawrence Martin. *From Behind the Red Line: An American Hockey Player in Russia* (9–adult). 1992, Macmillan $19.95 (0-02-548501-6). Memoir of a Harvard hockey player's year as the first North American to play for an elite Soviet Union team. (Rev: BL 5/15/92*) [796.962]

HERR, HUGH

4516 Osius, Alison. *Second Ascent: The Story of Hugh Herr* (9–adult). 1991, Stackpole $19.95 (0-8117-1794-1). A world champion mountain climber must cope with disability and guilt after he loses his legs in a climbing accident and a volunteer worker dies in the rescue effort. Awards: SLJ Best Book. (Rev: BL 8/91; SLJ 12/91) [796.5]

KRONE, JULIE

4517 Krone, Julie, and Nancy Ann Richardson. *Riding for My Life* (9–adult). 1995, Little, Brown $19.95 (0-316-50477-7). Jockey Krone's memoir about her struggle to achieve success in a male-dominated sport. (Rev: BL 4/15/95) [798.4]

LEWIN, TED

4518 Lewin, Ted. *I Was a Teenage Professional Wrestler* (7–12). 1993, Orchard/Richard Jackson LB $16.95 (0-531-08627-5); 1994, Hyperion paper $6.95 (0-7868-1009-2). Memoir of a children's book author/illustrator about his wrestling career in the 1950s, showing the human side of the sport. Awards: SLJ Best Book. (Rev: BL 6/1–15/93*; BTA; SLJ 7/93*; VOYA 10/93) [796.8]

PELE

4519 Arnold, Caroline. *Pele: The King of Soccer* (5–8). (First Book) 1992, Watts LB $11.90 (0-531-20077-9). Traces Pele's soccer career from early promise to international superstardom. (Rev: BL 10/1/92; MJHS) [796.334]

STARK, PETER

4520 Stark, Peter. *Driving to Greenland* (9–adult). 1994, Lyons & Burford $22.95 (1-55821-320-1). The author describes his adventures on skis, dogsled, and luge on mountains in Greenland and Iceland. (Rev: BL 9/1/94) [796.93]

TREVINO, LEE

4521 Gilbert, Thomas W. *Lee Trevino* (5–9). (Hispanics of Achievement) 1991, Chelsea House $17.95 (0-7910-1256-5). (Rev: BL 3/15/92) [796.352]

World Figures

Collective

4522 Ayer, Eleanor H., and others. *Parallel Journeys* (7–12). 1995, Atheneum $15 (0-689-31830-8). Personal narratives in alternative chapters of a Jewish woman and an ardent member of the Hitler Youth, who grew up a few miles from each other. Awards: Christopher. (Rev: BL 5/15/95*; SLJ 6/95) [943.086]

4523 Blue, Rose, and Corinne Naden. *People of Peace* (5–7). 1994, Millbrook LB $18.90 (1-56294-409-6). A collective biography of 10 peace activists, including Mohandas Gandhi, Jane Addams, and Desmond Tutu. (Rev: BL 12/15/94; SLJ 2/95)

4524 Boas, Jacob. *We Are Witnesses: The Diaries of Five Teenagers Who Died in the Holocaust* (7–12). 1995, Holt $15.95 (0-8050-3702-0). Boas, born in 1943 in a Nazi camp, tells about being a Holocaust survivor. (Rev: BL 5/15/95*) [940.53]

4525 Cantor, Norman F. *Medieval Lives: Eight Charismatic Men and Women of the Middle Ages* (9–adult). 1994, HarperCollins $23 (0-06-016989-3). Profiles, in the form of reconstructed dialogues, of 8 extraordinary ecclesiastic and powerful men and women who lived during the Middle Ages. (Rev: BL 3/1/94) [940.1]

4526 Fraser, Antonia. *The Wives of Henry VIII* (9–adult). 1992, Knopf $25 (0-394-58538-0). Portraits of the great Tudor king's 6 wives as dynamic individuals in their own right. (Rev: BL 10/1/92) [942.05]

4527 Graff, Nancy Price. *Where the River Runs: A Portrait of a Refugee Family* (5–7). Photos. 1993, Little, Brown $16.95 (0-316-32287-3). A photo-essay about the contemporary refugee experience, highlighting a Cambodian family who fled the civil war and arrived penniless in Boston. (Rev: BL 6/1–15/93) [973]

4528 Hoobler, Dorothy, and Thomas Hoobler. *Chinese Portraits: Images Across the Ages* (6–9). (Images Across the Ages) Illus. 1993, Raintree/Steck-Vaughn $15.96 (0-8114-6375-3). An illustrated collective biography of such Chinese notables as Confucius, Li Bo, Du Fu, Lin Xezu, and the Soong family. (Rev. BL 7/93; BTA) [920.051]

4529 Hoobler, Dorothy, and Thomas Hoobler. *Italian Portraits* (6–9). (Images Across the Ages) Illus. 1993, Raintree/Steck-Vaughn $15.96 (0-8114-6377-X). An illustrated collective biography of such Italian greats as Caesar, Dante, Galileo, Verdi, and Montessori. (Rev: BL 7/93) [920.045]

4530 Jacobs, William Jay. *World Government* (5–8). (Great Lives) 1992, Scribner $22.95 (0-684-19285-3). Biographies of 26 men and women who have shaped world events. (Rev: BL 10/15/92; MJHS) [909.8]

4531 Posner, Gerald L. *Hitler's Children: Sons and Daughters of Leaders of the Third Reich Talk about Their Fathers and Themselves* (9–adult). 1991, Random $20 (0-394-58299-3). The adult children of Nazi officials speak frankly about their fathers. (Rev: BL 1/1/91; SLJ 4/92) [943.086]

4532 Rabb, Theodore K. *Renaissance Lives: Portraits of an Age* (9–adult). 1993, Pantheon $27.50 (0-679-40781-2). Profiles 15 individuals who helped shape the Renaissance era. (Rev: BL 1/1/93; BTA; SHS; SLJ 11/93) [920.04]

4533 Salsitz, Norman, and Amalie Petranker Salsitz. *Against All Odds: A Tale of Two Survivors* (9–adult). 1991, Holocaust Publications

$24.95 (0-89604-148-4); paper $12.95 (0-89604-149-2). In these recollections of the Holocaust by 2 Polish Jews who married after the war, similar tales of Nazi brutality, false identities, clever escapes, and great endurance are told. (Rev: BL 9/15/91) [940.53]

4534 Schraff, Anne. *Women of Peace: Nobel Peace Prize Winners* (5–8). 1994, Enslow LB $17.95 (0-89490-493-0). The stories of 9 women who made tremendous sacrifices in pursuit of peace and justice. (Rev: BL 1/1/95; MJHS; SLJ 9/94) [327.1]

4535 Wakin, Edward. *Contemporary Political Leaders of the Middle East* (6–12). (Global Profiles) 1996, Facts on File LB $17.95 (0-8160-3154-1). A collection of biographies of 8 Middle Eastern leaders. (Rev: SLJ 3/96)

Africa

CLEOPATRA, QUEEN OF EGYPT

4536 Brooks, Polly Schoyer. *Cleopatra: Goddess of Egypt, Enemy of Rome* (7–10). 1995, HarperCollins LB $15.89 (0-06-023608-6). As much an account of the Roman struggle for power as a biography of the Egyptian queen, an intelligent and capable leader. (Rev: BL 11/1/95; SLJ 12/95; VOYA 4/96) [932]

4537 Nardo, Don. *Cleopatra* (8–12). (The Importance Of) 1994, Lucent LB $14.95 (1-56006-023-9). This illustrated biography discusses the life of the legendary queen in relation to the politics and power struggles of ancient Egypt and Rome. (Rev: BL 1/15/94; BTA; SLJ 3/94) [932]

MANDELA, NELSON

4538 Denenberg, Barry. *Nelson Mandela: "No Easy Walk to Freedom"* (6–12). 1991, Scholastic $12.95 (0-590-44163-9). A chronological accounting of Mandela's life as seen through Mandela's eyes, with the harshness of apartheid and black South African life always evident. (Rev: BL 3/1/91; SHS; SLJ 5/91) [324.268]

4539 Feinberg, Brian. *Nelson Mandela* (5–7). (Junior World Biographies) 1991, Chelsea House $12.95 (0-7910-1569-6). The story of the South African leader's fight against apartheid. (Rev: BL 9/1/91; SLJ 8/91) [324.268]

4540 Hoobler, Dorothy, and Thomas Hoobler. *Mandela: The Man, the Struggle, the Triumph* (6–12). 1992, Watts LB $13.90 (0-531-11141-5). A review of the last 5 years of South Africa and the struggle against apartheid. (Rev: BL 5/15/92; MJHS; SHS; SLJ 12/92) [968.06]

4541 Hughes, Libby. *Nelson Mandela: Voice of Freedom* (6–10). (People in Focus) 1992, Dillon LB $12.95 (0-87518-484-7). Integrates Mandela's political struggle against apartheid with his personal story. Extensive bibliography, photos. (Rev: BL 12/1/92; SLJ 1/93) [968.06]

4542 Mandela, Nelson. *Long Walk to Freedom* (9–adult). 1994, HarperCollins $25 (0-316-54585-6). A moving account of Mandela's life from his childhood to his inauguration as president of South Africa in May 1994. Awards: BL Editors' Choice. (Rev: BL 11/15/94*) [324.268]

4543 Otfinoski, Steven. *Nelson Mandela: The Fight Against Apartheid* (6–12). 1992, Millbrook $15.90 (1-56294-067-8). Relates the great leader's life to the history of the anti-apartheid struggle. (Rev: BL 2/15/92; SHS; SLJ 4/92; YR) [968.06]

Asia and the Middle East

ABU AHMAD FAMILY

4544 Gorkin, Michael. *Days of Honey, Days of Onion: The Story of a Palestinian Family in Israel* (9–adult). 1991, Beacon $24.95 (0-8070-6902-7). An account of an Arab family that describes the changes since the establishment of Israel and explores young people's ideas on Islamic fundamentalism, education, the role of women, and the chances for peace. (Rev: BL 10/15/91) [956.94]

ARAFAT, YASIR

4545 Ferber, Elizabeth. *Yasir Arafat: The Battle for Peace in Palestine* (7–12). 1995, Millbrook LB $16.90 (1-56294-585-8). A balanced presentation of Arafat's political career. (Rev: BL 10/1/95; SLJ 12/95) [956.04]

4546 Rubinstein, Danny. *The Mystery of Arafat* (9–adult). 1995, Steerforth $18 (1-883642-10-8). An Israeli journalist writes this biography of the PLO leader and considers his place in history. (Rev: BL 5/15/95) [956.04]

CHENG, NIEN

4547 Sommer, Robin Langley. *Nien Cheng: Prisoner in China* (5–7). (Library of Famous Women) 1993, Blackbirch LB $14.95 (1-56711-011-8). A simple portrait of this wealthy Chinese woman who was imprisoned during the Cultural Revolution. (Rev: BL 2/15/93) [951.05]

DALAI LAMA

4548 Perez, Louis G. *The Dalai Lama* (6–12). (World Leaders) 1993, Rourke (P.O. Box 3328, Vero Beach, FL 32964) $19.93 (0-86625-480-3). Tells of the Dali Lama's lonely childhood, nonviolent struggle for his people, years in exile, and current impact. (Rev: BL 12/1/93) [294.3]

DALOKAY, VEDAT

4549 Dalokay, Vedat. *Sister Shako and Kolo the Goat: Memories of My Childhood in Turkey* (5–7). Tr. by Güner Ener. 1994, Lothrop $13 (0-688-13271-5). The author, an architect and ex-mayor of Ankara, Turkey, fondly remembers his boyhood. Sister Shako is an elderly widow who had much to share with the young Dalokay. (Rev: BL 5/1/94; SLJ 6/94) [956.1]

DENG XIAOPING

4550 Evans, Richard. *Deng Xiaoping and the Making of Modern China* (9–adult). 1994, Viking $27.95 (0-670 84816-6). A biography of the most important political leader of the post-Mao era that chronicles the course of twentieth century Chinese history. (Rev: BL 3/1/94) [951]

FARMAN FARMAIAN, SATTAREH

4551 Farman Farmaian, Sattareh, and Dona Munker. *Daughter of Persia: A Woman's Journey from Her Father's Harem Through the Islamic Revolution* (9–adult). 1992, Crown $22 (0-517-58697-5). The daughter of a prominent Iranian recalls her privileged life in Tehran, her U.S. education, and her social reform work, which outraged Khomeini. (Rev: BL 1/1/92*; BTA; SHS) [955.05]

GANDHI, INDIRA

4552 Jayakar, Pupul. *Indira Gandhi: An Intimate Biography* (9–adult). 1993, Pantheon $27.50 (0-679-42479-2). Having been Gandhi's friend, Jayakar takes a personal look at Gandhi's relationships with her powerful father, neglected mother, philandering husband, grandfather, and sons. (Rev: BL 11/1/93) [954.04]

GANDHI, MOHANDAS

4553 Fisher, Leonard Everett. *Gandhi* (5–7). 1995, Atheneum $16 (0-689-80337-0). Many powerful black-and-white pictures enhance this unconventional story of Gandhi's role as a champion of Indian rights in South Africa. (Rev: BL 10/1/95; SLJ 10/95) [954.03]

HEE, KIM HYUN

4554 Hee, Kim Hyun. *The Tears of My Soul: The True Story of a North Korean Spy* (9–adult). 1993, Morrow $18 (0-688-12833-5). The former political activist Hee, who was recruited in college into the North Korean intelligence service, regretfully recalls her role in hiding the bomb aboard Korean Flight 858 in 1987 that caused the deaths of 115 people. (Rev: BL 10/15/93) [951.9]

HIROHITO, EMPEROR OF JAPAN

4555 Hoyt, Edwin. *Hirohito: The Emperor and the Man* (9–adult). 1992, Praeger $24.95 (0-275-94069-1). This biography presents the Japanese leader as a man of peace and goodwill. (Rev: BL 3/15/92) [952.03]

HUSSEIN, SADDAM

4556 Claypool, Jane. *Saddam Hussein* (6–12). (World Leaders) 1993, Rourke (P.O. Box 3328, Vero Beach, FL 32964) $19.93 (0-86625-477-3). Describes Hussein's violent childhood and rise to power and how he affected his nation. (Rev: BL 12/1/93; SLJ 1/94) [956.704]

4557 Stefoff, Rebecca. *Saddam Hussein: Absolute Ruler of Iraq* (7–12). 1995, Millbrook LB $15.90 (1-56294-475-4). A complex history of the Middle East is the backdrop for the biography of Hussein. (Rev: BL 3/15/95; SHS; SLJ 2/95) [956.704]

JESUS CHRIST

4558 *Jesus of Nazareth: A Life of Christ Through Pictures* (5–7). 1994, Simon & Schuster $16 (0-671-88651-7). (Rev: BL 1/1/95; SLJ 3/95) [232.9]

4559 *The Story of Jesus* (9–adult). 1993, Reader's Digest $33 (0-89577-472-0). A lavishly illustrated account of Jesus' life, portrayed in 200 selections, including biblical excerpts, prayers, stories, and poems. (Rev: BL 10/15/93; VOYA 2/94) [232.9]

KORDI, GOHAR

4560 Kordi, Gohar. *An Iranian Odyssey* (9–adult). 1993, Serpent's Tail paper $13.99 (1-85242-213-0). A memoir of a blind Iranian-born woman, who—without financial or emotional support from her parents—graduated from Teheran University in 1970. (Rev: BL 1/15/93; BTA) [955]

MIN, ANCHEE

4561 Min, Anchee. *Red Azalea* (9–adult). 1994, Pantheon $22 (0-394-25937-8). The hardships of Min's youth in Shanghai as a child of Mao's Cultural Revolution—a harsh portrait of China in the 1960s and 1970s. (Rev: BL 2/1/94) [951.05]

MORI, KYOKO

4562 Mori, Kyoko. *The Dream of Water: A Memoir* (9–adult). 1995, Holt $22.50 (0-8050-3260-6). An emotional memoir by a Japanese American woman who returns to her homeland after many years' absence. Awards: SLJ Best Book. (Rev: BL 1/1/95; SLJ 6/95) [813]

SASAKI, SADAKO

4563 Nasu, Masamoto. *Children of the Paper Crane: The Story of Sadako Sasaki and Her Struggle with the A-Bomb Disease* (9–adult). Tr. by Elizabeth W. Baldwin and others. 1991, M. E. Sharpe $19.95 (0-87332-715-2). A personal account of the legacy of the Hiroshima bombing that describes the devastating decline of one child and the effects on her family and all Japan. (Rev: BL 12/15/91) [362.1]

SULTANA (PSEUD.)

4564 Sasson, Jean. *Princess: A True Story of Life Behind the Veil in Saudi Arabia* (9–adult). 1992, Morrow $20 (0-688-11675-2). A member of the wealthy Saudi Arabian royal family recounts her life as an oppressed female in a male-dominated society. (Rev: BL 9/15/92) [305.42]

SUU KYI, AUNG SAN

4565 Parenteau, John. *Prisoner for Peace: Aung San Suu Kyi and Burma's Struggle for Democracy* (7–10). 1994, Morgan Reynolds $18.95 (1-883846-05-6). Chronicles Burma's struggle to be a democratic nation, focusing on the Nobel Prize winner's political activism and her subsequent arrest. (Rev: BL 11/1/94; BTA; SLJ 9/94; VOYA 4/95) [959.105]

4566 Suu Kyi, Aung San. *Freedom from Fear and Other Writings* (9–adult). 1991, Viking $25 (0-670-84560-4); Penguin paper $12 (0-14-017089-8). Speeches and essays on and interviews with the human rights activist and Nobel Peace Prize winner. (Rev: BL 2/15/92) [959.1]

TAJ AL-SALTANA

4567 Taj al-Saltana. *Crowning Anguish: Memoirs of a Persian Princess from the Harem to Modernity, 1884–1914* (9–adult). Edited by Abbas Amanat; Tr. by Anna Vanzan and Amin Neshati. 1993, Mage Publishers (1032 29th St. N.W., Washington, DC 20007) $29.95 (0-934211-35-3); paper $14.95 (0-934211-36-1). An Iranian princess's memoirs of her life in a sheik's palace that questions the traditions of this changing society. (Rev: BL 9/15/93) [955.05]

THAI, PAUL

4568 Fiffer, Sharon Sloan. *Imagining America: Paul Thai's Journey from the Killing Fields of Cambodia to Freedom in the U.S.A.* (9–adult). 1991, Paragon House $19.95 (1-55778-326-8). Comptemporary immigration story follow's one man's life from the killing fields of Cambodia to his hard-won success in the U.S. (Rev: BL 8/91; SHS) [325.21]

WEI-TIEN, HAN

4569 Pu Ning. *Red in Tooth and Claw: Twenty-Six Years in Communist Chinese Prisons* (9–adult). Tr. by Tung Chung-Hsuan and others. 1994, Grove/Atlantic $21 (0-8021-1454-7). A demonstration of the resiliency of the human body and spirit in the life of Han Wei-tien, a 26-year prisoner in China. (Rev: BL 4/15/94) [895.1]

ZHOU ENLAI

4570 Suyin, Han. *Eldest Son: Zhou Enlai and the Making of Modern China, 1898–1976* (9–adult). 1994, Hill & Wang $27.50 (0-8090-4151-0). An admiring portrait that relies heavily on the author's personal experiences of the Chinese leader and on anecdotes from those who knew him. (Rev: BL 2/1/94) [951.05]

Australia and the Pacific Islands

WARD, GLENYSE

4571 Ward, Glenyse. *Wandering Girl* (5–10). 1991, Holt $14.95 (0-8050-1634-1). A first-person account of a young aboriginal Australian girl and the prejudice and abuse she endured until she summoned the courage to strike out on her own. (Rev: BL 5/1/91; MJHS; SLJ 7/91) [305.8]

Europe

ACCOMANDO, CLAIRE HSU

4572 Accomando, Claire Hsu. *Love and Rutabaga: A Remembrance of the War Years* (9–adult). 1993, St. Martin's $19.95 (0-312-09330-6). A memoir of the years 1941–1944 in France, home of Accomando's mother's family. (Rev: BL 7/93) [944]

ALEXANDER III, KING OF MACEDONIA

4573 Stewart, Gail B. *Alexander the Great* (5–8). (The Importance Of) 1994, Lucent LB $14.95 (1-56006-047-6). (Rev: BL 8/94) [938.07]

ANDERSON, ANNA

4574 Lovell, James Blair. *Anastasia: The Lost Princess* (9–adult). 1991, Regnery Gateway $24.95 (0-89526-536-2). The story of the woman who claims to be the only surviving daughter of the last czar of Russia. (Rev: BL 8/91) [947.08]

ARTHUR, KING

4575 O'Neal, Michael. *King Arthur: Opposing Viewpoints* (6–10). (Great Mysteries: Opposing Viewpoints) 1992, Greenhaven LB $13.95 (0-89908-095-2). (Rev: BL 1/15/93; MJHS) [942.01]

AUBRAC, LUCIE

4576 Aubrac, Lucie. *Outwitting the Gestapo* (9–adult). 1993, Univ. of Nebraska $25 (0-8032-1029-9). Describes, in diary format, Aubrac's World War II French Resistance activities, the difficulties of wartime domestic life, and the underground in action. (Rev: BL 4/15/93) [940.53]

BERLAND-HYATT, FELICIA

4577 Berland-Hyatt, Felicia. *Close Calls: Memoirs of a Survivor* (9–adult). 1991, Holocaust Publications $13.95 (0-89604-150-6). A survivor's account of the Holocaust. (Rev: BL 1/15/92) [940.53]

BONAPARTE, NAPOLEON, EMPEROR OF THE FRENCH

4578 Carroll, Bob. *Napoleon Bonaparte* (5–8). 1994, Lucent $14.95 (1-56006-021-2). A discussion of Napoleon's life plus background on the French Revolution. (Rev: BL 5/15/94; SLJ 4/94) [944.05]

4579 Marrin, Albert. *Napoleon and the Napoleonic Wars* (7–12). 1991, Viking $14.95 (0-670-83480-7). Biography of one of the greatest military figures of all times, interspersed with a history of the French Revolution and its aftermath. Awards: SLJ Best Book. (Rev: BL 7/91; MJHS; SLJ 8/91*) [944.05]

BRACKEN, PAULINE

4580 Bracken, Pauline. *Light of Other Days: A Dublin Childhood* (9–adult). 1993, Dufour/Mercier paper $15.95 (1-85635-032-0). A childhood reminiscence in post–World War II Dublin. (Rev: BL 7/93) [823]

BREZNITZ, SCHLOMO

4581 Breznitz, Schlomo. *Memory Fields* (9–adult). 1993, Knopf $21 (0-679-40403-1). A Jewish psychologist recounts his childhood experiences as a converted Catholic hidden in a Czech convent/orphanage during World War II. (Rev: BL 12/15/92; SLJ 7/93) [943]

CATHERINE THE GREAT, EMPRESS OF RUSSIA

4582 Erickson, Carolly. *Great Catherine* (9–adult). 1994, Crown $25 (0-517-59091-3). A portrait of one of the world's great leaders that reads like a historical novel. (Rev: BL 5/15/94*; SLJ 1/95) [947]

CHURCHILL, WINSTON

4583 Rose, Norman. *Churchill: The Unruly Giant* (9–adult). 1995, Free Press $25 (0-02-874009-2). Charts Churchill's career and paints an image of the ambition, absorption, and pugnacity that won him both respect and resentment. (Rev: BL 7/95) [941.084]

DAMAN, HORTENSE

4584 Bles, Mark. *Child at War: The True Story of a Young Belgian Resistance Fighter* (9–adult). 1991, Mercury $20.95 (1-56279-004-8). (Rev: BL 3/1/91; SLJ 2/92) [940.53]

DE GAULLE, CHARLES

4585 Whitelaw, Nancy. *Charles de Gaulle: "I Am France"* (5–8). 1991, Dillon LB $12.95 (0-87518-486-3). Details the life and accomplishments of France's controversial leader. (Rev: BL 2/15/92) [944.083]

DESCHAMPS, HÉLÈNE

4586 Deschamps, Hélène. *Spyglass* (8–12). 1995, Holt $15.95 (0-8050-3536-2). Deschamps narrates her experiences as an agent for the World War II French Resistance from the age of 17, giving insight into the dangers of war. (Rev: BL 6/1–15/95) [940.54]

EICHENGREEN, LUCILLE

4587 Eichengreen, Lucille. *From Ashes to Life: My Memories of the Holocaust* (9–adult). 1994, Mercury paper $17.95 (1-56279-052-8). A young girl's harrowing experiences in the Nazi death camps end with liberation, followed by survivor guilt and search for meaning. Awards: SLJ Best Book. (Rev: SLJ 10/94)

ELIZABETH I, QUEEN OF ENGLAND

4588 Hibbert, Christopher. *The Virgin Queen: Elizabeth I, Genius of the Golden Age* (9–adult). 1991, Addison-Wesley $25 (0-201-15626-1). (Rev: BL 3/15/91; SHS) [941.085]

4589 Somerset, Anne. *Elizabeth I* (9–adult). 1991, Knopf $30 (0-394-54435-8). A highly detailed biography of the great monarch presenting fresh insights into the actions of Elizabeth as queen of Tudor England and as a woman. (Rev: BL 10/15/91) [942]

ELIZABETH II, QUEEN OF GREAT BRITAIN

4590 Auerbach, Susan. *Queen Elizabeth II* (6–12). (World Leaders) 1993, Rourke (P.O. Box 3328, Vero Beach, FL 32964) $19.93 (0-86625-481-1). (Rev: BL 12/1/93) [941.085]

FABERGÉ, CARL

4591 Habsburg-Lothringen, Geza von. *Carl Fabergé* (6–10). 1994, Abrams $19.95 (0-8109-3324-1). Presents the history of the creations of the Russian artisan known for his priceless Fabergé eggs, with color photos. (Rev: BL 7/94; SLJ 6/94) [739.2]

FILIPOVIC, ZLATA

4592 Filipovic, Zlata. *Zlata's Diary* (9–adult). 1994, Viking $16.95 (0-670-857-246). The personal journal of an accomplished 11-year-old Sarajevan girl whose world was shattered by the chaos and terror of war. (Rev: BL 3/1/94; BTA; MJHS; SLJ 7/94; VOYA 8/94) [949.7]

FRANK, ANNE

4593 Brown, Gene. *Anne Frank: Child of the Holocaust* (5–7). (Library of Famous Women) 1992, Rosen $14.95 (0-8239-1204-3). The life and death of a young Jewish girl who went into hiding with her family during World War II and wrote her now-famous diary. (Rev: BL 1/15/92) [940.53]

4594 Frank, Anne. *The Diary of a Young Girl: The Definitive Edition* (9–adult). Tr. by Susan Massotty. 1995, Doubleday $25 (0-385-47378-8). (Rev: BL 4/15/95; BTA; MJHS; SHS) [940.53]

4595 Lindwer, Willy. *The Last Seven Months of Anne Frank* (9–adult). 1992, Doubleday/Anchor paper $12 (0-385-42360-8). Moving testimony from 6 women interned in a concentration camp with Anne Frank relates the tragic conclusion of the diarist's life. (Rev: BL 3/15/91; SHS) [940.53]

FREEMAN, JOSEPH

4596 Freeman, Joseph. *Job: The Story of a Holocaust Survivor* (9–adult). 1995, Paragon House paper $9.95 (1-55778-738-7). A survivor tells what he witnessed in the Polish ghetto and at Auschwitz. (Rev: BL 9/15/95) [943.8]

GORBACHEV, MIKHAIL

4597 Sheehy, Gail. *The Man Who Changed the World: The Lives of Mikhail S. Gorbachev* (9–adult). 1990, HarperCollins $22.95 (0-06-016547-2). Provides insight into the Russian leader's personal life and political career. (Rev: BL 1/1/91; SHS) [947.085]

GÖRING, HERMANN

4598 Hoyt, Edwin. *Angels of Death: Goering's Luftwaffe* (9–adult). 1994, Tor/Forge $22.95 (0-312-85668-7). Traces the military career of Hermann Goering, the World War I fighter pilot who became leader of Hitler's air force. (Rev: BL 3/15/94) [940.54]

HENRY VIII, KING OF ENGLAND

4599 Weir, Alison. *The Six Wives of Henry VIII* (9–adult). 1992, Grove/Weidenfeld $24.95 (0-8021-1497-0). Well-documented portraits of each of King Henry the VIII's 6 wives. (Rev: BL 4/1/92; SLJ 8/92) [942.05]

HERZL, THEODOR

4600 Finkelstein, Norman H. *Theodor Herzl: Architect of a Nation* (7–12). 1991, Lerner LB

$15.95 (0-8225-4913-1). A respected playwright/journalist dedicates himself to helping the Jewish people obtain their own country. (Rev: BL 4/15/92; SLJ 7/92; YR) [320.5]

HITLER, ADOLF

4601 Heyes, Eileen. *Adolf Hitler* (6–12). 1994, Millbrook $16.90 (1-56294-343-X). Analyzes the führer's life and motivations. Examines Hitler's childhood, the Nazi party, and the Holocaust. (Rev: BL 10/15/94; SLJ 11/94; VOYA 5/95) [943.085]

4602 Ayer, Eleanor H. *Adolf Hitler* (7–12). (Importance Of) 1996, Lucent LB $16.95 (1-56006-072-7). This study of Hitler's rise includes analyses of the dictator's mental state, leadership qualities, and personality traits. (Rev: BL 3/15/95; SLJ 1/96)

ISABELLA I, QUEEN OF SPAIN

4603 Burch, Joann J. *Isabella of Castile: Queen on Horseback* (5–7). 1991, Watts LB $11.90 (0-531-20033-7). This sympathetic biography of the Spanish queen and empire builder contains a wide selection of engravings and portraits. (Rev: BL 10/15/91) [946]

IWENS, SIDNEY

4604 Iwens, Sidney. *How Dark the Heavens: 1400 Days in the Grip of Nazi Terror* (9–adult). 1990, Shengold $18.95 (0-88400-147-4). Diary entries recall time spent under Nazi control from 1941 until liberation in 1945. (Rev: BL 1/15/91) [940.53]

KEENAN, BRIAN

4605 Keenan, Brian. *An Evil Cradling: The Five-Year Ordeal of a Hostage* (9–adult). 1993, Viking $22.50 (0-670-85146-9); Penguin paper $10.95 (0-14-023641-4). Keenan's account of the 4-year ordeal of the Beirut hostages describes the beatings, illnesses, and torture they survived. Awards: Christopher. (Rev: BL 9/15/93) [956.9204]

KORN, ABRAM

4606 Korn, Abram. *Abe's Story: A Holocaust Memoir* (9–adult). 1995, Longstreet $18 (1-56352-206-3). The individuals who have survived ghettos and concentration camps never forgot that hope meant survival. (Rev: BL 4/15/95) [940.5318]

LEITNER, ISABELLA

4607 Leitner, Isabella. *The Big Lie: A True Story* (5–10). 1992, Scholastic $13.95 (0-590-45569-9). A simple, factual telling of the horrors experienced by a Hungarian Jewish family in Auschwitz, where Leitner's mother and baby sister were gassed. (Rev: BL 2/1/93*; SLJ 12/92) [940.53]

MILLER, RÉGINE

4608 Buchignani, Walter. *Tell No One Who You Are: The Hidden Childhood of Régine Miller* (7–12). 1994, Tundra $17.95 (0-88776-286-7). The story of Regine, 10, who was sent into hiding in 1942 to escape Nazi persecution, while her mother, father, and brother died in death camps. (Rev: BL 11/1/94; BTA; VOYA 2/96) [940.53]

MORRISSEY, MARTIN

4609 Morrissey, Martin. *The Changing Years* (9–adult). 1993, O'Brien Press paper $13.95 (0-86278-279-1). A humorous memoir of life in West Clare, Ireland, after World War II. (Rev: BL 7/93) [823]

MUSSOLINI, BENITO

4610 Hoyt, Edwin. *Mussolini's Empire: The Rise and Fall of the Fascist Vision* (9–adult). 1994, Wiley $24.95 (0-471-59151-3). Examines the career and personal life of Mussolini, and provides psychological insight into the Italian dictator's character. (Rev: BL 2/15/94) [945.09]

NICHOLAS II, CZAR OF RUSSIA

4611 Lieven, Dominic. *Nicholas II: Emperor of All the Russias* (9–adult). 1994, St. Martin's $24 (0-312-10510-X). A biography of the last Russian czar that portrays the doomed monarch as the inheritor of a government ill-prepared to deal with revolution. (Rev: BL 2/1/94) [947.08]

NIEMINEN, RAIJA

4612 Nieminen, Raija. *Voyage to the Island* (9–adult). 1990, Gallaudet Univ. $15.95 (0-930323-62-9). A hearing-impaired woman faces the challenge of adjusting to life in a foreign land. (Rev: BL 1/1/91) [362.4]

NOBEL, ALFRED

4613 Fant, Kenne. *Alfred Nobel* (9–adult). Tr. by Marianne Ruuth. 1993, Arcade $24.95 (1-55970-222-2). Two of Nobel's writings not released previously—a play and letters to his mistress—add a sense of gloominess to the story of his life. (Rev: BL 10/1/93)

PACK, AMY THORPE

4614 Lovell, Mary S. *Cast No Shadow: The Life of Betty Pack, the American Spy Who Changed the Course of World War II* (9–adult). 1992, Pantheon $22 (0-394-57556-3). An American socialite married to a British embassy official joins an intelligence organization and obtains secret information during World War II. (Rev: BL 3/1/92) [940.54]

RAYNER, RICHARD

4615 Rayner, Richard. *The Blue Suit* (9–adult). 1995, Houghton $19.95 (0-395-75288-4). A memoir of the author's past, when he got his kicks committing petty crimes. (Rev: BL 9/15/95) [813]

SCHINDLER, OSKAR

4616 Fensch, Thomas, ed. *Oskar Schindler and His List: The Man, the Book, the Film, the Holocaust and Its Survivors* (9–adult). 1995, Paul S. Eriksson $24.95 (0-8397-6472-3). A resource for film students studying the Holocaust, with articles, essays, and interviews related to the development of the book *Schindler's List*. (Rev: BL 9/15/95) [940.53]

4617 Roberts, Jack L. *Oskar Schindler* (7–12). (Importance Of) 1996, Lucent LB $16.95 (1-56006-079-4). A prosperous German turns his business into a safe haven for Jewish workers in contrast to the horrors of the Holocaust. (Rev: BL 3/15/95; SLJ 1/96)

STALIN, JOSEPH

4618 Conquest, Robert. *Stalin: Breaker of Nations* (9–adult). 1991, Viking $25 (0-670-84089-0). This biography of the Soviet dictator uses post-glasnost research to present evidence of the monstrous tyranny of the Stalin years. (Rev: BL 10/1/91)

4619 Otfinoski, Steven. *Joseph Stalin: Russia's Last Czar* (7–10). 1993, Millbrook $15.90 (1-56294-240-9). This introductory biography of Joseph Stalin includes many excerpts from his writings and speeches, as well as a chronology and black-and-white photos. (Rev: BL 11/1/93; SLJ 10/93; VOYA 2/94) [947.084]

4620 Volkogonov, Dmitri. *Stalin: Triumph and Tragedy* (9–adult). 1991, Grove/Weidenfeld $29.95 (0-8021-1165-3). A study of Russia's harsh, willful leader. (Rev: BL 8/91) [947.084]

4621 Whitelaw, Nancy. *Joseph Stalin: From Peasant to Premier* (6–10). (People in Focus) 1992, Dillon LB $13.95 (0-87518-557-6). (Rev: BL 1/15/93) [947.084]

SUTIN, JACK AND ROCHELLE

4622 Sutin, Jack, and Rochelle Sutin. *Jack and Rochelle: A Holocaust Story of Love and Survival* (9–adult). 1995, Graywolf $22.95 (1-55597-224-1). A story of love and resistance of Jewish partisans hiding out in the woods of Poland during the Holocaust. (Rev: BL 5/15/95) [940.53]

VAN BEEK, CATO BONTJES

4623 Friedman, Ina R. *Flying Against the Wind: The Story of a Young Woman Who Defied the Nazis* (6–10). 1995, Lodgepole Press (P.O. Box 1259, Brookline, MA 02146) paper $11.95 (1-886721-00-9). Tells the story of German Cato Bontjes van Beek, who grew up in a progressive household and was executed by the Nazis, along with her boyfriend, for joining an underground movement. (Rev: BL 7/95; VOYA 4/96) [940.53]

VICTORIA, QUEEN OF THE UNITED KINGDOM

4624 St. Aubyn, Giles. *Queen Victoria: A Portrait* (9–adult). 1992, Atheneum $29.95 (0-689-12141-5). An intimate portrait of the formidable queen that sympathetically treats her famous reserve, self-centeredness, and long bereavement following her husband's death. (Rev: BL 12/15/91) [941.081]

VOGEL, ILSE-MARGRET

4625 Vogel, Ilse-Margret. *Bad Times, Good Friends: A Personal Memoir* (8–12). 1992, Harcourt $16.95 (0-15-205528-2). Memoir of an ordinary German who hated Hitler, and what her family did to undermine the Nazi war effort. (Rev: BL 9/15/92; SLJ 1/93; YR) [943]

WAITE, TERRY

4626 Waite, Terry. *Taken on Trust* (9–adult). 1993, Harcourt $24.95 (0-15-187849-8). A chronicle of Waite's 5 years as a hostage in Beirut. Includes thoughts about his childhood and family, his survival, and how he became a hostage. (Rev: BL 9/15/93) [956.9204]

WALESA, LECH

4627 Lazo, Caroline. *Lech Walesa* (5–7). (Peacemakers) 1993, Dillon $13.95 (0-87518-525-8).

Discusses this Polish president's life, politics, position as leader of the Solidarity labor movement, and winning of the Nobel Peace Prize. (Rev: BL 12/15/93; SLJ 1/94) [943.805]

4628 Vnenchak, Dennis. *Lech Walesa and Poland* (7–12). 1994, Watts LB $14.84 (0-531-11288-8). As much a history of an era as an account of Walesa's life. (Rev: BL 3/1/95) [943.805]

WALLENBERG, RAOUL

4629 Linnéa, Sharon. *Raoul Wallenberg: The Man Who Stopped Death* (5–7). 1993, Jewish Publication Society $17.95 (0-8276-0440-8); paper $9.95 (0-8276-0448-3). A biography of the Swedish architect who risked his life to save thousands of Hungarian Jews from the Holocaust. (Rev: BL 6/1–15/93; SLJ 10/93) [940.54]

WALTER, JAKOB

4630 Walter, Jakob. *The Diary of a Napoleonic Foot Soldier* (9–adult). 1991, Doubleday $20 (0-385-41696-2). A firsthand account of the brutality of war by one of Napoleon's Grand Army soldiers. (Rev: BL 8/91*) [940.2]

WIESEL, ELIE

4631 Lazo, Caroline. *Elie Wiesel* (5–7). 1994, Dillon LB $13.95 (0-87518-636-X); paper $7.95 (0-382-24715-9). A chronicle of Wiesel's life, which bears witness to the Holocaust. (Rev: BL 2/15/95) [813]

4632 Schuman, Michael A. *Elie Wiesel: Voice from the Holocaust* (6–9). 1994, Enslow $17.95 (0-89490-428-0). This biography of the Nazi death camp survivor examines how the Holocaust shaped Wiesel's life and work, using interviews and excerpts from his writings. (Rev: BL 7/94; BTA; MJHS; SLJ 5/94; VOYA 8/94) [813]

YELTSIN, BORIS

4633 Miller, Calvin Craig. *Boris Yeltsin: First President of Russia* (6–9). 1994, Morgan Reynolds $18.95 (1-883846-08-0). (Rev: BL 12/1/94; BTA; SLJ 4/95; VOYA 2/95) [947.086]

4634 Morrison, John. *Boris Yeltsin: From Bolshevik to Democrat* (9–adult). 1991, Dutton $20 (0-525-93431-6). Focuses on the struggle to democratize the Soviet Union and the reformation efforts of the newly elected president of the Russian Republic. (Rev: BL 11/1/91; SHS) [947.085]

4635 Otfinoski, Steven. *Boris Yeltsin and the Rebirth of Russia* (7–12). 1995, Millbrook $15.90 (1-56294-478-9). The relationship between Yeltsin's political career and the rise of the Russian Republic. (Rev: BL 4/1/95; SHS; SLJ 3/95) [947.086]

North America (excluding the United States)

CASTRO, FIDEL

4636 Bentley, Judith. *Fidel Castro of Cuba* (7–12). (In Focus Biographies) 1991, Messner LB $13.98 (0-671-70198-3); paper $7.95 (0-671-70199-1). Relates the Cuban leader's personal story to a detailed history of his country, its problems and achievements, and the changing international scene. (Rev: BL 11/1/91; BY) [972.91]

4637 Beyer, Don E. *Castro!* (7–12). 1993, Watts $13.90 (0-531-13027-4). A highly critical biography of the Cuban dictator. (Rev: BL 5/1/93; SLJ 6/93; VOYA 10/93) [972.9106]

4638 Brown, Warren. *Fidel Castro: Cuban Revolutionary* (7–10). 1994, Millbrook $15.90 (1-56294-385-5). Focuses on Castro within the broad scope of Cuba's economic and political history. (Rev: BL 3/15/94; SLJ 5/94; VOYA 6/94) [972.9106]

CORTÉS, HERNÁN

4639 Lilley, Stephen R. *Hernando Cortes* (6–9). (Importance Of) 1996, Lucent LB $16.95 (1-56006-066-2). Biography of a Spanish explorer and how his exploits changed both Spain and Mexico. (Rev: BL 3/15/96; SLJ 1/96)

4640 Marks, Richard. *Cortés: The Great Adventurer and the Fate of Aztec Mexico* (9–adult). 1993, Knopf $27.50 (0-679-40609-3). This biography of Cortés portrays him neither as a hero nor as a murderer, instead presenting an unbiased account of the Spanish-Aztec meeting. (Rev: BL 9/15/93*) [972]

MALINCHE

4641 Durán, Gloria. *Malinche: Slave Princess of Cortez* (8–10). 1993, Shoe String/Linnet $17.50 (0-208-02343-7). The story of the Aztec mistress of and interpreter for Cortez, whom he declared the greatest help, after God, in his conquest. (Rev: BL 6/1–15/93; SLJ 7/93) [972]

MOWAT, FARLEY

4642 Mowat, Farley. *Born Naked* (9–adult). 1994, Houghton $21.95 (0-395-68927-9). In this affectionate memoir, the famous environmentalist remembers his Canadian childhood in the 1920s and 1930s. Awards: SLJ Best Book. (Rev: BL 1/1/94; MJHS; SLJ 10/94) [808.0092]

MUÑOZ MARÍN, LUIS

4643 Bernier-Grand, Carmen T. *Poet and Politician of Puerto Rico: Don Luis Muñoz Marín* (5–8). 1995, Orchard LB $15.99 (0-531-08737-9). A biography of Munóz Marín and a history of the island. (Rev: BL 5/15/95; SLJ 4/95) [972.9505]

RODRIGUEZ, ANA

4644 Rodriguez, Ana, and Glenn Garvin. *Diary of a Survivor: Nineteen Years in a Cuban Woman's Prison* (9–adult). 1995, St. Martin's $22.95 (0-312-13050-3). A former Cuban political prisoner of 19 years, Rodriguez details her experiences. (Rev: BL 5/15/95*) [365]

VILLA, FRANCISCO "PANCHO"

4645 Carroll, Bob. *Pancho Villa* (6–12). 1996, Lucent LB $16.95 (1-56006-069-7). Offers insight into the Mexican rebel's impact on history. (Rev: BL 3/15/96; SLJ 2/96)

4646 O'Brien, Steven. *Pancho Villa* (5–9). (Hispanics of Achievement) 1994, Chelsea House $18.95 (0-7910-1257-3). (Rev: BL 9/15/94; MJHS) [972.08]

Miscellaneous Interesting Lives

ALEXANDER, SALLY HOBART

4647 Alexander, Sally Hobart. *Taking Hold: My Journey into Blindness* (6–12). 1994, Macmillan $13.95 (0-02-700402-3). A true story of a third-grade teacher who lost her sight but found independence. Awards: Christopher. (Rev: BL 1/15/95; SLJ 4/95; VOYA 4/95) [362.4]

ALICEA, GIL C.

4648 Alicea, Gil C., and Carmine De Sena. *The Air Down Here: True Tales from a South Bronx Boyhood* (7–12). 1995, Chronicle $14.95 (0-8118-1048-8). An autobiographical account, in 115 short essays, of Puerto Rican Gil Alicea's experiences growing up in the Bronx. (Rev: BL 10/15/95; SLJ 3/96) [974.7]

ARCHER FAMILY

4649 Archer, Chalmers. *Growing Up Black in Rural Mississippi* (9–adult). 1992, Walker $19.95 (0-8027-1175-8). History of a Mississippi Delta family and the contributions they made to American culture. (Rev: BL 3/1/92) [976.2]

ARTHUR, ELIZABETH

4650 Arthur, Elizabeth. *Looking for the Klondike Stone* (9–adult). 1993, Knopf $23 (0-679-41894-6). A memoir of Arthur's life-altering summer camp experiences in Vermont's Green Mountains. (Rev: BL 6/1–15/93*) [818]

BARBER, PHYLLIS

4651 Barber, Phyllis. *How I Got Cultured: A Nevada Memoir* (9–adult). 1992, Univ. of Georgia $24.95 (0-8203-1413-7). Barber vividly recalls her Mormon childhood near Las Vegas in the 1950s with poetic language and keen insights. Awards: BL Editors' Choice. (Rev: BL 6/1/92) [979.3]

BARRON, SEAN

4652 Barron, Judy, and Sean Barron. *There's a Boy in Here* (9–adult). 1992, Simon & Schuster $20 (0-671-76111-0). One family's struggle with autism, told from both the parents' and child's points of view. (Rev: BL 2/1/92) [618.92]

BOYLE, FATHER GREG

4653 Fremon, Celeste. *Father Greg and the Homeboys: The Extraordinary Journey of Father Greg Boyle and His Work with the Latino Gangs of East L.A.* (9–adult). 1995, Hyperion $22.95 (0-7868-6089-8). This look at the intervention work of Father Greg Boyle with inner-city gangbangers features 10 of their autobiographies. (Rev: BL 6/1–15/95) [259]

BROWN, CECIL

4654 Brown, Cecil. *Coming Up Down Home: Memoir of a Sharecropper's Son* (9–adult). 1993, Ecco $22.95 (0-88001-293-5). A coming-of-age memoir of an African American in New York City in the 1940s and 1950s. (Rev: BL 7/93) [813]

BUTTINO, FRANK

4655 Buttino, Frank, and Lou Buttino. *A Special Agent: Gay and Inside the FBI* (9–adult). 1993, Morrow $23 (0-688-11958-1). Chronicles the sloppy investigation, termination, and still-pending lawsuit of a conservative, homosexual FBI agent whose work had been acknowledged as superior. (Rev: BL 6/1–15/93) [363.2]

CARY, LORENE

4656 Cary, Lorene. *Black Ice* (9–adult). 1991, Knopf $19.95 (0-394-57465-6). Cary was a 15-year-old black girl from Philadelphia who won a scholarship to an elite prep school in New England. She describes her transitions to an unfamiliar life and the racism over which she triumphs. Awards: SLJ Best Book; YALSA Best Book for Young Adults. (Rev: BL 2/15/91*; SLJ 8/91) [373.18]

CASTELLANO, CONSTANTINO PAUL

4657 O'Brien, Joseph F., and Andris Kurins. *Boss of Bosses: The Fall of the Godfather: The FBI and Paul Castellano* (9–adult). 1991, Simon & Schuster $22.95 (0-671-70815-5). (Rev: BL 4/15/91; SHS) [364.1]

CHAPELLE, DICKEY

4658 Ostroff, Roberta. *Fire in the Wind: The Life of Dickey Chapelle* (9–adult). 1992, Ballantine $21 (0-345-36274-8). Details the unusual life of a gutsy female combat photographer-reporter. (Rev: BL 2/1/92) [070.4]

CHASE, KEN

4659 Chase, Clifford. *The Hurry-Up Song: A Memoir of Losing My Brother* (9–adult). 1995, HarperSan Francisco $20 (0-06-251019-3). A memoir of an older brother's death from AIDS at age 37. (Rev: BL 2/15/95) [305.38]

CICIPPIO, JOSEPH

4660 Cicippio, Joseph, and Richard W. Hope. *Chains to Roses: The Joseph Cicippio Story* (9–adult). 1993, WRS (P.O. Box 21207, Waco, TX 76702-1207) $21.95 (1-56796-025-1). The experiences of this former comptroller for Beirut's American University as a hostage included being confined with an insane man and having a mysterious operation performed on him. (Rev: BL 12/15/93) [956.9204]

CISNEROS, SANDRA

4661 Cisneros, Sandra. *La casa en Mango Street* (6–12). Tr. by Elena Poniatowska. 1994, Random/Vintage $9 (0-679-75526-8). Vignettes—in the vernacular of Mexico—of Cisneros's Chicago Latino neighborhood and the poverty, racism, and difficulties experienced by her family and friends. English title: *The House on Mango Street*. (Rev: BL 6/1–15/95)

COLLINS, PAULINE

4662 Collins, Pauline. *Letter to Louise: A Loving Memoir to the Daughter I Gave Up for Adoption More Than Twenty-Five Years Ago* (9–adult). 1992, HarperCollins $20 (0-06-016589-8). British actress Collins's remembrances of childhood, early career struggles, and young-adult life, including an unwanted pregnancy. (Rev: BL 10/15/92) [362.83]

CROW DOG, LEONARD

4663 Crow Dog, Leonard, and Richard Erdoes. *Crow Dog: Four Generations of Sioux Medicine Men* (9–adult). 1995, HarperCollins $25 (0-06-016861-7). The family history and beliefs of a Sioux medicine man. (Rev: BL 4/15/95*) [929]

DEWEY, JENNIFER OWINGS

4664 Dewey, Jennifer Owings. *Cowgirl Dreams: A Western Childhood* (5–7). 1995, Boyds Mills $14.95 (1-56397-377-4). An "autobiographical narrative" of Dewey's childhood from ages 7 to 12—told simply and forcefully, but dark and disturbing in spots. (Rev: BL 10/15/95; SLJ 12/95)

DRUCKER, OLGA LEVY

4665 Drucker, Olga Levy. *Kindertransport* (6–12). 1992, Holt $14.95 (0-8050-1711-9). The author's 6 years in England as an evacuee from Nazi Germany and her eventual reunion with her parents in the U.S. after the war. Awards: YALSA Best Book for Young Adults. (Rev: BL 11/1/92; SLJ 11/92; YR) [940.53]

DULL KNIFE FAMILY

4666 Starita, Joe. *The Dull Knifes of Pine Ridge: A Lakota Odyssey* (9–adult). 1995, Putnam $24.95 (0-399-14010-7). The story of the Lakota Sioux as told through the life of one family, the Dull Knifes of Pine Ridge. (Rev: BL 3/15/95*) [973]

EQUIANO, OLAUDAH

4667 Cameron, Ann. *The Kidnapped Prince: The Life of Olaudah Equiano* (5–8). 1995, Knopf $16 (0-679-85619-6). This gripping story of an 11-year-old boy who spent 11 years as a slave in

England was a best-seller when it was first published in 1789. (Rev: BL 1/1/95; SLJ 2/95) [305.5]

FLIPPER, HENRY O.

4668 Pfeifer, Kathryn Browne. *Henry O. Flipper* (5–8). (African American Soldiers) 1993, Twenty-First Century LB $14.95 (0-8050-2351-8). Chronicles the life of the first African American to graduate from West Point. (Rev: BL 2/15/94; MJHS) [355]

FOSS, JOE

4669 Foss, Joe, and Donna Wild Foss. *A Proud American: The Autobiography of Joe Foss* (9–adult). 1992, Pocket $22 (0-671-75735-0). The autobiography of a World War II U.S. Marine pilot and Medal of Honor winner who served 2 terms as governor of South Dakota. (Rev: BL 11/15/92) [940.54]

FRANZESE, MICHAEL

4670 Franzese, Michael, and Dary Matera. *Quitting the Mob: How the "Yuppie Don" Left the Mafia and Lived to Tell All* (9–adult). 1992, HarperCollins $20 (0-06-016493-X). A Colombo crime family member—now out of the Mafia after reluctantly testifying against it to gain his freedom—provides a look at life inside La Cosa Nostra. (Rev: BL 12/1/91) [364.1]

GABRESKI, FRANCIS

4671 Gabreski, Francis, and Carl Molesworth. *Gabby: A Fighter Pilot's Life* (9–adult). 1991, Crown/Orion $20 (0-517-57801-8). The autobiography of America's highest-scoring living ace, covering wartime events from Pearl Harbor to Korea. (Rev: BL 9/1/91) [940.54]

GOLAN, LEW

4672 Golan, Lew. *Reading Between the Lips* (9–adult). 1995, Bonus $22.95 (1-56625-021-8). The author, deprived of his hearing as a child, records his observations of the deaf and hearing cultures. (Rev: BL 3/1/95*) [362.4]

GOLDSCHLAG, STELLA

4673 Wyden, Peter. *Stella* (9–adult). 1992, Simon & Schuster $22.50 (0-671-67361-0). The biography of Stella Goldschlag, a Jew who, after her arrest and torture, agreed to become a "catcher" of other Jews in Nazi Germany in order to survive. (Rev: BL 10/15/92*) [940.53]

GRIFFITH, BOBBY

4674 Aarons, Leroy. *Prayers for Bobby: A Mother's Coming to Terms with the Suicide of Her Gay Son* (9–adult). 1995, HarperSan Francisco $20 (0-06-251122-X). Presbyterian Mary Griffith told her son to pray to God for a cure when she found he was gay. After his suicide, she now tries to balance religion with his death. (Rev: BL 6/1–15/95) [305.38]

GUIBERT, HERVÉ

4675 Guibert, Hervé. *The Compassion Protocol* (9–adult). Tr. by James Kirkup. 1994, Braziller $20 (0-8076-1352-5). This journal of the author's final days fighting AIDS describes his pain and despair, the ecstasy of defying death by daring to live, and redemption through writing. (Rev: BL 3/1/94*) [843]

HAIZLIP, SHIRLEY TAYLOR

4676 Haizlip, Shirley Taylor. *The Sweeter the Juice: A Family Memoir in Black and White* (9–adult). 1994, Simon & Schuster $22 (0-671-79235-0). Haizlip, a woman of African American, white, and Native American heritage, tells how race shattered the lives of her relatives and how she's tried to pick up the pieces. (Rev: BL 12/1/93*) [929.2]

HOFFMAN, RICHARD

4677 Hoffman, Richard. *Half the House* (9–adult). 1995, Harcourt $20 (0-15-100174-X). Hoffman suffered for decades in secret shame over being sexually molested by a local baseball coach, which he reveals to his dad. (Rev: BL 9/15/95) [974.8]

HOFVENDAHL, RUSS

4678 Hofvendahl, Russ. *A Land So Fair and Bright: The True Story of a Young Man's Adventures Across Depression America* (9–adult). 1991, Sheridan House (145 Palisade St., Dobbs Ferry, NY 10522) $22.95 (0-924486-10-4). The real exploits of a teenager riding the rails, hitchhiking and hoboing across the U.S. during the Depression. (Rev: BL 8/91) [917.304]

JACOBSEN, DAVID

4679 Jacobsen, David, and Gerald Astor. *Hostage: My Nightmare in Beirut* (9–adult). 1991, Donald I. Fine $19.95 (1-55611-265-3). An ex-hostage recounts his captivity by Lebanese. (Rev: BL 6/1/91) [956.920]

JOHNSON, ISAAC

4680 Marston, Hope Irvin. *Isaac Johnson: From Slave to Stonecutter* (5–8). 1995, Dutton/Cobblehill $14.99 (0-525-65165-9). Based on Johnson's 1901 autobiography, *Slavery Days in Old Kentucky*, Marston brings the story of Isaac Johnson to life. (Rev: BL 9/15/95; SLJ 9/95) [976.9]

JOHNSON, LOU ANNE

4681 Johnson, Lou Anne. *My Posse Don't Do Homework* (9–adult). 1992, St. Martin's $19.95 (0-312-07638-X). Johnson—who taught non-English-speaking teens in an inner-city school—writes with concern about educational bureaucracy. This book was the basis for the movie and TV series *Dangerous Minds*. (Rev: BL 8/92; BTA; SLJ 12/92) [371.1]

JOHNSON, SAM

4682 Johnson, Sam, and Jan Winebrenner. *Captive Warriors: A Vietnam POW's Story* (9–adult). 1992, Texas A & M Univ. $24.50 (0-89096-496-3). A former fighter pilot recounts his experiences as a prisoner of war in North Vietnam. (Rev: BL 4/1/92) [959.704]

KLECKLEY, ELIZABETH

4683 Rutberg, Becky. *Mary Lincoln's Dressmaker: Elizabeth Kleckley's Remarkable Rise from Slave to White House Confidante* (6–10). 1995, Walker $15.95 (0-8027-8224-8). The story of a slave, a fine seamstress, who was freed and became Mary Todd Lincoln's dressmaker. (Rev: BL 10/15/95; SLJ 12/95; VOYA 12/95) [973.7]

KOSSMAN, NINA

4684 Kossman, Nina. *Behind the Border* (5–7). 1994, Lothrop $14 (0-688-13494-7). Vignettes of a Russian woman's early years living behind the Iron Curtain, before moving to the U.S. with her family. (Rev: BL 8/94; MJHS; SLJ 10/94) [947.085]

LAME DEER, ARCHIE FIRE

4685 Lame Deer, Archie Fire, and Richard Erdoes. *Gift of Power: The Life and Teachings of a Lakota Medicine Man* (9–adult). 1992, Bear & Co. (P.O. Box 2860, Santa Fe, NM 87504-2860) $21.95 (0-939680-87-4). A Lakota spiritual leader tells of his early life, discusses his role as tribal medicine man, and explains traditional beliefs. (Rev: BL 10/1/92) [978.3]

LEWIS, HELEN

4686 Lewis, Helen. *A Time to Speak* (9–adult). 1993, Blackstaff paper $16.95 (0-85640-491-8). Lewis recounts her wartime experiences in a Jewish ghetto and in Auschwitz, as well as her depression following liberation. (Rev: BL 3/1/93) [940.53]

LIUZZO, VIOLA

4687 Siegel, Beatrice. *Murder on the Highway: The Viola Liuzzo Story* (5–9). 1994, Four Winds $14.95 (0-02-782632-5). Viola Liuzzo was 39, white, the mother of 5, and murdered by the KKK for participating in the 1965 Selma-to-Montgomery civil rights march. This tells her story. (Rev: BL 12/15/93; SLJ 1/94; VOYA 2/94) [364.1]

LYON, MARY

4688 Rosen, Dorothy Schack. *A Fire in Her Bones: The Story of Mary Lyon* (5–7). 1995, Carolrhoda LB $13.13 (0-87614-840-2). This story of Mary Lyon's life and ambition to found the Mount Holyoke Female Seminary also gives a view of the hardships women faced in the nineteenth century. (Rev: BL 6/1–15/95; SLJ 4/95) [378.744]

MACKIN, ELTON

4689 Mackin, Elton E. *Suddenly We Didn't Want to Die: Memoirs of a World War I Marine* (9–adult). 1993, Presidio $19.95 (0-89141-498-3). Based on notes and tapes left to his son, this account details Mackin's life as a raw recruit, member of the American Expeditionary Force, and decorated World War I hero. (Rev: BL 10/15/93; BY) [940.4]

MCCLUNG, KEVIN

4690 McClung, Kevin, and Stephen J. Rivele. *Dark Genius: A Child Prodigy in the Shadow of the CIA* (9–adult). 1991, Knightsbridge $22.95 (1-56129-142-0). This autobiographical story of a gilfted child inventor whose work was monitored by the CIA reveals disturbing governmental machinations. (Rev: BL 10/1/91) [364.1]

MCDONALD, CHEROKEE PAUL

4691 McDonald, Cherokee Paul. *Blue Truth: Walking the Thin Blue Line—One Cop's Story of Life in the Streets* (9–adult). 1991, Donald I. Fine $18.95 (1-55611-246-7). A Fort Lauderdale police officer's job takes a heavy toll on his personal life. (Rev: BL 6/1/91) [363.2]

NELSON, JILL

4692 Nelson, Jill. *Volunteer Slavery: My Authentic Negro Experience* (9–adult). 1993, Noble Press (111 E. Chestnut, Suite 48A, Chicago, IL 60611) $21.95 (1-879360-24-1). The *Washington Post* Sunday magazine's first African American and first female writer recalls her 4-year stint there, revealing the tokenism she experienced. (Rev: BL 5/1/93*) [070.92]

NOVAK, MARIAN FAYE

4693 Novak, Marian Faye. *Lonely Girls with Burning Eyes: A Wife Recalls Her Husband's Journey Home from Vietnam* (9–adult). 1991, Little, Brown $19.95 (0-316-61323-1). A Vietnam veteran's wife recalls her struggles at home while her husband was fighting an unpopular war. (Rev: BL 1/15/91) [959.704]

PARRISH, ROBERT

4694 Parrish, Robert. *Combat Recon: My Year with the ARVN* (9–adult). 1991, St. Martin's $19.95 (0-312-05403-3). An infantryman's account of the year spent as an American adviser to a South Vietnamese battalion. (Rev: BL 1/15/91) [959.704]

PATRICK FAMILY

4695 Patrick, Sean. *Patrick's Corner* (9–adult). 1992, Pelican $15.95 (0-88289-878-7). The youngest of 6 boys fondly recalls his closeknit Irish Catholic family. (Rev: BL 3/15/92) [977]

PATTON FAMILY

4696 Patton, Robert H. *The Pattons: A Personal History of an American Family* (9–adult). 1994, Crown $25 (0-517-59068-9). General George Patton's grandson provides insight into his famous grandfather and the Patton family. (Rev: BL 3/1/94) [355]

PECK, SCOTT

4697 Peck, Scott. *All-American Boy: A Gay Son's Search for His Father* (9–adult). 1995, Scribner $22 (0-02-595362-1). An autobiography of a young, religious gay man in the military coming to terms with his sexuality. (Rev: BL 3/15/95) [305.38]

PURCELL, BEN AND ANNE

4698 Purcell, Ben, and Anne Purcell. *Love and Duty* (9–adult). 1992, St. Martin's $17.95 (0-312-07020-9). Autobiographical account of how an American officer and his wife coped with the colonel's 5 years of harsh captivity in a North Vietnamese prison camp. (Rev: BL 3/1/92) [959.704]

RAGONESE, PAUL

4699 Ragonese, Paul, and Berry Stainback. *The Soul of a Cop: The Story of One of America's Most Decorated Cops* (9–adult). 1991, St. Martin's $19.95 (0-312-04577-8). A celebrated former New York City police officer tells the very human story of the frustrations and rewards of being a member of the force. (Rev: BL 9/15/91) [363.2]

RICH, JOHN FRANCIS

4700 Rich, Kim. *Johnny's Girl: A Daughter's Memoir of Growing Up in Alaska's Underground* (9–adult). 1993, Morrow paper $15.95 (0-688-11836-4). A bittersweet memoir of Rich's childhood—the daughter of an Alaskan gambler/con man and a mentally unstable prostitute. (Rev: BL 3/1/93) [364.1]

RIVERS, LAFEYETTE AND PHAROAH

4701 Kotlowitz, Alex. *There Are No Children Here: The Story of Two Boys Growing Up in the Other America* (9–adult). 1991, Doubleday $21.95 (0-385-26526-3). A profile of squalid living conditions in a Chicago housing project and 2 brothers who live there. Awards: YALSA Best Book for Young Adults. (Rev: BL 1/15/91; SHS; SLJ 11/91) [305.23]

ROORBACH, BILL

4702 Roorbach, Bill. *Summers with Juliet* (9–adult). 1992, Houghton $19.95 (0-395-57323-8). An eight-year relationship, carried on only during the summer, grows toward a happy ending. (Rev: BL 1/15/92) [974]

ROSS, GLEN

4703 Ross, Glen. *On Coon Mountain: Scenes from a Childhood in the Oklahoma Hills* (9–adult). 1992, Univ. of Oklahoma $19.95 (0-8061-2405-9). Autobiographical essays depicting ways of life in Oklahoma between the Great Depression and World War II. (Rev: BL 3/1/92) [420]

SALZMAN, MARK

4704 Salzman, Mark. *Lost in Place: Growing Up Absurd in Suburbia* (9–adult). 1995, Random $22 (0-679-43945-5). A memoir of Salzman's adolescent years and his wonderfully quirky lifestyle, highlightled by his conversations with his father. (Rev: BL 9/1/95*; SLJ 12/95; VOYA 4/96) [813.54]

SHERBURNE, ANDREW

4705 Sherburne, Andrew. *The Memoirs of Andrew Sherburne: Patriot and Privateer of the American Revolution* (5–8). Edited by Karen Zeinert. Illus. 1993, Shoe String/Linnet $15.95 (0-208-02354-2). This excerpt from Sherburne's autobiography of the war years tells of his early life at sea and his capture and imprisonment by the British. (Rev: BL 5/15/93; SLJ 7/93) [973]

SHERR, LYNN

4706 Sherr, Lynn. *Failure Is Impossible: Susan B. Anthony in Her Own Words* (9–12). 1995, Times Books $23 (0-8129-2430-4). One woman's passionate belief in equal rights for all people chronicled in her own speeches, correspondence, and diary entries. (Rev: BL 2/1/95; SLJ 3/96)

STIVENDER, ED

4707 Stivender, Ed. *Still Catholic after All These Fears* (9–adult). 1995, August House $19.95 (0-87483-403-1). A look at a Catholic boyhood and the trials of growing up. (Rev: BL 4/1/95) [282]

STOFFEY, BOB

4708 Stoffey, Bob. *Cleared Hot! A Marine Combat Pilot's Vietnam Diary* (9–adult). 1992, St. Martin's $21.95 (0-312-06929-4). Memoir of a marine helicopter officer who flew 400-plus missions. (Rev: BL 2/15/92) [959.7]

SWAN, MADONNA

4709 Swan, Madonna, and Mark St. Pierre. *Madonna Swan: A Lakota Woman's Story* (9–adult). 1991, Univ. of Oklahoma $19.95 (0-8061-2369-9). In a series of interviews, a Lakota Sioux woman recounts her childhood on the reservation, her stay at a tuberculosis sanitarium, her marriage, family life, and college years. (Rev: BL 11/15/91) [973]

THOMPSON, FRANK (PSEUD.)

4710 Stevens, Bryna. *Frank Thompson: Her Civil War Story* (5–7). 1992, Macmillan $13.95 (0-02-788185-7). The story of Emma Edmonds, a Canadian woman who disguised herself as a man named Frank Thompson, joined the Union Army, and served as a nurse and spy during the Civil War. (Rev: BL 12/15/92; SLJ 10/92; YR) [973.7]

TOLL, NELLY S.

4711 Toll, Nelly S. *Behind the Secret Window: A Memoir of a Hidden Childhood* (6–9). 1993, Dial $15.99 (0-8037-1362-2). The harrowing account of the experiences of a Jewish family during World War II, based on a diary the author began at age 8. Awards: IRA Children's Book. (Rev: BL 3/15/93; BTA; MJHS) [940.5318]

WHITE, MEL

4712 White, Mel. *Stranger at the Gate: To Be Gay and Christian in America* (9–adult). 1994, Simon & Schuster $23 (0-671-88407-7). Drawing on his own experiences growing up religious, gay, and ashamed in a conservative Christian family, White exposes the homophobia of the religious right. (Rev: BL 4/1/94*) [262.1]

WHYTE, EDNA GARDNER

4713 Whyte, Edna Gardner, and Ann L. Cooper. *Rising above It: An Autobiography* (9–adult). 1991, Crown/Orion $20 (0-517-57685-6). In this autobiography of an early woman aviator, Whyte reflects on what drove her to succeed against great odds and documents the achievements of other female pilots. (Rev: BL 10/1/91; SLJ 4/92) [629.13]

WICKHAM, DE WAYNE

4714 Wickham, De Wayne. *Woodholme: A Black Man's Story of Growing Up Alone* (9–adult). 1995, Farrar $20 (0-374-29283-3). A reflection of life in the 1960s, when the author, an impressionable, orphaned African American teen, became a caddy at a prestigious country club. (Rev: BL 5/1/95) [973]

WILLIAMS, GREGORY HOWARD

4715 Williams, Gregory Howard. *Life on the Color Line: The True Story of a White Boy Who Discovered He Was Black* (9–adult). 1995, Dutton $22.95 (0-525-93850-8). Williams tells his riveting story of struggle against racism: Growing up white in segregated Virginia in the 1950s, he discovered at age 10 that he was black. Awards: SLJ Best Book. (Rev: BL 2/1/95; SLJ 7/95) [305.896]

WINGO, JOSETTE DERMODY

4716 Wingo, Josette Dermody. *Mother Was a Gunner's Mate* (9–adult). 1994, Naval Institute $24.95 (1-55750-924-7). An account of how Wingo left her blue-collar Irish family during World War II to join the WAVES. (Rev: BL 10/15/94) [940.54]

WINSTON, KEITH

4717 Winston, Keith. *Letters from a World War II G.I.* (8–12). Edited by Judith E. Greenberg and Helen Carey McKeever. 1995, Watts $13.93 (0-531-11212-8). A collection of letters home speaking of the hardships of life as a soldier. (Rev: BL 9/15/95; SLJ 9/95; VOYA 12/95) [940.54]

History and Geography

General History and Geography

Miscellaneous Works

4718 Davis, Kenneth C. *Don't Know Much about Geography: Everything You Need to Know about the World but Never Learned* (9–adult). 1992, Morrow $23 (0-688-10332-4). A survey of geography tied to world history and interspersed with passages from great historians, explorers, and travel writers. (Rev: BL 10/15/92; BTA; SHS) [910.76]

4719 Marshall, Bruce, ed. *The Real World: Understanding the Modern World Through the New Geography* (9–adult). 1991, Houghton $35 (0-395-52450-4). Presents the science of geography as a humane study linking broad concerns and interconnected issues. (Rev: BL 11/15/91) [910]

4720 Matthews, Rupert. *Explorer* (5–9). (Eyewitness Books) 1991, Knopf LB $15.99 (0-679-91460-9). (Rev: BL 12/1/91; MJHS) [910]

4721 Platt, Richard. *In the Beginning: The Nearly Complete History of Almost Everything* (5–7). 1995, Dorling Kindersley $19.95 (0-7894-0206-8). A vast compendium of information, including drawings/diagrams with 4-line factual comments. (Rev: BL 12/1/95; VOYA 4/96) [909]

Atlases, Maps, and Mapmaking

4722 Grant, Neil. *The Great Atlas of Discovery* (6–10). Illus. 1992, Knopf LB $21.99 (0-679-91660-1). Each double-page spread presents an area of world exploration and pinpoints voyages of an individual or group of explorers. (Rev: BL 8/92; MJHS; SLJ 2/93) [911]

4723 Jouris, David. *All over the Map: An Extraordinary Atlas of the United States* (9–adult). 1994, Ten Speed paper $9.95 (0-89815-649-1). A U.S. atlas that explores the history of the names of towns and cities, including such places as Peculiar, Ding Dong, Vendor, and Joy. (Rev: BL 7/94) [910]

4724 O'Shea, Richard, and David Greenspan. *Battle Maps of the Civil War* (9–adult). 1992, Council Oaks Books (1350 E.15th St., Tulsa, OK 74120-5801) $32.95 (0-933031-71-8). Includes many maps that were created for *American Heritage* in 1951: aerial photos, a summary of each battle/campaign, and brief biographies of Civil War generals. (Rev: BL 11/15/92) [973.73]

4725 Pratt, Paula Bryant. *Maps: Plotting Places on the Globe* (6–10). (Encyclopedia of Discovery and Invention) 1995, Lucent LB $15.95 (1-56006-255-X). Traces the evolution of mapmaking/cartography from ancient times to the present. (Rev: BL 4/15/95; SLJ 3/95) [912]

4726 Whitfield, Peter. *The Image of the World: 20 Centuries of World Maps* (9–adult). 1994, Pomegranate $29.95 (0-87654-080-9). Covers the monumental names in the history of world cartography. Includes 70 maps from the Middle Ages, the age of discovery, and modern times. (Rev: BL 11/15/94*) [912]

4727 Whitfield, Peter. *The Mapping of the Heavens* (9–adult). 1995, Pomegranate $29.95 (0-87654-475-8). This album of historical maps moves from Babylonian representations of the zodiac to the mid-nineteenth century and on to scientifically accurate modern maps. (Rev: BL 12/15/95) [525]

Paleontology

4728 Cohen, Daniel, and Susan Cohen. *Where to Find Dinosaurs Today* (5–7). 1992, Dutton/Cobblehill $15 (0-525-65098-9); Penguin/Puffin paper $7.99 (0-14-036154-5). Guide, by region, to museums, national monuments, businesses, etc. related to dinosaurs, e.g., Dinosaur National Monument and Smithsonian Institution. (Rev: BL 9/1/92; MJHS; YR) [567.9]

4729 Dewan, Ted. *Inside Dinosaurs and Other Prehistoric Creatures* (5–7). (Eyewitness Books) Illus. 1994, Doubleday $16.95 (0-385-31143-5). Colorful illustrations provide information about dinosaur skeletal system, dentition, respiration, and locomotion. (Rev: BL 3/15/94; SLJ 4/94) [667.9]

4730 Dixon, Dougal. *Dougal Dixon's Dinosaurs* (5–7). 1993, Boyds Mills/Bell Books LB $17.95 (1-56397-261-1). Facts on and illustrations of various species of dinosaurs. Awards: SLJ Best Book. (Rev: BL 9/15/93; SLJ 10/93*; VOYA 2/94)

4731 Eldredge, Niles. *The Miner's Canary: A Paleontologist Unravels the Mysteries of Extinction* (9–adult). 1991, Prentice-Hall $20 (0-13-583659-X). A paleontologist gives an account of episodes of mass extinction from the geological past, offers his own theory, and presents a pessimistic forecast for the future of Earth and its inhabitants. (Rev: BL 9/15/91) [575]

4732 Farlow, James O. *On the Tracks of Dinosaurs* (5–8). Illus. 1991, Watts LB $15.90 (0-531-10991-7). Explains how fossil tracks are formed, how scientists study and name them, and what they reveal about dinosaur behavior. (Rev: BL 5/1/91; SLJ 7/91) [567.9]

4733 Horner, John R., and Don Lessem. *The Complete Tyrannosaurus Rex* (9–adult). 1993, Simon & Schuster $25 (0-671-74185-3). This introduction to the species discusses its characteristics and probable habitat and documents a recent Montana dig. (Rev: BL 4/15/93) [567.9]

4734 Jacobs, Louis. *Quest for the African Dinosaur: The Ancient Roots of the Modern World* (9–adult). 1993, Villard $25 (0-679-41270-0). An account of fossil hunting in southern Africa, based on Jacobs's journal excerpts, filled with daily details of the dig, historical notes, and keen observations on contemporary life. (Rev: BL 2/1/93; BTA; VOYA 8/93) [567.9]

4735 Lambert, David. *The Ultimate Dinosaur Book* (9–adult). 1993, Dorling Kindersley $29.95 (1-56458-304-X). A handsomely illustrated survey of dinosaur anatomy and behavior, excavation and museum restoration techniques, and 55 dinosaur genera. (Rev: BL 10/15/93; MJHS; SLJ 3/94) [567.9]

4736 Lessem, Don. *Kings of Creation: How a New Breed of Scientists Is Revolutionizing Our Understanding of Dinosaurs* (9–adult). 1992, Simon & Schuster $25 (0-671-73491-1). Exciting survey of dinosaurs, including current theories about its evolution, behavior, extinction, and role in Earth's history. (Rev: BL 4/1/92) [567.9]

4737 Lindsay, William. *Barosaurio* (5–9). (Todo sobre los dinosaurios) Tr. by Manuel Pijoan i Rotgé. 1992, Plaza Joven (Barcelona, Spain) $11.95 (84-226-4358-8). Describes the life of the dinosaur barosaurus. Photos, drawings, and charts in color. English title: *Barosaurus*. (Rev: BL 4/1/94)

4738 Lindsay, William. *Barosaurus* (5–7). 1993, Dorling Kindersley $12.95 (1-56458-123-3). A paleontologist and museum curator outline the characteristics, daily life, and environs of the huge, gentle, vegetarian dinosaur. (Rev: BL 4/15/93; MJHS) [567.9]

4739 Lindsay, William. *Tyrannosaurus* (5–7). 1993, Dorling Kindersley $12.95 (1-56458-124-1). A paleontologist and museum curator outline the characteristics, daily life, and environs of the ferocious meat-eating dinosaur. (Rev: BL 4/15/93; MJHS) [567.9]

4740 Nardo, Don. *Dinosaurs: Unearthing the Secrets of Ancient Beasts* (6–10). (Encyclopedia of Discovery and Invention) 1995, Lucent LB $15.95 (1-56006-253-3). (Rev: BL 4/15/95) [567.9]

4741 Norell, Mark A, and others. *Discovering Dinosaurs in the American Museum of Natural History* (9–adult). 1995, Knopf $35 (0-679-43386-4). The curators of the ossuary in Central Park West discuss the largest collection of dinosaur bones in the world in question-and-answer format. (Rev: BL 5/15/95) [567.9]

4742 Parker, Steve. *The Practical Paleontologist* (9–adult). 1991, Simon & Schuster $24.95 (0-671-69308-5); paper $14.95 (0-671-69307-7). Overview of paleontology and how these specialists do their jobs. (Rev: BL 6/15/91) [560]

4743 Psihoyos, Louie, and John Knoebber. *Hunting Dinosaurs* (9–adult). 1994, Random $40 (0-679-43124-1). Outlines major dinosaur discoveries with humor. Interviews various paleontologists, including dino egg and dino dung experts. Awards: BL Editors' Choice. (Rev: BL 10/15/94; SHS; SLJ 4/96) [567.9]

4744 Sattler, Helen Roney. *The New Illustrated Dinosaur Dictionary* (5–9). Illus. 1990, Lothrop $24.95 (0-688-08462-1); paper $14.95 (0-688-10043-0). Handbook includes descriptions of more than 350 dinosaurs. Illustrated. (Rev: BL 1/1/91; MJHS) [567.9]

4745 Stein, Wendy. *Dinosaurs* (6–10). (Great Mysteries) 1994, Greenhaven LB $14.95 (1-56510-096-4). (Rev: BL 4/15/94; MJHS) [567.9]

4746 Thompson, Sharon Elaine. *Death Trap: The Story of the La Brea Tar Pits* (5–8). 1995, Lerner LB $16.13 (0-8225-2851-7). This describes the 40,000-year making of the La Brea Tar Pits in downtown Los Angeles, with color photos. (Rev: BL 6/1–15/95; SLJ 5/95) [560]

4747 Van Cleave, Janice. *Dinosaurs for Every Kid: Easy Activities That Make Learning Science Fun* (5–7). (Science for Every Kid) 1994, Wiley $22.95 (0-471-30813-7). Explores the known and unknown about dinosaurs, including how fossils are formed, the meanings of dinosaur names, theories about their skin, and how a their weight is determined. (Rev: BL 4/1/94; SLJ 7/94) [567.9]

4748 Whitfield, Philip. *Why Did the Dinosaurs Disappear?* (5–7). 1991, Viking $16.95 (0-670-84055-6). Interesting questions about dinosaurs and other forms of life are presented. Illustrations, glossary. (Rev: BL 1/1/92; SLJ 1/92) [567.9]

Anthropology and Evolution

4749 Angela, Alberto, and Piero Angela. *The Extraordinary Story of Human Origins* (9–adult). Tr. by Gabriele Tonne. 1993, Prometheus $26.95 (0-87975-803-1). A comprehensive presentation of our still-incomplete knowledge of human evolution, also discussing interesting unproven speculations and conflicting claims. (Rev: BL 6/1–15/93) [573.2]

4750 Bailey, Marilyn. *Evolution* (7–10). (Opposing Viewpoints) 1990, Greenhaven LB $13.95 (0-89908-078-2). Explains both Darwin's theory and the holes other scientists have found in it. Also shows how evolution can be reconciled with the presence of a divine creator. (Rev: BL 4/1/91; MJHS) [757]

4751 Garassino, Alessandro. *Life, Origins and Evolution* (5–8). 1995, Raintree/Steck-Vaughn LB $22.80 (0-8114-3335-8). Six books presenting scientific theories about "beginnings," from the Big Bang to the emergence of Homo sapiens. (Rev: BL 5/1/95) [575]

4752 Gould, Stephen Jay, ed. *The Book of Life* (9–adult). 1993, Norton $40 (0-393-03557-3). Traces the haphazard improvisations that resulted in the progression from fishes, to reptiles, to dinosaurs, to mammals, and finally to humans. 200 color illustrations. (Rev: BL 11/1/93*) [577.2]

4753 Gould, Stephen Jay. *Bully for Brontosaurus: Reflections in Natural History* (9–adult). 1991, Norton $22.95 (0-393-02961-1). A collection of essays discussing "evolutionary change and the nature of history" within the context of a wide range of topics. (Rev: BL 3/15/91; SHS) [508]

4754 Gould, Stephen Jay. *Dinosaur in a Haystack: Reflections in Natural History* (9–adult). 1996, Crown/Harmony $25 (0-517-70393-9). A collection of essays on evolution stimulated by thoughts from great lines in literature. (Rev: BL 12/1/95) [508]

4755 Gould, Stephen Jay. *Eight Little Piggies: Reflections in Natural History* (9–adult). 1993, Norton $22.95 (0-393-03416-X). Thirty-one essays on a wide range of subjects that present a picture of the humanism behind the best science and our place in the Darwinian scheme of things. (Rev: BL 10/15/92) [515.001]

4756 Johanson, Donald, and others. *Ancestors: The Search for Our Origins* (9–adult). 1994, Villard $27.50 (0-679-42060-6). This companion book to a PBS *Nova* series describes the latest excursions to discover the origins of humankind. (Rev: BL 2/15/94) [573.3]

4757 Leakey, Richard. *The Origin of Humankind* (9–adult). (Science Masters) 1994, Basic Books $20 (0-465-03135-8). Discusses evolutionary theory and the paleoanthropological discoveries that give clues to the origins of humankind. (Rev: BL 10/1/94; SHS) [573.2]

4758 Leakey, Richard, and Roger Lewin. *Origins Reconsidered: In Search of What Makes Us Human* (9–adult). 1992, Doubleday $25 (0-385-41264-9). Louis Leakey's son Richard takes us with his Hominid Gang of fossil hunters to Kenya, unraveling the mystery of "Turkana boy," who died 1.5 million years ago. (Rev: BL 9/1/92; SHS; SLJ 6/93) [573.2]

4759 Le Loeuff, Jean. *La aventura de la vida* (7–12). Illus. 1991, Ediciones Larousse $15.90 (1-56294-177-1). Introduces the principles of evolution. Includes high-quality photos, other illustrations, and diagrams in color. English title: *The Adventure of Life*. (Rev: BL 3/1/93)

4760 Lindsay, William. *Prehistoric Life* (5–9). (Eyewitness Books) 1994, Knopf LB $16.99 (0-679-96001-5). Prolific and colorful photos and illustrations of fossils, prehistoric plants, animals, and dinosaurs. (Rev: BL 10/15/94; MJHS) [560]

4761 Macdonald, Fiona. *How Would You Survive as an Aztec?* (5–7). (How Would You Survive) 1995, Watts LB $13.51 (0-531-14348-1). Takes the reader into the past as it explains what would be worn or eaten by Aztecs at the time. (Rev: BL 6/1–15/95) [972]

4762 Maybury-Lewis, David. *Millennium: Tribal Wisdom in the Modern World* (9–adult). 1992, Viking $45 (0-670-82935-8). An examination of nonindustrial civilizations and their contributions to society, based on the PBS series. (Rev: BL 3/15/92) [306]

4763 Niehoff, Arthur. *On Becoming Human: A Journey of 5,000,000 Years* (9–adult). 1995, Hominid (P.O. Box 1481, Bonsall, CA 92003-1481) paper $12.95 (0-9643072-1-9). An anthropologist traces the cultural history of human beings, beginning in Africa. (Rev: BL 3/15/95) [573.2]

4764 Peters, David. *From the Beginning: The Story of Human Evolution* (6–12). Illus. 1991, Morrow $14.95 (0-688-09476-7). An examination not just of human evolution but of all creatures, starting with single-celled organisms. Includes numerous clear, helpful illustrations. Awards: SLJ Best Book. (Rev: SLJS 1/92*)

4765 Raup, David M. *Extinction: Bad Genes or Bad Luck?* (9–adult). 1991, Norton $19.95 (0-393-03008-3). A look at how and why some species die out, with an emphasis on the extinction resistance of others. (Rev: BL 8/91) [575]

4766 Shreeve, James. *The Neandertal Enigma: Solving the Mystery of Modern Human Origins* (9–adult). 1995, Morrow $25 (0-688-09407-4); Avon paper $14 (0-380-72881-8). From the author of *Lucy's Child*, this narrative follows the replacement-versus-continuity debate regarding the relationship between Neandertals and Homo sapiens. (Rev: BL 9/1/95) [573.2]

4767 Thomas, Herbert. *Human Origins: The Search for Our Beginnings* (9–adult). (Discoveries) 1995, Abrams paper $12.95 (0-8109-2866-3). The search for human ancestry, from religious creation myths of the nineteenth century to a discussion of significant fossil finds. (Rev: BL 12/1/95) [569.9]

4768 Thomas, Peggy. *Talking Bones: The Science of Forensic Anthropology* (7–12). (Science Sourcebooks) 1995, Facts on File $17.95 (0-8160-3114-2). A forensic scientist examines mystery bones in the grisly but fascinating world of forensic anthropology. (Rev: BL 10/15/95; SLJ 1/96; VOYA 4/96) [614]

4769 Weiner, Jonathan. *The Beak of the Finch: A Story of Evolution in Our Time* (9–adult). 1994, Knopf $25 (0-679-40003-6). Following in Darwin's footsteps in the Galápagos were Peter and Rosemary Grant, who studied the features of the beaks of various species of finches and confirmed Darwin's theory of natural selection. (Rev: BL 4/15/94*) [590.8]

Archaeology

4770 Arnold, Caroline. *City of the Gods: Mexico's Ancient City of Teotihuacán* (5–7). Photos. 1994, Clarion $14.95 (0-395-66584-1). Explores the ruins of this ancient city and surmises what life was like for the people who lived there. (Rev: BL 12/15/94; SLJ 12/94) [972]

4771 Avi-Yonah, Michael. *Dig This! How Archaeologists Uncover Our Past* (5–8). (Buried Worlds) 1993, Lerner $22.95 (0-8225-3200-X). A history of the discipline of archaeology, an examination of excavating methods, and a look at several ancient civilizations. (Rev: BL 1/15/94; MJHS; SLJ 2/94) [930.1]

4772 Burenhult, Goran. *The First Humans: Human Origins and History to 10,000 B.C.* (9–adult). 1993, HarperCollins $40 (0-06-250265-4). As the first in a 5-volume series, this illustrated book traces human evolution from the perspective of anthropological archeology. (Rev: BL 11/15/93; SLJ 5/94) [573.2]

4773 David, Rosalie. *Discovering Ancient Egypt* (9–adult). 1994, Facts on File $22.95 (1-85479-114-1). Examines the reports of individuals from the time of Herodotus to the present who visited archaeological sites, then surveys the sites themselves. (Rev: BL 4/1/94) [932]

4774 Echo-Hawk, Roger C., and Walter R. Echo-Hawk. *Battlefields and Burial Grounds: The Indian Struggle to Protect Ancestral Graves in the United States* (7–10). 1994, Lerner $19.95 (0-8225-2663-8); paper $8.95 (0-8225-9722-5). A solid discussion of the conflict over Indian graves that have been plundered in the name of scientific research. Awards: Woodson Book. (Rev: BL 5/15/94; BTA; SLJ 7/94*) [393]

4775 Hansen, Jens Peder Hart, ed. *The Greenland Mummies* (9–adult). 1991, Smithsonian $39.95 (1-56098-045-1). Including numerous photos, this book describes "the oldest known find of well-preserved humans in the entire Arctic cultural community" and the history and lifestyle of the Inuit. (Rev: BL 9/1/91) [998.200497]

4776 Kirkpatrick, Sidney D. *Lords of Sipan: A Tale of Pre-Inca Tombs, Archaeology and Crime* (9–adult). 1992, Morrow $25 (0-688-10396-0). Chronicles a 1987 Peruvian tomb-looting and the role of archeologists who helped document and preserve the remains of the Moche civilization. (Rev: BL 10/1/92*; BTA) [985]

4777 La Pierre, Yvette. *Native American Rock Art: Messages from the Past* (5–8). 1994, Thomasson-Grant (One Morton Dr., Suite 500, Charlottesville, VA 22901) $16.95 (1-56566-064-1). Discusses the mediums used to make these pictures and speculates on their significance to their creators. (Rev: BL 12/1/94; SLJ 11/94) [709]

4778 Lessem, Don. *The Iceman* (5–7). 1994, Crown $14 (0-517-59596-6). Chronicles the discovery and study of a 5,300-year-old Copper Age man frozen in an Alpine glacier with tools, weapons, and clothes intact. (Rev: BL 11/1/94; MJHS; SLJ 7/94) [937]

4779 O'Neal, Michael. *Pyramids* (6–9). (Great Mysteries: Opposing Viewpoints) 1995, Greenhaven LB $14.95 (1-56510-216-9). The purpose and meaning of pyramids, concentrating more on the mystery than on opposing views. (Rev: BL 4/15/95; SLJ 3/95) [726]

4780 Pellegrino, Charles. *Unearthing Atlantis: An Archaeological Odyssey* (9–12). 1992, Random $23 (0-394-57550-4); Vintage paper $13 (0-

679-73407-4). Tantalizing clues suggest a possible explanation for the puzzling disappearance of the "lost city" of Atlantis. Awards: SLJ Best Book. (Rev: BL 6/15/90; SLJ 7/92)

4781 Perring, Stefania, and Dominic Perring. *Then and Now* (9–adult). 1991, Macmillan $24.95 (0-02-599461-1). Two archaeologists fabricate reconstructions of 20 famous ruins using illustrated transparent overlays and photos, as well as text that describes the individual civilizations. (Rev: BL 12/15/91) [930]

4782 Rachlin, Harvey. *Lucy's Bones, Sacred Stones, and Einstein's Brain: The Remarkable Stories Behind the Great Objects and Artifacts of History, from Antiquity to the Modern Era* (9–adult). 1996, Holt $25 (0-8050-3964-3). Some harmless fun as Rachlin presents 50+ objects made famous through mysterious origins. (Rev: BL 12/15/95) [909]

4783 Reeves, Nicholas. *The Complete Tutankhamun: The King, the Tomb, the Royal Treasure* (9–adult). 1990, Thames & Hudson $24.95 (0-500-05058-9). Detailed description of one of the richest archeological discoveries of the twentieth century. (Rev: BL 1/1/91; SHS) [932.014]

4784 Scheller, William. *Amazing Archaeologists and Their Finds* (6–10). 1994, Oliver Press (5707 W. 36th St., Minneapolis, MN 55416) $14.95 (1-881508-17-X). Presents the discoveries of 8 archeologists. Discusses the walls of Troy, the tomb of King Tut, Jericho, and Incan ruins. (Rev: BL 11/1/94; BTA; SLJ 2/95; VOYA 2/95) [930.1]

4785 Schick, Kathy D., and Nicholas Toth. *Making Silent Stones Speak: How the Dawn of Technology Changed the Course of Human Evolution Two and a Half Million Years Ago* (9–adult). 1993, Simon & Schuster $25 (0-671-69371-9). A fact-filled account of the first humanoid toolmakers and their crude but effective tools. (Rev: BL 3/1/93) [930.1]

4786 Smith, Norman F. *Millions and Billions of Years Ago: Dating Our Earth and Its Life* (8–12). (Venture) 1993, Watts LB $13.40 (0-531-12533-5). Records the history of our attempts to date artifacts, the Earth, the moon, and the universe and describes dating methods. (Rev: BL 1/1/94; SLJ 11/93) [551.7]

4787 Stiebing, William H. *Uncovering the Past: A History of Archaeology* (9–adult). 1993, Prometheus $24.95 (0-87975-764-7). Surveys the history of archaeology and documents the discoveries of numerous explorers. (Rev: BL 3/1/93) [930.1]

4788 Sullivan, George. *Slave Ship: The Story of the Henrietta Marie* (5–8). 1994, Dutton $15.95 (0-525-65174-8). Describes a slave ship that sank near Florida in the early 1700s and the underwater archaeological excavation. (Rev: BL 11/1/94; SLJ 12/94) [975.9]

4789 Wilcox, Charlotte. *Mummies and Their Mysteries* (5–7). 1993, Carolrhoda LB $22.95 (0-87614-767-8). Introduces mummies found in Egypt, Peru, the Far East, and in caves, ice, and bogs. Illustrated with riveting color photos. (Rev: BL 6/1–15/93*; SLJ 2/94) [393.3]

World History and Geography

General

4790 *América ayer y hoy* (5–10). 1992, Cultural, S.A. de Ediciones (Madrid, Spain) $100 (SET) (84-86732-91-3). This readable overview of the history of the Western Hemisphere, from 30,000 years ago to the twentieth century, provides information about key issues in the area's historical development. The nine large-format volumes include informative watercolor illustrations. The series comprises *A la sombra del cóndor* (*By the Shadow of the Condor*), by José Alcina Franch; *Así nació América* (*Thus Was America Born*), by Andrś Ciudad Ruiz; *Encuentro de dos mundos* (*Encounter of Two Worlds*), by Miguel León-Portilla; *América inglesa y francesa* (*British and French America*), by Manuel Lucena Salmoral; *La independencia americana* (*American Independence*), by Eduardo L. Bozzani; *América hoy* (*The Americas Today*), by Germán Vázquez Chamorro; *Mayos, aztecas, incas* (*Mayas, Aztecs, Incas*), by Germán Vázquez Chamorro; *Los pueblos del maíz* (*The Corn People*), by Germán Vázquez Chamorro; and *Los siglos coloniales* (*The Colonial Centuries*), by Pedro A. Vines Azancot and Josefa Vega. (Rev: BL 6/1–15/93)

4791 Asimov, Isaac. *Asimov's Chronology of the World* (9–adult). 1991, HarperCollins $35 (0-06-270036-7). This is a broadly based log of the events of world history, concentrating on dates, leaders, generals, and wars. (Rev: BL 9/1/91) [902]

4792 Cahill, Tim. *Pecked to Death by Ducks* (9–adult). 1993, Random $20 (0-679-40735-9). This travel book deals with such large subjects as animals, nature's grandeur, and risky adventures. (Rev: BL 11/15/92*) [814.54]

4793 *Chronicle of America* (9–12). 1995, DK $59.95 (0-7894-0124-X). Short articles discuss important political events, cultural milestones, and stories of human interest, organized by year. (Rev: SLJ 2/96; VOYA 4/96)

4794 Demko, George J., and others. *Why in the World: Geography for Everyone* (9–adult). 1992, Doubleday/Archer paper $10 (0-385-26629-4). A study of the influences geography has had on physical, political, human, and historical matters. Awards: BL Editors' Choice. (Rev: BL 4/15/92) [910]

4795 Fernández-Armesto, Felipe. *Millennium: A History of the Last Thousand Years* (9–adult). 1995, Scribner $35 (0-684-80361-5). Using 2 different viewpoints, the author relates the last 1,000 years of history. (Rev: BL 9/15/95*) [909]

4796 Rosenthal, Paul. *Where on Earth: A Geografunny Guide to the Globe* (5–7). Illus. 1992, Knopf/Borzoi LB $15.99 (0-679-90833-1); paper $11 (0-679-80833-7). Well-organized, very informative, lively, tongue-in-cheek guide to world geography (Rev: BL 1/15/93; SLJ 1/93) [910]

4797 Shenkman, Richard. *Legends, Lies, and Cherished Myths of World History* (9–adult). 1993, HarperCollins $20 (0-06-016803-X). Shenkman debunks many commonly held historical beliefs in this humorous take on world history. (Rev: BL 10/15/93; BTA) [902.07]

4798 Sobel, Dava. *Longitude: The True Story of a Lone Genius Who Solved the Greatest Scientific Problem of His Time* (9–adult). 1995, Walker $18 (0-8027-1312-2). Another sad tale of a struggle against rivalry to be rightfully credited for one's invention, in this case clockmaker John Harrison's development of the chronometer to measure longitude. (Rev: BL 9/1/95; SLJ 2/96) [526]

4799 Wood, A. J. *Errata: A Book of Historical Errors* (5–8). 1992, Simon & Schuster/Green Tiger $14 (0-671-77569-3). Challenges kids to find 10 mistakes or anachronisms in each of 12 color paintings of the history of various world cultures. (Rev: BL 9/1/92; SLJ 11/92) [930]

Ancient History

General and Miscellaneous

4800 Burrell, Roy. *Oxford First Ancient History* (5–7). 1994, Oxford Univ. $35 (0-19-521058-1). Surveys ancient civilizations, including the Egyptians, Sumerians, Chinese, Greeks, and Romans. Contains photos, maps, illustrations, and imaginary interviews with citizens. (Rev: BL 7/94; BTA; MJHS; VOYA 12/94) [930]

4801 Gonick, Larry. *The Cartoon History of the Universe II, Vols. 8–13* (9–adult). 1994, Doubleday paper $15.95 (0-385-42093-5). Continues the survey of the universe's history, starting with Alexander the Great and ending with the fall of Rome, using cartoons to depict major historical events. Part 2 of a multivolume set containing volumes 8–13. (Rev: BL 8/94*) [902.07]

4802 Langguth, A. J. *A Noise of War: Caesar, Pompey, Octavian and the Struggle for Rome* (9–adult). 1994, Simon & Schuster $25 (0-671-70829-5). This history of the decline of the Roman Empire focuses on Caesar and Cicero and their political intrigues and alliances. (Rev: BL 3/15/94) [937]

4803 Wilkinson, Phillip, and Michael Pollard. *The Magical East* (5–7). (Mysterious Places) 1994, Chelsea House $18.95 (0-7910-2754-6). This illustrated volume describes famous and relatively unknown sites in the ancient Oriental world. (Rev: BL 1/15/94; SLJ 4/94; VOYA 6/94) [930.1]

Greece

4804 Archibald, Zofia. *Discovering the World of the Ancient Greeks* (9–adult). 1991, Facts on File $29.95 (0-8160-2614-9). A recounting of classical Greek history (ca. 6500–2900 B.C. to A.D. 550), through archaeological discoveries. (Rev: BL 1/1/92; BTA; SLJ 3/92) [938]

4805 Nardo, Don. *Ancient Greece* (8–12). (World History) 1994, Lucent LB $14.95 (1-56006-229-0). Describes the lives and times of such ancient Greeks as Alexander the Great, Pericles, and Alcibiades. (Rev: BL 12/15/93; MJHS; SLJ 1/94) [938]

4806 Pearson, Anne. *Ancient Greece* (5–9). (Eyewitness Books) 1992, Knopf LB $15.99 (0-679-91682-2). Attractive layout covers the history, religion, people and customs, occupations and recreation, warfare, etc., of ancient Greeks. (Rev: BL 11/1/92; MJHS; SLJ 12/92) [938]

4807 Pearson, Anne. *¿Qué sabemos sobre los griegos?* (5–7). (¿Qué sabemos sobre . . . ?) Tr. by Jesús Valiente Malla. 1993, Ediciones SM (Madrid, Spain) $12.95 (84-348-3921-0). A brief, straightforward text highlighting significant Greeks and their way of life and special contributions, with color photos, maps, drawings, and charts. English title: *What Do We Know about the Greeks?* (Rev: BL 10/1/94)

Middle East

4808 Jenkins, Earnestine. *A Glorious Past: Ancient Egypt, Ethiopia and Nubia* (7–10). (Milestones in Black History) 1995, Chelsea House $18.95 (0-7910-2258-7); paper $7.95 (0-7910-2684-1). A social and political survey of ancient Egypt, Nubia, the civilization to the south, and present-day Ethiopia. (Rev: BL 4/15/95; SLJ 4/95) [932]

4809 Morley, Jacqueline. *How Would You Survive As an Ancient Egyptian?* (5–7). (How Would You Survive) 1995, Watts LB $13.51 (0-531-14345-7). Ranks readers' survival chances through knowledge of Ancient Egyptian culture. (Rev: BL 6/1–15/95; SLJ 8/95) [932]

4810 Smith, Carter. *The Pyramid Builders* (5–8). (Turning Points in World History) 1991, Silver Burdett LB $16.98 (0-382-24131-2); paper $8.95 (0-382-24137-1). A testimonial to a brilliant culture at its peak. (Rev: BL 3/15/92) [932]

Rome

4811 Ganeri, Anita. *How Would You Survive As an Ancient Roman?* (5–7). (How Would You Survive) 1995, Watts LB $13.51 (0-531-14349-X). Ranks readers' survival chances through knowledge of Ancient Roman culture. (Rev: BL 6/1–15/95; SLJ 8/95) [937]

4812 Howarth, Sarah. *Roman People* (5–7). (People and Places) 1995, Millbrook LB $14.90 (1-56294-650-1). Explores the daily lives of a variety of Roman people, including shopkeepers, the emperor, slaves, mothers, Christians, and centurions. (Rev: BL 7/95; SLJ 8/95) [937]

4813 Howarth, Sarah. *Roman Places* (5–7). 1995, Millbrook LB $14.90 (1-56294-651-X). Howarth presents facts about common Roman places, such as shrines, hospitals, colonies, baths, forums, forts, and vinyards. (Rev: BL 7/95; SLJ 8/95) [937]

4814 Nardo, Don. *Caesar's Conquest of Gaul* (7–12). (World History) 1996, Lucent LB $16.95 (1-56006-301-7). Detailed descriptions of battles, strategies, politics, and personalities that defined the event. (Rev: BL 2/15/96; SLJ 2/96)

4815 Nardo, Don. *The Punic Wars* (7–12). (World History) 1996, Lucent LB $16.95 (1-56006-417-X). Historical account of battles and strategies presented largely from the victors' perspective. (Rev: BL 2/15/96; SLJ 2/96)

4816 Nardo, Don. *The Roman Empire* (8–12). (World History) 1994, Lucent LB $14.95 (1-56006-231-2). Covers the Roman Empire from the Augustan Age to its fall, with descriptions of everyday lives and quotes from people of the time. (Rev: BL 12/15/93; SLJ 1/94) [937]

4817 Ochoa, George. *The Assassination of Julius Caesar* (5–8). (Turning Points in World History) 1991, Silver Burdett LB $16.98 (0-382-24130-4); paper $8.95 (0-382-24136-3). A study of the circumstances surrounding the murder of a Roman leader and its sociological impact. (Rev: BL 3/15/92; BTA) [937]

4818 Scarre, Chris. *Chronicle of the Roman Emperors: The Reign-by-Reign Record of the Rulers of Imperial Rome* (9–adult). 1995, Thames & Hudson $29.95 (0-500-05077-5). The story of emperors from Augustus to Romulus Augustulus is told through surviving annals of classical historians and photos of buildings attributed to them. (Rev: BL 10/15/95) [973.06]

Middle Ages Through the Renaissance (500–1700)

4819 Bayard, Tania. *A Medieval Home Companion: Housekeeping in the Fourteenth Century* (9–adult). 1991, HarperCollins $19.95 (0-06-016654-1). A translation and explication of a Parisian document, ca. 1393, in which an anonymous husband instructs his young bride on practical matters of homemaking and proper behavior. (Rev: BL 9/15/91) [640]

4820 Biel, Timothy Levi. *The Age of Feudalism* (8–12). (World History) 1994, Lucent LB $14.95 (1-56006-232-0). (Rev: BL 1/1/94) [321]

4821 Flowers, Sarah. *The Reformation* (8–12). (World History) 1996, Lucent LB $16.95 (1-56006-243-6). Provides background information about, causes and effects of, and important names from the Reformation. (Rev: BL 2/15/96; SLJ 3/96)

4822 Hanawalt, Barbara. *Growing Up in Medieval London: The Experience of Childhood in History* (9–adult). 1993, Oxford Univ. $27.50 (0-19-508405-5). Court records lend immediacy to the lives of London's children in the Middle Ages. Awards: SLJ Best Book. (Rev: SLJ 12/94)

4823 Howarth, Sarah. *The Middle Ages* (5–8). (See Through History) 1993, Viking $14.99 (0-670-85098-5). Looks at the day-to-day lives of people in the Middle Ages, including family, clothing, food, and status. (Rev: BL 12/15/93; MJHS; SLJ 2/94) [940.1]

4824 Howarth, Sarah. *Renaissance People* (5–7). 1992, Millbrook LB $13.90 (1-56294-088-0). Introduces Renaissance artisans, explorers, and alchemists by blending historical interpretation with quotations and art from the period. (Rev: BL 11/1/92; SLJ 1/93) [391]

4825 Howarth, Sarah. *Renaissance Places* (5–7). 1992, Millbrook LB $13.90 (1-56294-089-9). Renaissance cities, libraries, and workshops, among other topics, are discussed in this blend of art and quotations from the period. (Rev: BL 11/1/92; SLJ 1/93) [940.2]

4826 Jones, Madeline. *Knights and Castles* (6–9). (How It Was) 1991, Batsford $19.95 (0-7134-6352-X). Historical re-creation of castles and knights and the times in which they lived. (Rev: BL 1/15/92; SLJ 3/92) [941]

4827 Lace, William W. *The Battle of Hastings* (7–12). (The Battles) 1996, Lucent LB $19.95 (1-56006-416-1). Historical depiction of how William, Duke of Normandy, defeated King Harold and the lasting importance of the battle. (Rev: BL 3/1/96; SLJ 2/96)

4828 Lace, William W. *The Hundred Years' War* (8–12). (World History) 1994, Lucent LB $14.95 (1-56006-233-9). Gives a well-balanced presentation of the issues and personalities involved in the Hundred Years' War. (Rev: BL 1/1/94; MJHS; SLJ 3/94) [944]

4829 Lace, William W. *The Wars of the Roses* (8–12). (World History) 1996, Lucent LB $16.95 (1-56006-419-6). Provides background information about, causes and effects of, and important names from the War of the Roses. (Rev: BL 2/15/96; SLJ 3/96)

4830 Litvinoff, Barnet. *Fourteen Ninety Two: The Decline of Medievalism and the Rise of the Modern Age* (9–adult). 1991, Scribner $22.95 (0-684-19210-1). Uses historical hindsight concerning the life and times of Columbus to craft a cynical tale of self-interested and venal popes, rulers, and explorers. (Rev: BL 9/1/91) [940.2]

4831 Margeson, Susan M. *Viking* (5–9). (Eyewitness Books) 1994, Knopf LB $16.99 (0-679-96002-3). (Rev: BL 10/15/94; MJHS) [948]

4832 Morley, Jacqueline. *How Would You Survive as a Viking?* (5–7). (How Would You Survive) 1995, Watts LB $13.51 (0-531-14344-9). Ranks readers' survival chances based on their cultural knowledge of the Vikings. (Rev: BL 6/1–15/95) [948]

4833 Osman, Karen. *The Italian Renaissance* (8–12). (World History) 1996, Lucent LB $16.95 (1-56006-237-1). (Rev: BL 2/15/96; SLJ 3/96)

4834 Riley-Smith, Jonathan, ed. *The Oxford Illustrated History of the Crusades* (9–adult). 1995, Oxford Univ. $35 (0-19-820435-3). A history of the Crusades and their odd history of conquest and compassion. (Rev: BL 11/1/95) [909.7]

4835 Ross, Stewart. *Elizabethan Life* (6–9). (How It Was) 1991, Batsford $19.95 (0-7134-6356-2). Such historical sources as laws and journals of the period re-create a vivid picture of Elizabethan life. (Rev: BL 1/15/92) [941]

4836 Russell, Jeffrey Burton. *Inventing the Flat Earth: Columbus and Modern Historians* (9–adult). 1991, Praeger $12.95 (0-275-93956-1). The origin of the "flat Earth error" is explored in this examination of the persistent myth that Columbus proved to Europeans that the world is round. (Rev: BL 10/1/91)

4837 Wood, Tim. *The Renaissance* (5–8). (See Through History) 1993, Viking $14.99 (0-670-85149-3). Looks at the day-to-day lives of people in the Renaissance, including Far East trade, Italian city-states, women at court, art, and technology. (Rev: BL 12/15/93; MJHS; SLJ 2/94) [940.2]

4838 *The World in 1492* (5–9). Illus. 1992, Holt $19.95 (0-8050-1674-0). Six writers—e.g., Jean Fritz, Margaret Mahy, and Jamake Highwater—contemplate life in the late fifteenth century. Awards: ALSC Notable Children's Book; SLJ Best Book. (Rev: BL 11/1/92; SLJ 11/92*)

4839 Yue, Charlotte, and David Yue. *Armor* (5–7). 1994, Houghton $14.95 (0-395-68101-4). A succinct introduction to armor and the world in which it was used. (Rev: BL 11/15/94; MJHS; SLJ 12/94) [355.8]

Eighteenth Through Nineteenth Centuries (1700–1900)

4840 Marks, Jason. *Around the World in 72 Days: The Race Between Pulitzer's Nellie Bly and Cosmopolitan's Elizabeth Bisland* (9–adult). 1993, Gemittarius Press (P.O. Box 20151, New York, NY 10025-1511) $20 (0-9633696-1-X); paper $12.95 (0-9633696-2-8). An account of the 1889 publicity stunt by rival publishers sending 2 female reporters on a race to beat the fictional record of Jules Verne's Phileas Fogg. (Rev: BL 4/15/93) [070.92]

The Twentieth Century

General and Miscellaneous

4841 Harriss, John, ed. *The Family: A Social History of the Twentieth Century* (9–adult). 1991, Oxford Univ. $35 (0-19-520844-7). An overview of family life throughout the century in countries around the world. (Rev: BL 3/15/92; SHS) [306.85]

World War I

4842 Bosco, Peter. *World War I* (7–12). (America at War) 1991, Facts on File $17.95 (0-8160-2460-X). Highlights the major battles and personalities of World War I and discusses the events leading to a declaration of war, as well as the changes following the peace. (Rev: BL 10/15/91; MJHS; SHS; SLJ 8/91) [940.3]

4843 Brown, Gene. *Conflict in Europe and the Great Depression: World War I (1914–1940)* (5–8). (First Person America) 1994, Twenty-First Century LB $15.95 (0-8050-2585-5). (Rev: BL 5/15/94; MJHS) [973.9]

4844 Gay, Kathlyn, and Martin Gay. *World War I* (5–8). 1995, Twenty-First Century LB $15.98 (0-8050-2848-X). Combines personal eyewitness accounts with general background information. (Rev: BL 12/15/95) [940.3]

4845 Hull, Robert, ed. *A Prose Anthology of the First World War* (7–12). 1993, Millbrook LB $12.90 (1-56294-222-0). Primary source writings and photos, including excerpts from letters, diaries, and memoirs from those on opposite sides of the war. (Rev: BL 6/1–15/93; VOYA 8/93) [940.4]

4846 McGowen, Tom. *World War I* (5–7). 1993, Watts $12.40 (0-531-20149-X). A military history of the war, with dramatic photos, maps, fast-moving narrative, and facts and figures. (Rev: BL 6/1–15/93; MJHS) [940.3]

World War II and the Holocaust

4847 Aaseng, Nathan. *Paris* (6–12). (Cities at War) 1992, Macmillan/New Discovery LB $14.95 (0-02-700010-9). Remembrances from people who experienced World War II in Paris. (Rev: BL 10/15/92; MJHS) [944]

4848 Ambrose, Stephen E. *D-Day: June 6, 1944: The Climactic Battle of World War II* (9–adult). 1994, Simon & Schuster $30 (0-671-67334-3). Long, detailed, immediate, and readable, this history is for teens who can't get enough of World War II drama. (Rev: BL 4/1/94; SHS) [940.54]

4849 Ayer, Eleanor H. *Berlin* (6–12). (Cities at War) 1992, Macmillan/New Discovery LB $13.95 (0-02-707800-0). Photo-essay on what occurred in the lives of ordinary people in Berlin during World War II, with eyewitness quotes. (Rev: BL 6/15/92; MJHS; SLJ 9/92) [940.53]

4850 Bachrach, Susan D. *Tell Them We Remember: The Story of the Holocaust* (5–9). 1994, Little, Brown $19.95 (0-316-69264-6). Photohistory focusing on the young who struggled through the brutality of the Holocaust following the destruction of their world of family and friends. Awards: ALSC Notable Children's Book; BL Editors' Choice; SLJ Best Book; YALSA Best Book for Young Adults. (Rev: BL 7/94*; BTA; MJHS; SLJ 11/94; VOYA 12/94) [804.53]

4851 Berenbaum, Michael. *The World Must Know: A History of the Holocaust as Told in the United States Holocaust Memorial Museum* (9–adult). 1993, Little, Brown $40 (0-316-09135-9); paper $19.95 (0-316-09134-0). Includes moving photos of the Warsaw ghetto selected from the Holocaust Memorial Museum in Washington, D.C. (Rev: BL 3/1/93; BTA) [940.53]

4852 Black, Wallace B., and Jean F. Blashfield. *America Prepares for War* (5–7). (World War II 50th Anniversary) 1991, Macmillan/Crestwood LB $11.95 (0-89686-554-1). Photo-essay made up of B&W news photographs and details about Allied and enemy leaders, weapons, and vehicles. (Rev: BL 6/15/91; SLJ 9/91) [940.53]

4853 Black, Wallace B., and Jean F. Blashfield. *Bataan and Corregidor* (5–7). (World War II 50th Anniversary) 1991, Macmillan/Crestwood LB $12.95 (0-89686-557-6). East-to-follow details of the campaigns and strategies. (Rev: BL 12/1/91) [940.54]

4854 Black, Wallace B., and Jean F. Blashfield. *Battle of Britain* (5–7). 1991, Macmillan/Crestwood LB $11.95 (0-89686-553-3). Action-packed photo-essay includes news photos, maps, and facts about leaders, weapons, and vehicles. (Rev: BL 6/15/91; SLJ 9/91) [940.54]

4855 Black, Wallace B., and Jean F. Blashfield. *Battle of the Atlantic* (5–7). (World War II 50th Anniversary) 1991, Macmillan/Crestwood LB $12.95 (0-89686-558-4). Easty-to-follow details of the campaigns and strategies. (Rev: BL 12/1/91) [940.54]

4856 Black, Wallace B., and Jean F. Blashfield. *Blitzkrieg* (5–7). (World War II 50th Anniversary) 1991, Macmillan/Crestwood LB $11.95 (0-89686-552-5). Photo-essay includes B&W news photographs as well as facts about leaders, weapons, and vehicles. (Rev: BL 6/15/91; SLJ 9/91) [940.54]

4857 Black, Wallace B., and Jean F. Blashfield. *Flattops at War* (5–7). (World War II 50th Anniversary) 1991, Macmillan/Crestwood LB $12.95 (0-89686-559-2). (Rev: BL 12/1/91) [940.54]

4858 Black, Wallace B., and Jean F. Blashfield. *Pearl Harbor!* (5–7). 1991, Macmillan/Crestwood LB $11.95 (0-89686-555-X). News action photos comprise this pictoral history, which also includes maps and facts about Allied and enemy leaders, weapons, and vehicles. (Rev: BL 6/15/91; SLJ 9/91) [940.54]

4859 Black, Wallace B., and Jean F. Blashfield. *Russia at War* (5–7). (World War II 50th Anniversary) 1991, Macmillan/Crestwood LB $12.95 (0-89686-556-8). Easy-to-follow details of Russia's campaigns and strategies during World War II. (Rev: BL 12/1/91) [940.53]

4860 Block, Gay, and Malka Drucker. *Rescuers: Portraits of Moral Courage in the Holocaust* (9–adult). 1992, Holmes & Meier $49.95 (0-8419-1322-6); paper $29.95 (0-8419-1323-4). Profiles of 49 people who risked their lives to hide and protect Jews during the Holocaust. Awards: BL Editors' Choice. (Rev: BL 3/15/92) [940.53]

4861 Childers, Thomas. *Wings of Morning: The Story of the Last American Bomber Shot Down over Germany in World War II* (9–adult). 1995, Addison-Wesley $23 (0-201-48310-6). A re-creation of the lives of the 12-man crew of the bomber Black Cat, the last air casualty over Germany in World War II. (Rev: BL 4/15/95*) [940.54]

4862 Churchill, Winston S. *The Great Battles and Leaders of the Second World War: An Illustrated History* (9–adult). 1995, Houghton $40 (0-395-75516-6). A picture album with text excerpted from Churchill's classic 6-volume work *The Second World War*. (Rev: BL 12/1/95) [940.53]

4863 Clausen, Henry C., and Bruce Lee. *Pearl Harbor: Final Judgement* (9–adult). 1992, Crown $25 (0-517-58644-4). The prosecuting attorney appointed to investigate the 1941 Pearl Harbor attack explains why U.S. officials were unprepared. (Rev: BL 10/1/92) [940.54]

4864 Cross, Robin. *Children and War* (5–7). (World War II) 1994, Thomson Learning $14.95 (1-56847-180-7). An overview of how young people were affected by World War II. (Rev: BL 12/15/94; MJHS) [940.53]

4865 Daniels, Roger. *Prisoners Without Trial: Japanese Americans in World War II* (9–adult). 1993, Hill & Wang $19.95 (0-8090-7897-X); paper $7.95 (0-8090-1553-6). The shameful racist history of the internment of Japanese Americans in World War II. (Rev: BL 7/93; SLJ 6/94) [940.53]

4866 Devaney, John. *America Fights the Tide: 1942* (6–10). 1991, Walker $16.95 (0-8027-6997-7). Using a diary format and relying on anecdotal accounts, this volume focuses on America's entry into World War II in both the European and the Pacific theaters. (Rev: BL 10/15/91; SLJ 10/91) [940.54]

4867 Devaney, John. *America Goes to War: 1941* (5–8). 1991, Walker LB $17.85 (0-8027-6980-2). Each entry has a dateline in this illustrated day-by-day account that covers the personal and public events of the first year of World War II. (Rev: BL 10/1/91; SLJ 8/91) [940.53]

4868 Devaney, John. *America on the Attack: 1943* (6–10). (Walker's World War II) 1992, Walker LB $18.85 (0-8027-8195-0). (Rev: BL 12/1/92) [940.53]

4869 Dolan, Edward F. *America in World War II: 1941* (5–8). (America in World War II) 1991, Millbrook LB $12.90 (1-878841-05-X). An accessible account of the first year of World War II, with insets that introduce important figures and full-page illustrations. (Rev: BL 10/1/91; SLJ 9/91) [940.54]

4870 Dolan, Edward F. *America in World War II: 1942* (5–8). (America in World War II) 1991, Millbrook LB $13.90 (1-56294-007-4). (Rev: BL 10/1/91) [940.54]

4871 Dolan, Edward F. *America in World War II: 1943* (5–8). (America in World War II) 1992, Millbrook LB $15.90 (1-56294-113-5). Reviews the events of World War II up until 1943 and describes the events that took place that year. (Rev: BL 4/1/92) [940.54]

4872 Dolan, Edward F. *America in World War II: 1944* (5–8). (America in World War II) 1993, Millbrook LB $15.90 (1-56294-221-2). (Rev: BL 3/15/93) [940.54]

4873 Duffy, James P. *Hitler Slept Late and Other Blunders That Cost Him the War* (9–adult). 1991, Praeger $19.95 (0-275-93667-8). This examination of Hitler's military leadership analyzes specific decisions that had a significant impact on the outcome of World War II. (Rev: BL 8/91; SHS) [940.54]

4874 Dunnahoo, Terry. *Pearl Harbor: America Enters the War* (7–10). 1991, Watts LB $12.95 (0-531-11010-9). Compact history of the World War II attack, including profiles of key figures, both Japanese and American, involved in planning and counteracting the attack. (Rev: BL 6/15/91; SHS; SLJ 5/91) [940.54]

4875 Dwork, Deborah. *Children with a Star: Jewish Youth in Nazi Europe* (9–adult). 1991, Yale Univ. $25 (0-300-05054-2). Interviews with hundreds of Europeans and North Americans who lived through the Holocaust as children. (Rev: BL 3/1/91; SLJ 10/91) [940.53]

4876 Edmonds, Robin. *The Big Three: Churchill, Roosevelt, and Stalin in Peace and War* (9–adult). 1991, Norton $24.95 (0-393-02889-5). A first-rate examination of this often-rocky, ad hoc arrangement. (Rev: BL 3/1/91*; SHS) [940.53]

4877 Ford, Daniel. *Flying Tigers: Claire Chennault and the American Volunteer Group* (9–adult). (Smithsonian History of Aviation) 1991, Smithsonian $24.95 (1-56098-011-7). This study of the motley crew of Americans who flew for China early in World War II tells of their achievements in combat against heavy odds and in intolerable conditions. (Rev: BL 10/15/91) [940.54]

4878 Gay, Kathlyn, and Martin Gay. *World War II* (5–8). 1995, Twenty-First Century LB $15.98 (0-8050-2849-8). The causes, events, and consequences of this major conflict are presented, along with personal accounts by ordinary people who were there. (Rev: BL 12/15/95) [940.53]

4879 Gilbert, Martin. *The Day the War Ended: May 8, 1945—Victory in Europe* (9–adult). 1995, Holt $25 (0-8050-3926-0). In commemoration of the 50th anniversary of the end of World War II. Chronicles events leading up to and following the war in Europe. (Rev: BL 4/15/95) [940.54]

4880 Goldstein, Donald M., and others. *D-Day Normandy: The Story and Photographs* (9–adult). 1994, Brassey's $30 (0-02-881057-0). A collection of 400 photos by Robert Capa, ending with pictures of the permanent cemeteries on the high grounds just about the beaches. (Rev: BL 5/1/94) [940.54]

4881 Greenfeld, Howard. *The Hidden Children* (5–10). 1993, Ticknor & Fields $15.95 (0-395-66074-2). This account of what it was like to be a Jewish child hiding from the Nazis in World War II includes painful personal narratives of survivors. (Rev: BL 1/1/94*; MJHS; SLJ 5/94*; VOYA 6/94) [940.53]

4882 Gruhzit-Hoyt, Olga. *They Also Served: American Women in World War II* (9–adult). 1995, Birch Lane $19.95 (1-55972-280-0). Short profiles of women who served in World War II. (Rev: BL 5/1/95) [940.54]

4883 Hanmer, Trudy J. *Leningrad* (6–12). (Cities at War) 1992, Macmillan/New Discovery LB $14.95 (0-02-742615-7). (Rev: BL 10/15/92; MJHS) [947]

4884 Hartmann, Erich. *In the Camps* (9–adult). 1995, Norton $35 (0-393-03772-X). Enhanced by B&W photos showing the concentration camps, the stillness of the images reinforces the horror of their secrets. (Rev: BL 5/1/95) [940.54]

4885 Heide, Robert, and John Gilman. *Home Front America: Popular Culture of the World War II Era* (9–adult). 1995, Chronicle paper $17.95 (0-8118-0927-7). A volume wonderfully dependent on pictures that demonstrate the authors' devotion to World War II collectibles. (Rev: BL 8/95; VOYA 2/96) [973.917]

4886 Heydecker, Joe J. *The Warsaw Ghetto: A Photographic Record, 1941–1944* (9–adult). 1992, I. B. Tauris $29.95 (1-85043-155-8). A German eyewitness's photos and memories of what it was like in the Warsaw ghetto. (Rev: BL 3/15/92; SHS) [940.53]

4887 Heyes, Eileen. *Children of the Swastika: The Hitler Youth* (7–12). 1993, Millbrook LB $14.90 (1-56294-237-9). A study of the Hitler Youth's structure, purpose, inpact on the war effort, and effects on the youth. (Rev: BL 2/15/93; BTA) [324.243]

4888 Hilberg, Raul. *Perpetrators Victims Bystanders: The Jewish Catastrophe, 1933–1945* (9–adult). 1992, HarperCollins $25 (0-06-019035-3); 1993, paper $13 (0-06-099507-6). Profiles of 3 kinds of people who were willing and unwilling participants in the Nazi regime from 1933 to1945. (Rev: BL 9/15/92) [940.53]

4889 Holliday, Laurel. *Children in the Holocaust and World War II* (9–adult). 1995, Pocket $20 (0-671-52054-7). Excerpts from 23 World War II diaries provide glimpses into the lives and thoughts of teenagers. Awards: SLJ Best Book. (Rev: SLJ 9/95)

4890 Hoyt, Edwin. *The Airmen: The Story of American Fliers in World War II* (9–adult). 1991, McGraw-Hill $22.50 (0-07-030633-8). Highlights the experiences of numerous World War II airmen. A companion piece to *The GI's War*. (Rev: BL 1/1/91; SHS) [940.54]

4891 Hull, Robert, ed. *A Prose Anthology of the Second World War* (7–12). 1993, Millbrook LB $12.90 (1-56294-223-9). Primary source writings and photos, including excerpts from letters, diaries, and memoirs from those on opposite sides of the war. (Rev: BL 6/1–15/93; VOYA 8/93) [940.53]

4892 Isserman, Maurice. *World War II* (7–12). (America at War) 1991, Facts on File $17.95 (0-8160-2374-3). The major battles and personalities of World War II are highlighted, as well as events leading to war and discussion of changes following the conflict. (Rev: BL 10/15/91; MJHS; SLJ 8/92) [940.53]

4893 Kaplan, Phillip, and Jack Currie. *Round the Clock: The Experience of the Allied Bomber Crews Who Flew by Day and by Night from England in the Second World War* (9–adult). 1993, Random $50 (0-394-58921-1). The strategic bombing campaign waged by the U.S. Air Force and the British Royal Air Force is described with photos, first-person narratives, and quotations. (Rev: BL 1/1/94) [940.54]

4894 Keil, Sally Van Wagenen. *Those Wonderful Women in Their Flying Machines: The Unknown Heroines of World War II* (9–adult). Rev. ed. 1990, Four Directions Press (611 Broadway, New York, NY 10012) $24.95 (0-9627659-0-2). (Rev: BL 4/15/91; SHS) [940.54]

4895 Kelly, Mary Pat. *Proudly We Served: The Men of the USS Mason* (9–adult). 1995, Naval Institute $29.95 (1-55750-453-9). First-person narratives of the African American crew aboard a World War II destroyer that exposes the heroism and racism of naval combat. (Rev: BL 2/15/95; SLJ 8/95) [940.54]

4896 Kimmett, Larry, and Margaret Regis. *The Attack on Pearl Harbor: An Illustrated History* (9–adult). 1991, Navigator Publishing (P.O. Box 30548, Seattle, WA 98103) paper $15.95 (1-879932-00-8). An overview of the infamous assault, pieced together by numerous photos and maps of various attack centers. (Rev: BL 1/15/92) [940.54]

4897 Kodama, Tatsuharu. *Shin's Tricycle* (5–8). Tr. by Kazuko Hokumen-Jones. Illus. 1995, Walker LB $16.85 (0-8027-8376-7). The title stems from the tricycle the author's son wanted so badly and finally was able to acquire in spite of the wartime shortage of metal. The atom bomb exploded while his son was riding the tricycle. (Rev: BL 9/1/95*; SLJ 12/95) [940.54]

4898 Kronenwetter, Michael. *London* (6–12). (Cities at War) 1992, Macmillan/New Discovery LB $13.95 (0-02-751050-6). Photo-essay on what occurred in the lives of ordinary people in Berlin during World War II, with eyewitness quotes. (Rev: BL 6/15/92; MJHS; SLJ 9/92) [942.1084]

4899 Krull, Kathleen. *V Is for Victory: America Remembers World War II* (5–8). 1995, Knopf/Apple Soup $24 (0-679-86198-X). The events of World War II are explored with postcards, letters, posters, and photos that give a taste of the war from the home front, the battle field, and a political viewpoint. (Rev: BL 7/95; SLJ 10/95) [940.53]

4900 Landau, Elaine. *Nazi War Criminals* (9–12). 1990, Watts LB $11.95 (0-531-15181-6). Profiles of Nazi war criminals and the attempts made to bring them to justice. (Rev: BL 1/15/91; SHS) [364.1]

4901 Landau, Elaine. *The Warsaw Ghetto Uprising* (7–10). 1992, Macmillan/New Discovery LB $14.95 (0-02-751392-0). Recounts the horrors of the month-long battles between Nazis and young Jews in 1943 Poland. (Rev: BL 2/15/93; MJHS) [940.53]

4902 Landau, Ronnie S. *The Nazi Holocaust* (9–adult). 1994, Ivan R. Dee (1332 N. Halsted St., Chicago, IL 60622-2632) $27.50 (1-56663-054-1); paper $12.95 (1-56663-052-5). This study focuses on the Jewish experience during the Holocaust and explores global concerns regarding human relations and genocide. (Rev: BL 3/15/94) [940.53]

4903 Levine, Ellen. *A Fence Away from Freedom: Japanese Americans and World War II* (7–12). 1995, Putnam $17.95 (0-399-22638-9). Many voices tell of their bitter experiences as Japanese Americans illegally interned during World War II. Awards: Woodson Book. (Rev: BL 10/1/95; SLJ 12/95; VOYA 2/96) [940.53]

4904 Litoff, Judy Barrett, and David C. Smith, eds. *We're in This War, Too: World War II Letters from American Women in Uniform* (9–adult). 1994, Oxford Univ. $25 (0-19-507504-8). A collection of letters written by World War II service women that tell of their often unrecognized war experiences. (Rev: BL 7/94; SHS; SLJ 12/94) [940.54]

4905 McGowen, Tom. *World War II* (5–7). 1993, Watts $12.40 (0-531-20150-3). A military history of the war, with dramatic photos, maps, fast-moving narrative, and facts and figures. (Rev: BL 6/1–15/93; MJHS) [940.53]

4906 McKissack, Patricia, and Fredrick McKissack. *Red-Tail Angels: The Story of the Tuskegee Airmen of World War II* (7–12). 1995, Walker LB $20.85 (0-8027-8293-0). Account of a little-known squadron that served with distinction in segregated fighter groups under white commanding officers during World War II. (Rev: BL 2/15/96; SLJ 2/96; VOYA 4/96)

4907 Marshall, Robert. *In the Sewers of Lvov: A Heroic Story of Survival from the Holocaust* (9–adult). 1991, Scribner $22.95 (0-684-19320-5). Portrays the courage and the will to survive of a small group of Jews in German-occupied Poland. (Rev: BL 9/1/91) [940.53]

4908 Marx, Trish. *Echoes of World War II* (5–8). 1994, Lerner LB $14.96 (0-8225-4898-4). The stories of 6 children from various backgrounds whose lives were drastically altered by the war. Maps and documents help depict the agonies of each. (Rev: BL 9/15/94; SLJ 5/94) [940.53]

4909 Miller, Nathan. *War at Sea: A Naval History of World War II* (9–adult). 1995, Scribner $30 (0-684-80380-1). Miller, the author of 4 previous volumes of popular naval history, informally presents this history of naval power. (Rev: BL 9/1/95) [940.54]

4910 Miller, Russell, ed. *Nothing Less Than Victory: The Oral History of D-Day* (9–adult). 1994, Morrow $25 (0-688-10209-3). Four oral histories of members of the units that turned back a counterattack from the 21st Panzer division. (Rev: BL 5/1/94; SLJ 11/94) [940.54]

4911 Millu, Liana. *Smoke over Birkenau* (9–adult). Tr. by Lynne Sharon Schwartz. 1991, Jewish Publication Society $19.95 (0-8276-0398-3). Each story in this Holocaust survival anthology is both an individual portrait and a commentary on the concentration camp's perversion of significant events in a woman's life: childbirth, sexuality, motherhood, sisterhood, and death. (Rev: BL 10/15/91) [940.53]

4912 Morin, Isobel V. *Days of Judgment: The World War II War Crimes Trials* (7–12). 1995, Millbrook LB $15.90 (1-56294-442-8). A summary of the first Nuremberg trial plus other German and Japanese war crime trials. (Rev: BL 4/15/95; SHS; SLJ 3/95) [940.54]

4913 Mulvihill, Margaret. *Mussolini and Italian Fascism* (6–9). (World War II Biographies) 1990, Gloucester LB $11.91 (0-531-17253-8). Biography of the Italian leader includes illustrations of war campaigns and weapons systems. (Rev: BL 1/1/91)

4914 Newton, David E. *Tokyo* (6–12). (Cities at War) 1992, Macmillan/New Discovery LB $14.95 (0-02-768235-8). Remembrances from people who experienced World War II in Tokyo. (Rev: BL 10/15/92; MJHS) [952]

4915 Newton, Verne W. *The Cambridge Spies: The Untold Story of Maclean, Philby, and Burgess in America* (9–adult). 1991, Madison Books $24.95 (0-8191-8059-9). This detailed cold-war history focuses on an infamous trio of diplomatic spies. (Rev: BL 6/15/91) [327.1]

4916 Osmont, Marie-Louise. *The Normandy Diary of Marie-Louise Osmont: 1940–1944* (9–adult). 1994, Random $17 (0-679-43438-0). A rare civilian point of view of a woman in whose home were billeted pilots flying the 1940 blitz against Great Britain. Her home became a battlefield on D-Day. (Rev: BL 5/1/94) [940.54]

4917 Pfeifer, Kathryn Browne. *The 761st Tank Battalion* (5–8). (African American Soldiers) 1994, Twenty-First Century LB $14.95 (0-8050-3057-3). The history of an outfit of African American soldiers who served with distinction during World War II but were marginalized by racism. (Rev: BL 9/1/94; BTA; MJHS; SLJ 11/94) [940.54]

4918 Pietrusza, David. *The Battle of Normandy* (7–10). (Battles of World War II) 1996, Lucent LB $19.95 (1-56006-413-7). Review of the historic battle, from preparation through execution to hard-won success. (Rev: SLJ 2/96)

4919 Powers, Thomas. *Heisenberg's War: The Secret History of the German Bomb* (9–adult). 1993, Knopf $27.50 (0-394-51411-4). Details the Allied and Axis individuals, politics, and times in the race to build an atomic bomb, focusing on Heisenberg's role. (Rev: BL 1/15/93*) [355.8]

4920 Resnick, Abraham. *The Holocaust* (5–9). (Overview) 1991, Lucent LB $12.95 (1-56006-124-3). This history of Jewish genocide and its aftermath combines a sober account of the atrocities with personal testimony from survivors and observers and many affecting photos. (Rev: BL 10/15/91; SLJ 11/91) [940.53]

4921 Rice, Earle, Jr. *The Battle of Midway* (7–12). (The Battles) 1996, Lucent LB $19.95 (1-56006-415-3). Coverage of one of World War II's most important battles. (Rev: SLJ 2/96)

4922 Rittner, Carol, and John K. Roth, eds. *Different Voices: Women and the Holocaust* (9–adult). 1993, Paragon House $26.95 (1-55778-503-1); paper $19.95 (1-55778-504-X). Poignant assortment of memoirs, essays, and reflections by and about women who encountered the Holocaust through their own or their parents' experiences. (Rev: BL 2/15/93; SHS) [940.53]

4923 Rogers, James T. *The Secret War* (8–12). (World Espionage) 1991, Facts on File $16.95 (0-8160-2395-6). A well-supported thesis stating that the British and Americans were more successful at espionage, counterespionage, and detection than either the Germans or the Japanese. (Rev: BL 3/1/92; SHS) [940.54]

4924 Ross, Stewart. *Propaganda* (5–7). (World War II) 1993, Thomson Learning LB $14.95 (1-56847-080-0). Color and B&W photos enhance this discussion of the tactics used to influence public opinion during World War II. (Rev: BL 10/1/93; MJHS) [940.54]

4925 Ross, Stewart. *World Leaders* (5–7). (World War II) 1993, Thomson Learning LB $14.95 (1-56847-079-7). Presents biographies of Chamberlain, Chiang Kai-shek, Churchill, Franco, Hirohito, Hitler, Musolini, Roosevelt, Stalin, and Truman. (Rev: BL 10/1/93; MJHS) [940.54]

4926 Ross, Stewart. *World War II* (7–12). (Causes and Consequences) 1995, Raintree/Steck-Vaughn LB $25.69 (0-8172-4050-0). (Rev: BL 12/15/95) [940.53]

4927 Schapiro, Raya Czerner, and Helga Czerner Weinberg, eds. *Letters from Prague, 1939–1941* (9–adult). 1991, Academy Chicago $20 (0-89733-369-1). A collection of correspondence among a well-to-do Jewish family who were forced to separate offers personal insight into the Holocaust. (Rev: BL 12/1/91) [940.53]

4928 Sherrow, Victoria. *Amsterdam* (6–12). (Cities at War) 1992, Macmillan/New Discovery LB $13.95 (0-02-782465-9). Photo-essay on what occurred in the lives of ordinary people in Berlin during World War II, with eyewitness quotes. (Rev: BL 6/15/92; MJHS; SLJ 9/92) [940.53]

4929 Sherrow, Victoria. *Hiroshima* (6–12). 1994, Silver Burdett/New Discovery LB $14.95 (0-02-782467-5). Chronicles the birth of the atomic age, concluding in grisly descriptions of the

World War II bombing of Hiroshima. (Rev: BL 10/1/94; BTA; SLJ 11/94) [940.54]

4930 Silver, Eric. *The Book of the Just: The Unsung Heroes Who Saved Jews from Hitler* (9–adult). 1992, Grove/Weidenfeld $19.95 (0-8021-1347-8). Straightforward profiles of citizens who helped, sheltered, and saved Jews during World War II. (Rev: BL 9/15/92) [940.5318]

4931 Sloan, Frank. *Bismarck!* (5–8). 1991, Watts LB $11.90 (0-531-20002-7). Introduction to a landmark sea battle of World War II, when the British sank a great German battleship. (Rev: BL 6/15/91) [940.54]

4932 Smith, Page. *Democracy on Trial: The Japanese-American Evacuation and Relocation in World War II* (9–adult). 1995, Simon & Schuster $27.50 (0-684-80354-2). Smith uses archival research and survivor interviews in his study of World War II evacuation and relocation of Japanese Americans. (Rev: BL 8/95) [940.53]

4933 Spiegelman, Art. *Maus: A Survivor's Tale II: And Here My Troubles Began* (9–adult). 1991, Pantheon $18 (0-394-55655-0). Using a unique comic-strip-as-graphic-art format, the story of Vladek Spiegelman's passage through the Nazi Holocaust is told in his own words. Awards: YALSA Best Book for Young Adults. (Rev: BL 10/15/91) [940.53]

4934 Stein, R. Conrad. *World War II in Europe: "America Goes to War"* (5–7). (American War) 1994, Enslow LB $17.95 (0-89490-525-2). A succinct survey of the events of World War II in Europe. (Rev: BL 10/15/94; MJHS) [940.54]

4935 Stein, R. Conrad. *World War II in the Pacific: Remember Pearl Harbor* (5–7). (American War) 1994, Enslow LB $17.95 (0-89490-524-4). A sweeping overview of U.S. participation in the Pacific. (Rev: BL 7/94; MJHS; SLJ 7/94) [940.54]

4936 Steins, Richard. *The Allies Against the Axis: World War II (1940–1950)* (5–8). (First Person America) 1994, Twenty-First Century LB $15.95 (0-8050-2586-3). An introduction to World War II that includes excerpts from primary sources. (Rev: BL 5/15/94; MJHS) [940.53]

4937 Stewart, Gail B. *Hitler's Reich* (8–12). (World History) 1994, Lucent LB $14.95 (1-56006-235-5). An in-depth examination of Adolf Hitler and his henchmen. (Rev: BL 12/15/93; MJHS) [943.086]

4938 Stewart, Gail B. *Life in the Warsaw Ghetto* (6–12). (The Way People Live) 1995, Lucent LB $14.95 (1-56006-075-1). An in-depth history of the Warsaw ghetto told through witnesses. (Rev: BL 3/15/95*; SLJ 4/95) [943.8]

4939 Swiebocka, Teresa, ed. *Auschwitz: A History in Photographs* (9–adult). 1993, Indiana Univ. $59.95 (0-253-35581-8). More than 280 shocking photos taken by former Auschwitz prisoners and the Nazis who imprisoned them bear witness to death camp horrors. (Rev: BL 10/15/93) [940.53]

4940 Szulc, Tad. *The Secret Alliance: The Extraordinary Story of the Rescue of the Jews since World War II* (9–adult). 1991, Farrar $24.95 (0-374-24946-6). A historical account of the role played by American Jewry in the covert movement to Israel of Jews from Europe, North Africa, and the Middle East from the 1940s to the present. (Rev: BL 12/1/91) [325.5694]

4941 Travers, Paul Joseph. *Eyewitness to Infamy: An Oral History of Pearl Harbor* (9–adult). 1991, Madison Books $24.95 (0-8191-8058-0). The first-hand accounts of 43 survivors of the attack on Pearl Harbor on December 7, 1941. (Rev: BL 11/15/91) [940.54]

4942 Van der Vat, Dan. *The Pacific Campaign: World War II: The U.S.-Japanese Naval War, 1941–1945* (9–adult). 1991, Simon & Schuster $28 (0-671-73899-2). An analysis of the World War II Pacific naval campaign that offers insights into the leadership, strategies, and racial prejudices of both the United States and Japan. (Rev: BL 12/1/91) [940.54]

4943 Verges, Marianne. *On Silver Wings* (9–adult). 1991, Ballantine $20 (0-345-36534-8). The story of the 1,000+ women who flew noncombatant, stateside missions during World War II as U.S. Army pilots. (Rev: BL 9/15/91) [940.54]

4944 Verhoeven, Rian, and Ruud van der Rol. *Anne Frank: Beyond the Diary: A Photographic Remembrance* (5–12). Tr. by Tony Langham and Plym Peters. 1993, Viking $17 (0-670-84932-4). Includes photos of people and the places Anne lived and hid in, with excerpts from her diary text. Awards: ALSC Notable Children's Book; Christopher; SLJ Best Book; YALSA Best Book for Young Adults. (Rev: BL 10/1/93*; MJHS; SLJ 12/93*) [940.53]

4945 Weintraub, Stanley. *The Last Great Victory: The End of World War II, July/August 1945* (9–adult). 1995, Dutton/Truman Talley $32.95 (0-525-93687-4). An account of the last 30 days of World War II, including the bombings of Hiroshima and Nagasaki. (Rev: BL 4/15/95*) [940.54]

4946 Whitman, Sylvia. *Uncle Sam Wants You! Military Men and Women of World War II* (5–7). 1993, Lerner LB $13.13 (0-8225-1728-0). Covers the draft, boot camp, military job training, barracks life, battlefield conditions, and changing role of minorities because of their wartime participation. (Rev: BL 5/1/93; BTA; SLJ 6/93) [940.54]

4947 Whitman, Sylvia. *V Is for Victory: The American Home Front During World War II* (5–7). 1993, Lerner LB $13.13 (0-8225-1727-2). Provides entertaining glimpses of American daily life during World War II, with B&W photos. (Rev: BL 2/15/93; MJHS) [973.917]

4948 Zeinert, Karen. *Those Incredible Women of World War II* (6–9). 1994, Millbrook LB $16.90 (1-56294-434-7). An illustrated account of the contributions made by women during World War II. (Rev: BL 1/15/95; BTA; SLJ 2/95) [940.54]

Modern World History (1945–)

4949 Dudley, William, ed. *The Cold War* (10–12). (Opposing Viewpoints/American History) 1992, Greenhaven LB $17.95 (1-56510-009-3); paper $9.95 (1-56510-008-5). Provides scholarly material with a wide range of viewpoints and a long annotated bibliography. (Rev: BL 4/15/93; MJHS; SHS; SLJ 6/93) [327.73]

4950 Eyre, Ronald, and others. *Frontiers* (9–adult). 1991, Parkwest $31.95 (0-563-20701-9). Produced by the BBC in conjunction with the American release of the documentary series, these 8 essays examine territorial borders at crisis points worldwide and the concept of nationality. (Rev: BL 10/1/91) [824]

4951 Hills, Ken. *1960s* (6–8). (Take Ten Years) 1993, Raintree LB $15.96 (0-8114-3079-0). (Rev: BL 8/93) [909.82]

4952 Rieff, David. *Slaughterhouse: Bosnia and the Failure of the West* (9–adult). 1995, Simon & Schuster $22 (0-671-88118-3). A journalist's assessment of the killing or displacement of Bosnian Muslims. (Rev: BL 3/15/95*) [949.7]

4953 Sharman, Margaret. *1950s* (6–8). (Take Ten Years) 1993, Raintree LB $15.96 (0-8114-3078-2). (Rev: BL 8/93) [909.82]

Geographical Regions

Africa

General and Miscellaneous

4954 Ayo, Yvonne. *Africa* (5–9). (Eyewitness Books) 1995, Knopf LB $20.99 (0-679-97334-6). Interesting photographs and fascinating facts are laid out fabulously in this overview of Africa. (Rev: BL 12/15/95; SLJ 1/96) [960]

4955 Davidson, Basil. *The Black Man's Burden: Africa and the Curse of the Nation-State* (9–adult). 1992, Times Books $23 (0-8129-1998-X). A leading African historian argues against the nation-state as it relates to ethnicity, colonialism, and culture. (Rev: BL 4/15/92) [960.32]

4956 Englebert, Victor. *Wind, Sand and Silence: Travels with Africa's Last Nomads* (9–adult). 1992, Chronicle $35 (0-8118-0010-5). This illustrated volume provides a moving account of 26 years spent with nomads in North Africa. (Rev: BL 12/1/92) [305.9]

4957 Feelings, Tom. *The Middle Passage: White Ships/Black Cargo* (9–adult). 1995, Dial $45 (0-8037-1804-7). A cathartic text for the author, born of his need to escape the racial violence of the 1960s by traveling to Ghana where he could reaffirm his belief in humanity. Awards: Coretta Scott King. (Rev: BL 10/15/95; SLJ 2/96) [759.13]

4958 Harris, Eddy. *Native Stranger: A Black American's Journey into the Heart of Africa* (9–adult). 1992, Simon & Schuster $22 (0-671-74897-1). An African American explores the realities of Africa. (Rev: BL 2/1/92) [916]

4959 Houston, Dick. *Safari Adventure* (7–12). 1991, Dutton/Cobblehill $14.95 (0-525-65051-2). Bush safari guide chronicles Houston's journeys and poses questions regarding the destruction of Africa's wild places. (Rev: BL 8/91) [916.7604]

4960 Jones, Constance. *A Short History of Africa: 1500–1900* (8–12). 1993, Facts on File $16.95 (0-8160-2774-9). Jones describes the Islamic cultures of North Africa, the city-states and kingdoms of East Africa, the rich traditions of West Africa, and the roots of apartheid in South Africa. (Rev: BL 3/1/93; SLJ 10/93) [960]

4961 Wekesser, Carol, and Christina Pierce. *Africa* (7–12). (Opposing Viewpoints) 1992, Greenhaven LB $15.95 (0-89908-186-X); paper $8.95 (0-89908-161-4). The history of Africa, from politics to social issues. (Rev: BL 5/15/92; MJHS; SHS; SLJ 7/92) [960]

4962 Wepman, Dennis. *Africa: The Struggle for Independence* (7–10). 1993, Facts on File $16.95 (0-8160-2820-6). Focuses on the arbitrary division of the African continent by European countries and the struggle of various regions against colonial rule. (Rev: BL 2/15/94; MJHS; VOYA 6/94) [960]

Central and Eastern Africa

4963 Davidson, Basil. *The Search for Africa: History, Culture, Politics* (9–adult). 1993, Times Books $25 (0-8129-2278-6). Twenty wide-ranging essays that introduce major issues of African history, culture, politics, and economics. (Rev: BL 2/15/94; SHS) [967]

4964 Dorris, Michael. *Rooms in the House of Stone* (9–adult). 1993, Milkweed Editions (430 First Ave. N., Suite 400, Minneapolis, MN 55401) paper $4.95 (0-915943-70-0). Describes

Dorris's activities in and impressions of drought-plagued 1991 Zimbabwe as a member of the Save the Children Foundation. (Rev: BL 4/15/93) [362.87]

4965 Gaertner, Ursula. *Elmolo* (7–10). (Heritage Library of African Peoples) 1995, Rosen $15.95 (0-8239-1764-9). Looks at the customs, daily life, and values of the Elmolo tribe, which lives in Kenya. (Rev: BL 7/95; SLJ 5/95) [967.62]

4966 Holtzman, Jon. *Samburu* (7–10). (Heritage Library of African Peoples) 1995, Rosen $15.95 (0-8239-1759-2). Discusses in great detail the culture and lifestyle of the Samburu people of Kenya. (Rev: BL 7/95; SLJ 5/95) [960]

4967 Kabira, Wanjiku Mukabi. *Agikuyu* (7–10). (Heritage Library of African Peoples) 1995, Rosen $15.95 (0-8239-1762-2). Presents social and cultural aspects of the Agikuyu community of Kenya in ways that make them accessible to Western readers. (Rev: BL 7/95; SLJ 6/95) [306]

4968 Kurtz, Jane. *Ethiopia: The Roof of Africa* (5–9). (Discovering Our Heritage) 1991, Dillon LB $14.95 (0-87518-483-9). Conveys a lively sense of Ethiopian life through concrete descriptions. (Rev: BL 2/1/92; SLJ 5/92) [963]

4969 Latham, Aaron. *The Frozen Leopard* (9–adult). 1991, Prentice-Hall $20 (0-13-946021-7). Recounts the author's experiences with the Masai people, preservationists, animals, and culture of Kenya. (Rev: BL 9/1/91) [916.76204]

4970 Ogbaa, Kalu. *Igbo* (7–10). (Heritage Library of African Peoples) 1995, Rosen $15.95 (0-8239-1977-3). Explains the beliefs and worldview of the lgbo people and how these are reflected in their daily lives. (Rev: BL 9/15/95; SLJ 11/95) [966.9]

4971 Pateman, Robert. *Kenya* (5–7). (Cultures of the World) 1993, Marshall Cavendish $21.95 (1-85435-572-4). (Rev: BL 8/93) [967.62]

4972 Stewart, Gail B. *Ethiopia* (5–7). (Places in the News) 1991, Macmillan/Crestwood LB $10.95 (0-89686-601-7). (Rev: BL 9/1/91) [963]

4973 Zeleza, Tiyambe. *Akamba* (7–10). (Heritage Library of African Peoples) 1995, Rosen $15.95 (0-8239-1768-1). Presents social and cultural aspects of the Akamba community of Kenya in ways that make them accessible to Western readers. (Rev: BL 7/95; SLJ 6/95) [960]

4974 Zeleza, Tiyambe. *Mijikenda* (7–10). (Heritage Library of African Peoples) 1995, Rosen $15.95 (0-8239-1767-3). Combines history and anthropology to provide a portrait of the Mijikenda people. (Rev: BL 9/15/95; SLJ 11/95) [960]

North Africa

4975 Ayoub, Abderrahman, and others. *Umm El Madayan: An Islamic City Through the Ages* (7–10). Tr. by Kathleen Leverich. Illus. 1994, Houghton $16.95 (0-395-65967-1). This illustrated volume takes a fictional Islamic Arab city on the North African coast through 14 stages of its history. (Rev: BL 1/15/94; BTA; SLJ 4/94) [961]

4976 Diamond, Arthur. *Egypt: Gift of the Nile* (5–9). (Discovering Our Heritage) 1992, Dillon LB $14.95 (0-87518-511-8). An introduction to Egypt that includes recipes, folktales, maps, history, and a discussion of Egyptian immigrants in the United States. (Rev: BL 8/92; MJHS; SLJ 11/92) [962]

4977 Gottfried, Ted. *Libya: Desert Land in Conflict* (7–12). 1994, Millbrook LB $16.90 (1-56294-351-0). A focus on Libya's modern history, with some background of its earlier history. (Rev: BL 5/1/94; BTA; MJHS; SLJ 4/94; VOYA 6/94) [961.2]

4978 Malcolm, Peter. *Libya* (5–7). (Cultures of the World) 1993, Marshall Cavendish $21.95 (1-85435-573-2). (Rev: BL 8/93) [961.2]

4979 Reeves, Nicholas, and Nan Froman. *Into the Mummy's Tomb* (5–9). (Time Quest) 1992, Scholastic/Madison $15.95 (0-590-45752-7). This book on Howard Carter's discovery of Tutankhamen's tomb illustrates the richness of the find—both the treasure's opulence and in the knowledge gained. Awards: BL Editors' Choice; SLJ Best Book. (Rev: BL 10/15/92*; MJHS; SLJ 8/92*) [932]

South Africa

4980 Bradley, Catherine. *The End of Apartheid* (7–12). 1995, Raintree/Steck-Vaughn LB $25.69 (0-8172-4055-1). Crucial world political events are set within a historical context designed like a long magazine article, with maps and photos. (Rev: BL 12/15/95; SLJ 1/96) [305.8]

4981 Brandenburg, Jim. *Sand and Fog: Adventures in Southern Africa* (5–9). 1994, Walker LB $17.85 (0-8027-8233-7). A color photo-essay about the Namibian desert in southwest Africa by a photographer on assignment for *National Geographic*. (Rev: BL 3/1/94*; BTA; MJHS; SLJ 5/94) [968.81]

4982 Lanting, Frans. *Okavango: Africa's Last Eden* (9–adult). 1993, Chronicle $45 (0-8118-0527-1). The African wildlife photos in this collection were taken in a Botswana nature preserve. Also includes text describing this ecosystem. (Rev: BL 11/15/93; BTA) [508.6883]

4983 Lauré, Jason. *Botswana* (5–8). (Enchantment of the World) 1993, Children's Press $19.95 (0-516-02616-X). A sympathetic portrait of this independent African nation. (Rev: BL 11/1/93; MJHS; SLJ 4/94) [968.83]

4984 Lauré, Jason. *Namibia* (5–8). (Enchantment of the World) 1993, Children's Press LB $19.95 (0-516-02615-1). (Rev: BL 8/93) [968.81]

4985 Mallaby, Sebastian. *After Apartheid: The Future of South Africa* (9–adult). 1992, Times Books $22 (0-8129-1938-6). An in-depth view of South Africa now and in the near future. (Rev: BL 3/1/92; SLJ 1/93) [968.06]

4986 Pascoe, Elaine. *South Africa: Troubled Land* (7–12). 1992, Watts $13.40 (0-531-11139-3). This updated history of South Africa begins before whites "discovered" the Cape, discusses the role of Mandela and other leaders, and outlines the repeal of apartheid laws. (Rev: BL 10/15/92; MJHS; SLJ 12/92) [968]

4987 Pratt, Paula Bryant. *The End of Apartheid in South Africa* (6–8). (Overview) 1995, Lucent LB $14.95 (1-56006-170-7). (Rev: BL 7/95) [323.1]

4988 Rosmarin, Ike. *South Africa* (5–7). (Cultures of the World) 1993, Marshall Cavendish $21.95 (1-85435-575-9). (Rev: BL 8/93) [968]

4989 Sheehan, Sean. *Zimbabwe* (5–7). (Cultures of the World) 1993, Marshall Cavendish $21.95 (1-85435-577-5). (Rev: BL 8/93) [968.91]

4990 Smith, Chris. *Conflict in Southern Africa* (6–12). (Conflicts) 1993, Macmillan/New Discovery $13.95 (0-02-785956-8). An overview of the politics of southern Africa: Angola, Mozambique, Zambia, Namibia, and South Africa. (Rev: BL 7/93; BTA; SLJ 12/93) [968]

West Africa

4991 Barboza, Steven. *Door of No Return: The Legend of Goree Island* (5–7). 1994, Dutton/Cobblehill $14.99 (0-525-65188-8). Presents the brutal history of Goree Island, a former African slave trading post that is now a sunny paradise attracting tourists unaware of its dark past. (Rev: BL 7/94; SLJ 11/94) [966.3]

4992 Kennedy, Geraldine. *Harmattan: A Journey Across the Sahara* (9–adult). 1994, Clover Park (P.O. Box 5067, Santa Monica, CA 90409-5067) $22 (0-9628632-1-1). An account of 5 female Peace Corps volunteers who managed a nearly impossible Sahara crossing in 1964. (Rev: BL 1/1/94; BTA) [916.6]

4993 Koslow, Philip. *Yorubaland: The Flowering of Genius* (7–12). (The Kingdoms of Africa) 1995, Chelsea $14.95 (0-7910-3131-4); paper $7.95 (0-7910-3132-2). History of a lost African nation and its influence on present-day Nigeria. (Rev: BL 2/15/96; SLJ 2/96)

4994 Levy, Patricia. *Nigeria* (5–7). (Cultures of the World) 1993, Marshall Cavendish $21.95 (1-85435-574-0). (Rev: BL 8/93) [966.9]

4995 McKissack, Patricia, and Fredrick McKissack. *The Royal Kingdoms of Ghana, Mali, and Songhay: Life in Medieval Africa* (7–10). 1994, Holt $15.95 (0-8050-1670-8). Drawing on contemporary scholarship and the oral tradition, this volume describes the history of long-ignored cities of medieval West Africa. (Rev: BL 1/15/94; MJHS; SLJ 6/94) [966.2]

4996 Nugent, Rory. *Drums along the Congo: On the Trail of Mokele-Mbembe, the Last Living Dinosaur* (9–adult). 1993, Houghton $21.95 (0-395-58707-7); paper $10.95 (0-395-67071-3). Chronicles the explorer's journey to Lake Tele in the Congo to search for a fabled creature considered a powerful jungle deity. (Rev: BL 5/15/93) [916.751]

Asia

General and Miscellaneous

4997 Franck, Irene M., and David M. Brownstone. *Across Asia by Land* (6–10). (Travel and Trade Routes) 1991, Facts on File $17.95 (0-8160-1874-X). Specific trade and travel routes tell historical tales from ancient times to the present. (Rev: BL 1/15/91; SLJ 6/91) [380.1]

4998 Schmidt, Jeremy. *Himalayan Passage: Seven Months in the High Country of Tibet, Nepal, China, India and Pakistan* (9–adult). 1991, Mountaineers Books $22.95 (0-89886-262-0). The adventure-filled travels of 4 experienced mountaineers—on foot, by mountain bike, and in overcrowded buses and trucks—from Tibet to Sikkim. (Rev: BL 9/15/91) [915.49604]

China

4999 Ashabranner, Brent. *Land of Yesterday, Land of Tomorrow: Discovering Chinese Central*

Asia (5–12). Photos. 1992, Dutton/Cobblehill $16 (0-525-65086-5). A photo essay of Xinjiang, a province of China. (Rev: BL 5/1/92; MJHS; SLJ 6/92) [951]

5000 Brill, Marlene Targ. *Mongolia* (5–8). (Enchantment of the World) 1992, Children's Press LB $18.95 (0-516-02605-4). (Rev: BL 6/1/92; MJHS) [951.7]

5001 Ferroa, Peggy. *China* (5–7). (Cultures of the World) 1991, Marshall Cavendish LB $19.95 (1-85435-399-3). Summarizes the history and geography of China, with emphasis on its unique culture. (Rev: BL 2/15/92; SLJ 3/92) [951]

5002 Kort, Michael. *China under Communism* (9–12). 1995, Millbrook $16 (1-56294-450-9). This detailed history of the Communist movement in China offers opportunities for discussion from both historical and cultural perspectives. (Rev: BL 1/1/95; SLJ 3/95) [951.05]

5003 Murowchick, Robert E. *China: Ancient Culture, Modern Land* (9–adult). (Cradles of Civilization) 1994, Univ. of Oklahoma $34.95 (0-8061-2683-3). Follows the development of Chinese cultural history from ancient times to the present, tracing the evolution of religion, philosophy, government, land, and language. (Rev: BL 10/1/94; SHS) [951]

5004 Odijk, Pamela. *The Chinese* (5–7). (Ancient World) 1991, Silver Burdett LB $16.98 (0-382-09894-3). The rich history of a distinctive culture credited with introducing tea, medicines, and architectural styles to the world. (Rev: BL 1/15/92) [951]

5005 Terrill, Ross. *China in Our Time: The Epic Saga of the People's Republic from the Communist Victory to Tiananmen Square and Beyond* (9–adult). 1992, Simon & Schuster $25 (0-671-68096-X). A mixture of firsthand observation and historical facts, from a student trip by the author in the 1960s to the 1990s, presents an informal view of China's evolution. (Rev: BL 6/1/92; SHS) [951.05]

India, Pakistan, and Bangladesh

5006 Cumming, David. *The Ganges Delta and Its People* (5–8). (People and Places) 1994, Thomson Learning $15.95 (1-56847-168-8). (Rev: BL 10/15/94; MJHS) [954]

5007 Lauré, Jason. *Bangladesh* (5–8). (Enchantment of the World) 1992, Children's Press LB $19.95 (0-516-02609-7). This up-to-date look at Bangladesh features geological, historical, meteorological, and engineering aspects of the country, and also reflects on current problems. (Rev: BL 12/15/92; MJHS) [954.9]

Japan

5008 Avikian, Monique. *The Meiji Restoration and the Rise of Modern Japan* (5–8). (Turning Points in World History) 1991, Silver Burdett LB $13.98 (0-382-24132-0); paper $8.95 (0-382-24139-8). Examines the major factors that resulted in the establishment of a new social order in Japan. (Rev: BL 3/15/92) [952.03]

5009 Iyer, Pico. *The Lady and the Monk: Four Seasons in Kyoto* (9–adult). 1991, Knopf $22 (0-679-40308-6). In this autobiographical account of a year in Japan, the author describes the sights and philosophies he encountered and the evolution of his loving friendship with a Japanese woman. (Rev: BL 9/1/91) [952]

5010 Langone, John. *In the Shogun's Shadow: Understanding a Changing Japan* (6–12). Illus. 1994, Little, Brown $15.95 (0-316-51409-8). A discussion of the homogeneous Japanese culture and false stereotypes about it, as well as a candid look at American Japan-bashing and Japanese racism. (Rev: BL 1/15/94; BTA; SLJ 4/94; VOYA 6/94) [952]

5011 Nardo, Don. *Modern Japan* (8–12). (World History) 1995, Lucent LB $14.95 (1-56006-281-9). (Rev: BL 2/15/95) [952.03]

5012 Odijk, Pamela. *The Japanese* (5–7). (Ancient World) 1991, Silver Burdett LB $16.98 (0-382-09898-6). Japan's distinctive history highlighted through its culture, land, people, religion, and art. (Rev: BL 1/15/92) [952]

5013 Reingold, Edwin. *Chrysanthemums and Thorns: The Untold Story of Modern Japan* (9–adult). 1992, St. Martin's $24.95 (0-312-08160-X). An examination of modern Japanese society, focusing on the its economic magnetism and the challenges it faces in fulfilling its role as world leader. (Rev: BL 11/15/92) [952.04]

5014 Ross, Stewart. *Rise of Japan and the Pacific Rim* (7–12). (Causes and Consequences) 1995, Raintree/Steck-Vaughn LB $25.69 (0-8172-4054-3). Timely and informative presentation of modern Japan since World War II with details on political, social, and economic matters. (Rev: BL 12/15/95; SLJ 2/96) [330.952]

5015 Shelley, Rex. *Japan* (5–10). 1990, Marshall Cavendish $19.95 (1-85435-297-0). (Rev: BL 2/15/91; SLJ 6/91) [952]

5016 Zurlo, Tony. *Japan: Superpower of the Pacific* (5–9). (Discovering Our Heritage) 1991, Dillon LB $14.95 (0-87518-480-4). Highlights aspects of Japan's history and culture. (Rev: BL 2/1/92) [952]

Other Countries

5017 Ansary, Mir Tamim. *Afghanistan: Fighting for Freedom* (5–9). (Discovering Our Heritage) 1991, Dillon LB $14.95 (0-87518-482-0). (Rev: BL 2/1/92) [958.1]

5018 Borton, Lady. *After Sorrow: An American among the Vietnamese* (9–adult). 1995, Viking $23.95 (0-670-84332-6). Interviews and personal encounters with Vietnamese women convey a picutre of everyday life and resistance work for the Vietcong. (Rev: BL 4/15/95) [915.97044]

5019 Burbank, Jon. *Nepal* (5–7). (Cultures of the World) 1991, Marshall Cavendish LB $19.95 (1-85435-401-9). A review of Nepal's geography and history and highlights of its unique culture. (Rev: BL 2/15/92) [954.96]

5020 Chandler, David P. *The Land and People of Cambodia* (6–12). (Portraits of the Nations) 1991, HarperCollins LB $17.89 (0-06-021130-X). An up-to-date history and anaylsis of this country, with emphasis on its history from early Indianization with its Hindu and Buddhist influences. Awards: SLJ Best Book. (Rev: MJHS; SLJ 5/91*)

5021 Goodman, Jim. *Thailand* (5–10). (Cultures of the World) 1991, Marshall Cavendish LB $19.95 (1-85435-402-7). (Rev: BL 3/15/92) [959.3]

5022 Jones, Tristan. *To Venture Further* (9–adult). 1991, Hearst $19 (0-688-08022-7). An account of the seafaring adventures of a physically challenged captain and crew who make the first successful navigation of the Isthmus of Kra, Thailand. (Rev: BL 10/1/91) [915.93]

5023 Kendra, Judith. *Tibetans* (5–8). (Threatened Cultures) 1994, Thomson Learning $16.95 (1-56847-152-1). Discusses Tibetan culture and religion, with emphasis on minority rights. Follows the daily lives of 2 Tibetan children, one living in the country, one in the city. (Rev: BL 7/94; MJHS) [951]

5024 McNair, Sylvia. *Indonesia* (5–8). (Enchantment of the World) 1993, Children's Press $19.95 (0-516-02618-6). A bias-free look at the history, geography, economy, and culture, with abundant photographs. (Rev: BL 11/1/93; MJHS) [959.8]

5025 Marullo, Clara. *The Last Forbidden Kingdom: Mustang, Land of Tibetan Buddhism* (9–adult). Photos. 1995, Tuttle $40 (0-8048-3061-4). A survey of Mustang, a remote portion of western Tibet, which preserves Tibetan religious art and a Buddhist way of life that is swiftly being subsumed by China. (Rev: BL 9/1/95) [954.96]

5026 Nash, Amy K. *North Korea* (6–8). (Places and Peoples of the World) 1991, Chelsea House $14.95 (0-7910-0157-1). This survey of the geography and history of North Korea logically accents the period of Japanese annexation, World War II, and the Korean War. (Rev: BL 10/15/91) [951.93]

5027 Palmer, Alan. *The Decline and Fall of the Ottoman Empire* (9–adult). 1994, Evans $22.50 (0-87131-754-0). Traces the decline of the Ottoman Empire from 1683 to 1922 and explores the impact of its legacy on contemporary Middle Eastern society. (Rev: BL 2/1/94) [958.1]

5028 Sheehan, Sean. *Turkey* (5–7). (Cultures of the World) 1993, Marshall Cavendish $21.95 (1-85435-576-7). (Rev: BL 8/93) [956.1]

5029 Solberg, S. E. *The Land and People of Korea* (6–8). (Portraits of the Nations) 1991, HarperCollins LB $17.89 (0-397-32331-X). Awards: SLJ Best Book. (Rcv: MJHS; SLJS 8/91*)

5030 Stewart, Gail B. *The Philippines* (5–7). (Places in the News) 1991, Macmillan/Crestwood LB $11.95 (0-89686-659-9). (Rev: BL 1/15/92) [959.904]

5031 Tope, Lily Rose R. *Philippines* (5–7). (Cultures of the World) 1991, Marshall Cavendish LB $19.95 (1-85435-403-5). (Rev: BL 2/15/92) [959.9]

5032 *Vietnam—in Pictures* (5–8). 1994, Lerner LB $13.13 (0-8225-1909-7). Clear, readable, and up-to-date description that students will find useful for reports. (Rev: BL 11/1/94; MJHS) [915.97]

5033 Wanasundera, Nanda P. *Sri Lanka* (5–7). (Cultures of the World) 1991, Marshall Cavendish LB $19.95 (1-85435-397-7). (Rev: BL 2/15/92) [954.93]

5034 Weston, Mark. *The Land and People of Pakistan* (6–9). (Land and People Of) 1992, HarperCollins LB $17.89 (0-06-022790-7). The geography, ethnicity, and history—as well as an exploration of political, social, economic, and cultural life—is discussed. Awards: SLJ Best Book. (Rev: BL 8/92; MJHS; SLJ 12/92*) [954.91]

5035 Wright, David K. *Brunei* (5–8). (Enchantment of the World) 1991, Children's Press LB $18.95 (0-516-02602-X). (Rev: BL 2/1/92) [959.55]

5036 Zimmermann, Robert. *Sri Lanka* (5–8). (Enchantment of the World) 1992, Children's Press LB $18.95 (0-516-02606-2). (Rev: BL 6/1/92; MJHS) [954.93]

Australia and the Pacific Islands

5037 Arden, Harvey. *Dreamkeepers: A Spirit-Journey into Aboriginal Australia* (9–adult). 1994, HarperCollins $27.50 (0-06-016916-8). Arden's study of the heart of Australian Aboriginal culture discovered many similarities to Native American cultures. (Rev: BL 4/15/94) [299]

5038 Fox, Mary Virginia. *New Zealand* (5–8). (Enchantment of the World) 1991, Children's Press LB $17.95 (0-516-02728-X). (Rev: BL 10/1/91; MJHS) [993]

5039 Nile, Richard. *Australian Aborigines* (5–7). (Threatened Cultures) 1993, Raintree $14.94 (0-8114-2303-4). An oversize volume filled with interesting information, including the history of the Aborigines. (Rev: BL 8/93) [305.89]

5040 Rajendra, Vijeya, and Sundran Rajendra. *Australia* (5–7). (Cultures of the World) 1991, Marshall Cavendish LB $19.95 (1-85435-400-0). An overview of Australia's geography and history, with special emphasis on its cultural and ethnic diversity. (Rev: BL 2/15/92; SLJ 3/92) [994]

Europe

General and Miscellaneous

5041 Barstow, Anne Llewellyn. *Witchcraze: A New History of the European Witch Hunts* (9–adult). 1994, HarperSan Francisco/Pandora $25 (0-06-250049-X). A description and gender analysis of the Reformation-era European witch hunt in which 7 million women were persecuted, tortured, and/or executed. (Rev: BL 2/1/94) [133.4]

5042 *Cyprus—in Pictures* (5–8). (Visual Geography) 1992, Lerner LB $13.13 (0-8225-1910-0). (Rev: BL 2/1/93; MJHS) [956.45]

5043 Delouche, Frederic, ed. *Illustrated History of Europe: A Unique Portrait of Europe's Common History* (9–adult). Tr. by Richard Mayne. 1993, Holt $35 (0-8050-2707-6). Twelve eminent historians, each from a different country, present a view of European history that emphasizes the commonality of the European experience. (Rev: BL 1/1/94; SLJ 5/94) [940]

5044 Fox, Mary Virginia. *Cyprus* (5–8). (Enchantment of the World) 1993, Children's Press $19.95 (0-516-02617-8). The history, geography, economy, and culture of the country is discussed. Includes abundant and well-chosen photos and illustrations. (Rev: BL 11/1/93; MJHS) [956.93]

Eastern Europe and the Balkans

5045 Chicoine, Stephen, and Brent Ashabranner. *Lithuania: The Nation That Would Be Free* (5–8). 1995, Dutton/Cobblehill $16.99 (0-525-65151-9). Chicoine mixes his own experiences traveling in Lithuania with information on its history and current issues—e.g., environmental problems, persecution of Jews, and their Olympic triumph over Russia. (Rev: BL 7/95; SLJ 4/95) [947]

5046 *Czech Republic—in Pictures* (5–8). (Visual Geography) 1995, Lerner LB $14.21 (0-8225-1879-1). (Rev: BL 8/95) [943.7]

5047 Dizdarevic, Zlatko. *Sarajevo: A War Journal* (9–adult). Tr. by Anselm Hollo. 1993, Fromm International $19.95 (0-88064-149-5). This Sarajevo newspaper editor has put together over 50 of his columns from 1992–1993 describing the conflict from an insider's viewpoint. (Rev: BL 11/15/93; SLJ 5/94) [949.7]

5048 Gjelten, Tom. *Sarajevo Daily: A City and Its Newspaper under Siege* (9–adult). 1995, HarperCollins $22 (0-06-019052-3). A reporter for National Public Radio tells of his experience in Sarajevo and the depth of ethnic hatred. (Rev: BL 3/1/95) [079]

5049 Harbor, Bernard. *Conflict in Eastern Europe* (6–12). (Conflicts) 1993, Macmillan/New Discovery $13.95 (0-02-742626-2). An overview of events that led to the demise of the Soviet satellites in Eastern Europe and what has transpired since then. (Rev: BL 10/1/93; SLJ 12/93) [947]

5050 *Hungary—in Pictures* (5–8). (Visual Geography) 1993, Lerner LB $17.50 (0-8225-1883-X). (Rev: BL 12/1/93; MJHS) [943.9]

5051 Kronenwetter, Michael. *The New Eastern Europe* (7–12). 1991, Watts LB $13.90 (0-531-11066-4). This analysis of the recent changes in the region discusses the move to capitalism, the shifting power structure, and environmental concerns. (Rev: BL 9/15/91; SHS)

5052 Laufer, Peter. *Iron Curtain Rising: A Personal Journey Through the Changing Landscape of Eastern Europe* (9–adult). 1991, Mercury $19.50 (1-56279-015-3). An on-site examination of Eastern Europe during the first months following the collapse of the Berlin Wall. (Rev: BL 9/1/91) [914.704]

5053 Naythons, Matthew. *Sarajevo: A Portrait of the Siege* (9–adult). 1994, Warner $29.95 (0-446-51824-7). Stark B&W photos tell the grim story of the siege of Sarajevo. Awards: SLJ Best Book; YALSA Best Book for Young Adults. (Rev: BL 5/15/94; SHS) [949.742]

5054 Rudy, Martyn. *Collapse of Communism in Eastern Europe* (7–12). (Causes and Consequences) 1995, Raintree/Steck-Vaughn LB $25.69 (0-8172-4052-7). (Rev: BL 12/15/95) [940]

5055 Ricciuti, Edward R. *War in Yugoslavia: The Breakup of a Nation* (5–8). (Headliners) 1993, Millbrook $15.90 (1-56294-375-8). Describes the ethnic rivalries that led to Yugoslavia's breakup after the death of Tito and the wars in Croatia and Bosnia. (Rev: BL 6/1–15/93) [949.702]

5056 Rohr, Janelle, ed. *Eastern Europe* (7–12). (Opposing Viewpoints) 1990, Greenhaven LB $15.95 (0-89908-480-X); paper $8.95 (0-89908-455-9). Articles and speeches from 1989–90 by statesmen debating communisim, economic policies, the role of a united Germany, and European unification. (Rev: BL 2/1/91; MJHS) [947]

5057 *Romania—in Pictures* (5–8). (Visual Geography) 1993, Lerner $17.50 (0-8225-1894-5). (Rev: BL 9/1/93; MJHS) [[949.8]

5058 *Slovakia—in Pictures* (5–8). (Visual Geography) 1995, Lerner LB $14.21 (0-8225-1912-7). (Rev: BL 11/15/95) [[943.7305]

5059 Stewart, Gail B. *Romania* (5–7). (Places in the News) 1991, Macmillan/Crestwood LB $10.95 (0-89686-600-9). (Rev: BL 9/1/91) [949.8]

5060 Swick, Thomas. *Unquiet Days: At Home in Poland* (9–adult). 1991, Ticknor & Fields $19.95 (0-395-58563-5). A personal account of life in Poland during the early 1980s by an American journalist who moved to Warsaw after falling in love with a Polish woman. (Rev: BL 9/1/91) [943.805]

5061 Udovicki, Jasminka, and James Ridgeway, eds. *Yugoslavia's Ethnic Nightmare: The Inside Story of Europe's Unfolding Ordeal* (9–adult). 1995, Chicago Review/Lawrence Hill $24.95 (1-55652-215-0); paper $14.95 (1-55652-216-9). Essays by Muslim, Croatian, and Serbian journalists. (Rev: BL 4/1/95) [949.702]

France

5062 Benedict, Kitty C. *The Fall of the Bastille* (5–8). (Turning Points in World History) 1991, Silver Burdett LB $16.95 (0-382-24129-0); paper $8.95 (0-382-24135-5). A study of the event that symbolized a tremendous change in French society. (Rev: BL 3/15/92) [944.04]

5063 Corzine, Phyllis. *The French Revolution* (8–12). (World History) 1995, Lucent LB $14.95 (1-56006-248-7). (Rev: BL 2/15/95) [944.04]

5064 Gofen, Ethel Caro. *France* (5–7). (Cultures of the World) 1992, Marshall Cavendish $21.95 (1-85435-449-3). (Rev: BL 10/15/92) [944]

Germany and Austria

5065 Epler, Doris M. *The Berlin Wall: How It Rose and Why It Fell* (7–10). 1992, Millbrook $13.90 (1-56294-114-3). The history of the Berlin Wall from the rise of the Nazi regime between the world wars to the 1990 beginning of German reunification. (Rev: BL 12/1/91; MJHS; SLJ 3/92) [943.1]

5066 Fulbrook, Mary. *A Concise History of Germany* (9–adult). 1991, Cambridge Univ. $39.50 (0-521-36283-0); paper $10.95 (0-521-36836-7). Covers Germany from the medieval period and examines the political, social, and cultural context that led to reunification. (Rev: BL 2/15/91; SHS) [943]

5067 Fuller, Barbara. *Germany* (5–7). (Cultures of the World) 1992, Marshall Cavendish $21.95 (1-85435-530-9). (Rev: BL 1/1/93) [943]

5068 *Germany—in Pictures* (5–8). (Visual Geography) 1994, Lerner $14.21 (0-8225-1873-2). (Rev: BL 1/15/95) [943]

5069 Hargrove, Jim. *Germany* (5–8). (Enchantment of the World) 1991, Children's Press LB $18.95 (0-516-02601-1). (Rev: BL 2/1/92) [943]

5070 Mirable, Lisa. *The Berlin Wall* (5–8). (Turning Points in World History) 1991, Silver Burdett LB $16.98 (0-382-24133-9); paper $8.95 (0-382-24140-1). Chronicles the political, economic, and religious factors that led to a new social order in Germany. (Rev: BL 3/15/92; BTA) [943.1]

5071 Shales, Amity. *Germany: The Empire Within* (9–adult). 1991, Farrar $19.95 (0-374-

25605-5). A European correspondent for the *Wall Street Journal* mixes good and bad news as she surveys Germany's past, present, and future. (Rev: BL 1/15/91) [943]

5072 Sheehan, Sean. *Austria* (5–7). (Cultures of the World) 1992, Marshall Cavendish $21.95 (1-85435-454-X). (Rev: BL 10/15/92) [943.6]

5073 Spencer, William. *Germany Then and Now* (8–12). 1994, Watts LB $13.90 (0-531-11137-7). A history of Germany and its people, addressing such current issues as neo-Nazism and the problems created by combining capitalism with socialism. (Rev: BL 8/94; MJHS; SLJ 8/94; VOYA 10/94) [943]

5074 Yancey, Diane. *The Reunification of Germany* (6–8). (Overview) 1994, Lucent LB $14.95 (1-56006-143-X). A chronicle of this event written with objectivity, liberally illustrated with black-and-white photos and political cartoons. (Rev: BL 3/15/94; MJHS) [943.087]

Great Britain and Ireland

5075 Bland, Celia. *The Mechanical Age: The Industrial Revolution in England* (7–12). 1995, Facts on File LB $17.95 (0-8160-3139-8). Examines the technological and social advances of the Industrial Revolution in England, with detailed notes and an extensive bibliography. (Rev: BL 10/15/95; SLJ 11/95) [338.094]

5076 *A Day in the Life of Ireland: Photographed by 75 of the World's Leading Photojournalists on One Day, May 17, 1991* (9–adult). 1991, HarperCollins $45 (0-00-215951-1). A photographic tour of Ireland, with captions that lend insight into the people and culture. (Rev: BL 12/15/91) [941.5]

5077 Hibbert, Christopher. *Cavaliers and Roundheads: The English Civil War, 1642–1649* (9–adult). 1993, Scribner $27.50 (0-684-19557-7). A narrative account of the 1642 war touched off by the attempt of King James's son Charles to arrest his parliamentary antagonists. (Rev: BL 5/15/93; SLJ 1/94) [941.06]

5078 Lace, William W. *Elizabethan England* (8–12). (World History) 1995, Lucent LB $14.95 (1-56006-278-9). Elements of the period are discussed, including biographical details of the most able and successful queen in Great Britain's history. (Rev: BL 2/15/95) [942.05]

5079 *Northern Ireland—in Pictures* (5–8). (Visual Geography) 1991, Lerner LB $11.95 (0-8225-1898-8). (Rev: BL 2/15/92) [941.6]

5080 Pargeter, Edith. *A Bloody Field by Shrewsbury* (9–adult). 1991, Headline paper $8.95 (0-7472-3366-7). Details a fascinating but violent period in English history. (Rev: BL 2/1/92) [941.04]

5081 Parker, Tony. *May the Lord in His Mercy Be Kind to Belfast* (9–adult). 1994, Holt $25 (0-8050-3053-0). Testimonies that demonstrate how virtually all of Northern Ireland's citizens are touched by ongoing violence and hatred. (Rev: BL 3/1/94; SLJ 8/94) [941.6]

5082 Sauvain, Philip. *Hastings* (5–8). (Great Battles and Sieges) Illus. 1992, Macmillan/New Discovery $13.95 (0-02-781079-8). A description of the 1066 victory of Duke William of Normandy on the south coast of England that initiated Norman rule of Britain. (Rev: BL 10/1/92; SLJ 2/93)

5083 Seward, Desmond. *The Wars of the Roses: Through the Lives of Five Men and Women of the Fifteenth Century* (9–adult). 1995, Viking $26.95 (0-670-84258-3). The War of the Roses, told untraditionally from the perspective of 5 individuals differing in rank. (Rev: BL 10/1/95) [942]

5084 Weir, Alison. *The Wars of the Roses* (9–adult). 1995, Ballantine $24 (0-345-39117-9). This account of The War of the Roses chronicles the conflict between royal cousins and the events that preceded the war. (Rev: BL 8/95*) [942.04]

Greece

5085 Du Bois, Jill. *Greece* (5–7). (Cultures of the World) 1992, Marshall Cavendish $21.95 (1-85435-450-7). (Rev: BL 10/15/92) [949.5]

5086 *Greece—in Pictures* (5–8). (Visual Geography) 1992, Lerner LB $12.95 (0-8225-1882-1). (Rev: BL 10/1/92; MJHS) [949.5]

Italy

5087 Travis, David. *The Land and People of Italy* (6–9). (Land and People Of) 1992, HarperCollins LB $17.89 (0-06-022784-2). Includes handy facts, but is a thoroughly enjoyable travelogue-like read. (Rev: BL 8/92; MJHS; SLJ 11/92) [945]

5088 Winter, Jane Kohen. *Italy* (5–7). (Cultures of the World) 1992, Marshall Cavendish $21.95 (1-85435-453-1). (Rev: BL 10/15/92) [945]

The Netherlands and Belgium

5089 van Stegeren, Theo. *The Land and People of the Netherlands* (6–9). (Portraits of the Nations) 1991, HarperCollins LB $18.89 (0-06-022538-6). A comprehensive and useful book with aspects of the culture conveyed in the details of everyday life. (Rev: BL 9/1/91; SLJ 12/91) [949.2]

Russia and Other Former Soviet Republics

5090 *Armenia* (5–8). (Then and Now) 1992, Lerner LB $14.96 (0-8225-2806-1). (Rev: BL 2/1/93; MJHS) [956.6]

5091 *Azerbaijan* (5–8). (Then and Now) 1993, Lerner LB $14.96 (0-8225-2810-X). (Rev: BL 2/15/93; MJHS) [947]

5092 Barbour, William, and Carol Wekesser, eds. *The Breakup of the Soviet Union* (10–12). 1994, Greenhaven $17.95 (1-56510-068-9); paper $11.95 (1-56510-067 0). Focuses on recent history, with chapter prefaces setting up issues as well as questions for further discussion. (Rev: BL 3/1/94; MJHS; SLJ 3/94)

5093 *Belarus* (5–8). (Then and Now) 1993, Lerner LB $14.95 (0-8225-2811-8). (Rev: BL 5/15/93; MJHS) [947]

5094 Bradley, John. *Russia: Building Democracy* (6–8). (Topics in the News) 1995, Raintree/Steck-Vaughn LB $21.40 (0-8172-4177-9). Russian history from the ninth century to modern times. (Rev: BL 2/15/96; SLJ 3/96)

5095 Clark, Mary Jane Behrends. *The Commonwealth of Independent States* (6–8). (Headliners) 1992, Millbrook LB $15.90 (1-56294-081-3). Summarizes events in the formation of the CIS, created from 15 republics after the 1991 breakup of the Soviet Union. (Rev: BL 2/15/93; SLJ 1/93) [947.085]

5096 Cumming, David. *Russia* (5–8). 1994, Thomson Learning $15.95 (1-56847-240-4). A general introduction, emphasizing current conditions rather than cultural traditions and history. (Rev: BL 1/15/95; SLJ 3/95) [330.947]

5097 De Somma, Vincent V. *Union of Soviet Socialist Republics* (6–8). (Places and Peoples of the World) 1991, Chelsea House $14.95 (0-7910-1370-7). (Rev: BL 11/1/91) [947]

5098 Dunn, John M. *The Russian Revolution* (8–12). (World History) 1994, Lucent LB $14.95 (1-56006-234-7). A startling look at the reality of massacres, pogroms, famines, wars, and terrorist acts and the people involved. (Rev: BL 1/1/94; SLJ 3/94) [947.084]

5099 *Estonia* (5–8). 1992, Lerner LB $14.96 (0-8225-2803-7). Following an introduction about the fall of communism, provides an overview of the land and its peoples. (Rev: BL 2/1/93; MJHS; SLJ 12/92) [914.7]

5100 Harbor, Bernard. *The Breakup of the Soviet Union* (6–12). (Conflicts) 1993, Macmillan/New Discovery $13.95 (0-02-742625-4). An overview of the conflicts and change of the region. (Rev: BL 7/93) [947.08]

5101 Hawkes, Nigel. *Glasnost and Perestroika* (9–adult). (World Issues) 1990, Rourke LB $13.50 (0-86592-149-0). An outline of Soviet history and the contemporary changes that occurred under Gorbachev. (Rev: BL 1/1/91) [947.08]

5102 *Kazakhstan* (5–8). (Then and Now) 1993, Lerner $19.95 (0-8225-2815-0). (Rev: BL 9/1/93; MJHS) [958]

5103 Kort, Michael. *The Rise and Fall of the Soviet Union* (8–12). 1993, Watts $13.40 (0-531-11040-0). Provides a key to understanding current Russian and Eastern European issues by detailing the past promises and threats of Soviet communism. (Rev: BL 6/1–15/93; BTA) [947]

5104 Kort, Michael. *Russia* (7–12). (Nations in Transition) 1995, Facts on File LB $17.95 (0-8160-3061-8). A history of Russia from its beginnings through the Soviet period, including a clear explanation of the transition period after 1991, its problems, and prospects. (Rev: SLJ 3/96)

5105 *Latvia* (5–8). 1992, Lerner LB $14.96 (0-8225-2802-9). Following an introduction about the fall of communism, provides an overview of the land and its peoples. (Rev: BL 2/1/93; MJHS; SLJ 12/92) [947]

5106 *Lithuania* (5–8). (Then and Now) 1992, Lerner LB $14.96 (0-8225-2804-5). (Rev: BL 2/1/93; MJHS) [947]

5107 Loory, Stuart H., and Ann Imse. *CNN Reports: Seven Days That Shook the World: The Collapse of Soviet Communism* (9–adult). 1992, Turner $29.95 (1-878685-11-2); paper $19.95 (1-878685-12-0). The fall of communism told largely through photos. (Rev: BL 1/1/92) [947.085]

5108 Maclean, Fitzroy. *All the Russias* (9–adult). 1992, Smithmark $29.98 (0-8317-0278-8). A discussion of the enormous diversity of traditions, landscapes, and populations that are included in the immense area that was the Soviet Union. (Rev: BL 10/1/92) [947]

5109 *Moldova* (5–8). (Then and Now) 1992, Lerner LB $14.96 (0-8225-2809-6). (Rev: BL 2/1/93; MJHS) [947]

5110 Pipes, Richard. *A Concise History of the Russian Revolution* (9–adult). 1995, Knopf $30 (0-679-42277-3). A skillfully researched history and analysis of Russia's tragic revolution and the events that preceded and succeeded it. (Rev: BL 10/1/95*) [947.084]

5111 Richards, Susan. *Epics of Everyday Life: Encounters in a Changing Russia* (9–adult). 1992, Viking paper $12.50 (0-14-016929-6). (Rev: BL 4/15/91; SHS) [947.085]

5112 *Russia* (5–8). (Then and Now) 1992, Lerner LB $14.96 (0-8225-2805-3). (Rev: BL 2/1/93; MJHS) [947]

5113 Smith, Brenda J. *The Collapse of the Soviet Union* (6–8). (Overview) 1994, Lucent LB $14.95 (1-56006-142-1). Details of the Cold War, the Gorbachev years, and the breakup of the USSR are preceded by a brief summary of Karl Marx's ideas, the Bolshevik Revolution of 1917, and Soviet leadership through the decades. (Rev: BL 3/15/94; MJHS; SHS) [947]

5114 *Ukraine* (5–8). (Then and Now) 1992, Lerner LB $14.96 (0-8225-2808-8). (Rev: BL 2/1/93; MJHS) [947]

5115 Ulam, Adam B. *The Communists: The Story of Power and Lost Illusions: 1948–1991* (9–adult). 1992, Scribner $27.50 (0-684-19236-5). Analysis of Soviet communism and how the ideology disintegrated. (Rev: BL 2/1/92; SHS) [335.4]

5116 *Uzbekistan* (5–8). (Then and Now) 1993, Lerner LB $14.95 (0-8225-2812-6). (Rev: BL 5/15/93; MJHS) [958.7]

5117 Vadrot, Claude-Maria, and Victoria Ivleva. *Russia Today: From Holy Russia to Perestroika* (9–adult). Tr. by Harry Swalef. 1991, Atomium $31.95 (1-56182-004-0). A French photographer and Soviet photographer capture the essence of modern Russian life. (Rev: BL 7/91) [947.08]

5118 Vail, John J. *"Peace, Land, Bread!": A History of the Russian Revolution* (9–12). (World History Library) 1996, Facts on File LB $17.95 (0-8160-2818-4). Examines the uprising of 1917, including information on the events leading up to the rebellion and through the arrival of Lenin. (Rev: BL 2/15/96; SLJ 2/96; VOYA 4/96)

Scandinavia, Iceland, and Greenland

5119 Carlsson, Bo Kage. *Sweden* (5–8). (Modern Industrial World) 1995, Thomson Learning $15.95 (1-56847-436-9). (Rev: BL 12/15/95) [949.4]

5120 Charbonneau, Claudette, and Patricia Slade Lander. *The Land and People of Norway* (6–9). (Portraits of the Nations) Illus. 1992, HarperCollins LB $17.89 (0-06-020583-0). (Rev: BL 2/15/93; MJHS) [948.1]

5121 *Finland—in Pictures* (5–8). (Visual Geography) 1991, Lerner $11.95 (0-8225-1881-3). (Rev: BL 12/15/91) [948.97]

5122 Lasky, Kathryn. *Surtsey: The Newest Place on Earth* (5–9). Photos. 1992, Hyperion LB $15.89 (1-56282-301-9). Conveys the dramatic beginnings of the island of Surtsey, which sprang up off the coast of Iceland in 1963. Many full-page photos. Awards: SLJ Best Book. (Rev: BL 1/1/93*; SLJ 2/93*) [508.4912]

Spain and Portugal

5123 Champion, Neil. *Portugal* (5–8). (Modern Industrial World) 1995, Thomson Learning $15.95 (1-56847-435-0). (Rev: BL 12/15/95) [946.904]

5124 Gómez Cerdá, Alfredo. *Sin billete de vuelta* (7–9). Illus. 1994, Alfaguara (Madrid, Spain) paper $8.95 (84-204-4855-9). These sketches of 6 rural adolescents who moved to Barcelona portray the hard lives of poor rural workers in postwar Spain. English title: *Without a Return Ticket*. (Rev: BL 10/15/95)

5125 Kohen, Elizabeth. *Spain* (5–7). (Cultures of the World) 1992, Marshall Cavendish $21.95 (1-85435-451-5). (Rev: BL 10/15/92) [946]

5126 *Portugal—in Pictures* (5–8). (Visual Geography) 1991, Lerner $11.95 (0-8225-1886-4). (Rev: BL 12/15/91) [946.9]

5127 Shubert, Adrian. *The Land and People of Spain* (6–9). (Land and People of) 1992, HarperCollins LB $17.89 (0-06-020218-1). A comprehensive volume devoted to a detailed history of this country. (Rev: BL 8/92; MJHS) [946]

5128 *Spain—in Pictures* (5–8). (Visual Geography) 1995, Lerner LB $14.21 (0-8225-1887-2). (Rev: BL 11/15/95) [[914.6]

Middle East

General and Miscellaneous

5129 Abodaher, David J. *Youth in the Middle East: Voices of Despair* (6–12). 1990, Watts $12.40 (0-531-10961-5). Middle East politics are examined, with a focus on the suffering of its young people. (Rev: BL 1/15/91; SHS) [305.23]

5130 Dudley, William, ed. *The Middle East* (7–10). (Opposing Viewpoints) 1992, Greenhaven LB $15.95 (0-89908-185-1); paper $8.95 (0-89908-160-6). This updated edition examines causes of the Middle East conflicts and what the future may hold. (Rev: BL 6/15/92; MJHS; SHS; SLJ 7/92) [320.956]

5131 King, John. *Conflict in the Middle East* (6–12). (Conflicts) 1993, Macmillan/New Discovery $13.95 (0-02-785955-X). (Rev: BL 10/1/93; SLJ 12/93) [956.04]

5132 Wilkinson, Phillip, and Jacqueline Dineen. *The Lands of the Bible* (5–7). (Mysterious Places) Illus. 1994, Chelsea House $18.95 (0-7910-2752-X). Approaching ancient history through specific sites rather than whole civilizations, this book focuses on the most intriguing aspects of each place. (Rev: BL 1/15/94; SLJ 4/94) [220.9]

Egypt

5133 Brier, Bob. *Egyptian Mummies: Unraveling the Secrets of an Ancient Art* (9–adult). 1994, Morrow $20 (0-688-10272-7). Brier describes the research for his unusual forthcoming project, in which he wants to better understand the Egyptian mummification process by creating an actual mummy. (Rev: BL 10/1/94; SLJ 1/95) [932]

5134 Deem, James M. *How to Make a Mummy Talk* (5–7). 1995, Houghton $14.95 (0-395-62427-4). The author transforms our curiosity about mummies via a lively presentation of their background. (Rev: BL 9/15/95; SLJ 9/95) [393]

5135 Pateman, Robert. *Egypt* (5–7). (Cultures of the World) 1992, Marshall Cavendish $21.95 (1-85435-535-X). (Rev: BL 1/1/93) [962]

5136 Putnam, James. *Mummy* (5–9). (Eyewitness Books) Photos by Peter Hayman. 1993, Knopf LB $15.99 (0-679-93881-8). (Rev: BL 8/93; MJHS) [393]

Israel

5137 Du Bois, Jill. *Israel* (5–7). (Cultures of the World) 1992, Marshall Cavendish $21.95 (1-85435-531-7). (Rev: BL 1/1/93; MJHS) [956.94]

5138 Hersh, Seymour M. *The Samson Option: Israel's Nuclear Arsenal and American Foreign Policy* (9–adult). 1991, Random $23 (0-394-57006-5). A Pulitzer Prize–winning journalist reveals hitherto undocumented evidence of the development of a nuclear arsenal in Israel and the U.S. policy of ignoring the buildup. (Rev: BL 11/15/91) [956.94]

5139 Mozeson, I. E., and Lois Stavsky. *Jerusalem Mosaic: Young Voices from the Holy City* (6–12). 1994, Four Winds $15.95 (0-02-767651-X). Thirty-six lively monologues based on interviews with teenagers living in Jerusalem today—Jew and Arab, Muslim and Christian. (Rev: BL 12/1/94; BTA; SLJ 1/95) [305.23]

5140 Ross, Stewart. *Arab-Israeli Conflict* (7–12). (Causes and Consequences) 1995, Raintree/Steck-Vaughn LB $25.69 (0-8172-4051-9). Crucial world events are presented within a historical context in a magazine format, with maps and photos. (Rev: BL 12/15/95; SLJ 2/96) [956.9404]

5141 Sichrovsky, Peter. *Abraham's Children: Israel's Young Generation* (9–adult). Tr. by Jean Steinberg. 1991, Pantheon $19 (0-679-40419-8). A cross section of contemporary Israeli opinion on the political situation, internal economic problems, and external threats to the nation. (Rev: BL 11/1/91) [956.94]

5142 Tubb, Jonathan N. *Bible Lands* (5–9). (Eyewitness Books) 1991, Knopf LB $15.99 (0-679-91457-9). (Rev: BL 12/1/91; MJHS) [220.9]

Other Countries

5143 Foster, Leila Merrell. *Jordan* (5–8). (Enchantment of the World) 1991, Children's Press LB $18.95 (0-516-02603-8). (Rev: BL 2/1/92; MJHS) [956.95]

5144 Foster, Leila Merrell. *Lebanon* (5–8). (Enchantment of the World) 1992, Children's Press LB $18.95 (0-516-02612-7). A detailed look at Lebanon, from ancient history to recent civil unrest. (Rev: BL 12/1/92; MJHS) [956.92]

5145 Foster, Leila Merrell. *Saudi Arabia* (5–8). (Enchantment of the World) 1993, Children's Press LB $19.95 (0-516-02611-9). (Rev: BL 8/93; MJHS) [953.8]

5146 Fox, Mary Virginia. *Bahrain* (5–8). (Enchantment of the World) 1992, Children's Press LB $19.95 (0-516-02608-9). An in-depth introduction to Bahrain including geological, meteorological, historical, and engineering aspects. (Rev: BL 12/15/92; MJHS) [953.65]

5147 Fox, Mary Virginia. *Iran* (5–8). (Enchantment of the World) 1991, Children's Press LB $17.95 (0-516-02727-1). (Rev: BL 10/1/91; MJHS) [955]

5148 Hassig, Susan M. *Iraq* (5–7). (Cultures of the World) 1992, Marshall Cavendish $21.95 (1-85435-533-3). (Rev: BL 1/1/93) [956.7]

5149 Hiro, Dilip. *The Longest War: The Iran-Iraq Military Conflict* (9–adult). 1991, Routledge $49.95 (0-415-90406-4); paper $16.95 (0-415-90407-2). Detailed account of the 1980–88 war between Iran and Iraq. (Rev: BL 2/1/91; SHS) [955.05]

5150 Janin, Hunt. *Saudi Arabia* (5–7). (Cultures of the World) 1992, Marshall Cavendish $21.95 (1-85435-532-5). (Rev: BL 1/1/93) [953.8]

5151 Rajendra, Vijeya, and Gisela Kaplan. *Iran* (5–7). (Cultures of the World) 1992, Marshall Cavendish $21.95 (1-85435-534-1). (Rev: BL 1/1/93) [955]

5152 Reische, Diana. *Arafat and the Palestine Liberation Organization* (7–12). 1991, Watts LB $13.90 (0-531-11000-1). An outsider's controversial views of Arab nationalism in the Palestinian Liberation Organization. (Rev: BL 4/1/91; MJHS; SLJ 5/91) [322.4]

5153 Stewart, Gail B. *Iraq* (5–7). (Places in the News) 1991, Macmillan/Crestwood $11.95 (0-89686-657-2). An explanation of the background events in the Persian Gulf war. (Rev: BL 2/15/92) [956.7]

5154 *Yemen—in Pictures* (5–8). (Visual Geography) 1993, Lerner LB $17.50 (0-8225-1911-9). (Rev: BL 12/1/93; MJHS) [953.3]

North and South America (excluding the United States)

General History and Geography

5155 Dambrosio, Mónica, and Roberto Barbieri. *El nuevo mundo: Desde el descubrimiento hasta la indepedencia* (5–9). (Historia del hombre) Illus. 1991, Ediciones SM (Madrid, Spain) $12.95 (84-348-3449-9). This large-format book includes a straightforward narrative and full-page drawings, maps, charts, and color photos. Originally published in Italy. English title: *The New World: From Discovery to Independence.* (Rev: BL 6/1–15/93)

5156 Dambrosio, Mónica, and Roberto Barbieri. *El paso al mundo moderno* (5–9). (Historia del hombre) Illus. 1992, Ediciones SM (Madrid, Spain) $12.95 (84-348-3448-0). This large-format book includes a straightforward narrative and full-page drawings, maps, charts, and color photos. Originally published in Italy. English title: *To the Modern World.* (Rev: BL 6/1–15/93)

5157 Winn, Peter. *Americas: The Changing Face of Latin America and the Caribbean* (9–adult). 1993, Pantheon $40 (0-679-41169-0). This companion to a PBS series spotlights dramatic changes of the last 3 decades in Latin America and the Caribbean. (Rev: BL 1/1/93; SHS) [980]

North America

CANADA

5158 Beattie, Owen, and John Geiger. *Buried in Ice: The Mystery of a Lost Arctic Expedition* (5–7). (Time Quest) Illus. 1992, Scholastic/Madison LB $15.95 (0-590-43848-4). Discoveries of the disastrous expedition of Sir John Franklin come to light 120 years later. Awards: YALSA Best Book for Young Adults. (Rev: BL 4/1/92; MJHS; SLJ 4/92*) [919.804]

5159 Malcolm, Andrew. *The Land and People of Canada* (6–9). (Portraits of the Nations) 1991, HarperCollins LB $18.89 (0-06-022495-9). A historical, statistical, and analytical perspective for non-Canadians. (Rev: BL 9/1/91; MJHS) [971]

5160 Struzik, Edward. *Northwest Passage: The Quest for an Arctic Route to the East* (9–adult). 1991, Key Porter $29.95 (1-55013-181-8). Photographs and text illustrate the history of exploration in the region and provide a modern perspective. (Rev: BL 12/15/91) [910]

CENTRAL AMERICA

5161 Brill, Marlene Targ, and Harry R. Targ. *Guatemala* (5–8). (Enchantment of the World) 1993, Children's Press LB $19.95 (0-516-02614-3). (Rev: BL 8/93) [972.81]

5162 Hernandez, Xavier. *San Rafael: A Central American City Through the Ages* (5–7). Illus. 1992, Houghton $16.95 (0-395-60645-4). This oversize volume features 14 carefully detailed ink drawings that function like aerial photos, reconstructing the development of a fictitious but typical city in Central America, from Mayan times to the present. (Rev: BL 9/1/92; SLJ 9/92) [307.76]

5163 Krauss, Clifford. *Inside Central America: Its People, Politics and History* (9–adult). 1992, Simon & Schuster paper $11 (0-671-76072-6). (Rev: BL 3/1/91; SHS) [972.805]

5164 Vázquez, Ana María B. *Panama* (5–8). (Enchantment of the World) 1991, Children's Press LB $18.95 (0-516-02604-6). (Rev: BL 2/1/92; MJHS) [972.87]

MEXICO

5165 Avilés, Jaime. *Ignacio Cumplido, un impresor del siglo XIX* (8–10). (El tiempo vuela) 1992, Instituto de Investigaciones Dr. José María Luis Mora (Mexico) paper $6.95 (968-6382-57-7). Describes various aspects of life of the nineteenth-century publisher of Mexico's first modern newspaper. English title: *Ignacio Cumplido, a Printer of the nineteenth Century*. (Rev: BL 2/1/94)

5166 Baquedano, Elizabeth. *Aztec, Inca and Maya* (5–9). (Eyewitness Books) 1993, Knopf LB $15.99 (0-679-93883-4). A compare-and-contrast introduction to these ancient American civilizations. (Rev: BL 10/1/93) [972]

5167 Baquedano, Elizabeth. *Aztecas, incas y mayas* (5–9). (Biblioteca visual Altea) Photos. 1994, Santillana (Madrid, Spain) $18.95 (84-372-3779-3). Includes numerous close-up color photos and brief descriptions introducing readers to Aztec, Inca, and Mayan civilizations. English title: *Aztecs, Incas and Mayas*. (Rev: BL 10/1/94) [972]

5168 Escandón, Patricia. *Al servicio de su majestad imperial: Un oficial de húsares en México* (8–10). (El tiempo vuela) 1992, Instituto de Investigaciones Dr. José María Luis Mora (Mexico) paper $6.95 (968-6382-65-8). Describes various aspects of the political struggles between 2 opposing groups. English title: *At the Service of His Imperial Majesty: A Husar Officer in Mexico*. (Rev: BL 2/1/94)

5169 Molina, Silvia. *Los tres corazones: Leyendas totonacas de la creación* (5–7). Illus. 1992, Ediciones Corunda (Mexico) $13.95 (968-6044-49-3). Explains the legends of the Totonacan people of ancient Mexico: how the gods, sun, moon, Venus, humankind, and animals were created and how people learned to cultivate corn. Color illustrations. English title: *The Three Hearts: Creation Legends of the Totonacas*. (Rev: BL 6/1–15/93)

5170 Stefoff, Rebecca. *Independence and Revolution in Mexico, 1810–1940* (7–12). 1993, Facts on File $16.95 (0-8160-2841-9). The history of Mexico's 130-year struggle for independence is explored, highlighting notable events and people. (Rev: BL 12/1/93; BTA; MJHS) [972]

5171 Stein, R. Conrad. *The Mexican Revolution, 1910–1920* (7–9). 1994, Macmillan $14.95 (0-02-786950-4). An examination of significant political, emotional, economic, and belief issues of the period, with profiles of dominant leaders. (Rev: BL 3/1/94; MJHS; SLJ 8/94; VOYA 8/94) [972.08]

PUERTO RICO, CUBA, AND OTHER CARIBBEAN ISLANDS

5172 Abodaher, David J. *Puerto Rico: America's 51st State?* (6–9). 1993, Watts LB $12.90 (0-531-13024-X). A historical account of the island of Puerto Rico. (Rev: BL 8/93; MJHS; SLJ 6/93) [972.95]

5173 Hauptly, Dennis J. *Puerto Rico* (7–12). 1991, Atheneum $13.95 (0-689-31431-0). Traces the history of Puerto Rico from the first Arawak settlers to the present day, focusing on factors that have brought the nation its status as a U.S. commonwealth. (Rev: BL 9/1/91; SLJ 3/92) [972.95]

5174 Jacobs, Francine. *The Tainos: The People Who Welcomed Columbus* (6–9). 1992, Putnam $15.95 (0-399-22116-6). The history, culture, and annihilation of the people who welcomed Columbus when he first landed in the Americas in 1492. (Rev: BL 6/1/92; MJHS; SLJ 6/92*; YR) [972.9]

5175 Rice, Earle. *The Cuban Revolution* (8–12). (World History) 1995, Lucent LB $14.95 (1-56006-275-4). A historical account of the Cuban revolution. (Rev: BL 2/15/95) [972.9106]

5176 Smith, Wayne S., and Michael Reagan. *Portrait of Cuba* (9–adult). 1991, Turner $34.95 (1-878685-07-4). An overview of Cuban history and the significance to Cuban welfare of Castro's dictatorship, Soviet involvement, and continued U.S. hostility. (Rev: BL 12/1/91*) [972.91]

5177 Stewart, Gail B. *Cuba* (5–7). (Places in the News) 1991, Macmillan/Crestwood LB $11.95 (0-89686-658-0). (Rev: BL 1/15/92) [972.9106]

South America

5178 Fox, Geoffrey. *The Land and People of Venezuela* (6–9). (Portraits of the Nations) 1991, HarperCollins LB $18.89 (0-06-022477-0). An introduction to the geography, history, people, culture, economy, and culture of Venezuela. (Rev: BL 9/1/91; MJHS) [987]

5179 Gagnon, Mariano, and others. *Warriors in Eden* (9–adult). 1993, Morrow $23 (0-688-11796-1). "Gringo priest" Gagnon recalls his missionary work with Peru's Ashaninka Indians, who are threatened by drug traffickers, political terrorists, and a corrupt government. (Rev: BL 7/93) [266.0089]

5180 Garavaglia, Juan Carlos, and Raúl Fradkin. *Hombres y mujeres de la colonia* (9–12). 1992, Editorial Sudamericana (Buenos Aires, Argentina) paper $17.50 (950-07-0780-2). Includes the thoughts and feelings of 15 ordinary Argentine men and women of the eighteenth and nineteenth centuries. Each chapter contains a fictional biography, map, and text about different occupations, industries, and institutions. English title: *Men and Women from Colonial Times*. (Rev: BL 2/1/94)

5181 Ghinsberg, Yossi. *Back from Tuichi: The Harrowing Life-and-Death Story of Survival in the Amazon Rainforest* (9–adult). Tr. by Yael Politis and Stanley Young. 1994, Random $22 (0-679-42458-X). Ghinsberg recounts his experience of being lost with 2 others in the Bolivian rainforest. He was the only survivor of the party. (Rev: BL 12/1/93; BTA; VOYA 6/94) [918.4]

5182 Lepthien, Emilie U. *Peru* (5–8). (Enchantment of the World) 1992, Children's Press LB $19.95 (0-516-02610-0). An illustrated discussion of Peru's history, economy, and politics. (Rev: BL 2/1/93; MJHS) [985]

5183 Lourie, Peter. *Amazon: A Young Reader's Look at the Last Frontier* (5–7). Photos. 1991, Boyds Mills/Caroline House $17.95 (1-878093-00-2). This photographic chronicle of an expedition to the interior of Rondonia explores life in an area threatened by overdevelopment. (Rev: BL 12/1/91; SLJ 1/92) [918.1]

5184 Morrison, Marion. *The Amazon Rain Forest and Its People* (5–8). (People and Places) 1993, Thomson Learning LB $15.95 (1-56847-087-8). (Rev: BL 11/1/93) [333.75]

5185 Morrison, Marion. *Paraguay* (5–8). (Enchantment of the World) 1993, Children's Press $19.95 (0-516-02619-4). A historical, geographical, economical, and cultural discussion of Paraguay. (Rev: BL 11/1/93; MJHS) [989.2]

5186 Morrison, Marion. *Uruguay* (5–8). (Enchantment of the World) 1992, Children's Press LB $18.95 (0-516-02607-0). (Rev: BL 6/1/92; MJHS) [989.5]

5187 Myers, Lynne Born, and Christopher A. Myers. *Galápagos: Islands of Change* (5–7). 1995, Hyperion LB $16.89 (0-7868-2061-6). Discusses the formation of the islands, how they came to be inhabited, and evolutionary changes. Plate tectonics and Darwinian theory are explained in easy-to-understand terms. (Rev: BL 12/15/95; SLJ 11/95) [508.866]

5188 Popescu, Petru. *Amazon Beaming* (9–adult). 1991, Viking $25 (0-670-82997-8). A *National Geographic* writer/photographer recounts his dangerous adventures while searching for the Amazon's source. (Rev: BL 8/91) [981]

5189 Stewart, Gail B. *Colombia* (5–7). (Places in the News) 1991, Macmillan/Crestwood LB $10.95 (0-89686-603-3). (Rev: BL 9/1/91) [303.6]

Polar Regions

5190 Aldis, Rodney. *Polar Lands* (5–8). (Ecology Watch) 1992, Dillon LB $13.95 (0-87518-494-4). (Rev: BL 11/1/92) [574.5]

5191 Counter, S. Allen. *North Pole Legacy: Black, White and Eskimo* (9–adult). 1991, Univ. of Massachusetts $24.95 (0-87023-736-5). Supports Peary's claim as first to the North Pole while focusing on Peary's African-American partner Matthew Henson—a world-class explorer marginalized by white historians. Awards: YALSA Best Book for Young Adults. (Rev: BL 5/15/91; SHS) [998.2]

5192 Fisher, David. *Across the Top of the World: To the North Pole by Sled, Balloon, Airplane and Nuclear Icebreaker* (9–adult). 1992, Random $25 (0-679-41116-X). The author's experiences aboard a nuclear-powered Russian ship bound for the North Pole, including descriptions of the hazards faced by early polar explorers. (Rev: BL 11/1/92) [919.804]

5193 Hackwell, W. John. *Desert of Ice: Life and Work in Antarctica* (5–7). 1991, Scribner $14.95 (0-684-19085-0). A description of life on the last remaining large wilderness. (Rev: BL 3/15/91; SLJ 3/91) [919.8]

5194 Poncet, Sally. *Antarctic Encounter: Destination South Georgia* (5–7). 1995, Simon & Schuster $17 (0-02-774905-3). This photo-essay about a family's life studying birds on Antarctic islands includes color photos of native such birds as king penguins and albatrosses. (Rev: BL 6/1–15/95; SLJ 9/95) [508.97]

5195 Pringle, Laurence. *Antarctica: The Last Unspoiled Continent* (6–9). 1992, Simon & Schuster $15 (0-671-74684-7). This photo-essay shows how Antarctica's special conditions make it a research site for the study of evolution, geology, astronomy, botany, and geology. Awards: YALSA Best Book for Young Adults. (Rev: BL 11/15/92; MJHS) [919.8]

5196 Steger, Will, and Jon Bowermaster. *Crossing Antarctica* (9–adult). 1992, Knopf $25 (0-394-58714-6). Six adventurers attempt to cross Antarctica by dogsled in 7 months. (Rev: BL 1/15/92; SLJ 8/92) [919.8]

5197 Stewart, Gail B. *Antarctica* (5–7). (Places in the News) 1991, Macmillan/Crestwood LB $11.95 (0-89686-656-4). (Rev: BL 1/15/92) [998]

5198 Woods, Michael. *Science on Ice: Research in the Antarctic* (6–8). 1995, Millbrook $19.90 (1-56294-498-3). A description of Antarctica as a site for scientific research and its current importance to scientists worldwide. (Rev: BL 4/15/95; SLJ 6/95) [919.8]

United States

General History and Geography

5199 Adams, John Winthrop, ed. *Stars and Stripes Forever: The History of Our Flag* (9–adult). 1992, Smithmark $7.98 (0-8317-6658-1). A general history of the U.S. flag concentrating on colonial times. (Rev: BL 9/15/92)

5200 Faber, Harold. *From Sea to Sea: The Growth of the United States* (6–9). 1992, Scribner $16.95 (0-684-19442-2). Describes the growth of the United States in terms of its acquisition and control of land, from its birth to the present day. Includes new material on the Panama Canal Zone, Okinawa, and Micronesia. (Rev: BL 12/15/92; SLJ 1/93) [973]

5201 Gattuso, John, ed. *Insight Guides: Native America* (9–adult). 1992, Prentice-Hall paper $19.95 (0-13-467119-8). Includes descriptions of Indian peoples, places, and history as well as suggestions on appropriate tourist behavior in the Southwest. Illustrated. (Rev: BL 3/15/92) [970.00497]

5202 Katz, William Loren. *Exploration to the War of 1812, 1492–1814* (7–10). (History of Multicultural America) 1993, Raintree/Steck-Vaughn LB $15.96 (0-8114-6275-7). Discusses the United States before colonization, the development of the nation, and the debasement of women and minorities who helped create it. (Rev: BL 6/1–15/93; MJHS) [973]

5203 Lilliefors, Jim. *Highway 50: Ain't That America* (9–adult). 1993, Fulcrum $19.95 (1-55591-073-4). The author recounts his trip westward along U.S. 50 from Maryland to California. (Rev: BL 3/15/93*) [917.304]

5204 Lunardini, Christine. *What Every American Should Know about Women's History* (9–adult). (What Every American Should Know) 1994, Bob Adams $16 (1-55850-417-6). Deals with significant contributions made by women in America from the early seventeenth century to the present. (Rev: BL 12/1/94) [973]

5205 Reader's Digest, eds. *Discovering America's Past: Customs, Legends, History and Lore of Our Great Nation* (9–adult). 1993, Reader's Digest $33 (0-89577-520-4). Including vintage photos and artwork, this collection of anecdotal profiles forms a social history of the United States. (Rev: BL 1/1/94; VOYA 6/94) [973]

5206 Shenkman, Richard. *"I Love Paul Revere, Whether He Rode or Not"* (9–adult). 1991, HarperCollins $19.95 (0-06-016346-1). Further well-documented "revelations" on the same subject by the author of *Legends, Lies, and Cherished Myths of American History*. (Rev: BL 10/1/91) [973]

5207 Walker, Dave. *American Rock 'n' Roll Tour* (9–adult). 1992, Thunder's Mouth paper $13.95 (1-56025-041-0). A geographically arranged catalog of birthplaces, historic concerts, music memorabilia, etc. (Rev: BL 10/1/92) [781.66]

Historical Periods

INDIANS AND OTHER NATIVE AMERICANS

5208 Acatoz, Sylvio. *Pueblos: Prehistoric Indian Cultures of the Southwest* (9–adult). Tr. by Barbara Fritzemeier. 1990, Facts on File $45 (0-8160-2437-5). An illustrated study of early Indian culture in the American Southwest. (Rev: BL 4/15/91; SHS) [979]

5209 Arnold, Caroline. *The Ancient Cliff Dwellers of Mesa Verde* (5–7). Photos. 1992, Clarion $15.95 (0-395-56241-4). A history of the Anasazi people and a speculative account of their daily life. Awards: SLJ Best Book. (Rev: BL 5/1/92; SLJ 7/92*) [978.8]

5210 Ayer, Eleanor H. *The Anasazi* (6–9). 1993, Walker LB $14.85 (0-8027-8185-3). An in-depth look at the Anasazi Indians, who came to this country about 2,000 years ago. (Rev: BL 3/1/93; SLJ 11/93) [979]

5211 Bonvillain, Nancy. *The Inuit* (6–9). (Indians of North America) 1995, Chelsea House paper $8.95 (0-7910-0380-9). (Rev: BL 10/15/95; MJHS) [971]

5212 Bonvillain, Nancy. *The Sac and Fox* (6–9). (Indians of North America) 1995, Chelsea House $18.95 (0-7910-1684-6). (Rev: BL 7/95; MJHS) [977.1]

5213 Bonvillain, Nancy. *The Teton Sioux* (6–9). (Indians of North America) 1994, Chelsea House $18.95 (0-7910-1688-9). (Rev: BL 10/15/94; MJHS) [977]

5214 Bonvillain, Nancy. *The Zuni* (6–9). (Indians of North America) 1995, Chelsea House $18.95 (0-7910-1689-7); paper $8.95 (0-7910-3478-X). (Rev: BL 10/15/95; MJHS) [973]

5215 Bruchac, Joseph. *The Native American Sweat Lodge: History and Legends* (9–adult). 1993, Crossing $24.95 (0-89594-637-8); paper $12.95 (0-89594-636-X). Bruchac celebrates the importance of the sweat lodge in this overview of its history, meaning, and use to American Indians and other cultures. Includes 25 traditional Native American poems and stories. (Rev: BL 10/15/93) [391]

5216 Calloway, Colin G. *Indians of the Northeast* (6–10). (First Americans) 1991, Facts on File $18.95 (0-8160-2389-1). Focuses on the major tribes of the region. Coverage includes the French and Indian Wars and the government's policy toward Native Americans today. (Rev: BL 1/15/92; SHS) [974]

5217 Dial, Adolph L. *The Lumbee* (6–9). (Indians of North America) 1993, Chelsea House $18.95 (1-55546-713-X). (Rev: BL 4/15/94; MJHS) [973]

5218 Freedman, Russell. *An Indian Winter* (6–9). 1992, Holiday $21.95 (0-8234-0930-9); paper $12.95 (0-8234-1158-3). In words and pictures, a German naturalist/explorer and a Swiss artist recorded their 1832 observations of Mandan and Hidatsa Indian tribes in North Dakota. Awards: ALSC Notable Children's Book; Golden Kite; SLJ Best Book; Western Heritage; YALSA Best Book for Young Adults. (Rev: BL 6/1/92*; MJHS; SLJ 6/92*; YR) [917.804]

5219 Goetzmann, William H. *The First Americans: Photographs from the Library of Congress* (9–adult). 1991, Starwood Publishing (P.O. Box 40503, Washington, DC 20016) $30 (0-912347-96-1). This collection of turn-of-the-century commercial photos of Native Americans illustrates the "sentimental notions about the vanishing American" popular at the time. (Rev: BL 11/15/91; SHS) [973.0497]

5220 Hubbard-Brown, Janet. *The Shawnee* (6–9). (Indians of North America) 1995, Chelsea House $18.95 (0-7910-3475-5). (Rev: BL 7/95; MJHS) [973]

5221 Jones, Constance. *The European Conquest of North America* (7–12). 1995, Facts on File $17.95 (0-8160-3041-3). A detailed account of Native American cultures and the methods chosen by European conquerors to subdue them. (Rev: BL 5/1/95) [970.01]

5222 Josephy, Alvin M., ed. *America in 1492* (9–adult). 1992, Knopf $35 (0-394-56438-3). Illustrated essays on the history and cultures of American Indians. Covers geographic locations, languages, spiritual beliefs, customs, and art. (Rev: BL 1/1/92; SHS; SLJ 8/92) [970.01]

5223 Josephy, Alvin M. *500 Nations: An Illustrated History of North American Indians* (9–adult). 1994, Knopf $50 (0-679-42930-1). This companion to the television documentary gives a chronological overview of the history of North American Indians from ancient legends to the present. (Rev: BL 10/15/94; SHS) [970.004]

5224 Lacey, Theresa Jensen. *The Blackfeet* (6–9). (Indians of North America) 1995, Chelsea House $18.95 (0-7910-1681-1). (Rev: BL 7/95; MJHS) [970.004]

5225 Liptak, Karen. *Indians of the Southwest* (6–10). (First Americans) 1991, Facts on File $18.95 (0-8160-2385-9). Describes the first Indian inhabitants of the area and highlights their social, political, and religious life before and after contact with Europeans. (Rev: BL 1/15/92; SHS) [979]

5226 McCutchen, David. *The Red Record: The Wallam Olum of the Lenni Lenape* (9–adult). 1993, Avery paper $14.95 (0-89529-525-3). A translation/interpretation of the Wallam Olum, an ancient history of the Lenni Lenape (Delaware) Indians. (Rev: BL 2/15/93*; VOYA 10/93) [973]

5227 Medicine Crow, Joseph. *From the Heart of the Crow Country: The Crow Indians' Own Stories* (9–adult). (Library of the American Indian) 1992, Crown/Orion $17 (0-517-58839-0). The official historian of the Crow draws on personal experiences, his scholarship as an anthropologist, and traditional legends to tell the story of his people. (Rev: BL 10/1/92) [973]

5228 Nabokov, Peter, ed. *Native American Testimony: A Chronicle of Indian-White Relations from Prophecy to the Present* (9–adult). 1991, Viking $25 (0-670-83704-0). Compiled from primary documents and oral accounts, this anthology chronicles 500 years of Native American history from a tribal perspective. (Rev: BL 12/1/91; SHS) [970.004]

5229 Ortiz, Alfonso. *The Pueblo* (6–9). (Indians of North America) 1994, Chelsea House $18.95 (1-55546-727-X); paper $7.95 (0-7910-0396-5). (Rev: BL 1/1/94; MJHS) [979]

5230 Reedstrom, E. Lisle. *Apache Wars: An Illustrated Battle History* (9–adult). 1992, Sterling paper $19.95 (0-8069-7255-6). (Rev: BL 3/1/91; SHS) [973]

5231 Sattler, Helen Roney. *The Earliest Americans* (5–7). Illus. 1993, Clarion $16.95 (0-395-54996-5). Describes the controversy over the continent's earliest settlers and the more advanced forerunners of the Mayan and Incan civilizations. Awards: SLJ Best Book. (Rev: BL 5/1/93; BTA; MJHS; SLJ 6/93*; VOYA 8/93) [970.01]

5232 Smith, Carter. *Native Americans of the West: A Sourcebook on the American West* (9–12). 1991, Millbrook LB $16.90 (1-56294-131-3). A pictorial record of Indian-white relations from 1789 to 1890. (Rev: BL 5/15/92; SLJ 7/92) [978]

5233 Smith Baranzini, Marlene, and Howard Egger-Bovet. *Book of American Indians* (5–7). (Brown Paper School USKids History) 1994, Little, Brown $19.95 (0-316-96921-4). Focuses on several Native American peoples and their daily lives before the arrival of European settlers. (Rev: BL 10/1/94; SLJ 9/94) [970.004]

5234 Stein, Wendy. *Shamans* (6–10). (Great Mysteries) 1991, Greenhaven $13.95 (0-89908-088-X). Describes some of the past and present variations of Shamanism around the world. (Rev: BL 3/1/92; MJHS) [291]

5235 Tanner, Helen Hornbeck. *The Ojibwa* (6–9). (Indians of North America) 1991, Chelsea House paper $17.95 (1-55546-721-0). (Rev: BL 1/1/92; MJHS) [970.004]

5236 Trafzer, Clifford E. *The Nez Perce* (6–9). (Indians of North America) 1992, Chelsea House LB $17.95 (1-55546-720-2). (Rev: BL 10/1/92; MJHS) [973]

5237 Walens, Stanley. *The Kwakiutl* (6–9). (Indians of North America) 1992, Chelsea House LB $17.95 (1-55546-711-3). (Rev: BL 10/1/92; MJHS) [970.004]

5238 Warren, Scott. *Cities in the Sand: The Ancient Civilizations of the Southwest* (5–7). 1992, Chronicle $10.95 (0-8118-0012-1). Provides an in-depth look at the ancient cliff-dwelling cultures of the Anasazi, Hohokam, and Mogollon peoples of the Southwest. (Rev: BL 10/1/92; MJHS; SLJ 8/92) [979]

5239 Weatherford, Jack. *Native Roots: How the Indians Enriched America* (9–adult). 1991, Crown $20 (0-517-57485-3). This exposition of Native American influences on the nation's development demonstrates how deeply North America's real pioneers have affected aspects of our culture, from agriculture to warfare. (Rev: BL 10/15/91) [973]

5240 Williams, Jeanne. *Trails of Tears: American Indians Driven from Their Lands* (9–adult). 1992, Hendrick-Long (P.O. Box 12311, Dallas, TX 75225) $15.95 (0-937460-76-1). Details the U.S. government's forced removal of Comanche, Cheyenne, Apache, Navajo, and Cherokee from their native lands. (Rev: BL 6/1/92; MJHS) [973]

5241 Woodhead, Edward, ed. *The Woman's Way* (9–12). 1995, Time-Life $18.95 (0-8094-9729-8). Explains the traditional duties and customs of North American Indian women throughout history, with biographical sketches of some well-known Indian women. (Rev: BL 9/1/95; SLJ 11/95) [305.48]

5242 Wright, Ronald. *Stolen Continents: The Americans Through Indian Eyes since 1492* (9–adult). 1992, Houghton $22.95 (0-395-56500-6). A view of the past 500 years from the Native American perspective. (Rev: BL 1/15/92; SHS) [970.004]

DISCOVERY AND EXPLORATION

5243 Columbus, Christopher. *The Voyage of Christopher Columbus: Columbus' Own Journal of Discovery, Newly Restored and Translated* (9–adult). Tr. by John Cummins. 1992, St. Martin's $19.95 (0-312-07880-3). The log of this explorer's journey in plain-spoken English. (Rev: BL 5/15/92; SHS) [970.01]

5244 Faber, Harold. *The Discoverers of America* (6–12). 1992, Scribner LB $17.95 (0-684-19217-9). Discusses the exploration of North and South America, focusing on the period from Columbus to Lewis and Clark. (Rev: BL 5/15/92; MJHS; SLJ 6/92) [970.01]

5245 Huyghe, Patrick. *Columbus Was Last: From 200,000 B.C. to 1492, a Heretical History of Who Was First* (9–adult). 1992, Hyperion $22.95 (1-56282-940-8). Provides both documented and speculative historical and archaeological evidence that disputes the belief that Columbus was the first to discover America. (Rev: BL 10/1/92) [970.01]

5246 Jones, Mary Ellen, ed. *Christopher Columbus and His Legacy* (9–12). (Opposing Viewpoints) 1992, Greenhaven LB $17.95 (0-89908-196-7); paper $9.95 (0-89908-171-1). Offers differing opinions—from writers of various ethnic or national backgrounds—on Columbus and his impact on the New World. (Rev: BL 1/15/93; MJHS; SHS) [970.01]

5247 Lawrence, Bill. *The Early American Wilderness as the Explorers Saw It* (9–adult). 1991, Paragon House $23.95 (1-55778-145-1). Chronicles the experiences and impressions of early explorers; arranged by region. (Rev: BL 6/1/91) [970.01]

5248 Morgan, Ted. *Wilderness at Dawn: The Settling of the North American Continent* (9–adult). 1993, Simon & Schuster $27.50 (0-671-69088-4). This broad frontier survey describes Native American societies that existed before "discovery" and famous and obscure European settlers during the early 1800s. (Rev: BL 4/15/93) [970.01]

5249 Palmer, Colin. *The First Passage: Blacks in the Americas, 1502–1617* (7–12). 1995, Oxford Univ. $17.95 (0-19-509905-2). Details of the slave trade, the earliest black presence in the Americas, the roles blacks played in the New World, and the effect on growth in Europe. (Rev: BL 2/15/95) [973]

5250 Schouweiler, Thomas. *The Lost Colony of Roanoke* (6–10). (Great Mysteries) 1991, Greenhaven $13.95 (0-89908-093-6). Outlines known facts about the Lost Colony and poses questions about its unsolved mysteries. (Rev: BL 3/1/92; MJHS) [975.6]

5251 Viola, Herman J., and Carolyn Margolis, eds. *Seeds of Change: A Quincentennial Commemoration* (9–adult). 1991, Smithsonian $39.95 (1-56098-035-4); paper $24.95 (1-56098-036-2). Essays that reflect the reassessment of Columbus's "discovery" of America as a violent and destructive invasion of an existing culture. (Rev: BL 9/15/91; SLJ 4/92) [970.01]

5252 Yue, Charlotte, and David Yue. *Christopher Columbus: How He Did It* (5–8). Illus. 1992, Houghton $13.95 (0-395-52100-9). Includes basic history but concentrates more on the knowledge and technology that enabled him to do it. Includes maps, charts, diagrams. (Rev: BL 6/15/92*; SLJ 7/92; YR) [917.04]

COLONIAL PERIOD AND FRENCH AND INDIAN WARS

5253 Hakim, Joy. *Making Thirteen Colonies* (5–8). (History of US) 1993, Oxford Univ. LB $19.95 (0-19-507747-4); paper $9.95 (0-19-507748-2). The 2nd in the series explores the colonization of the New World, from Jamestown's founding (1607) to the opening of the Wilderness Road (1775). (Rev: BL 1/15/94; SLJ 2/94; VOYA 4/94) [973.2]

5254 Hill, Frances. *A Delusion of Satan: The Full Story of the Salem Witch Trials* (9–adult). 1995, Doubleday $23.95 (0-385-47255-2). A careful, analytical examination of the Salem witch hunts, in which a group of young girls accused innocent women of practicing witchcraft. (Rev: BL 11/1/95*) [133.4]

5255 Howarth, Sarah. *Colonial People* (5–8). 1994, Millbrook LB $14.90 (1-56294-512-2). Provides portraits of the work and lifestyles of selected individuals in the colonial era. (Rev: BL 5/15/95; SLJ 3/95) [973]

5256 Howarth, Sarah. *Colonial Places* (5–8). 1994, Millbrook LB $14.90 (1-56294-513-0). Describes several sites around which life in early America revolved. (Rev: BL 5/15/95; SLJ 3/95) [973]

5257 Lizon, Karen Helene. *Colonial American Holidays and Entertainment* (5–8). (Colonial America) 1993, Watts $12.90 (0-531-12546-7). (Rev: BL 1/1/94; MJHS; SLJ 12/93) [394.2]

5258 Nardo, Don. *Braving the New World, 1619–1784: From the Arrival of the Enslaved Africans to the End of the American Revolution* (7–10). (Milestones in Black History) 1995, Chelsea House $18.95 (0-7910-2259-5); paper $7.95 (0-7910-2685-X). How and why the slave trade became established in North America and the legacy of slave culture. (Rev: BL 4/15/95; BTA) [973]

5259 Scott, John Anthony. *Settlers on the Eastern Shore, 1607–1750* (7–12). (Library of American History) 1991, Facts on File $16.95 (0-8160-2327-1). A historical account of the early American settlers. (Rev: BL 5/15/91; SLJ 7/91) [973.2]

5260 Smith, Carter, ed. *The Arts and Sciences: A Sourcebook on Colonial America* (5–8). (American Albums from the Collections of the Library of Congress) 1991, Millbrook LB $14.90 (1-56294-037-6). (Rev: BL 1/1/92; MJHS) [973.2]

5261 Smith, Carter, ed. *Battles in a New Land: A Sourcebook on Colonial America* (5–8). (American Albums from the Collections of the Library of Congress) 1991, Millbrook LB $14.90 (1-56294-034-1). (Rev: BL 1/1/92; MJHS) [973.2]

5262 Smith, Carter, ed. *Daily Life: A Sourcebook on Colonial America* (5–8). (American Albums from the Collections of the Library of Congress) 1991, Millbrook LB $14.90 (1-56294-038-4). (Rev: BL 1/1/92; MJHS) [973.2]

5263 Smith, Carter, ed. *The Explorers and Settlers: A Sourcebook on Colonial America* (5–8). (American Albums) 1991, Millbrook LB $14.90 (1-56294-035-X). A visual history of the exploration and colonization of the United States, 1492–1775. (Rev: BL 1/1/92) [973.2]

5264 Smith, Carter, ed. *Governing and Teaching: A Sourcebook on Colonial America* (5–8). (American Albums from the Collections of the Library of Congress) 1991, Millbrook LB $14.90 (1-56294-036-8). (Rev: BL 1/1/92; MJHS) [973.2]

5265 Warner, John F. *Colonial American Home Life* (5–8). (Colonial America) 1993, Watts $12.90 (0-531-12541-6). Covers colonial clothing, food, work, school, homes, amusements and communications. (Rev: BL 1/1/94; MJHS; SLJ 2/94; VOYA 4/94) [973.2]

5266 Washburne, Carolyn Kott. *A Multicultural Portrait of Colonial Life* (7–12). (Perspectives) 1993, Marshall Cavendish LB $18.95 (1-85435-657-7). (Rev: BL 3/15/94; MJHS; SHS) [973.2]

5267 Wood, Peter H. *Strange New Land: African Americans, 1617–1776* (8–12). (Young Oxford History of African Americans) 1996, Oxford Univ. LB $21.00 (0-19-508700-3). The latest historical research on Africans in America in the pre-Revolutionary century. (Rev: SLJ 3/96)

REVOLUTIONARY PERIOD AND THE YOUNG NATION (1775–1809)

5268 Brenner, Barbara. *If You Were There in 1776* (5–8). 1994, Bradbury $14.95 (0-02-712322-7). The year 1776 in a world context, including a tour of the diverse populations of the colonies to such mundane topics as what children might be having for dinner. (Rev: BL 5/15/94; MJHS; SLJ 6/94) [973.3]

5269 Dolan, Edward F. *The American Revolution: How We Fought the War of Independence* (5–8). 1995, Millbrook LB $19.90 (1-56294-521-1). A well-researched volume on the war's battles that keeps its focus on the people and places involved. (Rev: BL 12/15/95) [973.3]

5270 Dudley, William, ed. *The American Revolution* (10–12). (Opposing Viewpoints/American History) 1992, Greenhaven LB $17.95 (1-56510-011-5); paper $9.95 (1-56510-010-7). Provides scholarly material with a wide range of viewpoints and a long annotated bibiography. (Rev: BL 4/15/93; SHS) [973.3]

5271 Egger-Bovet, Howard, and Marlene Smith-Baranzini. *Book of the American Revolution* (5–7). (Brown Paper School USKids History) 1994, Little, Brown $19.95 (0-316-96922-2). Brings the American Revolution to life through stories, plays, and personal accounts. Includes ideas for educational crafts and games. (Rev: BL 10/1/94; SLJ 9/94) [973.7]

5272 Fischer, David Hackett. *Paul Revere's Ride* (9–adult). 1994, Oxford Univ. $25 (0-19-508847-6). A reconstruction of the man and his role in the outbreak of war against the British. Awards: SLJ Best Book. (Rev: BL 4/15/94; SLJ 8/94) [973.3]

5273 Gay, Kathlyn, and Martin Gay. *Revolutionary War* (5–8). (Voices from the Past) 1995, Twenty-First Century LB $15.98 (0-8050-2844-7). Synopses of the causes, battles, and outcomes of the Revolutionary War. (Rev: BL 12/15/95) [973.3]

5274 Kent, Deborah. *The American Revolution: "Give Me Liberty or Give Me Death!"* (5–7). (American War) 1994, Enslow LB $17.95 (0-89490-521-X). Summarizes the American War for Independence, with quotations, maps, paintings, portraits, and a chronology of events. (Rev: BL 7/94; SLJ 7/94) [973.3]

5275 Leckie, Robert. *George Washington's War: The Saga of the American Revolution* (9–adult). 1992, HarperCollins $35 (0-06-016289-9). Traces the causes and events leading to the American Revolution, and analyzes the major political and military leaders, key battles, and foreign alliances. (Rev: BL 9/1/92; SHS) [973.3]

5276 Minks, Louise, and Benton Minks. *The Revolutionary War* (7–12). (America at War) 1992, Facts on File LB $17.95 (0-8160-2508-8). (Rev: BL 2/1/93; MJHS) [973.3]

5277 Smith, Carter, ed. *The Revolutionary War: A Sourcebook on Colonial America* (5–8). (American Albums from the Collections of the Library of Congress) 1991, Millbrook LB $14.90 (1-56294-039-2). (Rev: BL 1/1/92; MJHS) [973.38]

5278 Steins, Richard. *A Nation Is Born: Rebellion and Independence in America (1700–1820)* (5–8). (First Person America) 1993, Twenty-First Century LB $14.95 (0-8050-2582-0). A look at the American Revolution, including extracts from diaries, letters, and journals of individuals who lived during the period. (Rev: BL 2/1/94; MJHS) [973.3]

5279 Stokesbury, James L. *A Short History of the American Revolution* (9–adult). 1991, Morrow $23 (0-688-08333-1). Highlights of the Revolutionary War, beginning with a look at the causes and ending with the raising of the Stars and Stripes. (Rev: BL 6/15/91; SHS) [973.3]

5280 Tebbel, John. *Turning the World Upside Down: Inside the American Revolution* (9–

adult). 1993, Crown/Orion $27.50 (0-517-58955-9). This present-tense narrative history relies on firsthand accounts to debunk the myths surrounding the war and offers human perspectives from both sides. (Rev: BL 5/15/93; BTA; VOYA 12/93) [973.3]

5281 Zall, P. M. *Becoming American: Young People in the American Revolution* (8–12). 1993, Shoe String/Linnet $22.50 (0-208-02355-0). Letters, journal entries, and court testimonies by young people who observed events and social conditions from 1767 to 1789. (Rev: BL 5/1/93; BTA; VOYA 8/93) [973.3]

NINETEENTH CENTURY TO THE CIVIL WAR (1809–1861)

5282 Bial, Raymond. *The Underground Railroad* (5–7). 1995, Houghton $14.95 (0-395-69937-1). A photo-essay re-created from the few documentary records available. (Rev: BL 4/1/95; SLJ 4/95) [973.7]

5283 Bosco, Peter. *The War of 1812* (7–10). 1991, Millbrook LB $16.90 (1-56294-004-X). An in-depth study of military strategy in the war, with an emphasis on ships and sea battles. (Rev: BL 2/1/92; BTA; MJHS; SHS; SLJ 10/91; YR) [973.5]

5284 Chalfant, William Y. *Dangerous Passage: The Santa Fe Trail and the Mexican War* (9–adult). 1994, Univ. of Oklahoma $29.95 (0-8061-2613-2). A detailed account of the Santa Fe Trail during the Mexican War. (Rev: BL 2/1/94) [978]

5285 Cosner, Shaaron. *The Underground Railroad* (6–12). 1991, Watts $12.40 (0-531-12505-X). An overview of the groups and individuals who helped slaves gain freedom. (Rev: BL 1/1/92; MJHS) [973.7]

5286 Dudley, William, ed. *Slavery* (10–12). (Opposing Viewpoints/American History) 1992, Greenhaven LB $17.95 (1-56510-013-1); paper $9.95 (1-56510-012-3). Provides scholarly material with a wide range of viewpoints and a long annotated bibliography. (Rev: BL 4/15/93; SHS; SLJ 6/93) [973]

5287 Ellis, Jerry. *Walking the Trail: One Man's Journey along the Trail of Tears* (9–adult). 1991, Delacorte $19 (0-385-30448-X). The author, part Cherokee, retraces the route from Alabama to Indian Territory made by 18,000 Cherokees in 1838. (Rev: BL 11/1/91) [917.604]

5288 Fremon, David K. *The Trail of Tears* (7–12). (American Events) 1994, Macmillan/New Discovery $14.95 (0-02-735745-7). A political account of the history and achievements of the Cherokee Nation and the treachery that led to their forced removal from their Georgia territory. (Rev: BL 7/94; MJHS) [973]

5289 Gay, Kathlyn, and Martin Gay. *War of 1812* (5–8). (Voices from the Past) 1995, Twenty-First Century LB $15.98 (0-8050-2846-3). Synopses of the causes, battles, and outcomes of the War of 1812. (Rev: BL 12/15/95) [973.5]

5290 Katz, William Loren. *The Westward Movement and Abolitionism, 1815–1850* (7–10). (History of Multicultural America) 1993, Raintree/Steck-Vaughn LB $15.96 (0-8114-6276-5). Concentrates on the belief in Manifest Destiny and its impact on Native Americans, the rise of resistance to slavery, and efforts of early feminists. (Rev: BL 6/1–15/93; MJHS) [973.5]

5291 McKissack, Patricia C., and Fredrick L. McKissack. *Rebels Against Slavery: American Slave Revolts* (6–12). 1996, Scholastic $14.95 (0-590-45735-7). Explores slave revolts and the men and women who led them. (Rev: BL 2/15/96)

5292 Marks, Paula Mitchell. *Precious Dust: The American Gold Rush Era, 1848–1900* (9–adult). 1994, Morrow $30 (0-688-10566-1). A cultural, sociological, and historical chronicle of the American frontier during the Gold Rush period in the nineteenth century. (Rev: BL 3/15/94) [970.04]

5293 Nardo, Don. *The Mexican-American War* (9–12). (America's Wars) 1991, Lucent LB $16.95 (1-56006-402-1). A concise description of events and evaluations of the Mexican-American War. (Rev: BL 5/15/92; SHS) [973.6]

5294 Paulson, Timothy J. *Days of Sorrow, Years of Glory, 1831–1850: From the Nat Turner Revolt to the Fugitive Slave Law* (5–9). (Milestones in Black American History) 1994, Chelsea House $18.95 (0-7910-2263-3); paper $7.95 (0-7910-2552-7). An examination of the Underground Railroad, slave resistance, the Seminole Wars, and the abolition movement. (Rev: BL 11/1/94; BTA; MJHS; SLJ 4/95; VOYA 12/94) [973]

5295 Smith-Baranzini, Marlene, and Howard Egger-Bovet. *The Brown Paper School USKids History: Book of the New American Nation* (5–7). (Brown Paper School USKids History) 1995, Little, Brown $21.95 (0-316-96923-0); paper $12.95 (0-316-22206-2). Vignettes of those who helped develop the new American nation plus the issues they faced. (Rev: BL 8/95; SLJ 8/95) [973.5]

5296 Van Der Linde, Laurel. *The Pony Express* (5–8). 1993, Macmillan/New Discovery paper $14.95 (0-02-759056-9). A history of the Pony Express that discusses its beginnings, routes, riders, ponies, dangers, problems and successes, and the reasons for its demise. (Rev: BL 9/1/93; MJHS; SLJ 7/93) [383]

5297 Wallace, Anthony F. C. *The Long, Bitter Trail: Andrew Jackson and the Indians* (9–adult). 1993, Hill & Wang $19.95 (0-8090-6631-9); paper $7.95 (0-8090-1552-8). The story of the racist removal of Indians over the Trail of Tears to the Oklahoma Territory in the 1830s. (Rev: BL 7/93; SLJ 12/93) [323.1]

THE CIVIL WAR (1861–1865)

5298 Anders, Curt. *Hearts in Conflict: A One-Volume History of the Civil War* (9–adult). 1994, Birch Lane $29.95 (1-55972-184-7). A quick-reading journey through the battles and leaders of the Civil War. (Rev: BL 4/15/94) [973.7]

5299 Beller, Susan Provost. *Cadets at War: The True Story of Teenage Heroism at the Battle of New Market* (5–8). 1991, Betterway $9.95 (1-55870-196-6). Virginia Military Institute cadets, called to fight at the Battle of New Market in 1864, left a significant impact on the school and its traditions. (Rev: BL 8/91; SLJ 6/91) [973.7]

5300 Bennett, Barbara J. *Stonewall Jackson: Lee's Greatest Lieutenant* (5–7). (History of the Civil War) 1991, Silver Burdett LB $18.98 (0-382-09939-7); paper $8.95 (0-382-24048-0). (Rev: BL 9/1/91) [973.7]

5301 Bolotin, Norman, and Angela Herb. *For Home and Country: A Civil War Scrapbook* (5–8). 1995, Dutton/Lodestar $16.99 (0-525-67495-0). This sociological history of the Civil War provides a close-up of the everyday life of Civil War soldiers. (Rev: BL 10/1/95; VOYA 12/95) [973.7]

5302 Boritt, Gabor S., ed. *Lincoln's Generals* (9–adult). 1994, Oxford Univ. $21 (0-19-508505-1). Five essays examining the successes and failures of Generals McClellan, Hooker, Meade, Sherman, and Grant. (Rev: BL 9/1/94; SLJ 3/95) [973.7]

5303 Boritt, Gabor S., ed. *Why the Civil War Came* (9–adult). 1995, Oxford Univ. $25 (0-19-507941-8). A breakdown of the 1850s political processes on either side of the Mason-Dixon Line. (Rev: BL 10/15/95) [973.7]

5304 Bowers, John. *Chickamauga and Chattanooga: The Battles That Doomed the Confederacy* (9–adult). 1994, HarperCollins $28 (0-06-016592-8). Covers the 2 major battles of the Tennessee campaign in the fall of 1863. (Rev: BL 5/15/94) [973.7]

5305 Brophy, Ann. *John Ericsson: The Inventions of War* (5–7). (History of the Civil War) 1991, Silver Burdett LB $18.98 (0-382-09943-5); paper $8.95 (0-382-24052-9). (Rev: BL 9/1/91) [609.2]

5306 Burgess, Lauren Cook, ed. *An Uncommon Soldier* (9–adult). 1994, Minerva Center (20 Granada Rd., Pasadena, MD 21122-2708) $25 (0-9634895-1-8); 1996, Oxford Univ. paper $9.95 (0-19-510243-6). Letters of a New York farmer's daughter who disguised herself as a man to enlist in the Union Army in 1862—only the 2nd such published account. (Rev: BL 5/15/94) [973.7]

5307 Carter, Alden R. *Battle of the Ironclads: The Monitor and the Merrimack* (5–7). (First Book) 1993, Watts LB $12.90 (0-531-20091-4). The race to build the Confederate *Virginia* and the Union's *Monitor* during the Civil War and the ships' influence on the course of the war. (Rev: BL 1/15/94; MJHS) [973.7]

5308 Chang, Ina. *A Separate Battle: Women and the Civil War* (5–9). 1991, Dutton/Lodestar $15.95 (0-525-67365-2). The role women played in the Civil War and how it affected them. Includes profiles of Harriet Beecher Stowe, Harriet Tubman, and Clara Barton. Awards: ALSC Notable Children's Book. (Rev: BL 1/15/92; MJHS; SLJ 2/92*) [973.7]

5309 Cox, Clinton. *Undying Glory* (6–9). 1991, Scholastic $14.95 (0-590-44170-1). An account of the discrimination suffered by the all-black Massachusetts 54th Regiment in the Civil War campaign to capture Charleston uses quotations from participants. (Rev: BL 11/16/91; MJHS; SLJ 12/91) [973.7]

5310 Dubowski, Cathy East. *Robert E. Lee: The Rise of the South* (5–7). (History of the Civil War) 1991, Silver Burdett LB $18.98 (0-382-09942-7); paper $8.95 (0-382-24051-0). (Rev: BL 9/1/91) [973.7]

5311 Dudley, William, ed. *The Civil War* (9–12). (Opposing Viewpoints/American History) 1995, Greenhaven LB $17.95 (1-56510-225-8); paper $9.95 (1-56510-224-X). Primary sources and documentary evidence present differing views of issues and events surrounding the Civil War. (Rev: BL 7/95; SHS) [973.7]

5312 Furgurson, Ernest B. *Chancellorsville 1863: The Souls of the Brave* (9–adult). 1992, Knopf $25 (0-394-58301-9). This recounting of the many legendary episodes in the Chancellorsville campaign during the Civil War includes 15 maps. (Rev: BL 11/1/92*) [973.7]

5313 Gallman, J. Matthew. *The North Fights the Civil War: The Home Front* (9–adult). 1994, Ivan R. Dee (1332 N. Halsted St., Chicago, IL 60622-2632) $22.50 (1-56663-049-5). The changes wrought by the Civil War and their effects on the women, African Americans, and immigrants who lived in the North. (Rev: BL 4/1/94) [973.7]

5314 Gay, Kathlyn, and Martin Gay. *Civil War* (5–8). (Voices from the Past) 1995, Twenty-First Century LB $15.98 (0-8050-2845-5). An overview of the Civil War including excerpts from letters, diaries, and newspaper accounts. (Rev: BL 12/15/95) [973.7]

5315 Gettysburg. *Gettysburg* (8–12). (Voices of the Civil War) 1995, Time-Life $26.95 (0-7835-4700-5). The Battle of Gettysburg with close-up views showing the human dimension of battle. (Rev: BL 5/15/95) [973.7]

5316 Golay, Michael. *The Civil War* (7–12). (America at War) 1992, Facts on File LB $17.95 (0-8160-2514-2). (Rev: BL 10/15/92)

5317 Hall, Richard. *Patriots in Disguise: Women Warriors of the Civil War* (9–adult). 1993, Paragon House $21.95 (1-55778-438-8). Chronicle of the courageous exploits of numerous women who served in the Civil War as nurses, spies, and soldiers. (Rev: BL 1/1/93; SHS) [973.4]

5318 Hansen, Joyce. *Between Two Fires: Black Soldiers in the Civil War* (7–12). (African American Experience) 1993, Watts LB $13.40 (0-531-11151-2). Examines the forces against which African American soldiers had to battle: paternalism, blatant bigotry, unequal pay and health care, and the entrenched racism of their own side. (Rev: BL 5/15/93; BTA; MJHS; VOYA 8/93) [973.7]

5319 Haskins, Jim. *The Day Fort Sumpter Was Fired On: A Photo History of the Civil War* (5–8). 1995, Scholastic paper $6.95 (0-590-46397-7). This history of the Civil War and Reconstruction includes information on the roles of women and African Americans. Reproductions of original photos, engravings, posters, and records. (Rev: BL 7/95) [973.7]

5320 Hennessy, John. *Return to Bull Run: The Campaign and Battle of Second Manassas* (9–adult). 1992, Simon & Schuster $27.50 (0-671-79368-3). A guide to the Civil War battle of Second Manassas, compiled by the official battlefield historian. (Rev: BL 11/1/92) [973.7]

5321 Katcher, Philip. *The Civil War Source Book* (9–12). 1992, Facts on File $35 (0-8160-2823-0). Comprehensive coverage of major events, large issues, and small details of the Civil War. A resource that can be read cover to cover. Awards: SLJ Best Book. (Rev: SLJ 1/93*)

5322 Kennett, Lee. *Marching Through Georgia: The Story of Soldiers and Civilians During Sherman's Campaign* (9–adult). 1995, HarperCollins $27.50 (0-06-016815-3). The life of common soldiers and civilians caught up in Sherman's devastating march in 1864. (Rev: BL 3/15/95; SLJ 2/96) [973.7]

5323 Kent, Zachary. *The Civil War: "A House Divided"* (5–7). (American War) 1994, Enslow LB $17.95 (0-89490-522-8). Summarizes the American Civil War, detailing major battles. Presents the attitudes of individuals on each side. Includes early photos and a chronology of events. (Rev: BL 7/94; SLJ 9/94; VOYA 8/94) [973.7]

5324 Lawliss, Chuck. *The Civil War: A Traveler's Guide and Sourcebook* (9–adult). 1991, Crown/Harmony paper $18 (0-517-57767-4). A comprehensive guide to the Civil War's places, events, and personages. (Rev: BL 4/15/91; SHS; SLJ 4/92) [917.304]

5325 Logue, Larry M. *To Appomattox and Beyond: The Civil War Soldier in War and Peace* (9–adult). 1995, Ivan R. Dee (1332 N. Halsted St., Chicago, IL 60622-2632) $22.50 (1-56663-093-2). Logue traces Civil War veterans from the time they enlisted to their discharge and what followed afterward. (Rev: BL 10/15/95) [973.7]

5326 McPherson, James M. *Images of the Civil War: The Paintings of Mort Künstler* (9–adult). 1992, Gramercy Books $19.99 (0-517-07356-0). An album of 70 full-color paintings covering a wide range of Civil War subjects, with a brief outline of the war by a renowned historian. (Rev: BL 11/1/92; BTA; SLJ 5/93) [973.7]

5327 Malone, John. *The Civil War Quiz Book* (9–adult). 1992, Morrow/Quill paper $9 (0-688-11269-2). Year-by-year roundup of Civil War facts. (Rev: BL 2/15/92) [973]

5328 Markle, Donald E. *Spies and Spymasters of the Civil War* (9–adult). 1994, Hippocrene $24.95 (0-7818-0227-X). A history of Civil War espionage. (Rev: BL 5/1/94) [973.7]

5329 Masur, Louis P., ed. *"The Real War Will Never Get in the Books": Selections from Writers During the Civil War* (9–adult). 1993, Oxford Univ. $35 (0-19-506868-8). An intimate portrait of the Civil War through the writings of 14 literary artists of the era. (Rev: BL 7/93) [810.8]

5330 Murphy, Jim. *The Boys' War: Confederate and Union Soldiers Talk about the Civil War* (5–12). (Icarus World Issues) 1990, Clarion LB $15.95 (0-89919-893-7). Using soldiers' diaries, journals, and letters, Murphy describes the beginnings of the Civil War and the military role of the young soldiers, their life in the camps and field, and their return home. Awards: SLJ Best Book;

YALSA Best Book for Young Adults. (Rev: BL 12/1/90; SLJ 1/91*)

5331 Murphy, Jim. *The Long Road to Gettysburg* (6–9). 1992, Clarion $15.95 (0-395-55965-0). An account of the Civil War from both the Union and Confederate perspectives. Awards: BL Editors' Choice; Golden Kite; SLJ Best Book; YALSA Best Book for Young Adults. (Rev: BL 5/15/92*; MJHS; SLJ 6/92*) [973.7]

5332 O'Neal, Michael. *The Assassination of Abraham Lincoln* (6–10). (Great Mysteries) 1991, Greenhaven $13.95 (0-89908-092-8). Outlines known facts about the assassination and poses questions about the mysteries that remain unsolved. (Rev: BL 3/1/92; MJHS) [364.1]

5333 Phillips, Charles, and Alan Axelrod. *My Brother's Face: Portraits of the Civil War in Photographs, Diaries, and Letters* (9–adult). 1993, Chronicle $27.50 (0-8118-0369-4); paper $16.95 (0-8118-0162-4). A close-up view of Civil War soldiering, with photos, extracts from diaries and letters., etc. (Rev: BL 3/15/93; BTA; VOYA 8/93) [973.73]

5334 Piggins, Carol Ann. *A Multicultural Portrait of the Civil War* (7–12). (Perspectives) 1993, Marshall Cavendish LB $18.95 (1-85435-660-7). Concentrates on the events leading up to the Civil War and the crucial issue of slavery, as well as the continuing legacy of racism. (Rev: BL 3/15/94; MJHS; SLJ 4/94) [973]

5335 Ray, Delia. *Behind the Blue and Gray: The Soldier's Life in the Civil War* (5–10). (Young Readers' History of the Civil War) 1991, Dutton/Lodestar $15.95 (0-525-67333-4). This sequel to *A Nation Torn* tells the story of the Civil War from the perspective—and personal accounts—of common soldiers. (Rev: BL 9/1/91; MJHS; SLJ 8/91*) [973.7]

5336 Rickarby, Laura Ann. *Ulysses S. Grant and the Strategy of Victory* (5–7). (History of the Civil War) 1991, Silver Burdett LB $18.98 (0-382-09944-3); paper $8.95 (0-382-24053-7). (Rev: BL 9/1/91) [973.8]

5337 Robertson, James I. *Civil War! America Becomes One Nation* (6–10). 1992, Knopf LB $14 (0-394-92996-9). The basic history of the Civil War, with each chapter devoted to one calendar year of the conflict. (Rev: BL 4/1/92; BTA; SLJ 5/92) [973.7]

5338 Roth, David E. *The Illustrated History of the Civil War: 1861–1865* (9–adult). 1992, Smithmark $24.95 (0-8317-0775-5). This photo-essay brings the Civil War to life. (Rev: BL 9/15/92) [973.7]

5339 Shea, William L., and Earl J. Hess. *Pea Ridge: Civil War Campaign in the West* (9–adult). 1992, Univ. of North Carolina $29.95 (0-8078-2042-3). A comprehensive study of the 1862 Arkansas conflict that was the largest Civil War battle fought west of the Mississippi. (Rev: BL 11/1/92) [973.7]

5340 Shorto, Russell. *Abraham Lincoln: To Preserve the Union* (5–7). (History of the Civil War) 1991, Silver Burdett LB $18.98 (0-382-09937-0); paper $8.95 (0-382-24046-4). (Rev: BL 9/1/91) [973.7]

5341 Shorto, Russell. *David Farragut and the Great Naval Blockade* (5–7). (History of the Civil War) 1991, Silver Burdett LB $18.98 (0-382-09941-9); paper $8.95 (0-382-24050-2). (Rev: BL 9/1/91) [973.7]

5342 Smith, Carter, ed. *Behind the Lines: A Sourcebook on the Civil War* (5–8). (American Albums from the Collections of the Library of Congress) 1993, Millbrook LB $16.90 (1-56294-265-4). (Rev: BL 3/1/93; MJHS) [973.7]

5343 Smith, Carter, ed. *The First Battles: A Sourcebook on the Civil War* (5–8). (American Albums from the Collections of the Library of Congress) 1993, Millbrook LB $16.90 (1-56294-262-X). (Rev: BL 3/1/93; MJHS) [973.7]

5344 Smith, Carter, ed. *One Nation Again: A Sourcebook on the Civil War* (5–8). (American Albums from the Collections of the Library of Congress) 1993, Millbrook LB $16.90 (1-56294-266-2). (Rev: BL 3/1/93; MJHS) [973.8]

5345 Smith, Carter, ed. *Prelude to War: A Sourcebook on the Civil War* (5–8). (American Albums from the Collections of the Library of Congress) 1993, Millbrook LB $16.90 (1-56294-261-1). (Rev: BL 3/1/93; MJHS) [973.7]

5346 Smith, Carter, ed. *The Road to Appomattox: A Sourcebook on the Civil War* (5–8). (American Albums from the Collections of the Library of Congress) 1993, Millbrook LB $16.90 (1-56294-264-6). (Rev: BL 3/1/93; MJHS) [973.7]

5347 Steins, Richard. *The Nation Divides: The Civil War (1820–1880)* (5–8). (First Person America) 1993, Twenty-First Century LB $14.95 (0-8050-2583-9). A look at the Civil War including extracts from diaries, letters, and journals of individuals who lived through it. (Rev: BL 2/1/94; MJHS) [973.5]

5348 Stiles, T. J., ed. *In Their Own Words: Civil War Commanders* (9–adult). 1995, Putnam/Perigee paper $14 (0-399-51909-2). Writings by Civil War commanders from both the North and South chronicling decisive war events. (Rev: BL 3/15/95; SLJ 8/95) [973.7]

5349 Stokesbury, James L. *A Short History of the Civil War* (9–adult). 1995, Morrow $25 (0-688-11523-3). Highly readable, scholarly, presented with a dry wit, and shorter than most books on the Civil War, this text covers all the major events and personalities and discusses the origins of the war. (Rev: BL 10/15/95) [973.7]

5350 Trudeau, Noah Andre. *The Last Citadel: Petersburg, Virginia, June 1864–April 1865* (9–adult). 1991, Little, Brown $22.95 (0-316-85327-5). This volume of Civil War campaign history gives an account of the 9-month siege of Petersburg, Virginia. (Rev: BL 10/1/91) [973.7]

5351 Wheeler, Richard. *Lee's Terrible Swift Sword: From Antietam to Chancellorsville: An Eyewitness History* (9–adult). 1992, HarperCollins $30 (0-06-016650-9). Examination of a crucial segment of the Civil War, from the battle of Antietam to just before Gettysburg. (Rev: BL 4/15/92) [973.7]

WESTWARD EXPANSION AND PIONEER LIFE

5352 Beckstead, James H. *Cowboying: A Tough Job in a Hard Land* (9–adult). 1991, Univ. of Utah $45 (0-87480-357-8); paper $19.95 (0-87480-378-0). A retrospective of cowboy life in nineteenth- and early twentieth-century Utah, with rare antique sepia photos. (Rev: BL 12/1/91) [979.2]

5353 Bentley, Judith. *Brides, Midwives, and Widows* (6–9). (Settling the West) 1995, Twenty-First Century LB $16.98 (0-8050-2994-X). The story of the women who helped settle the West, recounting their struggles and successes from diaries and other primary sources. (Rev: BL 8/95; SLJ 9/95) [978]

5354 Bentley, Judith. *Explorers, Trappers, and Guides* (6–9). (Settling the West) 1995, Twenty-First Century LB $16.98 (0-8050-2995-8). Unusually well-told stories about lesser-known explorers derived from first-person accounts. (Rev: BL 8/95; SLJ 11/95) [979.5]

5355 Brown, Dee. *The American West* (9–adult). 1994, Scribner $25 (0-02-517421-5). Uses diaries, letters, and newspaper articles to describe Western conflicts and culture. Examines Indian wars, settlers' town life, and the gold rush. (Rev: BL 10/15/94*; SHS) [978]

5356 Brown, Dee. *Wondrous Times on the Frontier* (9–adult). 1991, August House $23.95 (0-87483-137-7). A series of humorous stories of the American West, including bawdy and outrageous tales of American Indian and Mexican confrontations with pioneer settlers. (Rev: BL 10/15/91) [978]

5357 Bryan, Howard. *Robbers, Rogues and Ruffians: True Tales of the Wild West* (9–adult). 1991, Clear Light (823 Don Diego, Santa Fe, NM 87501) $22.95 (0-940666-04-9). Includes accounts of lesser-known New Mexico Territory desperadoes and newspaper stories about and interviews with New Mexico's pioneers. (Rev: BL 12/1/91; SHS) [978.9]

5358 Cox, Clinton. *The Forgotten Heroes* (7–12). 1993, Scholastic $14.95 (0-590-45121-9). The story of African American U.S. Cavalrymen who were assigned to the frontier after the Civil War to protect white settlers and solve the "Indian problem." (Rev: BL 1/15/94; BTA; MJHS; VOYA 2/94) [978]

5359 Granfield, Linda. *Cowboy: An Album* (5–7). 1994, Ticknor & Fields $18.95 (0-395-68430-7). Cowboy lore describing the life of the historical and modern-day cowboy as well as the rise of the cowboy as popular media hero. (Rev: BL 2/1/94; BTA; SLJ 1/94) [636.2]

5360 Jones, Mary Ellen, ed. *The American Frontier* (9–12). (American History) 1994, Greenhaven LB $17.95 (1-56510-086-7); paper $9.95 (1-56510-085-9). Presents varied views of the pioneer, the Native American, mythic heroes, race and gender, and popular culture. (Rev: BL 3/1/94; MJHS) [978]

5361 Katz, William Loren. *Black Women of the Old West* (6–9). 1995, Atheneum $18 (0-689-31944-4). The role black women played in the settlement of the West is a topic virtually ignored in history books. (Rev: BL 12/15/95; SLJ 12/95; VOYA 4/96) [978]

5362 Katz, William Loren. *The Civil War to the Last Frontier: 1850–1880s* (7–9). (History of Multicultural America) 1993, Raintree/Steck-Vaughn $15.96 (0-8114-6277-3). A multicultural history of the United States during this period. (Rev: BL 9/1/93; MJHS) [973.5]

5363 Mancini, Richard. *American Legends of the Wild West* (9–adult). 1992, Running Press $19.98 (1-56138-119-5). Accounts of warriors and chiefs, cowboys and gunslingers, profusely illustrated with photos, paintings, and prints. (Rev: BL 6/15/92; SHS; SLJ 11/92) [978.02]

5364 Marrin, Albert. *Cowboys, Indians, and Gunfighters: The Story of the Cattle Kingdom* (6–10). 1993, Atheneum $22.95 (0-689-31774-3). An exciting account of the Old West, including Comanche vengeance, buffalo hunts, and frontier lawlessness. Awards: SLJ Best Book; Western Heritage. (Rev: BL 8/93; BTA; MJHS; SLJS 1/94*; VOYA 10/93) [978]

5365 Miller, Brandon Marie. *Buffalo Gals: Women of the Old West* (5–7). 1995, Lerner LB $14.21 (0-8225-1730-2). The daily life of nineteenth-century women of the Western frontier. (Rev: BL 5/1/95; SLJ 6/95) [978]

5366 Morgan, Ted. *A Shovel of Stars: The Making of the American West, 1800 to the Present* (9–adult). 1995, Simon & Schuster $30 (0-671-79439-6). Follows the history of each state after the colonial period. (Rev: BL 3/1/95) [978]

5367 Murdoch, David. *Cowboy* (5–9). (Eyewitness Books) 1993, Knopf LB $15.99 (0-679-94014-6). An illustrated history of cowboys in the American West and around the world. (Rev: BL 10/1/93; MJHS) [978]

5368 Press, Petra. *A Multicultural Portrait of the Move West* (7–12). (Perspectives) 1993, Marshall Cavendish LB $18.95 (1-85435-658-5). Told from the viewpoint of the people who lived there, this history challenges popular stereotypes of brave white explorers and cowboys "opening up" the empty Western frontier. (Rev: BL 4/1/94; MJHS; SLJ 4/94) [978]

5369 Rosa, Joseph G. *The Taming of the West: Age of the Gunfighter: Men and Weapons on the Frontier, 1840–1900* (9–adult). 1993, Smithmark $24.98 (0-8317-0381-4). This large-size volume introduces gunfighters from the West, with many color and B&W illustrations of rifles, pistols, and artifacts. (Rev: BL 10/15/93) [978]

5370 Ross, Stewart. *Cowboys* (5–7). (Fact or Fiction) 1995, Millbrook/Copper Beech LB $15.90 (1-56294-618-8). Looks at the myths and realities of life in the U.S. West in the late 1800s. (Rev: BL 7/95; SLJ 5/95) [978]

5371 Schultz, Duane. *Over the Earth I Come* (9–adult) 1992, St. Martin's $21.95 (0-312-07051-9). A riveting account of the brutal Great Plains Sioux uprising of 1862 and the public execution of 38 Indian men in Minnesota. (Rev: BL 4/1/92; SLJ 11/92) [973.7]

5372 Stewart, Gail B. *Cowboys in the Old West* (6–9). (The Way People Live) 1995, Lucent $14.95 (1-56006-077-8). An exploration of the life of the cowboy from 1865 to 1890. (Rev: BL 5/1/95; SLJ 5/95) [978]

5373 Underwood, Larry. *Love and Glory: Women of the Old West* (9–adult). 1991, Media Publishing (1102 Grand Blvd., Suite 2300, Kansas City, MO 64106-2305) paper $9.95 (0-939644-79-7). Lively biographies of 11 women of the Old West, drawn from diaries, memoirs, and other historical materials. (Rev: BL 6/15/91) [978]

5374 Welch, James, and Paul Stekler. *Killing Custer: The Battle of the Little Big Horn and the Fate of the Plains Indians* (9–adult). 1994, Norton $25 (0-393-03657-X). Examines Custer's death at Little Big Horn and the Great Sioux War from a Native American perspective. (Rev: BL 11/1/94; SHS) [973.8]

5375 Wexler, Sanford. *Westward Expansion* (9–adult). (Facts on File's Eyewitness History) 1991, Facts on File $40 (0-8160-2407-3). The entire territorial growth of the United States from 1754 to 1897 is described through first-person accounts taken from diaries, letters, and official documents . (Rev: BL 7/91; MJHS; SHS; SLJ 12/91) [973]

5376 *The Wild West* (9–12). 1993, Warner $49.95 (0-446-51761-5). This companion volume to the TV series contains hundreds of period photos, letters, diary entries, and artifacts. Awards: SLJ Best Book. (Rev: SLJ 8/93*)

RECONSTRUCTION TO WORLD WAR I (1865–1917)

5377 Bachrach, Deborah. *The Spanish-American War* (6–8). (America's Wars) 1991, Lucent LB $16.95 (1-56006-405-6). An overview of the war that solidified the United States as a world power. (Rev: BL 3/1/92; SLJ 5/92) [973.8]

5378 Blow, Michael. *A Ship to Remember: The Maine and the Spanish-American War* (9–adult). 1992, Morrow $25 (0-688-09714-6). An account of the destruction of the *Maine* and the subsequent events of the Spanish American War, with portraits of key figures on both sides. (Rev: BL 8/92; SHS) [973.8]

5379 Brown, Gene. *The Struggle to Grow: Expansionism and Industrialization (1880–1913)* (5–8). (First Person America) 1994, Twenty-First Century LB $14.95 (0-8050-2584-7). Covers the frontier, immigration, industry, and political reform during the period 1880–1913. (Rev: BL 2/1/94; MJHS; SLJ 3/94) [973.8]

5380 Fry, Annette R. *The Orphan Trains* (7–12). (American Events) 1994, Macmillan/New Discovery $14.95 (0-02-735721-X). Interviews, letters, and photos chronicle how slum children were sent on "orphan trains" to live in the West and how the move affected them. (Rev: BL 7/94; MJHS; SLJ 1/95) [362.7]

5381 Gay, Kathlyn, and Martin Gay. *Spanish-American War* (5–8). (Voices from the Past) 1995, Twenty-First Century LB $15.98 (0-8050-2847-1). Synopses of the causes, battles, and outcomes of the Spanish-American War. (Rev: BL 12/15/95) [973.8]

5382 Golay, Michael. *The Spanish-American War* (7–12). (America at War) 1995, Facts on File $17.95 (0-8160-3174-6). Chronicles the causes, major events, and crucial military strategies of the Spanish-American War. (Rev: BL 8/95; SLJ 12/95) [973.8]

5383 Lawrence, Jacob. *The Great Migration: An American Story* (5–7). 1993, HarperCollins LB $17.89 (0-06-023038-X). Using Lawrence's 60-panel *Migration* series from 1940–41, this picture book tells of the World War I migration of African Americans from the South to the industrialized North in search of a better life. Awards: SLJ Best Book. (Rev: BL 11/15/93*; BTA; MJHS; SLJ 12/93*) [759.13]

5384 Levinson, Nancy Smiler. *Turn of the Century: Our Nation One Hundred Years Ago* (5–7). 1994, Dutton/Lodestar $16.99 (0-525-67433-0). An overview of turn-of-the-century America covering immigration, the rise of cities, the organization of labor unions, the treatment of minorities, and more. (Rev: BL 11/15/94; SLJ 12/94) [973.8]

5385 Marrin, Albert. *The Spanish-American War* (6–10). 1991, Atheneum $14.95 (0-689-31663-1). Chronicles the years of Spanish domination in Cuba and the people's resistance. (Rev: BL 7/91; MJHS; SLJ 5/91) [973.8]

5386 Meltzer, Milton. *Bread and Roses: The Struggle of American Labor, 1865–1915* (7–12). 1991, Facts on File $16.95 (0-8160-2371-9). (Rev: BL 5/15/91; MJHS; SHS; SLJ 4/91) [331.88]

5387 Mettger, Zak. *Reconstruction: America after the Civil War* (5–8). (Young Readers' History of the Civil War) 1994, Dutton/Lodestar $16.99 (0-525-67490-X). Describes the Reconstruction period's social and economic struggles, including the fight for the civil rights of freed slaves. (Rev: BL 10/1/94; MJHS; SLJ 2/95) [973.8]

5388 Oliver, Carl R. *Panama's Canal* (8–12). 1990, Watts LB $13.90 (0-531-10958-5). A history of the Panama Canal, from the Spanish explorations through its construction in the early 1900s to the milestone agreeement with the U.S. in 1977. (Rev: BL 2/1/91; SHS) [972.87]

5389 Robinson, Charles M. *A Good Year to Die: The Story of the Great Sioux War* (9–adult). 1995, Random $27.50 (0-679-43025-3). A balanced narrative about the Great Sioux War (1876), where Custer, Crazy Horse, and George Crook were major figures. (Rev: BL 9/1/95) [973.8]

5390 Schlereth, Thomas J. *Victorian America: Transformations in Everyday Life, 1876-1915* (9–adult). 1991, HarperCollins $25 (0-06-016218-X). Perspectives on American lifestyles and the impact of technology, communications, and transportation between 1876 and 1915. (Rev: BL 7/91*; SHS) [973.8]

5391 Stalcup, Brenda. *Reconstruction* (9–12). (Opposing Viewpoints/American History) 1995, Greenhaven LB $17.95 (1-56510-227-4); paper $9.95 (1-56510-226-6). Primary documentary evidence represents opposing viewpoints of the Reconstruction. (Rev: BL 3/15/95; SHS) [973.8]

5392 Steele, Philip. *Little Bighorn* (5–8). (Great Battles and Sieges) Illus. 1992, Macmillan/New Discovery $13.95 (0-02-786885-0). A description of the battle in which Cheyenne and Sioux Indians defeated General Custer and the U.S. Army in 1876. (Rev: BL 10/1/92; SLJ 2/93) [973.8]

BETWEEN THE WARS AND THE GREAT DEPRESSION (1918–1941)

5393 Burg, David F. *The Great Depression: An Eyewitness History* (9–adult). 1996, Facts on File $45 (0-8160-3095-2). A variety of primary sources are culled for information that helps the reader experience the Great Depression within its historical context. (Rev: BL 12/15/95; VOYA 4/96) [973.91]

5394 Cooper, Michael L. *Bound for the Promised Land* (5–9). 1995, Dutton/Lodestar $15.99 (0-525-67476-4). A short history of the African Americans who left the South for better lives in the North and in the process changed the face of America. (Rev: BL 11/1/95; SLJ 12/95*; VOYA 4/96) [973]

5395 Dudley, William, ed. *The Great Depression* (7–12). (Opposing Viewpoints) 1994, Greenhaven LB $17.95 (1-56510-084-0). (Rev: BL 2/1/94; MJHS; SHS) [973.917]

5396 Farrell, Jacqueline. *The Great Depression* (7–12). (World History) 1996, Lucent LB $16.95 (1-56006-276-2). A comprehensive overview of the era, beginning with post–World War I and ending with the economic upswing resulting from World War II. (Rev: BL 2/15/96; SLJ 2/96)

5397 Hills, Ken. *1930s* (6–8). (Take Ten Years) 1992, Raintree/Steck-Vaughn LB $15.96 (0-8114-3076-6). A fast overview of a decade in a newspaper format, with double-page spreads, lots of headlines, and B&W photos. (Rev: BL 1/1/93; SLJ 6/93) [909.82]

5398 Katz, William Loren. *The New Freedom to the New Deal: 1913–1939* (7–9). (History of Multicultural America) 1993, Raintree/Steck-Vaughn $15.96 (0-8114-6279-X). (Rev: BL 9/1/93; MJHS) [973.91]

5399 Meltzer, Milton. *Brother, Can You Spare a Dime? The Great Depression, 1929–1933* (7–12). 1991, Facts on File $16.95 (0-8160-2372-7). (Rev: BL 5/15/91; SHS; SLJ 10/91) [330.973]

5400 Stanley, Jerry. *Children of the Dust Bowl: The True Story of the School at Weedpatch Camp* (5–8). 1992, Crown LB $15.99 (0-517-58782-3). Records the enormity of the Dust Bowl and migrants' desperate journey, followed by the founding of the Weedpatch School and the "Okie" children who built it. Awards: ALSC Notable Children's Book; BL Editors' Choice; Jefferson Cup Award; SLJ Best Book. (Rev: BL 9/1/92*; BTA; MJHS; SLJ 11/92*) [371.96]

5401 Stewart, Gail B. *The New Deal* (6–9). 1993, Macmillan/New Discovery $14.95 (0-02-788369-8). Explains the causes of the Great Depression and how President Roosevelt tried to turn the economy and national morale around through the New Deal. (Rev: BL 11/15/93; MJHS; VOYA 2/94) [973.917]

5402 Watkins, T. H. *The Great Depression: America in the 1930s* (9–adult). 1993, Little, Brown $24.95 (0-316-92453-9). Watkin explores the financial collapse and its effects on Americans, including its effect on our current society, with 100+ B&W photos. (Rev: BL 11/15/93; MJHS; SLJ 6/94) [973.917]

5403 Wormser, Richard. *Growing Up in the Great Depression* (6–12). 1994, Atheneum $15.95 (0-689-31711-5). Letters, photos, and interviews examine children's lives during the Great Depression. Includes accounts of job loss, child labor, and the struggles of African Americans. (Rev: BL 10/15/94; SHS; SLJ 12/94; VOYA 2/95) [973.91]

WORLD WAR II TO THE PRESENT (1945–)

5404 Abrams, Herbert L. *"The President Has Been Shot": Confusion, Disability, and the 25th Amendment in the Aftermath of the Attempted Assassination of Ronald Reagan* (9–adult). 1992, Norton $22.95 (0-393-03042-3). This account of the attempted assassination of Reagan analyzes the shooting, the president's medical treatment, and his subsequent mental competence. (Rev: BL 12/15/91) [973.927]

5405 Bullard, Sara. *Free at Last: A History of the Civil Rights Movement and Those Who Died in the Struggle* (6–10). 1993, Oxford Univ. $20 (0-19-508381-4). Following an overview of the history of African Americans, an in-depth look at the civil rights movement, with 40 biographies of influential participants. (Rev: BL 11/1/93; BTA; MJHS; SHS; VOYA 8/93) [323.1]

5406 Donnelly, Thomas, and others. *Operation Just Cause: The Invasion of Panama* (9–adult). 1991, Lexington $24.95 (0-669-24975-0). Various accounts of what actually occurred in Panama in December 1989, told by correspondents who offer us a soldier's point of view. (Rev: BL 9/15/91) [327.730728]

5407 Farber, David. *The Age of Great Dreams: America in the 1960s* (9–adult). 1994, Hill & Wang $25 (0-8090-2401-2). A scholarly analysis of the 1960s. (Rev: BL 4/15/94) [973.92]

5408 Fariello, Griffin. *Red Scare: Memories of the American Inquisition* (9–adult). 1995, Norton $29.95 (0-393-03732-0). Spanning the years 1945–1965, the memories of those who were accused of un-American activities. (Rev: BL 3/1/95) [973.92]

5409 Finkelstein, Norman H. *Thirteen Days/Ninety Miles: The Cuban Missile Crisis* (8–12). 1994, Messner $15 (0-671-86622-2). Declassified materials, letters, and memoirs describe the tension-filled crisis, documenting the actions and ideologies of Kennedy and Khrushchev and explaining how nuclear war was narrowly averted. (Rev: BL 7/94*; MJHS; SHS; SLJ 6/94) [973.992]

5410 Hills, Ken. *1940s* (6–8). (Take Ten Years) 1992, Raintree/Steck-Vaughn LB $15.96 (0-8114-3077-4). A fast overview of a decade in a newspaper format, with double-page spreads, lots of headlines, and B&W photos. (Rev: BL 1/1/93) [940.53]

5411 Johnson, Haynes. *Sleepwalking Through History: America in the Reagan Years* (9–adult). 1991, Norton $24.95 (0-393-02937-9). Analysis of what America's future holds following the Reagan administration. (Rev: BL 2/1/91; SHS) [973.927]

5412 Katz, William Loren. *The Great Society to the Reagan Era: 1964–1990* (7–9). (History of Multicultural America) 1993, Raintree/Steck-Vaughn $15.96 (0-8114-6282-X) (Rev: BL 9/1/93; MJHS) [973.92]

5413 Katz, William Loren. *World War II to the New Frontier: 1940–1963* (7–9). (History of Multicultural America) 1993, Raintree/Steck-Vaughn $15.96 (0-8114-6280-3). (Rev: BL 9/1/93; MJHS) [305.8]

5414 Lemann, Nicholas. *The Promised Land: The Great Black Migration and How It Changed America* (9–adult). 1991, Knopf $24.95 (0-394-56004-3). Focusing on individual experiences, the author traces the progress of blacks from the rural South to the promise of a new life in the urban North during the mid-twentieth century. (Rev: BL 3/1/91*) [973]

5415 Netzley, Patricia D. *The Assassination of President John F. Kennedy* (7–12). (American Events) 1994, Macmillan/New Discovery $14.95 (0-02-768127-0). (Rev: BL 7/94; MJHS) [973.922]

5416 Patterson, Charles. *The Civil Rights Movement* (6–12). (Social Reform Movement) 1995, Facts on File $17.95 (0-8160-2968-7). Chronicles the American civil rights movement, including a time line, chapter notes, and a reading list. (Rev: BL 11/15/95; SLJ 11/95; VOYA 12/95) [323.1196]

5417 Rochelle, Belinda. *Witnesses to Freedom: Young People Who Fought for Civil Rights* (5–7). 1993, Dutton/Lodestar $15.99 (0-525-67377-6). Stories of children who participated in the civil rights movement, including photos and discussion of the wider issues involved. (Rev: BL 11/1/93; MJHS; SLJ 5/94) [323.1]

5418 Steins, Richard. *The Postwar Years: The Cold War and the Atomic Age (1950–1959)* (5–8). (First Person America) 1994, Twenty-First Century LB $15.95 (0-8050-2587-1). An introduction to the Cold War that includes primary sources. (Rev: BL 5/15/94; MJHS) [973.92]

KOREAN, VIETNAM, AND GULF WARS

5419 Barr, Roger. *The Vietnam War* (9–12). (America's Wars) 1991, Lucent LB $16.95 (1-56006-410-2). A view of U.S. military involvement in Southest Asia. (Rev: BL 5/15/92; SLJ 6/92) [959.704]

5420 Becker, Elizabeth. *America's Vietnam War: A Narrative History* (9–12). 1992, Clarion $14.95 (0-395-59094-9). Emphasis on American policy during the Vietnam War years and the behind-the-scenes political power plays of the American and Vietnamese governments. (Rev: BL 4/15/92; BTA; MJHS; SLJ 11/92) [959.704]

5421 Bilton, Michael, and Kevin Sim. *Four Hours in My Lai: The Soldiers of Charlie Company* (9–adult). 1992, Viking $25 (0-670-84296-6). An investigation into the Vietnam massacre, including the cover-up, trials, sentencing, and press coverage. (Rev: BL 2/15/92) [959.704]

5422 Bratman, Fred. *War in the Persian Gulf* (7–10). 1991, Millbrook LB $14.90 (1-56294-051-1). This description of the Iraqi invasion of Kuwait and the Desert Storm operation also examines the causes behind the events. (Rev: BL 11/16/91; MJHS; SLJ 12/91) [955.05]

5423 Brown, Gene. *The Nation in Turmoil: Civil Rights and the Vietnam War (1960–1973)* (5–8). (First Person America) 1994, Twenty-First Century LB $15.95 (0-8050-2588-X). An overview of both aspects of American history including excerpts from letters, diaries, and speeches. (Rev: BL 5/15/94; MJHS) [973.92]

5424 Capps, Walter, ed. *The Vietnam Reader* (9–adult). 1991, Routledge $45 (0-415-90126-X); paper $14.95 (0-415-90127-8). Thirty-six authors, many of them veterans, have each contributed an essay on war experiences and the continuing effects of the Vietnam War. (Rev: BL 10/1/91) [959.704]

5425 Caraccilo, Dominic J. *The Ready Brigade of the 82nd Airborne in Desert Storm: A Combat Memoir by the Headquarters Company Commander* (9–adult). 1993, McFarland paper $16.95 (0-89950-829-4). Chronicles the company's 8 months in the desert—the moving, supplying, and setting up of troops and equipment. (Rev: BL 6/1–15/93; VOYA 10/93) [956.704]

5426 Cipkowski, Peter. *Understanding the Crisis in the Persian Gulf* (7–12). 1992, Wiley LB $19.89 (0-471-54815-4); paper $12.95 (0-471-54816-2). Covers the political history of the region, discusses the events that resulted in U.S. intervention, and provides information on postwar Iraq. (Rev: BL 9/15/92; MJHS) [956.704]

5427 Denenberg, Barry. *Voices from Vietnam* (7–12). 1995, Scholastic $16.95 (0-590-44267-8). Personal narratives and histories of the Vietnam War from the late 1940s to 1975. (Rev: BL 2/15/95*; SLJ 3/95) [959.704]

5428 Detzer, David. *An Asian Tragedy: America and Vietnam* (7–12). 1992, Millbrook $16.90 (1-56294-066-X). Tracing Vietnam's long history of strong resistance to foreign domination, Detzer examines America's controversial intervention in its civil war. (Rev: BL 9/1/92; MJHS; SLJ 8/92) [959.704]

5429 Dudley, William, and Stacey L. Tipp, eds. *Iraq* (9–12). (Current Controversies) 1991, Greenhaven LB $16.95 (0-89908-575-X); paper $9.95 (0-89908-581-4). A study of the Persian Gulf War that focuses on issues such as military lessons of the war and media coverage. (Rev: BL 6/15/92; MJHS) [956.704]

5430 Ebert, James R. *A Life in a Year: The American Infantryman in Vietnam, 1965–1972* (9–adult). 1993, Presidio $24.95 (0-89141-500-9). Using quotations from soldiers, Ebert looks at training, combat in the jungle, dealing with the Vietnamese, and U.S. sentiments about the conflict. (Rev: BL 10/1/93*) [959.704]

5431 Franklin, H. Bruce. *M.I.A.; or, Mythmaking in America* (9–adult). 1992, Chicago Review/

Lawrence Hill $17.95 (1-55652-118-9). A frank look at the popular belief that American servicemen are still being held in Southeast Asia and that the government is not doing enough to bring them back. (Rev: BL 2/15/92) [959.704]

5432 Friedman, Norman. *Desert Victory: The War for Kuwait* (9–adult). 1991, Naval Institute $24.95 (1-55750-254-4). Concludes that American strategy in the Persian Gulf War was largely successful, but that American intelligence failed to accurately gauge the strength and morale of Iraqi forces. (Rev: BL 10/15/91) [956.704]

5433 Gruner, Elliott. *Prisoners of Culture: Representing the Vietnam POW* (9–adult). 1993, Rutgers Univ. $37 (0-8135-1930-6); paper $14.95 (0-8135-1931-4). A history of the media image of POWs, discussing the multiplicity of Vietnam experiences and the need to end manipulation by orchestrated myths of guts and glory. (Rev: BL 5/15/93) [303.6]

5434 *In the Eye of Desert Storm: Photographers of the Gulf War* (9–adult). 1991, Abrams/Eastman Kodak $39.95 (0-8109-3460-4). This collection of nearly 200 color photos covers every aspect of the crisis: the buildup, the actual Persian Gulf War, and the liberation of Kuwait. (Rev: BL 11/1/91) [956.704]

5435 Isserman, Maurice. *The Korean War* (7–12). (America at War) 1992, Facts on File $17.95 (0-8160-2688-2). (Rev: BL 11/1/92; MJHS; SHS) [951.904]

5436 Isserman, Maurice. *The Vietnam War: America at War* (7–12). (America at War) 1992, Facts on File $17.95 (0-8160-2508-8). (Rev: BL 3/1/92; SHS) [959.7]

5437 Kent, Deborah. *The Vietnam War: "What Are We Fighting For?"* (5–7). (American War) 1994, Enslow LB $17.95 (0-89490-527-9). A good overview of the Vietnam War for students who know little or nothing about it. (Rev: BL 10/15/94; MJHS) [959.704]

5438 Kent, Zachary. *The Persian Gulf War: "The Mother of All Battles"* (5–7). (American War) 1994, Enslow LB $17.95 (0-89490-528-7). A clear, concise overview of the Persian Gulf War. (Rev: BL 4/15/95) [956.704]

5439 King, John. *The Gulf War* (7–10). 1991, Dillon LB $13.95 (0-87518-514-2). Factual account of the Iraqi invasion, wartime operations, and the conflict's aftermath. (Rev: BL 3/1/92; SLJ 4/92) [956.704]

5440 McConnell, Malcolm. *Inside Hanoi's Secret Archives: Solving the MIA Mystery* (9–adult). 1995, Simon & Schuster $25 (0-671-87118-8). An exploration of the whereabouts of MIAs from the Vietnam War. (Rev: BL 2/15/95; SHS) [959.7]

5441 Marrin, Albert. *America and Vietnam: The Elephant and the Tiger* (9–12). 1992, Viking $16 (0-670-84063-7). A historical review of Vietnam's fight for independence and the repercussions of America's involvement in the war. Awards: SLJ Best Book. (Rev: BL 3/1/92; BTA; SHS; SLJ 6/92*) [959.704]

5442 Olson, James, and Randy Roberts. *Where the Domino Fell: America in Vietnam, 1945–1990* (9–adult). 1991, HarperCollins $25 (0-06-016553-7). Detailed account of U.S. involvement in Vietnam from 1945 to the present. (Rev: BL 1/1/91) [959.704]

5443 Paschall, Rod. *Witness to War: Korea* (9–adult). 1995, Putnam paper $12 (0-399-51934-3). Firsthand accounts from soldiers and strategists who fought with the U.S. during the Korean War. (Rev: BL 5/1/95) [951.904]

5444 Pyle, Richard. *Schwarzkopf: The Man, the Mission, the Triumph* (9–adult). 1991, NAL/Signet paper $4.50 (0-451-17205-1). Profile of the commander's leadership during the Desert Shield and Desert Storm operations. (Rev: BL 7/91) [973.928]

5445 Sack, John. *Company C* (9–adult). 1995, Morrow $22 (0-688-11281-1). A journalist who accompanied the tank corps Company C during the Gulf War takes an intimate look at the experiences of the men during the conflict. (Rev: BL 5/15/95) [956.7044]

5446 Salzman, Marian, and Ann O'Reilly. *War and Peace in the Persian Gulf: What Teenagers Want to Know* (6–12). 1991, Peterson's Guides paper $5.95 (1-56079-135-7). Question-and-answer format presents information about the Gulf War that teenagers most want to know. (Rev: BL 6/15/91) [956.05]

5447 Sciolino, Elaine. *The Outlaw State: Saddam Hussein's Quest for Power and the War in the Gulf* (9–adult). 1991, Wiley $22.95 (0-471-54299-7). A *New York Times* diplomatic correspondent examines Saddam Hussein's effect on world politics and the events surrounding the Gulf War. (Rev: BL 7/91) [956.704]

5448 Sifry, Micah L., and Christopher Cerf, eds. *The Gulf War Reader: History, Documents, Opinions* (9–adult). 1991, Times Books paper $15 (0-812-91947-5). Writings by columnists, politicians, and political advisers concerning the 1990 events in Kuwait and Iraq. (Rev: BL 9/1/91; SHS) [956.704]

5449 Simon, Bob. *Forty Days* (9–adult). 1992, Putnam $22.95 (0-399-13760-2). CBS News' chief

Middle Eastern correspondent tells how he and his news team were captured by an Iraqi patrol and held for 40 days. (Rev: BL 4/1/92) [956.704]

5450 Simons, Donald L. *I Refuse: Memories of a Vietnam War Objector* (9–adult). 1992, Broken Rifle Press (P.O. Box 749, Trenton, NJ 08607) $27.50 (0-9620024-2-9); paper $13.95 (0-9620024-3-7). A graduate student explains why he became a conscientious objector to the Vietnam War. (Rev: BL 3/1/92) [355.224]

5451 Smith, Winnie. *American Daughter Gone to War: On the Front Lines with an Army Nurse in Vietnam* (9–adult). 1992, Morrow $22 (0-688-11188-2). A former member of the Army Nurse Corps in Vietnam recalls her tour of duty and her difficult adjustment to civilian life. (Rev: BL 9/1/92; SHS) [959.7]

5452 Stein, R. Conrad. *The Korean War: "The Forgotten War"* (5–7). (American War) 1994, Enslow LB $17.95 (0-89490-526-0). A clear, concise overview of the Korean War. (Rev: BL 4/15/95; MJHS) [951.904]

5453 Super, Neil. *Vietnam War Soldiers* (5–8). (African American Soldiers) 1993, Twenty-First Century LB $14.95 (0-8050-2307-0). A look at Africa American men and women from all branches of the services who served with distinction in the Vietnam War. (Rev: BL 2/15/94; MJHS; SLJ 4/94) [959.704]

5454 Taylor, Thomas. *Lightning in the Storm: The 101st Air Assault Division in the Gulf War* (9–adult). 1994, Hippocrene $29.50 (0-7818-0268-7). A mix of the anecdotal and the analytical in this history of the division's contributions in the Persian Gulf War. (Rev: BL 4/15/94) [956.704]

5455 Tomedi, Rudy. *No Bugles, No Drums* (9–adult). 1993, Wiley $24.95 (0-471-57232-2). A chronological narrative of the Korean War based on veterans' reminiscences. (Rev: BL 8/93; BTA) [951.9]

5456 Van Devanter, Lynda, and Joan A. Furey, eds. *Visions of War, Dreams of Peace: Writings of Women in the Vietnam War* (9–adult). 1991, Warner paper $9.95 (0-446-39251-0). Recollections from women who served in the Vietnam War. (Rev: BL 5/15/91; SHS) [811]

5457 Wiener, Robert. *Live from Baghdad: Gathering News at Ground Zero* (9–adult). 1992, Doubleday $22 (0-385-42165-6). A CNN executive explains how his network became the first to offer live coverage of war behind enemy lines. (Rev: BL 1/15/92) [070.4]

5458 Wormser, Richard. *Three Faces of Vietnam* (9–12). 1993, Watts $13.90 (0-531-11142-3). Examines the tragedy of the Vietnam War from a human perspective, narrating the personal histories of those who fought, those who protested, and Vietnamese civilians. (Rev: BL 2/15/94; BTA; SLJ 1/94; VOYA 2/94) [959.704]

5459 Wright, David. *Vietnam War* (7–12). (Causes and Consequences) 1995, Raintree/Steck-Vaughn LB $25.69 (0-8172-4053-5). (Rev: BL 12/15/95) [959.704]

Regions

MIDWEST

5460 Davis, Robert Murray. *Mid-Lands: A Family Album* (9–adult). 1992, Univ. of Georgia $19.95 (0-8203-1392-0). A nostalgic look at growing up in Missouri during the 1940s and 1950s. (Rev: BL 1/15/92) [977.8]

5461 Kerfoot, Justine. *Gunflint: Reflections on the Trail* (9–adult). 1990, Pfeifer-Hamilton (210 W. Michigan St., Duluth, MN 55802-1908) $16.95 (0-938586-43-2). Month-by-month meditations on life in the wilderness, drawn from over 60 years of experience. (Rev: BL 1/15/91) [917.76]

5462 Murphy, Jim. *The Great Fire* (5–9). 1995, Scholastic $16.95 (0-590-47267-4). This narrative of the great Chicago fire combines documents, personal accounts, illustrations, photos, and street maps to give an in-depth view of the disaster. Awards: SLJ Best Book. (Rev: BL 6/1–15/95; SLJ 7/95) [977.3]

MOUNTAIN AND PLAINS STATES

5463 Bauer, Erwin A. *Yellowstone* (9–adult). 1993, Voyageur Press (123 N. Second St., Stillwater, MN 55082) $29.95 (0-89658-177-2). An accessible text and beautiful color photos of the flora and fauna of our first national park. (Rev: BL 3/15/93) [917.87]

5464 Berger, Karen, and Daniel R. Smith. *Where the Waters Divide: A Walk Across America along the Continental Divide* (9–adult). 1993, Crown/Harmony $23 (0-517-58804-8). Chronicles the authors' meandering, 3000-mile, 9-month trek from Mexico to Canada along the Continental Divide Trail. (Rev: BL 6/1–15/93) [917.304]

5465 Heat-Moon, William Least. *PrairyErth (a Deep Map)* (9–adult). 1991, Houghton $24.95 (0-395-48602-5). An in-depth study of deceptively plain terrain in eastern Kansas covers geological information and describes the emotional attachment of the prairie natives to their land. (Rev: BL 8/91*) [917.81]

5466 Hillerman, Tony, ed. *The Best of the West: An Anthology of Classic Writing from the American West* (9–adult). 1991, HarperCollins $25 (0-06-016664-9). An extensive collection of Western fact and fiction, arranged by subject—e.g., explorers, settlers, cowboys, miners, women, Navajos. (Rev: BL 9/15/91; SHS) [978]

5467 Milner, Clyde A., and others, eds. *The Oxford History of the American West* (9–adult). 1994, Oxford Univ. $39.95 (0-19-505968-9). A collection of essays from seasoned academics on an area continually being redefined. (Rev: BL 4/15/94; SLJ 1/95) [979]

NORTHEASTERN AND MID-ATLANTIC STATES

5468 Diamonstein, Barbaralee. *Landmarks: Eighteen Wonders of the New York World* (8–12). Illus. 1992, Abrams $35 (0-8109-3565-1). The history and distinctive aspects of 18 New York City sites, among them Central Park, the Brooklyn Bridge, and Carnegie Hall. (Rev: BL 2/15/93; BTA) [720]

5469 Dunnahoo, Terry. *Boston's Freedom Trail* (5–7). 1994, Dillon LB $14.95 (0-87518-623-8); paper $7.95 (0-382-24762-0). A guidebook for young visitors to historical sites in Boston. (Rev: BL 1/1/95; SLJ 3/95) [917.44]

5470 Dwyer, Jim. *Subway Lives: 24 Hours in the Life of the New York City Subway* (9–adult). 1991, Crown $20 (0-517-58445-X). This day-in-the-life account of the New York City subway system provides portraits of subway workers and riders, as well as a history of the system's rise and near collapse. (Rev: BL 11/15/91) [388.4]

5471 Nylander, Jane C. *Our Own Snug Fireside: Images of the New England Home, 1760–1860* (9–adult). 1993, Knopf $30 (0-394-54984-8). A view of daily life in New England preceding the Civil War, based on probate records, journals, memoirs, etc. (Rev: BL 3/15/93) [974]

5472 Powledge, Fred. *Working River* (5–8). 1995, Farrar $15 (0-374-38527-0). This look at Maryland's Patuxent River goes into its archaeology, ecosystem, geography, pollution, and people in an attempt to inspire readers to be environmentally conscious. (Rev: BL 6/1–15/95; SLJ 11/95) [975.2]

5473 St. George, Judith. *Mason and Dixon's Line of Fire* (7–9). 1991, Putnam $16.95 (0-399-22240-5). Describes the background of the border territory between Maryland and Pennsylvania, with an in-depth look at the bloodshed in the area from frontier days to the Civil War. (Rev: BL 11/15/91; MJHS) [974.8]

5474 Shapiro, Mary J. *Ellis Island: An Illustrated History of the Immigrant Experience* (9–adult). 1991, Macmillan/Collier paper $49.95 (0-02-584441-5). This history of the island concentrates on the immigrants themselves, using photos, letters, memorabilia, and oral histories to demonstrate how they spread across the United States. (Rev: BL 10/15/91) [325]

PACIFIC STATES

5475 Maharidge, Dale. *Yosemite: A Landscape of Life* (9–adult). 1990, Yosemite Association (P.O. Box 545, Yosemite National Park, CA 95389) paper $14.95 (0-939666-56-1). An insightful look at the inner workings of the national park. (Rev: BL 1/15/91) [979.4]

5476 Miller, Luree, and Scott Miller. *Alaska: Pioneer Stories of a Twentieth-Century Frontier* (6–10). 1991, Dutton/Cobblehill $14.95 (0-525-65050-4). Contains the true-life adventures of various settlers in the "Last Frontier" and profiles 5 present-day Alaskans who embody the same pioneering spirit. (Rev: BL 9/1/91) [979.8]

5477 Salak, John. *The Los Angeles Riots: America's Cities in Crisis* (5–8). (Headliners) 1993, Millbrook LB $15.90 (1-56294-373-1). A look at the 1992 Los Angeles riots that examines the underlying social and economic problems that caused them. (Rev: BL 4/1/93; MJHS) [979.4]

5478 Tisdale, Sallie. *Stepping Westward: The Long Search for Home in the Pacific Northwest* (9–adult). 1991, Holt $19.95 (0-8050-1353-9). This meditation on living in the Pacific Northwest examines the pioneers' necessity of taming the wilderness, in contrast to our current environmental concerns. (Rev: BL 9/15/91) [917.9504]

5479 Walker, Tom. *Denali Journal: A Contemporary Look at the National Park* (9–adult). 1992, Stackpole paper $16.95 (0-8117-2437-9). A naturalist-photographer observes the changing character of a national park. (Rev: BL 2/1/92) [508.798]

SOUTH

5480 Branch, Muriel Miller. *The Water Brought Us: The Story of the Gullah-Speaking People* (5–9). 1995, Dutton/Cobblehill $16.99 (0-525-65185-3). About the Gullah people who live on the sea islands off the coast of South Carolina and Georgia and who are descendants of slaves. (Rev: BL 9/15/95; SLJ 10/95) [975.8]

5481 Bresee, Clyde. *How Grand a Flame: A Chronicle of a Plantation Family, 1813–1947* (9–adult). 1991, Algonquin Books of Chapel Hill (P.O. Box 2225, Chapel Hill, NC 27515-2225) $19.95 (0-945575-55-6). Based on original documents and personal remembrance, an illustrated reconstruction of family life on a South Carolina cotton plantation. (Rev: BL 10/1/91) [975.7]

5482 Cecelski, David S. *Along Freedom Road: Hyde County, North Carolina and the Fate of Black Schools in the South* (9–adult). 1994, Univ. of North Carolina $32.50 (0-8078-2126-8); paper $14.95 (0-8078-4437-3). The aftermath of desegregation in remote Hyde County, N.C., when white leaders threatened to close 2 historically black schools. (Rev: BL 2/15/94) [370.19]

5483 Lefkon, Wendy, ed. *Birnbaum's Walt Disney World for Kids by Kids* (5–7). 1994, Hyperion $9.95 (1-56282-750-2). Eight kids, ages 8–14, give their opinions about Disney World shopping, restaurants, accommodations, and attractions. (Rev: BL 1/1/94) [917.59]

5484 Reynolds, George P., ed. *Foxfire 10: Railroad Lore, Boardinghouses, Depression-Era Appalachia, Chairmaking, Whirligigs, Snake Canes, and Gourd Art* (9–adult). 1993, Doubleday/Anchor $30 (0-385-46910-1); paper $14 (0-385-42276-8). Offers first-person perspectives on such topics as how the Depression affected Appalachia and how the arrival of hydroelectric power changed the environment and people's lives. (Rev: BL 3/15/93; SHS) [975.8]

5485 Shroder, Tom, and John Barry. *Seeing the Light: Wilderness and Salvation: A Photographer's Tale* (9–adult). 1995, Random $30 (0-679-43282-5). Stunning photos of the Everglades made during a period of grief and loss in photographer Clyde Butcher's life with a hope of saving the Everglades' pristine beauty and his own troubled soul. (Rev: BL 11/15/95*) [770]

SOUTHWEST

5486 Rothschild, Mary Logan, and Pamela Claire Hronek. *Doing What the Day Brought: An Oral History of Arizona Women* (9–adult). 1992, Univ. of Arizona $40 (0-8165-1032-6); paper $16.95 (0-8165-1276-0). The role of women in the development of the American West, specifically Arizona pioneers. (Rev: BL 2/1/92) [305.4]

Physical and Applied Sciences

General and Miscellaneous

5487 Aaseng, Nathan. *Yearbooks in Science: 1930–1939* (5–8). 1995, Twenty-First Century $16.98 (0-8050-3433-1). An overview of human achievements in science and technology from 1930 to 1939. (Rev: BL 12/1/95; SLJ 1/96) [609]

5488 Ardley, Neil. *Diccionario de la ciencia* (5–9). Tr. by Ambrosio Garcia. 1994, Plaza & Janés (Barcelona, Spain) $29.95 (84-226-4818-0). Defines more than 2,000 important words and concepts in physics, chemistry, technology, and mathematics, with color photos, drawings, charts, and an index. English title: *Dictionary of Science*. (Rev: BL 10/15/95)

5489 Asimov, Isaac, and Janet Asimov. *Frontiers II: More Recent Discoveries about Life, Earth, Space, and the Universe* (9–adult). 1993, Dutton/Truman Talley $23 (0-525-93631-9). Asimov's last work, completed by his wife, contains his *Los Angeles Times* science columns. (Rev: BL 7/93) [500]

5490 Corben, Bert. *The Struggle to Understand: A History of Human Wonder and Discovery* (9–adult). 1992, Prometheus $29.95 (0-87975-683-7). How controversial science concepts evolved through history despite opposition. (Rev: BL 2/1/92) [509]

5491 *Del "big bang" a la electricidad* (5–8). (Biblioteca interactiva/Mundo maravilloso) Tr. from French by Fernando Bort. 1994, Ediciones SM (Madrid, Spain) $14.95 (84-348-4209-2). This "interactive" title includes numerous foldouts, flaps, and transparent plastic overlays with detailed color illustrations and a simple text. English title: *From the "Big Bang" to Electricity*. (Rev: BL 10/15/95)

5492 Duensing, Edward, and A. B. Millmoss. *Backyard and Beyond: A Guide for Discovering the Outdoors* (9–adult). 1992, Fulcrum paper $14.95 (1-55591-071-8). Descriptions of various animals, plants, and insects, with tips on how to observe and track them. (Rev: BL 3/15/92) [508.2]

5493 Flaste, Richard, ed. *The New York Times Book of Science Literacy: What You Need to Know from Newton to the Knuckleball* (9–adult). 1991, Times Books $24.95 (0-8129-1880-0). Articles from a weekly science column in the *New York Times* that explain what's happening in the science community and how it affects us. (Rev: BL 1/15/91; SHS) [500]

5494 Gallant, Roy A. *A Young Person's Guide to Science: Ideas That Change the World* (5–10). 1993, Macmillan $16.95 (0-02-735775-9). (Rev: BL 9/1/93; MJHS; SLJ 10/93) [500]

5495 Goodman, Billy. *Natural Wonders and Disasters* (5–7). (Planet Earth) 1991, Little, Brown $17.95 (0-316-32016-1). An explanation of earthquakes, volcanoes, floods, hurricanes, typhoons, with many photos. (Rev: BL 12/1/91; SLJ 1/92) [550]

5496 Hartmann, William. *The History of the Earth: An Illustrated Chronicle of an Evolving Planet* (9–adult). 1991, Workman $35 (1-56305-122-2); paper $19.95 (0-89480-756-0). Illustrated with paintings of often unseen sights, this story of the Earth's coming of age draws on the latest scientific theories. (Rev: BL 11/1/91) [525]

5497 Hawking, Stephen, ed. *Stephen Hawking's A Brief History of Time: A Reader's Companion* (9–adult). 1992, Bantam $25 (0-553-07772-4). A guide to help readers understand the complex ideas presented in Hawking's previous book. (Rev: BL 5/1/92; SHS) [523.1]

5498 Hehner, Barbara Embury. *Blue Planet* (7–12). (Wide World) 1992, Harcourt/Smithsonian $17.95 (0-15-200423-8). An examination of the interdependent systems that make up the planet Earth, including plate tectonics, volcanoes, weather, satellites, and the ozone layer. (Rev: BL 11/15/92; SLJ 10/92) [508]

5499 Kerrod, Robin. *Material Resources* (5–8). (World's Resources) 1994, Thomson Learning $15.95 (1-56847-176-9). Contains illustrated 2-page articles on metals, forest resources and products, plant and animal fibers, plastics, glass, and ceramics. (Rev: BL 2/1/95) [670]

5500 Kuttner, Paul. *Science's Trickiest Questions: 402 Questions That Will Stump, Amuse, and Surprise* (9–adult). 1994, Holt/Owl paper $10.95 (0-8050-2873-0). Clear, concise summaries provide entertaining reading. (Rev: BL 4/1/94; SHS) [502]

5501 McGowen, Tom. *Yearbooks in Science: 1900–1919* (5–8). 1995, Twenty-First Century $16.98 (0-8050-3431-5). An overview of human achievements in science and technology from 1900 to 1919. (Rev: BL 12/1/95; SLJ 1/96) [609]

5502 Newton, David E. *Yearbooks in Science: 1920–1929* (5–8). 1995, Twenty-First Century $16.98 (0-8050-3432-3). An overview of human achievements in science and technology from 1920 to 1929. (Rev: BL 12/1/95; SLJ 1/96) [609]

5503 Nye, Bill. *Bill Nye the Science Guy's Big Blast of Science* (5–8). 1993, Addison-Wesley paper $12.95 (0-201-60864-2). Science information presented in an entertaining manner, including such subjects as electricity, weather, space, matter, heat, light, fundamental forces, and scientific method. (Rev: BL 2/15/94) [507.8]

5504 Oleksy, Walter. *Science and Medicine* (6–12). (Information Revolution) 1995, Facts on File $17.95 (0-8160-3076-6). A summary of computer technology used in medicine and in science classrooms. (Rev: BL 11/15/95; SLJ 11/95) [502]

5505 Paul, Richard. *A Handbook to the Universe: Explorations of Matter, Energy, Space, and Time for Beginning Scientific Thinkers* (9–12). 1993, Chicago Review paper $14.95 (1-55652-172-3). A straightforward presentation of the principles of physics and astronomy that puts scientists and their work in a historic context. (Rev: BL 1/1/94; BTA) [500.2]

5506 Shroyer, Jo Ann. *Quarks, Critters, and Chaos: What Science Terms Really Mean* (9–adult). 1993, Prentice-Hall $25 (0-671-84744-9); paper $15 (0-671-84745-7). Provides accessible definitions of numerous scientific terms, theories, and discoveries. (Rev: BL 3/15/93) [501.4]

5507 Spangenburg, Ray. *The History of Science from 1895 to 1994* (7–12). 1994, Facts on File $18.95 (0-8160-2742-0). Surveys scientific progress, discussing atomic energy, relativity, space exploration, genetics, and the achievements of various scientists. (Rev: BL 9/1/94; SHS; VOYA 10/94) [509]

5508 Spangenburg, Ray, and Diane K. Moser. *The History of Science in the Eighteenth Century* (9–12). (On the Shoulders of Giants) 1993, Facts on File $17.95 (0-8160-2740-4). (Rev: BL 11/1/93; MJHS) [509]

5509 Stone, Judith. *Light Elements: Essays in Science from Gravity to Levity* (9–adult). 1991, Ballantine paper $8 (0-345-36608-5). (Rev: BL 4/15/91; SHS) [502]

5510 Tomb, Howard. *MicroAliens: Dazzling Journeys with an Electron Microscope* (6–10). Illus. 1993, Farrar $16 (0-374-34960-6). Tomb presents black-and-white photos of ordinary objects as seen through an electron microscope, as well as an introduction to the electron microscope's history. (Rev: BL 12/1/93; BTA; SLJ 1/94) [574]

5511 Trefil, James. *1,001 Things Everyone Should Know about Science* (9–adult). 1992, Doubleday $20 (0-385-24795-8). Descriptive entries on biology, physics, astronomy, and other fields of science, that contain science-related facts and interesting observations. (Rev: BL 12/15/91; SHS) [500]

5512 Wollard, Kathy. *How Come?* (5–9). 1993, Workman $10.95 (1-56305-324-1). Provides answers to some common and not-so-common questions about ordinary things. (Rev: BL 5/1/94) [500]

5513 Zimmerman, Barry E., and David J. Zimmerman. *Why Nothing Can Travel Faster Than Light . . . and Other Explorations in Nature's Curiosity Shop* (9–adult). 1993, Contemporary paper $10.95 (0-8092-3821-7). Designed to appeal to "scientific illiterates," this book covers the basics of scientific thought, from Newton to quantum mechanics. (Rev: BL 9/15/93) [500]

5514 Zotti, Ed. *Know It All! Everything They Should Have Told You in School but Didn't* (9–adult). 1993, Ballantine paper $8 (0-345-36232-2). Zotti provides no-nonsense, sometimes amusing answers to questions about animals, weather, space, time, and many other subjects. (Rev: BL 7/93) [031]

Experiments and Projects

5515 Berger, Joseph. *The Young Scientists: America's Future and the Winning of the Westinghouse* (9–adult). 1994, Addison-Wesley $21.95 (0-201-63255-1). Berger discusses the importance of science-oriented high schools in the United States and the success of students from these schools in the annual Westinghouse Science Talent Search. (Rev: BL 12/1/93; VOYA 6/94) [507.1]

5516 Bleifeld, Maurice. *Botany Projects for Young Scientists* (5–10). (Projects for Young Scientists) 1992, Watts LB $13.40 (0-531-11046-X). (Rev: BL 2/1/93; SHS) [581]

5517 Bochinski, Julianne Blair. *The Complete Handbook of Science Fair Projects* (7–12). 1991, Wiley paper $12.95 (0-471-52728-9). (Rev: BL 3/15/91; MJHS; SHS; SLJ 7/91) [507.9]

5518 Cash, Terry. *101 Physics Tricks: Fun Experiments with Everyday Materials* (5–7). 1993, Sterling $14.95 (0-8069-8786-3). Contains exercises that demonstrate laws of forces, air, and sound. (Rev: BL 3/1/93; MJHS; SLJ 2/94) [530]

5519 Cobb, Vicki. *Fun and Games: Stories Science Photos Tell* (5–7). (Stories Science Photos Tell) 1991, Lothrop LB $15.88 (0-688-09316-7). Organized according to scientific principle (gravity, mass, etc.), the text and photos bring 12 scientific phenomena to life. (Rev: BL 9/1/91) [507.8]

5520 Cobb, Vicki, and Josh Cobb. *Light Action: Amazing Experiments with Optics* (5–8). 1993, HarperCollins LB $14.89 (0-06-021437-6). Basic principles of optics and activities for demonstration. (Rev: BL 1/15/94; MJHS; VOYA 6/94) [535]

5521 Dashefsky, H. Steven. *Zoology: 49 Science Fair Projects* (8–12). 1994, TAB $19.95 (0-07-015682-4); paper $10.95 (0-07-015683-2). (Rev: BL 1/15/95; SHS; SLJ 3/95) [591]

5522 Dashefsky, H. Steven. *Zoology: High School Science Fair Experiments* (7–12). 1995, TAB paper $12.95 (0-07-015687-5). Twenty zoology experiments are presented in the categories of people-related, biocides, animal lives, and animals and the environment. (Rev: BL 6/1–15/95; SHS) [591]

5523 Drake, Jane, and Ann Love. *The Kids' Summer Handbook* (5–7). Illus. 1994, Ticknor & Fields $15.95 (0-395-68711-X). A book of outdoor activities and indoor rainy-day craft projects. (Rev: BL 4/1/94; MJHS; SLJ 6/94) [790.1]

5524 Dykstra, Mary. *The Amateur Zoologist: Explorations and Investigations* (6–10). (Amateur Science) 1994, Watts LB $12.90 (0-531-11162-8). (Rev: BL 9/15/94; MJHS) [591]

5525 Gardner, Robert. *Experimenting with Energy Conservation* (7–10). (Venture) 1992, Watts LB $12.90 (0-531-12538-6). Offers 31 energy conservation investigations, many of which will make good science fair projects. (Rev: BL 3/15/93; MJHS; SLJ 7/93) [621.042]

5526 Gardner, Robert. *Experimenting with Light* (9–12). (Venture) 1991, Watts LB $12.40 (0-531-12520-3). The author offers avenues for exploring light through playful activities as well as through more goal-oriented experiments. (Rev: BL 5/15/91; MJHS; SHS; SLJ 7/91) [535]

5527 Gardner, Robert. *Experimenting with Sound* (9–12). (Venture) 1991, Watts $12.40 (0-531-12503-3). Presents a wide range of activities for investigating such properties of sound as speed, resonance, frequency, intensity, and acoustics. (Rev: BL 12/15/91; MJHS; SHS; SLJ 2/92) [534]

5528 Gardner, Robert. *Experimenting with Water* (7–12). (Venture) 1993, Watts LB $13.40 (0-531-12549-1). The unusual properties of water are described in these simple experiments and "puzzlers" that provide clear explanations of scientific concepts. (Rev: BL 2/15/94; MJHS; SLJ 4/94) [546]

5529 Gardner, Robert. *Famous Experiments You Can Do* (6–12). 1990, Watts LB $12.90 (0-531-10883-X). Most of the equipment needed for these experiments—once performed by the likes of Galileo, Newton, Lavoisier, and Harvey—can be found in the home. (Rev: BL 2/15/91; MJHS; SHS; SLJ 4/91) [530]

5530 Gardner, Robert. *Robert Gardner's Favorite Science Experiments* (5–8). 1993, Watts LB $12.90 (0-531-11038-9); paper $6.95 (0-531-15255-3). This how-to manual outlines materials, defines terms, and explains the methods used in over 30 easy-to-perform experiments. (Rev: BL 5/15/93; MJHS) [507.8]

5531 Gardner, Robert. *Science Projects about Chemistry* (6–9). 1994, Enslow LB $17.95 (0-89490-531-7). Gardner conveys the fun of learning in this volume about the uses of chemistry. (Rev: BL 1/1/95; MJHS; SLJ 2/95) [540]

5532 Gardner, Robert, and Eric Kemer. *Making and Using Scientific Models* (9–12). (Experimental Science) 1993, Watts $13.40 (0-531-10986-0). The authors discuss specific models in the fields of astronomy, physics, biology, chemistry, and engineering and encourage students to think creatively and analytically about designing models for science fairs. (Rev: BL 9/1/93; MJHS) [507.8]

5533 Goodwin, Peter H. *Physics Projects for Young Scientists* (9–12). (Projects for Young Scientists) 1991, Watts LB $12.90 (0-531-11070-2). This brief introduction to physics focuses on mechanics, molecules, and electricity. Includes science fair project guidelines. (Rev: BL 1/1/92; MJHS; SLJ 2/92) [530]

5534 Gutnik, Martin J. *Experiments That Explore Acid Rain* (5–8). (Investigate!) Illus. 1992, Millbrook LB $13.90 (1-56294-115-1). (Rev: BL 2/1/92; MJHS) [628.5]

5535 Gutnik, Martin J. *Experiments That Explore Oil Spills* (5–8). (Investigate!) 1991, Millbrook LB $13.90 (1-56294-012-0). A study of water ecology and the problems of separating oil from water, with related experiments. (Rev: BL 12/1/91) [551.52]

5536 Gutnik, Martin J. *Experiments That Explore the Greenhouse Effect* (5–8). (Impact) 1991, Millbrook LB $13.90 (1-56294-013-9). An exploration of the properties of air, the causes of the greenhouse effect, and the results of global warming, with related experiments. (Rev: BL 12/1/91) [363.7]

5537 Harlow, Rosie, and Gareth Morgan. *Cycles and Seasons* (5–7). (Fun with Science) 1991, Watts LB $12.90 (0-531-19123-0). (Rev: BL 3/15/92) [525.5]

5538 Harlow, Rosie, and Gareth Morgan. *Trees and Leaves* (5–7). (Fun with Science) 1991, Watts LB $12.90 (0-531-19126-5). (Rev: BL 3/15/92) [582.16]

5539 Haslam, Andrew. *Building* (5–7). (Make It Work!) 1994, Thomson Learning $15.95 (1-56847-259-5). Instructions for building projects using common materials, including designs for tents, igloos, model bridges, and model cablecars. (Rev: BL 10/15/94; SLJ 11/94) [624.1]

5540 Iritz, Maxine Haren. *Blue-Ribbon Science Fair Projects* (7–12). 1991, TAB $23.95 (0-8306-7615-5); paper $14.95 (0-8306-3615-3). A variety of science fair projects for the novice are presented with charts, graphs, photos, and a chapter on choosing a topic. (Rev: BL 9/15/91) [507.8]

5541 Joyce, Katherine. *Astounding Optical Illusions* (5–7). 1994, Sterling $12.95 (0-8069-0431-3). Explains optical illusions and how they are perceived by the brain. Includes many illustrations containing hidden pictures. (Rev: BL 8/94) [153.74]

5542 Lawlor, Elizabeth P. *Discover Nature at Sundown: Things to Know and Things to Do* (9–adult). 1995, Stackpole paper $12.95 (0-8117-2527-8). Sensory awareness for nature lovers to track and observe creatures at night. (Rev: BL 2/15/95) [591.5]

5543 Leon, George de Lucenay. *Electronics Projects for Young Scientists* (9–12). (Projects for Young Scientists) 1991, Watts LB $12.90 (0-531-11071-0). An introduction to the electronics field, including a brief history and basic principles. Illustrated instructions for a series of progressively difficult projects. (Rev: BL 1/1/92; SLJ 4/92) [621.381]

5544 Markle, Sandra. *Science to the Rescue* (5–7). 1994, Atheneum $15.95 (0-689-31783-2). Following an explanation of the scientific method, the author identifies 8 problematic areas facing people today and provides a solution, called a science rescue. (Rev: BL 3/15/94; SLJ 4/94) [507.8]

5545 Mebane, Robert C., and Thomas R. Rybolt. *Adventures with Atoms and Molecules, Vol. 5: Chemistry Experiments for Young People* (7–10). 1995, Enslow LB $16.95 (0-89490-606-2). A basic user's guide to start young people thinking scientifically, with ideas for science fair projects. (Rev: BL 12/1/95) [540]

5546 Mebane, Robert C., and Thomas R. Rybolt. *Adventures with Atoms and Molecules, Vol. 3: Chemistry Experiments for Young People* (5–8). 1991, Enslow LB $16.95 (0-89490-254-7). Beginning chemistry experiments, with lists of materials needed, an outline of procedures, and discussion questions. (Rev: BL 6/1/91; MJHS; SLJ 7/91) [540]

5547 Millspaugh, Ben. *Aviation and Space Science Projects* (7–12). 1991, TAB $16.95 (0-8306-2157-1); paper $9.95 (0-8306-2156-3). A series of experiments for young people who want to learn more about aviation and spaceflight. (Rev: BL 1/15/92) [507]

5548 Newton, David E. *Consumer Chemistry Projects for Young Scientists* (9–12). (Projects for Young Scientists) 1991, Watts LB $12.90 (0-531-11011-7). Suitable experiments designed to answer questions about chemicals found in household products, such as foods, detergents, personal-care products, and medicines. (Rev: BL 6/15/91; MJHS; SLJ 11/91) [540]

5549 Newton, David E. *Making and Using Scientific Equipment* (9–12). (Experimental Science) 1993, Watts $13.40 (0-531-11176-8). (Rev: BL 9/1/93; VOYA 2/94) [681]

5550 Newton, David E. *Science/Technology/Society Projects for Young Scientists* (9–12). (Projects for Young Scientists) 1991, Watts $12.90 (0-531-11047-8). An examination of science and technology issues that relate to everyday life, with suggestions for projects on such topics as population, nutrition, and environmental pollution. (Rev: BL 12/15/91; SHS; SLJ 3/92) [507.8]

5551 Nye, Bill, and Ian Saunders. *Bill Nye the Science Guy's Consider the Following: A Way Cool Set of Science Questions, Answers, and Ideas to Ponder* (5–7). 1995, Disney LB $13.89 (0-7868-5035-3); paper $9.95 (0-7868-4054-4). A conversational tone directs the reader to the question that heads up each 4-page section. (Rev: BL 12/1/95) [507.8]

5552 Parker, Steve. *How the Body Works* (5–7). 1994, Reader's Digest $25 (0-89577-575-1). (Rev: BL 11/15/94*; SLJ 10/94) [612]

5553 Rainis, Kenneth G. *Exploring with a Magnifying Glass* (7–12). 1991, Watts LB $12.40 (0-531-12508-4). An introduction to how magnification works and a series of projects exploring photos, plants, minerals, fabrics, and more. (Rev: BL 1/15/92; SLJ 4/92) [507.8]

5554 Richards, Roy. *101 Science Tricks: Fun Experiments with Everyday Materials* (5–8). Illus. 1992, Sterling $14.95 (0-8069-8388-4). Fun, easy-to-perform science and math activities, with notes for parents and teachers. (Rev: BL 2/1/92; SLJ 1/92) [507.8]

5555 Rybolt, Thomas R., and Robert C. Mebane. *Environmental Experiments about Land* (5–7). (Science Experiments for Young People) 1993, Enslow LB $16.95 (0-89490-411-6). Presents activities dealing with land, including materials, procedures, observations, discussion, and other things to try. (Rev: BL 12/15/93; MJHS; SLJ 2/94) [631.4]

5556 Rybolt, Thomas R., and Robert C. Mebane. *Environmental Experiments about Life* (5–7). (Science Experiments for Young People) 1993, Enslow LB $16.95 (0-89490-412-4). Presents activities dealing with life, including materials, procedures, observations, discussion, and other things to try. (Rev: BL 12/15/93; SLJ 2/94) [574.5]

5557 Sheldrake, Rupert. *Seven Experiments That Could Change the World: A Do-It-Yourself Guide to Revolutionary Science* (9–adult). 1995, Putnam/Riverhead $23.95 (1-57322-014-0). Allows nonscientists to participate in the dialogue that frequently challenges conventional science. (Rev: BL 9/1/95) [507]

5558 Smith, Bruce, and David McKay. *Geology Projects for Young Scientists* (5–10). (Projects for Young Scientists) 1992, Watts LB $13.40 (0-531-11012-5). (Rev: BL 3/1/93; MJHS; SHS) [550]

5559 Van Cleave, Janice. *Janice Van Cleave's A+ Projects in Biology: Winning Experiments for Science Fairs and Extra Credit* (6–10). 1993, Wiley paper $12.95 (0-471-58628-5). Offers a variety of experiments in 3 general areas: botany, zoology, and the human body. (Rev: BL 1/15/94; BTA) [574]

5560 Van Cleave, Janice. *Janice Van Cleave's A+ Projects in Chemistry: Winning Experiments for Science Fairs and Extra Credit* (6–10). 1993, Wiley $24.95 (0-471-58631-5); paper $12.95 (0-471-58630-7). Thirty experiments that investigate such topics as calories, acids, and electrolytes, among others. (Rev: BL 12/1/95; BTA; SLJ 4/94)

5561 Van Cleave, Janice. *Janice Van Cleave's Electricity: Mind-Boggling Experiments You Can Turn into Science Fair Projects* (5–7). 1994, Wiley paper $9.95 (0-471-31010-7). Twenty experiments with electricity, including experiments with molecules, gravity, and magnets. (Rev: BL 12/1/94; SLJ 11/94)

5562 Van Cleave, Janice. *Janice Van Cleave's Volcanoes: Mind-Boggling Experiments You Can Turn into Science Fair Projects* (5–7). (Van Cleave's Spectacular Science Projects) 1994, Wiley paper $9.95 (0-471-30811-0). Step-by-step instructions for performing 20 experiments that explore volcanic eruptions, all using common materials found at home or in school. (Rev: BL 7/94; SLJ 8/94) [551.2]

5563 Wong, Ovid K. *Experimenting with Electricity and Magnetism* (7–12). 1993, Watts LB $12.90 (0-531-12547-5). (Rev: BL 8/93; SLJ 7/93; VOYA 10/93) [537]

5564 Wood, Robert W. *Physics for Kids: 49 Easy Experiments with Electricity and Magnetism* (5–7). 1990, TAB $16.95 (0-8306-8412-3); paper $9.95 (0-8306-3412-6). (Rev: BL 2/15/91; MJHS) [537]

5565 Zubrowski, Bernie. *Making Waves: Finding Out about Rhythmic Motion* (5–8). (Boston Children's Museum Activity Book) 1994, Morrow/Mulberry LB $13.96 (0-688-11787-2). Suggests ways to explore and experiment with waves, including instructions on building a simple wave machine. Shows how to observe waves in water, cloth materials, and string. (Rev: BL 7/94; MJHS; SLJ 8/94) [532]

Astronomy and Space Science

General and Miscellaneous

5566 Asimov, Isaac. *Isaac Asimov's Guide to Earth and Space* (9–adult). 1991, Random $20 (0-679-40437-6). Explains the workings of supernovas, comets, stars, planets, galaxies, and other cosmic phenomena. (Rev: BL 10/15/91; SHS) [520]

5567 Berman, Bob. *Secrets of the Night Sky: The Most Amazing Things in the Universe You Can See with the Naked Eye* (9–adult). 1995, Morrow $23 (0-688-12727-4). Berman makes it clear that what we see in the night sky is a wonderful collection of heavenly bodies. (Rev: BL 2/15/95) [520]

5568 Dauber, Philip M., and Richard A. Muller. *The Three Big Bangs: Comet Crashes, Exploding Stars, and the Creation of the Universe* (9–adult). 1996, Addison-Wesley $25 (0-201-40752-3). A description of the 3 main events that brought life to planet Earth. (Rev: BL 12/1/95) [523.1]

5569 Dickinson, Terence, and Alan Dyer. *The Backyard Astronomer's Guide* (9–adult). 1991, Camden House $39.95 (0-921820-11-9). Gives detailed reviews of optical equipment and discusses techniques of observation and astrophotography. (Rev: BL 11/1/91) [520]

5570 Goldsmith, Donald. *The Astronomers: Companion Book to the PBS Television Series* (9–adult). 1991, St. Martin's $24.95 (0-312-05380-0). (Rev: BL 3/15/91; SHS) [520]

5571 Gustafson, John. *Planets, Moons and Meteors: The Young Stargazer's Guide to the Galaxy* (5–8). 1992, Messner LB $12.98 (0-671-72534-3); paper $6.95 (0-671-72535-1). This guidebook tells how and when to make observations of the solar system and provides basic facts on the planets. (Rev: BL 11/1/92) [523]

5572 Hatchett, Clint. *Discover Planetwatch: A Year-Round Viewing Guide to the Night Sky with a Make-Your-Own Planetfinder* (9–adult). 1993, Hyperion paper $9.95 (1-56282-874-6). Projects, some without telescopes, for serious amateur astronomers. (Rev: BL 7/93) [523.2]

5573 Hathaway, Nancy. *The Friendly Guide to the Universe* (9–adult). 1994, Viking $21.95 (0-670-83944-2). An examination of the solar system, black holes, quasars, and the accomplishments of such scientists as Hawking and Hubble. (Rev: BL 3/15/94) [520.2]

5574 Lancaster-Brown, Peter. *Skywatch: Eyes-on Activities for Getting to Know the Stars, Planets and Galaxies* (6–9). 1993, Sterling $14.95 (0-8069-8627-1). A discussion of astronomy, including information about light, heavenly bodies, historical discoveries, and purchasing viewing equipment. (Rev: BL 3/1/94; SLJ 1/94) [523]

5575 Lightman, Alan. *Time for the Stars: Astronomy in the 1990s* (9–adult). 1992, Viking $19 (0-670-83976-0). This history of astronomy points to the 1990s and beyond as a period of unparalleled discovery. (Rev: BL 12/1/91) [520]

5576 North, John. *The Norton History of Astronomy and Cosmology* (9–adult). (Norton History of Science) 1994, Norton $35 (0-393-03656-1); paper $18.95 (0-393-31193-7). Examines the sciences of astronomy and cosmology from ancient Egypt to the present and the evolution beyond myth and superstition. (Rev: BL 8/94; SHS) [520]

5577 Rasmussen, Richard Michael. *Mysteries of Space* (6–10). (Great Mysteries) 1994, Greenhaven LB $14.95 (1-56510-097-2). (Rev: BL 4/15/94; MJHS) [520]

5578 Savage, Marshall T. *The Millennial Project: Colonizing the Galaxy—in 8 Easy Steps* (9–adult). 1993, Empyrean (1616 Glenarm Place, Suite 101, Denver, CO 80202) $24.95 (0-9633914-8-8); paper $18.95 (0-9633914-9-6). An 8-step program, from space colonies in the sea through orbiting space colonies. (Rev: BL 1/15/93*) [629.47]

5579 Schaaf, Fred. *The Amateur Astronomer: Explorations and Investigations* (6–10). (Amateur Science) 1994, Watts LB $12.90 (0-531-11138-5). (Rev: BL 9/15/94; MJHS) [520]

5580 Steele, Philip. *Astronomy* (5–8). (Pocket Facts) 1991, Macmillan/Crestwood LB $10.95 (0-89686-586-X). This introduction to astronomy includes easily understandable facts and photos. (Rev: BL 3/15/92) [520]

5581 Tyson, Nell De Grasse. *Universe Down to Earth* (9–adult). 1994, Columbia Univ. $29.95 (0-231-07560-X). Tyson translates the fundamental meaning of various scientific models of the cosmos into language comprehensible to the general reader. (Rev: BL 5/1/94) [523.1]

Astronautics and Space Exploration

5582 Arnold, H. J. P., ed. *Man in Space: An Illustrated History of Space Flight* (9–adult). 1993, Smithmark $29.98 (0-8317-4491-X). (Rev: BL 8/93; BTA; MJHS) [629.4]

5583 Becklake, Sue. *Space, Stars, Planets and Spacecraft* (5–7). (See and Explore Library) Illus. 1991, Dorling Kindersley LB $12.99 (1-879431-29-7). Explains how spacecraft and satellites work, what they do, and their importance to life on Earth. (Rev: BL 3/1/92; SLJ 5/92) [629.4]

5584 Berliner, Don. *Our Future in Space* (5–7). 1991, Lerner LB $14.95 (0-8225-1592-X). Scientific research is emphasized in this discussion of space stations, trips to the moon and Mars, communication with extraterrestrials, and other topics. (Rev: BL 9/15/91; SLJ 8/91) [629.4]

5585 Booth, Nicholas. *Space: The Next 100 Years* (9–adult). 1990, Crown $21.95 (0-517-57764-X). A British aerospace journalist speculates on possible achievements in space over the next century. (Rev: BL 2/1/91; SHS) [629.4]

5586 Chaisson, Eric J. *The Hubble Wars: Astrophysics Meets Astropolitics in the Two Billion Dollar Struggle over the Hubble Space Technology* (9–adult). 1994, HarperCollins $27.50 (0-06-017114-6). The troubles between the Science Institute and the Goddard Space Flight Center, which worked on the Hubble. More than 100 photos. (Rev: BL 4/15/94) [522]

5587 Dolan, Terrance. *Probing Deep Space* (6–9). (World Explorers) 1993, Chelsea House $19.95 (0-7910-1326-X). (Rev: BL 10/1/93; MJHS) [520]

5588 Harris, Alan, and Paul Weissman. *The Great Voyager Adventure: A Guided Tour Through the Solar System* (5–8). 1990, Messner LB $14.98 (0-671-72538-6). Two scientists introduce novices to the missions, paths, and discoveries of the Voyager spacecraft. (Rev: BL 2/1/91; MJHS; SLJ 2/91) [523.4]

5589 Herbst, Judith. *Star Crossing: How to Get Around the Universe* (7–12). 1993, Atheneum $16.95 (0-689-31523-6). Explains rocket history, Einsteinian theory, the atomic bomb, quantum physics, time travel, black holes, and other factors that could influence interstellar travel. (Rev: BL 11/15/93; MJHS; SLJ 2/94; VOYA 2/94) [919.9]

5590 Kennedy, Gregory P. *Apollo to the Moon* (6–9). (World Explorers) 1992, Chelsea House LB $18.95 (0-7910-1322-7). (Rev: BL 9/1/92; MJHS) [629.45]

5591 Kettelkamp, Larry. *Living in Space* (5–7). 1993, Morrow $14 (0-688-10018-X). After looking at past and current space efforts, the future of the U.S. space exploration program, including colonization of Mars, is speculated upon. (Rev: BL 10/1/93; MJHS) [629.4]

5592 Lovell, Jim, and Jeffrey Kluger. *Lost Moon: The Perilous Voyage of Apollo 13* (9–adult). 1994, Houghton $22.95 (0-395-67029-2). The astronaut chronicles his harrowing, nearly fatal, failed mission to the moon, describing his crew's ingenuity in returning safely to Earth. (Rev: BL 9/15/94; SHS) [629.4]

5593 McCormick, Anita Louise. *Space Exploration* (6–8). (Overview) 1994, Lucent $14.95 (1-56006-149-9). (Rev: BL 7/94; MJHS) [919.9]

5594 Markle, Sandra. *Pioneering Space* (5–8). 1992, Atheneum $14.95 (0-689-31748-4). Presents basic information about space travel and spacecraft operation and speculates on how people will live in space. (Rev: BL 9/1/92; SLJ 2/93) [629.4]

5595 Maurer, Richard. *Rocket! How a Toy Launched the Space Age* (5–9). 1995, Crown $17 (0-517-59628-8). A discussion of the early science fiction speculations of rocket travel to the scientific trials and errors of 3 important scientists. (Rev: BL 4/15/95*; SLJ 6/95) [621.43]

5596 Neal, Valerie, and others. *Spaceflight: A Smithsonian Guide* (9–adult). (Smithsonian Guide) 1995, Macmillan $24.95 (0-02-860007-X); paper $18 (0-02-860040-1). The history of space flight beginning with Sputnik, as well as photos of missions, launches, landings, and designs. (Rev: BL 6/1–15/95) [629.4]

5597 Ordway, Frederick I., III, and Randy Liebermann, eds. *Blueprint for Space: Science Fiction to Science Fact* (9–adult). 1992, Smithsonian $60 (1-56098-072-9); paper $24.95 (1-56098-073-7). Over 20 contemporary authors tell the tale of space travel from the imaginings of ancient people to the real-life, present-day missions. (Rev: BL 2/1/92; SLJ 11/92) [629.4]

5598 Sagan, Carl. *Pale Blue Dot: A Vision of the Human Future in Space* (9–adult). 1994, Random $35 (0-679-43841-6). Examines space exploration and humankind's evolutionary urge to explore frontiers and search for our place in the universe. (Rev: BL 10/15/94*; SHS)

5599 Scott, Elaine. *Adventure in Space: The Flight to Fix the Hubble* (5–7). 1995, Hyperion LB $16.89 (0-7868-2031-4). The 1993 *Endeavor* mission to fix the Hubble telescope is explored with full-color photos and descriptions of the problem, the astronauts, the launch, flight, and completion of the mission. Awards: SLJ Best Book. (Rev: BL 7/95*; SLJ 4/95) [522]

5600 Scott, Phil. *The Shoulders of Giants: A History of Human Flight to 1919* (9–adult). 1995, Addison-Wesley $23 (0-201-62722-1). Charts the development of flight from 1400 B.C. to the end of World War I, including portraits of Octave Chanute, Otto Lilienthal, Hiram Maxim, Clement Ader, and the Wright Brothers. (Rev: BL 7/95) [629.13]

5601 Shepard, Alan, and Deke Slayton. *Moon Shot: The Inside Story of America's Race to the Moon* (9–adult). 1994, Turner $21.95 (1-878685-54-6). Two of America's most respected astronauts recall the space program and portray the great bond uniting the original Mercury Seven. (Rev: BL 3/15/94; BTA; SHS) [629.45]

5602 Steele, Philip. *Space Travel* (5–8). (Pocket Facts) 1991, Macmillan/Crestwood LB $10.95 (0-89686-585-1). An introduction to space flight, packed with facts and photos. (Rev: BL 3/15/92) [629.4]

5603 Verba, Joan Marie. *Voyager: Exploring the Outer Planets* (6–12). 1991, Lerner LB $14.95 (0-8225-1597-0). Details the travels of Voyagers 1 and 2, launched in 1977. Includes information on images taken of Jupiter, Saturn, Uranus, and Neptune. (Rev: BL 1/1/92; SLJ 11/91; YR) [523.4]

5604 Vogt, Gregory. *Magellan and the Radar Mapping of Venus* (6–10). (Missions in Space) 1992, Millbrook LB $15.90 (1-56294-146-1). (Rev: BL 8/92; MJHS) [523]

5605 Vogt, Gregory. *Viking and the Mars Landing* (6–10). 1991, Millbrook LB $14.90 (1-878841-32-7). (Rev: BL 3/1/91; MJHS) [629.4354]

5606 Walter, William J. *Space Age* (9–adult). 1992, Random $30 (0-679-40295-0). A companion volume to the PBS series celebrating space exploration and pioneers. Many color photos. (Rev: BL 9/1/92; BTA) [629.4]

Comets, Meteors, and Asteroids

5607 Gallant, Roy A. *The Day the Sky Split Apart: Investigating a Cosmic Mystery* (7–12). 1995, Atheneum $16 (0-689-80323-0). An examination of the Tunguska meteorite that exploded over Siberia in 1908 and subsequent research on this "cosmic mystery." (Rev: BL 12/1/95; SLJ 11/95; VOYA 4/96) [523.5]

5608 Hutchinson, Robert, and Andrew Graham, eds. *Meteorites* (9–adult). 1994, Sterling paper $10.95 (0-8069-0489-5). An illustrated presentation in question-and-answer format of information on natural objects that fall from space. (Rev: BL 1/1/94; MJHS; SLJ 5/94) [523.5]

5609 Kraske, Robert. *Asteroids: Invaders from Space* (5–7). 1995, Atheneum $15 (0-689-31860-X). Presents facts about asteroids, including past collisions, future collision scenarios, and land formations created by asteroids. (Rev: BL 7/95; SLJ 9/95) [523.4]

5610 Yeomans, Donald. *Comets: A Chronological History of Observation, Science, Myth, and Folklore* (9–adult). 1991, Wiley $35 (0-471-61011-9). Examines the origins of comets and current scientific theories surrounding them. (Rev: BL 2/1/91; SHS) [523.6]

Earth and the Moon

5611 Comins, Neil F. *What If the Moon Didn't Exist? Voyages to Worlds the Earth Might Have*

Been (9–adult). 1993, HarperCollins $20 (0-06-016864-1). Comins demonstrates the importance of the moon to Earth's structure by contrasting our world to hypothetical Earths where there is no moon, the moon is closer to the Earth, and other scenarios. (Rev: BL 11/15/93*) [523.2]

5612 Haddock, Patricia. *Mysteries of the Moon* (6–10). (Great Mysteries: Opposing Viewpoints) 1992, Greenhaven LB $13.95 (0-89908-094-4). (Rev: BL 2/15/93; MJHS) [523.3]

5613 Ride, Sally, and Tam O'Shaughnessy. *The Third Planet: Exploring the Earth from Space* (5–7). 1994, Crown LB $15.99 (0-517-59362-9). Uses color photos and diagrams to explore Earth's oceans, deserts, rain forests, atmosphere, storms, and clouds from a unique perspective. Awards: BL Editors' Choice. (Rev: BL 7/94*; MJHS; SLJ 7/94) [525]

5614 Strain, Priscilla, and Frederick Engle. *Looking at Earth* (9–adult). 1992, Turner $39.95 (1-878685-24-4). Nine major areas of Earth are shown in detailed color photos and satellite images, with descriptive text. (Rev: BL 10/1/92) [525]

Sun and the Solar System

5615 Beebe, Reta. *Jupiter: The Giant Planet* (9–adult). 1994, Smithsonian $29.95 (1-56098-417-1). Provides information on our solar system's largest planet, including its Great Red Spot, sunlike properties, rings, moon, atmosphere, and magnetic field. (Rev: BL 9/1/94; SHS) [523.4]

5616 Cattermole, Peter. *Mars: The Story of the Red Planet* (9–adult). 1992, Chapman & Hall $35 (0-412-44140-3). A detailed, technical look at the scientific study of the planet, filled with photos, graphs, and charts. (Rev: BL 10/1/92) [523.43]

5617 Cooper, Henry S. F. *The Evening Star: Venus Observed* (9–adult). 1993, Farrar $22 (0-374-15000-1). An account of the 1989 Magellan spacecraft launched to gather data on Venus. (Rev: BL 7/93) [523.4]

5618 Corrick, James A. *Mars* (8–12). 1991, Watts LB $12.40 (0-531-12528-9). Information on Martian geology, water, and climate, as well as on NASA's exploration missions to the "red planet." (Rev: BL 6/1/91; SLJ 9/91) [523.4]

5619 Dickinson, Terence. *Other Worlds: A Beginner's Guide to Planets and Moons* (5–8). 1995, Firefly Books LB $19.95 (1-895565-71-5); paper $9.95 (1-895565-70-7). A handy guide, more personal and enthusiastic than most astronomy books. (Rev: BL 11/15/95) [523.4]

5620 Evans, Barry. *The Wrong Way Comet and Other Mysteries of Our Solar System: Essays* (9–adult). 1992, TAB $22.95 (0-8306-2679-4); paper $14.95 (0-8306-2670-0). An introduction to mysteries of the solar system in a series of informal essays. (Rev: BL 3/15/92) [523.2]

5621 Lauber, Patricia. *Journey to the Planets* (5–8). 1990, Crown LB $16.99 (0-517-58125-6). Information and insights into the solar system, including facts gathered after the Voyager fly-by of Neptune in 1989. (Rev: BL 1/1/91; MJHS) [523.4]

5622 Maurer, Richard. *The NOVA Space Explorer's Guide: Where to Go and What to See* (5–7). Rev. ed. 1991, Crown $18 (0-517-57758-5). A companion to the PBS television series. (Rev: BL 12/15/91) [919.9]

5623 Vogt, Gregory. *The Solar System: Facts and Exploration* (5–8). 1995, Twenty-First Century LB $18.98 (0-8050-3249-5). A readable guide to the planets and moons and other bodies in the solar system. Includes images from the Hubble telescope and explanations of terms. (Rev: BL 12/1/95; SLJ 11/95; VOYA 4/96) [523.2]

Stars

5624 Gustafson, John. *Stars, Clusters and Galaxies: The Young Stargazer's Guide to the Galaxy* (5–8). (Young Stargazer's Guide to the Galaxy) 1993, Simon & Schuster LB $12.98 (0-671-72536-X); paper $6.94 (0-671-72537-8). Introduces stars, binary stars, star clusters, nebulae, and galaxies and provides tips for viewing the night sky through binoculars and telescopes. (Rev: BL 7/93; BTA; SLJ 6/93; VOYA 10/93) [523.8]

Universe

5625 Barrow, John D. *The Origin of the Universe* (9–adult). (Science Masters) 1994, Basic Books $20 (0-465-05354-8). Explains how astronomers have used discoveries, including the expanding-universe theory and infrared radiation, to form a picture of the "big bang." (Rev: BL 10/1/94) [523.1]

5626 Bartuslak, Marcia. *Through a Universe Darkly: A Cosmic Tale of Ancient Ethers, Dark Matter, and the Fate of the Universe* (9–adult). 1993, HarperCollins $27.50 (0-06-018310-1). Describes science's investigation of the physical universe, from earliest history to the present-day search for astronomical dark matter. (Rev: BL 6/1–15/93) [523.1]

5627 Ferguson, Kitty. *Black Holes in Spacetime* (7–12). 1991, Watts LB $12.40 (0-531-12524-6). Presents evidence of the existence of black holes, traces the life cycle of a star, and takes readers on an imaginary journey of discovery. (Rev: BL 9/1/91; MJHS; SLJ 8/91) [523.8]

5628 Glover, David. *Universe* (5–7). (Make It Work! Science) 1995, Thomson Learning LB $15.95 (1-56847-348-6). (Rev: BL 10/15/95) [520]

5629 Gribbin, John. *In the Beginning: After COBE and Before the Big Bang* (9–adult). 1993, Little, Brown $22.95 (0-316-32833-2). Links terrestrial biological evolution to background microwave radiation, the observational proof of the big bang's existence. (Rev: BL 6/1–15/93; BTA) [523.1]

5630 Halpern, Paul. *Cosmic Wormholes: The Search for Interstellar Shortcuts* (9–adult). 1992, Dutton $21 (0-525-93477-4). Based on concepts and ideas from books, films, TV, and scientific theories, a case is made for instantaneous travel through time and space. (Rev: BL 9/15/92) [523.0]

5631 Hawking, Stephen. *Black Holes and Baby Universes and Other Essays* (9–adult). 1993, Bantam $21.95 (0-553-09523-4). (Rev: BL 8/93; BTA) [530.1]

5632 Lerner, Eric J. *The Big Bang Never Happened* (9–adult). 1991, Times Books $21.95 (0-8129-1853-3). (Rev: BL 3/15/91; SHS) [523.1]

5633 Miotto, Enrico. *The Universe: Origins and Evolution* (5–8). (Beginnings) 1995, Raintree/Steck-Vaughn LB $22.80 (0-8114-3334-X). (Rev: BL 4/15/95) [523.1]

5634 Overbye, Dennis. *Lonely Hearts of the Cosmos* (9–adult). 1991, HarperCollins $25 (0-06-015964-2). Cosmologists search for the origin and destiny of the universe. (Rev: BL 1/15/91; SHS) [523.1]

5635 Ronan, Colin A. *The Natural History of the Universe from the Big Bang to the End of Time* (9–adult). 1991, Macmillan $39.95 (0-02-604511-7). Current scientific theories on the creation of the universe are presented in this comprehensive review of astronomical events, as well as discussions of relativity theory, curved space-time, quasars, and the chemical essence of life. (Rev: BL 10/15/91; SHS) [520]

5636 Smoot, George, and Keay Davidson. *Wrinkles in Time* (9–adult). 1994, Morrow $25 (0-688-12330-9). Following post-Einsteinian thought, this experimental astrophysicist clears up misconceptions about the big bang, explains wrinkles in time, and tells us we're traveling at 600 km/sec toward a "supercluster." (Rev: BL 11/15/93*; BTA) [523.1]

5637 *Viaja por el universo* (5–8). (Biblioteca interactiva/Mundo maravilloso) Tr. from French by Fernando Bort. 1993, Ediciones SM (Madrid, Spain) $12.95 (84-348-4108-8). This "interactivo" title includes numerous foldouts, flaps, and transparent plastic overlays; detailed color illustrations; and a simple explanation of the universe. English title: *Travel Through the Universe*. (Rev: BL 10/1/94)

5638 *The Visual Dictionary of the Earth* (5–9). 1993, Dorling Kindersley $15.95 (1-56458-335-X). Double-page illustrated spreads describe the heavenly bodies in our universe, telescopes, and space and lunar exploration equipment. (Rev: BL 12/15/93; MJHS; SLJ 2/94) [550]

Biological Sciences

General and Miscellaneous

5639 Bowler, Peter J. *The Norton History of the Environmental Sciences* (9–adult). 1993, Norton $35 (0-393-03535-2); paper $15.95 (0-393-31042-6). Historical highlights and development of the environmental sciences. (Rev: BL 7/93) [363.7]

5640 Evans, Howard Ensign. *Pioneer Naturalists: The Discovery and Naming of North American Plants and Animals* (9–adult). 1993, Holt $22.50 (0-8050-2337-2). Contains brief biographical information on 75 naturalists and discusses the naming of North American plant and animal species. (Rev: BL 10/15/93) [508.7]

5641 Hoagland, Mahlon, and Bert Dodson. *The Way Life Works* (9–adult). 1995, Times Books $35 (0-8129-2020-1). A collaboration between Hoagland, a molecular biologist, and Dodson, an artist, emphasizing the unity of life rather than its diversity. (Rev: BL 12/1/95) [574]

5642 Horn, Bob, and W. P. Chips. *Dimension-5: Everything You Didn't Know You Didn't Know* (9–adult). 1992, Fithian (P.O. Box 1525, Santa Barbara, CA 93102) paper $9.95 (1-56474-007-2). Thought-provoking essays, both humorous and serious, on scientific, religious, and philosophical issues. (Rev: BL 2/15/92) [500]

5643 Lerner, Carol. *A Desert Year* (5–7). 1991, Morrow LB $13.88 (0-688-09383-3). An introduction to North American desert mammals, birds, reptiles, amphibians, arthropods, and plants of each season. (Rev: BL 11/1/91; SLJ 11/91) [574.5]

5644 Levin, Ted. *Blood Brook: A Naturalist's Home Ground* (9–adult). 1992, Chelsea Green Publishing (P.O. Box 428, White River Junction, VT 05001) $21.95 (0-930031-56-3); paper $14.95 (0-930031-60-1). Descriptions of natural environments and life in Vermont. (Rev: BL 9/15/92) [508.743]

5645 Markle, Sandra. *Exploring Autumn: A Season of Science Activities, Puzzlers, and Games* (5–7). 1991, Atheneum $14.95 (0-689-31620-8). Combines technical scientific information with history, myth, anecdotes, seasonal festival activities, and quizzes. (Rev: BL 11/1/91) [574.5]

5646 Murray, John A., ed. *American Nature Writing* (9–adult). 1994, Sierra Club paper $12 (0-87156-479-3). The first of what promises to be an annual anthology of writings (including poetry) about nature. (Rev: BL 4/15/94) [810]

5647 Murray, John A., ed. *Nature's New Voices* (9–adult). 1992, Fulcrum paper $15.95 (1-55591-117-X). Personal literary observations on natural history by contemporary generation of nature essayists. (Rev: BL 10/1/92) [508.73]

5648 Patent, Dorothy Hinshaw. *The Vanishing Feast: How Dwindling Genetic Diversity Threatens the World's Food Supply* (6–10). 1994, Harcourt $17.95 (0-15-292867-7). Explains the importance of maintaining plant and animal diversity. Describes experiments with genetic engineering and factory farming. (Rev: BL 10/1/94; BTA; SHS; SLJ 12/94; VOYA 4/95) [338.1]

5649 Peck, Robert McCracken. *Land of the Eagle: A Natural History of North America* (9–adult). 1991, BBC Books $30 (0-671-75596-X). A descriptive celebration of the North American terrain and animal and plant life as experienced by its native people and European settlers. (Rev: BL 11/15/91; SLJ 4/92) [508.7]

5650 Quinn, John R. *Wildlife Survivors: The Flora and Fauna of Tomorrow* (9–adult). 1994,

TAB $22.95 (0-8306-4346-X); paper $12.95 (0-8306-4345-1). A serious study that attempts to determine that plants and animals will continue to survive despite the encroachment of human civilization. (Rev: BL 3/1/94; SHS) [574.5]

5651 Sagan, Carl, and Ann Druyan. *Shadows of Forgotten Ancestors: A Search for Who We Are* (9–adult). 1992, Random $23 (0-394-53481-6). Traces the evolutionary ladder from microorganisms to more complex creatures, including humans. Awards: BL Editors' Choice. (Rev: BL 9/15/92*; SHS) [304.4]

5652 Sandak, Cass R. *Living Fossils* (5–9). (First Book) 1992, Watts LB $11.90 (0-531-20048-5). Discusses the complex idea of living fossils and their place in evolution and then considers particular species, from insects to fish to mammals. (Rev: BL 6/15/92; SLJ 7/92) [574]

5653 Whipple, A. B. C. *Critters: Adventures in Wildest Suburbia* (9–adult). 1994, St. Martin's $18.95 (0-312-10445-6). A lighthearted look at animals that coexist with humans and often invade their property. (Rev: BL 3/1/94; BTA; SLJ 7/94) [591.52]

5654 *The Wildlife Year* (9–adult). 1993, Reader's Digest $35 (0-276-42012-8). A nature picture-book that follows happenings in the natural world on a month-to-month basis. Drawings and color photos. (Rev: BL 9/15/93; VOYA 2/94) [591]

Botany

General and Miscellaneous

5655 Ross, Bill. *Straight from the Bear's Mouth: The Story of Photosynthesis* (6–9). 1995, Atheneum $16 (0-689-31726-3). Young people at a science camp are asked to develop hypotheses and test them out while gaining knowledge about chemistry, physics, and botany. (Rev: BL 12/1/95; SLJ 12/95) [581.1]

Foods

GENERAL AND MISCELLANEOUS

5656 Bodanis, David. *The Secret Garden: Dawn to Dusk in the Astonishing Hidden World of the Garden* (9–adult). 1992, Simon & Schuster $25 (0-671-66353-4). Describes in detail the complex interrelationship between garden microorganisms, insects, and plants. Illustrated. (Rev: BL 10/1/92) [574.5]

5657 Koch, Frances King. *Mariculture: Farming the Fruits of the Sea* (5–8). 1992, Watts LB $15.90 (0-531-11116-4). This photo-essay discusses the development of mariculture, what crops are currently being produced, and its potential to alleviate world hunger. (Rev: BL 10/15/92; MJHS; SLJ 12/92) [639]

5658 McCoy, J. J. *How Safe Is Our Food Supply?* (7–12). 1990, Watts LB $12.90 (0-531-10935-6). An outline of modern procedures, issues, and conflicts within the food industry. (Rev: BL 2/1/91; SHS; SLJ 1/91) [363.19]

5659 Powell, Jillian. *Food* (5–7). (Traditions Around the World) 1995, Thomson Learning LB $16.95 (1-56847-346-X). (Rev: BL 9/15/95) [394.1]

5660 Staten, Vince. *Can You Trust a Tomato in January?* (9–adult). 1993, Simon & Schuster $18 (0-671-76941-3). A humorous compilation of information about the manufacturing, packaging, and processing of common food items. (Rev: BL 6/1–15/93) [641.3]

5661 Tennyson, Jeffrey. *Hamburger Heaven: The Illustrated History of the Hamburger* (9–adult). 1993, Hyperion $29.95 (1-56282-982-3). A bounty of pictures and documented memorabilia of America's favorite food. (Rev: BL 8/93; BTA) [338.4]

5662 Tesar, Jenny. *Food and Water: Threats, Shortages and Solutions* (5–9). (Our Fragile Planet) 1992, Facts on File/Blackbirch LB $18.95 (0-8160-2495-2). (Rev: BL 6/1/92; MJHS) [333.91]

VEGETABLES

5663 Meltzer, Milton. *The Amazing Potato: A Story in Which the Incas, Conquistadores, Marie Antoinette, Thomas Jefferson, . . . and French Fries All Play a Part* (5–8). 1992, HarperCollins LB $14.89 (0-06-020807-4). The title says it all! Includes photos. Awards: ALSC Notable Children's Book; BL Editors' Choice; SLJ Best Book. (Rev: BL 7/92*; MJHS; SLJS 1/93*) [635]

5664 Phillips, Roger, and Martyn Rix. *The Random House Book of Vegetables* (9–adult). (Random House Garden) 1994, Random paper $25 (0-679-75024-X). Provides descriptions of vegetable families, the history of vegetables, and advice on cultivation, fertilization, and pest control. (Rev: BL 2/15/94) [635]

Forestry and Trees

5665 Aldis, Rodney. *Rainforests* (5–8). (Ecology Watch) 1991, Dillon $13.95 (0-87518-495-2). A study of how rain forests have matured, highlighting how plants and animals depend on each other for survival in this delicate ecosystem. (Rev: BL 3/1/92; SLJ 4/92) [574.5]

5666 Forsyth, Adrian. *How Monkeys Make Chocolate: Foods and Medicines from the Rainforests* (5–8). 1995, Firefly Books/Owl Books $16.95 (1-895688-45-0); paper $9.95 (1-895688-32-9). A conservation biologist presents a narrative with a sense of wonder for the interdependence of plants, animals, and humans. (Rev: BL 12/1/95) [581.6]

5667 Gallant, Roy A. *Earth's Vanishing Forests* (6–10). 1991, Macmillan $14.95 (0-02-735774-0). A carefully researched examination of the reasons for the destruction of the planet's forests and the implications of their loss. (Rev: BL 10/1/91; SLJ 5/92) [333.75]

5668 Goodman, Billy. *The Rain Forest* (5–7). (Planet Earth) 1992, Little, Brown $17.95 (0-316-32019-6). The beauty of the rain forests, their value, and the results of their destruction on humanity are described. (Rev: BL 2/15/92) [574.5]

5669 Jorgenson, Lisa. *Grand Trees of America: Our State and Champion Trees* (5–7). 1992, Roberts Rinehart (P.O. Box 666, Niwot, CO 80544) paper $8.95 (1-879373-15-7). Tells about the official tree of each state—its history, uses, and distinctive features—and the background and history of the National Register of Big Trees. (Rev: BL 2/15/93) [582.16]

5670 Little, Charles E. *The Dying of the Trees: The Pandemic in America's Forests* (9–adult). 1995, Viking $22.95 (0-670-84135-8). A sobering chronicle of dying trees across our country, emphasizing the need for concern in opposition to the current trend toward denial and backlash. (Rev: BL 8/95) [634.9]

5671 Mallory, Kenneth. *Water Hole: Life in a Rescued Tropical Forest* (5–8). (New England Aquarium Endangered Habitats) 1992, Watts LB $15.90 (0-531-11154-7). Describes the successful reclamation of a Costa Rican tropical forest by following the raccoonlike coati. Introduces other indigenous plants and animals. (Rev: BL 5/1/93) [574.5]

5672 Miller, Christina G., and Louise A. Berry. *Jungle Rescue: Saving the New World Tropical Rain Forests* (5–8). 1991, Atheneum $13.95 (0-689-31487-6). Gives a thorough description of the ecology of a tropical rain forest with clear explanations of unfamiliar terms. (Rev: BL 3/15/91; SLJ 7/91) [574.5]

5673 Russo, Monica. *The Tree Almanac: A Year-Round Activity Guide* (5–7). Photos. 1993, Sterling $14.95 (0-8069-1252-9). Provides tree families and species, development throughout the seasons, diseases and insects, and close-ups of leaves and bark. (Rev: BL 12/15/93; SLJ 1/94) [582.16]

5674 Silcock, Lisa, ed. *The Rainforests: A Celebration* (9–adult). 1990, Chronicle $35 (0-87701-790-5). Rain forest experts explain various aspects of life in this habitat. Illustrated. (Rev: BL 2/1/91; SHS) [508.315]

5675 Siy, Alexandra. *The Brazilian Rain Forest* (5–8). (Circle of Life) 1992, Dillon LB $13.95 (0-87518-470-7). Offers general information about the fragile rain forest and the delicate interconnectedness of life on Earth. (Rev: BL 9/1/92; SLJ 10/92) [574.5]

Plants and Flowers

5676 *Diccionario visual Altea de las plantas* (5–12). 1992, Santillana (Madrid, Spain) $24.95 (84-372-4529-X). This large-format dictionary includes more than 200 detailed, eye-catching photos and drawings in color, with brief texts explaining the interior and exterior of plants. Index. English title: *The Visual Dictionary of Plants*. (Rev: BL 4/1/94)

5677 Dowden, Anne Ophelia. *Poisons in Our Path: Plants That Harm and Heal* (5–7). Illus. 1994, HarperCollins LB $16.89 (0-06-020862-7). Combines botany, folklore, and history to study plants important for their physical properties, including medicinal and poisonous plants and those associated with magic. (Rev: BL 7/94; MJHS; SLJ 6/94) [581.6]

5678 Garassino, Alessandro. *Plants: Origins and Evolution* (5–8). (Beginnings) 1995, Raintree/Steck-Vaughn LB $22.80 (0-8114-3332-3). (Rev: BL 4/15/95) [581.3]

5679 Halpern, Robert R. *Green Planet Rescue: Saving the Earth's Endangered Plants* (5–8). (Cincinnati Zoo Book) 1993, Watts LB $15.90 (0-531-11095-8). A balanced study of the future of the plant kingdom that encourages involvement in environmental activities, with examples of forest destruction worldwide. (Rev: BL 3/15/94; MJHS; SLJ 4/94) [581.5]

5680 Huxley, Anthony. *Green Inheritance: The World Wildlife Fund Book of Plants* (9–adult).

1991, Four Walls Eight Windows (39 W. 14th St., Suite 503, New York, NY 10011) paper $26.95 (0-941423-70-0). A prominent botanist warns against further damaging the already fragile ecosystem. (Rev: BL 2/1/92) [581.6]

5681 Johnson, Sylvia A. *Roses Red, Violets Blue: Why Flowers Have Colors* (5–8). Illus. 1991, Lerner LB $14.95 (0-8225-1594-6). An examination of the role of flower color in the life of plants and the function of color in reproduction and communication. Photos and drawings. (Rev: BL 12/1/91; SLJ 1/92*) [582.13]

5682 Joyce, Christopher. *Earthly Goods: Medicine-Hunting in the Rainforest* (9–adult). 1994, Little, Brown $22.95 (0-316-47408-8). Explores the biodiversity of rain forests, detailing the medicinal properties of their plants, and profiles several "green knights," individuals devoted to finding plant-based pharmaceuticals. (Rev: BL 7/94*) [615]

5683 Julivert, María Angels. *La vida de las plantas* (5–9). (Mundo invisible/Invisible World) Illus. 1993, Parramón (Barcelona, Spain) $9.95 (84-342-1465-2). Explains the functions of plants, including photosynthesis, through full-color drawings and diagrams and easy texts. Glossary. English title: *The Life of Plants*. (Rev: BL 4/1/94)

5684 Nielsen, Nancy J. *Carnivorous Plants* (5–8). (Full Color First Books) 1992, Watts LB $11.90 (0-531-20056-6). Discusses flesh-eating plants, such as Venus-flytraps, sundews, and pitcher plants, with focus on how they catch and digest their prey. (Rev: BL 6/1/92; MJHS; SLJ 7/92) [581.5]

5685 Parsons, Alexandra, and Claire Watts. *Plants* (5–7). (Make It Work! Science) 1995, Thomson Learning LB $15.95 (1-56847-470-9). (Rev: BL 10/15/95) [581]

5686 Pope, Joyce. *Practical Plants* (5–8). (Plant Life) 1990, Facts on File $15.95 (0-8160-2424-3). Outlines the uses of plants ranging from oxygen providers to supplying humans with food, medicine, and fiber. (Rev: BL 6/15/91; SLJ 8/91) [581.6]

5687 Reading, Susan. *Plants of the Tropics* (5–8). (Plant Life) 1990, Facts on File $15.95 (0-8160-2423-5). A tour of the rain forest, noting a variety of plants, their means of survival, and their partnership with animals. (Rev: BL 6/15/91; SHS; SLJ 8/91) [581.909]

5688 Taylor, Barbara. *La pradera* (5–8). (Mira de cereal) Tr. by Juan Manuel Ibeas. Photos. 1993, Grupo Anaya (Madrid, Spain) $15.95 (84-207-4856-0). For young scientists-to-be, this volume includes a simple text and spectacular color photos, including close-up views of animals and plants in their natural habitats. English title: *Meadow*. Other titles in the series: *El desierto (Desert), La selva tropical (Jungle),* and *Arrecige de coral (Coral Reef)*. (Rev: BL 2/1/94)

Seeds

5689 Ausubel, Kenny. *Seeds of Change: The Living Treasure* (9–adult). 1994, HarperSan Francisco paper $18 (0-06-250008-2). A critique of the state of agribusiness, from planting to packaging, by the founder of a leading organic seed company. (Rev: BL 2/15/94) [631.5]

Zoology

General and Miscellaneous

5690 Aaseng, Nathan. *Invertebrates* (5–9). 1993, Watts LB $13.40 (0-531-12550-5). A discussion of the 95 percent of the world's population made up of invertebrates. (Rev: BL 3/15/94; BTA; MJHS; SLJ 3/94) [592]

5691 Aaseng, Nathan. *Vertebrates* (5–9). 1993, Watts LB $13.40 (0-531-12551-3). Discusses backboned animals, including fish, amphibians, reptiles, birds, and mammals. (Rev: BL 3/15/94; BTA; MJHS; SLJ 3/94) [596]

5692 Ackerman, Diane. *The Moon by Whale Light: And Other Adventures among Bats, Penguins, Crocodilians, and Whales* (9–adult). 1991, Random $20 (0-394-58574-7). A poet and nature writer accompanies animal experts on adventurous close-up investigations of alligators, whales, penguins, and bats in their native habitats. Awards: SLJ Best Book. (Rev: BL 10/1/91*; SLJ 2/92) [591]

5693 Cohen, Daniel. *Animal Rights: A Handbook for Young Adults* (6–9). 1993, Millbrook $15.90 (1-56294-219-0). Discusses the use of animals for medical experimentation, conditions in zoos, marine theme parks, rodeos, factory farming and hunting, puppy mills, and classroom dissection. (Rev: BL 7/93; BTA; MJHS; VOYA 2/94) [179]

5694 Day, Nancy. *Animal Experimentation: Cruelty or Science?* (7–12). (Issues in Focus) 1994, Enslow LB $17.95 (0-89490-578-3). A balanced discussion of experiments that benefit from testing with animals, presenting alternatives to the arguably cruel practice. (Rev: BL 11/1/94; MJHS; SLJ 4/95; VOYA 2/95) [179]

5695 *Diccionario visual Altea de los animales* (5–12). 1992, Santillana (Madrid, Spain) $24.95 (84-372-4525-7). This large-format dictionary includes more than 200 detailed, eye-catching photos and drawings in color, with brief texts explaining the interior and exterior of animals. Index. English title: *The Visual Dictionary of Animals*. (Rev: BL 4/1/94)

5696 Facklam, Howard, and Margery Facklam. *Parasites* (5–7). (Invaders) 1994, Twenty-First Century LB $15.95 (0-8050-2858-7). Covers such creatures as leeches, tapeworms, and pinworms. (Rev: BL 1/1/95; SLJ 3/95) [574.5]

5697 Gelman, Rita Golden. *Dawn to Dusk in the Galápagos: Flightless Birds, Swimming Lizards, and Other Fascinating Creatures* (5–7). Photos. 1991, Little, Brown $16.95 (0-316-30739-4). (Rev: BL 4/1/91; SLJ 7/91) [591.9866]

5698 Hecht, Jeff. *Vanishing Life: The Mystery of Mass Extinctions* (7–12). 1993, Scribner $15.95 (0-684-19331-0). A study of mass extinctions throughout history. Discusses how geological evidence supports or discredits current theories. (Rev: BL 1/15/94; MJHS; SLJ 2/94; VOYA 2/94) [575]

5699 Margulis, Lynn. *Diversity of Life: The Five Kingdoms* (7–10). 1992, Enslow LB $16.95 (0-89490-278-4). An explanation of how living organisms are divided into groups, taxonomy, the history of classification, and the characteristics of the 5 kingdoms. (Rev: BL 11/15/92; SLJ 11/92) [574]

5700 Natural History Museum, London, England. *Creepy Crawlies: Ladybugs, Lobsters and Other Amazing Arthropods* (5–7). 1991, Sterling $14.95 (0-8069-8336-1). This informational text on arthropods is profusely illustrated with photos of crustaceans, myriapods, insects, and arachnids. (Rev: BL 10/1/91; SLJ 4/92) [595]

5701 Owen, Marna. *Animal Rights: Yes or No?* (6–10). 1993, Lerner LB $17.50 (0-8225-2603-4). A discussion of the various positions on animal rights. (Rev: BL 1/15/94; SLJ 3/94) [179]

5702 Parker, Steve. *Inside the Whale and Other Animals* (5–8). Illus. 1992, Doubleday $16 (0-385-30651-2). Presents 21 animals, including bat, scorpion, octopus, shark, crocodile, and kangaroo, in double-page spreads, illustrated with pen-and-ink or watercolor drawings. Awards: Mother Goose. (Rev: BL 7/92; MJHS; SLJ 7/92) [591.4]

5703 Parker, Steve. *Natural World* (6–12). 1994, Dorling Kindersley $29.95 (1-56458-719-3). (Rev: BL 12/1/94; SLJ 1/95; VOYA 5/95) [591]

5704 Patterson, Charles. *Animal Rights* (6–10). 1993, Enslow LB $17.95 (0-89490-468-X). Presents a thorough examination of the topic, including a history of animal rights movements. (Rev: BL 10/15/93; MJHS; SLJ 11/93; VOYA 2/94) [179]

5705 Taylor, Barbara. *Arctic and Antarctic* (5–9). (Eyewitness Books) 1995, Knopf $17 (0-679-87257-4). Spectacular photos and diagrams explain ice formations, tundra, and plant, sea, and wildlife of each region. (Rev: BL 8/95) [508.311]

Amphibians and Reptiles

GENERAL AND MISCELLANEOUS

5706 Allen, Missy, and Michel Peissel. *Dangerous Reptilian Creatures* (9–12). (Encyclopedia of Danger) 1993, Chelsea House $19.95 (0-7910-1789-3). Covers 25 deadly snakes from around the world. (Rev: BL 9/1/93) [597.9]

5707 Clarke, Barry. *Amphibian* (5–9). (Eyewitness Books) Photos. 1993, Knopf LB $15.99 (0-679-93879-6). (Rev: BL 8/93; MJHS) [597.6]

5708 Massare, Judy A. *Prehistoric Marine Reptiles* (5–8). 1991, Watts $14.90 (0-531-11022-2). Surveys sea life during the Mesozoic era. Includes many photos, drawings, and maps. (Rev: BL 2/15/92; SLJ 2/92) [567.9]

ALLIGATORS AND CROCODILES

5709 Glasgow, Vaughn L. *A Social History of the American Alligator: The Earth Trembles with His Thunder* (9–adult). 1991, St. Martin's $29.95 (0-312-06288-5). A thorough examination of the facts and folklore surrounding our largest reptile, formerly an endangered species, today considered a crop to be harvested. (Rev: BL 9/1/91) [398]

5710 Stoops, Erik D., and Debbie Lynne Stone. *Alligators and Crocodiles* (5–7). 1995, Sterling $14.95 (0-8069-0422-4). After giving an explanation of the difference between the two, the authors describe both animal behavior and anatomy—including what a croc does just before biting you. (Rev: BL 1/1/95; SLJ 3/95) [597.98]

FROGS AND TOADS

5711 White, William. *All about the Frog* (5–8). (Sterling Color Nature) 1992, Sterling $14.95 (0-8069-8274-8). White defines and gives a brief history of the frog, followed by discussion of anatomy, reproduction, food, adaptations, and likely future. (Rev: BL 7/92; SLJ 9/92) [597.8]

SNAKES AND LIZARDS

5712 Mattison, Chris. *The Encyclopedia of Snakes* (9–adult). 1995, Facts on File $35 (0-8160-3072-3). A large-scale study of snakes and how they differ from other reptiles, including their use in mythology. Many color photos. (Rev: BL 8/95; SLJ 2/96) [597.96]

TORTOISES AND TURTLES

5713 White, William. *All about the Turtle* (5–8). (Sterling Color Nature) 1992, Sterling $14.95 (0-8069-8276-4). White defines and gives a brief history of the turtle, followed by discussion of anatomy, reproduction, food, adaptations, and likely future. (Rev: BL 7/92; SLJ 8/92) [597.9]

Animal Behavior

GENERAL AND MISCELLANEOUS

5714 Brooks, Bruce. *Predator!* (5–8). (Knowing Nature) 1991, Farrar $13.95 (0-374-36111-8). Examines the food chain, with explanations of how and why animals hunt and protect themselves. Awards: YALSA Best Book for Young Adults. (Rev: BL 1/1/92; SLJ 2/92*, YR) [591.53]

5715 Cooke, John. *The Restless Kingdom: An Exploration of Animal Movement* (9–adult). 1991, Facts on File $39.95 (0-8160-1205-9). A study of how animals move on land, in air and water. (Rev: BL 2/1/91; SHS; SLJ 10/91) [591.1]

5716 Flegg, Jim, and others. *Animal Helpers* (5–7). 1991, Millbrook LB $10.90 (1-878137-06-9). Examines the cooperative hunting methods of lions and pelicans, the social order of ants, and the group defense systems of elephants. (Rev: BL 7/91; SLJ 7/91) [591.57]

5717 Flegg, Jim, and others. *Animal Hunters* (5–7). (Wild World) 1991, Millbrook LB $10.90 (1-878137-04-2). Describes the hunting techniques of sharks, pirhanas, wasps, and other animals. (Rev: BL 7/91; SLJ 7/91) [591.51]

5718 Flegg, Jim. *Animal Movement* (5–7). (Wild World) Illus. 1991, Millbrook/Newington LB $11.90 (1-878137-22-0). Eye-catching photos effectively demonstrate the methods by which various animals get around. (Rev: BL 11/1/91) [591.18]

5719 Flegg, Jim. *Animal Senses* (5–7). (Wild World) Illus. 1991, Millbrook/Newington LB $11.90 (1-878137-21-2). (Rev: BL 11/1/91) [591.51]

5720 Halliday, Tim, ed. *Animal Behavior* (9–adult). 1994, Univ. of Oklahoma $25.95 (0-8061-2647-7). This basic book on how animals are born, live, and die contains its share of cuddly creatures but does not shy away from portraying (with photos) their place in the food chain. (Rev: BL 5/1/94) [591.51]

5721 Herbst, Judith. *Animal Amazing* (5–9). 1991, Atheneum $13.95 (0-689-31556-2). The author recounts unusual events about unexplained phenomena in the animal world. (Rev: BL 4/1/91; MJHS; SLJ 6/91) [591]

5722 Jordan, William. *Divorce among the Gulls: An Uncommon Look at Human Nature* (9–adult). 1997, Farrar paper $11 (0 86547-500-8). (Rev: BL 2/15/91*) [591.5]

5723 Morris, Desmond. *Animalwatching* (9–adult). Illus. 1990, Crown $35 (0-517-57859-X). A study of how animals form social groups, outsmart predators, feed, use tools, handle conflicts, mate, and parent. (Rev: BL 2/1/91; SHS; SLJ 4/91) [591.51]

5724 Presnall, Judith Janda. *Animals That Glow* (5–7). 1993, Watts $12.40 (0-531-20071-X). Introduces the phenomenon of bioluminescence and describes how, when, and why it occurs in the animal kingdom. (Rev: BL 5/15/93; SLJ 6/93) [591.19]

5725 Quiri, Patricia Ryon. *Metamorphosis* (5–8). (First Book) 1991, Watts LB $11.90 (0-531-20042-6). A discussion of animal metamorphosis, detailing the transformation of butterflies, flies, frogs, and marine animals. Color photos. (Rev: BL 12/15/91; SLJ 5/92) [591.3]

5726 Sinclair, Sandra. *Extraordinary Eyes: How Animals See the World* (5–8). 1992, Dial LB $14.89 (0-8037-0806-8). An investigation of animal sight organs, explaining eye positioning, the connection between sight and the brain, and various eye adaptations. (Rev: BL 10/15/92; SLJ 12/92) [591.1]

5727 Stidworthy, John. *Animal Behavior* (5–8). (Prentice Hall World of Nature) 1992, Prentice-Hall LB $15 (0-13-033390-5). (Rev: BL 10/15/92) [591.51]

CAMOUFLAGE

5728 Ferrari, Marco. *Colors for Survival: Mimicry and Camouflage in Nature* (9–adult). 1993, Thomasson-Grant (One Morton Dr., Suite 500, Charlottesville, VA 22901) $29.95 (1-56566-048-X). This book presents full-color photographs and text showing how mimicry and camouflage in nature can ensure survival. (Rev: BL 12/15/93; BTA) [591.57]

COMMUNICATION

5729 Brooks, Bruce. *Making Sense: Animal Perception and Communication* (5–8). (Knowing Nature) 1993, Farrar $17 (0-374-34742-5). Brooks looks at each of the senses and shows how they affect the behavior of animals. (Rev: BL 12/1/93; BTA; MJHS; SLJ 1/94) [591.1]

5730 Flegg, Jim. *Animal Communication* (5–7). (Wild World) Illus. 1991, Millbrook/Newington LB $11.90 (1-878137-23-9). (Rev: BL 11/1/91) [591.59]

5731 Masson, Jeffrey Moussaieff, and Susan McCarthy. *When Elephants Weep: The Emotional Lives of Animals* (9–adult). 1995, Delacorte $22.95 (0-385-31425-6). A psychoanalyst's fact-filled look at "human" feelings in animals. (Rev: BL 5/15/95; SLJ 4/96) [591.51]

5732 Morton, Eugene S., and Jake Page. *Animal Talk: Science and the Voices of Nature* (9–adult). 1992, Random $22 (0-394-58337-X). Analysis of the origins and nature of animal communication. (Rev: BL 4/15/92) [591.59]

HOMES

5733 Brooks, Bruce. *Nature by Design* (5–8). (Knowing Nature) 1991, Farrar $13.95 (0-374-30334-7). A study of animal "architecture" and intelligence. Glossary. (Rev: BL 1/1/92; SLJ 2/92*; YR) [591.56]

5734 Flegg, Jim, and others. *Animal Builders* (5–7). 1991, Millbrook LB $10.90 (1-878137-05-0). Presents several kinds of nest-building birds, papermaking wasps, web-spinning spiders, and tunnel-digging animals (including humans). (Rev: BL 7/91; SLJ 7/91) [591.564]

5735 Goodman, Billy. *Animal Homes and Societies* (5–7). (Planet Earth) 1992, Little, Brown $17.95 (0-316-32018-8). An introduction to the social habits of wild animals. (Rev: BL 2/15/92) [591.5]

5736 Lauber, Patricia. *Fur, Feathers, and Flippers: How Animals Live Where They Do* (5–8). 1994, Scholastic $16.95 (0-590-45071-9). This photo-essay shows how animals adapt to their habitats. (Rev: BL 12/1/94*; SLJ 12/94) [591.5]

MIGRATION

5737 Flegg, Jim, and others. *Animal Travelers* (5–7). (Natural History) 1991, Millbrook LB $10.90 (1-878137-07-7). Describes how animals of different species—including birds, whales, butterflies, and even parasites—get from one place to another. (Rev: BL 7/91; SLJ 7/91) [591.525]

REPRODUCTION AND BABIES

5738 Richardson, Nan, and Catherine Chermayeff. *Wild Babies* (9–adult). 1994, Chronicle $14.95 (0-8118-0477-1). This photo-essay describes parenting among wild mammals, birds, amphibians, and insects, showing both the beauty and ferocity of nature. (Rev: BL 3/15/94; BTA) [591.3]

TRACKS

5739 Rezendes, Paul. *Tracking and the Art of Seeing: How to Read Animal Tracks and Signs* (9–adult). 1992, Camden House $29.95 (0-944475-33-7); paper $19.95 (0-944475-29-9). Experts explain how examining animal tracks and signs can reveal much information about that creature. (Rev: BL 9/15/92) [599]

Animal Species

GENERAL AND MISCELLANEOUS

5740 Pringle, Laurence. *Jackal Woman: Exploring the World of Jackals* (5–7). Illus. 1993, Scribner $14.95 (0-684-19435-X). Zoologist Patricia Moehlman's work with the golden and silver-backed jackal in Africa is described with color photos. (Rev: BL 11/1/93; MJHS; SLJ 12/93) [599.74]

5741 Runtz, Michael W. P. *Moose Country: Saga of the Woodland Moose* (9–adult). 1991, North Word (2520 Hwy. 51, Minocqua, WI 54548) $39 (1-55971-132-9). The giant moose is observed in its northern woodland habitat. Color photos. (Rev: BL 1/15/92) [599.73]

5742 *The Sierra Club Book of Small Mammals* (5–7). 1993, Sierra Club $16.95 (0-87156-525-0). Oversized, illustrated introduction to small mammals of the world, grouped by type: insect eaters, canids, rodents, and others. (Rev: BL 3/15/93; MJHS; SLJ 6/93) [599]

5743 Stodart, Eleanor. *The Australian Echidna* (5–7). 1991, Houghton $14.95 (0-395-55992-8). The natural history of an unusual Australian mammal, which is similar to a porcupine. (Rev: BL 6/15/91; SLJ 8/91) [599.1]

5744 Yancey, Diane. *Camels for Uncle Sam* (5–7). 1995, Hendrick-Long (P.O. Box 12311, Dallas, TX 75225) $14.95 (0-937460-91-5). Built on a little-known fact that camels once roamed the Southwest and were used in an army experiment. (Rev: BL 9/15/95) [357]

APE FAMILY

5745 Galdikas, Biruté M. F. *Reflections of Eden: My Years with the Orangutans of Borneo* (9–adult). 1995, Little, Brown $24.95 (0-316-30181-7). (Rev: BL 1/1/95*) [599.8]

5746 Montgomery, Sy. *Walking with the Great Apes: Jane Goodall, Dian Fossey, Biruté Galdikas* (9–adult). 1991, Houghton $19.95 (0-395-51597-1). Awards: YALSA Best Book for Young Adults. (Rev: BL 3/15/91*; SHS) [599.88]

5747 Peterson, Dale, and Jane Goodall. *Visions of Caliban: On Chimpanzees and People* (9–adult). 1993, Houghton $22.95 (0-395-53760-6). Contains vivid, haunting images of chimpanzees brutally snared for experiments or caged for pets. (Rev: BL 1/15/93*) [599.88]

5748 Redmond, Ian. *Gorilla* (5–9). (Eyewitness Books) 1995, Knopf LB $20.99 (0-679-97332-X). (Rev: BL 12/15/95) [599.8]

BEARS

5749 Lawter, William Clifford. *Smokey Bear 20252: A Biography* (9–adult). 1994, Lindsay Smith (P.O. Box 30312, Alexandria, VA 22310-8312) $26.95 (0-9640017-0-5); paper $16.95 (0-9640017-1-3). Outlines the history of Smokey Bear (a real bear, rescued from a forest fire and sent to the National Zoo), the famous poster, and the costumes worn by the nation's forest services. (Rev: BL 5/1/94) [363.377]

CATS (LIONS, TIGERS, ETC.)

5750 Bolgiano, Chris. *Mountain Lion: An Unnatural History of Pumas and People* (9–adult). 1995, Stackpole $19.95 (0-8117-1044-0). Details the mythological history and the impact of the mountain lion, from its use in Native American tales to its uses in modern advertising. (Rev: BL 8/95) [599.74]

5751 McCall, Karen, and Jim Dutcher. *Cougar: Ghost of the Rockies* (9–adult). 1992, Sierra Club $30 (0-87156-564-1). The parallel stories of one female cougar and her offspring and the filming of the same. (Rev: BL 11/1/92; SHS) [599.74]

5752 Montgomery, Sy. *Spell of the Tiger: The Man-Eaters of Sundarbans* (9–adult). 1995, Houghton $21.95 (0-395-64169-1). (Rev: BL 1/15/95*) [398]

5753 Patterson, Gareth. *Last of the Free* (9–adult). 1995, St. Martin's $21.95 (0-312-13109-7). After the murder of *Born Free's* George Adamson, the author relocated 3 of Adamson's lion cubs to the bushlands. (Rev: BL 4/15/95) [599.74]

5754 Schneider, Jost. *Lynx* (5–7). 1994, Carolrhoda LB $14.95 (0-87614-844-5). Full-color photos reveal hunting, mating, and other behaviors in documentary style. (Rev: BL 1/15/95; SLJ 3/95) [599.74]

COYOTES, FOXES, AND WOLVES

5755 Brandenburg, Jim. *To the Top of the World: Adventures with Arctic Wolves* (5–7). 1993, Walker LB $17.85 (0-8027-8220-5). An award-winning *National Geographic* author-photographer describes his experiences living close to an Arctic wolf pack on a remote island. Awards: SLJ Best Book. (Rev: BL 1/1/94*; BTA; SLJ 12/93*) [599.74]

5756 Busch, Robert. *The Wolf Almanac* (9–adult). 1995, Lyons & Burford $25 (1-55821-351-1). An introduction to wolves, with 100 illustrations. (Rev: BL 5/1/95) [599.74]

5757 Busch, Robert, ed. *Wolf Songs: The Classic Collection of Writing about Wolves* (9–adult). 1994, Sierra Club $15.95 (0-87156-411-4). Personal essays about the misunderstood wolf, each arguing that wolves have the right to free existence in nature. (Rev: BL 10/15/94; SLJ 6/95; VOYA 4/95) [599.74]

5758 Mech, L. David. *The Way of the Wolf* (9–adult). 1991, Voyageur Press (123 N. Second St., Stillwater, MN 55082) $27.50 (0-89658-163-2). Demonstrates wolves' place in the natural order and their similarity to domesticated dogs, dispels the myth that they attack people, and makes the case for their preservation. (Rev: BL 10/1/91) [599.75]

5759 Mech, L. David. *Wolves of the High Arctic* (9–adult). 1992, Voyageur Press (123 N. Second St., Stillwater, MN 55082) $29.95 (0-89658-213-2). The author, who has lived with and studied the same wolf pack for many years, presents a study of the species that consists of informatively captioned photos. (Rev: BL 11/1/92; MJHS) [599.74]

5760 Steinhart, Peter. *The Company of Wolves* (9–adult). 1995, Knopf $25 (0-679-41881-4). Explores the tenuous relationship between the enigmatic wolf and humans. (Rev: BL 4/15/95) [599.74]

DEER

5761 Cox, Daniel J. *Elk* (9–adult). 1992, Chronicle paper $12.95 (0-87701-828-6). This photo-filled essay acquaints readers with the North American elk. (Rev: BL 4/15/92) [599.73]

ELEPHANTS

5762 Barkhausen, Annette, and Franz Geiser. *Elephants* (5–7). (Animal Families) 1994, Gareth Stevens $13.95 (0-8368-1001-5). This photo-essay provides facts on the evolution of the elephant, its classification, its behavior, and its reproductive process. (Rev: BL 7/94) [599.6]

5763 Caras, Roger A. *A Most Dangerous Journey: The Life of an African Elephant* (5–8). 1995, Dial $14.99 (0-8037-1880-2). Based on a composite picture of an elephant culled from Caras's observations in Africa. His point is clear in his critical comments about poachers and corrupt officials in search of ivory. (Rev: BL 10/15/95; SLJ 10/95; VOYA 4/96) [599.4]

5764 Chadwick, Douglas H. *The Fate of the Elephant* (9–adult). 1992, Sierra Club $25 (0-87156-635-4). A revealing report on the impending extinction of the elephant. (Rev: BL 9/15/92; SHS; SLJ 5/93) [599.6]

5765 Di Silvestro, Roger L. *The African Elephant: Twilight in Eden* (9–adult). 1991, Wiley $34.95 (0-471-53207-X). The social behavior of Earth's largest land mammal, now endangered because of the ivory trade, and its association with humans from prehistory to the present day. (Rev: BL 10/15/91) [333.95]

5766 Douglas-Hamilton, Iain, and Oria Douglas-Hamilton. *Battle for the Elephants* (9–adult). 1992, Viking $30 (0-670-84003-3). Noted elephant experts graphically document the slaughter of African elephants and relate their battle to protect the animals from poachers. (Rev: BL 4/15/92) [333.95]

5767 Gavron, Jeremy. *King Leopold's Dream: Travels in the Shadow of the African Elephant* (9–adult). 1993, Pantheon $24 (0-679-41998-5). A British journalist chronicles his African journeys tracking elephants in sanctuaries and natural habitats. Includes interviews with conservationists on wildlife management. (Rev: BL 4/15/93) [916.04]

5768 Owens, Delia, and Mark Owens. *The Eye of the Elephant: An Epic Adventure in the African Wilderness* (9–adult). 1992, Houghton $22.95 (0-395-42381-3). A description of the practical realities involved in the authors' efforts to save Zambian elephants from poachers. (Rev: BL 10/1/92) [639.9]

5769 Redmond, Ian. *Elephant* (5–9). (Eyewitness Books) Photos. 1993, Knopf LB $15.99 (0-679-83880-5). (Rev: BL 8/93; MJHS) [599]

MARSUPIALS

5770 Phillips, Ken. *Koalas: Australia's Ancient Ones* (9–adult). 1994, Prentice-Hall $27.50 (0-671-79777-8). A study of the beloved marsupial that provides detailed information, chronicles koala rescues, and describes the growth of the Koala Hospital. (Rev: BL 10/1/94) [599.2]

5771 Triggs, Barbara. *Wombats* (5–7). 1991, Houghton $14.95 (0-395-55993-6). A profile of an unusual Australian animal with an in-depth explanation of how and why it digs its many burrows. (Rev: BL 6/15/91; SLJ 7/91) [599.2]

PANDAS

5772 Laidler, Keith, and Liz Laidler. *Pandas: Giants of the Bamboo Forest* (9–adult). 1994, Parkwest/BBC $29.95 (0-563-36361-4). How the familiar black-and-white giant panda and its obscure foxlike cousin, the red panda, live in the bamboo forests of China. Color photos. (Rev: BL 5/1/94; SHS; SLJ 10/94) [599.74443]

5773 Schaller, George B. *The Last Panda* (9–adult). 1993, Univ. of Chicago $24.95 (0-226-73628-8). A noted field biologist recounts his experiences researching the giant panda in the wilds of China. (Rev: BL 3/15/93; BTA) [599.74]

Birds

GENERAL AND MISCELLANEOUS

5774 Adler, Bill. *Impeccable Birdfeeding: How to Discourage Scuffling, Hull-Dropping, Seed-Throwing, Unmentionable Nuisances and Vulgar Chatter at Your Birdfeeder* (9–adult). 1992, Chicago Review/A Cappella paper $9.95 (1-55652-157-X). Discusses birdbaths, birdfeeders, and birdhouses, and rates food and bird species on the basis of mess potential. (Rev: BL 10/1/92) [598]

5775 Buff, Sheila. *The Birdfeeder's Handbook: An Orvis Guide* (9–adult). 1991, Lyons & Burford paper $9.95 (1-55821-123-3). This manual offers basic information on birdfeeding, birdhouses, and avian behavior, including feeder manners, territories, courtship, breeding, and migration. (Rev: BL 9/1/91) [598]

5776 Friedman, Judi. *Operation Siberian Crane: The Story Behind the International Effort to Save an Amazing Bird* (5–7). 1992, Dillon $13.95 (0-87518-515-0). Describes the life of the Siberian crane, efforts to breed them, and difficulties involved in trying to save them experienced by the International Crane Foundation. Awards:

SLJ Best Book. (Rev: BL 1/15/93; MJHS; SLJ 1/93*) [639.9]

5777 Hara. *Flamingo: A Photographer's Odyssey* (9–adult). 1992, Abrams paper $29.95 (0-8109-2511-7). The author's adventures on an expedition to the Rift Valley of Tanzania and Kenya provide the source for this collection of high-quality bird photos. (Rev: BL 11/1/92) [508.676]

5778 Katz, Barbara. *So Cranes May Dance: A Rescue from the Brink of Extinction* (9–adult). 1993, Chicago Review $19.95 (1-55652-171-5). An illustrated history of the International Crane Foundation. (Rev: BL 7/93) [639.9]

5779 Patent, Dorothy Hinshaw. *Feathers* (5–7). Photos. 1992, Dutton/Cobblehill $15 (0-525-65081-4) An almost encyclopedic discussion of feathers, their role in human history, their 6 varieties, the scientific explanation for their colors, and more. Color photos. Awards: SLJ Best Book. (Rev: BL 5/15/92; MJHS; SLJ 7/92*) [598.2]

5780 Toops, Connie. *Hummingbirds: Jewels in Flight* (9–adult). 1992, Voyageur Press (123 N. Second St., Stillwater, MN 55082) $29.95 (0-89658-161-6). The author recounts her trips to observe hummingbirds in the Southwest and along the Gulf Coast and provides information on plants that attract them. (Rev: BL 11/1/92) [598.8]

5781 Walters, Mark Jerome. *A Shadow and a Song: Extinction of the Dusky Seaside Sparrow* (9–adult). 1992, Chelsea Green Publishing (P.O. Box 428, White River Junction, VT 05001) $21.95 (0-930031-58-X). Traces the rapid, tragic demise of a unique bird species at the hands of environmentalists, bird-watchers, NASA, and Disney World through callousness and political infighting. (Rev: BL 10/1/92) [598]

BEHAVIOR

5782 Burton, Robert. *Bird Flight: An Illustrated History of Birds' Aerial Mastery* (9–adult). 1990, Facts on File $24.95 (0-8160-2410-3). A look at the bird as a flying machine—how it controls power and speed, different flying skills, various ways of flying and airborne behavior. Illustrated with color photos and diagrams. (Rev: BL 1/1/91*; SHS) [598.2]

5783 Dunning, Joan. *Secrets of the Nest: The Family of North American Birds* (9–adult). 1994, Houghton $29.95 (0-395-62035-X). The author uses pen-and-ink drawings to illustrate the nesting behavior of robins, hummingbirds, ducks, egrets, the California condor, and other birds. (Rev: BL 3/15/94) [598.256]

5784 Short, Lester L. *The Lives of Birds: The Birds of the World and Their Behavior* (9–adult). (American Museum of Natural History: Animal Behavior) 1993, Holt $25 (0-8050-1952-9). Describes how birds find mates, stake out territories, reproduce, navigate over long distances, what they eat, and why they sing. (Rev: BL 6/1–15/93; BTA) [598.2]

DUCKS AND GEESE

5785 Lorenz, Konrad, and others. *Here I Am—Where Are You? The Behavior of the Greylag Goose* (9–adult). Tr. by Robert D. Martin. 1991, Harcourt $26.95 (0-15-140056-3). Offers intimate observations of the social behavior of the greylag goose, and covers decades of scientific inquiry by a pioneering expert on ducks and geese. (Rev: BL 10/15/91)

EAGLES, HAWKS, AND OTHER BIRDS OF PREY

5786 Arnold, Caroline. *On the Brink of Extinction: The California Condor* (5–7). (Gulliver Green Books) Photos. 1993, Harcourt/Gulliver LB $17.95 (0-15-257990-7); paper $8.95 (0-15-257991-5). Although in 1986 there was only one breeding pair of California condors left in the wild, scientists and others struggled to save the bird from extinction. Color photos. Awards: SLJ Best Book. (Rev: BL 4/15/93; SLJ 6/93*)

5787 Houle, Marcy. *The Prairie Keepers: Secrets of the Grasslands* (9–adult). 1995, Addison-Wesley $20 (0-201-60843-X). A memoir of a field biologist's 6-month study of hawks in an Oregon prairie. (Rev: BL 4/1/95*) [598.9]

5788 Olsen, Penny. *Falcons and Hawks* (5–8). 1992, Facts on File LB $17.95 (0-8160-2843-5). Offers detailed information on 70 birds of prey, with color photos. (Rev: BL 3/1/93; MJHS; SLJ 5/93) [598.9]

5789 Patent, Dorothy Hinshaw. *Ospreys* (5–7). Photos. 1993, Clarion $14.95 (0-395-63391-5). Discusses the physical characteristics, behavior, nesting and feeding habits, and life cycle of these birds of prey, often called fish hawks. (Rev: BL 6/1–15/93; MJHS) [598]

5790 Savage, Candace. *Peregrine Falcons* (9–adult). 1992, Sierra Club $30 (0-87156-504-8). A detailed discussion of the tragic effects of pesticide pollution on peregrine falcons. (Rev: BL 11/1/92; SHS) [598.9]

5791 Silverstein, Alvin, and others. *The Peregrine Falcon* (5–7). (Endangered in America) 1995, Millbrook LB $15.40 (1-56294-417-7). Tells how pesticides and hunting have jeopardized the peregrine falcon, and describes programs to save it. (Rev: BL 6/1–15/95) [598.9]

OWLS

5792 Sutton, Patricia, and Clay Sutton. *How to Spot an Owl* (9–adult). 1994, Chapters Publishing (2031 Shelburne Rd., Shelburne, VT 05482) $24.95 (1-881527-35-2); paper $14.95 (1-881527-36-0). A good starter book on owling, in 2 sections: "An Introduction to Owling" and "The Owls of North America." (Rev: BL 4/15/94) [598.9]

PENGUINS

5793 Barkhausen, Annette, and Franz Geiser. *Penguins* (5–7). (Animal Families) 1994, Gareth Stevens $13.95 (0-8368-1002-3). This photo-essay provides facts on penguin evolution, classification, behavior, and reproduction. (Rev: BL 7/94) [598.4]

5794 Vernon, Adele. *The Hoiho, New Zealand's Yellow-Eyed Penguin* (6–12). Photos. 1991, Putnam $15.95 (0-399-21686-3). Photo-essay focuses on the endangered hoiho penguin, found only in New Zealand. (Rev: BL 6/1/91) [598]

Environmental Protection and Endangered Species

5795 Ackerman, Diane. *The Rarest of the Rare: Vanishing Animals, Timeless Worlds* (9–adult). 1995, Random $23 (0-679-40346-9). Ackerman writes with eloquence about endangered species and our close connection with their fate. (Rev: BL 9/1/95) [574.5]

5796 Adams, Jonathan S., and Thomas O. Shane. *The Myth of Wild Africa* (9–adult). 1992, Norton $21.95 (0-393-03396-1). Debunks traditional African conservation methods and explores ways to save the environment through positive coexistence of conservation and development. (Rev: BL 10/1/92) [333.95]

5797 Amdur, Richard. *The Fragile Earth* (9–12). 1994, Chelsea House $19.95 (0-7910-1572-6). A discussion of the origin of the universe and the interdependence of life in understandable terms. (Rev: BL 5/1/94; MJHS; VOYA 6/94) [363.7]

5798 Aylesworth, Thomas G. *Government and the Environment* (5–8). 1993, Enslow LB $17.95 (0-89490-398-5). (Rev: BL 8/93; SLJ 5/93; VOYA 8/93) [363.7]

5799 Barton, Miles. *Vanishing Species* (5–8). (Green Issues) 1991, Gloucester LB $11.90 (0-531-17306-2). (Rev: BL 11/1/91) [363.95]

5800 Bernards, Neal, ed. *The Environmental Crisis* (7–12). (Opposing Viewpoints) 1991, Greenhaven LB $15.95 (0-89908-175-4); paper $8.95 (0-89908-150-9). (Rev: BL 5/15/91; MJHS; SLJ 8/91) [363.7]

5801 Bierhorst, John. *The Way of the Earth: Native America and the Environment* (7–12). 1994, Morrow $15 (0-688-11560-8). Explores the mythologic and folkloric patterns of many Native American belief systems. (Rev: BL 5/15/94; MJHS; SLJ 5/94) [179]

5802 Bramwell, Martyn. *The Environment and Conservation* (5–8). (Prentice Hall World of Nature) 1992, Prentice-Hall LB $15 (0-13-280090-X). (Rev: BL 10/15/92) [333.72]

5803 Challand, Helen J. *Vanishing Forests* (5–8). (Saving Planet Earth) 1991, Children's Press LB $18.95 (0-516-05505-4). Interactive study of an alarming environmental problem. (Rev: BL 3/1/92; SLJ 3/92) [333.75]

5804 Clark, Margaret Goff. *The Endangered Florida Panther* (5–8). 1993, Dutton/Cobblehill $14.99 (0-525-65114-4). Summarizes what little is known about the rare, endangered Florida panther and the ways that wildlife biologists study it in its natural environment. (Rev: BL 4/1/93; SLJ 12/93) [599.74]

5805 Dolan, Edward F. *The American Wilderness and Its Future: Conservation Versus Use* (7–12). 1992, Watts LB $13.90 (0-531-11062-1). A history of the use of federal wilderness areas and the current controversies surrounding them. (Rev: BL 5/1/92; BTA; MJHS; SHS; SLJ 12/92) [333.78]

5806 Ehrlich, Paul R., and others. *Birds in Jeopardy: The Imperiled and Extinct Birds of the United States and Canada, Including Hawaii and Puerto Rico* (9–adult). 1992, Stanford Univ. $39.95 (0-8047-1967-5); paper $17.95 (0-8047-1981-0). Lists the endangered and extinct birds of North America. Includes information on nesting, food, and breeding. (Rev: BL 2/1/92) [333.95]

5807 Erickson, Jon. *Dying Planet: The Extinction of Species* (9–adult). 1991, TAB $16.95 (0-8306-7615-5); paper $9.95 (0-8306-3615-3). A look at the various causes of extinction throughout the ages. (Rev: BL 6/1/91; SHS) [575]

5808 Fleisher, Paul. *Ecology A to Z* (6–10). 1994, Dillon $14.95 (0-87518-561-4). Defines words and phrases related to ecology and to our interaction with the environment. (Rev: BL 4/1/94; MJHS; SLJ 5/94; VOYA 6/94) [363.7]

5809 Gardner, Robert. *Celebrating Earth Day: A Sourcebook of Activities and Experiments* (5–9). 1992, Millbrook LB $15.90 (1-56294-070-8). Discusses such global problems as solid waste, water conservation, overpopulation, and acid rain. Includes easy experiments. (Rev: BL 12/1/92; SLJ 11/92) [333.7]

5810 Gartner, Robert. *Working Together Against the Destruction of the Environment* (7–12). (Library of Social Activism) 1995, Rosen $14.95 (0-8239-1774-6). (Rev: BL 4/15/95) [363.7]

5811 Gay, Kathlyn. *Caretakers of the Earth* (6–9). (Better Earth) 1993, Enslow LB $17.95 (0-89490-397-7). Profiles environmental-protection activists and programs. (Rev: BL 4/1/93; SLJ 5/93) [363.7]

5812 Henley, Don, and Dave Marsh, eds. *Heaven Is under Our Feet* (9–adult). 1991, Longmeadow $18.95 (0-681-41129-5). This volume benefits the Walden Woods Project—created to preserve the site made famous by Thoreau—and consists of celebrity essays about the environment. (Rev: BL 12/15/91) [333.7]

5813 Herda, D. J. *Environmental America: The North Central States* (5–7). 1991, Millbrook LB $12.90 (1-878841-08-4). A focus on environmental issues in the central United States, including a discussion of current agricultural and industrial practices and how people can improve the environment. (Rev: BL 8/91; SLJ 7/91) [639.9]

5814 Herda, D. J. *Environmental America: The Southeastern States* (5–7). 1991, Millbrook LB $12.90 (1-878841-07-6). A look at environmental issues in the southern United States, specifically how pollution has affected the area's wetlands as well as human health. (Rev: BL 8/91; SLJ 7/91) [639.9]

5815 Krensky, Stephen. *Four Against the Odds: The Struggle to Save Our Environment* (5–8). 1992, Scholastic paper $2.95 (0-590-44743-2). Introduces the work of 4 people who fought to raise public awareness about important environmental issues: John Muir, Chico Mendes, Rachel Carson, and Lois Gibb. (Rev: BL 6/1/92; SLJ 10/92) [363.7]

5816 Landau, Elaine. *Endangered Plants* (5–8). (Full Color First Books) 1992, Watts LB $11.90 (0-531-20134-1). Describes various endangered plants—such as species of cactus, sunflower, and lily—why they are endangered, and what's being done to preserve them. (Rev: BL 6/1/92; MJHS; SLJ 7/92) [581.5]

5817 Landau, Elaine. *Environmental Groups: The Earth Savers* (5–8). 1993, Enslow LB $17.95 (0-89490-396-9). (Rev: BL 8/93; VOYA 8/93) [363.7]

5818 Langone, John. *Our Endangered Earth: What We Can Do to Save It* (6–9). 1992, Little, Brown $13.95 (0-316-51415-2). Discusses pollution, deforestation, endangered species, poverty, overpopulation, and energy sources, as well as possible solutions. (Rev: BL 12/1/91; MJHS; SLJ 1/92) [363.7]

5819 Liptak, Karen. *Saving Our Wetlands and Their Wildlife* (5–7). 1991, Watts LB $11.90 (0-531-20092-2). Examines the unique ecosystems of wetlands, swamps, marshes, bogs, and bottomlands. Includes lists of wetlands to visit and organizations concerned with protecting them. (Rev: BL 1/1/92; SLJ 1/92) [333.91]

5820 McClung, Robert M. *Lost Wild America: The Story of Our Extinct and Vanishing Wildlife* (5–8). Rev. ed. Illus. 1993, Shoe String $25 (0-208-02359-3). This history of American wildlife management from pioneer days to the present includes information on extinct and endangered species. (Rev: BL 1/1/94; BTA; MJHS; SLJ 2/94; VOYA 2/94) [591.5]

5821 Mann, Charles C., and Mark L. Plummer. *Noah's Choice: The Future of Endangered Species* (9–adult). 1995, Knopf $24 (0-679-42002-9). Detailed overview of the biological, economic, and political considerations influencing the Endangered Species Act. (Rev: BL 2/15/95) [574.4]

5822 Middleton, Susan, and David Liittschwager. *Here Today: Portraits of Our Vanishing Species* (9–adult). 1991, Chronicle $35 (0-8118-0041-5); paper $19.95 (0-8118-0028-8). Portraits of disappearing plant and animal species. (Rev: BL 2/1/92) [574.5]

5823 O'Neill, Mary. *Nature in Danger* (5–7). Illus. 1991, Troll LB $9.89 (0-8167-2285-4); paper $2.95 (0-8167-2286-2). Historical background shows why our natural resources are suffering. (Rev: BL 6/15/91) [333.7]

5824 Palmer, Tim. *The Snake River: Window to the West* (9–adult). 1991, Island Press (1718 Connecticut Ave. N.W., Suite 300, Washington, DC 20009) $34.95 (0-933280-59-9); paper $17.95 (0-933280-60-2). A history of the Snake River is combined with a detailed report on the ecological issues surrounding it. (Rev: BL 8/91) [333.91]

5825 Patent, Dorothy Hinshaw. *The Challenge of Extinction* (7–12). (Environmental Issues) 1991, Enslow LB $15.95 (0-89490-268-7). (Rev: BL 9/1/91; MJHS) [574.5]

5826 Patent, Dorothy Hinshaw. *Habitats: Saving Wild Places* (7–9). 1993, Enslow LB $17.95 (0-89490-401-9). (Rev: BL 8/93; SLJ 5/93) [333.95]

5827 Porritt, Jonathon. *Save the Earth* (9–adult). 1991, Turner $29.50 (1-878685-05-8). Commentaries by celebrity environmentalists, with photos and color graphics, that illustrate the problem of pollution and suggest remedies. (Rev: BL 10/1/91; SHS) [333.7]

5828 Pyle, Robert Michael. *The Thunder Tree: Lessons from an Urban Wildland* (9–adult). 1993, Houghton $19.95 (0-395-46631-8). An ecologist's essays recalling his boyhood along Colorado's High Line Canal and musing on the relationship of humans to the natural world. (Rev: BL 5/1/93) [508.788]

5829 Reisner, Marc. *Game Wars: The Undercover Pursuit of Wildlife Poachers* (9–adult). 1992, Viking Penguin paper $11 (0-14-008768-0). An action-packed account of 3 U.S. Fish and Wildlife Service undercover operations. (Rev: BL 3/15/91*; SHS) [363.2]

5830 Shabecoff, Philip. *A Fierce Green Fire: The American Environmental Movement* (9–adult). 1992, Hill & Wang $25 (0-8090-8459-7). Explores the evolution of environmentalism, what the movement has accomplished, and what still needs to be done. (Rev: BL 3/1/93) [363.7]

5831 Sherrow, Victoria. *Endangered Mammals of North America* (5–8). 1995, Twenty-First Century LB $18.98 (0-8050-3253-3). An informative, attractive volume on endangered species, with habitat maps and photos. (Rev: BL 12/1/95; VOYA 4/96) [599]

5832 Sholly, Dan R., and Steven M. Newman. *Guardians of Yellowstone: An Intimate Look at the Challenges and Risks of Protecting America's Foremost Wilderness Park* (9–adult). 1991, Morrow $23 (0-688-09213-6). Threats facing the country's national parks are revealed in this detailed report by the chief ranger at Yellowstone Park. (Rev: BL 6/15/91) [634.9]

5833 Silverstein, Alvin, and others. *The Black-Footed Ferret* (5–7). (Endangered in America) 1995, Millbrook LB $15.90 (1-56294-552-1). Explains the physical features and daily lives of these animals. (Rev: BL 10/15/95) [333.95]

5834 Silverstein, Alvin, and others. *The Manatee* (5–7). (Endangered in America) 1995, Millbrook LB $15.90 (1-56294-551-3). Excellent photos help reveal how these animals live and why they became endangered. (Rev: BL 10/15/95) [599.5]

5835 Silverstein, Alvin, and others. *Saving Endangered Animals* (6–8). (Better Earth) 1993, Enslow LB $17.95 (0-89490-402-7). Practical information about saving threatened animal species and reintroducing them into their native environments. (Rev: BL 5/1/93; MJHS; SLJ 5/93) [333.95]

5836 Stefoff, Rebecca. *The American Environmental Movement* (7–10). 1995, Facts on File $17.95 (0-8160-3046-4). A study of environmental activities from the fifteenth century to the present, with discussion of the prominent figures and incidents in the movement. (Rev: BL 9/1/95; SLJ 9/95) [363.7]

5837 Stefoff, Rebecca. *Extinction* (9–12). 1991, Chelsea House $19.95 (0-7910-1578-5). A history of vanished species and how humans have, in some cases, accelerated the process of extinction. (Rev: BL 2/1/92; BTA; SLJ 11/91) [333.95137]

5838 Tesar, Jenny. *Endangered Habitats* (5–9). (Our Fragile Planet) 1992, Facts on File/Blackbirch LB $18.95 (0-8160-2493-6). A succinct overview of food chains and ecosystems, and an account of environmental problems, extinction, and endangered species. (Rev: BL 6/1/92; MJHS) [333.95]

5839 Tudge, Colin. *Last Animals at the Zoo: How Mass Extinction Can Be Stopped* (9–adult). 1992, Island Press $22 (1-55963-158-9). Explains what zoos have accomplished in the area of conservation breeding. (Rev: BL 3/1/92) [639.9]

5840 Turner, Tom. *Sierra Club: 100 Years of Protecting Nature* (9–adult). Photos. 1991, Abrams $49.50 (0-8109-3820-0). A commemoration of the Sierra Club that provides a history of the organization, its mission, and its accomplishments. (Rev: BL 11/15/91; SHS) [333.9516]

5841 Wallace, Aubrey. *Eco-Heroes: Twelve Tales of Environmental Victory* (9–adult). 1993, Mercury paper $12.50 (1-56279-033-1). The intriguing stories of 12 crusaders whose efforts have helped the environment. (Rev: BL 3/1/93) [363.7]

5842 Whitman, Sylvia. *This Land Is Your Land: The American Conservation Movement* (5–7). 1994, Lerner LB $14.21 (0-8225-1729-9). This historical overview traces the movement from its beginnings in 1870 to the present day, and discusses our major concerns—recycling, oil spills, and nuclear disaster. (Rev: BL 12/15/94; SLJ 12/94) [363.7]

Farms and Ranches

GENERAL AND MISCELLANEOUS

5843 Bial, Raymond. *Portrait of a Farm Family* (5–7). 1995, Houghton $15.95 (0-395-69936-3). Photos and text reflect the hard work and many complex decisions that comprise farm life. (Rev: BL 9/1/95*; SLJ 12/95) [338.1]

5844 Paulsen, Gary. *Clabbered Dirt, Sweet Grass* (9–adult). 1992, Harcourt $19.95 (0-15-118101-2). Paulsen eloquently describes modern farm life: spring calves, summer gardens, harvest, and winter solitude. (Rev: BL 9/1/92; SHS) [813]

ANIMALS AND CROPS

5845 Damerow, Gail. *Your Chickens: A Kid's Guide to Raising and Showing* (5–7). 1993, Storey/Garden Way paper $12.95 (0-88266-823-4). Covers a multitude of aspects of raising and showing chickens. (Rev: BL 5/15/94; SLJ 1/94) [636.5]

5846 Damerow, Gail. *Your Goats: A Kid's Guide to Raising and Showing* (5–7). 1993, Storey/Garden Way paper $12.95 (0-88266-825-0). An everything-you-want-to-know book with a sense of humor about raising and showing goats. (Rev: BL 5/15/94; SLJ 1/94) [636.3]

Insects and Arachnids

GENERAL AND MISCELLANEOUS

5847 Baker, Wendy, and others. *Insects* (5–7). (Make It Work!) 1994, Thomson Learning $15.95 (1-56847-257-9). (Rev: BL 10/15/94) [372.3]

5848 Baker, Wendy, and Andrew Haslam. *Los insectos* (5–8). (Make It Work!) Tr. by Fernando Bort. Photos. 1993, Ediciones SM (Madrid, Spain) $19.95 (84-348-3996-2). Simple explanations and clear color photos allow children to experience insects in flight, how they obtain food, and their defense mechanisms. English title: *Insects*. Other titles in the series: *La electricidad (Electricity), El sonido (Sound), La Tierra (Earth), Las Máquinas (Simple Machines),* and *Las plantas (Plants)*. (Rev: BL 2/1/94)

5849 Facklam, Howard, and Margery Facklam. *Insects* (5–7). 1994, Twenty-First Century LB $15.95 (0-8050-2859-5). (Rev: BL 1/1/95; SLJ 3/95) [595]

5850 Hubbell, Sue. *Broadsides from the Other Order: A Book of Bugs* (9–adult). 1993, Random $23 (0-679-40062-1). A rich, informative survey of insects by an acclaimed nature writer and beekeeper. (Rev: BL 3/15/93*; SLJ 10/93) [595.7]

5851 Pringle, Laurence. *Scorpion Man: Exploring the World of Scorpions* (5–7). 1994, Scribner $15.95 (0-684-19560-7). (Rev: BL 1/15/95; SLJ 3/95) [595.4]

BEES AND WASPS

5852 Whynott, Douglas. *Following the Bloom: Across America with Migratory Beekeepers* (9–adult). 1991, Stackpole $19.95 (0-8117-1944-8). (Rev: BL 2/15/91*) [638]

BUTTERFLIES, MOTHS, AND CATERPILLARS

5853 Lasky, Kathryn. *Monarchs* (5–7). (Gulliver Green Books) Photos. 1993, Harcourt LB $16.95 (0-15-255296-0); paper $8.95 (0-15-255297-9). Lasky examines the life and unusual migration cycle of the monarch butterfly. Awards: SLJ Best Book. (Rev: BL 11/15/93; SLJS 1/94*)

5854 Lavies, Bianca. *Monarch Butterflies: Mysterious Travelers* (5–7). 1992, Dutton LB $14.99 (0-525-44905-1). Chronicles an expedition to the recently discovered Mexican site where monarch butterflies summer and the butterfly's cycle from egg to adult. Color photos. Awards: SLJ Best Book. (Rev: BL 1/15/93; MJHS; SLJS 6/93*) [595.78]

SPIDERS

5855 Dewey, Jennifer Owings. *Spiders Near and Far* (5–7). 1993, Dutton LB $14.99 (0-525-44979-5). Discusses 2 main types of spiders—web builders and wanderers—how they subdue and kill prey, body structures, reproduction, and other characteristics. (Rev: BL 2/15/93; SLJ 5/93) [595.4]

Marine and Freshwater Life

GENERAL AND MISCELLANEOUS

5856 Curtis, Patricia. *Aquatic Animals in the Wild and in Captivity* (5–7). 1992, Dutton/Lodestar $16 (0-525-67384-9). An insightful look at the homes and habits of aquatic animals in and out of the wild. Illustrated. (Rev: BL 9/15/92; SLJ 5/92) [590]

5857 Downer, Ann. *Don't Blink Now! Capturing the Hidden World of Sea Creatures* (5–8). 1991, Watts LB $13.90 (0-531-11072-9). An introduction to the world of marine animals, covering hunting techniques, survival, reproduction, and possible fates of these creatures. Includes dramatic underwater photography. (Rev: BL 1/1/92; SLJ 2/92) [591.92]

5858 Holmes, Martha. *Sea Trek* (9–adult). 1993, Parkwest/BBC $29.95 (0-563-36091-7). An underwater journey to 5 ocean sites, with beautiful color photos. A companion to the BBC/National Geographic TV series. (Rev: BL 3/1/93; SLJ 7/93) [551.46]

5859 Kaufman, Les, and others. *Alligators to Zooplankton: A Dictionary of Water Babies* (5–7). 1991, Watts LB $14.90 (0-531-10995-X). Introduction to the undersea world, arranged alphapbetically. Illustrated with spectacular color photography. (Rev: BL 6/15/91; SLJ 7/91) [591.92]

5860 Sargent, William. *Night Reef: Dusk to Dawn on a Coral Reef* (5–7). (New England Aquarium Books) 1991, Watts LB $13.90 (0-531-11073-7). Examination of a wide range of nocturnal marine life. (Rev: BL 2/1/92; SLJ 2/92*) [591.9]

5861 Sherrow, Victoria. *Seals, Sea Lions, and Walruses* (5–7). 1991, Watts LB $11.90 (0-531-20028-0). An illustrated informational text on pinnipeds, including discussions of environmental pollution, fishing industry problems, and protection efforts. (Rev: BL 12/15/91) [599.74]

5862 Taylor, Barbara. *La charca* (5–8). (Mira de cereal) Tr. by Nuria Hernández de Larenzo. Photos. 1993, Grupo Anaya (Madrid, Spain) $15.95 (84-207-4751-3). For young scientists-to-be, this volume includes a simple text and spectacular color photos, including close-up views of animals and plants in their natural habitats. English title: *Pond Life*. Other titles in the series: *El desierto (Desert), La selva tropical (Jungle),* and *Arrecige de coral (Coral Reef)*. (Rev: BL 2/1/94)

CORALS AND JELLYFISH

5863 Gowell, Elizabeth Tayntor. *Sea Jellies: Rainbows in the Sea* (5–8). 1993, Watts LB $15.90 (0-531-11152-0). Their unusual life cycles, varied means of movement, and ability to sting make these animals engrossing subjects. Well-labeled color photos expand the text. Awards: SLJ Best Book. (Rev: BL 9/1/93; MJHS; SLJ 8/93*) [591]

FISHES

5864 Guiberson, Brenda Z. *Salmon Story* (5–7). 1993, Holt $14.95 (0-8050-2754-8). A description of the dramatic life cycle of the Pacific salmon, its precarious status, and a rescue plan being carried out by scientists and farmers. (Rev: BL 1/1/94; SLJ 4/94) [597]

SHARKS

5865 Cerullo, Mary M. *Sharks: Challengers of the Deep* (5–9). 1993, Dutton/Cobblehill $15 (0-525-65100-4). Packed with information and photos on sharks' physical characteristics, behavior, ecology, and survival. Awards: SLJ Best Book. (Rev: BL 1/15/93; MJHS; SLJ 2/93*) [597]

5866 Cousteau, Jean-Michel, and Mose Richards. *Cousteau's Great White Shark* (9–adult). 1992, Abrams $39.95 (0-8109-3181-8). Chronicles the real-life undersea investigations of an expedition headed by Jacques-Yves Cousteau's son. Illustrations. (Rev: BL 10/15/92) [597]

5867 MacQuitty, Miranda. *Shark* (5–9). (Eyewitness Books) 1992, Knopf LB $15.99 (0-679-91683-0). (Rev: BL 11/1/92) [597]

5868 MacQuitty, Miranda. *Tiburones* (5–10). (Biblioteca visual Altea) 1992, Santillana (Madrid, Spain) $18.95 (84-372-3770-X). Contains a clear, concise text on sharks, with close-up photos, charts, and drawings in color. English title: *Sharks*. (Rev: BL 2/1/94)

WHALES, DOLPHINS, AND OTHER SEA MAMMALS

5869 Dietz, Tim. *The Call of the Siren: Manatees and Dugongs* (9–adult). 1992, Fulcrum paper $15.95 (1-55591-104-8). A consciousness-raising description of the fight to save 2 endangered species, the gentle manatees and the dugongs, from extinction. (Rev: BL 10/1/92) [599.8]

5870 Ellis, Richard. *Men and Whales* (9–adult). 1991, Knopf $40 (0-394-55839-1). Describes families of whales in detail and covers the history of the whaling industry, as well as the current, belated "save the whales" movement. (Rev: BL 10/15/91*) [639.2]

5871 Gourley, Catherine. *Hunting Neptune's Giants: True Stories of American Whaling* (5–8). 1995, Millbrook LB $19.90 (1-56294-534-3). A look at the whaling industry's history through diaries and books by the men and women involved in this once important industry. (Rev: BL 11/1/95*; SLJ 12/95) [639.3]

5872 Grace, Eric S. *Seals* (5–10). (Wildlife Library) Photos. 1991, Little, Brown/Sierra Club

$14.95 (0-316-32279-2). An introduction to the lives of seals, sea lions, and walruses. (Rev: SLJ 2/92*)

5873 Hand, Douglas. *Gone Whaling: A Search for Orcas in the Northwest Waters* (9–adult). 1994, Simon & Schuster $20 (0-671-76840-9). The orca, a gentle beast known as the "killer whale," is examined in its natural habitat and in captivity. (Rev: BL 7/94) [599.5]

5874 Hoyt, Erich. *Meeting the Whales: The Equinox Guide to Giants of the Deep* (5–10). Illus. 1991, Camden House $17.95 (0-921820-23-2); paper $9.95 (0-921820-23-2). This guide to 19 whale species describes their origins and habits. Includes discussion of whale watching and photography. (Rev: BL 8/91) [599.5]

5875 Morton, Alexandra. *In the Company of Whales: From the Diary of a Whale Watcher* (6–9). 1993, Orca $15.95 (1-55143-000-2). A committed whale watcher living on an island off the coast of British Columbia provides an intimate view of the creature's behavior. (Rev: BL 2/1/94) [599.5]

5876 Norris, Kenneth S. *Dolphin Days: The Life and Times of the Spinner Dolphin* (9–adult). 1991, Norton $21.95 (0-393-02945-X). This researcher's account of a dolphin society explains the dolphin's language and navigational skills and provides an unsettling eyewitness report of the deadly disorientation and fear caused by tuna netting. (Rev: BL 9/1/91) [599.5]

5877 Obee, Bruce. *Guardians of the Whales: The Quest to Study Whales in the Wild* (9–adult). 1992, Alaska Northwest $34.95 (0-88240-428-8). Profiles the scientists largely responsible for saving whales from near extinction and explains how research on the marine mammals is conducted. (Rev: BL 10/15/92) [599.50451]

5878 Papastavrou, Vassili. *Whale* (5–9). (Eyewitness Books) 1993, Knopf LB $15.99 (0-679-93884-2). (Rev: BL 10/1/93) [599.5]

5879 Payne, Roger. *Among Whales* (9–adult). 1995, Macmillan $25 (0-02-595245-5). The anatomy, habits, and characteristics of whales by one of the world's leading marine mammal experts. (Rev: BL 4/15/95*) [599.5]

5880 Silverstein, Alvin, and others. *The Sea Otter* (5–7). (Endangered in America) 1995, Millbrook LB $15.40 (1-56294-418-5). Shows how the fur trade and oil spills have jeopardized the sea otter and describes current rescue efforts. (Rev: BL 6/1–15/95) [599.74]

Microbiology and Biotechnology

5881 Facklam, Howard, and Margery Facklam. *Bacteria* (5–7). (Invaders) 1994, Twenty-First Century LB $15.95 (0-8050-2857-9). (Rev: BL 1/1/95; SLJ 3/95) [589.9]

5882 Margulis, Lynn, and Dorion Sagan. *What Is Life?* (9–adult). 1995, Simon & Schuster $40 (0-684-81326-2). Explores the multifaceted answers to the question the title poses. A microscopic complement to Stephen Gould's macroscopic paleobiology in his *Book of Life*. (Rev: BL 9/1/95) [577]

5883 Nardo, Don. *Germs: Mysterious Microorganisms* (6–8). (Encyclopedia of Discovery and Invention) 1991, Lucent LB $15.95 (1-56006-214-2). Explains the history of germ theory and "useful" germs, as well as those that cause disease. (Rev: BL 12/1/91; MJHS) [616]

Pets

GENERAL AND MISCELLANEOUS

5884 Hearne, Vicki. *Animal Happiness* (9–adult). 1994, HarperCollins $20 (0-06-019016-7). An animal trainer/poet/philosopher presents a collection of vignettes about the sentiments inspired by animals. (Rev: BL 1/1/94) [636]

5885 Taylor, Michael. *Pot Bellied Pigs as a Family Pet* (9–adult). 1993, TFH (211 Sylvania Ave., Neptune, NJ 07553) $29.95 (0-86622-081-X). Includes what to feed pot-bellies, how they are related to other swine, and legal restrictions on ownership. (Rev: BL 4/15/93) [636.4]

CATS

5886 Allan, Eric, and Lynda Bonning. *Everycat: The Complete Guide to Cat Care, Behaviour and Health* (9–adult). 1993, Allen & Unwin paper $24.95 (1-86373-307-8). Specifics on feline health, including illnesses, first aid, infectious diseases, pregnancy and newborn care, and nutrition. (Rev: BL 5/15/93) [636.8]

5887 Altman, Roberta. *The Quintessential Cat* (9–adult). 1994, Prentice-Hall $27.50 (0-671-85008-3). Feline tales, trivia, and tips. Discusses specific breeds and their abilities and cat-loving celebrities, such as Robert De Niro. (Rev: BL 10/1/94) [599.74]

5888 Caras, Roger A. *The Cats of Thistle Hill: A Mostly Peaceable Kingdom* (9–adult). 1994, Simon & Schuster $22 (0-671-75462-9). Anecdotes about the personalities and behaviors of the dozens of cats—and countless other animals—that share Caras's home and grounds. (Rev: BL 5/1/94) [636.8]

5889 Clutton-Brock, Juliet. *Cat* (5–9). (Eyewitness Books) 1991, Knopf LB $15.99 (0-679-91458-7). (Rev: BL 12/1/91; MJHS) [599.74]

5890 Damian, Jacqueline. *Sasha's Tail: Lessons from a Life with Cats* (9–adult). 1995, Norton $19.95 (0-393-03731-2). A discussion of feline personality and behavior. (Rev: BL 3/1/95) [808.8]

5891 Denny, D. Michael. *How to Get a Cat to Sit in Your Lap: Confessions of an Unconventional Cat Person* (9–adult). 1995, Andiron (136 River Rd., East Hanover, NJ 07936) paper $14.95 (0-9645799-0-1). Thirty years of living with cats lets Denny humorously tell of cat evolution, anatomy, behavior, naming, hunting, eating, and more. (Rev: BL 6/1–15/95) [636.8]

5892 Fogle, Bruce. *Know Your Cat: An Owner's Guide to Cat Behavior* (9–adult). 1991, Dorling Kindersley $19.95 (1-879431-04-1). A veterinarian provides insights into a cat's behavior, with 350 color photos. (Rev: BL 1/1/92; MJHS; SHS) [636.8]

5893 Hammond, Sean, and Carolyn Usrey. *How to Raise a Sane and Healthy Cat* (9–adult). 1994, Howell Book $22 (0-87605-797-0). Answers questions regarding the many facets of cat care and ownership, including choosing a cat, nutrition, and stray-cat care. (Rev: BL 7/94) [636.8]

5894 Herriot, James. *James Herriot's Cat Stories* (9–adult). 1994, St. Martin's $16.95 (0-312-11342-0). A small collection of cat tales, ranging from the informative and scientific to the humorous and poignant. (Rev: BL 7/94) [636.8]

5895 Huxley, Sally. *The Cat Who Had Two Lives* (9–adult). 1994, Donald I. Fine $18.95 (1-55611-386-2). The true tale of Pip, a stray cat who entered the life of the formerly prejudiced author and found a happy, loving home. (Rev: BL 1/15/94) [636.8]

5896 Lumpkin, Susan. *Small Cats* (5–8). (Great Creatures of the World) 1993, Facts on File LB $17.95 (0-8160-2848-6). (Rev: BL 2/15/93; MJHS) [599.74]

5897 McGinnis, Terri. *The Well Cat Book: The Classic Comprehensive Handbook of Cat Care* (9–adult). 2nd ed. 1993, Random $23 (0-394-58769-3). An updated, authoritative guide by a veterinarian, covering feline anatomy, preventive medicine, diagnosis, home care, breeding, reproduction, and choosing a doctor. (Rev: BL 6/1–15/93) [636.808]

5898 Maggitti, Phil. *Owning the Right Cat* (9–adult). 1993, Tetra $24.95 (1-56465-111-8). Provides information on feeding, grooming, breeding, showing, laws, history, health care, and genetics. Color photos and illustrations. (Rev: BL 11/1/93) [636.8]

5899 Moravec, Randy. *Claude* (9–adult). 1992, Putnam $14.95 (0-399-13792-0). A series of 2-page spreads combining a photograph of the author's pet cat with observations on feline behavior. (Rev: BL 11/1/92) [636.8]

5900 Oates, Joyce Carol, and Daniel Halpern, eds. *The Sophisticated Cat: A Gathering of Stories, Poems, and Miscellaneous Writings about Cats* (9–adult). 1992, Dutton $23 (0-525-93522-3). Feline prose and poetry from nearly 100 writers throughout history, from Aesop to Oates and Halpern themselves. (Rev: BL 10/15/92) [808.8]

5901 Steiger, Brad. *Cats Incredible! True Stories of Fantastic Feline Feats* (9–adult). 1994, NAL/Plume paper $7.95 (0-452-27159-2). This amusing cat miscellany provides many feline factoids and believe-it-or-not anecdotes. (Rev: BL 3/15/94) [636.8]

5902 Zistel, Era. *A Gathering of Cats* (9–adult). 1993, J. N. Townsend Publishing (12 Greenleaf Dr., Exeter, NH 03833) paper $11.95 (1-880158-00-0). Zistel tells the stories of various members of her pride of cats. (Rev: BL 11/1/93) [636.8]

DOGS

5903 Alexander, Sally Hobart. *Mom's Best Friend* (5–8). Photos. 1992, Macmillan $14.95 (0-02-700393-0). This photo-essay begins with the death of the author's first guide dog and tells of her trip to get a new dog and the adjustment period following. (Rev: BL 11/1/92; SLJ 12/92) [362.4]

5904 Caras, Roger A. *A Dog Is Listening: The Way Some of Our Closest Friends View Us* (9–adult). 1992, Summit $20 (0-671-70249-1). The president of the ASPCA explains the evolution of the dog and clears up common misconceptions. (Rev: BL 1/15/92; SHS) [636.7]

5905 Clutton-Brock, Juliet. *Dog* (5–9). (Eyewitness Books) 1991, Knopf LB $15.99 (0-679-91459-5). (Rev: BL 12/1/91) [599.74]

5906 Fogle, Bruce. *ASPCA Complete Dog Care Manual* (9–adult). 1993, Dorling Kindersley $24.95 (1-56458-168-3). Illustrated information and instructions for novice owners on diet, housebreaking, obedience, grooming, and health. (Rev: BL 5/1/93; SHS) [636.7]

5907 Fogle, Bruce. *The Encyclopedia of the Dog* (9–12). 1995, DK $39.95 (0-7894-0149-5). (Rev: BL 10/1/95; SLJ 3/96; VOYA 4/96)

5908 Fogle, Bruce. *Know Your Dog: An Owner's Guide to Dog Behavior* (9–adult). 1992, Dorling Kindersley $22.95 (1-56458-080-6). Color photos enhance Fogle's introduction to dog characteristics and behavior in this large-format book. (Rev: BL 1/1/93; MJHS; SHS) [636.7]

5909 Johns, Bud, ed. *Old Dogs Remembered* (9–adult). 1993, Carroll & Graf $19.95 (0-88184-928-6). Some nineteenth- and twentieth-century writers' remembrances of dog friends, including those of E. B. White, James Thurber, and John Updike. (Rev: BL 6/1–15/93) [814]

5910 Maggitti, Phil. *Owning the Right Dog* (9–adult). 1993, Tetra $24.95 (1-56465-110-X). Provides information on feeding, grooming, breeding, showing, and training. Color illustrations. (Rev: BL 11/1/93) [636.7]

5911 Ogden, Paul. *Chelsea: The Story of a Signal Dog* (9–adult). 1992, Little, Brown $18.95 (0-316-63375-5). This personal account of a deaf professor of communications and his signal dog describes the training and the experience of living with his canine companion. (Rev: BL 11/15/91; SLJ 5/92) [636.7]

5912 Scalisi, Danny, and Libby Moses. *When Rover Just Won't Do: Over 2000 Suggestions for Naming Your Puppy* (9–adult). 1993, Howell paper $10 (0-87605-691-5). This collection of names for dogs includes more than 2,000 ideas, from Fajita to Rocky and Bullwinkle. (Rev: BL 11/1/93) [636.7]

5913 Squire, Ann. *Understanding Man's Best Friend: Why Dogs Look and Act the Way They Do* (5–7). 1991, Macmillan $14.95 (0-02-786590-8). Beginning with the wolf connection, this guide offers a history and analysis of dog breeds and behavior. (Rev: BL 6/15/91; SLJ 9/91) [636.7]

5914 White, Betty, and Tom Sullivan. *The Leading Lady* (9–adult). 1991, Bantam $20 (0-553-07395-8). After serving as a singer's guide dog for 12 years, a golden retriever retires and spends the rest of her life as actress Betty White's house pet. (Rev: BL 8/91) [636.7]

FISHES

5915 Levine, Joseph S. *The Complete Fishkeeper: Everything Aquarium Fish Need to Be Happy, Healthy and Alive* (9–adult). 1991, Hearst $30 (0-688-10146-1). Discusses fish anatomy and provides information on the doctoring, feeding, and chemistry of aquarium fish and plants and aquarium maintenance. (Rev: BL 11/15/91) [639.3]

5916 Quinn, John R. *Our Native Fishes: The Aquarium Hobbyist's Guide to Observing, Collecting, and Keeping Them* (9–adult). 1991, Countryman paper $14.95 (0-88150-181-6). Tips for fish hobbyists on maintaining aquarium specimens as well as advice on bringing fish from local waters indoors. (Rev: BL 1/15/91) [639.3]

HORSES

5917 Clutton-Brock, Juliet. *Caballos* (5–10). (Biblioteca visual Altea) 1992, Santillana (Madrid, Spain) $18.95 (84-372-3766-1). Originally published in Great Britain, this volume contains a clear, concise text on horses, with close-up photos, charts, and drawings in color. English title: *Horses*. (Rev: BL 2/1/94)

5918 Clutton-Brock, Juliet. *Horse* (5–9). (Eyewitness Books) 1992, Knopf LB $15.99 (0-679-91681-4). (Rev: BL 6/1/92; MJHS) [636.1]

5919 Edwards, Elwyn Hartley. *The Ultimate Horse Book* (9–adult). 1991, Random/Dorling Kindersley $29.95 (1-879431-03-3). This illustrated guide introduces more than 80 breeds of horses and ponies, describes their relationship with humans, and discusses equine ownership and care. (Rev: BL 12/1/91; MJHS) [636.1]

5920 Meltzer, Milton. *Hold Your Horses! A Feedbag Full of Fact and Fable* (5–8). 1995, HarperCollins LB $14.89 (0-06-024478-X). The last of Meltzer's books from the trilogy on vegetable-mineral-animal and the 3 kingdoms of nature. Focuses on how people have used horses in work, war, sports, and art. (Rev: BL 11/15/95; SLJ 12/95*) [636.1]

5921 Van Der Linde, Laurel. *The White Stallions: The Story of the Dancing Horses of Lipizza* (6–8). 1994, Macmillan/New Discovery $14.95 (0-02-759055-0). The history of the famous Austrian Lipizzans, including how the horses were protected during World War II. (Rev: BL 5/1/94; BTA; MJHS; SLJ 6/94) [636.1]

Zoos, Aquariums, and Animal Care Shelters

5922 Benyus, Janine M. *Beastly Behaviors: A Zoo Lover's Companion: What Makes Whales Whistle, Cranes Dance, Pandas Turn Somersaults, and Crocodiles Roar* (9–adult). 1992, Addison-Wesley $29.95 (0-201-57008-4). This companion to zoo visits details the physical characteristics and social, feeding, parenting, and sexual behaviors of more than 20 captive animals. (Rev: BL 10/1/92; SHS) [591.51]

5923 Curtis, Patricia. *Animals and the New Zoos* (5–7). 1991, Dutton/Lodestar $15.95 (0-525-67347-4). An examination of the new philosophy of housing for zoo animals that stresses a more natural habitat and more humane treatment. (Rev: BL 10/1/91; SLJ 10/91) [590]

5924 Dewey, Jennifer Owings. *Wildlife Rescue: The Work of Dr. Kathleen Ramsay* (5–7). 1994, Boyds Mills $16.95 (1-56397-045-7). Profiles Dr. Ramsey's National Wildlife Center, dedicated to healing injured animals that are returned to the wild when they recover. Awards: SLJ Best Book. (Rev: BL 9/1/94; SLJ 9/94) [639.95]

5925 Smith, Roland. *Inside the Zoo Nursery* (5–7). Photos. 1993, Dutton/Cobblehill $15 (0-525-65084-9). A clear presentation, with color photos, of the care of animal babies in zoos. Awards: SLJ Best Book. (Rev: BL 1/15/93; SLJ 1/93*)

5926 Stretch, Mary Jane, and Phyllis Hobe. *The Swan in My Bathtub and Other Adventures in the Aark* (9–adult). 1991, Dutton $19.95 (0-525-24999-0). An animal rehabilitator seeks to enlighten people about the impact they have on nature. (Rev: BL 6/1/91; SHS) [639.9]

5927 Yancey, Diane. *Zoos* (5–8). (Overview) 1995, Lucent LB $14.95 (1-56006-163-4). Looks into the history and controversy over zoos and species survival plans from an ecologically friendly approach. (Rev: BL 6/1–15/95; SLJ 3/95) [590]

Chemistry

General and Miscellaneous

5928 Atkins, P. W. *The Periodic Kingdom: A Journey into the Land of the Chemical Elements* (9–adult). (Science Masters) 1995, Basic Books $20 (0-465-07265-8). Looks at the chemical elements by weight, density, and ionization energies, describing their properties and the chemists who isolated them. (Rev: BL 6/1–15/95) [541.2]

5929 Brock, William H. *The Norton History of Chemistry* (9–adult). 1993, Norton $35 (0-393-03536-0); paper $15.95 (0-393-31043-4). Historical highlights and development of the science of chemistry. (Rev: BL 7/93) [540.9]

5930 Cooper, Christopher. *Matter* (5–8). (Eyewitness Science) 1992, Dorling Kindersley LB $15.95 (1-879431-88-2). Clear explanations and color photos provide a wealth of information on the origins, principles, and history of the study of matter. (Rev: BL 1/15/93; MJHS; SLJ 12/92) [530]

5931 Galas, Judith C. *Plastics: Molding the Past, Shaping the Future* (6–10). (Encyclopedia of Discovery and Invention) 1995, Lucent LB $15.95 (1-56006-251-7). (Rev: BL 4/15/95) [668.4]

5932 Hoffman, Roald, and Vivian Torrence. *Chemistry Imagined: Reflections on Science* (9–adult). 1993, Smithsonian $19.95 (1-56098-214-4). Celebrates the wonders of chemistry, from alchemy to synthetics, in history, anecdote, poetry, and art. (Rev: BL 4/15/93; SLJ 12/93) [540.2]

Geology and Geography

Earth and Geology

5933 Beautier, François. *Descubrir la tierra* (7–12). Illus. 1991, Ediciones Larousse $15.90 (1-56294-175-5). Introduces the diversity of shapes and forms found on Earth. Includes high-quality color photos and other illustrations. English title: *Discovering the Earth*. (Rev: BL 3/1/93)

5934 Brown, Kenneth. *Cycles of Rock and Water: At the Pacific Edge* (9–adult). 1993, HarperCollins $23 (0-06-016056-X). A guided tour of the San Andreas Fault, from Baja California to the Aleutian Islands, describing the region's instability and its animal, marine, and vulnerable human life. (Rev: BL 5/1/93*) [557.9]

5935 Erickson, Jon. *Marine Geology: Undersea Landforms and Life Forms* (9–adult). 1996, Facts on File $24.95 (0-8160-3354-4). An examination of the dynamics of the ocean floor and its geologic history plus a discussion of deep-sea research. (Rev: BL 12/1/95) [551.46]

5936 Erickson, Jon. *Plate Tectonics: Unraveling the Mysteries of the Earth* (9–adult). (Changing Earth) 1992, Facts on File $24.95 (0-8160-2588-6). Deals with new ideas related to the plate movement theory. (Rev: BL 4/15/92) [551.1]

5937 Officer, Charles, and Jake Page. *Tales of the Earth* (9–adult). 1993, Oxford Univ. $21 (0-19-507785-7). This introduction to earth science presents accounts of natural castastrophes: volcanoes, floods, earthquakes, meteorites and comets, profound climatic change, and mass extinctions. (Rev: BL 5/1/93) [550]

5938 Sattler, Helen Roney. *Our Patchwork Planet: The Story of Plate Tectonics* (5–8). Illus. 1995, Lothrop LB $15.93 (0-688-09313-2). A look at the planet in a new way via the motion that is constantly going on. (Rev: BL 2/15/95; SLJ 4/95) [551.1]

5939 Wiggers, Raymond. *The Amateur Geologist: Explorations and Investigations* (6–10). (Amateur Science) 1993, Watts LB $12.90 (0-531-11112-1). Introduces the fundamentals of geology and suggests activities for exploration of the subject. (Rev: BL 1/15/94; SLJ 3/94) [550]

Earthquakes and Volcanoes

5940 Bisel, Sara C. *The Secrets of Vesuvius: Exploring the Mysteries of an Ancient Buried City* (5–7). (Time Quest) 1991, Scholastic/Madison $15.95 (0-590-43850-6). A physical anthropologist pieces together physical evidence to recreate an ancient Roman city destroyed in the violent eruption of Mount Vesuvius in A.D. 79. (Rev: BL 7/91; MJHS; SLJ 2/91) [937]

5941 Booth, Basil. *Earthquakes and Volcanoes* (5–8). 1992, Macmillan/New Discovery LB $13.95 (0-02-711735-9). The interrelationship between earthquakes and volcanoes is explored in picture-essay form. (Rev: BL 9/15/92; MJHS; SLJ 10/92) [551.2]

5942 Chiesa, Pierre. *Volcanes y terremotos* (7–12). Illus. 1991, Ediciones Larousse $15.90 (1-56294-176-3). Introduces readers to ancient and modern volcanoes and earthquakes. High-quality color photos and other illustrations. English title: *Volcanoes and Earthquakes*. (Rev: BL 3/1/93)

5943 Dineen, Jacqueline. *Volcanoes* (5–8). (Natural Disasters) 1991, Gloucester $11.90 (0-531-17338-0). Studies the power and unpredictability of volcanic activity and describes some recent erruptions, including Mt. St. Helens. (Rev: BL 1/15/92) [551.2]

5944 Erickson, Jon. *Quakes, Eruptions and Other Geologic Cataclysms* (9–adult). 1994, Facts on File $26.95 (0-8160-2949-0). Describes the physical mechanisms causing such geologic cataclysms as earthquakes, volcanoes, landslides, mudflows, and dust storms. (Rev: BL 8/94; SLJ 11/94) [550]

5945 Levy, Matthys, and Mario Salvadori. *Why the Earth Quakes* (9–adult). 1995, Norton $25 (0-393-03774-6). All about earthquakes and safety precautions in case there is one. (Rev: BL 9/15/95) [551.2]

5946 McPhee, John. *Assembling California* (9–adult). 1993, Farrar $20 (0-374-10645-2). The final volume in a 4-part series on geologic principles, emphasizing plate tectonics. (Rev: BL 12/1/92*) [557.94]

5947 Thro, Ellen. *Volcanoes of the United States* (7–10). 1992, Watts LB $12.40 (0-531-12522-X). Focuses on volcanic activity in Alaska, Hawaii, and the Pacific Northwest, including history, related thermal activities, environmental impact, and modern scientific methods of study. (Rev: BL 7/92; SHS; SLJ 8/92) [551.2]

5948 van Rose, Susanna. *Volcanes* (5–10). (Biblioteca visual Altea) 1992, Santillana (Madrid, Spain) $18.95 (84-372-3773-4). Contains a clear, concise text on volcanoes, with close-up color photos, charts, and drawings. English title: *Volcanoes*. (Rev: BL 2/1/94)

5949 van Rose, Susanna. *Volcano and Earthquake* (5–9). (Eyewitness Books) 1992, Knopf LB $15.99 (0-679-91685-7). (Rev: BL 11/1/92; MJHS) [551.2]

5950 Walker, Jane. *Earthquakes* (5–8). (Natural Disasters) 1992, Gloucester LB $11.90 (0-531-17360-7). (Rev: BL 9/15/92) [551.2]

Icebergs and Glaciers

5951 Green, Bill. *Water, Ice and Stone: Science and Memory on the Antarctic Lakes* (9–adult). 1995, Crown/Harmony $23 (0-517-58759-9). A geochemist combines lyrical musings with scientific passion in an exploration of the chemistry of the Antarctic lakes. (Rev: BL 5/1/95*) [551.48]

Physical Geography

5952 Arritt, Susan. *The Living Earth Book of Deserts* (9–adult). 1993, Reader's Digest $30 (0-89577-519-0). This guided tour through the world's deserts combines history with explanations of scientific phenomena, geological information, and plant and animal life. (Rev: BL 2/15/94; VOYA 6/94) [508.315]

5953 Collinson, Alan. *Mountains* (5–8). (Ecology Watch) 1992, Dillon LB $13.95 (0-87518-493-6). (Rev: BL 11/1/92) [574.5]

5954 Duffy, Trent. *The Vanishing Wetlands* (7–12). 1994, Watts LB $13.40 (0-531-13034-7). Defines the wetland environment, explains its destruction, and suggests what can be done to preserve wetland ecosystems. (Rev: BL 7/94; MJHS; SHS; SLJ 7/94) [574.5]

5955 Lourie, Peter. *Everglades: Buffalo Tiger and the River of Grass* (5–7). 1994, Boyds Mills $16.95 (1-878093-91-6). This first-person account, told through Miccosukee Indian guide Buffalo Tiger, provides insight into what the region has meant to his people, as Lourie and Buffalo Tiger travel through this beautiful region. (Rev: BL 12/1/94*; SLJ 10/94) [574.4]

5956 MacQuitty, Miranda. *Desert* (5–9). (Eyewitness Books) 1994, Knopf LB $16.99 (0-679-96003-1). (Rev: BL 10/15/94; MJHS) [910]

5957 Schultz, Ron. *Looking Inside Caves and Caverns* (5–8). (X-Ray Vision) 1993, John Muir paper $9.95 (1-56261-126-7). (Rev: BL 1/1/94; SLJ 2/94) [551.4]

5958 Steele, Philip. *Deserts* (5–8). (Pocket Facts) 1991, Macmillan/Crestwood LB $10.95 (0-89686-588-6). Concise introduction to deserts, featuring easy-to-understand facts and photos. (Rev: BL 3/15/92) [508.315]

5959 Steele, Philip. *Mountains* (5–8). (Pocket Facts) 1991, Macmillan/Crestwood LB $10.95 (0-89686-587-8). Easy-to-understand facts about mountains, with many photos. (Rev: BL 3/15/92) [910]

5960 Twist, Clint. *Deserts* (5–8). (Ecology Watch) 1991, Dillon $13.95 (0-87518-490-1). Traces the evolution of deserts, explains why they are threatened, and offers possible solutions to specific problems. (Rev: BL 3/1/92; SLJ 4/92) [574.5]

Rocks, Minerals, and Soil

5961 Barrow, Lloyd H. *Adventures with Rocks and Minerals: Geology Experiments for Young People* (7–10). (Adventures with Science) 1995, Enslow LB $16.95 (0-89490-624-0). A beginner's guide to learning about sedimentary rocks and fossils. (Rev: SLJ 2/96; VOYA 2/96)

5962 Bates, Robert L. *The Challenge of Mineral Resources* (7–12). (Environmental Issues) 1991, Enslow LB $15.95 (0-89490-245-8). Overview of 3 major mineral resources and their impact on modern society. (Rev: BL 6/15/91; SLJ 7/91) [533]

5963 Erickson, Jon. *An Introduction to Fossils and Minerals: Seeking Clues to the Earth's Past* (9–adult). 1992, Facts on File $24.95 (0-8160-2587-8). An overview of how rocks, fossils, and minerals are moved naturally. (Rev: BL 4/15/92; SHS) [560]

5964 Erickson, Jon. *Rock Formations and Unusual Geologic Structures: Exploring the Earth's Surface* (9–adult). 1993, Facts on File $24.95 (0-8160-2589-4). A detailed explanation of the forces that created our landscape, including the logistics of continental rift and drift. (Rev: BL 5/1/93) [550]

5965 Meltzer, Milton. *Gold: The True Story of Why People Search for It, Mine It, Trade It, Fight for It, Mint It, . . . Steal It, and Kill for It* (5–9). 1993, HarperCollins $15 (0-06-022983-7). This discussion of the role of gold in history, science, economics, and art connects the past with contemporary technology and exploitation. (Rev: BL 1/1/94; BTA; MJHS; SLJ 2/94) [553.4]

5966 Oliver, Ray. *Rocas y fósiles* (7–12). (Mis aficiones) 1993, Editorial Debate (Madrid, Spain) $12.99 (84-7444-644-9). Includes simple explanations, numerous practical suggestions, and photos, charts, and drawings in color. Large format. English title: *Rocks and Fossils*. Previous series titles: *Observación de pájaros (Bird Watching)* and *Sellos (Stamps)*. (Rev: BL 4/1/94)

5967 Oliver, Ray. *Rocks and Fossils* (5–7). (Hobby Handbooks) 1993, Random LB $13.99 (0-679-92661-5); paper $13 (0-679-82661-0). Includes simple explanations, numerous practical suggestions, and photos, charts, and drawings in color. (Rev: BL 10/1/93) [552]

5968 Van Cleave, Janice. *Janice Van Cleave's Rocks and Minerals: Mind-Boggling Experiments You Can Turn into Science Fair Projects* (6–8). (Spectacular Science Projects) 1996, Wiley paper $9.95 (0-471-10269-5). Guide to student science projects includes B&W how-to diagrams. (Rev: BL 3/15/96; SLJ 3/96)

5969 Wilhelms, Don E. *To a Rocky Moon: A Geologist's History of Lunar Exploration* (9–adult). 1993, Univ. of Arizona $29.95 (0-8165-1065-2). Profiles the principal participants in the race to the moon and describes every phase of the journey and our understanding of the moon's geologic cycle. (Rev: BL 5/1/93) [559.9]

Mathematics

General and Miscellaneous

5970 Guillen, Michael. *Five Equations That Changed the World: The Power and Poetry of Mathematics* (9–adult). 1995, Hyperion $22.95 (0-7868-6103-7). A philosophical, biographical, and historical trip through 2 centuries of changing scientific thought and the scientists who shaped the future: Newton, Bernoulli, Faraday, Clausius, and Einstein. (Rev: BL 9/1/95) [530.1]

5971 Osserman, Robert. *Poetry of the Universe: A Mathematical Exploration of the Cosmos* (9–adult). 1995, Doubleday/Anchor $18.95 (0-385-47340-0). A look at various mathematical concepts, with useful examples and illustrations. (Rev: BL 2/15/95) [530.1]

5972 Stewart, Ian. *Nature's Numbers: The Unreal Reality of Mathematical Imagination* (9–adult). (Science Masters) 1995, Basic Books $20 (0-465-07273-9). Explains such mathematical concepts as calculus, waves, and chaos theory. (Rev: BL 6/1–15/95) [510]

Algebra, Numbers, and Number Systems

5973 Clawson, Calvin C. *The Mathematical Traveler: Exploring the Grand History of Numbers* (9–adult). 1994, Plenum $25.95 (0-306-44645-6). A mathematical adventure about the history of numbers as a reflection of the evolution of culture, from the Chinese, Mayans, and Greeks to the modern day. (Rev: BL 5/1/94) [513.2]

5974 Humez, Alexander, and others. *Zero to Lazy Eight: The Romance of Numbers* (9–adult). 1993, Simon & Schuster $21 (0-671-74282-5). A collection of brain games using prime numbers, square roots, sequences, base-2 arithmetic, and other concepts. (Rev: BL 6/1–15/93) [513.2]

Geometry

5975 Ross, Catherine Sheldrick. *Circles: Fun Ideas for Getting A-Round in Math* (5–7). Illus. 1993, Addison-Wesley paper $9.95 (0-201-62268-8). An elementary introduction to the mathematics, physics, lore, and multicultural history of circles, disks, spheres, cylinders, cones, and spirals. (Rev: BL 6/1–15/93) [516]

Mathematical Games and Puzzles

5976 Sloane, Paul, and Des MacHale. *Challenging Lateral Thinking Puzzles* (9–adult). 1993, Sterling paper $4.95 (0-8069-8671-9). More than 90 brainteasers, with clues leading the reader through a "lateral thinking" mode, and answers. (Rev: BL 5/1/93) [793.73]

5977 Smullyan, Raymond. *Satan, Cantor, and Infinity and Other Mind-Boggling Puzzles* (9–adult). 1992, Knopf $21 (0-679-40688-3). Brainteasers, from the simple to the near-impossible, set on the Island of Knights and Knaves, with the Sorcerer as the guide. (Rev: BL 11/15/92; BTA) [793.7]

5978 Tahan, Malba. *The Man Who Counted: A Collection of Mathematical Adventures* (9–adult). 1993, Norton $19.95 (0-393-03430-5); paper $9.95 (0-393-30934-7). Regales readers with delightful mathematical adventures featuring beautiful princesses, viziers, sultans, and Tahan himself. (Rev: BL 2/15/93*; BTA) [793.7]

5979 Townsend, Charles Barry. *World's Hardest Puzzles* (9–adult). 1993, Sterling paper $4.95 (0-8069-8516-X). Challenging scenarios and illustrations having a historical theme, with solutions. (Rev: BL 5/1/93; BTA) [793.73]

5980 Townsend, Charles Barry. *World's Most Baffling Puzzles* (5–12). 1992, Sterling $12.95 (0-8069-5832-4). Nearly 100 word and number brainteasers, with answers provided. (Rev: BL 1/15/92) [793.73]

5981 Weaver, Charles. *Hidden Logic Puzzles* (9–adult). 1993, Sterling paper $4.95 (0-8069-8334-5). Over 150 cryptograms and conundrums that require logical thinking and math skills for solution, with answers. (Rev: BL 5/1/93) [793.7]

Trigonometry and Calculus

5982 Berlinski, David. *A Tour of the Calculus* (9–adult). 1996, Pantheon $25 (0-679-42645-0). With a goal to explain the mystery of motion and the area and volume of irregular shapes, Berlinski kindles interest in calculus. (Rev: BL 12/1/95) [515]

Meteorology

General and Miscellaneous

5983 Bilger, Burkhard. *Global Warming* (9–12). (Earth at Risk) 1991, Chelsea House LB $17.95 (0-7910-1575-0). A well-researched book that explains the scientific, political, and social issues concerning global warming, which is occurring as a result of human activity. (Rev: BL 4/1/92) [363.73]

5984 Newton, David E. *The Ozone Dilemma* (9–12). (Contemporary World Issues) 1995, ABC-Clio LB $39.50 (0-87436-719-0). A scientific explanation of how the ozone layer is being depleted. (Rev: SLJ 1/96; VOYA 4/96)

Air

5985 Fisher, Marshall. *The Ozone Layer* (9–12). (Earth at Risk) 1991, Chelsea House $19.95 (0-7910-1576-9). Covers the historical and scientific background and discusses the steps that have been taken to counteract the depletion of the ozone layer. (Rev: BL 2/1/92; MJHS) [363.73]

5986 Hoff, Mary, and Mary M. Rodgers. *Atmosphere* (5–7). (Our Endangered Planet) 1995, Lerner LB $16.13 (0-8225-2509-7). A general overview of how atmospheric gases affect Earth and how the actions of people are changing the atmosphere's composition. (Rev: BL 8/95) [363.73]

5987 Johnson, Rebecca L. *Investigating the Ozone Hole* (5–8). 1994, Lerner $17.96 (0-8225-1574-1). A discussion of the ozone hole above Antarctica and the continued threat of further ozone depletion. (Rev: BL 3/1/94; MJHS) [551.5]

5988 Nance, John J. *What Goes Up: The Global Assault on Our Atmosphere* (9–adult). 1991, Morrow $20 (0-688-08952-6). Scientists discover that chlorofluorocarbons (CFCs) are destroying the earth's ozone layer. (Rev: BL 6/1/91) [363.73]

Storms

5989 Dineen, Jacqueline. *Hurricanes and Typhoons* (5–8). (Natural Disasters) 1991, Gloucester $11.90 (0-531-17339-9). A look at the power and destruction of tropical storms. Prediction, tracking, and precautions are also discussed. (Rev: BL 1/15/92) [551.55]

5990 Fisher, David E. *The Scariest Place on Earth: Eye to Eye with Hurricanes* (9–adult). 1994, Random $23 (0-679-43566-2). Investigates the nature, history, causes, and dynamics of hurricanes. Documents the devastation of Hurricane Andrew, among others. (Rev: BL 8/94; SHS) [363.3]

5991 Twist, Clint. *Hurricanes and Storms* (5–8). (Repairing the Damage) 1992, Macmillan/New Discovery LB $13.95 (0-02-789685-4). (Rev: BL 9/15/92) [551.55]

Water

5992 Cossi, Olga. *Water Wars: The Fight to Control and Conserve Nature's Most Precious Resource* (6–12). 1993, Macmillan/New Discovery

$13.95 (0-02-724595-0). Discusses the sources and uses of fresh water and examines the reasons for drought, water quality problems, and how to conserve water. (Rev: BL 11/1/93; BTA; SLJ 2/94; VOYA 4/94) [333.91]

5993 Hoff, Mary, and Mary M. Rodgers. *Groundwater* (5–7). 1991, Lerner $14.95 (0-8225-2500-3). Discusses the supply, access, uses, and pollution of groundwater throughout the world. (Rev: BL 6/15/91; MJHS; SLJ 5/91) [333.91]

5994 Morgan, Sally, and Adrian Morgan. *Water* (5–7). (The Designs in Science) 1994, Facts on File $14.95 (0-8160-2982-2). Explores the impact of water on society, discussing water storage, conservation, and filtering. Suggests experiments using simple materials. (Rev: BL 7/94; MJHS; VOYA 8/94) [533.7]

5995 Ocko, Stephanie. *Water: Almost Enough for Everyone* (5–10). 1995, Atheneum $16 (0-689-31797-2). Ocko traces the interconnectedness of the earth's ecosystems, which can cause floods or droughts when humans mistreat it. The author provides ways people can conserve water and care for the environment. (Rev: BL 6/1–15/95; SLJ 6/95; VOYA 12/95) [363.3]

5996 Vogel, Carole Garbuny. *The Great Midwest Flood* (5–8). 1995, Little, Brown $15.95 (0-316-90248-9). The Mississippi River flood in 1993 was a castastrophe in slow motion. Vogel digs up unusual bits of information—such as how to deal with snakes in your basement—along with a discussion of floodplain management. (Rev: BL 12/15/95) [363.3]

Weather

5997 McVey, Vicki. *The Sierra Club Book of Weatherwisdom* (5–7). Illus. 1991, Little, Brown/Sierra Club $15.95 (0-316-56341-2). General information about the earth's atmosphere and climate told through stories about children in different parts of the world. (Rev: BL 7/91; SLJ 7/91) [551.5]

5998 Tyson, Peter. *Acid Rain* (9–12). (Earth at Risk) 1991, Chelsea House LB $17.95 (0-7910-1577-7). Objective coverage of the nature, distribution, and dangers of acid rain and the prospects for its reduction. (Rev: BL 4/1/92) [363.73]

5999 Waters, John. *Flood!* (5–7). (Nature's Disaster) 1991, Macmillan/Crestwood LB $10.95 (0-89686-596-7). Real-life examples demonstrate how floods are caused by weather and/or the failure of technology. (Rev: BL 8/91) [551.48]

Oceanography

General and Miscellaneous

6000 Gorman, James. *Ocean Enough and Time: Discovering the Waters Around Antarctica* (9–adult). 1995, HarperCollins $25 (0-06-016620-7). A travelogue with reflections on natural history, the McMurdo Research Station, and life on board a Coast Guard icebreaker. (Rev: BL 4/15/95) [551.4689]

6001 Hirschi, Ron. *Save Our Oceans and Coasts* (6–10). Photos. 1993, Delacorte $17.95 (0-385-31077-3); paper $9.95 (0-385-31126-5). Examines why various plant and animal species are endangered, and spotlights efforts to counter their decline. (Rev: BL 3/15/94; MJHS) [574.5]

6002 Johnson, Rebecca L. *The Great Barrier Reef: A Living Laboratory* (5–8). 1992, Lerner $15.95 (0-8225-1596-2). A look at the world's largest coral reef, off the coast of Australia. (Rev: BL 5/15/92; SLJ 7/92; YR) [574.9943]

6003 MacQuitty, Miranda. *Ocean* (5–9). (Eyewitness Books) 1995, Knopf LB $20.99 (0-679-97331-1). Two-page entries illustrated with full-color photos introduce the oceans of the world. (Rev: BL 12/15/95) [551.46]

6004 Siy, Alexandra. *The Great Astrolabe Reef* (5–8). (Circle of Life) 1992, Dillon LB $13.95 (0-87518-499-5). Offers general information about the fragile coral ecosystem and the delicate interconnectedness of life on Earth. (Rev: BL 9/1/92; SLJ 11/92) [574.5]

6005 Tesar, Jenny. *Threatened Oceans* (5–9). (Our Fragile Planet) 1991, Facts on File $18.95 (0-8160-2494-4). Covers basic material for general reading and for research. (Rev: BL 12/1/91; MJHS) [333.91]

6006 Twist, Clint. *Seas and Oceans* (5–8). (Ecology Watch) 1991, Dillon $13.95 (0-87518-491-X). Discusses how the seas and oceans evolved and how and why they are now threatened. (Rev: BL 3/1/92) [333.95]

6007 Weber, Michael, and Judith Gradwohl. *The Wealth of Oceans* (9–adult). 1995, Norton $25 (0-393-03764-9). New discoveries in marine ecology are discussed with regard to the stresses imposed by human societies. (Rev: BL 4/1/95) [333.71]

6008 Whitfield, Philip. *Oceans* (5–7). (Strange and Amazing Worlds) 1991, Viking $15.95 (0-670-84176-5). Concise descriptions of marine life and explanations of tides, hurricanes, and deep-sea vents. (Rev: BL 3/1/92) [551.46]

6009 Wu, Norbert. *Life in the Oceans* (5–7). 1991, Little, Brown $17.95 (0-316-95638-4). A look at oceanic life: coral reefs, kelp forests, and the deep ocean, as well as a discussion of environmental threats. (Rev: BL 12/1/91; SLJ 1/92) [574.92]

Underwater Exploration and Sea Disasters

6010 Ballard, Robert D. *The Lost Wreck of the Isis* (5–8). Illus. 1990, Scholastic/Madison $15.95 (0-590-43852-2). Fascinating account of the excavation of an ancient Roman shipwreck by a marine geologist. (Rev: BL 1/15/91; SLJ 1/91) [930.1]

6011 Ballard, Robert D., and Rick Archbold. *The Discovery of the Bismarck* (9–adult). 1990, Warner/Madison Press $35 (0-446-51386-5). Historical background on the German battleship that sank in 1941 and an account of an expedition that tried to locate the vessel in 1988. (Rev: BL 1/15/91; SHS) [940.54]

6012 Ballard, Robert D., and Rick Archbold. *Exploring the Bismarck* (5–7). 1991, Scholastic $15.95 (0-590-44268-6). A description of the destruction of the German battleship in 1941 and the men aboard, and of the ship's discovery on the ocean floor in 1989. (Rev: BL 11/1/91; MJHS; SLJ 8/91) [940.54]

6013 Ballard, Robert D., and Rick Archbold. *The Lost Ships of Guadalcanal* (9–adult). 1993, Warner $39.95 (0-446-51636-8). With underwater photos and other illustrations, this history documents the bloody World War II battles near Guadalcanal. (Rev: BL 10/15/93) [995.93]

6014 Ballard, Robert D., and Spencer Dunmore. *Exploring the Lusitania: Probing the Mysteries of the Sinking That Changed History* (9–adult). 1995, Warner $45 (0-446-51851-4). The sinking of the luxury liner *Lusitania*, its history, speculations on why it sank so quickly, and the remains that Ballard found on the ocean floor. (Rev: BL 11/1/95) [940.4]

6015 Cone, Joseph. *Fire under the Sea: The Discovery of Hot Springs on the Ocean Floor and the Origin of Life* (9–adult). 1991, Morrow $23 (0-688-09834-7). Scientists study active volcanoes on the sea floor that are pumping hot lava from deep inside the earth. (Rev: BL 7/91*) [551.2]

6016 Heyer, Paul. *Titanic Legacy: Disaster as Media Event and Myth* (9–adult). 1995, Praeger $39.95 (0-275-95352-1). Traces the events of the sinking, the heroes and villains, and how the media reported the disaster. (Rev: BL 12/1/95) [363.12]

6017 Lynch, Don. *Titanic: An Illustrated History* (9–adult). 1992, Hyperion $60 (1-56282-918-1). Paintings reconstruct what life was like aboard the *Titanic* and illustrate its sinking, the 1985 discovery, and the exploration of the ship's remains. (Rev: BL 10/15/92) [910]

6018 Nalepka, James, and Steven Callahan. *Capsized* (9–adult). 1992, HarperCollins $22 (0-06-017961-9). A novice sailor describes his experiences with 3 companions surviving aboard an overturned trimaran adrift in the Pacific for 119 days. (Rev: BL 10/1/92) [910.91648]

6019 *Sunk! Exploring Underwater Archaeology* (5–8). (Buried Worlds) 1994, Lerner LB $17.21 (0-8225-3205-0). Provides a general overview of how archaeologists interpret aspects of ancient trade, commerce, and history through underwater discoveries. (Rev: BL 10/15/94; MJHS) [930.1]

Physics

General and Miscellaneous

6020 Davies, Paul. *About Time: Einstein's Unfinished Revolution* (9–adult). 1995, Simon & Schuster $24 (0-671-79964-9). Time warps, black holes, Einstein's theory of relativity, quantum time, and imaginary time are among the topics covered. (Rev: BL 3/1/95) [530.1]

6021 Davies, Paul, and John Gribbin. *The Matter Myth: Dramatic Discoveries That Challenge Our Understanding of Physical Reality* (9–adult). 1992, Simon & Schuster/Touchstone paper $12 (0-671-72841-5). Astrophysicists reveal recent discoveries that make obsolete the traditional scientific notions of how the world works. (Rev: BL 1/15/92*; BTA) [530.2]

6022 Lederman, Leon, and Dick Teresi. *The God Particle: If the Universe Is the Answer, What Is the Question?* (9–adult). 1993, Houghton $24.95 (0-395-55849-2). Lederman puts his witty spin on quantum physics in an enlightening account for older teens. (Rev: BL 2/1/93*) [523.1]

6023 Rosen, Joe. *The Capricious Cosmos: Universe Beyond Law* (9–adult). 1992, Macmillan $19.95 (0-02-604931-7). An outline of the nature of science and metaphysics as well as the impact of modern science on humankind. (Rev: BL 2/15/92; BTA) [523.1]

6024 Swisher, Clarice. *Relativity* (6–10). (Opposing Viewpoints) 1990, Greenhaven LB $13.95 (0-89908-076-6). A concise overview of thought about the universe, from the development of prehistoric rituals, through myth and religion, to the early and modern scientific theories, with the main focus on Einstein's theory of relativity. (Rev: BL 9/1/91; MJHS) [531.1]

6025 Thorne, Kip S. *Black Holes and Time Warps: Einstein's Outrageous Legacy* (9–adult). 1994, Norton $25 (0-393-03505-0). A physicist explains the concepts he helped develop in this book for lay people. (Rev: BL 2/15/94*; SHS) [530.1]

Energy and Motion

6026 Gutnik, Martin J. *The Energy Question: Thinking about Tomorrow* (6–12). (Better Earth) 1993, Enslow $17.95 (0-89490-400-0). Discusses alternate energy sources, including nuclear fusion and solar and wind power. Energy laws and incentives, use of public transportation, and recycling are recommended. (Rev: BL 11/1/93; SLJ 10/93; VOYA 2/94) [333.79]

General and Miscellaneous

6027 Lafferty, Peter. *Force and Motion* (5–8). (Eyewitness Science) 1992, Dorling Kindersley $15.95 (1-879431-85-8). (Rev: BL 1/15/93; MJHS) [531]

6028 Polesetsky, Matthew, and Charles Cozic, eds. *Energy Alternatives* (9–12). (Current Controversies) 1991, Greenhaven LB $16.95 (0-89908-577-6); paper $9.95 (0-89908-583-0). (Rev: BL 6/15/92; SHS) [333.79]

Nuclear Energy

6029 Andryszewski, Tricia. *What to Do about Nuclear Waste* (7–12). 1995, Millbrook LB

$16.40 (1-56294-577-7). Up-to-date information on this urgent problem. Discussion of the Manhattan Project, nuclear power's heyday in the 1950s, the Three Mile Island and Chernobyl meltdowns, and a review of controversial solutions. (Rev: BL 11/1/95; SLJ 12/95; VOYA 4/96) [363.72]

6030 Cheney, Glenn Alan. *Chernobyl: The Ongoing Story of the World's Deadliest Nuclear Disaster* (7–12). 1993, Macmillan/New Discovery $13.95 (0-02-718305-X). This account of the Chernobyl disaster discusses current problems and the potential for similar occurrences in other Russian nuclear power plants. (Rev: BL 1/15/94; MJHS; SLJ 3/94; VOYA 2/94) [363.17]

6031 Galperin, Anne. *Nuclear Energy/Nuclear Waste* (9–12). 1991, Chelsea House $19.95 (0-7910-1585-8). The pros and cons of nuclear energy are examined, along with the political and technological problems of radioactive waste disposal. (Rev: BL 2/1/92; MJHS) [333.792]

6032 Read, Piers Paul. *Ablaze: The Story of Chernobyl* (9–adult). 1993, Random $25 (0-679-40819-3). Lengthy, readable account of the 1986 Chernobyl nuclear accident that humanizes the tragedy. (Rev: BL 3/15/93) [363.17]

Light, Color, and Laser Science

6033 Billings, Charlene W. *Lasers: The New Technology of Light* (9–12). (Science Sourcebooks) 1992, Facts on File LB $17.95 (0-8160-2630-0). A concise overview of lasers, their development, uses, types, and how they are revolutionizing communications, surgery, industry, scientific research, and other fields. (Rev: BL 1/15/93; BTA; MJHS; SHS) [621.36]

6034 Burnie, David. *Light* (5–8). (Eyewitness Science) 1992, Dorling Kindersley LB $15.95 (1-879431-79-3). Clear explanations and color photos provide a wealth of information on the origins, principles, and history of the study of light. (Rev: BL 1/15/93; BTA; MJHS; SLJ 11/92) [535]

6035 Heifetz, Jeanne. *When Blue Meant Yellow: How Colors Got Their Names* (7–12). 1994, Holt $14.95 (0-8050-3178-2). Explores the origins of 191 color terms—from apricot to zinnaber green. (Rev: BL 1/1/95; SLJ 2/95) [535.6]

6036 Zubrowski, Bernie. *Mirrors: Finding Out about the Properties of Light* (5–7). Illus. 1992, Morrow/Boston Children's Museum Activity Book $13.95 (0-688-10592-0). A hands-on approach to the science of light. (Rev: BL 7/92; MJHS; SLJ 8/92) [535]

Magnetism and Electricity

6037 Billings, Charlene W. *Superconductivity: From Discovery to Breakthrough* (5–8). 1991, Dutton/Cobblehill $15.95 (0-525-65048-2). A discussion of the research that led to the development of superconductors. (Rev: BL 5/1/91) [537.6]

6038 Gardner, Robert. *Electricity and Magnetism* (6–9). (Yesterday's Science, Today's Technology) Illus. 1994, Twenty-First Century LB $16.95 (0-8050-2850-1). Discusses magnets, electric charges, the future of electric power, and other topics. (Rev: BL 12/1/95; MJHS; SLJ 11/94) [537]

6039 Parker, Steve. *Electricity* (5–8). (Eyewitness Science) 1992, Dorling Kindersley $15.95 (1-879431-82-3). (Rev: BL 1/15/93; MJHS) [537]

6040 Parsons, Alexandra. *Electricity* (5–7). (Make It Work! Science) 1995, Thomson Learning LB $15.95 (1-56847-469-5). (Rev: BL 10/15/95) [537]

6041 Souza, D. M. *Northern Lights* (5–7). 1994, Carolrhoda $17.50 (0-87614-799-6); paper $7.95 (0-87614-629-9). The mysterious beauty of the Northern Lights and the physics that lie behind their mystery are introduced in this photo-essay. (Rev: BL 12/1/95)

6042 Stwertka, Albert. *Superconductors: The Irresistible Future* (6–10). (Venture) 1991, Watts LB $12.40 (0-531-12526-2). A description of the history, development, and molecular activity of superconducting materials and an explanation of their potential use. (Rev: BL 6/15/91; MJHS; SHS; SLJ 8/91) [621.3]

Nuclear Physics

6043 Asimov, Isaac. *Atom: Journey Across the Subatomic Cosmos* (9–adult). 1991, Dutton $21.95 (0-525-24990-7). (Rev: BL 4/1/91; SHS) [539.7]

6044 Lampton, Christopher. *Particle Physics: The New View of the Universe* (7–12). 1991, Enslow LB $15.95 (0-89490-328-4). Scientists look for one theory to explain everything from the essential nature of matter to the origin of the universe. (Rev: BL 8/91; MJHS; SLJ 8/92) [539.7]

6045 Stwertka, Albert. *The World of Atoms and Quarks* (6–10). 1995, Twenty-First Century $18.98 (0-8050-3533-8). A book, more readable than most, that traces the history of atomic theory in physics over the past 100 years. (Rev: BL 12/1/95; SLJ 2/96) [539.7]

6046 Taubes, Gary. *Bad Science: The Short Life and Very Hard Times of Cold Fusion* (9–adult). 1993, Random $25 (0-394-58456-2). Documents the bizarre 1989 episode of 2 scientists who announced they had created a sustained nuclear-fusion reaction at room temperature and the ensuing scandal. (Rev: BL 5/15/93*) [539.7]

Sound

6047 Lampton, Christopher. *Sound: More Than What You Hear* (7–12). 1992, Enslow LB $16.95 (0-89490-327-6). Explains what sound is, how it's transmitted, and some of the latest developments in recording and using it. (Rev: BL 6/15/92; SHS) [534]

6048 Morgan, Sally, and Adrian Morgan. *Using Sound* (5–7). (Designs in Science) 1994, Facts on File $14.95 (0-8160-2981-4). Discusses, among other topics, how animals and humans produce sound and, although we cannot see sound, how it is measured by instrumentation. (Rev: BL 7/94; MJHS) [534]

Technology and Engineering

General Works and Miscellaneous Industries

6049 Abrams, Malcolm, and Harriet Bernstein. *More Future Stuff: More Than 250 Inventions That Will Change Your Life by 2001* (9–adult). 1991, Penguin paper $10.95 (0-14-014523-0). This sequel describes further technological wonders and gadgets-to-come, from the frivolous to the utilitarian. (Rev: BL 10/1/91) [338]

6050 Bailey, Janet. *The Good Servant: Making Peace with the Bomb at Los Alamos* (9–adult). 1995, Simon & Schuster $22 (0-684-80939-7). A look at how Los Alamos scientists are currently recycling bomb technology. (Rev: BL 9/15/95) [507]

6051 Brackin, A. J. *Clocks: Chronicling Time* (6–10). (Encyclopedia of Discovery and Invention) 1991, Lucent LB $15.95 (1-56006-208-8). (Rev: BL 4/15/92) [681.1]

6052 Cardwell, Donald. *The Norton History of Technology* (9–adult). (Norton History of Science) 1994, Norton $35 (0-393-03652-9); paper $18.95 (0-393-31192-9). An overview of mankind's technological progress, from simple tools to computers and satellites. Focuses on such key areas as transportation, medicine, and energy. (Rev: BL 8/94; SHS) [609]

6053 Colman, Penny. *Toilets, Bathtubs, Sinks, and Sewers: A History of the Bathroom* (5–8). 1994, Atheneum $14.95 (0-689-31894-4). A well-written book that provides interesting facts about the history of personal cleanliness and hygiene. (Rev: BL 1/1/95; MJHS; SLJ 3/95) [643]

6054 Duncanson, Neil. *Sports Technology* (6–8). (Technology in Action) 1992, Bookwright LB $12.40 (0-531-18401-3). (Rev: BL 8/92; MJHS) [688.7]

6055 Endacott, Geoff. *Discovery and Inventions* (5–7). (Strange and Amazing Worlds) 1991, Viking $15.95 (0-670-84177-3). Covers such diverse topics as "The Printed Word," "Building Bridges," and "Famous Fashions." (Rev: BL 3/1/92; SLJ 4/92) [608]

6056 Flatow, Ira. *They All Laughed . . . : From Light Bulbs to Lasers: The Fascinating Stories Behind the Great Inventions* (9–adult). 1992, HarperCollins $20 (0-06-016445-X). Examines the unusual beginnings of common inventions and discoveries, such as the lightning rod, Teflon, and xerography. (Rev: BL 7/92; SHS) [609]

6057 Friedel, Robert. *Zipper: An Exploration in Novelty* (9–adult). (Perspectives) 1994, Norton $23 (0-393-03599-9). Describes the people who created and manufactured the zipper and their marketing struggles and patent wars. (Rev: BL 3/15/94) [609]

6058 Hine, Thomas. *The Total Package: The Evolution and Secret Meanings of Boxes, Bottles, Cans, Tubes, and Other Persuasive Containers* (9–adult). 1995, Little, Brown $24.95 (0-316-36480-0). The history, development, failures, and successes of modern packaging. (Rev: BL 3/15/95) [658.5]

6059 Kerr, Daisy. *Keeping Clean: A Very Peculiar History* (5–7). (A Very Peculiar History) 1995, Watts LB $14.42 (0-531-14353-8). Looks at the history of sanitation from ancient times to the present, including pictures of bathing devices and short factoids. (Rev: BL 6/1–15/95) [613]

6060 Lampton, Christopher. *DNA Fingerprinting* (7–10). 1991, Watts $12.90 (0-531-13003-7). An introduction to DNA fingerprinting and a discussion of its part in crime solving, wildlife management, evolutionary biology, and paternity testing. (Rev: BL 12/1/91; MJHS; SHS; SLJ 2/92) [614]

6061 Macdonald, Anne L. *Feminine Ingenuity: Women and Invention in America* (9–adult). 1992, Ballantine $22.50 (0-345-35811-2). (Rev: BL 4/15/92*; SHS) [609.2]

6062 *Machines and Inventions* (5–9). (Understanding Science and Nature) 1993, Time-Life $17.95 (0-8094-9704-2). Using a question-and-answer format, this covers historic inventions as well as modern machines and electronic equipment. (Rev: BL 1/15/94; SLJ 6/94) [621.8]

6063 Morgan, Sally, and Adrian Morgan. *Materials* (5–7). (Designs in Science) 1994, Facts on File $14.95 (0-8160-2985-7). The authors define materials: natural vs. manufactured, soft vs. brittle, those that can withstand heat or chemicals or not, and those that can be grouped only by like properties. (Rev: BL 7/94; MJHS) [620.1]

6064 Nachtigall, Werner. *Exploring with the Microscope: A Book of Discovery and Learning* (7–12). Tr. by Elizabeth Reinersmann. 1995, Sterling $19.95 (0-8069-0866-1). A very complete book about microscopes and their use, with 100 color slides, diagrams, and black-and-white photos. (Rev: BL 10/1/95; SLJ 11/95) [578]

6065 Noonan, Jon. *Nineteenth-Century Inventors* (7–10). (American Profiles) 1992, Facts on File $16.95 (0-8160-2480-4). (Rev: BL 11/15/91) [609.2]

6066 Parker, Steve. *The Random House Book of How Things Work* (5–12). 1991, Random LB $19.99 (0-679-90908-7); paper $14.95 (0-679-80908-2). (Rev: BL 5/15/91; MJHS; SLJ 7/91) [600]

6067 Patton, Phil. *Made in U.S.A.: The Secret Histories of the Things That Made America Great* (9–adult). 1992, Grove/Weidenfeld $19.95 (0-8021-1276-5). An examination of classic objects of American culture, such as the Golden Arches and airstream trailers. (Rev: BL 1/15/92; SHS) [609.73]

6068 Platt, Richard. *El asombroso libro del interior del las cosas* (5–12). Illus. 1992, Santillana (Madrid, Spain) $23.95 (84-372-4524-9). Detailed cross-section drawings in color and brief texts describe the functions and operations of a medieval castle, an observatory, a submarine, an airplane, the Empire State Building, a car factory, a coal mine, and other architectural and technological wonders. English title: *The Incredible Cross Section Book*. (Rev: BL 4/1/94)

6069 Regis, Ed. *Nano: The Emerging Science of Nanotechnology* (9–adult). 1995, Little, Brown $23.95 (0-316-73858-1). An introduction to nanotechnology (whole technology based on molecular machines) by controversial pioneer L. Eric Drexler. (Rev: BL 3/1/95) [620.4]

6070 Skurzynski, Gloria. *Almost the Real Thing: Simulation in Your High-Tech World* (5–9). 1991, Bradbury $16.95 (0-02-778072-4). This explanation of physical and computer simulation covers everything from the Wright brothers' wind tunnel to virtual reality and space age technological innovations. Awards: SLJ Best Book. (Rev: BL 10/15/91; MJHS; SLJ 10/91*) [620]

6071 Stewart, Gail B. *Microscopes: Bringing the Unseen World into Focus* (6–10). (Encyclopedia of Discovery and Invention) 1992, Lucent LB $15.95 (1-56006-211-8). (Rev: BL 12/15/92; MJHS; SHS) [502]

6072 Tchudi, Stephen. *Lock and Key: The Secrets of Locking Things Up, In and Out* (5–8). 1993, Scribner $14.95 (0-684-19363-9). The world of locks is explored in this book, including history, how they work, lock-picking, etymologies, and both current and future security. (Rev: BL 12/1/93; MJHS; SLJ 12/93) [683]

6073 Tesar, Jenny. *Scientific Crime Investigation* (7–10). 1991, Watts $12.90 (0-531-12500-9). An introduction to the latest forensic laboratory tools and techniques, including fingerprinting, autopsies, voice prints, and polygraph tests. (Rev: BL 12/1/91; MJHS) [363.2]

6074 Tucker, Tom. *Brainstorm! The Stories of Twenty American Kid Inventors* (5–7). 1995, Farrar $15 (0-374-30944-2). Twenty stories show kid inventors who have had a passion for creative tinkering over 3 centuries. (Rev: BL 8/95; SLJ 10/95; VOYA 2/96) [609.2]

6075 Vare, Ethlie Ann, and Greg Ptacek. *Women Inventors and Their Discoveries* (6–10). 1993, Oliver Press (5707 W. 36th St., Minneapolis, MN 55416) LB $14.95 (1-881508-06-4). (Rev: BL 10/15/93; SLJ 1/94; VOYA 2/94) [609.2]

6076 Werth, Barry. *The Billion-Dollar Molecule: One Company's Quest for the Perfect Drug* (9–adult). 1994, Simon & Schuster $25 (0-671-72327-8). An examination of the founding of the biotechnology company Vertex and its shift from the search for the ultimate immunosuppressant to a drive for venture capital. (Rev: BL 1/15/94) [615]

Building and Construction

6077 Darling, David. *Spiderwebs to Skyscrapers: The Science of Structures* (5–8). 1991, Dillon LB $13.95 (0-87518-478-2). Discusses foundations, building materials, styles of construction, and animal architecture. Includes experiments and color illustrations. (Rev: BL 6/1/92; MJHS; SLJ 3/92) [624.1]

6078 Dunn, Andrew. *Bridges: Structures* (5–7). (Structures) 1993, Thomson Learning $13.95 (1-56847-028-2). (Rev: BL 8/93; MJHS) [624]

6079 Dunn, Andrew. *Dams: Structures* (5–7). (Structures) 1993, Thomson Learning $13.95 (1-56847-029-0). (Rev: BL 8/93; MJHS) [627]

6080 Dunn, Andrew. *Tunnels: Structures* (5–7). (Structures) 1993, Thomson Learning $13.95 (1-56847-026-6). Discusses the reasons for tunnel construction, how tunnels are built, and the future of the technology. (Rev: BL 6/1–15/93; MJHS) [725.9]

6081 Hawkes, Nigel. *Structures: The Way Things Are Built* (9–adult). 1990, Macmillan $39.95 (0-02-549105-9). An illustrated look at some of the marvels of civil engineering throughout the world. (Rev: BL 1/15/91; MJHS) [624.09]

6082 Platt, Richard. *Stephen Biesty's Incredible Cross-Sections* (5–12). Illus. 1992, Knopf $20 (0-679-81411-6). Highly detailed cross-sections of 18 buildings and other structures, such as the *Queen Mary*, a steam train, an oil rig, an automobile factory, and a 747. (Rev: BL 9/1/92)

6083 Trefil, James. *A Scientist in the City* (9–adult). 1994, Doubleday $22.50 (0-385-24797-4). An examination of the technological wonder that is the urban ecosystem, viewed as a natural combination of inanimate structures and living organisms. (Rev: BL 1/1/94; BTA; SLJ 9/94) [307.76]

6084 Wilkinson, Philip. *Building* (5–9). (Eyewitness Books) 1995, Knopf $17 (0-679-87256-6). The history of building techniques, materials, and philosophy through the years. (Rev: BL 8/95) [690]

Computers and Automation

6085 Billings, Charlene W. *Supercomputers: Shaping the Future* (7–12). (Science Sourcebooks) 1995, Facts on File $17.95 (0-8160-3096-0). Looks at a topic not often covered—the silicon revolution—focusing on the mega-machines that are the most powerful computers in the world. (Rev: BL 10/15/95; SLJ 4/96) [004.1]

6086 Bortz, Fred. *Mind Tools: The Science of Artificial Intelligence* (7–12). 1992, Watts $12.90 (0-531-12515-7). A concise overview of the controversy surrounding the science of artificial intelligence, new computer technologies, and the field's pioneers. (Rev: BL 11/1/92; BTA; MJHS; SHS) [006.3]

6087 *Computadoras al instante* (8–12). (Aprender a simple vista) 1993, Prentice-Hall Career & Technology paper $14.95 (0-13-178872-8). This user-friendly manual to computers contains simple explanations, cartoon characters, and clear color illustrations. English title: *Computers Simplified*. (Rev: BL 2/1/95)

6088 Freedman, Alan. *Diccionario de computacíon* (8–12). Tr. by Gloria Elizabeth Rosas Lopetegui. 1994, McGraw-Hill (Colombia) paper $14.95 (958-600-203-9). This new translation of *Computer Words You Gotta Know!* explains more than 2,000 English computer-related terms. Includes a list of Spanish terms with English translations. English title: *Dictionary of Computing*. (Rev: BL 10/1/94)

6089 Hafner, Katie, and John Markoff. *Cyberpunk: Outlaws and Hackers on the Computer Frontier* (9–adult). 1991, Simon & Schuster $22.95 (0-671-68322-5). Three computer whizzes turn their hobby into illegal activities, ranging from breaking into corporate computers to accessing classified government information. (Rev: BL 7/91) [364.1]

6090 Herz, J. C. *Surfing on the Internet: A Nethead's Adventures On-Line* (9–adult). 1995, Little, Brown $19.95 (0-316-35958-0). A guided tour that explores online culture, including sexuality. (Rev: BL 2/15/95) [004.6]

6091 Manger, Jason J. *The Essential Internet Information Guide* (9–adult). 1994, McGraw-Hill paper $27.95 (0-07-707905-1). Detailed and well-organized manual. Assumes computer experience, but can be used by some beginners. (Rev: BL 2/15/95) [005.7]

6092 Moody, Fred. *I Sing the Body Electronic: A Year with Microsoft on the Multimedia Frontier* (9–adult). 1995, Viking $24.95 (0-670-84875-1). Follows the development of a new software for children and the dynamics of teamwork, creative processes, and the corporate world. (Rev: BL 9/1/95) [338.7]

6093 *MS-DOS 6.2 al instante* (8–12). (Aprender a simple vista) 1993, Prentice-Hall Career &

Technology paper $14.95 (0-13-123282-7). This user-friendly manual to the computer-operating system MS-DOS contains simple explanations, cartoon characters, and clear color illustrations. English title: *MS-DOS 6.2 Simplified*. (Rev: BL 2/1/95)

6094 Mungo, Paul, and Bryan Clough. *Approaching Zero: The Extraordinary Underworld of Hackers, Phreakers, Virus Writers and Keyboard Criminals* (9–adult). 1993, Random $22 (0-679-40938-6). A fast-paced history of computer hackers and virus writers. (Rev: BL 2/1/93; BTA; VOYA 10/93) [364.1]

6095 Pearson, Olen R. *Personal Computer Buying Guide: Foolproof Advice on How to Buy Computer Software and Hardware* (9–adult). 1990, Consumers Union paper $10.95 (0-89043-336-4). (Rev: BL 2/15/91; SHS) [004.16]

6096 Peterson, Ivars. *Fatal Defect: Chasing Killer Computer Bugs* (9–adult). 1995, Times Books $23 (0-8129-2023-6). Peterson, a reporter for *Science News*, describes the work of "bug hunters," software experts who investigate and analyze computer problems. (Rev: BL 6/1–15/95) [005.3]

6097 Pouts-Lajus, Serge. *Robots y ordenadores* (7–12). 1991, Ediciones Larousse $15.90 (1-56294-178-X). Introduces the world of computers and robots. Includes high-quality photos, diagrams, and other illustrations in color. English title: *Robots and Computers*. (Rev: BL 3/1/93)

6098 Rheingold, Howard. *Virtual Reality* (9–adult). 1991, Summit $22.95 (0-671-69363-8). A look at comptuer-generated artificial worlds and how they will affect everyday life. (Rev: BL 6/15/91; SHS) [501]

6099 Ryan, Ken. *Computer Anxiety? Instant Relief!* (9–adult). 1991, Castle Mountain Press (P.O. Box 190913, Anchorage, AK 99519-0913) paper $9.95 (1-879925-04-4). Using subtle humor, this work attempts to simplify an intimidating subject for novice users. It offers definitions of computer terms and illustrations of difficult concepts. (Rev: BL 9/1/91) [004]

6100 Salzman, Marian, and Robert Pondiscio. *Kids On-Line: 150 Ways for Kids to Surf the Net for Fun and Information* (5–9). 1995, Avon paper $5.99 (0-380-78231-6). A leap into cyberspace for both adults and youth, with valuable information plus etiquette for on-line users. (Rev: BL 10/15/95) [004.69]

6101 Thro, Ellen. *Robotics: The Marriage of Computers and Machines* (7–12). (Science Sourcebooks) 1993, Facts on File $17.95 (0-8160-2628-9). Presents this complicated subject in understandable, interesting terms, covering robots that work underground, in factories, and in space exploration, as well as artificial intelligence. (Rev: BL 7/93; MJHS; SHS) [629.8]

6102 White, Ron. *How Computers Work* (9–adult). 1992, Ziff-Davis $22.95 (1-56276-094-7). Cutaway diagrams and sequenced photos combine with concise, informative text to give an inside-out view of computers and how they work. (Rev: BL 11/15/92; BTA; MJHS) [004.16]

6103 Wood, Lamont. *The Net after Dark* (9–adult). 1994, Wiley paper $16.95 (0-471-10347-0). Topically organized how-to book that introduces terminology and "netiquette." (Rev: BL 2/15/95) [005.7]

Electronics

6104 Bridgman, Roger. *Electronics* (5–8). (Eyewitness Science) 1993, Dorling Kindersley LB $15.95 (1-56458-324-4). Describes the changes in machines from pre-electric times to the modern world of computers and other technological innovations. (Rev: BL 11/15/93; MJHS) [621.381]

Telecommunications

6105 Coe, Lewis. *The Telegraph: A History of Morse's Invention and Its Predecessors in the United States* (9–adult). 1993, McFarland $25.95 (0-89950-736-0). This concise history of the telegraph and its uses focuses on its impact on American society. (Rev: BL 3/1/93) [621.383]

6106 Lampton, Christopher. *Telecommunications: From Telegraphs to Modems* (7–12). (Venture) 1991, Watts LB $12.40 (0-531-12527-0). A discussion of various kinds of electronic communication, from basic waves to digital systems. (Rev: BL 7/91; MJHS; SHS; SLJ 8/91) [621.382]

6107 Skurzynski, Gloria. *Get the Message: Telecommunications in Your High-Tech World* (5–7). 1993, Bradbury $16.95 (0-02-778071-6). (Rev: BL 8/93*; BTA; MJHS; SLJ 6/93) [621.382]

6108 Webb, Marcus. *Telephones: Words over Wires* (6–10). (Encyclopedia of Discovery and Invention) 1992, Lucent LB $15.95 (1-56006-219-3). Covers the early history of the telephone to present-day mass communication—including fax machines, communication satellites, and deregulation of the telephone industry—and looks to the future and the effect such technologies as fiber optics will have. (Rev: BL 12/15/92)

Television, Motion Pictures, Radio, and Recording

6109 Calabro, Marian. *Zap! A Brief History of Television* (7–12). 1992, Four Winds $13.95 (0-02-716242-7). Explores the many aspects of television, its cultural and global impact, its business side, and the development of the major broadcast networks. (Rev: BL 1/15/93; MJHS; SLJ 2/93) [384.55]

6110 Helms, Harry. *All about Ham Radio* (9–adult). 1992, HighText $19.95 (1-878707-04-3). An illustrated how-to manual for those wanting their license and a new hobby. (Rev: BL 9/1/92; BTA) [621]

Transportation

General and Miscellaneous

6111 Bartimus, Tad, and Scott McCartney. *Trinity's Children: Living along America's Nuclear Highway* (9–adult). 1991, Harcourt $21.95 (0-15-167719-0). This chronicle of a "military highway"—I–25, from White Sands, New Mexico, to the Wyoming MX missile sites—describes governmental authority at the expense of ordinary citizens. (Rev: BL 10/15/91) [355.8]

6112 Bourne, Russell. *Floating West: The Erie and Other American Canals* (9–adult). 1992, Norton $24.95 (0-393-03044-X). Popular account of the building of the Erie and other American canals. (Rev: BL 4/15/92) [386]

6113 Spangenburg, Ray, and Diane K. Moser. *The Story of America's Bridges* (5–9). (Connecting a Continent) 1991, Facts on File $18.95 (0-8160-2259-3). Historical information, descriptions of key technological innovations, and brief stories are used to present a picture of the country's bridges. (Rev: BL 11/15/91; MJHS) [624]

6114 Spangenburg, Ray, and Diane K. Moser. *The Story of America's Roads* (5–9). (Connecting a Continent) 1991, Facts on File $18.95 (0-8160-2255-0). Brief stories, biographies, and charts are used to trace the development of the nation's road system. Includes a discussion of Roman roads and Indian trails. (Rev: BL 11/15/96; MJHS) [388]

6115 Spangenburg, Ray, and Diane K. Moser. *The Story of America's Tunnels* (5–9). (Connecting a Continent) 1992, Facts on File LB $18.95 (0-8160-2258-5). (Rev: BL 2/15/93; MJHS) [624]

6116 Wilson, Anthony. *The Dorling Kindersley Visual Timeline of Transportation* (5–8). 1995, Dorling Kindersley $16.95 (1-56458-880-7). The history of transportation on land and water, from 10,000 B.C. to future trends. (Rev: BL 12/15/95; VOYA 4/96) [629.04]

6117 Yepsen, Roger. *Humanpower: Cars, Planes and Boats with Muscles for Motors* (5–8). 1992, Macmillan $14.95 (0-02-793615-5). A history of the development of human-powered bicycles, cars, planes, and boats and speculation on the future of other human-powered vehicles. (Rev: BL 9/15/92) [629.04]

Airplanes, Aeronautics, and Ballooning

6118 Aaseng, Nathan. *Breaking the Sound Barrier* (6–9). 1992, Messner LB $12.98 (0-671-74212-4); paper $7.95 (0-671-74213-2). The events that led to Chuck Yeager's breaking the sound barrier in 1947, including the efforts of early pilots to achieve greater air speed. (Rev: BL 11/15/92; BTA; MJHS) [626.132]

6119 Brenlove, Milovan S. *Vectors to Spare: The Life of an Air Traffic Controller* (9–adult). 1993, Iowa State Univ. $24.95 (0-8138-0471-X). Conveys the flavor of the job of aerial cop, describing arrogant pilots, boom-lowering supervisors, career politics, and actual crashes and near misses. (Rev: BL 6/1–15/93) [629.136]

6120 Briggs, Carole S. *At the Controls: Women in Aviation* (5–8). 1991, Lerner LB $14.95 (0-8225-1593-8). (Rev: BL 4/15/91; MJHS; SLJ 6/91) [629.1]

6121 Coonts, Stephen. *The Cannibal Queen: An Aerial Odyssey Across America* (9–adult). 1992, Pocket $22 (0-671-74884-X). The author recounts how his appreciation for the American way of life grew while touring the U.S. in a biplane. (Rev: BL 5/1/92) [917]

6122 Hart, Philip S. *Flying Free: America's First Black Aviators* (5–9). 1992, Lerner LB $14.96 (0-8225-1598-9). The contributions of African Americans who succeeded against great odds to become aerial performers, combat pilots, and aviation instructors. (Rev: BL 10/15/92; MJHS; SLJ 1/93) [629.13]

6123 Jaspersohn, William. *A Week in the Life of an Airline Pilot* (5–9). 1991, Little, Brown $14.95 (0-316-45822-8). (Rev: BL 3/15/91; SLJ 5/91) [629.132]

6124 Lopez, Donald S. *Aviation: A Smithsonian Guide* (9–adult). (Smithsonian Guide) 1995, Macmillan $24.95 (0-02-860006-1); paper $18 (0-02-860041-X). Looks at aviation principles, personalities, and history with 2-page, full-color photos of famous planes. (Rev: BL 6/1–15/95) [629.13]

6125 Nader, Ralph, and Wesley J. Smith. *Collision Course: The Truth about Airline Safety* (9–adult). 1993, TAB $21.95 (0-8306-4271-4). Outlines the development of the commercial aviation industry and examines each aspect of the "system" that controls it. (Rev: BL 7/93) [363.12]

6126 Neely, William. *Pilots: The Romance of the Air: Pilots Speak about the Triumphs and Tragedies, Fears and Joys of Flying* (9–adult). 1991, Simon & Schuster $19.95 (0-671-70257-2). Dozens of pilots describe in their own words what its like to be up in the air. (Rev: BL 7/91) [629.13]

6127 Paulson, Tim. *How to Fly a 747* (7–12). (Masters of Motion) 1992, John Muir $14.95 (1-56261-043-0); paper $9.95 (1-56261-061-9). Contains information about the principles of flight, how planes are built, how their various parts work, what pilots do, and more. (Rev: BL 2/1/93; SLJ 1/93) [629.132]

6128 Reiss, Bob. *Frequent Flyer: One Plane; One Passenger; The Spectacular Feat of Commercial Flight* (9–adult). 1994, Simon & Schuster $23 (0-671-77650-9). Describes the author's experiences flying on a Delta Airlines Tristar, learning how commercial aviation works and gaining knowledge of pilots, crew, and the airplane itself. (Rev: BL 1/1/94) [387.7]

6129 Ryan, Craig. *The Pre-Astronauts: Manned Ballooning on the Threshold of Space* (9–adult). 1995, Naval Institute $29.95 (1-55750-732-5). A chronicle of the achievements of those involved in the dangerous, postwar, manned balloon programs. (Rev: BL 5/1/95) [629.13]

6130 Sullivan, George. *Modern Bombers and Attack Planes* (7–12). (Military Aircraft) 1993, Facts on File LB $17.95 (0-8160-2354-9). (Rev: BL 3/1/93; MJHS) [358.4]

6131 Sullivan, George. *Modern Fighter Planes* (7–12). (Military Aircraft) 1991, Facts on File $17.95 (0-8160-2352-2). The history of 11 warplanes conceived and tested over the last 30 years. Black-and-white photos, glossary. (Rev: BL 1/15/92; SLJ 3/92) [358.4]

6132 Taylor, Richard L. *The First Flight Across the United States: The Story of Calbraith Perry Rogers and His Airplane, the Vin Fiz* (5–7). 1993, Watts LB $12.90 (0-531-20159-7). Historical photos give the reader a flavor of the time. (Rev: BL 4/15/94; MJHS; SLJ 2/94) [629.13]

6133 Taylor, Richard L. *The First Solo Flight Around the World: The Story of Wiley Post and His Airplane, the Winnie Mae* (5–7). 1993, Watts LB $12.90 (0-531-20160-0). For young aviation enthusiasts, this biography of Wiley Post captures the excitement of the early days of aviation. (Rev: BL 4/15/94; MJHS) [629.13]

6134 Tessendorf, K. C. *Wings Around the World: The American World Flight of 1924* (5–9). 1991, Atheneum $14.95 (0-689-31550-3). An account of man's first flight around the world in 1924. (Rev: BL 1/15/92; SLJ 11/91) [910.4]

6135 *Volar, el sueño del hombre* (5–8). (Biblioteca interactiva/Mundo maravilloso) Tr. from French by Fernando Bort. 1995, Ediciones SM (Madrid, Spain) $14.95 (84-348-4506-7). This "interactive" title includes numerous foldouts, flaps, and transparent plastic overlays with detailed color illustrations and simple text on flying. English title: *To Fly: Man's Dream*. (Rev: BL 10/15/95)

Automobiles and Trucks

6136 *Diccionario visual Altea de los automóviles* (5–12). 1992, Santillana (Madrid, Spain) $24.95 (84-372-4530-3). This large-format dictionary includes more than 200 detailed, eye-catching photos and drawings in color, with brief texts explaining the interior and exterior of automobiles. Index. English title: *The Visual Dictionary of Cars*. (Rev: BL 4/1/94)

6137 Gaston, Jim. *When There's No Mechanic: A General Guide to Driving, Maintenance, and Car Repair* (9–adult). 1992, CoNation Publications (703 Ninth St., Suite 236, Durham, NC 27705) paper $12.95 (1-879699-10-9). A basic, practical car and driving manual giving safety, maintenance, and repair information. (Rev: BL 12/15/91) [629.287]

6138 Makower, Joel. *The Green Commuter* (9–adult). 1992, National Press Books (7200 Wisconsin Ave., Suite 212, Bethesda, MD 20814) $9.95 (0-915765-95-0). Tips on how to make a car less damaging to the environment. Includes lists of environmental organizations, government resources, and U.S. addresses of major car manufacturers. (Rev: BL 2/1/92) [363.73]

6139 Parker, Steve. *The Car* (5–8). 1994, Gloucester LB $12.40 (0-531-17415-8). Describes the evolution of the automobile from its prototypes in the late eighteenth century to the proposed electric- and solar-powered vehicles. (Rev: BL 4/1/94; MJHS) [629.222]

6140 Perrin, Noel. *Solo: Life with an Electric Car* (9–adult). 1992, Norton $18.95 (0-393-03407-0). An account of a California-to-Vermont trip in an electric car by an environmental-studies teacher. Also provides a capsule history of research on alternative models. (Rev: BL 10/1/92) [629.25]

6141 Schleifer, Jay. *Corvette: America's Sports Car* (6–10). (Cool Classics) 1992, Macmillan/Crestwood LB $13.95 (0-89686-697-1). Presents information on styling, engine development, suspension and braking advances, and other technical matters. Color photos of various Corvette models. (Rev: BL 10/15/92) [629.222]

6142 Schleifer, Jay. *Ferrari: Red-Hot Legend* (6–10). (Cool Classics) 1992, Macmillan/Crestwood LB $13.95 (0-89686-700-5). Presents information on styling, engine development, suspension and braking advances, and other technical matters. Color photos of various Ferrari models. (Rev: BL 10/15/92; SLJ 1/93) [629.222]

6143 Schleifer, Jay. *Mustang: Power-Packed Pony* (6–10). (Cool Classics) 1992, Macmillan/Crestwood LB $13.95 (0-89686-699-8). Presents information on styling, engine development, suspension and braking advances, and other technical matters. Color photos of various Mustang models. (Rev: BL 10/15/92) [629.222]

6144 Schleifer, Jay. *Porsche: Germany's Wonder Car* (6–10). (Cool Classics) 1992, Macmillan/Crestwood LB $13.95 (0-89686-703-X). Presents information on styling, engine development, suspension and braking advances, and other technical matters. Color photos of various Porsche models. (Rev: BL 10/15/92; SLJ 1/93) [629.222]

6145 Schultz, Mort. *Car Care Q and A: The Auto Owner's Complete Problem-Solver* (9–adult). 1992, Wiley $29.95 (0-471-54478-7); paper $17.95 (0-471-54479-5). Based on *Popular Mechanics* columns, this car maintenance guidebook is filled with practical tips. (Rev: BL 4/15/92) [629.28]

6146 Sclar, Deanna. *The Auto Repair for Dummies Glove Compartment Guide to Emergency Repair* (9–adult). 1991, Ten Speed paper $4.95 (0-89815-435-9). This compact reference guide for motorists gives environmentally friendly advice on safety consciousness, breakdown prevention, and unexpected repairs. (Rev: BL 10/1/91) [629.28]

6147 Sikorsky, Robert. *From Bumper to Bumper: Robert Sikorsky's Automotive Tips* (9–adult). 1991, TAB $16.95 (0-8306-2134-2); paper $9.95 (0-8306-2134-2). Practical advice on automobile maintenance, driving techniques, buying tips, and motoring information. (Rev: BL 11/1/91; SHS) [629.28]

Cycles

6148 Lafferty, Peter, and David Jefferis. *Superbikes: The History of Motorcycles* (5–7). 1990, Watts LB $11.90 (0-531-14039-3). (Rev: BL 5/15/91; MJHS; SLJ 5/91) [629.227]

6149 Wilson, Hugo. *Encyclopedia of the Motorcycle* (9–12). 1995, DK $39.95 (0-7894-0150-9). Pictures 1,000 motorcyles and scooters and lists more than 3,000 manufacturers. (Rev: BL 11/15/95; SLJ 2/96)

Railroads

6150 Coiley, John. *Train* (5–9). (Eyewitness Books) 1992, Knopf LB $15.99 (0-679-91684-9). (Rev: BL 11/1/92; MJHS) [625.1]

6151 Coiley, John. *Trenes* (5–10). (Biblioteca visual Altea) 1992, Santillana (Madrid, Spain) $18.95 (84-372-3772-6). Originally published in Great Britain, this volume contains a clear, concise text on trains, with close-up color photos, charts, and drawings. English title: *Trains*. (Rev: BL 2/1/94)

6152 Fisher, Leonard Everett. *Tracks Across America: The Story of the American Railroad, 1825–1900* (6–10). 1992, Holiday $17.95 (0-8234-0945-7). The history of the railroad, from the steam engine to the Civil War and the western expansion of the nation. (Rev: BL 5/15/92; SLJ 8/92; YR) [385]

6153 Jefferis, David. *Trains: The History of Railroads* (5–7). (Wheels) 1991, Watts LB $11.90 (0-531-14192-6). (Rev: BL 11/15/91) [625.1]

6154 Spangenburg, Ray, and Diane K. Moser. *The Story of America's Railroads* (5–9). (Connecting a Continent) 1991, Facts on File $18.95 (0-8160-2257-7). This history of the railways incorporates stories, biographies, time lines, and charts to provide a description of their influence on the development of the nation. (Rev: BL 11/15/91) [625]

6155 Warburton, Lois. *Railroads: Bridging the Continents* (6–10). (Encyclopedia of Discovery and Invention) 1991, Lucent LB $15.95 (1-56006-216-9). (Rev: BL 4/15/92) [385]

6156 Withuhn, William L. *The Spirit of Steam: The Golden Age of North American Steam* (9–adult). 1995, Smithmark $15.98 (0-8317-5511-3). A curator at the Smithsonian tells the story, through black-and-white photos, of the former importance of steam locomotives as the economic lifeline for towns both small and large. (Rev: BL 10/15/95) [385.3]

6157 Wormser, Richard. *The Iron Horse: How Railroads Changed America* (6–9). 1993, Walker LB $18.85 (0-8027-8222-1). From the robber barons to the Gold Rush and immigrant influx, this discusses the economic and social impact of the railroad between 1830 and 1900. (Rev: BL 12/15/93; BTA; SLJ 1/94; VOYA 4/94) [385]

Ships and Boats

6158 *Diccionario visual Altea de naves y navegación* (5–12). 1992, Santillana (Madrid, Spain) $24.95 (84-372-4526-5). This large-format dictionary includes more than 200 detailed, eye-catching photos and drawings in color, with brief texts explaining the interior and exterior of ships. Index. English title: *The Visual Dictionary of Ships and Sailing*. (Rev: BL 4/1/94)

6159 Gillmer, Thomas C. *Pride of Baltimore: The Story of the Baltimore Clippers, 1800–1990* (9–adult). 1992, International Marine $24.95 (0-87742-309-1). A ship designer traces the history of early American shipbuilding, in particular, a schooner known as the *Baltimore Clipper*. (Rev: BL 3/15/92; SLJ 7/92) [387.2]

6160 Grady, Sean M. *Ships: Crossing the World's Oceans* (6–10). (Encyclopedia of Discovery and Invention) 1992, Lucent LB $15.95 (1-56006-220-7). (Rev: BL 12/15/92) [387.2]

6161 Graham, Ian. *Boats, Ships, Submarines and Other Floating Machines* (5–7). (How Things Work) 1993, Kingfisher LB $10.95 (1-85697-868-0); paper $5.95 (1-85697-867-2). Introductory information on such topics as buoyancy, wind power, and marine vehicles, including hydrofoils, hovercrafts, and submarines. (Rev: BL 6/1–15/93; MJHS; SLJ 5/93) [623.8]

6162 Kentley, Eric. *Barcos* (5–10). (Biblioteca visual Altea) 1992, Santillana (Madrid, Spain) $18.95 (84-372-3769-6). Contains a clear, concise text on boats, with close-up photos, charts, and drawings in color. English title: *Boats*. (Rev: BL 2/1/94)

6163 Macaulay, David. *Ship* (5–8). 1993, Houghton $19.95 (0-395-52439-3). This narrative describes the present-day discovery and recovery of artifacts from a caravel that sank in the Caribbean 500 years ago. (Rev: BL 10/15/93*; MJHS; SLJ 11/93) [387.2]

6164 Nalder, Eric. *Tankers Full of Trouble: The Perilous Journey of Alaskan Crude* (9–adult). 1994, Grove/Atlantic $23 (0-8021-1458-X). A Pulitzer Prize–winning investigative reporter describes life aboard a massive oil tanker and discusses the ecological threat posed by them. (Rev: BL 2/1/94*) [387.2]

6165 Platt, Richard. *El asombroso libro del interior de un barco de guerra del siglo XVIII* (5–12). Tr. by Juan Génova Sotil. Illus. 1993, Santillana (Madrid, Spain) $22.95 (84-372-4536-2). This large-format book includes detailed, cross-section color drawings and brief texts based on the battleship HMS *Victory*, built in England in 1765 and used in the Battle of Trafalgar. English title: *Cross-Sections: Man-of-War*. (Rev: BL 10/1/94)

6166 Platt, Richard. *Stephen Biesty's Cross-Sections: Man-of-War* (5–12). Illus. 1993, Dorling Kindersley $16.95 (1-56458-321-X). This visual representation of an eighteenth-century British man-of-war presents detailed cutaways with text describing life at sea. (Rev: BL 10/1/93; SLJ 1/94; VOYA 2/94) [359.1]

6167 Stillwell, Paul. *Battleship Arizona: An Illustrated History* (9–adult). 1991, Naval Institute $48.95 (0-87021-023-8). The story of Pearl Harbor's most famous "victim." (Rev: BL 1/15/92) [359.3]

Weapons and Submarines

6168 Calvert, James F. *Silent Running: My Years in a World War II Attack Submarine* (9–adult). 1995, Wiley $27.95 (0-471-12778-7). A memoir of Calvert's career in submarines, with accounts of the women in his life. (Rev: BL 11/1/95) [940.54]

6169 Clancy, Tom. *Submarine: A Guided Tour Inside a Nuclear Warship* (9–adult). 1993, Berkley paper $14.95 (0-425-13873-9). An in-depth look at submarines, including their history, design, weapons, tactics, crew, and scenarios showing their continued value. (Rev: BL 9/15/93) [623.812]

6170 Goldstein, Donald M., and Katherine V. Dillon. *Rain of Ruin: A Photographic History of Hiroshima and Nagasaki* (9–adult). 1995, Brassey's $31.95 (1-57488-033-0). More than 400 black-and-white photos and text generally support the bombing of Hiroshima and Nagasaki. (Rev: BL 8/95) [940.54]

6171 Gonen, Rivka. *Charge! Weapons and Warfare in Ancient Times* (5–9). (Buried Worlds) 1993, Lerner $22.95 (0-8225-3201-8). Traces the evolution of primitive weapons from sticks and stones for hunting to increasingly sophisticated tools for warfare and defense. (Rev: BL 2/1/94; SLJ 2/94) [355.8]

6172 Grady, Sean M. *Explosives: Devices of Controlled Destruction* (6–10). (Encyclopedia of Discovery and Invention) 1995, Lucent LB $15.95 (1-56006-250-9). (Rev: BL 4/15/95) [662]

6173 Landau, Elaine. *Chemical and Biological Warfare* (7–10). 1991, Dutton/Lodestar $14.95 (0-525-67364-4). This history of chemical and biological weapons discusses the moral, ethical, and environmental risks involved in their use and the difficulty of their disposal. (Rev: BL 11/15/91; SHS; SLJ 12/91) [353]

6174 Lanier-Graham, Susan D. *The Ecology of War: Environmental Impacts of Weaponry and Warfare* (9–adult). 1993, Walker $22.95 (0-8027-1262-2). Covers agent orange effects, Gulf War oil spills and fires, unexploded ammunition in the Pacific, and pollution around military bases. (Rev: BL 5/1/93) [363.73]

6175 Maddox, Robert James. *Weapons for Victory: The Hiroshima Decision Fifty Years Later* (9–adult). 1995, Univ. of Missouri $19.95 (0-8262-1037-6). The author argues that President Truman dropped the bomb to end the war, contrary to arguments made by revisionist historians. (Rev: BL 8/95) [940.54]

6176 Pringle, Laurence. *Chemical and Biological Warfare: The Cruelest Weapons* (7–12). 1993, Enslow LB $17.95 (0-89490-280-6). Describes the horrors of chemical/biological warfare, with detailed information on weaponry development. (Rev: BL 7/93; SLJ 5/93; VOYA 8/93) [358]

6177 Rhodes, Richard. *Dark Sun: The Making of the Hydrogen Bomb* (9–adult). 1995, Simon & Schuster $30 (0-684-80400-X). Examines the history of the hydrogen bomb, from the race to be the first to develop it to the moral implications of its existence. (Rev: BL 7/95*) [623.4]

6178 Sagan, Scott D., and Kenneth N. Waltz. *The Spread of Nuclear Weapons: A Debate* (9–adult). 1995, Norton $16.95 (0-393-03810-6). Two educators debate the nuclear weapons issue. (Rev: BL 4/1/95) [355.02]

6179 Takaki, Ronald. *Hiroshima: Why America Dropped the Atomic Bomb* (9–adult). 1995, Little, Brown $19.95 (0-316-83122-0). A discussion of the decision makers and their motivations for bombing Hiroshima. (Rev: BL 8/95) [940.54]

6180 Taylor, C. L., and L. B. Taylor. *Chemical and Biological Warfare* (7–12). Rev. ed. 1992, Watts LB $13.40 (0-531-13029-0). This revision of the 1985 edition includes Saddam Hussein's use of CB weapons against Kurds and the threat of their use in the Gulf War. (Rev: BL 3/1/93; SHS) [358]

6181 Yamazaki, James N., and Louis B. Fleming. *Children of the Atomic Bomb: An American Physician's Memoir of Nagasaki, Hiroshima, and the Marshall Islands* (9–adult). 1995, Duke Univ. $16.95 (0-8223-1658-7). Yamazaki, a pediatrician and a Nisei, writes this poignant memoir of his journey to Japan for the first time to gather firsthand accounts of the attack on Nagasaki. (Rev: BL 8/95) [618.92]

Recreation and Sports

Crafts, Hobbies, and Pastimes

General and Miscellaneous

6182 Adkins, Jan. *String: Tying It Up, Tying It Down* (5–8). 1992, Scribner $13.95 (0-684-18875-9). Entertaining step-by-step directions for tying knots. (Rev: BL 4/15/92; SLJ 6/92) [677]

6183 Bawden, Juliet. *101 Things to Make: Fun Craft Projects with Everyday Materials* (5–7). 1994, Sterling $14.95 (0-8069-0596-4). Provides clear illustrations and instructions for crafting models, textiles, puppets, patchwork, masks, and more. (Rev: BL 9/1/94) [746.5]

6184 Besmehn, Bobby. *Juggling Step-by-Step* (5–8). 1995, Sterling $17.95 (0-8069-0814-9). Juggling explained by a professional juggler. (Rev: BL 4/15/95; SLJ 3/95) [793.8]

6185 Boswell, Thom, ed. *The Kaleidoscope Book: A Spectrum of Spectacular Scopes to Make* (9–adult). 1992, Sterling $19.95 (0-8069-8370-1). Kaleidoscopes viewed as an art form, with instructions for readers who would like to construct their own. (Rev: BL 4/1/92) [688.7]

6186 Cassin-Scott, Jack. *Amateur Dramatics* (9–adult). 1993, Cassell $24.95 (0-304-34146-0). An overview of play production, including chapters on set design, lighting and sound, make-up and wigs, costumes, and props. (Rev: BL 5/15/93) [792.02]

6187 Cook, Amber. *Nature Crafts for All the Seasons* (9–adult). 1994, Sterling $24.95 (0-8069-8602-6). A selection of projects for making decorative seasonal items using natural materials, such as seashells, vines, and twigs. (Rev: BL 2/1/94) [745.5]

6188 Deshpande, Chris. *Festival Crafts* (5–7). 1994, Gareth Stevens $13.95 (0-8368-1153-4). Demonstrates how to make papier-mâché Mardi Gras maracas and other crafts for the Mexican celebration of All Soul's Day. (Rev: BL 3/1/95; SLJ 1/95) [745.594]

6189 Diehn, Gwen, and Terry Krautwurst. *Kid Style Nature Crafts: 50 Terrific Things to Make with Nature's Materials* (5–7). 1995, Sterling $19.95 (0-8069-0996-X). An unusual collection of projects, with discussions of different aspects of nature. (Rev: BL 11/15/95; SLJ 10/95) [745.5]

6190 Diehn, Gwen, and Terry Krautwurst. *Nature Crafts for Kids* (5–8). 1992, Sterling/Lark $19.95 (0-8069-8372-8). Offers ideas for every season that combine challenging projects with scientific lore. (Rev: BL 7/92; SLJ 7/92) [745.5]

6191 Guerrier, Charlie. *A Collage of Crafts* (5–7). (Young Artisan) Illus. 1994, Ticknor & Fields $12.95 (0-395-68377-7). Projects are usually 1 or 2 to a page, illustrated with color photos of materials needed and finished products. (Rev: BL 4/1/94; MJHS; SLJ 3/94) [745.5]

6192 Herald, Jacqueline. *World Crafts* (9–adult). 1993, Lark Books (50 College St., Asheville, NC 28801) $35 (0-937274-66-6). (Rev: BL 8/93; BTA) [745]

6193 Jans, Martin. *Stage Make-up Techniques* (9–adult). 1993, Players Press paper $23.95 (0-88734-621-9). A primer of basic makeup techniques (including children's makeup), with detailed illustrations of all aspects of the craft. (Rev: BL 11/1/92) [792]

6194 Kenzle, Linda Fry. *Dazzle: Creating Artistic Jewelry and Distinctive Accessories* (9–adult). 1995, Chilton paper $21.95 (0-8019-8638-9). How to create 30 design patterns that customize and personalize outfits. (Rev: BL 10/1/95) [745.594]

6195 McCormick, Anita Louise. *Shortwave Radio Listening for Beginners* (9–adult). 1993, TAB paper $10.95 (0-8306-4135-1). Explains shortwave reception, profiles major broadcasters, summarizes necessary equipment for hobbyists, and includes tables with band frequencies of stations. (Rev: BL 5/15/93) [621.3841]

6196 MacLeod-Brudenell, Iain. *Animal Crafts* (5–7). (World Wide Crafts) 1994, Gareth Stevens $13.95 (0-8368-1151-8). Crafts from cultural traditions from around the world. (Rev: BL 3/1/95; SLJ 1/95) [745.5]

6197 *Nature Craft* (9–adult). 1993, North Light paper $14.95 (0-89134-542-6). Based on the British crafts magazine *Creative Hands*, projects in basketry, woodworking, flowers, and gardening are presented. (Rev: BL 11/15/93; SLJ 1/94) [745.5]

6198 Taylor, Carol. *Creative Bead Jewelry* (9–adult). 1995, Sterling $18.95 (0-8069-1306-1). This book, with 70 examples from 38 bead artists, is guaranteed to send one off to the nearest bead emporium. (Rev: BL 11/15/95) [745.594]

6199 Treinen, Sara Jane, ed. *Better Homes and Gardens Incredibly Awesome Crafts for Kids* (5–8). 1992, Meredith $24.95 (0-696-01924-8); paper $19.95 (0-696-01984-1). More than 75 projects are explained step by step and illustrated with color photos. (Rev: BL 4/15/92) [745.5]

American Historical Crafts

6200 Gadia-Smitley, Roselyn. *Wearable Quilts: Sewing Timeless Fashions Using Traditional Patterns* (9–adult). 1993, Sterling paper $14.95 (0-8069-8800-2). Garment patterns, including instructions for appliqué, trapunto (stuffed quilting), English or wadded quilting, and traditional patchwork. (Rev: BL 5/15/93) [746.9]

6201 Hanson, Joan. *Calendar Quilts* (9–adult). 1991, That Patchwork Place (P.O. Box 118, Bothell, WA 98041-0118) paper $16.95 (0-943574-77-3). A pattern book of 12 quilted wall hangings with seasonal themes, each designed to teach a different quilting technique. (Rev: BL 10/1/91) [746.46]

6202 Lawther, Gail. *The Complete Quilting Course* (9–adult). 1992, Chilton $27.95 (0-8019-8358-4). Includes graphed templates and photos of finished products. (Rev: BL 12/1/92) [746.46]

6203 Margaret, Pat Maixner, and Donna Ingram Slusser. *Watercolor Quilts* (9–adult). 1993, That Patchwork Place (P.O. Box 118, Bothell, WA 98041-0118) paper $24.95 (1-56477-031-1). A guide to using color values to achieve striking effects in the creation of quilts suitable for wall hanging. (Rev: BL 1/1/94) [746.3]

6204 Marston, Gwen, and Joe Cunningham. *Quilting with Style: Principles for Great Pattern Design* (9–adult). 1993, American Quilter's Society $24.95 (0-89145-814-X). Methods of planning the cable, fan, and feather of a quilt are described, with more than 75 color photos of traditional quilts and traceable full-sized figures. (Rev: BL 11/1/93) [746.9]

6205 Mumm, Debbie. *Quick Country Quilting: Over 80 Projects Featuring Easy, Timesaving Techniques* (9–adult). 1991, Rodale $23.95 (0-87857-984-2). An expert quilter offers 80 sewing projects for the enthusiast who has already mastered some of the basic techniques. (Rev: BL 2/1/92) [746.46]

6206 Reidy, Elaine. *Quilt Blocks: Fast and Easy Projects Using Interchangeable Squares* (9–adult). 1991, Sterling/Main Street $24.95 (0-8069-7423-0); paper $14.95 (0-8069-7422-2). Quick, simple, and inexpensive projects using interchangeable cloth squres. Illustrated. (Rev: BL 7/91) [746.9]

6207 Stevens, Bernardine S. *Colonial American Craftspeople* (5–8). (Colonial America) 1993, Watts $12.90 (0-531-12536-X). A description of colonial trades and the apprenticeship system, illustrated with period engravings and paintings. (Rev: BL 1/1/94; MJHS; SLJ 2/94) [680]

6208 Swain, Gwenyth. *Bookworks: Making Books by Hand* (5–7). 1995, Carolrhoda LB $16.13 (0-87614-858-5). After tracing the history of the book and printing, directions are given for making paper and books with fold-ups, pop-ups, and windows. (Rev: BL 7/95; SLJ 8/95) [745.5]

Clay Modeling and Ceramics

6209 Wensley, Doug. *Pottery: A Manual of Techniques* (9–adult). 1991, Trafalgar Square/Crowood $34.95 (1-85223-176-9). (Rev: BL 4/15/91; SHS) [738]

Cooking

6210 Albyn, Carole Lisa, and Lois Sinaiko Webb. *The Multicultural Cookbook for Students* (6–9). 1993, Oryx $25.95 (0-89774-735-6). Provides 337 authentic recipes from 122 countries, arranged geographically. (Rev: BL 2/15/94; MJHS; SHS; SLJ 10/93) [641.59]

6211 Benning, Lee Edwards. *The Cook's Tales: Origins of Famous Foods and Recipes* (9–adult). 1992, Globe Pequot paper $15.95 (0-87106-229-1). An alphabetized history of favorite foods, with anecdotal notes and 50 recipes for such classics as Waldorf salad, Toll House cookies, and Yorkshire pudding. (Rev: BL 10/1/92) [641]

6212 *Betty Crocker's Everything Chocolate* (9–adult). 1993, Prentice-Hall $16 (0-671-84718-X). Recipes for beginning and more experienced cooks. (Rev: BL 3/15/93) [641.6]

6213 *Betty Crocker's Great Chicken Recipes* (9–adult). 1993, Prentice-Hall paper $8 (0-671-84689-2). Contains more than 100 recipes, color photos, food ideas, boxed tips, and practical hints. (Rev: BL 3/1/93) [641.6]

6214 *Betty Crocker's Holiday Baking* (9–adult). 1993, Prentice-Hall paper $8 (0-671-86961-2). More than 100 simple recipes for the holiday season, including nutritional information for classic and revamped favorites. Color photos and sidebar tips make directions easy to follow. (Rev: BL 10/1/93) [641.7]

6215 *Betty Crocker's Homemade Quick Breads: Muffins, Biscuits and More* (9–adult). 1993, Prentice-Hall $16 (0-671-84717-1). Recipes for beginning and more experienced cooks. (Rev: BL 3/15/93) [641.8]

6216 *Betty Crocker's Low-Calorie Cooking* (9–adult). 1993, Prentice-Hall paper $8 (0-671-84690-6). Contains more than 100 recipes, color photos, food ideas, boxed tips, and practical hints. (Rev: BL 3/1/93) [641.5]

6217 *Betty Crocker's Mexican Made Easy* (9–adult). 1993, Prentice-Hall paper $8 (0-671-84691-4). Contains more than 100 recipes, color photos, food ideas, boxed tips, and practical hints. (Rev: BL 3/1/93) [641.5972]

6218 *Betty Crocker's New Choices Cookbook* (9–adult). 1993, Prentice-Hall $23 (0-671-86767-9). More than 500 health-conscious recipes are each labeled as low calorie, low fat, low cholesterol, low sodium, or high fiber to make eating right easy. (Rev: BL 10/1/93) [641.5]

6219 *Betty Crocker's Quick Dinners: In 30 Minutes or Less* (9–adult). 1993, Prentice-Hall paper $8 (0-671-84692-2). Contains more than 100 recipes, color photos, food ideas, boxed tips, and practical hints. (Rev: BL 3/1/93) [641.5]

6220 *Betty Crocker's Soups and Stews* (9–adult). 1993, Prentice-Hall paper $8 (0-671-86960-4). Soups and stews of more than 100 varieties are presented with color photos, sidebar explanations and tips, and nutritional information. (Rev: BL 10/1/93) [641.5]

6221 Copage, Eric V. *Kwanzaa: An African-American Celebration of Culture and Cooking* (9–adult). 1991, Morrow $23 (0-688-10939-X). Drawing on sources from Angola to the United States, this collection of recipes and stories celebrates the relatively new African American tradition of Kwanza. Awards: SLJ Best Book. (Rev: BL 10/15/91; SLJ 4/92) [641.59]

6222 Cox, Beverly, and Martin Jacobs. *Spirit of the Harvest: North American Indian Cooking* (9–adult). 1991, Stewart, Tabori & Chang $35 (1-55670-186-1). Native American experts have aided the authors in this book that contains recipes of various North American tribes, adapted for modern kitchens and substituting readily available ingredients when required. (Rev: BL 9/15/91) [641.59]

6223 Damerow, Gail. *Ice Cream! The Whole Scoop* (9–adult). 1991, Glenbridge Publishing (4 Woodland Lane, Macomb, IL 61455) $24.95 (0-944435-09-2). This collection of recipes is also a thorough survey of all types of frozen desserts. Includes technical information on ingredients, techniques, and special equipment. (Rev: BL 9/1/91) [641.8]

6224 Davis, William C. *The Civil War Cookbook* (9–adult). 1993, Running Press $12.98 (1-56138-287-6). Drawing on anecdotes and quotes from soldiers and sailors, Davis presents more than 40 updated Civil War–era recipes. (Rev: BL 11/1/93) [973.78]

6225 Elliot, Rose. *The Classic Vegetarian Cookbook* (9–adult). 1994, Dorling Kindersley $24.95 (1-56458-486-0). Describes how to prepare nutritious vegetarian meals representing various international cuisines. (Rev: BL 7/94; SLJ 9/94; VOYA 2/95) [641.5]

6226 Fandre, Donovan Jon. *Real Food Microwave: 200 Recipes from Television's "Microwave Master" That Taste As If They Were Made the Old-Fashioned Way* (9–adult). 1992, Morrow $20 (0-688-09115-6). A television microwave chef teaches easy-to-use recipes and gives "zap tips" for the average cook. (Rev: BL 2/15/92) [641.5]

6227 Herbst, Sharon Tyler. *The Food Lover's Tiptionary* (9–adult). 1994, Morrow paper $15 (0-688-12146-2). Tips on buying, storing, cooking, preparing, and serving food and drink. (Rev: BL 3/15/94) [641.3]

6228 Kirlin, Katherine S., and Thomas Kirlin. *Smithsonian Folklife Cookbook* (9–adult). 1991,

Smithsonian $35 (1-56098-091-5); paper $15.95 (1-56098-089-3). The contributors to these historical recipes, which have been demonstrated at the Smithsonian's Festival of American Folklife, reveal bygone cultural mores and eating habits. (Rev: BL 9/15/91; SLJ 2/92) [641.5973]

6229 Kreschollek, Margie. *The Guaranteed Goof-Proof Microwave Cookbook for Kids* (5–9). 1992, Bantam paper $9.50 (0-553-35255-5). A step-by-step guide for young people on how to "nuke" all kinds of food, from main dishes to desserts. (Rev: BL 2/1/92) [641.5]

6230 Lemlin, Jeanne. *Quick Vegetarian Pleasures* (9–adult). 1992, HarperCollins $30 (0-06-055324-3); paper $15 (0-06-096911-3). Tasty, easy-to-prepare meatless recipes ranging from appetizers to entrées. (Rev: BL 3/1/92) [641.5]

6231 Levin, Karen A. *Twenty-Minute Chicken Dishes: Delicious, Easy-to-Prepare Meals Everyone Will Love!* (9–adult). 1991, Contemporary paper $7.95 (0-8092-4033-5). This collection of quick, simple chicken dishes includes familiar favorites and ethnic specialties. (Rev: BL 12/1/91) [641.6]

6232 Luchetti, Cathy. *Home on the Range: A Culinary History of the American West* (9–adult). 1993, Random paper $25 (0-679-74484-3). A complete picture of the role food preparation and meals played in nineteenth-century daily life on the frontier. With photos, diary extracts, and recipes. (Rev: BL 7/93; SLJ 12/93) [394.1]

6233 Medearis, Angela Shelf. *The African-American Kitchen: Cooking from Our Heritage* (9–adult). 1994, Dutton $23.95 (0-525-93834-6). Contains more than 250 recipes from Africa, the Caribbean, and the United States, including Tanzanian baked bananas, pumpkin meat loaf, and baked ham. (Rev: BL 9/15/94) [641.59]

6234 Moll, Lucy. *Vegetarian Times Complete Cookbook* (9–adult). 1995, Macmillan $29.95 (0-02-621745-7). A former editor of *Vegetarian Times* presents more than 600 recipes in what she hopes will be the standard vegetarian cookbook. Includes nutritional breakdowns for each recipe. (Rev: BL 11/15/95) [641.5]

6235 Moore, Marilyn M. *The Wooden Spoon Cookie Book: Favorite Home-Style Recipes from the Wooden Spoon Kitchen* (9–adult). 1994, Atlantic Monthly paper $15 (0-87113-601-5). Over 100 recipes for cookies and sweets, from animal crackers to rosy rhubarb squares. (Rev: BL 7/94) [641.8]

6236 Norman, Jill. *The Complete Book of Spices* (9–adult). 1991, Viking/Studio $21.95 (0-670-83437-8). These recipes from Ghana are divided into 3 levels of difficulty. (Rev: BL 3/1/91; SHS) [641.3]

6237 Osseo-Asare, Fran. *A Good Soup Attracts Chairs: A First African Cookbook for American Kids* (5–9). 1993, Pelican $18.95 (0-88289-816-7). (Rev: BL 10/15/93; MJHS) [641.5966]

6238 Peters, Colette. *Colette's Cakes: The Art of Cake Decorating* (9–adult). 1991, Little, Brown $24.95 (0-316-70205-6). A guide to creative cake design and decorating, not just a cake cookbook, with step-by-step instructions for assembling elaborate baked desserts. (Rev: BL 9/1/91) [641.8]

6239 Purdy, Susan G. *Have Your Cake and Eat It, Too: 200 Luscious Low Fat Cakes, Pies, Cookies, Pudding, and Other Desserts You Thought You Could Never Eat Again* (9–adult). 1993, Morrow $25 (0-688-11110-6). Using ingredients like fruits, egg whites, nonfat milk, and less sugar and butter, Purdy presents 200 healthful recipes. (Rev: BL 11/1/93) [641.8]

6240 Ralph, Judy, and Ray Gompf. *The Peanut Butter Cookbook for Kids* (5–7). Illus. 1995, Hyperion LB $14.89 (0-7868-2110-8). Brief, step-by-step recipes for those with a passion for peanut butter in almost any combination. (Rev: BL 10/1/95; SLJ 9/95) [641.6]

6241 Rani. *Feast of India* (9–adult). 1991, Contemporary paper $11.95 (0-8092-4095-5). This beginner's guide to Indian cuisine includes recipes for traditional Indian curries, kabobs, pilao, and dals, with modern cooking techniques. (Rev: BL 11/15/91) [641.5954]

6242 Rosin, Arielle. *Eclairs and Brown Bears* (5–7). Illus. 1994, Ticknor & Fields $12.95 (0-395-68380-7). This cookbook, imported from France, includes recipes for éclairs, butter cookies, tarts, pies, brownies, and more. (Rev: BL 4/1/94; MJHS; SLJ 3/94) [641.8]

6243 Rosin, Arielle. *Pizzas and Punk Potatoes* (5–7). Illus. 1994, Ticknor & Fields $12.95 (0-395-68381-5). The recipes in this cookbook, imported from France, focus on apples, potatoes, and pizza. (Rev: BL 4/1/94; MJHS; SLJ 3/94) [641.5]

6244 Scobey, Joan. *The Fannie Farmer Junior Cookbook* (6–10). Illus. 1993, Little, Brown $19.95 (0-316-77624-6). Recipes covering a wide range of tastes. Includes definitions and illustrations of terms, appliances, pans, and other tools. (Rev: BL 11/15/93; MJHS; SLJ 11/93; VOYA 2/94) [641.5]

6245 Seelig, Tina L. *Incredible Edible Science* (5–8). 1994, W. H. Freeman $19.95 (0-7167-6501-2); paper $13.95 (0-7167-6507-1). Explores the science behind various foods and recipes, for example, the difference between white and dark meat. (Rev: BL 7/94; SLJ 8/94) [641.5]

6246 Shaw, Maura D., and Synda Altschuler Byrne. *Foods from Mother Earth* (6–10). 1994, Shawangunk Press (8 Laurel Park Rd., Wappingers Falls, NY 12590) paper $9.95 (1-885482-02-7). Most of the recipes in this vegetarian cookbook can be prepared in 3 or 4 easy steps. (Rev: BL 1/15/95; SLJ 2/95) [641.5]

6247 Sparks, Pat, and Barbara Swanson. *Tortillas!* (9–adult). Illus. 1993, St. Martin's paper $10.95 (0-312-08912-0). Everything from traditional Mexican recipes to moo shu burritos. (Rev: BL 3/15/93) [641.8]

6248 Van Cleave, Jill. *Big, Soft, Chewy Cookies* (9–adult). 1991, Contemporary paper $7.95 (0-8092-3969-8). Fifty-eight varieties of cookies with clear instructions for beginning cooks. (Rev: BL 11/15/91) [641.8]

6249 *Vegetarian Cooking Around the World* (5–7). (Easy Menu Ethnic Cookbook) 1992, Lerner LB $11.21 (0-8225-0927-X). Includes vegetarian recipes from all over the world. (Rev: BL 2/15/93; MJHS) [641.5]

6250 Walter, Carole. *Great Cakes* (9–adult). 1991, Ballantine $25 (0-345-36473-2). The emphasis is on correct technique in this collection of more than 250 recipes, with at-a-glance information for each cake. (Rev: BL 9/15/91) [641.8]

6251 Wayne, Marvin A., and Stephen R. Yarnall. *The New Dr. Cookie Cookbook: Dessert Your Way to Health with More Than 150 Scrumptious Cookies, Cakes, and Treats* (9–adult). 1994, Morrow/Quill paper $14 (0-688-12222-1). Using substitutions and deletions, these 2 Pacific Northwest doctors present more than 150 sweets along with nutritional information such as calorie and fat counts. (Rev: BL 12/15/93) [641.8]

6252 Wedman, Betty. *Quick and Easy Diabetic Menus: More Than 150 Delicious Recipes for Breakfast, Lunch, Dinner, and Snacks* (9–adult). 1993, Contemporary paper $10.95 (0-8092-3853-5). These recipes are useful for both diabetics and anyone watching his or her weight. (Rev: BL 7/93) [641.5]

6253 Weiner, Leslie, and Barbara Albright. *Quick Chocolate Fixes: 75 Fast and Easy Recipes for People Who Want Chocolate . . . in a Hurry!* (9–adult). 1995, St. Martin's paper $6.95 (0-312-13153-4). Describes 75 quick recipes, all loaded with chocolate, including flourless chocolate cake, gorp clusters, brownie cheese cake, and S'mores ice cream pie. (Rev: BL 7/95) [641.6]

6254 Woods, Sylvia, and Christopher Styler. *Sylvia's Soul Food: Recipes from Harlem's World-Famous Restaurant* (9–adult). 1992, Hearst $17 (0-688-10012-0). A Harlem restaurateur and her chef present more than 100 recipes from her kitchen, all representative of African American culture. (Rev: BL 10/15/92) [641.59]

6255 Yockelson, Lisa. *Brownies and Blondies* (9–adult). 1992, HarperCollins $12.50 (0-06-016751-3). Fifty brownie recipes, including some vanilla varieties (blondies), by a veteran cookbook author. (Rev: BL 10/15/92) [641.8]

6256 Zisman, Honey, and Larry Zisman. *The 55 Best Brownies in the World: The Recipes That Won the Nationwide Great American Brownie Bake* (9–adult). 1991, St. Martin's paper $6.95 (0-312-05862-4). Contains recipes for everything from raspberry truffle brownies to brownie pizza. (Rev: BL 7/91) [641.8]

Costume Making, Dress, and Fashion

6257 Baker, Patricia. *Fashions of a Decade: The 1940s* (7–12). (Fashions of a Decade) Illus. 1992, Facts on File LB $16.95 (0-8160-2467-7). Each book in the Fashions of a Decade series connects political and social history with the reasons people chose particular modes of dress. (Rev: BL 4/1/92; MJHS) [391]

6258 Carnegy, Vicky. *Fashions of a Decade: The 1980s* (7–12). 1990, Facts on File $16.95 (0-8160-2471-5). (Rev: BL 2/15/91; MJHS; SLJ 5/91) [391]

6259 Connikie, Yvonne. *Fashions of a Decade: The 1960s* (7–12). 1990, Facts on File $16.95 (0-8160-2469-3). (Rev: BL 2/15/91; SLJ 5/91) [391]

6260 Constantino, Maria. *Fashions of a Decade: The 1930s* (7–12). (Fashions of a Decade) 1992, Facts on File LB $16.95 (0-8160-2466-9). (Rev: BL 4/1/92) [391]

6261 Feldman, Elane. *Fashions of a Decade: The 1990s* (7–12). (Fashions of a Decade) 1992, Facts on File LB $16.95 (0-8160-2472-3). (Rev: BL 12/15/92; MJHS) [391]

6262 Herald, Jacqueline. *Fashions of a Decade: The 1970s* (7–12). (Fashions of a Decade) 1992, Facts on File LB $16.95 (0-8160-2470-7). (Rev: BL 12/15/92; MJHS) [391]

6263 MacLeod-Brudenell, Iain. *Costume Crafts* (5–7). 1994, Gareth Stevens $13.95 (0-8368-

1152-6). Creative explorations of cultural traditions, including silhouette portraits—decorated paper hand patterns as practiced in India. (Rev: BL 3/1/95; SLJ 1/95) [745.5]

6264 Parks, Carol. *Make Your Own Great Vests: 90 Ways to Jazz Up Your Wardrobe* (9–adult). 1995, Sterling $24.95 (0-8069-0972-2). A showcase for tailoring unusual vests. (Rev: BL 4/15/95) [646.4]

6265 Peacock, John. *The Chronicle of Western Fashion: From Ancient Times to the Present Day* (9–adult). 1991, Abrams $29.95 (0-8109-3953-3). A former BBC costume designer offers a quick review of Western fashion from ancient Egypt to 1980. (Rev: BL 6/1/91; SHS) [391]

6266 Rowland-Warne, L. *Costume* (5–10). (Eyewitness Books) 1992, Knopf $15 (0-679-81680-1). (Rev: BL 8/92; MJHS) [391]

6267 Rowland-Warne, L. *Trajes* (5–10). (Biblioteca visual Altea) 1992, Santillana (Madrid, Spain) $18.95 (84-372-3768-8). Contains a clear, concise text on costumes, with close-up color photos, charts, and drawings. English title: *Costumes*. (Rev: BL 2/1/94)

6268 Schnurnberger, Lynn. *Let There Be Clothes* (9–adult). 1991, Workman paper $19.95 (0-89480-833-8). An overview of fashion history from cave dwellers to the present. (Rev: BL 1/15/92; SHS; SLJ 12/91) [391]

6269 Sensier, Danielle. *Costumes* (5–7). (Traditions Around the World) 1994, Thomson Learning $16.95 (1-56847-227-7). Introduces the ritual and traditional uses of costumes worldwide and offers well-chosen information about the ways climate, natural resources, and religious beliefs influence clothing. (Rev: BL 2/1/95; SLJ 3/95) [391]

Dolls and Other Toys

6270 Hall, Dorothea, ed. *Rag Dolls and How to Make Them* (9–adult). 1994, Running Press $14.98 (1-56138-352-X). This illustrated guide to rag-doll making contains step-by-step instructions and projects suitable for novices. (Rev: BL 3/15/94) [745.592]

6271 King, Patricia. *Making Dolls' House Furniture* (9–adult). 1993, Sterling/Guild of Master Craftsmen paper $14.95 (0-946819-24-6). A how-to guide for using found household objects to create furnishings for every room of an English nineteenth-century dollhouse. (Rev: BL 5/15/93) [745.5]

6272 Lord, M. G. *Forever Barbie: The Unauthorized Biography of a Real Doll* (9–adult). 1994, Morrow $25 (0-688-12296-5). Examines the creative, commercial, and sociological aspects of the world's most famous doll. Designers, critics, and collectors are interviewed. (Rev: BL 10/1/94*) [688.7]

6273 McGraw, Sheila. *Dolls Kids Can Make* (6–12). 1995, Firefly LB $19.95 (1-895565-75-8); paper $9.95 (1-895565-74-X). A guide best suited for adult-child teams to construct dolls from a variety of materials. (Rev: BL 11/15/95; SLJ 3/96)

6274 Rivers, Beverly, ed. *Better Homes and Gardens Country Dolls* (9–adult). 1991, Meredith paper $9.95 (0-696-01916-7). Contains directions for creating a wide variety of country dolls using found objects from nature, with full-size patterns for dolls and doll clothing. (Rev: BL 12/1/91) [745.59221]

Drawing and Painting

6275 Albert, Greg, and Rachel Wolf, eds. *Basic Watercolor Techniques* (9–adult). 1991, North Light paper $14.95 (0-89134-387-3). Encourages experimentation while giving illustrated information on basic painting methods and materials, and on how to paint specific subjects. (Rev: BL 10/1/91) [751.42]

6276 Allen, Anne, and Julian Seaman. *Fashion Drawing: The Basic Principles* (9–adult). 1993, Trafalgar Square paper $24.95 (0-7134-7096-8). A large-format paperback that explains techniques in this stylized tradition. Traceable examples of clothing and accessories are given. (Rev: BL 9/15/93) [746.92]

6277 Clinch, Moira. *The Watercolor Painter's Pocket Palette: Instant, Practical Visual Guidance on Mixing and Matching Watercolors to Suit All Subjects* (9–adult). 1991, North Light $15.95 (0-89134-401-2). A guide to mixing watercolors. (Rev: BL 1/1/92) [751.422]

6278 Du Bosque, Doug. *Learn to Draw 3-D* (5–8). 1992, Peel Productions (P.O. Box 546, Columbus, NC 28722-0546) paper $8.95 (0-939217-17-1). This step-by-step interactive text explains the mechanics and logic associated with 1- and 2-point perspectives. (Rev: BL 1/1/93; SLJ 11/92) [742]

6279 Gautier, Dick. *Drawing and Cartooning 1,001 Faces* (9–adult). 1993, Putnam/Perigee paper $10.95 (0-399-51767-7). A manual on drawing profiles, caricatures, and cartoons that offers specifics on capturing features, ages, and facial shapes. (Rev: BL 11/15/92; BTA) [743]

6280 Johnson, Cathy. *Painting Watercolors* (9–adult). 1995, North Light paper $18.99 (0-89134-616-3). A book for beginners. (Rev: BL 9/15/95) [751.42]

6281 Lloyd, Elizabeth Jane. *Watercolor Still Life* (9–adult). (DK Art School) 1994, Dorling Kindersley $16.95 (1-56458-490-9). Practical advice for beginners and amateurs looking for fresh ideas and inspiration. (Rev: BL 12/15/94; SHS; SLJ 4/95) [751.42]

6282 Martin, Judy. *The Encyclopedia of Pastel Techniques* (9–adult). 1992, Running Press $24.95 (1-56138-087-3). Hands-on guide to pastel techniques and their use in landscape drawing. (Rev: BL 9/15/92) [741.235]

6283 Moran, Pat. *Painting the Beauty of Flowers with Oils* (9–adult). 1991, North Light $27.95 (0-89134-382-2). Photos of each phase of creation are a key element of this book that gives step-by-step instructions for flower painting. (Rev: BL 10/1/91)

6284 Nice, Claudia. *Creating Textures in Pen and Ink with Watercolor* (9–adult). 1995, North Light $27.99 (0-89134-595-7). Instructions for rendering specific objects and materials, with the focus on texture. (Rev: BL 9/15/95) [751.4]

6285 Seslar, Patrick. *Wildlife Painting Step by Step* (9–adult). 1995, North Light $28.99 (0-89134-584-1). A guide to the art of careful observation and meticulous execution as well as a celebration of nature. (Rev: BL 9/15/95) [751.4]

6286 Sheppard, Joseph. *Realistic Figure Drawing* (9–adult). 1991, North Light $19.95 (0-89134-374-1). Sheppard's drawings capture figures in rest and in motion, and he instructs the reader on the use of different materials and approaches. (Rev: BL 5/15/91; SLJ 10/91) [143]

6287 Smith, Ray. *Drawing Figures* (9–adult). (DK Art School) 1994, Dorling Kindersley $16.95 (1-56458-666-9). Provides many photos of materials, examples of techniques, and reproductions of portraits of the very young and the old. (Rev: BL 12/15/94; SHS; SLJ 4/95) [743]

6288 Snazaroo. *Five-Minute Faces: Fantastic Face-Painting Ideas* (5–8). 1992, Random LB $10.99 (0-679-92810-3); paper $7.99 (0-679-82810-9). This introduction to face painting offers basic advice on makeup application, with instructions for 30 character ideas, including a clown, pirate, cat, and Dracula. (Rev: BL 6/15/92; SLJ 7/92) [745.5]

6289 Waters, Elizabeth, and Annie Harris. *Painting: A Young Artist's Guide* (5–8). (Young Artist) 1993, Dorling Kindersley/Royal Academy of Arts $14.95 (1-56458-348-1). Reproductions of art masterpieces are used to illustrate basic painting techniques and discussions about fundamental visual elements and design principles. (Rev: BL 1/15/94; SLJ 3/94; VOYA 8/94) [751.4]

6290 Welton, Jude. *Drawing: A Young Artist's Guide* (5–8). 1994, Dorling Kindersley $14.95 (1-56458-676-6). (Rev: BL 1/15/95; SLJ 3/95) [741.2]

6291 Wilcox, Michael. *The Wilcox Guide to the Best Watercolor Paints* (9–adult). 1991, Artways (P.O. Box 396, Rockport, MA 01966) paper $24.95 (0-89134-409-8). A list of the names, strengths, and weaknesses of more than 2,000 watercolors. (Rev: BL 1/1/92) [751.422]

Gardening

6292 Holmes, Anita. *Flowers for You: Blooms for Every Month* (5–7). Illus. 1993, Bradbury $16.95 (0-02-744280-2). Provides novice gardeners with guidelines for growing 12 common flowering plants. Watercolor illustrations and a glossary. (Rev: BL 3/1/93) [635.9]

6293 McHoy, Peter, and others. *The Complete Book of Container Gardening* (9–adult). 1994, Trafalgar Square (P.O. Box 257, North Pomfret, VT 05053) $29.95 (0-943955-66-1). Provides advice on planting in all kinds of containers, instructions for building planters, and a guide to suitable plants to grow. (Rev: BL 1/1/94) [635.9]

6294 Merser, Cheryl. *A Starter Garden: The Guide for the Horticulturally Hapless* (9–adult). 1994, HarperPerennial paper $13 (0-06-096933-4). A humorous look at the pitfalls of beginner gardening. Glossary. (Rev: BL 1/15/94) [639.5]

6295 Nick, Jean M. A., and Fern Marshall Bradley. *Growing Fruits and Vegetables Organically: The Complete Guide to a Great-Tasting, More Bountiful, Problem-Free Harvest* (9–adult). 1994, Rodale $26.95 (0-87596-586-5). Basic gardening techniques and an alphabetical guide to growing more than 200 fruits, vegetables, herbs, nuts, and grains. (Rev: BL 1/15/94) [635]

6296 Ogden, Shepherd. *Step by Step to Organic Vegetable Gardening* (9–adult). Rev. ed. 1992, HarperCollins $23 (0-06-016668-1). Revised edition of a popular guide to successfully planning, planting, and cultivating organic gardens. (Rev: BL 9/15/92) [635]

6297 Swain, Roger B. *Groundwork: A Gardener's Ecology* (9–adult). 1994, Houghton $18.95 (0-395-68400-5). Ten essays by the host of PBS's *Victory Garden* that reflect the author's respect for nature, wildlife, organic gardening, and environmental issues. (Rev: BL 3/15/94) [635]

6298 Time-Life, eds. *Time-Life Books Complete Guide to Gardening and Landscaping* (9–adult). 1991, Prentice-Hall $30 (0-13-028614-1). Comprehensive guide to outdoor gardening and landscaping, with checklists and troubleshooting tips. (Rev: BL 1/15/92) [712]

Home Repair

6299 Charnow, Will. *Paint Your House Like a Pro: Tips from A to Z on Painting Your House Inside and Out* (9–adult). 1991, Globe Pequot paper $13.95 (0-87106-306-9). An alphabetically arranged collection of house-painting tips. (Rev: BL 9/1/91) [698]

Kite Making and Flying

6300 Morgan, Paul, and Helene Morgan. *The Ultimate Kite Book* (9–adult). 1992, Simon & Schuster $19.95 (0-671-74443-7). Instructions for novices and experts alike on how to make, fly, and fight with kites. (Rev: BL 4/1/92; SHS) [629.133]

Magic Tricks

6301 Bird, Malcolm, and Alan Dart. *The Magic Handbook* (5–8). 1992, Chronicle paper $12.95 (0-8118-0284-1). Using colorful cartoons, this book presents some magic tricks that use water and others that use a magic wand. (Rev: BL 11/1/92; SLJ 1/93) [793.8]

6302 Day, Jon. *Let's Make Magic* (5–7). Illus. 1992, Kingfisher Books (95 Madison Ave., New York, NY 10016) paper $9.95 (1-85697-806-0). The secrets behind 40 magic tricks, using objects found at home. With illustrated instructions for practice and presentation. (Rev: BL 10/15/92; SLJ 7/93) [793.9]

6303 Ginn, David. *Clown Magic* (9–adult). 1993, Piccadilly Books (P.O. Box 25203, Colorado Springs, CO 80936) $16.95 (0-941599-21-3). Advice for new clowns, including skits, gags, magic tricks, and specifics on creating and using surprise-filled props. (Rev: BL 4/15/93) [793.8]

6304 McGill, Ormond. *Voice Magic: Secrets of Ventriloquism and Voice Conjuring* (5–8). Illus. 1992, Millbrook LB $12.90 (1-56294-137-2). Analyzes the art of ventriloquism, with advice on perfecting various techniques. (Rev: BL 4/1/92; SLJ 5/92) [793.8]

6305 Randi, James. *Conjuring* (9–adult). 1992, St. Martin's $29.95 (0-312-08634-2). This history of the craft of illusion focuses on both the artists and their tricks and guides readers through the profession without revealing secrets. (Rev: BL 11/15/92) [793.8]

Masks and Mask Making

6306 Gelber, Carol. *Masks Tell Stories* (5–7). (Beyond Museum Walls) 1993, Millbrook $14.90 (1-56294-224-7). An account of masks that have been used in various cultures through the years. (Rev: BL 8/93; SLJ 7/93) [391]

Model Making

6307 Spohn, Terry, ed. *Scale Model Detailing: Projects You Can Do* (9–adult). 1995, Kalmbach paper $14.95 (0-89024-209-7). Modelers who have already developed their skills will find this a comprehensive resource for honing their skills. Includes 20 projects from *FineScale Modeler*. (Rev: BL 9/1/95) [745.5]

6308 Townsley, John. *Getting Started with Model Trains* (5–12). 1991, Sterling $14.95 (0-8069-7362-5). For novices starting railroad collections. Includes lists of manufacturers, hobby organizations, and museums. (Rev: BL 1/15/92) [625]

Paper Crafts

6309 Churchill, E. Richard. *Fabulous Paper Airplanes* (5–8). Illus. 1991, Sterling $14.95 (0-8069-8342-6). How to create 29 types of paper airplanes, most from only one piece of paper. (Rev: BL 1/15/92; SLJ 4/92) [745.592]

6310 Dawson, Sophie. *The Art and Craft of Papermaking* (9–adult). 1992, Running Press $24.95 (1-56138-158-6). This illustrated, practical guide to papermaking includes an explanation of how paper has been made around the world throughout the ages. (Rev: BL 10/1/92) [676.22]

6311 Irvine, Joan. *How to Make Super Pop-ups* (5–7). Illus. 1992, Morrow/Beech Tree paper $6.95 (0-688-11521-7). A treasury of ideas and directions for making 3-dimensional paper constructions with parts that move slide, snap, and pop up. Awards: SLJ Best Book. (Rev: BL 1/15/93; SLJS 6/93*) [745.592]

6312 Jackson, Paul. *The Encyclopedia of Origami and Papercraft* (9–adult). 1991, Running Press $24.95 (1-56138-063-6). Provides technical information on 3-dimensional paper creations from simple folded forms to sculptures using papier-mâché, paper pulp, and castings. (Rev: BL 12/1/91; SHS) [736.98]

6313 Johnston, Malinda. *The Book of Paper Quilling: Techniques and Projects for Paper Filigree* (9–adult). 1994, Sterling $21.95 (0-8069-0598-0). The craft of paper quilling demonstrated in 70 projects with step-by-step procedures and explanation of necessary tools. (Rev: BL 4/15/94) [745.54]

6314 Leland, Nita, and Virginia Lee Williams. *Creative Collage Techniques* (9–adult). 1994, North Light $27.95 (0-89134-563-9). Step-by-step instructions for creating collages. Lists materials that can be used, including fabric, photos, newspaper, ink, and acrylics. (Rev: BL 10/15/94) [702]

6315 *Paper Craft* (9–adult). 1993, North Light paper $14.95 (0-89134-541-8). Taken from the British crafts publication *Creative Hands*, this explains marbling, making boxes and jewelry, and more. Includes colorful drawings and photos. (Rev: BL 11/15/93; SLJ 1/94) [745.54]

6316 Rich, Chris. *The Book of Paper Cutting: A Complete Guide to All the Techniques—with More Than 100 Project Ideas* (9–adult). 1993, Sterling $21.95 (0-8069-0285-X). Includes clear instructions, photos, and many project ideas and patterns. (Rev: BL 3/1/93; MJHS; SLJ 8/94) [796]

6317 Thomas, Denise, and Mary Fox. *Practical Decoupage* (9–adult). 1993, Trafalgar Square (P.O. Box 257, North Pomfret, VT 05053) $24.95 (0-943955-78-5). This guide to the simple, decorative craft of decoupage is filled with photos and step-by-step drawings. For beginners and the more experienced. (Rev: BL 10/15/93) [745.546]

Photography, Video, and Film Making

6318 Andersen, Yvonne. *Make Your Own Animated Movies and Videotapes* (6–12). Rev. ed. 1991, Little, Brown $19.95 (0-316-03941-1). Awards: SLJ Best Book. (Rev: BL 4/15/91; MJHS; SLJ 5/91*) [778.5]

6319 Cheshire, David. *The Book of Video Photography: A Handbook for the Amateur Movie-Maker* (9–adult). 1990, Knopf $29.95 (0-394-58744-8). (Rev: BL 1/15/91; SHS) [778.59]

6320 Gleason, Roger. *Seeing for Yourself: Techniques and Projects for Beginning Photographers* (7–12) 1993, Chicago Review paper $14.95 (1-55652-159-6). Emphasizes pinhole camera techniques and the basics of more advanced cameras. (Rev: BL 12/1/92; SLJ 6/93) [771]

6321 Hughes, Jerry. *The World's Simplest Photography Book* (9–adult). 1993, Phillips Lane (5430 LBJ Freeway, Suite 1600, Dallas, TX 75240) $17.95 (0-9634348-0-2). For casual photographers, shows the changing effects of shooting angles, lenses, film and shutter speeds, and printing. (Rev: BL 6/1–15/93) [771]

6322 Joyner, Harry M. *Roll 'em! Action! How to Produce a Motion Picture on a Shoestring Budget* (9–adult). 1994, McFarland paper $30 (0-89950-860-X). Provides advice on producing and directing film and video projects on a low budget. (Rev: BL 3/15/94) [791.43]

6323 Levy, Edmond. *Making a Winning Short: How to Write, Direct, Edit, and Produce a Short Film* (9–adult). 1994, Holt paper $14.95 (0-8050-2680-0). Gives advice and instruction on the creation of short films. (Rev: BL 10/1/94) [070.1]

6324 Morgan, Terri, and Shmuel Thaler. *Photography: Take Your Best Shot* (5–8). (Media Workshop) 1991, Lerner LB $14.95 (0-8225-2302-7). Includes basic information on cameras, film, developing, composition, lighting, special effects, and display, as well as discussing career opportunities. (Rev: BL 10/1/91; SLJ 11/91) [771]

6325 Schaefer, John P. *Basic Techniques of Photography* (9–adult). 1992, Little, Brown $50 (0-8212-1801-8); paper $29.95 (0-8212-1882-4). An introduction to photography, with information on techniques, film development, and equipment. (Rev: BL 2/15/92) [771]

6326 Schwartz, Perry. *How to Make Your Own Video* (6–10). 1991, Lerner $14.95 (0-8225-2301-9). Demonstrates the making of a video, with tips on script development, lighting, sound, and the editing process. (Rev: BL 2/15/92; BTA; BY; YR) [791.45]

Sewing and Other Needle Crafts

6327 Theiss, Nola, and Chris Rankin. *Great Crocheted Sweaters in a Weekend* (9–adult). 1993, Sterling/Lark $24.95 (0-8069-0441-0). Fifty classic sweater styles that can be crocheted over one weekend, with directions, charts, and color photos. (Rev: BL 10/15/93) [746.9]

Stamp, Coin, and Other Types of Collecting

6328 Briggs, Michael. *Stamps* (7–10). 1993, Random $13 (0-679-82664-5). An introduction for the beginning hobbyist. (Rev: BL 8/93; MJHS) [769]

6329 Lewis, Brenda Ralph. *Coins and Currency* (5–7). (Hobby Handbooks) 1993, Random LB $13.99 (0-679-92662-3); paper $13 (0-679-82662-9). A look at the history of money, how it's made, mistakes and forgeries, and how to begin and maintain a collection. (Rev: BL 10/1/93; MJHS) [737]

6330 Lewis, Brenda Ralph. *Stamps! A Young Collector's Guide* (5–8). 1991, Dutton/Lodestar $14.95 (0-525-67341-5). The basics of stamp collecting are introduced in this comprehensive guide. (Rev: BL 1/15/91; SLJ 6/91) [769.56]

Woodworking and Carpentry

6331 Key, Ray. *The Woodturner's Workbook* (9–adult). 1993, Batsford $29.95 (0-7134-6667-7). A text for upgrading skills rather than learning basic techniques, with sections on choosing wood, effects various woods display, and exotic woods. (Rev: BL 9/15/93) [684]

6332 McGuire, Kevin. *Woodworking for Kids: 40 Fabulous, Fun and Useful Things for Kids to Make* (6–8). 1993, Sterling $19.95 (0-8069-0429-1). Detailed instructions, illustrations, and color photos describe how to make woodworking projects of differing difficulty, although adult supervision in intended. (Rev: BL 12/1/93; SLJ 2/94) [684]

6333 Nelson, John A. *52 Weekend Woodworking Projects* (9–adult). 1991, Sterling paper $12.95 (0-8069-8300-0). A collection of short-term projects from the very simple to the intricate, including toys, mirrors, clocks, and furniture. (Rev: BL 11/1/91) [684]

6334 Strom, Mark, and Lee Rankin. *Woodworking Projects for the Kitchen: 50 Useful Easy-to-Make Items* (9–adult). 1993, Sterling/Lark paper $14.95 (0-8069-0396-1). Directions to beginners for making kitchen items suitable for gifts or everyday use. (Rev: BL 10/1/93) [684]

Mysteries, Curiosities, and Controversial Subjects

6335 Aaseng, Nathan. *Science Versus Pseudoscience* (7–12). 1994, Watts LB $13.40 (0-531-11182-2). Explains the difference between true scientific theory and pseudoscience, discussing ESP, near-death experiences, creation science, and cold fusion. (Rev: BL 8/94; MJHS; SLJ 9/94) [500]

6336 Allen, Eugenie. *The Best Ever Kids' Book of Lists* (5–8). 1991, Avon/Camelot paper $2.95 (0-380-76357-5). Brief lists of the biggest, smallest, strangest, ugliest, etc., with humorous drawings. (Rev: BL 12/15/91) [031.02]

6337 Arvey, Michael. *The End of the World* (6–10). (Great Mysteries: Opposing Viewpoints) 1992, Greenhaven LB $13.95 (0-89908-096-0). (Rev: BL 1/15/93; MJHS) [001.9]

6338 Arvey, Michael. *Miracles* (9–adult). (Great Mysteries) 1990, Greenhaven LB $13.95 (0-89908-084-7). Explores mostly Christian miracles, including healings and the appearance of religious images. (Rev: BL 1/1/91, MJHS) [231.7]

6339 Ballinger, Erich. *Monster Manual: A Complete Guide to Your Favorite Creatures* (5–8). 1994, Lerner LB $14.21 (0-8225-0722-6). (Rev: BL 12/1/94; SLJ 3/95) [001.9]

6340 Boller, Paul F. *Not So! Popular Myths about America from Columbus to Clinton* (9–adult). 1995, Oxford Univ. $19.95 (0-19-509186-8). Disproves or challenges 44 myths people generally consider truth, such as Columbus's notion of a round earth being uncommon and that FDR knew in advance about Pearl Harbor. (Rev: BL 7/95) [973]

6341 Bunson, Matthew. *The Vampire Encyclopedia* (9–adult). 1993, Crown paper $16 (0-517-88100-4). Enough ghoulish lore to satisfy the bloodthirstiest vampire enthusiast. Awards: SLJ Best Book. (Rev: SLJ 3/94)

6342 Cavendish, Richard. *The World of Ghosts and the Supernatural* (9–adult). 1994, Facts on File $22.95 (0-8160-3209-2). Describes encounters with the spirit world and other paranormal phenomena, including reports of ghosts haunting the Tower of London. (Rev: BL 8/94; SHS; SLJ 6/95) [133.1]

6343 Cohen, Daniel. *The Ghost of Elvis and Other Celebrity Spirits* (5–7). 1994, Putnam $14.95 (0-399-22611-7). Examines tales of celebrity-ghost sightings. Spirits allegedly seen include those of Elvis Presley, Rudolph Valentino, and Abraham Lincoln. (Rev: BL 7/94; SLJ 8/94) [133.1]

6344 Cohen, Daniel. *Ghostly Tales of Love and Revenge* (6–8). 1992, Putnam $14.95 (0-399-22117-4). Thirteen eerie legends revolving around ill-fated love and revenge, some of them based on the lives of real people. (Rev: BL 8/92; SLJ 7/92; YR) [398.25]

6345 Cohen, Daniel. *Ghosts of the Deep* (5–7). 1993, Putnam $14.95 (0-399-22435-1). Cohen uses a journalistic style to relate sightings of ghosts at sea, including exact dates and names of those involved. (Rev: BL 11/15/93; MJHS; SLJ 3/94; VOYA 12/93) [133.1]

6346 Cohen, Daniel. *Prophets of Doom* (7–10). 1992, Millbrook $15.90 (1-56294-068-6). An analysis of those who predicted the end of the world, along with the methods they used. (Rev:

BL 2/15/92; MJHS; SLJ 5/92; VOYA; YR) [133.3]

6347 Cohen, Daniel. *Werewolves* (6–9). 1996, Cobblehill $14.99 (0-525-65207-8). Includes legends from around the world and discussions on rare diseases and hallucinogens that may have caused belief in werewolves. (Rev: SLJ 3/96)

6348 Cohen, Daniel. *Young Ghosts* (5–8). 1994, Dutton $13.99 (0-525-65154-3). "True" accounts of ghost children. Rosalie, for example, is summoned in seances by her mother. Also includes tales of ghosts that appear to children. (Rev: BL 9/1/94; SLJ 10/94) [133.1]

6349 Craig, Roy. *UFOs: An Insider's View of the Official Quest for Evidence* (9–adult). 1995, Univ. of North Texas $24.95 (1-57441-005-9); paper $18.95 (0-929398-94-7). The controversial investigation of UFOs in the late 1960s is reviewed by a chemist and field investigator who was there. (Rev: BL 10/1/95; MJHS) [001.9]

6350 Crystall, Ellen. *Silent Invasion: The Shocking Discoveries of a UFO Researcher* (9–adult). 1992, Paragon House $19.95 (1-55778-446-9); paper $12.95 (1-55778-493-0). A leading UFO researcher describes her personal encounters with aliens and offers explanations for a variety of space mysteries. (Rev: BL 2/1/92) [001.9]

6351 Deem, James M. *How to Catch a Flying Saucer* (5–7). Illus. 1991, Houghton $15.95 (0-395-51958-6). A solid look at the UFO phenomenon and how theories surrounding sightings need to be tested. (Rev: BL 8/91; MJHS; SLJ 9/91) [001.9]

6352 Deem, James M. *How to Read Your Mother's Mind* (5–7). Illus. 1994, Houghton $15.95 (0-395-62426-6). An introduction to ESP that offers anecdotal material and provides opposing viewpoints and experiments to test one's powers. (Rev: BL 3/1/94) [133.8]

6353 Duncan, Lois, and William Rool. *Psychic Connections: A Journey into the Mysterious World of Psi* (6–10). 1995, Delacorte paper $12.95 (0-385-32072-8). After her daughter's murder, Duncan used psychics to learn more about it. Here she joins Psychical Research Foundation project director Rool in this comprehensive look at psychic phenomena. (Rev: BL 6/1–15/95; SLJ 5/95) [133]

6354 Eberhart, George M., ed. *The Roswell Report: A Historical Perspective* (9–adult). 1991, Hynek Center of UFO Studies (2457 W. Peterson Ave., Chicago, IL 60659) paper $12 (0-929343-59-X). Essays about the 1947 flying saucer sightings in Roswell, New Mexico, that put events in perspective. Discusses investigations, with documents and photos. (Rev: BL 12/15/91) [001.942]

6355 Ellis, Richard. *Monsters of the Sea* (9–adult). 1994, Knopf $30 (0-679-40639-5). Examines whales, octopuses, giant squid, sharks, and manatees, once believed to be sea serpents, leviathans, and mermaids. (Rev: BL 11/1/94*; SHS) [591.92]

6356 Feldman, David. *Do Penguins Have Knees?* (9–adult). 1991, HarperCollins $19 (0-06-016294-5). Another of the volumes on "imponderables," in which the author wittily poses and answers perplexing questions. (Rev: BL 10/1/91) [031.02]

6357 Felton, Bruce. *One of a Kind: A Compendium of Unique People, Places, and Things* (9–adult). 1992, Morrow paper $9 (0-688-10815-6). Unique trivia on meaningless topics. (Rev: BL 3/15/92) [973]

6358 Fleming, Robert Loren, and Robert F. Boyd. *The Big Book of Urban Legends* (9–adult). 1994, DC Comics/Paradox paper $12.95 (1-56389-165-4). A collection of 200 urban legends in comic strip format. (Rev: BL 3/1/95) [741.5]

6359 Floyd, E. Randall. *Great American Mysteries* (9–adult). 1991, August House $18.95 (0-87483-171-7); paper $9.95 (0-87483-170-9). Thirty-eight well-known mysteries, such as the Salem witchcraft trials, the Lizzie Borden case, the Bermuda Triangle, ghosts, and psychics. (Rev: BL 3/1/91; MJHS; SLJ 8/91) [001.94]

6360 Frazier, Kendrick, ed. *The Hundredth Monkey and Other Paradigms of the Paranormal* (9–adult). 1991, Prometheus paper $17.95 (0-87975-655-1). Scientists offer rational explanations for many mysterious phenomena, presenting facts to counterbalance claims of paranormal experiences. (Rev: BL 6/15/91) [133]

6361 Gardner, Martin. *On the Wild Side: The Big Bang, ESP, the Beast 666, Levitation, Rain Making, Trance-Channeling, Seances and Ghosts, and More* (9–adult). 1992, Prometheus $24.95 (0-87975-713-2). A collection of articles that examine, expose, and debunk many offbeat scientific theories, cults, and beliefs. (Rev: BL 2/15/92) [500]

6362 Giblin, James Cross. *The Truth about Unicorns* (5–7). Illus. 1991, HarperCollins LB $14.89 (0-06-022479-7). An extensively researched history of belief about the one-horned animal and a description of its hold on the human imagination. Awards: SLJ Best Book. (Rev: BL 11/1/91*; SLJ 12/91*) [398.24]

6363 Guiley, Rosemary Ellen. *The Encyclopedia of Ghosts and Spirits* (9–12). 1993, Facts on File paper $19.95 (0-8160-2846-X). Comprehensive coverage—400 entries and many photos—of the spirit world. Awards: SLJ Best Book. (Rev: SLJ 6/93*)

6364 Guiley, Rosemary Ellen, and J. B. Macabre. *The Complete Vampire Companion* (9–adult). 1994, Macmillan paper $16 (0-671-85024-5). Discusses vampires in myth, folklore, and entertainment, our fascination with them, and claims about their real-life existence. (Rev: BL 10/1/94) [133.4]

6365 Hoobler, Dorothy, and Thomas Hoobler. *Lost Civilizations* (5–7). 1992, Walker LB $15.85 (0-8027-8153-5). A look at Stonehenge and missing civilizations from history. (Rev: BL 5/1/92; SLJ 9/92) [930]

6366 Hoobler, Dorothy, and Thomas Hoobler. *Vanished!* (7–12). (Fact or Fiction Files) 1991, Walker LB $15.85 (0-8027-8149-7). This examination of famous unsolved disappearances combines background information with possible scenarios for hypothetical solutions. (Rev: BL 12/15/91; SLJ 5/92) [909]

6367 Hubbard-Brown, Janet. *The Curse of the Hope Diamond* (5–7). (History Mystery) 1991, Avon/Camelot paper $2.99 (0-380-76222-6). Using a mystery-story style to introduce historical information, this book explores the tragedies experienced by the owners of the famous blue diamond. (Rev: BL 12/15/91) [736]

6368 Hubbard-Brown, Janet. *The Secret of Roanoke Island* (5–7). (History Mystery) 1991, Avon/Camelot paper $2.99 (0-380-76223-4). An investigation of the disappearance of the 1587 colony off the coast of North Carolina, told in the style of a mystery story. (Rev: BL 12/15/91) [975.6]

6369 Jacobs, David M. *Secret Life: Firsthand Accounts of UFO Abductions* (9–adult). 1992, Simon & Schuster $21 (0-671-74857-2). A respected university professor examines evidence of UFO abductions. (Rev: BL 3/15/92) [001.9]

6370 Kohut, John, and Roland Sweet. *News from the Fringe: True Stories of Weird People and Weirder Times* (9–adult). 1993, NAL/Plume paper $8 (0-452-27095-2). A collection of 500 outrageous, hilarious, and bizarre stories originally published in newspapers from around the world. (Rev: BL 10/15/93) [031.02]

6371 Larsen, Anita. *Psychic Sleuths* (5–7). 1994, Macmillan/New Discovery $14.95 (0-02-751645-8). Profiles psychic detectives who use paranormal means to solve real-life mysteries. Debunks frauds and explains how reputable crime-solving psychics work. (Rev: BL 10/1/94; SLJ 11/94) [363.2]

6372 Macklin, John. *World's Most Bone-Chilling "True" Ghost Stories* (5–8). 1994, Sterling paper $3.95 (0-8069-0390-2). "True" tales of the supernatural from the mid-1800s to 1960, featuring ghosts, witches, UFOs, mummies, and cats. (Rev: BL 9/1/94) [133.1]

6373 Moore, Laurence A. *Lightning Never Strikes Twice and Other False Facts* (9–adult). 1994, Avon paper $10 (0-380-77477-1). Trivia and all manner of things that everybody knows. (Rev: BL 5/15/94) [031.02]

6374 Norman, Michael, and Beth Scott. *Historic Haunted America* (9–adult). 1995, Tor $24.95 (0-312-85752-7). The authors spent 18 years collecting this huge volume of old-fashioned ghost tales ranging from the typical to the very elaborate. (Rev: BL 10/15/95; VOYA 4/96) [133.1]

6375 O'Neal, Michael. *Haunted Houses* (6–10). (Great Mysteries) 1994, Greenhaven LB $14.95 (1-56510-095-6). (Rev: BL 4/15/94; MJHS) [133.1]

6376 O'Neill, Terry, and Stacey Tipp, eds. *Paranormal Phenomena* (7–12). (Opposing Viewpoints) 1991, Greenhaven $15.95 (0-89908-487-7); paper $8.95 (0-89908-462-1). Various opinions on the controversial issue of paranormal events are presented. (Rev: BL 6/1/91; SHS; SLJ 8/91) [133]

6377 Panati, Charles. *Panati's Parade of Fads, Follies, and Manias: The Origins of Our Most Cherished Obsessions* (9–adult). 1991, HarperCollins $25 (0-06-055191-7); paper $12.95 (0-06-096477-4). A panorama of Americana that describes a century of media trends, fashions, crazes, expositions, songs, and dances and explores the origins of mass culture. (Rev: BL 11/15/91) [306]

6378 Randle, Kevin, and Donald R. Schmitt. *The Truth about the UFO Crash at Roswell* (9–adult). 1994, Evans $19.95 (0-87131-761-3). A sequel to their *Crash at Roswell*, this text adds new witnesses and a revised chronology for the alleged crash of a UFO at Roswell, New Mexico, in July 1947. (Rev: BL 5/15/94) [001.9]

6379 Randles, Jenny. *UFOs and How to See Them* (9–adult). 1993, Sterling paper $14.95 (0-8069-0297-3). This illustrated field guide includes a history of the UFO mystery, identification of objects often mistaken for UFOs, and advice on organizing a skywatch. (Rev: BL 4/15/93) [001.942]

6380 Scavone, Daniel C. *Vampires* (7–10). (Opposing Viewpoints) 1990, Greenhaven LB $13.95 (0-89908-080-4). (Rev: BL 4/1/91; MJHS) [809]

6381 Schouweiler, Thomas. *Life after Death* (6–9). (Great Mysteries) 1990, Greenhaven LB

$13.95 (0-89908-082-0). The question is examined from several viewpoints, including reincarnation, heaven and hell, and annihilation. (Rev: BL 1/1/91; MJHS) [133.9]

6382 Sellier, Charles E. *Miracles and Other Wonders* (9–adult). 1994, Dell paper $5.99 (0-440-21804-7). Chronicles miraculous rescues by concerned people, dogs, ghosts, and CB radios. (Rev: BL 11/1/94) [291.2]

6383 Skal, David J. *V Is for Vampire: The A–Z Guide to Everything Undead* (9–adult). 1995, NAL/Plume paper $15.95 (0-452-27173-8). The comprehensive guide to vampiredom. All the expected entries are here, with a few unexpected ones. (Rev: BL 10/1/95) [398]

6384 Steiger, Brad, and Sherry Hansen Steiger. *Montezuma's Serpent and Other True Supernatural Tales of the Southwest* (9–adult). 1992, Paragon House $22.95 (1-55778-474-4). The mysterious deserts of the Southwest are the setting for a variety of tales about the abnormal and supernatural. (Rev: BL 9/15/92) [398.25]

6385 Stein, Wendy. *Witches* (6–9). (Great Mysteries: Opposing Viewpoints) 1995, Greenhaven LB $14.95 (1-56510-240-1). A discussion of the real nature of witches. (Rev: BL 4/15/95; SLJ 3/95) [133.4]

6386 Sutton, Caroline, and Kevin Markey. *More How Do They Do That? Wonders of the Modern World Explained* (9–adult). 1993, Morrow $18 (0-688-10129-1). Answers a lot of questions you may or may not have considered, e.g., how do they make shredded wheat? (Rev: BL 2/1/93; SHS; SLJ 7/93) [031.02]

6387 Underwood, Peter. *Ghosts and How to See Them* (9–adult). 1995, Trafalgar Square/Anaya paper $16.95 (1-85470-194-0). Experiencing the paranormal and photographing it. (Rev: BL 2/15/95) [133.1]

6388 Walker, Paul Robert. *Bigfoot and Other Legendary Creatures* (5–7). Illus. 1992, Harcourt $15.95 (0-15-207147-4). Speculations on whether 7 fabled creatures really exist. (Rev: BL 2/15/92; MJHS; SLJ 3/92) [001.9]

6389 Williams, Ben, and others. *The Black Hope Horror: The True Story of a Haunting* (9–adult). 1991, Morrow $19 (0-688-05176-6). An account of a 6-year ordeal undergone by the Williams family, who unknowingly built their house over a graveyard. (Rev: BL 5/15/91; SLJ 11/91) [133.1]

Sports and Games

General and Miscellaneous

6390 Aaseng, Nathan. *The Locker Room Mirror: How Sports Reflect Society* (7–10). 1993, Walker LB $15.85 (0-8027-8218-3). Argues that problems in professional sports today—cheating, drug abuse, violence, commercialization, discrimination—are reflections of society at large. (Rev: BL 6/1–15/93; BTA; MJHS; SLJ 5/93) [306.4]

6391 Berlow, Lawrence H. *Sports Ethics* (7–12). (Contemporary World Issues) 1995, ABC-CLIO LB $39.50 (0-87436-769-7). Covers major issues concerning children in sports, college athletics, the Olympics, professionals, women, drug abuse, and media relations. (Rev: BL 8/95; SLJ 1/95)

6392 Boswell, Tom, ed. *The Best American Sports Writing, 1994* (9–adult). 1994, Houghton $24.95 (0-395-63326-5); paper $11.95 (0-395-63325-7). Collects 25 of the best sports articles published in 1993, including stories about Alaskan surfing; gambler and baseball player Len Dykstra; and boxer Muhammad Ali. (Rev: BL 10/15/94)

6393 Burgett, Gordon. *Treasure and Scavenger Hunts: How to Plan, Create, and Give Them* (9–adult). 1994, Communication Unlimited (P.O. Box 6405, Santa Maria, CA 93456) paper $9.95 (0-910167-25-7). While focusing on adult recreation, also includes suggestions for teens. (Rev: BL 3/15/94) [796.1]

6394 Cook, Jeff. *The Triathletes: A Season in the Lives of Four Women in the Toughest Sport of All* (9–adult). 1992, St. Martin's $19.95 (0-312-08184-7). A description of the background, training, dedication, and personality of 4 top women athletes as they prepared for the 1989 Hawaiian Ironman Triathlon. (Rev: BL 10/1/92) [796.4]

6395 Deford, Frank, ed. *The Best American Sports Writing, 1993* (9–adult). 1993, Houghton $21.95 (0-395-60340-4); paper $10.95 (0-395-60341-2). This anthology of sports stories includes pieces by such writers as Dave Barry, George Plimpton, and David Halberstam. (Rev: BL 11/15/93) [070.44]

6396 Dolan, Ellen M. *Susan Butcher and the Iditarod Trail* (5–7). 1993, Walker LB $16.85 (0-8027-8212-4). A combination of history, outdoor adventure, animal lover's tale, and biography, centering on the Iditarod sled dog race. (Rev: BL 4/1/93; MJHS) [798.8]

6397 Dudley, William, ed. *Sports in America* (7–12). (Opposing Viewpoints) 1994, Greenhaven paper $9.95 (1-56510-104-9). (Rev: BL 5/15/94; MJHS; SHS) [796]

6398 Dunningan, James F. *The Complete Wargames Handbook: How to Play, Design and Find Them* (9–adult). 1992, Morrow/Quill paper $12.95 (0-688-10368-5). Includes suggestions for single and doubles play, a game bibliography, and a listing of computer war games. (Rev: BL 12/1/92) [793.9]

6399 *Family Fun and Games* (9–adult). 1992, Sterling $24.95 (0-8069-8776-6). An encyclopedic illustrated guide to more than 800 games. (Rev: BL 11/1/92) [793]

6400 Feinberg, Jeremy R. *Reading the Sports Page: A Guide to Understanding Sports Statistics* (7–10). 1992, Macmillan/New Discovery $12.95 (0-02-734420-7). Explains how to read baseball, basketball, football, hockey, and tennis stats in a newspaper's sports pages. (Rev: BL 1/15/93; MJHS; SLJ 1/93) [796]

6401 Finnigan, Dave. *The Joy of Juggling* (9–adult). 1993, Jugglebug (One Sportime Way, Atlanta, GA 30340) paper $4.95 (0-9615521-3-1). Finnigan describes and provides illustrations for 25 juggling routines, then discusses plagiarism of others' acts and gives performance tips for various audiences. (Rev: BL 12/15/93) [793.8]

6402 Firestone, Roy, and Scott Ostler. *Up Close: And in Your Face with the Greats, Near-Greats, and Ingrates of Sports* (9–adult). 1993, Hyperion $19.95 (1-56282-869-X). Collects behind-the-scenes anecdotes from Firestone's career of interviewing sports celebrities. (Rev: BL 6/1–15/93) [796]

6403 Halberstam, David, ed. *The Best American Sports Writing, 1991* (9–adult). 1991, Houghton $21.95 (0-395-57043-3); paper $9.95 (0-395-57044-1). The first of an annual collection of excellent sports writing, including pieces by such authors as Stephen King and Frank Conroy, with biographical information on each writer. (Rev: BL 10/1/91) [796]

6404 Hall, Godfrey. *Games* (5–7). (Traditions Around the World) 1995, Thomson Learning LB $16.95 (1-56847-345-1). (Rev: BL 6/1–15/95) [790.1]

6405 Hinkson, Jim. *Lacrosse Fundamentals* (9–adult). 1993, Firefly Books/Warwick Publishing paper $15.95 (1-895629-11-X). Tips and techniques in stick selection, cradling, grip, catching, passing, offense and defense, shooting, face-offs, and goal-tending. (Rev: BL 11/15/93) [796.34]

6406 Jenkins, Dan, ed. *The Best American Sports Writing, 1995* (9–adult). 1995, Houghton $24.95 (0-395-70070-1); paper $12.95 (0-395-70069-8). From short to lengthy essays, this collection has something for nearly every sports fan. (Rev: BL 9/15/95) [796.0973]

6407 Judson, Karen. *Sports and Money: It's a Sellout!* (7–12). (Issues in Focus) 1995, Enslow LB $17.95 (0-89490-622-4). (Rev: BL 11/15/95) [796.0619]

6408 Kahn, Roger. *Games We Used to Play: Four Decades of Sports Writing* (9–adult). 1992, Ticknor & Fields $19.95 (0-395-59351-4). Magazine essays and profiles by a leading sports journalist concentrate on baseball but include other sports as well. (Rev: BL 12/15/91) [796]

6409 Langley, Andrew. *Sports and Politics* (9–adult). (World Issues) 1990, Rourke LB $13.50 (0-86592-117-2). A look at how politics influence sports. (Rev: BL 1/1/91) [796]

6410 Leifer, Neil. *Sports* (9–adult). 1992, HarperCollins $45 (0-00-255108-X). An oversized collection of photos of sports legends. (Rev: BL 12/1/92) [779]

6411 Marchon-Arnaud, Catherine. *A Gallery of Games* (5–7). (Young Artisan) Illus. 1994, Ticknor & Fields $12.95 (0-395-68379-3). Projects are usually 1 or 2 to a page, illustrated with color photos of materials needed and finished products. Includes rules of play. (Rev: BL 4/1/94; MJHS; SLJ 3/94) [745.592]

6412 Nash, Bruce, and Allan Zullo. *The Basketball Hall of Shame* (9–adult). (Hall of Shame) 1991, Pocket paper $9 (0-671-69414-6). Brief, humorous basketball stories, including battles with referees, strange shots, and weird happenings. (Rev: BL 11/1/91) [796.323]

6413 Nuwer, Hank. *Sports Scandals* (7–12). 1994, Watts LB $13.90 (0-531-11183-0). Profiles contemporary sports stars who have fallen from grace because of scandals ranging from gambling to sexual misconduct. (Rev: BL 8/94; MJHS; SLJ 8/94; VOYA 12/94) [796]

6414 Paulsen, Gary. *Winterdance: The Fine Madness of Running the Iditarod* (9–adult). 1994, Harcourt $21.95 (0-15-126227-6). This survival adventure describes the author's experiences running with his dog team in the 1,180-mile Alaskan Iditarod race. Awards: SLJ Best Book; YALSA Best Book for Young Adults. (Rev: BL 2/15/94; BTA; MJHS; VOYA 10/94) [798.8]

6415 Pejcic, Bogdan, and Rolf Meyer. *Pocket Billiards: Fundamentals of Technique and Play* (9–adult). Tr. by Elisabeth E. Reinersmann. 1994, Sterling paper $8.95 (0-8069-0458-5). An illustrated introduction to the sport of billiards, providing insight into equipment, rules, and playing techniques. (Rev: BL 2/15/94) [794.7]

6416 Press, David P. *A Multicultural Portrait of Professional Sports* (7–12). (Perspectives) 1993, Marshall Cavendish LB $18.95 (1-85435-661-5). (Rev: BL 3/15/94) [306.4]

6417 Ryan, Joan. *Little Girls in Pretty Boxes: The Making and Breaking of Elite Gymnasts and Figure Skaters* (9–adult). 1995, Doubleday $22.95 (0-385-47790-2). Portrays women's gymnastics and figure skating as forms of physical and psychological child abuse, causing permanent bone damage and weight problems. (Rev: BL 6/1–15/95; SLJ 11/95) [796.44]

6418 Schultz, Ron. *Looking Inside Sports Aerodynamics* (5–8). (X-Ray Vision) Illus. 1992, John Muir paper $9.95 (1-56261-065-1). Uses what scientists know about air (effects of gravity, turbulence, drag, lift) to explain what happens when we throw or hit all kinds of balls and other objects. (Rev: BL 1/15/93; MJHS; SLJ 2/93) [796]

6419 Sheff, David. *Game Over: How Nintendo Zapped an American Industry, Captured Your Dollars, and Enslaved Your Children* (9–adult). 1993, Random $25 (0-679-40469-4). Overview of Nintendo, both the company and the people responsible for its huge success. (Rev: BL 3/15/93) [338.7]

6420 Sherman, Eric. *365 Amazing Days in Sports: A Day-by-Day Look at Sports History* (7–12). 1990, Little, Brown/Sports Illustrated for Kids paper $10.85 (0-316-78537-7). This almanac lists memorable moments in sports for each day of the year. (Rev: BL 1/1/91; SLJ 3/91) [796]

6421 Sherwonit, Bill. *Iditarod: The Great Race to Nome* (9–adult). 1991, Alaska Northwest paper $19.95 (0-88240-411-3). This history of the 1,180-mile dogsled race and its leading participants contains photos of the action. (Rev: BL 12/15/91; SHS; SLJ 6/92) [798]

6422 Sifakis, Carl. *Three Men on Third and Other Wacky Events from the World of Sports* (9–adult). 1994, Prentice-Hall paper $12 (0-671-86502-1). Wacky anecdotes from more than 100 years of sports history. (Rev: BL 3/15/94) [796]

6423 Silverman, Al, and Brian Silverman, eds. *The Twentieth Century Treasury of Sports* (9–adult). 1992, Viking $30 (0-670-84662-7). Eighty sports articles, essays, poems, and book excerpts chosen "to convey the diverse excellence of writing." (Rev: BL 9/1/92*) [810.8]

6424 Weiss, Ann E. *Money Games: The Business of Sports* (7–12). 1993, Houghton $14.95 (0-395-57444-7). Reviews the place of sport throughout history and examines the financial forces that shape modern sports: profit motive, league control, TV rights, gambling, endorsement contracts, etc. (Rev: BL 4/1/93; MJHS; SLJ 6/93; VOYA 8/93) [796]

6425 Young, Perry Deane. *Lesbians and Gays and Sports* (8–12). (Issues in Lesbian and Gay Life) 1995, Chelsea House $24.95 (0-7910-2611-6); paper $12.95 (0-7910-2951-4). Looks at the effect homosexuality has had on the sports community, with biographies of Kopay, Tilden, King, and Navratilova. (Rev: BL 6/1–15/95) [796]

6426 Zinsser, Nate. *Dear Dr. Psych* (5–7). 1991, Little, Brown/Sports Illustrated for Kids paper $5.95 (0-316-98898-7). A sports psychologist gives advice on methods of achieving success in athletic pursuits, including positive self-talk and imaging. (Rev: BL 11/1/91) [796]

Automobile Racing

6427 Gaillard, Frye, and Kyle Petty. *200 M.P.H.: A Sizzling Season in the Petty/NASCAR Dynasty* (9–adult). 1993, St. Martin's $19.95 (0-312-09732-8). Petty describes NASCAR racing from the viewpoint of a third-generation driver, especially the camaraderie between drivers, crews, and families. (Rev: BL 10/1/93) [796.72]

6428 Golenbock, Peter. *American Zoom: Stock Car Racing—from the Dirt Tracks to Daytona* (9–adult). 1993, Macmillan $24 (0-02-544615-0). Presents the history of the sport from the mouths of drivers, mechanics, crew chiefs, and promoters. (Rev: BL 9/15/93*) [796.7]

6429 Rubel, David. *How to Drive an Indy Race Car* (7–12). (Masters of Motion) 1992, John Muir paper $9.95 (1-56261-062-7). Offers detail on a wide range of aspects of Indy car racing—and with a touch of comedy. (Rev: BL 2/1/93) [796.7]

6430 Stephenson, Sallie. *Autocross Racing* (5–12). (Fast Track) 1991, Macmillan/Crestwood $11.95 (0-89686-692-0). A brief history of the race, with car and racecourse descriptions. (Rev: BL 1/15/92; SLJ 4/92) [796.7]

6431 Stephenson, Sallie. *Circle Track Racing* (5–12). 1991, Macmillan/Crestwood $11.95 (0-89686-693-9). A brief history of the sport, with car and racecourse descriptions. (Rev: BL 1/15/92) [796.7]

6432 Stephenson, Sallie. *Rally Racing* (5–12). 1991, Macmillan/Crestwood $11.95 (0-89686-694-7). An overview of the sport, along with car and racecourse descriptions and advice on how to start racing. (Rev: BL 1/15/92; MJHS; SLJ 4/92) [796.7]

6433 Stephenson, Sallie. *Winston Cup Racing* (5–12). 1991, Macmillan/Crestwood $11.95 (0-89686-695-5). A brief history of the race, along with car descriptions and racecourse descriptions. (Rev: BL 1/15/92) [796.7]

6434 Taylor, Rich. *Indy: Seventy-Five Years of Racing's Greatest Spectacle* (9–adult). 1991, St. Martin's $39.95 (0-312-05447-5). A detailed history of the event from its beginning in 1911 through its seventy-fifth running, with more than 500 photos. (Rev: BL 5/15/91; SHS) [796.7]

Baseball

6435 Aldridge, Gwen, and Bret Wills. *Baseball Archaeology: Artifacts from the Great American Pastime* (9–adult). 1993, Chronicle $29.95 (0-8118-0365-1). Artifacts from baseball's history—many from the Baseball Hall of Fame in Cooperstown, New York—are displayed in color photos with explanatory text. (Rev: BL 11/15/93; SLJ 1/94) [796.357]

6436 Baker, Dusty, and others. *You Can Teach Hitting: A Systematic Approach to Hitting for Parents, Coaches and Players* (9–adult). 1993, Bittinger paper $24.95 (0-940279-73-8). Presents systematic instruction on hitting a baseball, including drills and situational tips. (Rev: BL 12/1/92*) [796.357]

6437 Boswell, Tom. *Cracking the Show* (9–adult). 1994, Doubleday $23 (0-385-47286-2). A collection of pieces by a *Washington Post* baseball columnist, grouped by subject. (Rev: BL 3/15/94) [796.357]

6438 Cooper, Michael L. *Playing America's Game: The Story of Negro League Baseball* (5–7). 1993, Dutton/Lodestar $15.99 (0-525-67407-1). An overview of the key figures in Negro League baseball, with many black-and-white photos. (Rev: BL 2/15/93; MJHS) [796.357]

6439 Coyle, Daniel. *Hardball: A Season in the Projects* (9–adult). 1994, Putnam $22.95 (0-399-13867-6). The 1992 Little League season at the Cabrini Green Homes in Chicago is portrayed, including tensions between white coaches, African American players, gangs, and the League's founders. (Rev: BL 12/15/93) [796.357]

6440 Curran, William. *Strikeout: A Celebration of the Art of Pitching* (9–adult). 1995, Crown $23 (0-517-58841-2). An anecdotal history of baseball pitching. (Rev: BL 2/15/95) [796.357]

6441 Dewey, Donald, and Nick Acocella. *The All-Time All-Star Baseball Book* (9–adult). 1992, Brown & Benchmark paper $10.95 (0-697-14594-8). Baseball data grouped into imaginative categories. (Rev: BL 4/15/92) [796.357]

6442 Dixon, Phil, and Patrick J. Hannigan. *The Negro Baseball Leagues: A Photographic History* (9–adult). 1992, Amereon House $34.95 (0-8488-0425-2). Celebrates the defunct Negro Baseball Leagues with anecdotes, newspaper accounts, and hundreds of photos. (Rev: BL 10/1/92) [796.357]

6443 Fimrite, Ron, ed. *Birth of a Fan* (9–adult). 1993, Macmillan $20 (0-02-537760-4). Fifteen essays by well-known writers such as Roger Angell and Roy Blount who relate their first encounters with baseball and how they came to love the game. (Rev: BL 3/1/93) [796.357]

6444 Fimrite, Ron. *The World Series: A History of Baseball's Fall Classic* (9–adult). 1993, Oxmoor $40 (0-8487-1155-6). An overview of the World Series, with profiles of great players and teams and 130 photos. (Rev: BL 7/93) [796.357646]

6445 Fremon, David K. *The Negro Baseball Leagues* (7–12). (American Events) 1994, Silver Burdett LB $14.95 (0-02-735695-7); paper $7.95 (0-382-24730-2). (Rev: BL 3/15/95) [796.357]

6446 Galt, Margot Fortunato. *Up to the Plate: The All American Girls Professional Baseball League* (6–9). (Sports Legacy) 1995, Lerner LB $17.21 (0-8225-3326-X). This history of the All-American Girls Professional Baseball League includes personal interviews with the players and their reactions to the movie *A League of Their Own*. (Rev: BL 7/95; SLJ 6/95) [796.357]

6447 Gardner, Robert, and Dennis Shortelle. *The Forgotten Players: The Story of Black Baseball in America* (5–8). 1993, Walker LB $13.85 (0-8027-8249-3). Detailed information on the day-to-day life of African American baseball players in the Negro Leagues. (Rev: BL 2/15/93; MJHS) [796.357]

6448 Gershman, Michael. *Diamonds: The Evolution of the Ballpark* (9–adult). 1993, Houghton $40 (0-395-61212-8). Describes the history of some of the most famous ballfields, with anecdotes and photos. (Rev: BL 10/1/93) [796.357]

6449 Gilbert, Bill. *They Also Served: Baseball and the Home Front, 1941–1945* (9–adult). 1992, Crown $20 (0-517-58522-7). Baseball as a focal point for world and social history during World War II. (Rev: BL 1/15/92; SLJ 2/93) [796.357]

6450 Golenbock, Peter. *Fenway: An Unexpurgated History of the Boston Red Sox* (9–adult). 1992, Putnam $24.95 (0-399-13713-0). Chronological history of the Boston Red Sox baseball team. (Rev: BL 2/15/92) [796.357]

6451 Gutman, Dan. *World Series Classics* (5–8). 1994, Viking $14.99 (0-670-85286-4). A play-by-play look at the 1912, 1924, 1947, 1974, and 1991 World Series games, including anecdotes and baseball trivia. (Rev: BL 9/15/94; SLJ 11/94; VOYA 4/95) [796.357]

6452 Hanmer, Trudy J. *The All-American Girls Professional Baseball League* (7–12). (American Events) 1994, Silver Burdett LB $14.95 (0-02-742595-9); paper $7.95 (0-382-24731-0). (Rev: BL 3/15/95) [796.357]

6453 Lamb, David. *Stolen Season: A Journey Through America and Baseball's Minor Leagues* (9–adult). 1991, Random $20 (0-394-57608-X). (Rev: BL 3/1/91*) [796.357]

6454 Layden, Joe. *The Great American Baseball Strike* (5–8). (Headliners) 1995, Millbrook LB $16.40 (1-56294-930-6). (Rev: BL 11/15/95) [331.89]

6455 Macy, Sue. *A Whole New Ballgame: The Story of the All-American Girls Professional Baseball League* (6–10). 1993, Holt $14.95 (0-8050-1942-1). Celebrates the women who played in the All-American Girls Professional Baseball League, started by P. K. Wrigley during World War II. Awards: SLJ Best Book; YALSA Best Book for Young Adults. (Rev: BL 3/15/93; BTA; MJHS; SLJ 5/93*; VOYA 12/93) [796.357]

6456 Margolies, Jacob. *The Negro Leagues: The Story of Black Baseball* (7–12). (African American Experience) 1993, Watts LB $13.90 (0-531-11130-X). The history of African American baseball from the 1880s through the birth of the Negro Leagues in the 1920s and their demise in the 1950s. (Rev: BL 2/15/94; VOYA 6/94) [793.357]

6457 Nash, Bruce, and Allan Zullo. *The Baseball Hall of Shame's Warped Record Book* (9–adult) 1991, Macmillan/Collier paper $8.95 (0-02-029485-9). An amusing collection of unusual baseball "records," such as "longest time trapped in a bathroom during a game" and other weird or embarrassing incidents. (Rev: BL 9/15/91) [796.357]

6458 Nauen, Elinor, ed. *Diamonds Are a Girl's Best Friend: Women Writers on Baseball* (9–adult). 1994, Faber & Faber $22 (0-571-19819-8). Poems, essays, and fiction by more than 70 women writers on baseball-related topics. (Rev: BL 1/15/94) [810]

6459 Nemec, David. *The Great American Baseball Team Book* (9–adult). 1992, NAL/Plume paper $14 (0-452-26781-1). Assessments of the best, worst, and weirdest baseball teams from 1876 to 1991. (Rev: BL 4/1/92) [796.357]

6460 Nemec, David. *The Rules of Baseball* (9–adult). 1994, Lyons & Burford $24.95 (1-55821-279-5). An annotated version of the official rules of the game, with plain English explanations and examples. (Rev: BL 3/15/94) [796.357]

6461 Obojski, Robert. *Baseball Memorabilia* (7–12). 1992, Sterling paper $8.95 (0-8069-7289-0). Provides information about valuable and not-so-valuable baseball collectibles, as well as baseball trivia. (Rev: BL 6/1/92; BY)

6462 Reichler, Joseph L. *The Great All-Time Baseball Record Book* (9–adult). 1992, Macmillan $23 (0-02-603101-9). Includes a comprehensive record of statistics through the 1991 season. (Rev: BL 4/15/92) [796.357]

6463 Schenin, Richard. *Field of Screams: The Dark Underside of America's National Pastime* (9–adult). 1994, Norton paper $12.95 (0-393-31138-4). A chronologically arranged collection of items from the "underside" of baseball history. (Rev: BL 3/15/94) [796.357]

6464 Schlain, Bruce. *Baseball Inside Out: The Unspoken Rules of the Game* (9–adult). 1992, Viking $20 (0-670-83506-4). Strategy behind the game revealed through the perspectives of players, managers, and fans. Awards: BL Editors' Choice. (Rev: BL 2/1/92) [796.357]

6465 Schmidt, Mike, and Rob Ellis. *The Mike Schmidt Study: Hitting Theory, Skills and Techniques* (9–adult). 1994, McGriff & Bell (P.O. Box 1622, Grand Rapids, MI 49501) paper $15.95 (0-9634-6092-7). Designed to help coaches teach Little Leaguers how to hit, Schmidt explains the 3 major systems and the mental aspects involved. (Rev: BL 12/15/93) [796.35726]

6466 Wallace, Joseph, ed. *The Baseball Anthology: 125 Years of Stories, Poems, Articles, Photographs, Drawings, Interviews, Cartoons, and Other Memorabilia* (9–adult). 1994, Abrams $39.95 (0-8109-3135-4). (Rev: BL 12/15/94; SHS) [796.357]

6467 Ward, Geoffrey, and others. *Who Invented the Game?* (5–8). (Baseball, the American Epic) 1994, Knopf LB $16.99 (0-679-96750-8). (Rev: BL 12/15/94) [796.357]

6468 Ward, Geoffrey, and Ken Burns. *Baseball: An Illustrated History* (9–adult). 1994, Knopf $60 (0-679-40459-7). A history of the game, published in conjunction with a PBS documentary, presenting essays, facts, and over 500 photos. (Rev: BL 7/94*; BTA) [796.357]

6469 Winfield, Dave. *Ask Dave: Dave Winfield Answers Kids' Questions about Baseball and Life* (5–7). 1994, Andrews & McMeel paper $7.95 (0-8362-8057-1). Compiles newspaper columns by the Minnesota Twins baseball player about his life, celebrity, and other players. Also provides playing tips. (Rev: BL 9/1/94) [796.375]

6470 Zack, Bill. *Tomahawked: The Inside Story of the Atlanta Braves' Tumultuous Season* (9–adult). 1993, Simon & Schuster $20 (0-671-86878-0). This recap of the 1992 season illustrates how the baseball team fine-tuned itself after the 1991 World Series loss, describing relationships between managers and players. (Rev: BL 4/15/93) [796.357]

Basketball

6471 Bjarkman, Peter C. *The Encyclopedia of Pro Basketball Team Histories* (9–adult). 1994, Carroll & Graf $24 (0-7867-0126-9). (Rev: BL 12/1/94; SHS) [796.323]

6472 Blais, Madeleine. *In These Girls, Hope Is Muscle* (9–adult). 1995, Atlantic Monthly $21.95 (0-87113-572-8). Covers the championship season of a girls' high school basketball team. (Rev: BL 12/1/94; SLJ 11/95; VOYA 5/95) [797.323]

6473 Frey, Darcy. *The Last Shot: City Streets, Basketball Dreams* (9–adult). 1994, Houghton $19.95 (0-395-59770-6). Chronicles a group of teenagers playing for one of the best high school teams in New York City. (Rev: BL 12/1/94; SHS) [796.323]

6474 George, Nelson. *Elevating the Game: Black Men and Basketball* (9–adult). 1992, HarperCollins $23 (0-06-016723-8). The role of African American players in the evolution of basketball. (Rev: BL 1/15/92) [796.323]

6475 Guffey, Greg. *The Greatest Basketball Story Ever Told: The Milan Miracle, Then and Now* (9–adult). 1993, Indiana Univ. $24.95 (0-253-32688-5); paper $12.95 (0-253-32689-3). The real-life events that inspired the movie *Hoosiers* are explored in this look at the 1954 Milan High School basketball team and changes since then. (Rev: BL 12/1/93) [796.323]

6476 Jackson, Phil, and Hugh Delehanty. *Scared Hoops: Spiritual Lessons of a Hardwood Warrior* (9–adult). 1995, Hyperion $22.95 (0-7868-6206-8). Jackson, head coach of the Chicago Bulls, offers the coaching philosophy that has helped him get his team to pull together spiritually and attain a common goal. (Rev: BL 9/1/95) [796.323]

6477 Keown, Tim. *Skyline: One Season, One Team, One City* (9–adult). 1994, Macmillan $20 (0-02-562305-2). An intimate view of one season with Oakland's "melting pot" Skyline High School basketball team and their idealistic, dedicated rookie coach. Awards: BL Editors' Choice. (Rev: BL 3/15/94*) [796.323]

6478 Lazenby, Roland. *The Lakers: A Basketball Journey* (9–adult). 1993, St. Martin's $22.95 (0-312-09840-5). This history of the team focuses on the Lakers' performance when led by Magic Johnson in the 1980s. (Rev: BL 11/1/93) [796.323]

6479 Miller, Reggie, and Gene Wojciechowski. *I Love Being the Enemy: A Season on the Court with the NBA's Best Shooter and Sharpest Tongue* (9–adult). 1995, Simon & Schuster $23 (0-684-81389-0). Miller's diary kept during the 1994–95 season reveals a side of him not often seen. (Rev: BL 12/1/95) [796.323]

6480 Mullin, Chris, and Brian Coleman. *The Young Basketball Player* (5–7). 1995, Dorling Kindersley $15.95 (0-7894-0220-3). Many photos of players, basketballs, and hoops create the background for this how-to book for young basketball players. (Rev: BL 11/1/95) [796.323]

6481 Pitino, Rick, and Dick Weiss. *Full-Court Pressure* (9–adult). 1992, Hyperion $22.95 (1-56282-931-9). University of Kentucky's head basketball coach recalls past seasons with the Wildcats. (Rev: BL 9/15/92) [796.323]

6482 Pluto, Terry. *Falling from Grace: Can Pro Basketball Be Saved?* (9–adult). 1995, Simon & Schuster $23 (0-684-80766-1). An examination of a declining sport with comments from 52 experts bolstering Pluto's assertion that the trash-talking and in-your-face culture of disrespect dominates pro basketball. (Rev: BL 11/15/95) [796.323]

6483 Sullivan, George. *All about Basketball* (5–8). 1991, Putnam paper $6.95 (0-399-21793-2). Surveys the history of basketball from its beginnings in 1891 through the NBA 1991 playoffs. (Rev: BL 1/1/92; YR) [796.323]

6484 Vancil, Mark. *NBA Basketball Basics* (5–9). 1995, Sterling $16.95 (0-8069-0927-7). A book of basics for young people. Loaded with full-color photos. (Rev: BL 4/15/95) [796.323]

6485 Vitale, Dick, and Dick Weiss. *Holding Court: Reflections on the Game I Love* (9–adult). 1995, Masters Press (2647 Waterfront Pkwy. E. Dr., Indianapolis, IN 46214-2041) $22.95 (1-57028-037-1). College basketball's voice on ESPN and a coach himself, Vitale discusses various topics, including the intense pressure on coaches to win. (Rev: BL 12/1/95) [796.323]

Bicycling, Motorcycling, etc.

6486 Abt, Samuel. *Tour de France: Three Weeks to Glory* (9–adult). 1991, Bicycle Books (1282 Seventh Ave., San Francisco, CA 94122-2526) $22.95 (0-933201-39-7); paper $12.95 (0-933201-40-0). Overview of the world's largest, most prestigious bicycle race, its origins, and the sport's leading riders. (Rev: BL 6/1/91; SHS) [796.62]

6487 Ballantine, Richard, and Richard Grant. *Richards' Bicycle Repair Manual* (9–adult). 1994, Dorling Kindersley paper $8.95 (1-56458-484-4). An illustrated handbook for the home bicycle mechanic, covering routine and preventive maintenance and emergency repairs. (Rev: BL 3/15/94; BTA; SLJ 9/94; VOYA 2/95) [629.28]

6488 Ballantine, Richard, and Richard Grant. *Richards' Ultimate Bicycle Book* (9–adult). 1992, Dorling Kindersley $29.95 (1-56458-036-9). Informative overview of bicycles and bicycling. Color photos. (Rev: BL 4/1/92; SHS; SLJ 7/92) [629.227]

6489 Bennett, Jim. *The Complete Motorcycle Book* (9–adult). 1995, Facts on File $24.95 (0-8160-2899-0). (Rev: BL 12/15/94; SLJ 6/95) [629.28]

6490 Nye, Peter. *The Cyclist's Sourcebook* (9–adult). 1991, Putnam/Perigee paper $16.95 (0-399-51705-7). A catalog of information and equipment for recreational bicyclists, including names, addresses, and price data. (Rev: BL 9/1/91) [796.6]

6491 van der Plas, Rob. *Mountain Bike Magic* (9–adult). 1991, Bicycle Books (1282 Seventh Ave., San Francisco, CA 94122-2526) paper $14.95 (0-933201-41-9). One of the sport's pioneers gives a detailed look at all-terrain bicycling in this illustrated introduction to the world of fat tires. (Rev: BL 9/1/91) [796.64]

6492 Wilson, Hugo. *The Ultimate Motorcycle Book* (9–adult). 1993, Dorling Kindersley $29.95 (1-56458-303-1). Color photos of over 200 bikes illustrate this guide to U.S. and imported motorcycles, their history, World War II use, racing, touring, motocross, and customizing. (Rev: BL 11/1/93; MJHS) [629.227]

Boxing and Wrestling

6493 Anderson, Dave. *In the Corner: Great Boxing Trainers Talk about Their Art* (9–adult). 1991, Morrow $19.95 (0-688-09446-5). A collection of reminiscences by 12 of the best trainers in their time. (Rev: BL 4/1/91; SHS) [796.8]

6494 Douglas, Bobby. *Take It to the Mat* (9–adult). 1993, Sigler Press (413 Northwestern, Ames, IA 50010) paper $15.95 (0-9635812-0-1). U.S. Olympic wrestler/coach Douglas presents an introductory guide to competitive wrestling. Includes photos of holds and escapes, as well as diet guidelines. (Rev: BL 9/15/93) [796.8]

Camping, Hiking, Backpacking, and Mountaineering

6495 Bangs, Richard. *Peaks: Seeking High Ground Across Six Continents* (9–adult). 1994, Taylor $34.95 (0-87833-856-X). Describes the author's exploration of mountainous regions around the world. Includes color photos. (Rev: BL 10/1/94) [910]

6496 Cook, Charles. *The Essential Guide to Hiking in the United States* (9–adult). 1991, Michael Kesend (1025 Fifth Ave., New York, NY 10028) paper $14.95 (0-935576-41-X). Contains information on such hiking essentials as shoes, clothing, safety, and the best areas for hiking and the trails in each state. (Rev: BL 12/1/91) [917.3]

6497 McManners, Hugh. *The Complete Wilderness Training Book* (9–adult). 1994, Dorling Kindersley $29.95 (1-56458-488-7). Survival techniques for the hardcore survivalist in familiar as well as extreme environments. This British import is more international in scope than American versions. (Rev: BL 5/15/94; BTA; VOYA 12/94) [613.6]

6498 Randall, Glenn. *The Backpacker's Handbook: An Environmentally Sound Guide* (9–adult). 1994, Lyons & Burford paper $14.95 (1-55821-248-5). Tells "how to be comfortable in the wilderness while leaving it untouched for the enjoyment of the next visitor" by giving tips on clothing, packing, safety, and more. (Rev: BL 12/1/93) [796.5]

6499 Scott, Doug. *Himalayan Climber: A Lifetime's Quest to the World's Greatest Ranges* (9–adult). 1992, Sierra Club $35 (0-87156-599-4). A pictorial diary captures the thrill of mountain climbing . (Rev: BL 9/15/92; BTA) [796.5]

6500 Seaborg, Eric, and Ellen Dudley. *Hiking and Backpacking* (9–adult). 1994, Human Kinetics paper $12.95 (0-87322-506-6). An introduction to hiking and backpacking, covering safety gear, safe travel, and the best places to go. (Rev: BL 3/15/94; VOYA 12/94) [796.5]

6501 Waterman, Jonathan. *In the Shadow of Denali: Life and Death on Alaska's Mt. McKinley* (9–adult). 1994, Dell/Laurel Leaf paper $5.99 (0-440-21530-7). This first-person narrative explores the psychology of climbers who attempt to scale the nation's highest mountain. (Rev: BL 3/1/94) [796.5]

Chess, Checkers, and Other Board and Card Games

6502 Hochberg, Burt, ed. *The 64-Square Looking Glass: The Great Game of Chess in World Literature* (9–adult). 1992, Times Books $23 (0-8129-1929-7). Forty-plus essays and fiction pieces on chess, including contributions from Samuel Beckett, Woody Allen, and Kurt Vonnegut. (Rev: BL 11/15/92) [809]

6503 Sheinwold, Alfred. *101 Best Family Card Games* (5–12). Illus. 1993, Sterling paper $4.95 (0-8069-8635-2). Card games for all ages, from 5 to adulthood. (Rev: BL 2/15/93) [795.4]

Fishing and Hunting

6504 Arnosky, Jim. *Fish in a Flash! A Personal Guide to Spin-Fishing* (5–9). 1991, Bradbury $14.95 (0-02-705854-9). Covers tackle, casting techniques with various lures, and fishing conditions, all in the context of the author's personal experiences. (Rev: BL 9/15/91; MJHS; SLJ 10/91) [799.1]

6505 Buckland, John. *The Game Fishing Bible* (9–adult). 1991, Prentice-Hall $40 (0-13-521691-5). Information, tips, and techniques on fly-fishing for the beginner. (Rev: BL 2/1/92) [799.1]

6506 Capstick, Peter Hathaway. *Sands of Silence* (9–adult). 1991, St. Martin's $35 (0-312-06459-4). The author muses on life and death in the wild in this story of elephant hunting near the edge of the African Kalahari desert, with an in-depth report on the lives of the region's natives. (Rev: BL 10/15/91) [799.2]

6507 Greene, Laura Offenhartz. *Wildlife Poaching* (7–12). 1994, Watts LB $13.93 (0-531-13007-X). Tackles the problems of game poaching from a historical perspective and explores the differences between big-game hunting in North America and in Africa and Asia. (Rev: BL 2/1/95; SHS) [364.1]

6508 Margolis, Jon, and Jeff MacNelly. *How to Fool Fish with Feathers* (9–adult). 1992, Simon & Schuster/Fireside paper $9.95 (0-671-75943-4). The basics of fly-fishing. (Rev: BL 1/15/92) [799.1]

6509 Migdalski, Edward C. *The Inquisitive Angler* (9–adult). 1991, Lyons & Burford $27.95 (1-55821-132-2). A serious fishing text with information on taxonomy, habitat, limnology, and anatomy, designed to improve sports skills. (Rev: BL 12/15/91) [799.1]

6510 Morey, Shaun. *Incredible Fishing Stories* (9–adult). 1991, World Publications (P.O. Box 2306, Sausalito, CA 94966-2306) paper $12.95 (0-944406-09-2). A collection of tall tales and case histories from saltwater anglers. (Rev: BL 11/15/91) [799.1]

6511 Morris, Holly, ed. *Uncommon Waters: Women Write about Fishing* (9–adult). 1991, Seal Press paper $14.95 (1-878067-10-9). This book, the first published collection of fishing stories by women, includes everything from trout and deep-sea fishing exploits to a classic by a fifteenth-century nun. (Rev: BL 10/15/91) [810.8]

6512 Patent, Dorothy Hinshaw. *A Family Goes Hunting* (5–8). Photos. 1991, Clarion $14.95 (0-395-52004-5). A balanced exploration of the hunting, with information on weapons, licenses, gun cleaning, hunting dogs, and safety measures. (Rev: BL 12/15/91; SLJ 11/91) [799.29786]

6513 Paulsen, Gary. *Father Water, Mother Woods: Essays on Fishing and Hunting in the North Woods* (6–12). 1994, Delacorte $16.95 (0-385-32053-1). Essays concerning the author's deep love for the wilderness, describing his adventures hunting, fishing, canoeing, and camping. (Rev: BL 7/94; BTA; SHS; SLJ 8/94; VOYA 10/94) [799]

6514 Poortvliet, Rien. *Journey to the Ice Age: Mammoths and Other Animals of the Wild* (9–adult). Tr. by Karin H. Ford. 1994, Abrams $39.95 (0-8109-3648-8). Hunting stories from the Netherlands, featuring child-eating wolves, wild boars, bears, hawks, and Ice Age woolly mammoths. (Rev: BL 11/1/94) [599.09492]

6515 Swan, James A. *In Defense of Hunting* (9–adult). 1994, HarperSan Francisco $20 (0-06-251029-0). Defends the right to hunt, citing moral, ecological, and historical justifications. Attempts to debunk arguments made by animal-rights activists. (Rev: BL 11/1/94) [799.2]

6516 Walker, Spike. *Working on the Edge: Surviving in the World's Most Dangerous Profession: King Crab Fishing on Alaska's High Seas* (9–adult). 1991, St. Martin's $19.95 (0-312-06002-5). Seamen risk their lives in hurricane-force winds, 50-foot waves, and blinding fog to make a fortune crab fishing. (Rev: BL 6/1/91) [639]

Football

6517 Anastasia, Phil. *Broken Wing, Broken Promise: A Season Inside the Philadelphia Eagles* (9–adult). 1993, Camino Books (P.O. Box 59026, Philadelphia, PA 19102-9026) $18 (0-940159-20-1). Reporter Anastasia chronicles the Eagles' 1992 season, including Jerome Brown's death, mistrust of coach Kotite, and the division of team loyalty between 2 quarterbacks. (Rev: BL 10/1/93) [796.332]

6518 Carucci, Vic. *The Buffalo Bills and the Almost-Dream Season* (9–adult). 1991, Simon & Schuster $20 (0-671-74850-5). This account of a pro football team during one nearly victorious season profiles several of its key personalities and examines the team's relationship with its hometown. (Rev: BL 9/15/91) [796.332]

6519 Denlinger, Ken. *For the Glory: College Football Dreams and Realities Inside Paterno's Program* (9–adult). 1994, St. Martin's $22.95 (0-312-11436-2). Journalist Denlinger, granted access to Coach Paterno's Penn State football program, tracks the lives and development of a freshman class through 5 years of playing. (Rev: BL 9/15/94) [796.332]

6520 Harrington, Denis J. *The Pro Football Hall of Fame: Players, Coaches, Team Owners and League Officials, 1963–1991* (9–adult). 1991, McFarland $25.95 (0-89950-550-3). Thumbnail profiles of football greats, organized by position. (Rev: BL 1/15/92; SHS) [796.332]

6521 King, Peter. *Inside the Helmet: A Player's Eye View of the NFL* (9–adult). 1993, Simon & Schuster $21 (0-671-74704-5). A look at football from the players' perspective. Interviews, anecdotes, and strategy analysis explain the rigors involved. (Rev: BL 9/15/93) [796.332]

6522 Korch, Rick. *The Truly Great: The 200 Best Pro Football Players of All Time* (9–adult). 1993, Taylor paper $15.95 (0-87833-831-4). The editor of *Pro Football Weekly* ranks the greatest football players of all time, with rationales from ex-players, writers, coaches, and others. (Rev: BL 9/15/93) [796.332]

6523 Lott, Ronnie, and Jill Lieber. *Total Impact: Straight Talk from Football's Hardest Hitter* (9–adult). 1991, Doubleday $19.50 (0-385-42055-2). A professional memoir by one of the best defensive backs in football, in which Lott analyzes players, teams, coaches, owners, and the NFL. (Rev: BL 10/15/91) [796.332]

6524 Mooney, Chuck. *The Recruiting Survival Guide* (10–12). 1991, 21st Century Press (3460 Dryden, Suite 2052, Fort Worth, TX 76109) paper $9.95 (0-9630239-0-X). A former college ball player explains how recruiters work and what pitfalls and rewards await the targeted athlete. (Rev: BL 4/15/92) [796.33]

6525 Oppenheimer, Judy. *Dreams of Glory: A Mother's Season with Her Son's High School Football Team* (9–adult). 1991, Summit $19.50 (0-671-68754-9). A humorous, upbeat examination of high school football in an affluent suburb. (Rev: BL 9/1/91) [796.332]

6526 Sperber, Murray. *Shake Down the Thunder: The Creation of Notre Dame Football* (9–adult). 1993, Holt $22.50 (0-8050-1874-3). (Rev: BL 10/15/93*) [796.332]

6527 Wiebusch, John, and Brian Silverman, eds. *A Game of Passion: The NFL Literary Companion* (9–adult). 1994, Turner $21.95 (1-57036-115-0); paper $10.95 (1-57036-106-1). Forty essays championing football and the NFL. Includes pieces about former Giants coach Steve Owen and Super Bowl memories. (Rev: BL 10/15/94) [810.8]

Golf

6528 Campbell, Malcolm. *The Random House International Encyclopedia of Golf: The Definitive Guide to the Game* (9–adult). 1991, Random $60 (0-394-58893-2). A comprehensive reference for golf enthusiasts highlighting courses, equipment, and past tournament winners. (Rev: BL 1/15/92) [796.352]

6529 Feinstein, John. *A Good Walk Spoiled: Days and Nights on the PGA Tour* (9–adult). 1995, Little, Brown $23.95 (0-316-27720-7). An overview of the inner and outer lives of pro golf athletes. (Rev: BL 5/15/95*) [796.352]

6530 Glenn, Rhonda. *The Illustrated History of Women's Golf* (9–adult). 1991, Taylor $34.95 (0-87833-743-1). Examines the women's amateur golf circuit from the 1920s through the 1950s. Includes a complete list of golf records. (Rev: BL 1/1/92) [796.352]

6531 Kroen, William C. *The Why Book of Golf* (9–adult). 1992, Price/Stern/Sloan paper $8.95 (0-8431-2982-4). Golf trivia and tips on equipment, the course, and rules of the game. (Rev: BL 2/1/92) [796.35202]

6532 Penick, Harvey, and Bud Shrake. *For All Who Love the Game: Lessons and Teachings for Women* (9–adult). 1995, Simon & Schuster $20

(0-684-80058-6). Goal-directed tips for golfers' swings. (Rev: BL 4/15/95) [796.352]

6533 Pepper, George. *Grand Slam Golf* (9–adult). 1991, Abrams $49.50 (0-8109-3359-4). Descriptions of 30 golf courses in the United States and the United Kingdom that have hosted the tournaments that make up the Grand Slam. (Rev: BL 1/15/92) [796.352]

6534 Waggoner, Glen. *Divots, Shanks, Gimmes, Mulligans, and Chili Dips: A Life in Eighteen Holes* (9–adult). 1993, Villard $21 (0-394-58005-2). A loving memoir of a golfing addict about his experiences as a reporter on the pro tour and his career as a lifetime hacker. (Rev: BL 4/15/93) [796.352]

Gymnastics

6535 Jackman, Joan. *The Young Gymnast* (5–7). 1995, Dorling Kindersley $15.95 (1-56458-677-4). Includes many color photos (mostly of female gymnasts), a brief history of the sport, discussion of skills required, a glossary, and useful addresses. (Rev: BL 9/1/95) [796.44]

6536 Whitlock, Steve. *Make the Team: Gymnastics for Girls* (5–8). 1991, Little, Brown $13.95 (0-316-99794-3); paper $5.95 (0-316-88793-5). Step-by-step guide to beginning gymnastics for girls, including program selection, training, conditioning, and competitions. (Rev: BL 1/15/92; MJHS; SLJ 5/92) [796.44]

Hockey

6537 Diamond, Dan, ed. *The Official National Hockey League 75th Anniversary Commemorative Book* (9–adult). 1991, Firefly Books $50 (0-7710-6727-5). Essays on the NHL, with profiles of Wayne Gretzky and Bobby Hull. Illustrated. (Rev: BL 1/1/92) [796.962]

6538 Hunter, Douglas. *A Breed Apart: An Illustrated History of Goaltending* (9–adult). Illus. 1995, Triumph Books (644 S. Clark St., Suite 2000, Chicago, IL 60605) $28.95 (1-57243-048-6). Hunter tracks goaltending from its earliest years, but mostly after 1943. Includes portraits of the most renowned goalies. (Rev: BL 10/1/95*)

Horse Racing and Horsemanship

6539 Best, David Grant. *Portrait of a Racetrack: A Behind the Scenes Look at a Racetrack Community* (9–adult). 1992, Best Editions (7841 Leary Way, Redmond, WA 98052) paper $24.95 (0-9634241-0-6). A black-and-white photo-essay of the horses, jockeys, grooms, and trainers at a Seattle racetrack. (Rev: BL 12/1/92*) [798.400]

6540 Draper, Judith. *Practical Showjumping* (6–10). (Ward Lock Riding School) 1994, Sterling $14.95 (0-7063-7135-6). Provides information on showing horses, focusing on horse selection, training, and competition. (Rev: BL 9/1/94) [798.2]

6541 Johnson, Dirk. *Biting the Dust: The Wild Ride and Dark Romance of the Rodeo Cowboy and the American West* (9–adult). 1994, Simon & Schuster $22 (0-671-79221-0). Describes a year on the rodeo circuit, the adventurous lifestyles of its personalities, and their reasons for competing. (Rev: BL 10/1/94) [791.8]

6542 Kirksmith, Tommie. *Ride Western Style: A Guide for Young Riders* (5–8). 1991, Howell Book $16.95 (0-87605-895-0). Background information and step-by-step instructions for youth interested in learning to ride horses Western style. (Rev: BL 4/1/92; SLJ 7/92) [798.2]

6543 McBane, Susan. *Tack and Clothing* (6–10). (Ward Lock Riding School) 1994, Sterling $14.95 (0-7063-7145-3). Explains the function and maintenance of the equipment required to outfit a horse properly. (Rev: BL 9/1/94) [798.2]

6544 Norbury, Rosamond. *Behind the Chutes: The Mystique of the Rodeo Cowboy* (9–adult). 1993, Mountain Press Publishing (P.O. Box 2399, Missoula, MT 59806) paper $17 (0-87842-287-0). Realistic sepia tone photos illustrate this celebratory history of the rodeo lifestyle. (Rev: BL 5/1/93) [791.8]

6545 Rodenas, Paula. *The Random House Book of Horses and Horsemanship* (5–8). 1991, Random LB $18.99 (0-394-98705-5). (Rev: BL 5/1/91; SLJ 6/91) [636.1]

6546 Roughton, Sheila. *Breaking and Training Your Horse* (9–adult). 1994, Ward Lock $24.95 (0-7063-7123-2). Suggests training routines for equestrian competition, giving tips on preventing a horse's boredom. (Rev: BL 11/1/94) [798.2]

6547 Schwartz, Jane. *Ruffian: Burning from the Start* (9–adult). 1991, Ballantine $18 (0-345-36017-6). The author uses a doomed horse's life as a basis for a pointed look inside thoroughbred racing. (Rev: BL 9/1/91) [636.1]

Ice Skating

6548 Gutman, Dan. *Ice Skating: From Axels to Zambonis* (5–8). 1995, Viking $14.99 (0-670-86013-1). Chronicles the early history of skating, with biographies of famous skaters. (Rev: BL 10/1/95; SLJ 12/95; VOYA 2/96) [796.91]

In-Line Skating

6549 Powell, Mark, and John Svensson. *In-Line Skating: The Skills for Fun and Fitness on Wheels* (9–adult). 1992, Human Kinetics paper $12.95 (0-87322-399-3). A step-by-step guide to the popular sport, geared to all abilities. (Rev: BL 9/1/92; BTA; VOYA 10/93) [796]

6550 Sullivan, George. *In-Line Skating: A Complete Guide for Beginners* (5–12). 1993, Dutton/Cobblehill $13.99 (0-525-65124-1). Describes the new sport's invention, equipment selection, and demonstration and racing techniques. Awards: SLJ Best Book. (Rev: BL 4/1/93; MJHS; SLJ 7/93*) [796.2]

Martial Arts

6551 Goedecke, Christopher J. *The Wind Warrior: The Training of a Karate Champion* (5–7). Photos. 1992, Four Winds $15.95 (0-02-736262-0). Describes a typical karate lesson, the various forms the art can take, tournaments, clothing, equipment, and the history and philosophy of the sport. (Rev: BL 6/1/92; BTA; MJHS; SLJ 7/92) [796.8]

6552 Metil, Luana, and Jace Townsend. *The Story of Karate: From Buddhism to Bruce Lee* (6–9). 1995, Lerner LB $17.21 (0-8225-3325-1). (Rev: BL 7/95; MJHS) [796.8]

6553 Turner, Karyn, and Mark Van Schuyver. *Secrets of Championship Karate* (9–adult). 1991, Contemporary paper $11.95 (0-8092-4052-1). Suggestions and advice for karate competitors looking for a physical and mental edge. (Rev: BL 6/1/91) [796.8]

Olympic Games

6554 Arnold, Caroline. *The Olympic Summer Games* (5–7). (First Book) 1991, Watts LB $11.90 (0-531-20052-3). This illustrated description of Olympic events includes notes about the origin of the games and their politicalization in modern times. (Rev: BL 11/15/91; MJHS; SLJ 2/92) [796.48]

6555 Arnold, Caroline. *The Olympic Winter Games* (5–7). (First Book) 1991, Watts LB $11.90 (0-531-20053-1). Photographs enliven this description of Olympic individual and team events, with thumbnail profiles of several modern Olympic champions. (Rev: BL 11/15/91; MJHS; SLJ 2/92) [796.98]

6556 Brown, Fern G. *Special Olympics* (5–7). 1992, Watts LB $11.90 (0-531-20062-0). Recounts the history of the Special Olympics, designed to help developmentally/physically challenged individuals participate in organized athletics. (Rev: BL 6/1/92; MJHS; SLJ 7/92) [796]

6557 Guttmann, Allen. *The Olympics: A History of the Modern Games* (9–adult). 1992, Univ. of Illinois $24.95 (0-252-01701-3). History of the Olympics from the first games in Athens in 1896 through the 1988 contests. (Rev: BL 4/15/92; SHS) [796.48]

6558 Knight, Theodore. *The Olympic Games* (5–8). 1991, Lucent LB $12.95 (1-56006-119-7). A thorough examination of all facets and issues of the Olympics. (Rev: BL 4/15/92; MJHS; SLJ 8/92) [796.48]

6559 Kristy, Davida. *Coubertin's Olympics: How the Games Began* (5–8). 1995, Lerner LB $17.21 (0-8225-3327-8). How the Olympic games began and much more about the life of Baron Pierre de Coubertin, their founder. (Rev: BL 8/95; SLJ 11/95) [338.4]

6560 Malley, Stephen. *The Kids' Guide to the 1994 Winter Olympics* (5–8). 1994, Bantam paper $9.99 (0-553-48159-2). Presents historical and explanatory information about skating, sledding, and skiing. (Rev: BL 2/15/94) [796.98]

Running and Jogging

6561 Henderson, Joe. *Think Fast: Mental Toughness Training for Runners* (9–adult). 1991, NAL/Plume paper $10.95 (0-452-26610-6). Detailed training book for serious runners who want to increase their mental toughness. (Rev: BL 7/91) [796.42]

6562 Higdon, Hal. *Boston: A Century of Running* (9–adult). 1995, Rodale $40 (0-87596-283-1). From the senior writer for *Runner's World* and a marathon runner himself, a history of the marathon and information on current runners. (Rev: BL 11/1/95) [796.42]

Sailing, Boating, and Canoeing

6563 Anderson, Scott. *Distant Fires* (8–12). Illus. 1990, Pfeifer-Hamilton (210 W. Michigan St., Duluth, MN 55802-1908) paper $12.95 (0-938586-33-5). Journal of a 1,700-mile canoe trip from Minnesota to Canada's Hudson's Bay. (Rev: BL 1/15/91; SLJ 4/91) [797.122]

6564 Cheripko, Jan. *Voices of the River: Adventures on the Delaware* (6–9). 1994, Boyds Mills $15.95 (1-56397-325-1). The author's 10-day canoeing trip down the Delaware River with a 14-year-old boy. (Rev: BL 1/15/94; SLJ 2/94) [974.9]

6565 Conner, Dennis, and Michael Levitt. *Learn to Sail* (9–adult). 1994, St. Martin's $22.95 (0-312-11020-0). A beginner's guide for the novice sailor. (Rev: BL 5/15/94; MJHS; SHS) [797.1]

6566 Goodman, Di, and Ian Brodie. *Learning to Sail: The Annapolis Sailing School Guide for All Ages* (9–adult). 1994, International Marine paper $12.95 (0-07-024014-0). Provides instruction for novices on how to begin recreational sailing. Includes nautical jargon, safety tips, and helpful drawings. (Rev: BL 7/94) [797.1]

6567 Henderson, Richard. *Hand, Reef and Steer: A Practical Handbook on Sailing* (9–adult). Rev. ed. 1991, Contemporary paper $11.95 (0-8092-4010-6). Features information on sail materials, hull types, navigational aids, anchors, and boating rules and defines nautical terms for new boat owners. (Rev: BL 9/1/91) [797.1]

6568 Kentley, Eric. *Boat* (5–9). (Eyewitness Books) 1992, Knopf LB $15.99 (0-679-91678-4). (Rev: BL 6/1/92; MJHS) [623.8]

6569 Kimber, Robert. *A Canoeist's Sketchbook* (9–adult). 1991, Chelsea Green Publishing (P.O. Box 428, White River Junction, VT 05001) $21.95 (0-930031-50-4); paper $12.95 (0-930031-45-8). These literary sketches reflect the author's love of wilderness boating and provide a wealth of practical tips and canoeing lore. (Rev: BL 10/15/91) [797.1]

6570 Kuhne, Cecil. *Whitewater Rafting: An Introductory Guide* (9–adult). 1995, Lyons & Burford paper $16.95 (1-55821-317-1). An introduction to white-water rafting including pretrip checklists and a list of classic whitewater rafting spots in the country. (Rev: BL 2/15/95) [796.1]

6571 Ray, Slim. *The Canoe Handbook: Techniques for Mastering the Sport of Canoeing* (9–adult). 1992, Stackpole paper $15.95 (0-8117-3032-8). Handbook covering canoeing fundamentals, including paddling techniques, styles, maneuvers, design, equipment. (Rev: BL 2/15/92; MJHS) [797.1]

Skateboarding

6572 Andrejtschitsch, Jan, and others. *Action Skateboarding* (6–12). 1993, Sterling paper $10.95 (0-8069-8500-3). Provides a history, gives an overview of equipment, and defines styles and terrains of skateboarding, with tips on tricks and maneuvers. (Rev: BL 6/1–15/93; MJHS; SLJ 7/93) [795.2]

Skiing and Snowboarding

6573 Bennett, Jeff, and Scott Downey. *The Complete Snowboarder* (9–adult). 1994, McGraw-Hill/Ragged Mountain paper $14.95 (0-07-005142-9). Presents tips for prospective snowboarders, with diagrams and illustrations. (Rev: BL 9/15/94) [796.9]

Soccer

6574 Bauer, Gerhard. *Soccer Techniques, Tactics and Teamwork* (9–adult). 1993, Sterling paper $14.95 (0-8069-8730-8). Basic soccer training and skill development, with color photos. (Rev: BL 7/93*) [796.344]

6575 Gardner, Paul. *The Simplest Game* (9–adult). Rev. ed. 1994, Macmillan/Collier paper $12 (0-02-043225-9). Provides historical perspective on the World Cup and a detailed analysis of soccer. (Rev: BL 2/15/94; BTA) [796.334]

6576 Lauffer, Butch, and Sandy Davie. *Soccer Coach's Guide to Practices, Drills and Skill Training* (9–adult). 1992, Sterling $17.95 (0-8069-8218-7). Basic soccer guide, with skills broken down into age groups to help players develop their potential. (Rev: BL 2/1/92) [796.334]

Surfing, Water Skiing, and Other Water Sports

6577 McCallum, Paul. *The Scuba Diving Handbook: A Complete Guide to Salt and Fresh Water Diving* (9–adult). 1991, Betterway paper $19.95 (1-55870-180-X). This comprehensive guide to scuba diving covers all aspects of the sport. (Rev: BL 6/15/91; SHS; SLJ 1/92) [797.2]

Tennis and Other Racquet Games

6578 Ashe, Arthur, and Alexander McNab. *Arthur Ashe on Tennis: Strokes, Strategy, Traditions, Players, Psychology, and Wisdom* (9–adult). 1995, Knopf $20 (0-679-43797-5). An instructional guide which also expresses much admiration for Ashe the man and his struggle with a heart condition and then AIDS. (Rev: BL 3/1/95) [796.342]

6579 Gilbert, Brad, and Steve Jamison. *Winning Ugly: Mental Warfare in Tennis—Tales from the Tour and Lessons from a Master* (9–adult). 1993, Birch Lane $18.95 (1-55972 169-3) Tips for competetive tennis players on how to maximize one's game through mental strategies. (Rev: BL 6/1–15/93) [796.342]

6580 *International Book of Tennis Drills* (9–adult). 1993, Triumph Books (644 S. Clark St., Suite 2000, Chicago, IL 60605) paper $14.95 (1-880141-36-1). This resource from the U.S. Professional Tennis Registry presents more than 100 tennis drills with accompanying diagrams to build basic skills. (Rev: BL 11/15/93) [796.342]

6581 Jennings, Jay, ed. *Tennis and the Meaning of Life: A Literary Anthology of the Game* (9–adult). 1995, Breakaway $24 (1-55821-378-3). A collection of well-known writers on tennis-related stories and poetry. (Rev: BL 5/15/95) [808.8]

6582 Kittleson, Stan. *Racquetball: Steps to Success* (9–adult). 1991, Human Kinetics paper $13.95 (0-88011-440-1). An instructional text for beginning players on mastering 18 basic racquetball skills, each with appropriate drills. (Rev: BL 10/1/91; MJHS) [796.34]

6583 Mewshaw, Michael. *Ladies of the Court: Grace and Scandal on the Women's Tennis Tour* (9–adult). 1993, Crown $21 (0-517-58758-0). An outsider's view of the competitive sport of women's pro tennis, based on interviews with players, coaches, and others. (Rev: BL 3/15/93) [796.342]

6584 Singleton, Skip. *The Junior Tennis Handbook: A Complete Guide to Tennis for Juniors, Parents, and Coaches* (5–12). 1991, Betterway paper $12.95 (1-55870-192-3). This comprehensive tennis guide offers instruction in training to beginners 10 years old and up. (Rev: BL 8/91; MJHS) [796.342]

6585 Turner, Ed, and Woody Clouse. *Winning Racquetball: Skills, Drills, and Strategies* (9–adult). 1995, Human Kinetics paper $16.95 (0-87322-721-2). Includes drills to develop recommended shots, strategies, and tips on conditioning. (Rev: BL 12/1/95) [796.34]

Volleyball

6586 Crisfield, Deborah. *Winning Volleyball for Girls* (5–7). 1995, Facts on File $22.95 (0-8160-3033-2). An author who takes her sport seriously presents everything you need to know about playing a competitive game of volleyball. (Rev: BL 9/1/95) [796.32]

Author Index

Authors are arranged alphabetically by last name. Authors' and joint authors' names are followed by book titles—which are also arranged alphabetically—and the text entry number. All fiction titles are indicated by (F), following the entry number.

Title Index

References are to entry numbers, not page numbers. All fiction titles are indicated by (F), following the entry number.

Subject/Grade Level Index

All entries are listed within specific subjects and then according to grade level suitability (see the key at the foot of pages for grade level designations). Subjects are arranged alphabetically and subject heads may be subdivided into nonfiction (e.g., "Adoption") and fiction (e.g., "Adoption—Fiction"). Reference to entries are by entry numbers, not pages.

A

IJ = Intermediate–Junior High IS = Intermediate–Senior High
JS = Junior–Senior High S = Senior High SA = Senior High–Adult

IJ = Intermediate–Junior High IS = Intermediate–Senior High
JS = Junior–Senior High S = Senior High SA = Senior High–Adult

IJ = Intermediate–Junior High IS = Intermediate–Senior High
JS = Junior–Senior High S = Senior High SA = Senior High–Adult

IJ = Intermediate–Junior High IS = Intermediate–Senior High
JS = Junior–Senior High S = Senior High SA = Senior High–Adult

IJ = Intermediate–Junior High IS = Intermediate–Senior High
JS = Junior–Senior High S = Senior High SA = Senior High–Adult

IJ = Intermediate–Junior High IS = Intermediate–Senior High
JS = Junior–Senior High S = Senior High SA = Senior High–Adult

IJ = Intermediate–Junior High IS = Intermediate–Senior High
JS = Junior–Senior High S = Senior High SA = Senior High–Adult

B

IJ = Intermediate–Junior High IS = Intermediate–Senior High
JS = Junior–Senior High S = Senior High SA = Senior High–Adult

IJ = Intermediate–Junior High IS = Intermediate–Senior High
JS = Junior–Senior High S = Senior High SA = Senior High–Adult

IJ = Intermediate–Junior High IS = Intermediate–Senior High
JS = Junior–Senior High S = Senior High SA = Senior High–Adult

IJ = Intermediate–Junior High IS = Intermediate–Senior High
JS = Junior–Senior High S = Senior High SA = Senior High–Adult

C

IJ = Intermediate–Junior High IS = Intermediate–Senior High
JS = Junior–Senior High S = Senior High SA = Senior High–Adult

IJ = Intermediate–Junior High IS = Intermediate–Senior High
JS = Junior–Senior High S = Senior High SA = Senior High–Adult

IJ = Intermediate–Junior High IS = Intermediate–Senior High
JS = Junior–Senior High S = Senior High SA = Senior High–Adult

IJ = Intermediate–Junior High IS = Intermediate–Senior High
JS = Junior–Senior High S = Senior High SA = Senior High–Adult

IJ = Intermediate–Junior High IS = Intermediate–Senior High
JS = Junior–Senior High S = Senior High SA = Senior High–Adult

IJ = Intermediate–Junior High IS = Intermediate–Senior High
JS = Junior–Senior High S = Senior High SA = Senior High–Adult

IJ = Intermediate–Junior High IS = Intermediate–Senior High
JS = Junior–Senior High S = Senior High SA = Senior High–Adult

D

IJ = Intermediate–Junior High IS = Intermediate–Senior High
JS = Junior–Senior High S = Senior High SA = Senior High–Adult

IJ = Intermediate–Junior High IS = Intermediate–Senior High
JS = Junior–Senior High S = Senior High SA = Senior High–Adult

E

IJ = Intermediate–Junior High IS = Intermediate–Senior High
JS = Junior–Senior High S = Senior High SA = Senior High–Adult

IJ = Intermediate–Junior High IS = Intermediate–Senior High
JS = Junior–Senior High S = Senior High SA = Senior High–Adult

F

IJ = Intermediate–Junior High IS = Intermediate–Senior High
JS = Junior–Senior High S = Senior High SA = Senior High–Adult

G

IJ = Intermediate–Junior High IS = Intermediate–Senior High
JS = Junior–Senior High S = Senior High SA = Senior High–Adult

H

IJ = Intermediate–Junior High IS = Intermediate–Senior High
JS = Junior–Senior High S = Senior High SA = Senior High–Adult

IJ = Intermediate–Junior High IS = Intermediate–Senior High
JS = Junior–Senior High S = Senior High SA = Senior High–Adult

IJ = Intermediate–Junior High IS = Intermediate–Senior High
JS = Junior–Senior High S = Senior High SA = Senior High–Adult

I

IJ = Intermediate–Junior High IS = Intermediate–Senior High
JS = Junior–Senior High S = Senior High SA = Senior High–Adult

IJ = Intermediate–Junior High IS = Intermediate–Senior High
JS = Junior–Senior High S = Senior High SA = Senior High–Adult

IJ = Intermediate–Junior High IS = Intermediate–Senior High
JS = Junior–Senior High S = Senior High SA = Senior High–Adult

J

IJ = Intermediate–Junior High IS = Intermediate–Senior High
JS = Junior–Senior High S = Senior High SA = Senior High–Adult

K

IJ = Intermediate–Junior High IS = Intermediate–Senior High
JS = Junior–Senior High S = Senior High SA = Senior High–Adult

IJ = Intermediate–Junior High IS = Intermediate–Senior High
JS = Junior–Senior High S = Senior High SA = Senior High–Adult

IJ = Intermediate–Junior High IS = Intermediate–Senior High
JS = Junior–Senior High S = Senior High SA = Senior High–Adult

M

IJ = Intermediate–Junior High IS = Intermediate–Senior High
JS = Junior–Senior High S = Senior High SA = Senior High–Adult

IJ = Intermediate–Junior High IS = Intermediate–Senior High
JS = Junior–Senior High S = Senior High SA = Senior High–Adult

IJ = Intermediate–Junior High IS = Intermediate–Senior High
JS = Junior–Senior High S = Senior High SA = Senior High–Adult

IJ = Intermediate–Junior High IS = Intermediate–Senior High
JS = Junior–Senior High S = Senior High SA = Senior High–Adult

IJ = Intermediate–Junior High IS = Intermediate–Senior High
JS = Junior–Senior High S = Senior High SA = Senior High–Adult

N

IJ = Intermediate–Junior High IS = Intermediate–Senior High
JS = Junior–Senior High S = Senior High SA = Senior High–Adult

O

P

IJ = Intermediate–Junior High IS = Intermediate–Senior High
JS = Junior–Senior High S = Senior High SA = Senior High–Adult

IJ = Intermediate–Junior High   IS = Intermediate–Senior High
JS = Junior–Senior High   S = Senior High   SA = Senior High–Adult

IJ = Intermediate–Junior High IS = Intermediate–Senior High
JS = Junior–Senior High S = Senior High SA = Senior High–Adult

IJ = Intermediate–Junior High IS = Intermediate–Senior High
JS = Junior–Senior High S = Senior High SA = Senior High–Adult

IJ = Intermediate–Junior High IS = Intermediate–Senior High
JS = Junior–Senior High S = Senior High SA = Senior High–Adult

Q

IJ = Intermediate–Junior High IS = Intermediate–Senior High
JS = Junior–Senior High S = Senior High SA = Senior High–Adult

R

IJ = Intermediate–Junior High IS = Intermediate–Senior High
JS = Junior–Senior High S = Senior High SA = Senior High–Adult

IJ = Intermediate–Junior High IS = Intermediate–Senior High
JS = Junior–Senior High S = Senior High SA = Senior High–Adult

S

IJ = Intermediate–Junior High IS = Intermediate–Senior High
JS = Junior–Senior High S = Senior High SA = Senior High–Adult

IJ = Intermediate–Junior High IS = Intermediate–Senior High
JS = Junior–Senior High S = Senior High SA = Senior High–Adult

IJ = Intermediate–Junior High IS = Intermediate–Senior High
JS = Junior–Senior High S = Senior High SA = Senior High–Adult

IJ = Intermediate–Junior High IS = Intermediate–Senior High
JS = Junior–Senior High S = Senior High SA = Senior High–Adult

T

IJ = Intermediate–Junior High IS = Intermediate–Senior High
JS = Junior–Senior High S = Senior High SA = Senior High–Adult

IJ = Intermediate–Junior High IS = Intermediate–Senior High
JS = Junior–Senior High S = Senior High SA = Senior High–Adult

U

IJ = Intermediate–Junior High IS = Intermediate–Senior High
JS = Junior–Senior High S = Senior High SA = Senior High–Adult

IJ = Intermediate–Junior High IS = Intermediate–Senior High
JS = Junior–Senior High S = Senior High SA = Senior High–Adult

IJ = Intermediate–Junior High IS = Intermediate–Senior High
JS = Junior–Senior High S = Senior High SA = Senior High–Adult

V

IJ = Intermediate–Junior High   IS = Intermediate–Senior High
JS = Junior–Senior High   S = Senior High   SA = Senior High–Adult

W

IJ = Intermediate–Junior High IS = Intermediate–Senior High
JS = Junior–Senior High S = Senior High SA = Senior High–Adult

IJ = Intermediate–Junior High IS = Intermediate–Senior High
JS = Junior–Senior High S = Senior High SA = Senior High–Adult

IJ = Intermediate–Junior High IS = Intermediate–Senior High
JS = Junior–Senior High S = Senior High SA = Senior High–Adult

IJ = Intermediate–Junior High IS = Intermediate–Senior High
JS = Junior–Senior High S = Senior High SA = Senior High–Adult

IJ = Intermediate–Junior High   IS = Intermediate–Senior High
JS = Junior–Senior High   S = Senior High   SA = Senior High–Adult

Y